THIRD CANADIAN EDITION

PSYCHOLOGY

John W. Santrock
University of Texas at Dallas

John O. Mitterer
Brock University

McGraw-Hill
Ryerson

Toronto Montréal Boston Burr Ridge, IL Dubuque, IA Madison, WI
New York San Francisco St. Louis Bangkok Bogotá Caracas
Kuala Lumpur Lisbon London Madrid Mexico City Milan
New Delhi Santiago Seoul Singapore Sydney Taipei

Psychology
Third Canadian Edition

Copyright © 2006, 2004, 2001 by McGraw-Hill Ryerson Limited, a Subsidiary of The McGraw-Hill Companies. Copyright © 2003, 2000, 1997 by The McGraw-Hill Companies, Inc. All rights reserved. No part of this publication may be reproduced or transmitted in any form or by any means, or stored in a data base or retrieval system, without the prior written permission of McGraw-Hill Ryerson Limited, or in the case of photocopying or other reprographic copying, a licence from The Canadian Copyright Licensing Agency (Access Copyright). For an Access Copyright licence, visit www.accesscopyright.ca or call toll free to 1-800-893-5777.

Statistics Canada information is used with the permission of the Minister of Industry, as Minister responsible for Statistics Canada. Information on the availability of the wide range of data from Statistics Canada can be obtained from Statistics Canada's Regional Offices, its World Wide Web site at http://www.statcan.ca, and its toll free access number 1-800-263-1136.

ISBN: 0-07-095570-0

1 2 3 4 5 6 7 8 9 10 VH 0 9 8 7 6

Printed and bound in the United States of America

Care has been taken to trace ownership of copyright material contained in this text; however, the publisher will welcome any information that enables it to rectify any reference or credit for subsequent editions.

Executive Sponsoring Editor: James Buchanan
Marketing Manager: Marc Trudel
Developmental Editor: Jodi Lewchuk
Editorial Associate: Marina Seguin
Manager, Editorial Services: Kelly Dickson
Supervising Editor: Joanne Limebeer
Copy Editor: Gillian Scobie
Senior Production Coordinator: Paula Brown
Cover Design: Greg Devitt
Page Layout: Liz Harasymczuk
Printer: Von Hoffmann Press, Inc.

Library and Archives Canada Cataloguing in Publication Data

Santrock, John W.
        Psychology / John W. Santrock, John O. Mitterer. — 3rd Canadian ed.

Includes bibliographical references and index.
ISBN 0-07-095570-0

        1. Psychology—Textbooks. I. Mitterer, John Otto, 1950- II. Title.

BF121.S267 2006   150   C2005-906301-7

With special appreciation to my wife, Mary Jo

John Santrock

*For my father, Otto, whom I lost in late 2004,
my mother, Elizabeth, and my wife, Heather*

John Mitterer

About the Authors

JOHN W. SANTROCK received his Ph.D. from the University of Minnesota in 1973. He taught at the University of Charleston and the University of Georgia before joining the psychology department at the University of Texas at Dallas. He has been a member of the editorial board of *Developmental Psychology*. His research on father custody is widely cited and used in expert witness testimony to promote flexibility and alternative considerations in custody disputes. John has also authored these exceptional McGraw-Hill texts: *Child Development*, tenth edition, *Life-Span Development*, ninth edition, *Children*, eighth edition, *Adolescence*, tenth edition, and *Educational Psychology*, second edition.

JOHN O. MITTERER holds a B.A. from the University of Calgary and a Ph.D. from McMaster University. He is currently a Professor of Psychology at Brock University, where he has taught over 20,000 introductory psychology students. As a scholar of teaching, John has been involved in the production of a wide range of pedagogical materials, from learning objects and CD-ROMs to textbooks. He has also spoken across Canada and the United States on the pedagogy of post-secondary education. John is the recipient of several teaching awards, including a 3M Teaching Fellowship and the Canadian Psychological Association Award for Distinguished Contributions to Education and Training in Psychology.

Brief Contents

Contents

CHAPTER 4   Human Development   116

CHAPTER 5   Sensation and Perception   174

CHAPTER 12   Personality   470

CHAPTER 13   Psychological Disorders   508

CHAPTER 14   Therapies   552

CHAPTER 15 · Stress, Coping, and Health 592

CHAPTER 16 · Social Psychology 634

Preface

If you are reading this preface you are almost certainly either a student who is using this book as part of a course in introductory psychology or the instructor of an introductory psychology course. Regardless, thank you for taking the time to read this preface. I invite you to read all of my comments, whether they are directed to students or instructors.

I've been teaching introductory psychology at Brock University, in St. Catharines, Ontario, since 1981 and have long admired John Santrock's introductory psychology textbooks. John, who has been teaching introductory psychology since 1967, and I both share a deep motivation and love for imparting psychology as a relevant science—one that is empirically sound yet meaningful for people's lives. In no other discipline (we are admittedly biased) will you find so many opportunities to better understand yourself and the people around you than in the discipline of psychology. This belief has not only been a foundation of our teaching introductory psychology for a long time, but is also the heart of this book.

To the Student

Welcome to *Psychology,* Third Canadian Edition, one textbook that I hope you will actually enjoy reading. And since you are almost certainly reading this textbook as part of a course in psychology, I trust that it will also help you reach your educational goals. The key is realizing that this is not just any type of book. Unlike a novel, which is written to be read and enjoyed, a textbook is written to be read and studied. As I like to put it, a good textbook is composed of content + pedagogy.

Content refers to the material you are expected to understand and remember. In this case, the content is an introductory survey of the richness of the discipline of psychology. If you finish this textbook understanding and remembering most of what you read, you will have a thorough foundation in the discipline of psychology. *Pedagogy* refers to the tools the textbook offers to help you reach your learning goals. Those tools—and the general study skills, which are used by all good students—are so important that I discuss them in their own section of Chapter 1 entitled *How to Get the Most Out of Psychology.*

If you are chomping at the bit to get started, good luck and off you go to Chapter 1. If you are curious to learn more about the design of this textbook, then feel free to read the remainder of this preface, which is entitled *To the Instructor* but contains much of interest for you, the student, as well.

To the Instructor

Welcome to *Psychology,* Third Canadian Edition. I am writing to you as a student of psychology, an author of this book, and a fellow instructor who has been teaching introductory psychology to classes of 1,000 students for over 20 years. I am grateful for the ongoing opportunity to coauthor this textbook, now in its third edition, because it allows me to create more effective learning materials for my students, and yours, to use as they engage our fascinating discipline. In this section I want to introduce you to my rationale for the design of this textbook.

My main design goal has been to create a book that students can read and understand without requiring extensive instructor support. That way, my lectures are less tethered to the textbook or the need to "cover" all of the course content. In my view, this goal is best served with a mid-level introductory textbook that is written in a more accessible style. The U.S. version of this book has repeatedly been assessed as upper-mid-level (Griggs, 1999; Koenig & others, 2004) and my coauthor, John Santrock, is well known for his accessible writing, textbook qualities I have sought to strengthen in this Canadian edition.

Ultimately, a good introductory textbook must be judged a success or failure based on how well it fosters student learning of its subject matter. It is my deep belief that good content is a necessary, but not sufficient, condition for effective student learning. The missing piece is the pedagogical framework. As I wrote in my comments to the students, textbook = content + pedagogy. As such, a good introductory textbook both presents well-organized up-to-date content and does so in a pedagogically sound way.

The Contents of This Book

Three heuristics guided my approach to content in this edition: coverage, relevance, and readability. If a textbook covers the information students need to learn, and does so in ways that students find relevant and readable, the textbook has a good chance of playing its proper role in your course curriculum.

Coverage — Focus on Key Ideas

I have taken care to ensure that *Psychology,* Third Canadian Edition covers the key ideas in introductory psychology (e.g., Nairn & others, 2003). One measure of those key ideas is the glossary terms, which are bold-faced, defined in the margin, and listed and page-referenced at the end of each chapter. All key terms and their definitions are also collected together in the Glossary at the end of the book along with a reference to the page on which the term is introduced. Other important terms are italicized throughout the book. Another measure of the key ideas covered in the book can be found in the Chapter Review section, which gives high-level summaries for each section of that chapter.

This edition continues to stress the scientific nature of the discipline. A hallmark of the book has always been its focus on research, the foundation of all sciences. Here the latest research findings are discussed, along with the classic studies that established psychology as an objective science. More than 1,000 citations come from sources published since January 2000, including many from 2006.

The growing emphasis on neuroscience and genetics as the means of understanding the effects of biology on behaviour is also reflected in this edition. Evolutionary psychology, another area of increasing interest, receives increased attention as well. Knowing that students often have difficulty understanding why it is important to learn biology in a course on psychology, I have taken particular care to present these topics in a psychological context and to underscore the complex relationship between biology, environment, and behaviour wherever appropriate.

Finally, I continue to stress positive psychology because psychology has much to offer to those of us interested in living joyful lives. Proponents of positive psychology, notably Mihaly Csikszentmihalyi, share the belief that for much of the twentieth century the discipline of psychology concentrated on the negative aspects of life and that it is time to emphasize the positive side of psychology. I concur. Positive psychology offers all of us the opportunity to take control of our lives and find balance. For this edition, I have again revised many of the chapter-opening vignettes and examples in the text to highlight positive outcomes.

Relevance

Many students come into the introductory psychology class asking why they should study psychology when their major is physics or computer science or French. To a psychologist the answer is obvious: It will help you to understand yourself and others better. Psychology is relevant to almost every aspect of daily life. What psychologists have learned from memory research, for example, can be used to study more effectively, no matter what the subject is. Principles of learning can be applied to change undesirable behaviour in children. Knowledge of sensation and perception can be used to design computers more effectively. Research on stress, coping, and health can help people to live fuller, happier lives.

But students often need help to realize this. Student focus groups reviewing earlier editions of the original U.S. edition on which this book is based identified relevance as their number one concern. In fact, this finding, more than any other single factor, is what persuaded me to undertake a Canadian edition — to make the book I ask my students to use as relevant as possible. Making sure a textbook is relevant is one way of making it easier for students to connect what they learn in the textbook with what they already know from their life experience. As I argue below in my description of the pedagogy in this book, relevance leads to more elaboration and hence better comprehension and memory.

While *Psychology,* Third Canadian Edition remains grounded in John Santrock's original writing, I have extensively updated and adapted it in order to increase the relevance of psychology to our Canadian students. However, as in previous editions, this adaptation does not parade Canadian psychology at the expense of coverage of American and European psychology.

Without forgetting that we Canadians and Americans share much in common, in a number of cases American examples and statistics were replaced with Canadian ones. Canadian statistics from Statistics Canada and Health Canada, Canadian examples of creative and prominent people, and hypothetical scenarios relevant to Canadians, serve to unobtrusively sharpen relevant Canadian perspectives without creating an overly Canadian focus. We also draw attention to Canadian research in psychology by including hundreds of references to work by influential Canadian researchers like Endel Tulving, John Berry, Robert Ladouceur, Sandra Witelson, Robert Hare, Douglas Wahlsten, Norman Endler, Donald Saklofske, Kenneth Dion, Donald Meichenbaum, Sampo Paunonen, Fergus Craik, and many, many others.

Readability

A more readable text is also easier for students to assimilate. The tone of this book has deliberately been chosen so it is more personal and colloquial than that found in journal articles. This tone contributes to the relevance of the textbook, speaking as it does directly to the student. Also, a cognitive map at the beginning of each major chapter section provides a visual preview of the section, and a cognitive map of the entire chapter appears at the end of each chapter.

The Pedagogy of This Book

So much of the learning in an introductory psychology course involves explicit declarative memory, such as memory for core concepts, important theories, and key experiments. Influenced by Jean Piaget's idea of the child as actively constructing knowledge, David Ausubel (1963) proposed the subsumption theory to explain the effective formation of meaningful explicit memories, a theory I consulted in my extensive redesign of the pedagogy in this third Canadian edition. The basic idea of this theory is that the learner will be most successful when he or she subsumes new material under existing knowledge structures. Two empirically well-established cognitive principles underlie successful subsumption: advance organizers and elaboration (J. R. Anderson, 2005).

Advance Organizers

An advance organizer (Ausubel, 1968) is a reference frame for encountering new information. Reading an unfamiliar passage is easier and results in better comprehension and memory when we have some advance idea of what we are about to read.

The most common form of advance organizer is a table of contents. Glancing at the *Chapter Outline* for any chapter in *Psychology* will give the student some idea of the three to six key ideas he or she will encounter in that chapter. Each major heading in the chapter outline has an associated *Chapter Question* that the student should be able to answer after reading that chapter section. Questions, especially self-generated questions, have been shown to be especially powerful advance organizers (Frase, 1975; Ausubel, 1978). Content maps of the section and subsection headings also accompany the chapter question at the beginning of each major section. Finally, another advance organizer, a chapter-opening vignette, introduces the main themes of each chapter.

The chapter questions reappear at several places in the chapter: as a rephrased question at the beginning of a new section, and in declarative form in a *Reflect and Review* box at the end of each major section and again in the *Chapter Review* at the end of the chapter. Together with a complete chapter map at the end of the chapter, the section maps and reappearing chapter questions provide a visual and verbal guide to the core concepts in each chapter.

Elaboration

Elaboration refers to how extensively information has been processed (see Chapter 8). The more varied the processing the better, as the information will be associated with other bits of information and thus will be more easily retrieved via one or the other retrieval cue. Students' academic success has been linked to their use of elaboration (e.g., Gadzella, 1995).

The most powerful form of elaboration is self-reference. Throughout this book, the tone is personal. The student is invited to relate the content to what he or she already knows. In a classic study (Rogers, Kuiper, & Kirker, 1977), participants were given instructions like those used in levels-of-processing research. They were asked to judge words based on their physical, acoustic, or semantic characteristics. In addition, some words were judged based on self-reference: whether the word could be applied to the participants themselves. Self-reference produced superior recall. According to Klein and Kihlstrom (1986), this is because relating new information to the rich and organized knowledge structures involving the self increases the organization of the information to be remembered.

This textbook includes several opportunities for students to elaborate their understanding. Within each chapter students will encounter a *Critical Reflections* box, which elaborates on a particular contemporary controversy in psychology. Further, each chapter includes a *Personal Reflections* box, asking the student to apply some chapter information to his or her own life. Both of these features end with critical thinking questions.

Throughout every chapter, main sections end with a *Reflect and Review* box. The reflection component is especially designed to foster further elaboration of the just-read material through the presentation of critical thinking questions. Finally, at the end of each chapter the student will encounter a *Chapter Reflections* section, including an *Apply Your Knowledge* section and a *Connections* section. For students who have access to the Web, the end-of-chapter exercises usually include at least one Web-based activity.

To help students make the best use of the student supplements, notes in the margins of the text remind students where to go to check their grasp of key concepts and ideas or to find practice quizzes, weekly news updates, and links to additional resources. Incorporating the learning goals and maps in the student supplements reinforces the lessons from the text and eliminates the confusion many students have about how to use the supplements to boost their performance in the course.

PQ4R

In order to make these pedagogical features more accessible to the student, I have created a variation of the popular PQ4R (Thomas & Robinson, 1972) method. This heuristic is already in widespread use and many students will already be familiar with it. I describe this method to the student in more detail in the *How to Get the Most out of Psychology* section of Chapter 1 and also briefly cover it again in the memory chapter (Chapter 8). The PQ4R method proposes that students work through the material in a textbook chapter or chapter section in a series of steps rather than just diving in to begin reading, then setting the chapter aside after finishing. These steps are:

Preview: Before reading the actual chapter material, the student is encouraged to read the *Chapter Preview*, a chapter-opening vignette that introduces the student to the main themes of the chapter, and the *Chapter Outline*, the chapter table of contents. These serve as advance organizers that, like a map, give the student some idea in advance of what the chapter will cover.

Question: Similarly, before beginning to read the chapter the student is encouraged to look at the *Chapter Questions* and to formulate any additional questions he or she would be interested in answering.

Read: In this step the student reads the main chapter. He or she checks to see if the chapter fits the expectations developed from the initial preview step and answers any of the questions from the question step. Notes should be taken, preferably in the student's own words. Underlining is discouraged as a less active form of processing.

Reflect: After reading, the student is encouraged to reflect on the material in order to elaborate it. This step includes many opportunities for self-reflection, considering the material relevance to his or her own life. Several textbook features support elaboration, as mentioned above. In each chapter, the student will encounter a *Critical Reflections* box, which elaborates on a particular contemporary controversy in psychology. Further, each chapter includes a *Personal Reflections* box, asking the student to apply some chapter information to his or her own life. Throughout every chapter, main sections end with a *Reflect and Review* box. The reflection component is especially designed to foster further elaboration of the just-read material. Finally, at the end of each chapter the student will encounter a *Chapter Reflections* section.

Recite: After reading and reflecting, recitation is encouraged as a form of consolidation and further elaboration. The student is encouraged to minimize rote repetition in favour of rewording, explaining the concepts to other students, and inventing mnemonics.

Review: The student is urged to go back over the material repeatedly throughout the term. Chapter summaries are useful here, as is trying to recall the material, self-testing, and working with study partners. The review step, along with the multi-pass nature of the PQ4R system, encourages distributed practice (spacing effect), which refers to the well-established finding that repeatedly studying material produces better memory than does studying it all at once, which is referred to as mass practice (e.g., Reynolds & Glaser, 1964; J. R. Anderson, 2005). If nothing else, the student who conscientiously follows the PQ4R method in studying this book will benefit from distributed practice as he or she works though the material in several different ways.

One last point — aside from the distributed practice effect mentioned above, do any of these pedagogical devices actually help students learn better? There is considerable controversy on this point (Gurung, 2004), but until now, most of the research has looked primarily at the relationship between spontaneous student compliance and course grades. In my experience, it is much more helpful for the instructor to stress the importance of using these aids as a way to increase the likelihood of their use (see also Gurung, 2003). I spend time at the beginning of my course explaining the value of using these pedagogical devices and have even offered marks for their use. For example, I have taken the learning questions from the beginnings of chapters and used them as exam questions. Please consider alerting your students to the value of the pedagogy in this book. As I mentioned previously, making students explicitly aware of the importance of the pedagogy in this book is, to my mind, so important that I have made it a separate section of Chapter 1 (*How to Get the Most Out of Psychology*). (**Note to any students still reading this:** Seriously, use these tools if you want to be a more effective learner, not just in your psychology course, but in all of your courses!)

In closing, I wish you the best in teaching your course and trust that this book and accompanying materials will make your job a bit easier.

Changes in Coverage

Instructors who have used the previous edition of this text will find much in *Psychology,* Third Canadian Edition that's different as well as much that hasn't changed. The book has been extensively updated. In addition to an increased emphasis on neuroscience, genetics, evolutionary psychology, and positive psychology, this edition contains increased coverage of diversity, controversies, and careers in psychology. This material is presented, where appropriate, throughout the book.

The table of contents and chapter sequence remain the same as in the previous edition, with human development near the beginning of the book (chapter 4). Thus instructors can cover a topic of high student interest early in the course, while the principles of genetics (chapter 3) are still fresh in students' minds, and later incorporate the material in their discussions of learning, cognition, and language.

Although the number of chapters and their topics are unchanged, the substance and presentation in each chapter have been revised thoroughly. Some of the detail that is less

relevant today than it once was has been pruned to make room for cutting-edge research, and some of the presentation was reconceptualized to focus on the key ideas in psychology. Although there isn't enough space here to list all of the changes in this edition, here are some highlights:

Chapter 1: What Is Psychology?

- Introduces the distinction between folk psychology and psychology as a science
- Ascribes Structuralism as a label more accurately to Titchener rather than Wundt
- Treats gestalt psychology as one of the early scientific approaches to psychology
- Mentions Albert Bandura's Canadian roots
- New table better summarizes the six contemporary approaches to psychology
- Extensively rewrites the section entitled *How to Get the Most Out of Psychology* to better invite students to make use of the updated pedagogical features in this edition

Chapter 2: Psychology's Scientific Methods

- Rewrites the opening chapter vignette around the current student interest in forensic psychology and the popular *CSI* television series to better motivate the discussion of research methods
- Discusses the work of John Yuille and his colleagues in developing the Step-Wise Interview for forensic interviewing of children, as an example of scientific curiosity
- Introduces another popular television show, *Numb3rs,* to show the need for statistical methods in psychology
- Uses research by Pierette Bouchard and her colleagues at Université Laval to illustrate the interpretation of statistical significance
- Updates the coverage of CPA ethics guidelines through mention of the Tri-Council Policy Statement

Chapter 3: Biological Foundations of Behaviour

- Describes the case of Bryan Kolb, of the University of Lethbridge, who suffered a stroke and wrote about it in the *Canadian Journal of Psychology,* as the basis of the chapter-opening vignette
- Adds functional specialization to complexity, integration, and adapability as characteristics of the nervous system
- Updates the section *How the Brain and Nervous System are Studied,* which now occurs earlier in the chapter. CAT, PET, and MRI scans are treated in separate subsections. Canadian research is used as examples of the research carried out with these methods
- Identifies nuclei as parts of neural networks
- Mentions recent work suggesting that glial cells may modulate synaptic transmission
- Clarifies the section on neural functioning
- Highlights the use of hybrid robots (hybrots) to study the functioning of neural networks in the *Critical Reflections* box

- Updates treatment of sex differences in the human brain
- Updates description of The Human Genome Project

Chapter 4: Human Development

- Focuses on the phenomenon of delayed adulthood in the chapter-opening vignette
- Clarifies the description of Piaget's stage of cognitive development
- Discusses Lev Vygotsky's zone of proximal development with illustrated example
- Highlights the issue of parental pampering and excessively high self-esteem in children in the *Critical Reflections* box
- Adds a section on childcare after the discussion of parenting
- Discusses research on gender schema development by Lisa Serbin at Concordia University
- Restructures coverage of the section on adolescence to be more consistent with other major chapter sections
- Discusses work by Donald Taylor of McGill University on ethnic adolescents
- Covers recent concerns about the dangers of hormone replacement therapy
- Discusses the Victoria Longitudinal Study
- Covers death and dying in new section

Chapter 5: Sensation and Perception

- Focuses on the phenomenon of synaesthesia in the chapter-opening vignette
- Updates treatment of subliminal perception
- Reintroduces Stratton's 1897 prism studies to the book as a compelling example of sensory adaptation
- Rewrites and expands the treatment of dorsal and ventral visual pathways, including a discussion of blindsight
- Updates *Critical Reflections* box on claims of extrasensory perception
- Discusses telepresence and haptic interfaces more completely in the section *Exploring Touch in Life*
- Offers neuromatrix theory of Ronald Melzack (McGill University) as an explanation of phantom limb pain
- Identifies umami as a possible fifth basic taste quality
- Discusses the work of Laurence Harris and Michael Jenkin of York University on immersive visual environments

Chapter 6: States of Consciousness

- Distinguishes first-person and third-person perspectives on consciousness in the chapter-opening vignette
- Completely rewrites the opening section, *Levels of Awareness*, and following section, *Consciousness and the Brain*. These sections now draw heavily on work by Donald Stuss of the University of Toronto and Vicki Anderson of the University of Melbourne, linking levels of conscious awareness with different brain areas
- Introduces capgrass syndrome as a dramatic example of the disruption of awareness resulting from frontal lobe damage

- Updates and rewrites section entitled *Circadian Rhythms and Biological Clocks*
- Notes the role of both REM and NREM sleep in memory formation
- Discusses the possibility of distinguishing hypnotic from other states via brain imaging
- Updates the discussion of the forensic value of hypnosis in the *Critical Reflections* box
- Updates all drug-use statistics in this chapter

Chapter 7: Learning

- Rewrites opening vignette on the work of Shepard Segal, of McMaster University, on classically conditioned compensatory tolerance to drugs
- Rewrites *Critical Reflections* box, *Will Sparing the Rod Spoil the Child?*, with a sharper focus on recent developments in Canada and around the world
- Discusses the entertainment–education strategy as an extension of Albert Bandura's approach to observational learning
- Updates *Personal Reflections* box, *Mentors and Mentees*
- Uses example of the use of conditioned taste aversion to prevent crows from eating the eggs of endangered species

Chapter 8: Memory

- Highlights the work of psychologist Dr. Brian Richards, of Toronto's Baycrest Hospital, with patients stricken by anterograde amnesia in a new chapter-opening vignette
- Discusses the use of neural networks to simulate human memory phenomena
- Rewrites the discussion of tip-of-the-tongue states
- Notes that state-dependent memory is produced by drug use
- Discusses U.S. President George Bush's false flashbulb memory of 9/11/2001
- Updates *Critical Reflections* box, *Recovered Memories or False Memories*, and the section on eyewitness testimony
- Updates the treatment of transience in long-term memory

Chapter 9: Thinking and Language

- Updates chapter-opening vignette on Williams syndrome
- Clarifies extensively the section on the cognitive revolution in psychology, about the differences between how brains and computers process information, and critiques early analogies between the two. Two different approaches to AI are contrasted later in the chapter.
- Discusses thin-slicing, rapid intuitive processing in new *Critical Reflections* box, *Is Mindful the Opposite of Intuitive?*, as outlined in Malcolm Gladwell's 2005 book, *Blink*
- Rewrites section on the Whorfian hypothesis to acknowledge that Whorf's claims about the plenitude of Inuit (relative to English) words for snow were exaggerated
- Presents Michael Tomasello's views that much of language is learned

- Critiques the idea that there are critical periods for language acquisition
- Rewrites and updates material on bilingualism

Chapter 10: Intelligence

- Covers the neuroscience of intelligence more extensively
- Updates discussion of the roles of environment and heredity. The Human Genome project is mentioned and the sections dealing with environmental influences have been extensively reworked
- Explores Steven Johnson's (2004) creative proposal that the Flynn effect can be explained by the increasing complexity of popular culture in a new *Critical Reflections* box, *Are television and computer games making us smarter?*
- Mentions University of California anthropologist John Ogbu's argument that lower IQ scores among African Americans stem from a cultural bias against "acting white"
- Presents the contemporary view that "race" is not a useful biological category
- Updates treatment of gender differences in intelligence

Chapter 11: Motivation and Emotion

- Expands the opening vignette on the remarkable motivation shown by Canadians Terry Fox and Rick Hansen
- Clarifies the treatment of the trade-off between intrinsic and extrinsic motivation
- Updates the section on the biology of hunger. For example, a discussion of the role of ghrelin is now included
- Updates the section on homosexuality. For example, the views of Anthony Bogaert, of Brock University, are now discussed
- Discusses Claude Aaronson's notion of stereotype threat as a motivational factor underlying poor achievement by minority groups
- Discusses alexithymia in the *Critical Reflections* box, *What Difference Does It Make If You Can't Name Your Emotions?*

Chapter 12: Personality

- Adds Nelson Mandela to the list of great world leaders whose personalities are discussed in the chapter-opening vignette
- Updates section on locus of control
- Discusses the work of Michael Ashton, of Brock University, and Kibeom Lee, of the University of Calgary, on HEXACO, a new six-factor trait model, in the section on trait theories
- Updates the treatment of the situationist view of personality with a discussion of Walter Mishel's idea of if…then…personality signatures
- Updates the discussion of suicide

Chapter 13: Psychological Disorders

- Eulogizes York University's Norman Endler and extends coverage of his experience of depression in the chapter-opening vignette
- Updates mental health statistics throughout the chapter
- Updates the sections on the etiology of panic disorder and social phobia
- Updates section on PTSD
- Mentions the proposal by John Abela, of McGill University, that insecure attachment is related to depression

Chapter 14: Therapies

- Updates treatment of biological therapies
- Updates discussion of ECT
- Discusses the applications of VR in therapy in the *Critical Reflections* box, *Virtual Reality Therapy*. An example of the treatment of arachniphobia is given
- Expands the coverage of meta-analyses to evaluate therapies

Chapter 15: Stress, Coping, and Health

- Features Norman Cousins and the origins of psychoneuroimmunology in the chapter-opening vignette
- Reworks the first section of this chapter extensively to define both the medical model and the biopsychosocial model. The two models are contrasted in a new table, and this distinction is reflected throughout the chapter.
- Updates coverage of the topic of hardiness
- Notes the role of positive emotions in the release of immunoglobulin A
- Contrasts the usual account of the placebo effect with the newer notion of meaning response, which stresses the importance of nonspecific factors in healing, in the *Critical Reflections* box, *Positive Emotions and Health: Placebo Effect or Meaning Response?*
- Reworks the section on meditation extensively. Now distinguishes between concentrative and mindfulness meditation
- Updates discussion of the role of the Internet in loneliness

Chapter 16: Social Psychology

- Highlights the remarkable story of Canadian General Romeo Dallaire's struggle to protect innocent civilians in Rwanda in the face of orders from his superiors to abandon them to slaughter in the new chapter-opening vignette
- Rewrites section on conformity for greater clarity
- Updates and rewrites section on stereotypes, which now includes a discussion of stereotype threat
- Updates treatment of attractiveness

Stay Focused and Learn

Psychology's unique learning system keeps students focused on key ideas, helping them learn and remember fundamental psychological concepts.

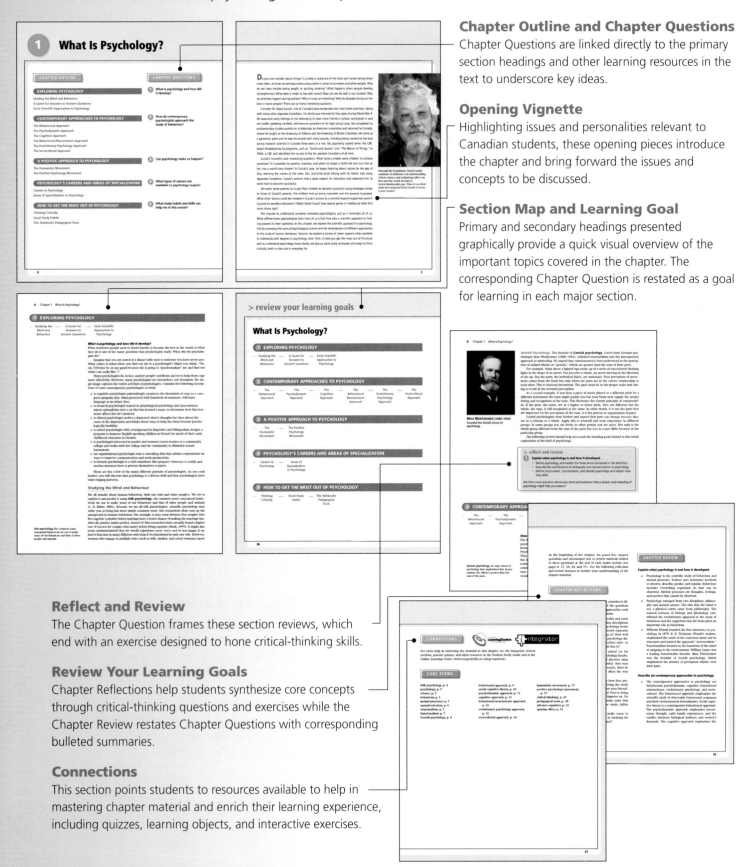

Chapter Outline and Chapter Questions
Chapter Questions are linked directly to the primary section headings and other learning resources in the text to underscore key ideas.

Opening Vignette
Highlighting issues and personalities relevant to Canadian students, these opening pieces introduce the chapter and bring forward the issues and concepts to be discussed.

Section Map and Learning Goal
Primary and secondary headings presented graphically provide a quick visual overview of the important topics covered in the chapter. The corresponding Chapter Question is restated as a goal for learning in each major section.

Reflect and Review
The Chapter Question frames these section reviews, which end with an exercise designed to hone critical-thinking skills.

Review Your Learning Goals
Chapter Reflections help students synthesize core concepts through critical-thinking questions and exercises while the Chapter Review restates Chapter Questions with corresponding bulleted summaries.

Connections
This section points students to resources available to help in mastering chapter material and enrich their learning experience, including quizzes, learning objects, and interactive exercises.

Find Balance

Balance scientific research with real-world experience and applications.

Research

Critical Reflections boxes in each chapter highlight current debates in psychology and pose thought-provoking questions to encourage students to examine evidence on both sides of an issue.

Clearly labelled graph and explanatory captions help students become familiar with visual data presentation.

FIGURE 4.20

Pubertal Growth Spurt
On average, the pubertal growth spurt begins and peaks about 2 years earlier for girls (starts at 9, peaks at 11) than for boys (starts at 11, peaks at 13).

Applications

In each chapter, a **Personal Reflections** feature invites students to apply what they've learned to their own lives.

Descriptions and photos of psychologists at work illustrate applications of psychology in various settings plus different career options for psychology majors.

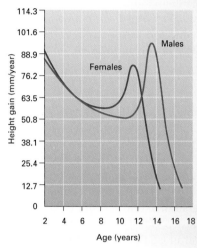

Comprehensive Support for Instructors and Students

To help instructors and students meet today's teaching and learning challenges, *Psychology*, Third Canadian Edition, offers a complete, integrated supplements package.

Superior Service

Service takes on a whole new meaning with McGraw-Hill Ryerson and *Psychology*. More than just bringing you the textbook, we have consistently raised the bar in terms of innovation and educational research. These investments in learning and the educational community have helped us to understand the needs of students and educators across the country and allowed us to foster the growth of truly innovative, integrated learning.

Integrated Learning

Your Integrated Learning Sales Specialist is a McGraw-Hill Ryerson representative who has the experience, product knowledge, training, and support to help you assess and integrate any of our products, technology, and services into your course for optimum teaching and learning performance. Whether it's using our test bank software, helping your students improve their grades, or putting your entire course online, you *i*Learning Sales Specialist is there to help you do it. Contact your local *i*Learning Sales Specialist today to learn how to maximize all of McGraw-Hill Ryerson's resources!

*i*Learning Services Program

McGraw-Hill Ryerson offers a unique *i*Services package designed for Canadian faculty. Our mission is to equip providers of higher education with superior tools and resources required for excellence in teaching. For additional information visit http://www.mcgrawhill.ca/highereducation/iservices.

Teaching, Technology, & Learning Conference Series

The educational environment has changed tremendously in recent years, and McGraw-Hill Ryerson continues to be committed to helping you acquire the skills you need to succeed in this new milieu. Our innovative Teaching, Technology, & Learning Conference Series brings faculty together from across Canada with 3M Teaching Excellence award winners to share teaching and learning best practices in a collaborative and stimulating environment. Pre-conference workshops on general topics such as teaching large classes and technology integration are also offered. In addition, we will work with you at your own institution to customize workshops that best suit the needs of your faculty.

Instructor Supplements

The *i*ntegrator

This pioneering instructional resource from McGraw-Hill Ryerson is your road map to all the other elements of your text's support package. Keyed to the chapters and topics of your McGraw-Hill Ryerson textbook, the *i*ntegrator ties together all of the elements in your resource package, guiding you to where you'll find corresponding coverage in each of the related support package components!

Online Learning Centre

The Online Learning Centre includes a password-protected Web site for instructors (www.mcgrawhill.ca/college/santrock). The site offers downloadable supplements, Web links, and other teaching resources.

Instructor's CD-ROM

This CD-ROM contains all the necessary instructor supplements, fully adapted to accord with the Third Canadian Edition of *Psychology*:

- An **Instructor's Course Planner** that provides for each chapter teaching objectives, ideas and outlines for lectures, recommendations for class discussions and activities, and suggested readings and video/film selections.
- A **Computerized Test Bank** that contains more than 5,000 multiple choice, true/false, fill-in-the-blank, and essay questions keyed to the appropriate page number in the textbook.
- **Microsoft® PowerPoint® Slides** that accompany each chapter, highlighting key concepts and including charts and graphs from the text.

McGraw-Hill Media Resources for Teaching Psychology CD-ROM/DVD

Providing wide-ranging media resources across the field of psychology, from *Anagrams* (Thinking and Language) to *The Stroop Effect* (Sensation and Perception) to *Beautiful Minds: An Interview with John Nash and Son* (Psychological Disorders), this two-disc set provides over 60 topics, including 48 video segments from the Discovery Channel, as well as animations and activities.

McGraw-Hill Introduction to Psychology Video Clips (VHS)

Clips on topics such as Gestalt Theories with Demonstrations (Sensation and Perception), Eyewitness Testimony (Memory), and Understanding Schizophrenia (Psychological Disorders) enhance students' classroom experience.

In-Class Activities Manual

Geared to instructors of large introductory psychology courses, this manual covers every major topic in the course, with activities ranging from simple to in-depth.

Overhead Transparencies

The *Introductory Psychology Transparency Set* provides more than 100 additional images illustrating key concepts in general psychology.

Taking Sides: Clashing Views on Controversial Psychological Issues

This debate-style reader carefully examines issues with pro and con essays representing the arguments of leading scholars and commentators.

Annual Editions: Psychology

This collection of annually updated articles examines the latest research and thinking in the field of psychology.

Sources: Notable Selections in Psychology

A selection of classic articles, book excerpts, and research studies illustrate how psychology—and our understanding of it—have been shaped.

eInstruction's Classroom Performance System (CPS)

CPS is a student response system using wireless connectivity. It gives instructors and students immediate feedback from the entire class. The response pads are remotes that are easy to use and serve several purposes: increase student preparation, interactivity, and active learning; allow for administration of quizzes and tests and provide immediate grading; evaluate classroom attendance and activity. Please contact your *i*Learning Sales Specialist for more information on how you can integrate CPS into your social psychology classroom.

Course Management

Visit www.mhhe.com/pageout to create a Web page for your course using our resources. PageOut is the McGraw-Hill Ryerson Web site development centre. This Web-page-generation software is free to adopters and is designed to help faculty create an online course, complete with assignments, quizzes, links to relevant Web sites, and more—all in a matter of minutes.

In addition, content cartridges are available for the course management systems **WebCT** and **Blackboard.**

These platforms provide instructors with user-friendly, flexible teaching tools. Please contact your local McGraw-Hill Ryerson *i*Learning Sales Specialist for details.

Student Supplements

Online Learning Centre

The Online Learning Centre for the text offers chapter outlines, practice quizzes, flashcards, interactive exercises, Internet activities, relevant Web links, a searchable Glossary, a career appendix, and a statistics primer. Visit www.mcgrawhill.ca/college/santrock.

Learning Objects

McGraw-Hill Ryerson has developed a library of learning objects, designed to provide an interactive, audio-visual learning environment for topics that prove challenging for students. Visit the Online Learning Centre to access the Learning Objects for the text.

Study Guide—Now Online and Interactive

The online interactive Study Guide is a valuable resource that provides students with a comprehensive set of activities for each chapter, including learning goals, chapter overview, review questions, in-your-own-words exercise, correcting-the-incorrect quiz, and a multiple-choice practice test. Please contact your *i*Learning Sales Specialist for details on how to make this online learning resource available for your students.

InPsych Student CD-ROM

InPsych sets a new standard for introductory psychology multimedia. This CD-ROM is organized according to the text chapter outlines and features more than 60 interactive exercises chosen to illustrate core introductory psychology concepts.

PowerWeb

PowerWeb extends the learning experience beyond the core textbook by offering all the latest news and developments pertinent to your course via the Internet, without all the clutter and dead links of a typical online search.

PowerWeb offers current articles, curriculum-based materials, weekly updates with assessment information, timely world news, and refereed Web links. In addition, PowerWeb provides an array of helpful learning aids, including self-grading quizzes and interactive glossaries and exercises. Students may also access study tips, conduct online research, and learn about different career paths. To learn more, visit the PowerWeb site at http://dushkin.com/powerweb.

Acknowledgements

U.S. Acknowledgements

Many people guided the U.S. edition of *Psychology,* on which this Canadian edition is based, including the McGraw-Hill team of Steve DeBow, President; Thalia Dorwick, Editor in Chief; Steve Rutter, Publisher; Melissa Mashburn, Senior Editor; and Chris Hall, Senior Marketing Manager.

In-Depth Reviewers of the U.S. Seventh Edition

We benefited considerably from the advice and analysis provided by a number of in-depth reviewers of the U.S. book's seventh edition. The following individuals provided this input:

Mihaly Csikszentmihalyi, Claremont Graduate University (positive psychology)

Larry Cauller, University of Texas at Dallas (neuroscience)

Susan Swithers, Purdue University (chapters 3 and 5 and author of end-of-chapter exercises)

John Mitterer, Brock University (author of many of the *Critical Controversy* boxes)

Meredith Stanford-Pollack, University of Massachusetts at Lowell (diversity)

Saera Khan, Western Washington University (illustrations)

Reviewers of the U.S. Seventh Edition

The following psychologists also helped to make the U. S. seventh edition a much better text through their thoughtful reviews:

Richard Anderson, Bowling Green State University; Jim Backlund, Kirtland Community College; Stella B. Baldwin, Wake Technical Community College; Pearl Berman, Indiana University of Pennsylvania; Joy L. Berrenberg, University of Colorado at Denver; Frederick M. Brown, Penn State University; Richard Cavasina, California University of Pennsylvania; George A. Cicala, University of Delaware; Pamela Costa, Tacoma Commmunity College; Donna Dahlgren, Indiana University Southeast; Leta Fenell, Chesapeake College; Roseanne L. Flores, Hunter College; Bety Jane Fratzke, Indiana Wesleyan University; Robert Gallen, Indiana University of Pennsylvania; J. P. Garofalo, University of Pittsburgh; Michael Kaye Garza, Brookhaven College; Roderick C. Gillis, University of Miami; Leslie Grout, Hudson Valley Community College; Arthur Gutman, Florida Institute of Technology; Christine Harness, University of Wisconsin, Milwaukee; James R. Heard, Antelope Valley College; Paul Hernandez, South Texas Community College; Karen Jordan, University of Illinois at Chicago; Kevin Keating, Broward Community College; Saera Khan, Western Washington University; Brian Kim, University of Maryland, College Park; Michele K. Lewis, Northern Virginia Community College, Annandale; Wanda McCarthy, Northern Kentucky University; Diane Martichuski, University of Colorado at Boulder; Glenn E. Meyer, Trinity University; Fred Miller, Oregon Health Sciences University, Portland Community College; Richard Miller, Western Kentucky University; Ann Miner, Indiana University of Pennsylvania; Arthur G. Olguin, Santa Barbara City College; Barbara Radigan, Community College of Allegheny County, Allegheny Campus; Pamela Regan, California State University, Los Angeles; Bob Riesenberg, Whatcom Community College; Susan J. Shapiro, Indiana University East; John E. Sparrow, University of New Hampshire, Manchester; Meredith Stanford-Pollock, University of Massachusetts at Lowell; Susan Swithers, Purdue University; Jeremy Turner, The University of Tennessee at Martin; David Wasieeski, Valdosta State University; Marek Wosinski, Arizona State University

Canadian Acknowledgements

I mean it when I say that McGraw-Hill Ryerson is truly a collection of first-rate people dedicated to bringing excellent educational products to the Canadian marketplace. I will always remain grateful to MHR for allowing me the opportunity to make my own little contribution to the education of budding Canadian psychologists.

In particular, James Buchanan, my Executive Sponsoring Editor, has been tremendously supportive of my efforts on this new edition. I am also especially grateful to Jodi Lewchuk, my Developmental Editor, for her expert and patient input and supervision. I also want to thank Joanne Limebeer, Supervising Editor; Paula Brown, Production Coordinator; Liz Harasmyczuk, Designer; and Gillian Scobie, Copy Editor. This edition is far stronger for all of their hard work.

I also want to thank the McGraw-Hill Ryerson *i*Learning Sales Specialists whose job it is to bring this book to Canadian teachers and students of psychology and to bring back their comments to McGraw-Hill Ryerson and to me.

I again owe a debt of gratitude to my students and colleagues at Brock University. Many of my colleagues at Brock yet again patiently provided their expert advice, including Karen Arnell, Michael Ashton, Kathy Belicki, Tony Bogaert, Angela Book, Stefan Brudzynski, Kimberly Cote, Drew Dane, Nancy DeCourville, David DiBattista, Jane Dywan, Dawn Good, Carolyn Hafer, Gordon Hodson, Harry Hunt, Nancy Johnston, Zopito Marini, Tanya Martini, Cheryl McCormick, Cathy Mondloch, Cameron Muir, Tim Murphy, Linda Rose-Krasnor, Stan Sadava, Sid Segalowitz, Paul Tyson, and Teena Willoughby.

Finally, I want to thank my immediate family: my wife, Heather Hagerman-Mitterer, and my step-daughters, Kendra and Kayleigh Hagerman, for their tolerant and loving support. There were, as you might imagine, many, many late nights.

In-Depth Reviewers of the Third Canadian Edition

Several reviewers offered incredibly thoughtful comments on an earlier draft of *Psychology,* Third Canadian Edition. In the process they demonstrated their own mastery of psychology and their deep commitment to the education of Canadian students through their careful and thorough feedback:

Jeffrey Adams, Trent University
Elizabeth Bowering, Mount Saint Vincent University
Michael T. Bradley, University of New Brunswick
Ken Cramer, University of Windsor
Kathy Denton, Douglas College
Jillian Esmonde-Moore, Georgian College
Verian Farnsworth, Kwantlen University College
Ken Fowler, Memorial University of Newfoundland
Karen Fraser, Loyalist College
David Furrow, Mount Saint Vincent University
Crystal Kotow-Sullivan, St. Clair College of Applied Arts and Technology
Richard Kruk, University of Manitoba
Elizabeth Levin, Laurentian University
Rick Maddigan, Memorial University of Newfoundland
Keith F. Mauthe, Lethbridge Community College
James D. A. Parker, Trent University
Sara Pawson Herrington, Kwantlen University College
Suzanne Prior, St. Thomas University
David Reagan, Camosun College
Donald Sharpe, University of Regina
Harry Strub, University of Winnipeg

Many others (some Americans and many Canadians) were warmly supportive of my efforts to create this new edition. Canadian psychology has much to be proud of and I thank the following people for their gracious assistance:

Shimon Amir, Concordia University
Sibylle Artz, University of Victoria
Andreas Arvanitogiannis, Concordia University
John Berry, Queens University (retired)
Ellen Bialystok, York University
Ramona Bobocel, University of Waterloo
Roger Broughton, University of Ottawa
Joseph De Koninck, University of Ottawa
Natalie Durand-Bush, University of Ottawa
Joan Durrant, University of Manitoba
Victoria Esses, University of Western Ontario
Raymond Fancher, York University
Nancy Galambos, University of Alberta

Robert Gifford, University of Victoria
Vinod Goel, York University
Christopher Green, York University
Leslie S. Greenberg, York University
Laurence Harris, York University
N. C. Higgins, St. Thomas University
Ron Holden, Queen's University
Michaela Hynie, York University
Larry Jacoby, Washington University in St. Louis
Herbert Jenkins, McMaster University (retired)
Laurence Kirmayer, McGill University
Barbara Kisilevsky, Queen's University
Raymond Klein, Dalhousie University
Bryan Kolb, University of Lethbridge
Robert Ladouceur, Université Laval
Raymond Lam, University of British Columbia
Antoon Leenaars, University of Windsor
Alex McKay, The Sex Information and Education Council of Canada
Donald Meichenbaum, University of Waterloo
Sean Moore, Mount Saint Vincent University
Moris Moscovitch, University of Toronto
Patrick O'Neill, Acadia University (retired)
David Olson, Ontario Institute for Studies in Education
Linda Parker, Wilfrid Laurier University
Sampo Paunonen, University of Western Ontario
Jeff Pfeifer, University of Regina
John Pinel, University of British Columbia
Peter Pirolli, XEROX Parc
Janet Polivy, University of Toronto
Steve Potter, Georgia Institute of Technology and Emory University
Tim Pychyl, Carleton University
Sandra Pyke, York University (retired)
Jillian Roberts, University of Victoria
William Roberts, University of Western Ontario
Donald Saklofske, University of Saskatchewan
Mark Schaller, University of British Columbia
Chip Scialfa, University of Calgary
Allison Sekuler, McMaster University
Shepard Siegel, McMaster University
Cannie Stark, University of Regina
Diane Ste-Marie, University of Ottawa
Michael Stones, Lakehead University
Cornelia Wieman, University of Toronto and McMaster University
Margo Wilson, McMaster University
Mark Zanna, University of Waterloo

Finally, I wish to thank all of the other people whose earlier input continues to be reflected in this new edition.

John Mitterer
Brock University
February 2006

1 What Is Psychology?

CHAPTER QUESTIONS

1 What is psychology and how did it develop?

2 How do contemporary psychologists approach the study of behaviour?

3 Can psychology make us happier?

4 What types of careers are available to psychology majors?

5 What study habits and skills can help me in this course?

Do you ever wonder about things? Curiosity is surely one of the traits we human beings share most often. And we are perhaps most curious when it comes to ourselves and other people. Why do we have trouble losing weight or quitting smoking? What happens when people develop schizophrenia? What does it mean to live with stress? How can we do well in our studies? Why do atrocities happen during warfare? Why is music so interesting? Why do disasters bring out the best in some people? There are so many interesting questions.

Consider Dr. David Suzuki, one of Canada's best-recognized and most loved scientists. Along with many other Japanese-Canadians, his family was interned for four years during World War II. He overcame early feelings of not belonging to have many friends in school, participate in and win public speaking contests, and become president of his high school class. He completed his postsecondary studies quickly on scholarships to American universities and returned to Canada, where he taught at the University of Alberta and the University of British Columbia. His fame as a geneticist grew and he was honoured with many awards, including being named as the best young research scientist in Canada three years in a row. His popularity soared when the CBC began broadcasting his programs, such as "Quirks and Quarks" and "The Nature of Things." In 2004, a CBC poll identified him as one of the ten greatest Canadians of all time.

Suzuki's triumphs raise interesting questions: What factors enable some children to achieve greatness? Is it possible for parents, teachers, and others to shape a child's life and turn him or her into a world-class thinker? In Suzuki's case, he began learning about nature by the age of four, learning the names of the trees, fish, and birds while fishing with his father. Like many Japanese-Canadians, Suzuki's parents had a great respect for education and expected him to work hard to become successful.

Yet when some parents try to get their children to become successful using strategies similar to those of Suzuki's parents, the children end up being miserable and the parents frustrated. What other factors could be involved in Suzuki's success as a scientist beyond supportive parenting and an excellent education? Might David Suzuki have special genes or intellectual skills that most others lack?

The impulse to understand ourselves motivates psychologists, just as it motivates all of us. What differentiates psychologists from most of us is that they take a scientific approach to finding answers to their questions. In this chapter, we explore the scientific approach to psychology, first by surveying the roots of psychological science and the development of different approaches to the study of human behaviour. Second, we explore a variety of career opportunities available to individuals with degrees in psychology. And, third, to help you get the most out of this book and to understand psychology more clearly, we discuss some study strategies and ways to think critically, both in class and in everyday life.

Through his foundation, David Suzuki continues to influence our understanding of how science and technology affect our lives and the world around us (www.davidsuzuki.org). *What do you think might have motivated David Suzuki to become a great scientist?*

① EXPLORING PSYCHOLOGY

— Studying the   — A Quest for   — Early Scientific
   Mind and   Answers to   Approaches to
   Behaviour   Ancient Questions   Psychology

What is psychology and how did it develop?

What motivates people such as David Suzuki to become the best in the world at what they do is one of the many questions that psychologists study. What else do psychologists do?

Imagine that you are seated at a dinner table next to someone you have never met. What comes to mind when you find out she is a psychologist? Might you think, "Uh, oh, I'd better be on my guard because she is going to "psychoanalyze" me and find out what I am really like."?

Many psychologists do, in fact, analyze people's problems and try to help them cope more effectively. However, many psychologists are researchers, not therapists. No single image captures the varied activities of psychologists. Consider the following descriptions of some contemporary psychologists at work:

- A cognitive psychologist painstakingly constructs the thousands of steps in a computer program that, when presented with hundreds of sentences, will learn language as an infant does.
- A research psychologist trained in physiological psychology and neuroscience injects epinephrine into a rat that has learned a maze, to determine how that hormone affects the rat's memory.
- A clinical psychologist probes a depressed client's thoughts for clues about the cause of the depression and thinks about ways to help the client become psychologically healthier.
- A school psychologist with a background in linguistics and bilingualism designs a program to immerse English-speaking children in French for much of their early childhood education in Ontario.
- A psychologist interested in gender and women's issues teaches at a community college and works with her college and the community to eliminate sexual harassment.
- An organizational psychologist runs a consulting firm that advises corporations on ways to improve communication and work productivity.
- A forensic psychologist is a trial consultant who prepares witnesses to testify and teaches attorneys how to present themselves to jurors.

These are but a few of the many different portraits of psychologists. As you read further, you will discover that psychology is a diverse field and that psychologists have wide-ranging interests.

Studying the Mind and Behaviour

We all wonder about human behaviour, both our own and other people's. We try to explain it and predict it using **folk psychology**, the common-sense conceptual framework we use to make sense of our behaviour and that of other people and animals (L. R. Baker, 2001). Because we are all folk psychologists, scientific psychology may strike you as being just more simple common sense. But researchers often turn up the unexpected in human behaviour. For example, it may seem obvious that couples who live together (cohabit) before marriage have a better chance of making the marriage last. After all, practice makes perfect, doesn't it? But researchers have actually found a higher rate of success for couples who marry before living together (Nock, 1995). It might also seem commonsensical that we would experience more stress and be less happy if we had to function in many different roles than if we functioned in only one role. However, women who engage in multiple roles (such as wife, mother, and career woman) report

folk psychology The common-sense conceptual framework we use to make sense of our behaviour and that of other people and animals.

Peanuts reprinted by permission of United Feature Syndicate, Inc.

more satisfaction with their lives than women who engage in a single role or fewer roles (such as wife or wife and mother; Watkins & Subich, 1995). As you can see, psychology doesn't accept assumptions at face value, however reasonable they sound. Instead, psychology is a rigorous discipline that tests assumptions (Pittenger, 2003).

Formally defined, **psychology** is the scientific study of behaviour and mental processes. There are three key terms in this definition: science, behaviour, and mental processes. To understand what psychology is, you need to know what each of these terms means.

Unlike folk psychology, scientific methods are not casual. As a **science**, psychology uses systematic methods to observe, describe, predict, and explain behaviour. Researchers carefully and precisely plan and conduct their studies (Kantowitz, Roediger, & Elmes, 2005). In psychology, it is desirable to obtain results that describe the behaviour of many different people. For example, researchers might construct a questionnaire on sexual attitudes and give it to hundreds of individuals. They might spend considerable time devising the questions and determining the backgrounds of the people chosen to participate in the survey. The researchers might try to predict the sexual activity of university students based on whether their attitudes are liberal or conservative or on their sexual knowledge, for example. After the psychologists have analyzed their data, they will also want to explain their results. If the researchers found that university students are less sexually active than they were a decade ago, for example, they might ask, "Is the reason an increased fear of sexually transmitted diseases?" Because psychologists use the same research methods as physicists, biologists, and other scientists, psychology is a scientific discipline.

Let's now examine what behaviour and mental processes are. **Behaviour** is everything we do that can be directly observed—two people kissing, a baby crying, a university student going on a ski trip.

Mental processes are trickier to define than behaviour; they are the thoughts, feelings, and motives that each of us experiences privately but that cannot be observed directly. Though we cannot directly see thoughts and feelings, they are nonetheless real. They include *thinking* about kissing someone, a baby's *feelings* when its mother leaves the room, and a student's *memory* of a ski trip.

Controversy is also a part of science. As scientists conduct research and uncover new findings, they refine or even discard ideas. Healthy debate characterizes the field of psychology. A new psychological perspective has sometimes arisen when one scientist questions the views of another. Ongoing debate and controversy are signs that psychology today is a vigorous, healthy discipline, both in Canada and worldwide (Dobson, 1995). In each chapter of this text, you will find a Critical Reflections box that focuses on a current debate in psychology.

A Quest for Answers to Ancient Questions

Though scientific psychology is little more than a hundred years old, it seeks to answer questions that people have been asking for thousands of years:

How do our senses perceive the world?
What is the connection between what we think and how we behave?

psychology The scientific study of behaviour and mental processes.

science In psychology, the use of systematic methods to observe, describe, predict, and explain behaviour.

behaviour Everything we do that can be directly observed.

mental processes The thoughts, feelings, and motives that each of us experiences privately but that cannot be observed directly.

How do we learn? What is memory?

Are we in conscious control of our lives or is our behaviour determined by unconscious forces?

Why does one person grow and flourish whereas another person struggles in life?

What makes some people smarter than others?

Do dreams matter?

Why do some children so strongly resemble their parents in how they think and act? How do some children turn out so differently?

Can people learn to be happier and more optimistic?

The questions are old, but the science is young. From the time human language included the word *why* and became rich enough to let people talk about the past, we have been creating myths to explain why things are the way they are. Ancient myths attributed most important events to the pleasure or displeasure of the gods: When a volcano erupted, the gods were angry; if two people fell in love, they had been hit by Cupid's arrows. Gradually, myths gave way to philosophy, the rational investigation of the underlying principles of being and knowledge. People attempted to explain events in terms of natural rather than supernatural causes (Viney & King, 2003).

Historians believe that the idea of an independent human mind may have developed around the sixth century B.C. In India, for example, the Buddha said that it was our own sensations and perceptions that combined to form our human thoughts. The Chinese sage Confucius (551–479 B.C.) believed that the power of thought and decision lay within us (Hunt, 1993).

In the Western tradition, philosophy came of age in ancient Greece in the fourth and fifth centuries B.C. Socrates, Plato, Aristotle, and others debated the nature of thought and behaviour, including the possible link between the mind and the body (Green & Groff, 2003). Later philosophers, especially René Descartes, argued that the mind and body were completely separate, and focused their attention on the mind. Psychology grew out of this tradition of thinking about the mind as distinct from the body (Danziger, 1997; Benjafield, 2004).

Psychology did not emerge only from philosophy. Psychology also has roots in the natural sciences of biology and physiology (Green, Shore & Teo, 2001). The intellectual atmosphere when psychology emerged as a science in the late nineteenth century was dominated by the work of the British naturalist Charles Darwin (1809–1882).

In 1859, Darwin published his ideas in *On the Origin of Species*. He proposed the principle of **natural selection**, an evolutionary process that favours organisms that are best adapted to reproduce and survive. He believed that organisms reproduce at rates that would cause enormous increases in the populations of most species, yet noted that populations remain nearly constant. Darwin reasoned that an intense, constant struggle for food, water, and resources must occur among the young born in each generation, because many of the young do not survive. Those that do survive to adulthood pass their genes on to the next generation. Darwin concluded that organisms with biological features that led to more successful reproduction were better represented in subsequent generations. Over the course of many generations, organisms with these characteristics would constitute an ever-growing percentage, producing a gradual modification of the whole population. If environmental conditions changed, however, other characteristics might become favoured by natural selection, moving the process in a different direction.

Psychology has recently rediscovered Darwin's evolutionary theory and applied it to behaviour. There is an especially strong interest today in interpreting behaviour in terms of its adaptive value and evolutionary development (Cosmides & others, 2003; Larsen & Buss, 2005), including social behaviour (Schaller & Crandall, 2004).

In addition to Darwin's influence on psychology's emergence, physiologists in the mid-nineteenth century, such as the German Johannes Müller, were already proposing that the brain's role is to associate incoming sensory information with appropriate motor responses.

Thus, by the late nineteenth century, conditions were ripe for psychology to emerge as a scientific discipline, a hybrid offspring of philosophy and natural science. Indeed, as

natural selection The principle that the organisms best adapted to their environment are the most likely to survive, reproduce, and pass on their genes to their offspring.

we will see shortly, it was a philosopher-physician who put the pieces of the philosophy–natural science puzzle together to create the academic discipline of psychology.

Early Scientific Approaches to Psychology

The German physiologist Wilhelm Wundt (1832–1920) is most often regarded as the founding father of modern psychology. Students trained by Wundt formed the first generation of North American psychologists. James Mark Baldwin, trained in the Wundtian tradition, established the first psychological laboratory in Canada at the University of Toronto in 1889 (Green, 2004). The most influential of Wundt's students was E. B. Titchener (1867–1927), an Englishman, who put his own spin on Wundt's psychology of consciousness after he immigrated to the United States to teach psychology at Cornell University in Ithaca, New York.

Some historians like to say that modern psychology was born in December 1879 at the University of Leipzig, when Wundt and two young students performed an experiment to measure the time lag between the instant at which a person heard a sound and the instant at which that person actually pressed a telegraph key to signal that he had heard. The experiment was one of many attempts to measure human behaviour through physiological measurement.

What was so special about this experiment? Wundt's experiment was about the workings of the brain: he was trying to measure the amount of time it took the human brain and nervous system to translate information into action. At the heart of this experiment was the idea that mental processes could be studied quantitatively—that is, that mental processes could be measured. This focus ushered in the new science of psychology.

Structuralism **Structuralism** is the label given to the search for the basic elements or "structures" of mental life (Hergenhahn, 2001). For example, the structuralists described three different dimensions of *feeling*: pleasure/displeasure, tension/relaxation, and excitement/depression. Although Wundt himself is often described as a structuralist, it is historically more accurate to ascribe that label to the approach of his student, E. B. Titchener (Danziger, 1980).

The most common method used in the study of mental structures was *introspection* (literally, "looking inside"). For this type of experiment, a person was placed in a laboratory setting and was asked to think (introspect) about what was going on as various events took place. For example, the individual might be subjected to a sharp, repetitive clicking sound and asked to report whatever conscious feelings the clicking produced. What made this method scientific was the systematic, detailed self-reports required of the person in the controlled laboratory setting.

These studies focused mainly on sensation and perception because they were the easiest processes to break down into component parts. For example, Titchener used the introspective method to study taste. He trained participants to identify and record their taste sensations. The outcome was the identification of four components of taste: bitter, sweet, salty, and sour. In the long run, though, conscious introspection was not a very productive method of exploring the basic elements of human behaviour.

Functionalism In contrast to structuralism, which focused on describing the components of the mind, **functionalism** emphasized the functions of mind and behaviour in adapting to the environment. The structuralists were less interested in the person's interaction with the environment, a major theme of the functionalists. Thus, in a way, the structuralists were looking *inside* the mind, searching for its structures, whereas the functionalists were looking more at what was going on in the person's interaction with the *outside* world.

The American psychologist William James (1842–1910) and other functionalists did not believe in the existence of elementary, rigid structures of the mind. James saw the mind as flexible and fluid, characterized by constant change and adaptation in response to a flow of information. He called this flow a *stream of consciousness*.

WILHELM WUNDT (1832–1920)
Founded the first psychology laboratory (with his co-workers) in 1879 at the University of Leipzig in Germany.

WILLIAM JAMES (1842–1910)
What was his functionalist approach like?

structuralism An early school of psychology that attempted to discover the basic elements (structures) of the human mind.

functionalism An early school of psychology that emphasized the interaction between the mind and the outside environment.

MAX WERTHEIMER (1880–1943)
Founded the Gestalt school of
psychology.

Gestalt Psychology   The founder of **Gestalt psychology**, Czech-born German psychologist Max Wertheimer (1880–1943), criticized structuralism and the introspection approach as misleading. He argued that consciousness is best understood as the perception of unified wholes or "gestalts," which are greater than the sum of their parts.

For example, think about a lighted sign made up of a series of successively flashing lights in the shape of an arrow. You perceive a whole, an arrow moving in the direction of the tip. But the parts, the individual lights, are stationary. Your perception of movement comes from the brain but only when the parts are in the correct relationship to each other. This is *relational determinism*. The parts must be in the proper order and timing to result in the intended perception.

As a second example, if you hear a piece of music played at a different pitch by a different instrument the tune might puzzle you but your brain may supply the proper timing and recognition of the tune. This illustrates the Gestalt principle of *transposability*. If the parts, the notes, are at a higher or lower pitch, they are different but the whole, the tune, is still recognized as the same. In other words, it is not the parts that are important for the perception of the tune, it is the pattern or organization of parts.

Gestalt psychologists went further and argued that parts can change because they are in a relation to a whole. Apply this to yourself and your experience in different groups. In some groups you are lively, in other groups you are quiet. Not only is the whole group different from the sum of the parts but you as a part differ because of the particular group.

The following review should help you reach the learning goals related to this initial exploration of the field of psychology.

> ## > reflect and review
>
> **1 Explain what psychology is and how it developed.**
> - Define psychology, and explain the three terms contained in the definition.
> - Describe the contributions of philosophy and natural science to psychology.
> - Define structuralism, functionalism, and Gestalt psychology and explain how they differ.
>
> *Are there some questions about your mind and behaviour that a deeper understanding of psychology might help you answer?*

② CONTEMPORARY APPROACHES TO PSYCHOLOGY

The Behavioural Approach	The Psychodynamic Approach	The Cognitive Approach	The Behavioural Neuroscience Approach	The Evolutionary Psychology Approach	The Sociocultural Approach

Gestalt psychology An early school of psychology that emphasized that, in perception, the whole is greater than the sum of the parts.

How do contemporary psychologists approach the study of behaviour?

The three approaches we have just discussed—structuralism, functionalism, and Gestalt psychology—are no longer considered to be contemporary approaches to psychology. However, contemporary psychology has absorbed some aspects of these approaches. Psychologists still have an interest in the structures of the brain and how they function. They also stress the importance of the person's interaction with the environment and the importance of the interaction of parts to perceive the whole. Psychologists today realize that human thought and behaviour are influenced by many factors, including common biological heritage, biological variations from person to person, and experience. In addition to immediate environmental influences, such as our physical and social surroundings, psychologists also recognize the broader influence of culture.

Efforts to understand the complexity of mental processes and behaviour have given rise to a number of broad approaches in psychology. The following sections will introduce six contemporary approaches: behavioural, psychodynamic, cognitive, behavioural neuroscience, evolutionary psychology, and sociocultural. Knowing about these approaches is important because many of the debates and controversies in psychology reflect differences in researchers' perspectives. In addition, much of the research discussed later in the text can be understood more clearly against the background of one or more of these approaches.

As you consider the six approaches and how they might illuminate human thought and behaviour, keep three ideas in mind:

1. Although psychology may often seem to focus on the individual, human beings are profoundly social. They need other people to satisfy their wants and needs. Parents, teachers, peers, friends, and partners in close relationships play important roles in our socially connected lives (Borstein & Bradley, 2003; Collins & others, 2003). How we treat others and they us, whether caring or hurting, stirs our thoughts and emotions.
2. Theories can help us to understand human behaviour in general, but there is still enormous individual variation. No two lives play out in the same way. Roommates, parents and children, teachers and students, and friends and lovers soon discover their differences. One task of psychology is to chart not only our commonalities but also what makes us unique (Stanovich, 2004). Your mixture of genes and experiences cannot be duplicated. Even in these days of animal cloning and the potential for human cloning, experience uniquely imprints each person's life (Gottlieb, 2002a; Moore, 2001).
3. Keep in mind that one approach is not necessarily better than another. Some approaches are more useful in some situations and at certain times in the development of the field. Individual psychologists may become invested in a particular approach, but all six approaches provide valid ways of looking at human behaviour. Just as blueprints, floor plans, and photographs are all valid ways of looking at a house, some approaches are better for some purposes than others. For instance, a floor plan is more useful than a photograph for deciding how much lumber to buy. Similarly, the behavioural neuroscience approach is more useful than the sociocultural approach for explaining the fundamental aspects of perception. At the same time, the sociocultural approach is more useful than the behavioural neuroscience approach for understanding how to reduce prejudice and discrimination.

The Behavioural Approach

The **behavioural approach** emphasizes the scientific study of observable behavioural responses and their environmental determinants. In other words, the behavioural approach focuses on interactions with the environment that can be seen and measured. The principles of the behavioural approach also have been widely applied to help people change their behaviour for the better. The psychologists who adopt this approach are called *behaviourists*. Under the intellectual leadership of John B. Watson (1878–1958) and B. F. Skinner (1904–1990), behaviourism dominated psychological research during the first half of the twentieth century (Benjafield, 2004; Mills, 1998).

While many studies with a behavioural approach take place in experimental laboratories under carefully controlled conditions, some take place in natural settings, such as schools and homes. Skinner himself often conducted applied research and even studied the effect of a controlled environment called an Air-Crib on his own daughter.

Skinner emphasized that what we *do* is the ultimate test of who we are, not what we think. He believed that rewards and punishments determine our behaviour. For example, a child might behave in a well-mannered fashion because her parents have rewarded this behaviour. An adult might work hard at a job because of the money he gets for his effort. We do these things, say behaviourists, not because of an inborn

behavioural approach Emphasizes the scientific study of behaviour and asserts that behaviour is shaped by the environment.

B. F. Skinner was a tinkerer who liked to make new gadgets. The younger of his two daughters, Deborah, spent some time in Skinner's enclosed Air-Crib. Some critics accused Skinner of monstrous experimentation with his children; however, the early controlled environment has not had any noticeable harmful effects. Debbie, shown here as a child with her parents, is currently a successful artist, is married, and lives in London. *In what ways would a controlled environment (such as the Air-Crib) for very young children help their development?*

motivation to be competent people but rather because of the environmental conditions we have experienced and continue to experience (Skinner, 1938).

Contemporary behaviourists still emphasize the importance of observing behaviour to understand an individual and continue to use the rigorous sorts of experimental methods advocated by Watson and Skinner (Martin & Pear, 2003; Watson & Tharp, 2003). They also continue to stress the importance of environmental determinants of behaviour (Baldwin & Baldwin, 2001; Spiegler & Guerremont, 2003). However, not every behaviourist accepts the earlier behaviourists' rejection of thought processes (often called cognition).

Social cognitive theory stresses that behaviour is determined not only by environmental conditions but also by how thoughts modify the effects of environment on behaviour (Bandura, 1986, 2001). Social cognitive theory was proposed by Albert Bandura, who was born in Alberta, received his undergraduate education at the University of British Columbia, and has since gone on to become one of the ten most *cited* psychologists (a *citation* occurs when one scholar makes note of the work of another scholar; in this paragraph, we are citing Bandura's work). Bandura believes that imitation is one of the main ways in which we learn about our world. To reproduce a model's behaviour, we must enter and store the information in memory, which is a mental (cognitive) process. Thus social cognitive theorists have broadened the scope of behaviourism to include not only observed behaviour but also the ways in which the mind processes information about the environment.

In one of Bandura's classic experiments (Bandura, 1965), children watched a film in which a model was rewarded, punished, or experienced no consequences for being aggressive. Bandura observed how aggressive the children were after they watched the film. He found that children who watched the model being rewarded for being aggressive were subsequently more aggressive themselves than children who saw the model being punished or receiving no consequences for being aggressive.

What can the behavioural approach tell us about David Suzuki? Behaviourists would tell us not to look inside David Suzuki to try to find out what makes him a great scientist. According to behaviourists, motives and feelings cannot be directly observed so

social cognitive theory Stresses that behaviour is determined not only by environmental conditions but also by how thoughts modify the impact of environment on behaviour.

they really won't help us understand his behaviour. Behaviourists would examine Suzuki's learning history. They would note his practice for, and participation in, public-speaking contests. As well, they would note the praise he earned from his parents and teachers for his achievements in school. Social cognitive theorists, like Bandura, would stress that Suzuki developed his scientific skills through extensive observational learning. They would also suggest that David Suzuki developed positive expectations and the self-confidence to become a great scientist through his interactions with others.

The Psychodynamic Approach

The **psychodynamic approach** emphasizes unconscious thought, conflict between biological instincts and society's demands, and early family experiences. This approach argues that unlearned biological instincts, especially sexual and aggressive impulses, influence the way people think, feel, and behave. These instincts, buried deep within the unconscious mind, are often at odds with society's demands. Although Sigmund Freud (1856–1939), the founding father of the psychodynamic approach, saw much of psychological development as instinctual, he believed that early relationships with parents are the chief forces that shape an individual's personality. Freud's (1917) theory was the basis for the therapeutic technique that he termed *psychoanalysis*. His approach was controversial when he introduced it in Vienna at the beginning of the twentieth century. However, his ideas played a major role in shaping 20th century thought, and many psychologists still find his insights about human behaviour valuable (Gedo, 2002).

SIGMUND FREUD (1856–1939)
What was the nature of his psychoanalytic approach?

Unlike the behavioural approach, the psychodynamic approach focuses almost exclusively on clinical applications rather than on experimental research. For this reason, psychodynamic theories always have been controversial and difficult to validate. Nonetheless, they are an important part of psychology. Today's psychodynamic theories tend to place less emphasis on sexual instincts and more on cultural experiences as determinants of behaviour.

What can the psychodynamic approach tell us about David Suzuki? The psychodynamic approach suggests that David Suzuki is likely to be unaware of why he became a prominent scientist and popularizer of science and why he behaves the way he does. It also suggests that his early experiences with his parents likely formed his outgoing personality and ability to get along with others.

The Cognitive Approach

According to cognitive psychologists, your brain hosts or embodies a "mind," whose mental processes allow you to remember, make decisions, plan, set goals, and be creative (J. A. Anderson, 2005; Sternberg, 2003a). The **cognitive approach**, then, emphasizes the mental processes involved in knowing: how we direct our attention, how we perceive, how we remember, and how we think and solve problems. For example, cognitive psychologists want to know how we solve algebraic equations, why we remember some things for only a short time but remember others for a lifetime, and how we can use imagery to plan for the future (Benjafield, 1997; Bruning & others, 2004).

Cognitive psychologists view the mind as an active and aware problem-solving system (Baddeley, 2000, 2003). This positive view contrasts with the behavioural view, which portrays behaviour as controlled by external environmental forces. The cognitive view also contrasts with pessimistic views (such as those of Freud) that see human behaviour as being controlled by instincts or other unconscious forces. In the cognitive view, an individual's mental processes control behaviour through memories, perceptions, images, and thinking (Solso, MacLin, & MacLin, 2005).

One area of cognitive research that occasionally gets attention in news coverage of criminal trials is eyewitness identification (e.g., Yuille & Daylen, 1998). The potential bias in eyewitness identification was revealed in a classic experiment in which students

psychodynamic approach Emphasizes the unconscious aspects of the mind, conflict between biological instincts and society's demands, and early family experiences.

cognitive approach Focuses on the mental processes involved in knowing: how we direct our attention, perceive, remember, think, and solve problems.

in an introductory psychology class were asked to view 10 "criminals" (actually graduate and senior undergraduate white males) for 25 seconds each (Brown, Deffenbacher, & Sturgill, 1977). The experimenter told the class to observe the "criminals" carefully because they would later have to pick out the "criminals" from mug shots. Ninety minutes later the students looked at 15 mug shots and were asked whether each person had appeared earlier in front of the class. Five of the 15 mug shots were of people who actually had appeared. These five "criminals" were correctly identified 72 percent of the time. However, the ten "noncriminals" were incorrectly identified as having appeared in front of the class 45 percent of the time. This study indicates that people in mug shots might be falsely accused and reflects how inaccurate our memories can sometimes be.

What can the cognitive approach tell us about David Suzuki? Cognitive psychologists would be impressed with David Suzuki's ability to process information, especially his ability to concentrate and focus his attention. They would also be interested in his ability to remember the volume of scientific information he encounters every day. Cognitive psychologists might be intrigued by Suzuki's ability to solve problems and make decisions, not only while working in the laboratory or for his foundation, but in his daily life as well.

The Behavioural Neuroscience Approach

The **behavioural neuroscience approach** emphasizes that the brain and nervous system are central to understanding behaviour, thought, and emotion. Neurobiologists believe that thoughts have a physical basis in the brain (Kolb & Whishaw, 2003; Rains, 2002). They also believe that when injury and disease assault the brain, its powerful role in influencing behaviour becomes apparent (Melzack, 1989; Mitchell, 1989). The human brain and nervous system constitute the most complex, intricate, and elegant system imaginable. The human brain is only a 1.5-kilogram lump of matter, but in this lump are more than 100 billion interconnected nerve cells. Electrical impulses zoom through our brain cells, and chemical substances are released as we think, feel, and act.

Behavioural neuroscience originated with the 1949 publication, by McGill University psychologist D. O. Hebb, of *The Organization of Behaviour*. Hebb stressed the need for an interdisciplinary approach to brain and behaviour, emphasized the central problem of internal mental processes, critiqued then-current theories of learning and perception, and proposed a broad and imaginative theory of his own (Fentress, 1999).

Much of what we know about the brain comes from research on animals that have simpler brains with far fewer nerve cells than humans (Changeux & Chavillion, 1995; Wicks, Roehrig, & Rankin, 1996). Consider the memory of the sea slug, a tiny snail with only about 10,000 nerve cells. The sea slug is a slow creature, but if given an electric shock to its tail, it withdraws the tail quickly—and even more quickly if the tail was previously shocked. In a primitive way, the sea slug remembers. The memory is written in chemical code, called a *neurotransmitter*. Shocking the sea slug's tail releases a neurotransmitter that reminds the organism that the tail was previously shocked. This memory informs the nerve cells to send out chemical commands to retract the tail (Kandel & Schwartz, 1982). As nature builds complexity out of simplicity, so the mechanism used by the sea slug may work in the human brain as well. In humans, the memory might come from the sight of a close friend, a dog's bark, or the sound of a car horn. Thus, neurotransmitters are the ink with which memories are written.

What can the behavioural neuroscience approach tell us about David Suzuki? Neuroscientists are intrigued by the neural circuitry that underlies virtually all behaviours. They would be interested in the brain processes that underlie David Suzuki's intellectual and social skills. They would attempt to explain how Suzuki's brain coordinates so many things so quickly to allow him to function as a top-flight scientist and communicator.

behavioural neuroscience approach Views understanding the brain and nervous system as central to understanding behaviour, thought, and emotion.

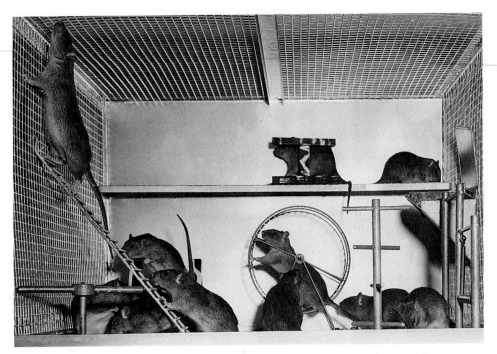

In one research study, an "enriched" environment rewired the brains of rats by dramatically increasing their neural connections and neurochemical activity (Rosenzweig, Bennett, & Diamond, 1972). In psychology and life, both biological and environmental processes matter. *Can you think of other ways scientists might study how "enriched" environments might influence behaviour?*

The Evolutionary Psychology Approach

Although Darwin introduced the theory of evolution by natural selection in the middle of the nineteenth century, his ideas about evolution have only recently became a popular framework for explaining behaviour. One of psychology's newest approaches, the **evolutionary psychology approach** emphasizes the importance of adaptation, reproduction, and "survival of the fittest" in explaining behaviour (Barkow, 2005). Evolution favours organisms that are best adapted to survive and reproduce in a particular environment. The evolutionary psychology approach focuses on the conditions that allow individuals to survive or fail. In this view, natural selection favours behaviours that increase an organism's reproductive success and ability to pass its genes to the next generation (Daly & Wilson, 1983).

David Buss (2004) argues that, just as evolution shapes our physical features, such as body shape and height, it also pervasively influences how we make decisions, how aggressive we are, our fears, and our mating patterns. Thus it is argued that the way we adapt in our world today can be traced to problems that animals and early humans faced in adapting to their evolutionary environments.

Steven Pinker (1999, 2002) also believes that evolutionary psychology is an important approach to understanding behaviour. According to Pinker, the way the mind works can be summarized by three points: (1) the mind computes, (2) the mind was designed to compute by evolution, and (3) these computations are performed by specialized brain systems that natural selection has designed to achieve specific kinds of goals, such as survival. Thus, in Pinker's view, the mind analyzes sensory input in ways that would have benefitted prehistoric human hunters and gatherers. People with minds that understood causes and effects, who could build tools, set traps, and avoid poisonous mushrooms, had the best chance of surviving and having offspring that would some day invent mathematics and make movies about robots.

Evolutionary psychologists believe that their approach provides an umbrella that unifies the diverse fields of psychology. Not all psychologists agree. Some argue that it is unlikely that one approach can unify the diverse, complex field of psychology

Neuroscientists have studied the memory of the sea slug, a tiny snail with only about 10,000 nerve cells. *How did they investigate the sea slug's memory?*

evolutionary psychology approach Emphasizes the importance of functional purpose and adaptation in explaining why behaviours are formed, are modified, and survive.

In Xinjiang, China, a woman prepares for horseback courtship. Her suitor must chase her, kiss her, and evade her riding crop—all on the gallop. A new marriage law took effect in China in 1981. The law sets a minimum age for marriage—22 years for males, 20 years for females. Late marriage and late childbirth are critical efforts in China's attempt to control population growth. *What do you think about such laws?*

The tapestry of Canadian culture has changed with the increasing ethnic diversity of Canada's citizens. According to Statistics Canada, by 1996 only 20 percent of Canadians had their origins in the British Isles or France. The rest have come from around the globe, with visible minorities making up the fastest-growing group. Two of psychology's challenges are to become more sensitive to race and ethnic origin and to provide improved services to ethnic minority individuals. *What might these communication strategies be like?*

(Graziano, 1995). Others stress that the evolutionary approach does not adequately account for cultural diversity (Paludi, 2002). But the evolutionary psychology approach is young, and its future may be fruitful (Cosmides & others, 2003).

What can the evolutionary psychology approach tell us about David Suzuki? The evolutionary approach would stress that David Suzuki's scientific abilities are the result of a long evolutionary process in which genes involving excellent intellectual capacities survived and were passed down from generation to generation. This approach would also call attention to the adaptive behaviour that allows Suzuki to function competently in his world.

The Sociocultural Approach

The **sociocultural approach** examines the ways in which the social and cultural environments influence behaviour. The sociocultural approach argues that a full understanding of a person's behaviour requires knowing about the cultural context in which the behaviour occurs. For instance in some cultures, such as in Canada, it is entirely acceptable for a woman to be assertive, but in another culture, such as in Iran, the same behaviour may be considered inappropriate (e.g., Berry & Triandis, 2004).

The sociocultural approach focuses not only on comparisons of behaviour across countries but also on the behaviour of people from different ethnic and cultural groups within a country, such as the behaviour of Aboriginal Canadians. One such area of interest is in the acculturation of immigrants in their new countries. (Berry & others, 2005; Sam & Berry, 2004). Thus, there is increasing interest in the behaviour of new Canadians from third-world countries, especially in terms of the factors that have restricted or enhanced their ability to acculturate and cope with living in a predominantly English- and French-speaking society (e.g., Attaca & Berry, 2002).

sociocultural approach Emphasizes social and cultural influences on behaviour.

Approach	Emphasis	A Sample Question the Approach Might Ask About David Suzuki
Behavioural	The scientific study of observable behavioural responses and their environmental determinants. Social cognitive theory is a contemporary behavioural approach	Why has Suzuki found science so rewarding ever since he was a young child?
Psychodynamic	Unconscious thought, early family experiences, and the conflict between biological instincts and society's demands	How much of Suzuki's ambition derives from his mother's and father's differing early influences on him?
Cognitive	The mental processes involved in knowing	How does Suzuki's memory store information about scientific research?
Behavioural Neuroscience	The centrality of the brain and nervous system in understanding behaviour	How does Suzuki's brain allow him to notice patterns in nature?
Evolutionary Psychology	The importance of adaptation, reproduction, and "survival of the fittest"	How has the evolution of the brain made possible Suzuki's analytic scientific skills?
Sociocultural	The social and cultural determinants of behaviour	Does Suzuki's ethnic background matter in his life and career as a scientist?

FIGURE 1.1 Questions about David Suzuki Derived from Six Psychological Approaches

The growing diversity of Canadian culture promises not only the richness that diversity produces but also difficult challenges in extending fuller opportunities to all ethnic-minority individuals (Berry, 1999). Queen's University cross-cultural psychologist John Berry (1993) suggests that our low population density, cultural, social, and linguistic dualism (French and English), and growing cultural pluralism requires a uniquely Canadian response (e.g., Preuger & Rogers, 1993).

Religion is also an important area of cultural study in psychology (Altemeyer, 2004a; Altemeyer & Hunsberger, 2004; Peterson, 1999). Similarly, a special concern of feminist writers is that, in much of its history psychology has portrayed human behaviour with a "male-dominant" theme (Pyke, 1997).

What can the sociocultural approach tell us about David Suzuki? The sociocultural approach would be especially interested in David Suzuki's ethnic background and how this might have hindered or helped the development of his skills and behaviour. Suzuki has been sustained throughout his life by a strong sense of values, which he learned from his family and from Japanese-Canadian culture. These values allowed him to rise above the pain inflicted on him by the internment of Japanese-Canadians in the Second World War and by racial discrimination to become one of the best-recognized and best-loved Canadians. The sociocultural approach would also be interested in the achievement context of Canadian culture and how this influenced his motivation. Figure 1.1 can help you remember the emphasis of the sociocultural approach and how psychologists with a sociocultural approach would think about David Suzuki as a scientist. For comparison, the figure also includes the emphases of psychologists who adopt a different approach and examples of the questions they might pose about Suzuki.

The sociocultural approach can provide insights into behaviour that other approaches do not adequately explain, such as altruism. See the Critical Reflections box for a discussion of this topic.

Can Humans Really Be Altruistic?

If there was a silver lining in the dark days following the Asian tsunami of December 26, 2004, it was that many people, including emergency personnel, local residents and tourists, altruistically risked their own lives to help other people caught up in the onrushing waves. In the following weeks, millions more around the globe contributed their time and money to send much-needed aid to stricken areas. Altruistic behaviour is often defined as voluntary behaviour that is intended to benefit others and is not motivated by any expectation of personal gain. The most extreme form of altruism is giving one's life to save someone else, as some of those who responded to the December 26 tsunami did.

Altruism poses an important problem for the evolutionary psychology approach (Caporael, 2001). According to Charles Darwin's theory of evolution, behaviours that favour an organism's reproductive success are likely to be passed on to future generations. In fact, altruistic behaviour *reduces* a person's chances of

A volunteer carries a box containing clothes to be sent as relief supplies for victims, in Bangalore, India, of the December 26, 2004 Asian tsunami. *Why are humans altruistic?*

reproductive success. Therefore, altruists should be at a clear disadvantage compared with those who act more selfishly, ensuring the propagation of their own genes. Over many generations, selfish behaviour should be favoured and altruistic behaviour should die out.

Referring to altruistic behaviour among social insects, Darwin (1859/1979) wrote about one circumstance that is difficult for evolutionary theory to explain. Worker bees, born without the ability to reproduce, spend their lives caring for the offspring of the queen bee in their hive. Natural selection predicts that sterile worker bees should become extinct over time. How, then, could there be such a thing as a sterile worker bee?

Seen through the Darwinian lens of the "survival of the fittest," human altruism also appears implausible. The concept of *kin selection* provides one way to reconcile altruism with evolutionary theory. According to this concept, our genes survive not just when we reproduce but also when our relatives reproduce. Kin selection includes the idea of *inclusive fitness*, which is measured by the number of our direct descendants and those of our relatives, in proportion to their degree of relationship with us. The worker bees in a hive turn out to be genetically related to the queen bee and, therefore to all the other bees in the hive, including any eggs the queen bee lays. Thus, even though a worker bee has no direct offspring, its inclusive fitness is high when the hive thrives. The theory of kin selection can explain why some people forego having their own children and choose instead to care for relatives and relatives' children. What this theory cannot explain is altruism directed toward people outside the family, especially toward strangers.

To deal with this difficulty, evolutionary psychologists have begun to explore the evolutionary bases of *reciprocity*. This idea is that we may have evolved to help other people, even total strangers, in the

expectation that, at some future time, we may get help in return (Field, 2002).

In contrast to the evolutionary psychology approach, the sociocultural approach attempts to explain altruistic behaviour as being the result of social and cultural experiences (Dovidio & Penner, 2001). According to this approach, each of us is a product of many culturally and socially derived relationships, which continually unfold over time. Because our relationships within our culture are open-ended and adaptable rather than rigidly determined by our genes, genuine acts of altruism are possible. Simply put, if our culture teaches us to be kind without regard for our own gain, then we can become true altruists.

By providing a theory that emphasizes the importance of adaptation and natural selection in explaining all behaviour, the evolutionary psychology approach has much to recommend it (Belk & Ruse, 2000). It forces us to look at our capacity for selfishness and to refine our notions of kindness and altruism. Yet the sociocultural approach is also attractive, because it stresses that people can be genuinely altruistic. This possibility is what we think about when we think about the rescuers who risked, and sometimes lost, their lives on December 26, 2004 and the millions who contributed aid in the weeks that followed. In the end, this contrast in views may well serve to sharpen our understanding of what it is to be fully human.

What do you think?

- Are people ever truly altruistic? Or are they always operating according to selfish motives?
- Have you ever acted in a truly altruistic fashion? Or could your behaviour be explained by theories of kin selection?
- What kind of research might settle the question of whether humans are capable of genuine altruism?

> **reflect and review**

2 **Describe six contemporary approaches to psychology.**

- Define each of the six approaches in your own words.
- Some approaches emphasize what is going on inside of the person. Others focus on the outside environment. Compare the approaches.

Suppose you could talk with a psychologist from each of the six approaches. Think about the members of your family and other people you know. Write down at least one question you might want to ask each of the psychologists about the thoughts and behaviours of these people.

3 A POSITIVE APPROACH TO PSYCHOLOGY

— The Humanistic Movement   — The Positive Psychology Movement

Can psychology make us happier?

If you are like most people, you probably associate psychology with problems such as depression, violence, and eating disorders. Psychologists, too, sometimes think that their field focuses too much on the negative and not enough on the positive aspects of behaviour.

Psychology deals with both the positive and negative aspects of life. When the tone of psychology was believed to be too negative, two movements emerged to focus on the positive effects psychology can have on people's lives. One of these movements (humanistic) appeared in the middle of the twentieth century; the other (positive psychology) began gaining momentum at the beginning of the twenty-first century. Let's explore these two movements.

The Humanistic Movement

The **humanistic movement** emphasizes a person's positive qualities, capacity for positive growth, and freedom to choose a destiny. Humanistic psychologists stress that people have the ability to control their lives and avoid being manipulated by the environment (Maslow, 1971; Rogers, 1961). They believe that, rather than being driven by unconscious sexual and aggressive impulses, as the psychodynamic approach dictates, or by external rewards, as the behavioural approach emphasizes, people can choose to live by higher human values, such as altruism and free will. Humanistic psychologists also think that people have a tremendous potential for conscious self-understanding and that the way to help others achieve self-understanding is by being warm, nurturant, and supportive of them. Many aspects of this optimistic approach to defining human nature appear in clinical practice today.

The Positive Psychology Movement

The end of an old century and the beginning of a new one can stimulate reflections on what has been and visions of what could be and should be. In 2000, two influential American psychologists, Mihaly Csikszentmihalyi and Martin Seligman, edited a special issue of the journal *American Psychologist* on the theme of positive psychology (Seligman & Csikszentmihalyi, 2000).

Their analysis of psychology in the twentieth century was that it had become far too negative, focusing on what can go wrong in people's lives rather than on what they

Humanists believe that we have a natural tendency to be loving toward each other and that each of us has the capacity to be a loving person.

humanistic movement An emphasis on a person's capacity for personal growth, freedom to choose a destiny, and positive qualities.

positive psychology movement A strong emphasis on the experiences that people value subjectively (such as happiness), positive individual traits (such as the capacity for love), and positive group and civic values (such as responsibility).

Mihaly Csikszentmihalyi, one of the main architects of the current positive psychology movement.

can do competently. Too often, they said, psychology has characterized people as passive and victimized.

Seligman, Csikszentmihalyi, and others hope to usher in a new focus on the positive things that psychology can accomplish (Diener, 2000; Nakamura & Csikszentmihalyi, 2003; Seligman, 2002). They describe the **positive psychology movement** as giving a stronger emphasis to and conducting more research on three general topics (Seligman & Csikszentmihalyi, 2000):

1. Experiences that people value subjectively, such as hope, optimism, and happiness
2. Positive individual traits, such as the capacity for love, work, creativity, talent, and interpersonal skills
3. Positive group and civic values, such as responsibility, nurturance, civility, and tolerance

This is a worthwhile goal. Throughout this book we talk about the positive potential of psychology and the ways in which it can enable individuals and groups to take more control of their own lives and to live them in a more fulfilling way. We also frequently link theory with specific applications that demonstrate psychology's contributions in these positive settings.

> ## > reflect and review

3 **Describe two movements that reflect a positive approach to psychology.**

- Explain the nature of the humanistic movement.
- Describe the positive psychology movement.

Think about what you read in the newspaper and see on television and at the movies. Does the information focus more on the negative or the positive aspects of people's lives? Why might the media present more negative than positive stories? Are they just giving their readers and viewers what they want? Are there ways in which the positive psychology movement could help to change the media's negative orientation?

4 PSYCHOLOGY'S CAREERS AND AREAS OF SPECIALIZATION

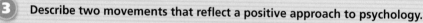

Careers in Psychology   —   Areas of Specialization in Psychology

What types of careers are available to psychology majors?

Psychologists don't spend all of their time in a laboratory, white-smocked with clipboard in hand, observing rats and crunching numbers. Some psychologists spend their days seeing people with problems; others teach at universities and conduct research. Still others work in business and industry, designing more efficient criteria for hiring. In short, psychology is a field with many areas of specialization.

Careers in Psychology

Have you ever thought about majoring in psychology? Students who major in psychology often find that the subject matter is highly interesting. You have already encountered some interesting topics in this chapter, including the brain's role in behaviour and analyzing the lives of people such as David Suzuki from a psychological perspective. In the remaining chapters of this book, you will encounter hundreds more truly fascinating inquiries in psychology.

Not only do you gain considerable knowledge and understanding of the mind and behaviour by majoring in psychology, but majoring in psychology also equips you with

Business	Social/Human Services	Research
• personnel administrator	• case worker	• research assistant
• public relations	• youth counsellor	• trainee for product research companies
• sales representative	• employment counsellor	• marketing researcher
• admissions recruiter	• fundraising specialist	• grant and report writer
• textbook representative	• alumni affairs coordinator	• information specialist/researcher
• advertising	• mental health aide	• research analyst
• insurance agent	• parent educator	• statistical assistant
• management trainee	• drug abuse counsellor	
• retail sales management		
• loan officer		

FIGURE 1.2 Some Job Possibilities for Students with an Undergraduate Degree in Psychology

a rich and diverse portfolio of skills that will serve you well in many different types of work, both practical and professional. A major in psychology helps you improve your skills in research, measurement and computing, problem solving and critical thinking, and writing (Hayes, 1997). Integrating these skills, which span the arts and sciences, provides you with unique qualifications. Even if you are not a psychology major and do not plan to major in psychology, this course and others in psychology can give you a richer, deeper understanding of many areas of life.

Psychology also pays reasonably well (Sternberg, 1997c). Psychologists earn well above the median salary in North America. It is unlikely that you would live in a palatial mansion because you majored in psychology, but it is also unlikely that you would go broke. A major in psychology enables you to improve peoples' lives, to understand yourself and others, possibly to advance the state of knowledge in the field, and to have an enjoyable time while you are doing these things.

An undergraduate degree in psychology can give you access to a variety of jobs. For a list of some of the job possibilities in business, social and human services, and research, see figure 1.2. If you choose a career in psychology, you can greatly expand your opportunities (and your income) by getting a graduate degree, either a master's or a doctorate. Born in Canada, Peter Pirolli obtained his undergraduate degree from Trent University and his Ph.D. in cognitive psychology from Carnegie-Mellon. Now a principal scientist at the Xerox Palo Alto Research Center in California, Pirolli investigates how people use computers, for example to find information on the World Wide Web (Pirolli, 2003, in press). Anna Marie Apanovitch, who has a Ph.D. in experimental psychology, is now a senior marketing analyst at Bayer Corporation (O'Connor, 2001). She is part of a team that does objective, cost-effective analysis of different marketing programs for various drugs, such as aspirin.

Where do psychologists work? Slightly more than one-third are teachers, researchers, or counsellors at colleges or universities. Most other psychologists work in clinical and private practice settings (see figure 1.3).

Areas of Specialization in Psychology

If you were to go to graduate school to earn an advanced degree in psychology, you would be required to specialize in a particular area. Following is a list of some of the specialties: clinical and counselling; experimental; behavioural neuroscience and comparative; developmental; social; personality; health; community; school and educational; industrial and organizational; environmental; cross-cultural; psychology of women; forensic; and sport. Some of these categories are not mutually exclusive. For example, some social psychologists are also experimental psychologists.

Anna Marie Apanovitch obtained a Ph.D. in experimental psychology and today is a senior marketing analyst for Bayer Corporation. Psychology provides excellent training for a wide range of careers, as exemplified by Anna Marie Apanovitch's job. She believes that it is important for students to think about their long-term career options and the skills they will need in performing those jobs and then to work on building up the skills at every opportunity. *Are there some careers in psychology that interest you?*

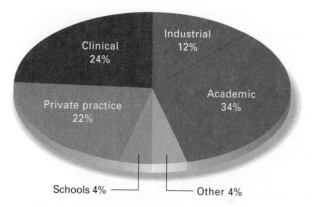

FIGURE 1.3 Settings in Which Psychologists Work
More psychologists work in academic settings (34%), such as colleges and universities, than any other. However, clinical (24%) and private practice (22%) settings, both contexts in which many psychologists in the mental health professions work, together make up almost half the total settings.

Clinical and Counselling Psychology Clinical and counselling psychology is the most widely practised specialization in psychology. Clinical and counselling psychologists diagnose and treat people with psychological problems (Corey & Corey, 2002; James & Gilliland, 2003). Counselling psychologists sometimes deal with people who have less serious problems. For instance, counselling psychologists may work with students, advising them about personal problems and career planning.

While there are some differences in training between Canada and the U.S. (e.g., regarding dealing with cultural diversity; Bowman, 2000; Hertzsprung & Dobson, 2000), a clinical psychologist typically has a doctoral degree in psychology, which requires three to four years of graduate work and one year of internship in a mental health facility. Clinical psychologists are different from psychiatrists. *Psychiatry* is a branch of medicine practised by physicians with a doctor of medicine (M.D.) degree who subsequently specialize in abnormal behaviour and psychotherapy. Clinical psychologists and psychiatrists alike are interested in improving the lives of people with mental health problems. One important distinction is that psychiatrists can prescribe drugs, whereas clinical psychologists cannot.

Some clinical psychologists specialize in working with a certain age group. Leslie Greenberg, a clinical psychologist at York University, focuses on emotional aspects of change processes in individual and marital therapy with adults (Greenberg, Korman, & Paivio, 2001; Greenberg & Bolger, 2001). Luis Vargas is a clinical child psychologist at the University of New Mexico Children's Psychiatric Hospital. He is interested in cultural issues that affect the assessment and treatment of children from diverse backgrounds.

Experimental Psychology Experimental psychologists use an experimental strategy in their work and often conduct basic research. Among the key aspects of behaviour that experimental psychologists study are sensation and perception, cognitive processes (such as memory), learning, motivation, and emotion (Klein, 2004, 2005; Myers, 2003).

Jim Stevenson, a blind experimental psychologist at NASA, focuses on how sound can be added to graphic displays and the different ways in which we hear patterns. Annabel Cohen, of the University of Prince Edward Island, studies the psychology of music, including how the music helps to create our emotional response to movies (Cohen, 2000, 2001).

Behavioural Neuroscience and Comparative Psychology Behavioural neuroscientists and comparative psychologists focus on biological processes, especially the brain's role in behaviour (Pinel, 2006; Kolb & Whishaw, 2005; Rains, 2002). Many of these scientists use animals in their research and investigate a range of topics, from how

"Well, you don't look like an experimental psychologist to *me.*"

© The New Yorker Collection 1994 Sam Gross from Cartoonbank.com.
All rights reserved.

the brain processes information to the effects of hormones on behaviour. Comparative psychology is a branch of psychology that studies animal behaviour.

Joseph LeDoux, a neuroscientist at New York University, studies how the brain forms, stores, and retrieves memories of life's significant events, especially traumatic ones (LeDoux, 2002; Debiec & Ledoux, 2004). Sandra Witelson, a neuroscientist at McMaster University, has conducted extensive research on communication between the two hemispheres of the brain (e.g., Witelson & Kigar, 1992) and on the difference between the brains of men and women (e.g. Hall, Witelson & others, 2004). A collector of human brains, Witelson has even studied parts of Einstein's brain (Witelson, Kigar, & Harvey, 1999).

Neuroscientist Sandra Witelson has conducted extensive research on communication between the two hemispheres of the brain.

Developmental Psychology Developmental psychology is concerned with how people become who they are, from conception to death. In particular, developmental psychologists focus on the biological and environmental factors that contribute to human development. For many years the major emphasis of developmentalists was on child development. However, an increasing number of today's developmental psychologists show a strong interest in adult development and aging (Santrock & others, 2005). Their inquiries range across the biological, cognitive, and social domains of life.

Developmental psychologist Sibylle Artz is director of the University of Victoria's School of Child and Youth Care. According to Artz (1998, 2004, 2005), we are seeing more and more young females respond to potent social pressures—to be popular, sexy, and powerful—by turning to violence to achieve those goals. Laura Carstensen, director of the Institute for Gender and Women at Stanford University, has documented that older adults become more selective about the people with whom they interact (Fung & Carstensen, 2004; Löckenhoff & Carstensen, 2004).

Social Psychology Social psychology deals with people's social interactions, relationships, social perceptions, and attitudes (Aronson, Wilson, & Akert, 2005). Social psychologists believe we can better understand mind and behaviour if we know something about how people function in groups.

Mark Zanna, a social psychologist at the University of Waterloo, has focused on understanding prejudice (e.g., Zanna, 1994; Jordan, Spencer & Zanna, 2005). Roy Baumeister, of Case Western Reserve University, has studied the importance of self-esteem (Baumeister & others, 2003) and the psychology of hate (Baumeister & Butz, 2005).

Sibylle Artz is a developmental psychologist who studies young women who resort to violence.

Personality Psychology Personality psychology focuses on the relatively enduring traits and characteristics of individuals. Personality psychologists study such topics as self-concept, aggression, moral development, gender roles, and inner or outer directedness (Ashcroft, 2003; Feist & Feist, 2006).

William Revelle, a personality psychologist at Northwestern University, studies the biological foundations of personality (Baehr, Revelle, & Eastman, 2000) and how personality is linked to motivation and cognition (Yovel, Revelle & Mineka, 2005). N. C. Higgins, of St. Thomas University, studies how individual differences in people's causal explanation style differences are linked to helping behaviours, retaliatory aggression, risk behaviours and negative life events (Higgins & Shaw, 1999; Higgins & Hay, 2003).

Health Psychology Health psychology is a multidimensional approach to health that emphasizes psychological factors, lifestyle, and the nature of the health care delivery system. Many health psychologists study the roles of stress and coping in people's lives (Brannon & Feist, 2004). Health psychologists may work in physical or mental health areas. Some are members of multidisciplinary teams that conduct research or provide clinical services.

James Parker, a health psychologist at Trent University, is especially interested in the relationship of our emotions to our health. He has studied emotional intelligence (Parker, 2000; Parker & others, 2005) and its relationship to academic achievement in high school (Parker, Creque & others, 2004) and in the transition from high school to university (Parker, Summerfeldt & others, 2004). Jeannette Ickovics, of Yale University,

James Parker is a health psychologist interested in the relationship between emotion and health.

focuses on the behaviours that place adolescent girls at risk for pregnancy and sexually transmitted diseases (Meade & Ickovics, 2005; Kershaw, Ickovics & others, 2004).

Community Psychology   Community psychology focuses on providing accessible care for people with psychological problems. Community-based mental health centres are one means of delivering such services as outreach programs to people in need, especially those who have traditionally been underserved by mental health professionals (Campbell & Murray, 2004; Murray & others, 2004). Community psychologists view human behaviour in terms of how people adapt to resources and the specific situation. They work to create communities that are more supportive of residents by pinpointing needs, by providing needed services, and by teaching people how to gain access to resources that are already available. Community psychologists are also concerned about *prevention*. They try to prevent mental health problems by identifying high-risk groups and then intervening with appropriate services and by stimulating new opportunities in the community.

Patrick O'Neill is a community psychologist at Acadia University in Nova Scotia. He has focused on cognitive processes in community consultation (O'Neill, 2000) and ethical issues in community psychology (O'Neill, 1999; 2005). South African-born Catharine Campbell is a community psychologist at the London School of Economics. She retains strong research links with the University of KwaZulu-Natal in South Africa where she studies how to strengthen local community responses to the AID/HIV epidemic (Campbell, 2004; Campbell & Foulis, 2004).

School and Educational Psychology   School and educational psychology is concerned with children's learning and adjustment in school. School psychologists in elementary and secondary school systems test children, make recommendations about educational placement, and work on educational planning teams. Educational psychologists work at colleges and universities, teach classes, and do research on teaching and learning (Santrock & others, 2004).

Donald Saklofske, an educational psychologist at the University of Saskatchewan, is interested in school psychology (Saklofske and others, 2000) and especially psychoeducational assessment (Andrews, Saklofske & Janzen, 2001; Prifitera, Saklofske & Weiss, 2005). Michael Pressley, at Notre Dame University, has found that children's reading improves when they use effective reading strategies, such as monitoring what they have read (Pressley, 2000; Pressley & Hilden, 2005).

Industrial and Organizational Psychology   Industrial and organizational psychology (I/O psychology) centres on the workplace, both on the workers and on the organizations that employ them. I/O psychology is often partitioned into industrial psychology and organizational psychology. Industrial psychology involves personnel and human resource management. Industrial psychology is increasingly referred to as personnel psychology. Organizational psychology examines the social and group influences of the organization (Goldstein & Ford, 2002; Muchinsky, 2003).

Ramona Bobocel, an I/O psychologist at the University of Waterloo, studies issues concerning justice in the workplace (Bobocel & others, 2002; Peters, van den Bos & Bobocel, 2004). Leaetta Hough, the 2005–6 president of the Society for Industrial and Organizational Psychology, helps businesses develop better resources for their employees. She is interested in the relevance of personality variables in the world of work (Hough & Furnham, 2003).

I/O psychologist Ramona Bobocel studies the effects of judgments of justice in the workplace on attitudes.

Environmental Psychology   Environmental psychology is the study of transactions between people and the physical environment. Environmental psychologists explore the effects of physical settings in most major areas of psychology, including perception, cognition, learning, development, abnormal behaviour, social relations, and others (Gifford, 2002). Topics that an environmental psychologist might study range from how different building and room arrangements influence behaviour to strategies for getting people to reduce behaviour that harms the environment.

Roberta Feldman is an environmental psychologist whose research and applied interests focus on the design of buildings and communities that people sense are their own (Feldman, 1999). Robert Gifford, of the University of Victoria, also studies environmental psychology (Gifford, 2002), focusing on a variety of topics such as people's beliefs about the effects of lighting (Veitch & Gifford, 1996) and predicting the use of public transportation (Heath & Gifford, 2002).

Cross-Cultural Psychology Cross-cultural psychology is the study of culture's role in understanding behaviour, thought, and emotion (Lehman, Chiu, & Schaller, 2004; Schaller & Crandall, 2004). Cross-cultural psychologists compare the nature of psychological processes in different cultures, with a special interest in whether psychological phenomena are universal or culture-specific. The International Association for Cross-Cultural Psychology promotes research on cross-cultural comparisons and awareness of culture's role in psychology.

Harry Triandis is an emeritus cross-cultural psychologist at the University of Illinois. His research reveals that North Americans are oriented more toward the individual and are more competitive with other people than many people from Asian countries, who are oriented more toward the needs of a group (Triandis, 2001, 2005). Sampo Paunonen, of the University of Western Ontario, is interested in both nonverbal (Paunonen & Ashton, 2002) and verbal (Paunonen & others, 2003) measures of personality suitable for cross-cultural research.

Psychology of Women The psychology of women emphasizes the importance of promoting research on women, and the study of women. This field emphasizes the importance of integrating information about women with current psychological knowledge and beliefs and applying the information to society and its institutions (Worell, 2002). The Section on Women and Psychology (SWAP), now the second-largest section of the Canadian Psychological Association, was formed in 1976.

Cannie Stark, of the University of Regina, has studied women's issues throughout her career. She has focused on the role of women in Canadian psychology (Stark, 2000) and sexism in research (Stark-Adamec, 1992). Rosalind Barnett, of the Murray Research Center of Radcliffe College, is especially interested in how work and family demands and challenges affect the lives of women (Barnett, 2002, 2004, 2005).

Cannie Stark has studied women's issues throughout her career in psychology.

Forensic Psychology Forensic psychology is the field of psychology that applies psychological concepts to the legal system (Wrightsman & others, 2002; Ogloff, 2004). Social and cognitive psychologists increasingly conduct research on topics related to psychology and law. Forensic psychologists are hired by legal teams to provide input about many aspects of a trial. For example, forensic psychologists were members of the legal teams in the trials of O. J. Simpson and Timothy McVeigh.

Don Dutton is a forensic psychologist at the University of British Columbia. He conducts research on family violence (Dutton, 1998; Winters, Clift, & Dutton, 2004) and counsels intimate abusers, who are not always men (Nichols & Dutton, 2001). He has served as an expert witness in trials involving intimate violence, including testimony for the prosecution in the O. J. Simpson trial.

Sport Psychology Sport psychology is the field of psychology that applies psychology's principles to improving sport performance and enjoying sport participation (LeUnes & Nation, 2002). Sport psychology is a relatively new field, but it is rapidly gaining acceptance. At recent Olympics, psychologists worked with athletes and coaches from Canada, the U.S., and many other countries.

The research of Diane Ste-Marie, of the University of Ottawa, on biases in sport judgments (Ste-Marie, 1996; Findley & Ste-Marie, 2004), is especially relevant in light of the judging scandal at the 2002 Winter Olympics, which resulted in the awarding of extra gold medals to Canadian figure skaters Jamie Salé and David Pelletier.

To reflect on whether a career in psychology might be in your future, see the Personal Reflections box.

Sport psychologists are likely to play a role in improving the quality of judging in figure skating, after the judging scandal at the 2002 Winter Olympics involving Canadians Jamie Salé and David Pelletier.

Is Psychology in Your Future?

Instructions

Students who are successful as psychology majors have a profile that is related to the questions below. Answer true or false to each item.

	True	False
1. I often think about what makes people do what they do.	___	___
2. I like reading about new findings that scientists have discovered while doing behavioural research.	___	___
3. I am often skeptical when someone tries to persuade me about behavioural claims, unless there is evidence to back up the claim.	___	___
4. I like the prospect of measuring behaviour and doing statistics to determine meaningful differences.	___	___
5. I can usually come up with multiple explanations to account for behaviour.	___	___
6. I think I could come up with ideas to research to help explain behaviours I am curious about.	___	___
7. I am often approached by others who want me to listen to their problems and share my ideas about what to do.	___	___
8. I don't get especially frustrated if I can't get answers to my questions.	___	___
9. I am usually careful with details.	___	___
10. I enjoy writing and speaking about things I am learning.	___	___
11. I like to solve puzzles.	___	___
12. I feel comfortable that psychology can provide me with an education that will lead to a good job.	___	___

Scoring and Interpretation

If you answered "true" to a majority of the items, psychology is a major that likely matches up well with your interests. Although the items are not a perfect predictor of whether you will enjoy majoring in and pursuing a career in psychology, they can give you an indication of whether you might benefit from finding out more about what psychologists do and what is involved in becoming a psychologist. Your psychology professor or a career counsellor at your university can likely inform you about the best way to pursue a career in psychology.

> **reflect and review**

 Evaluate careers and areas of specialization in psychology.

- Describe the kinds of career opportunities that are available to people with an undergraduate degree in psychology.
- List and discuss the areas of specialization in psychology.

Think of a career other than psychology that you might enter. In what ways might studying psychology be useful in that career?

---

⑤ HOW TO GET THE MOST OUT OF PSYCHOLOGY

- Thinking Critically
- Good Study Habits
- This Textbook's Pedagogical Tools

What skills and study habits can help me in this course?

Very likely you are taking other courses besides psychology. You will have a lot of reading and studying to do, and you will probably have to take a number of tests. What are some good strategies for succeeding in this and other courses?

Thinking Critically

Thinking critically is an important aspect of psychology, as it is in all disciplines. The ability to critically evaluate information is essential to all areas of daily life (Halpern, 2002, 2003). For example, if you were planning to buy a car, you might want to collect information about different makes and models and evaluate their features and costs before deciding which one to test-drive. This would be an exercise in critical thinking.

Critical thinking is not a spectator sport (Halpern, 1998). You need to regularly practise your critical thinking skills on a wide variety of problems to keep them sharp. Let's practise them.

What Is Critical Thinking?

People don't change.
Love is blind.
Birds of a feather flock together.
Communicating with spirits is possible.

Such statements about human nature spark the psychologist's curiosity and skepticism, which is the tendency to doubt the validity of claims in the absence of evidence. Psychologists try to sort fact from fancy by critically questioning the nature of mind and behaviour.

What does it mean to be a critical thinker? Understanding the complex nature of mind and behaviour requires **critical thinking**, the process of thinking reflectively and productively and evaluating the evidence. Thinking critically means asking yourself how you know something. Too often we have a tendency to recite, define, describe, state, and list rather than analyze, infer, connect, synthesize, criticize, create, evaluate, think, and rethink (Brooks & Brooks, 2001). Following is a brief sampling of some thinking strategies that can stimulate you to think reflectively and productively:

- *Be open-minded.* Explore options and avoid narrow thinking.
- *Be intellectually curious.* Wonder, probe, question, and inquire. Also be alert for problems and inconsistencies.
- *Be intellectually careful.* Check for inaccuracies and errors, be precise, and be organized.
- *Look for multiple determinants of behaviour.* People have a tendency to explain things as having a single cause. After all, that's a lot easier than having to analyze the complexity of, say, mind and behaviour and come up with multiple explanations. However, one of psychology's important lessons is that mind and behaviour have multiple determinants. For example, if someone asked what causes a person to be a good critical thinker, the person might respond, "Being open-minded." Having an open mind is one of critical thinking's multiple dimensions, but it does not cause critical thinking. When another person is asked what causes critical thinking, the individual might respond, "Practice." Yet another person might say, "An inquiring, critical-thinking mentor." Like all aspects of mind and behaviour, critical thinking has many dimensions.
- *Think like a scientist.* Neil Agnew and Sandra Pyke (1993) stress that thinking like a scientist about human minds and behaviours can be learned. Scientific thinkers examine the available evidence about some aspect of mind and behaviour, evaluate how strongly the data (information) supports their hunches, analyze disconfirming evidence, and carefully consider whether they have explored all of the possible factors and explanations (Agnew & Pyke, 1993). It is important to underscore how critical it is to look for biases in the way people think and behave. For example, a person who is wildly enthusiastic about the remarkable effects of exercise on health when responding to survey questions about health awareness might sell exercise videos on the side. In the discussion of the scientific method in the next chapter, we explore more systematically how to think like a scientist. And in the next section, you will read about the healthy skepticism of

critical thinking The process of thinking reflectively and productively, as well as evaluating evidence.

scientific thinkers and how they require sound evidence before accepting information as valid.

Maintaining a Healthy Skepticism The failure to think critically ranges from taking advice based on horoscopes to believing that eating a ground-up portion of a tiger's sexual organ will increase the human male's sexual potency. Critical thinking expert Diane Halpern (1998, 2003) explained why she is concerned that so many people fail to engage in critical thinking. Approximately 75 percent of North Americans read their horoscope, and many of them believe that it is personally meant for them (Lister, 1992). Some phone their psychics and pay exorbitant fees for advice that ranges from how to invest their money to whether or not a loved one should be disconnected from life-support systems. They spend large sums of money on remedies for which there is no evidence of effectiveness or safety. In a survey of university students, most students believed in at least one of the following (Messer & Griggs, 1989):

- channelling (the ability to enter a trance state and communicate with someone in another place and time, even centuries ago)
- clairvoyance (the ability to perceive remote events that are not visible to normal sight)
- precognition ("knowing" events before they occur)
- telepathy (the extrasensory transfer of thought from one person to another)
- psychic healing (performing miracle cures instantaneously through contact with a higher spiritual being)
- psychic surgery (a brand of faith healing in which sleight of hand is relied on to achieve a "miracle," such as removing dead or diseased tissue)
- crystal power (use of quartz crystals for healing)
- psychokinesis (being able to move objects without actually touching them)
- astral travel
- levitation
- the Bermuda Triangle mystery
- unidentified flying objects (UFOs)
- plant consciousness
- auras
- ghosts

If you believe in any of these phenomena, psychologists urge you to be more skeptical. Remember that thinking like a scientist means that you demand to see the evidence for such phenomena as channelling, crystal power, and plant consciousness. There is no scientific evidence for the existence of any of the previously listed phenomena, only personal anecdotes and coincidences—and those do not meet science's criteria of objectivity and public verifiability.

When you think like a scientist, you will be skeptical of astrology, channelling, crystal power, and anything else that claims access to wondrous powers and supernatural forces (Ward & Grashial, 1995). If something sounds too good to be true, think through the claims logically and demand to see the evidence. A failure to think critically and to demand scientific evidence often underlie our purchase and use of highly touted, ineffective health care products (Halpern, 1998, 2003). For example, there is a widespread belief around the world today that a man who ingests the ground penis of a tiger will have more sexual potency. This belief is so pervasive that it has resulted in rare wild tigers and other endangered species being poached. Males who believe that this works think like this: Tigers (presumably) have a great sex life; thus eating a tiger's sexual organ will improve my sex life. You should be able to see what is wrong with this kind of thinking, especially when there is no evidence to support it.

Thinking Critically About Controversies As we indicated earlier in the chapter, psychology is full of controversies. How might psychology benefit from these controversies? Psychology has advanced as a field because it does not accept simple explanations and because psychologists do not always agree with each other about why mind

Why should you be skeptical when you hear that eating a ground-up penis of a tiger will increase the human male's sexual potency?

Why does the science of psychology urge you to be skeptical of astrology?

and behaviour work the way they do: We have reached a more accurate understanding of mind and behaviour *because* psychology fosters controversies and *because* psychologists think deeply and reflectively and examine the evidence on both sides.

What are some of psychology's controversies? Here is a brief sample:

- Are memories of sexual abuse real or imagined?
- Can intelligence be increased?
- Is alcoholism a biologically based disease or a learned behaviour?
- Is it better to treat depression with drugs or with psychotherapy?

Controversies are usually not totally resolved on one side or the other. Often the resolution comes down to a matter of degree. For example, some cases of sexual abuse may be imagined, whereas others are real; and certain aspects of abuse are more likely to be imagined than others.

In this book we call your attention to a number of controversies. Because it is important for you to think critically about controversies, each chapter has a Critical Reflections box that presents a controversial issue in contemporary psychology.

Good Study Habits

Mastering good study habits will help you not only in psychology and in school but also in your career and personal life. Here we focus on five important strategies for success: time management, study environment, reading effectiveness, attentiveness in class, and test preparation.

Plan and Manage Your Time Effectively Learning takes time. You will benefit enormously in this course and others if you become a great time manager. If you waste too much time, for instance, you will find yourself poorly prepared the night before an important exam. Procrastination is one of the most important ways in which students can end up wasting time (Schouwenburg & others, 2004; Blunt & Pychyl, 2005). If you manage time well, you will have time to relax before exams and other deadlines. Time management can help you to be more productive and less stressed, so you have a better balance between work and play.

You might find it helpful to fill out the dates for the tests in your courses in a term calendar. Many students benefit from keeping a weekly calendar to see how they are

FIGURE 1.4
Example of a To-Do List

To Do

The Most Important:

1. Study for Psychology Test

Next Two:

2. Go to English and History classes

3. Make appointment to see advisor

Task	Time	Done
Study for psychology test	Early morn., night	
Call home	Morning	
Go to English class	Morning	
Buy test book	Morning	
Call Ann about test	Morning	
Make advisor appt.	Afternoon	
Go to history class	Afternoon	
Do exercise workout	Afternoon	

allocating their time. Students who consistently get A's in courses often report that they study 2 to 3 hours outside class for every hour they are in class (Santrock & Halonen, 2006). Thus, if you are in class 15 hours a week and you want to get A's, a rule of thumb is to study 30 to 45 hours a week outside of class.

A good strategy for managing your time is to space out your study in a particular course rather than cramming it all into one or two study sessions just before the test. On a weekly schedule, block out at least 1 hour a day for 6 days to read this book and study your notes for this course. Then you will be better prepared when the time comes for each test, and you won't have to cram.

It is a good idea to plan not only for the term and the week but also for tomorrow. Great time managers identify the most important things to do each day and allocate enough time to get them done. Figuring out what is most important involves setting priorities. An effective way to set priorities is to create a manageable to-do list. Set a goal of making a to-do list for the next day every night or, at the latest, early in the morning. Figure 1.4 shows one student's to-do list.

Choose the Most Effective Study Environment Too many distractions can keep you from studying or remembering what you have studied. Select your place of study carefully, paying close attention to the features of the environment that will let you do your best work.

Some students find that their studying is more effective when they do it in the same place. Ideally, the area should be well lighted, without glare, and should be a comfortable temperature. A quiet location will let you concentrate much better than a noisy one. Noise is a major distraction to effective study. Turn off the stereo, radio, or TV while you are studying to minimize distraction.

Maximize Your Reading Effectiveness Studying involves a lot of reading, from course outlines to textbooks to research articles. Many students approach the challenge of reading as just so many pages to plow through. But there is a difference between reading to read (to complete the required number of pages) and reading to learn. Reading to learn improves your understanding if you approach your reading as a conversation the author is having with you, about the requirements for passing your course, about the concepts of psychology, or about a specific piece of research. As in any effective conversation, you must pay attention, figure out how the parts of the conversation fit together, and make some judgments as you go about understanding the author's intent.

The following strategies can help you maximize your ability to understand and retain what you read (we offer more detailed strategies for using this textbook in the next section, *This Textbook's Pedagogical Tools*):

- **Preview and plan.** Look at the number of pages you have to read and plan how to read the assignment. If the task is very long, determine at what points it would be appropriate to take breaks. For example, we have divided each chapter of this textbook into three to five main sections, so a good time to take a break in your reading might be after you have read one or two main sections.
- **Survey.** Spend a short time beforehand skimming the reading assignment and determine what main ideas will be covered. Look at any main headings. When you skim, you begin to build a foundation for the main ideas of the reading, even if it is a course outline or an exam.
- **Read to comprehend.** There is no easy way around the effort and hard work involved in understanding what you read. However, there are some things you can do to increase your understanding of what you read:
  1. Pay attention to the sections of what you are reading as meaningful units. Take one section at a time. Read each one until you are satisfied that you know the ideas.
  2. Don't skip over what you don't understand. On exams, take time to make sure you understand the question before writing out an answer. We find that students often fail to earn full grades on examinations, not because they don't know the material but because they misread the questions and wrote down an inappropriate answer. When it is not an exam and it is appropriate, consider finding a classmate who is willing to discuss the challenging ideas.
  3. Work on your reading speed. Practise taking in more words as your eyes sweep the line of print. Don't mouth the words as you read—that only slows you down.
- **Read to retain.** Most students need to read reading assignments more than once if they are going to learn the material. Thinking about personal examples that illustrate concepts is a good memory aid. Periodically ask yourself the meaning of what you have been reading.
- **Review.** After you have used the aforementioned strategies, you may need to review the material you have read several times. This is a normal part of reading for retention. Just because you have read a chapter once, don't think that you will be able to remember everything in it that is important. At the end of each major section in this book, for example, you will find review questions and, at the end of the chapter, a summary of the chapter's main ideas for an overall review.

Be a Good Listener and Concentrate in Class You need to do more than just memorize or passively absorb new information in class. To do well in most classes, including this one, you need to go to class, listen carefully, and take good notes.

A good strategy is to treat each and every class hour as an important learning experience. To carry out this strategy, you obviously have to be there. It also helps to prepare for the class by reading about the topic(s) that will be covered prior to the class.

In preparing for a lecture, motivate yourself by telling yourself that it is important for you to stay alert and listen carefully. Make sure you get sufficient sleep the night before so that you will be able to maximize your learning in class the next day. Many students find that a regular exercise program increases their alertness and ability to concentrate in class and when they are studying.

Take notes in class, but don't try to write down everything the instructor says. As you listen to a lecture, focus on the main ideas and take notes about them. If you miss an idea, get together later with one or more students in the class to find out what the idea was. Many students find it helpful to review their notes right after class, because the material in the lecture will be fresher in their minds than if they wait several days or more to review them.

Prepare Effectively for the Test In most cases, your grade in a course will depend on how well you do on the exams given periodically during the term. At the beginning of the term, find out what kinds of tests your instructor will be giving. Will they be all multiple-choice items? Will there be essay questions? Will the exams be a mixture of these or include other types of items, such as true-false?

A good strategy is to complete all of your textbook reading well before the exam. All of your classroom notes should be in order so you can easily review them. If you have been studying on a regular basis, you should be in a good position to consolidate what you have learned for the test.

Some students find it helpful to develop their own questions about what they think will be covered on the test and practise answering them. You may also find it helpful to study in a small group with other students in the class, who may be able to contribute information that you missed or did not adequately understand.

When you take a test, you will have to remember information. If you have practised good study skills day after day and week after week leading up to the test, your ability to remember information will be enhanced when you take the test. In chapter 8, we discuss a number of strategies for remembering effectively.

Getting the most out of psychology involves remembering ideas and concepts. It also involves thinking critically about these ideas and concepts.

This Textbook's Pedagogical Tools

You may have noticed that we already talked about this textbook's **pedagogical tools** in both the student and instructor prefaces prior to this chapter. Studying the student preface will give you an understanding of how to learn more effectively from this book. We are briefly reviewing these tools to underscore their importance. To reiterate, your understanding of, and memory for, what you read depends on the active, constructive processing effort you put into it. A good textbook supports your effort by presenting the content you need to learn in the context of helpful pedagogical tools. Remember, a *textbook = content + pedagogy*.

We strongly recommend that you make use of the pedagogical tools we have used to structure this textbook. If you do so, your understanding of the textbook content will be enhanced, giving you a more elaborated understanding of psychology and a better memory for what you have learned. We are so confident about these principles that we also invite you to apply them to all your text-based learning. We know it is extra work but believe that the benefits far outweigh the costs.

FIGURE 1.5
Chapter Opening Pedagogical Tools

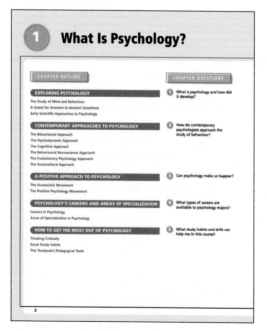

pedagogical tools Activities that aid in the active construction of knowledge or skill.

Integrated Pedagogical Tools The pedagogical tools in this textbook form an integrated system that can produce powerful results for you when approached through the PQ4R system. At the beginning of each chapter, you will see a Chapter Preview that introduces you to the main themes of the chapter and a Chapter Outline, a table of contents for the chapter. You will also see three to six Chapter Questions, one for each chapter section (see figure 1.5).

Following each main heading in the chapter, you will again come across the relevant chapter question and will see a map that includes the main heading and subheadings for that particular section (see figure 1.6a). This provides a visual preview of what you will be reading in the section.

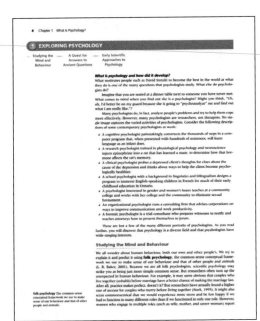

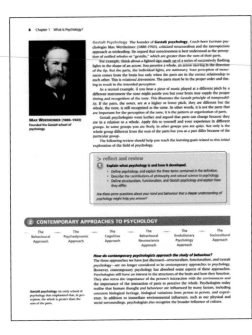

FIGURE 1.6
Chapter Section Pedagogical Tools

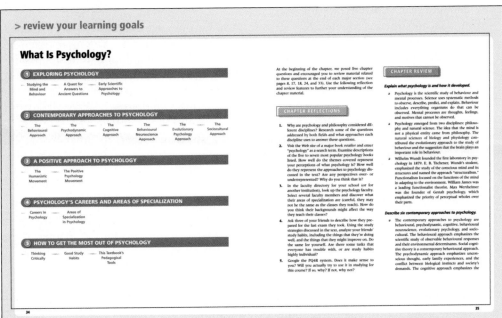

FIGURE 1.7
Chapter Ending Pedagogical Tools

At the end of each major section, you will come to the heading Reflect and Review (see figure 1.6b). The first part presents further elaborative reflections on the material you just read and the second part restates the section's chapter question and asks you to review each of the main topics in the section. The bulleted review statements are correlated with the map at the beginning of the section.

Finally, at the end of the chapter, a map of the entire chapter gives you a visual reminder of the main topics (see figure 1.7). Here, a section called Chapter Review restates the chapter questions and summarizes the material related to each question. This information is provided in bulleted form and matches up in a one-to-one fashion with the bulleted statements in each of the chapter's section reviews. Identifying the core concepts in this textbook is also easier through the Core Terms, which are listed and page-referenced at the end of the chapter. These terms are also bold-faced and defined in the margin when they are first presented. In the Glossary at the end of the book you will find definitions for all core terms, along with a reference to the page on which the term is introduced (see figure 1.7).

Finally, the book offers several additional tools to deepen your thinking about psychology. The Critical Reflections boxes elaborate on a particular contemporary controversy in psychology. We urge that you always ask if what you are reading is relevant to your own life, an activity we encourage with the Personal Reflections Boxes. Further, both the Reflect and Review and the Chapter Reflections tools encourage you to further elaborate what you have just read. Finally, in the margins of the book you will see notes directing you to other resources can also help you reflect and review your growing understanding of psychology. These resources include the Student Study Guide and the Online Learning Centre for the book. These resources include quizzes, Internet activities, and many other activities. A general reminder about the additional available study resources also appears at the end of the chapter.

Systematic Study Through PQ4R We have chosen to present these pedagogical tools as a variation of the PQ4R (Preview, Question, Read, Reflect, Recite, Review) system with which you may already be familiar (Thomas & Robinson, 1972). Systems like this (e.g. PQ3R, SQ4R) are very useful for deepening your understanding of, and improving your memory for textual material for several reasons.

First, the *Preview* and *Question* steps serve as **advance organizers** (Ausubel, 1968). Most students find that reading an unfamiliar passage is easier and results in better comprehension and memory when they have some advance idea about what they are about to read (Ausubel, 1978).

Second, the *Reflect* and *Recite* steps serve to encourage elaboration, which refers to how extensively information has been processed (see Chapter 8). The more extensive and varied your processing, the better. Students' use of elaboration has been linked to their academic success (e.g., Gadzella, 1995). *Self-reference* is an especially powerful form of elaboration (Rogers, Kuiper, and Kirker, 1977). Throughout this textbook, we will often invite you to relate the content to your own life experiences.

Third, if you follow this system, including repeating the *Review* step, you will be engaging in distributed practice, resulting in a **spacing effect**. In other words, the PQ4R system encourages a more efficient distribution of study time, resulting in better understanding and memory (Reynolds & Glaser, 1964).

Preview. We recommend that you start each chapter by working through the first two pages of the chapter. You will find a Chapter Preview, introducing you to the main themes of the chapter, and a Chapter Outline, a table of contents for the chapter. These are advance organizers that, like a map, give you a good idea of what the chapter will cover (see figure 1.5).

Question. Similarly, before beginning to read the chapter, we recommend that you think about the Chapter Questions that encapsulate the chapter's main themes and underscore the most important ideas in the chapter (see figure 1.5). Also, feel free to formulate any additional questions you would be interested in answering. Reading with some questions already in mind, especially if you have formulated those questions yourself is an especially effective advance organizer (Frase, 1975).

Read. You are now better prepared to understand what you are about to read. As you read the chapter, periodically check to see if it fits with the expectations you developed from your initial preview and answers any of your questions from the question step. A good time to do this is between chapter sections. Each section begins with a restatement of the preview information relevant to that section and ends with some reflection and review information (see figure 1.6). We encourage you to take notes, especially in your own words. But avoid underlining as it is a much less active form of processing.

Reflect. Both while you are reading and after finishing a section, we encourage you to reflect on what you have read to elaborate your understanding. The Critical Reflections boxes elaborate on a particular contemporary controversy in psychology. We urge that you always ask if what you are reading is relevant to your own life, an activity we

advance organizer A reference frame for encountering new information that results in better comprehension and memory for textual material.

spacing effect The finding that for a given amount of study time, it is better to distribute studying across time than to mass it together.

encourage with the Personal Reflections Boxes. Finally, both the Reflect and Review and the Chapter Reflections tools encourage you to further elaborate what you have just read.

Recite. After you have read and reflected on a chapter or chapter section, we recommend that you recite what you have learned. This is a good time to put together your study notes for this material. This activity helps you consolidate and further elaborate your understanding. Try to minimize rote repetition in favour of rewording, explaining the concepts to other students, and inventing mnemonics (see Chapter 8).

Review. Finally, we urge you to revisit your notes repeatedly throughout the term. Chapter Reviews are useful here (see figure 1.7). Keep in mind that, although the Chapter Reviews offer an organized, systematic review of the entire chapter, they are not a substitute for reading and studying the chapter. Use them, rather, as guides to help you organize your study of the chapters. Also, consider repeatedly recalling the material, self-testing, and working with study partners. As we mentioned previously, reviewing helps to distribute your practice, a much more efficient study strategy.

> **> reflect and review**
>
> **Apply some strategies that will help you succeed in psychology.**
>
> - Describe the nature of critical thinking.
> - Discuss some good study habits.
> - Identify the study tools in this book.
>
> *Why do you think so many people believe in astrology?*
> *What good study habits do you already use? What could you do to improve them?*

What Is Psychology?

① EXPLORING PSYCHOLOGY

— Studying the Mind and Behaviour — A Quest for Answers to Ancient Questions — Early Scientific Approaches to Psychology

② CONTEMPORARY APPROACHES TO PSYCHOLOGY

— The Behavioural Approach — The Psychodynamic Approach — The Cognitive Approach — The Behavioural Neuroscience Approach — The Evolutionary Psychology Approach — The Sociocultural Approach

③ A POSITIVE APPROACH TO PSYCHOLOGY

— The Humanistic Movement — The Positive Psychology Movement

④ PSYCHOLOGY'S CAREERS AND AREAS OF SPECIALIZATION

— Careers in Psychology — Areas of Specialization in Psychology

⑤ HOW TO GET THE MOST OUT OF PSYCHOLOGY

— Thinking Critically — Good Study Habits — This Textbook's Pedagogical Tools

At the beginning of the chapter, we posed five chapter questions and encouraged you to review material related to these questions at the end of each major section (see pages 8, 17, 18, 24, and 33). Use the following reflection and review features to further your understanding of the chapter material.

CHAPTER REFLECTIONS

1. Why are psychology and philosophy considered different disciplines? Research some of the questions addressed by both fields and what approaches each discipline uses to answer these questions.

2. Visit the Web site of a major book retailer and enter "psychology" as a search term. Examine descriptions of the five to seven most popular psychology books listed. How well do the themes covered represent your perceptions of what psychology is? How well do they represent the approaches to psychology discussed in the text? Are any perspectives over- or underrepresented? Why do you think that is?

3. In the faculty directory for your school (or for another institution), look up the psychology faculty. Select several faculty members and discover what their areas of specialization are (careful, they may not be the same as the classes they teach). How do you think their backgrounds might affect the way they teach their classes?

4. Ask three of your friends to describe how they prepared for the last exam they took. Using the study strategies discussed in the text, analyze your friends' study habits, including the things that they're doing well, and the things that they might improve on. Do the same for yourself. Are there some tasks that everyone has trouble with, or are study habits highly individual?

5. Google the PQ4R system. Does it make sense to you? Will you actually try to use it in studying for this course? If so, why? If not, why not?

CHAPTER REVIEW

Explain what psychology is and how it developed.

- Psychology is the scientific study of behaviour and mental processes. Science uses systematic methods to observe, describe, predict, and explain. Behaviour includes everything organisms do that can be observed. Mental processes are thoughts, feelings, and motives that cannot be observed.

- Psychology emerged from two disciplines: philosophy and natural science. The idea that the mind is not a physical entity came from philosophy. The natural sciences of biology and physiology contributed the evolutionary approach to the study of behaviour and the suggestion that the brain plays an important role in behaviour.

- Wilhelm Wundt founded the first laboratory in psychology in 1879. E. B. Titchener, Wundt's student, emphasized the study of the conscious mind and its structures and named the approach "structuralism." Functionalism focused on the functions of the mind in adapting to the environment. William James was a leading functionalist theorist. Max Wertheimer was the founder of Gestalt psychology, which emphasized the priority of perceptual wholes over their parts.

Describe six contemporary approaches to psychology.

- The contemporary approaches to psychology are behavioural, psychodynamic, cognitive, behavioural neuroscience, evolutionary psychology, and sociocultural. The behavioural approach emphasizes the scientific study of observable behavioural responses and their environmental determinants. Social cognitive theory is a contemporary behavioural approach. The psychodynamic approach emphasizes unconscious thought, early family experiences, and the conflict between biological instincts and society's demands. The cognitive approach emphasizes the mental processes involved in knowing. The behavioural neuroscience approach emphasizes that the brain and nervous system are central to understanding behaviour. The evolutionary psychology approach stresses the importance of adaptation, reproduction, and "survival of the fittest." The sociocultural approach focuses on the social and cultural determinants of behaviour.

- John B. Watson and B. F. Skinner were important early behaviourists. Sigmund Freud was the founding father of the psychodynamic approach.

- Psychodynamic, cognitive, behavioural neuroscience, and evolutionary psychology approaches emphasize what is going on inside a person. Behavioural and sociocultural approaches focus on the outside environment.

Describe two movements that reflect a positive approach to psychology.

- The humanistic movement emphasizes a person's capacity for positive growth, freedom to choose a destiny, and positive qualities.

- The positive psychology movement is a recent one. It argues that psychology has been too negative and needs to focus more on the positive aspects of people, such as their optimism, creativity, and civic values.

Evaluate careers and areas of specialization in psychology.

- Majoring in psychology can open up many career opportunities. Careers range from conducting therapy with people who have mental problems to teaching and conducting research at a university to advertising and public relations.

- Areas of specialization in psychology include clinical and counselling psychology, experimental psychology, behavioural neuroscience and comparative psychology, developmental psychology, social psychology, personality psychology, health psychology, community psychology, school and educational psychology, industrial and organizational psychology, environmental psychology, cross-cultural psychology, the psychology of women, forensic psychology, and sport psychology.

Apply some strategies that will help you succeed in psychology.

- Critical thinking involves thinking reflectively and productively and evaluating the evidence. It is important to maintain a healthy skepticism about anything that appears to be magical and wondrous. Demand to see the logical evidence before believing in something involving psychology. Psychology is full of controversies, and it is important to think critically about these controversies. Most controversies are not completely resolved on one side or the other.

- Developing good study habits includes planning and time management, choosing a conducive study environment, maximizing reading effectiveness, being a good listener and concentrating in class, and preparing effectively for tests.

- This book's pedagogical tools include a chapter questions and chapter map system, questions to encourage reflection, core terms and the PQ4R system.

For extra help in mastering the material in this chapter, see the integrator, review sections, practice quizzes, and other resources in the Student Study Guide and at the Online Learning Centre (www.mcgrawhill.ca/college/santrock).

CORE TERMS

folk psychology, p. 4
psychology, p. 5
science, p. 5
behaviour, p. 5
mental processes, p. 5
natural selection, p. 6
structuralism, p. 7
functionalism, p. 7
Gestalt psychology, p. 8

behavioural approach, p. 9
social cognitive theory, p. 10
psychodynamic approach, p. 11
cognitive approach, p. 11
behavioural neuroscience approach, p. 12
evolutionary psychology approach, p. 12
sociocultural approach, p. 14

humanistic movement, p. 17
positive psychology movement, p. 17
critical thinking, p. 25
pedagogical tools, p. 30
advance organizer, p. 32
spacing effect, p. 32

2 Psychology's Scientific Methods

CHAPTER QUESTIONS

1. What makes psychology a science?

2. What are the three types of research that are used in psychology?

3. What is the difference between descriptive statistics and inferential statistics?

4. What are some research challenges that involve ethics, bias, and information?

Did you watch "Bomb," the *CSI: Crime Scene Investigation* episode that starts with a bomb going off in a briefcase in the reception area of an office building? As always, the CSI forensics crew begins dutifully collecting data. Gil Grissom carries out a neat little study as he blows up three bombs to measure the resulting scatter and determine the composition of the pipe at the heart of the bomb. Warrick tests a whole bunch of tools to see which one was used to inscribe the letters "FP" on that pipe. At the heart of the show is a scientific attitude, with Grissom usually telling his crew that only the evidence can clarify the truth. He is forever running little studies and collecting physical evidence: lifting fingerprints, locating DNA, analyzing bullets and, his favourite, collecting insects from decomposing bodies to establish a timeline for murder.

At the same time, like any good murder mystery, theories are put forward, to be tested against the available data. Several suspects usually need to be evaluated in order to confirm the identity of the perpetrator. In "Bomb," the obvious suspect is a security guard who left the building only moments before the bomb exploded. He makes his own bombs and even has some suspicious bomb-making parts in his possession. But Grissom is forever warning against a premature rush to judgment of accepting a theory before the data fully support it. That particular theory can be ruled out when another bomb goes off while the prime suspect is in jail. As usual, the real perpetrator is eventually caught and must now pay for his crimes.

In this same episode, Nick gets entangled with a woman who is murdered. As members of his team try to exonerate him, they encounter conflict of interest issues. Are they investigating a homicide or protecting a friend? Gil Grissom is forever telling his team to keep personal matters separate from their professional work, just one example of the kinds of ethical issues that provide a dash of humanity to this award-winning dramatic series.

Psychologists face the same kinds of problems as the CSI team. We also collect data and also put forward theories. Often, psychological theories seem so commonsensical, having arisen in folk psychology, that we are tempted to accept them as true on the face of it. But, like Grissom, a psychologist will remain skeptical, sorting out theoretical alternatives by carefully collecting relevant evidence. Also, psychologists face ethical issues around their detective work as well, being required to treat research participants appropriately and to be careful about allowing their own values to bias their research.

Aside from being entertaining, *CSI* episodes like this one remind us that the key to learning about science and psychology is knowing and using scientific methods. Scientific methods are what differentiate a discipline like psychology from a discipline like philosophy. Philosophers seek truth by thinking about thinking and by discussing thinking. Psychologists use scientific methods. In this chapter, we explore the scientific method and some of the specific types of research methods used by psychologists to test their theories. We also explore some of the challenges involved in psychological research, including research ethics.

William Petersen plays Gil Grissom, a scientifically minded crime scene investigator on *CSI: Crime Scene Investigations*.

① EXPLORING PSYCHOLOGY AS A SCIENCE

— A Scientific — Collaboration — The Scientific
   Approach   Method

What sets psychology and other sciences apart from other disciplines?

Science is not defined by *what* it investigates but by *how* it investigates. Whether you study underwater life, the conservation of koala bears, the Martian surface, or the reasons that people enjoy extreme sports, the way you study the question is what makes your approach scientific or not. You can obtain a better understanding of science by knowing what it means to take a scientific approach, realizing the importance of collaboration, and learning about the scientific method.

A Scientific Approach

Central to the scientific approach are four attitudes: curiosity, skepticism, objectivity, and a willingness to think critically.

Being curious is basic to science. UBC's John Yuille was curious about how to conduct forensic interviews with children that could stand up in court and yet minimize the traumatic impact on the child (Yuille & others, 1993). He and his colleagues developed the Step-Wise Interview, which is now in wide use throughout Canada (Hardy & van Leeuwen, 2004).

Being skeptical is also essential to science. Skeptical people question things that other people take for granted. Skeptical people ask what evidence there is for an idea and question whether the evidence is really strong enough to be accepted as accurate and factual. Psychologists are trained to be skeptical.

Science is not defined by what it studies but by how it investigates it. Underwater life, koala bears, the surface of Mars, and human behaviour all can be studied in a scientific manner. *What are some areas of psychology other than extreme sports that science can appropriately be used to investigate?*

Science also means *being objective*. Scientists believe that one of the best ways to be objective is to conduct research studies (Pittenger, 2003). The opening episode of "Numb3rs," a recent CSI-style television series, featured the use of geographic profiling. The location of the crime scenes of a serial killer were computer-analyzed to predict where he lived and worked, making it easier to finally arrest him. A joint British-Canadian team of forensic psychologists, including Brent Snook of Memorial University of Newfoundland and Craig Bennell of Carleton University, wanted to test the effectiveness of various geographical profiling strategies. They were able to show that more complex geographic profiling strategies are not necessarily better (Snook & others, 2005) and that it is possible to train people to perform just as well as computer-based techniques (Snook, Taylor & Bennell, 2004).

It is sometimes said that experience is the most important teacher. We do get a great deal of knowledge from subjective, personal experience. We generalize from what we observe and frequently turn memorable encounters into lifetime "truths;" parts of our "common sense" folk psychology. But how valid are these conclusions? As individuals, we often misinterpret what we see and hear. You can probably think of many situations in which you thought other people read you the wrong way, just as they might have felt that you misread them. Our personal judgments are often based on a need to protect our egos and self-esteem (McMillan, 2004a; McMillan & Wergin, 2002).

Being objective means trying to see things as they really are, not just as we would like them to be or as we think they should be. It means using methods of decision making that keep us in touch with the real world.

Last but not least, science involves *thinking critically*. In chapter 1, we saw that thinking critically consists of thinking reflectively, thinking productively, and evaluating the evidence. Critical thinkers question what some people say are "facts." They test the "facts." They examine research to see how sound its support of an idea really is.

These four attitudes are all ideals. No scientist possesses them all at every moment in life. But the more closely we embrace these attitudes, the better we are able to use the basic tools of scientific theory and objective observation. They reduce the likelihood that information will be based on unreliable personal beliefs, opinions, emotions, and folk psychology. As you go through this book, practise these scientific attitudes. You would also do well to call on these attitudes whenever you hear people discussing "facts" and arguing about issues.

Collaboration

Science is a collaborative effort. Even when different groups of scientists seem to be competing to answer a particular question first, they are part of a collective effort to increase an overall body of knowledge. More than that, no scientific finding has much impact until a community of scientists agrees through the process of peer review that the finding is true and important.

Within colleges and universities, psychologists share their findings with their colleagues and open their research to evaluation. Conferences conducted by national and international societies also allow psychologists to share and discuss their findings.

Research psychologists also share their work by publishing it in scientific and academic journals. Some journals, including *Canadian Psychology*, *American Psychologist*, and *Psychological Review*, focus on psychology in general. Others focus on more specific areas. These more specialized journals include *Behavioral Neuroscience*, *Developmental Psychology*, *Journal of Abnormal Psychology*, *Journal of Personality and Social Psychology*, *Gender Roles*, and *Canadian Journal of Community Mental Health*.

In psychology, many journal articles are reports of original research. A number of journals also include, or focus exclusively on, reviews of research or theoretical ideas. Many journals are highly selective about what they publish. Every journal has a board of experts that evaluates articles submitted for publication. The best journals maintain high standards. Some accept only 10 to 20 percent of the articles that are submitted to them.

Research journals are the core of information in virtually every academic discipline. Those shown here are among the increasing number of research journals that publish information about psychology. *What are the main parts of a research article that present findings from original research?*

The Scientific Method

One of the hallmarks of taking a scientific approach involves adopting the scientific method in studying topics in psychology (Langston, 2005; Shaughnessy & others, 2006). Indeed, most of the studies psychologists publish in research journals follow the scientific method. The scientific method is essentially a four-step process:

1. Conceptualize a problem.
2. Collect research information (data).
3. Analyze data.
4. Draw conclusions.

This process is based on two key ideas: theory and hypothesis. A **theory** is a broad idea or set of closely related ideas that attempt to explain certain observations. Theories try to explain why certain things have happened. They can also be used to make predictions about future observations. If your friend's new computer crashes, you might have a theory to explain why it happened. Your theory probably includes the idea that there are many hardware components inside the computer and that the computer uses an operating system to run software. Your theory might also include the idea that computer viruses can infect computers, preventing them from operating properly. This theory gives you a framework for trying to figure out why your friend's computer isn't running.

In psychology, theories serve a similar purpose. They help to organize and connect observations and research. The overall meaning of the large numbers of research studies that are always being conducted in psychology would be difficult to grasp if theories did not provide a structure for summarizing and understanding them and putting them in a context with other research studies. In addition, good, testable theories generate interesting research questions and allow researchers to make observations that might answer those questions.

The second key idea underlying the scientific method is central to the process of testing a theory. A **hypothesis** is an idea that is arrived at logically from a theory. It is a prediction that can be tested. For example, if your theory about the computer includes the idea of antivirus software, you can test the hypothesis that a computer virus caused the computer to stop. You would simply run some antivirus software. If you observe that the computer runs properly after you tried the antivirus software, you might

theory A broad idea or set of closely related ideas that attempt to explain and predict observations.

hypothesis An idea that is a testable prediction, often arrived at logically from a theory.

conclude that your hypothesis is correct. If not, you might consider a different hypothesis (perhaps the operating system was improperly installed).

The relationship between theories and hypotheses is not necessarily as straightforward as this simple example indicates. A theory can generate many hypotheses. If more and more hypotheses related to a theory turn out to be supported by observations, the theory gains in credibility. One reason that so many scientists hold the theory of evolution in high esteem is that it has been able to generate many hypotheses that, in turn, predict many observations.

On the other hand, if some of the hypotheses derived from a theory are not supported by observation, the theory will have to be revised. In fact, entirely new theories have arisen when researchers have found that no existing theory explains the facts that they have observed. Sigmund Freud's theory that no significant changes take place in adulthood is an example of a theory that has been revised. For example, Erik Erikson (1968) observed that changes take place throughout the adult years, beginning with an increased motivation for intimacy during the 20s and 30s.

Essentially, then, the scientific method is a process of developing and testing theories. Scientists do not regard theories as being exactly, entirely, and permanently correct. A theory is judged by its ability to generate hypotheses that predict important events and behaviours. Depending on how well it predicts, a theory gains or loses support. Some theories sound great at first, but testing shows them to be worthless. Other theories start out sounding less useful but are shaped and improved in the course of testing.

A good example of the links between theory and hypothesis and the research process that binds them together is the work of James Pennebaker, a research psychologist at the University of Texas at Austin. He is interested in the connection between emotions and health (Pennebaker, Kiecolt-Glaser, & Glaser, 1988; Pennebaker & Graybeal, 2001; Pennebaker, 2004). You may be interested to learn how some of his research proceeded through the four steps of the scientific method. Notice how deeply theory and hypothesis were integrated in Pennebaker's research.

1. Conceptualize a Problem Pennebaker's thinking about emotions and health began in a very personal way. He had gotten married just after finishing university, and a few years later his marriage was in trouble. After about a month of deep depression and emotional isolation, he began to write privately every day about his problems. After about a week of writing, he says, "I noticed my depression lifting. For the first time in years—perhaps ever—I had a sense of meaning and direction. I fundamentally understood my deep love for my wife and the degree to which I needed her" (Pennebaker, 1997b).

Some years later, he looked back on that experience and wondered why his private writing had helped him. He became interested in a theory of catharsis that had been developed by Freud and the psychodynamic psychologists nearly a hundred years before.

As we will see in chapters 11 and 14, the theory of catharsis says that by expressing pent-up emotions, a person can often eliminate those emotions, along with unwanted physical symptoms of stress and anxiety. This is one important premise of psychotherapy—a process in which individuals experience relief by talking about their problems with a therapist.

Pennebaker's personal experience led him to ask whether this theory of catharsis should perhaps be modified. For example, to experience the benefits of emotional release, was it really necessary to talk to a psychotherapist? (After all, therapists can be expensive!) In fact, was it really necessary to be speaking to anyone at all? Could people with emotional troubles achieve the same relief by writing? And could people actually improve their physical health simply by writing about their problems?

To explore these ideas further, Pennebaker needed to express his questions in more specific and concrete terms. He began by developing a hypothesis that he could test through concrete, objective observations. For example, exactly what did he mean

James Pennebaker (*right*) discussing the value of writing about emotional experiences with participants in one of his research studies.

by "writing about emotions"? Also, what did he mean by "physical health"? He needed to translate these ideas into operational definitions. An **operational definition** is an objective description of how a research variable is going to be observed and measured. Operational definitions eliminate some of the fuzziness and loose ends that easily creep into thinking about a problem. By being very specific about what measurements define concepts, operational definitions also clarify concepts for other scientists.

In 1986, Pennebaker and a graduate student, Sandra Beall, decided to test the following hypothesis:

> If people write about their negative emotions and the situations that caused them, people will reduce their stress and be more healthy in the future.

To operationally define writing about emotions, they decided to instruct student volunteer participants to write continuously for 15 minutes each day on 4 consecutive days about an upsetting or traumatic experience and to express how they felt about the experience when it happened and how they felt about it while writing. To operationally define health, they decided to record the number of illness visits that their participants made to the student health centre before, during, and after the study (Pennebaker & Beall, 1986).

2. Collect Research Information (Data) The second step of the scientific method is to actually collect research information (data). Among the important decisions to be made about collecting data are whom to choose as the participants and which research methods to use. We explore a number of research methods in some detail shortly, so we focus here on the research participants.

Will the participants be people or animals? Will they be children, adults, or both? Will they be females, males, or both? Will they be of a single ethnicity, such as Anglo-Canadian, or will they come from diverse ethnic groups?

When psychologists conduct a study, they usually want to be able to draw conclusions that will apply to a larger group of people (or animals) than the participants they actually study. Thus an investigator might conduct a study of 300 married couples in Vancouver in which the husband shows a history of abusing the wife, but the researcher may have the goal of applying the results to all married couples in Canada in

operational definition A circumstance or behaviour defined in such a way that it can be objectively observed and measured.

which husbands abuse their wives. The entire group about which the investigator wants to draw conclusions is the **population**. In this particular study of spousal abuse, the population is all couples in Canada in which husbands abuse their wives. The subset of the population chosen by the investigator for study is a **sample**. In this spousal abuse study, the sample is the 300 couples in Vancouver. By surveying a sample of the population, the researcher avoids the difficulties involved in trying to find and survey all Canadian husbands who abuse their wives.

The target population to which the investigator wants to generalize varies with the study. For example, in a study of the effects of televised violence on children's aggression, the population might be all 3- to 5-year-old children in North America. In a study of how people think critically, the population might be all humans. In a study of whether chimpanzees have language, the population might be all chimpanzees. Generalization from the sample to the population can be made only if the sample is representative—or "typical"—of the population. For example, a disproportionate number of the 300 couples in the study of spousal abuse might have income in the poverty range and be European Canadians. We would have to be cautious about generalizing the results of this study to the entire Canadian population of couples in which the husbands abuse their wives, especially to such couples in higher income brackets and from other ethnic groups.

One way to more closely mirror the population is to use a **random sample**, a sample that gives every member of the population an equal chance of being selected. In the study of spousal abuse, a random sample would be more likely to reflect the population's age, socioeconomic status, age at marriage, geographic location, religion, and so forth. As a consequence, the sample would be more representative of the population. For this reason random sampling provides a much better basis for generalizing the results to a population than a nonrandom sample.

Investigators do not always use appropriate sampling methods (Leary, 2004). Surveys by newspapers and magazines often ask people to mail or call in their opinions. However, the people who respond probably feel more strongly about the issue than those who do not respond. In addition, the readers may feel differently about an issue than the population as a whole. For example, when a magazine such as *Playboy* asks its Canadian readers for their opinions on sexual attitudes, the results are likely to show far more permissiveness than if a random sample of adults in Canada were asked about their sexual attitudes.

You may be getting the impression that psychological research is worthless if it is not based on a random sample. However, though random sampling is important in some types of research, it is much less important in others. If a researcher wants to know how often spousal abuse occurs in Canada, obtaining a random sample is important. However, in many research studies, psychologists are interested in studying specific aspects of behaviour under specific conditions, in which case they deliberately do not obtain a random sample. In these studies, they might want people with certain characteristics to be well represented. Say that a researcher is interested in discovering whether having been married before is related to the incidence and nature of spousal abuse that a wife experiences. That researcher might study 50 couples in which the wife had been married before and 50 couples in which the wife had not, without worrying about whether these couples represent all the couples in Canada.

It also should be pointed out that in many areas of psychology, generalization comes from similar findings across a number of studies rather than from random sampling within a single study. Imagine five or six studies conducted with varied samples—maybe one in Winnipeg with low-income and middle-income ethnic minority participants; another in Charlottetown, with middle-income white participants; and others with somewhat similar or different participant characteristics. If all the studies find that frequent conflict and one or more incidents of physical abuse in a previous marriage are related to spousal abuse, then we gain confidence that these findings can be generalized to the population as a whole.

population The entire group that the investigator wants to learn about.

sample The subset of the population that the investigator has chosen for study.

random sample A sample in which every member of the population has an equal chance of being selected.

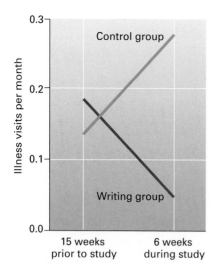

FIGURE 2.1

Health Centre Visits Before and After Writing About Emotional Experiences

Pennebaker's sample was not random (Pennebaker, Kiecolt-Glaser, & Glaser, 1988). At the time of this research, he was teaching at Southern Methodist University in Dallas, Texas, where introductory psychology students were given credit for participating in psychological research. His sample was a group of 46 students who volunteered to be his participants. Because a sample of students at Southern Methodist is not likely to be very representative of people in general, Pennebaker needed to be cautious about generalizing from the sample. Whatever results he got from this research, he would want to try similar experiments on other samples (for example, older people, nonstudents, people in other countries) before he generalized about most humans.

3. Analyze Data Once psychologists collect measurable research data, they use statistical procedures to understand what the data mean (Gravetter & Wallnau, 2004; Howell, 2004). Later in the chapter, we examine two types of statistical procedures in some detail.

In his research, Pennebaker used a number of statistical procedures to determine whether students' health benefitted from writing about emotional experiences. For example, he analyzed information about how often the students who wrote about their emotional experiences used the health centre. As shown in figure 2.1, the two groups—the group who wrote about their emotional experiences and those who did not (control group)—visited the health centre about equally prior to the experiment. However, after the writing group wrote about their emotional experiences, they visited the health centre considerably less than the control group. Psychologists often use graphs, like the one shown in figure 2.1, to illustrate their results.

4. Draw Conclusions Pennebaker's research was set up so he could draw conclusions by comparing two groups: a group of students who wrote about their emotional trauma and another group of students who wrote about other things. When he and Sandra Beall examined their results, they found that the participants who wrote about their feelings made significantly fewer illness visits to the student health centre afterward than those who did not write about their emotions.

Conclusions might also be made by connecting the research findings back to the hypothesis and its underlying theory. The results of Pennebaker's study were exciting. They confirmed the hypothesis and suggested that emotional "cathartic" writing actually causes improvements in a person's physical health. The results also suggested that the general theory of emotional catharsis should be modified to account for the fact that it can be achieved through writing, as well as talking, and does not require the presence of a therapist.

It is important to keep in mind that a theory is usually revised only after a number of studies produce similar results. Before we change a theory, we want to be sure that the research is reliable. *Reliability* is the extent to which scientific research yields a consistent, reproducible result. In the case of Pennebaker's work, reliability would not be established until other experiments were performed to test the same basic idea under different conditions and with different samples of participants.

Pennebaker and others performed later studies with further interesting results. One study redefined "health" operationally in terms of certain measurements of participants' blood samples (Pennebaker, Kiecolt-Glaser, & Glaser, 1988). It found that the emotional writing led to improvements in the immune system. Another study involved a group of unemployed middle-aged engineers who were deeply angry after having been suddenly fired by a corporation for which some of them had worked 30 years (Spera, Buhrfeind, & Pennebaker, 1994). This study found that emotional writing led many of the engineers to overcome their frustration and find new jobs, whereas engineers who did not do the writing remained angry and unemployed.

Other studies have shown that writing about emotions does not necessarily have the same results for everyone. Emotional writing may or may not work for you as an individual. But, if you are interested, the Personal Reflections box on page 47, "Writing Might Improve Your Health," gives suggestions about how to do it.

Summarize the scientific method applied to James Pennebaker's study of emotional writing and health. *Do you think writing about your emotional experiences might improve your health? Explain.*

Personal Reflections: Writing Might Improve Your Health

Research by James Pennebaker and others has demonstrated that writing about your emotions can improve your physical health. Pennebaker (1997a, b; 2004) suggests that you experiment to find a method that works best for you. Maintaining a blog (weblog) is currently a popular approach to personal writing. Some researchers have even suggested that blogging can help develop your sense of self (Hevern, 2004). However, the kind of writing Pennebaker is describing is best kept private, so if your goal is improving your health, blogging may not be the best approach.

What to Write

You don't need to write about the biggest trauma in your life. Write about issues that currently bother you and preoccupy your thinking. Write about things that you may not be telling others out of fear of embarrassment or punishment. Write as objectively as you can about an experience that troubled you. Express your emotions. Write as deeply as you can about your feelings.

How to Write It

Just start and keep writing. Don't worry about spelling or making good sentences. If you get stuck, go back and repeat what you were writing before you got stuck.

When and Where to Write

Emotional writing is not the same as keeping a blog or journal of various events and thoughts as they occur. Write when you feel like writing. Write when you feel prepared to get into the writing on an emotional level. Find a place where you won't be interrupted or distracted.

What to Do with Your Writing

Keep the writing to yourself. Don't plan to show it to anyone. Don't write for an audience, online or otherwise, which may cause you to hold back or feel that you need to justify yourself.

What to Expect

Writing about your emotions is not a cure-all. It's not a substitute for tackling problems that may keep you angry, sad, or frustrated. If you are in the midst of turmoil over the death of a loved one or the end of a long-term relationship, your writing may not make you instantly feel better, but it probably will help you see things in better perspective. You may feel sad or depressed for a few hours or even a day or so after writing. However, most people feel relieved, happier, and more content soon after.

> ## reflect and review

 Explain what makes psychology a science.

- Discuss the four attributes of a scientific attitude.
- Explain the need for collaboration in science.
- Name and describe the four main steps in the scientific method. Include the role of theory and hypothesis in your description.

Create an operational definition of happy. List several measurements that you might use to assess happiness.

---

2 TYPES OF RESEARCH

| Descriptive | Correlational | Experimental |
| Research | Research | Research |

How do psychologists collect research data?

As you have seen, collecting research information (or data) is an important step in the scientific method. The collection of data is the fundamental means of testing hypotheses. Today even the Internet is used for data collection purposes (Andrews & others, 2003; Birnbaum, 2004). Like crime scene investigators, psychologists rely on a variety of data collection methods, matching the method to the research hypothesis as required. This section describes the major ways that data about behaviour and mental processes can be gathered. There are three basic types of research used in psychology: descriptive, correlational, and experimental. Each has strengths and weaknesses.

THE FAR SIDE   By GARY LARSON

"For crying out loud; gentlemen! That's us! Someone's installed the one-way mirror in backward!"

THE FAR SIDE ©1985 FARWORKS, INC. Used by permission. All rights reserved.

Descriptive Research

Some important psychological theories have grown out of descriptive research, which serves the purpose of observing and recording behaviour. For example, a psychologist might observe the extent to which people are altruistic or aggressive toward each other. By itself, descriptive research cannot prove what causes some phenomena, but it can reveal important information about people's behaviours and attitudes. Descriptive research methods include observation, surveys and interviews, standardized tests, and case studies.

Observation   Scientific observation requires an important set of skills. Unless we are trained observers and practise our skills regularly, we might not know what to look for, we might not remember what we saw, we might not realize that what we are looking for is changing from one moment to the next, and we might not communicate our observations effectively (Billman, 2003).

Recall how James Pennebaker's interest in catharsis grew out of his own experience during a time of depression. Suppose we had been observing him back then and it was up to us to decide whether or not he was truly depressed. What constitutes depressed behaviour? How do we know it when we see it? Does it involve a blank emotionless stare, a saddened look? To distinguish a person who is depressed from a person who is not, how long should we say that the person's blank stares and saddened looks must last?

For observations to be effective, they have to be systematic (Leary, 2004). We have to have some idea of what we are looking for. We have to know whom we are observing, when and where we will observe, and how the observations will be made. And in what form will they be recorded? In writing? Tape recording? Video?

To see the importance of observing systematically, consider the story of a clever horse named Hans that lived in Germany in the early 1900s (Benjafield, 2004). A retired math teacher, Mr. von Osten, trained Hans to communicate by tapping his forefoot and moving his head. A head nod meant "yes," a shake "no." Mr. von Osten developed a code for verbal information in which each letter was represented by a pair of numbers. The letter A was coded as one tap, pause, one tap; the letter I was three taps, pause, two taps. Once Hans learned to tap his foot or move his head when questioned, he was given simple math problems and then fed a piece of bread or carrot for correct responses. By the end of his training, Hans could spell words spoken to him, and he excelled in math.

Hans became a hero in Germany—his picture was on liquor bottles and toys. Experts were so impressed that an official commission of 13 scientists, educators, and public officials examined the horse, testing him to see if he really could do all of the things claimed. They came away even more impressed and issued a statement saying that there was no evidence of any intentional influence or aid on the part of Hans's questioners. According to the experts, Hans could reason and "talk."

But one scientist was not so sure that Hans was as intelligent as he had been portrayed. Oskar von Pfungst, a very sharp observer, had detected that Hans always faced his questioner. Von Pfungst hypothesized that this positioning might have something to do with Hans's math ability.

He set up a very simple experiment to test this hypothesis. He wrote numbers on a card and held them up one at a time, asking Hans to tap out the numbers written on each card. Half of the cards von Pfungst held so that only Hans, not von Pfungst, could see what was on them. With the cards von Pfungst could see, Hans was his usual brilliant self, getting 92 percent of the answers correct. But for the numbers von Pfungst could not see, Hans was no longer a brilliant horse, getting only 8 percent correct.

Von Pfungst repeated the experiment over and over again with nearly the same results. He then carefully observed Hans with his other questioners, including Hans's owner, Mr. von Osten. As soon as they stated the problem to Hans, most questioners would turn their heads and upper bodies slightly. When Hans had made the correct number of foot taps, the questioners would move their heads upward.

When he learned of these observations, Mr. von Osten was stunned. Despite his years of work with the horse, he had never dreamed that Hans had learned to "read" him. Instead he believed that Hans could actually spell and do math. Von Osten commented that he was actually angry at the horse and felt betrayed by him.

Thus we can see that what sometimes seems to be the truth may be a false impression. Furthermore, even experts can be fooled if they don't make appropriate use of other research procedures to check their observations.

If we are going to make observations, where should we make them? We have two choices: the laboratory and the everyday world.

Laboratory Observation. When we observe scientifically, we often need to control certain factors that determine behaviour but are not the focus of our inquiry (Salkind, 2003; D. W. Martin, 2004) For this reason much of psychology's research is conducted in a *laboratory*, a controlled setting with many of the complex factors of the "real world" removed.

A researcher codes the behaviour of children in a play group as part of a research study. *What are some advantages and disadvantages of laboratory research?*

An experiment conducted by Albert Bandura (1965), in which children behaved more aggressively after observing a model being rewarded for aggression, was briefly described in chapter 1. Bandura conducted this study in a laboratory with adults the child did not know. He thus controlled when the child witnessed aggression, how much aggression the child saw, and what form the aggression took. Bandura would not have had as much control over the experiment or as much confidence in the results if the study had been conducted in the children's homes and if familiar people had been present, such as the child's parents, siblings, or friends.

Laboratory research does have some drawbacks. First, it is almost impossible to conduct research without the participants' knowing they are being studied. Second, the laboratory setting is unnatural and therefore can cause the participants to behave unnaturally.

Another drawback of laboratory research is that people who are willing to come to a university laboratory may not fairly represent groups from diverse cultural backgrounds. Those who are unfamiliar with university settings and with the idea of "helping science" may be intimidated by the setting.

Still another problem is that some aspects of mind and behaviour are difficult if not impossible to examine in the laboratory. Laboratory studies of certain types of stress, for example, may even be unethical.

Naturalistic Observation. Naturalistic observation provides insight that we sometimes cannot achieve in the laboratory (Langston, 2005). **Naturalistic observation** means observing behaviour in real-world settings, making no effort to manipulate or control the situation. Psychologists conduct naturalistic observations at sporting events, day-care centres, work settings, malls, and other contexts people live in, such as families (Pence, 1988). Suppose you wanted to study the level of civility on your campus. Most likely, you would want to include some naturalistic observation of how people treat one another in places like the cafeteria or the library reading room.

Naturalistic observation was used in one study that focused on the relationship between caregiving behaviour and the positive development of toddlers from 18 to 30 months of age (Wachs & others, 1993). The study was conducted in Egypt. Twice a month, researchers observed children and the caregivers in the children's homes for a period of 30 minutes, noting such behaviours as how frequently the caregivers talked with the children and guided their play. They also observed the number of vocalizations made by the children and the amount of time they spent playing with objects (Pence, 1989). As had been found in studies of Western families, the more the Egyptian caregivers talked with and guided young children's play, the more alert, vocal, and actively involved in play the children were (Bukatko & Daehler, 2001).

naturalistic observation Observations of behaviour in real-world settings with no effort made to manipulate or control the situation.

Jane Goodall was a young woman when she made her first trip to the Gombe Research Centre in Tanzania, Africa. Fascinated by chimpanzees, she dreamed about a career that would allow her to explore her hunches about the nature of chimpanzees. A specialist in animal behaviour, she embarked on a career in the bush that involved long and solitary hours of careful, patient observation. Her observations spanned 30 years, years that included her marriage, the birth of her son, untold hardship, and inestimable pleasure. Due to her efforts, our understanding of chimpanzees in natural settings dramatically improved. *What are some other aspects of behaviour that could be studied by using naturalistic observation?*

Surveys and Interviews   Sometimes the best and quickest way to get information about people is to ask them for it. One technique is to interview them directly. A related method that is especially useful when information from many people is needed is the survey, sometimes referred to as a questionnaire. A standard set of questions is used to obtain people's self-reported attitudes or beliefs about a particular topic. In a good survey, the questions are clear and unbiased, allowing respondents to answer unambiguously.

Surveys and interviews can be used to study a wide range of topics from religious beliefs to sexual habits to attitudes about gun control. Surveys and interviews can be conducted in person or over the telephone. Some surveys are also now being conducted over the Internet.

Some survey and interview questions are unstructured and open-ended, such as "Could you elaborate on your optimistic tendencies?" or "How fulfilling would you say your marriage is?" They allow for unique responses from each person surveyed. Other survey and interview questions are more structured and ask about more specific things. For example, a structured survey or interview question might ask, "How many times have you talked with your partner about a personal problem in the past month: 0, 1–2, 3–5, 6–10, 10–30, every day?"

Durrant, Broberg & Rose-Krasnor, (1999) conducted one example of a survey. They asked 97 Swedish and 103 Canadian mothers about their attitudes toward physical punishment. Swedish mothers reported that they were less likely to have been punished as children and were also less likely to physically punish their own children than Canadian mothers. The Swedish sample was randomly selected from mothers in the city of Gothenburg. The Canadian sample came from daycare centres and university classes in Winnipeg and the Niagara Peninsula of Ontario. When surveys are conducted on a national basis, as this survey was, random sampling is considered to be an important aspect of the survey process.

As another example, David Clark, a clinical psychologist at the University of New Brunswick in Fredericton, studies the cognitive aspects of anxiety and depression (e.g., Clark, 2004, 2005). He also makes extensive use of surveys in his research. For example, Byers, Purdon, & Clark (1998) surveyed 171 college students about their sexual intrusive

"Would you say Attila is doing an excellent job, a good job, a fair job, or a poor job?"

Drawing by Chas Addams; ©1982 The New Yorker Magazine, Inc.

thoughts. They found that men experienced more sexual intrusive thoughts that were more varied and sexually arousing than women did. The pattern of results indicated that sexual intrusive thoughts did not reflect psychological distress.

One problem with surveys and interviews is the tendency of participants to answer questions in a way that they think is socially acceptable or desirable rather than telling what they truly think or feel. For example, a person might exaggerate the amount of communication that goes on in a relationship in order to impress the interviewer.

Standardized Tests A **standardized test** requires people to answer a series of written or oral questions or sometimes both. A standardized test has two distinct features: an individual's answers are tallied to yield a single score, or set of scores, that reflects something about that individual; and the individual's score is compared with the scores of a large group of similar people to determine how the individual responded relative to others (Aiken, 2006; Cohen & Swerdlik, 2005). One widely used standardized test in psychology is the Stanford-Binet intelligence test, which is described in chapter 10.

Scores on standardized tests are often stated in percentiles. Suppose you scored in the 92nd percentile on the WAIS-III, another intelligence test. This score would mean that 92 percent of a large group of individuals who previously took the test received scores lower than yours.

The main advantage of standardized tests is that they provide information about individual differences among people (Walsh & Betz, 2001; Kaplan & Saccuzzo, 2005). One problem with standardized tests is that they do not always predict behaviour in nontest situations. Another problem is that standardized tests are based on the belief that a person's behaviour is consistent and stable, yet personality and intelligence—two primary targets of standardized testing—can vary with the situation. For example, a person may perform poorly on a standardized intelligence test in a final examination setting but score much higher at home, where he or she is less anxious.

This criticism is especially relevant for members of minority groups, some of whom have been inaccurately classified as mentally retarded on the basis of their scores on intelligence tests (Valencia & Suzuki, 2001). In addition, cross-cultural psychologists caution that while many psychological tests developed in Western cultures might work reasonably well in Western cultures, they might not always be appropriate in other cultures (Cushner, 2003). People in other cultures may have had experiences that cause them to interpret and respond to questions much differently from the people on whom the test was standardized.

University of New Brunswick clinical psychologist David Clark makes extensive use of surveys in his clinical research on the role of cognition in anxiety and depression.

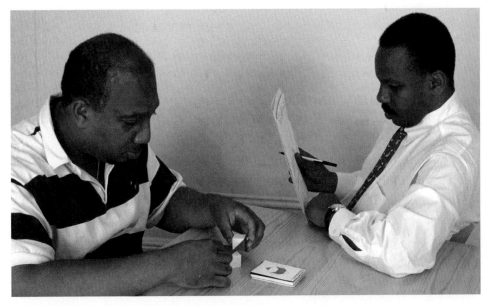

Standardized tests require individuals to answer a series of written or oral questions. The individual on the left is being given a standardized test of intelligence.

standardized test An oral or written assessment for which an individual receives a score indicating how the individual responded relative to others.

Mahatma Gandhi was the spiritual leader of India in the middle of the twentieth century. Erik Erikson conducted an extensive case study of his life to determine what contributed to his identity development. *What are some limitations of the case study approach?*

Case Study A **case study**, or case history, is an in-depth look at a single individual. Case studies are performed mainly by clinical psychologists when, for either practical or ethical reasons, the unique aspects of an individual's life cannot be duplicated and tested in other individuals (Dattilio, 2001). A case study provides information about one person's fears, hopes, fantasies, traumatic experiences, upbringing, family relationships, health, or anything that helps the psychologist understand the person's mind and behaviour. For example, we could have observed Pennebaker during the period of his deep depression and used our observations as the basis of a case study.

Traumatic experiences have produced some truly fascinating case studies in psychology. Consider the following: A 26-year-old schoolteacher met a woman with whom he fell intensely in love. But several months after their love affair began, the schoolteacher became depressed, drank heavily, and talked about suicide. The suicidal ideas progressed to images of murder and suicide. His actions became bizarre. On one occasion he punctured the tires of his beloved's car. On another he stood on the side of the road where she passed frequently in her car, extending his hand in his pocket so that she would think he was holding a gun. Only eight months after meeting her, the teacher shot her while he was a passenger in the car that she was driving. Soon after the act, he ran to a telephone booth to call his priest. The girlfriend had died (Revitch & Schlesinger, 1978).

This case reveals how depressive moods and bizarre thinking can precede violent acts, such as murder. Other vivid case studies appear later in this book, among them a modern-day wild child named Genie, who lived in near isolation during her childhood, and a woman named Eve with three personalities. They don't indicate how everyone will react in similar circumstances, but they give us an idea of the range of possibilities in human behaviour and some of the effects of different experiences.

Another, more positive example of a case study is the analysis of India's spiritual leader Mahatma Gandhi by psychodynamic theorist Erik Erikson (1969). Erikson studied Gandhi's life in great depth to discover insights about how his positive spiritual identity developed, especially during his youth. In putting the pieces of Gandhi's identity development together, Erikson described the contributions of culture, history, family, and various other factors that might affect the way other people develop an identity.

Case histories provide dramatic, in-depth portrayals of people's lives, but remember that we must be cautious when generalizing from this information. The subject of a case study is unique, with a genetic makeup and personal history that no one else shares. In addition, case studies involve judgments of unknown reliability. Psychologists who conduct case studies rarely check to see whether other psychologists agree with their observations.

Correlational Research

In **correlational research**, the goal is to describe the strength of the relationship between two or more events or characteristics. The more strongly the two events are correlated (related or associated), the more effectively we can predict one event from the other (Vernoy & Kyle, 2003). This form of research is a key method of data analysis, which, you may recall, is the third step in the scientific method.

The degree of relationship between two variables can be expressed as a numerical value called a *correlational coefficient*. Let's assume that we have data on the relationship between how long your instructor lectures (the X variable) and the number of times students yawn (the Y variable). For the sake of this example, let's assume these data produce a correlation coefficient (represented by the letter r) of +.70. Remember this number, as it will soon be used to illustrate what a correlation coefficient tells you about the relationship between two events or characteristics.

For the moment, however, you need to know only that the number tells you the strength of the relationship between the two factors. The rule is simple: The closer the number is to 1.00, the stronger the correlation; conversely, the closer the number is to .00, the weaker the correlation. Figure 2.2 offers guidelines for interpreting correlational values. But perhaps you are wondering about the significance of the plus sign in the correlation coefficient of +.70 that we have calculated in our classroom study.

case study An in-depth look at a single individual.

correlational research Research with the goal of describing the strength of the relationship between two or more events or characteristics.

Positive and Negative Correlations The numeric value of a correlation coefficient always falls within the range from +1.00 to −1.00, but the negative numbers do not indicate a lower value than positive numbers. A correlation of −.65 is just as strong as a correlation of +.65. The plus and minus sign do have different meanings, however, which you will learn about in a moment. The most important point is that you must avoid the temptation to attach value judgments to correlational values. A positive correlation is not "good" or "desirable" and a negative correlation is not "bad" or "undesirable."

As you can see, there are two parts to a correlation coefficient: the number and the sign. Remember that the plus or minus sign tells you nothing about the strength of the correlation. A correlation coefficient of −.87 is closer to −1.00, and thus indicates a stronger correlation, than the coefficient of +.45 is to +1.00.

What the plus or minus sign does tell you is the direction of the relationship between the two variables. A *positive correlation* is a relationship in which the two factors vary in the same direction. Both factors tend to either increase together or decrease together. Either relationship represents a positive correlation. A *negative correlation,* in contrast, is a relationship in which the two factors vary in opposite directions. As one factor increases, the other factor decreases. Thus a correlation of +.15 would indicate a weak positive correlation, and a -.74 would indicate a strong negative correlation. Examples of scatter plots showing positive and negative correlations appear in figure 2.3.

Let's return to the example about the relationship between how long your professor lectures and the number of times students yawn. As mentioned earlier, those two variables produced a correlation coefficient of +.70. What does the number .70 tell us? That these two factors happen together frequently. And what does the positive sign indicate? That the two factors vary in the same direction. As the amount of time your professor lectures increases, so does the number of yawns.

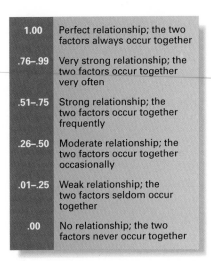

1.00	Perfect relationship; the two factors always occur together
.76–.99	Very strong relationship; the two factors occur together very often
.51–.75	Strong relationship; the two factors occur together frequently
.26–.50	Moderate relationship; the two factors occur together occasionally
.01–.25	Weak relationship; the two factors seldom occur together
.00	No relationship; the two factors never occur together

FIGURE 2.2

Guidelines for Interpreting Correlational Values

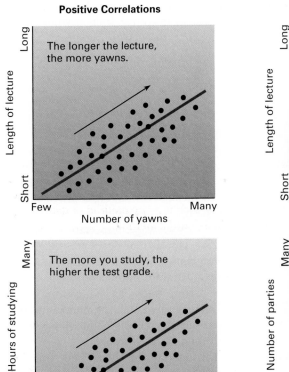

Positive Correlations

The longer the lecture, the more yawns.

Length of lecture (Short → Long)

Number of yawns (Few → Many)

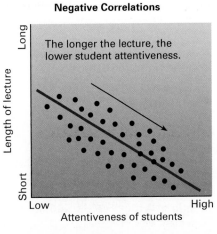

Negative Correlations

The longer the lecture, the lower student attentiveness.

Length of lecture (Short → Long)

Attentiveness of students (Low → High)

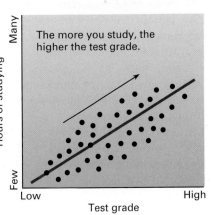

The more you study, the higher the test grade.

Hours of studying (Few → Many)

Test grade (Low → High)

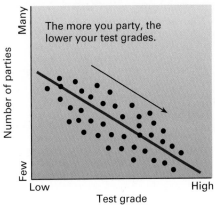

The more you party, the lower your test grades.

Number of parties (Few → Many)

Test grade (Low → High)

FIGURE 2.3

Scatter Plots Showing Positive and Negative Correlations

A positive correlation is a relationship in which two factors vary in the same direction, as shown in the two scatter plots on the left. A negative correlation is a relationship in which two factors vary in opposite directions, as shown in the two scatter plots on the right.

An example of a negative correlation in this situation might be the relationship between how long your instructor lectures and the level of student attentiveness. As the length of time your instructor lectures increases, the level of student attentiveness decreases. These two factors vary in opposite directions and thus have a negative correlation.

Correlation and Causation In trying to make sense of the world, people often make a big mistake about correlation. Look at the terms in bold type in the following newspaper headlines:

Researchers **Link** Coffee Consumption to Cancer of Pancreas
Scientists Find **Connection** Between Ear Hair and Heart Attacks
Psychologists Discover **Relationship** Between Marital Status and Health
Researchers Identify **Association** Between Loneliness and Social Skills
Parental Discipline **Tied** to Personality Disorders in Children

Reading these headlines, the general public would tend to jump to the conclusion that coffee causes cancer, ear hair causes heart attacks, and so on. But all of the words in bold type are synonymous only with correlation, not with causality. *Correlation does not equal causation.*

As you read about the findings of psychological studies, or findings in other sciences, guard against making the same mistake. Remember, correlation means only that two factors seem to occur together. Being able to predict one event based on the occurrence of another event does not necessarily tell us anything about the cause of either event (Silverthorne, 2004). Only experimental research allows the inference of causation.

Why, then, do researchers even bother doing correlational studies? Why don't they simply conduct experiments, which provide the most compelling evidence of causality? There are several reasons. For instance, it would be unethical to carry out an experiment in which expectant mothers are directed to drink varying numbers of alcoholic beverages to see how alcohol affects birth weight and fetal activity level. Also, the issue under investigation may be post hoc (after the fact) or historical, such as studying the childhood backgrounds of people who are abusive parents. Further, sometimes the factors simply cannot be manipulated experimentally, such as the effects on the residents of Prince Edward Island of building a bridge from the mainland.

Correlational methods permit research in situations that cannot be experimentally manipulated, such as the effects on residents of public works projects like the 1997 completion of the Confederation Bridge to Prince Edward Island. *What are some other examples of situations for which correlational methods might be well suited?*

To ensure that you understand the difference between correlation and causation, let's consider another example. Imagine a study in which it is found that people who make a lot of money have higher self-esteem than their counterparts who make less money. We could interpret this correlation to mean that making a lot of money causes high self-esteem. But we need to consider two other interpretations (see figure 2.4). One is that developing high self-esteem causes people to make a lot of money. Another interpretation is that a third factor, such as education, social upbringing, or genetic tendencies, causes the correlation between making a lot of money and high self-esteem.

Throughout this book you will read about numerous correlational research studies. Keep in mind how easy it is to assume causality when two events or characteristics are merely correlated.

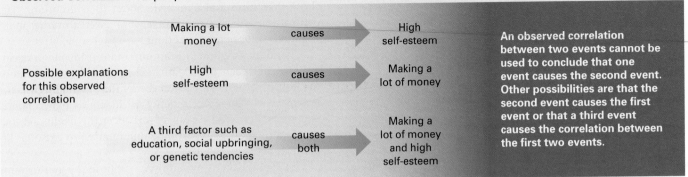

Observed Correlation: As people make a lot of money, their self-esteem increases.

Possible explanations for this observed correlation

Making a lot money → causes → High self-esteem

High self-esteem → causes → Making a lot of money

A third factor such as education, social upbringing, or genetic tendencies → causes both → Making a lot of money and high self-esteem

An observed correlation between two events cannot be used to conclude that one event causes the second event. Other possibilities are that the second event causes the first event or that a third event causes the correlation between the first two events.

FIGURE 2.4

Guidelines for Interpreting Correlation Coefficients

Experimental Research

James Pennebaker used experimental research to find answers to their questions about human behaviour. So do many other research psychologists who are interested in determining causes of behaviour—that is, why people do what they do (Aron, Aron & Coups, 2006). An **experiment** is a carefully regulated procedure in which one or more factors believed to influence the behaviour being studied are manipulated while all other factors are held constant.

If the behaviour under study changes when a factor is manipulated, we say that the manipulated factor has caused the behaviour to change. In other words, the experiment has demonstrated cause and effect. The cause is the factor that was manipulated, and the effect is the behaviour that changed because of the manipulation. Nonexperimental research methods (descriptive and correlational research) cannot establish cause and effect because they do not involve manipulating factors in a controlled way.

Independent and Dependent Variables Experiments have two types of changeable factors, or variables: independent and dependent. An **independent variable** is a manipulated, influential, experimental factor. It is a potential cause. The label independent is used because this variable can be manipulated independently of other factors to determine its effect. Researchers have a vast array of options open to them in selecting independent variables, and one experiment may include several independent variables (Bordens & Barrington, 2005).

In Pennebaker's first experiment, the independent variable was writing about emotions. Pennebaker manipulated this variable by asking different participants to write about their problems in different ways. For example, he asked some participants to write objectively about an emotional situation, without indulging their feelings. He asked other participants to both describe an experience and write how they felt about it. He also asked other participants to write about a topic that was unrelated to emotional events.

A **dependent variable** is a factor that can change in an experiment in response to changes in the independent variable. As researchers manipulate the independent variable, they measure the dependent variable for any resulting effect.

In Pennebaker's first experiment, the dependent variable was the number of visits that the student made to the health centre during the several months after writing about an emotional experience. Pennebaker found that the number of visits depended on the sort of writing that the student was asked to do.

Experimental and Control Groups Experiments can involve one or more experimental groups and one or more control groups. An **experimental group** is a group whose experience is manipulated. A **control group** is as much like the experimental group as possible and is treated in every way like the experimental group except for the independent variable or manipulated factor. The control group thus serves as a baseline against which the effects of the manipulated condition can be compared.

experiment A carefully regulated procedure in which one or more factors believed to influence the behaviour being studied are manipulated and all other factors are held constant.

independent variable The manipulated, influential, experimental factor in an experiment.

dependent variable The factor that can change in an experiment in response to changes in the independent variable.

experimental group A group in a research study whose experience is manipulated.

control group A comparison group that is treated in every way like the experimental group except for the manipulated factor.

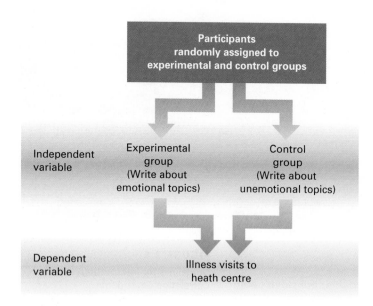

FIGURE 2.5
Random Assignment and Experimental Design

In Pennebaker's studies, the experimental groups were those that were asked to write about their emotions. The control groups were those that were asked to write about some other, nonemotional topic.

Random assignment is an important principle in deciding whether each participant will be placed in the experimental group or in the control group. **Random assignment** means that researchers assign participants to experimental and control groups by chance. It reduces the likelihood that the experiment's results will be due to any pre-existing differences between groups.

In Pennebaker's experiment, suppose the participants had not been randomly assigned but had been allowed to choose which group they would join—either the group that would write about emotions or the group that would write about something else. In that situation, people who were comfortable expressing their emotions might choose to join the first group, and people who were not comfortable expressing their emotions might choose to be in the second group. As a result, any difference between the groups in terms of health at the end of the experiment might owe nothing to the effects of writing but simply reflect the effects of a person's comfort in expressing emotions (see figure 2.5).

Pennebaker randomly assigned each participant to either the experimental group that wrote about emotional experiences or a control group that wrote about a nonemotional topic. The independent variable (which is always the manipulated variable) was the type of writing the students did (about the emotion situation or about something else). The dependent variable was the number of illness visits that students paid to the health centre after the writing. The design of this experiment allowed Pennebaker to argue that the emotional writing caused better health.

Some Cautions About Experimental Research Although experimental research is a powerful tool for discovering the causes of behaviour, experimental research must be done cautiously, with safeguards (Kantowitz, Roediger, & Elmes, 2005). Expectations and biases on the part of the people involved in the experiment can tarnish results (Rosnow & Rosenthal, 2002).

Experimenter Bias. Experimenters may subtly (and often unknowingly) influence their research participants. **Experimenter bias** occurs when the experimenter's expectations influence the outcome of the research.

In a classic study, Robert Rosenthal (Rosenthal & Lawson, 1964) turned university students into experimenters. They were randomly assigned rats from the same litter. However, half of the students were told that their rats were "maze bright," whereas the other half were told that their rats were "maze dull." Because of the random assignment, there were no actual differences between the two groups of rats. The students then conducted experiments to test their rats' ability to navigate mazes. The results were stunning. The so-called maze-bright rats were more successful than the maze-dull rats at running the mazes. Since there were no preexisting differences between the two groups of rats, the only explanation for the results is that the university students' expectations affected the performance of the rats. In other studies, researchers have demonstrated that experimenters' expectations influence not only rodent behaviour but human behaviour as well (Rosenthal, 1968, 1994).

Research Participant Bias and the Placebo Effect. Like the experimenters, research participants may have expectations about what they are supposed to do and how they should behave that affect the results of experiments (Shaughnessy & others, 2006). **Research participant bias** occurs when the behaviour of research participants during the experiment is influenced by how they think they are supposed to behave.

For example, in one study, the researchers first assessed participants' sensitivity to pain (Levine, Gordon, & Fields, 1979). Then they gave the participants an injection of a

random assignment Assignment of participants to experimental and control groups by chance.

experimenter bias The influence of the experimenter's own expectations on the outcome of the research.

research participant bias The influence of research participants' expectations on their behaviour within an experiment.

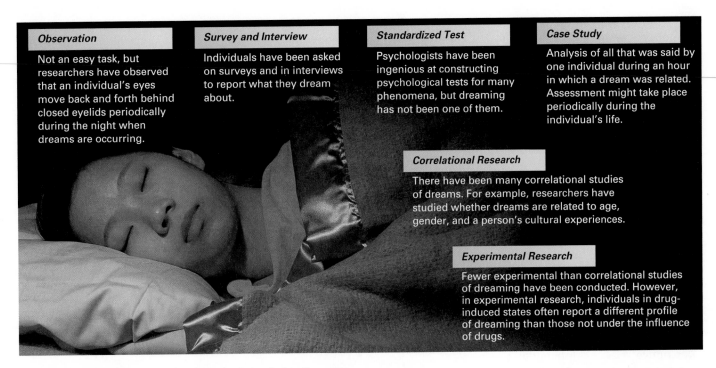

Observation

Not an easy task, but researchers have observed that an individual's eyes move back and forth behind closed eyelids periodically during the night when dreams are occurring.

Survey and Interview

Individuals have been asked on surveys and in interviews to report what they dream about.

Standardized Test

Psychologists have been ingenious at constructing psychological tests for many phenomena, but dreaming has not been one of them.

Case Study

Analysis of all that was said by one individual during an hour in which a dream was related. Assessment might take place periodically during the individual's life.

Correlational Research

There have been many correlational studies of dreams. For example, researchers have studied whether dreams are related to age, gender, and a person's cultural experiences.

Experimental Research

Fewer experimental than correlational studies of dreaming have been conducted. However, in experimental research, individuals in drug-induced states often report a different profile of dreaming than those not under the influence of drugs.

FIGURE 2.6 Psychology's Research Methods Applied to Dreaming

painkiller, or so the participants thought. Actually, they received a **placebo**, an innocuous, inert substance that has no specific physiological effect. (A placebo can be given to participants instead of the presumed active agent, such as a drug, to determine if it produces the effects thought to characterize the active agent.) Subsequently, when the experimenter administered painful stimuli, the participants perceived less pain than they had in the earlier assessment of their sensitivity to pain. This experiment demonstrated a **placebo effect**, which occurs when participants' expectations, rather than the experimental treatment, produce an experimental outcome.

In many studies, the researchers deliberately make use of the placebo effect to test a drug's effectiveness (Wilens & others, 2001). For example, in one study, 204 adults with social phobia (having an intense fear of being humiliated or embarrassed in social situations) were randomly assigned either to an experimental group in which the participants were given a drug, sertraline, or to a control group, in which they received a placebo (Van Ameringen & others, 2001). After 20 weeks, those who took sertraline showed less social phobia than their counterparts who took the placebo. In this case, the drug was judged effective exactly because it was more effective than a placebo.

Another way to make sure that neither the experimenter's nor the participants' expectations affect the outcome is to design a **double-blind experiment**. In this design, neither the experimenter nor the participants are aware of which participants are in the experimental group and which are in the control group until the results are calculated. The study of drug treatment for social phobia just described was conducted in a double-blind manner (Van Ameringen & others, 2001). Both the experimenter, who administered the drug, and the participants were kept in the dark about which individuals were receiving the drug and which were receiving a placebo that merely looked like the drug. Thus the experimenter could not make subtle gestures signaling who was receiving the drug and who was not. This was the same method that Oskar von Pfungst used to ensure that he was not subtly signalling the horse Hans to respond in a certain way to the number written on a card. A double-blind study allows researchers to tease apart the actual effects of the independent variable from the possible effects of the experimenter's and the participants' expectations about it.

At this point you have read about several different types of research in psychology. For another look how these research methods differ, see figure 2.6.

placebo An innocuous, inert substance or condition that may be given to participants instead of a presumed active agent, such as a drug, to determine if it produces effects similar to those of the active agent.

placebo effect The influence of participants' expectations, rather than the experimental treatment, on experimental outcome.

double-blind experiment An experiment that is conducted so that neither the experimenter nor the participants are aware of which participants are in the experimental group and which are in the placebo control group until after the results are calculated.

> **reflect and review**

② **Discuss the three types of research that are used in psychology.**

- Name and describe four kinds of descriptive research and identify at least one advantage of each kind of study.
- State the goal of correlational research and explain the significance of the correlation coefficient.
- Discuss the experimental method, including its components. Include in your discussion the potential pitfalls of the experimental method and how to avoid them.

You have learned that correlation does not equal causation. Develop an example of two variables (two sets of observations) that are correlated but that you believe almost certainly have no causal tie between them.

③ ANALYZING AND INTERPRETING DATA

— Descriptive — Inferential
   Statistics   Statistics

How do psychologists analyze and interpret research data?

As you saw in the preceding discussion of the scientific method, after psychologists collect data, they analyze and interpret it. To do this, they call on statistics, which are mathematical methods used to report data. The uniqueness of individual human beings means that no two people will respond identically to any given situation. In order to uncover regularities in human behaviour it is, therefore, necessary to collect data from a large sample of individuals and use statistics to isolate any regular patterns in the data. The relatively new CSI-style television series, "Numb3rs," revolves around a mathematician who uses various mathematical techniques to isolate the patterns underlying criminal behaviour. To do their research, psychologists must rely on statistics as well.

There are two basic categories of statistics: descriptive statistics, which are used to describe and summarize data, and inferential statistics, which are used to draw conclusions about those data (Aron, Aron & Coups, 2005).

Descriptive Statistics

Most psychological studies generate considerable numerical data. Just simply listing all the scores generated by a study—for each individual in the study—is often not very meaningful. **Descriptive statistics** are the mathematical procedures researchers have developed to describe and summarize sets of data in a meaningful way. Descriptive statistics show us the "big picture"—that is, the overall characteristics of the data and the significant variations among them (Wilson, 2005).

Measures of Central Tendency If you want to describe an "average" value for a set of scores, you would use a measure of central tendency. A *measure of central tendency* is a single number that tells you something about the middle point of a set of data. The three measures of central tendency are the mean, the median, and the mode.

The **mean** is what people often think of as the average, although it is only one type of average. The mean is calculated by adding all the scores and then dividing by the number of scores. It is a good indicator of the central tendency for a group of scores; it is the measure of central tendency that is used most often.

The mean is not as helpful, however, when a group of scores contains a few extreme scores. Consider the annual earnings for the two groups of five people shown

descriptive statistics Mathematical procedures that are used to describe and summarize samples of data in a meaningful way.

mean A statistical measure of central tendency that is calculated by adding all the scores and then dividing by the number of scores.

in the table that follows. Group 1 lists the earnings of five ordinary people. Group 2 is composed of the earnings of four ordinary people plus the approximate earnings of Shania Twain. Now look at the means that have been calculated for the two groups. The vast difference between them is due to the one extreme score. In such a situation, one of the other two measures of central tendency, median or mode, would give a more accurate picture of the data overall.

The **median** is the score that falls exactly in the middle of the distribution of scores after they have been arranged (or ranked) from highest to lowest. When you have an odd number of scores (say, 5 or 7 scores), the median is the score with the same number of scores above it as below it. In the table, each group has a median income of $23,000. Notice that, unlike the mean, the median is unaffected by extreme scores. The medians are the same for both groups ($23,000), but their means are extremely different ($22,000 versus $12,017,000). Of course, if there is an even number of scores, there is no "middle" score. This problem is dealt with by averaging the scores that "share" the middle location.

Mean $22,000

Group 1	Group 2
$19,000	$19,000
19,000	19,000
23,000	23,000
24,000	24,000
25,000	60,000,000
Mean $22,000	Mean $12,017,000
Median $23,000	Median $23,000
Mode $19,000	Mode $19,000

The **mode** is the score that occurs most often in a set of data. In our present example, the mode is $19,000, which occurs twice in each group. All the other annual incomes occur only once. The mode is the least used measure of central tendency. The mode can be useful, however, in cases in which information is desired about preference or popularity. Consider a teacher who wants to know the most popular child in her classroom. She might create a questionnaire and ask students which of their classmates they like the most. The most frequently nominated child would be the mode in these instances.

Measures of Variability In addition to revealing the central characteristics of a sample, statistics can also give us *measures of variability*, which describe how much the scores in a sample vary from one another (Davis & Smith, 2005). Imagine that you are the owner of three music stores that all have the same annual earnings of $1,200,000. However, these three stores fluctuate widely in their monthly earnings. Store 1 consistently produces a monthly income of about $10,000. Store 2 generates no income some months but produces $200,000 of income in other months. Store 3 loses money the first 9 months of every year but makes enormous profits during October, November, and December. You would be correct in saying that the mean annual earnings of each of your stores is $1,200,000. But business planning would be easier if you could also represent the individual fluctuations in the earnings of your three stores. Measures of variability can be very helpful in this regard.

Two common measures of variability are the range and the standard deviation. The **range** is the distance between the highest and the lowest scores. The ranges in the monthly incomes of your three stores could be something like this:

Store 1: $10,500 − $9,500 = $1,000
Store 2: $200,000 − $0 = $200,000
Store 3: $500,000 − (−$50,000) = $550,000

median A statistical measure of central tendency that falls exactly in the middle of a distribution of scores after they have been arranged (or ranked) from highest to lowest.

mode A statistical measure of central tendency, the score that occurs most often.

range A statistical measure of variability that is the distance between the highest and lowest scores.

The difference between $1,000 and $550,000 a month—and thus the range of monthly earnings at your stores—is huge. The differences reflect the vastly different cash flow at each of the three stores.

Generally speaking, the range is a rather simplistic estimate of variability, or dispersion, for a group of scores. More important, because the range takes into account only the lowest and highest scores, it can produce a misleading picture of the variability in your data.

A more informative measure of variability, and the one most commonly used in psychology research, is the **standard deviation**. It measures how much the scores vary on the average around the mean of the sample. Put another way, it indicates how closely scores are clustered around the mean. The smaller the standard deviation, the less variability from the mean.

A simple example will illustrate how standard deviation is calculated. Consider the following four race scores for each of three cross-country skiers:

	Skier 1	Skier 2	Skier 3
Race 1	44 minutes	40 minutes	32 minutes
Race 2	36 minutes	40 minutes	48 minutes
Race 3	44 minutes	40 minutes	32 minutes
Race 4	36 minutes	40 minutes	48 minutes
Mean Time	40 minutes	40 minutes	40 minutes
Standard Deviation	4 minutes	0 minutes	8 minutes

Notice that all three skiers had the same mean race time of 40 minutes. But skier 1 and skier 3 each had race times that varied from race to race, whereas skier 2 had exactly the same time for each of the four races. This variability from race to race, or the lack of it, is expressed by the three different standard deviations. Because skier 2 had no variability from race to race, that person's standard deviation is 0. Skier 1's race time varied 4 minutes on average from his mean of 40 minutes. (Calculate the difference between each skier's mean time and race time, and then divide by the four races.) In other words, skier 1 had a standard deviation of 4 minutes for his race times. Skier 3's race times varied 8 minutes on average from her mean time of 40 minutes. Thus, skier 3 had a standard deviation of 8 minutes for her race times. The different standard deviations tell you that skier 2 had no variability among his race scores, skier 1 had some variability among his race scores, and skier 3 had even more variability among her race scores. Thus the standard deviation tells you how consistently each skier performed.

Why do psychologists use the standard deviation so frequently in their research? Because it tells them how far away a measured score is from the mean in a distribution of scores (Aron, Aron & Coups, 2006). In chapter 8, you will see that such information is especially helpful in determining a person's intelligence.

Inferential Statistics

Imagine that you have conducted a naturalistic observation investigating whether boys play more aggressively than girls. You have followed all the procedures for a good research design to eliminate or minimize any bias or any other factors that might distort the data you have collected. When you calculate the descriptive statistics comparing the aggressive behaviour of boys with that of girls, you find differences between the two groups. How large do those differences have to be before you are willing to conclude confidently that the differences are significant, that boys truly do play more aggressively than girls? Small differences between the boys and girls could easily arise through chance factors you were not aware of or had no control over. Perhaps, for example, a few of the boys in your study happened to have just came back from hockey practice

standard deviation A statistical measure of variability that involves how much the scores vary on the average around the mean of the sample.

and were still feeling more aggressive than usual. Thus any small difference in the descriptive statistics may represent only the small differences you are likely to find among any group of individuals or the circumstances in which you are observing each group. Inferential statistics can help determine the significance of the scores you have collected.

Inferential statistics are statistical methods used to draw conclusions about data that have been collected. More specifically, inferential statistics indicate whether or not data sufficiently support or confirm a research hypothesis (Aron, Aron & Coups, 2006).

The idea behind inferential statistics is relatively simple. Measures of inferential statistics tell us how likely differences observed between two or more groups were due simply to chance. If a probability statement tells you that the odds are 5 out of 100 (or .05) or less that the differences are due to chance, the results are considered statistically significant. In statistical language, this is referred to as the .05 *level of statistical significance*. Put another way, statistical significance means that the differences observed between two groups are so large that it is highly unlikely that those differences are due merely to chance.

The .05 level of statistical significance is considered the minimum level of probability that scientists will accept to conclude that the differences observed are real, thereby supporting a hypothesis. In some types of research it may be particularly important to be careful about concluding that an observed difference is truly significant. For example, we would want to be especially conservative drawing conclusions about the effectiveness of a new heart medication with troublesome side effects since if we were wrong many heart patients might suffer those side effects without experiencing any real benefit from the drug. In such cases, researchers prefer to use more rigorous levels of statistical significance, such as the .01 level of statistical significance (1 out of 100 odds or less that the differences are due to chance) or the .001 level of statistical significance (1 out of 1,000 odds or less).

A word of caution is in order about interpreting statistical significance. A statistically significant difference in a research study does not always translate into a difference that has meaning in everyday life. Before assuming that a finding is significant both statistically and in everyday life, it is wise to examine the actual differences involved. For example, although the media in Canada and other industrialized nations commonly report that boys have more trouble in school than girls, the research does not strongly support this conclusion (Bouchard & others, 2003). As one example, Bouchard and St-Amant (1996) studied 2,200 senior high school students in Quebec. They found that 51 percent of the lowest achievers were boys (and 49 percent girls) but that 48 percent of the highest achievers were boys (and 52 percent girls). In other words, the difference in achievement between the boys and girls is not just a fluke. But because the average difference is only a few percent, it may have little practical importance.

> **reflect and review**

3 **Distinguish between descriptive statistics and inferential statistics.**

- Identify three measures of central tendency and two measures of variability and understand the purpose of each.
- Discuss the concept of statistical significance and its importance in data interpretation.

Why is it important for you to develop a basic understanding of statistics?

inferential statistics Mathematical methods that are used to draw conclusions about data.

④ FACING UP TO RESEARCH CHALLENGES

— Conducting
  Ethical
  Research

— Minimizing
  Bias

— Being a Wise
  Consumer of
  Information
  About Psychology

What are some research challenges that involve ethics, bias, and information?
The scientific and statistical foundation of psychological research helps to minimize the effect of individual researchers' biases and to maximize the objectivity of the results. Still, some subtle challenges remain to be fully resolved. One is to ensure that research is conducted in an ethical way; another is to recognize and try to overcome researchers' deeply buried personal biases. Researchers are not the only ones who face challenges, however. So do you. Every time you encounter information about psychology, whether in the popular media or in academic journals, you face the challenge of evaluating the information objectively and making sure that you are not jumping to the wrong conclusions.

Conducting Ethical Research

Ethics is an important part of your understanding of the science of psychology. Even if you never have any formal exposure to psychology after you take this course, you will find that scientific research in psychology and related disciplines affects your everyday life. For one thing, decision makers in business, government, schools, and many other institutions use the results of psychological research to help people lead happier, healthier, more productive lives.

Psychological research affects our pocketbooks as well, at least indirectly. Very often, psychological research is supported by federal government grants. Because the allocation of grant money is highly competitive—not only within the scientific community but also between science and other government-sponsored projects—our society as a whole must continually decide which lines of research are the most beneficial. In recent years, for example, our priorities have shifted to educational research in the face of problems experienced by youth and an explosion in educational technology.

In addition, the explosion in other technologies has forced society to grapple with looming ethics questions that were unimaginable only a few decades ago (Kimmel, 1996). For example, stem-cell research raises hopes for thousands of people with spinal cord injuries, for whom Christopher Reeve was a spokesperson until his death in 2004. Also, this research offers the possibility of new therapies for a host of diseases from Parkinson's Disease to macular degeneration. However, this same line of research has led to the "harvesting" of stem cells from aborted human embryos or embryos taken from a mother undergoing in vitro fertilization. Should embryos left over from such procedures be used in such ways?

Ethics in psychological research may affect you more personally if you serve at some point, as is quite likely, as a participant in a study. In that event, you need to know about your rights as a participant and about the responsibilities researchers have in ensuring that those rights are safeguarded. Participants' experiences can have life-altering consequences for them if researchers fail to consider their well-being. For example, one investigation of young dating couples asked them to complete a questionnaire that coincidentally stimulated some of the participants to think about potentially troublesome issues (Rubin & Mitchell, 1976). One year later, when the researchers followed up with the original sample, 9 of 10 participants said they had discussed their answers with their dating partners. In most instances, the discussions helped to strengthen the relationships. But in some cases, the participants used the questionnaire as a springboard to discuss problems or previously hidden concerns. One participant said, "The study definitely played a role in ending my relationship with Larry." In this case, the couple had different views about how long they expected to be together. She was thinking of a short-term dating relationship only, whereas he was thinking in terms of a lifetime. Their answers to the questions brought the disparity in their views to the surface and led to the end of their relationship. Researchers have a responsibility to anticipate the personal problems their study might cause and to at least inform the participants of the possible fallout.

If you ever become a researcher in psychology yourself, you need an even deeper understanding of ethics. You may never become a researcher in the field of psychology, but you may carry out one or more experimental projects in psychology courses. Even smart, conscientious students frequently do not consider the rights of the participants who serve in their experiments. A student might think, "I volunteer in a home for the mentally retarded several hours a week. I can use the residents of the home in my study to see if a particular treatment helps improve their memory for everyday tasks." But without proper permissions, the most well-meaning, kind, and considerate studies still violate the rights of the participants. In this case, the residents may feel coerced into participating out of fear that the student volunteer will treat them badly if they do not comply or give the "right" answers.

Ethics Guidelines   Safeguarding the rights of research participants is a challenge because the potential harm is not always obvious. At first glance, you might not imagine that a questionnaire on dating relationships among university students would have any substantial impact or that an experiment involving treatment of memory loss would be anything but beneficial. But psychologists increasingly recognize the lasting harm that might come to the participants in a psychological study.

Today, colleges and universities have review boards that evaluate the ethical nature of research conducted at their institutions. Proposed research plans must pass the scrutiny of a research ethics committee before the research can be initiated.

In 2001, the Interagency Advisory Panel on Research Ethics (PRE) was formed to integrate the ethical standards guiding research funded by the three major federally supported Canadian granting agencies that fund psychological research, Canadian Institutes of Health Research (CIHR), the Natural Sciences and Engineering Research Council (NSERC) and the Social Sciences and Humanities Research Council (SSHRC). PRE and the three funding agencies have published a joint statement to guide the ethics of Canadian research on human subjects (Tri-Council Policy Statement, 2003).

In addition, the Canadian Psychological Association (CPA) has developed comparable ethics guidelines for its members (Canadian Psychological Association, 2000; Sinclair, 1998; Hadjistavropoulos & others, 2002). The code of ethics instructs psychologists to protect their participants from mental and physical harm. The participants' best interests need to be kept foremost in the researcher's mind. Contemporary ethics guidelines address four important issues:

- **Informed consent**. All participants must know what their participation will involve and what risks might develop. For example, participants in a study on dating should be told beforehand that a questionnaire might stimulate thoughts about issues in their relationships that they have not considered. Participants should also be informed that in some instances a discussion of the issues might improve their relationships but that in others it might worsen the relationships and even end them. Even after informed consent is given, participants must retain the right to withdraw from the study at any time and for any reason.
- **Confidentiality**. Researchers are responsible for keeping all the data they gather on individuals completely confidential and, when possible, completely anonymous.
- **Debriefing**. After the study has been completed, participants should be informed of its purpose and the methods that were used. In most cases, the experimenter can also inform participants in a general manner beforehand about the purpose of the research without leading participants to behave in a way that they think that the experimenter is expecting. When preliminary information about the study is

likely to affect the results, participants can at least be debriefed after the study has been completed.

- **Deception**. This is an ethical issue that psychologists debate extensively (Shaughnessy & others, 2006). In some circumstances, telling the participants beforehand what the research study is about substantially alters the participants' behaviour and invalidates the researcher's data. For example, suppose a psychologist wants to know whether bystanders will report a theft. A mock theft is staged, and the psychologist observes which bystanders report it. Had the psychologist informed the participants beforehand that the theft was staged and that the study was intended to discover the percentage of bystanders who will report a theft, the whole study would have been undermined. And so the researcher deceives participants about the purpose of the study, perhaps leading them to believe that it has some other purpose. In all cases of deception, however, the psychologist must ensure that the deception will not harm the participants and that the participants will be told the true nature of the study (debriefed) as soon as possible after the study is completed (Chastain & Landrum, 1999).

The Ethics of Research with Animals For generations, psychologists have used animals in some research. Animal studies have provided a better understanding of and solutions for many human problems (Cozby, 2004). Neal Miller, who has made important discoveries about the effects of biofeedback on health, listed the following areas in which animal research has benefitted humans (Miller, 1985):

- Psychotherapy techniques and behavioural medicine
- Rehabilitation of neuromuscular disorders
- Alleviation of the effects of stress and pain
- Drugs to treat anxiety and severe mental illness
- Methods for avoiding drug addiction and relapse
- Treatments to help premature infants gain weight so they can leave the hospital sooner
- Methods used to alleviate memory deficits in old age

Relatively few CPA members use animals in their psychological research. When animals *are* used in research, they are almost always rats and mice. Further, all research with animals in Canada is governed by a set of standards for housing, feeding, and maintaining the psychological and physical well-being of their animal subjects (Canadian Psychological Association, 1996). Researchers are required to weigh potential benefits of the research against possible harm to the animal and to avoid inflicting unnecessary pain. Simply put, whether animals or humans are the subjects in psychological research, stringent ethical guidelines must be followed (Herzog, 1995).

Values Questions are asked not only about the ethics of psychology but also about its values, its standards for judging what is worthwhile and desirable (Pettifor, 1998). Some psychologists argue that psychology should be value-free and morally neutral. From their perspective, the psychologist's role as a scientist is to present facts as objectively as possible.

Others believe that because psychologists are human, they cannot possibly be value-free, even if they try to be. Indeed, some people even argue that psychologists should take stands on value-laden issues (Neufeldt, 1989). For example, if research were to show that day care in the first year of life is harmful to children's development, shouldn't psychologists support reforms to improve day care or support mandates to have businesses give parents up to a year of paid leave after their child is born? The underlying question is of psychologists' scientific responsibilities versus their responsibilities to society as a whole. To think further about psychology and values, see the Critical Reflections box.

Is Psychology Value-Free?

The relationship between science and values is one of the most controversial questions psychologists face today. On the one hand, the scientific psychologist embraces objectivity. In the pure world of science, there is no place for values. As a science, psychology is dedicated to discovering facts about behaviour and creating theories to explain those facts. On the other hand, some critics question whether a view of science as value-free is realistic (Seligman, Olson, & Zanna, 1996). We are all human and have our all-too-human points of view. For example, do you agree or disagree with the following statements?

	Agree	Disagree
1. Human beings are basically good.	✓	
2. By changing the environment, you can change people's behaviour.	✓	
3. Intelligence is the most important human trait.	✓	
4. People are too concerned about themselves.	✓	
5. Physical attraction is important in choosing a mate.	✓	
6. Women are becoming too assertive.		✓
7. Divorce is wrong.	`	✓
8. Religion is not an appropriate area of study for psychologists.		✓
9. Money can bring happiness.	✓	
10. It is okay to cheat if you don't get caught.		✓

The way you responded to these items provides insight about your values. If you decide to become a psychologist, might your views on these topics, as well as others, influence the area you choose to research? How about the views of particular psychologists? A divorced woman might decide to study the inadequate involvement and support of noncustodial fathers in their children's lives rather than the increased role of fathers in caring for children because of her soured relationship with her ex-husband. An Asian-Canadian might choose to study the importance of conformity to a group's goals rather than an individual's unique contributions to a project because he or she believes that getting along with others in a group is more important than an individual's achievement.

More importantly, how can you be sure that your values have not resulted in biased research? The history of psychology offers many troubling examples. Psychological research has been used to support the idea that women are inferior to men (Tavris, 1992) and that some races are inferior to others (Gould, 1981). In many cases, the biases were introduced into the research through unconscious experimenter bias and research participant bias.

When psychologists are called on as experts, they may make statements and recommendations that are laden with values.

A psychologist interviewed in *Maclean's* magazine or testifying in a court of law may have certain values concerning parents' responsibility in an adolescent's use of cocaine. For example, one psychologist might stress that parents should be held financially responsible for any crimes committed by their cocaine-addicted offspring, whereas another might insist the parents don't need to take any responsibility at all.

Clinical psychologists' values may affect the advice they give to clients. Psychotherapists who people consult about problems may have certain personal values concerning self-esteem, marriage, sexual conduct, and other topics that influence the advice they give (Dobson & Breault, 1998). For example, one psychotherapist might perceive a client's sexual behaviour as "sick," whereas another might think of it as an adaptive sexual variation.

Similarly, psychology professors' values may influence the topics they choose to discuss in class and how they respond to students' questions. Psychology professors may have certain values about gender, moral behaviour, religion, child rearing, and how to get ahead in life that might influence what they communicate in their lectures and how they respond to students' questions. For example, one professor might perceive that a female's assertive behaviour is too aggressive, whereas another might think of the behaviour as being competent.

This values debate is often focused on one question: Can psychologists be objective in spite of their values? Critics argue that, although psychologists often strive to reduce the role of values as they seek to discover facts about behaviour, in the court of life, which is psychology's setting, values and psychology are difficult to disentangle (Evans, 1997). Others even argue that psychologists should take stands on value-laden issues rather than pretend to some sort of objective neutrality. (Neufeldt, 1989).

Perhaps "CSI: Crime Scene Investigation's" Gil Grissom has it right when he stresses both the ideal of objectivity and yet urges his team to be realistic by being on guard to identify and avoid bias in every possible way. It is, after all, a disservice if a crime scene investigator allows his or her biases to taint a criminal investigation and perhaps lead to a wrongful conviction. Similarly, we do the science of psychology a disservice if we allow our values to bias our psychological research. One especially helpful way to disentangle objectivity and values is for individual psychologists to clarify their own values and attempt to become more aware of their own unconscious biases.

What do you think?
- Is psychology value-free? Explain.
- How might the culture in which psychologists grow up influence their values, and how might those values in turn affect their choice of research topics and the advice they give to clients in psychotherapy?
- Are religious values appropriate study material for psychologists? How might psychologists study religious values?

Minimizing Bias

The debate over the place of values in psychology continues. But psychologists have generally come to agree that another type of personal objectivity is desirable when doing research. Psychological studies are most useful when they are conducted without bias or prejudice toward any particular group of people—especially biases based on sex or gender and on culture or ethnicity.

Gender Bias For centuries, Western society has had a strong gender bias, a preconceived notion about the abilities of women and men that prevented women from pursuing their own interests and achieving their potential. Historically women have faced barriers in the academic world and in their careers. But gender bias has also had a less obvious effect within psychology (Etaugh & Bridges, 2004).

Too often psychological research has had a gender bias (Hyde, 2004; Stark-Adamec & Kimball, 1984; Stark, 1992). Researchers have traditionally been male. It has not always been easy for women to become researchers in psychology (O'Connell & Russo, 1983) although this situation has recently changed (Wright & Myers, 1982). Similarly, research participants have traditionally been male. Despite this, conclusions were often drawn about "human" attitudes and behaviour and then generalized to females.

Even when men and women are included in studies, if gender differences are found, they are often unduly magnified (Bouchard & others, 2003; Denmark & others, 1988). For example, a researcher might report in a study that 74 percent of the men had high achievement expectations versus only 67 percent of the women and go on to talk about the differences in some detail. In reality, this might be a rather small difference. It might also disappear if the study were repeated or if the study were found to have methodological problems that don't allow such strong interpretations.

In response to such problems, Stark-Adamec & Kimball (1984) proposed a set of guidelines for the conduct of nonsexist research that the Canadian Psychological Association adopted as policy in 1983. They argued that only nonsexist research can improve the status and quality of life of women. In contrast, sex bias in psychological research is largely unintentional and due to a persistent lack of awareness of the issues and factors involved. Given the implications of such research for women—in terms of quality of life, physical and psychological health, and equal opportunity—the support, conduct, and publication of sex-biased research is unscientific and unethical.

If we are concerned about equal rights in research, then we should consider questions such as the following (Tetreault, 1997; Stark-Adamec, 1992):

- How might gender bias influence the choice of hypotheses, participants, and research design? For example, the most widely known theory of moral development was proposed by a male (Lawrence Kohlberg) in a male-dominant society (the United States), and males were the main participants in research used to support the theory for many years.
- How might research on traditionally female topics, such as relationships, feelings, and empathy, challenge existing theory and research? For example, in the study of moral development, the highest level has often been portrayed as based on a principle of "justice for the individual" (Kohlberg, 1976). However, more recent theorizing notes that individuality and autonomy tend to be male concerns and suggests that a principle based on relationships and connections with others be added to our thinking about high-level moral development (Gilligan, 1982, 1996, 2003).
- How has research that has exaggerated gender differences between females and males influenced the way people think about females? For example, some researchers believe that gender differences in mathematics have often been exaggerated and have been fuelled by societal bias (Hyde & Mezulis, 2002). Such exaggeration of differences can lead to negative expectations for females' math performance, even among females themselves.

Cultural and Ethnic Bias The realization that psychological research needs to include more people from diverse ethnic groups has also been building (Graham, 1992;

Guthrie, 2004). Historically, people from ethnic minority groups (for example, Aboriginal peoples, or North Americans of Chinese or West Indian descent) have been discounted from most research in North America and are simply thought of as variations from the norm, or average. Because their scores don't always fit neatly into measures of central tendency, minority individuals have been viewed as confounds, or "noise" in data. Consequently, researchers have deliberately excluded them from the samples they have selected. Given the fact that individuals from diverse ethnic groups have been excluded from psychological research for so long, we might reasonably conclude that people's real lives are perhaps more varied than research data have indicated in the past (Pope-Davis & others, 2003; Ponterotto & others, 2001).

Researchers have also tended to overgeneralize about ethnic groups. **Ethnic gloss** is using an ethnic label, such as "Aboriginal" or "Asian," in a superficial way that portrays an ethnic group as being more homogeneous than it really is. For example, a researcher might describe a research sample like this: "The 20 Aboriginal participants were of Mi'kmaq origin and were equally divided into four groups of five: one group was from Fort Folly, New Brunswick, another group was from Pictou Landing First Nation, in Trenton, Nova Scotia, a third was from the Abegweit Band, in Cornwall, Prince Edward Island. The fourth group was off-reserve, living and working in the greater Halifax area. All participants were functionally trilingual (Mi'kmaq, English, French) and were born on one of the three reserves mentioned here." Of course, a similarly detailed description of European Canadian groups would also be appropriate. Ethnic gloss can cause researchers to obtain samples of ethnic groups that are not representative of the group's diversity, which can lead to overgeneralization and stereotyping.

Many psychologists are interested in obtaining better research information about gender and ethnicity (Reid & Zalk, 2001). Victoria Esses, of the University of Western Ontario, is especially interested in ethnic relations and our attitudes towards immigration and immigrants. Her research with her colleague Lynn Jackson, of Ryerson Polytechnic University in Toronto, focuses on factors that promote negative attitudes toward immigrants (Esses & others, 2001, in press). For example, Jackson & Esses (2000) found that many people prefer to maintain economic advantages over immigrants, thus making it difficult for empowering help to be offered to new immigrants. This may be because people perceive immigrants as creating competition for scarce resources (Esses, Jackson, & Armstrong, 1998).

Being a Wise Consumer of Information About Psychology

Television, radio, newspapers, and magazines all frequently report on psychological research that is likely to be of interest to the general public. Much of the information has been published in professional journals or presented at national meetings, and most major colleges and universities have a media relations department that contacts the press about current research by their faculty.

You should be aware, however, that not all psychological information that is presented for public consumption comes from professionals with excellent credentials and reputations at colleges or universities or in applied mental health settings (Stanovich, 2004). Because journalists, television reporters, and other media personnel are not usually trained in psychological research, they often have trouble sorting through the widely varying material they find and making sound decisions about the best information to present to the public.

In addition, the media often focus on sensationalistic and dramatic psychological findings to capture your attention. They tend to go beyond what actual research articles and clinical findings really say.

Even when the media present the results of excellent research, they have trouble adequately informing people about what has been found and the implications for people's lives. For example, this entire book is designed to carry out the task of carefully introducing, defining, and elaborating on key concepts and issues, research, and clinical findings. The media, however, do not have the luxury of so much time and space to

Look at the two photographs, one of all white males, the other of a diverse group of females and males from different ethnic groups, including some white individuals. Consider a topic in psychology, such as parenting, love, or cultural values. *If you were conducting research on this topic, might the result of the study be different depending on whether the participants in your study were the individuals in the photograph on the left or those on the right?*

ethnic gloss Involves using an ethnic label, such as "Aboriginal" or "Asian," in a superficial way that portrays the ethnic group as more homogeneous than it really is.

Victoria Esses, of the University of Western Ontario, focuses her research effort on stereotypes, prejudice, and discrimination.

detail and specify the limitations and qualifications of research. They often have only a few minutes or a few lines to summarize as best they can the complex findings of a study or a psychological concept.

In the end, you have to take responsibility for evaluating the reports on psychological research that you encounter in the media. To put it another way, you have to consume psychological information wisely. Here are five guidelines that you may find helpful:

Distinguish Between Group Results and Individual Needs People who learn about psychological research through the media are likely to apply the results to their individual circumstances. Yet most research focuses on groups, and individual variations in participants' responses are seldom emphasized. As a result, the ill-informed consumer of psychological research may get the wrong idea about the "normality" of his or her circumstances. For example, researchers interested in the effects of divorce on an adult's ability to cope with stress might conduct a study of 50 divorced women and 50 married women. They might conclude that the divorced women, as a group, cope more poorly with stress than the married women in the study do. In this particular study, however, some of the divorced women were likely to be coping better than some of the married women. Indeed, of the 100 women in the study, the two or three women who were coping the best with stress may have been divorced women. It would be accurate to report the findings as showing that divorced women (as a group) coped less effectively with stress than married women (as a group) did. But it would not be sensible to conclude, after reading a summary of the results of the study, that your divorced sister may not be coping with stress as well as she thinks and recommend that she see a therapist.

The failure of the media to distinguish adequately between research on groups and the individual needs of consumers is not entirely their fault. Researchers have not made the difference clear, either. They often fail to examine the overlap in the data on the groups they are comparing and look for only the differences. And then too often they highlight only these differences in their reports as well.

Remember, if you read a report in a research journal or the media that states that the divorced women coped more poorly with stress than the married women did, you cannot conclude that *all* divorced women coped more poorly with stress. The only conclusion that you can reasonably draw is that *more* married women coped better than divorced women did.

Overgeneralizing from a Small or Unrepresentative Sample Media presentations of psychological information often don't have the space or time to go into details about the nature of the sample used in the study. Sometimes you will get basic information about the sample's size—whether it is based on 10, 50, or 200 participants, for example. If you can't learn anything else about the sample, at least pay attention to its number.

Small or very small samples require caution in generalizing to a larger population of individuals. For example, a sample of only 10 or 20 divorced women may have some unique characteristics that would make the study's finding inapplicable to many women, especially if there are further questions about the representativeness of the sample. The women in the sample might all have high incomes, be English-Canadian, be childless, live in a small town in Manitoba, or be undergoing psychotherapy. Divorced women who have moderate to low incomes, are from other ethnic backgrounds, have children, are living in different contexts, or are not undergoing psychotherapy might have given very different responses.

Look for Answers Beyond a Single Study The media might identify an interesting piece of research or a clinical finding and claim that it is something phenomenal with far-reaching implications. Although such pivotal studies do occur, they are rare. It is safer to assume that no single study will provide conclusive answers to an important question, especially answers that apply to all people. In fact, in most psychological domains that prompt many investigations, conflicting results are common. Answers to questions in research usually emerge after many scientists have conducted similar investigations that yield similar conclusions.

If one study reports that a particular therapy conducted by a particular therapist has been especially effective with divorced adults, you should not conclude that the therapy will work as effectively with all divorced adults and with other therapists until more studies are conducted. Remember that you should not take a report of one research study as the absolute, final answer to a question.

Attributing Causes Where None Have Been Found   Drawing causal conclusions from correlational studies is one of the most common mistakes made by the media. When a true experiment has not been conducted—that is, when participants have not been randomly assigned to treatments or experiences—two variables or factors might have only a noncausal relationship to each other (Cozby, 2004). Remember from the discussion of correlation earlier in the chapter that causal interpretations cannot be made when two or more factors are simply correlated. We cannot say that one causes the other.

In the case of divorce, imagine that you read this headline: "Low income causes divorced women to have a high degree of stress." You can instantly conclude that the story is about a correlational study, not an experimental study. The word "causes" is used in error. Why? Because, for ethical and practical reasons, women participants cannot be randomly assigned to become divorced or stay married, and divorced women cannot be randomly assigned to be poor or rich. A more accurate heading would probably be "Low-income divorced women have a high degree of stress," meaning that the researchers found a correlation between being divorced, having a low income, and having a lot of stress. Be skeptical of words indicating causation until you know more about the research they are describing.

Consider the Source of Psychological Information   Remember that the rest of the research community does not automatically accept studies conducted by psychologists. The researchers must usually submit their findings to a journal for review by their colleagues, who make a decision about whether to publish the paper or not depending on the care taken in conducting the research. Although the quality of research and findings is not uniform among all psychology journals, in most cases journals submit the findings to far greater scrutiny than the popular media do (Stanovich, 2004).

Within the media, though, you can usually draw a distinction. The reports of psychological research in respected newspapers, such as *The Globe and Mail* and the *National Post*, as well as in credible magazines such as *Time* and *Maclean's*, are far more trustworthy than reports in tabloids, such as the *National Enquirer*. But regardless of the source—serious publication, tabloid, or even academic journal—you are responsible for reading the details of the research behind the findings that are presented and analyzing the study's credibility.

> ## reflect and review

 Discuss some research challenges that involve ethics, bias, and information.

- Describe researchers' ethical responsibilities to the humans and animals they study.
- Explain how gender, cultural, and ethnic bias can affect the outcome of a research study.
- Make a list of the things to keep in mind when you come across information pertaining to psychological research.

In the next few days, look through several newspapers and magazines for reports about psychological research. Also notice what you see and hear on television about psychology. Try applying the guidelines for being a wise consumer of information about psychology to these media reports.

Psychology's Scientific Methods

1 EXPLORING PSYCHOLOGY AS A SCIENCE

— A Scientific   — Collaboration   — The Scientific
    Approach   Method

2 TYPES OF RESEARCH

— Descriptive   — Correlational   — Experimental
    Research   Research   Research

3 ANALYZING AND INTERPRETING DATA

— Descriptive   — Inferential
    Statistics   Statistics

4 FACING UP TO RESEARCH CHALLENGES

— Conducting   — Minimizing   — Being a Wise
    Ethical   Bias   Consumer of
    Research   Information
                                                About Psychology

At the beginning of the chapter, we posed four chapter questions and encouraged you to review material related to these questions at the end of each major section (see pages 47, 58, 61, and 69). Use the following reflection and review features to further your understanding of the chapter material.

CHAPTER REFLECTIONS

1. Look back at the section Maintaining a Healthy Skepticism, in chapter 1 (p. 26). Find a Web site dedicated to one of the phenomena listed in this section. Using the four attributes of a scientific attitude, critically examine the claims made on the Web site. Describe the theory, the hypothesis, the data, and the analysis. Can you find all of this information on the Web site? If not, how would a scientist respond to the Web site?

2. Consider the following questions that might interest a psychologist. Describe a study you would use to address each of these questions, including what kind of research method you would employ.
   a. What percentage of people wash their hands after using the washroom?
   b. Does background music make people buy more at the grocery store?
   c. Is there a relationship between anger and car accidents?
   d. Do antidepressants work?

3. Visit the library at your school and find an article in a psychology journal. Describe what kind of study was done—was it descriptive, correlational, or an experiment? If it was an experiment, what were the independent and dependent variables? What kind of statistics did the researchers use? Can you tell if the results are statistically significant?

4. Much of the experimental research in psychology has been conducted using undergraduate students. How might this choice influence the interpretation of the results to other groups, such as children or older adults? Describe some of the special ethical issues that might be involved in using children and older adults in psychological experiments.

5. Visit Hanover College's website dedicated to psychological research on the Internet (http://psych.hanover.edu/research/exponnet.html). Browse the available studies and consider participating in some as a way to experience psychological research as a research participant. As you do, make note of the research methodology and how ethical concerns are dealt with.

6. After completing this chapter watch an episode of "CSI: Crime Scene Investigations" or "Numb3rs." Is the analogy between what a crime scene investigator does with what a scientific psychologist does a reasonable one?

CHAPTER REVIEW

Explain what makes psychology a science.

- A scientific attitude involves being curious, being skeptical, being objective, and thinking critically.

- Science is a collaborative effort in which colleagues share their findings, making them open for evaluation. Research psychologists usually publish their work in academic journals.

- The scientific method is essentially a four-step process: (1) conceptualize a problem, (2) collect research information (data), (3) analyze data, and (4) draw conclusions. Step 1 often involves a theory, which is a possible explanation for past observations that also can be used to predict future observations. Using a theory to generate a hypothesis or testable assumption, a researcher can collect and analyze data and then draw conclusions about the validity of the hypothesis.

Discuss the three types of research that are used in psychology.

- Descriptive research has the purpose of systematically observing and recording behaviour. Four types of descriptive research are observation (in a laboratory or a naturalistic setting), surveys based on questionnaires and interviews, standardized tests, and case studies.

In correlational research, the goal is to describe the strength of the relationship between two or more events or characteristics. A correlation coefficient is the numerical value that expresses the degree of relationship between two variables. An important point to remember is that correlation does not equal causation.

Experimental research involves conducting an experiment, a systematic controlled study in which one or more factors believed to influence the behaviour being studied are manipulated while all other factors are held constant. An experiment can determine cause and effect. An independent variable in an experiment is a manipulated, influential, experimental factor. A dependent variable is a factor that can change in an experiment in response to changes in the independent variable. Experiments can involve one or more experimental groups and one or more control groups. The experimental group is the group whose experience is being manipulated. The control group is a comparison group that is treated in every way like the experimental group except for the factor being manipulated. In random assignment, researchers assign participants to experimental and control groups by chance. Experimenter and research participant bias are potential pitfalls in experimental research. To reduce research participant bias, researchers may give a placebo to some participants. In a double-blind experiment, neither the experimenter nor the participant is aware of which participants are in the experimental or the control group until the results are analyzed.

Distinguish between descriptive statistics and inferential statistics.

Descriptive statistics are used to describe and summarize samples of data in a meaningful way. Two types of descriptive statistics are measures of central tendency (mean, median, and mode) and measures of variability (range and standard deviation).

Inferential statistics are used to draw conclusions about the data that have been collected. Inferential statistics aim to uncover statistical significance, which means that the differences observed between two groups are so large that they are highly unlikely to be the result of mere chance.

Discuss some research challenges that involve ethics, bias, and information.

Researchers' ethical responsibilities include seeking participants' informed consent; ensuring their confidentiality; debriefing them about the purpose and potential personal consequences of participating; and avoiding unnecessary deception of participants. In animal research, ethical responsibilities include protecting subjects from unnecessary pain and discomfort while weighing the potential benefits of research against the possible harm to the animals.

Psychologists need to guard against gender, cultural, and ethnic bias in research. Research in which only males or only middle-socioeconomic-status European Canadians participated cannot be generalized to the population as a whole. Gender bias and ethnic bias can lead to inaccurate conclusions in psychological studies.

Being a wise consumer of information about psychology means distinguishing between group results and individual needs; not overgeneralizing based on a small sample; understanding that a single study is usually not the defining word about an issue or a problem; not making causal conclusions from correlational studies; and evaluating the source of the information and its credibility.

For extra help in mastering the material in this chapter, see the integrator, review sections, practice quizzes, and other resources in the Student Study Guide and at the Online Learning Centre (www.mcgrawhill.ca/college/santrock).

CORE TERMS

theory, p. 42
hypothesis, p. 42
operational definition, p. 44
population, p. 45
sample, p. 45
random sample, p. 45
naturalistic observation, p. 49
standardized test, p. 51
case study, p. 52
correlational research, p. 52

experiment, p. 55
independent variable, p. 55
dependent variable, p. 55
experimental group, p. 55
control group, p. 55
random assignment, p. 56
experimenter bias, p. 56
research participant bias, p. 56
placebo, p. 57
placebo effect, p. 57

double-blind experiment, p. 57
descriptive statistics, p. 58
mean, p. 58
median, p. 59
mode, p. 59
range, p. 59
standard deviation, p. 60
inferential statistics, p. 61
ethnic gloss, p. 67

3

Biological Foundations of Behaviour

CHAPTER QUESTIONS

1. What are the characteristics and organization of the nervous system?

2. What are neurons and synapses and how they process information?

3. What are the brain's levels and structures and what are their functions?

4. In what ways is the brain adaptable?

5. What is the endocrine system and how it influence behaviour?

6. How do genetics and evolutionary psychology increase our understanding of behaviour?

On the morning of January 9, 1986, BK noticed that something was wrong. Everything looked darker as he began to feed his cat. He was startled to find he could not see his left hand. BK had lost most of the vision in the upper left hand quadrant of his visual field. A hospital visit confirmed that he had suffered a stroke, a blockage of a blood vessel in his brain, which had damaged part of the right occipital lobe of his cerebral cortex. In the months that followed, BK battled depression and panic attacks as he came to terms with his injury. He suffered from a variety of visual disturbances including a persistent left *visual field neglect*. He couldn't see things that were actually present just in front of him on his left side. For example, he once completely missed seeing a colleague sitting on his left talking on the phone. When reading, he once misread the word "telephone" as "lephone" and wondered what it meant. To compensate, he began to deliberately scan to his left further than usual and was often surprised by what he saw. Once, when he went skiing, he actually ran into a tree in his good right visual field because he was overcompensating for a bush some distance away in his neglected left visual field. Over time, he regained some visual ability in parts of the affected area and was more or less been able to resume his previous lifestyle.

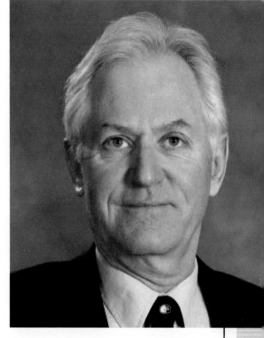

University of Lethbridge neuroscientist Bryan Kolb suffered some loss of vision from a right occipital stroke, which he correctly self-diagnosed. He then wrote about his recovery in the *Canadian Journal of Psychology*.

BKs story is particularly interesting because he is Dr. Bryan Kolb. At the time of his stroke he was, and still is today, a neuroscientist at the University of Lethbridge. An expert, he immediately diagnosed himself and actually had to argue with hospital staff about his own diagnosis, which was eventually confirmed. He became his own case study and wrote a fascinating scientific paper relating his experience to the scientific literature on recovery from occipital stroke (Kolb, 1990).

Bryan Kolb's case study highlights our absolute dependency upon the healthy functioning of our complex nervous systems. Different parts of our brains specialize in controlling different psychological functions and yet work together to orchestrate every detail of our rich lives. Our nervous systems constantly change to allow us to successfully adapt to our environments, even showing plasticity in response to damage.

It is not by coincidence that the human brain is so versatile. It has evolved over millions of years from a small, fairly primitive organ into a very complex network capable of coordinating our body functions, our thoughts, our emotions, and our behaviours. From the point of view of evolutionary psychology, the human brain has evolved because its increased complexity in some individuals enabled them to behave in ways that gave them and their descendants a better chance of survival—for example, by being able to anticipate adversity and plan for ways to avoid it or cope with it.

In this chapter we explore the all-important biological foundations of human behaviour. The main focus is the nervous system and its command centre—the brain. We also explore the genetic and evolutionary processes that have a significant influence on who we are as individuals and how we behave.

① THE NERVOUS SYSTEM

Characteristics — How the Brain and Nervous System Are Studied — Divisions of the Nervous System — Pathways in the Nervous System

What is the nervous system and what does it do?

Likely the most intricately organized aggregate of matter on planet Earth, the human **nervous system** is a vast chemical communication ciruitry made up of billions of cells (Campbell, Reece, & Mitchell, 2002). A single cubic centimetre of the human brain consists of well over 50 million nerve cells, each of which communicates with thousands of other nerve cells. Neurons operate electrically but communicate with each other chemically via neurotransmitters. The resulting information-processing network makes the most elaborate digital computer seem primitive.

The field that studies the nervous system is called *neuroscience*, and the people who study it are *neuroscientists* (Kolb & Whishaw, 2005).

Characteristics

Several extraordinary characteristics allow the nervous system to direct our behaviour: complexity, functional specialization, integration, and adaptability.

Complexity Over the last century, anatomists and physiologists have marvelled at the complexity of the nervous system as they have distinguished many different levels of the brain, specific brain areas, types of neurons, and types of neurotransmitters (Johnson, 2003). The orchestration of these components allows us to see, to hear, to touch, to dream, to study, to plan, to dance, to skate, to write, to love (Schall, 2003). In fact, the incredible complexity of human behaviour is mirrored in the complexity of the human brain and nervous system (Clark, Boutros, & Mendez, 2005). Even social behaviour has a neural basis (Insel & Fernald, 2004). As Bryan Kolb prepares a neuroscience lecture, his brain is carrying out a huge number of tasks—involved in breathing, seeing, thinking, moving, reading, writing—in which extensive assemblies of nerve cells are participating.

Functional Specialization The sheer complexity of the nervous system does not, however, make it impossible to decipher. Fortunately, specific functions are frequently allocated to specific brain regions (Kolb & Whishaw, 2003). Bryan Kolb's case, for example, suggests that the damaged part of his right occipital lobe is somehow specialized to carry out the function of vision in the upper left-hand quadrant of the visual field. Many other scientific observations had already suggested this conclusion, which is what allowed Kolb to correctly diagnose his own condition. Accordingly, attempting to localize specific functions in specific brain areas has been a major research strategy in neuroscience (Harrington, 2006). It should be possible, then, to identify which areas of the brain are responsible for each of the tasks carried out by Bryan Kolb's brain as he prepares his lecture.

Integration Although the brain is composed of many different levels and functionally specialized regions, the specializations complement each other (Bryden, 1986), resulting in a brain that operates in a highly integrated fashion. Brain activity is integrated through countless interconnections of brain cells and extensive pathways that link different parts of the brain. Each nerve cell communicates, on average, with thousands of others, making up many kilometres of connections (Kalat, 2004). Consider what happens when a mosquito bites your arm. How does your brain know you were bitten and where? Bundles of interconnected nerve cells relay information about the bite from your arm through the nervous system in a very orderly fashion to the highest levels of your brain.

nervous system The body's electrochemical communication circuitry, made up of billions of neurons.

Indeed, behaving in just about any way requires many interconnections in your brain. Working out the interplay of specialized brain areas as they produce behaviour has been another major research strategy in neuroscience (Friston, 2005). It should also be possible, then, to describe how the various specialized brain areas, each responsible for a particular function, cooperate to allow Bryan Kolb to prepare his lecture.

Adaptability   The world around us is constantly changing. To survive, we must adapt to new conditions. Together, our brain and nervous system serve as our agent in adapting to the world. Although nerve cells reside in certain brain regions, they are not fixed and immutable structures. They have a hereditary, biological foundation, but they are constantly adapting to changes in the body and the environment (Wilson, 2003).

The term **plasticity** denotes the brain's special capacity for modification and change (Kolb, Gibb, & Robinson, 2003). The experiences that we have contribute to the wiring or rewiring of the brain (Blair, 2002; Greenough, 2000; Scharfman, 2002). For example, each time a baby tries to touch an object or gazes intently at a face, electrical impulses and chemical messengers shoot through the baby's brain, knitting brain cells together into pathways and networks.

The brain's plasticity is evident in Bryan Kolb's case. In the years following his stroke, he experienced many improvements including improvements in his reading speed, eye-hand coordination, and ability to recognize faces. These occurred as his brain adapted to compensate for the lost functions of the damaged brain area.

How the Brain and Nervous System Are Studied

How can we study something as complex as the human nervous system? Much of our knowledge of the human brain comes from clinical case studies of individuals who suffered brain damage from injury or disease (like Bryan Kolb) or who had brain surgery to relieve another condition. Discoveries have also benefitted from sophisticated techniques, including some that enable researchers to "look inside" the brain while it is at work (Harrington, 2006). Let's examine some of these techniques.

Staining   Identifying the pathways of connectivity in the brain and nervous system that allow information to get from one place to another is a central interest in neuroscience (B. K. Sorensen & others, 2002). Unravelling the anatomy of these pathways is not an easy task because of the complexity and extent of the interconnections. Much of the progress in charting these neural networks has come about through the use of stains, or dyes, that are selectively absorbed by neurons. One commonly used stain is horseradish peroxidase. A stain will coat only a small portion of neurons so that neuroscientists, using high-powered microscopes, can see which neurons absorb the stains and determine how they are connected.

Brain Lesioning   Brain lesioning is an abnormal disruption in the tissue of the brain resulting from injury, disease, or deliberate damage. Lesioning is commonly used to localize function; the part of the brain with the lesion is related to the psychological or behavioural function that has been disrupted as a result.

The study of naturally occurring brain lesions in humans has provided considerable information about how the brain functions, as in Bryan Kolb's case. Neuroscientists also deliberately produce lesions in laboratory animals to determine the effects on the animals' behaviour (Krauss & Jankovic, 2002). These lesions may be made by surgically removing brain tissue, applying a strong electrical current, destroying tissue with a laser, or eliminating tissue by injecting it with a drug. Administering a drug that temporarily inactivates an area of the brain can sometimes make transient lesions. The organism's behaviour can be studied while the area is inactivated; after the effects of the drug have worn off, brain activity in the area returns to normal (Gazzaniga, Ivry, & Mangun, 2002).

plasticity The brain's special capacity for modification and change.

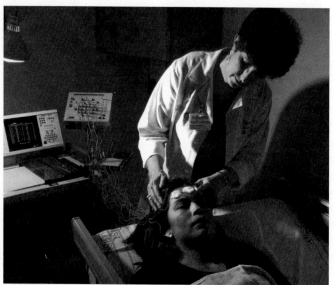

FIGURE 3.1

An EEG Recording
The electroencephalograph (EEG) is widely used in sleep research. It has led to some major breakthroughs in understanding sleep by showing how the brain's electrical activity changes during sleep.

Electrical Recording and Stimulation Because neuronal functioning is electrical in nature, it is possible to use electricity to study the nervous system. One widely used method is the *electroencephalograph* (*EEG*), which records the electrical activity of the brain. Electrodes placed on the scalp detect brain-wave activity, which is recorded on a chart known as an electroencephalogram (see figure 3.1). The resulting pattern of activity has been used to assess brain damage, epilepsy, and other problems (Aldenkamp & Arends, 2004; Wallace & others, 2001).

An EEG measurement is crude because it measures the pooled activity of many millions of neurons beneath each electrode. In contrast, in single-unit recording—a measure of a single neuron's electrical activity—a thin wire or *microelectrode* is inserted in or near an individual neuron (Heekeren & others, 2004). The neuron's activity is transmitted to an *oscilloscope*, which visually displays information about the activity (Harrington, 2006).

Microelectrodes inserted into the brain can also be used to deliver an electric current to surrounding brain tissue. If the current is mild, the result is electrical stimulation of that part of the brain. If the current is stronger, the result is a lesion. This method is also commonly used to localize function in the brain. Researchers can electrically stimulate parts of the brain and see what changes in behaviour result.

CAT Scans The use of microelectrodes to electrically record from, stimulate, or lesion parts of the brain require surgery and is too invasive to use in most human experimentation. In contrast, for years x-rays have been used to reveal damage noninvasively inside or outside our bodies, both in the brain and in other locations. But a single x-ray of the brain is hard to interpret because it shows a two-dimensional image of the three-dimensional interior of the brain (Goel, 1995). A newer technique called *computerized axial tomography* (*CAT scan*) produces a three-dimensional image obtained from x-rays of the head that are assembled into a composite image by a computer. The CAT scan is a noninvasive method that provides valuable information about the localization of function, including the extent of damage involving stroke, language disorder, or loss of memory (e.g., Lehtonen & others, 2005).

PET Scans While CAT scans can reveal details of internal brain structures, they yield no information about brain activity. In contrast, *positron-emission tomography* (*PET scan*) measures the amount of glucose in various areas of the brain, then sends this information to a computer for analysis. Because glucose levels vary with the levels of activity throughout the brain, tracing the amounts of glucose generates a picture of activity levels throughout the brain (Siebner & others, 2002). Recently, Molina and his colleagues (2005) have used PET scans to show that schizophrenics suffer damage to parts of the brain involved in thinking (prefrontal cortex), likely due to overactivity in the emotion-processing circuitry (the limbic system). Figure 3.2 shows PET scans of people's brain activity while they are hearing, seeing, speaking, and thinking.

MRI and fMRI The newest and most powerful imaging technique is *magnetic resonance imaging* (*MRI*), which involves creating a magnetic field around a person's body and using radio waves to construct images of the person's tissues. An extension of the MRI technique, fMRI (functional MRI), can even provide images of biochemical activities (or functions) in the brain. MRI and fMRI provide very detailed pictures of the brain's interior structure and function, do not require injecting the brain with a substance, and, unlike x-rays, do not pose the problem of radiation overexposure (Kolb & Whishaw, 2005).

Vinod Goel, of York University, uses fMRI to study human reasoning. He has shown, for example, that different parts of the front of the brain (prefrontal cortex) are involved in deductive and inductive reasoning. (Goel & Dolan, 2004). Goel (2005b) describes another study, which examined two theories of deductive reasoning. One, which he calls *mental logic theory*, holds that deductive reasoning involves processing language-based representations.

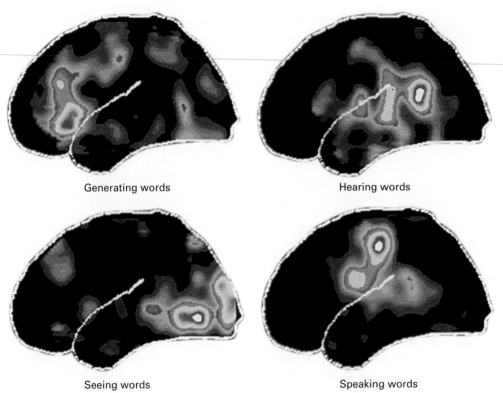

Generating words   Hearing words

Seeing words   Speaking words

FIGURE 3.2
PET Scan
This PET scan of the left half of the brain contrasts the different areas used in aspects of language activity: generating words, hearing words, seeing words, and speaking words.

Accordingly, language regions of the left side of the brain (frontal and temporal lobes) should be active during deductive reasoning. The other theory, *mental model theory,* holds that deductive reasoning involves processing mental images. Visual processing regions in the back of the brain (parietal lobes) should be more active during deductive reasoning. Figure 3.3 presents fMRIs images of participants engaged in a deductive reasoning task. According to Goel (2005b), brain areas associated with both models are active, indicating that deductive reasoning is best described by some sort of *dual-mechanism model* which incorporates elements of both the mental logic theory and the mental model theory.

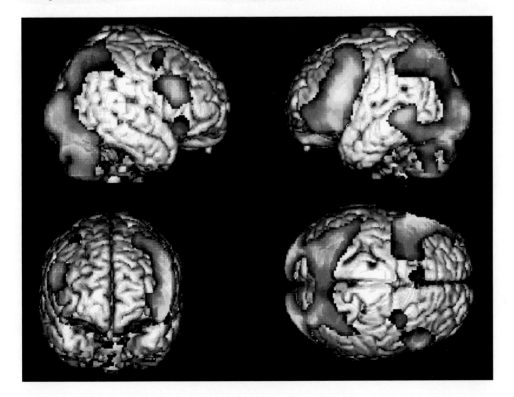

FIGURE 3.3
fMRI Scan
This composite fMRI reveals that many different parts of the brain, including both language areas and visual areas, work together during deductive reasoning

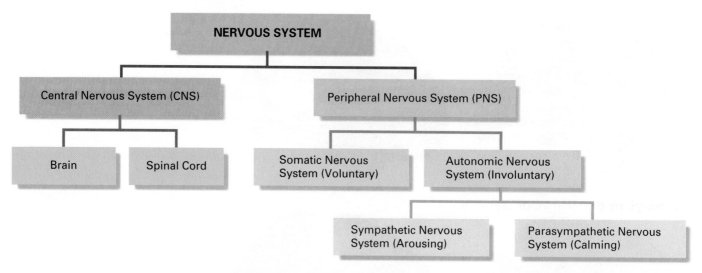

FIGURE 3.4 **Major Divisions of the Human Nervous System**

In another study, Brian Levine and his colleagues at the Rotman Research Institute at the University of Toronto conducted a fMRI study of participants who attempted to recall autobiographical information as well as general information. A unique pattern of brain activation was observed during autobiographical recall, lending strength to the theory that autobiographical recall is a distinct form of human memory (Levine & others, 2004).

Divisions of the Nervous System

When the nineteenth-century American poet and essayist Ralph Waldo Emerson said, "The world was built in order and the atoms march in tune," he must have had the human nervous system in mind. This truly elegant system is highly ordered and organized for effective function.

Figure 3.4 shows the two primary divisions of the human nervous system: the central nervous system and the peripheral nervous system. The **central nervous system (CNS)** is made up of the brain and spinal cord. More than 99 percent of all nerve cells in our body are located in the CNS. The **peripheral nervous system (PNS)** is the network that connects the brain and spinal cord to other parts of the body. The functions of the peripheral nervous system are to bring information to and from the brain and spinal cord and to carry out the commands of the CNS to execute various muscular and glandular activities.

The peripheral nervous system itself has two major divisions: the **somatic nervous system** and the **autonomic nervous system**. The somatic nervous system consists of sensory nerves, whose function is to convey information from the skin and muscles to the CNS about conditions such as pain and temperature; and motor nerves, whose function is to tell muscles what to do. The function of the autonomic nervous system is to take messages to and from the body's internal organs, monitoring such processes as breathing, heart rate, and digestion. The autonomic nervous system is also divided into two parts: the **sympathetic nervous system** arouses the body and the **parasympathetic nervous system** calms the body.

To better understand the various divisions of the nervous system, let's see what they do in a particular situation. Imagine that you are preparing to ask a judge to dismiss a parking ticket. As you are about to enter the courtroom, you scan a note card one last time to remember what you plan to say. Your *peripheral nervous system* carries the written marks from the note card to your *central nervous system*. Your central nervous system processes the marks, interpreting them as words, and allows you to memorize key points and plan ways to keep the judge friendly. After studying the notes several minutes longer, you jot down an additional joke that you hope will amuse her.

central nervous system (CNS) The brain and spinal cord.

peripheral nervous system (PNS) The network of nerves that connects the brain and spinal cord to other parts of the body. It is divided into the somatic nervous system and the autonomic nervous system.

somatic nervous system Division of the PNS consisting of sensory nerves, whose function is to convey information to the CNS, and motor nerves, whose function is to transmit information to the muscles.

autonomic nervous system Division of the PNS that communicates with the body's internal organs. It consists of the sympathetic and parasympathetic nervous systems.

sympathetic nervous system The division of the autonomic nervous system that arouses the body.

parasympathetic nervous system The division of the autonomic nervous system that calms the body.

Again your *peripheral nervous system* is at work, conveying to the muscles in your arm and hand the information from your brain that enables you to make the marks on the paper.

The information that is being transmitted from your eyes to your brain and to your hand is handled by the *somatic nervous system*. This is your first ticket hearing, so you are a little anxious. Your stomach feels queasy, and your heart begins to thump. This is the sympathetic division of the *autonomic nervous system* functioning as you become aroused. You regain your confidence after reminding yourself that you were parked in a legal spot. As you relax, the *parasympathetic* division of the *autonomic nervous system* is working.

Pathways in the Nervous System

As we interact with and adapt to the world, the brain and the nervous system receive and transmit sensory input, integrate the information received from the environment, and direct the body's motor activities. Information flows into the brain through sensory input, becomes integrated within the brain, and then moves out of the brain to be connected with motor output (Enger & Ross, 2005). This flow of information through the nervous system occurs in specialized pathways, called nerves or tracts, which interconnect brain areas that are adapted for different functions.

As we shall see in more detail in the next section, every nerve cell has an axon, a long, thin fibre that carries information to other nerve cells. A bundle of axons carrying information from one cluster of nerve cells to another is called a **nerve** when it occurs outside of the brain and a **tract** when it occurs inside the brain. Thus the optic nerve is a bundle of axons carrying information from the retina to the brain. Once the optic nerve has entered the brain it is called the optic tract.

Three major types of pathways are afferent nerves, efferent nerves, and neural networks. Nerves that carry information from the body to the brain are called **afferent nerves**, or sensory nerves. The word *afferent* comes from the Latin word meaning "bring to." These sensory pathways communicate information about external and bodily environments from sensory receptors into and throughout the brain. For example, sense receptors in the ear translate incoming sound into neural signals that are sent to the brain via the auditory nerve.

Efferent nerves, or motor nerves, carry the brain's output back to the body. The word *efferent* is derived from the Latin word meaning "bring from." These motor pathways communicate information from the brain to the hands, feet, and other areas of the body that allow a person to engage in motor behaviour. In order to deliberately move even a single muscle, signals from the brain must be sent to the muscle via the appropriate efferent nerve.

Most information processing occurs when information moves through **neural networks** in the central nervous system. Visual inspection of the brain reveals areas of *grey matter* and areas of *white matter*. Grey areas contain clusters of specialized nerve cells, called **nuclei** (one cluster is called a **nucleus**). The nerve cells of a given nucleus may be richly interconnected as well as sending out one or more bundles of white-coloured axons to carry information to nuclei in other parts of the brain. Thus, anatomical analysis reveals the neural networks of the brain to be composed of many nuclei richly interconnected via a web of tracts (Passingham, Stephan, & Kötter, 2002). Neural networks make up most of the brain.

The function of these networks of nerve cells is to integrate sensory input and motor output (Peng, Qiao, & Xu, 2002). For example, as you read your class notes, the afferent input from your eye is transmitted to your brain, then passed through many neural networks, which translate (process) your black pen scratches into neural codes for letters, words, associations, and meaning (van Vreeswijk, in press). Some of the information is stored in the neural networks for future associations, and, if you read aloud, some is passed on as efferent messages to your lips and tongue.

nerve A collection of axons carrying information from one cluster of neurons to another outside the brain.

tract A collection of axons carrying information from one cluster of neurons to another inside the brain.

afferent nerves Sensory nerves that transport information to the brain.

efferent nerves Motor nerves that carry the brain's output.

neural networks Clusters of neurons that are interconnected to process information.

nucleus (pl. nuclei) A cluster of specialized nerve cells in the brain or spinal cord.

> **reflect and review**

1 **Identify the fundamental characteristics of the brain and nervous system.**

- Specify six techniques that are used to study the brain and the nervous system.
- Identify the divisions of the nervous system and explain their role in behaviour
- Name and describe the pathways that allow the nervous system to carry out its three basic functions.

Try this exercise without looking at Figure 3.1. Suppose you (1) saw a person coming toward you, (2) realized it was someone famous, (3) got excited, (4) waved and shouted, (5) suddenly realized it was not a famous person, and (6) became suddenly calm again. Which part of your nervous system would have been heavily involved at each of these six points?

2 NEURONS AND SYNAPSES

Specialized Cell Structure	The Neural Impulse	Synapses and Neurotransmitters	Neural Networks

What are neurons and how do they communicate?

Within each division of the nervous system, much is happening at the cellular level. Nerve cells, chemicals, and electrical impulses work together to transmit information at speeds of up to 530 kilometres per hour. As a result, information can travel from your brain to your hands (or vice versa) in a matter of milliseconds (Krogh, 2003; Martini, 2004). There are two types of cells in the nervous system: neurons and glial cells.

Neurons are the nerve cells that actually handle the information processing function. The human brain contains about 100 billion neurons. The average neuron is quite complex, with thousands of synaptic connections with other cells. To have even the merest thought requires millions of neurons acting simultaneously (Kolb & Whishaw, 2005).

There are many more **glial cells** in the nervous system than there are neurons. Glial cells are not specialized to process information in the way that neurons are, although recent evidence suggests that they can play a role in modulating synaptic transmission (Oliet & others, 2004). Glial cells do, however, provide support and nutritional functions in the nervous system (Lemke, 2001; Meller & others, 2002). In one study, neurons placed in a solution containing glial cells grew more rapidly and prolifically than neurons floating in the same solution without glial cells (Ullian & others, 2001). This study indicates that glial cells function in a supportive or nutritive role for neurons.

Specialized Cell Structure

Not all neurons are alike. They are specialized to handle different information-processing functions. However, all neurons do have some common characteristics. Most neurons are created very early in life, but their shape, size, and connections can change throughout the life span. The way neurons function thus reflects a major characteristic of the nervous system that we described at the beginning of the chapter: plasticity. They are not fixed and immutable but can change. Every neuron has a cell body, dendrites, and axon (see figure 3.5).

The **cell body** contains the nucleus, which, as in any other cell, directs the manufacture of substances that the neuron needs for growth and maintenance.

Dendrites receive and orient information toward the cell body. One of the most distinctive features of neurons is the tree-like branching of their dendrites. Most nerve

neuron Nerve cell that is specialized for processing information. Neurons are the basic units of the nervous system.

glial cells Provide support and nutritional functions in the nervous system.

cell body Part of the neuron that contains the nucleus, which directs the manufacture of substances that the neuron needs for growth and maintenance.

dendrites Branches of a neuron that receive and orient information toward the cell body; most neurons have numerous dendrites.

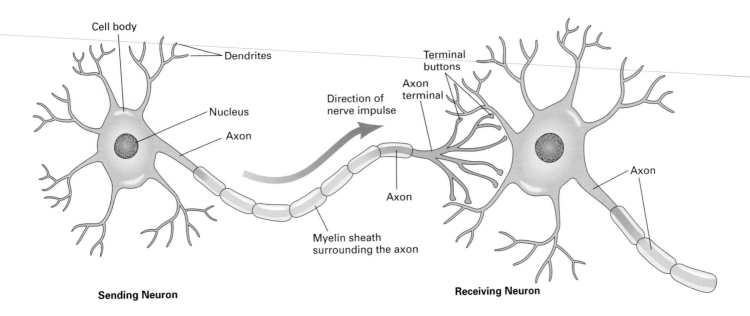

FIGURE 3.5

The Neuron
The drawing shows the parts of a neuron and the connection between one neuron and another. Note the cell body, branching of dendrites, and the axon with a myelin sheath.

cells have numerous dendrites, which increase their surface area, allowing each neuron to receive input from many other neurons.

The **axon** is the part of the neuron that carries information away from the cell body toward other cells. Although very thin (1/25,000 of a centimetre), axons can be very long, with many branches. In fact, some extend more than a metre—all the way from the top of the brain to the base of the spinal cord.

The surface of each neuron, including its dendrites and axon, is made up of a very thin cellular membrane. Like human skin, neuronal membranes are semipermeable, meaning that they contain tiny gates, or *channels*, that control the passage of certain substances into and out of the neurons.

A **myelin sheath**, a layer of fat cells, encases and insulates most axons. It is the myelin sheath that gives tracts of axons within the brain their characteristic white colour. By insulating axons, myelin sheaths speed up the transmission of nerve impulses (Mattson, 2002; Paus & others, 2001). Multiple sclerosis, a degenerative disease of the nervous system in which a destruction of myelin tissue occurs, disrupts neuronal communication (Archibald & Fisk, 2000). The deterioration of myelin sheaths in certain brain areas may also be related to Alzheimer's disease (Bartzokis & others, 2004).

The myelin sheath developed as the brain evolved. As brain size increased, it became necessary for information to travel over longer distances in the nervous system. Axons without myelin sheaths are not very good conductors of electricity. Myelin sheaths are insulated, so they transmit electrical impulses and convey information much more rapidly. We can compare the myelin sheath's development to the evolution of freeways as cities grew. A freeway is a shielded road. It keeps fast-moving, long-distance traffic from getting snarled by slow, local traffic.

The Neural Impulse

A neuron sends information through its axon in the form of brief impulses, or waves, of electricity. In old movies you might have seen telegraph operators tapping out messages one click at a time over a telegraph wire to the next telegraph station. That is what neurons do. To transmit information to other neurons, a neuron sends impulses ("clicks") through its axon to the next neuron. As you reach to turn this page, hundreds of such impulses will stream down the axons in your arm to tell your muscles just when to flex and how vigorously. By changing the rate and timing of the signals or "clicks," the neuron can vary its message.

How does a neuron—a living cell—generate electrical impulses? To answer this question, we need to further examine the nature of a neuron and the fluids in which it

axon The part of the neuron that carries information away from the cell body to other cells; each neuron has only one axon.

myelin sheath A layer of fat cells that encases and insulates most axons. The myelin sheath speeds up the transmission of nerve impulses.

FIGURE 3.6

The Resting Potential

An oscilloscope measures the difference in electrical potential between two electrodes. When one electrode is placed inside an axon at rest and one is placed outside, the electrical potential inside the cell is −70 millivolts (mV) relative to the outside. This potential difference is due to the separation of positive (+) and negative (−) charges along the membrane.

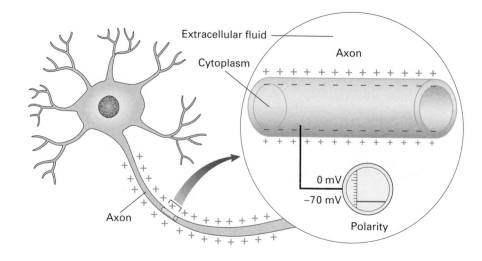

FIGURE 3.7

The Action Potential

An action potential is a wave of localized depolarization that travels down the axon as the ion channels in the axon membrane open and close. (*a*) The action potential causes a change in electrical potential as it moves along the axon. (*b*) The movements of sodium ions (Na⁺) and potassium ions (K⁺) into and out of the axon cause the electrical changes.

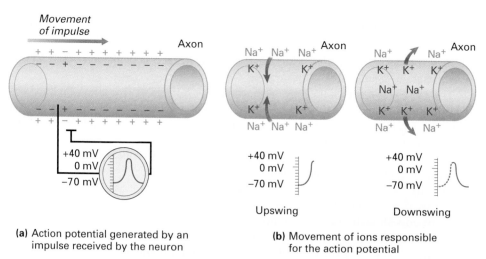

(a) Action potential generated by an impulse received by the neuron

(b) Movement of ions responsible for the action potential

is bathed. Electrically charged particles called *ions* float in both the fluid outside the neuron (*the extracellular fluid*) and the fluid inside the neuron (*the cytoplasm*). Some of these ions, notably sodium (Na+) and potassium (K+), carry positive charges. Some, notably chlorine (Cl−), carry negatively charged ions. Other elements are also present.

The neuron creates various electric potentials by controlling the flow of positive and negative ions back and forth through its semipermeable membrane. How does the movement of ions across the membrane occur? Embedded in the membrane are hundreds of thousands of small gates, known as *ion channels*, that open and close to let various ions pass into and out of the cell.

As long as the neuron is inactive (not transmitting information) or at *rest*, the membrane's ion channels prevent positive ions from flowing into the cell. This results in more negative ions inside the neuron cytoplasm than there are in the surrounding extracellular fluid. This difference creates a stable, negative electrical charge, called the **resting potential**, that the resting neuron uses in order to generate electrical impulses (see figure 3.6). That potential, by the way, is about –70 millivolts, which is about one-fourteenth of a volt, so fourteen neurons could make up a one-volt battery. An electric eel's 8,400 neurons could generate 600 volts!

A neuron becomes activated when an incoming impulse, in reaction to, say, a pinprick or the sight of someone's face, raises the neuron's voltage threshold, and the sodium channels at the base of the axon open briefly. This action allows positively charged sodium ions to flow into the neuron, creating a more positively charged neuron and *depolarizing* the membrane by decreasing the charge difference between the fluids inside and outside of the neuron. Then potassium channels open, and positively charged potassium ions move out through the neuron's semipermeable membrane.

resting potential The stable, negative charge of an inactive neuron.

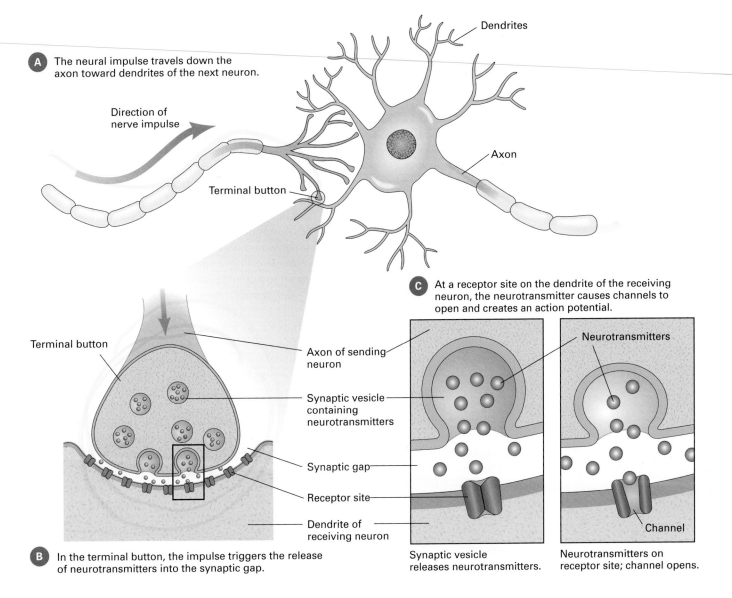

A The neural impulse travels down the axon toward dendrites of the next neuron.

Dendrites

Direction of nerve impulse

Axon

Terminal button

C At a receptor site on the dendrite of the receiving neuron, the neurotransmitter causes channels to open and creates an action potential.

Terminal button

Axon of sending neuron

Synaptic vesicle containing neurotransmitters

Synaptic gap

Receptor site

Dendrite of receiving neuron

Neurotransmitters

Channel

B In the terminal button, the impulse triggers the release of neurotransmitters into the synaptic gap.

Synaptic vesicle releases neurotransmitters.

Neurotransmitters on receptor site; channel opens.

This returns the neuron to a negative charge. Then the same process occurs as the next group of channels flip open briefly. And so it goes all the way down the axon, just like a long row of cabinet doors opening and closing in sequence (see figure 3.7).

The brief wave of positive electrical charge that sweeps down the axon is called an **action potential**. It lasts only about one-thousandth of a second, because the sodium channels stay open for only a very brief time. They quickly close again and become reset for the next action potential. When a neuron sends an action potential down the axon, it is commonly said to be "firing."

The action potential abides by the **all-or-none principle**: Once incoming electrical impulses reach a certain level of intensity, the neuron fires and the action potential moves all the way down the axon without losing any of its intensity. The impulse travelling down an axon can be compared to a burning fuse. It doesn't matter whether a match or blowtorch was used to light the fuse, once the fuse has been lit, the spark travels quickly and with the same intensity down the fuse.

Synapses and Neurotransmitters

What happens when a neural impulse reaches the end of the axon? Neurons do not touch each other directly, but they manage to communicate. The story of the connection between one neuron and another is one of the most intriguing and highly

FIGURE 3.8

How Synapses and Neurotransmitters Work
(*A*) The axon of the *presynaptic* (sending) neuron meets dendrites of the *postsynaptic* (receiving) neuron. (*B*) This is an enlargement of one synapse, showing the synaptic gap between the two neurons, the terminal button, and the synaptic vesicles containing a neurotransmitter. (*C*) This is an enlargement of the receptor site. Note how the neurotransmitter opens the channel on the receptor site, triggering the neuron to fire.

action potential The brief wave of electrical charge that sweeps down the axon during the transmission of a nerve impulse.

all-or-none principle Once an electrical impulse reaches a certain level of intensity, it fires and moves all the way down the axon without losing any of its intensity.

researched areas of contemporary neuroscience (Bi & Poo, 2001). Figure 3.8 gives an overview of how this connection between neurons takes place.

Synaptic Transmission **Synapses** are tiny junctions between neurons; the gap between neurons is referred to as a *synaptic gap*. Most synapses lie between the axon of one neuron and the dendrites or cell body of another neuron. Before the electrical impulse can cross the synaptic gap, it must be converted into a chemical signal.

Each axon branches out into many *axon terminals*, each of which ends in structures called *terminal buttons*. Stored in minute *synaptic vesicles (sacs)* within the terminal buttons are substances called **neurotransmitters**. As their name suggests, neurotransmitters transmit or carry information across the synaptic gap to the next neuron. When a nerve impulse reaches the terminal button, synaptic vesicles move to the neuronal membrane, triggering the release of neurotransmitter molecules from the vesicles. The neurotransmitter molecules flood the synaptic gap. Their movements are random, but some of them bump into receptor sites on the next neuron. If the shape of the receptor site corresponds to the shape of the neurotransmitter molecule, the neurotransmitter acts like a key to open an ion channel at the receptor site, triggering the inflow or outflow of positive ions, and possibly an action potential in the receiving neuron.

Think of the synapse as a river that blocks a road. A mail truck (the action potential) arrives at one bank of the river, the mail is unloaded and crosses by ferry, where it is loaded on another mail truck and is sent on its way. Similarly, a message in the brain is "ferried" across the synapse by a neurotransmitter, which pours out of the terminal button when the message approaches the synapse.

Neurochemical Messengers There are many different neurotransmitters. Each one plays a specific role and function in specific pathways. Whereas some neurotransmitters stimulate or excite neurons to fire, others can inhibit neurons from firing (Heim & Nemeroff, 2002). Some neurotransmitters are both excitatory and inhibitory, depending on what is needed. Thousands of neurons can synapse with any particular neuron. As various combinations of excitatory and inhibitory neurotransmitters move across the synaptic gap, they excite and inhibit electrical activity in any particular neuron.

Most neurons secrete only one type of neurotransmitter, but often many different neurons are simultaneously secreting different neurotransmitters into the synaptic gaps of a single neuron. At any given time, a neuron is receiving a mixture of messages from the neurotransmitters. At its receptor sites, the chemical molecules bind to the membrane and either excite the neuron, bringing it closer to the threshold at which it will fire, or inhibit the neuron from firing. The job of the neuron is to integrate the excitatory and inhibitory inputs into a decision to launch an action potential. This usually occurs when more excitatory rather than inhibitory neurotransmitters move across the synaptic gap. Usually the binding of an excitatory neurotransmitter from one neuron will not be enough to trigger an action potential in the receiving neuron. Triggering an action potential often takes a number of neurons sending excitatory messages simultaneously or fewer neurons sending rapid-fire excitatory messages.

So far, researchers have identified more than 50 neurotransmitters, each with a unique chemical makeup. The rapidly growing list likely will grow to more than 100 (Johnson, 2003). In organisms ranging from snails to whales, neuroscientists have found the same neurotransmitter molecules that our own brains use. Many animal venoms, such as that of the black widow spider, are actually neurotransmitter-like substances that do their harm by disturbing neurotransmission. To get a better sense of what neurotransmitters do, let's consider just six that have major effects on our behaviour.

Acetylcholine *Acetylcholine* (ACh) usually stimulates the firing of neurons and is involved in the action of muscles, learning, and memory (Devi & Silver, 2000; McIntyre & others, 2002). ACh is found throughout the central and peripheral nervous systems.

synapses Tiny junctions between two neurons, generally where the axon of one neuron meets the dendrites or cell body of another neuron.

neurotransmitters Chemicals that carry information across the synaptic gap from one neuron to the next.

The venom of the black widow spider causes ACh to gush through the synapses between the spinal cord and skeletal muscles, producing violent spasms. The drug curare, which some South American Aboriginals apply to the tips of poison darts, blocks receptors for ACh, paralyzing muscles. In contrast, nicotine stimulates acetylcholine receptors. Individuals with Alzheimer's disease, a degenerative brain disorder that involves a decline in memory, have an acetylcholine deficiency. Some of the drugs that alleviate the symptoms of Alzheimer's disease do so by compensating for the loss of the brain's supply of acetylcholine (Lambert & Kinsley, 2005).

GABA *GABA* (gamma aminobutyric acid) is found throughout the central nervous system. It is believed to be the neurotransmitter in as many as one-third of the brain's synapses. GABA is important in the brain because it keeps many neurons from firing (Bou-Flores & Berger, 2001; Ryan, 2001). In this way it helps to control the preciseness of the signal being carried from one neuron to the next. Low levels of GABA are linked with anxiety. Valium and other antianxiety drugs increase the inhibiting effects of GABA.

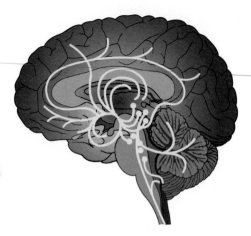

FIGURE 3.9
Serotonin Pathways
Each of the neurotransmitters in the brain has specific pathways in which they function. Shown here are the pathways for serotonin.

Norepinephrine *Norepinephrine* usually inhibits the firing of neurons in the central nervous system, but it excites the heart muscle, intestines, and urogenital tract. Stress stimulates the release of norepinephrine (Zaimovic & others, 2000). This neurotransmitter also helps to control alertness. Too little norepinephrine is associated with depression, too much, with agitated, manic states. For example, amphetamines and cocaine cause hyperactive, manic states of behaviour by rapidly increasing brain levels of norepinephrine.

Recall from the beginning of the chapter that one of the most important characteristics of the brain and nervous system is integration. In the case of neurotransmitters, they may work in teams of two or more. For example, norepinephrine works with acetylcholine to regulate states of sleep and wakefulness.

Dopamine *Dopamine* mainly inhibits. It helps to control voluntary movement (Jakel & Marangos, 2000). Dopamine also affects sleep, mood, attention, and learning. Stimulant drugs, such as cocaine and amphetamines, produce excitement, alertness, elevated mood, decreased fatigue, and, sometimes, increased motor activity, mainly by activating dopamine receptors.

Low levels of dopamine are associated with Parkinson's disease, in which physical movements deteriorate (Malapani, Deweer, & Gibbon, 2002). Although Alberta-born actor Michael J. Fox contracted Parkinson's disease in his late 20s, the disease is uncommon before the age of 30. It becomes more common as people age. High levels of dopamine are associated with schizophrenia, a severe mental disorder that is discussed in chapter 14.

Serotonin *Serotonin* also primarily inhibits. Serotonin is involved in the regulation of sleep, mood, attention, and learning. In regulating states of sleep and wakefulness, it teams with acetylcholine and norepinephrine. Lowered levels of serotonin are associated with depression (Kanner & Balabanov, 2002; Wagner & Ambrosini, 2001). The antidepressant drug Prozac works by increasing brain levels of serotonin. Figure 3.9 shows the brain pathways for serotonin.

Endorphins *Endorphins* are natural opiates that mainly stimulate the firing of neurons. Endorphins shield the body from pain and elevate feelings of pleasure. A long-distance runner, a woman giving birth, and a person in shock after a car wreck all have elevated levels of endorphins (Jamurtas & others, 2000).

As early as the fourth century B.C., the Greeks used wild poppies to induce euphoria. More than 2000 years later, the magical formula behind opium's addictive action was finally discovered. In the early 1970s, scientists found that opium plugs into the sophisticated system of endorphins that lies deep within the brain's pathways (Pert & Snyder, 1973; Spetea & others, 2002). Morphine, an opiate that is sometimes used as a painkiller, mimics the action of endorphins by stimulating receptors in the brain involved with pleasure and pain.

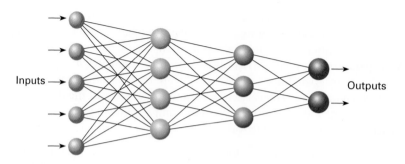

FIGURE 3.10

An Example of a Neural Network
Inputs (information from the environment and sensory receptors—as when someone looks at a person's face) become embedded in extensive connections between neurons in the brain, which leads to outputs (such as remembering the person's face).

Drugs and Neurotransmitters Most drugs that influence behaviour do so mainly by interfering with the work of neurotransmitters (McGuigan, 2004; Mader, 2004). Drugs can mimic or increase the effects of a neurotransmitter, or they can block those effects. An **agonist** is a drug that mimics or increases a neurotransmitter's effects. For example, morphine mimics the actions of endorphins by stimulating receptors in the brain associated with pleasure and pain. An **antagonist** is a drug that blocks a neurotransmitter's effects. For example, alcohol blocks serotonin activity (Fils-Aime & others, 1996).

Neural Networks

So far in our coverage of neurons, we have focused mainly on how a single neuron functions and on how a nerve impulse travels from one neuron to another. Now let's look at how large numbers of neurons normally work together to integrate incoming information and coordinate outgoing information.

At the beginning of the chapter, we briefly described neural networks as clusters of neurons that are interconnected to process information. Some neurons have short axons and communicate with other nearby neurons. Other neurons have long axons and communicate with circuits of neurons some distance away. Figure 3.10 shows a simplified drawing of a neural network or pathway (McIntosh, 2000). By looking at this diagram, you can get an idea of how the activity of one neuron is linked with many others.

Any piece of information, such as a name, might be embedded in hundreds or even thousands of connections between neurons (Lee & Farhat, 2001). In this way, such human activities as being attentive, memorizing, and thinking are distributed over a wide range of interconnected neurons (Rogers & McClelland, 2004). The strength of these connected neurons determines how well you remember the information (Krause & others, 2000).

Researchers have found that these neural networks are not static (Pinel, 2006). They can be altered through changes in the strength of synaptic connections. Changing patterns of synaptic connections strengths may well be how the brain carries out the functions of learning and memory.

Let's see how the neural network concept might explain a typical memory, such as the name of a new acquaintance. Initially, the processing of the person's face might activate a small number of weak neuronal connections that make you remember a general category ("interesting woman" or "attractive man"). However, repeated experience with that person will increase the strength and possibly the number of those connections. So you may remember the person's name as the neurons activated by the name become connected with the neurons that are activated by the face. Chapter 8 explores the nature of memory at greater length. To look more deeply into current research on neural networks, see the Critical Reflections box.

agonist A drug that mimics or increases a neurotransmitter's effects.

antagonist A drug that blocks a neurotransmitter's effects.

Studying Neural Networks with Hybrots

While it seems obvious that complex brain functions must be carried out by networks of neurons, rather than single neurons, neural networks have proven difficult to study. Recording from a single neuron *in vivo* (within a living organism) is difficult enough. The animal must be kept anaesthetized, surgery is required, it is difficult to locate neurons to record from, and neurons often die within moments once recording begins.

Because the direct study of living neural networks has proven so difficult, controversial alternatives have sprung up. One major approach, called *parallel distributed processing*, uses computers to simulate neural networks (Rogers & McClelland, 2004). A network, like that pictured in Figure 3.7, can be described by a computer program. Running the program simulates the operation of the neural network. Such computer simulations have produced some interesting results, especially in the study of human memory (see chapter 8). However, they have never been widely accepted by neuroscientists who insist that such computer simulations rest on oversimplifications of real neural networks.

Enter the *hybrot*, a hybrid robot composed of artifical components mixed with living brain tissue (Potter, Wagenaar, & DeMaarse, in press). The foundation of a hybrot is a multi-electrode array—a grid of 60 electrodes interconnected with a computer and an electrical stimulation device. Thousands of living neurons in a nutrient bath are poured over the electrodes. Especially when glial cells are added (Ullian & others, 2001), the resulting layer of neurons will not only live for quite some time, the neurons will develop synapses with each other. Each electrode in the array is capable of recording electrical activity in one or more nearby neurons and is also capable of electrically stimulating the same neuron(s).

Using the computer and electrical stimulation device, it is possible to apply complex patterns of electrical stimulation to the living neural network and to simultaneously record the activity of sixty or more neurons in the network. Incoming patterns of electrical stimulation serve as the hybrot's afferent, or "sensory" inputs and patterns of electrical activity recorded in response serve as efferent or "motor" outputs.

By using patterns of outputs from the neural network as feedback to change the pattern of "sensory" inputs it has proven possible to induce the networks to change their pattern of synaptic connections. In this way, hybrots have learned to control actual mechanical robots, acting as their "brains." One hybrot controlling a robot learned to follow another robot around. Another hybrot, Meart (Multi-Electrode Array art), learned to create simple drawings (Bakkum & others, 2004).

Hybrots have an exciting future. They may be able to learn to help damaged human brains control prosthetic devices or fly unmanned airplanes. While these potential applications are very exciting, the critical question neuroscientists are asking is whether or not hybrots can be used to study the process of learning in living neural networks (Wagenaar & others, 2005). It is possible that the study of how hybrot input-output patterns change will yield deeper insights into the functioning of natural neural networks. Will hybrots be another oversimplification or will they lead us to a much deeper understanding of how our plastic brains allow us to adapt to the world around us?

What do you think?

- Computer simulations of the weather are in common use today despite the fact they routinely oversimplify the complexity of real weather phenomena. Is it fair for neuroscientists to reject the use of computers to simulate neural networks because they also oversimplify real neural networks?
- How can hybrots increase our understanding of the functioning of real neural networks?
- Can you think of any other applications of hybrot technologies?

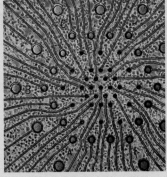

FIGURE 3.11 Hybrot
This "Brain in a Dish" is composed of a grid of electrodes and a growing, living neural network.

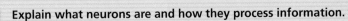

> **reflect and review**

2 **Explain what neurons are and how they process information.**

- Differentiate between neurons and glial cells, and describe the functions of the parts of a neuron.
- Explain what a neural impulse is and how it is generated.
- Discuss how a neural impulse is transmitted from one neuron to another.
- Describe the function of neural networks.

Why is it important to have so many connections and to have integration between neurons?

③ FUNCTIONAL SPECIALIZATION OF THE BRAIN

Levels of Organization in the Brain	The Cerebral Cortex	The Cerebral Hemispheres	Integration of Function in the Brain	Are There "His" and "Hers" Brains?

How is the brain organized?

The extensive and intricate networks of neurons that we have just studied form larger structures at various levels within the brain. This section explores the structures, functions, and levels of the brain. Special attention is given to the cerebral cortex, the highest region of the brain.

Levels of Organization in the Brain

As a human embryo develops inside its mother's womb, the nervous system begins forming as a long, hollow tube on the embryo's back. At three weeks or so after conception, the cells making up the tube differentiate into a mass of neurons, most of which then develop into three major regions of the brain: the hindbrain, which is adjacent to the top part of the spinal cord; the midbrain, which rises above the hindbrain; and the forebrain, which is the uppermost region of the brain (see figure 3.12).

Hindbrain The **hindbrain**, located at the rear of the skull, is the lowest, and evolutionarily oldest, portion of the brain. The three main parts of the hindbrain are the medulla, cerebellum, and pons. Figure 3.13 shows the location of these brain structures.

The *medulla* begins where the spinal cord enters the skull. It helps to control our breathing and regulates reflexes that allow us to maintain an upright posture.

The *cerebellum* extends from the rear of the hindbrain, just above the medulla. It consists of two rounded structures thought to play important roles in motor coordination (Middleton & Strick, 2001). Leg and arm movements are coordinated by the cerebellum, for example. When we play golf, practise the piano, or learn a new dance, the cerebellum is hard at work. If a higher portion of the brain commands us to write the number 7, it is the cerebellum that integrates the muscular activities required. Damage

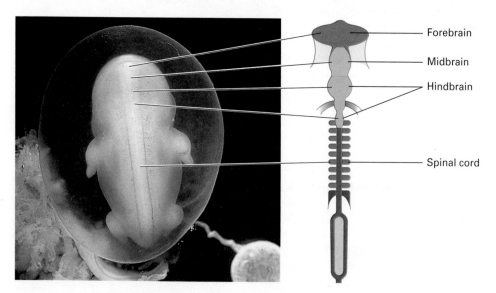

— Forebrain

— Midbrain

— Hindbrain

— Spinal cord

FIGURE 3.12 Embryological Development of the Nervous System
The photograph shows the primitive, tubular appearance of the nervous system at 6 weeks in the human embryo. The drawing shows the major brain regions and spinal cord as they appear early in the development of a human embryo.

hindbrain The lowest, and evolutionarily oldest, level of the brain, consisting of the medulla, cerebellum, and pons.

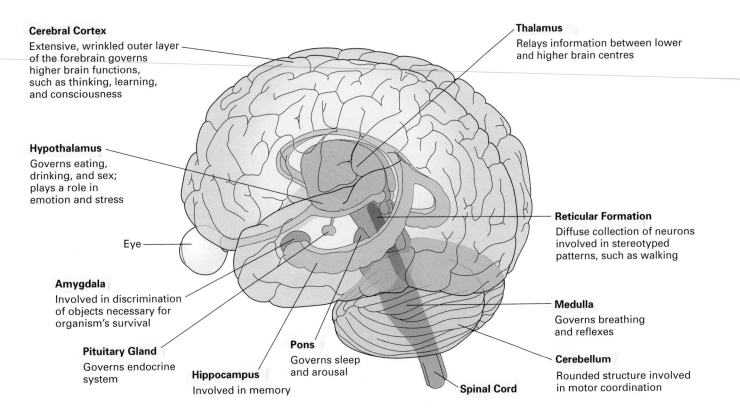

Cerebral Cortex
Extensive, wrinkled outer layer of the forebrain governs higher brain functions, such as thinking, learning, and consciousness

Thalamus
Relays information between lower and higher brain centres

Hypothalamus
Governs eating, drinking, and sex; plays a role in emotion and stress

Eye

Amygdala
Involved in discrimination of objects necessary for organism's survival

Pituitary Gland
Governs endocrine system

Hippocampus
Involved in memory

Pons
Governs sleep and arousal

Spinal Cord

Reticular Formation
Diffuse collection of neurons involved in stereotyped patterns, such as walking

Medulla
Governs breathing and reflexes

Cerebellum
Rounded structure involved in motor coordination

FIGURE 3.13
Structure and Regions in the Human Brain

to the cerebellum impairs the performance of coordinated movements. When this damage occurs, people's movements become uncoordinated and jerky. Extensive damage to the cerebellum even makes it impossible to stand up.

The *pons* is a bridge in the hindbrain. It contains several clusters of fibres involved in sleep and arousal.

Midbrain The **midbrain**, located between the hindbrain and forebrain, is an area in which many nerve-fibre systems ascend and descend to connect the higher and lower portions of the brain. In particular, the midbrain relays information between the brain and the eyes and ears. Visual attention, for example, is linked to one midbrain nucleus, the *superior colliculus*. Parkinson's disease, a deterioration of movement that produces rigidity and tremors, damages the *substantia nigra*, a small nucleus near the bottom of the midbrain.

Two systems in the midbrain are of special interest. One is the **reticular formation** (see figure 3.13), a diffuse collection of neurons involved in stereotyped patterns of behaviour such as walking, sleeping, or turning to attend to a sudden noise (Soja & others, 2001). The other system consists of nuclei that use the neurotransmitters serotonin, dopamine, and norepinephrine. Although these groups contain relatively few cells, they send their axons to a remarkable variety of brain regions, perhaps explaining their involvement in high-level, integrative functions (Shier, Butler, & Lewis, 2003).

A region called the **brain stem** includes much of the hindbrain (it does not include the cerebellum) and midbrain and is so-called because it looks like a stem. Embedded deep within the brain, the brain stem connects with the spinal cord at its lower end and then extends upward to encase the reticular formation in the midbrain. The most ancient part of the brain, the brain stem evolved more than 500 million years ago (Kolb & Whishaw, 2005). It is much like the entire brain of present-day reptiles and thus is often referred to as the "reptilian brain." Nuclei in the brain stem determine alertness and regulate basic survival functions such as breathing, heartbeat, and blood pressure.

Forebrain You try to understand what all of these terms and parts of the brain mean. You talk with friends and plan a party for this weekend. You remember that it has been six months since you went to the dentist. You are confident you will do well on the next

midbrain Located between the hindbrain and forebrain, a region in which many nerve-fibre systems ascend and descend to connect the higher and lower portions of the brain.

reticular formation A midbrain system that consists of a diffuse collection of neurons involved in stereotypical behaviours such as walking, sleeping, or turning to attend to a sudden noise.

brain stem The region of the brain that includes most of the hindbrain (excluding the cerebellum) and the midbrain.

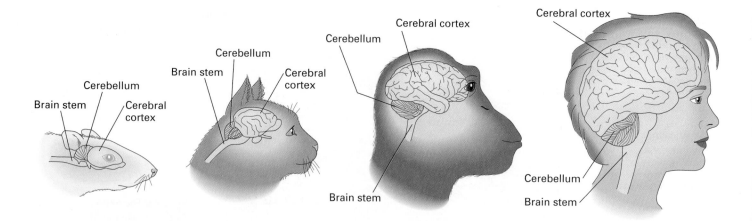

FIGURE 3.14

The Brain in Different Species
Note how much larger the cerebral cortex becomes as we go from the brain of a rat to the brain of a human.

exam in this course. All of these experiences, and millions more, would not be possible without the **forebrain**, the highest, and most recently evolved, level of the human brain.

Before we explore the structures and function of the forebrain, though, let's stop for a moment and examine how the brain evolved. The brains of the earliest vertebrates were smaller and simpler than those of later animals (Shettleworth, 1998). Genetic changes during the evolutionary process were responsible for the development of more complex brains with more parts and more interconnections (Carlson, 2005). Figure 3.14 compares the brains of a rat, cat, chimpanzee, and human. In the chimpanzee's brain, and especially the human's brain, the hindbrain and midbrain structures are covered by a forebrain structure called the cerebral cortex (Goldsmith & Zimmerman, 2001). The human hindbrain and midbrain are similar to those of other animals, so it is the forebrain structures, and especially the cerebral cortex, that mainly differentiate the human brain from the brains of animals such as rats, cats, and monkeys. The human forebrain's most important structures are the limbic system, thalamus, basal ganglia, hypothalamus, and cerebral cortex.

Limbic System   The **limbic system**, a loosely connected network of structures under the cerebral cortex, is important in both memory and emotion (Panksepp, 2004). Its two principal structures are the amygdala and hippocampus (see figure 3.13).

The *amygdala* (from the Latin for "almond" shape) is involved in the discrimination of objects that are necessary for the organism's survival, such as appropriate food, mates, and social rivals. Neurons in the amygdala often fire selectively at the sight of such stimuli, and lesions in or stimulation of the amygdala can cause animals to attempt to eat, fight, or mate with inappropriate objects such as chairs. The amygdala is also involved in emotional awareness and expression through its many connections with higher and lower regions of the brain (Davidson, 2000).

The *hippocampus* has a special role in the storage of memories (Bannerman & others, 2002). Individuals who suffer extensive hippocampal damage cannot retain any new conscious memories after the damage. It is fairly certain, though, that memories are not stored "in" the limbic system. Instead, the limbic system seems to determine what parts of the information passing through the cortex should be "printed" into durable, lasting neural traces in the cortex.

Thalamus   The **thalamus** is a forebrain structure that sits at the top of the brain stem in the central core of the brain (see figure 3.13). It serves as a very important relay station, functioning much like a server in a computer network. That is, an important function of the thalamus is to sort information and send it to the appropriate places in the forebrain for further integration and interpretation (Castro-Alamancos & Calcagnotto, 2001). For example, one area of the thalamus receives information from the cerebellum and projects it to the motor area of the cerebral cortex. Indeed, most neural input to the cerebral cortex goes through the thalamus. While one area of the thalamus works to direct information from the sense receptors (hearing, seeing, and so on), another

forebrain The highest, and most recently evolved level of the brain. Key structures in the forebrain are the limbic system, thalamus, basal ganglia, hypothalamus, and cerebral cortex.

limbic system Loosely connected network of structures—including the amygdala and hippocampus—that play important roles in memory and emotion.

thalamus Forebrain structure that functions as a relay station to sort input and direct it to different areas of the cerebral cortex. It also has ties to the reticular formation.

region, with ties to the reticular formation, seems to be involved in sleep and wakefulness.

Basal Ganglia   Above the thalamus and under the cerebral cortex lie large clusters, or *ganglia*, of neurons called basal ganglia. The **basal ganglia** work with the cerebellum and the cerebral cortex to control and coordinate voluntary movements. The basal ganglia enable people to engage in habitual behaviours such as riding a bicycle. Individuals with damage to the basal ganglia suffer from either unwanted movement, such as constant writhing or jerking of limbs, or too little movement, as in the slow and deliberate movements of those with Parkinson's disease (Boraud & others, 2002; Addis & others, 2004).

Hypothalamus   The **hypothalamus**, a small forebrain structure located just below the thalamus, monitors three pleasurable activities—eating, drinking, and sex—as well as emotion, stress, and reward (see figure 3.13 for the location of the hypothalamus). As is discussed later, the hypothalamus also helps direct the endocrine system. Perhaps the best way to describe the function of the hypothalamus is as a regulator of the body's internal state. It is sensitive to changes in the blood, as well as to neural input, and it responds by influencing the secretion of hormones and neural outputs. For example, if the temperature of circulating blood near the hypothalamus is increased by just one or two degrees, certain cells in the hypothalamus start increasing their rate of firing. As a result, a chain of events is set in motion. Increased circulation through the skin and sweat glands occurs immediately to release this heat from the body. The cooled blood circulating to the hypothalamus slows down the activity of some of the neurons there, stopping the process when the temperature is just right—37.1° Celsius. These temperature-sensitive neurons function like a finely tuned thermostat to maintain the body in a balanced state.

The hypothalamus is also involved in emotional states, playing an important role as an integrative location for handling stress. Much of this integration is accomplished through the hypothalamus's action on the pituitary gland, an important endocrine gland located just below the hypothalamus.

If certain areas of the hypothalamus are electrically stimulated, a feeling of pleasure results. In a classic experiment, McGill researchers James Olds and Peter Milner (1954) implanted an electrode in the hypothalamus of a rat's brain. When the rat ran to a corner of an enclosed area, a mild electric current was delivered to its hypothalamus. The researchers thought the electric current would cause the rat to avoid the corner. Much to their surprise, the rat kept returning to the corner. Olds and Milner believed they had discovered a pleasure centre in the hypothalamus. Olds (1958) conducted further experiments and found that rats would press bars until they dropped over from exhaustion just so they could continue to receive a mild electric shock to their hypothalamus. One rat pressed a bar more than 2,000 times an hour over a 24 hour period to receive the stimulation to its hypothalamus (see figure 3.15). Today researchers agree that the hypothalamus is involved in pleasurable feelings but that other areas of the brain, such as the limbic system and a bundle of fibres in the forebrain, are also important in the link between the brain and pleasure (Milner, 1991).

The Olds studies have implications for drug addiction. In the Olds studies, the rat pressed the bar mainly because it produced a positive, rewarding effect (pleasure), not because it wanted to avoid or escape a negative effect (pain). Cocaine users, for instance, talk about the drug's ability to heighten pleasure in food, in sex, and in a variety of activities, highlighting the reward aspects of the drug.

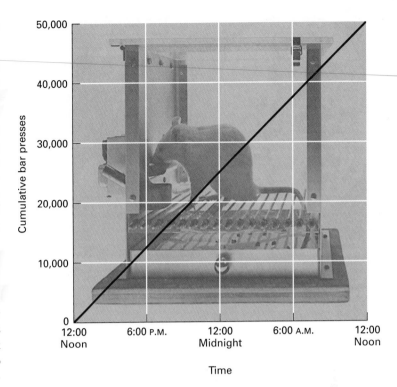

FIGURE 3.15

Results of the Experiment by Olds (1958) on the Role of the Hypothalamus in Pleasure
The graphed results for one rat show that it pressed the bar more than 2000 times an hour for a period of 24 hours to receive stimulation to its hypothalamus. One of the rats in Olds and Milner's experiments is shown pressing the bar.

basal ganglia Located above the thalamus and under the cerebral cortex, these large clusters of neurons work with the cerebellum and the cerebral cortex to control and coordinate voluntary movements.

hypothalamus Forebrain structure involved in regulating eating, drinking, and sex; directing the endocrine system through the pituitary gland; and monitoring emotion, stress, and reward.

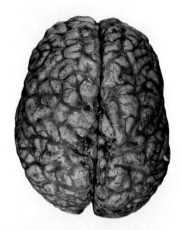

FIGURE 3.16

The Human Brain's Hemispheres
The two halves (hemispheres) of the human brain can be seen clearly in this photograph.

The Cerebral Cortex

The **cerebral cortex** is the highest region of the forebrain and is the most recently evolved part of the brain. The highest mental functions, such as thinking and planning, take place in the cerebral cortex. The neural tissue that makes up the cerebral cortex is, by volume the largest part of the brain (about 80 percent) and covers the lower portions of the brain like a large cap. In humans, the cerebral cortex is greatly convoluted with many grooves and bulges, which considerably enlarge its surface area (compared to a brain with a smooth surface). The cerebral cortex is highly connected with other parts of the brain. Millions of axons connect the neurons of the cerebral cortex with those located elsewhere in the brain.

Lobes The wrinkled surface of the cerebral cortex is divided into two halves called *hemispheres* (see figure 3.16). Each hemisphere is subdivided into four regions—the frontal lobe, the parietal lobe, the temporal lobe, and the occipital lobe (see figure 3.17).

The **occipital lobe**, at the back of the head, responds to visual stimuli (Milner & Goodale, 1995). Different areas of the occipital lobes are connected to process information about such aspects of visual stimuli as their colour, shape, and motion (Olshausen & Field, 2005). A stroke or wound in the occipital lobe can cause blindness or, at a minimum, wipe out a portion of the person's visual field, just as it did in the case of Bryan Kolb.

The **temporal lobe**, the portion of the cerebral cortex just above the ears, is involved in hearing, language processing, and memory. The temporal lobes have a number of connections to the limbic system. For this reason, people with damage to the temporal lobes cannot file experiences into long-term memory.

The **frontal lobe**, the portion of the cerebral cortex behind the forehead, is involved in the control of voluntary muscles, intelligence, and personality. One fascinating case study illustrates how damage to the frontal lobe can significantly alter personality. Phineas T. Gage, a 25-year-old foreman who worked for the Rutland and Burlington Railroad, met with an accident on September 13, 1848. Phineas and several co-workers were using blasting powder to construct a roadbed. The crew drilled holes in the rock and gravel, poured in the blasting powder, and then tamped down the powder with an iron rod. While Phineas was still tamping it down, the powder blew up, driving

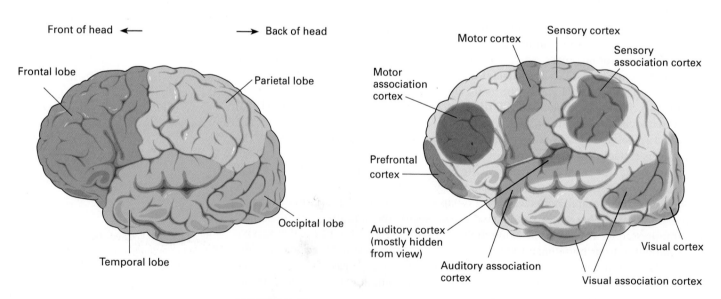

FIGURE 3.17

The Cerebral Cortex's Lobes and Association Areas
The cerebral cortex (*left*) is roughly divided into four lobes: occipital, temporal, frontal, and parietal. The cerebral cortex (*right*) also consists of the motor cortex and sensory cortex. Further, the cerebral cortex includes association areas, such as the visual association cortex, auditory association cortex, and sensory association cortex.

the iron rod up through the left side of his face and out through the top of his head. Though the wound in his skull healed in a matter of weeks, Phineas became a different person. He had been a mild-mannered, hardworking, emotionally calm individual prior to the accident, well liked by all who knew him. Afterward, he became obstinate, moody, irresponsible, selfish, and incapable of participating in any planned activities. Damage to the frontal lobe of his brain dramatically altered Phineas's personality.

Without intact frontal lobes, humans are emotionally shallow, distractible, listless, and so insensitive to social contexts that they may belch with abandon at dinner parties (Hooper & Teresi, 1993). Individuals with frontal lobe damage become so distracted by irrelevant stimuli that they often cannot carry out some basic directions. In one such case, an individual, when asked to light a candle, struck a match correctly but instead of lighting the candle, he put the candle in his mouth and acted as if he was smoking it (Luria, 1973).

The frontal lobes of humans are especially large when compared with those of other animals. For example, the frontal cortex of rats barely exists; in cats, it occupies a paltry 3.5 percent of the cerebral cortex; in chimpanzees, 17 percent; and in humans, approximately 30 percent. Some neuroscientists maintain that the frontal cortex is an important index of evolutionary advancement (Hooper & Teresi, 1993). Fergus Craik and his colleagues from the Rotman Institute at the University of Toronto (Craik & others, 1999) have even presented evidence that the self and self-concept might be represented in the right frontal lobe.

An important part of the frontal lobes is the *prefrontal cortex*, which is at the front of the motor cortex (see figure 3.17). The prefrontal cortex is believed to be involved in higher cognitive functions, such as planning and reasoning (Goel, 2005a; Manes & others, 2002). Some neuroscientists refer to the prefrontal cortex as an executive control system because of its role in monitoring and organizing thinking (Owen, 1997).

The **parietal lobe**, located at the top and toward the rear of the head, is involved in registering spatial location, attention, and motor control. The parietal lobes are at work when you are judging how far you have to throw a ball to get it to someone else, when you shift your attention from one activity to another (turn your attention away from the TV to a noise outside), and when you turn the pages of this book. Albert Einstein said that his reasoning was often best when he imagined objects in space. It turns out that his parietal lobes were 15 percent larger than average (Witelson, Kigar, & Harvey, 1999).

Motor Cortex and Sensory Cortex Two other important regions of the cerebral cortex are the motor cortex and the sensory cortex (see figure 3.17). The **motor cortex**, part of the frontal lobes, processes information about voluntary movement and sends outputs to various muscles throughout the body. The **sensory cortex**, part of the parietal lobes, processes information about body sensations (such touch) based on inputs from the various parts of the body.

The map in figure 3.18 shows which parts of the motor and sensory cortex are associated with different parts of the body. It is based on research first done by Wilder Penfield (1947), a neurosurgeon at the Montreal Neurological Institute. He often performed surgery to remove portions of the brains of patients with severe epilepsy.

However, he was concerned that removing a portion of the brain might impair some of his patients' functions. Penfield's solution was to map the cortex during surgery by stimulating different cortical areas and observing the responses of the patients, who were given a local anesthetic so they would remain awake during the operation. He found that different parts of a patient's body moved when he stimulated certain areas of the motor cortex. He also found that patients reported feeling sensations in different parts of their bodies when he stimulated certain areas of the sensory cortex.

For both motor and sensory areas, there is a point-to-point relation between a part of the body and a location on the cerebral cortex. In figure 3.16, the face and hands are given proportionately more space than other body parts because the face and hands are capable of finer perceptions and movements than other body areas and, therefore, need more cerebral cortex representation (Penfield & Rasmussen, 1950).

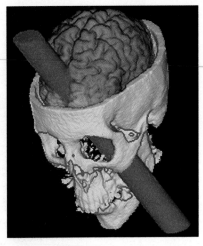

This is a computerized reconstruction of Phineas T. Gage's accident, based on measurements taken of his skull.

cerebral cortex Highest level of the forebrain, where the highest mental functions, such as thinking and planning, take place.

occipital lobe The part of the cerebral cortex at the back of the head that is involved in vision.

temporal lobe The portion of the cerebral cortex just above the ears that is involved in hearing, language processing, and memory.

frontal lobe The part of the cerebral cortex just behind the forehead that is involved in the control of voluntary muscles, intelligence, and personality.

parietal lobe Area of the cerebral cortex at the top of the head that is involved in registering spatial location, attention, and motor control.

motor cortex Area of the frontal lobe that processes information about voluntary movement.

sensory cortex Area of the parietal lobe that processes information about body sensations.

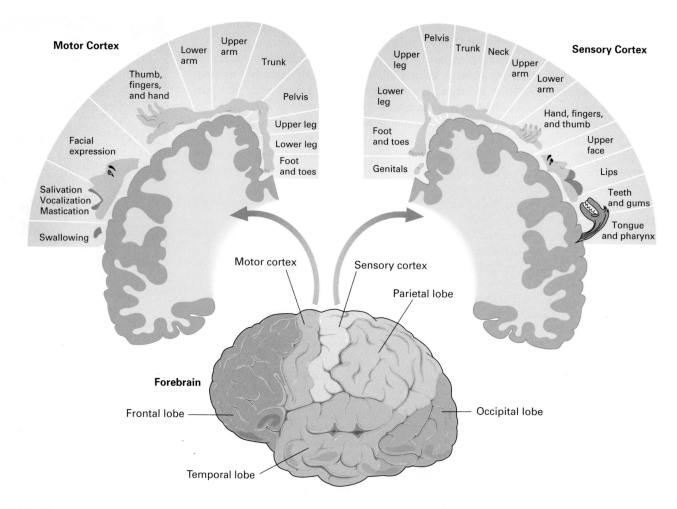

FIGURE 3.18

Disproportionate Representation of Body Parts in the Motor and Sensory Areas of the Cortex
The amount of cortex allotted to a body part is not proportionate to the body part's size. Instead, the brain has more space for body parts that require precision and control. Thus the thumb, fingers, and hand require more brain tissue than does the arm.

The point-to-point mapping of sensory fields onto the cortex's surface is the basis of our orderly and accurate perception of the world (Cheyne & others, 1998; Fox, 2004). When something touches your lip, for example, your brain knows what body part has been touched because the nerve pathways from your lip are the only pathways that project to the lip region of the sensory cortex.

Siamese cats are a familiar example of what happens when these neural pathways get connected the wrong way. Many Siamese cats have a genetic defect that causes the pathways from the eyes to connect to the wrong parts of the visual cortex during development. The result is that these cats spend their lives looking at things cross-eyed in an effort to "straighten out" the visual image of their visual cortex.

The Association Cortex Located in the brain's lobes, the association cortex makes up 75 percent of the cerebral cortex (see figure 3.17). Processing information about sensory input and motor output is not all that is taking place in the cerebral cortex. The **association cortex** (sometimes called *association areas*) is the region of the cerebral cortex that integrates this information. The highest intellectual functions, such as thinking and problem solving, occur in the association cortex.

Interestingly, damage to a specific part of the association cortex often does not result in a specific loss of function. With the exception of language areas (which are localized), loss of function seems to depend more on the extent of damage to the association cortex than on the specific location of the damage. By observing brain-damaged individuals and using a mapping technique, scientists have found that the association cortex is involved in linguistic and perceptual functioning.

The largest portion of the association cortex is located in the frontal lobe, directly under the forehead. Damage to this area does not lead to sensory or motor loss. Indeed, it is this area that may be most directly related to thinking and problem solving. Early

association cortex Region of the cerebral cortex in which the highest intellectual functions, including thinking and problem solving, occur (also called as sociation areas).

studies even referred to the frontal lobe as the centre of intelligence, but research suggests that frontal lobe damage may not result in a lowering of intelligence. Planning and judgment are often associated with the frontal lobe. Personality may also be linked to the frontal lobe. Recall the misfortune of Phineas Gage, whose personality radically changed after he experienced frontal lobe damage.

In closing this discussion of the cerebral cortex's lobes, a word of caution is in order about going too far in localizing function within a particular lobe. Although we have attributed specific functions to a particular lobe (such as vision in the occipital lobe), there is considerable integration and connection between any two or more lobes and between lobes and other parts of the brain.

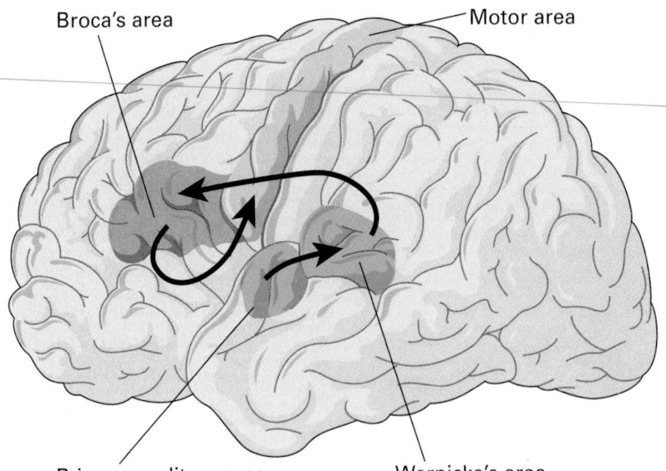

The Cerebral Hemispheres

At the beginning of the discussion of the cerebral cortex, we indicated that it is divided into two halves—left and right (see figure 3.16). Do these hemispheres have different functions?

Hemispheric Differences In 1861, French surgeon Paul Broca saw a patient who had injured the left side of his brain about 30 years earlier. The patient became known as Tan, because *Tan* was the only word he could speak. Tan suffered from *aphasia*, a loss of language ability associated with brain damage. Tan died several days after Broca evaluated him. An autopsy revealed that the injury was to a precise area of the left hemisphere. Today we refer to this area of the brain as *Broca's area*, and we know that it plays an important role in the expression of speech. Patients with damage to Broca's area suffer from *Broca's aphasia*. They know what they want to say but have great difficulty expressing themselves in spoken language (hence the alternate designation of *expressive aphasia*), speaking painfully slowly in uneven bursts of inappropriate words or nonsense words.

Another area of the brain's left hemisphere that has an important role in language is *Wernicke's area*, which, if damaged, causes problems in receiving language. Patients with damage to Wernicke's area suffer from *Wernicke's aphasia*. These patients have great difficulty understanding spoken language (hence the alternate designation of *receptive aphasia*), seeming to speak fluently, but in often-meaningless sentences, because they cannot understand what they are hearing. More recently, the Wernicke-Geschwind model (see figure 3.19) has been proposed to explain how these two areas collaborate with others when a spoken word is presented and the individual repeats the word out loud (Geschwind & Galaburda, 1987).

Models like this help us to understand how the functions of specialized brain areas like Broca's and Wernicke's areas are integrated, in this case to allow us to process human language. If you revisit the PET scan images in Figure 3.2, you can see that when we are speaking words, Broca's area and motor cortex are most active and when we are hearing words, the primary auditory area and Wernicke's area are most active. This is consistent with the Wernicke-Geschwind model.

The Wernicke-Geschwind model assigns some responsibility for verbal processing exclusively to the left hemisphere. Following are the main functions the brain tends to allocate to one hemisphere or the other (Gazzaniga, Ivry, & Mangun, 2002; Springer & Deutsch, 1998):

- *Verbal processing.* The most extensive research on the brain's two hemispheres has focused on language. Speech and grammar are localized to the left hemisphere. A common misconception, though, is that all language processing is carried out in the brain's left hemisphere. However, such aspects of language as appropriate use of language in different contexts, metaphor, and much of our sense of humour are found in the right hemisphere.

FIGURE 3.19

The Wernicke-Geschwind Model
When a word is heard and repeated aloud, the ear sends action potentials to the primary auditory area, where the sound is first analyzed. It then goes to Wernicke's area where a sound-based code is retrieved and the word is understood. Next, it goes to Broca's area where the instructions to speak the word are assembled. Finally, these instructions are sent to the motor cortex, which activates the appropriate parts of the speech system. *How would damage to Broca's area interfere with repeating a heard word? How about Wernicke's area?*

- *Nonverbal processing.* The right hemisphere is more dominant in processing nonverbal information, such as spatial perception, visual recognition, and emotion (Corballis, Funnell, & Gazzaniga, 2002). While the evidence is open to question (Kampf, Babkoff, & Nachson, 2005), according to current opinion it is the right hemisphere that is mainly at work when we are processing information about people's faces (Kanwisher & Moscovitch, 2000). The right hemisphere may also be more involved in processing information about emotions, as when we express emotions ourselves and when we recognize others' emotions (Heller & others, 1997).

Because differences in the functioning of the brain's two hemispheres are known to exist, people commonly use the phrases *left-brained* and *right-brained* as a way of categorizing themselves and others. Such generalizations have little scientific basis. The most common myth about hemispheric specialization is that the left brain is logical and the right brain is creative. To most scientists, the concept of the brain as split into two tidy halves—one being the source of creativity, the other the source of logical thinking—is simplistic. For example, while Roger Sperry did discover that the left hemisphere is superior in the logic used to prove geometric theorems, in everyday life our problems involve integrating information and drawing conclusions. In these instances, the right hemisphere is crucial.

Sandra Witelson, a neuroscientist at McMaster University, points out that no complex function—music, art, reading, or whatever—can be assigned to one single hemisphere or the other. Complex thinking in normal people involves *complementary specialization* (Bryden, 1986) and communication between both sides of the brain. In reading, for example, the left hemisphere comprehends syntax and grammar, which the right does not. However, the right brain is better at understanding a story's intonation and emotion. The same is true for music and art. In some musical skills, such as recognizing chords, the right hemisphere is better. In others, such as distinguishing which of two sounds came first, the left hemisphere takes over. The real issue is the degree to which the bihemispheric representation of functions may vary in left-handers versus right-handers (Witelson, 1985), women versus men (Witelson & Kigar, 1992), geniuses versus normal people (Witelson, Kigar, & Harvey, 1999), and even homosexual versus heterosexual people (McCormick & Witelson, 1994).

One positive side effect of the left-brain–right-brain myth is a perception that more "right-brain" activities and exercises should be incorporated into school programs. In schools that rely heavily on rote learning to instruct students, children would probably benefit from exercises in intuitive thought and holistic thinking. But a deficiency in school curricula has nothing at all to do with left-brain, right-brain specialization (Segalowitz, 1983).

In sum, some specialization of functions exists in both the left hemisphere (processing of certain verbal information) and the right hemisphere (processing of certain nonverbal information) of the brain. However, in many complex tasks in which humans engage in their everyday lives, integration across the hemispheres is common.

The Split-Brain Today, there continues to be considerable interest in the degree to which the brain's left hemisphere or right hemisphere is involved in various aspects of thinking, feeling, and behaviour (Corballis, Funnell, & Gazzaniga, 2002; Spence & others, 2002). How, for example, does communication between the two hemispheres occur? What would happen if it were disrupted? For many years scientists speculated that the **corpus callosum**, the large bundle of axons that connects the brain's two hemispheres, had something to do with relaying information between the two sides (see figure 3.20). Roger Sperry (1974) confirmed this in an experiment in which he cut the corpus callosum in cats. He also severed certain nerves leading from the eyes to the brain. After the operation, Sperry trained the cats to solve a series of visual problems with one eye blindfolded. After the cat learned the task, say with only its left eye uncovered, its other eye was blindfolded and the animal was tested again. The "split-brain" cat behaved as if it had never learned the task. It seems that the memory was stored only

corpus callosum A large bundle of axons that connect the brain's two hemispheres.

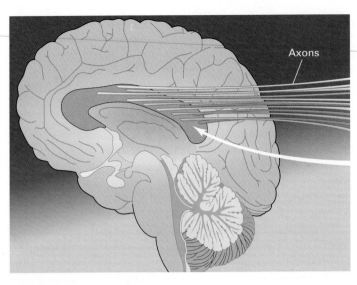
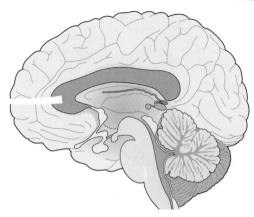

Axons

FIGURE 3.20 The Corpus Callosum

The corpus callosum is a thick band of about 80 million axons that connect the brain cells in one hemisphere to those in the other. In healthy brains, the two sides engage in a continuous flow of information via this neural bridge.

in the left hemisphere, which could no longer directly communicate with the right hemisphere.

On rare occasions, the corpus callosum of human beings has been severed in order to treat serious illnesses. The nervous system works effectively in most people to allow us to think and act. However, when the nervous system is short-circuited, as in the case of *epilepsy*, the flow of information is disrupted, the brain is unable to channel information accurately, and the person cannot effectively engage in mental processing and behaviour. Epileptic seizures are the result of abnormal electrical discharges in the brain. Just as an electrical surge during a lightning storm can disrupt the circuits in a computer, the electrical surge that produces an epileptic seizure disrupts the brain's information processing circuits. The brains of individuals with epilepsy work effectively to process information between seizures, unless the seizures occur with such regularity that they cause brain damage. In about 75 percent of epilepsy cases, seizures do not cause structural damage to the brain.

Epileptic seizures begin on one side of the brain. Nerve cells there become overactive and, across the corpus callosum, stimulate overactivity in nerve cells on the other side. The excess stimulation produces a seizure in which the individual loses consciousness and goes into convulsions. In severe cases, seizures can occur numerous times during the day and can threaten the person's life. In one famous case, neurosurgeons severed the corpus callosum of an epileptic patient now known as W. J. in a final attempt to reduce his unbearable seizures. Sperry (1968) examined W. J. and found that the corpus callosum functions the same in humans as in animals—cutting the corpus callosum seemed to leave the patient with "two separate minds" that learned and operated independently.

The right hemisphere, it turns out, receives information only from the left side of the body, and the left hemisphere receives information only from the right side of the body. When you hold an object in your left hand, for example, only the right hemisphere of your brain detects the object. When you hold an object in your right hand, only the left hemisphere of the brain detects the object (see figure 3.21). If you have a normal corpus callosum, both hemispheres receive this information.

Integration of Function in the Brain

How do all the regions of the brain cooperate to produce the wondrous complexity of thought and behaviour that characterizes humans? Neuroscience still doesn't have

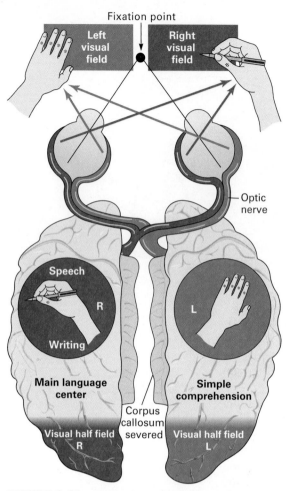

FIGURE 3.21 **Visual Information in the Split Brain**
In a split-brain patient, information from the visual field's left side projects only to the right hemisphere. Information from the visual field's right side projects only to the left hemisphere. Because of these projections, stimuli can be presented to only one of a split-brain patient's hemispheres.

answers to such questions as how the brain solves a murder mystery or writes a poem or essay. But we can get a sense of integrative brain function by considering something like the act of escaping from a burning building.

Imagine you are sitting at your desk writing some e-mails when fire breaks out behind you. The sound of crackling flames is relayed from your ear, through the thalamus, to the auditory cortex, and on to the auditory association cortex. At each stage, the stimulus is processed to extract information, and, at some stage, probably at the association cortex level, the sounds are finally matched with something like a neural memory representing sounds of fires you have heard previously. The association "fire" sets new machinery in motion. Your attention (guided in part by the reticular formation) shifts to the auditory signal being held in your association cortex, and on to your auditory association cortex, and simultaneously (again guided by reticular systems) your head turns toward the noise. Now your visual association cortex reports in: "Objects matching flames are present." In other regions of the association cortex, the visual and auditory reports are synthesized ("We have things that look and sound like fire"), and neural associations representing potential actions ("flee") are activated. However, firing the neurons that code the plan to flee will not get you out of the chair. The basal ganglia must become engaged, and from there the commands will arise to set the brain stem, motor cortex, and cerebellum to the task of actually transporting you out of the room.

Which part of your brain did you use to escape? Virtually all systems had a role; each was quite specific, and together they generated the behaviour. By the way, you would probably remember this event because your limbic circuitry would likely have started the memory formation process when the significant association "fire" was first triggered. The next time the sounds of crackling flames reach your auditory association cortex, the associations triggered would include those of this most recent escape. In sum, considerable integration of function takes place in the brain (Gevins, 1999; Miller & Cohen, 2001).

Are There "His" and "Hers" Brains?

We have just seen that the human brain is very complex. Different parts of the brain are specialized for different functions, from the hindbrain right up through to the cerebral cortex. At the same time, all of these specialized areas are richly interconnected to produce a highly integrated network that allows us to adapt our behaviour to the world around us. But we do not all behave in the same ways. Could it be that different people have different patterns of functional specialization or different patterns of integration across the brain?

For example, does sex matter when it comes to brain structure and function? Many differences between the brains of men and women have been reported, both cortically (Kimura, 1999; Goldstein & others, 2001) and subcortically (Raz & others, 2001; Swaab & others, 2001). The interpretation of these differences, however, is quite controversial. One interesting recent argument states that differences between the brains of women and men do not mean that one sex's brain is better, any more than one sex's genitals are better. People can be different without being unequal in ability (Halpern, 2001).

In one study, consistent with this argument, women were more likely to use both brain hemispheres to process language, whereas men were more likely to use only the left hemisphere (Shaywitz & others, 1995). Despite this difference, the two sexes performed equally well on the task, which involved sounding out words. The researchers concluded that nature has given the brain different routes to the same ability.

A similar conclusion was reached in a recent study of intelligence (Haier & others, 2004, 2005). While the men and women in this study had similar IQs, MRIs revealed major differences in the parts of their brains involved in intelligence. In general, the men had more grey matter (neuron cell bodies) while the women had more white matter (neuron axons). Both the grey and white matter of the women was more concentrated in their frontal lobes than the men's. In contrast, the men's grey matter was split between the frontal and parietal lobes while their white matter was concentrated in the temporal lobe. Whatever else these differences mean, they show that the human brain may be integrated in different ways to arrive at the same capabilities.

One related hypothesis is that these sorts of differences in the ways in which men's and women's brains function evolved over time. Some of the differences may be the result of a division of labour dating to early hunter-gatherer civilizations, in which men ventured away from home to hunt and women stayed closer to home as they cared for children and gathered food. For example, men are better than women at spatial-navigational skills, such as map reading, judging distances, and dart throwing (Kimura, 1999; Majeres, 1999). In one recent neuroimaging study, an area of the parietal lobe that functions in visuospatial skills was larger in men than in women (Frederikse & others, 2000). Women, on the other hand, have a better memory for words and objects and are better at fine motor skills (Halpern, 2001). These abilities may have evolved through making clothes and preparing food. Neither of these behavioural patterns requires more intelligence, just a different integration of intelligence throughout the brain.

But are these brain differences truly innate, driven by "nature" through evolution, genetic programming, and hormones in the womb? Neuroscientist Doreen Kimura (1999), originally from the University of Western Ontario but now in retirement at the University of Victoria, has explored how hormones actually "reorganize" the brain early in life. Drawing upon behavioural, neurological, and endocrinological studies, she theorizes how the sexes end up with distinct problem-solving abilities. Or might brain differences be more a consequence of environment, the result of societal influences that stereotypically define sex-specific roles and characteristics, in effect shaping our brains in accordance with these roles? Some psychologists argue that the latter explanation accounts for male/female differences in math and verbal achievement (Eagly, 2001; Eagly, Beall, & Sternberg, 2004).

It is also important to remember that many questions regarding men's and women's brains are exceedingly complex and likely cannot be answered by strictly biological or environmental arguments. Besides, debate continues to flourish about whether there are gender differences at all and about how big or small the differences are for many human skills. In many cases observed differences are small and the differences do not mean that all men are better or worse than all women at such tasks (Hyde & Mezulis, 2002).

> **reflect and review**

 Identify the brain's levels and structures, and summarize the functions of its structures.

- Outline the levels of organization in the human brain.
- Discuss the areas of the cerebral cortex and their functions.
- Explain how split-brain research has increased our understanding of the way the cerebral hemispheres function.
- Describe the integration of function in the brain. Do male and female brains achieve their integration in different ways and for different purposes?

In your experience, does human behaviour differ in important ways from the behaviour of other animals? What tasks are human brains able to accomplish that other animals may not be able to?

4 ADAPTABILITY OF THE BRAIN

The Brain's — The Brain's — Brain Tissue
Plasticity   Capacity   Implants
            for Repair

In what ways is the brain adaptable?

Recall from the discussion of the brain's important characteristics earlier in the chapter that plasticity is the term used to describe the brain's remarkable adaptability. While the plasticity of the immature brain has been appreciated for some time, it is only recently that we have come to understand that the adult brain can exhibit plasticity as well (Kolb, Gibb, & Robinson, 2003).

The study of brain plasticity includes how the brain changes when learning, when remembering, when becoming addicted, and when recovering from damage. Brain damage can produce horrific effects, including paralysis, sensory loss, memory loss, and personality deterioration. When such damage occurs, can the brain recover some or all its functions? Recovery from brain damage varies considerably from one case to another depending on the age of the individual and the extent of the damage (Sofroniew, Howe, & Mobley, 2001).

The Brain's Plasticity

Your brain changes on a day-to-day basis. Every time you learn a new skill, that learning must be reflected in a change in the brain. Every time you commit some information to long-term memory, that memory must be consolidated in the form of a long-term change in the brain. For example, Kolb, Gibb & Gorny (2003) raised rats in both a complex environment and a standard laboratory environment. They found longer dendrites and more synapses in the motor and sensory cortices of adult and aged animals living in complex environments compared with those living in standard environments. In response to experience, then, dendrites in our brain grow longer and form more synapses in order to encode those experiences. Intriguingly, Kolb, Gibb & Gorny (2003) reported that the brains of younger rats were also enriched by living in complex environments, but not in the same way as those of older rats.

One notable form of brain plasticity occurs among chronic drug abusers. Many psychoactive drugs exert their effects at the synaptic level and, with repeated use, can change the brain's structure. According to Kolb, Gibb & Robinson (2003), changes in the brain induced by long-term drug abuse can remain for years after the use of the drug has been discontinued. Apparently there are limits to the brain's plasticity.

The Brain's Capacity for Repair

Plasticity is especially evident if the brain is damaged through injury or illness, as it can sometimes show a dramatic capacity to repair itself. The human brain shows the most plasticity in young children before the functions of the cortical regions become entirely fixed (Kolb, 1989). For example, if the speech areas in an infant's left hemisphere are damaged, the right hemisphere assumes much of this language function. However, after age five or six, damage to the left hemisphere can permanently disrupt language ability (Kolb & others, 1998).

Brandi Binder is one dramatic example of the plasticity of the young child's brain. At age six, surgeons at the University of California at Los Angeles removed the entire right side of her cerebral cortex in an effort to subdue frequent seizures caused by very severe and uncontrollable epilepsy. As we saw previously, physicians have discovered that by severing the connection between the two sides of the brain or by removing the side of the brain in which the overactivity originates, they can eliminate the seizures or at least reduce their severity. Although not without risks and disadvantages, such surgery may greatly improve an individual's quality of life.

After her surgery, Brandi Binder had almost no control over muscles on the left side of her body, the side controlled by the right side of her brain. She needed years of therapy to regain abilities she had lost with the right side of her brain (Nash, 1997; Stuss, Winocur, & Robertson, 1999). At age 13, however, Brandi was an A student. She also loved music, math, and art, all of which are commonly associated with the brain's right side.

Brandi's story illustrates how amazingly adaptive and flexible the brain is, especially at an early age. In Brandi's case, the left side of her brain took over functions that are based on the right side. Although her recuperation has not been 100 percent—she never regained the use of her left arm, for example—her recovery is remarkable. Her story shows that if there is a way to compensate for damage, the brain will find it (Nash, 1997). The brain's plasticity is further discussed in chapter 4 on development throughout the life span.

A key factor in recovery is whether some or all of the neurons in an affected area are just damaged or completely destroyed (Black, 1998; Carlson, 2005). If the neurons have not been destroyed, brain function often becomes restored over time.

There are three ways in which repair of the damaged brain might take place:

- *Collateral sprouting*, in which the axons of some healthy neurons adjacent to damaged cells grow new branches (Chung & Chung, 2001).
- *Substitution of function*, in which the damaged region's function is taken over by another area or areas of the brain. This is what happened to Brandi Binder.
- *Neurogenesis*, the term given to the generation of new neurons. One of the long-standing beliefs in neuroscience regarding plasticity was that all the neurons an individual will ever have are present soon after birth. However, neuroscientists have recently found that human adults can generate new neurons (Pinel, 2006). Researchers also discovered that adult monkeys' brains can create thousands of new neurons each day (Gould & others, 1999). Some researchers believe there is good evidence that neurogenesis is much more pervasive than previously thought (Hsu & others, 2001). However, other neuroscientists argue that the evidence is weak (Rakic, 2002). If researchers can discover how new neurons are generated, possibly the information can be used to fight degenerative diseases of the brain, such as Alzheimer's disease and Parkinson's disease (Gage, 2000).

Brandi Binder is evidence of the brain's great power, flexibility, and resilience. Despite having had the right side of her cortex removed, Brandi engages in many activities often portrayed as right-brain activities. She loves music, math, and art; she is shown here working on one of her paintings.

Brain Tissue Implants

While some people, like Brandi Binder and Bryan Kolb, benefit from the brain's natural plasticity, other people are less fortunate. The brain naturally recovers some functions lost following damage, but not all. There is hope that one day surgeons will be able to implant healthy tissue and restore function lost as a result of illness or injury. In recent years, considerable excitement has been generated about *brain grafts*, implants of healthy tissue into damaged brains (Rossi, Saggiorato, & Strata, 2002).

The potential success of brain grafts is much better when brain tissue from the fetal stage (an early stage in prenatal development) is used. The neurons of the fetus are still growing and have a much higher probability of making connections with other neurons than the neurons of adults do. In a number of studies, researchers have damaged part of an adult rat's (or some other animal's) brain, waited until the animal recovered as much as possible by itself, then assessed its behavioural deficits. Then they took the corresponding area of a fetal rat's brain and transplanted it into the damaged brain of the adult rat. In these studies, the rats that received the brain transplants demonstrated considerable behavioural recovery (Dunnett, 1989).

Might such brain grafts be successful with humans suffering from brain damage? Research suggests that they might. One study examined individuals who have Parkinson's disease, which affects about 200,000 people in Canada. In one recent study, grafting embryonic dopamine neurons from aborted fetuses into the brains of individuals with Parkinson's disease resulted in a decrease of negative symptoms in individuals under 60 years of age but not in patients over 60 (Freed & others, 2001).

In another study, neuronal cells were transplanted into stroke victims (Kondziolka & others, 2000). The motor and cognitive skills of 12 patients who had experienced strokes improved markedly after the healthy neuronal cells were implanted in the midbrain.

The potential for brain grafts also exists for individuals with Alzheimer's disease, which is characterized by a progressive decline in intellectual functioning resulting from the degeneration of neurons that function in memory. Such degenerative changes can be reversed in rats (Gage & Bjorklund, 1986). As yet, though, no successful brain grafts have been reported for Alzheimer's patients.

Brain graft research holds promise for many people, but it is also controversial (Lindvall, 2001). The major sources of human fetal tissue are aborted fetuses and fetal stem cells. The use of such tissue raises serious and still unresolved ethical issues.

> **reflect and review**

4 **Discuss the brain's plasticity during learning, while remembering, and when addicted.**

- State the factors that favour recovery of function in damaged brains and list three ways in which the brain may recover.
- Discuss the possibility of repairing damaged brains with tissue grafts.

Suppose someone has suffered a mild form of brain damage. What questions might you ask to determine whether the person's brain will likely be able to either compensate or repair itself?

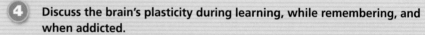

5 THE ENDOCRINE SYSTEM

What is the endocrine system and how does it affect behaviour?

The **endocrine system** is a set of glands that regulate the activities of certain organs by releasing their chemical products into the bloodstream. In the past, the endocrine system was considered separate from the nervous system. However, today neuroscientists know that these two systems are often interconnected.

Hormones are the chemical messengers that are manufactured by the endocrine glands. Hormones travel more slowly than nerve impulses. The bloodstream conveys hormones to all parts of the body, and the membrane of every cell has receptors for one or more hormones.

The endocrine glands consist of the pituitary gland, the thyroid and parathyroid glands, the adrenal glands, the pancreas, and the ovaries in women and the testes in men (see figure 3.20). In much the same way that the brain's control of muscular activity is constantly monitored and altered to suit the information received by the brain, the action of the endocrine glands is continuously monitored and changed by nervous, hormonal, and chemical signals (Mader, 2004). Recall from earlier in the chapter that the autonomic nervous system regulates processes such as respiration, heart rate, and digestion. The autonomic nervous system acts on the endocrine glands to produce a number of important physiological reactions to strong emotions such as rage and fear.

The **pituitary gland**, a pea-sized gland that sits at the base of the skull, controls growth and regulates other glands. The anterior (front) part of the pituitary is known as the master gland, because almost all its hormones direct the activity of target glands elsewhere in the body. In turn, the anterior pituitary gland is controlled by the hypothalamus.

The **adrenal glands** are instrumental in regulating moods, energy level, and the ability to cope with stress. Each adrenal gland secretes epinephrine (also called adrenaline) and norepinephrine (also called noradrenaline). Unlike most hormones, epinephrine and norepinephrine act quickly. Epinephrine helps a person get ready for an

endocrine system A set of glands that regulates the activities of certain organs by releasing hormones into the bloodstream.

hormones Chemical messengers manufactured by the endocrine glands.

pituitary gland An important endocrine gland at the base of the skull that controls growth and regulates other glands.

adrenal glands Important endocrine glands that are instrumental in regulating moods, energy level, and the ability to cope with stress.

emergency by acting on smooth muscles, the heart, stomach, intestines, and sweat glands. In addition, epinephrine stimulates the reticular formation, which in turn arouses the sympathetic nervous system, which subsequently excites the adrenal glands to produce more epinephrine. Norepinephrine also alerts the individual to emergency situations by interacting with the pituitary and the liver. You may remember that norepinephrine functions as a neurotransmitter when it is released by neurons. In the adrenal glands, norepinephrine is released as a hormone. In both instances, norepinephrine conveys information—in the first instance to neurons, in the second to glands (Raven & Johnson, 2002).

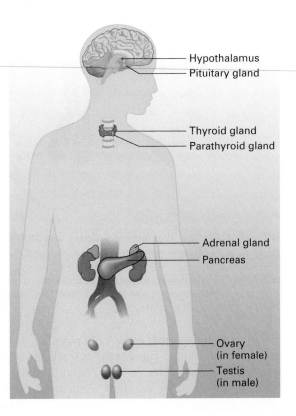

FIGURE 3.22
The Major Endocrine Glands
The pituitary gland releases hormones that regulate the hormone secretions of the other glands. The pituitary gland is itself regulated by the hypothalamus.

> **reflect and review**

5 **State what the endocrine system is and how it affects behaviour.**

• Describe the endocrine system, its glands, and their functions.

Is the behaviour of animals such as rats, rabbits, and bulls more likely to be strongly controlled by hormones than human behaviour is? As you answer this question, think about the differences in the structures of the brains of humans and the animals that were described earlier in the chapter.

6 GENETIC AND EVOLUTIONARY BLUEPRINTS OF BEHAVIOUR

— Chromosomes, — The Study — Genetics
   Genes,   of Genetics   and Evolution
   and DNA

How do genetics and evolutionary psychology increase our understanding of behaviour?

As you saw at the beginning of this chapter, genetic and evolutionary processes favour organisms that have adapted for survival. Successful adaptations can be physical, as in the case of the brain's increasing complexity, or behavioural, as in choosing a suitable mate to raise a family.

Chromosomes, Genes, and DNA

You began life as a single cell, a fertilized human egg, weighing about one 700-thousandth of a gram. From this single cell, you developed into a human being made up of trillions of cells. The nucleus of each human cell contains 46 **chromosomes**, which are

chromosomes Threadlike structures that contain genes and DNA. Humans have 23 chromosome pairs in the nucleus of every cell. Each parent contributes one chromosome to each pair.

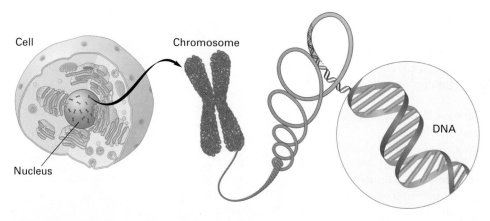

FIGURE 3.23 **Cells, Chromosomes, Genes, and DNA**
(*Left*) The body contains trillions of cells, which are the basic structural units of life. Each cell contains a central structure, the nucleus. (*Middle*) Chromosomes and genes are located in the nucleus of the cell. Chromosomes are made up of threadlike structures composed mainly of DNA molecules. (*Right*) A gene is a segment of DNA that contains the hereditary code. The structure of DNA resembles a spiral ladder.

threadlike structures that come in 23 pairs, one member of each pair coming from each parent. Chromosomes contain the remarkable substance **deoxyribonucleic acid**, or **DNA**, a complex molecule that contains genetic information. **Genes**, the units of hereditary information, are short segments of chromosomes, composed of DNA. Genes act like blueprints for cells. They enable cells to reproduce and manufacture the proteins that are necessary for maintaining life. The relationship among chromosomes, genes, and DNA is illustrated in figure 3.23.

When the approximately 30,000 genes from one parent combine at conception with the same number of genes from the other parent, the number of possibilities is staggering. Although scientists are still a long way from unravelling all the mysteries about the way genes work, some aspects of the process are well understood, starting with the fact that every person has two genes for each characteristic governed by principles of heredity (Lewis, 2005).

In some gene pairs, one gene is dominant over the other. If one gene of a pair is dominant and one is recessive, according to the **dominant-recessive genes principle**, the dominant gene overrides the recessive gene. A recessive gene exerts its influence only if both genes of a pair are recessive. If you inherit a recessive gene from only one parent, you may never know you carry the gene. In the world of dominant-recessive genes, brown eyes, farsightedness, and dimples rule over blue eyes, nearsightedness, and freckles. If you inherit a recessive gene for a trait from both of your parents, you will show the trait. That's why two brown-eyed parents can have a blue-eyed child: Each parent would have a dominant gene for brown eyes and a recessive gene for blue eyes. Because dominant genes override recessive genes, the parents have brown eyes. However, the child can inherit a recessive gene for blue eyes from each parent. With no dominant gene to override them, the recessive genes make the child's eyes blue.

Unlike eye colour, complex human characteristics such as personality and intelligence are likely influenced by many different genes. The term *polygenic inheritance* is used to describe the influences of multiple genes on behaviour.

The Study of Genetics

Historically speaking, genetics is a relatively young science. Its origins go back to the mid-nineteenth century, when an Austrian monk named Gregor Mendel studied heredity in generations of pea plants. By cross-breeding plants with different characteristics and noting the characteristics of the offspring, Mendel discovered predictable patterns of heredity and laid the foundation for modern genetics. Today researchers

deoxyribonucleic acid (DNA) A complex molecule that contains genetic information; makes up chromosomes.

genes The units of hereditary information. They are short segments of chromosomes, composed of DNA.

dominant-recessive genes principle If one gene of a pair governing a given characteristic (such as eye colour) is dominant and one is recessive, the dominant gene overrides the recessive gene. A recessive gene exerts its influence only if both genes in a pair are recessive.

continue to apply Mendel's methods, as well as modern technology, in their quest to expand our knowledge of genetics. This section discusses three ways to study genetics: selective breeding, molecular genetics, and behavioural genetics.

Selective Breeding *Selective breeding* is a genetic method in which organisms are chosen for reproduction based on how much of a particular trait they display. Mendel developed this technique in his studies of pea plants. A more recent example involving behaviour is the classic selective breeding study conducted by Robert Tryon (1940). He chose to study maze-running ability in rats. After he trained a large number of rats to run a complex maze, he then mated the rats that were the best at maze running (*maze-bright*) with each other and the ones that were the worst (*maze-dull*) with each other. He continued this process with 21 generations of rats. As can be seen in figure 3.24, after several generations, the maze-bright rats significantly outperformed the maze-dull rats.

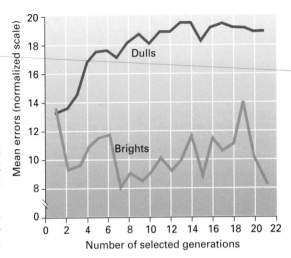

FIGURE 3.24
Results of Tryon's Selective Breeding Experiment with Maze-Bright and Maze-Dull Rats

Selective breeding studies have demonstrated that genes are an important influence on behaviour, but that does not mean that experience is unimportant (Pinel, 2006). For example, in another classic study, maze-bright and maze-dull rats were reared in one of two environments: (1) an impoverished environment that consisted of a barren wire-mesh group cage, or (2) an enriched environment that contained tunnels, ramps, visual displays, and other stimulating objects (Cooper & Zubeck, 1958). When they reached maturity, only the maze-dull rats, which had been reared in an impoverished environment, made more maze-learning errors than the maze-bright rats.

Selective breeding of human beings is also practised. For example, Dr. Robert Graham founded the Repository for Germinal Choice in California, as a sperm bank for Nobel Prize winners and other bright individuals, with the intent of producing geniuses. The sperm is available to women whose husbands are infertile. What are the odds that the sperm bank will yield that special combination of factors required to produce a creative genius? Twentieth-century Irish-born playwright George Bernard Shaw once told a story about a beautiful woman who wrote to him, saying that, with her body and his mind, they could produce wonderful offspring. Shaw responded by saying that, unfortunately, the offspring might get his body and her mind!

What do you think about the Nobel Prize winners' sperm bank? Is it right to breed humans for intelligence? Does it raise visions of attempts throughout human history at *eugenics*, the selective breeding of human beings? In one notorious example, the German genetics program of the 1930s and 1940s was based on the Nazis' belief that certain traits were superior. The Nazis tried to produce children with such traits and killed people who didn't have them, in their attempt to create a so-called "master race." Or does the sperm bank merely provide a social service for couples who cannot conceive a child, couples who want to maximize the probability that their offspring will have good genes?

Molecular Genetics Recent advances in technology have given rise to the field of *molecular genetics*, which involves the direct study of genes to determine their effect on behaviour (Marcus, 2004). There is currently a great deal of enthusiasm about the use of molecular genetics to discover the specific locations on genes that determine an individual's susceptibility to many diseases and other aspects of health and well-being (Mader, 2004).

The term *genome* is used to describe the complete set of instructions for making an organism. It contains the master blueprint for all cellular structures and activities for the life span of the organism. The human genome was completely determined in 2003 (U.S. Department of Energy Human Genome Project, 2003). To read about the Human Genome Project and its possible relevance to your own life, see the Personal Reflections box.

The Human Genome Project and Your Genetic Future

The Human Genome Project, begun in the 1970s, was completed in 2003, when it succeeded in determining the sequence of the 3 billion chemical base pairs that make up the human genome and identifying all of the genes in human DNA. But the drama of this moment is overshadowed by what lies ahead. Only about 30,000 genes were identified, the same number as the laboratory mouse and only about one-third as many as expected. Further, the functions of more than half the identified genes are currently unknown. Intriguingly, these genes comprise only about 2 percent of the human genome. Most of the rest of the genome, including an amazing 50 percent devoted to repeated sequences, is still poorly understood (U.S. Department of Energy Human Genome Project, 2003).

The Human Genome Project has already linked specific DNA variations with an increased risk of a number of diseases and conditions, including Huntington's disease (in which the central nervous system deteriorates), some forms of cancer, asthma, diabetes, hypertension, and Alzheimer's disease (Davies, 2001). Other documented DNA vari-

A positive result from the Human Genome Project. Shortly after Andrew Gobea was born, his cells were genetically altered to prevent his immune system from failing.

ations affect the way people react to certain drugs. Every individual carries a number of DNA variations that might predispose that person to a serious physical disease or mental disorder. Identifying these flaws could enable doctors to estimate an individual's disease risks, recommend healthy lifestyle regimens, and prescribe the safest and most effective drugs. A decade or two from now, prospective parents might be able to obtain a full genome analysis of their baby while it is still in the womb that reveals various disease risks. Based on this information, parents might then make decisions about abortion or future health care options.

However, mining DNA variations to discover health risks might increasingly threaten an individual's ability to obtain and hold jobs, obtain insurance, and keep genetic profiles private. For example, should an airline pilot or neurosurgeon who may one day develop a disorder that makes the hands shake be required to leave that job early?

Answering the following questions should encourage you to think further about some of the issues involved in our genetic future:

1. Would you want yourself or a loved one to be tested for a gene that increases your risk for a disease but does not determine whether you will actually develop the disease?
2. Would you want yourself and your mate tested before having offspring to determine your risk for having a child who is likely to contract various diseases?
3. Should testing of fetuses be restricted to traits that are commonly considered to have negative outcomes, such as Huntington's disease?
4. Should altering a newly conceived embryo's genes to improve qualities such as intelligence, appearance, and strength be allowed?
5. Should employers be permitted access to your genetic information?
6. Should life insurance companies have access to your genetic information?

Behaviour Genetics *Behaviour genetics* is the study of the degree and nature of heredity's influence on behaviour. Behaviour genetics is less invasive than molecular genetics and selective breeding. Using methods such as the *twin study*, behaviour geneticists examine the extent to which individuals are shaped by their heredity and their environmental experiences (Wahlsten, 2000).

In the most common type of twin study, the behavioural similarity of identical twins is compared with the behavioural similarity of fraternal twins. *Identical twins* develop from a single fertilized egg that splits into two genetically identical embryos, each of which becomes a person. *Fraternal twins* develop from separate eggs and separate sperm, making them genetically no more similar than nontwin siblings. They may even be of different sexes.

By comparing groups of identical and fraternal twins, behaviour geneticists capitalize on the fact that identical twins are more similar genetically than fraternal twins. In one twin study, 7,000 pairs of Finnish identical and fraternal twins were compared on the personality traits of extroversion (being outgoing) and neuroticism (being psychologically unstable; Rose & others, 1988). The identical twins were much more alike than the fraternal twins on both these personality traits, suggesting that genes influence both traits.

The Jim twins: how coincidental? Springer (*right*) and Lewis were unaware of each other for 39 years.

One problem with twin studies is that adults might stress the similarities of identical twin children more than those of fraternal twins, and identical twins might perceive themselves as a "set" and play together more than fraternal twins do. If so, observed similarities in identical twins might be more strongly influenced by environmental factors than usually thought.

In another type of twin study, researchers evaluate identical twins who have been reared in separate environments (Bouchard, Jr., 2004). If their behaviour is similar, the assumption is that heredity has played an important role in shaping their behaviour. This strategy is the basis for the Minnesota Study of Twins Reared Apart, directed by Thomas Bouchard Jr. and his colleagues (1996). They brought together identical twins from all over the world who had been reared apart to study their behaviour. They asked thousands of questions about the twins' family and childhood environment, personal interests, vocational orientation, and values. Detailed medical histories were obtained, including information about the twins' diet, smoking, and exercise habits.

One pair of twins made famous by the Minnesota study, Jim Springer and Jim Lewis, were separated at four weeks of age and did not see each other again until they were 39 years old. They had an uncanny number of similarities, even though they had lived apart. For example, they both worked as part-time deputy sheriffs, had vacationed in Florida, had owned Chevrolets, had dogs named Toy, and had married and divorced women named Betty. Both liked math but not spelling. Both were good at mechanical drawing. Both put on 10 pounds at about the same time in their lives, and both started suffering headaches at 18 years of age. They did have a few differences. For example, one expressed himself better verbally, whereas the other was more proficient at writing. One parted his hair over his forehead, the other wore his hair slicked back, and had sideburns.

Critics argue that some of the separated twins in the Minnesota study had been together several months prior to their adoption, that some had been reunited prior to their testing (in some cases for a number of years), that adoption agencies often put identical twins in similar homes, and that even strangers who spend several hours together are likely to come up with some coincidental similarities (Adler, 1991). Still, even in the face of such criticism, it seems unlikely that all the similarities in the identical twins reared apart could be due to experience alone.

Behaviour geneticists also use *adoption studies* to try to determine whether the behaviour of adopted children is more like that of their biological parents or their

Calvin and Hobbes

by Bill Watterson

CALVIN AND HOBBES ©Watterson. Reprinted with permission of UNIVERSAL PRESS SYNDICATE. All rights reserved.

adoptive parents. Another type of adoption study compares biological and adopted siblings. In one study, the educational levels attained by the biological parents were better predictors of the adopted children's IQ scores than the IQs of the children's adoptive parents (Scarr & Weinberg, 1983). Because of the stronger genetic link between the adopted children and their biological parents, the implication is that heredity plays an important role in intelligence. However, there are numerous studies that document the critical role of environment in intelligence, as well (Sternberg, 1997b).

Genetics and behaviour, especially the way heredity and environment interact, are discussed further in chapter 4. The interaction of heredity and behaviour in determining human intelligence is discussed further in chapter 10.

Genetics and Evolution

Often we can see the effects of genetics by observing family resemblances. For example, you might have your mother's dark hair and your father's long legs. Evolutionary influences are not as easy to see, because we share physical and psychological characteristics with every other human, such as a cerebral cortex in our brain that allows us to think and plan. We also share certain problems that we have to solve and adapt to, such as how to protect ourselves from harm, how to nourish our bodies, how to find a compatible mate, and how to rear our children. In the evolutionary scheme, some individuals were more successful than others at solving these problems and adapting effectively (Cummings, 2003; Goldsmith & Zimmerman, 2001). Those who were successful passed on their genes to the next generation. Those who were less successful did not.

In the evolutionary psychology view, psychological functions evolved to become specialized. Thus, just as the cerebellum became functionally specialized in coordinating movement, so it might be that specialized psychological functions evolved (Buss, 2004). Among the specialized psychological functions that evolutionary psychologists study are:

- Development of a fear of strangers between 3 and 24 months of age, as well as fears of snakes, spiders, heights, open spaces, and darkness (Marks, 1987)
- Perceptual adaptations for tracking motion (Ashida, Seiffert, & Osaka, 2001)
- Children's imitation of high-status rather than low-status models (Bandura, 1977)
- The worldwide preference for mates who are kind, intelligent, and dependable (Buss & others, 1990)

Evolutionary psychologists believe that these specialized functions developed because they helped humans adapt and solve problems in past evolutionary environments (Cosmides & others, 2003). According to Martin Daly, Margo Wilson, and Denys deCatanzaro of McMaster University, these problems include parenthood (Daly & Wilson, 1998), infanticide (Wilson & Daly, 2002), murder (Daly & Wilson, 2001), and motivation and emotion (deCatanzaro, 1999). In later chapters, we examine what evolutionary psychologists have to say about other psychological topics.

Evolutionary psychology is not without its critics, who believe it places too much emphasis on biological foundations of behaviour. For example, Albert Bandura (2001), whose social cognitive theory was described in chapter 1, acknowledges the importance of human adaptation and change. However, he rejects what he calls "one-sided evolutionism," in which social behaviour is the product of evolved biology. Bandura recommends a bidirectional view. In this view, evolutionary pressures created changes in biological structures for the use of tools, which enabled organisms to manipulate, alter, and construct new environmental conditions. Environmental innovations of increasing complexity, in turn, produced new selection pressures for the evolution of specialized biological systems for consciousness, thought, and language.

Human evolution gave us body structures and biological potentialities, not behavioural dictates, according to scientists such as Steven Jay Gould (1981). Having evolved, advanced biological capacities can be instrumental in producing diverse cultures—aggressive or peaceful, for example (Janicki & Krebs, 1998). And Russian-American scientist Theodore Dobzhansky (1977) reminds us that the human species has selected for learnability and plasticity, which allows us to adapt to diverse contexts. Most, if not all, psychologists would agree that the interaction of biology and environment is the basis for our own development as human beings. McGill psychologist Donald Hebb used to offer a useful analogy: what is the relevant contribution of height and width to the area of a rectangle? Of course both dimensions are absolutely essential; if either is reduced to zero, there is no rectangle any more. Similarly, if an attractive, popular, intelligent girl is elected president of her senior high school class, her success is due to both heredity and the environment. Chapter 4 further explores the influence of biology and environment on human development.

> ## > reflect and review

 Explain how genetics and evolutionary psychology increase our understanding of behaviour.

- Discuss the structures and functions of chromosomes, genes, and DNA.
- Describe three methods for studying genetics.
- Explain how evolution might direct human behaviour.

What ethical issues regarding genetics and behaviour might arise in the future?

Biological Foundations of Behaviour

1 THE NERVOUS SYSTEM

Characteristics — How the Brain and Nervous System Are Studied — Divisions of the Nervous System — Pathways in the Nervous System

2 NEURONS AND SYNAPSES

Specialized Cell Structure — The Neural Impulse — Synapses and Neurotransmitters — Neural Networks

3 FUNCTIONAL SPECIALIZATION OF THE BRAIN

Levels of Organization in the Brain — The Cerebral Cortex — The Cerebral Hemispheres — Integration of Function in the Brain — Are There "His" and "Hers" Brains?

4 ADAPTABILITY OF THE BRAIN

The Brain's Plasticity — The Brain's Capacity for Repair — Brain Tissue Implants

5 THE ENDOCRINE SYSTEM

6 GENETIC AND EVOLUTIONARY BLUEPRINTS OF BEHAVIOUR

Chromosomes, Genes, and DNA — The Study of Genetics — Genetics and Evolution

At the beginning of the chapter, we posed six chapter questions and encouraged you to review material related to these questions at the end of each major section (see pages 82, 89, 101, 104, 105, and 111). Use the following reflection and review features for further your understanding of the chapter material.

CHAPTER REFLECTIONS

1. Consider the four characteristics of the nervous system. Suppose you had to do without one of them. Which would you choose, and what would be the consequences for your behaviour?

2. Do a search on the World Wide Web for "nutrition" and "the brain." Examine the claims made by one or more of the Web sites. Based on what you learned in the chapter about how the nervous system works, how could nutrition affect brain function? Based on what you know about being a scientist, how believable are the claims on the Web site?

3. Imagine that you could make one part of your brain twice as big as it is right now. Which part would it be, and how do you think your behaviour would change as a result? What if you had to make another part of your brain half its current size? Which part would you choose to shrink, and what would the effects be?

4. Ephedra is a drug contained in a number of formulas marketed to enhance athletic performance. Among the actions of ephedra is stimulation of areas that normally respond to epinephrine and norepinephrine. Think about the two different kinds of actions (neurotransmitter and hormone) these chemicals normally have in the nervous system, and describe the kinds of side effects you might expect from taking ephedra. In particular, why might taking ephedra be very dangerous?

5. Visit the U. S. Department of Energy Web site devoted to genomics and the Human Genome Project (http://www.doegenomes.org/). From there you can reach a particularly good primer (http://www.ornl.gov/sci/techresources/Human_Genome/publicat/primer2001/primer2001/index.shtml). Can you find any information on the genetic basis for psychological disorders? Does any of this information invite you to think differently than you did before about people with psychological disorders?

CHAPTER REVIEW

Discuss the nature and basic functions of the nervous system.

- The nervous system is the body's electrochemical communication circuitry. Four important characteristics of the brain and nervous system are complexity, functional specialization, integration, and adaptability. The brain's special ability to adapt and change is called plasticity.

- The main techniques used to study the brain are staining, brain lesioning, electrical recording and stimulation, and brain imaging techniques, including CAT scans, PET scans, and MRI and fMRI.

- The nervous system is divided into two main parts: central (CNS) and peripheral (PNS). The CNS consists of the brain and spinal cord. The PNS has two major divisions: somatic and autonomic. The autonomic nervous system consists of two main divisions: sympathetic and parasympathetic.

- The flow of information in the nervous system occurs in specialized pathways of nerve cells. These pathways can be categorized as sensory input, motor output, and neural networks.

Explain what neurons are and describe how they process information.

- Neurons are cells that specialize in processing information. They make up the communication network of the nervous system. Glial cells perform supportive and nutritive functions for neurons. The three main parts of the neuron are the cell body, dendrite (receiving part), and axon (sending part). A myelin sheath encases and insulates most axons and speeds up transmission of neural impulses.

- Resting potential is the term given to the stable, slightly negative charge of an inactive neuron. When incoming electrical signals exceed a certain activation threshold, positively charged sodium ions rush into the neuron, causing it to send information along its axon in the form of brief electric impulses. The brief wave of electrical charge that sweeps down the axon is called the action potential. The neuron returns to the resting potential as positively charged potassium ions move out of it, returning the neuron to a negative charge. The action potential abides by the all-or-none principle: Its strength does not change during transmission.

- To go from one neuron to another, information must be converted from an electrical impulse to a chemical messenger called a neurotransmitter. At the synapse where neurons meet, neurotransmitters are released into the narrow gap that separates them. There, some neurotransmitter molecules attach to receptor sites on the receiving neuron, where they influence another electrical impulse. Neurotransmitters can be excitatory or inhibitory depending on the nature of the neural impulse. Neurotransmitters include acetylcholine, GABA, norepinephrine, dopamine, serotonin, and endorphins. Most drugs that influence behaviour do so mainly by mimicking neurotransmitters or interfering with their activity.

- Neural networks are clusters of neurons that are interconnected to process information.

Identify the brain's levels and structures and the functions of its structures.

- The three major levels of the brain are the hindbrain, midbrain, and forebrain. The hindbrain is the lowest portion of the brain. The three main parts of the hindbrain are the medulla (involved in controlling breathing and posture), cerebellum (involved in motor coordination), and pons (involved in sleep and arousal).

- From the midbrain, many nerve-fibre systems ascend and descend to connect to higher and lower levels of the brain. The midbrain contains the reticular formation, which is involved in stereotypical patterns of behaviour (such as walking, sleeping, or turning to a sudden noise), and small groups of neurons that communicate with many areas in the brain. The brain stem consists of much of the hindbrain (excluding the cerebellum) and the midbrain.

- The forebrain is the highest level of the brain. The key forebrain structures are the limbic system, thalamus, basal ganglia, hypothalamus, and cerebral cortex. The limbic system is involved in memory and emotion through its two structures, the amygdala (which plays roles in survival and emotion) and the hippocampus (which functions in the storage of memories). The thalamus is a forebrain structure that serves as an important relay station for processing information. The basal ganglia are forebrain structures that help to control and coordinate voluntary movements. The hypothalamus is a forebrain structure that monitors eating, drinking, and sex; directs the endocrine system through the pituitary gland; and is involved in emotion, stress, and reward.

- The cerebral cortex makes up most of the outer layer of the brain. Higher mental functions, such as thinking and planning, take place in the cerebral cortex. The wrinkled surface of the cerebral cortex is divided into hemispheres. Each hemisphere is divided into four lobes: occipital, temporal, frontal, and parietal. There is considerable integration and connection between the brain's lobes. The sensory cortex processes information about body sensations. The motor cortex processes information about voluntary movement. Penfield (1947) pinpointed specific areas in the brain that correspond to specific parts of the body and also mapped sensory fields onto the cortex's surface. The association cortex, which makes up 75 percent of the cerebral cortex, is instrumental in integrating information, especially about the highest intellectual functions.

- A controversial topic is the extent to which the left and right hemispheres of the brain are involved in different functions. Two areas in the left hemisphere that involve specific language functions are Broca's area (speech) and Wernicke's area (comprehending language). The corpus callosum is a large bundle of fibres that connects the two hemispheres. Researchers have studied what happens when the corpus callosum has to be severed, as in some cases of severe epilepsy. Research suggests that the left brain is more dominant in processing verbal information (such as language), and the right brain in processing nonverbal information (such as spatial perception, visual recognition, and emotion). Nonetheless, in a normal individual whose corpus callosum is intact, both hemispheres of the cerebral cortex are involved in most complex human functioning.

- It is extremely important to remember that generally brain function is integrated and involves connections between different parts of the brain. Pathways of neurons involved in a particular function, such as memory, are integrated across different parts and levels of the brain. Male and female brains may integrate functions differently, although the differences are small and neither is better than the other.

State what the endocrine system is and how it affects behaviour.

- The endocrine glands release hormones directly into the bloodstream for distribution throughout the body. The pituitary gland is the master endocrine gland. The adrenal glands play important roles in moods, energy level, and ability to cope with stress.

Describe the brain's capacity for recovery and repair.

- On a day-to-day basis the brain changes while learning, while remembering, and when becoming addicted.

- The damaged human brain has considerable plasticity, although this plasticity is greater in young children than later in development. Three ways in which a damaged brain might repair itself are collateral sprouting, substitution of function, and neurogenesis.

- Brain grafts are implants of healthy tissue into damaged brains. Brain grafts are more successful when fetal tissue is used.

Explain how genetics and evolutionary psychology increase our understanding of behaviour.

- Chromosomes are threadlike structures that come in 23 pairs, one member of each pair coming from each parent. Chromosomes contain the genetic substance deoxyribonucleic acid (DNA). Genes, the units of hereditary information, are short segments of chromosomes composed of DNA. The dominant-recessive genes principle states that if one gene of a pair is dominant and one is recessive, the dominant gene overrides the recessive gene.

- Three methods that are used to study heredity's influence are molecular genetics, selective breeding, and behaviour genetics. Two methods used by behaviour geneticists are twin studies and adoption studies.

- Several key points in evolutionary psychology centre on the idea that nature selects behaviours that increase an organism's reproductive success, the importance of adaptive behaviour, and specialization of functions. Evolutionary psychologists believe that just as parts of the brain have become specialized in function through the process of evolution, so have mental processes and behaviour. Critics stress that it is important to recognize how evolutionary advances allow humans to choose and select their environments, rather than being completely under the control of their evolutionary past.

CONNECTIONS Online **LearningCentre** with POWERWEB **i-ntegrator**

For extra help in mastering the material in this chapter, see the integrator, review sections, practice quizzes, and other resources in the Student Study Guide and at the Online Learning Centre (www.mcgrawhill.ca/college/santrock).

CORE TERMS

nervous system, p. 76
plasticity, p. 77
central nervous system (CNS), p. 80
peripheral nervous system (PNS), p. 80
somatic nervous system, p. 80
autonomic nervous system, p. 80
sympathetic nervous system, p. 80
parasympathetic nervous system, p. 80
nerve, p. 81
tract, p. 81
afferent nerves, p. 81
efferent nerves, p. 81
neural network, p. 81
nucleus, p. 81
neuron, p. 82
glial cells, p. 82
cell body, p. 82
dendrite, p. 82

axon, p. 83
myelin sheath, p. 83
resting potential, p. 84
action potential, p. 85
all-or-none principle, p. 85
synapses, p. 86
neurotransmitters, p. 86
agonist, p. 88
antagonist, p. 88
hindbrain, p. 90
midbrain, p. 91
reticular formation, p. 91
brain stem, p. 91
forebrain, p. 92
limbic system, p. 92
thalamus, p. 92
basal ganglia, p. 93
hypothalamus, p. 93

cerebral cortex, p. 95
occipital lobe, p. 95
temporal lobe, p. 95
frontal lobe, p. 95
parietal lobe, p. 95
motor cortex, p. 95
sensory cortex, p. 95
association cortex, p. 96
corpus callosum, p. 98
endocrine system, p. 104
hormones, p. 104
pituitary gland, p. 104
adrenal glands, p. 104
chromosomes, p. 105
deoxyribonucleic acid (DNA), p. 106
genes, p. 106
dominant-recessive genes principle,
   p. 106

4 Human Development

CHAPTER QUESTIONS

1. How do psychologists think about development?

2. How do children develop from conception to adolescence?

3. What are the most important changes that occur in adolescence?

4. How do adults develop and what are the positive dimensions of aging?

Are you a "twixter," trapped in an eternal adolescence between childhood and adulthood? You might be if you are in your late twenties, still live at home, are unmarried, childless, and not yet committed to a career. If you think you belong in this category, are you enjoying a few extra years of freedom so you can explore your identity by travelling, dating widely, and trying out different jobs, or are you ducking your adult responsibilities by letting your parents pamper you, being casual in your sexual relationships, and postponing the inevitable career choice? Demographic trends in many Westernized countries, including Canada, confirm that people are, in fact, taking longer to complete their educations, move away from home, get married, have children, and start their careers (Arnett, 2000, 2002, 2004). In fact, the Canadian edition of *Time* magazine featured twixters in its January 24, 2005 issue under the headline "They Just Won't Grow Up."

The period of emerging adulthood is growing longer as more and more young people live at home well into their twenties. *Are you a twixter?*

Jeffrey Arnett, of the University of Maryland, one of the first psychologists to study the phenomenon he has termed *emerging adulthood* (Arnett, 2000), takes a positive view. He argues that the transition from adolescence to the responsibilities of adulthood has always been marked by a period of exploration and choice; it is just that the affluence of Westernized cultures allows people to take longer to construct the identities that will guide them through their adult lives (Arnett, 2004).

Others have been less positive. James Coté, a University of Western Ontario sociologist, described the phenomenon as "arrested adulthood" (Coté, 2000). Similarly, University of Alberta psychologist Nancy Galambos has presented evidence that some twixters may be caught in a "maturity gap" (Galambos, Barker & Tilton-Weaver, 2003), one not as common in other cultures (Arnett & Galambos, 2003).

The phenomenon of emerging adulthood and the accompanying academic discussion typifies many of the concerns of developmental psychology. To what extent do our cognitive, emotional, and social experiences play a role in the process of maturation? Are twixters simply immature? Or have socioeconomic conditions encouraged or even enforced a shift in developmental patterns? Arnett argues that emerging adulthood is neither universal nor unchangeable. It is, rather, a cultural construction that exists only in societies that allow adolescents to take their time in assuming adult roles. Similarly, are our early life experiences crucial or can later life experiences also be important in forming our adult selves? Did the parents of twixters make some sort of parenting mistake when their children were young? Or does the experimentation of the emerging adulthood years, as Arnett argues, play an important role in the development of the adult self?

Our experiences allow us to develop skills in three areas of development—physical, cognitive, and socioemotional. In this chapter, development is divided into three main time frames: childhood, adolescence, and adulthood. As you read each section, pay attention to how each aspect (physical, cognitive, and socioemotional) of development typically changes from one phase of life to another. And keep in mind that some people may develop slower or faster or to a different degree in these areas than others.

① EXPLORING HUMAN DEVELOPMENT

What Is Development?	How Do Nature and Nurture Influence Development?	Do Early Experiences Rule Us for Life?	Positive Psychology and Optimal Experiences

How do psychologists think about development?

Although not every young adult has the luxury of taking time to assume his or her adult role, as human beings we all travel some common paths. For example, whether you are likely to become a famous person or simply a good one, most likely you walked at about the age of one, talked at about the age of two, engaged in fantasy play as a young child, and began to think more logically as an older child. Yet each of us is also unique. No one else in the world has the same fingerprints as you, for example. Let's explore the reasons for these differences.

What Is Development?

Development refers to the pattern of change in human capabilities that begins at conception and continues throughout the life span. Most development involves growth, although it also consists of decline (for example, older adults become slower at processing information). Researchers who study development are intrigued by its universal characteristics and individual variations (Muir & Slater, 2003). The pattern of development is complex because it is the product of several processes:

- *Physical processes* involve changes in an individual's biological nature. Genes inherited from parents; the hormonal changes of puberty and menopause; changes throughout life in the brain, height and weight, and motor skills all reflect the developmental role of biological processes. Psychologists refer to such biological growth processes as *maturation*. Whereas you might think that emerging adults have completed their physical maturation, Diamond (2002) reviews evidence that the prefrontal cortex, critical to higher cognitive functions, takes more than 20 years to mature.
- *Cognitive processes* involve changes in an individual's thought, intelligence, and language. For example, Jim Enns and his colleagues at the University of British Columbia have studied age-related changes in our ability to selectively attend to aspects of our environment (Enns & Trick, in press; Burack & others, 2000). One common observation about today's emerging adults is that they often study longer at college or university than their parents did, to acquire the cognitive skills necessary for many careers in modern society.
- *Socioemotional processes* involve changes in an individual's relationships with other people, changes in emotions, and changes in personality. An infant's smile in response to her mother's touch, a girl's development of assertiveness, an adolescent's joy at the senior prom, a young man's aggressiveness in sport, and an older couple's affection for each other all reflect the role of socioemotional processes. Exploring different relationships may help emerging adults form deeper relationships throughout the remainder of their adult lives.

Remember as you read about physical, cognitive, and socioemotional processes that they are intricately interwoven, as figure 4.1 shows. For example, socioemotional processes shape cognitive processes, cognitive processes promote or restrict socioemotional processes, and physical processes influence cognitive processes. Although the three processes of development are discussed in separate sections of the chapter, keep in mind that you are studying the development of an integrated human being whose body, mind, and emotions are interdependent.

development The pattern of change in human capabilities that begins at conception and continues throughout the life span.

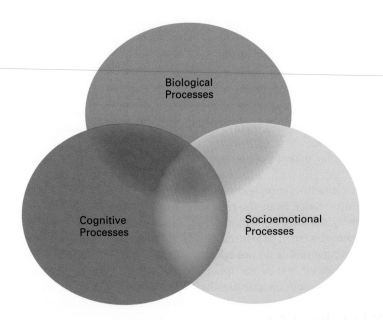

FIGURE 4.1 .

Developmental Changes Are the Result of Biological, Cognitive, and Socioemotional Processes
These processes are interwoven as individuals develop.

How Do Nature and Nurture Influence Development?

In chapter 3 we examined the relationship between genetics and behaviour. Although genes play an important role in human behaviour, genes alone do not determine who we are. Genes exist within the context of a complex environment which is necessary for an organism to even exist. Environment includes all the surrounding physical and social conditions and influences that affect the development of living things. Biologists who study even the simplest animals agree that separating the effects of the animals' genes from the effects of their environment is virtually impossible (Lewis, 2005).

Genotype and Phenotype Genetic material may be expressed differently depending on the environment. Thus a person's observable and measurable characteristics might not reflect his or her genetic heritage very precisely because of the experiences that person has had.

To account for this gap between genes and behaviour, scientists make a distinction between genotype and phenotype. **Genotype** is the individual's genetic heritage, the actual genetic material. **Phenotype** is the way an individual's genotype is expressed in observable, measurable characteristics. Phenotypes include physical characteristics (such as height, weight, and eye colour) and psychological characteristics (such as intelligence and personality).

For each genotype, a range of phenotypes can be expressed. An individual can inherit the genetic potential to grow very tall, but good nutrition will also be important in achieving that potential. Or suppose we could identify all the genes that contribute to making a person introverted (shy) or extraverted (outgoing). Would knowledge of specific genes allow us to predict *measured* introversion or extroversion, that is, the extent to which someone will be extraverted or introverted? The answer is no, because introversion and extraversion are characteristics that are influenced not only by heredity but also by experience. For example, parents might guide a shy child to become more social.

Exploring Nature and Nurture Related to the distinction between genotype and phenotype is a broader distinction between nature and nurture. The term **nature** is often used to refer to an organism's biological inheritance. The term **nurture** is often used to refer to an organism's environmental experiences. The interaction of nature and nurture, of genes and environment, influences, to a degree, every aspect of mind and behaviour. Neither operates alone (Gottlieb, 2002b; Mader, 2004).

genotype An individual's genetic heritage, the actual genetic material.

phenotype The expression of an individual's genotype in observable, measurable characteristics.

nature An organism's biological inheritance.

nurture An organism's environmental experience.

At one time, psychologists argued about what percentage of human development was due to nature and what percentage was due to nurture. That debate no longer seems productive (Johnson, 2003; Lewis, 2005). Nor is it accurate to say that our genes "turn on" all at once, around conception or birth, after which we take our genetic legacy into the world to see how far it carries us. Throughout the life span, in many different environments, either genes produce the proteins that affect experience and human development or they don't, depending on how harsh or how nourishing those environments are.

Psychologists are starting to agree that many complex behaviours have some genetic loading that makes people likely to develop in a particular way. At the same time, our actual development also depends on what we experience in our environment. And that environment is complex, as is the mixture of genes that we inherit. Environmental influences range from the things we lump together under "nurture" (such as parenting, family dynamics, peer relations, schooling, and neighbourhood quality) to biological encounters (such as viruses, birth complications, and even cellular activities).

Most developmentalists do not take an extreme position on nature versus nurture. Development is not all one or the other (Lerner, 2002). It is an *interaction* of the two. Heredity and environment operate together to produce temperament, height, weight, the ability to pitch a baseball, reading ability, and so on (Gottlieb, 2002a,b; Santrock, 2004).

Do Early Experiences Rule Us for Life?

As psychologists study development, they debate whether early experiences or later experiences are more important (Santrock, 2005a). Some psychologists believe that unless infants experience warm, nurturant caregiving in the first year or so of life, they will not develop to their full potential (Bowlby, 1989; Shaver & Mikulincer, 2005). These psychologists are not the only ones who think that way. The ancient Greek philosopher Plato was sure that infants who were rocked frequently became better athletes. Nineteenth-century New England ministers told parents in Sunday sermons that the way they handled their infants would determine their children's future character. This *early-experience* doctrine suggests that after a period of early development, we become relatively fixed and permanent in our makeup. This doctrine rests on the belief that each life is like an unbroken trail on which a psychological quality can be traced back to its origin (Kagan, 1992, 2000).

In contrast, some psychologists emphasize the power of later experience and liken development in later years to the ebb and flow of the tides. The *later-experience* advocates argue that children are malleable and that sensitive caregiving is just as important later as it is earlier. A number of life-span developmentalists, who focus on both children and adults, stress that too little attention has been given to adult development (Baltes & Kunzmann, 2003; Birren & Schaie, 2001). They argue that although early experiences are important contributors to development, they are not necessarily more important than later experiences.

The life of Alice Walker provides one example of the ability to continue developing past childhood. She grew up knowing the brutal effects of poverty and racism. Born in 1944, she was the eighth child of Georgia sharecroppers who earned $300 a year. When Walker was 8, her brother accidentally shot her in the left eye with a BB gun. By the time her parents got her to the hospital a week later (they did not have a car), she was blind in that eye, and it had a disfiguring layer of scar tissue.

As an adolescent, Walker became acutely aware of the bias and discrimination shown toward her and her family. She had a dream of going to Senegal, Africa, to search for her roots and an identity. As the civil rights movement grew in the United States in the late 1950s and early 1960s, she shifted her focus, seeking her identity by putting herself into the heart and heat of the movement. In that context, her identity flourished and expanded. Despite the early counts against her, Walker went on to become an essayist, poet, award-winning novelist, short-story writer, and social activist. Like her characters (especially the women), she overcame her pain and anger. Walker turned poverty and trauma into a rich literary harvest, including a Pulitzer Prize-winning book, *The Color Purple*.

Undoubtedly, Alice Walker's early experiences helped to provide a foundation for her compassionate view of humanity and motivated many of her efforts. But her harsh experiences early in life did not prevent her from continuing to grow and eventually achieving great success as a writer.

Recall from chapter 2 that case studies such as that of Alice Walker have unique aspects that are often difficult to generalize to many people. So let's explore correlational research that addresses the early/later experience issue, focusing on adolescent depression. One classic study examined the link between parents' relationships with their young daughters between the ages of three to five and the daughters' depression in adolescence (Gjerde, Block, & Block, 1991). It found that the adolescent girls were more likely to be depressed when the parents had been overly controlling, had demanded high achievement, and had not adequately nurtured the girls when they were three to five years of age. These results demonstrate the importance of early experience. But other research studies show that stressful experiences in adolescence—such as making low grades, breaking up with a boyfriend, or dealing with a parent's death—are also related to depression in adolescent girls (Compas & others, 2001). Depression in adolescent girls thus appears to be linked to both early and later experiences.

As with the question on nature versus nurture, most developmentalists do not take extreme positions on the issue of early versus later experience (Shaffer, Wood, & Willoughby, 2005). They believe that, although early experience can create a foundation for later experience, both make important contributions to development.

Alice Walker won the Pulitzer Prize for her book *The Color Purple*. Like many of the characters in her book (especially the women), Walker overcame early experiences with poverty and pain to become a very competent adult.

Positive Psychology and Optimal Experiences

Some psychologists believe we can optimize what our genetic inheritance and our environment give us. They argue that a key aspect of development involves seeking optimal experiences in life (Massimini & Delle Fave, 2000). They cite examples of people who go beyond simple biological adaptation to actively pick and choose from the environment the things that serve their purposes. These individuals construct their own lives, authoring a unique developmental path (Sheldon, 2004), especially as they grow older (Sheldon, in press).

In our effort to experience our lives in optimal ways, we develop *life themes* that involve activities, social relationships, and life goals (Csikszentmihalyi & Beattie, 1979; Nakamura & Csikszentmihalyi, 2002). One example of an optimal life theme is to make the decision to grow beyond selfish reproduction and competition in order to foster understanding, tolerance, and cooperation among all human beings (Gable & others, 2004; Cloninger, 2004).

Some people are more successful at constructing optimal life experiences than others. Among individuals who have succeeded are Albert Schweitzer, Mother Teresa, Martin Luther King, Jr., and Mahatma Gandhi. These people looked for and found meaningful life themes as they developed. Their lives were not restricted to simple biological survival or passive acceptance of environmental dictates.

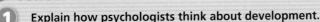

> **reflect and review**

1 **Explain how psychologists think about development.**

- Name and describe the three main developmental processes.
- Evaluate the influences of nature and nurture on development.
- Discuss the influence of early and later experiences on human development.
- What is the positive psychology perspective on development?

Evaluate the influences of nature and nurture on development.
Your development as a human being is determined by multiple factors. Think about what you are like as a person today and reflect on the processes in your development that made you who you are.

② CHILD DEVELOPMENT

Prenatal	Physical	Cognitive	Socioemotional	Positive
Development	Development	Development	Development	Psychology
	in Childhood	in Childhood	in Childhood	and Children's
				Development

How do children develop from conception to adolescence?

How children develop has special importance because children are the future of any society. Our journey through childhood begins with conception and continues through the elementary school years. The focus of this section is on the three fundamental developmental processes—physical, cognitive, and socioemotional. The nature and nurture theme is revisited along the journey, and the importance of taking a positive view of childhood is explored.

Prenatal Development

Many special things have taken place in your life since you were born. But imagine ... at one time you were a microscopic organism floating in a sea of fluid in your mother's womb. As the 19th century poet-essayist Samuel Taylor Coleridge remarked, "The history of man for nine months preceding his birth is probably far more interesting and contains more stunning events than all the years that follow."

The Course of Prenatal Development   *Conception* occurs when a single sperm cell from the male penetrates the female's ovum (egg). This process is also called *fertilization*. Prenatal development is divided into three periods:

- *Germinal period: the first 3 weeks*. The germinal period begins with conception. The fertilized egg, or *zygote*, is a single cell with 23 chromosomes from the mother and 23 from the father. After one week and many cell divisions, the zygote is made up of 100 to 150 cells. By the end of two weeks, the mass of cells attaches to the uterine wall.
- *Embryonic period: weeks 4 through 8*. Before most women even know they are pregnant, the rate of cell differentiation intensifies, support systems for the cells form, and the beginnings of organs appear. In the third week the neural tube, which eventually becomes the spinal cord, starts to form. At about 21 days, eyes begin to appear, and by 24 days the cells of the heart begin to differentiate. During the fourth week, arm and leg buds emerge (see figure 4.2a). At five to eight weeks, the heart begins to beat, arms and legs become more differentiated, the face starts to form, and the intestinal tract appears (see figure 4.2b).
- *Fetal period: months 3 through 9*. Organs mature to the point at which life can be sustained outside the womb, and muscles begin their first exercises (see figure 4.2c). The mother feels the fetus move for the first time. At six months after conception, the eyes and eyelids are completely formed, a fine layer of hair covers the fetus, the grasping reflex appears, and irregular breathing begins. By seven to nine months, the fetus is much longer and weighs considerably more. In addition, various organs become more functional.

In nine short months, a single cell has developed the capacity to live and function as a human being, with the potential for further physical, cognitive, and socio-emotional changes. Sometimes, however, normal development is disrupted (Golden, 2005).

Threats to the Fetus   Some pregnant women tiptoe about in the belief that everything they do has a direct effect on their unborn child. Others behave more casually, assuming their experiences have little effect. The truth lies somewhere between these extremes. Although it floats in a comfortable, well-protected environment, the fetus is not totally immune to the larger environment surrounding the mother (Fifer & Grose-Fifer, 2002).

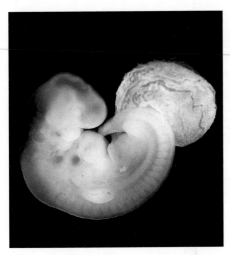 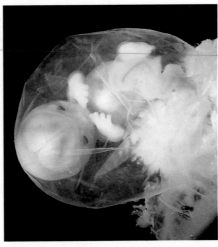 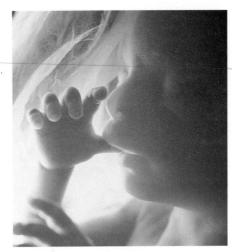

a.   b.   c.

For example, many chemical substances are *teratogens* (from the Greek word *tera*, meaning "monster"), agents that cause an embryo or fetus to be malformed. Many chemical pollutants, such as polychlorinated biphenyls (PCBs) and dioxins are especially harmful to developing fetuses. Prescription drugs can also be teratogens. For example, women taking medication for epilepsy (Duchowny, 2004) or for bipolar disorder (Yonkers, & others, 2004) must be careful to balance their own health concerns with the health of their unborn child. Many non-prescription drugs, from nicotine to heroin, are also teratogens. Babies born to users of heroin can die, and are at risk for many problems, including premature birth, low birth weight, physical defects, and breathing problems.

Heavy drinking by pregnant women can also have devastating effects on their offspring (Golden, 2005). *Fetal alcohol syndrome* (*FAS*) is a cluster of abnormalities that occur in children born to mothers who are heavy drinkers. These abnormalities include a small head (microcephaly) and defective limbs, face, and heart. Most FAS children are also below average in intelligence and suffer from attention deficits (Hausknecht & others, 2005).

Concern has increased about the well-being of the fetus when pregnant women drink even small amounts of alcohol. The best advice is that a woman who is pregnant or anticipates becoming pregnant should not drink any alcohol. This obvious advice may not be easy for all expectant mothers to follow, however. Recent evidence suggests that women whose mothers drank heavily during pregnancy are at greater risk for drinking heavily during their own pregnancies (Rouleau, Levichek, & Koren, 2003).

A variety of other problems may short-circuit prenatal development. Full-term infants, who have grown in the womb for 38 to 42 weeks between conception and delivery, have the best chances of normal development in childhood. A *preterm infant*, who is born prior to 38 weeks after conception, is at greater risk for developmental problems, such as learning difficulties (Rennie, 2005). In addition, the parents of preterm infants generally experience considerable parenting stress (Robson, 1997). Very small preterm infants and those who grow up in poverty are more likely to have problems than those who are larger or live in higher socioeconomic conditions. Indeed, many larger preterm infants from middle- and high-income families do not have developmental problems. Nonetheless, more preterm infants than full-term babies have learning disorders.

Researchers are continuing to study ways to improve the lives of preterm infants. Tiffany Field's (2001, 2003) research has led to a surge of interest in the role that massage might play in improving the developmental outcomes of premature infants. In one classic study, massaging infants for 15 minutes three times a day led to 47 percent more weight gain than standard medical treatment (Field & others, 1986) (see figure 4.3). The massaged infants also were more active and alert, and they performed better on

FIGURE 4.2

From Embryo to Fetus
(*a*) At about four weeks, an embryo is less than one centimetre long. The head, eyes, and ears begin to show; the head and neck are half the length of the body; the shoulders will be located where the whitish arm buds are attached.

(*b*) At eight weeks the developing individual is about four centimetres long and has reached the end of its embryonic phase. It has become a fetus. Everything that will be found in the fully developed human being has now begun to form. The fetal stage is a period of growth and perfection of detail. The heart has been beating for a month, and the muscles have just begun their first exercises.

(*c*) At four-and-a-half months, the fetus is about 18 centimetres long. When the thumb comes close to the mouth, the head may turn, and lips and tongue begin their sucking motions—a reflex for survival.

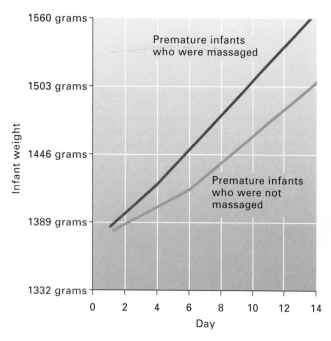

FIGURE 4.3 **Weight Gain Comparison of Premature Infants Who Were Massaged or Not Massaged** The graph shows that the mean daily gain of premature infants who were massaged was greater than that of premature infants were not massaged.

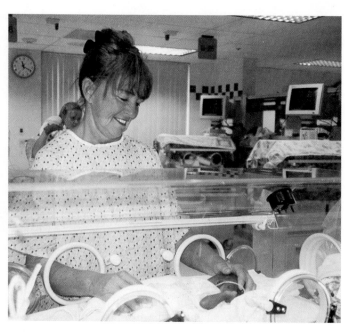

Tiffany Field massages a newborn infant. Her research has demonstrated the power of massage in improving the developmental outcome of at-risk infants. Under her direction, the Touch Research Institute in Miami, Florida, investigates the role of touch in a number of domains of health and well-being.

developmental tests. Field and her colleagues have also demonstrated the benefits of massage therapy with cocaine babies (Scafidi & Field, 1996) and with infants of depressed mothers (Field & others, 1996).

Prenatal and newborn development sets the stage for development in childhood. The changes in every realm of childhood—physical, cognitive, and socioemotional—set the foundation for our development as adults.

Physical Development in Childhood

People grow and develop physically throughout life, but at no other time will so many physical changes occur as fast as during infancy (the developmental period from birth to about 18 to 24 months of age; Hetherington, Parke &, Schmuckler, 2005). During infancy, children change from virtually immobile beings to creatures who toddle as fast as their legs can carry them.

Reflexes Newborns are not empty headed (Blythe, 2004). They come into the world equipped with several genetically "wired" reflexes. For example, they have no fear of water and naturally hold their breath and contract their throats to keep water out.

Some of the reflexes that newborns possess persist throughout life—coughing, blinking, and yawning, for example. Others disappear in the months following birth as higher brain functions mature and infants develop voluntary control over many behaviours (McDonnell, Corkum, & Wilson, 1989).

Some reflexes that weaken or disappear by six or seven months of age are:

- *Grasping*. When the infant's palms are touched, the infant grasps tightly with its fingers (although not the thumb).
- *Sucking*. When an object touches the infant's mouth, the infant automatically begins sucking.
- *Stepping*. When the infant is held above a surface with its feet lowered to touch the surface, the infant moves its feet as if to walk.
- *Startle*. When sudden stimulation occurs, such as hearing a loud noise or being

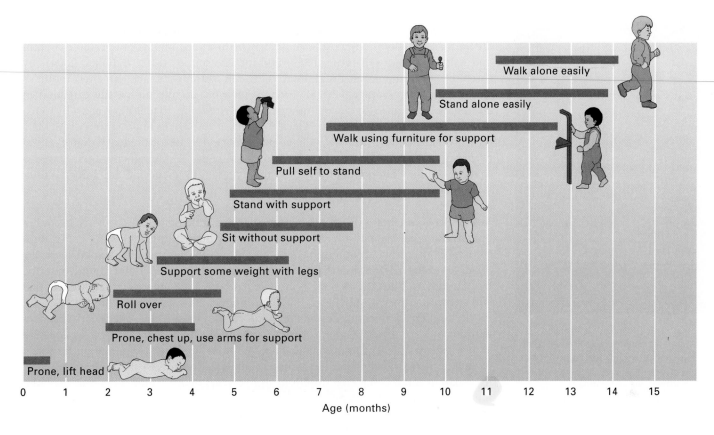

Walk alone easily

Stand alone easily

Walk using furniture for support

Pull self to stand

Stand with support

Sit without support

Support some weight with legs

Roll over

Prone, chest up, use arms for support

Prone, lift head

| 0 | 1 | 2 | 3 | 4 | 5 | 6 | 7 | 8 | 9 | 10 | 11 | 12 | 13 | 14 | 15 |

Age (months)

dropped, the infant startles, arches its back, throws back its head, and flings out its arms and legs and then rapidly closes them to the centre of its body.

Motor and Perceptual Skills At birth, the newborn has, relative to the rest of the body, a gigantic head that flops around uncontrollably. Within 12 months, the infant becomes capable of sitting upright, standing, stooping, climbing, and often walking. During the second year, growth decelerates, but rapid gains occur in such activities as running and climbing. Figure 4.4 shows the average ages at which infants reach various motor milestones.

The study of motor development has seen a renaissance in the past decade. Historically, researchers such as Arnold Gesell (1934), assumed that motor milestones were like the ones shown in figure 4.4, unfolding as part of a genetic plan. However, psychologists now recognize that motor development is not the consequence of nature or nurture alone. The focus of research has shifted to discovering how motor skills develop and away from simply describing the age at which they develop (Lochman, 2000).

In addition, when infants are motivated to do something, they may create a new motor behaviour (Thelen, 2000). That new behaviour is the result of many converging factors: the developing nervous system, the body's physical properties and its movement possibilities, the goal the infant is motivated to reach, and environmental support for the skill.

Psychologists also believe that motor skills and perceptual skills are vitally linked (Smitsman, 2001). Babies are continually coordinating their movements with information they perceive through their senses to learn how to maintain their balance, reach for objects in space, and move across various surfaces and terrains (Gershkoff-Stowe & Thelen, 2004). Action also educates perception. For example, watching an object while holding and touching it helps infants to learn about its texture, size, and hardness. Moving from place to place in the environment teaches babies how objects and people look from different perspectives and whether surfaces will support their weight (Gibson, 2001).

Canadian researchers, such as Darwin Muir and Barbara Kisilevsky of Queen's University, have made many significant contributions to our understanding of the

FIGURE 4.4

Developmental Accomplishments in Gross Motor Skills During the First 15 Months

Darwin Muir, of Queen's University, studies infant perception, including sensitivity to adult tactile stimulation and vocal and facial expressions of emotions during social interactions with infants.

development of the infant's senses. Infants respond to acoustic information before they are born (Kisilevsky & others, 2004). Before the first year, infants can perceive rhythm and tempo (Trehub & Thorpe, 1989) and localize sounds (Muir & Hains, 2004). By three months, infants can discriminate between a stranger's face and their mother's face (Mondloch & others, 2003). By five months, infants notice the direction of another person's gaze (Symons & others, 1998). The ability to tell things apart by touch also develops during this period (Stack & Tsonis, 1999). Dauphne Maurer, of McMaster University, and her colleagues have presented evidence for the existence of critical periods in early perceptual experience (Maurer, Lewis, & Mondloch, 2005; Lewis, & Maurer, 2005). Children deprived of visual experiences at specific times during their infancy show visual processing deficits later in life.

The Brain   As an infant walks, talks, runs, shakes a rattle, smiles, and frowns, his or her brain is changing dramatically. At birth and in early infancy, the brain's 100 billion neurons have only minimal connections. But, as the infant ages from birth to two years, the dendrites of the neurons branch out, and the neurons become far more interconnected (see figure 4.5). The infant's brain is literally ready and waiting for the experiences that will create the connections (Eliot, 2001; Greenough, 2001; Johnson, 2003).

Recall from chapter 3 that a *myelin sheath* encases most axons. The sheath insulates neurons and helps nerve impulses travel faster. Myelination, the process of encasing axons with fat cells, begins prenatally and continues after birth. Myelination for visual pathways occurs rapidly after birth and is completed in the first six months. Auditory myelination is not completed until four to five years of age. Some aspects of myelination continue into adolescence.

Another important aspect of the brain's development in childhood is the dramatic increase in *synaptic connections* (Ramey & Ramey, 2000). Recall from chapter 3 that a synapse is a gap between neurons that is bridged by chemical neurotransmitters. Researchers have discovered that nearly twice as many synapses are available as will ever be used (Huttenlocher & Dabholkar, 1997). The connections that are made become stronger and will survive; the unused ones will be replaced by other neural pathways or disappear. In the language of neuroscience, these unused connections will be *pruned*. Figure 4.6 vividly illustrates the dramatic growth of synapses during infancy in the visual, auditory, and prefrontal cortex areas of the brain and their later pruning.

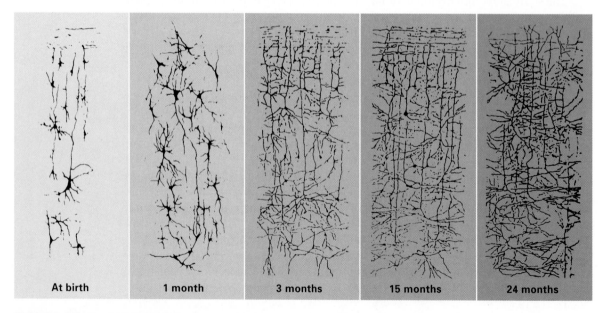

| At birth | 1 month | 3 months | 15 months | 24 months |

FIGURE 4.5 Dendritic Spreading
Note the increase in connections among neurons over the course of the first two years of life.

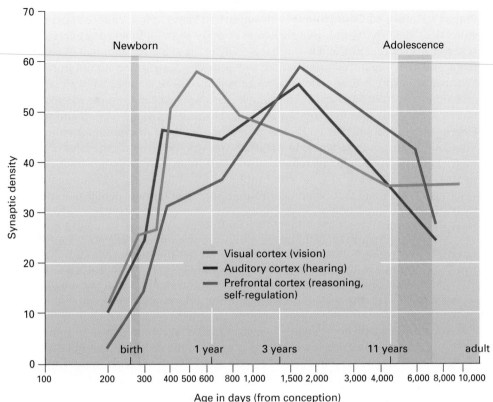

FIGURE 4.6

Synaptic Density in the Human Brain from Infancy to Adulthood
The graph shows the dramatic increase and then pruning in synaptic density in three regions of the brain: visual cortex, auditory cortex, and prefrontal cortex. Synaptic density is believed to be an important indication of the extent of connectivity between neurons.

Brain scanning techniques, such as MRI and CAT (which were discussed in chapter 3), are improving the detection of developmental changes in the brain (Spelke, 2002). Using these techniques, scientists have recently discovered that children's brains undergo dramatic anatomical changes between the ages of 3 and 15 (Thompson & others, 2000; Palmer & others, 2004). By repeatedly obtaining brain scans of the same children for up to four years, they found that the amount of brain material in some areas can nearly double within as little as a year, followed by a drastic loss of tissue as unneeded cells are purged and the brain continues to reorganize itself. The overall size of the brain did not show dramatic growth, but local patterns within the brain changed dramatically. From three to six years of age the most rapid growth takes place in the frontal lobe areas, which are involved in planning and organizing new actions and in maintaining attention to tasks (Thompson & others, 2000).

Of course, if the dendrites and synapses are not being stimulated by a wealth of new experiences, children's brains are less likely to develop normally (Blair, 2002). Thus, as in other areas of development, nature and nurture operate together.

Cognitive Development in Childhood

As amazing as physical development is in childhood, it is easily matched by cognitive development. As you read earlier in the chapter, cognitive processes involve thought, intelligence, and language. Cognitive development refers to how these processes change as people mature.

Until the mid–twentieth century, North American psychologists had no useful theory for explaining how children's minds change as they age. Psychologists who were interested in the topic had to view it through the lens of behaviourism, which emphasizes that children merely receive information from the environment, or through the lens of the IQ testing approach, which emphasizes individual differences in children's intelligence. But then Jean Piaget (1896–1980), the famous Swiss developmental psychologist, changed the way we think about children's minds. When Piaget's ideas were introduced in North America in the 1960s, psychologists here embraced his view that children *actively construct* their cognitive world as they go through a series of stages.

Piaget's Theory of Cognitive Development In Piaget's view, children actively construct their cognitive world, using schemas to make sense of what they experience. A **schema** is a concept or framework that already exists at a given moment in a person's mind and that organizes information and provides a structure for interpreting it. Schemas are expressed as various behaviours and skills that the child can exercise in relation to objects or situations. For example, sucking is an early, simple schema. Later, more complex schemas might include licking, blowing, crawling, hiding, and so forth. Piaget's interest in schemas had to do with how they help in organizing and making sense out of current experience. In chapter 8 you will see how schemas also help us to understand why people don't remember the past in an exact way but instead reconstruct it.

Piaget (1952) said that two processes are responsible for how people use and adapt their schemas:

- **Assimilation** occurs when individuals incorporate new information into existing knowledge. That is, people *assimilate* the environment into an existing schema. For example, a schema in the child's mind might provide the information that some objects can be picked up. The first time a child realizes that she might pick up a set of keys, she is assimilating the category "keys" into the schema of "picking up."
- **Accommodation** occurs when individuals adjust their schemas to new information. That is, people *accommodate* their schemas to the environment. For example, a child might possess the schema of "picking up." With experience, the child might learn that some things can be picked up easily between two fingers, that other things might require both hands and strong use of the arms, and that still other things cannot be picked up at all because they are too hot, for example, or too heavy. Thus the schema "picking up" becomes differentiated into schemas that *accommodate* the realities of different types of objects.

Through accommodation, schemas develop over time and many repetitions of experience. Consider the schema of "sucking." Newborns reflexively suck everything that touches their lips. Their experience in sucking various objects allows them to assimilate those objects into other schemas of taste, texture, shape, and so on. After several months of experience, though, they accommodate the sucking schema by being more selective with it. For example, they discover that some objects, such as fingers and the mother's breasts, can be sucked, whereas others, such as fuzzy blankets, are better not.

Another important element of Piaget's theory is his observation that we go through four stages in understanding the world (see figure 4.7). Each of the stages is age-related and consists of distinct ways of thinking. In Piaget's view, it is not simply knowing more information that makes a child's thinking more advanced with each stage. Rather, it is the different way of understanding the world that makes one stage more advanced than another. The child's cognition is qualitatively different from one stage to the next.

Sensorimotor Stage The first Piagetian stage, the **sensorimotor stage**, lasts from birth to about two years of age. In this stage, infants construct an understanding of the world by coordinating sensory experiences (such as seeing and hearing) with motor (physical) actions—hence the term *sensorimotor*. As newborns they have little more than reflexive patterns with which to work. They cannot create mental representations. Can you imagine the last cup of coffee you drank? Your imagining is a symbol, a mental representation. By the end of this stage, two-year-olds show complex sensorimotor patterns and are beginning to use symbols in their thinking.

Imagine how you might experience the world if you were a five-month-old infant. You are in a playpen filled with toys. One of the toys, a monkey, falls out of your grasp and rolls behind a larger toy, a hippopotamus. Would you know the monkey is behind the hippopotamus, or would you think it is completely gone? At this point you could not create a mental symbol to represent the monkey and so could not keep the monkey "in mind" when it was out of your sight. Accordingly, you could not have reached for

schema A concept or framework that already exists at a given moment in a person's mind and that organizes and interprets information.

assimilation Occurs when individuals incorporate new information into existing knowledge.

accommodation Occurs when individuals adjust their schemas to new information.

sensorimotor stage The first Piagetian stage of cognitive development (birth to about two years of age), in which infants construct an understanding of the world by coordinating sensory experiences (such as seeing and hearing) with motor (physical) actions.

Sensorimotor Stage	**Preoperational Stage**	**Concrete Operational Stage**	**Formal Operational Stage**
The infant constructs an understanding of the world by coordinating sensory experiences with physical actions. An infant progresses from reflexive, instinctual action at birth to the beginning of symbolic thought toward the end of the stage.	The child begins to represent the world with words and images. These words and images reflect increased symbolic thinking and go beyond the connection of sensory information and physical action.	The child can now reason logically about concrete events and classify objects into different sets.	The adolescent reasons in more abstract, idealistic, and logical ways.
Birth to 2 Years of Age	*2 to 7 Years of Age*	*7 to 11 Years of Age*	*11 Years of Age Through Adulthood*

FIGURE 4.7
Piaget's Four Stages of Cognitive Development

the monkey when it fell behind the hippopotamus. As Piaget put it, "out of sight" is literally "out of mind" for young infants. By eight months of age, though, infants begin to understand that out of sight is not out of mind. At this point, you probably would have reached behind the hippopotamus to search for the monkey, coordinating your senses with your movements through the mental symbol you have created to represent the monkey.

Object permanence is Piaget's term for this crucial accomplishment: understanding that objects and events continue to exist even when they cannot be seen, heard, or touched directly. The most common way to study object permanence is to show an infant an interesting toy and then cover the toy with a sheet or a blanket. If infants understand that the toy still exists, they try to uncover it (see figure 4.8). Object permanence continues to develop throughout the sensorimotor period. For example, when infants initially understand that objects exist even when out of sight, they look only briefly for them. By the end of the sensorimotor stage, infants engage in a more prolonged and sophisticated search for an object.

From sensorimotor cognition—which involves the ability to organize and coordinate sensations with physical movements and includes the realization of object permanence—we move on to a second, more symbolic cognitive stage.

Preoperational Stage   Piaget's second stage of cognitive development, the **preoperational stage**, lasts from approximately two to seven years of age. Preoperational thought is more symbolic than sensorimotor thought. In preschool years, children

FIGURE 4.8   Object Permanence
Piaget thought that object permanence was one of infancy's landmark cognitive accomplishments. For this five-month-old boy, out of sight is literally out of mind. The infant looks at the toy dog (*left*), but when his view of the toy is blocked (*right*), he does not search for it. In a few more months, he will search for hidden toys, reflecting the presence of object permanence.

preoperational stage The second Piagetian stage of cognitive development (approximately two to seven years of age) in which thought becomes more symbolic, egocentric, and intuitive rather than logical; but the child cannot yet perform operations.

FIGURE 4.9

Piaget's Conservation Task
The beaker test determines whether a child can think operationally—that is, can mentally reverse actions and understand conservation of the substance. (*a*) Two identical beakers are presented to the child, each containing the same amount of liquid. As the child watches, the experimenter pours the liquid from B into C, which is taller and thinner than A and B. (*b*) The experimenter then asks the child whether beakers A and C have the same amount of liquid. The preoperational child says no. When asked to point to the beaker that has more liquid, the child points to the tall, thin beaker.

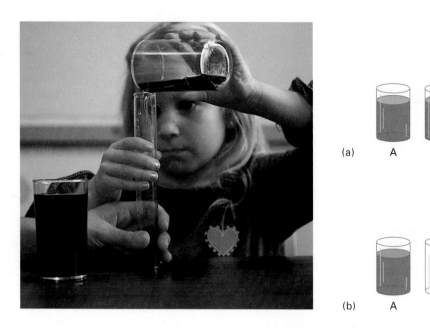

begin to mentally represent their world with words, images, and drawings. Thus their thoughts begin to exceed simple connections of sensory information and motor action.

The type of symbolic thinking that children are able to accomplish during this stage is limited, however. While they can create mental representations, they still cannot perform mental *operations*, by which Piaget meant the ability to manipulate their mental representations. For example, imagine pouring your last cup of coffee into another cup. Now imagine pouring it back again. You just applied a mental operation to your mental representation of your cup of coffee and then reversed that mental operation. Preoperational children have difficulty understanding that reversing an action may restore the original conditions from which the action began. For example, the preoperational child may know that 4 plus 2 equals 6 but not understand that the reverse, 6 minus 2 equals 4, is also necessarily true according to the principle of reversibility. Or a preoperational child may walk a short distance to his friend's house each day but always gets a ride home. If you asked him to walk home one day he would probably reply that he did not know the way because he had never walked home before.

A well-known test of whether a child can think "operationally" is to present a child with two identical beakers, A and B, filled with liquid to the same height (see figure 4.9). Next to them is a third beaker, C. Beaker C is tall and thin, whereas beakers A and B are short and wide. The liquid is poured from B into C, and the child is asked whether the amounts in A and C are the same. The four-year-old child invariably says that the amount of liquid in the tall, thin beaker (C) is greater than that in the short, wide beaker (A). The eight-year-old child consistently says the amounts are the same. The four-year-old child, a preoperational thinker, cannot mentally reverse the pouring action; that is, she cannot imagine the liquid going back from container C to container B. Piaget said that such a child has not grasped the concept of *conservation*, in this case conservation of volume, a belief in the permanence of certain attributes of objects or situations in spite of superficial changes.

The child's thought in the preoperational stage is also limited in that it is egocentric. By *egocentrism*, Piaget meant the inability to distinguish between one's own perspective and someone else's perspective. Piaget and Barbel Inhelder (1969) initially studied young children's egocentrism by devising the three-mountains task (see figure 4.10). The child walks around the model of the mountains and becomes familiar with what the mountains look like from different perspectives. The child can see that different objects are on the mountains as well. The child is then seated on one side of the table on which the mountains are placed. The experimenter takes a doll and moves it to different locations around the table, at each location asking the child to

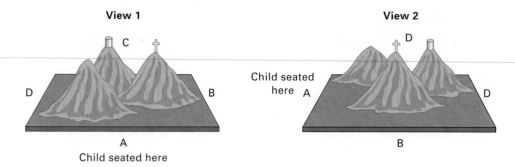

View 1

C
+
D
B

A
Child seated here

View 2

Child seated here A

D
+
D

B

FIGURE 4.10

The Three-Mountains Task
View 1 shows the child's perspective from where he or she is sitting. View 2 is an example of a photograph the child would be shown mixed in with others from different perspectives. The experimenter asks the child to identify the photograph in which the view of the mountains looks as it would look from position B. To correctly identify the photo, the child has to take the perspective of a person sitting at spot B. Invariably, a child who thinks in a preoperational way cannot perform this task. When asked what a view of the mountains looks like from position B, the child selects a photograph taken from location A, the child's own view at the time.

select one photo from a series of photos that most accurately reflects the view the doll is seeing. Children in the preoperational stage often pick the photo that shows the view they have rather than the view the doll has. To take the doll's view requires a mental operation.

Another limitation of preoperational thought that Piaget identified is that it is *intuitive*. When he asked children why they knew something, often they did not give logical answers but instead offered personal insights or guesses. Preoperational children do not seem to be bothered by the absence of logic in their thinking. As Piaget observed, they often seem very sure that they know something, even though they do not use logical reasoning to arrive at the answer.

Overall, then, preoperational thought is more symbolic than sensorimotor thought, but it is egocentric and intuitive rather than logical, and it does not include the ability to perform operations. But in reaching a basic level of operational understanding, the child progresses to the third of Piaget's cognitive stages.

Concrete Operational Stage Piaget's **concrete operational stage** occurs from approximately 7 to 11 years of age. Concrete operational thought involves using operations and replacing intuitive reasoning with logical reasoning in concrete situations. Classification skills are present, but abstract thinking is not yet developed.

Earlier you read about the conservation of volume task, which preoperational children cannot do. Another well-known conservation task is conservation of mass. Also used for demonstrating operational thinking, it involves two identical balls of clay (see figure 4.11). As the child watches, the experimenter rolls one ball into a long, thin rod and leaves the other ball in its original spherical shape. The child is then asked if there is more clay is in the ball or in the long, thin rod. By the time children reach seven to eight years of age, most answer that the amount of clay is the same. To solve this problem correctly, children have to recall that the ball was rolled into the shape of a rod and imagine the rod being returned to its original round shape—imagination that involves a reversible mental action. In this experiment and in the beaker experiment, the child who performs concrete operational thinking is able to mentally coordinate several characteristics or dimensions of an object rather than focusing on a single one. In the clay example, the preoperational child is likely to focus on either height or width. The child who has reached the stage of concrete operational thought coordinates information about both dimensions.

Many of the concrete operations identified by Piaget are related to properties of objects. One important skill at this stage of reasoning is the ability to classify or divide things into different sets or subsets and to consider their interrelations. Figure 4.12 shows an example of a classification task that concrete operational children can perform.

In sum, concrete operational thought involves operational thinking, classification skills, and logical reasoning in concrete, but not abstract, contexts. According to Piaget, reasoning in abstract contexts develops in the fourth and final cognitive stage.

Formal Operational Stage In Piaget's theory, individuals enter the **formal operational stage** of cognitive development at 11 to 15 years of age, and this stage continues through the adult years. Formal operational thought is more abstract, idealistic, and logical than concrete operational thought.

concrete operational stage The third Piagetian stage of cognitive development (approximately 7 to 11 years of age) in which thought becomes operational, replacing intuitive thought with logical reasoning in concrete situations.

formal operational stage The fourth and final Piagetian stage of cognitive development (emerging from about 11 to 15 years of age) in which thinking becomes more abstract, idealistic, and logical.

Initial Presentation

Two identical balls of clay are shown to the child. The child agrees that they are equal.

Manipulation

The experimenter changes the shape of one of the balls and asks the child whether they still contain equal amounts of clay.

Preoperational Child's Answer

No, the longer one has more.

Concrete Operational Child's Answer

Yes, they still have equal amounts.

FIGURE 4.11

Preoperational and Concrete Operational Children: The Clay Example

Unlike elementary school children, adolescents are no longer limited to actual concrete experience as the anchor of thought. They can conceive hypothetical possibilities, which are purely abstract.

Thought also becomes more idealistic. Adolescents often compare themselves and others to ideal standards. And they think about what an ideal world would be like, wondering if they couldn't carve out a better world than the one the adult generation has handed to them.

At the same time adolescents are thinking more abstractly and idealistically, they also think more logically. Adolescents begin to think more the way a scientist thinks, devising plans to solve problems and systematically testing solutions. Piaget gave this type of problem solving an imposing title: *hypothetical-deductive reasoning.* The phrase denotes adolescents' ability to develop hypotheses, or best hunches, about ways to solve problems, such as an algebraic equation. It also denotes their ability to systematically deduce or conclude the best path to follow to solve the problem. In contrast, prior to adolescence, children are likelier to solve problems in a trial-and-error fashion.

Thus, over the course of Piaget's four developmental stages, a child progresses from sensorimotor cognition to abstract, idealistic, and logical thought. Piaget based his stages on careful observation of children's behaviour, but there is always room to evaluate theory and research. Let's consider the current thinking about Piaget's ideas about the development of cognition.

FIGURE 4.12

Classification Involving a Family Tree

One way to determine if children possess classification skills is to see if they can understand a family tree of four generations (Furth & Wachs, 1975). This family tree suggests that the grandfather (A) has three sons (B, C, & D), each of whom has two sons (E through J), and that one of these sons (J) has three sons (K, L, & M). A child who comprehends this classification system can move up and down a level (vertically), across a level (horizontally), and up and down and across a level (obliquely) within the system. A child who thinks in a concrete operational way understands that person J can, at the same time, be father, brother, and grandson, for example. A preoperational child cannot perform this classification and says that a father cannot fulfill the other roles.

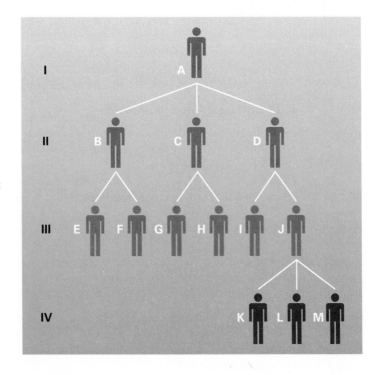

Evaluating Piaget Piaget opened up a new way of looking at how children's minds develop. We owe him for a long list of masterful concepts that have enduring power and fascination (Scholnick, 1999). These include the concepts of schemas, assimilation, accommodation, cognitive stages, object permanence, egocentrism, and conservation. We are also indebted to Piaget for the currently accepted vision of children as active constructive thinkers who manufacture (in part) their own development.

But just as other psychological theories have been criticized and amended, so have Piaget's (Bjorklund, 2004; Smith, 2002). For example, researchers have found that some cognitive abilities emerge earlier in some children than Piaget thought (Bremner, 2005; Lacerda, Von Hofsten, & Heimann, 2000). Renee Baillargeon (1997, 2004) has documented that infants as young as four months of age know that objects continue to exist even when hidden (which Piaget did not think was possible until eight months of age). Also, memory and other forms of symbolic activity occur by at least the first half of the first year, much earlier than Piaget thought possible (Mandler, 1998). Nor does formal operational thought emerge as consistently in early adolescence as Piaget envisioned. Many adolescents and even adults do not reason as logically as Piaget proposed. Infants are thus more cognitively competent than Piaget thought, and adolescents and adults are less competent.

Piaget has also been criticized on broader grounds. He was interested in examining the human species and the general ways in which all people go through cognitive stages at particular ages. Not surprisingly, he has been criticized for ignoring individual differences.

In another broad criticism, information-processing psychologists like Robbie Case (Case, 1991; Case & others, 2001) argue that Piaget's view places too much emphasis on grand stages and not enough on smaller, precise steps in solving problems. Information-processing psychologists believe that children's minds can be best understood by focusing more on strategies and skills, as well as how fast and efficiently people process information (Keenan, Olson, & Marini, 1998; Siegler, 2004).

The sociocultural perspective gives us yet another view of the shortcomings of Piaget's work. Piaget did not believe that culture and education play important roles in children's cognitive development. However, researchers have found that the age at which children acquire conservation skills is related to some extent on whether or not their culture provides relevant practice (Cole, 1999; Cole, Cole, & Lightfoot, 2005). The Russian psychologist Lev Vygotsky (1978) recognized that cognitive development does not occur in a sociocultural vacuum. In fact, a major goal of cognitive development is to learn the skills that will allow you to be competent in your culture. Thus it is important to be guided and assisted by skilled members of the culture.

According to Vygotsky, development occurs when children encounter situations they cannot handle by themselves but are not impossible to master if assistance is available from someone who already knows how to deal with that situation. He called this the **zone of proximal development**, the gap between what is already known and what, with assistance, can be learned (LeBlanc & Bearison, 2004). For example, suppose you were going to help someone improve her tennis game. Which would be best: 1) hitting the ball too softly and right at her every time, so that she is not challenged, 2) hitting the ball too hard and away from her, so that she can never reach it, or 3) hitting the ball just at the edge of her current ability, forcing her to stretch herself? According to Vygotsky, she will learn best if you play at the edge of her ability. Vygotsky's view has become increasingly popular in educational psychology because of its emphasis on collaborative learning through interaction with skilled others (Edwards, 2005).

Today, children's cognitive development is approached from several perspectives (Flavell, Miller, & Miller, 2002; Thomas, 2001, Pascual-Leone & Johnson, 1999, 2004). Yet, even though some of his ideas have been modified, Piaget still stands head and shoulders above all others in this field. It was his great work that let us see that children's minds change and develop in orderly, sequential ways (Scholnick & others, 1999).

Jean Piaget, the famous Swiss developmental psychologist, changed the way we think about the development of children's minds.

zone of proximal development According to Vygotsky, the gap between what is already known and what, with assistance, can be learned.

Erik Erikson with his wife, Joan, an artist. Erikson generated one of the most important developmental theories of the twentieth century.

Socioemotional Development in Childhood

As children grow and develop, they are socialized by and socialize others, such as parents, siblings, peers, and teachers. Their small world widens as they grow older. In this section, you will learn about these aspects of children's socioemotional development: Erikson's theory of socioemotional development, attachment between infants and their caregivers, temperament, parenting, the wider social world, Kohlberg's theory of moral development, and gender development.

Erikson's Theory of Socioemotional Development Erik Erikson (1902–1994) spent his early life in Europe. After working as a psychoanalyst under Sigmund Freud's direction, he went to the United States and taught at Harvard University. Although he accepted some of Freud's beliefs, he disagreed with others. For example, Freud argued that *psychosexual* stages (see chapter 12) are the key to understanding development; Erikson said that *psychosocial* stages are the key. In addition, Freud stressed that personality is shaped mainly in the first five years of life. By contrast, Erikson emphasized lifelong development.

Erikson's theory of life-span development proposes eight psychosocial stages of development, from infancy through old age. In Erikson's (1968) view, the first four stages take place in childhood, the last four in adolescence and adulthood (see figure 4.13). Each stage represents a developmental task or crisis that a person must negotiate. Each stage also marks a potential turning point toward greater personal competence or greater weakness and vulnerability. The more successfully people resolve the issues at each stage, the more competent they are likely to become.

Erikson's Childhood Stages Erikson's adolescence and adult stages are examined later in the chapter. His four childhood stages are as follows:

1. Trust versus mistrust occurs approximately during the first one-and-a-half years of life. Trust is built when a baby's basic needs—such as comfort, food, and warmth—are met. If responsive, sensitive caregivers do not meet infants' needs, the result is mistrust. Trust in infancy sets the stage for a lifelong expectation that the world will be a good and pleasant place to live.
2. Autonomy versus shame and doubt occurs from about one-and-a-half through three years of age. In this stage children can develop either a positive sense of independence and autonomy or negative feelings of shame and doubt. In seeking autonomy, they are likely to develop a strong sense of independence.
3. Initiative versus guilt occurs from three to five years of age, the preschool years. During these years, children's social worlds are widening, and they are being challenged to develop purposeful behaviour to cope with the challenges. When asked to assume more responsibility for themselves, children can develop initiative. When allowed to be irresponsible or made to feel anxious, they can develop too much guilt. But Erikson believed that young children are resilient. He said that a sense of accomplishment quickly compensates for most guilt feelings.
4. Industry versus inferiority occurs from about the age of six until puberty. Children can achieve industry by mastering knowledge and intellectual skills. When they do not, they can feel inferior. For example, Erikson believed that at the end of the period of expansive imagination that occurs in early childhood, children are ready to turn their energy to learning academic skills. If they do not, they can develop a sense of being incompetent and unproductive.

Erikson did not believe that the proper resolution to a stage is always completely positive. For example, developing trust is good, but one cannot trust all people under all circumstances and survive. However, for optimal development to take place, positive resolutions should dominate.

Evaluating Erikson's Theory At a time when people believed that most development takes place in childhood, Erikson charted development as a lifelong challenge. His insights also helped to move us away from Freud's focus on sexuality and toward an

Erikson's Stages	Developmental period	Characteristics
Trust versus mistrust	Infancy (Birth–1 ½ years)	A sense of trust requires a feeling of physical comfort and a minimal amount of fear about the future. Infants' basic needs are met by responsive, sensitive caregivers.
Autonomy versus shame and doubt	Toddlerhood (1 ½–3 years)	After gaining trust in their caregivers, infants start to discover that they have a will of their own. They assert their sense of autonomy, or independence. They realize their will. If infants are restrained too much or punished too harshly, they are likely to develop a sense of shame and doubt.
Initiative versus guilt	Early childhood (preschool years, ages 3–5)	As preschool children encounter a widening social world, they are challenged more and need to develop more purposeful behaviour to cope with these challenges. Children are now asked to assume more responsibility. Uncomfortable guilt feelings may arise, though, if the children are irresponsible and are made to feel too anxious.
Industry versus inferiority	Middle and late childhood (elementary school years, 6 years–puberty)	At no other time are children more enthusiastic than at the end of early childhood's period of expansive imagination. As children move into the elementary school years, they direct their energy toward mastering knowledge and intellectual skills. The danger at this stage involves feeling incompetent and unproductive.
Identity versus identity confusion	Adolescence (10–20 years)	Individuals are faced with finding out who they are, what they are all about, and where they are going in life. An important dimension is the exploration of alternative solutions to roles. Career exploration is important.
Intimacy versus isolation	Early adulthood (20s, 30s)	Individuals face the developmental task of forming intimate relationships with others. Erikson described intimacy as finding oneself yet losing oneself in another person.
Generativity versus stagnation	Middle adulthood (40s, 50s)	A chief concern is to assist the younger generation in developing and leading useful lives.
Integrity versus despair	Late adulthood (60s–)	Individuals look back and evaluate what they have done with their lives. The retrospective glances can either be positive (integrity) or negative (despair).

understanding of the importance of successfully resolving different socioemotional tasks at different points in our lives. Erikson's ideas changed the way we think about some periods of development (Marcia, 2002). For example, Erikson encouraged us to look at adolescents not just as sexual beings, but as individuals seeking to find out who they are and searching to find their niche in the world.

But Erikson's theory, like Piaget's, has also been criticized. As was mentioned in chapter 2, Erikson himself mainly practised case study research. Although critics argue that a firm research base has not been developed, researchers have successfully used Erikson's theory to guide research on both normal (e.g., Westermeyer, 2004) and abnormal (e. g. Drapeau, 2004) development.

FIGURE 4.13
Erikson's Eight Stages of Human Development

FIGURE 4.14

Contact Time with Wire and Cloth Surrogate Mothers
Regardless of whether the infant monkeys were fed by a wire or a cloth mother, they overwhelmingly preferred to spend contact time with the cloth mother.

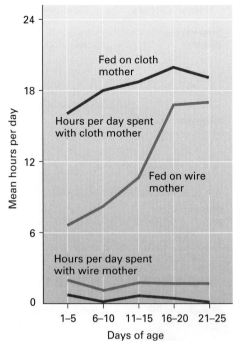

Critics also say that Erikson's attempt to capture each stage with a single concept sometimes leaves out other important developmental tasks. For example, Erikson said that the main task for young adults is to resolve the conflict between intimacy and isolation. However, another important developmental task in early adulthood involves careers and work.

Such criticisms do not tarnish Erikson's monumental contributions, however. His theory remains the most popular overarching developmental theory. Erikson, like Piaget, is a giant in developmental psychology.

Attachment in Infancy The word *attachment* usually refers to a strong relationship between two people in which each person does a number of things to continue the relationship. Many types of people are attached: relatives, lovers, a teacher and a student. In the language of developmental psychology, however, **attachment** is the close emotional bond between the infant and its caregiver.

Theories about infant attachment abound. Freud believed that the infant becomes attached to the person or object who feeds the infant and thus provides oral satisfaction. For most infants, this is the mother.

But researchers have questioned the importance of feeding in infant attachment. Harry Harlow (Harlow & Zimmerman, 1959) separated infant monkeys from their mothers at birth and placed them in cages in which they had access to two artificial "mothers." One of the mothers was made of wire, the other of cloth. Each mother could be outfitted with a feeding mechanism. Half the infant monkeys were fed by the wire mother, half by the cloth mother. The infant monkeys nestled close to the cloth mother and spent little time on the wire one, even if it was the wire mother that gave them milk (see figure 4.14). This study clearly demonstrates that what the researchers described as *contact comfort*, not feeding, is the crucial element in the attachment process.

Another famous study grew out of the field of *ethology*, which involves the study of the function and evolution of behaviour. One of ethology's founders was the European zoologist Konrad Lorenz (1903–1989). Lorenz (1965) examined attachment behaviour in geese. He separated the eggs laid by one goose into two groups. He returned one group of eggs to the goose to be hatched; the other group was hatched in an incubator. The goslings in the first group performed as predicted; they followed their mother as soon as they hatched. But those in the second group, who first saw Lorenz after hatching, followed him everywhere as if he were their mother. Lorenz marked the goslings and then placed both groups under a box. Mother goose and "mother" Lorenz stood

attachment The close emotional bond between an infant and its caregiver.

FIGURE 4.15

Canadian Bill Lishman Leads a Flock of Imprinted Canada Geese on Their First Southward Migration.
Inspired by Konrad Lorenz, Lishman (along with Joseph Duff) experimented with helping orphaned Canada geese learn to migrate. Lishman's work was described in his autobiography, *Father Goose*, and was the subject of the film *Fly Away Home*.

nearby as the box was lifted. Each group of goslings went directly to its "mother." Lorenz called this process **imprinting**, the tendency of an infant animal to form an attachment to the first moving object it sees and/or hears. More recently, Canadian Bill Lishman has led Canada geese imprinted on him on their migration (see figure 4.15).

For goslings, the critical period for imprinting is the first 36 hours after birth. Human infants appear to have a longer, more flexible "sensitive period" for attachment. A number of developmental psychologists believe that attachment to the caregiver during the first year provides an important foundation for later development (Bridges, 2003). John Bowlby (1969, 1989), for instance, believes that the infant and the mother instinctively form an attachment. He believes the newborn is innately equipped to stimulate the caregiver to respond; it cries, clings, smiles, and coos. Later the infant crawls, walks, and follows the mother. The infant's goal is to keep the mother nearby. Research on attachment supports Bowlby's view that the infant's attachment to its caregiver intensifies at about six to seven months (Schaffer & Emerson, 1964).

Some babies have more positive attachment experiences than others (Levy, 1999). Mary Ainsworth (1979) believes that the difference depends on how sensitive the caregiver is to the infant's signals (Pederson & others, 1998). She uses the term **secure attachment** to describe how infants use the caregiver, usually the mother, as a secure base from which to explore the environment. Infants who are securely attached are likelier to have mothers who are responsive and accepting and who express affection toward them than infants who are insecurely attached. The securely attached infant moves freely away from the mother but also keeps tabs on her location by periodically glancing at her. The securely attached infant responds positively to being picked up by others and, when put back down, happily moves away to play. An insecurely attached infant, in contrast, avoids the mother or is ambivalent toward her. The insecurely attached infant fears strangers and is upset by minor, everyday sensations.

Not all developmentalists believe that a secure attachment in infancy is the only path to competence in life. Jerome Kagan (1998, 2000, 2003), for example, believes that infants are highly resilient and can adapt to wide variations in parenting style. Kagan and others stress that genetics and temperament play more important roles in a child's social competence. For example, inheriting a low tolerance for stress, rather than forming an insecure attachment bond, might be responsible for a child's inability to get along with peers.

Another criticism of attachment theory is that it ignores the evidence that in some cultures infants show strong attachments to many people, not just their primary caregiver (Thompson, 2000). In the African Hausa culture, both grandmothers and siblings provide a significant amount of care to infants (Harkness & Super, 2002). Infants in agricultural societies tend to form attachments to older siblings, who are assigned a major responsibility for younger siblings' care. The attachments formed by infants in group care in Israeli kibbutzim provide another variation.

In general, however, psychologists accept the importance of competent, nurturant caregivers in an infant's development (Bornstein & Tamis-LeMonda, 2001). Accordingly,

In the Hausa culture, siblings and grandmothers provide a significant amount of care for infants. *How might this practice affect attachment?*

imprinting The tendency of an infant animal to form an attachment to the first moving object it sees and/or hears.

secure attachment An important aspect of socioemotional development in which infants use the caregiver, usually the mother, as a secure base from which to explore the environment.

attachment theory has been used to develop therapies for a wide variety of attachment disorders (Brisch & Kronenberg, 2002). Recently, Schore (2003) has proposed that attachment failures lead to an inability of the right hemisphere to regulate affect, and, thus, to many psychopathologies.

Temperament Some psychologists believe that one of the factors critical to understanding child development is **temperament**, which refers to an individual's behavioural style and characteristic way of responding. Psychiatrists Alexander Chess and Stella Thomas (1977) identified three basic types or clusters of temperament in children:

- The *easy child*, who is generally in a positive mood, quickly establishes regular routines in infancy, and adapts easily to new experiences
- The *difficult child*, who tends to react negatively and cry frequently, engages in irregular daily routines, and is slow to accept new experiences
- The *slow-to-warm-up child*, who has a low activity level, is somewhat negative, shows low adaptability, and displays a low mood intensity

Other researchers propose different dimensions as the core of temperament, such as *emotionality* (tendency to be distressed), *sociability* (tendency to prefer the company of others to being alone), and *activity level* (tempo and vigour of movement; Buss & Plomin, 1987). Psychologists have not reached agreement about the basic core dimensions of temperament (Sanson, Hemphill, & Smart, 2002; Wachs & Kohnstamm, 2001). Regardless, Australian psychologist Ann Sanson and her colleagues have linked temperament differences to differences in social development (Sanson, Hemphill & Smart, 2004).

Many parents don't believe in the importance of temperament until they have their second child (Putnam, Sanson, & Rothbart, 2002). Parents typically view the firstborn child's behaviour as a result of the way they have raised the child. However, management strategies that worked with the first child might be frustratingly ineffective with the second child. Such differences in children's temperament, which appear very early in their lives, support the belief that nature as well as nurture influence development.

Parenting Even though many North American children spend a great deal of time in child care in their early years and nearly all North American children spend many hours in school as they grow older, parents are still the main caregivers for most children. Despite this, Harris (1998) argued that children's genes and their peers are far more important than parents in children's development. One argument is that humans evolved to learn from any source, not just parents (Rowe, 1994). Such a general learning mechanism means that children might learn cultural innovations even if their parents do not. For example, the children of immigrants learn a second language faster and more completely than their parents do .

Critics reply that Harris ignored research studies documenting the importance of parents in children's development (Collins & others, 2003). For example, Rose-Krasnor and her colleagues (1996) trace the origins of social competence in children to early positive relationships with their mother. Conversely, many studies reveal that when parents abuse their children, the children have problems in regulating their emotions, in becoming securely attached to others, in developing competent peer relations, and in adapting to school. Such children also develop anxiety and depression disorders as children (Azar, 2002; Shea & others, 2005) and later, as adults (Schore (2003).

Studies of positive intervention especially can show whether parenting plays an important role in children's development (Bornstein & Bradley, 2003; Collins & others, 2003). In one study, parents' participation in 16-week discussion groups on effective parenting just prior to their children's entry into kindergarten resulted in better school adjustment and higher academic achievement for their children than for children whose parents attended discussion groups without the effective parenting emphasis (Cowan & Cowan, 2001).

temperament An individual's behavioural style and characteristic way of responding.

Parenting Styles Ideas about the best way to rear children have undergone many changes over the years and may vary across cultures. At one time, and in some cultures still, parents were advised to impose strict discipline along the lines of such adages as "Spare the rod and spoil the child" and "Children should be seen and not heard." But attitudes toward children—and how best to parent them—have changed to encompass more nurturing and caring (Smetana & Campione, 2003).

Diana Baumrind (1971, in press) believes parents interact with their children in one of four basic ways:

- **Authoritarian parenting** is a restrictive, punitive style in which the parent exhorts the child to follow the parent's directions and to value hard work and effort. The authoritarian parent firmly limits and controls the child, with little verbal exchange. In a difference of opinion about how to do something, for example, the authoritarian parent might say, "You do it my way or else. No backtalk." Authoritarian parenting is associated with children's social incompetence. Children of authoritarian parents often fail to initiate activity, have poor communication skills, and compare themselves with others.
- **Authoritative parenting** encourages children to be independent but still places limits and controls on their behaviour. Extensive verbal give-and-take is allowed, and parents are warm and nurturant toward the child. An authoritative parent might put his arm around the child in a comforting way and say, "You know you shouldn't have done that; let's talk about how you can handle the situation better next time." Children whose parents are authoritative tend to be socially competent, self-reliant, and socially responsible.
- **Neglectful parenting** is a style in which parents are uninvolved in their child's life. Ask such parents, "It's 10 p.m. Do you know where your child is?" and they are likely to answer, "No." Yet children have a strong need for their parents to care about them. Children whose parents are neglectful might develop a sense that other aspects of the parents' lives are more important than they are. Children whose parents are neglectful tend to be less competent socially, not to handle independence well, and, especially, to show poor self-control.
- **Indulgent parenting** is a style in which parents are involved with their children but place few limits on them. Such parents let their children do what they want. Some parents deliberately rear their children in this way because they believe the combination of warm involvement with few restraints will produce a creative, confident child. But children whose parents are indulgent often rate poorly in social competence. They often fail to learn respect for others, expect to get their own way, and have difficulty controlling their behaviour. Are today's parents too indulgent? To examine this issue further, see the Critical Reflections Box.

Figure 4.16 summarizes Baumrind's parenting styles and their child outcomes.

Style	Parental Behaviour	Common Outcome in Children
Authoritarian	Restrict and punish. Orders not to be questioned. Little verbal exchange.	Anxiety about social comparison, lack of initiative, poor communication skills.
Authoritative	Encourage independence within limits. Extensive verbal give-and-take. Warmth, nurturance.	Social competence, self-reliance, social responsibility.
Neglectful	Little involvement in the child's life. Unaware of what the child is doing.	Anxiety about social comparison, lack of initiative, poor communication skills.
Indulgent	Involved with the child but without placing demands. Highly permissive.	Anxiety about social comparison, lack of initiative, poor communication skills.

FIGURE 4.16 Parenting Styles and Child Outcomes

authoritarian parenting A restrictive, punitive style in which the parent exhorts the child to follow the parent's directions and value hard work and effort.

authoritative parenting A parenting style that encourages children's independence (but still places limits and controls on their behaviour), includes extensive verbal give-and-take, and warm and nurturant interactions with the child.

neglectful parenting A parenting style in which parents are uninvolved in their child's life.

indulgent parenting A parenting style in which parents are involved with their children but place few limits on them.

critical reflections

Are We Spoiling Our Children?

With the publication of *Pampered Child Syndrome*, by Ottawa clinical psychologist Maggie Mamen, the whole issue of indulgent parenting has re-entered the public spotlight (Mamen, 2004). Mamen's thesis is that many parents want to adopt a more humane parenting style. As a consequence they believe that placing few limits on their children will empower them. They believe that giving children everything they want will make their children feel special. Unfortunately, as Mamen points out, these parents' best intentions may have backfired, resulting in children who have developed unrealistic expectations and an over-blown sense of self. In other words, indulgent parenting produces spoiled children.

Yet in another recent book, entitled *The Road to Whatever: Middle-Class Culture and the Crisis of Adolescence*, University of California professor Elliot Currie argues that North American adolescents are in a crisis caused by punitive and uncaring parents (Currie, 2005). The result is an epidemic of teen drug use and crime. While Mamen and Currie agree that children and adolescents are experiencing difficulties, they disagree about the role of parents. Are parents too indulgent or too uncaring?

As an example of the difference between these two styles, while both types of parent might allow a five-year-old to dig in a backyard flowerbed unsupervised, an indulgent parent might pronounce the resulting damage to the flowerbeds a "masterpiece" and a neglectful parent might simply use a shovel to level out the flowerbed again. In contrast, an authoritarian parent might not allow a five-year-old to dig in the flowerbed at all and an authoritative parent might be right there with guidance and gardening gloves on.

Research shows that the children of indulgent parents frequently lack self-control (Baumrind, in press). For example, one boy whose parents deliberately reared him in an indulgent manner moved his parents out of their bedroom suite and took it over for himself. At nearly

Maggie Mamen is a practising clinical psychologist in Ottawa, Ontario. She claims that children today are too pampered. *Do you agree?*

18 years old he had still not learned to control his behaviour; when he couldn't get something he wanted, he still threw temper tantrums. As you might expect, he wasn't popular with his peers. Perhaps children who are pampered when they are young develop too strong a sense of entitlement, which may be accepted inside the family but becomes a liability in the wider social world. Such children may become self-indulgent, engaging in drug use or exercise their inappropriate sense of entitlement through criminal activity.

On the other hand, perhaps the problem is not so much one of indulgent parenting, as Mamen suggests, but of neglectful parenting, as Currie suggests. Children of neglectful parents do, in fact, also tend to lack self-control (Kilgore, Snyder, & Lentz, 2000). Further, these children are definitely at risk for delinquency, drug abuse, and sexual misconduct (Weiss & Schwarz, 1996).

So which is it? Are today's parents indulgent or neglectful? One way to resolve this debate is to recognize that both parenting styles are relatively uninvolved, whereas the authoritative style is relatively involved. Modern life has definitely made it more difficult for parents to spend enough time with their children and to be aware of any issues their children may be facing. This basic lack of involvement may be more important than any other variable in creating the situation children face today.

What do you think?

- Is there a problem with parenting today? If so, is the problem indulgent parenting or neglectful parenting? Or is it something else?
- Do you think parental involvement may be a critical factor or are other factors (peer pressure, poor schooling, cultural influences) more important in creating difficulties for children and adolescents?

Although Baumrind's findings are useful, they leave many questions about parenting unanswered. There is more to understanding parent-child relationships than parenting style, such as the importance of fathers in parenting (Videon, 2005). One key issue is whether parenting style is really a product of the parents alone. For many years the socialization of children was viewed as a straightforward, one-way matter of indoctrination—telling small children about the use of spoons and potties, the importance of saying thank you, and being nice to the baby brother. The basic philosophy was that children had to be trained to fit into the social world, so their behaviour had to be shaped into that of a mature adult. However, as research on temperament suggests, the young child is not like the inanimate blob of clay from which a sculptor builds a statue. Through the process of *reciprocal socialization*, children socialize their parents just as parents socialize their children. For example, children's smiles usually elicit positive overtures by parents. However, when children are difficult and aggressive, their parents are more likely to punish them. Or consider adolescents: They promote guilt feelings in parents, just as parents promote guilt feelings in them. In other words, parenting styles may be influenced by children's behaviour.

Divorce Many children are highly vulnerable to stress when their parents divorce (Kitzmann & Gaylord, 2002). Research shows that children from divorced families are more poorly adjusted (are more likely to have psychological problems, such as being overly aggressive or depressed) than their counterparts from nondivorced families (Wallerstein & Lewis, 2004). Those who have experienced multiple divorces are at even greater risk. Recent research has even shown that children whose grandparents divorced are more likely to experience marital discord and divorce (Amato & Cheadle, 2005).

What percentage of children from divorced families have adjustment problems? Many researchers agree that it is 20 to 25 percent, compared with only 10 percent of children in nondivorced families (Hetherington & Kelly, 2002). Remember, however, that approximately 80 percent of children in divorced families do not have adjustment problems, which runs counter to stereotypical beliefs about children of divorce. Among the factors that predict better adjustment for children in divorced families are harmony between the divorced parents, authoritative parenting, good schools, and whether the child possesses an easy rather than a difficult temperament (Hetherington & Kelly, 2002).

Positive Parenting You have already examined some important aspects of positive parenting, especially an authoritative parenting style. Another aspect is recognizing that parenting takes time and effort (Laird & others, 2003; Edwards & Liu, 2002; Teti & Candelaria, 2002). For example, Simons-Morton & colleagues (2004) found that while friends can influence adolescents to start smoking, ongoing parental involvement can be instrumental in preventing smoking progression. Similarly, Laird & colleagues (2003) found that the children of parents who were more knowledgable about their adolescent's activities and whereabouts were less likely to report delinquent behaviour.

According to Lynn Katz, of the University of Washington, and her colleagues, another aspect of positive parenting is coaching children about how to control their emotions (Katz & Windecker-Nelson, 2004). "Emotion-coaching parents" monitor their children's emotions, view their children's negative emotions as opportunities for teaching about emotion, and provide guidance in effectively dealing with emotions. In research, emotion-coaching parents have been observed to reject their children less, praise them more, and be more nurturant toward them than "emotion-dismissing parents" (Gottman, Katz, & Hooven, 1997). The children of the emotion-coaching parents in this research were better at toning down the intensity of their negative emotions and at focusing their attention and had fewer behaviour problems than the children of emotion-dismissing parents.

A final aspect of positive parenting is using strategies for raising a moral child (Grusec & others, 2000). The goal is to raise a child who is considerate of others, understands the difference between right and wrong, and is less likely to lie, cheat, or steal (Noddings, 2005). For example, parents who intervene in their children's most intense disputes prompt an increase in more sophisticated negotiation (Perlman & Ross, 1997). Following are the positive parenting strategies that have most often been found to be helpful in raising a moral child (Eisenberg & Valiente, 2002).

- Parents are warm and supportive rather than punitive.
- Parents use reasoning the child can understand when disciplining.
- Parents provide opportunities for the child to learn about others' perspectives and feelings.
- Parents involve children in family decision making and thinking about moral decisions.
- Parents model moral behaviours and thinking themselves and provide their children with opportunities to engage in such moral behaviours and thinking.

The Wider Social World The family is one social context in which children's development occurs. But the broader culture, the child's peer relations, school influences, and the quality of the neighbourhood in which the child lives are also important (Bronfenbrenner, 2000; Harkness & Super, 2002).

Today, psychologists are especially interested in improving the lives of children who live in impoverished neighbourhoods and attend ineffective schools (Blyth,

Children's development is influenced not only by their family experiences but also by their experiences with peers, in the neighbourhood, at school, and in the culture. A special concern is the effect of poverty on children's development. Poverty is especially high in ethnic minority families.

2000; Booth & Crouter, 2000). For example, Sobolewski & Amato (2005) have found that poverty can negatively affect children even after they have grown into adulthood. Psychologists are also increasingly interested in studying children from ethnic minority groups. Although many ethnic minority families are not poor, poverty contributes to the stressful life experiences of many minority children, creating a double disadvantage for them (Ceballo, McLoyd & Toyokawa, 2004): prejudice, discrimination, and bias because of their ethnic minority background, and the stressful effects of poverty.

Developmental psychologists are also intrigued by cultural comparisons of North American children with those of other countries. For example, parents in the United States tend to rear their children to be more independent than their counterparts in Japan and other Asian countries (Matsumoto, 2000). Similarly, by the time they get to university, young Canadians have more of an uncertainty orientation than young Japanese students, who are less tolerant of uncertainty (Shuper & others, 2004). Such cross-cultural variations reflect the nurture part of the nature versus nurture issue.

Childcare While it is normal for older children to spend considerable time in the wider social world, the same has not been historically true for younger children. Yet, as more women return to school or the workforce after pregnancy, and more of them are single parents, more families are relying on nonparental care for their infants and young children. At the same time, parents and researchers often worry about the impact of childcare on their children (Vandell, 2004; Vandell, Pierce, & Dadisman, 2005).

Canadian researchers have long been interested in the quality of childcare in Canada (Clifford & others, 1992; Goelman, 2000; Goelman & others, 2003; Pence, 1989). The emerging consensus is that high-quality childcare does no harm and can sometimes even help children.

For example, Schliecker, White, and Jacobs (1991) found that child-care quality was related to vocabulary development, implicating lower-quality child-care settings. They also found that this effect was greater for single-parent mother-headed households. Turned around, high-quality child care may make a significant contribution to the development of a child's vocabulary, especially when that child comes from a single-parent family. The Canadian Transition to Child Care Study (McKim & others, 1999) examined the effect of childcare on infant attachment. This study found that high-quality childcare can actually counter the tendency of infants with a difficult temperament to experience insecure mother-infant attachment.

The issues of childcare and early education have received national attention in Canada with the signing in 2000 of the First Ministers Early Childhood Development Agreement, which included a federal government commitment to provide $2.2 billion dollars over five years beginning in 2001–2. In 2004, premiers from throughout Canada, with the exception of Quebec, agreed on four principles to inform the creation of a national program. The four principles are **Q**uality, **U**niversal inclusivity, **A**ccessibility, and **D**evelopmental focus, or QUAD. Available data (Hertzman, Goelman, & Kershaw, 2005) have already suggested that each of the four principles are not yet fully realized in the current climate of child care in Canada.

Moral Development   Moral development involves changes with age in thoughts, feelings, and behaviours regarding the principles and values that guide what people should do (Killen & Smetana, 2005). Moral development has both an intrapersonal dimension (a person's basic values and sense of self) and an interpersonal dimension (what people should do in their interactions with other people; Nucci, 2001; Walker & Pitts, 1998).

Psychologists have studied how people reason and think about moral matters, how they feel about them, and how they actually behave. Their greatest interest in recent years has been moral reasoning and thinking. Much of their work has revolved around Lawrence Kohlberg's theory of moral development and reactions to it.

Lawrence Kohlberg, who created a provocative theory of moral development. In his view, "Moral development consists of a sequence of qualitative changes in the way an individual thinks."

Kohlberg's Theory   Kohlberg (1958) began his study of moral thinking by creating 11 stories and asking children, adolescents, and adults questions about the stories. One of the stories (set in Europe) goes like this:

> A woman was near death from a special kind of cancer. There was one drug that the doctors thought might save her. It was a form of radium that a druggist in the same town had recently discovered. The drug was expensive to make, but the druggist was charging ten times what the drug cost him to make. He paid $200 for the radium and charged $2,000 for a small dose of the drug. The sick woman's husband, Heinz, went to everyone he knew to borrow the money, but he could get together only $1,000. He told the druggist that his wife was dying and asked him to sell it cheaper or let him pay later. But the druggist said, "No. I discovered the drug, and I am going to make money from it." Desperate, Heinz broke into the man's store to steal the drug for his wife (Kohlberg, 1969).

After reading the story, the interviewee was asked a series of questions about the moral dilemma. Should Heinz have stolen the drug? Was stealing it right or wrong? Why? Is it a husband's duty to steal a lifesaving drug for his wife if he can get it in no other way? Would a good husband do it? Did the druggist have the right to charge so much in the absence of a law setting a limit on the price? Why or why not? Based on the answers that people gave to the questions about this and other moral dilemmas, Kohlberg constructed a theory.

Kohlberg (1986) proposed that moral development consists of three levels with two stages at each level (see figure 4.17).

1. The *preconventional* level is based primarily on punishments (stage 1) or rewards (stage 2) that come from the external world. In regard to the Heinz story, at stage 1 an individual might say that Heinz should not steal the drug because he might get caught and sent to jail. At stage 2, the person might say he should not steal the drug because the druggist needs to make a profit on the drug.
2. At the *conventional* level, the individual abides by standards, such as those learned from parents (stage 3) or society's laws (stage 4). At stage 3, an individual might say that Heinz should steal the drug for his wife because that is what people expect a good husband would do. At stage 4, the person might say that it is natural for Heinz to want to save his wife but that the law says it still is always wrong to steal.
3. At the *postconventional* level, the individual recognizes alternative moral courses, explores the options, and then develops a personal moral code. The code reflects the principles generally accepted by the community (stage 5) or it reflects more abstract principles for all of humanity (stage 6). At stage 5, a person might say that the law was not set up for these circumstances, so Heinz can steal the drug. It is not really right, but he is justified in doing it. At stage 6, the individual evaluates alternatives but recognizes that Heinz's wife's life is more important than a law.

LEVEL 1 Preconventional Level No Internalization	LEVEL 2 Conventional Level Intermediate Internalization	LEVEL 3 Postconventional Level Full Internalization
Stage 1 Heteronomous Morality *Individuals pursue their own interests but let others do the same. What is right involves equal exchange.*	**Stage 3** Mutual Interpersonal Expectations, Relationships, and Interpersonal Conformity *Individuals value trust, caring, and loyalty to others as a basis for moral judgments.*	**Stage 5** Social Contract or Utility and Individual Rights *Individuals reason that values, rights, and principles undergird or transcend the law.*
Stage 2 Individualism, Purpose, and Exchange *Children obey because adults tell them to obey. People base their moral decisions on fear of punishment.*	**Stage 4** Social System Morality *Moral judgments are based on understanding and the social order, law, justice, and duty.*	**Stage 6** Universal Ethical Principles *The person has developed moral judgments that are based on universal human rights. When faced with a dilemma between law and conscience, a personal, individualized conscience is followed.*

FIGURE 4.17

Kohlberg's Three Levels and Six Stages of Moral Development

Kohlberg believed that these levels and stages develop in a sequence and are age-related. Some evidence for the sequence of Kohlberg's stages has been found, although few people reach stage 6 (Colby & others, 1983). Children are often in stages 1 and 2, although in the later elementary school years they may be in stage 3. Most adolescents are at stage 3 or 4.

Kohlberg also believed that advances in moral development take place because of the maturation of thought (especially in concert with Piaget's stages), opportunities for role taking, and opportunities to discuss moral issues with a person who reasons at a stage just above one's own. In Kohlberg's view, parents contribute little to children's moral thinking because parent-child relationships are often too power-oriented.

Evaluating Kohlberg's Theory Kohlberg's ideas stimulated a great deal of interest in the field of moral development. His provocative view continues to promote considerable research about how people think about moral issues (e.g., Comunian, 2004).

At the same time, his theory has numerous critics. One criticism is that moral *reasoning* does not necessarily mean moral *behaviour*. When people are asked about their moral reasoning, what they say might fit into Kohlberg's advanced stages, but their actual behaviour might be filled with cheating, lying, and stealing. The cheaters, liars, and thieves might know what is right and what is wrong but still do what is wrong.

Carol Gilligan, who argues that Kohlberg's view does not give adequate attention to relationships. In Gilligan's view, "Many girls seem to fear, most of all, being alone—without friends, family, and relationships."

Another major criticism is that Kohlberg's view does not adequately reflect interpersonal relationships and concerns for others; that it focuses too much on the intrapersonal dimension of moral development. Kohlberg's theory is thus a *justice perspective* concerned with the rights of "the individual," who stands alone and independently makes moral decisions. In contrast, the *care perspective*, which lies at the heart of Carol Gilligan's (1982, 2003) theory of moral development, views people in terms of their connectedness with others and focuses on interpersonal communication, relationships, and concern for others. Gilligan faults Kohlberg for greatly underplaying the care perspective in moral development. She believes he may have done so because he is a male, because most of his research was with males rather than females, and because he used male responses as a model for his theory. However, not everyone adopts Gilligan's view either, and even she argues that at the highest level of moral development the individual and relationship aspects of moral reasoning are likely to be integrated.

Gender Development Carol Gilligan's view of moral development points up another important aspect of socioemotional development in childhood: gender. Recall from chapter 1 that *gender* refers to the social and psychological aspects of being female and male. Gilligan's view of moral development provides some good examples of the differences between girls' and boys' experiences as they grow up and the potential lasting effects of those experiences. For instance, Gilligan (1996, 1998) says that at the edge of adolescence—at about 11 to 12 years of age—girls become aware that their intense interest in intimacy is not prized by the male-dominated culture, even though society values females as caring and altruistic. The dilemma, says Gilligan, is that girls are presented with a choice that makes them appear either selfish (if they become independent and self-sufficient) or selfless (if they remain responsive to others), neither of which may be desirable. As young adolescent girls experience this dilemma, Gilligan says, they increasingly "silence" their distinctive voices. They become less confident and more tentative in offering their opinions, behaviour that may persist into adulthood. Some researchers believe this self-doubt and ambivalence may translate into depression and eating disorders among adolescent girls (Piran, 2002).

Gilligan's work is only one aspect of psychology's intense interest in gender development. Other avenues of research include how strongly biology shapes gender, how strongly social experiences with parents and others influence the way girls and boys behave, and how gender and cognition are linked.

Biology and Gender Development Researchers did not confirm the existence of human sex chromosomes, the genetic material that determines our sex, until the 1920s. Anatomical differences were obvious, of course, but not the underlying biological elements that differentiate the sexes. Humans normally have 46 chromosomes arranged in pairs. The 23rd pair may have two X-shaped chromosomes, which produces a female, or it may have both an X-shaped and a Y-shaped chromosome, which produces a male (see figure 4.18).

However, in the first few weeks after conception, male and female embryos look alike. When the Y chromosome in the male embryo triggers the secretion of **androgens**, the main class of male sex hormones, male sex organs start to differentiate from female sex organs. (As noted in chapter 3, hormones are powerful chemical substances secreted by the endocrine glands and carried by the blood throughout the body.) Low levels of androgen in a female embryo allow the normal development of female sex organs. The developing genitals cannot be observed externally until about the seventh week after conception. Long after conception, hormones can still play a powerful role in shaping sex characteristics and possibly in influencing gender-related behaviours (Tobach, 2002). Later in this chapter you will read about the hormonal changes that take place in androgens and **estrogens**, the main class of female sex hormones, during puberty and adulthood.

In rare instances, an imbalance in the secretion of hormones occurs during prenatal development. Insufficient androgens in the male embryo or an excess of androgens in the female embryo creates a hermaphrodite: an individual with both male and female sex organs. When genetically female (XX chromosomes) infants are born with masculine-looking genitals, surgery can achieve a genital-genetic match. Prior to puberty these females often behave in more aggressive, "tomboyish" ways than most girls (Berenbaum & Hines, 1992; Ehrhardt, 1987).

Is the gender behaviour of these surgically corrected girls due to their prenatal hormones or is it the result of their social experience? Experiments with different animal species reveal that, when male hormones are injected into female embryos, the females develop masculine physical traits and behave more aggressively (Hines, 1982). However, as we move from animals to humans, hormones exert less control over behaviour. Perhaps because these girls looked more masculine, they were treated more like boys and so adopted their tomboyish ways. Thus, as with other aspects of development, in gender behaviour both biology and experience are likely at work.

Evolutionary psychologists emphasize the importance of biology, however (as you may recall from chapter 1). In the evolutionary psychology view of gender, differences in gender behaviour are the product of gradual genetic adaptations (Buss, 2004). Evolutionary psychologists argue that women and men have faced different pressures throughout human evolution (Bjorklund, Yunger, & Pellegrini, 2002; Mealey, 2000). They stress that the sexes' different status in reproduction is the key to understanding how this evolution took place (Mealey, 2000).

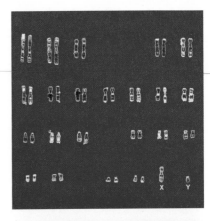

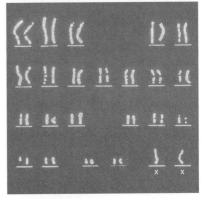

FIGURE 4.18

The Genetic Difference Between Males and Females

The chromosome structures of a male (*top*) and female (*bottom*). The 23rd pair is shown at bottom right. Notice that the male's Y chromosome is smaller than his X chromosome. To obtain pictures of chromosomes, a cell is removed from a person's body, usually from inside the mouth, and the chromosomes are photographed under magnification.

androgens The main class of male sex hormones.

estrogens The main class of female sex hormones.

cathy®   by **Cathy Guisewite**

Cathy © Cathy Guisewite. Reprinted with permission of UNIVERSAL PRESS SYNDICATE. All rights reserved.

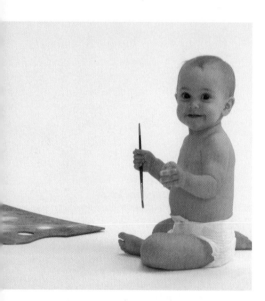

First imagine that this is a photograph of a baby girl. *What expectations would you have for her?* Then imagine that this is a photograph of a baby boy. *What expectations would you have for him?*

In this view, male competition led to a reproductive advantage for dominant males. Men adopted short-term mating practices because this allowed them to increase their reproductive advantage by fathering more children. In contrast, women devoted more effort to parenting and chose mates who could provide their offspring with resources for protection. Because men competed with other men for access to women, men have evolved dispositions that favour violence and risk taking. Women have developed a preference for long-term mates who can support a family. Men strive to acquire more resources than other men in order to attract more women, and women seek to attract successful, ambitious men who can provide these resources.

Critics of evolutionary psychology theory argue that humans have the decision-making ability to change their gender behaviour and thus are not locked into their evolutionary past. They cite extensive cross-cultural variation in gender behaviour and mate preference as proof that social experience affects gender behaviour (Wood, 2001). For instance, in Alice Eagly's (2000, 2001) *social roles* view of gender, it is indeed social experiences that have caused differences in gender behaviour. She stresses that as women were forced to adapt to roles with less power and less status in society, they showed more cooperative and less dominant profiles than men. Following are some ways in which social experiences might influence gender behaviour.

Social Experience and Gender Development   As children grow up, they adopt **gender roles**, which involve expectations as to how females and males should think, act, and feel (Denmark, Rabinowitz, & Sechzer, 2005). Some cultures emphasize that children should be reared to adopt traditional gender roles (Best, 2002). Boys are reared to be "masculine" (powerful, aggressive, and independent, for example) and girls are brought up to be "feminine" (sensitive to others, good at relationships, and less assertive, for example). Other cultures, especially in recent times, have placed more emphasis on rearing boys and girls to be more similar—girls being raised to be just as assertive as boys and boys being raised to be just as caring toward others as girls, for example. Egypt and China are two of the countries in which traditional gender roles continue to dominate, but Canada and the United States are moving toward more diversity in gender roles. Still, much socialization in our culture is gender based (Lott & Maluso, 2002).

In a gendered society, parents often apply the "pink" and "blue" treatment to infants. Boys are dressed in blue, girls in pink. Boys are given trucks to play with, girls are given dolls. Parents let boys be more aggressive and require girls to be more reserved. These social experiences inevitably influence the behaviour of these individuals when they get older (Brannon, 2005).

Peers also play an important role in gender development. Especially during middle and late childhood (6 to 10 or 11 years of age or until puberty begins), peer groups are often highly segregated into boy groups and girl groups. Peers are stricter than most parents in rewarding what is considered gender-appropriate behaviour in the culture and punishing gender-inappropriate behaviour.

Interestingly, tolerance of gender-inappropriate behaviour is itself gendered. North Americans tend to disapprove more of boys engaging in feminine behaviour (playing with dolls and crying, for example) than of girls displaying masculine behaviour (being

gender roles Expectations for how females and males should think, act, and feel.

a tomboy and being assertive, for example). In other words, female gender roles are somewhat more flexible than male gender roles.

Cognition and Gender   How do children learn what girls and boys are supposed to be like? And do girls and boys actually think differently? Both of these questions link cognitive development to gender development.

Recall from our discussion of Piaget's theory earlier in the chapter that a schema is a mental framework that organizes and guides an individual's thoughts. A recent theory proposes that children develop a gender schema based on what is considered appropriate behaviour for females and males in their culture (Martin & Dinella, 2001; Martin & Ruble, 2004). They actively search for gender cues to construct a gender schema, which then serves as a cognitive framework for interpreting further experiences related to gender. As their gender schema develops, children knit together all sorts of things with gender, such as "girls are expected to be nurturant," "boys are expected to be independent," and so on.

According to Lisa Serbin, and her colleagues, of Concordia University, gender schemas are already beginning to develop by the second year of life (Serbin & others, 2002; Poulin-Dubois & others, 2002). In one study, twenty-four month old infants were shown photographs of male and female adults engaged in either gender neutral or gender stereotyped behaviours (Serbin & others, 2002). The infants spent longer looking at photos depicting behaviour inconsistent with gender stereotypes (e.g., a man putting on lipstick) than they did photos depicting gender neutral behaviours (e.g., a picture of a woman reading').

The research that has focused on differences between the cognitive skills of older boys and girls are has mainly examined math skills, visuospatial skills, and verbal skills (Halpern, 2004). According to Diane Halpern, of California's Claremont McKenna College, in math and visuospatial skills—the kinds of skills an architect needs to design a building's angles and dimensions—boys tend to perform better than girls, although the differences are usually small. In the area of verbal skills, 20 years ago researchers found that girls often had better verbal ability (such as a better vocabulary) than boys, but in most verbal areas that difference has not held up over the years (Hyde & Mezulis, 2002).

In other parts of this book, you will learn more about gender. It is one of the most frequently examined factors in psychological research. For example, chapter 16 ("Social Psychology") examines gender in relationships, gender in aggression, and gender in altruism.

Positive Psychology and Children's Development

We cannot fully understand children's development without examining their competence and adaptive capabilities. The concept of resilient children highlights this competence and adaptability.

Resilient Children   Despite hardship, time and time again resilient children grow up to be capable adults, just as Alice Walker did. But why does one person who is subjected to poverty or racism or the divorce of parents remain mired in lifelong misfortune whereas another rises above those obstacles to succeed in business, the community, or family life?

Researchers have found that *resilient* children have one or more advantages that help them to overcome their disadvantages (Masten, 2001; Masten & Reed, 2002). These advantages include individual factors (such as good intellectual functioning), family factors (such as a close, caring relationship with at least one parent), and extrafamilial factors (such as bonds to supportive, competent adults outside the family; see figure 4.19). Not all of them need to be present to help a child develop successfully. If a child does not have responsible, caring parents, then high self-esteem and a bond to a caring adult outside the home could make the child resilient enough to overcome negative family factors. Educators are also developing programs to enhance young children's resilience (Israelashvili & Wegman-Rozi, 2003).

The study of resilient children raises questions about what optimal functioning in children is like and which factors contribute to positive development. The same characteristics that show up in resilient children are those that appear in competent children who don't face adverse circumstances.

Source	Characteristic
Individual	Good intellectual functioning
	Appealing, sociable, easygoing disposition
	Self-confidence, high self-esteem
	Talents
	Faith
Family	Close relationship to caring parent figure
	Authoritative parenting: warmth, structure, high expectations
	Socioeconomic advantages
	Connections to extended supportive family networks
Extrafamilial Context	Bonds to caring adults outside the family
	Connections to positive organizations
	Attending effective schools

FIGURE 4.19

Characteristics of Resilient Children and Their Contexts

Improving the Lives of Children Unfortunately, however, many children living in at-risk circumstances—characterized by such factors as poverty, lack of quality parenting, inadequate schools, and high-crime neighbourhoods—are not resilient. Today, between 15 and 20 percent of all children in Canada live in poverty. Rates are higher for ethnic minority children and are over 50 percent for children of lone-parent mothers (Ross, Scott, & Smith, 2000). According to a 2005 UNICEF study, these percentages place Canada 19th among 26 industrialized countries (UNICEF Innocenti Research Centre, 2005).

These children desperately need prevention and intervention programs that give them an opportunity to become competent—for example, health education and help in developing both cognitive and socioemotional skills, including self-control, stress management, and communication (Compas & others, 2001; Powell, 2001). Competence enhancement programs for children living in poverty are increasingly two-generational: They help parents find good jobs and obtain quality health care, in addition to helping the child (McLoyd, 2000; Weissberg & Greenberg, 1998).

At the beginning of the twenty-first century, the well-being of children is one of Canada's foremost challenges. Children who do not reach their potential, who are unable to contribute to society, and who do not take their place as productive adults diminish the vitality of society's future.

> **reflect and review**

2 **Describe children's development from conception to adolescence.**

- Identify the stages of prenatal development and describe the risks associated with this period.
- Summarize the physical changes after birth that make possible rapid cognitive and socioemotional growth in childhood.
- Explain Piaget's theory of cognitive development and the key criticisms of the theory..
- Discuss Erikson's theory of psychosocial development and other key research on specific factors believed to have an influence on children's socioemotional development.
- Describe the contributions of positive psychology to our understanding of children's development.

Is there a best way to parent? Explain.

3 ADOLESCENCE

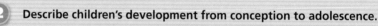

Physical Development in Adolescence — Cognitive Development in Adolescence — Socioemotional Development in Adolescence — At-Risk Youth — Positive Psychology and Adolescents

What are the most important physical, cognitive, and socioemotional changes in adolescence?

Adolescence is the developmental period of transition from childhood to adulthood. It begins around 10 to 12 years of age and ends at 18 to 21 years of age. As with every stage of development, in exploring adolescence it is important to balance the positive side with the negative side and to examine the search for an identity that every adolescent pursues.

Remember too that adolescents do not make up a homogeneous group (Santrock, 2005b). Ethnic, cultural, historical, gender, socioeconomic, and lifestyle variations characterize their actual life trajectories. Our image of adolescents should take into account the particular adolescent or group of adolescents we are considering.

Physical Development in Adolescence

The signature physical change in adolescence is **puberty**, a period of rapid skeletal and sexual maturation that occurs mainly in early adolescence. In general, we know when an individual is going through puberty, but we have a hard time pinpointing its beginning and its end. A spurt in height and weight are among the most obvious markers of pubertal change. This growth spurt occurs about two years earlier for girls than for boys (see figure 4.20). Today, in North America, the mean beginning of the growth spurt is 9 years of age for girls and 11 years of age for boys. The peak of pubertal change occurs at an average age of 11 for girls and 13 for boys.

Except for *menarche* (girls' first menstrual cycle), no single marker defines puberty. For boys, the first whisker or first wet dream could mark its appearance, but both may go unnoticed. In North America, the age at which menarche begins has declined on average from 14.2 years in 1900 to about 12.45 years today, a decline of about three months per decade for the past century, likely as a result of increasingly higher levels of nutrition and health.

Hormonal changes lie at the core of pubertal development (Cobb, 2004). The concentrations of certain hormones increase dramatically during puberty. *Testosterone*, an androgen, is associated in boys with the development of genitals, an increase in height, and voice change. *Estradiol*, an estrogen, is associated in girls with breast, uterine, and skeletal development. In one study, testosterone levels doubled in girls but increased eighteenfold in boys during puberty; similarly, estradiol doubled in boys but increased eightfold in girls (Nottelmann & others, 1987).

Are concentrations of hormones and adolescents' behaviour linked? Developmental psychologists believe that hormonal changes account for at least some of the emotional ups and downs of adolescence (Archibald, Graber, & Brooks-Gunn, 2003). Researchers have found that higher levels of androgens, such as testosterone, are associated with violence and other problems in boys (van Goozen & others, 1998). There is also some indication that increased levels of estrogens, such as estradiol, are linked with depression in adolescent girls (Angold & others, 1998).

But hormones alone are not responsible for adolescent behaviour (Susman & Rogol, 2003). For example, in one study, social factors (such as stress, getting bad grades, and relationship problems) accounted for two to four times as much variance as hormonal factors in young girls' depression and anger (Brooks-Gunn & Warren, 1989). Keep in mind, too, that social factors such as stress, eating patterns, or sexual activity can either activate or suppress hormones. Hormones may also interact with other factors. Brumberg (1997) argues that the recent decline in the average age of menarche, a hormonal change, is not matched by the earlier development of emotional or cognitive skills. The resulting development gap can put young girls at risk for depression and early sexual activity.

Cognitive Development in Adolescence

Adolescents undergo some significant cognitive changes. One is their advance to Piaget's stage of formal operational thinking, which was described earlier in the chapter. Another change has to do with adolescent egocentrism.

Adolescence is a time of evaluation, decision making, and commitment, as adolescents seek to find out who they are and carve out a place for themselves in the world.

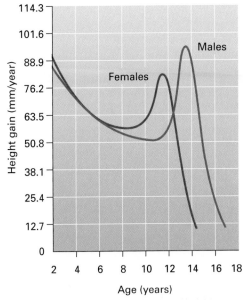

FIGURE 4.20

Pubertal Growth Spurt
On average, the pubertal growth spurt begins and peaks about 2 years earlier for girls (starts at 9, peaks at 11) than for boys (starts at 11, peaks at 13).

puberty A period of rapid skeletal and sexual maturation that occurs mainly in early adolescence.

From *Penguin Dreams and Stranger Things* by Berke Breathed. Copyright © 1985 by The Washington Post Company. By permission of Little, Brown and Company.

Piaget's Formal Operational Stage Piaget said that adolescents enter a fourth and most advanced stage of cognitive development, which he called the formal operational stage, at about 11 to 15 years of age. It is characterized by thought that is abstract, idealistic, and logical.

The abstract quality of thought at the formal operational level is evident in the adolescent's new verbal problem-solving ability. The concrete operational thinker would need to see the concrete elements, A, B, and C, to be able to make the logical inference that if A = B = C, then A = C. But the formal operational thinker can solve this problem merely through verbal presentation.

Another indication of the abstract quality of adolescents' thought is their increased tendency to think about thought itself. One adolescent commented, "I began thinking about why I was thinking what I was. Then I began thinking about why I was thinking about why I was thinking about what I was." If this sounds abstract, it is.

Formal operational thought is also full of idealism and possibilities. Children often think in concrete ways or in terms of what is real and limited. Adolescents begin to engage in extended speculation about the qualities they desire in themselves and in others. In search of the ideal, adolescents' thoughts may take fantasy flights into future possibilities. It is not unusual for adolescents to become impatient with these newfound ideals, however, and become perplexed over which of many ideal standards to adopt.

At the same time adolescents begin to think more abstractly and idealistically, they begin to think more logically about problems and possible solutions. This hypothetical-deductive reasoning, as Piaget called it, refers to the ability to develop hypotheses, or best hunches, about ways to solve problems, and then to deduce or conclude the best way to solve the problem.

In actuality, not all adolescents engage in formal operational thought, especially in hypothetical-deductive reasoning (Flavell, Miller, & Miller, 2002). Some adolescents and adults remain at Piaget's concrete operational stage. Others may be overwhelmed at times by their idealistic thinking and may not reason very logically.

Adolescent Egocentrism Especially in early adolescence, adolescent thought is egocentric. In the classic formulation, *adolescent egocentrism* involves the belief that others are as preoccupied with the adolescent as he or she is, the belief that one is unique, and the belief that one is invincible (Elkind, 1978). Notice that adolescent egocentrism does not mean feeling "conceited" or superior to others.

Adolescent egocentrism does mean that adolescents perceive others to be noticing and watching them more than actually is the case. They have an *imaginary audience*. Imagine the grade 8 boy who has just finished exercising and believes that everyone will notice the tiny change in his biceps. The same imaginary audience can magnify self-criticism, as, for example, when the same boy believes that everyone else is horrified at the tiny pimple on his face.

In addition to worrying about the imaginary audience, the adolescent also tells a personal fable about his or her *uniqueness*. An example might be the adolescent girl who says, "My mother has no idea about how much pain I'm going through. She has never been hurt like I have. Why did he break up with me?"

The aspect of adolescent egocentrism that can produce the most harm is a sense of *invincibility*, which may lead to risky behaviour like jumping off the roof of a house on a skateboard, to drug use, or to sexually transmitted diseases or adolescent pregnancy. Imagine that an adolescent girl hears that a friend of hers has become pregnant. She may exclaim, "I won't ever let that happen to me," and then goes out and has unprotected sex the next week. Her sense of invincibility causes her to behave in a high-risk manner. It is worth pointing out that not all adolescent high-risk behaviour can be attributed to the feeling of invincibility. Frankenberger (2004) has shown that while feelings of invincibility are involved in adolescent smoking onset, long-time teen smokers are well aware of the risks. On a positive note, the adolescent's sense of invincibility may also lead to courageous efforts to save people's lives in hazardous circumstances, as when someone is drowning or is trapped in a burning car.

"Do you have any idea who I am?"

© The New Yorker Collection 1988. Edward Koren from cartoonbank.com. All rights reserved.

Socioemotional Development in Adolescence

The increase in abstract and idealistic thought during adolescence serves as a foundation for exploring one's identity. Many aspects of socioemotional development—such as relationships with parents, peer interaction and friendships, and cultural and ethnic values—contribute to an adolescent's identity development. Erikson's theory addresses the manner in which adolescents seek their identities.

Erikson's Theory and Identity Development   As you learned in the section on socioemotional development in children, Erik Erikson's life-span theory states that people go through eight psychosocial stages of development. Within the eight stages that Erikson (1968) proposed, his ideas about the formation of identity during adolescence are among his most important contributions to psychology. They changed the way we think about adolescence (Marcia, 2002). Erikson encouraged us to look at adolescents, not just as hormone-driven beings, but as individuals finding out who they are and searching for their niche in the world. He also encouraged us to appreciate the psychological price adolescents can pay when they encounter difficulties in their quest (Crawford & others, 2004).

Erikson's theory characterizes the main concern of the fifth stage of socioemotional development as **identity versus identity confusion**. In seeking an identity, adolescents face the challenges of finding out who they are, what they are all about, and where they are going in life. Adolescents are confronted with many new roles and adult statuses—from the vocational to the romantic. If they do not adequately explore their identities during this stage, they emerge with a sense of confusion about who they are. Therefore, Erikson argues, parents should allow adolescents to explore many different roles and paths within a particular role and not push an identity on them.

Erikson described adolescence as a moratorium, a temporal and psychological gap between the security of childhood and the autonomy of adulthood. Adolescents who use the moratorium to explore alternatives can reach some resolution of the identity crisis and emerge with a new sense of self that is both refreshing and acceptable; those who do not successfully resolve the crisis become confused, suffering what Erikson calls identity confusion. This confusion is expressed in one of two ways: Either individuals withdraw, isolating themselves from peers and family, or they lose themselves in the crowd.

Erikson noted that in North American culture, adolescents want to decide freely for themselves such matters as what careers they will pursue, whether they will go to college or university, and whether they will marry. In other words, they want to free themselves from the control of their parents and other adults and make their own choices. At the same time, many deeply fear making the wrong decisions and failing. In some cases the problem may be simply that adolescents have not yet realized their own

identity versus identity confusion Erikson's fifth psychological stage in which adolescents face the challenge of finding out who they are, what they are all about, and where they are going in life.

Michelle Chin, age 16, reflecting on her identity, commented, "Parents do not understand that teenagers need to find out who they are, which means a lot of experimenting, a lot of mood swings, a lot of emotions and awkwardness. Like any teenager, I am facing an identity crisis. I am still trying to figure out whether I am a Chinese North American or a North American with Asian eyes."

growing cognitive abilities. One strength that equips them to effectively pursue their identities is that their thoughts have become more abstract and logical, and they are able to reason in increasingly sophisticated ways.

With such high stakes, perhaps it is no accident that more and more young people are extending their emerging adulthood, as we saw at the beginning of this chapter. Some may even be trying to avoid it altogether. One recent study of "street kids" in Montreal found that they do not have a meaningful set of longer-term goals, do not trust authorities, and do not have stable friendships (Taylor & others, 2004). It is tempting to describe these young adults as suffering from extreme identity diffusion, a concept we will explore in the next section.

Identity Status   Building on Erikson's ideas, James Marcia of Simon Fraser University proposed the concept of *identity status* to describe a person's position in the development of an identity (Marcia, 1980, 2002). In his view, two dimensions of identity are important. *Exploration* refers to a person's exploring various options for a career and for personal values. *Commitment* involves making a decision about which identity path to follow and making a personal investment in attaining that identity.

Various combinations of exploration and commitment give rise to one of four identity statuses (see figure 4.21):

- *Identity diffusion.* A person has not yet explored meaningful alternatives and also has not made a commitment. Many young adolescents have a diffuse identity status. They have not yet begun to explore different career options and personal values.
- *Identity foreclosure.* A person makes a commitment to an identity before adequately exploring various options. For example, an adolescent might say that she wants to be a doctor because that is what her parents want her to be, rather than exploring career options and then deciding on her own to be a doctor.
- *Identity moratorium.* A person is exploring alternative paths but has not yet made a commitment. Many university students are in a moratorium status with regard to a major field of study or a career. Another way to describe the period of emerging adulthood is as an extended period of identity moratorium.
- *Identity achievement.* A person has explored alternative paths and made a commitment. For example, an individual might have examined a number of careers over an extended period of time and finally decided to pursue one wholeheartedly.

Ethnic Identity   In a multicultural society like Canada's, developing an identity in adolescence can be especially challenging for individuals from ethnic minority groups (Day, 2000; Kymlicka, 1998; D. M. Taylor, 2002). For these individuals, the already daunting challenge of identity formation is complicated by the challenge of biculturalism—identifying in some ways with their ethnic minority group, in other ways with the majority culture, whether English or French.

As they mature cognitively, many adolescents become acutely aware of the evaluation of their ethnic group by the majority culture. According to McGill psychologist Donald Taylor, when the minority ethnic group is not valued by the majority culture, the collective identity of the minority group is damaged (Taylor, 1997). As a result, the

Position on Occupation and Ideology	Identity Status			
	Identity diffusion	Identity foreclosure	Identity moratorium	Identity achievement
Exploration	Absent	Absent	Present	Present
Commitment	Absent	Present	Absent	Present

FIGURE 4.21   **Marcia's Four Statuses of Identity**

Jillian Roberts, shown here with her children, teaches counsellors to counsel HIV-positive students with dignity, responsible caring, integrity, and responsibility to society.

ability of minority group adolescents to incorporate their minority group values in their identities is compromised. The result is *acculturative stress* (see chapter 15) that pushes them toward *assimilation*, when individuals relinquish their ethnic cultural identity, and away from *integration*, when individuals combine elements of both the majority culture and the ethnic minority culture (Berry, 1980).

Unfortunately, if adolescents from ethnic minority groups do reject their ethnic identities in favour of assimilating into the majority culture, they may face additional difficulties. For example, Kevin Wong, of Brandon University, found that Chinese Canadians are less likely to become delinquents if they adhere to Chinese culture (Wong, 1999) or become bilingual (Wong, 2001) than if they assimilate to North American values.

At-Risk Youth

Although adolescence is best viewed positively as a time of decision-making and commitment rather than a time of crisis and pathology, for a large subset of adolescents it is a time of risk. This risk limits the likelihood that they will become productive adults.

Four key aspects of risk are delinquency, substance abuse, unprotected sex and adolescent pregnancy (Maticka-Tyndale, 2001), and school-related problems (Dryfoos, 1990). Estimates are that as many as 25 percent of adolescents have three or more of these problems. Given the far-reaching effects of at-risk behaviour by adolescents, a number of programs for helping individuals navigate adolescence have been established. Some are more effective than others. In her analysis, Joy Dryfoos (1990) found that the greatest success has come from individualized attention and community-wide programs.

In successful individualized programs, at-risk youths are paired with responsible adults who pay attention to the adolescents' specific needs. For example, in substance abuse programs, a student-assistance counsellor might be available full time for individual counselling. In delinquency prevention, a family worker might give intensive support to a predelinquent and the family so that they will make the necessary changes to avoid repeated delinquent acts.

School counsellors can play an important role in detecting which students need individualized psychological services and intervention. Jillian Roberts, of the University of Victoria, focuses on the counselling of children and families with chronic and/or terminal illnesses such HIV/AIDS (Roberts, 2000). She helps train counsellors to work with HIV-positive children (Roberts & Marshall, 2001). Her work includes adapting the Canadian Psychological Association Guidelines for Non-Discriminatory Practice (Roberts & others, 2000). She stresses respect for the dignity of persons, responsible caring, integrity in relationships, and responsibility to society.

The basic concept of community-wide programs is that improving the lives of at-risk youth requires a number of interrelated programs and services (O'Donnell & others, 1999). For example, a substance abuse program might feature community-wide health promotion through local media and community events in conjunction with a substance abuse prevention curriculum in the schools. A neighbourhood development program in which local residents cooperate with schools, police, courts, gang leaders, and the media might address delinquency problems. The goal, as with individualized attention, is to ensure that the minority of adolescents who do experience a rocky youth have a better chance of developing into successful, productive adults.

Positive Psychology and Adolescents

Too often adolescents have been stereotyped as abnormal and deviant. For example, Freud described adolescents as sexually driven and conflicted. Young people of every generation have seemed radical, unnerving, and different to adults—different in how they look, how they behave, and even the music they enjoy.

However, thinking of adolescence as a time of rebellion, crisis, pathology, and deviation does little good and can do considerable disservice to adolescents. It is far more accurate to view adolescence as a time of evaluation, a time of decision making, and a time of commitment as young people carve out their place in the world (Santrock, 2005b). It is an enormous error to confuse the adolescent's enthusiasm for trying on new identities and enjoying moderate amounts of outrageous behaviour with hostility toward parents and society. Searching for an identity is a time-honoured way in which adolescents move toward accepting, rather than rejecting, parental and societal values.

How competent adolescents will eventually become often depends on their access to legitimate opportunities for growth, such as a quality education, community and societal support for achievement and involvement, and access to good jobs. Especially important in adolescents' development is long-term support from adults who deeply care about them.

As evidence that the majority of adolescents develop more positively than is commonly believed, consider the research study conducted by Daniel Offer and his colleagues (1988). They sampled the self-images of adolescents around the world—in Australia, Bangladesh, Hungary, Israel, Italy, Japan, Taiwan, Turkey, the United States, and West Germany. About three of every four of these adolescents had healthy self-images. Most were happy, enjoyed life, and believed they had the ability to cope effectively with stress. They valued school and work.

But what about the one in four adolescents who did not have positive self-images? What might be done to help them negotiate adolescence? According to Larson (2000), adolescents need more opportunities to develop the capacity for initiative, defined as becoming self-motivated and expending effort to reach challenging goals. Too often adolescents find themselves bored with life. To counter this boredom and help adolescents develop more initiative, Mahoney, Larson & Eccles (2005) recommend structured voluntary activities such as sports, the arts, and participation in organizations.

For all adolescents and young adults, developing a positive identity is an important life theme. To further explore your development of a positive identity, see the Personal Reflections box.

Developing a Positive Identity

Following are some questions to help you think about developing a positive identity:

- *Do you think your identity is simple or complex?*

Be aware that your identity is complex and takes a long time to develop. Your identity has many components. One of your main identity tasks is to integrate all these parts into a meaningful whole. Your identity does not spring forth in a sudden burst of insight. It is achieved in bits and pieces over your lifetime. What are some of the bits and pieces of your identity development?

- *How important are your college or university years in developing your adult identity?*

Make the most of your college or university years. For many people, these years are an important time for identity development. College and university by their very nature encourage exploration and exposure to a wide variety of ideas and values. Your views will likely be challenged by instructors and classmates, which may motivate you to change some aspects of your identity. Can you think of some examples where this has happened to you? What was the outcome?

- *Is your current identity your own or is it your parents'?*

Some college and university students have foreclosed on an identity without adequately considering alternatives. Identity foreclosure occurs especially when individuals accept their parents' views without deeply questioning whether they want to be just like their parents. Individuals might come to an identity similar to that of their parents, but while evaluating different paths, a more suitable identity may be discovered. Have you adequately developed an identity that is your own?

- *Will your identity change?*

Expect your identity to change. Even people who think they have achieved the identity they want could find it changing in the future. Your world will change and you will change, especially if you explore new opportunities and face new challenges. What do you expect your identity to be like after you finish college or university? Different from what it is now? The same?

> ## reflect and review

3 **Identify the most important changes that occur in adolescence.**

- Discuss the nature of puberty.
- Describe the key aspects of cognitive development during adolescence.
- Explain these aspects of adolescent socioemotional development: identity development and
- Discuss risk factors for youths.
- Explore the contribution of positive psychology to our thinking about adolescent development.

Are Marcia's identity statuses useful to you in thinking about your own identity development? To explore this question, return to figure 4.22 and evaluate your levels of exploration and commitment in regard to career and personal values. Into which identity status would you place yourself?

---

④ ADULT DEVELOPMENT AND AGING

| — | Physical Development in Adulthood | — | Cognitive Development in Adulthood | — | Socioemotional Development in Adulthood | — | Positive Psychology and Aging | — | Death and Dying |

What are the main physical, cognitive, and socioemotional changes in adults?

Development does not end with adolescence. It continues throughout the roughly 50 (and often more) years of adulthood. Developmental psychologists identify three approximate periods in adult development: early adulthood (20s and 30s), middle adulthood (40s and 50s), and late adulthood (60s until death). Each phase features some distinctive physical, cognitive, and socioemotional changes.

What are some physical changes that women go through as they age?

Physical Development in Adulthood

Singer-actress Bette Midler said that after 30 a body has a mind of its own. A line in a Leonard Cohen song goes "I ache in the places where I used to play." How do we age physically as we go through the adult years?

Physical Changes in Early Adulthood Most adults reach their peak physical development during their 20s and are also their healthiest then. For athletes—not only at the Olympic level but also the average athlete—performance peaks in the 20s, especially for strength and speed events such as weight lifting and the 100-metre dash (Schultz & Curnow, 1988). The main exceptions are female gymnasts and swimmers, who often peak in adolescence, and marathon runners, who tend to peak in their late 30s.

Unfortunately, early adulthood is also when many skills begin to decline. The decline in strength and speed is often noticeable in the 30s.

Perhaps because of their robust overall health and physical skills, young adults rarely recognize that bad eating habits, heavy drinking, and smoking in early adulthood can impair their health as they age. Despite warnings on packages and in advertisements that cigarettes are hazardous to health, individuals actually increase their use of cigarettes as they enter early adulthood (Johnston, Bachman, & O'Malley, 1989). They also increase their use of alcohol, marijuana, amphetamines, barbiturates, and hallucinogens.

A special concern is heavy drinking by high school and university students (Aboud & Dennis, 1998). According to Schulenberg & Maggs (2002), heavy drinking is associated with the stresses of making the transition from adolescence to adulthood. In one Canadian study, 52 percent of males and 35 percent of females aged 15 to 19 said they had engaged in binge drinking (drinking five or more drinks in a row) at least once in the previous year (Galambos & Tilton-Weaver, 1998). In a U.S. study, 40 percent of college students admitted binge drinking at least once a week in the two weeks before they were surveyed (Wechsler, 2000). In one study of 140 colleges, binge drinking was associated with class absences, physical injuries, troubles with police, and unprotected sex (Wechsler & others, 1994).

Fortunately, by the time individuals reach their mid-20s, many have reduced their use of alcohol and drugs, according to a study of 33,000 individuals from high school through their mid-20s (Bachman, 1997). This study also found that:

- University students drank more than their counterparts who ended their education after high school.
- Those who did not go to university were more likely to smoke.
- Single adults used marijuana more than married adults.
- Drinking was heaviest among single and divorced adults. Becoming engaged, married, or remarried quickly reduced alcohol use.

As you can see, living arrangements and marital status are key factors in alcohol and drug use rates during a person's 20s.

Physical Changes in Middle Adulthood Middle adulthood is generally a healthy time when most physical changes do not cause any disability (Lachman, 2004). One of the most visible physical changes in middle adulthood is appearance. By the 40s or 50s, the skin begins to wrinkle and sag because of a loss of fat and collagen in underlying tissues. Small, localized areas of pigmentation in the skin produce age spots, especially in areas exposed to sunlight, such as the hands and face. Hair becomes thinner and greyer due to a lower replacement rate and a decline in melanin production.

Individuals actually begin to lose height in middle age, and many gain weight. Adults lose about a centimetre of height per decade beginning in their 40s (Memmler & others, 1995). Fat generally accounts for about 10 percent of body weight in adolescence but for 20 percent or more in middle age.

Perhaps because the signs of aging are all too visible to us, we become more acutely concerned about our health in our 40s. In fact, we do experience a general decline in physical fitness throughout middle adulthood and some deterioration in health. The three greatest health concerns at this age are heart disease, cancer, and weight. Cancer related to smoking often surfaces in middle adulthood.

Because North American culture values a youthful appearance, the physical deterioration that takes place in middle adulthood—greying hair, wrinkling skin, and a sagging body—can be difficult to handle. Many middle-aged adults dye their hair and join weight reduction programs; some even undergo cosmetic surgery to look young.

For women, entering middle age also means that menopause will soon occur. Usually in the late 40s or early 50s a woman's menstrual periods cease completely. The median age at which women have their last period is 50-52, but there is also wide variability (Rossi, 2004).

With menopause comes a dramatic decline in the production of estrogen by the ovaries. Estrogen decline produces some uncomfortable symptoms in some menopausal women, such as hot flashes (sudden brief flushing of the skin and a feeling of elevated body temperature), nausea, fatigue, and rapid heartbeat. Some menopausal women report depression and irritability, but in some instances these feelings are related to other circumstances in their lives, such as becoming divorced, losing a job, or caring for a sick parent (Dickson, 1990). Research reveals that menopause does not produce psychological or physical problems for most women (Avis, 1999).

Although menopause is not the negative experience for most women that it was once thought to be, the loss of fertility is an important marker for women: Its approach means that they have to make final decisions about having children (Sommer, 2002). Women in their 30s who have not had children sometimes speak about being "up against the biological clock" because they cannot postpone the decision much longer.

Although estrogen replacement therapy was popular for a number of years it has recently been increasingly called into question (Stefanick, 1999; Marriott & Wenk, 2004). According to the Canadian Task Force on Preventive Health Care (Wathen & others, 2004),

- Given the balance of harms and benefits, the Canadian Task Force on Preventive Health Care recommends against the use of combined estrogen–progestin therapy and estrogen-only therapy for the primary prevention of chronic diseases in menopausal women.
- For women who wish to alleviate menopausal symptoms using hormone replacement therapy (HRT), a discussion between the woman and her physician about the potential benefits and risks of HRT is warranted.

Do men go through anything like the menopause that women experience? Men do experience *andropause*, as sex-related hormones decline in their 50s and 60s, but they are usually not as precipitous as women's estrogen decline (King, 2005).

Physical Changes in Late Adulthood The concept of a period called "late adulthood" is a recent one: Until the twentieth century, most individuals died before they were 65. Many societies around the world have become less youthful, however, and so need to develop a better understanding of the later years of life (Whitbourne, 2005; Masoro & Austad, 2001).

Developmentalists distinguish between life span and life expectancy. The term *life span* is used to describe the upper boundary of a species' life, the maximum number of years an individual can expect to live. The maximum number of years human beings can live is about 120. As can be seen in figure 4.22, *Homo sapiens* is believed to have one of the longest life spans, if not the longest.

The term *life expectancy* is used to describe the number of years that the average person born in a particular year will probably live. Improvements in medicine, nutrition, exercise, and lifestyle have increased our life expectancy 30 additional years since 1900 (see figure 4.23). The life expectancy of individuals born today in Canada is 79.7 years—82.1 for women, 77.2 for men (Statistics Canada, 2002a). One in three women born today is expected to live to be 100 or more. The world's population of individuals

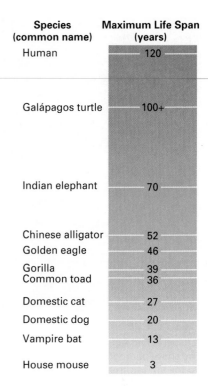

FIGURE 4.22

Maximum Recorded Life Spans of Various Species

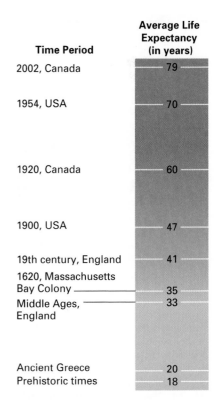

FIGURE 4.23

Human Life Expectancy at Birth from Prehistoric to Contemporary Times

FIGURE 4.24
Telomeres and Aging
The above photograph shows telomeres lighting up the tips of chromosomes.

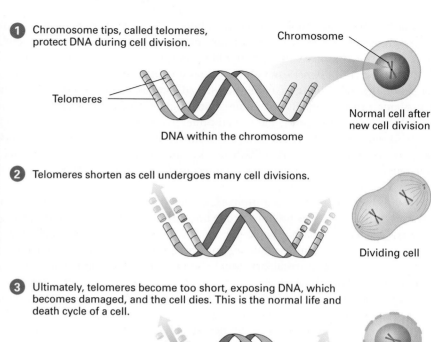

1 Chromosome tips, called telomeres, protect DNA during cell division.

Chromosome

Telomeres

DNA within the chromosome

Normal cell after new cell division

2 Telomeres shorten as cell undergoes many cell divisions.

Dividing cell

3 Ultimately, telomeres become too short, exposing DNA, which becomes damaged, and the cell dies. This is the normal life and death cycle of a cell.

Cell death

Frenchwoman Jeanne Louise Calumet pushed the upper boundary of the human life span, dying in 1997 at the age of 122. Asked on her 120th birthday about the kind of future she expected, Calumet replied, "A very short one." Greater ages have been claimed, but scientists say that the human life span is approximately 120 years of age. However, as genetic engineering continues to make progress, the possibility of altering cellular functioning to increase the human life span is raised. Some biologists even have brought up the possibility that in the future humans might live 400 years! *What kinds of ethical issues are involved in genetically engineering cellular functioning to increase the human life span?*

65 years and older doubled from 1950 to 1990, and the fastest growing segment of the population is 85 years and older.

Although life expectancy has increased dramatically, life span does not seem to have increased since the beginning of recorded history. Even if we are remarkably healthy through our adult lives, we begin to age at some point.

Biological Theories of Aging Many biological theories of aging have been proposed, but two that especially merit attention are the cellular-clock theory and the free-radical theory. Both of these theories look within the body's cells for causes of aging. The *cellular-clock theory* is Leonard Hayflick's (1997) view that cells can divide a maximum of about 100 times and that, as we age, our cells become less capable of dividing. Hayflick found that cells extracted from adults in their 50s to 70s had divided fewer than 100 times. The total number of cell divisions was roughly related to the age of the individual. Based on the way cells divide, Hayflick places the upper limit of the human life span at about 120 years.

In the past decade, scientists have tried to explain why cells lose their ability to divide (Shay & Wright, 2000). The answer may lie at the tips of chromosomes. Each time a cell divides, the *telomeres* that protect the ends of chromosomes become shorter and shorter (see figure 4.24). After about 100 replications, the telomeres are dramatically reduced, and the cell can no longer reproduce. In one recent study, age-related telomere erosion was linked with an inability to recover from stress and an increase in cancer (Rudolf & others, 1999).

Another biological theory of aging is the *free-radical theory*, which states that people age because unstable oxygen molecules known as "free radicals" are produced inside their cells. The damage done by free radicals may lead to a range of disorders, including cancer and arthritis. These molecules create oxidative stress, damaging DNA and other cellular structures (Knight, 2000; Skinner & Turker, 2005). According to Saretzki & von Zglinicki (2002), one way free radicals may affect aging is by prematurely shortening the telomeres.

Physical Changes and Health Even without the development of disease, the aging process produces many physical changes. Changes in physical appearance become more pronounced in older adults, including wrinkles and aging spots. Whereas weight often increases in middle age, it frequently declines after the age of 60 because of muscle loss. Blood pressure often rises in older adults but can be treated by exercise and/or drugs.

Normal aging involves some bone tissue loss from the skeleton, and in some instances the loss can be severe, as in osteoporosis (Whitbourne, 2005). Almost two-thirds of women over 60 are affected to some degree by osteoporosis. Estrogen replacement therapy can reduce bone loss for women, and a program of weight lifting can help (Nelson & others, 1994).

Chronic diseases—characterized by a slow onset and long duration—are rare in early adulthood, increase in middle adulthood, and become more common in late adulthood. The most common chronic disorder in late adulthood is arthritis; the second most common is hypertension (high blood pressure).

This list of physical deteriorations may sound rather dismal. However, a substantial portion of individuals even over the age of 85 are still robust and active. Consider Sadie Halperin, who at age 85 had been working out for 11 months at a rehabilitation centre for the aged, lifting weights and riding a stationary bicycle. She said that before she started working out, almost everything she did—shopping, cooking, walking—was a major struggle. She felt wobbly and had to hold on to a wall when she walked. After starting to exercise. she walked down the centre of the hallways and reported that she felt great. Sadie's exercise routine increased her muscle strength and helped her to battle osteoporosis by slowing the calcium loss in her bones (Ubell, 1992). Researchers continue to document how effective exercise is in slowing the aging process and helping older adults function in society (Burke & others, 2001).

Eighty-five-year-old Sadie Halperin doubled her strength in exercise after just 11 months. Before developing an exercise routine, she felt wobbly and often had to hold on to a wall when she walked. Now she walks down the middle of hallways and says she feels wonderful.

Another important factor in the health of older adults is their sense of control over their lives. In a classic experimental study, Judith Rodin and Ellen Langer (1977) found that the sense of control, a cognitive factor, was linked not only with the health of nursing home residents but even with their survival. The researchers encouraged one group of elderly nursing home residents to make more day-to-day choices and thus to feel more responsible and have more control over their lives. They were allowed to decide on such matters as what they ate, when visitors could come, what movies to see, and who could come to their rooms. A similar group in the same nursing home was told by the administrator how caring the nursing home was and how much the staff wanted to help. However, they were given no opportunities to be responsible and make their own decisions. Eighteen months later, the nursing home residents who were given responsibility and control were more alert, active, and happier, and they were likelier to still be alive than residents who were encouraged to be dependent on the nursing staff. Perceived control and responsibility for oneself, then, may be literally a matter of life or death. Researchers continue to document the importance of perceived control over their world in the health and well-being of older adults (Lachman & Firth, 2004; DeVellis & DeVellis, 2001).

The Brain and Alzheimer's Disease Just as the aging body has been found to have a greater capacity for renewal than previously believed, so has the aging brain (Gage, 2004). For decades, scientists believed that no new brain cells are generated past the early childhood years. However, as mentioned in chapter 3, researchers recently discovered that adults can grow new brain cells throughout their lives (Gould & others, 1999). In one study, the growth of dendrites (the receiving, branching part of the neuron or nerve cell) continued through the 70s, although no new dendritic growth was discovered in people in their 90s (Coleman, 1986).

Even in late adulthood, the brain has remarkable repair capability. Stanley Rapaport (1994), chief of the neurosciences laboratory at the U.S. National Institute of Aging, compared the brains of younger and older adults when they were engaged in the same tasks. The older adults' brains literally rewired themselves to compensate for losses. If one neuron was not up to the job, neighbouring neurons helped to pick up the slack. Rapaport concluded that as brains age, they can actually shift responsibilities for a given task from one region to another.

Alzheimer's disease—a progressive, irreversible brain disorder that is characterized by gradual deterioration of memory, reasoning, language, and eventually physical

Canadian painter Joyce Wieland poses with a self-portrait, painted to "find out what I look like." She died of Alzheimer's in Toronto in 1998.

FIGURE 4.25

Two Brains: Normal Aging and Alzheimer's Disease
(Left) A slice of a normally aging brain. (Right) A slice of a brain ravaged by Alzheimer's disease. Notice the deterioration and shrinking in the Alzheimer's diseased brain.

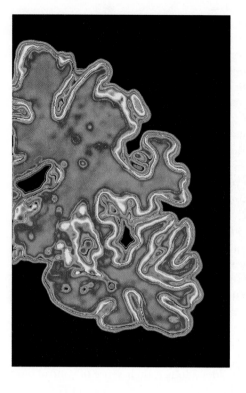
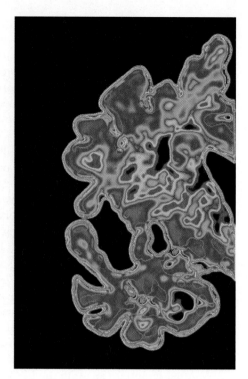

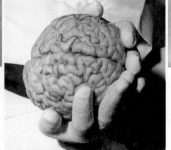

FIGURE 4.26

The Brains of the Mankato Nuns
At 90 years old, nun study participant Sister Rosella Kreuzer, SSND, remains an active, contributing member of her community of sisters. Sister Rosella designed the nun study logo, *That You May Have Life to the Full. Inset:* A neuroscientist holds a brain donated by one of the Mankato nun study participants.

functioning—does not present such encouraging prospects (Lindsay & Anderson, 2003). About 300,000 Canadians have this disease, a number that is expected to rise to 500,000 by 2031 as the Canadian population ages. Alzheimer's disease currently afflicts 1 in 13 people older than 65, and about 1 in 3 of those older than 85.

As Alzheimer's disease progresses, the brain deteriorates and shrinks (Salmon, 2000). Figure 4.25 strikingly contrasts the brain of a normal aging individual with the brain of an individual who has Alzheimer's disease. Among the main characteristics of Alzheimer's disease are the increasing number of tangles (tied bundles of proteins that impair the function of neurons) and plaques (deposits that accumulate in the brain's blood vessels). The formation of tangles and plaques is a normal part of aging, but it is far more pronounced in Alzheimer's disease.

Alzheimer's disease also involves a deficiency in the important brain messenger chemical acetylcholine, which you read about in chapter 3 (Hodges, 2000). This neurotransmitter plays an important role in memory. The drugs currently used to treat Alzheimer's disease are cholinesterase inhibitors, which work by blocking the enzymes that ordinarily cut acetylcholine apart. However, such drugs do not prevent the brain from continuing to deteriorate in Alzheimer's patients.

Research on the aging brain does give cause for hope. An intriguing ongoing study involves nearly 700 nuns in a convent in Mankato, Minnesota (Snowden, 1997, 2001; see figure 4.26). The nuns are the largest group of brain donors in the world. By examining the nuns' donated brains, as well as others, neuroscientists have documented the remarkable ability of the aging brain to grow and change. Even the oldest Mankato nuns lead intellectually challenging lives, and neuroscientists believe that stimulating mental activities increase dendritic branching. The researchers are also intrigued to find that the nuns show almost no signs of Alzheimer's disease. Indeed, researchers have consistently found support for the "use it or lose it" concept: The cognitive skills of older adults benefit considerably when they engage in challenging intellectual activities (Schaie & Willis, 2001).

Cognitive Development in Adulthood

Earlier in the chapter, you learned that considerable changes take place in children's cognitive development. What kinds of cognitive changes occur in adults?

Cognition in Early Adulthood Piaget believed that formal operational thought is the highest level of thinking, and he argued that no new qualitative changes in cognition take place in adulthood (but see Commons & Richards, 2003). He didn't believe that a person with a Ph.D. in physics thinks any differently than a young adolescent who has reached the stage of formal operational thought. The only difference is that the physicist has more knowledge in a specific scientific domain. The physicist and the young adolescent both use logical thought to develop alternatives for solving a problem and to deduce a solution from the options.

Piaget was right about some adolescents and some adults—but not about all of them. As you learned earlier, some adolescents are not formal operational thinkers, and many adults never reach that stage either.

Yet some experts on cognitive development argue that the typical idealism of Piaget's formal operational stage is replaced in young adulthood by more realistic, pragmatic thinking (Labouvie-Vief, 1986). Also, adolescents tend to think in absolute terms—things are either all this way or that way. As they go through the college and university years, individuals often begin to think in more relative and reflective ways. In sum, for the most part, intellectual skills are strong in early adulthood (Berg, 2000). Do they begin to decline in middle age?

Cognition in Middle Adulthood In a now-classic formulation, John Horn proposed that some intellectual abilities begin to decline in middle age, whereas others increase (Horn & Donaldson, 1980). He argued that **crystallized intelligence**, an individual's accumulated information and verbal skills, increases in middle adulthood. By contrast, **fluid intelligence**, one's ability to reason abstractly, begins to decline in middle adulthood (see figure 4.27).

Horn's view is based on data he collected in a *cross-sectional study*, which assesses a number of people all at one point in time. A cross-sectional study, for example, might assess the intelligence of six hundred 40-, 50-, and 60-year-olds in a single evaluation, say in September 2005. In a cross-sectional study, differences on intelligence tests might be due to *cohort effects*, the effects of living through a certain historical time in a certain culture, rather than to age. The 40-year-olds and the 60-year-olds were born in different eras, which offered different economic, educational, and health opportunities. For example, as the 60-year-olds grew up, they likely had fewer educational opportunities than the 40-year-olds had, which may influence their performance on intelligence tests.

In contrast, a *longitudinal study* assesses the same participants over a lengthy period. A longitudinal study of intelligence in middle adulthood might consist of giving the same intelligence test to the same individuals over a 20-year time span, when they are 40, 50, and 60 years of age. As discussed next, whether data on intelligence are collected cross-sectionally or longitudinally can make a difference in the results.

K. Warner Schaie (1983, 1996, 2005) is conducting the Seattle Longitudinal Study, an extensive and long-term study of intellectual abilities in adulthood. Five hundred individuals were initially tested in 1956. Individuals are retested and new waves of participants are added every seven years. Data are now available for 1956: 1963, 1970, 1977, 1984, 1991, and 1998. The main abilities tested by Schaie are

- Vocabulary (ability to encode and understand ideas expressed in words)
- Verbal memory (ability to encode and recall meaningful language units, such as a list of words)
- Number (ability to perform simple mathematical computations such as addition, subtraction, and multiplication)
- Spatial orientation (ability to visualize and mentally rotate stimuli in two- and three-dimensional space)

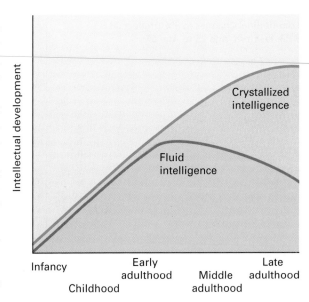

FIGURE 4.27

Fluid and Crystallized Intellectual Development Across the Life Span
According to Horn, crystallized intelligence (based on cumulative learning experiences) increases throughout the life span, but fluid intelligence (the ability to perceive and manipulate information) steadily declines from middle adulthood.

crystallized intelligence An individual's accumulated information and verbal skills.

fluid intelligence One's ability to reason abstractly.

FIGURE 4.28

Longitudinal Changes in Six Intellectual Abilities from Age 25 to Age 67

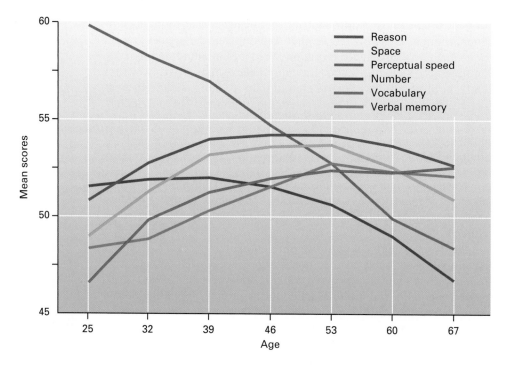

FIGURE 4.29

Cross-Sectional and Longitudinal Comparisons of Reasoning Ability Across the Adulthood Years
In Schaie's most recent research, the cross-sectional approach revealed declining scores with age; the longitudinal approach showed a slight rise of scores in middle adulthood and only a slight decline beginning in the early part of late adulthood.

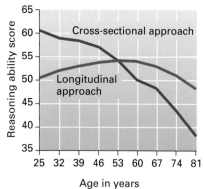

- Inductive reasoning (ability to recognize and understand patterns and relationships in a problem and use this understanding to solve other instances of the problem)
- Perceptual speed (ability to quickly and accurately make simple discriminations in visual stimuli)

As shown in figure 4.28, the highest level of functioning for four of the six intellectual abilities—vocabulary, verbal memory, inductive reasoning, and spatial orientation—occurred in middle adulthood (Schaie & Willis, 2001; Willis & Schaie, 1999). Only two of the six abilities—numerical ability and perceptual speed—declined in middle age. Perceptual speed showed the earliest decline, beginning in early adulthood.

Those are encouraging results, but should we accept them uncritically? When Schaie (1994) assessed intellectual skills both cross-sectionally and longitudinally, he found more decline in middle age in the cross-sectional assessment. For example, as shown in figure 4.29, when he assessed inductive reasoning longitudinally, it increased until the end of middle adulthood, at which point it began a slight decline. By contrast, when he assessed it cross-sectionally, inductive reasoning was already declining at the beginning of middle adulthood.

Interestingly, Schaie found middle adulthood to be a time of peak performance for some aspects of both crystallized intelligence (vocabulary) and fluid intelligence (spatial orientation and inductive reasoning). John Horn, as you may recall, found that fluid intelligence peaks in early adulthood and crystallized intelligence in middle age. Schaie concluded, based on the longitudinal data he has collected so far, that middle adulthood, not early adulthood, is when many people reach their peak for many intellectual skills (Schaie, 2005).

Cognition in Late Adulthood At age 74, one of Canada's most prominent scholars, Northrop Frye, was awarded the Governor General's Literary Award for Non-Fiction for his book *Northrop Frye on Shakespeare*. At age 76, Anna Mary Robertson, better known as Grandma Moses, took up painting and became internationally famous. When Pablo Casals reached 95 years of age, a reporter called him the greatest cellist who ever lived but wondered why he still practised six hours a day. Casals replied, "Because I feel like I am making progress."

Claims about intellectual functioning through the late adult years are provocative. Many contemporary psychologists believe that, as with middle adulthood, some dimensions of intelligence decline in late adulthood, whereas others are maintained or may even increase (Salthouse, 2004; Dixon, Bäckman, & Nilsson, L.-G., 2004).

One of the most consistent findings is that, when speed of processing information is involved, older adults do more poorly than their younger counterparts (figure 4.30; Craik & Salthouse, 2000; Salthouse, 2004; Dixon, & others, 2003). This decline in speed of processing is apparent in middle-aged adults and becomes more pronounced in older adults.

One common stereotype is that older adults tend to do more poorly than younger adults in many areas of memory (Backman, Small, & Wahlin, 2001). A large-scale Canadian longitudinal study of cognitive aging has examined this stereotype in some detail. Roger Dixon, of the University of Alberta and the University of Victoria, and his colleagues, have been conducting the Victoria Longitudinal Study for 15 years (Dixon & de Frias, 2004). Older adults have poorer episodic memories; they do not remember the "where" and "when" of life's happenings as well as younger adults (Tulving, 2000; see chapter 8). However, using a longitudinal, rather than cross-sectional design, Dixon & his colleagues found only modest declines as a function of age (Dixon & others, 2004). In contrast, semantic memory, a person's general knowledge of the world, showed little or no decline with age (Cabeza, Nyberg & Park, 2005). Similarly although older adults may have difficulty remembering the directions to the home of a new acquaintance (a task requiring new learning), they do not forget how to drive a car (a well-established motor pattern), (Hoyer, Rybash & Roodin, 2004). Finally, in the important area of memory in which individuals manipulate and assemble information to solve problems and make decisions, decline occurs in older adults (Zelazo, Craik, & Booth, 2004; Salthouse, 2000, 2004).

However, some aspects of cognition might actually improve with age. One candidate is **wisdom**, expert knowledge about the practical aspects of life (Kramer, 2003). Wisdom may increase with age because of the build-up of life experiences we have. However, not every older person has wisdom (Baltes, Lindenberger, & Staudinger, 1998; Baltes & Kunzmann, 2003). Individual variations characterize all aspects of our cognitive lives (Belsky, 1999).

Do we all face the prospect, then, of gradually becoming less competent intellectually? Not necessarily, as the study of the Mankato nuns suggests. Even for those aspects of cognitive aging that decline, such as memory, educating and training older adults can improve their cognitive skills (Park, Nisbett, & Hedden, 1999; Schaie & Willis, 2001). Researchers have demonstrated that training older adults to use certain strategies can even improve their memories (Baltes, 1993; Willis & Schaie, 1994). However, many experts on aging believe that older adults are less able to change and adapt than younger adults and thus are limited in how much they can improve their cognitive skills (Baltes, 2000).

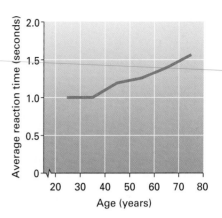

FIGURE 4.30

The Relation of Age to Reaction Time
In one study, the average reaction time began to slow in the 40s and this decline accelerated in the 60s and 70s (Salthouse, 1984). The task used to assess reaction time required individuals to match numbers with symbols on a computer screen.

Older adults might not be as quick with their thoughts as younger adults, but wisdom may be an entirely different matter. This woman shares the wisdom of her experiences with a classroom of children.

Socioemotional Development in Adulthood

As both Sigmund Freud and the nineteenth-century Russian novelist Leo Tolstoy observed, adulthood's two most important themes are work and love. The study of socioemotional development in the adult years largely bears them out. Psychologists have proposed different theories about adult socioemotional development. Most theories address themes of work and love, career and intimacy. But before examining what psychologists have learned about these themes, let's return to Erikson's stage theory of life-span development.

Erikson's Adult Stages   Recall that Erikson's eight stages of the human life span include one stage for early adulthood, one for middle adulthood, and one for late adulthood (Marcia, 2002). Erikson (1968) said that individuals enter his sixth stage of *intimacy*

wisdom Expert knowledge about the practical aspects of life.

"Your son has made a career choice, Mildred. He's going to win the lottery and travel a lot."

© 1985; Reprinted courtesy of Bunny Hoest.

Desired Skills	
Oral communication skills	4.7
Interpersonal skills	4.6
Analytical skills	4.5
Teamwork skills	4.4
Flexibility	4.3
Leadership skills	4.2
Proficiency in field of study	4.2
Written communication skills	4.2
Computer skills	4.1

FIGURE 4.31

Desired Skills of an Ideal Job Candidate As Described by Employers

versus isolation during early adulthood. At this time, people face the developmental task of either forming intimate relationships with others or becoming socially isolated. Erikson describes intimacy as both finding oneself and losing oneself in another. If the young adult develops healthy friendships and an intimate close relationship with a partner, intimacy will likely be achieved.

Generativity versus stagnation, Erikson's seventh stage, occurs in middle adulthood. A main concern in middle adulthood is to assist and guide the younger generation in developing and leading useful lives—this is what Erikson means by generativity (Pratt & others, 2001; de St Aubin, McAdams, & Kim, 2004). The feeling of having done nothing to help the next generation is stagnation.

Integrity versus despair, Erikson's eighth stage, occurs in late adulthood. In the later years of life, we look back and evaluate what we have done with our lives. If the older adult has resolved many of the earlier stages negatively, looking back likely will produce doubt or gloom—the despair Erikson speaks of. But if the older adult has successfully negotiated most or all of the previous stages of development, the looking back will reveal a picture of a life well spent, and the person will feel a sense of satisfaction—integrity will be attained (Sheldon & Kasser, 2001).

Careers and Work A few people seem to have had their careers chosen—to have known what they wanted to be—ever since childhood. But for many of us, choosing an occupation involves exploring a number of options during college or university and even beyond. And establishing oneself in a job and then a career is one of the central concerns of people in their 20s and 30s.

Career interests continue to be an important dimension of life for many middle-aged adults. Midlife is a time when many people examine what they have accomplished in their careers and become concerned about the limited amount of time remaining to accomplish what they want. However, many reach the highest satisfaction in their careers during middle age (Lachman, 2004), and only about 10 percent of North Americans change careers at midlife. Some change careers against their wills, of course. Middle-aged adults may be forced to reexamine their career choices because of the downsizing and early-retirement programs at many companies that are experiencing financial troubles. Similarly, adult immigrants may experience difficulty in finding the same kind of professional work they did in their former countries.

Whether you are changing careers or just beginning one, you may be interested in what research has shown to be the most important job skills. In one survey, employers rated a list of skills that they want in a job candidate on a scale of 1 (extremely unimportant) to 5 (extremely important; Collins, 1996). Figure 4.31 shows the results. Notice how important communication skills—oral, interpersonal, teamwork, written—are to today's employers.

Work defines individuals in fundamental ways (Osipow, 2000). People identify with their work, and the work shapes many aspects of their lives. It is an important influence on their financial standing, leisure activities, where they live, friendships, and health. Work also eats up big chunks of people's time. More Canadians and Americans work very long hours (Wong & Picot, 2001). Furthermore, this devotion to the job is impacting on family life. Although single-earner married families still make up a sizable minority of families, the era of the stay-at-home mom has given way to the era of dual-earner couples (Barnett, 2002), who have often been inappropriately negatively stereotyped (but see Barnett, 2005)

The increasing career commitment on the part of women has led to new work-related issues, such as the division of work and family responsibilities in dual-career couples. Until recently, it had been assumed that men show less interest in home and family matters than women do. However, more recent research (Barnett, 2002) suggests that, although women still bear most of the load at home:

- *Men are increasing their responsibility for maintaining the home.* Men in dual-career families do about 45 percent of the housework. The decreasing gap between the time women and men spend in household and child-care tasks is mainly due to large increases in time spent by men.
- *Women are increasing their responsibility for breadwinning.* In terms of hourly earnings, a growing percentage of wives earn as much as or more than their husbands. This role reversal is present in about one-third of dual-earner couples.
- *Men are showing greater interest in family and parenting.* The twenty-first century is the first time that young men are reporting that family is at least as important to them as work. Among men with more egalitarian attitudes, fatherhood is linked with a decrease of 9 hours per week at work, while among men with more traditional views, fatherhood is associated with an increase of almost 11 hours per week.

John Gottman, who has conducted extensive research on what makes marriages work.

Lifestyles, Commitment, and Marriage Should I get married? If I wait any longer, will it be too late? Should I stay single or is it too lonely a life? If I get married, do I want to have children? How will children affect my marriage? These are questions that many young adults ask themselves as they try to figure out what they want their lives to be like.

Until about 1930, a stable marriage was accepted as a legitimate end point of adult development. In the past 70 years, however, we have seen the desire for personal fulfillment—both inside and outside a marriage—become an equally legitimate goal. Unfortunately, the quest for personal fulfillment may destabilize a marriage.

As a result, in the 1990s, adults were remaining single longer than was the case a few decades before. In the early 1990s, about 38 percent of Canadian marriages ended in divorce (Statistics Canada, 2001) and U.S. rates were even higher. The divorce rate, which increased astronomically in the 1970s, has begun to slow down, although it still remains very high. The number of divorces in Canada in 2002, the last year for which statistics are available, was about 70,000, down from the 1987 all-time high of 96,000 divorces (Statistics Canada, 2004a).

One explanation of the high divorce rate is the overly idealistic expectations of marriage that many people have. We expect our spouse to be simultaneously a lover, a friend, a confidant, a counsellor, a career person, and a parent. Many myths about marriage contribute to these unrealistic expectations (Markman, 2000).

One myth that especially deserves mention is the notion that "men and women are from different planets." According to a popular book by John Gray (1992), men and women have serious relationship problems because he is "from Mars" and she is "from Venus." Gender differences may contribute to marital problems, but they do not usually cause them. The research shows that whether wives or husbands feel satisfied with the sex, romance, and passion in their marriage depends on the extent to which the couple are good friends (Gottman & Silver, 1999) and spend time together (Driver & Gottman, 2004).

What makes a marriage work? John Gottman (1994; Gottman & Silver, 1999; Gottman & others, 1998; Gottman & others, 2002) has been studying married couples' lives since the early 1970s. He interviews couples about the history of their marriage, their philosophy about marriage, and their views of their parents' marriages. He videotapes them talking with each other about how their day went and evaluates what they say about the good and bad times of their marriages. He uses physiological measures to assess their heart rates, blood flow, blood pressure, and immune functioning moment by moment while they discuss these topics. He also checks back with the couples every year to see how their marriages are faring. Currently, he and his colleagues are following 700 couples in seven different studies.

In his exceptionally thorough research, Gottman has found these four principles at work in successful marriages:

- *Nurturing fondness and admiration.* In successful marriages, partners sing each other's praises. When couples put a positive spin on their talk with and about each other, the marriage tends to work.

- *Turning toward each other as friends.* In good marriages, partners see each other as friends and turn toward each other for support in times of stress and difficulty.
- *Giving up some power.* Bad marriages often involve one partner who is a power monger. This is more common in husbands, but some wives have this problem as well.
- *Solving conflicts together.* In successful marriages, couples work to solve problems, regulate their emotion during times of conflict, and compromise to accommodate each other (Driver & others, 2003).

Many myths are also associated with being single, ranging from the "swinging single" to the "desperately lonely, suicidal single." Most singles are somewhere between these two extremes. The pluses of being single include time to make decisions about one's life, time to develop personal resources to meet goals, freedom to make one's own decisions and pursue one's own schedule and interests, opportunities to explore new places and try out new things, and privacy. Common problems of single adults include a lack of intimate relationships with others, loneliness, and feelings of being out of step in a marriage-oriented society. Generalizing about singles is hard. Some single adults would rather remain single; others would rather be married.

Throughout most of Canada people think of *cohabitation*, living together in a sexual relationship without being married, as a halfway step between being single and being married. This is only partly true, however. In Quebec, cohabiting unions are seen as a valid alternative for family life (Le Bourdais & Lapierre-Adamcyk, 2004). Also, many older Canadians cohabit after the failure of a first marriage (Wu & Schimmele, 2005). In 2001, 16 percent of Canadian couples were living together in common law relationships (Statistics Canada, 2002b), twice the U.S. rate but only half the rate in Sweden. These arrangements are often short-lived; one-third of them lasts less than a year (Hyde & DeLamater, 2006). An important question that has been asked about cohabitation is whether it leads to more successful marriages. The weight of the correlational evidence says "probably not" (Nock, 1995). When couples cohabit before marriage, they tend to be less happy in marriage, and the marriage is likelier to end in a divorce than the marriages of couples who did not cohabit (Statistics Canada, 2001).

Midlife Crises In his best-selling book, *The Seasons of a Man's Life*, Daniel Levinson (1978) described the results of his extensive interviews with middle-aged men in a variety of occupations: hourly workers, academic biologists, business executives, and novelists. Although Levinson's original participants were all men, he subsequently reported that the midlife issues he uncovered in his research affect women as well (Levinson, 1996). Levinson argued that, by age 40, people reach a stable point in their careers, outgrow their earlier, more tenuous status as adults, and begin to define the kind of lives they will lead in middle age. He believes the transition period is a time of crisis that lasts about five years.

In Levinson's view, the change to middle adulthood requires individuals to come to grips with four major conflicts that have existed since adolescence:

- being young versus being old
- being destructive versus being constructive
- being masculine versus being feminine
- being attached to others versus being separated from them

"Goodbye, Alice, I've got to get this California thing out of my system."

Leo Cullum © 1984 from The New Yorker Collection. All Rights Reserved.

This is an interesting view, but research on middle-aged adults reveals that few experience midlife in the tumultuous way described by Levinson. Individuals vary extensively in how they cope with and perceive midlife (Santrock & others, 2005). However, in one large-scale study, the portrait of midlife was mainly positive (Brim, 1999). Only about 10 percent of individuals described themselves as experiencing a midlife crisis. In fact, middle-aged individuals (40–65 years old) had lower anxiety levels and worried less than people under 40. The middle-aged individuals did report more negative life events than people under 40, but they showed considerable resilience and good coping skills in facing these stresses. The midlife individuals generally had few illnesses but their physical fitness was poor.

More accurate than the phrase "midlife crisis" might be the phrase "midlife consciousness" (Santrock & others, 2005). That is, during middle age, people do become aware of the gap between being young and being old and the shrinking time left in their lives. They do think about their role in contributing to the next generation. They do contemplate the meaning of life. But for most people, midlife consciousness does not become tumultuous and take on crisis proportions.

What is the nature of social relationships among older adults?

Meaning in Life and Life Themes One of the negative events that people begin to experience in middle adulthood is death, especially the deaths of parents and older relatives. Also faced with less time in their lives, many individuals think more deeply about what life is all about and what they want the rest of their lives to be like.

Austrian psychiatrist Victor Frankl confronted this issue personally and then shared his insights with the rest of us. His mother, father, brother, and wife died in the concentration camps and gas chambers in Auschwitz, Poland. Frankl survived the camp and went on to write *Man's Search for Meaning* (1946/1984), in which he emphasized each person's uniqueness and the finiteness of life. If life were not finite, said Frankl, we could spend our lives doing just about anything we please because time would go on forever. Frankl proposed that people need to ask themselves such questions as why they exist, what they want from life, and what the meaning of their life is.

Frankl's ideas fit with the concept of *life themes* introduced earlier in this chapter. Recall that life themes involve people's efforts to cultivate meaningful, optimal experiences (Massimini & Delle Fave, 2000). Thus some people who have spent much of their adult lives trying to make a lot of money and succeed in a career turn their attention in middle age to more selfless pursuits. They devote more energy to helping others by volunteering or to spending more time with young people in their effort to contribute something meaningful to the next generation. These efforts can shepherd people into a positive and meaningful old age.

Socioemotional Aspects of Aging Although we are in the evening of our lives in late adulthood, there is no reason to live out our remaining years lonely and unhappy. The more active and involved older people are, the more satisfied they are, and the more likely they are to stay healthy (Antonucci, 2001). Researchers have found that older people who go to church, attend meetings, take trips, and exercise are happier than those who simply sit at home (George, 2001; Stones & Kozma, 1989).

However, older adults may become more selective about their social networks, according to one theory (Löckenhoff & Carstensen, 2004). Because they place a high value on emotional satisfaction, older adults are often motivated to spend more time with familiar individuals—close friends and family members—with whom they have had rewarding relationships. They may deliberately withdraw from social contact with individuals on the fringes of their lives. This narrowing of social interaction maximizes positive emotional experiences and minimizes emotional risks as individuals become older. Researchers have found support for this theory (Fung & Carstensen, 2004).

Researchers have also found that the emotional lives of older adults are more positive than previously believed (Ryan & LaGuardia, 2000). In one study of everyday emotions in individuals from early through late adulthood, researchers gave participants electronic pagers to carry for one week (Carstensen, Pasupathi, & Mayr, 1998). The participants were paged at random 35 times, and they recorded their emotions at each paging. Positive emotions (such as joy) were reported about equally across the adult years. Negative emotions (such as anger) were highest in young adults and lowest in older

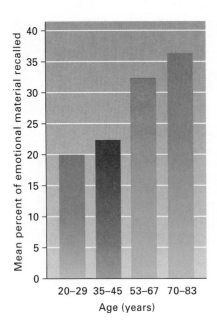

FIGURE 4.32

Remembering Emotional Material
In one study of memory, individuals from 20 to 83 years of age were asked to recall a passage from a popular novel (Carstensen & Turk-Charles, 1994). Younger adults remembered more than older adults did, but only the neutral material. As shown above, when memory for emotional material from the novel was assessed, the percentage remembered increased with age. The reason given for this increase is that older adults likely gave greater attention to emotional information when they were reading the novel than younger adults did.

adults. In another study, the percentage of emotional material that individuals recalled increased with age (see figure 4.32).

Positive Psychology and Aging

Until fairly recently, middle-aged and older adults were perceived as enduring a long decline in physical, cognitive, and socioemotional functioning, and the positive dimensions of aging were ignored (Antonucci and others, 2000; Rowe & Kahn, 1997). Throughout this section, however, you have seen examples and evidence of successful aging. The earlier stereotypes of aging are being overturned as researchers discover that being a middle-aged or older adult has many positive aspects (Wong, 1989).

Once developmentalists began focusing on the positive aspects of aging, they discovered that far more robust, healthy middle-aged and older adults are among us than they previously envisioned. A longitudinal study of aging documented some of the ways that positive aging can be attained (Vaillant, 2002). Individuals were assessed at age 50 and then again at 75 to 80 years of age. As shown in figure 4.33, when individuals at 50 years of age were not heavy smokers, did not abuse alcohol, had a stable marriage, engaged in exercise, maintained a normal weight, and had good coping skills, they were more likely to be alive and happy at 75 to 80 years of age. To put it the other way around, people who were happy-well at 75–80 were more likely to not have smoked heavily or abused alcohol, to have got some exercise, had a stable marriage, maintained a normal weight, and had good coping skills when they were 50 than people who were sad-sick at 75–80 or had died before that age.

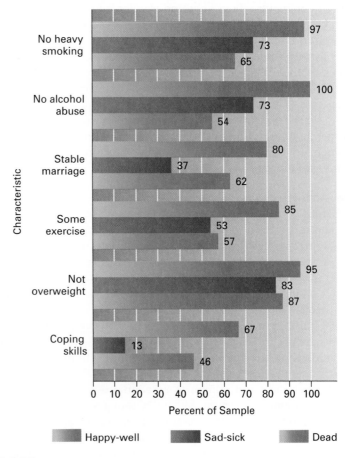

FIGURE 4.33

Linkage Between Characteristics at Age 50 and Health and Happiness at Age 75 to 80
In a longitudinal study, the characteristics shown at age 50 were related to whether individuals were happy-well, sad-sick, or dead at age 75 to 80 (Vaillant, 2002).

Death and Dying

Every life ends in death. Yet death was virtually a taboo topic until Elizabeth Kübler-Ross published *On Death and Dying* (Kübler-Ross, 1969). In recognition of her contribution, Kübler-Ross, who died in August of 2004, was named one of the 100 greatest minds of the 20th century by *Time Magazine*. Kübler-Ross (1969) proposed a five-stage model of the experience of dying patients, progressing from denial to anger, bargaining for time, depression, to acceptance. At first the dying person experiences denial, "this isn't happening to me." Then he or she feels anger, "why is this happening to me," bargaining, "I promise to mend my ways if I can live longer," and depression, "I no longer care." In the end, the dying person finds acceptance, "I am ready for what is to come." Her views have become widespread, although there is some debate about whether each patient experiences these stages in the same order or even experiences all of them (Corr, 1993).

Perhaps more importantly, Kübler-Ross's pioneering work gave prominence to the modern *hospice* movement initiated by Dr. Cecily Saunders, who, in 1967, founded St. Christopher's Hospice, in London, England. Hospices emerged as an alternative to hospitalization for terminally ill patients and their families (Kleespies, 2004). The father of one of your authors (JM) died in late 2004 at Hospice House, in Vernon, BC. Hospice House staff worked with the family to help the patient die an "appropriate death" as free from physical, emotional, social, and spiritual pain as possible. The result was a positive death in which a resilient human being was able to end his life with dignity (Nakashima & Canda, 2005). Pastoral counsellors can also play an important role as a patient's death draws near (Paulson, 2004).

Many ethical issues still surround death and dying (Kleespies, 2004). One particularly thorny debate surrounds *euthanasia*, especially physician-assisted suicide. Anywhere from 4–10 percent of physicians have intentionally helped a patient die (Magnusson, 2004). Untold others, usually family members, have also helped someone end his or her own life. Magnusson (2004) argues that it is better to regulate physician-assisted suicide than to drive it underground. In any event, as the field of *thanatology*, the study of death and dying, matures, issues like these will likely receive further scrutiny.

> **reflect and review**

 Discuss adult development and the positive dimensions of aging.

- Describe physical development throughout adulthood.
- Identify major changes in cognitive development in adulthood.
- Discuss the main aspects of socioemotional development in adulthood.
- Summarize the positive view of aging that now exists.
- Describe the stages of dying and the hospice movement.

Summarize the positive view of aging that now exists.
Suppose that you wanted to construct a test for "wisdom" that would be fair to adults of all ages. Write down two or three questions or items that you would want to include in your test.

Human Development

1 EXPLORING HUMAN DEVELOPMENT

What Is Development? — How Do Nature and Nurture Influence Development? — Do Early Experiences Rule Us for Life? — Positive Psychology and Optimal Experiences

2 CHILD DEVELOPMENT

Prenatal Development — Physical Development in Childhood — Cognitive Development in Childhood — Socioemotional Development in Childhood — Positive Psychology and Children's Development

3 ADOLESCENCE

Physical Development in Adolescence — Cognitive Development in Adolescence — Socioemotional Development in Adolescence — At-Risk Youth — Positive Psychology and Adolescents

4 ADULT DEVELOPMENT AND AGING

Physical Development in Adulthood — Cognitive Development in Adulthood — Socioemotional Development in Adulthood — Positive Psychology and Aging — Death and Dying

At the beginning of the chapter, we posed four chapter questions and encouraged you to review material related to these questions at the end of each major section (see pages 121, 148, 155, and 169). Use the following reflection and review features for further your understanding of the chapter material.

CHAPTER REFLECTIONS

1. The possibility of human cloning has received extensive media coverage. If you could clone yourself, your clone would have the same genetic makeup as you have. Take a quick survey of some of your friends to ask whether they would clone themselves if they were given the opportunity. Ask them to explain their answers and critically examine their reasons, keeping in mind the lessons on nature and nurture in the text. Do you think the phenotype of your clone would most resemble you physically, cognitively, or socioemotionally?

2. Find a copy of a popular child-rearing book. Read a few pages and comment on how the perspective on children's development in the popular book relates to the scientific perspectives on children's development in the text. Are all perspectives represented, or does one view dominate?

3. The text discusses development during childhood, adolescence, and adulthood. How are the boundaries across these periods defined, and how would you decide which phase of development best describes you?

4. Visit Health Canada's Aging and Seniors Web site (www.hc-sc.gc.ca/seniors-aines) and examine the article "Challenges of an aging society" (http://www.naca-ccnta.ca/beyond1999/toc_e.htm) How well do these trends correspond to your perception of what happens as we age?

5. Recent genetic advances have offered the possibility of expanding the human life span. Consider the physical, cognitive, and socioemotional changes of adulthood described in the text, and discuss what might happen to these psychological functions if the human life span increases significantly.

CHAPTER REVIEW

Explain how psychologists think about development.

- Development refers to the pattern of change in human capabilities that begins at conception and continues throughout the life span. Important developmental processes are biological (the person's physical nature), cognitive (thought, intelligence, and language), and socioemotional (relationships, emotion, and personality).

- Both nature (biological inheritance) and nurture (environmental experience) influence development extensively. However, people are at the mercy of neither their genes nor their environment when they actively construct optimal experiences.

- Developmental psychologists debate the extent to which early experience (as in infancy or early childhood) is more important than later experience in development. Most agree that both early and later experiences influence development.

- According to positive psychology, optimizing our life through life themes is a key aspect of development.

Describe children's development from conception to adolescence.

- Prenatal development progresses through the germinal, embryonic, and fetal periods. Certain drugs, such as alcohol, can have an adverse effect on the fetus. Preterm birth is another potential problem, especially if the infant is very small or grows up in an adverse environment.

- The newborn comes into the world with several genetically "wired" reflexes, including grasping and sucking. The infant's physical development is dramatic in the first year, and a number of motor milestones are reached in infancy. Motor behaviours are assembled for perceiving and acting, drawing on the infant's physical abilities, perceptual skills, and factors in the environment. Extensive changes in the brain, including denser connections between synapses, take place in infancy and childhood.

- In Piaget's view, children use schemas to actively construct their world, either assimilating new information into existing schemas or adjusting schemas to accommodate it. Piaget also said that people go through four stages of cognitive development: (1) the sensorimotor stage (birth to 2 years of age), (2) the preoperational stage (2 to 7 years of age, (3) the concrete operational stage (7 to 11 years of age), and (4) the formal operational stage (11 to 15 years of age through adulthood). Piaget opened up new ways of looking at how children's minds develop, and he gave us the model of a child as an active, constructivist thinker. However, critics believe that Piaget's stages are too rigid and do not adequately take into account the influence of culture and education on cognitive development.

- Erikson presented a major, eight-stage psychosocial view of life-span development; its first four stages occur in childhood. In each stage, the individual seeks to resolve a particular socioemotional conflict. Other researchers have focused on specific aspects of socioemotional development in childhood. For instance, Bowlby and Ainsworth theorized that the first year of life is crucial for the formation of a secure attachment between infant and caregiver. Development also depends on temperament, an individual's behavioural style or characteristic way of responding. Among the important aspects of parenting are parenting style, divorce, and positive parenting. The family is an important context for children's development, but other social contexts such as peers, schools, neighbourhood quality, and culture are also important. Kohlberg proposed a major cognitive-developmental theory of moral development with three levels (preconventional, conventional, and postconventional) and two stages at each level. Gilligan presented an alternative view of moral development that emphasizes interpersonal relationships more heavily than Kohlberg's theory does. Finally, gender development includes biology, social experience, and cognitive factors.

- Positive psychology emphasizes children's resilience and focuses on improving children's lives.

Identify the most important changes that occur in adolescence.

- Puberty is a period of rapid skeletal and sexual maturation that occurs mainly in early adolescence. It occurs about two years earlier in girls than in boys. Hormonal changes lie at the core of pubertal development.

- According to Piaget, cognitive development in adolescence is characterized by the appearance of formal operational thought, the final stage in his theory. He believed that children enter this stage between 11 and 15 years of age. This stage involves abstract, idealistic, and logical thought. Hypothetical-deductive reasoning is Piaget's term for adolescents' logical thought. Another key feature of cognitive development, especially in early adolescence, is egocentric thought.

- One of the most important aspects of socioemotional development in adolescence is identity. Erikson's fifth stage of psychosocial development is identity versus identity confusion. Marcia proposed four statuses of identity based on crisis and commitment. A special concern is the development of ethnic identity.

- Successful programs for intervening in adolescent problems involve individual attention and community-wide interventions.

- Positive psychology views adolescence as a time of evaluation, decision making, and commitment. Adolescents are not all alike, but the majority of them develop competently.

Discuss adult development and the positive dimensions of aging.

- Most adults reach their peak physical performance during their 20s and are also the healthiest then. However, physical skills begin to decline during the 30s. Changes in physical appearance are among the most visible signs of aging in middle adulthood. Menopause, which also takes place during middle adulthood, has been stereotyped as more negative than it actually is. The cellular-clock and free-radical theories are two important cellular theories of aging. Alzheimer's disease is a special concern. Even in late adulthood, the brain has remarkable repair capacity and plasticity.

- Piaget argued that no new cognitive changes occur in adulthood. However, some psychologists have proposed that the idealistic thinking of adolescents is replaced by the more realistic, pragmatic thinking of young adults. Horn argued that crystallized intelligence increases in middle age, whereas fluid intelligence declines. Schaie conducted a longitudinal study of intelligence and found that many cognitive skills reach their peak in middle age. Overall, older adults do not do as well on memory and other cognitive tasks and are slower to process information than younger adults. But older adults may have greater wisdom than younger adults.

• Erikson's three stages of socioemotional development in adulthood are intimacy versus isolation (early adulthood), generativity versus stagnation (middle adulthood), and integrity versus despair (late adulthood). Career and work become central themes in the life of young adults. Lifestyles, marriage, and commitment also become important aspects of adult life for most people. In middle adulthood, people begin to realize the limits of their ideals and dreams. Levinson proposed that a majority of people experience midlife crises as a result, but researchers have found that only a small percentage of middle-aged adults experience such a crisis. Nevertheless, a special concern, beginning in the 50s, is understanding the meaning of life. Researchers have found that remaining active increases the likelihood that older adults will be happier and healthier. They have also found that older adults often reduce their general social affiliations. Instead, they are motivated to spend more time with close friends and family members.

• The positive dimensions of aging were largely ignored until recently. Developmentalists now recognize that many adults can sustain or even improve their functioning as they age.

CONNECTIONS

For extra help in mastering the material in this chapter, see the integrator, review sections, practice quizzes, and other resources in the Student Study Guide and at the Online Learning Centre (www.mcgrawhill.ca/college/santrock).

CORE TERMS

development, p. 118
genotype, p. 119
phenotype, p. 119
nature, p. 119
nurture, p. 119
schema, p. 128
assimilation, p. 128
accommodation, p. 128
sensorimotor stage, p. 128
preoperational stage, p. 129

concrete operational stage, p. 131
formal operational stage, p. 131
zone of proximal development, p. 133
attachment, p. 136
imprinting, p. 137
secure attachment, p. 137
temperament, p. 138
authoritarian parenting, p. 139
authoritative parenting, p. 139
neglectful parenting, p. 139

indulgent parenting, p. 139
androgens, p. 145
estrogens, p. 145
gender role, p. 146
puberty, p. 149
identity versus identity confusion, p. 151
crystallized intelligence, p. 161
fluid intelligence, p. 161
wisdom, p. 163

5 Sensation and Perception

CHAPTER QUESTIONS

1. What are the basic principles of sensation and perception?

2. How does the visual system enable us to see and, by communicating with the brain, to perceive the world?

3. How does the auditory system register sound and how does it connect with the brain to perceive sound?

4. How do the skin, chemical, and kinesthetic and vestibular senses work?

5. What do human factors psychologists study?

What does music look like? For one possible answer, look at *Composition 1916*. The artist, Russian abstract expressionist Wassili Kandinsky (1866-1944), claimed he could see colours associated with certain musical notes and sounds. He even titled many of his paintings "Compositions" or "Improvisations." Kandinsky is not unique. For M.W., the taste of spiced chicken is pointy, for C.S., pain is orange, and for H.G., voices trigger both colours and taste (Dixon, Smilek & Merikle, 2004). For E.J., the note C sharp is blue and for M.B., the shape of a hamburger patty is bitter (Ramachandran, & Hubbard, 2003).

These individuals experience *synaesthesia*, the effect of one sense provoking a response in another (Robertson & Sagiv, 2005). The term comes from the Latin syn (together) and *aesthesia* (to sense or perceive). Different synaesthetes experience different types of synaesthesia. For example, C. is a grapheme-colour synaesthete, the most common type. When she sees a single number written in black, she automatically and consistently experiences a particular colour (Dixon & others, 2000). According to Mike Dixon and Daniel Smilek and their colleagues at the University of Waterloo, while rare, synaethesia has been accepted as a genuine perceptual phenomenon (Blake & others, 2005) and has become a focus of psychological investigation (Smilek & Dixon, 2002).

What does synaesthesia teach us about sensation and perception? According to one theory, all infants experience sensory inputs in an undifferentiated fashion. In other words, we were all synesthetes as babies. Sensory development consists in differentiating the various senses and adult synesthetes have for some reason retained links between various sensory/perceptual brain areas, allowing for cross-modal transfers the rest of us cannot experience. A link with creativity has even been proposed, since synesthesia is more common among creative people. Perhaps synesthesia and metaphor are related (Ramachandran, & Hubbard, 2003); when Kandinsky made that *"colour is the keyboard"* comment, he may have been describing his experiences literally while the rest of us must be content to understand him metaphorically.

Phenomena like synaesthesia challenge us to better understand the processes of sensation and perception, which we explore in this chapter. We need to learn more about the neural pathways that bring information to the brain from the senses and how the brain combines these inputs into our perceptions and, ultimately, into our experience of ourselves and the world around us. We begin this chapter with a general introduction to basic concepts of sensation and perception, leading to a detailed discussion of vision, the sense that scientists know the most about. Then we examine hearing, the skin senses, taste and smell, and the kinesthetic and vestibular senses. Finally, we touch on the area of human factors to see how it applies information about sensation and perception to design equipment and machines that are more compatible with human capabilities.

Composition 1916 (1913), by Wassili Kandinsky. Kandinsky once remarked "Color is the keyboard, the eyes are the harmonies, the soul is the piano with many strings. The artist is the hand that plays, touching one key or another, to cause vibrations in the soul."

1 HOW WE SENSE AND PERCEIVE THE WORLD

| Detecting, Processing, and Interpreting Experiences | Sensory Receptors and the Brain | Thresholds | Signal Detection Theory | Perceiving Sensory Stimuli | Sensory Adaptation |

How do we detect and perceive the world around us?

When the hand of an artist like Wassili Kandinsky touches a paint brush, his brain recognizes the sensation and directs his fingers and hand to move the brush, and he begins to paint. The brain automatically interprets the information it receives from the fingers and hand as they feel the brush and, through it, the canvas, and responds to its sensation. What may seem like the simple act of painting one stroke on canvas, however, is really the outcome of two complex, virtually inseparable processes: sensation and perception.

Detecting, Processing, and Interpreting Experiences

Sensation is the process of receiving stimulus energies from the external environment. Stimuli in the environment give rise to physical energy. For example, a light pattern is given off by the night sky and sound waves are produced by the singer at a hockey game. Physical energy arising from stimuli is detected by specialized receptor cells in the sense organs—eyes, ears, skin, nose, and tongue. In a process called **transduction**, physical energy falling upon a sense receptor is transformed to an electrochemical impulse. Transduction results in an action potential that relays information about the stimulus through the nervous system to the brain. When it reaches the brain, the information travels to the appropriate areas of the cerebral cortex (Sekuler & Blake, 2006).

The brain gives meaning to sensation through perception. **Perception** is the process of organizing and interpreting sensory information to give it meaning. Receptor cells in our eyes respond in certain patterns, but they do not "see" Northern lights; receptor cells in our ears vibrate in a particular way, but they do not "hear" *O Canada*. Finding meaningful patterns in sensory information is perception. Sensing and perceiving give us three-dimensional views of the setting sun, the sounds of a hiphop concert, the touch of soft caresses, the taste of sweets, and the smells of flowers and peppermint.

Bottom-Up and Top-Down Processing Psychologists distinguish between bottom-up and top-down processing in sensation and perception. In **bottom-up processing**, sensory receptors register information about the external environment and send it up to the brain for analysis and interpretation. Bottom-up processing is initiated by stimulus input (Sun, 2002; Sussman & others, 2001). **Top-down processing** starts out with cognitive processing at the higher levels of the brain (Miyashita & Hayashi, 2000). These cognitive processes include knowledge, beliefs, and expectations. Even our cultural experiences shape our processing of incoming information (Berry 1996; Segall & others, 1990). Thus top-down processing does not start with the detection of a stimulus, as bottom-up processing does.

When an artist like Wassili Kandinsky looks at a stroke of paint he has just completed on the canvas, bottom-up processing is taking place. When he sees it is not quite what he wanted and adjusts his next stroke, based on his plan for the painting, top-down processing is occurring. Clearly, both bottom-up and top-down processing take place in sensing and perceiving the world (Whiting & others, 2005). By themselves, our eyes provide only incoming information about light in the environment. We must consider both what the eyes sense (bottom-up processing) and what the brain interprets (top-down processing) to fully understand how we perceive our visual world.

Let's look at another example in which bottom-up and top-down processing might be involved: a jigsaw puzzle. If you have ever tried to put together a jigsaw puzzle without the puzzle's original box, you understand how difficult it is to finish the puzzle without knowing what the finished picture looks like. Basically, you have to proceed on

sensation The process of receiving stimulus energies from the environment.

transduction The process of transforming physical energy into electrochemical energy.

perception The brain's process of organizing and interpreting sensory information to give it meaning.

bottom-up processing Processing that begins with sensory receptors registering environmental information and sending it to the brain for integration and cognitive processing.

top-down processing Processing of perceptual information that starts out with cognitive processing at the higher levels of the brain.

Anableps microlepis, a fish with four eyes. Two eyes allow it to observe the world above water, two the world below water, as it swims just at the surface of the water. *Why was this evolutionary adaptation developed?*

the basis of the shapes and colours of the pieces to determine how they fit together. That is bottom-up processing. However, if you have a picture of the finished product, you can select a particular area to work on. For example, if you know that there will be a tiger on the right side of the puzzle, you can go through the pieces and pick out in advance those that look like they are part of the tiger. That makes your task of fitting the pieces together much easier—you have fewer to work with and have a general idea of how they should look once they are put together. Your selection process based on prior knowledge is an example of top-down processing.

In everyday life, the two processes of sensation and perception are virtually inseparable. The brain automatically perceives the information it receives from the sense organs. For this reason, most psychologists refer to sensation and perception as a unified information processing system (Goldstein, 2002).

The Purpose of Perception   Important insights about perception can be gained by asking the simple question What is its purpose? According to a leading expert in this field, David Marr (1982), the purpose of perception is to represent information from the outside world internally. For example, the purpose of vision is to create a three-dimensional representation or map of the surrounding environment in the brain.

From an evolutionary perspective, the purpose of sensation and perception is adaptation to improve a species' chances for survival. An organism must be able to sense and respond quickly and accurately to events in the immediate environment, such as the approach of a predator, the presence of prey, or the appearance of a potential mate. Thus it is not surprising that most animals—from goldfish to elephants to humans—can see, hear, and touch, as well as sense chemicals (smell and taste). However, a close comparison of sensory systems in animals reveals that each species is exquisitely adapted to the habitat in which it evolved (Shettleworth, 1998).

A marvellous example of evolutionary accomplishment appears in a fish called *Anableps microlepis*, which has four eyes! To survive, *Anableps microlepis* swims just at the surface of the water, with two aerial eyes monitoring the visual field above the water and two aquatic eyes monitoring the visual field underwater. This remarkable adaptation enables *Anableps microlepis* to search for food while watching for predators.

Sensory Receptors and the Brain

All sensation begins with sensory receptors. **Sensory receptors** are specialized cells that detect and transmit stimulus information to sensory (afferent) nerves and the brain (Sekuler & Blake, 2006). They are the windows through which the brain and nervous

Sensory receptors Specialized cells that detect and transmit stimulus information to sensory neurons and the brain.

FIGURE 5.1
Sensory Receptor Cells
These cells are specialized to detect particular stimuli.

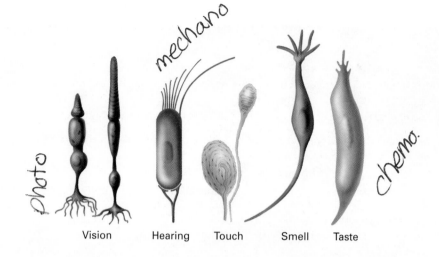

Vision   Hearing   Touch   Smell   Taste

system experience the world. Figure 5.1 shows the types of sensory receptors for each of the five senses in humans.

The sensory receptors of every animal species have evolved to fit their environments. For example, the sensory receptors that a bat uses to find food are very different from, but no more specialized, than those that an eagle uses. Bats use sound to locate prey at night, whereas eagles hunt with their eyes from great heights to avoid being detected by their potential prey.

Figure 5.2 depicts the general flow of information from the environment to the brain. Sensory receptors trigger action potentials in sensory neurons, which carry that information to the central nervous system. Recall from chapter 3 that an action potential is the brief wave of electrical activity that sweeps down the axon of a neuron for possible transmission to another neuron. The action potentials of all sensory nerves are alike, which raises an intriguing question: How can an animal distinguish sight, sound, odour, taste, and touch? The answer is that sensory receptors are selective and have different neural pathways. They are specialized to absorb a particular type of energy—light energy, mechanical energy (such as sound vibrations), or chemical energy, for example—and transduce (convert) it into the electrochemical energy of an action potential.

Humans have multiple receptors that provide a rich tapestry of sensations (Coren, Ward & Enns, 2004). Your skin, for example, contains 4 million pain receptors, 500,000 pressure receptors, 150,000 receptors for cold, and 16,000 receptors for heat. Specialized receptors in the joints, ligaments, and muscles produce information that is combined with information from other sensory receptors, such as those in the eyes and ears, to give us a sense of where certain body parts are in relation to other body parts. Thus—although vision, hearing, touch, taste, and smell are the five most commonly described senses—the nervous system blends these into a wider spectrum of sensations.

FIGURE 5.2
Information Flow in Senses
The diagram shows a general flow of sensory information from energy stimulus to sensory receptor cells to sensory neuron to sensation and perception.

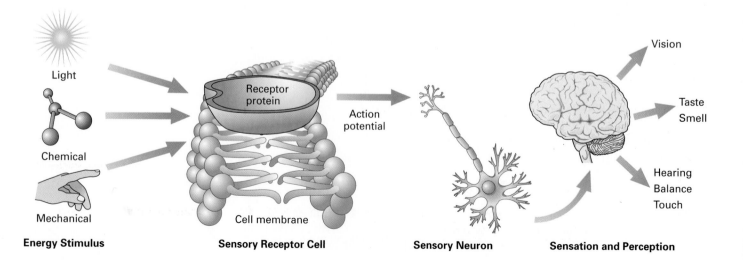

Light

Chemical

Mechanical

Energy Stimulus

Receptor protein

Action potential

Cell membrane

Sensory Receptor Cell

Sensory Neuron

Vision

Taste
Smell

Hearing
Balance
Touch

Sensation and Perception

The sense organs and sensory receptors fall into several main classes based on the type of energy that is transmitted. These include

- *Photoreception*, the detection of light, perceived as sight
- *Mechanoreception*, the detection of pressure, vibration, and movement perceived as touch, hearing, and equilibrium
- *Chemoreception*, the detection of chemical stimuli detected as smell and taste

Thus, when an artist like Wassili Kandinsky begins to paint, sensory receptors in his eyes pick up visual information in the form of light and transduce it into electrochemical energy, which his brain perceives as the sight of his canvas.

In the brain, nearly all sensory signals go through the thalamus. Recall from chapter 3 that the thalamus is the brain's great relay station. From the thalamus, the signals go to the sensory areas of the cerebral cortex, where they are processed and distributed throughout a vast network of neurons.

Also recall from chapter 3 that certain areas of the cerebral cortex are specialized to handle different sensory functions. Visual information is processed mainly in the occipital lobes, hearing in the temporal lobes, and pain, touch, and temperature in the parietal lobes. Keep in mind, however, that the interactions and pathways of sensory information are complex, and the brain must coordinate and interpret extensive information, both within senses and across them (Kolb & Whishaw, 2003). The senses have evolved to help animals solve important problems, such as knowing when to flee and understanding how to build a shelter. Large numbers of sensory neurons make this behaviour possible. As they do so, they allow us to perceive the world in a unified way. One question raised by the phenomenon of synaesthesia is exactly how the brain achieves the integration of information across senses, both in normal individuals and in synaesthetes.

An important part of perception is figuring out what the sensory messages mean (Sekuler & Blake, 2006). Many top-down factors determine this meaning, including signals from different parts of the brain, prior learning, the person's goals, and how aroused the person is. Moving in the opposite direction, bottom-up signals from a sensory area may help other parts of the brain maintain arousal, form an image of where the body is in space, or regulate movement.

Thresholds

How close does an approaching bumblebee have to be before you can hear it buzzing? How far away from a brewing coffeepot can you be and still detect the smell of coffee? How different does the percentage of fat in the "low-fat" and "regular" versions of your favourite ice cream have to be for you to taste a difference?

Questions like these are answered by **psychophysics**, the field that studies links between the physical properties of stimuli and a person's experience of them. For example, an experiment in psychophysics might examine the relation between the rate at which a light flashes and a participant's ability to see individual flashes.

Absolute Threshold Any sensory system must have the ability to detect varying degrees of energy in the environment. This energy can take the form of light, sound, chemical, or mechanical stimulation. How much energy from a stimulus is necessary for you to see, hear, taste, smell, or feel something? One way to address this question is to assume that there is an **absolute threshold**, or minimum amount of energy that a person can detect. When the energy of a stimulus falls below this absolute threshold, we cannot detect its presence; when the energy of the stimulus rises above the absolute threshold, we can detect the stimulus. An experiment with a clock will help you understand the principle of absolute threshold. Find a clock that ticks. Put it on a table and walk far enough across the room so that you no longer hear it ticking. Then gradually move toward the clock. At some point you will begin to hear it ticking. Hold your position and notice that occasionally the ticking fades, and you may have to move forward to reach the threshold; at other times the ticking may become loud, and you can move backward.

psychophysics The field that studies links between the physical properties of stimuli and a person's experience of them.

absolute threshold The minimum amount of stimulus energy that people can detect.

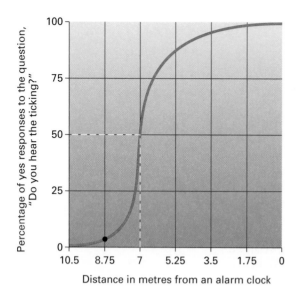

FIGURE 5.3

Measuring Absolute Threshold
Absolute threshold is the minimum amount of energy we can detect. To measure absolute threshold, psychologists have arbitrarily decided to use the criterion of detecting the stimulus 50 percent of the time. In this graph, the person's absolute threshold for detecting the ticking clock is at a distance of 7 metres.

In this experiment, if you measure your absolute threshold several times, you will likely record several different distances for detecting the stimulus. For example, the first time you try it, you might hear the ticking at 8 metres from the clock. But you probably won't hear it every time at 8 metres. Maybe you hear it only 38 percent of the time at this distance, but you hear it 50 percent of the time at 7 metres away and 65 percent of the time at 6 metres. Also, people have different thresholds, because some people have better hearing than others and some people have better vision than others. Figure 5.3 shows one person's measured absolute threshold for detecting a clock's ticking sound. Psychologists have arbitrarily decided that absolute threshold is the point at which the individual detects the stimulus 50 percent of the time—in this case 7 metres away. Using the same clock, another person might have a measured absolute threshold of 8.1 metres, and yet another, 5.5 metres. The approximate absolute thresholds of five different senses are listed in figure 5.4.

Under ideal circumstances, our senses have very low absolute thresholds, and so we can be remarkably good at detecting small amounts of stimulus energy. You can demonstrate this to yourself by using a sharp pencil point to carefully lift a single hair on your forearm. Most people can easily detect this tiny bit of pressure on the skin. You might be surprised to learn that the human eye can see a candle flame at 50 kilometres on a dark, clear night. But our environment seldom gives us ideal conditions to detect stimuli. If the night is cloudy or the air is polluted, for example, you would have to be much closer to see the flicker of a candle flame. And other lights on the horizon—car or house lights—would hinder your ability to detect the candle's flame. **Noise** is the term given to irrelevant and competing stimuli. For example, suppose someone speaks to you from the doorway of the room in which you are sitting. You might fail to respond because your roommate is talking on a cellphone and your MP3 player is blaring out your favourite song. We usually think of noise as being auditory, but the psychological meaning of noise also involves other senses. Air pollution, cloudiness, car lights, and house lights are forms of visual noise that hamper your ability to see a candle flame from a great distance.

Subliminal Perception   Is it possible to experience sensations at levels below your absolute threshold without being aware of them? **Subliminal perception**—the ability to detect information below the level of conscious awareness—fascinates us. For example, we spend millions of dollars every year on subliminal motivational tapes. Even golfer Tiger Woods played such tapes while he was asleep at night as a young boy in the hope that they would improve his golf game.

In 1973, subliminal perception became the focus of popular attention with the publication of Canadian professor Wilson Bryan Key's book, *Subliminal Seduction: Ad Media's Manipulation of a Not So Innocent America*. Key (1973, 2003) and others (e.g., Shrum, 2004) have repeatedly asserted that subliminal messages hidden in advertisements are used to shape consumer behaviour. In a bizarre moment in the 2000 U.S. presidential

noise Irrelevant and competing stimuli.

subliminal perception The ability to detect information below the level of conscious awareness.

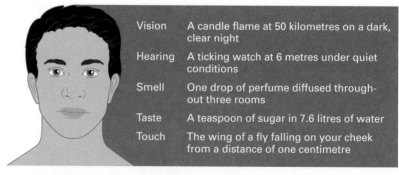

Vision	A candle flame at 50 kilometres on a dark, clear night
Hearing	A ticking watch at 6 metres under quiet conditions
Smell	One drop of perfume diffused throughout three rooms
Taste	A teaspoon of sugar in 7.6 litres of water
Touch	The wing of a fly falling on your cheek from a distance of one centimetre

FIGURE 5.4 Approximate Absolute Thresholds for Five Senses

campaign, someone took a close look at a Republican TV commercial criticizing then Vice President Al Gore's Medicare proposal. The word "RATS" flashed for 1/30 of a second across the phrase "The Gore prescription plan: Bureaucrats decide." Presidential candidate George W. Bush's campaign team did its best to make light of the situation, but, clearly, someone in the Bush campaign had intended to broadcast an unflattering subliminal label for the Democratic candidate. Another bizarre controversy arose a number of years ago when claims surfaced that the recordings of some rock groups, when played backward, contain satanic messages. In theory, when the record is played normally (forward), the messages cannot be consciously perceived, but they influence our behaviour in a subliminal way.

But do subliminal messages work? Research has failed to find much evidence that subliminal motivational tapes work (Moore, 1995). As for backwards subliminal messages, researchers have been unable to find any evidence whatsoever that such messages exist or, if they do, that they influence our behaviour (McIver, 1988). In one study, Begg, Needham, & Bookbinder (1993) presented subjects with digitized statements played backwards or forwards and then tested the subject's recognition. While subjects did have some ability to recognize backward statements, they showed no evidence that they understood them. Thus, the forward meaning of the backward statements does not "leak" through even when the backward statements are, in themselves, memorable. Investigators have found that people's perceptions of whether or not these messages exist are largely a function of what they expect to hear. In one experiment, when told beforehand that a message of a satanic nature would influence them, participants were likely to hear the message. With no such expectation, participants did not hear the message (Vokey & Read, 1985).

Although the question of subliminal perception remains controversial (Erdelyi, 2004), researchers from the University of Waterloo have argued that subliminal perception can occur under some circumstances (Merikle, Smilek, & Eastwood, 2001). An experiment by Mack & Rock (1998) provides some supportive evidence. In this study, participants were asked to make judgments about crosses rapidly displayed on a screen. Although words were also presented on some trials, participants often failed to see them. On those trials when participants failed to see a word, they were nevertheless able to choose the word from among a set of five alternatives with almost 50 percent accuracy, much better than if they had just guessed. These results suggest that subliminal perception is possible. Other research has also confirmed that people's performance can be affected by stimuli that are too faint to be recognized at a conscious level (Allen, Kraus, & Bradlow, 2000; Monahan, Murphy, & Zajonc, 2000).

One interesting approach has been to study the memories of people under general anesthesia for surgery (Merikle & Daneman, 1996). You might be interested in just how this sort of research is carried out. For example, Bonebakker and colleagues (1996) presented words via headphones to patients under anesthesia during surgery for elective procedures. Early reports suggested that positive comments during anesthesia could speed up postoperative recovery. Subsequent research, however, has failed to support this idea. On the other hand, specific information is remembered following surgery, as long as testing occurs within 36 hours (Merikle & Daneman, 1996).

What can we make, then, of the claims of subliminal perception enthusiasts and of the research conducted by experimental psychologists? First, weak sensory stimuli can be registered by sensory receptors and are possibly encoded in the brain at a level beneath conscious awareness. Second, no evidence supports the claims of advertisers and rock music critics that such sensory registry and neural encoding have any influence on our thoughts and behaviour. Rather, evidence suggests that we are influenced extensively by those sounds and views we are consciously aware of and can attend to efficiently (Smith & Rogers, 1994).

Difference Threshold   In addition to studying how much energy is required for a stimulus to be detected, psychologists investigate the degree of *difference* that must exist between two stimuli before the difference is detected. This is the **difference threshold**, or *just noticeable difference*. An artist might appreciate the difference between two

difference threshold Also called just noticeable difference, this concept refers to the smallest difference in stimulation required to discriminate one stimulus from another 50 percent of the time.

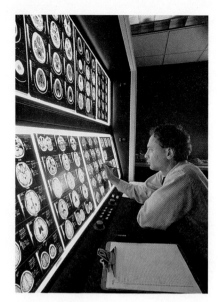

What is the nature of signal detection theory? How might signal detection theory be applied to a physician's decision making?

— fatigue
— urgency

similar shades of colour. A wine taster might savour the difference between two vintages of wine. How different must the colours and tastes be to notice the difference? Just as the absolute threshold is determined by a 50 percent detection rate, the difference threshold is the smallest difference in stimulation required to discriminate one stimulus from another 50 percent of the time.

An important aspect of difference thresholds is that the threshold increases with the magnitude of the stimulus. When music is playing softly, you may notice when your roommate increases the volume by even a small amount. But you may not notice if he or she turns the volume up an equal amount when the music is playing very loudly. More than 150 years ago, E. H. Weber, a German psychologist, noted that, regardless of their magnitude, two stimuli must differ by a constant proportion to be detected. **Weber's law** is the principle that two stimuli must differ by a constant minimum percentage, rather than a constant amount, to be perceived as different. Weber's law generally holds true. For example, we add 1 candle to 60 candles and notice a difference in the brightness of the candles; we add 1 candle to 120 candles and do not notice a difference. We discover, though, that adding 2 candles to 120 candles does produce a difference in brightness. Adding 2 candles to 120 candles is the same proportionately as adding 1 candle to 60 candles. The exact proportion varies with the stimulus involved. For example, a change of 3 percent in a tone's pitch can be detected, but a 20 percent change is required for a person to detect a difference in taste, and a 25 percent change in smell is required.

Signal Detection Theory

Nearly all reasoning and decision making takes place with some degree of uncertainty. One theory about perception—**signal detection theory**—focuses on decision making about stimuli in the presence of uncertainty. According to signal detection theory, the detection of sensory stimuli depends on a variety of factors besides the physical intensity of the stimulus and the sensory abilities of the observer. These factors include individual and contextual variations such as fatigue, expectancy, and the urgency of the moment (Kiernan & others, 2001; Coren, Ward, & Enns, 2004).

Consider the case of two air traffic controllers with exactly the same sensory ability to detect blips on a radar screen. One is monitoring the radar screen while working overtime late into the night and feeling fatigued. The other is watching the screen in the morning after having a good night's sleep. The fatigued radar operator fails to see a blip indicating that a small private plane is flying too close to a large passenger jet, and the two almost collide in mid-air. However, in a similar situation, the well-rested controller easily detects a private plane intruding into the air space of a large passenger jet and contacts the small private plane's pilot, who then changes course. Consider also the circumstance of two individuals at a dentist's office. One begins to "feel" pain the instant the drill touches the tooth's surface; the other doesn't "feel" pain until the dentist drills deep into a cavity.

Signal detection theory provides a precise language and graphic representation for analyzing decision making in the presence of uncertainty. To see how signal detection theory works, consider the following medical context (Heeger, 2003). A radiologist is scanning an image of the brain created by magnetic resonance imaging (MRI) to determine if a tumour is present. Either there is a tumour (signal present) or there is not (signal absent). Either the radiologist sees the tumour (responding "yes") or does not (responding "no"). This leads to four possible outcomes: (1) hit (tumour present and radiologist says, "Yes, I see it"), (2) miss (tumour present and radiologist says, "No, I don't see it"), (3) false alarm (tumour absent and radiologist says, "Yes, I see it"), and (4) correct rejection (tumour absent and radiologist says, "No, I don't see it;" see figure 5.5).

There are two main components to the decision-making process in signal detection theory: information acquisition and criterion. In terms of *information acquisition*, the question is: What information is in the image produced by the brain scan? For example, a healthy brain has a characteristic shape. The presence of a tumour might distort that

Weber's law The principle that two stimuli must differ by a constant minimum percentage (rather than a constant amount) to be perceived as different.

signal detection theory Focuses on decision making about stimuli in the presence of uncertainty; detection depends on a variety of factors besides the physical intensity of the stimulus and the sensory abilities of the observer.

FIGURE 5.5
Four Outcomes in Signal Detection

	Observer's Response	
	"Yes, I see it"	*"No, I don't see it"*
Signal Present	Hit (correct)	Miss (mistake)
Signal Absent	False alarm (mistake)	Correct rejection (correct)

shape. Tumours might have different image characteristics, such as brightness or darkness or a difference in texture.

The *criterion* component of signal detection theory is the basis for making a judgment about the information that is available. That is, responses depend on the criterion that decision makers set for determining whether a stimulus is present or not. The criterion depends on more than the information provided by the environmental stimuli. For example, in addition to relying on technology or testing to provide information, radiologists also make judgments about the information. They may feel that different types of errors are not equal. For example, a radiologist may believe that missing an opportunity for early diagnosis may mean the difference between life and death, whereas a false alarm may simply result in a routine biopsy operation. This type of radiologist may err on the side of "yes" (tumour present) decisions. However, other radiologists may believe that unnecessary surgeries, even routine biopsies, should not be done because of the expense, the stress, and so on. This type of radiologist may tend to be more conservative and say "no" (tumour absent) more often. This type of radiologist may miss more tumours but will reduce unnecessary surgeries. The conservative radiologist may also believe that if a tumour is present, it will be detected in time on the next checkup.

Perceiving Sensory Stimuli

As we just saw, the perception of stimuli is influenced by more than the characteristics of the environmental stimuli themselves. Two important factors in perceiving sensory stimuli are attention and perceptual set.

Attention The world holds a lot of information to perceive. When you drive a car, you focus on the roadway ahead of you. A horn sounds and you look into the rear-view mirror. You want to turn left so you check the left-hand lane before turning. You read a street sign looking for a particular street where a friend lives. In each of these circumstances, you engaged in **selective attention**, which involves focusing on a specific aspect of experience while ignoring others (Trick & Enns, 2004). A familiar example of selective attention is the ability to focus on one voice among many in a crowded room or a noisy restaurant. Psychologists call this common occurrence the "cocktail party effect."

Not only is attention selective, but it is also *shiftable*. For example, if someone calls your name in a crowded room, you can shift your attention to that person. Or if you go to an art museum, you look at one painting, then another, then others, moving your attention from one painting to the next. Our capacity to shift our attention is itself limited. Karen Arnell, of Brock University, and her colleagues have studied this limitation using a rapid serial visual presentation (RSVP) task in which visual stimuli are quickly presented one after another at the same location on a computer screen. They found that paying attention to one stimulus makes it harder to attend to a subsequent stimulus and that this difficulty persists for an interval of about half a second (Arnell & Jenkins, 2004; Raymond & others, 1992). They have also shown that this attentional blink occurs in our sense of hearing as well (Arnell & Jolicoeur, 1999). Researchers from Dalhousie University have also shown that the *attentional blink* is more severe when more effort is required to process the first stimulus (Shore & others, 2001). It is worth noting that this effect depends upon the relationship of the two stimuli. For example, Todd Mondor, of

selective attention Focusing on a specific aspect of experience while ignoring others.

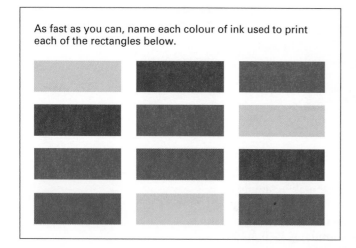

As fast as you can, name each colour of ink used to print each of the rectangles below.

Now, as fast as you can, name the colour of ink used to print each word shown below, ignoring what each word says.

GREEN   BLUE   RED
RED   GREEN   BLUE
YELLOW   RED   YELLOW
BLUE   YELLOW   GREEN

FIGURE 5.6 The Stroop Effect

Before reading further, read the instructions above and complete the tasks. Now, you probably had little or no difficulty naming the colours of the rectangles in the set on the left. However, you likely stumbled more when you were asked to name the colour of ink used to print each word in the set on the right. This demonstration of automaticity in perception is the Stroop effect.

the University of Manitoba, has shown that the processing of a second stimulus can be speeded up if it is sufficiently similar to the first stimulus (Mondor & Lacey, 2001).

Why do we pay attention to some aspects of our experience and block out others? Your motivation and interests influence what you attend to. If tattooing is one of your interests, you will be more likely to attend to an advertisement for a tattoo parlour than someone who has no interest in tattoos. A person who is interested in extreme sports is more likely to attend to an announcement that a program on skydiving will be on TV tonight than someone who is not interested in extreme sports. Certain features of stimuli also cause people to attend to them. Novel stimuli (those that are new, different, or unusual) often attract our attention. If one of those new, environmentally friendly Smart cars whizzes by, you are more likely to notice it than you would a Ford. Size, colour, and movement also influence our attention. Objects that are large, vividly coloured, or moving are more likely to grab our attention than objects that are small, dull-coloured, or stationary.

Highly practised and familiar stimuli, such as your own name, are often perceived so automatically that it is almost impossible to ignore them. The *Stroop effect* is an example of an automatic perception whereby it is difficult to name the colours in which words are printed when the words name different colours (Monsell, Taylor, & Murphy, 2001). To experience the Stroop effect, see figure 5.6. Most of the time, the highly practised and almost automatic perception of word meaning makes reading easier. However, this same automaticity makes it hard to ignore the meaning of the words for colours (such as blue) when they are printed in a different colour (such as orange) (MacLeod, 1992; Besner & Stolz, 1999; Roberts & Besner, 2005). Thus the Stroop effect represents a failure of selective attention. Interestingly, highly suggestible participants who were hypnotized and told they cannot read do not suffer Stroop intereference. Apparently hypnosis can allow us to access deeper than normal levels of the control over selective attention (MacLeod & Sheehan, 2003).

Psychologists are also interested in the top-down and bottom-up processing aspects of attention (Whiting, Madden & others, 2005; Pashler, Johnston, & Ruthruff, 2001). For example, the Stroop effect is an example not only of selective attention but also of *bottom-up processing*, in which attention is stimulus driven (Monahan, 2001). However, attention also involves *top-down processing*, in which attention is not stimulus driven but rather is due to decisions people make to initiate attention. Thus, you can make a decision to look at your watch to see how much more time you have to study this book today.

Perceptual Set Place your hand over the playing cards on the right in the illustration below and look at the playing cards on the left. As quickly as you can, count how many aces of spades you see. Then place your hand over the cards on the left and count the number of aces of spades among the cards on the right.

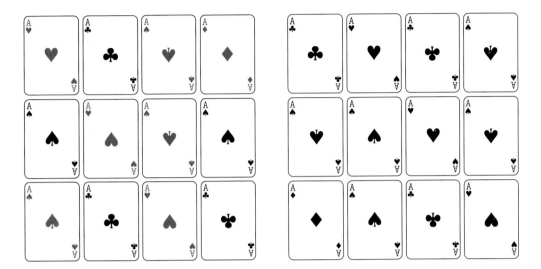

Most people report that they see two or three aces of spades in the set of 12 cards on the left. However, if you look closely, you'll see that there are five. Two of the aces of spades are black and three are red. When people look at the set of 12 cards on the right, they are more likely to count five aces of spades. Why do we perceive the two sets of cards differently? We expect the ace of spades to be black because it is always black in a regular deck of cards. We don't expect it to be red, so we skip right over the red ones. Our expectations influence our perceptions.

Psychologists refer to a predisposition or readiness to perceive something in a particular way as a **perceptual set**. Perceptual sets act as "psychological" filters in processing information about the environment. Interpretation is another consequence of a perceptual set. Interpretation can occur even before a stimulus or signal appears, as in the case of a runner waiting for a starting signal.

Interestingly, young children are more accurate at the task involving the ace of spades than adults are. Why? Because they have not built up the perceptual set that aces of spades are black. The underestimation of aces of spades in the left set of 12 cards reflects the concept of top-down processing.

Sensory Adaptation

Turning out the lights in your bedroom at night, you stumble across the room to your bed, completely blind to the objects around you. Gradually you *dark adapt*, as the objects in your room reappear and become more and more clear. The ability of the visual system to dark adapt is an example of **sensory adaptation**—a change in the responsiveness of the sensory system based on the average level of surrounding stimulation (Durgin, 2000). You have experienced sensory adaptation countless times in your life—adapting to the water in an initially "freezing" swimming pool, or to the smell of the Thanksgiving dinner that is wonderful to the arriving guests but almost undetectable to the cook who spent all day over it. Although all senses adapt to prolonged stimulation, we use vision as an example to illustrate this topic.

We used the example of adapting to the dark. When you turn out the lights, everything is black. Conversely, when you step out into the bright sunshine after spending some time in a dark basement, your eyes are flooded with light, everything appears too light, and you must *light adapt*. An important function of the eye is to get a good picture of the world. Good pictures have sharp contrasts between dark and light parts. The pupil of the eye adjusts the amount of light that gets into the eye and therefore helps to

perceptual set A predisposition or readiness to perceive something in a particular way.

sensory adaptation A change in the responsiveness of the sensory system based on the average level of surrounding stimulation.

preserve the contrast between dark and light areas in our picture. Additionally, structures throughout the visual system adapt. You may have noticed that the change in the size of the pupil as you dim or brighten the lights happens very quickly. You may also have noticed that when you turn out the lights in your bedroom, the contrast between dark and light continues to improve for nearly 45 minutes. The reason is that the sensory receptors in your visual system adapt or adjust their response rates on the basis of the average light level of the surrounding room. This adaptation takes longer than it does for the pupil to adjust. All of these mechanisms allow the visual system to preserve contrast over an extremely large range of background illumination conditions. We do, however, pay for our ability to adapt to the average level of light in our environment. It takes precious time to adapt, say when driving out of a dark tunnel under a mountain into the glistening and blinding reflection of the sun off the snow.

Our sensory systems are remarkably adaptable (Marotta, Keith, & Crawford, 2005). In one classic study, Stratton (1897) wore upside-down prisms for several weeks. At first he could make no sense of the world around him but after a few weeks he adapted so that he could function normally. Of course, when he finally took the prisms off, the world appeared upside-down to him again and he had to go through the adaptation process all over again.

> **reflect and review**

1 **Discuss basic principles of sensation and perception.**

- Explain what sensation and perception mean.
- Outline the sensory reception process and define three types of sensory reception.
- Distinguish between absolute threshold and difference threshold, and evaluate subliminal perception.
- Understand how signal detection theory accounts for the effect of uncertainty on perception.
- Discuss these aspects of perception: attention and perceptual set.
- Describe sensory adaptation.

Try the absolute threshold experiment described on p. xxx. Discuss your results with others in your class who tried the experiment.

2 THE VISUAL SYSTEM

The Visual Stimulus and the Eye — Visual Processing in the Brain — Colour Vision — Perceiving Shape, Depth, Motion, and Constancy — Illusions

How do we see the world and know what we are seeing?

Dr. P. was a distinguished musician who also taught music. However, he began having difficulty in visually perceiving his world. Sometimes he would fail to recognize his students, whom he had taught for many years, until they spoke. Dr. P. knew who they were by their voices. Aware that there was something wrong with the way he was seeing his world, Dr. P. went to see an ophthalmologist. Dr. P. was told that there was nothing wrong with his eyes but that he should see a neurologist. Dr. P. was referred to neurologist Oliver Sacks (1985), who wrote about him in *The Man Who Mistook His Wife for a Hat*. By the time he saw Sacks, nothing was familiar to Dr. P. He actually did confuse his wife with a hat. When shown a glove, Dr. P. said it was a container of some sort, maybe a five-chambered change purse. Visually, he was lost in a world of lifeless

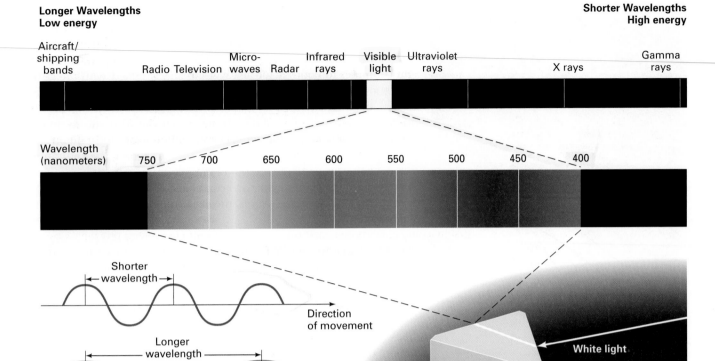

FIGURE 5.7

The Electromagnetic Spectrum and Visible Light
(*Top*) Visible light is only a narrow band in the electromagnetic spectrum. Visible light wavelengths range from about 400–700 nm. X-rays are much shorter, radio waves much longer. (*Bottom*) The two graphs show how waves vary in length between successive peaks. Shorter wavelengths are higher in frequency, as reflected in blue colours; longer wavelengths are lower in frequency, as reflected in red colours.

abstractions. He could no longer recognize familiar people and objects; Dr. P. suffered from visual agnosia, a failure to interpret visual information. While his eyes detected visual information in the world, his brain failed to make any sense of it. Only when we consider both what the eyes see and how the brain interprets what the eyes see can we fully understand how people visually perceive the world. The next section explores the physical foundations of the visual system.

The Visual Stimulus and the Eye

Our ability to detect visual stimuli depends on the sensitivity of our eyes to differences in light. This section covers some basic facts about light energy and the complex structure of the eye.

Light *Light* is a form of electromagnetic energy that can be described in terms of wavelengths. Like ocean waves moving toward the beach, light travels through space in waves. The *wavelength* of light is the distance from the peak of one wave to the peak of the next. Wavelengths of visible light range from about 400 to 700 nanometres (a nanometre is 1-billionth of a metre and is abbreviated nm). Outside the range of visible light are longer radio and infrared radiation waves and shorter ultraviolet and x-rays (see figure 5.7). These other forms of electromagnetic energy continually bombard us, but we do not see them. Why do we see only the narrow band of electromagnetic energy with wavelengths between 400 and 700 nanometres? The likeliest answer is that our visual system evolved in the sun's light. Thus our visual system is able to perceive the range of

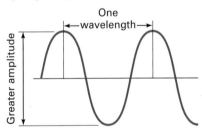
Light waves of greater amplitude make up brighter light.

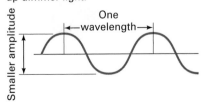
Light waves of smaller amplitude make up dimmer light.

FIGURE 5.8

Light Waves of Varying Amplitude

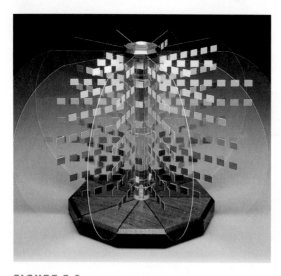

FIGURE 5.9

A Colour Tree Showing Colour's Three Dimensions: Hue, Saturation, and Brightness
Hue is represented around the colour tree, saturation horizontally, and brightness vertically.

energy emitted by the sun. By the time sunlight reaches the earth's surface, it is strongest in the 400 to 700 nanometre range. The wavelength of light that is reflected by a visual stimulus determines its hue, or perceived colour.

Two other characteristics of light waves are amplitude and purity. *Amplitude* refers to the height of a wave, and is linked with the perceived brightness of a visual stimulus (see figure 5.8). Purity, the mixture of wavelengths in light, is related to the perceived saturation or richness of a visual stimulus. The colour tree shown in figure 5.9 can help you to understand saturation. Colours that are very pure have no white light in them. They are located on the outside of the colour tree. Notice how the saturation of a colour changes toward the interior of the colour tree. The closer we get to the centre, the more white light has been added to the single wavelength of a particular colour. In other words, the deep colours at the edge fade into pastel colours toward the centre.

The Structure of the Eye The eye, not unlike a camera, is constructed to get the best possible "picture" of the world. Let's see how the eye performs this task.

Getting the Best "Picture" of the World A good picture is in focus, is not too dark or too light, and has good contrast between the dark and light parts. Each of several structures in the eye plays an important role in this process. If you look closely at your eyes in the mirror, you will notice three parts—the sclera, iris, and pupil (figure 5.10). The *sclera* is the white outer part of the eye that helps to maintain the shape of the eye and to protect it from injury. The *iris* is the coloured part of the eye, which might be light blue in one individual and dark brown in another. The *pupil*, which appears black, is the opening in the centre of the iris. To get a good picture of the world, the eye needs to be able to adjust the amount of light that enters. The iris contains muscles that control the size of the pupil and, hence, the amount of light that gets into the eye. In this sense, the pupil acts like the aperture of a camera, opening to let in more light when it is needed and closing to let in less light when there is too much. This allows the eye to function optimally under different conditions of illumination, which can range in the course of a normal day from the darkest moonless night to the brightest summer sunshine. In other words, we dark adapt and light adapt, in part, by changing the size of our pupils.

You can demonstrate changes in the size of the pupil by looking at your eyes in the mirror and turning the room lights up and down. (You need to try this experiment in a room with sufficient light to be able to see your eyes even when the lights are turned all the way down.) As you dim the light, your pupils will begin to enlarge to let in more light;

FIGURE 5.10

Parts of the Eye
Note that the image of the butterfly on the retina is upside down. The brain allows us to see the image right side up.

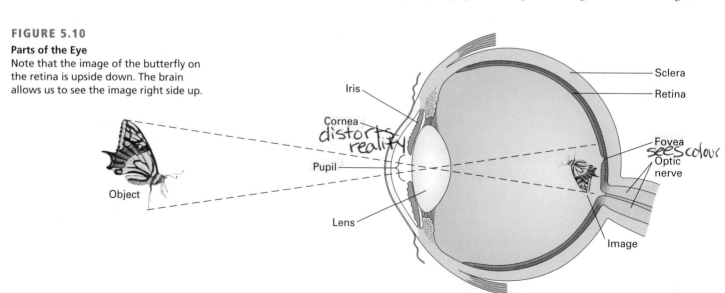

as you turn the room lights back up, the pupil opening will shrink to let in less light.

If the eye acts like a camera, then, in addition to having the right amount of light, the image has to be in focus at the back of the eye. Two structures serve this purpose: the *cornea*, which is a clear membrane just in front of the eye, and the *lens* of the eye, which is a transparent and somewhat flexible disk-shaped structure filled with a gelatinous material. The function of both these structures is to bend the light falling on the surface of the eye just enough to focus it at the back of the eye. The curved surface of the cornea does most of this bending, while the lens fine-tunes the focus. When you are looking at faraway objects, attached muscles pull the lens into a relatively flat shape, because the light reaching the eye from faraway objects is parallel and the bending power of the cornea is sufficient to keep things in focus. However, the light reaching the eye from objects that are close is more scattered, so the light needs to bend more to achieve focus.

Without this ability of the lens to change its curvature, the eye would have a tough time focusing on objects that are close to us, as in activities like needlework or reading. As we age, we may develop *presbyopia*. The lens of our eye loses its flexibility and, hence, its ability to change from its normal flattened shape to the rounder shape needed to bring objects into close focus. This is why many people whose vision is normal throughout their young adult lives require reading glasses when they get older.

Recording Images on the Retina   The parts of the eye that have been discussed so far work together to get the best possible picture of the world. All of this effort, however, would be for naught without a method for keeping or "recording" the images we take of the world (Enns, 2004). In a camera, film serves just such a purpose. Film is made of a material that responds to light. The multilayered **retina** at the back of the eye is the light-sensitive surface that records what we see and converts it to neural impulses for processing in the brain.

Making an analogy between the film of a camera and the retina, however, vastly underestimates the complexity and elegance of the retina's design. The retina is, in fact, the primary mechanism of sight, but even after decades of intense study, the full marvel of this structure is far from understood (Masland & Raviola, 2000).

Because the retina is so important to vision, we need to study its makeup in some detail. Earlier in this chapter, we discussed transduction, the conversion of one form of energy into another. In sensation, stimulus energy is transduced into neural impulses (Reid, 2000). How does transduction occur in vision?

The human retina has approximately 126 million receptor cells. They turn the electromagnetic energy of light into a form of energy that can be processed by the nervous system. There are two kinds of visual receptor cells: rods and cones. Rods and cones are involved in different aspects of vision, and they differ both in how they respond to light and in their patterns of distribution on the surface of the retina (Blake, 2000). **Rods** are the receptors in the retina that are sensitive to light, but they are not very useful for colour vision. Thus they function well under low illumination; as you might expect, they are hard at work at night (Field, Alapakkam, & Rieke, 2005). Humans have about 120 million rods. **Cones** are the receptors that we use for colour perception. Like the rods, cones are light sensitive. However, they require a larger amount of light than the rods do to respond, and so they operate best in daylight or under high illumination. There are about six million cone cells in human eyes. Figure 5.11 shows what rods and cones look like.

The most important part of the retina is the fovea, a minute area in the centre of the retina where vision is most acute (see figure 5.10). The fovea contains mainly cones and is vitally important to many visual tasks (try reading out of the corner of your eye!). By contrast, rods are found mainly on the periphery (outer boundary) of the retina around the central fovea. Because rods require little light, they work best under conditions of low illumination. This light sensitivity and the rods' location on the retina give us the ability to detect fainter spots of light on the peripheral retina than at the fovea. Thus, if you want to see a very faint star, you should gaze slightly away from the star.

— Rod

— Cone

FIGURE 5.11
Rods and Cones

retina The light-sensitive surface in the back of the eye that houses light receptors called rods and cones.

rods The receptors in the retina that are sensitive to light but are not very useful in colour vision.

cones The receptors in the retina that process information about colour.

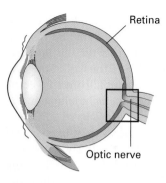

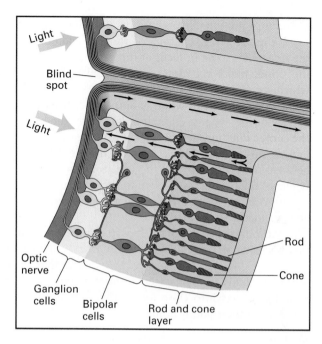

FIGURE 5.12 **Direction of Light in the Retina**

After light passes through the cornea, pupil, and lens, it falls on the retina. Three layers of specialized cells in the retina convert the image into a neural signal that can be transmitted to the brain. First, light triggers a reaction in the rods and cones at the back of the retina, transducing light energy into electrochemical neural impulses. The neural impulses activate the bipolar cells, which in turn activate the ganglion cells. Then light information is transmitted to the optic nerve, which conveys it to the brain. The arrows indicate the sequence in which light information moves in the retina.

Light striking the rods and cones at the back of the retina is transduced by breaking down a chemical (*rhodopsin* in rods and *iodopsin* in cones) to produce electrochemical impulses (Sandell, 2000; Sakmar & others, 2002). This signal is transmitted to the bipolar cells and then moves on to another layer of specialized cells called *ganglion* cells (see Figure 5.12). The axons of the ganglion cells make up the optic nerve that carries the visual information to the brain for further processing.

There is one place on the retina that contains neither rods nor cones. Not surprisingly, this area is called the *blind spot*; it is the place on the retina where the optic nerve leaves the eye on its way to the brain (see figure 5.12). We cannot see anything that reaches only this part of the retina. To prove to yourself that you have a blind spot, see figure 5.13. A summary of the characteristics of rods and cones is presented in figure 5.14.

FIGURE 5.13 **The Eye's Blind Spot**

There is a normal blind spot in your eye, a small area where the optic nerve leads to the brain. To find your blind spot, hold this book at arm's length, cover your left eye, and stare at the red pepper on the left with your right eye. Move the book slowly toward you until the yellow pepper disappears. To find the blind spot in your left eye, cover your right eye, stare at the yellow pepper, and adjust the book until the red pepper disappears.

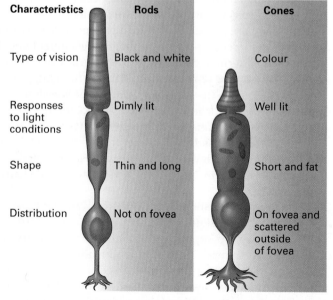

FIGURE 5.14 **Characteristics of Rods and Cones**

Characteristics	Rods	Cones
Type of vision	Black and white	Colour
Responses to light conditions	Dimly lit	Well lit
Shape	Thin and long	Short and fat
Distribution	Not on fovea	On fovea and scattered outside of fovea

Visual Processing in the Brain

Recall the case of Dr. P., the musician who lost the ability to recognize familiar people and objects on sight. The eyes are just the beginning of visual perception. The next step occurs when neural impulses generated in the retina are dispatched to the brain for analysis and integration.

The optic nerve leaves the eye, carrying information about light toward the brain. Light travels in a straight line; therefore, stimuli in the left visual field are registered in the right half of the retina in both eyes, and stimuli in the right visual field are registered in the left half of the retina in both eyes (see figure 5.15). In the brain, at a point called the *optic chiasm*, the optic nerve fibres divide, and approximately half the nerve fibres cross over the midline of the brain. As a result, the visual information originating in the right halves of the two retinas is transmitted to the left side of the occipital lobe in the cerebral cortex, and the visual information coming from the left halves of the retinas is transmitted to the right side of the occipital lobe. These crossings mean that what we see in the left side of our visual field is registered in the right side of the brain, and what we see in the right visual field is registered in the left side of the brain (see figure 5.15). This information is then processed and combined into a recognizable object or scene in the visual cortex.

The Visual Cortex The *visual cortex*, located in the occipital lobe of the brain, is the part of the cerebral cortex that functions in vision. Most visual information travels to the primary visual cortex, where it is processed, before moving to other visual areas for further analysis (Milner & Goodale, 2002).

An important aspect of visual information processing is the specialization of neurons. Like the cells in the retina, many cells in the primary visual cortex are highly specialized. **Feature detectors** are neurons in the brain's visual system that respond to particular features of a stimulus. Canadian David Hubel and Swede Torsten Wiesel (1965) won a Nobel Prize for their research on feature detectors. By recording the activity of *single* neurons in cats while they looked at patterns that varied in size, shape, colour, and movement, they found that the visual cortex has neurons that are individually sensitive to different types of lines and angles. One neuron might show a sudden burst of activity when stimulated by lines of a particular angle; another neuron might fire only when moving stimuli appear; yet another neuron might be stimulated when the object in the visual field has a combination of certain angles, sizes, and shapes.

Parallel Processing According to Melvyn Goodale, of the University of Western Ontario, *What?* and *Where?* are two of the basic questions that need to be answered in visual perception. Not only must people realize what they are looking at, but they also need to know where it is so they can respond appropriately. The elegantly organized brain has two pathways—dubbed "what" and "where"—to handle these important vision tasks (see figure 5.16; Ungerleider & Mishkin, 1982; Goodale & Humphrey, 2001; Deco, Rolls, & Horwitz, 2004). The *ventral pathway* in the temporal lobe processes *what* information about the object, including its colour, form, and texture. The *dorsal pathway* processes *where* information about an object's location, including information about movement and the depth of the object. This pathway is located in the parietal lobe.

As you might have guessed, Dr. P., the musician with visual agnosia, likely suffered damage somewhere along the ventral pathway in the temporal lobe. A peculiar form of visual agnosia, called *prosopagnosia*, arises from localized damage to an area along the ventral pathway that is activated when we try to recognize someone's face. In the rare

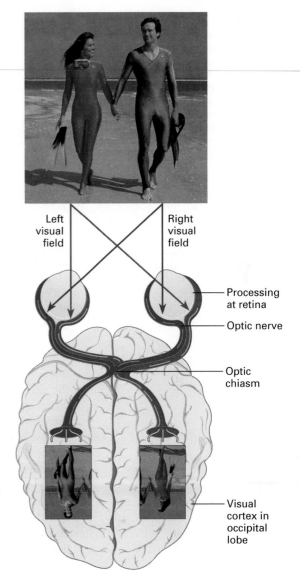

FIGURE 5.15

Visual Pathways to and Through the Brain
Light from each side of the visual field falls on the opposite side of each eye's retina. Visual information then travels along the optic nerve to the optic chiasm, where most of the visual information crosses over to the other side of the brain. From there, visual information goes to the occipital lobe at the rear of the brain. All these crossings mean that what we see in the left side of our visual field (here, the woman) is registered in the right side of our brain, and what we see in the right visual field (the man) is registered in the left side of our brain.

feature detectors Neurons in the brain's visual system that respond to particular lines or other features of a stimulus.

FIGURE 5.16

**The What and Where Pathways
for Visual Information**
These parallel neural pathways process
information about an object's
characteristics ("what") and location
("where"). Note the interconnecting
arrows between the pathways. As the
what and where pathways carry information to other areas of the cerebral
cortex, they are not completely
isolated: Connections between them
contribute to the integration of "what"
and "where" information.

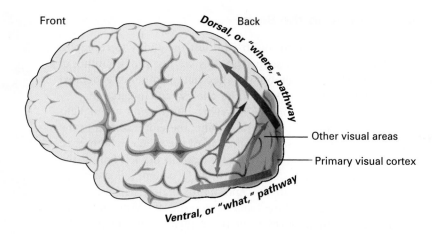

cases in which these areas are damaged, individuals have difficulty recognizing the person whose face they are seeing, even though they know they're seeing a face (Marotta,
McKeeff, & Behrmann, 2002; Behrmann & others, in press). What happens if someone
suffers damage to the dorsal pathway? In a rare case, a woman with damage in an area
of the parietal lobe that is activated by movement had great difficulty crossing the street.
While she could recognize cars, she could not distinguish approaching cars from parked
cars (Zeki, 1991).

The phenomenon of *blindsight* is perhaps the strongest evidence supporting the distinction between the ventral and dorsal pathways. Goodale and his colleagues describe
the case of D.F., who suffered damage to her ventral pathway, resulting in a severe
visual agnosia (Goodale & others, 1991; James & others, 2003). While she could not
recognize objects, she was nevertheless able to successfully grasp them. In one test, she
was asked to insert a card in a slot at a particular angle. While she could not describe the
orientation of the slot, she could skillfully insert a card into it. According to Goodale and
his colleagues, her ventral pathway damage left her, in a sense, *blind* to the slot but her
intact dorsal pathway still allowed her enough sight to guide her actions. In other
words, it is the *where* pathway that guides reaching and grasping.

The dorsal and ventral pathways are examples of **parallel processing**, the simultaneous distribution of information across different neural pathways. Parallel processing helps sensory information travel rapidly through the brain. A sensory system
designed to process information about sensory qualities serially or consecutively (such
as the shapes of images, their colours, their movements, their locations, and so on)
would be too slow to keep us current with a rapidly changing world. There is some evidence suggesting that parallel processing also occurs for sensations of touch and hearing (Kalat, 2004).

Binding Although the ventral and dorsal pathways work in parallel, connections
between them serve to unify sensory information into a complete picture of the what
and where of all we see. For instance, if you were to look at a parrot, visual information
about the parrot would enter the visual system through your eyes as a complete object.
However, as we have seen, the sensory system breaks down this visual information and
transmits it in distributed pathways and to specific neurons. Seeing the whole parrot
requires reassembling the information (Crick & Koch, 1998).

An exciting topic in visual perception today is what neuroscientists call **binding**,
the bringing together and integration of what is processed by different pathways or cells
(Robertson, 2003). Binding involves the coupling of the activity of various cells and
pathways, thus allowing information about the parrot's shape, size, location, colour,
motion, and so on to be integrated into a complete image of the parrot in the cerebral
cortex. One way to describe the failure of object recognition in visual agnosia is as a failure to bind information about the shape, texture, and size of objects. According to
Robertson (2003), one possible explanation for synaesthesia, which we discussed at the
beginning of this chapter, is that inappropriate cross-sensory binding occurs across connections between brain areas.

parallel processing The simultaneous
distribution of information across
different neural pathways.

binding The bringing together and
integration of what is processed through
different pathways or cells.

Researchers have found that all the neurons throughout pathways that are activated by a visual object fire together at the same frequency (Engel & Singer, 2001; Singer & Gray, 1995). Within the vast network of cells in the cerebral cortex, this set of neurons appears to *bind* together all the features of the objects into a unified perception. Exactly how binding occurs is not completely known at this time, but the process is a major focus of research in the neuroscience of visual perception today.

Colour Vision

We don't have to be synesthetes, like artist Wassili Kandinsky, to appreciate our colour vision. Imagine how dull a world without colour would be. Natural wonders such as the Rocky Mountains of British Columbia and Alberta or the coastline of Newfoundland would lose much of their beauty for us if we could not see their rich colours. The ability to see colour evolved because it provides many advantages to animals, including the ability to detect and discriminate various objects (Kingdom, 2003; Gegenfurtner & Kiper, 2003). For example, the edibility of foods depends on ripeness, which is reflected in colour.

Different wavelengths of light give rise to different patterns of neural responses, which, in turn, generate colour vision (Sekuler & Blake, 2006). The study of human colour vision using psychological methods is well-developed (Kaiser & Boynton, 1996). A full century before the methods existed to study the anatomical and neurophysiological bases of colour perception, psychological studies had discovered many of the basic principles of our colour vision system. These studies produced two main theories: trichromatic theory and opponent-process theory. Both turned out to be correct.

The **trichromatic theory** states that colour perception is produced by three types of receptors (cone cells in the retina) that are particularly sensitive to different, but overlapping, ranges of wavelengths. The three different types of cone (called *red, green,* and *blue*) each rely upon a different iodopsin which is best broken down when it absorbs a different wavelength of visible light. The trichromatic theory of colour vision was proposed by Thomas Young in 1802 and extended by Hermann von Helmholtz in 1852. The theory is based on the results of experiments on human colour-matching abilities, which show that a person with normal vision can match any colour in the spectrum by combining three other wavelengths. In this type of experiment, individuals are given a light of a single wavelength and are asked to combine three other single-wavelength lights to match the first light. They can do this by changing the relative intensities of the three lights until the colour of the combination light is indistinguishable from the colour of the first light. Young and Helmholtz reasoned that if the combination of any three wavelengths of different intensities is indistinguishable from any single pure wavelength, the visual system must base its perception of colour on the relative responses of three receptor systems.

Further support for the trichromatic theory is found in the study of defective colour vision, or what is commonly referred to as colour blindness (see figure 5.17). The term *colour blind* is somewhat misleading because it suggests that a colour-blind person cannot see colour at all. That condition occurs only when all three kinds of cone are not functioning in that person. Complete colour blindness is rare; most people who are colour blind, the vast majority of whom are men, are better described as *colour deficient,* since they can see some colours but not others (Coren, Ward, & Enns, 2004). The nature of colour deficiency depends on which of the three kinds of cones is inoperative. *Monochromats* are people with only one kind of cone. *Dichromats* are people with only two kinds of cones. In the most common form of colour blindness, red-green colour blindness, the green cone or red cone system malfunctions in some way, rendering green indistinguishable from certain combinations of blue and red. Colour-matching experiments performed by people with this form of colour deficiency show that they need only two other colours to match a pure colour and thus have dichromatic colour perception. Incidentally, you may have heard that dogs are colour blind. Actually they are dichromats, with colour vision like that of a red-green colour blind human. *Trichromats* have all three kinds of cone receptors and normal colour vision.

trichromatic theory Colour perception is based on the existence of three types of receptors that are maximally sensitive to different, but overlapping, ranges of wavelengths.

FIGURE 5.17

Examples of Stimuli Used to Test for Colour Blindness
People with normal vision see the number 16 in the left circle and the number 8 in the right circle. People with red-green colour blindness may see just the 16, just the 8, or neither. A complete colour blindness assessment involves the use of fifteen stimuli.

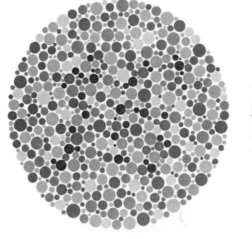
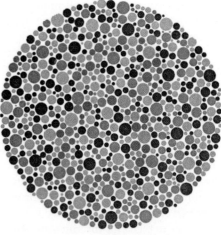

FIGURE 5.18

Negative Afterimage— Complementary Colours
If you gaze steadily at the dot in the coloured panel on the left for a few moments, then shift your gaze to the grey box on the right, you will see the original hues' complementary colours. The blue appears as yellow, the red as green, the green as red, and the yellow as blue. This pairing of colours has to do with the fact that colour receptors in the eye are apparently sensitive as pairs: When one colour is turned off (when you stop staring at the panel), the other colour in the receptor is briefly turned on. The afterimage effect is especially noticeable with bright colours.

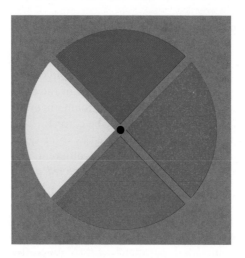
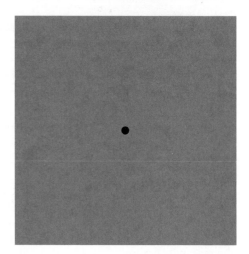

opponent-process theory Cells in the visual system respond to red-green and blue-yellow colours; a given cell might be excited by red and inhibited by green, whereas another might be excited by yellow and inhibited by blue.

In 1878, the German physiologist Ewald Hering observed that some colours cannot exist together, whereas others can. For example, it is easy to imagine a greenish blue or a reddish yellow, but nearly impossible to imagine a reddish green or a bluish yellow. Hering also noticed that trichromatic theory could not adequately explain *afterimages*, sensations that remain after a stimulus is removed (see figure 5.18 to experience an afterimage). Colour afterimages are common and involve complementary colours. One example of afterimages occurs after prolonged exposure to older computer screens with green lettering, such as those still used in some businesses. Working with a screen like this all day can cause white objects and walls to appear reddish. Conversely, if you look at red long enough, eventually a green afterimage will appear. And, if you look at yellow long enough, eventually a blue afterimage will appear. Such afterimages are examples of bottom-up processing.

Hering's observations led him to propose that the visual system treats colours as complementary pairs: red-green and blue-yellow. Hering's view is called **opponent-process theory**, which states that cells in the visual system respond to red-green and blue-yellow colours; a given cell might be excited by red and inhibited by green, whereas another cell might be excited by yellow and inhibited by blue. Researchers have found that opponent-process theory does indeed explain afterimages (Enns, 2004; Jameson & Hurvich, 1989). If you stare at red, for instance, your red-green system seems to "tire," and when you look away, it rebounds and gives you a green afterimage. Also, if you mix equal amounts of opponent colours, such as blue and yellow, you see grey; figure 5.19 illustrates this principle.

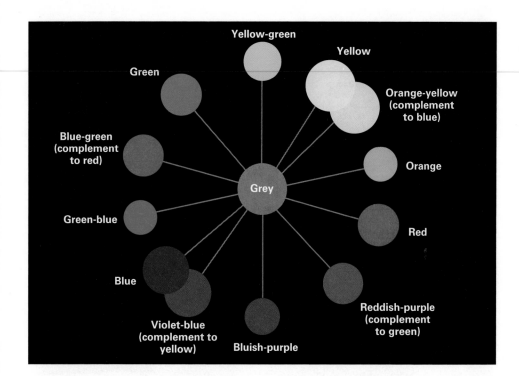

FIGURE 5.19
Colour Wheel
Colours opposite each other produce the neutral grey in the centre when they are mixed.

If the trichromatic theory of colour perception is correct and we do in fact have three kinds of cone receptors like those predicted by Young and Helmholtz, then how can the opponent-process theory also be correct? The answer is that the red, blue, and green cones in the retina are connected to retinal ganglion cells in such a way that the three-colour code is immediately translated into the opponent-process code (see figure 5.20). For example, a green cone might inhibit and a red cone might excite a particular ganglion cell. Thus, *both* the trichromatic and opponent-process theories are correct—the eyes and the brain use both methods to code colours.

This discussion of theories of colour vision illustrates an important feature of psychology that we described in chapter 1. Science often progresses when conflicting ideas are posed and investigated. In many instances, as with colour vision, seemingly conflicting ideas or systems may actually work, and even work best, together.

THE FAR SIDE   By GARY LARSON

" . . . And please let Mom, Dad, Rex, Ginger, Tucker, me and all the rest of the family see color."

THE FAR SIDE © FARWORKS, Inc. Used by permission. All rights reserved.

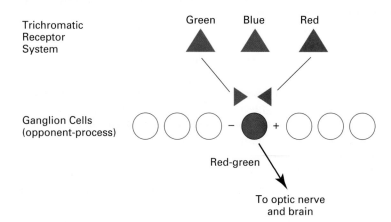

FIGURE 5.20 Trichromatic and Opponent-Process Theories: Transmission of Colour Information in the Retina Cones responsive to green, blue, or red light form a trichromatic receptor system in the retina. As information is transmitted to the retina's ganglion cells, opponent-process cells are activated. As shown here, a retinal ganglion cell is inhibited by a green cone (−) and excited by a red cone (+), producing red-green colour information.

FIGURE 5.21

Reversible Figure-Ground Pattern
Do you see the silhouette of a goblet
or a pair of faces in profile?

FIGURE 5.22 **Sophisticated Use of the Figure-Ground Relationship in Escher's Woodcut**
Relativity **(1938)**

Perceiving Shape, Depth, Motion, and Constancy

Perceiving visual stimuli means organizing and interpreting the fragments of information that the eye sends to the visual cortex. Information about the dimensions of what
we are seeing is critical to this process. Among these dimensions are shape, depth,
motion, and constancy.

Think about the world of shapes—buildings against the sky, boats on the horizon,
letters on this page. We see these shapes because they are marked off from the rest of
what we see by *contour*, a location at which a sudden change of brightness occurs (Feldman & Singh, 2005). As you look at this page, you see letters, which are shapes, in a
field or background, the white page. The **figure-ground relationship** is the principle
by which we organize the perceptual field into stimuli that stand out (*figure*) and those
that are left over (*background*). Generally, this principle works well for us, but some figure-ground relationships are highly ambiguous, and it may be difficult to tell what is
figure and what is ground. A well-known ambiguous figure-ground relationship is
shown in figure 5.21. As you look at the figure, your perception is likely to shift from
seeing two faces to seeing a single goblet. The work of artist M. C. Escher, which does
not provide consistent spatial location and depth cues, also illustrates figure-ground
ambiguity (see figure 5.22).

One school of psychology has been especially intrigued by how we perceive shapes.
According to **gestalt psychology**, people naturally organize their perceptions according
to certain patterns (*gestalt* is German for "configuration" or "form"). The concept of
"pattern" reflects one of gestalt psychology's main underlying principles: The whole is

figure-ground relationship People
organize the perceptual field into stimuli
that stand out (figure) and those that are
left over (background).

gestalt psychology People naturally
organize their perceptions according to
certain patterns.

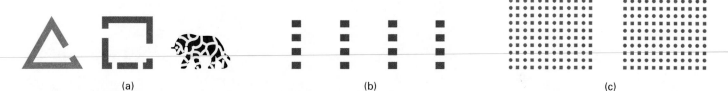

FIGURE 5.23 **Gestalt Principles of Closure, Proximity, and Similarity**
(a) Closure: When we see disconnected or incomplete figures, we fill in the spaces and see them as complete figures. *(b) Proximity:* When we see objects that are near each other, they tend to be seen as a unit. You are likely to perceive the grouping as 4 columns of 4 squares, not 1 set of 16 squares. *(c) Similarity:* When we see objects that are similar to each other, they tend to be seen as a unit. Here, you are likely to see vertical columns of circles and squares in the left box but horizontal rows of circles and squares in the right box.

different from the sum of its parts (Palmer, 2003). Thus, from the thousands of tiny coloured dots ("parts") that make up an image in a newspaper or on a computer screen, we perceive a "whole" image, such as the face of Brad Pitt or Halle Berry. Similarly, when you watch one of these actors in a movie, the "motion" you see in the film cannot be found in the film itself; if you examine it, you see only separate frames. When you watch the film, the frames move past a light source at a rate of 24 per second, and you perceive a whole that is very different from the separate frames that are the film's parts.

The figure-ground relationship is also a gestalt principle. Three other gestalt principles are closure, proximity, and similarity. The principle of *closure* states that when individuals see a disconnected or incomplete figure, they fill in the spaces and see it as a complete figure (see figure 5.23a). The principle of *proximity* states that when individuals see objects close to each other, they tend to group them together (see figure 5.23b). The principle of *similarity* states that when objects are similar, individuals tend to group them together (see figure 5.23c).

Depth Perception Images appear on our retinas in two-dimensional form, yet remarkably we see a three-dimensional world. **Depth perception** is the ability to perceive objects three-dimensionally. Look around you. You don't see your surroundings as flat. You see some objects farther away, some closer. Some objects overlap each other. The scene and objects that you are looking at have depth. How do you see depth? To see a world of depth, we use two kinds of information, or cues—binocular and monocular.

Because we have two eyes, we get two views of the world, one from each eye (Howard & Rogers, 2001a). **Binocular cues** are depth cues that depend on the combination of the images in the left and right eyes and on the way the two eyes work together. The pictures are slightly different because the eyes are in slightly different positions. Try holding your hand about 25 centimetres from your face. Alternately close and open your left and right eyes, so that only one eye is open at a time. The image of your hand will appear to jump back and forth because the image of your hand is in a slightly different place on the left and right retinas. The *disparity*, or difference between the images in the two eyes, is the cue the brain uses for binocular vision, also known as *stereopsis* (Howard & Rogers, 2001b). The combination of the two images in the brain, and the disparity between them in the eyes, gives us information about the three-dimensionality of the world (Howard & Rogers, 2001 a,b; Cumming & DeAngelis, 2000).

In the late nineteenth century, *stereograms*, pairs of slightly different images, became popular. Viewing a stereogram through a stereoviewer, which displays one image to each eye, results in a strong three-dimensional experience. More recently, Chris Tyler (1983) popularized the *autostereogram*, which presents stereoscopic information in a single two-dimensional image (figure 5.24).

In addition to using binocular cues to get an idea of the depth of objects, we use a number of **monocular cues**, or depth cues, available from the image in one eye, either right or left. These are powerful cues and under normal circumstances can provide a very compelling impression of depth. Try closing one eye—your perception of the world

depth perception The ability to perceive objects three dimensionally.

binocular cues Depth cues that are based on the combination of the images on the left and right eyes and on the way the two eyes work together.

monocular cues Depth cues that can be extracted from the images in either eye.

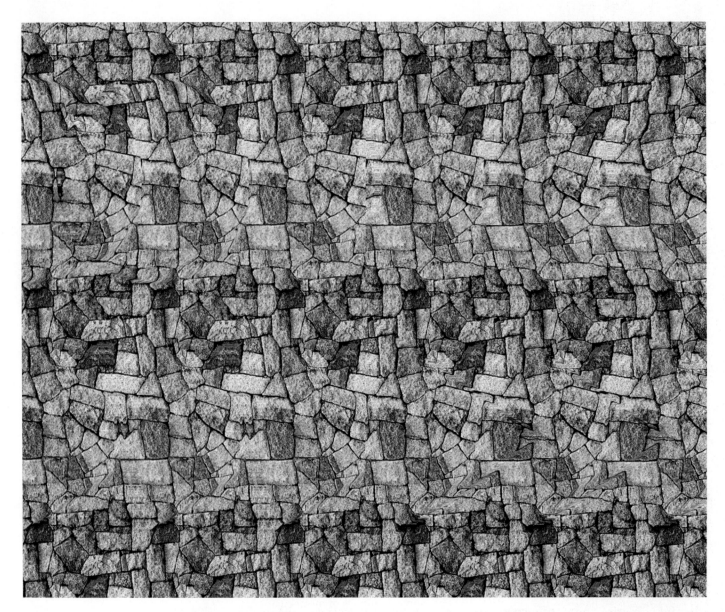

FIGURE 5.24 **A Stereogram**

Seen in the right way, this figure contains 3 three-dimensional objects: a sphere in the top left, a pyramid in the top right, and a curved pointed conical figure in the centre at the bottom. It may take a moment or two to see them, but when you do, they will be astoundingly clear. There are two ways to see the three-dimensional objects in this figure. *Technique 1:* Cross your eyes by holding your finger up between your face and the figure. Look at the tip of your finger, and then slowly move your finger back and forth, toward and away from the figure, being careful to maintain focus on your finger. When the correct distance is reached, the three-dimensional objects will pop out at you. *Technique 2:* Put your face very close to the figure, so that it is difficult to focus or converge your eyes. Wait a moment, and begin to pull your face very slowly back from the figure. The picture should appear blurred for a bit, but when the right distance is reached should snap into three dimensionality. Regardless of the technique you try, be patient! You may have to try one or both of these techniques a few times. The difficulty is that your eyes will try to converge at the distance of the page (very sensible of them!)—so you must trick them into converging elsewhere, such as in front of the page, as in technique 1, or into staying perfectly parallel and unconverged, as in technique 2. Note: Some people will not be able to see the three dimensionality in these figures at all, for one of several reasons. First, some of us have eyes too well adapted to the real world to be convinced to converge in the "wrong place," given the image data appearing on the retinas. Second, some very common visual deficits that can yield appreciable differences between the quality of the image on the left and right retinas can affect the development of normal binocular vision. The brain requires comparable image quality from the two eyes in the first few years of life to develop a high degree of stereoacuity. When this fails to happen, the development of binocular neural mechanisms, which need to compare information in the two eyes, can be affected and can pose problems in processing pure stereoscopic information, as in this figure. The information here is purely stereoscopic because other, monocular, kinds of cues to depth, such as shading and perspective, are not available.

FIGURE 5.25   An Artist's Use of the Monocular Cue of Linear Perspective
Lawren Harris, of Canada's Group of Seven, used linear perspective to give the perception of depth to his painting *Miners' Houses, Glace Bay.* AGO No. 69/122.

still retains many of its three-dimensional qualities. Some examples of monocular cues are as follows:

1. *Familiar size.* This cue to the depth and distance of objects is based on what we have learned from experience about the standard sizes of objects. We know how large oranges tend to be, so we can tell something about how far away an orange is likely to be by the size of its image on the retina.

2. *Height in the field of view.* All other things being equal, objects positioned higher in a picture are seen as farther away.

3. *Linear perspective.* Objects that are farther away take up less space on the retina. As shown in figure 5.25, as an object recedes into the distance, parallel lines in the scene appear to converge.

4. *Overlap.* An object that partially conceals or overlaps another object is perceived as closer.

5. *Shading.* This cue involves changes in perception due to the position of the light and the position of the viewer. Consider a laptop computer under a desk lamp. If you walk around the desk, you will see different shading patterns on the laptop.

6. *Texture gradient.* Texture becomes denser and finer the farther away it is from the viewer (see figure 5.26).

FIGURE 5.26
Texture Gradient
The gradients of texture create an impression of depth on a flat surface.

FIGURE 5.27

Movement Aftereffects
This is an example of a geometric pattern that produces afterimages in which motion can be perceived. Stare at the centre of the pattern for about 10 seconds, then look at a white sheet of paper. You should perceive rotary motion on the paper.

FIGURE 5.28

Size Constancy
Even though our retinal images of the hot air balloons vary, we still realize the balloons are approximately the same size. This illustrates the principle of size constancy.

apparent movement The perception that a stationary object is moving.

perceptual constancy Recognition that objects are constant and unchanging even through sensory input about them is changing.

Depth perception is especially intriguing to painters, who have to paint a three-dimensional world on a two-dimensional canvas. Painters often use monocular cues to give the feeling of depth to their paintings. Indeed, monocular cues have become so widely used by artists that they are also called *pictorial cues*.

Motion Perception Motion perception plays an important role in the lives of many species. Indeed, for some animals motion perception is critical for survival. Both predators and their prey depend on being able to quickly detect motion. Frogs and some other simple vertebrates may not even see an object unless it is moving. For example, if a dead fly is dangled motionlessly in front of a frog, the frog cannot sense its winged meal. The "bug detecting" cells in the frog's retinas are wired only to sense movement. It is understandable, then, that dragonflies have evolved to camouflage their motion from their predators (Mizutani, Chahl, & Srinivasan, 2003).

Whereas the retinas of frogs can detect movement, the retinas of humans and other primates cannot. According to one neuroscientist, "the dumber the animal, the 'smarter' the retina" (Baylor, 2001). In humans, the brain takes over the job of analyzing motion through highly specialized pathways. Recall from our discussion of the brain pathways in vision that the where pathway is involved in motion detection.

How do humans perceive motion? First, we have neurons that are specialized to detect motion. Second, feedback from our body tells us whether we are moving or whether someone else or an object is moving, for example, moving your eye muscles as you watch a ball coming toward you. Third, the environment we see is rich in cues that give us information about movement (Royden, 2000). For example, when we run, what's around us appears to be "moving."

Psychologists are interested in both real movement and **apparent movement**, which occurs when an object is stationary, but we perceive it as moving. A dramatic example of apparent movement can be experienced at an IMAX theatre. Specially produced films are shown on six-storey-tall screens that fill your entire visual field. Airplanes, whales, jaguars, or spacecraft appear to move right out of the screen toward the audience. Scenes filmed from roller coasters or cars induce strong sensations of "movement" in the audience as well. A powerful sound system broadcast in surround sound enhances the experience. More recently, 3-D films have been produced for the IMAX screen, compounding the intensity of the experience.

Two forms of apparent motion are stroboscopic motion and movement aftereffects. *Stroboscopic motion* is the illusion of movement created when a rapid stimulation of different parts of the retina occurs. Motion pictures are a form of stroboscopic motion. *Movement aftereffects* happen when we watch continuous movement and then look at another surface, which then appears to move in the opposite direction. Figure 5.27 provides an opportunity to experience movement aftereffects.

Perceptual Constancy Retinal images are constantly changing. Yet, even though the stimuli that fall on the retinas of our eyes change as we move closer to or farther away from objects or look at objects from different orientations and in light or dark settings, our perception of them remains stable. **Perceptual constancy** is the recognition that objects are constant and unchanging even though sensory input about them is changing.

FIGURE 5.29 **Shape Constancy**
The various projected images from an opening door are quite different, yet you perceive a rectangular door.

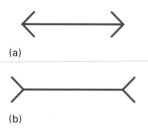

(a)

(b)

FIGURE 5.30

Müller-Lyer Illusion
The two lines are exactly the same length, although (b) looks longer than (a). This illusion was created by Franz Müller-Lyer in the late nineteenth century.

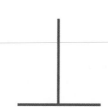

FIGURE 5.31

The Horizontal-Vertical Illusion
The vertical line looks longer than the horizontal line, but they are the same length.

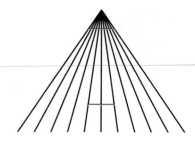

FIGURE 5.32

Ponzo Illusion
The top line looks much longer than the bottom line, but they are the same length.

We experience three types of perceptual constancy: size constancy, shape constancy, and brightness constancy. *Size constancy* is the recognition that an object remains the same size even though the retinal image of the object changes (see figure 5.28). Shape constancy is the recognition that an object retains the same shape even though its orientation to us changes. Look around. You probably see objects of various shapes—chairs and tables, for example. If you walk around the room, you see these objects from different sides and angles. Even though the pattern of light falling on the retina, the retinal image of the object, changes as you walk, you still perceive the objects as having the same shape (see figure 5.29). *Brightness constancy* is the recognition that an object retains the same degree of brightness even though different amounts of light fall on it. For example, regardless of whether you are reading this book indoors or outdoors, the white pages and the black print do not look any different to you in terms of their whiteness or blackness.

How are we able to resolve the discrepancy between a retinal image of an object and its actual size, shape, and brightness? Experience is important. For example, no matter how far away you are from your car, you know how large it is. Not only is familiarity important in size constancy, so are binocular and monocular depth cues. Even if we have never seen an object before, these cues provide us with information about an object's size. Many visual illusions are influenced by our perception of size constancy.

© Sidney Harris

Illusions

Our perceptual interpretations are usually correct. For example, on the basis of differences in colour or texture, we can conclude that a dog is on the rug. On the basis of a continuous increase in size, we conclude that a train is coming toward us. Sometimes, though, our interpretations or inferences are wrong, and the result is an illusion.

A **visual illusion** occurs when there is a discrepancy or incongruency between reality and the perceptual representation of it. Illusions are incorrect, but they are not abnormal. They can provide insight into how our perceptual processes work (Gregory, 2000). More than 200 different types of illusions have been discovered. Following are six of them.

One of the most famous visual illusions is the Müller-Lyer illusion, illustrated in figure 5.30. The two horizontal lines are exactly the same length, although (b) looks longer than (a). Another illusion is the horizontal-vertical illusion, in which a vertical line looks longer than a horizontal line even though the two are equal (see figure 5.31). In the Ponzo illusion, the top line looks much longer than the bottom line (see figure 5.32).

Why do these illusions trick us? One reason is that we mistakenly use certain cues for maintaining size constancy. For example, in the Ponzo illusion we see the upper line as being farther away (remember that objects higher in a picture are perceived as being farther away). The Müller-Lyer illusion, though, is not so easily explained. We might make judgments about the lines by comparing incorrect parts of the figures. The magnitude of the illusion varies as we direct our attention to different aspects of the Müller-Lyer illusion (Predebon, 2004).

visual illusion A discrepancy or incongruency between reality and the perceptual representation of it.

FIGURE 5.33

Moon Illusion
When the moon is on the horizon, it looks much larger than when it is high in the sky, directly above us. *Why does the moon look so much larger on the horizon?*

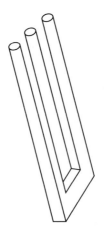

FIGURE 5.34

Devil's Tuning Fork
An example of a two-dimensional representation of an impossible three-dimensional figure.

FIGURE 5.35

Why Does This Famous Face Look So Different When You Turn the Book Upside Down?

Another well-known illusion is the moon illusion (see figure 5.33). The moon is 3200 kilometres in diameter and 465,000 kilometres away. Because both the moon's size and its distance from us are beyond our own experience, we have difficulty judging just how far away it really is (Ross & Plug, 2002). When the moon is high in the sky, directly above us, we have little information to help us judge its distance— for example, no texture gradients or stereoscopic cues exist. But when the moon is on the horizon, we can judge its distance in relation to familiar objects—trees and buildings, for example—which make it appear farther away. The result is that we estimate the size of the moon as much larger when it is on the horizon than when it is overhead.

The devil's tuning fork is another fascinating illusion. Look at figure 5.34 for about 30 seconds, then close the book. Now try to draw the tuning fork. You undoubtedly found this a difficult, if not impossible, task. Why? Look carefully at the figure again. You'll see that the figure's depth cues are ambiguous.

In our final example of an illusion, a "doctored" face seen upside down goes unnoticed. Look at figure 5.35—you probably recognize this famous face as Jean Chrétien's. In what seems to be an ordinary portrait, however, the mouth and eyes have been cut out from the original and pasted back on upside down. If you turn this book upside down, the horrific look is easily seen. The Chrétien illusion may take place because the mouth is so far out of alignment that we simply cannot respond to its expression; it is still a fearsome face, but we do not see that, and we may have a difficult time figuring out what really is the top of the mouth in the picture.

> **reflect and review**

2 **Explain how the visual system enables us to see and, by communicating with the brain, to perceive the world.**

- Explain the nature of light and how it is detected and transduced into neural impulses in the human eye.
- Describe how neural impulses are processed in the brain and reassembled into a single image.
- Discuss the trichromatic and opponent-process theories of colour vision.
- State how shape, depth, motion, and perceptual constancy enable us to transform flat images into three-dimensional objects and scenes.
- Give an explanation for visual illusions and cite examples.

Try to think of at least one perceptual illusion involving a sense other than vision.

③ THE AUDITORY SYSTEM

What is the auditory system and how does it process sound so that the brain can hear it?

Just as light provides us with information about the environment, so does sound. What would your life have been like without music, the rushing sound of ocean waves, or the voices of your parents and friends? Sounds tell us about the approach of a person behind us, an oncoming car, the force of the wind outside, or the mischief of a two-year-old; perhaps most important, sounds enable us to communicate through language and song (Yost, 2000).

The Nature of Sound and How We Experience It

At a music concert you may have felt the throbbing pulse of the music or sensed the air vibrating around you. Bass instruments are especially effective at creating mechanical pulsations, even causing the floor to vibrate. When the bass is played loudly, we can sense air molecules being pushed forward in waves from the speaker. How does sound generate these sensations?

Sounds, or *sound waves*, are vibrations in the air that are processed by the auditory (or hearing) system. Remember that we described light waves as being much like the waves in the ocean moving toward the beach. Sound waves are similar. Sound waves also vary in wavelength. Wavelength determines the *frequency* of the sound wave, or the number of cycles (full wavelengths) that pass through a point in a given time. Frequency is measured in *Hertz* (*Hz*), sometimes also called *cps* (*cycles per second*). Pitch is the perceptual interpretation of the frequency of a sound. High-frequency sounds are perceived as having a high pitch, low-frequency sounds as having a low pitch. A soprano voice sounds high-pitched. A bass voice has a low pitch. As in the case of vision, human sensitivity is limited to a range of sound frequencies—about 20–20,000 Hz (Coren, Ward, & Enns, 2004). Dogs can hear higher frequencies than humans can.

Sound waves vary not only in frequency but also in amplitude (see figure 5.8). *Amplitude* of a sound wave, measured in *decibels* (*dB*), is the amount of pressure produced by a sound wave relative to a standard. The typical standard—zero decibels—is the weakest sound the human ear can detect. *Loudness* is the perception of the sound wave's amplitude. In general, the higher the amplitude of the sound wave, or the higher the decibel level, the louder the sound is perceived to be. In the world of amplitude, this means that the air is pressing more forcibly against you and your ears during loud sounds and more gently during quiet sounds.

So far we have been describing a single sound wave with just one frequency. A single sound wave is similar to the single wavelength of pure coloured light we discussed in the context of colour matching. Most sounds, including those of speech and music, are *complex sounds*, those in which numerous frequencies of sound blend together. *Timbre* is the tone saturation or the perceptual quality of a sound (Singh & Bregman, 1997). Timbre is responsible for the perceptual difference between a trumpet and a trombone playing the same note and for the differences in quality we hear in human voices. Complex sounds themselves combine to produce more complex sequences, such as musical melodies (Cuddy, 1997; Hébert & Cuddy, 2002). Figure 5.36 illustrates the physical differences in sound waves that produce the different qualities of sounds.

Structures and Functions of the Ear

What happens to sound waves once they reach your ear? How do various structures of the ear transform sound waves into signals that the brain will recognize as sound?

FIGURE 5.36
Physical Differences in Sound Waves and the Qualities of Sound They Produce

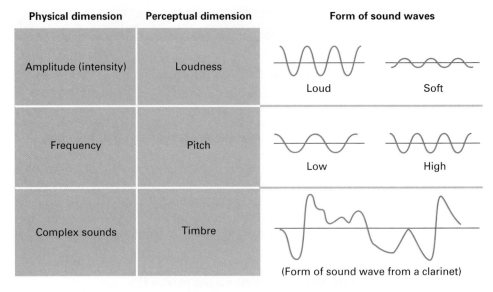

Physical dimension	Perceptual dimension	Form of sound waves
Amplitude (intensity)	Loudness	Loud / Soft
Frequency	Pitch	Low / High
Complex sounds	Timbre	(Form of sound wave from a clarinet)

FIGURE 5.37
The Outer, Middle, and Inner Ear
On entering the outer ear, sound waves travel through the auditory canal, where they generate vibrations in the eardrum. These vibrations are transferred via the hammer, anvil, and stirrup to the fluid-filled cochlea in the inner ear. There the mechanical vibrations are converted to an electrochemical signal that the brain will recognize as sound.

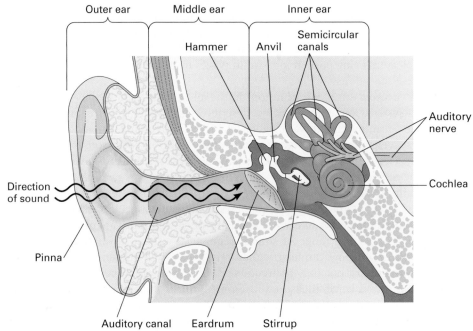

Functionally, the ear is analogous to the eye. The ear serves the purpose of transducing and transmitting a high-fidelity version of sounds to the brain for analysis and interpretation. Just as an image needs to be in focus and sufficiently bright for the brain to interpret it, a sound needs to be transmitted in a way that preserves information about its location; its frequency, which helps us distinguish the voice of a child from that of an adult; its amplitude, which helps us tell how loud a sound is; and its timbre, which allows us to identify the voice of a friend on the cellphone.

The ear is divided into three parts: *outer ear, middle ear,* and *inner ear* (see figure 5.37).

Outer Ear The **outer ear** consists of the pinna and the external auditory canal. The funnel-shaped *pinna* (plural, *pinnae*) is the outer visible part of the ear. (Elephants have very large pinnae). The pinna collects sounds and channels them into the interior of the ear. The pinnae of many animals, such as cats, are movable and serve a more important role in sound localization than the pinnae of humans do. Cats turn their ears in the direction of a faint and interesting sound.

Middle Ear After passing the pinna, sound waves move through the auditory canal to the middle ear. The **middle ear** channels the sound through the eardrum (*tympanic*

outer ear Consists of the pinna and the external auditory canal.

middle ear Consists of eardrum, hammer, anvil, and stirrup.

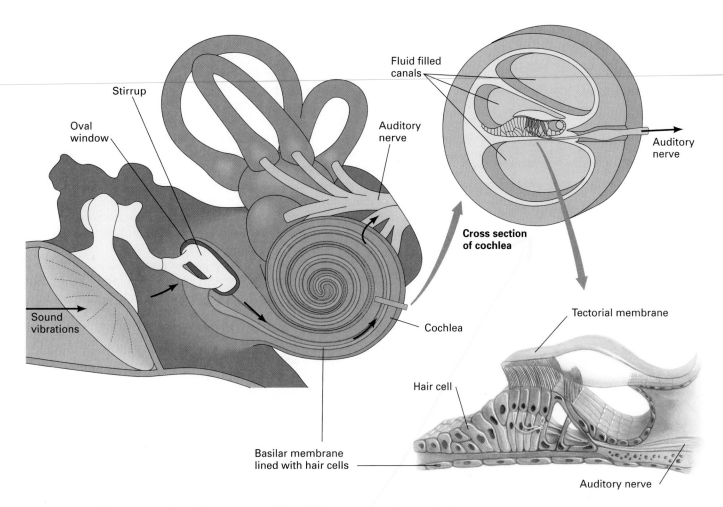

Cross section
of cochlea

FIGURE 5.38

The Cochlea
The cochlea is a spiral structure consisting of fluid-filled canals. When the stirrup vibrates against the oval window, the fluid in the canals vibrates. Vibrations along portions of the basilar membrane correspond to different sound frequencies. The vibrations exert pressure on the hair cells (between the basilar and tectorial membranes); the hair cells in turn push against the tectorial membrane, which bends the hairs. This triggers an action potential in the auditory nerve.

membrane), hammer (*malleus*), anvil (*incus*), and stirrup (*stapes*) to the inner ear. The eardrum is a membrane that vibrates in response to sound. It is the first structure that sound touches in the middle ear. The *hammer, anvil,* and *stirrup* are a connected chain of the three smallest bones in the human body. When they vibrate, they transmit sound waves to the fluid-filled inner ear.

Sound waves entering the ear travel in air until they reach the inner ear. At this border between air and fluid, sound meets the same kind of resistance encountered by shouts directed at an underwater swimmer when they hit the surface of the water. To compensate, the hammer, anvil, and stirrup also amplify the sound waves before they reach the fluid-filled inner ear.

Inner Ear The function of the **inner ear**, which includes the oval window, cochlea, and basilar membrane, is to transduce sound waves into neural impulses and send them on to the brain (Zwislocki, 2002). The stirrup is connected to the membranous *oval window*, which transmits sound waves to the cochlea. The *cochlea* is a tubular fluid-filled structure that is coiled up like a snail (see figure 5.38). The *basilar membrane* lines the inner wall of the cochlea and runs its entire length. It is narrow and rigid at the base of the cochlea but widens and becomes more flexible at the tip: The variation in width and flexibility allows different areas of the basilar membrane to vibrate more intensely when exposed to different sound frequencies. For example, the high-pitched tinkle of a bell stimulates the narrow region of the basilar membrane at the base of the cochlea, whereas the low-pitched tones of a foghorn stimulate the wide end.

In humans and other mammals, hair cells line the basilar membrane (see figure 5.38). These *hair cells* are the sensory receptors of the ear. They are called hair cells because of the tufts of fine bristles, or cilia, that sprout from the top of them. The movement of the hair cells against the *tectorial membrane*, a jelly-like flap above them, generates resulting impulses that are interpreted as sound by the brain.

inner ear Consists of oval window, cochlea, and basilar membrane.

Theories of Hearing

One important question is how the inner ear registers the frequency of sound. Two theories have been proposed: place theory and frequency theory. **Place theory** states that each frequency produces vibrations at a particular spot on the basilar membrane. Georg von Békésy (1960) studied the effects of vibration applied at the oval window on the basilar membrane of human cadavers. Through a microscope, he saw that this stimulation produced a travelling wave on the basilar membrane. A travelling wave is like the ripples that appear in a pond when you throw in a stone. However, because the cochlea is a long tube, the ripples can travel in only one direction, from the oval window at one end of the cochlea to the far tip of the cochlea. High-frequency vibrations create travelling waves that maximally displace, or move, the area of the basilar membrane next to the oval window; low-frequency vibrations maximally displace areas of the membrane closer to the tip of the cochlea. Békésy won a Nobel Prize in 1961 for his research on the basilar membrane.

Place theory adequately explains high-frequency sounds but not low-frequency sounds. A high-frequency sound stimulates a very precise area on the basilar membrane. By contrast, a low-frequency sound causes such a large part of the basilar membrane to be displaced that it is hard to localize the maximal displacement. Because humans can hear low-frequency sounds better than can be predicted by looking at the basilar membrane's response to these sounds, some other factors must be involved. **Frequency theory** addresses this problem by stating that the perception of a sound's frequency depends on how often the auditory nerve fires. Higher frequency sounds cause the auditory nerve to fire more often than do lower frequency sounds. One limitation of frequency theory is that a single neuron has a maximum firing rate of about 1000 times per second. Therefore, frequency theory cannot be applied to tones with frequencies that would require a neuron to fire more rapidly.

To deal with this limitation, a modification of frequency theory called the **volley principle** states that a cluster of nerve cells can fire neural impulses in rapid succession, producing a volley of impulses. Individual neurons cannot fire faster than 1000 times per second. But if the neurons team up and alternate their neural firing, they can attain a combined frequency above that rate. Frequency theory thus better explains the perception of sounds below 1000 times per second, whereas a combination of frequency and place theory is needed for sounds above 1000 times per second.

Auditory Processing in the Brain

As you saw in the discussion of the visual system, once energy from the environment is picked up by our receptors, it must be transmitted to the brain for processing and interpretation. An image on the retina does not a painting make—likewise, a pattern of receptor responses in the cochlea does not a symphony make. In the retina, we saw that the responses of the rod and cone receptors feed into ganglion cells in the retina and leave the eye via the optic nerve. In the auditory system, information about sound moves from the hair cells of the inner ear to the **auditory nerve**, which carries neural impulses to the brain's auditory areas. Remember that it is the movement of the hair cells that transforms the physical stimulation of sound waves into the action potential of neural impulses.

Auditory information moves up the auditory pathway via electrochemical transmission in a more complex manner than visual information does in the visual pathway. Many synapses occur in the ascending auditory pathway, with most fibres crossing over the midline between the hemispheres of the cerebral cortex, although some proceed directly to the hemisphere on the same side as the ear of reception. This means that most of the auditory information from the left ear goes to the right side of the brain, but some also goes to the left side of the brain. The auditory nerve extends from the cochlea to the brain stem, with some fibres crossing over the midline. The cortical destination of most of these fibres is the temporal lobes of the brain (beneath the temples of the head). As in the case of visual information, researchers have found that features are extracted from auditory information and transmitted along parallel what and where pathways in the brain (Feng & Ratnam, 2000; Rubel & Fritzsch, 2002).

place theory A theory of hearing that states that each frequency produces vibrations at a particular spot on the basilar membrane.

frequency theory Perception of a sound's frequency is due to how often the auditory nerve fires.

volley principle A cluster of nerve cells can fire neural impulses in rapid succession, producing a volley of impulses.

auditory nerve Carries neural impulses to the brain's auditory area.

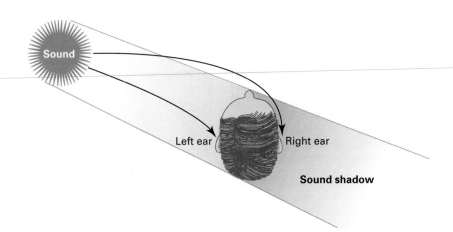

FIGURE 5.39
The Sound Shadow
The sound shadow is caused by the listener's head, which forms a barrier that reduces the sound's intensity. Here the sound is to the person's left, so the sound shadow will reduce the intensity of the sound that reaches the right ear.

Localizing Sound

Imagine that you set your cellphone down somewhere in the room and now it begins to ring. How do you know where the ring is coming from? The basilar membrane gives us information about the frequency, pitch, and complexity of a sound, but it doesn't tell us where a sound is located.

Earlier in the chapter, we indicated that because our two eyes see slightly different images, we can determine how near or far away an object is. Similarly, having two ears helps us to localize a sound because they receive somewhat different stimuli from the sound source. A sound coming from the left has to travel different distances to the two ears. So if the cellphone ring is to your left, your left ear receives the sound sooner than your right ear. Also, in this case, your left ear will receive a slightly more intense sound than your right ear. The sound reaching one ear is more intense than the sound reaching the other ear for two reasons: (1) it has travelled less distance and (2) the other ear is in what is called the *sound shadow* of the listener's head, which provides a barrier that reduces the sound's intensity (see figure 5.39). The sound shadow is one means that blind individuals use to orient themselves in the world.

Thus, differences in both the *timing* of the sound and the *intensity* of the sound help us to localize a sound. Humans often have difficulty localizing a sound that is coming from a source that is directly in front of them because it reaches both ears simultaneously. The same is true for sounds directly above your head or directly behind you.

Compared with some animals, humans aren't very accurate at locating sounds. For example, barn owls can hunt mice at night because their auditory systems are capable of highly accurate sound localization (Kubke, Massoglia, & Carr, 2002). Bats are also able to hunt insects at night. Unlike owls, bats achieve their success with a highly developed sensitivity to their own echoes. They emit sounds and then listen to the echoes coming back. Using this system—called *echolocation*—bats can fly through their environment at high speeds, avoid predators, and find prey. Why has evolution provided owls and bats with such exquisite hearing? The answer is simple: vision requires light, and owls and bats are nocturnal animals. Any method of building internal representations of the environment that depends primarily on light would not be an effective perceptual system for owls or bats.

Humans do not need such accurate hearing because we do not hunt at night. Instead, we use our eyes to pursue food by day. Nonetheless, we are fairly accurate at localizing sounds.

How do bats navigate through their environment?

Noise Pollution

Earlier in the chapter, we discussed the effect of noise on the absolute threshold. It is also important to think about noise as a significant environmental influence on behaviour. Usually auditory noise has little effect on us when it is at low volume or when we are doing simple, routine tasks. However, under some conditions noise can annoy us and disrupt our behaviour (Bronzaft, 2002; Ramirez, Alvarado, Santisteban, 2004).

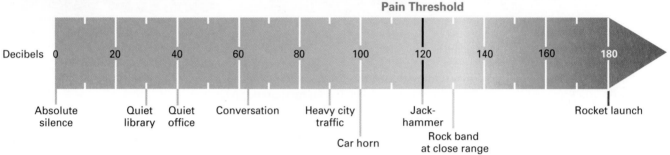

Pain Threshold

| Decibels | 0 | 20 | 40 | 60 | 80 | 100 | 120 | 140 | 160 | 180 |

Absolute silence — Quiet library — Quiet office — Conversation — Heavy city traffic — Car horn — Jack-hammer — Rock band at close range — Rocket launch

FIGURE 5.40

Sounds Around Us

Shown here are the decibel (dB) levels of a number of sounds in our world. Every increase of 6 dB doubles a sound's intensity. For example, a 40-dB sound is twice as intense as a 34-dB sound. Noise rated at 80 dB or higher, if heard for prolonged periods of time, can cause permanent hearing loss. According to one comment, "The human ear was not made to handle the racket of modern civilization." By one estimate, machinery is making the Western world noisier by about 1 dB a year.

Noise rated at 80 decibels or higher, if heard for prolonged periods of time, can cause permanent hearing loss. However, there are other consequences of constant, or even intermittent, noise at lower decibels. In a quiet library the noise level is about 30 decibels. The sound of a car horn is about 100 decibels, a heavy metal band at close range 130 decibels, and a rocket launching 180 decibels. The decibel levels of various sounds are shown in figure 5.40. Because noise levels throughout the environment have risen in recent years, noise pollution is a concern for an increasing number of people, even in national parks (Mace, Bell, & Loomis, 2004).

Noise is especially bothersome when we cannot do anything to control it, and too often in today's urban environments we do not have control over noise. This was the case for some children living in a New York City high-rise apartment building right next to a busy highway (Cohen, Glass, & Singer, 1973): Children who lived on the bottom floors (who were exposed to a high level of noise) did considerably worse on reading tests than children living on the upper floors (who were exposed to a much lower level of noise). In another classic study, children who lived in the corridor of the Los Angeles International Airport were compared with children living in a quieter neighbourhood away from the air corridor (Cohen & others, 1981). Every day, more than 300 jets roared over the children in the air corridor. The children in the high-noise corridor had higher blood pressure and were more easily distracted at tasks than their counterparts who lived in the low-noise neighbourhood.

Loud music is another modern development that can be physically harmful. The damage begins with the hair cells in the inner ear, which develop blister-like bulges that eventually pop. The tissue beneath the hair cells swells and softens until the hair cells, and sometimes the neurons leaving the cochlea, become scarred and degenerate (Lewis, 2004).

Following are some symptoms of possible hearing loss that could be caused by loud noise or music:

- Ringing or buzzing in ears
- Slight muffling of sounds
- Difficulty in understanding speech—hearing the words but not understanding them
- Problems hearing conversations in groups of people when there is background noise or in rooms with poor acoustics

To find out how well you protect your hearing, see the Personal Reflections box.

Love Your Ears

H.E.A.R. (Hearing Education and Awareness for Rockers) was founded by rock musicians whose hearing had been damaged by their exposure to high volumes of rock music. Such hearing loss is common among musicians and limits what they are able to do later in their lives. At the H.E.A.R. Web site (www.hearnet.com), artists ranging from Pete Townsend of *The Who* to Jack Black, who starred in the comedy film *School of Rock*, speak out about the need to protect your hearing.

Other noisy environments such as production factories and aviation grounds may also pose threats to your hearing.

To determine how well you protect your hearing, answer the following questions:

- Do you work in a noisy environment? If so, ask your employer to inform you about the level of noise and company policy on protecting your hearing.
- If you use power equipment, are you using earmuffs or earplugs to protect your ears?
- Do you listen to music on headphones? If you listen to loud music often, go to a hearing specialist, get your hearing tested, and listen to the specialist's advice.
- Do you go to music concerts? According to H.E.A.R., the sound levels at a music concert can be as high as 140 dB in front of the speakers, which can damage hearing, and above 100 dB behind the speakers, still very loud and potentially dangerous.

Lars Ulrich of Metallica says, "Three of the four members of Metallica wear earplugs. Some people think earplugs are for wimps. But if you don't want to hear records in 5 or 10 years, that's your decision."

> ### > reflect and review

 Understand how the auditory system registers sound and how it connects with the brain to perceive it.

- Describe the nature of sound and how it is experienced.
- Identify the structures of the ear and their functions.
- Discuss three theories of hearing.
- Explain how auditory signals are transmitted to the brain for processing.
- Describe sound localization.
- Discuss the effects of noise pollution on behaviour.

Suppose you were in an accident and, in order to survive, had to sacrifice either your vision or hearing. Which sense would you preserve? Why?

④ OTHER SENSES

— The Skin Senses   — The Chemical Senses   — The Kinesthetic and Vestibular Senses

How do the skin, chemical, kinesthetic, and vestibular senses work?

Now that the visual and auditory systems have been described in some detail, let's take a look at our other sensory systems. You are familiar with the skin senses and the chemical senses (smell and taste). The lesser known kinesthetic and vestibular senses enable us to stay upright and to coordinate our movements.

Should We Believe the Claims of Psychics?

A woman says she is a psychic (a person who claims to have extrasensory perception). She reports that she has power over the goldfish in a 50-gallon tank, claiming that she can will them to swim to either end of the tank.

Under the careful scrutiny of James Randi, this woman's account turned out to be just another fish story. The woman had written Randi, a professional magician who has a standing offer of $1,000,000 to anyone whose psychic claims withstand his analysis. In the case of the woman and her goldfish, Randi received a letter from her priest validating her extraordinary power. Randi talked with the priest, who told him that the woman would put her hands in front of her body and then run to one end of the tank. The fish soon swam to that end of the tank. Since the fish could see out of the tank just as we could see into it, Randi suggested that the woman put opaque brown wrapping paper over one end of the tank and then try her powers. The woman did and called Randi to tell him that she had discovered something new about her powers: Her mind could not penetrate brown paper. The woman, believing she had magical powers, completely misunderstood why Randi had asked her to place the brown paper over the fish tank.

To date, no one has met Randi's $1,000,000 challenge, but he has investigated hundreds of reports of supernatural and occult powers. On September 3, 2001, on CNN's *Larry King Live*, Randi invited prominent psychic Sylvia Browne to accept his challenge, which she did. Sylvia's Clock, at Randi's *James Randi Educational Foundation* Web site, continues to tick as she has not, to date, actually undertaken any tests of her "powers" in a controlled setting.

In response to the claims of prominent psychics like Sylvia Browne and John Edwards, Randi has recently evaluated cold-reading, a popular technique among psychics. When *cold-reading*, the psychic tells the person nothing but makes guesses, puts out suggestions, and asks questions. For example, if the "reader" says, "I am visualizing an older woman," the person usually gives some reaction. It may be just a nod, somebody's name, or even identification of a sister, aunt, mother, or grandmother. The important point is that this information is supplied by the person, not the reader. Of course, almost everyone will show some reaction to such a general statement, giving the reader new information to incorporate into subsequent comments or

Magician James Randi (right) has investigated a large number of psychics' claims. No one has yet won Randi's standing offer of $1,000,000 to anyone whose psychic claims withstand his analysis.

questions. Alternatively, the reader may say, "Mary? Do you recognize this person?" If there is a Mary, the person will give more helpful information to the reader. If no Mary is immediately recognized, the reader moves on. If "Mary" is remembered later, she is incorporated into the reader's comments. The reader can try many names, confident that the person will likely remember only suggested names that are meaningful to him or her. In this way, the person may well end up volunteering what he or she wants to hear.

According to Randi, cold-readers often interview people while they are waiting to get into the show. Then, when the show begins, they can choose to work with people they have already talked to. Suppose a person approaches the reader before the show and says he has a question about his deceased wife. That person can later be selected during the show and be asked, "Is your question about your dead wife?" To other people who are not aware of the previous conversation, the reader's question can seem miraculous.

Randi also says that when cold-readers are not allowed to speak to anyone in advance, or to be asked or told anything in advance, and people are allowed to answer only "yes" or "no" when asked direct questions, they fail miserably. In general, according to Randi, cold-readers have a way of leading people to believe that they knew something they didn't.

Randi (1997) makes a distinction between the tricks of magicians like him, and the work of psychics and others who claim extraordinary ESP powers. He says that magic is done to entertain, the other to swindle. Read more about the Amazing Randi's skeptical approach to supernatural phenomena at his Web site, www.randi.org.

What do you think?

- Do you think the Amazing Randi's $1,000,000 prize will ever be claimed? Why or why not?
- Why do you think people continue to believe in psychic phenomena when confronted with contradictory evidence produced by Randi and others?
- What kind of research would be necessary to establish that a particular psychic phenomenon is genuine? Visit the Web site of the Institute for Noetic Sciences (www.noetic.org) for some possible examples.

Some people also claim to have another "sense" that enables them to read other people's minds, for example, or foresee the future. Such claims have not held up under scientific scrutiny, but many people continue to believe in so-called psychic powers (Alcock, 2003; Alcock, Burns, & Freeman, 2003). To learn about one man's efforts to expose fraudulent psychics, see the Critical Reflections box.

The Skin Senses

You know when a friend has a fever by putting your hand to her head; you know how to find your way to the light switch in a darkened room by groping along the wall; and you know whether or not a pair of shoes is too tight by the way the shoes touch different parts of your feet when you walk. Many of us think of our skin as a fashion accessory rather than a sense. We pierce it and colour it with cosmetics, dyes, and tattoos. But the skin is our largest sensory system, draped over the body with receptors for touch, temperature, and pain. These three kinds of receptors form the *cutaneous* senses.

A large variety of important information comes to us through our ability to detect touch.

Touch   *Touch* is a sense we often take for granted. Yet our ability to respond to touch is astounding.

Processing Information About Touch   What do we detect when we feel "touch"? What kind of energy does our sense of touch pick up from our external environment? In vision, we detect light energy. In audition, we detect the vibrations of air or sound waves pressing against our eardrums. In touch, we detect mechanical energy, or pressure against the skin. The lifting of a single hair causes pressure on the skin around the shaft of hair. This tiny bit of mechanical pressure at the base of the hair is sufficient for us to detect the touch of a pencil point. More commonly, we detect the mechanical energy of the pressure of a car seat against our buttocks or the pressure of a fork in our hands. Is this kind of energy so different from the kind of energy we detect in vision or audition? Sometimes the only difference is one of intensity—the sound of a rock band playing softly is an auditory stimulus, but at the high volumes that make a concert hall reverberate, this auditory stimulus is also *felt*, as mechanical energy pressing against our skin.

How does information about touch travel from the skin through the nervous system? Sensory fibres arising from receptors in the skin enter the spinal cord. From there the information travels to the brain stem, at which point most fibres from each side of the body cross over to the opposite side of the brain. Then the information about touch moves on to the thalamus, which serves as a relay station. The thalamus then projects the map of the body's surface onto the somatosensory areas of the parietal lobes in the cerebral cortex (Andersen & Bruneo, 2002).

As in the visual and auditory systems, both feature detection and parallel processing occur when information about touch is processed. Some cells in the somatosensory cortex respond to specific aspects of touch, such as movement across the skin. Also, such features of tactile (touch) sensation as pressure, temperature, and movement may be recombined in the somatosensory cortex through reassembly in the same manner as in vision (Kalat, 2004).

Just as the visual system is more sensitive to images on the fovea than to images in the peripheral retina, our sensitivity to touch is not equally good across all areas of the skin. As you might expect, human toolmakers need to have excellent touch discrimination in their hands, but they require much less touch discrimination in other parts of the body, such as the torso or legs. Because of this, the brain devotes more space to analyzing touch signals coming from the hands than from the legs (Penfield & Rasmussen, 1950; see figure 3.16 on page 94).

Exploring Touch in Life   Touch is important in many aspects of day-to-day life. For example, when a surgeon operates, she relies extensively on feedback from her sense of touch to help her control her scalpel while she is cutting. Anything, including wearing surgical gloves, which hampers this feedback, can make the surgery more difficult and, therefore, more dangerous. Recently, surgeons have begun to use *telepresence surgery*, in which the surgeon is at a different location than the patient. The surgeon might be manipulating controls at a computer console while the actual surgical instruments are at the end of small tubes inserted into the patient's body several feet (or even thousands of miles) away.

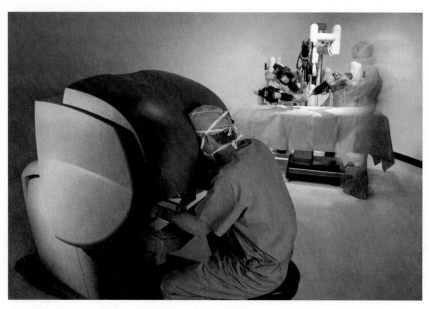

In telepresence surgery, the surgeon and the patient can be separated by great distances. *Will this separation make surgery more difficult? Why?*

Today, *telepresence* is increasingly used in other settings, such as the control of bomb-disposal robots and remote manipulator arms like the one on the space shuttle. Despite the obvious benefits, remote manipulation is very difficult because touch feedback is dramatically reduced.

Psychologists Susan Lederman of Queen's University and Roberta Klatsky of Carnegie-Mellon University are working to develop a better understanding of the sense of touch and to apply that understanding to improving the design of *haptic interfaces*, systems designed to provide touch feedback in telepresence systems. (Lederman & Klatsky, 1998; 2004; Lederman & others, 2004). This research focuses mainly on the hands because the fingertips contain the highest densities of tactile receptors. In one study, Lederman and Klatsky tested individuals' ability to perform several tasks with and without feedback to their index fingers (Lederman & Klatsky, 1998). They measured people's ability to feel vibrations, to sense whether they could feel two distinct objects or just one, and to detect the presence of a thin nylon hair. They also tested perceptual abilities, such as the ability to judge how rough a surface was and to compare the roughness of the two surfaces. To simulate a no-feedback situation, they covered participants' fingertips with a fibreglass sheath. The sheath had a dramatic impact on the participants' perceptual judgments. For example, their ability to sense the thin hair declined 73 percent, and their skill in detecting two objects as opposed to one dropped 32 percent.

Lederman & Klatsky (2004) found that using thin control rods, a common design in current haptic interfaces, limits touch feedback. They recommended using designs that provide feedback at more than one contact point, preferably on more than one finger, to improve the use of touch information to control remote grasping.

Another important aspect of touch is its role in infant development. Can newborns feel your caress when you touch them? Yes, they can. Indeed, they can feel touch better than they can see, hear, or even taste (Eliot, 2001). Newborn girls are more sensitive to touch than their male counterparts, a gender difference that persists throughout life. Psychologists believe that the sense of touch is especially helpful to infants, as it helps them detect and explore the physical world and is also important for health and emotional well-being. As was shown in chapter 4, touch is a key aspect of attachment to a caregiver (Ferber, 2004). Massage therapy has been effective in helping preterm infants become healthier.

Temperature Beyond the need to sense physical pressure on the skin, we need to detect temperature, even in the absence of direct contact with the skin. **Thermoreceptors**, which are located under the skin, respond to increases and decreases in temperature at or near the skin and also provide input to keep the body's temperature at 37 degrees Celsius. There are two types of thermoreceptors. Warm thermoreceptors respond to the warming of the skin, and cold thermoreceptors respond to the cooling of the skin (Okazawa & others, 2002).

Somewhat surprisingly, when warm and cold receptors that are close to each other in the skin are stimulated simultaneously, we experience the sensation of hotness. Figure 5.41 illustrates this "hot" experience, which arises because your brain is confused by the two conflicting messages and tries to combine them into a single consistent interpretation.

thermoreceptors Located under the skin, they respond to increases and decreases in temperature.

Pain   When skin contact takes the form of a sharp pinch, our sensation of mechanical pressure changes from touch to pain. When a pot handle is so hot that it burns your hand, your sensation of temperature becomes one of pain. Many kinds of stimuli can cause pain. Intense stimulation of any sense can produce pain—too much light, very loud sounds, or very spicy food, for example. Our ability to sense pain is vital to our survival as a species. **Pain** is the sensation that warns us of damage to our bodies. It functions as a quick-acting system that tells the motor systems of the brain that they must act to minimize or eliminate this damage. A hand touching a hot stove must be pulled away and ears should be covered up when one walks by a loud pavement drill.

Pathways of Pain   Pain receptors are dispersed widely throughout the body—in the skin, in the sheath tissue surrounding muscles, in internal organs, and in the membranes around bone (Turk & Melzack, 2001). Although all pain receptors are anatomically similar, they differ in the type of physical stimuli to which they best respond. Mechanical pain receptors respond mainly to pressure, such as when a sharp object is encountered. Heat pain receptors respond primarily to strong heat that is capable of burning tissue. Other pain receptors have a mixed function, responding to both types of painful stimuli. Many pain receptors are chemically sensitive and respond to a range of pain-producing substances.

Pain receptors have a much higher threshold for firing than receptors for temperature and touch (McMahon & Koltzenburg, 2005). Pain receptors react mainly to physical stimuli that distort them, or to chemical stimuli that "irritate" them into action. Inflamed joints or sore, torn muscles produce *prostaglandins*, which stimulate the receptors and cause the experience of pain. Drugs such as aspirin likely reduce the feeling of pain by reducing the body's production of prostaglandins.

Two different neural pathways transmit pain messages to the brain: a fast pathway and a slow pathway (McMahon & Koltzenburg, 2005). In the *fast pathway*, fibres connect directly with the thalamus, then to the motor and sensory areas of the cerebral cortex. This pathway transmits information about sharp, localized pain, as when you cut your skin. The fast pathway may serve as a warning system, providing immediate information about an injury—it takes less than a second for the information in this pathway to reach the cerebral cortex. In the *slow pathway*, pain information travels through the limbic system, a detour that delays the arrival of information at the cerebral cortex by seconds. The unpleasant, nagging pain that characterizes the slow pathway may function to remind the brain that an injury has occurred, that normal activity needs to be restricted, and that the pain needs to be monitored.

An influential theory of pain perception that offers insight into how cognitive and emotional factors might exert such dramatic influences on the experience of pain was developed by McGill psychologist Ronald Melzack and neuroscientist Patrick Wall of University College, London, (1965). They proposed the **gate-control theory of pain**, which states that the spinal column contains a neural gate that can be opened (allowing the perception of pain) or closed (blocking the perception of pain). The brain can send signals downward to the spinal cord to close the gate and thus suppress the sensation of pain. The gate-control theory was proposed as an explanation for the effects of *acupuncture*, a technique in which thin needles are inserted at specific points in the body to produce various effects, such as local anesthesia (see figure 5.42). Gate-control theory assumes that the presence of acupuncture needles somehow manages to shut the pain gate, inhibiting the experience of pain. The process of turning pain signals on and off is probably a chemical process that involves *endorphins*, which were discussed in chapter 3. Recall that endorphins are neurotransmitters that function as natural opiates in producing pleasure and pain. It is believed that endorphins are released mainly in the synapses of the slow pathway (McMahon & Koltzenburg, 2005).

The phenomenon of *phantom limb pain* raises questions about the completeness of gate-control theory (Hunter, Katz, & Davis, 2003). Amputees usually retain an awareness of a limb, including sometimes excruciating sensations of pain, long after the limb has been amputated. Phantom limb pain cannot be emanating from the missing limb and, thus, cannot be flowing up to the brain through a pain gate. Melzack has proposed

Warm water   Cold water

FIGURE 5.41

A "Hot" Experience
When two pipes, one containing cold water and the other warm water, are braided together, a person touching the pipes feels a sensation of "hot." The perceived heat coming from the pipes is so intense that a person cannot touch them for longer than a couple of seconds.

pain The sensation that warns us that damage to our bodies is occurring.

gate-control theory of pain The spinal column contains a neural gate that can be open (allowing the perception of pain) or closed (blocking the perception of pain).

FIGURE 5.42

Acupuncture
(*Left*) This woman is being treated for pain by an acupuncturist. (*Right*) Acupuncture points are carefully noted on this nineteenth-century Japanese papier-mâché figure. In their adaptation of the Chinese methodology, the Japanese identified 660 points.

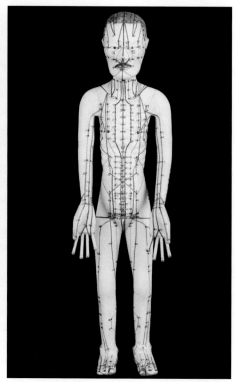

neuromatrix theory, a revision of gate-control theory, to explain phantom limb pain. (Melzack, 1993, 1999). Melzack proposes that the brain encodes a body image called the *neuromatrix,* which ultimately creates our sense of bodily self. While amputation may remove a limb, it does not remove the body image of that limb from the brain-based neuromatrix. Even through direct pain signals from the amputated limb are no longer available, the neuromatrix may continue to interpret other sensory information as pain coming from the amputated limb. In other words, while the experience of pain often originates in signals coming through the spinal cord gate, ultimately the brain generates the experience of pain.

Perception of pain is complex and often varies from one person to the next. Some people rarely feel pain; others seem to be in great pain if they experience a minor bump or bruise (Edwards & others, 2003). To some degree these individual variations may be physiological. A person who experiences considerable pain even with a minor injury may have a neurotransmitter system that is deficient in endorphin production.

However, perception of pain goes beyond physiology. Although it is true that sensations are affected by factors such as motivation and expectation, the perception of pain is especially susceptible to these factors (Philips & Rachman, 1996). Cultural and ethnic contexts can also greatly determine the degree to which an individual experiences pain (Davidhizar & Giger, 2004; Callister, 2003). For example, one pain researcher described a ritual performed in India in which a chosen person travels from town to town delivering blessings to the children and the crops while suspended from metal hooks embedded in his back (Melzak, 1973). Apparently, the chosen person reports no sensation of pain and appears to be in ecstasy (see figure 5.43).

Nowhere is cultural variation more pronounced than in the perception of pain in childbirth. In some cultures, women do not expect childbirth to be painful. They may have their babies and in a matter of hours go back to performing their normal daily activities. However, in Canada and most other Western cultures, women expect childbirth to involve considerable pain. The Lamaze method of childbirth (natural childbirth) seeks to reduce this fear of pain by training women's muscle tone and breathing patterns. Women who use the Lamaze method experience reduced perception of pain in childbirth.

Pain Control and Treatment Most acute pain decreases over time when activity is avoided or with analgesic medication. Treatment of chronic pain is often more complex. Often the most successful treatment of pain involves a combination of physical and psychological techniques. Accordingly, a pain clinic may select one or more of the following techniques to treat an individual's pain: surgery, drugs, acupuncture, electrical stimulation, massage, exercise, hypnosis, relaxation, and thought distraction (Gatchel, 2005). Hypnosis is discussed further in chapter 6 and relaxation techniques in chapter 15.

Let's further explore several strategies for reducing acute pain:

- *Distraction.* When you get an injection, do you focus on the needle as it is about to plunge into your flesh, or do you avert your eyes and concentrate on something else? Distraction is usually the best way to reduce pain, because attention to the sensation can magnify it. You might focus your attention on something pleasant that you plan to do this weekend, for example.
- *Focused breathing.* The next time you stub your toe, try panting—short, fast breaths (similar to the breathing practised in Lamaze childbirth). Focused breathing may successfully close the pain gate and diminish your agony.
- *Counterstimulation.* If you pinch your cheek in the aftermath of a bad cut, itwill likely mute your pain. This may close the pain gate. Applying ice to a sprained or swollen area not only reduces the pain but can also keep the swelling down.

The Chemical Senses

The information impinging on our senses comes in many diverse forms: electromagnetic energy in vision, sound waves in audition, and mechanical pressure and temperature in the cutaneous senses. The two senses presented in this section are responsible for processing chemicals in our environment (Rouby, Schaal, & Holley, 2002). With taste we detect chemicals that have been dissolved in saliva (Northcutt, 2004) and with the sense of smell we detect airborne chemicals (Stockhorst & Pietrowsky, 2004). Sometimes we realize the strong links between the two senses only when a nasty cold and nasal congestion seem to take the pleasure out of eating. Our favourite foods become "tasteless" without the smells that characterize them. Despite this link, taste and smell are indeed two distinct systems.

Taste What would life be with no sense of *taste*? For anyone who has tried to diet, "not worth living" is a common response. The thought of giving up a favourite taste, such as maple syrup or butter, can be very depressing. We use our sense of taste to select food and to regulate our food intake. Although it is not so easy to see or smell mould on a blueberry, a small taste is enough to prompt you to sense that the fruit is no longer fit for consumption. Beyond that, the pleasure associated with the taste of food depends on many aspects of our body's need for a particular food (Bartoshuk & Beauchamp, 1994). The taste of devil's food cake can be very pleasurable when we are hungry but downright revolting after eating a banana split.

It is not the prettiest sight you've ever seen, but try this anyway. Take a drink of milk and allow it to coat your tongue. Then go to a mirror, stick out your tongue, and look carefully at its surface. You should be able to see rounded bumps above the surface of your tongue. Those bumps, called **papillae**, contain taste buds, which are the receptors for taste. About 10,000 of these taste buds are located on your tongue. As with all the other sensory systems discussed in this chapter, the information picked up by these receptors is transmitted to the brain for analysis and, when necessary, response (spitting something out, for example).

The taste qualities we respond to can be categorized as sweet, sour, bitter, salty, and umami (Lindemann, 2001). You may not be familiar with umami (after the Japanese *umai*, for "delicious"), the taste of "savouryness." Umami is associated with meats, cheeses and other foods high in the amino acid l-glutamate. Monosodium glutamate (MSG) is often used to enhance the savoury quality of food. Though all areas of the

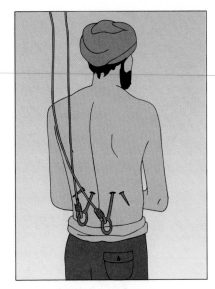

FIGURE 5.43

Hook-Swinging Ceremony
(*Top*) Two steel hooks are shown hanging from the back of an Asian Indian participating in a hook-swinging ceremony. (*Bottom*) The man hangs on to ropes as a cart takes him from village to village. After he blesses each child and farm field in the village, he swings freely, suspended by the hooks in his back (after Kosambi, 1965).

papillae Bumps on the tongue that contain taste buds, the receptors for taste.

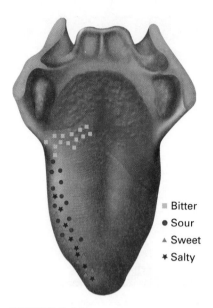

FIGURE 5.44

Location on the Tongue of Sensitivity to Sweet, Salty, Sour, and Bitter Substances

■ Bitter
● Sour
▲ Sweet
✱ Salty

tongue can detect each of the five tastes, different regions of the tongue are more sensitive to some tastes than others. The tip of the tongue is the most sensitive to sweet and salty substances, the sides to sour, and the rear to bitter (see figure 5.44; Bloom & others, 2001). All regions of the tongue appear to be equally sensitive to umami.

Today, many neuroscientists believe that the breakdown of taste into five independent, elementary categories is overdrawn. The taste fibres leading from a taste bud to the brain often respond strongly to a range of chemicals that span multiple taste elements, such as salty and sour (Smith & Margolskee, 2001). The brain processes these somewhat ambiguous incoming signals and integrates them into a perception of taste.

Although people often still categorize taste sensations along the five dimensions of sweet, bitter, salty, sour, and umami, our tasting ability goes far beyond them. Most of us pride ourselves on being able to distinguish different brands of ice cream; caffeinated and decaffeinated soda, coffee, and tea; and the many variations of product substitutes that are supposed to be better for us than the standard high-cholesterol, high-sugar, and high-fat culinary pleasures. Think of the remarkable range of tastes you have that are generated by variations and combinations of sweet, sour, bitter, salty, and umami.

Smell   A good way to begin the discussion of *smell* is to consider the many functions it serves. It is often easier to understand the importance of smell when we think about animals with more sophisticated senses of smell than our own. A dog, for example, can use its sense of smell to find its way back from a lone stroll, to distinguish friend from foe, or even (with practice) to detect illegal drugs concealed in a suitcase. In fact, dogs can detect odours in concentrations 100 times lower than those detectable by humans. Given the nasal feats of the average dog, we might be tempted to believe that the sense of smell has outlived its usefulness in humans. What do we use smell for? For one thing, humans need the sense of smell to decide what to eat. We can distinguish rotten food from fresh food and remember (all too well) which foods have made us ill in the past. The smell of a food that has previously made us ill is often, by itself, enough to make us feel nauseated. Second, although tracking is a function of smell that we often associate only with animals, humans are competent odour trackers. We can follow the smell of smoke to a fire, the smell of a hot apple pie to a windowsill, or the smell of dirty hockey socks to the equipment bag in a locker.

What physical equipment do we use to process information about odour? Just as the eyes scan the visual field for objects of interest and the pinnae prick up to direct

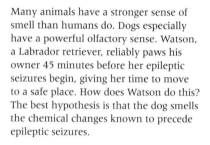

Many animals have a stronger sense of smell than humans do. Dogs especially have a powerful olfactory sense. Watson, a Labrador retriever, reliably paws his owner 45 minutes before her epileptic seizures begin, giving her time to move to a safe place. How does Watson do this? The best hypothesis is that the dog smells the chemical changes known to precede epileptic seizures.

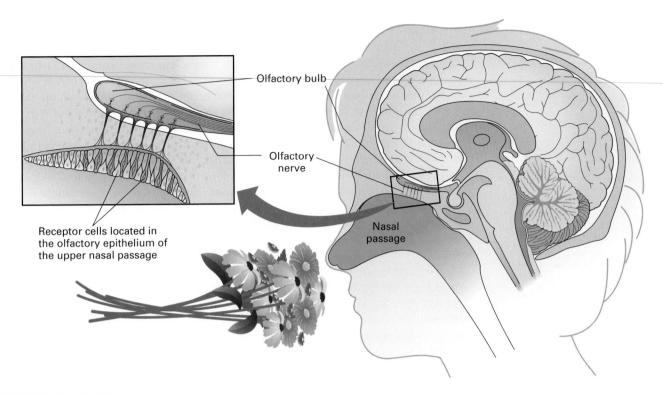

Olfactory bulb

Olfactory nerve

Nasal passage

Receptor cells located in the olfactory epithelium of the upper nasal passage

FIGURE 5.45 **The Olfactory Sense**
Airborne molecules of an odour reach tiny receptor cells in the roof of the nasal cavity. The receptor cells form a mucous-covered membrane called the olfactory epithelium. Then the olfactory nerve carries information about the odour to the brain for further processing.

attention to sounds of interest, the nose is not a passive instrument. We actively sniff when we are trying to track down the source of a fire or of a burned-out fluorescent light. The **olfactory epithelium**, lining the roof of the nasal cavity, contains a sheet of receptor cells for smell (see figure 5.45), so sniffing has the effect of maximizing the chances of detecting an odour (Doty & Muller-Schwarze, 1992). The receptor cells are covered with millions of minute hair-like antennae, or cilia, that project through the mucus in the top of the nasal cavity and make contact with air on its way to the throat and lungs (Laurent & others, 2001). Interestingly, unlike the neurons of most sensory systems, the neurons in the olfactory epithelium tend to replace themselves after injury (Stockhorst & Pietrowsky, 2004).

What is the neural pathway for information about smell? Although all other sensory pathways pass through the thalamus, the pathway for smell does not. In smell, the neural pathway first goes to the olfactory areas of the cerebral cortex in the temporal lobes and then projects to various brain regions, especially the limbic system, which is involved in emotion and memory. For many people, smells have a way of generating memories—often emotion-laden ones—undoubtedly because of the neural pathways that smell takes through the limbic system (Gnatkovsky, Uva, & de Curtis, 2004).

The Kinesthetic and Vestibular Senses

You know the difference between walking and running and between lying down and sitting up. To perform even the simplest acts of motor coordination, such as reaching out to take a book off a library shelf or getting up out of a chair, the brain must be constantly receiving and coordinating information from every part of the body (Lackner & DiZio, 2005). Your body has two kinds of senses that provide information about your movement and orientation in space, as well as helping to maintain balance. The **kinesthetic senses** provide information about movement, posture, and orientation. The **vestibular sense** provides information about balance and movement.

olfactory epithelium Located in the roof of the nasal cavity, a sheet of receptor cells for smell.

kinesthetic senses Provide information about movement, posture, and orientation.

vestibular sense Provides information about balance and movement.

No specific organ contains the kinesthetic senses. Instead, they are embedded in muscle fibres and joints. As we stretch and move, these receptors signal the state of the muscle. Kinesthesia is a sense that you often do not even notice until it is gone. Try walking when your leg is "asleep," or smiling (never mind talking) when you've just come from a dentist's office and you are still under the effects of novocaine. Perhaps the sophistication of kinesthesis can be best appreciated when we think of it in terms of memory. Even a mediocre typist can bang out 20 words per minute—but how many of us could write down the order of the letters on a keyboard without looking? Typing is a skill that relies on very coordinated sensitivity to the orientation, position, and movements of our fingers. We say that our fingers remember the positions of the keys. Likewise, the complicated movements a ballet dancer uses to perform cannot be written down or communicated easily using language. They involve nearly every muscle and joint in the body. Most information about the kinesthetic sense is transmitted from the joints and muscles along the same pathways to the brain as information about touch.

The vestibular sense tells us whether our head (and hence usually our body) is tilted (e.g., Zikovitz & Harris, 1999), moving, slowing down, or speeding up. It works in concert with the kinesthetic senses to coordinate our *proprioceptive feedback*, which is information about the position of our limbs and body parts in relation to other body parts. Consider the combination of sensory abilities involved in the motion of a hockey player skating down the ice cradling the puck and pushing it forward with the hockey stick. The hockey player is responding simultaneously to a multitude of sensations, including those produced by the slickness of the ice, the position of the puck, the speed and momentum of the forward progression, and the requirements of the play to turn and to track the other players on the ice.

The **semicircular canals**, located in the inner ear, contain the sensory receptors that detect head motion caused when we tilt or move our heads and/or bodies (see figure 5.46). These canals consist of three fluid-filled circular tubes that lie in

FIGURE 5.46

The Semicircular Canals and Vestibular Sense
The semicircular canals provide feedback to the gymnast's brain as his head and body tilt in different directions. Any angle of head rotation is registered by hair cells in one or more semicircular canals in both ears. (*Inset*) The semicircular canals.

semicircular canals Located in the inner ear; contain the sensory receptors that detect head motion.

© King Features. Reprinted with special permission of King Features Syndicate.

the three planes of the body—right-left, front-back, and up-down. We can picture these as three intersecting rings. As you move your head, the fluid of the semicircular canals flows in different directions and at different speeds (depending on the force of the head movement). The movements of these receptor cells determine our perception of head movement and position. This ingenious system of using the motion of fluid in tubes to sense head position is not unlike the auditory system found in the inner ear. However, the fluid movement in the cochlea is caused by the pressure sound exerts on the oval window, whereas the movements in the semicircular canals reflect physical movements of the head and body. Vestibular sacs in the semicircular canals contain hair cells embedded in a gelatin-like mass, and, just as the hair cells in the cochlea trigger hearing impulses in the brain, the hair cells in the semicircular canals are involved in transmitting information about balance and movement.

The brain pathways for the vestibular sense begin in the auditory nerve, which contains both the cochlear nerve (with information about sound) and the vestibular nerve (which contains information about balance and movement). Most of the axons of the vestibular nerve connect with the medulla, although some go directly to the cerebellum. There also appear to be vestibular projections to the temporal cortex, although their specific pathways have not been fully charted. Most neuroscientists believe that the projections to the cerebral cortex are responsible for dizziness, whereas the connections to the lower brain stem produce the nausea and vomiting that accompany motion sickness (Carlson, 2005).

Laurence Harris, Michael Jenkin, and their colleagues, of York University, have recently built IVY, the Immersive Visual Environment at York (Robinson & others, 2002). IVY is used to study the applications of *virtual reality technology* as well as to conduct more basic research on the combination of kinesthetic and vestibular senses and how it is supplemented by information from vision (Harris & Jenkin, 1998). This simple principle has recently been turned to making a profit. When you go to a motion ride movie, you sit on a moving platform while you watch the movie. The combination of motion information and visual information makes for an exciting and compelling experience (Allison & others, 2000). An exciting new area of research involves the role of kinesthetic cues in the exploration and creation of virtual environments, computer-generated worlds, which may be best experienced while wearing 3-D stereo goggles (Harris, Jenkin, & Zikovitz, 1999, Allison & others, 2000).

> **reflect and review**

4 **Know how the skin, chemical, kinesthetic, and vestibular senses work.**

- Explain how the skin monitors touch, temperature, and pain
- Discuss the chemical senses of taste and smell
- Describe how the kinesthetic and vestibular senses function

Why can some individuals stand more pain than others?

⑤ PERCEPTION AND HUMAN FACTORS PSYCHOLOGY

What are some applications of research in perception?

After completing his Ph.D. in experimental psychology at the University of Waterloo, Robert McCann went on to become a human factors psychologist for NASA. He has worked on projects like retrofitting space shuttle cockpits with liquid-crystal displays that provide much more flexibility in displaying information than current displays provide (McCann, 2001). He hopes the new displays will increase the safety of space shuttle missions by providing astronauts with better awareness of information with less mental effort. In our discussion of the kinesthetic and vestibular senses, we just described the research of Laurence Harris & Michael Jenkin, who have been working on integrating kinesthetic, vesibular and visual information in virtual reality systems. Similarly, in our discussion of touch, we described the research of Susan Lederman and Roberta Klatsky (1998, 2004; Lederman & others, 2004), who have been working on improving haptic interfaces to provide touch feedback in telepresence systems.

This sort of research falls into the area of psychology known as "human factors" (in North America) or "ergonomics" (in Europe). Human factors psychology involves designing equipment and arranging environments in which humans function to improve them in various ways, such as making them safer and more efficient (Gamache, 2004; Buxton, 2001; Wise & Hopkins, 2000). Human factors psychology is often associated with the field of industrial and organizational psychology. Human factors psychologists make the dials and controls on the instrument panel of your car easier to read, easier to handle, and minimally distracting. They also help to design computer interface software and devices to make them more "user friendly."

Human factors psychologists spend considerable time designing displays (Payne, Lang, & Blackwell, 1995). One of the initial decisions they have to make is which sensory modality to use. Typically, displays are visual. However, auditory and tactile displays might be used, depending on the situation and the information that needs to be monitored. Consider the routine operation of a car. You get visual feedback about the speed at which you are driving, the temperature of the engine, and the oil pressure. You might hear a beeping sound if a door is not completely closed. You might forget to latch your seatbelt and then hear a buzzer that signals you to latch it (Buxton & others, 2000).

Air safety is one field to which human factors psychologists have made many contributions. Research in this field includes classic work. For example, what an airplane

Robert McCann, a human factors psychologist, at work at NASA.

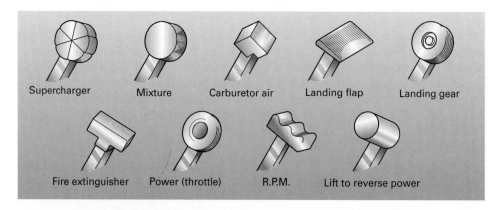

Supercharger   Mixture   Carburetor air   Landing flap   Landing gear

Fire extinguisher   Power (throttle)   R.P.M.   Lift to reverse power

FIGURE 5.47 Shape-Coded Controls

Controls need to be clearly coded to assure their correct and rapid identification. One way to accomplish this is to shape code the controls. Each knob on a console might be a recognizably different shape, which allows for rapid visual identification of the correct control. It also allows tactual identification in the dark or when the operator's eyes must focus somewhere else. An effective way of shape coding controls is to design the control so that its shape represents or symbolizes its function.

pilot can see through the cockpit window varies considerably due to weather conditions and the amount of glare and degree of brightness (Hawkins, 1987). These changing factors can sometimes cause hazardous perceptual illusions. Illusions of apparent motion can also be a hazard as pilots wait for or initiate a takeoff. Human factors psychologists seek to find ways to minimize these illusions. Human factors psychologists have long advocated designing controls that provide information without interfering with the task. For example, the landing flap controls on many airplanes are shaped like the landing flaps themselves, so that pilots can manage the controls without looking at them (see figure 5.47).

More recently, human factors psychologists have begun to evaluate the safety of a new generation of 3-D flight displays (Alexander, & Wickens, & Merwin, 2005) and the use of 3-D audio for cockpit warning (Oving, Veltman, & Bronkhorst, 2004). Human factors psychologists also study other aspects of commercial flying. For example, in the cockpit, they assess pilot fatigue and sources of error, such as miscommunication among the flight crew (Hancock & Desmond, 2000). In the passenger cabin, they might examine influences on the anxiety level, safety, and behaviour of passengers. Opportunities are even opening up for the study of human factors in the aerospace industry (Suedfeld, 2004).

> **reflect and review**

5 **Describe what human factors psychologists study.**

- Define human factors psychology and discuss some of its benefits.

Come up with some aspects of life other than those described in the text in which human factors research might improve functioning.

Sensation and Perception

1 HOW WE SENSE AND PERCEIVE THE WORLD

Detecting, Processing, and Interpreting Experiences — Sensory Receptors and the Brain — Thresholds — Signal Detection Theory — Perceiving Sensory Stimuli — Sensory Adaptation

2 THE VISUAL SYSTEM

The Visual Stimulus and the Eye — Visual Processing in the Brain — Colour Vision — Perceiving Shape, Depth, Motion, and Constancy — Illusions

3 THE AUDITORY SYSTEM

The Nature of Sound and How We Experience It — Structures and Functions of the Ear — Theories of Hearing — Auditory Processing in the Brain — Localizing Sound — Noise Pollution

4 OTHER SENSES

The Skin Senses — The Chemical Senses — The Kinesthetic and Vestibular Senses

5 PERCEPTION AND HUMAN FACTORS PSYCHOLOGY

At the beginning of the chapter, we posed five chapter questions and encouraged you to review material related to these questions at the end of each major section (see pages 186, 202, 209, 219, and 221). Use the following reflection and review features to further your understanding of the chapter material.

CHAPTER REFLECTIONS

1. Find a partner and test your absolute detection threshold for sugar. Have your partner set up the following sugar-and-water mixtures. Mix 2 teaspoons of sugar in 1 litre of water. Label this solution "Solution A." Take half a litre of "Solution A," add half a litre of water, and label this solution "Solution B." Then, take half a litre of "Solution B" and add half a litre of water and label this "Solution C." Continue taking half a litre from each successive solution until there is a total of eight solutions, making sure to keep track of which solution is which. When you're done, the concentration of the solutions should be equivalent to a teaspoon of sugar in each of the following amounts of water: A) 0.5 litre, B) 1 litre, C) 2 litres, D) 4 litres, E) 8 litres, F) 16 litres, G) 32 litres, and H) 64 litres. Your partner should place a sample of one of the solutions in a cup and a sample of plain water in another, identical cup. You should taste the solution in each cup and decide which one is the sugar solution. Do this with all the solutions until you can decide what your absolute detection threshold is according to the definition in the text. Do you think your detection threshold would vary depending on what you have eaten recently? Why or why not?

2. Imagine that you have two sets of dominoes. Each set contains 100 dominoes. With the first set, you make a straight line of 100. With the second set, you make an arrangement in which tipping a single domino causes five separate lines of dominoes to fall down simultaneously. Which set of dominoes will fall the fastest? How is this set of dominoes similar to the way we process visual information?

3. Compare and contrast the consequences of losing vision in one eye versus losing hearing in one ear.

4. You smell a delicious aroma coming from the kitchen, so you head that way, but you manage to stub your toe on your roommate's backpack and then hit your head on the table as you bend down to rub your toe. Your roommate hands you what looks like a brownie; it smells pretty good, so you take a big bite. First it tastes good; then, suddenly, your mouth feels as if it is on fire, so you grab the glass of ice water sitting on the table and take a big gulp of it. Describe the different kinds of sensory signals that your brain has processed during this episode and the different kinds of receptors you have used to make sense of what's happened.

5. Many Web sites are easy to use and navigate, but some would benefit from some design help from human factors psychologists. Browse the Web and find sites that have good human factors designs and others that have bad human factors designs. Can you identify aspects of the good designs that are missing in the bad designs (or vice versa)?

6. Speaking of Web sites, try Michael Darnell's Web site, Bad Human Factors Designs (http://www.baddesigns.com/). What is your favourite example of a bad human factors design?

CHAPTER REVIEW

Discuss basic principles of sensation and perception.

- Sensation is the process of receiving stimulus energies from the environment. Perception is the process of organizing and interpreting sensory information to give it meaning. Sensation and perception are integrated. Perceiving the world involves both bottom-up and top-down processing.

- All sensation begins with sensory receptors, which are specialized cells that detect and transmit information about a stimulus to sensory neurons and the brain. Sensory receptors are selective and have different neural pathways. The three main classes of sense organs and receptors are photoreception, mechanoreception, and chemoreception.

- Psychophysics, the field that studies links between the physical properties of stimuli and a person's experience of them, defines absolute threshold as the minimum amount of energy that people can detect. There is no evidence that subliminal perception—the ability to detect information below the level of conscious awareness—has any substantial influence on our thoughts and behaviour. The difference threshold, or just noticeable difference, is the smallest difference in stimulation required to discriminate one stimulus from another 50 percent of the time. Weber's law holds that two stimuli must differ by a constant minimum percentage to be perceived as different.

- Signal detection theory focuses on decision making about stimuli in the presence of uncertainty. In this theory, detection of sensory stimuli depends on many other factors than the physical properties of the stimuli, and differences in these other factors may lead different people to make different decisions about identical stimuli.

- What we perceive depends in part on which stimuli engage our attention and on a tendency to perceive things according to our beliefs and expectations. Selective attention involves focusing on a specific aspect of experience while ignoring others. Attention may involve bottom-up or top-down processing. A perceptual set is a collection of experiences and expectations that influence perception.
- Sensory adaptation is a change in the responsiveness of the sensory system based on the average level of surrounding stimulation.

Explain how the visual system enables us to see and, by communicating with the brain, to perceive the world.

- Light is a form of electromagnetic energy that can be described in terms of wavelengths. Three characteristics of light are hue, amplitude, and purity. The eye responds to light within a narrow range of wavelengths (400–700 nm). Light passes through the cornea and lens to the retina, a light-sensitive surface in the back of the eye that houses light receptors called rods (which function in low illumination) and cones (which react to colour). The fovea of the retina contains only cones and serves to sharpen detail in an image. Ganglion cells interpret incoming visual information and send it to the brain.
- The optic nerve transmits neural impulses to the brain. There it diverges at the optic chiasm, so that what we see in the left visual field is registered in the right side of the brain and vice versa. In the occipital lobes of the cerebral cortex, the information is integrated. Visual information processing involves feature detection, parallel processing, and binding.
- The trichromatic theory of colour perception stipulates that three types of colour receptors in the retina allow us to perceive three colours (green, red, and blue). The opponent-process theory states that cells in the visual system respond to red-green and blue-yellow colours. Both theories are probably correct—the eye and the brain use both methods to code colours.
- Shape perception is the ability to distinguish objects from their background. This figure-ground relationship is a principle of gestalt psychology, which emphasizes that people naturally organize their per-

ceptions according to patterns. Depth perception is the ability to perceive objects three-dimensionally. Depth perception depends on binocular cues and monocular cues. Motion perception by humans depends on specialized neurons, feedback from the body, and environmental cues. Psychologists are interested in both real and apparent movement. Perceptual constancy is the recognition that objects are stable despite changes in the way we see them. Three types of perceptual constancy are size constancy, shape constancy, and brightness constancy.

- A visual illusion is the result of a discrepancy between reality and the perceptual representation of it. Examples are the Müller-Lyer illusion, the moon illusion, the horizontal-vertical illusion, the Ponzo illusion, and the devil's tuning fork.

Understand how the auditory system registers sound and how it connects with the brain to perceive it.

- Sounds, or sound waves, are vibrations in the air that are processed by the auditory system. Sound waves vary in wavelength. Wavelength determines frequency. Pitch is the perceptual interpretation of frequency. Amplitude, measured in decibels, is perceived as loudness. Complex sounds involve a blending of frequencies. Timbre is the tone saturation or perceptual quality of a sound.
- The outer ear consists of the pinna and external auditory canal and acts to funnel sound to the middle ear. In the middle ear, the eardrum, hammer, anvil, and stirrup vibrate in response to sound and transfer the vibrations to the inner ear. Important parts of the fluid-filled inner ear are the oval window, cochlea, and basilar membrane. The movement of hair cells between the basilar membrane and the tectorial membrane generates nerve impulses.
- Place theory states that each frequency produces vibrations at a particular spot on the basilar membrane. Place theory adequately explains high-frequency sounds but not low-frequency sounds. Frequency theory states that the ability to perceive a sound's frequency depends on how often the auditory nerve fires. A modification of frequency theory, the volley principle, states that a cluster of neurons can fire impulses in rapid succession, producing a volley of impulses.
- Information about sound moves from the hair cells to the auditory nerve, which carries information to the brain's auditory areas. The cortical destination of most fibres is the temporal lobes of the cerebral cortex.

- Localizing sound involves both the timing of the sound and the intensity of the sound arriving at each ear.
- Noise pollution is a special concern, because it can have a negative effect on behaviour. Noise at 80 decibels or higher, if heard for prolonged periods of time, can damage hearing.

Know how the skin, chemical, kinesthetic, and vestibular senses work.

- Touch is the detection of mechanical energy, or pressure, against the skin. Touch information travels through the spinal cord, brain stem, and thalamus, and on to the somatosensory areas of the parietal lobes. Psychologists are studying the role of touch in various jobs and in infant development. Thermoreceptors under the skin respond to increases and decreases in temperature. Pain is the sensation that warns us about damage to our bodies. Two different neural pathways transmit information about pain: a fast pathway and a slow pathway. One theory of pain is gate-control theory. Many physical and psychological techniques are used to control pain.

- Taste and smell enable us to detect and process chemicals in the environment. Papillae are bumps on the tongue that contain taste buds, the receptors for taste. The taste qualities we respond to are categorized as sweet, sour, bitter, salty, and umami, although our tasting ability goes beyond these five qualities. The olfactory epithelium contains a sheet of receptor cells for smell in the roof of the nose.
- The kinesthetic sense provides information about movement, posture, and orientation. The vestibular sense provides information about balance and movement. Receptors for the kinesthetic sense are embedded in muscle fibres and joints. The semicircular canals in the inner ear contain the sensory receptors that detect head motion.

Describe what human factors psychologists study.

- Human factors psychologists design equipment and arrange environments in which humans function to improve those environments, for example, by designing displays to make them safer and more efficient.

CONNECTIONS

For extra help in mastering the material in this chapter, see the integrator, review sections, practice quizzes, and other resources in the Student Study Guide and at the Online Learning Centre (www.mcgrawhill.ca/college/santrock).

CORE TERMS

sensation, p. 176
transduction, p. 176
perception, p. 176
bottom-up processing, p. 176
top-down processing, p. 176
sensory receptors, p. 177
psychophysics, p. 179
absolute threshold, p. 179
noise, p. 180
subliminal perception, p. 180
difference threshold, p. 181
Weber's law, p. 182
signal detection theory, p. 182
selective attention, p. 183
perceptual set, p. 185
sensory adaptation, p. 185

retina, p. 189
rods, p. 189
cones, p. 189
feature detectors, p. 191
parallel processing, p. 192
binding, p. 192
trichromatic theory, p. 193
opponent-process theory, p. 194
figure-ground relationship, p. 196
gestalt psychology, p. 196
depth perception, p. 197
binocular cues, p. 197
monocular cues, p. 197
apparent movement, p. 200
perceptual constancy, p. 200
visual illusion, p. 201

outer ear, p. 204
middle ear, p. 204
inner ear, p. 205
place theory, p. 206
frequency theory, p. 206
volley principle, p. 206
auditory nerve, p. 206
thermoreceptors, p. 212
pain, p. 213
gate-control theory of pain, p. 213
papillae, p. 215
olfactory epithelium, p. 217
kinesthetic senses, p. 217
vestibular sense, p. 217
semicircular canals, p. 218

6 States of Consciousness

CHAPTER QUESTIONS

1 What is the nature of consciousness?

2 What is the nature of sleep and dreams?

3 What is hypnosis?

4 What are the uses and types of psychoactive drugs?

The nature of consciousness is one of the great mysteries of human existence and one of modern psychology's most intriguing topics. In a classic essay entitled *What is it like to be a bat?* philosopher Thomas Nagel framed the problem as one of perspective (Nagel, 1974). From a third-person, or objective, point of view, bats, as we saw in the previous chapter, use echolocation to hunt for insects at night. But this tells us nothing about the bat's first-person, or subjective, point of view. Have you ever wondered what it is like to be a bat (or your pet dog or cat)? What does music sound like to them? Are their dreams as weird as ours? Do they ever imagine themselves in improbable situations? Or feel sad? Nagel claimed we cannot know what it is like, subjectively, to be a bat, although he suspected that it must be like something to be a bat. On the other hand, he suspected it is like nothing to be a rock. Whatever else, consciousness is associated with the subjective point of view. The inner experience of your own consciousness does not appear to be accessible to anyone else.

What do you think it is like to be this bulldog?

Philosophers from Plato to Thomas Nagel have reflected on the subjective nature of consciousness for thousands of years. For most of that time, consciousness was considered impossible to study from an objective point of view. As we saw in the opening chapter, early psychologists, and especially the structuralists, also relied on introspection, "looking inside," to offer first-person accounts of mental processes. In fact, for Wundt there were only two sciences: physics, the study of our experience of the external world, and psychology, the study of our experience of our interior world. However, introspection failed to provide a solid foundation for the new science of psychology and was soon replaced by behaviourism, the study of observable behaviour. The subjective first-person point of view gave way to the objective third-person point of view. For fifty years, behaviourism contented itself to study behaviour; it is only recently that scientific psychology has once again turned its attention to the topic of consciousness.

So we return to the ancient questions about the nature of consciousness but we do so from the objective third-person perspective of science. What can the third-person point of view contribute to our understanding of a quintessentially first-person phenomenon? While modern psychology cannot yet explain the subjective nature of consciousness, much progress has been made. We begin this chapter with a discussion of different levels of awareness, or consciousness, and go on to have a look at consciousness and the brain (Grossenbacher, 2001). Second, we delve into the realm of sleep and dreams, in which most of us spend a great deal of time. The third topic is the mysterious and controversial topic of hypnosis. Fourth, we discuss the altered states of consciousness produced by psychoactive drugs and some of the reasons that people become addicted to them.

① THE NATURE OF CONSCIOUSNESS

— Levels of — Consciousness
Awareness and the Brain

What is consciousness?

In the late nineteenth and early twentieth centuries, psychology pioneers such as Sigmund Freud and William James took great interest in the study of the conscious and unconscious mind. However, for much of the twentieth century, psychologists shunned the slippery, subjective trappings of consciousness. Instead, they focused on behaviours and the rewards and punishments that determined those behaviours (Skinner, 1938; Watson, 1913). In the past decade, though, the study of consciousness has gained widespread respectability in psychology (Koch, 2004). And, for the first time in many decades, psychologists from many different fields are interested in consciousness (Baruss, 2003; Lehar, 2002), including evolutionary psychologists (Bering & Shackelford, 2004).

One difficulty with the study of consciousness is that it may not be a unitary phenomenon amenable to a simple explanation. It has often been proposed that there are different types or levels of consciousness, or awareness (H. T. Hunt, 1995; Whitehead, 2004). You are aware of some of the processing, unaware of other processing. Although there is still disagreement about how consciousness should be defined, here we define **consciousness** as the awareness of external events and internal sensations, including awareness of the self and thoughts about your experiences. Externally, you might be aware that your best friend just cracked a joke about his latest body piercing, that the car in front of you just swerved to miss a dog, and that your sunglasses fell off your nose as you leapt back to the curb. Internally, you might be aware that your headache just returned, that you are breathing too fast, that your stomach is rumbling because you missed breakfast, and that you are relieved that the weekend is almost here.

Information moves rapidly in and out of consciousness as the contents of our awareness change from moment to moment. William James (1890/1950) described the mind as a **stream of consciousness**—a continuous flow of changing sensations, images, thoughts, and feelings. Our minds can race from one topic to the next—from thinking about the person approaching us, to how well we feel, to what we are going to do tomorrow, to where we are going for lunch, and so on.

Levels of Awareness

The flow of sensations, images, thoughts, and feelings that James spoke of can occur at different levels of awareness. We discuss five levels of awareness here: no awareness, subconscious awareness, primary awareness, self-awareness, and altered states of awareness (see figure 6.1).

No Awareness The term *unconscious* is generally applied to someone who has been knocked out by a blow, anaesthetized, or fallen into a deep, prolonged unconscious state. Even in such a state, most patients show some degree of basic arousal, or reactivity. The Glasgow coma scale is used to measure basic reactivity, such as a patient's ability to open an eye as well as give verbal and motor responses (e.g. De Guise & others, 2005). Without a minimal degree of arousal, no higher level of awareness is possible.

However, Sigmund Freud (1917) used the term *unconscious* in a very different way. At about the same time that William James was charting the shifting nature of our stream of consciousness, Freud concluded that most of our thoughts are unconscious. **Unconscious thought**, said Freud, is a reservoir of unacceptable wishes, feelings, and thoughts that are beyond conscious awareness.

According to Freud, unconscious thoughts are too laden with anxiety and other negative emotions for consciousness to admit them. For example, if a young man is nervous around women and breaks into a cold sweat when a woman approaches him,

consciousness Awareness of external events and internal sensations, including awareness of the self and thoughts about one's experiences.

stream of consciousness James's concept that the mind is a continuous flow of sensations, images, thoughts, and feelings.

unconscious thought Freud's concept of a reservoir of unacceptable wishes, feelings, and thoughts that are beyond conscious awareness.

Level of Awareness	Description		
No Awareness	Refers to both low levels of arousal and to Freud's belief that some unconscious thoughts are too laden with anxiety and other negative emotions for consciousness to admit them.		The woman on the couch is undergoing psychoanalytic therapy to reveal her unconscious thoughts.
Subconscious Awareness	Can occur when people are awake, as well as when they are sleeping and dreaming.		All of us dream while we sleep, but some of us dream more than others.
Primary Awareness	Involves uncontrolled awareness, including automatic processing and daydreaming, as well as more effortful controlled awareness, in which individuals focus their efforts on a goal.		This woman is an experienced computer operator. Her manoeuvres with the keyboard are automatic, requiring minimal awareness.
Self-Awareness	Involves being cognizant of one's own awareness, including metacognition, which is recognition of one's own cognitive process.		This student is thinking about how well she is understanding what she is reading, which requires metacognition.
Altered States of Awareness	Can be produced by drugs, trauma, fatigue, possibly hypnosis, and sensory deprivation.		These people, who are drinking alcohol, are in an altered state of consciousness.

he might be unconscious that his fear of women springs from the cold, punitive way his mother treated him when he was a child. Freud believed that one of psychotherapy's main goals was to bring unconscious thoughts into conscious awareness so they could be addressed and treated.

Freud's concept of the unconscious mind, especially its pervasiveness, is controversial. Whether or not we accept his view of the unconscious mind, we owe a debt to Freud for recognizing the complexity of consciousness.

Subconscious Awareness In chapter 5, you learned that a great deal of brain activity is going on beneath the level of conscious awareness. Psychologists are increasingly interested in the subconscious processing of information, which can take place while we are asleep or while we are awake (Damasio, 2001).

Sleep and Dreams Although we are relatively unreactive to outside stimuli during sleep and dreams, they should not be regarded as the absence of consciousness but as low levels of consciousness.

Consider the German chemist August Kekulé, who, in 1865, had a dream of a snake swallowing its own tail and, upon waking, developed the insight that the benzene molecule might be shaped like a ring (Benjafield, 2004). If he had remained awake, Kekulé may well have rejected as ridiculous the idea of a link between snakes and benzene molecules. However, in his subconscious mind rational thought could not censor the connection, so when Kekulé woke up he could not ignore its possibility. It may be that irrelevant connections fade away and disappear but that those that are robust survive long enough to eventually emerge into consciousness (Csikszentmihalyi, 1996).

FIGURE 6.1
Levels of Awareness

"If you ask me, all three of us are in different states of awareness."

© The New Yorker Collection 1983 Edward Frascino from cartoonbank.com. All Rights Reserved.

Researchers have found that when people are asleep they still remain aware of external stimuli to some degree. In one classic study, people who were clearly asleep (as determined by physiological monitoring devices) were nevertheless able to respond to faint tones by pressing a handheld button (Ogilvie & Wilkinson, 1988). In another study, the presentation of pure auditory tones to sleeping individuals activated auditory processing regions of the brain, whereas participants' names activated language areas, the amygdala, and the prefrontal cortex (Stickgold, 2001). Sleep and dreams are covered more thoroughly in the next section.

Waking Subconscious Awareness According to creativity experts, insights often occur when a subconscious connection between ideas is so strong that it is forced to "pop out" into awareness, somewhat like the way a cork held underwater bobs to the surface as soon as it is released (Csikszentmihalyi (1996; Kaufman & Baer, 2005).

Csikszentmihalyi believes that creative ideas often "incubate" for some time below the threshold of conscious awareness before they emerge. When an idea is incubating, our minds may be processing information even though we are not aware of it. Perhaps, in the absence of conscious connections, ideas simply combine more or less randomly beneath the level of awareness.

Evidence that we are not always aware of the processing of information in our brains also comes from studies of individuals with certain neurological disorders. One example is the phenomenon of *blindsight*, which we encountered in chapter 5. A woman who suffered neurological damage was unable to describe or report the shape or size of objects in her visual field, though she was capable of describing other physical perceptions she had (Milner & Goodale, 1995). Yet when she reached for an object she could accurately adjust the size of her grip to allow her to grasp the object. Thus she did possess some subconscious knowledge of the size and shape of objects, even though she had no awareness of this knowledge.

Subconscious information processing can occur simultaneously in a distributed manner along many *parallel* tracks. (Recall the discussion of parallel processing of visual information in chapter 5. For example, when you look at a cat running down the street, you are consciously aware of the event but not of the subconscious processing of the object's identity (a cat), its colour (black), its movement (fast), and so on. In contrast, conscious processing is *serial*. That is, it occurs in sequence and is slower than much subconscious processing.

Primary Awareness If there is a "normal" level of awareness it is surely the one we experience while we are awake and going about our business more or less aware of our surroundings (Farthing, 1992). It was this level of awareness William James described as a stream of consciousness. Within this level of awareness, we can distinguish between uncontrolled and controlled awareness

Uncontrolled Awareness It is a beautiful spring day. You are soaking up the sunlight for the first time since last summer. You are not focusing and your mind begins to wander. You think about your vacation last summer, an exam coming up in one of your courses, what you might do on the weekend, whether or not to get a drink, and so on. You are not attempting to control your awareness. William James described this flow of loosely connected thoughts as being like the flights and perchings of a bird. Uncontrolled levels of awareness include automatic processes and the familiar state of daydreaming.

Automatic Processes We spend a significant proportion of every day in relatively automatic levels of awareness. A few weeks after acquiring her cell phone, Maria flips it open and places a call in the middle of a conversation with you. Her fingers fly almost automatically across the buttons. She doesn't have to concentrate on dialing now and hardly seems aware of the gadget against her cheek as she continues to talk on it while finishing her lunch. For her, cell phone dialing has reached the point of automatic processing. **Automatic processes** are states of consciousness that require minimal attention and do not interfere with other ongoing activities. In memory, this means remembering without deliberately trying (Jacoby, 1998). Automatic processes require less

automatic processes States of consciousness that require little attention and do not interfere with other ongoing activities.

conscious effort than controlled awareness. When we are awake, our automatic behaviours occur at a lower level of awareness than controlled processes, but they are still conscious behaviours. Maria pushed the right buttons, so apparently at some level she was aware of what she was doing.

Daydreaming   Another state of awareness that involves a lower level of conscious effort, *daydreaming* lies somewhere between controlled awareness and dreaming while we are asleep. It is a little like dreaming while we are awake. Mind wandering is probably the most obvious type of daydreaming. Sometimes it occurs even when we are supposed to be concentrating on some task. In this event, as Scottish psychologist Jonathan Smallwood and his colleagues have shown, performance on the task at hand usually suffers (Smallwood & others, 2003).

More often, daydreams begin spontaneously when we are doing something that requires less than our full attention. We regularly take brief side trips into our own private kingdoms of imagery and memory while reading, listening, or working. When we daydream, we drift into a world of fantasy. We imagine ourselves on dates, at parties, on television, in faraway places, at another time in our lives, and so on. Sometimes our daydreams are about ordinary, everyday events, such as paying the rent, getting our hair done, or dealing with somebody at work.

Daydreams can result in a variety of consequences. According to Langens & Schmalt (2002), people with a high fear of failure can find themselves repeatedly drawn in to positive daydreams, which leads to negative feelings once they come back to a more controlled awareness. On the other hand, the semiautomatic flow of daydreaming can be useful. As you daydream while you shave, iron a pair of pants, or walk to the store, you may make plans, solve a problem, or come up with a creative idea. Daydreams can remind us of important things ahead. Daydreaming keeps our minds active while helping us to cope, create, and fantasize (Klinger, 2000).

Controlled Awareness   After hours of gameplay you have reached the final level of a new computer game, one last life-and-death boss fight away from victory. In that moment, you are paying such close attention that the outside world ceases to exist. This is controlled, or focused, awareness.

Richard Schiffrin and Walter Schneider proposed an influential distinction between controlled and automatic processes. **Controlled processes** represent the most alert states of human consciousness, in which individuals actively focus their efforts toward a goal (Shiffrin & Schneider, 1977; Cooper & others, 2002). In memory, this means being aware that you are trying to remember (Kelley & Jacoby, 1996). Watch Maria as she struggles to master the unfamiliar buttons on her new ten-function cell phone. She doesn't hear you humming to yourself or notice the intriguing shadow on the wall. Her state of focused awareness is a controlled process.

In the previous chapter, we discussed the role of attention in perception. Controlled processes require selective attention, the ability to focus on a specific aspect of experience while ignoring others (Pashler, Johnston, & Ruthruff, 2001). Perhaps the most extreme forms of controlled awareness are found in meditation. In concentrative meditation, associated with Hinduism, attention is deliberately focused an object, thought or sound (*mantra*) in order to clear consciousness of all other thoughts. In mindfulness meditation, associated with Buddhism, attention is deliberately opened to whatever goes through the mind to become calmer, clearer, and less reactive. Valentine & Sweet (1999) have shown that both types of meditators perform better on tests of sustained attention than nonmeditators do.

Self-Awareness   You are busily working on writing a paragraph for an essay. You find yourself thinking that you are writing this paragraph particularly well. You notice your creative use of adjectives and how well you got across the main theme of the paragraph. You determine to keep it up for the remainder of the essay. Your awareness has shifted from the essay to your writing of the essay. In this particular case you were engaged in *metacognition*, thinking about your own thinking processes, a type of "minding your mind" (Bogdan, 1999; Maibom, 2004). This is self-awareness, perhaps the highest form of awareness.

controlled processes The most alert states of consciousness.

Both the mindful meditation practised by Zen Buddhist monks (*top*) and the concentrative meditation practised by Hindu Yogis (*bottom*) are highly controlled forms of conscious awareness. *Have you ever considered meditation?*

Self-awareness need not always be positive. Some people can just go to a party and be drawn into the experience. A more introspective person might find herself feeling like she is on the outside, observing the other people having a good time but unable to let herself do the same. She is being *self-conscious*.

We are not born self-aware but must develop it, a process that begins sometime after the first year of life. In one study, children did not recognize themselves in a mirror, a rudimentary form of self-awareness, until after 12 months of age (Nielsen, Dissanayake, & Kashima, 2003).

Altered States of Awareness   *Altered states of awareness or consciousness* are mental states that are noticeably different from normal awareness. They can be produced by drugs, trauma, fatigue, possibly hypnosis, and sensory deprivation (Vaitl & others, 2005). Meditation is often treated as an altered state of awareness. Interestingly, it is possible that new media, such as television, video games, the Internet, and virtual reality can also alter consciousness (Preston, 1998). In some cases, drug use may create a higher level of awareness. The popularity of coffee and other beverages that contain caffeine, a stimulant drug, provides evidence of the widespread belief that caffeine increases alertness. Awareness may also be altered to a lower level. Alcohol has this effect. Later in the chapter, we discuss drugs, as well as hypnosis, which some psychologists believe involves an altered state of consciousness.

Consciousness and the Brain

One of the great unanswered questions about consciousness concerns its relationship to the brain. Does consciousness stand alone (located in what might be called "mind"), separate in some way from the brain, or is it an intrinsic aspect of the brain's functioning? From the viewpoint of scientific psychology, consciousness is a brain function, just like sensation, perception, memory, and cognition. Thus, it makes sense to ask where it is located (Tulving, 1999b; Tulving & Lepage, 2000). If consciousness is in the brain, is there a particular location that is the seat of consciousness or if there are different levels of consciousness, is consciousness distributed across different areas of the brain?

According to Donald Stuss of the University of Toronto and Vicki Anderson of the University of Melbourne, different levels of awareness are associated with different brain areas and higher levels of awareness are associated with the frontal lobes (Stuss & Anderson, 2004). In general, low levels of awareness are associated with evolutionarily older brain structures in the hindbrain and higher levels of awareness are associated with evolutionarily newer structures in the forebrain (Striedter, 2005).

Basic arousal, without which higher levels of consciousness are not possible, is controlled by lower brain structures in the brainstem. Severe damage to these areas generally results in death or coma. Less severe damage can result in *stupor*, a general lack of arousability.

Intermediate and higher levels of awareness are produced by the activity of a number of separate distributed processing systems. Depending on what a person is aware of at a particular point in time, different areas of the brain "light up," or are activated (Alkire, Haier, and James, 1998; Kosslyn, 1994). Along with other activity, visual experiences will produce some activity in the visual cortex, auditory experiences will produce activity in the temporal lobe, and so forth. One view is that neural networks or assemblies become more or less active depending on what the consciousness of the situation demands (Greenfield, 1996).

Consider, for example, the awareness of visual stimuli. As we saw in chapter 5, damage to the medial, or "what," pathway results in visual agnosia; the patient is unaware of the identity of objects directly in front of him. Notice that the damage does not make the person totally unaware. Rather, the lack of awareness is modular and related to the specific brain area that was damaged. Dr. P., who we met in the last chapter, remained highly aware except for his agnosia. Intriguingly, Dr. P. tended not to be aware of his agnosia.

Higher levels of awareness definitely involve activity in the cerebral cortex, especially its association areas and frontal lobes (Stuss & Knight, 2002, Damasio & Anderson, 2003). It is likely that the integration of information from the senses, along with information about emotions and memories in the frontal lobes, creates primary awareness (Kalat, 2004). One of the highest levels of awareness is controlled awareness. According to Stuss & Anderson (2004), the frontal lobes are involved in the deliberate integration of information, one of the goals of controlled awareness. Damage to this part of the brain produces a different deficit in awareness.

For example, Alexander, Stuss, & Benson (1979) describe *Capgras* syndrome, which results from bilateral frontal lobe damage. One patient suffering from this kind of damage convalesced in the hospital for a year. In the interim, his family grew a year older, his wife changed her hair style and purchased a new car. During his convalescence, the patient insisted that he had a "new" second family, virtually identical to, but somehow different from, his "old" family. Even though he agreed it was implausible that these could actually be two nearly identical but different families, he could not shake the feeling that they were, well, *different*. His ability to deliberately integrate information from his senses, his memory, and his emotions had been damaged; he could not become aware of the identity of his own family.

Finally Stuss and his colleagues assign a special role in self-awareness to the right frontal lobe and its connections with the limbic system (Stuss and others, 2001; Stuss & Anderson, 2004). Two patients with right frontal lobe damage performed well on tests of controlled awareness. Despite this, they could not function effectively. They knew what their problems were but blamed others. They knew how to fix their problems but didn't act on their knowledge. While these patients had a good understanding of the rest of the world, their sense of self was disturbed, leaving them without a clear purpose.

> ## > reflect and review

 Discuss the nature of consciousness.

- Define consciousness and describe five levels of awareness.
- Explain the brain's role in consciousness.

How many different states of awareness have you experienced? In one or two sentences each, describe the nature of your experience in each state.

② SLEEP AND DREAMS

Biological Rhythms and Sleep	Why Do We Need Sleep?	Sleep Stages	Sleep and Disease	Sleep Disorders	Dreams

What is the nature of sleep and dreams?

Sleep claims about one-third of our time, more than any other pursuit. Despite this, many of us are not getting enough sleep to function optimally. What is sleep and why is it so important? This section explores the answers to these questions, as well as the fascinating world of dreams. First, let's look at one type of internal biological rhythm—sleep.

Biological Rhythms and Sleep

Biological rhythms are periodic physiological fluctuations in the body. We are unaware of many biological rhythms, such as the rise and fall of hormones in the bloodstream, accelerated and decelerated cycles of brain activity, and highs and lows in body

biological rhythms Periodic physiological fluctuations in the body.

temperature, but they can influence our behaviour. These rhythms are controlled by biological clocks, which include

- Annual or seasonal cycles, such as the migration of birds, the hibernation of bears, and the seasonal fluctuations of humans' eating habits
- Twenty-eight day cycles, such as the female menstrual cycle which averages 28 days
- Twenty-four hour cycles, such as the sleep/wake cycle and temperature changes in the body

Let's explore the 24-hour cycles further.

Circadian Rhythms A **circadian rhythm** is a daily behavioural or physiological cycle (Antle & Mistlberger, 2005). The term *circadian* comes from the Latin words *circa*, meaning "about," and *dies*, meaning "day." Daily circadian rhythms influence the sleep/wake cycle, body temperature, blood pressure, and blood sugar level. For example, body temperature fluctuates about 1.7° Celsius in a 24-hour day, peaking in the afternoon and reaching its lowest point between 2 a.m. and 5 a.m. Recent research suggests that circadian rhythms even modulate memory performance and the control of attention (Hasher, Goldstein, & May, 2005).

A number of biological clocks or pacemakers are involved in regulating circadian rhythms (Ruby & others, 2002; Dawson, 2004). Of these, the **suprachiasmatic nucleus (SCN)** is the master clock (Panda & Hogenesch, 2004). The SCN is a small structure in the hypothalamus that synchronizes its own rhythm with the daily cycle of light and dark based on input from the retina (Arvanitogiannis & others, 2000). Output from the SCN allows the hypothalamus to regulate daily rhythms such as temperature and hunger and the reticular formation to regulate daily rhythms of sleep and wakefulness (see figure 6.2).

Understandably, many individuals who are totally blind experience sleeping problems for their entire lives because their retinas cannot detect light. The result is a kind of permanent jet lag because their circadian rhythms often do not follow a 24-hour cycle (U.S. National Institute of Neurological Disorders and Stroke, 2004).

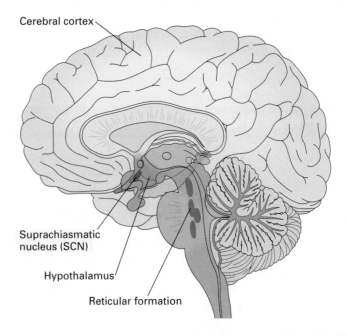

circadian rhythms Daily behavioural or physiological cycles, such as the sleep/wake cycle.

suprachiasmatic nucleus (SCN) A small structure in the hypothalamus that registers changes in light.

FIGURE 6.2 Suprachiasmatic Nucleus
The suprachiasmatic nucleus plays an important role in keeping our biological clock running on time. The SCN is located in the hypothalamus. It receives information from the retina about light, which is the external stimulus that synchronizes the SCN. Output from the SCN is distributed to the rest of the hypothalamus and to the reticular formation.

How accurate are the biological clocks that control circadian rhythms? To answer this question, researchers have completely isolated individuals from all *zeitgebers* (in German literally "time givers"): clocks, calendars, night, the moon, the sun, and other indices of time. A number of experiments have focused on such isolation experiences (Kales, 1970; Siffre, 1975). For example, French scientist Michael Siffre entered Midnight Cave near Del Rio, Texas, on February 14, 1972. A small nylon tent deep within the cave was Siffre's home for six months. Because Siffre could not see or sense the sun rising and setting while he was in the cave, he began to live by circadian cycles instead of by days.

Siffre referred to each of his sleep/wake cycles as a day. He and other individuals who have been isolated judge a day to be about 25 hours. However, in recently conducted studies that exercised better control of the light participants' experience, a day was judged to vary from 24 hours by only a few minutes (Lavie, 2001).

In northern countries like Canada the short days of mid-winter and the long days of mid-summer can disrupt circadian rhythms. Short winter days can lead to *seasonal affective disorder* (*SAD*), a seasonal form of depression accompanied by increased appetite and hypersomnia, or excessive sleepiness. Perhaps not surprisingly, some patients can suffer from summer SAD when days get especially long. The symptoms are the opposite of those reported in winter SAD: decreased appetite and insomnia. As you might imagine, the effects of winter and summer SAD become exacerbated the further north you live. People who live north of the Arctic Circle can face months of endless night and months of endless day. Winter SAD can be treated, either with medication or with daily exposure to white light (Tam, Lam, & Levitt 1995; Neumeister, 2004). Using light bulbs that emit the full spectrum of sunlight may be especially helpful.

What are the effects of jet travel across a number of time zones and working night shifts on individuals' biological clocks?

Desynchronizing the Biological Clock   Biological clocks can become desynchronized, or thrown off their regular schedules. Some sleep disturbances can be traced to the desynchronization of internal circadian clocks with external environmental cycles. These disturbances include *delayed sleep phase syndrome*, in which the internal clocks run abnormally slow, and *advanced sleep phase syndrome*, in which the internal clocks run abnormally fast (Zisapel, 2001). Among the circumstances of modern life that can introduce irregularities in our sleep are jet travel and changing work shifts (Albrecht, 2002). What effects might such irregularities have on circadian rhythms?

If you fly from Vancouver to Halifax and then go to bed at 11 p.m. Atlantic Time, you may have trouble falling asleep because your body is still on Pacific Time. Even if you sleep for eight hours that night, you may find it hard to wake up at 7 a.m. Atlantic Time, because your body thinks it is 3 a.m. and you may experience excessive sleepiness the next day. However, if you stay in Halifax for several days, your body will adjust to the new schedule.

The jet lag you experienced when you flew from Vancouver to Halifax occurred because your body time was out of phase, or synchronization, with clock time (Herxheimer & Waterhouse, 2003). When this occurs, two or more body rhythms are usually out of sync. You normally go to bed when your body temperature begins to drop, but in your new location you might be trying to go to sleep when it is rising. In the morning, your adrenal glands release large doses of the hormone cortisol to help you wake up. In your new geographical time zone, the glands may be releasing this chemical just as you are getting ready for bed at night.

Circadian rhythms may also become desynchronized when shift workers change their work hours (Ahasan & others, 2001; Lac & Chamoux, 2004). Shift rotation may have been one of the causes of the nuclear accident at Three Mile Island, Pennsylvania, in 1979 (Moore-Ede, Sulzman, & Fuller, 1982). The team of workers monitoring the nuclear plant when the accident took place had been placed on the night shift just after a six-week period of constant shift rotation.

Shift-work problems most often affect night-shift workers, who never fully adjust to sleeping in the daytime after their work shifts, may fall asleep at work, and are at increased risk for heart disease and gastrointestinal disorders (Quinlin, Mayhew, &

Bohle, 2001; Takeyama & others, 2005). Not all shift workers are affected equally, though (Monk, 1993). A small proportion actually prefer shift work. Individuals older than 50, those who require more than nine hours of sleep a night, and those with a tendency to be "morning types" (get up early, go to bed early) are the most adversely affected by shift work.

Resetting the Biological Clock If your biological clock for sleeping and waking becomes desynchronized, how can you reset it? Concordia University psychologists Andreas Arvanitogiannis and Shimon Amir have found that the circadian clock can be reset, mainly by the use of ultra-short light flashes (Arvanitogiannis & Amir, 1999, 2001).

With regard to jet lag, if you take a transoceanic flight and arrive at your destination during the day, it is a good idea to spend as much time outside in the daylight as possible. Bright light during the day, especially in the morning, increases wakefulness, whereas bright light at night delays sleep (Oren & Terman, 1998).

Melatonin, a hormone that is produced in greater quantities at night in humans, is also being studied for its possible effects in reducing jet lag (Sharkey & Eastman, 2002). A number of recent studies have shown that a small dosage of melatonin can reduce jet lag by advancing the circadian clock, which makes it useful for eastward jet lag but not westward jet lag (Suhner & others, 2001). However, the potential side effects of melatonin are still largely unknown, and negative long-term effects have not yet been adequately studied (U. S. National Institute of Neurological Disorders and Stroke, 2004).

Strategies for shift workers who need to reset their biological clocks include splitting sleep between after-work morning naps and before-work late-afternoon naps to increase the number of hours of sleep, brighter light in the workplace, and sleeping in complete darkness. Sedatives do not affect circadian realignment, and their long-term use is inadvisable for shift workers.

Why Do We Need Sleep?

Everyone sleeps, and when we do not get enough sleep, we often do not function well, physically and mentally. The important benefits of sleep include restoration, adaptation, growth, and memory.

Because all animals require sleep, it seems that sleep is a fundamental mechanism for survival. Examining the evolutionary basis for sleep, scientists have proposed that sleep restores, replenishes, and rebuilds our brains and bodies, which can become worn out or used up by the day's waking activities. This idea fits with the feeling of being "worn out" or tired before we go to sleep and "restored" when we wake up.

In support of the restorative function of sleep, many bodily cells show increased protein metabolism during deep sleep (U.S. National Institute of Neurological Disorders and Stroke, 2004). Protein molecules are the building blocks needed for cell growth and for repair of damages from factors such as stress. Also, some neuroscientists believe that sleep gives neurons that are used while we are awake a chance to shut down and repair themselves (U.S. National Institute of Neurological Disorders and Stroke, 2004). Without sleep, neurons might become so depleted in energy or so polluted by the by-products of cellular activity that they begin to malfunction.

In addition to having a restorative function, sleep may also have an adaptive evolutionary function. Sleep may have developed because animals needed to protect themselves. For example, for some animals the search for food and water is easier and safer when the sun is up. When it is dark, it is adaptive for these animals to save energy, avoid getting eaten, and avoid falling off a cliff that they cannot see. In general, animals that serve as food for other animals sleep the least. Figure 6.3 portrays the average amount of sleep per day for different animals.

Sleep may also be beneficial to physical growth and increased brain development in infants and children. For example, deep sleep is associated with the release of growth hormone in children (U.S. National Institute of Neurological Disorders and Stroke, 2004).

**Hours of sleep per
24-hour period**

Bat	19.9
Armadillo	18.5
Cat	14.5
Fox	9.8
Rhesus monkey	9.6
Rabbit	8.4
Human	8.0
Cow	3.9
Sheep	3.8
Horse	2.9

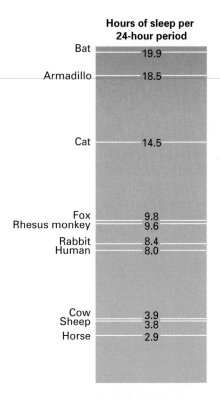

FIGURE 6.3

**From Bats to Horses: The Wide
Range of Sleep in Animals**

Sleep is now also thought to play an important role in the storage and maintenance of long-term memory. One possible explanation is that during sleep the cerebral cortex is not busy with processing sensory input, active awareness, and motor functions. Therefore, it is free to conduct activities that strengthen memory associations so that memories formed during recent waking hours can be integrated into long-term memory storage. In one recent study, the stage of sleep called **REM sleep** (rapid-eye-movement sleep) was linked with the formation of emotional memories in humans (Wagner, Gais, & Born, 2001). Another series of studies demonstrated a link between nonREM sleep (also called slow-wave sleep) and the formation of declarative memories (see chapter 8; Gais & Born, 2004). One possibility is that both nonREM and REM sleep play different roles in long-term memory; nonREM sleep may reactivate information learned earlier in the day and REM sleep may then consolidate that information into long-term memory (Smith, Aubrey, & Peters, 2004; Cartwright, 2004).

Are you thinking about pulling an all-nighter for the next test in one of your classes? You might want to think again. In one study, a good night's sleep helped the brain to store the memory of what had been learned during the day (Stickgold & Hobson, 2000). In the study, the memory of individuals who stayed up all night on one of the nights during the study was inferior to the memory of individuals who got a good night's sleep every night during the study. The conclusion: Lost sleep often results in lost memories.

The Effects of Chronic Sleep Deprivation Testing the limits of his capacity to function without sleep, one 17-year-old high school student, Randy Gardner, went without sleep for over 264 hours (about 11 days). Still the longest observed period of total sleep deprivation on record, he did it as part of a science fair project (Dement, 1978). Randy, who was carefully monitored by sleep researchers, did suffer some hallucinations, as well as speech and movement problems. However, on the last night, Gardner played arcade games with sleep researcher William Dement and consistently beat him. Randy recovered fully, as well as could be detected, after a 14-hour, 40-minute restorative sleep. Randy's story is exceptional in that he was able to maintain a high level of physical activity and in that he received national TV coverage, which helped him to stay awake. Even so, he almost fell asleep several times, but his observers would not let him close his eyes. In more normal circumstances, individuals have far more difficulty staying awake all night, especially between 3 a.m. and 6 a.m.

Sleep researchers record Randy Gardner's (he's the person doing push-ups) behaviour during his 264-hour period of sleep deprivation. Most people who try to stay up even one night have difficulty remaining awake from 3 A.M. to 6 A.M. *Why shouldn't you follow Gardner's sleep deprivation example?*

REM sleep (Rapid-eye-movement sleep)
Stage 5 of sleep, in which most dreaming occurs.

Roger Broughton is a Senior Scientist with the Ottawa Health Research Institute at the University of Ottawa. His research focuses on excessive daytime sleepiness and narcolepsy. He is interested in the circadian regulation of sleep and the value of the afternoon nap zone. Broughton points out that "Excessive daytime sleepiness is a major clinical symptom which has significant socioeconomic impact and is a leading cause of vehicular, occupational, and home accidents."

What are some developmental changes in sleep patterns during adolescence? How might this influence alertness at school?

Although Randy Gardner was able to go about 11 days without sleep, the following discussion should convince you that even getting 60 to 90 minutes less sleep than you need at night can harm your ability to perform optimally the next day. As you will also see, it does not take very long for sleep deprivation to play havoc with our lives.

In a recent analysis of sleep patterns (C. Williams, 2001) 47 percent of Canadians over 15 said they cut down on their sleep in order to extend their days and 15 percent say they got fewer than 6.5 hours of sleep a night. About 25 percent reported regularly having trouble falling asleep, a figure that rose to 40 percent for those who are severely time stressed. While mid-afternoon snoozes are not popular, many Canadians report trying to catch up on their sleep on the weekend.

According to the University of Ottawa's Roger Broughton, excessive daytime sleepiness is a major clinical problem. With adequate sleep you give yourself the opportunity to perform at peak level the next day (Dement, 1999). A sleep debt can build quickly, not unlike finance charges on an unpaid credit card balance, when you are burning the candle at both ends (Coren, 1996). Consider a medical technician who tried to get by on 4 hours of sleep a night—ironically, while working at a sleep-disorders centre—so she could take care of her infant daughter during the day. Before long, she developed heart palpitations, dizziness, a fear of driving, and wide mood swings from being awake 20 hours a day. She was even at risk for becoming violent (Broughton & Shimsu, 1995).

An increasing number of research studies underscore that optimal performance is enhanced by sleeping more than eight hours a night and reduced by sleeping less. At one sleep-disorders research centre, the alertness of eight-hour sleepers who claimed to be well rested increased when they added two more hours to their nightly sleep total (Roehrs & Roth, 1998). In one study, brain scans revealed that sleep deprivation decreased brain activity in the thalamus and the prefrontal cortex (Thomas & others, 2001). Alertness and cognitive performance declined, along with brain activity. In another study, sleep deprivation was linked with an inability to sustain attention (Doran, Van Dongen, & Dinges, 2001). In yet another study, EEGs of individuals who experienced total sleep deprivation for 24 hours revealed a decline in the complexity of brain activity (Jeong & others, 2001).

Sleep deprivation can also affect decision-making. Sleepiness is a factor in about 20 percent of traffic accidents (Philip, 2005). One review of studies on this topic concluded that the following aspects of decision-making are affected especially adversely by sleep deprivation: dealing with the unexpected, innovation, revising plans, and effective communication (Harrison & Horne, 2000).

Why are we getting too little sleep? Work pressures, school pressures, family obligations, and social obligations often lead to long hours of wakefulness and irregular sleep/wake schedules. Not having enough hours to do all we want to do in a day, we cheat on our sleep. Most people need to get 60 to 90 minutes more sleep each night than they get now.

Sleep Deprivation in Adolescents and Older Adults There has recently been a surge of interest in adolescent sleep patterns. This interest focuses on the belief that many adolescents are not getting enough sleep, that there are physiological underpinnings to adolescents' desires to stay up later at night and sleep longer in the morning, and that these findings can help understand when adolescents learn most effectively in school (Eliasson & others, 2002; Gau & Soong, 2003).

Mary Carskadon and her colleagues (Carskadon, Acebo, & Seifer, 2001; Carskadon & others, 1998, 1999) have conducted a number of research studies on adolescent sleep patterns. They have found that adolescents sleep an average of 9 hours and 25 minutes when given the opportunity to sleep as long as they like. Most adolescents get considerably less sleep than this, especially during the week. The result is a sleep debt, which adolescents often try to make up for on the weekend. The researchers found that older adolescents (16–18 years old) are often sleepier during the day than younger adolescents (13–15 years old) are. Carskadon believes this developmental change is not due to factors such as academic work and social pressures. Rather, her research suggests that adolescents' biological clocks undergo a hormonal shift as they get older that pushes the time of wakefulness to an hour later than when they were younger adolescents. In her research, Carskadon found that this shift was caused by a delay in the nightly release of melatonin. Melatonin is secreted at about 9:30 p.m. in younger adolescents, but it is produced approximately one hour later in older adolescents, delaying the onset of sleep.

Carskadon determined that early school starting times can result in grogginess and lack of attention in class and poor performance on tests. Based on this research, in 1997, schools in Edina, Minnesota, made the decision to start classes at 8:40 a.m. instead of the former starting time of 7:15 a.m. Under this later starting time, there have been fewer referrals for discipline problems and fewer illnesses. Test scores have also improved among high school students, but not middle school students, an outcome that supports Carskadon's conclusion that earlier school starting times are more detrimental to older adolescents than to younger adolescents.

Sleep patterns also change as people age through the middle-adult (40s and 50s) and late-adult (60s and older) years. Many adults go to bed earlier at night and wake up earlier in the morning. Thus, a clear reversal occurs in the time at which individuals go to bed—later to bed as adolescents, earlier to bed in middle age. Beginning in their 40s, individuals report that they are less likely to sleep through the entire night than when they were younger (Ohayon, 2004). Middle-aged adults also spend less time in the deepest sleep stage than when they were younger. And almost one-half of individuals in late adulthood report that they experience some degree of insomnia.

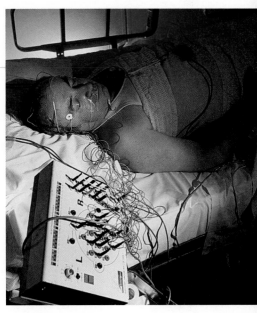

An individual being monitored by an EEG in a sleep experiment.

Sleep Stages

Have you ever been awakened from your sleep and been totally disoriented? Have you ever awakened in the middle of a dream and gone right back into the dream as if it were a movie that is running just under the surface of your consciousness? These two circumstances reflect two distinct stages in the sleep cycle (Broughton & Ogilvie, 1992).

According to Brock University psychologist Robert Ogilvie, stages of sleep correspond to massive electrophysiological changes that occur throughout the brain as the fast, irregular, and low amplitude electrical activity of wakefulness is replaced by the slow, regular, high amplitude waves of deep sleep (Ogilvie, 1993; Ogilvie & Harsh, 1994). Using the electroencephalograph (EEG) to monitor the brain's electrical activity during waking and sleep states, scientists have discovered five distinct stages of sleep and two stages of wakefulness.

When people are awake, their EEG patterns exhibit two types of waves: beta and alpha. *Beta waves* reflect wakefulness and controlled processing. These waves are the highest in frequency and lowest in amplitude. They are also more *desynchronous* than other waves. Desynchronous waves do not form a very consistent pattern. Inconsistent patterning makes sense given the extensive variation in sensory input and activities we experience when we are awake. When we are relaxed but still awake, our brain waves slow down, increase in amplitude, and become more *synchronous*, or regular. These waves are called *alpha* waves.

The five stages of sleep are differentiated by the types of wave patterns that can be detected with an EEG. The depth of sleep varies from one stage to another.

Stages 1–4 *Stage 1 sleep* is characterized by *theta waves*, which are even slower in frequency and greater in amplitude than alpha waves. The difference between just being relaxed and stage 1 sleep is gradual. Figure 6.4 shows the EEG pattern of stage 1 sleep, along with the EEG patterns for the other four sleep stages and beta and alpha waves.

In *stage 2 sleep*, theta waves continue but are interspersed with a defining characteristic of stage 2 sleep: *sleep spindles*. These involve a sudden increase in wave frequency (Gottselig, Bassetti, & Achermann, 2002). Stages 1 and 2 are both relatively light stages of sleep, and if people awaken during one of these stages, they often report not having been asleep at all.

"MY PROBLEM HAS ALWAYS BEEN AN OVERABUNDANCE OF ALPHA WAVES"

© 1990 by Sidney Harris.

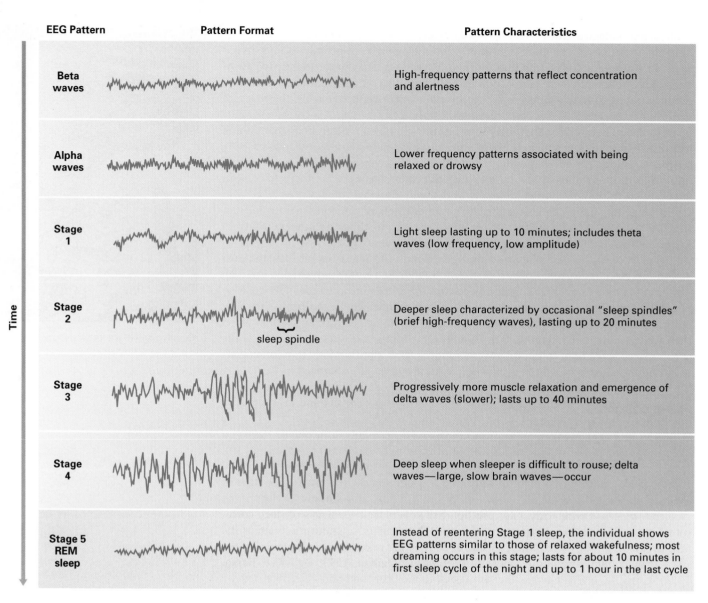

EEG Pattern	Pattern Format	Pattern Characteristics
Beta waves		High-frequency patterns that reflect concentration and alertness
Alpha waves		Lower frequency patterns associated with being relaxed or drowsy
Stage 1		Light sleep lasting up to 10 minutes; includes theta waves (low frequency, low amplitude)
Stage 2	sleep spindle	Deeper sleep characterized by occasional "sleep spindles" (brief high-frequency waves), lasting up to 20 minutes
Stage 3		Progressively more muscle relaxation and emergence of delta waves (slower); lasts up to 40 minutes
Stage 4		Deep sleep when sleeper is difficult to rouse; delta waves—large, slow brain waves—occur
Stage 5 REM sleep		Instead of reentering Stage 1 sleep, the individual shows EEG patterns similar to those of relaxed wakefulness; most dreaming occurs in this stage; lasts for about 10 minutes in first sleep cycle of the night and up to 1 hour in the last cycle

FIGURE 6.4 Characteristics and Formats of EEG Recordings During Stages of Sleep

Stage 3 and *stage 4* sleep are characterized by *delta waves*, the slowest and highest amplitude brain waves during sleep. These two stages are often referred to as delta sleep. Distinguishing between stage 3 and stage 4 is difficult, although typically stage 3 is characterized by delta waves occurring less than 50 percent of the time and stage 4 by delta waves occurring more than 50 percent of the time. Delta sleep is our deepest sleep, the time when our brain waves are least like waking brain waves. It is during delta sleep that it is the most difficult to wake sleepers. When they are awakened during this stage, they usually are confused and disoriented.

REM Sleep After going through stages 1 through 4, sleepers drift up through the sleep stages toward wakefulness. But, instead of reentering stage 1, they enter stage 5, a different form of sleep called *REM (rapid-eye-movement)* sleep. REM sleep is an active stage of sleep during which dreaming occurs. During REM sleep, the EEG pattern shows fast waves similar to those of relaxed wakefulness, and the sleeper's eyeballs move up and down and from left to right (see figure 6.5). REM sleep is sometimes also referred to as *paradoxical sleep* because of the curious combination of brain activity and sleep immobility. Stages 1–4 are referred to as *non-REM sleep*. Non-REM sleep is characterized by a lack of rapid eye movement and little dreaming.

A person who is awakened during REM sleep is more likely to report having dreamed than when awakened at any other stage. Even people who claim they rarely dream frequently report dreaming when they are awakened during REM sleep. The longer the period of REM sleep, the more likely it is that the person will report dreaming. Dreams also occur during slow-wave or non-REM sleep. These dreams are uncommon (Takeuchi & others, 2001) and produce a different EEG pattern than dreams in REM sleep (Takeuchi & others, 2003). Reports of dreaming by individuals awakened from REM sleep are typically longer, more vivid, more motorically animated, more emotionally charged, and less related to waking life than reports by those awakened from non-REM sleep (Hobson, Pace-Schott, & Stickgold, 2000).

The amount of time we spend in REM sleep changes over the life span. As shown in figure 6.6, the percentage of total sleep during a 24-hour period that consists of REM sleep is especially large during early infancy (almost 8 hours). Older adults engage in less than 1 hour of REM sleep per 24-hour period. Figure 6.6 also reveals how the total amount of sleep changes from approximately 16 hours per 24-hour period for young infants to fewer than 6 hours for older adults.

These dramatic developmental changes in sleep, especially REM sleep, raise questions about the function of sleep. For young infants, REM sleep may play a role in stimulating the brain and contributing to its growth. Because such a large percentage of an infant's life is spent in sleep, REM sleep may be nature's way of stimulating the brain.

As was mentioned above, REM sleep likely also contributes to memory (Wagner, Gais & Born, 2001). For example, Carlyle Smith of Trent University and his colleagues have studied what they call the paradoxical sleep window, during which REM sleep is required for learning (Legault, Smith, & Beninger, 2004).

Sleep Cycling Through the Night   The five stages of sleep described here make up a normal cycle of sleep. As shown in figure 6.7, one of these cycles lasts about 90 to 100 minutes and recurs several times during the night. The amount of deep sleep (stages 3 and 4) is much greater in the first half of a night's sleep than in the second

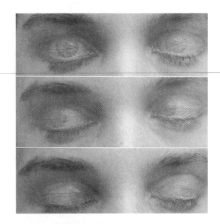

FIGURE 6.5

REM Sleep
During REM sleep, our eyes move rapidly. Although rapid eye movements are not like the eye movements we make when scanning an image, they do suggest that we are observing the images we see moving in our dreams.

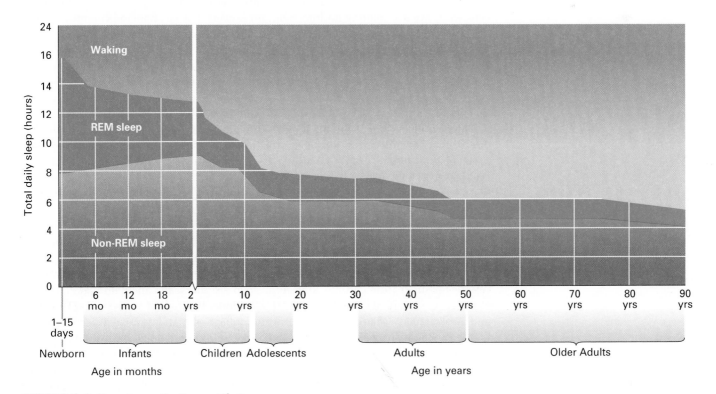

FIGURE 6.6 **Sleep Across the Human Life Span**

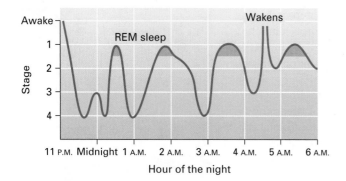

FIGURE 6.7

Cycling Through a Night's Sleep
During a night's sleep, we go through several cycles. Depth of sleep decreases and REM sleep (shown in darker yellow) increases as the night progresses. In this graph, the person is depicted as awakening at about 5 a.m. and then going back to sleep for another hour.

half. Most REM sleep takes place toward the end of a night's sleep, when the REM stage becomes progressively longer. The night's first REM stage might last for only 10 minutes, and the final REM stage might continue for as long as an hour. During a normal night of sleep, individuals will spend about 60 percent of sleep in light sleep (stages 1 and 2), 20 percent in delta or deep sleep, and 20 percent in REM sleep (Webb, 2000).

Sleep and the Brain The five sleep stages are associated with distinct patterns of neurotransmitter activity initiated in the reticular formation, the core of the brain stem. In all vertebrates, the reticular formation plays a crucial role in sleep and arousal (see figure 6.2). Damage to the reticular formation can result in coma and death.

Three important neurotransmitters involved in sleep are serotonin, epinephrine, and acetylcholine. As sleep begins, the levels of neurotransmitters sent to the forebrain from the reticular formation start dropping, and they continue to fall until they reach their lowest levels during the deepest sleep stage—stage 4. REM sleep (stage 5) is initiated by a rise in acetylcholine, which activates the cerebral cortex while the rest of the brain remains relatively inactive. REM sleep is terminated by a rise in serotonin and norepinephrine, which increase the level of forebrain activity nearly to the awakened state. You are most likely to wake up just after a REM period. If you don't wake up then, the level of the neurotransmitters begins to fall again, and you enter another sleep cycle.

Sleep and Disease

Sleep plays a role in a large number of diseases and disorders (U.S. National Institute of Neurological Disorders and Stroke, 2004). For example, stroke and asthma attacks are more common during the night and in the early morning, probably because of changes in hormones, heart rate, and other characteristics associated with sleep.

Neurons that control sleep interact closely with the immune system (Pollmacher & others, 2000). As anyone who has had the flu knows, infectious diseases make us sleepy. The probable reason is that chemicals called cytokines, produced by the body's cells while we are fighting an infection, are powerful sleep-inducing chemicals. Sleep may help the body conserve energy and other resources that the body needs to overcome infection.

Sleep problems afflict most people who have mental disorders, including those with depression (Blais & others, 2001). Individuals with depression often awaken in the early hours of the morning and cannot get back to sleep, and they often spend less time in delta wave or deep sleep than nondepressed individuals (Armitage & others, 2001).

Sleep problems are common in many other disorders as well, including Alzheimer's disease, stroke, and cancer. In some cases, however, such as Parkinson's disease, these problems may be due not to the disease itself but to the drugs used to treat the disease (Lauterbach, 2004).

Sleep Disorders

According to Pegram and his colleagues (2004), 40 percent of adults will experience a sleep disorder during their lifetime. According to Sleep/Wake Disorders Canada, more than two million Canadians suffer from sleep disorders. Each year, at least 40 million Americans suffer from chronic, long-term sleep disorders, and an additional 20 million experience occasional sleep problems (U.S. National Institute of Neurological Disorders and Stroke, 2004). Many people suffer from undiagnosed and untreated sleep disorders that leave them struggling through the day feeling unmotivated and exhausted (U.S. National Commission on Sleep Disorders Research, 1993). Some of the major sleep problems are insomnia, sleepwalking and sleep talking, nightmares and night terrors, narcolepsy, and sleep apnea. To determine whether you are having sleep problems, see the Personal Reflections box.

Do You Get Enough Sleep?

Many college and university students do not get enough sleep. In a survey of more than 200,000 first-year students, more than 80 percent said they stayed up all night at least once during the year (Sax & others, 1995). Howell, Jahrig & Powell, (2004) reported that among college students carrying a full course load, poor reported sleep quality predicted poorer academic performance. Kelly (2004) even found that college students who report having less sleep also report having lower life satisfaction. To evaluate whether you are sleep deprived, answer the following questions with yes or no.

Yes	No	
_____	_____	I need an alarm clock to wake up at the appropriate time.
_____	_____	It's a struggle for me to get out of bed in the morning.
_____	_____	I feel tired, irritable, and stressed out during the week.
_____	_____	I have trouble concentrating.
_____	_____	I have trouble remembering.
_____	_____	I feel slow with critical thinking, problem solving, and being creative.
_____	_____	I often fall asleep watching TV.
_____	_____	I often fall asleep in boring meetings or lectures in warm rooms.
_____	_____	I often fall asleep after heavy meals or after low doses of alcohol.
_____	_____	I often fall asleep within five minutes of getting into bed.
_____	_____	I often feel drowsy while driving.
_____	_____	I often sleep extra hours on weekend mornings.
_____	_____	I often need a nap to get through the day.
		I have dark circles around my eyes.

According to sleep expert James Maas (1998), who developed this quiz, if you responded "yes" to three or more of these items, you are probably not getting enough sleep.

If you are not getting enough sleep, the following behavioural strategies might help you:

1. Reduce stress as much as possible.
2. Exercise regularly, but not just before you go to bed.
3. Keep mentally stimulated during the day.
4. Become a good time manager.
5. Eat a proper diet.
6. Stop smoking.
7. Reduce caffeine intake.
8. Avoid alcohol, especially near bedtime.
9. Take a warm bath before bed.
10. Maintain a relaxing atmosphere in the bedroom.
11. Clear your mind at bedtime.
12. Before going to bed, engage in a relaxation technique such as listening to a tape designed for relaxation.
13. Learn to value sleep.
14. If necessary, contact the health service at your college or university for advice about your sleeping problem.

Insomnia A common sleep problem is *insomnia*, the inability to sleep (Sateia & Nowell, 2004). Insomnia can involve a problem in falling asleep, waking up during the night, or waking up too early (Harvey, 2001; Mahendran, 2001). According to Sleep/Wake Disorders Canada, insomnia may affect one-third of the general Canadian population. It is more common among women and older adults, as well as people who are thin, stressed, or depressed (Devries, 1998).

For short-term insomnia, most physicians prescribe sleeping pills. In 1997, about one million Canadians over the age of 11 used sleeping pills (Health Canada, 1999). However, most sleeping pills stop working after several weeks of nightly use, and their long-term use can actually interfere with good sleep. Simply practising good sleep habits can often reduce mild insomnia. In more serious cases of insomnia, researchers are experimenting with light therapy, melatonin supplements, and other ways to alter circadian cycles (S. I. Cohen, 2002; Kennaway & Wright, 2002). Also, in one recent study, behavioural changes helped insomniacs increase their sleep time, as well as to awaken less frequently in the middle of the night (Edinger & others, 2001). In this study, insomniacs were restricted from taking a nap during the day, even if they were exhausted, and they were required to set an alarm and to force themselves to get out of bed in the morning. Thus the longer the insomniacs stayed awake during the day, the better they were able to sleep at night.

Sleepwalking and Sleep Talking *Somnambulism* is the formal term for sleepwalking, which occurs during the deepest stages of sleep. For many years, experts believed that somnambulists were just acting out their dreams. But somnambulism occurs during stages 3 and 4, usually early in the night, at the time when a person is unlikely to be dreaming (Stein & Ferber, 2001). Except for the danger of accidents due to wandering around in the dark, and very rare cases of sleepwalkers being acquitted of murder charges (e.g., Broughton and others, 1994), there is nothing really abnormal about sleepwalking. Despite superstition, it is safe to awaken sleepwalkers; in fact, they probably should be awakened, as they may harm themselves wandering around in the dark (Swanson, 1999).

Another quirky night behaviour is sleep talking (Hublin & others, 2001). If you interrogate sleep talkers, can you find out what they did, for instance, last Thursday night? Probably not. Although sleep talkers will talk with you and make fairly coherent statements, they are soundly asleep. So even if a sleep talker mumbles a response to your question, don't count on its accuracy.

Nightmares and Night Terrors A *nightmare* is a frightening dream that awakens a dreamer from REM sleep. The nightmare's content invariably involves danger—the dreamer is chased, robbed, raped, murdered, or thrown off a cliff. Nightmares are common. Most of us have had them, especially when we were young children (Mindell & Owens, 2003). Nightmares peak at three to six years of age and then decline, although the average college or university student experiences four to eight nightmares a year (Hartmann, 1993) and 10 percent of 70-year-olds report nightmares (Asplund, 2003). Reported increases in nightmares or worsening nightmares are often associated with an increase in stress in people's lives, such as the loss of a relative, conflict, or some type of negative event (Belicki, Chambers, & Ogilvie, 1997).

A *night terror* is characterized by sudden arousal from sleep and intense fear. Night terrors are accompanied by a number of physiological reactions, such as rapid heart rate and breathing, loud screams, heavy perspiration, and movement (Thiedke, 2001). Night terrors are less common than nightmares. Unlike nightmares, night terrors occur during slow-wave, non-REM sleep. Night terrors are more common in childhood (Kataria, 2004).

Narcolepsy The overpowering urge to sleep is called *narcolepsy*. The urge is so strong that the person may fall asleep while talking or standing up. Narcoleptics immediately enter REM sleep rather than moving through the sleep stages (Mignot, 2001; Mignot & Thorsby, 2001). Researchers suspect that narcolepsy is inherited (Chabas & others, 2003). Narcoleptics experience severe embarrassment, academic decline, and feelings of loss of self-worth (Broughton & Broughton, 1994). Treatment usually involves counselling to discover the potential causes of the excessive sleepiness.

Sleep Apnea *Sleep apnea* is a sleep disorder in which individuals stop breathing because the windpipe fails to open or because brain processes involved in respiration fail to work properly. People with sleep apnea experience numerous brief awakenings during the night so that they can breathe better, although usually they are not aware of being awake. During the day these people may feel sleepy because they were deprived of sleep at night.

Sleep apnea affects 2 percent of children, 4 percent of middle-aged adults and 10 percent of older adults (G. Miller, 2004). Sleep apnea also occurs more frequently among obese individuals (Davidson & Callery, 2001). Untreated, sleep apnea can cause high blood pressure, strokes, and impotence. In addition, the daytime sleepiness it causes can result in accidents, lost productivity, and relationship problems (Billmann & Ware, 2002).

Dreams

Ever since the dawn of language, dreams have been imbued with historical, personal, and religious significance. As early as 5000 B.C., Babylonians recorded and interpreted their dreams on clay tablets. Egyptians built temples in honour of Serapis, the god of dreams. People occasionally slept in these temples in the hope that Serapis would appear in their dreams and either heal them or tell them what to do to be healed. Dreams are described at length in more than 70 passages in the Bible.

Many people in modern societies, such as in Canada, view dreams as separate from reality and usually as having little importance to their waking lives. However, in some societies dreams are often thought of as an extension of reality. For example, in one account, an African chief dreamed that he had visited England. On awakening, he ordered a wardrobe of European clothes. As he walked through the village in his new wardrobe, he was congratulated for having made the trip. Similarly, Cherokees who dreamed of being bitten by snakes were treated for the snakebite. The Inuit who live in the Arctic region of North America believe that dreams provide a vehicle for entering the spiritual world.

In terms of dream content, small traditional societies show a higher percentage of animal characters in their dreams, and variations exist from culture to culture in the percentage of aggressive actions in dreams (Domhoff, 1999). For example, in one study, Palestinian children living under the threat of violence reported more themes of persecution and aggression in their dreams than Finnish or Palestinian children living in more peaceful surroundings (Punamaki & Joustie, 1998). In the Colombian village of Arimatima, many dreams are thought to symbolize the deaths of relatives.

Not only are there cultural variations in dreaming, but there are also differences in the dreams of men and women (Kolchakian & Hill, 2002). Men are more likely to dream about sexual experiences and physical aggression while women dream more often about someone alive being dead, being a member of the opposite sex, and failing an exam (Schredl & others, 2004).

Why do we dream? Many theorists and researchers have attempted to explain dreaming. But because dreams are written in the mind with little or no conscious participation, it is indeed difficult to unravel their mysteries (A. T. Beck, 2004). The most prominent theories of dreams are derived from Freud's theory, cognitive theory, and activation-synthesis theory.

Dreams as Wish Fulfillment Sigmund Freud (1900/1953) thought that the reason we dream is **wish fulfillment**, an unconscious attempt to fulfill needs (especially for sex and aggression) that cannot be expressed or that go ungratified during waking hours. In this view, for example, people who are sexually inhibited while awake would likely have dreams with erotic content. Those who have strong aggressive tendencies but suppress anger while awake would be inclined to have dreams filled with violence and hostility.

Freud also stressed that dreams often contain memories of infant and child experiences, especially events associated with parents. Additionally, he believed that our dreams frequently contain information from a day or two preceding the dream. In his view, many of our dreams reflect combinations of distant early experiences with our parents and more recent daily events. Freud said that the task of dream interpretation is a difficult one because we successfully disguise wish fulfillment when we dream. Note that the term *wish fulfillment* does not mean that dreams reflect only hopes; some reflect fears.

Freud distinguished between a dream's manifest content and its latent content. **Manifest content** is the dream's surface content, which contains dream symbols that distort and disguise the dream's true meaning. **Latent content** is the dream's hidden content, its unconscious meaning. For example, if a person had a dream that included snakes and neckties, the snakes and neckties would be the dream's manifest content. Another person might dream about a king or a president. Freud believed that such dreams symbolize underlying latent content. In these examples, the snakes and neckties symbolize a male's genitals and the king or president symbolizes a father or the therapist. Freud thought that once the therapist understood a client's symbolism, the nature of the dream could be interpreted (Auld, Hyman, & Rudzinski, 2005). As shown in figure 6.8, artists have sometimes incorporated the symbolic world of dreaming in their paintings.

A final point about Freud's dream theory involves its scientific merit. Although symbolic interpretation can be fascinating, researchers have found it very difficult to devise appropriate methods to even attempt to verify his dream theory. His theory has largely given way to newer theories of dreams.

Subconscious Cognitive Processing The **cognitive theory of dreaming** proposes that dreaming can be understood by relying on the same cognitive concepts that are used

wish fulfillment Freud's concept of dreaming as an unconscious attempt to fulfill needs (especially for sex and aggression) that cannot be expressed, or that go ungratified, while awake.

manifest content In Freud's view, the dream's surface content, which contains symbols that distort and disguise the dream's true meaning.

latent content In Freud's view, the dream's hidden content; its unconscious meaning.

cognitive theory of dreaming Proposes that dreaming can be understood by relying on the same cognitive processes that are used in studying the waking mind.

FIGURE 6.8

Artists' Portrayals of Dreams
Through the centuries, artists have been adept at capturing the enchanting or nightmarish characteristics of our dreams. (*Left*) Dutch painter Hieronymus Bosch (1450–1516) captured both the enchanting and frightening world of dreams in *Garden of Earthly Delights*. (*Right*) Marc Chagall painted a world of dreams in *I and the Village*.

in studying the waking mind. That is, dreaming involves processing information, memory, and problem solving. In the cognitive theory of dreaming there is little or no search for the hidden, symbolic content of dreams that Freud sought (Foulkes, 1993, 1999).

Rather than being an arena for playing out our unsatisfied needs, dreams might be a mental realm in which we can solve problems and think creatively (White & Taytroe, 2003). For example, Robert Louis Stevenson claimed that he got the idea for his book, *Dr. Jekyll and Mr. Hyde*, in a dream. Elias Howe, attempting to invent a machine that sewed, reportedly dreamed that he was captured by savages carrying spears with holes in their tips. On waking, he realized that he should place the hole for the thread at the end of the needle, not in the middle. Dreams may spark such gifts of inspiration because, in unique and creative ways, they weave together current experiences with the past.

Criticisms of the cognitive theory of dreaming focus on skepticism about the ability to resolve problems during sleep and the lack of attention to the roles of brain structures and activity in dreaming, the main emphasis of the activation-synthesis theory of dreams.

Finding Logic in Random Brain Activity In a classic paper, Hobson & McCarley (1977) proposed **activation-synthesis theory**, which states that dreaming occurs when the cerebral cortex synthesizes neural signals generated from activity in the lower part of the brain. In this view, dreams reflect the brain's efforts to make sense out of neural activity that takes place during sleep.

When we are awake and alert, the contents of our conscious experience tend to be driven by external stimuli that result in specific motor behaviour. During sleep, according to activation-synthesis theory, conscious experience is driven by internally generated stimuli that have no apparent behavioural consequence. A key source of this internal stimulation is spontaneous neural activity in the reticular formation of the limbic system (Hobson, 2000).

Recently, proponents of activation-synthesis theory have suggested that neural networks in other areas of the forebrain play a key role in dreaming (Hobson & others, 2000). Specifically, they believe that the same regions of the forebrain that are involved in certain waking behaviours also function in particular aspects of dreaming. Thus, the primary motor and sensory areas of the forebrain would be activated in the sensorimotor aspects of the dream; the parietal lobe would be activated in the spatial organization of the dream; the visual aspects of the dream in the visual association cortex; the amygdala, hippocampus, and frontal lobe would be activated in the emotional aspects of a dream, and so on.

activation-synthesis theory States that dreaming occurs when the cerebral cortex synthesizes neural signals emanating from activity in the lower part of the brain.

The sudden, uncoordinated eye movements of REM sleep make the dream world move in odd ways. For instance, a dream might include magic carpets flying over an undulating landscape. Dreams tend to truncate, dissolve, or shift suddenly in midstream. Freud explained this phenomenon as the dreamer's attempt to elude the unpleasant and the taboo. Activation-synthesis theorists say that this shifting is due to normal cycles of neural activation (Hobson, 2000). As levels of neurotransmitters rise and fall during the stages of sleep, some neural networks are activated, and others shut down. As a new cycle is activated, a new dream landscape emerges. In sum, in the activation-synthesis view, dreams are merely a glitzy sideshow, not the main event (Hooper & Teresi, 1993).

Like all dream theories, activation-synthesis theory has its critics. Among their criticisms are the belief that the brain stem is not the only starting point for neural activity in dreaming and that life experiences stimulate and shape dreaming more than activation-synthesis theory acknowledges (Domhoff, 2001; Solms, 1997).

> ## > reflect and review
>
> **2** **Explain the nature of sleep.**
>
> - Describe the relationship between biological rhythms and sleep.
> - Summarize the benefits of sleep and the effects of sleep deprivation.
> - Describe the five stages of sleep and changes in the level of activity in the brain during sleep.
> - Explain the links between sleep and disease.
> - Name and describe five types of sleep disorders.
> - Describe the nature of dreams, including theories of why people dream.
>
> *Do you know someone who might have a diagnosed or undiagnosed sleep disorder? What might he or she be able to do about it?*

3 HYPNOSIS

— **The Nature of Hypnosis**   —   **Explaining Hypnosis**   —   **Applications of Hypnosis**

Is hypnosis an altered state of consciousness?

A young cancer patient is about to undergo a painful bone marrow transplant. Her doctor directs the girl's attention, asking her to breathe and listen carefully. Soon the girl is absorbed in a pleasant fantasy in which she is snowboarding down a snow-capped mountain peak at Sunshine Village near Banff, Alberta, jumping moguls and carving turns around snow-covered pine trees. Minutes later the procedure is over. The girl is relaxed and feels good about her self-control. The doctor has successfully used hypnosis as a technique to help the patient control pain by reducing her perception of it.

Hypnosis is defined as a psychological state of possibly altered attention and awareness in which the individual is unusually receptive to suggestions. Basic hypnotic techniques have been used since the beginning of recorded history in association with religious ceremonies, magic, the supernatural, and many erroneous theories (Spanos & Chaves, 1991).

In the late nineteenth century, the Austrian physician Friedrich Anton Mesmer cured patients of various problems by passing magnets over their bodies. Mesmer said the problems were cured by "animal magnetism," an intangible force that passes from therapist to patient. In reality, the cures were due to some form of hypnotic suggestion. A committee was appointed by the French Academy of Science to investigate Mesmer's claims. The committee agreed that his treatment was effective. However, they disputed his theory about animal magnetism and prohibited him from practising in Paris. Mesmer's theory was called "mesmerism," and even today we use the term mesmerized to mean hypnotized or enthralled.

hypnosis A psychological state or possibly altered attention and awareness in which the individual is unusually responsive to suggestions.

The brain activity of a hypnotized individual is being monitored. *How is hypnosis different from sleep?*

Today, hypnosis is recognized as a legitimate process in psychology and medicine, although we still have much to learn about how it works. In addition, as is discussed shortly, there is still debate about whether or not hypnosis truly is an altered state of consciousness (Chaves, 2000; Kallio & Revonsuo, 2003).

The Nature of Hypnosis

In our discussion of sleep, we described the five different stages of sleep and the distinctive brain waves associated with each stage. A common misconception is that the hypnotic state is much like a sleep state. However, unlike sleepers, hypnotized individuals are aware of what is happening and remember the experience later unless they are instructed to forget what happened. Researchers have found that individuals in a hypnotic state showed a predominance of alpha and beta waves, characteristic of persons in a waking state, when monitored by an EEG (Williams & Gruzelier, 2001). Further, evidence from EEG studies documents that during hypnosis individuals show different patterns of brain activity than they do when they are not under hypnosis (Isotani & others, 2001; Jensen & others, 2001). Similarly, Alan Hobson, of Harvard University, has proposed that hypnosis can be distinguished from other states of consciousness, based on an examination of PET and fMRI data (Hobson, 2001; Kahn & Hobson, 2003).

The Four Steps in Hypnosis Successful hypnosis involves four steps:

1. Distractions are minimized; the person to be hypnotized is made comfortable.
2. The hypnotist tells the person to concentrate on something specific, such as an imagined scene or the ticking of a watch.
3. The hypnotist tells the person what to expect in the hypnotic state, such as relaxation or a pleasant floating sensation.
4. The hypnotist suggests certain events or feelings he or she knows will occur or observes occurring, such as "Your eyes are getting tired." When the suggested effects occur, the person interprets them as being caused by the hypnotist's suggestions and accepts them as an indication that something is happening. This increase in the person's expectations that the hypnotist will make things happen in the future makes the person even more suggestible.

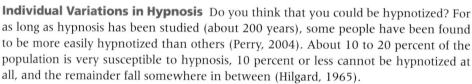

Individual Variations in Hypnosis Do you think that you could be hypnotized? For as long as hypnosis has been studied (about 200 years), some people have been found to be more easily hypnotized than others (Perry, 2004). About 10 to 20 percent of the population is very susceptible to hypnosis, 10 percent or less cannot be hypnotized at all, and the remainder fall somewhere in between (Hilgard, 1965).

There is no simple way to tell beforehand who can be hypnotized. But if you have the capacity to immerse yourself in imaginative activities—listening to a favourite piece of music or reading a novel, for example—you are a likely candidate. People susceptible to hypnosis become completely absorbed in what they are doing, removing the boundaries between themselves and what they are experiencing in their environment. Nonetheless, such absorption is best described as a weak rather than a strong predictor of a person's likelihood of being hypnotized (Nash, 2001; Nash & Nadon, 1997).

Hypnosis and Will If you are in a hypnotic state, can the hypnotist make you do something against your will? Individuals being hypnotized abdicate their responsibility to the hypnotist and follow the hypnotist's suggestions. However, they are unlikely to do anything in a hypnotic state that violates their morals or that is dangerous.

Explaining Hypnosis

Ever since Anton Mesmer proposed his theory of animal magnetism, psychologists have been trying to figure out why hypnosis works. Contemporary theorists are divided on their answers to the question: Is hypnosis a dissociated state of consciousness or is it simply a form of learned social behaviour?

A Dissociated State of Consciousness Ernest Hilgard (1986, 1992) proposed that hypnosis involves a special *dissociated*, or divided, state of consciousness, a sort of splitting of consciousness into separate components. One component follows the hypnotist's commands, while another component acts as a "hidden observer."

In one situation, Hilgard placed one arm of hypnotized individuals in a bucket of ice-cold water and told them that they would not feel any pain but that another part of their minds—the hidden part that is aware of what is going on—could signal any true pain by pressing a key with the hand that was not submerged (see figure 6.9). The individuals under hypnosis reported afterward that they did not experience any pain, but, while their arms were submerged in the ice-cold water, they had indeed pressed the key with their nonsubmerged hands, and they pressed it more frequently the longer their arms were in the cold water. Thus, in Hilgard's view, in hypnosis, consciousness has a hidden part that stays in contact with reality and feels pain while another part of consciousness feels no pain.

According to University of Waterloo psychologists Erik Woody and Ken Bowers, this dissociation is achieved through the inhibition of the normal functioning of the frontal cortex (Woody & Bowers, 1994; Jamieson & Sheehan, 2004).

Social Cognitive Behaviour Some experts are skeptical that hypnosis is truly an altered state of consciousness (Chaves, 2000; Kallio & Revonsuo, 2003). Carleton professor Nick Spanos was a major architect of an alternative theory of hypnosis. In the **social cognitive behaviour view of hypnosis**, hypnosis is a normal state in which the hypnotized person behaves the way he or she believes a hypnotized person should behave (Gwynn & Spanos, 1996; Spanos, 1991). In this view, the important questions about hypnosis focus on cognitive factors—the attitudes, expectations, and beliefs of good hypnotic participants—and on the social context in which hypnosis occurs (Spanos & Chaves, 1989).

It may be that hypnosis is both a dissociated state and a normal state. Aside from hypnosis, other situations, like daydreaming and some forms of meditation, also produce an inhibition of the normal functioning of the frontal cortex (Farvolden & Woody, 2004). It may be quite normal for us to be able to "turn off" our controlled awareness in a variety of circumstances.

Applications of Hypnosis

Hypnosis is widely used in psychotherapy, medicine, and dentistry, in criminal investigations, and in sports. Hypnosis has been used in psychotherapy to treat alcoholism, somnambulism, suicidal tendencies, overeating, and smoking (Eimer, 2000; Yapko, 2001). Among the least effective, but most common, applications of hypnosis are those intended to help people stop overeating or quit smoking. Hypnotists direct individuals to stop these behaviours, but dramatic results are rarely achieved unless these individuals are already motivated to change. Hypnosis is most effective when combined with psychotherapy (Borckardt, 2002).

A long history of research and practice has clearly demonstrated that hypnosis can reduce the experience of pain (Keefe, Abernethy, & Campbell, 2005; Patterson, 2004; Langenfeld, Cipani, & Borckardt, 2002). However, not everyone is hypnotizable enough to benefit from this effect. Moreover, there is no evidence that hypnosis increases muscular strength and endurance, or sensory thresholds (Druckman & Bjork, 1994).

Hypnosis has sometimes been used in attempts to enhance people's ability to accurately recall forgotten events (Coleman, Stevens, & Reeder, 2001). Therapists sometimes use hypnosis to age-regress patients back to an earlier stage in life in order to help them work through long-forgotten, painful experiences. Also, police departments sometimes arrange to have eyewitnesses to crimes hypnotized in the hope that this will significantly improve their recall of the crime (Risen, Quas, & Goodman, 2002). To read about the research on this topic and the issues involved in whether forensic hypnosis is trustworthy, see the Critical Reflections box.

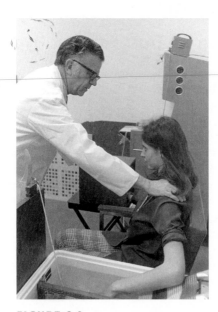

FIGURE 6.9
Divided Consciousness
Ernest Hilgard tests a participant in the study in which he had individuals place one arm in ice-cold water. *Why did Hilgard believe this study demonstrated the presence of divided consciousness?*

social cognitive behaviour view of hypnosis Views hypnosis as a result of social factors associated with the hypnotic context, coupled with cognitive events involved in the efforts of the hypnotized person to immerse himself or herself in the role of the hypnotized person.

Can We Trust Forensic Hypnosis?

Hypnosis is sometimes used to enhance people's ability to recall forgotten events (Nash, 2001; Stafford & Lynn, 2002). Police departments occasionally use forensic hypnosis to help eyewitnesses remember forgotten crime scene details. In 1976, for example, a school bus carrying 26 schoolchildren from Chowchilla, California disappeared. It turned out that three armed men kidnapped the bus driver and the children, and buried them alive in a trailer in a gravel quarry some distance away. After 16 hours underground, they were rescued. When the school bus driver was hypnotized, he recalled all but one digit of the licence plate on the vehicle driven by the kidnappers. This memory proved critical in tracking down the suspects (Loftus, 1979).

But forensic hypnosis is not always so successful. In 1977, two nurses were accused of poisoning nine patients at a Veterans Administration Hospital in Ann Arbor, Michigan. Two of the patients died. At first no clear evidence was found to link the nurses to the crime. In an attempt to prove their case, FBI agents hypnotized the surviving victims and several staff members. Under hypnosis, one victim gradually began to remember the presence of one of the two nurses in his room. Were the memories of this witness accurate? How do we know whether events recalled under hypnosis actually happened as people recall them? While this critical testimony resulted in a conviction, a judge ordered a new trial and the prosecution chose not to retry the case (Loftus, 1979).

Research suggests that improvements in memory due to hypnosis may often be more apparent than real (Lynn, Rhue, & Spanos, 1994). In a classic study, participants watched a videotape of a mock armed robbery and then recalled specific crime details six times: twice immediately after seeing the videotape, twice one week after seeing the videotape, once during hypnosis, and once after hypnosis (Nadon, Laurence, & Perry, 1991). High-hypnotizability participants, in fact, recovered more memories of specific crime details under hypnosis than they did just before hypnosis, while low-hypnotizability participants did not. Unfortunately, high-hypnotizability participants also recovered more pseudomemories—false memories that are confidently believed to be real—than low-hypnotizability participants did. In other words, when people are hypnotized, they may remember more information that is correct *and* incorrect.

Unfortunately for police and judges, in most real-life circumstances it may be impossible to discriminate between correct and incorrect memories. In the Chowchilla case mentioned above, corroborating evidence confirmed the accuracy of the bus driver's hypnotic recall. In the Ann Arbor case, with no corroborating evidence, it was impossible to confirm or disconfirm the accuracy of the victim's recovered memory.

One explanation of this result is that hypnosis may make participants more willing than normal to report whatever comes into their mind. This uncertainty about the accuracy of memories recalled under hypnosis is magnified by the tendency of hypnotized participants to be influenced by leading questions. For example, after viewing a photo, hypnotized individuals might be asked, "What colour was that person's moustache?" The individuals then often create an image of the person they saw and supply the person with a moustache, even though the photo did not show a moustache. Later they might confidently recall the person as having a moustache.

Also, a number of studies have shown that hypnotized witnesses are more confident about the inaccurate aspects of their recall or about misidentifications than non-hypnotized witnesses are (Orne, 1959). In a court of law, hypnotized witnesses have so much confidence in their pseudomemories that they are effectively immune against cross-examination (Orne, 1959). Jane Dywan (1995) has proposed that increased confidence in memories recovered under hypnosis is due to an illusion of familiarity that hypnosis helps to produce.

Because of the mixed evidence, in Canada hypnotic testimony can, at best, be used as corroborative evidence. In some American states, it has actually been banned. If hypnotic testimony is allowed in court, extreme caution must be exercised to obtain corroborating evidence and to minimize the risk of implanting pseudomemories when questioning victims and witnesses under hypnosis (Lynn, Neuschatz, & Fite, 2002).

There is some evidence that it may not be necessary to hypnotize eyewitnesses to help them remember more details about a crime. In one study, although individuals sometimes recalled new information following a hypnotic interview, they also sometimes recalled new information when motivated by nonhypnotic instructions (Frischoltz, 1995). One promising technique is focused meditation, which seems to enhance recall without increasing false recall (Wagstaff & others, 2004). However, even nonhypnotic methods of improving memory are vulnerable to the same problems, leading to the same concerns about the accuracy of recovered memories (Loftus, 1979).

What do you think?

- Why should extreme caution be exercised when evaluating memories generated by hypnotic testimony?
- Might age regression be a valuable therapeutic technique regardless of the risk of generating pseudomemories?
- Why might hypnosis cause someone to report recalled events inaccurately?

> **reflect and review**

3 **Describe hypnosis.**

- Explain what hypnosis is.
- Discuss two theoretical explanations of hypnosis.
- Identify some applications of hypnosis.

Do you think you are a good candidate for hypnosis? Why or why not?

4 PSYCHOACTIVE DRUGS

Uses of Psychoactive Drugs — Types of Psychoactive Drugs — Addiction

What are psychoactive drugs and how do they affect behaviour?

In 1885, the American druggist John Pemberton introduced a new medicine based on alcohol, the coca plant, and the kola nut that he called *Pemberton's French Wine Coca*. Like Sigmund Freud, he was enthusiastic about the health benefits of cocaine, the active ingredient in the coca plant. Ironically, under pressure from the temperance movement, he eliminated the alcohol and named the resulting medicine *Coca-Cola*, after the two main remaining ingredients. By 1902, the amount of coca was dramatically reduced and Coca-Cola became coca-free in 1929. Cocaine is just one of many drugs taken to alter consciousness.

Illicit drug use is a global problem. More than 200 million people worldwide abuse drugs (UNDCP, 2003). The images span all segments of society: the urban professional snorting cocaine in a downtown nightclub, the farmer addicted to the opium poppy he grows, the teenage ecstasy user in a comfortable suburban home.

The use of illegal drugs among young people is a particular problem. The Centre for Addiction and Mental Health, in affiliation with the University of Toronto, has been surveying drug use among Ontario adolescents every two years since 1977. *OSDUS*, the *Ontario Student Drug Use Survey* has revealed that, overall, drug use among Ontario adolescents increased in the 1970s, then decreased in the 1980s, but rose once again in the 1990s (Adlaf & Paglia, 2003). A recent comparison of the OSDUS data with data from a similar American survey showed similar trends, except that usage levels were generally higher among the Canadian students (Centre for Addiction and Mental Health, 2004). The most recent OSDUS surveys have found that, except for cocaine, which has increased, drug use has declined in the first few years of this decade (Adlaf & Paglia, 2003). Later, when we discuss specific drugs, we describe trends in adolescents' use of specific drugs.

Uses of Psychoactive Drugs

Psychoactive drugs are substances that act on the nervous system to alter states of consciousness, modify perceptions, and change moods. Most psychoactive drugs, among other effects, increase dopamine levels in the brain's reward pathways (U.S. National Institute on Drug Abuse, 2001). This reward pathway is located in the *ventral tegmental area (VTA)* and *nucleus accumbens* (see figure 6.10). Only the limbic and prefrontal areas of the brain are directly activated by dopamine, which comes from the VTA (Kandel, Schwartz, & Jessell, 2003).

Perhaps because they influence reward pathways, people are attracted to the use of psychoactive drugs use to help them adapt to an ever-changing environment. Drinking, smoking, and taking drugs reduce tension, relieve boredom and fatigue, and in some

psychoactive drugs Drugs that act on the nervous system to alter consciousness, modify perceptions, and change moods.

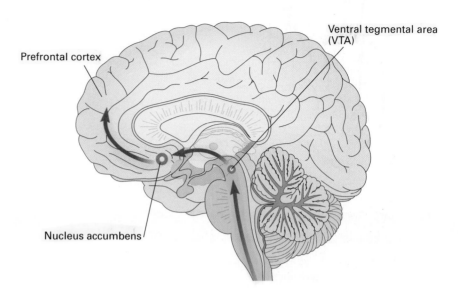

FIGURE 6.10 The Brain's Reward Pathway for Psychoactive Drugs
The ventral tegmental area (VTA) and nucleus accumbens are important locations in the reward pathway for psychoactive drugs. Information travels from the VTA to the nucleus accumbens and then up to the prefrontal cortex. The VTA is located in the midbrain just above the pons, and the nucleus accumbens is located in the forebrain, just beneath the prefrontal cortex.

cases help people to escape from the harsh realities of the world. Some people take drugs because they are curious about their effects. Others may take drugs for social reasons, for example to feel more at ease and happier in interacting with others.

Unfortunately, the overuse of psychoactive drugs for personal gratification and temporary adaptation can carry a high price tag: drug dependence, personal disarray, and a predisposition to serious, sometimes fatal, diseases (Goldberg, 2003). For example, drinking alcohol may initially help people relax and forget about their worries. But if they turn more and more to alcohol to escape reality, they may develop a dependence that can destroy relationships, careers, and their bodies. All psychoactive drugs have the potential to cause health or behaviour problems or both. To evaluate whether you abuse drugs, see figure 6.11.

Continued use of psychoactive drugs leads to **tolerance**, which is the need to take increasing amounts of a drug to get the same effect. For example, the first time someone takes 5 milligrams of the tranquilizer Valium, the drug will make them feel very relaxed. However, after taking the pill every day for six months, the person may need to take 10 milligrams to achieve the same calming effect.

Continuing drug use can also result in **physical dependence**, the physiological need for a drug that causes unpleasant *withdrawal* symptoms, such as physical pain and a craving for the drug, when it is discontinued. **Psychological dependence** is the strong desire to repeat the use of a drug for emotional reasons, such as a feeling of well-being and reduction of stress. Experts on drug abuse use the term *addiction* to describe either a physical or psychological dependence, or both, on the drug (Carroll, 2003). Both physical and psychological dependence mean that the psychoactive drug is exerting a powerful influence over the person's behaviour.

Types of Psychoactive Drugs

tolerance The need to take increasing amounts of the drug to produce the same effect.

physical dependence The physical need for a drug, accompanied by unpleasant withdrawal symptoms when the drug is discontinued.

psychological dependence The strong desire and craving to repeat the use of the drug for emotional reasons.

From a neurobiological perspective, psychoactive drugs act by influencing the activity of one or more major neurotransmitters, such as serotonin, norepinephrine, and dopamine. Different drugs have different mechanisms of action. Recall from chapter 3 that when a drug mimics a particular neurotransmitter or blocks its reuptake, it is referred to as an *agonist*. In contrast, when a drug blocks a neurotransmitter or diminishes its release, it is called an *antagonist*. Three main categories of psychoactive drugs are depressants, stimulants, and hallucinogens.

Respond yes or no to the following items:

Yes	No	
_____	_____	I have gotten into problems because of using drugs.
_____	_____	Using alcohol or other drugs has made my university life unhappy at times.
_____	_____	Drinking alcohol or taking other drugs has been a factor in my losing a job.
_____	_____	Drinking alcohol or taking other drugs has interfered with my studying for exams.
_____	_____	Drinking alcohol or taking drugs has jeopardized my academic performance.
_____	_____	My ambition is not as strong since I've been drinking a lot or taking drugs.
_____	_____	Drinking or taking drugs has caused me to have difficulty sleeping.
_____	_____	I have felt remorse after drinking or taking drugs.
_____	_____	I crave a drink or other drugs at a definite time of the day.
_____	_____	I want a drink or other drug in the morning.
_____	_____	I have had a complete or partial loss of memory as a result of drinking or using other drugs.
_____	_____	Drinking or using other drugs is affecting my reputation.
_____	_____	I have been in the hospital or another institution because of my drinking or taking drugs.

University students who responded yes to items similar to these on the Rutgers Collegiate Abuse Screening Test were more likely to be substance abusers than those who answered no. If you responded yes to just 1 of the 13 items on this screening test, consider going to your university health or counselling centre for further screening.

FIGURE 6.11 Do You Abuse Drugs?

Depressants **Depressants** are psychoactive drugs that slow down mental and physical activity. Among the most widely used depressants are alcohol, barbiturates, tranquillizers, and opiates.

Alcohol We do not always think of alcohol as a drug, but it is a powerful one. Alcohol acts on the body primarily as a depressant and slows down the brain's activities. This might seem surprising, as people who normally tend to be inhibited may begin to talk, dance, and socialize after a few drinks. However, people "loosen up" after a few drinks because the areas of the brain involved in inhibition and judgment slow down. As people drink more, their inhibitions become reduced even further, and their judgment becomes increasingly impaired. Activities that require intellectual functioning and motor skills, such as driving, become increasingly impaired as more alcohol is consumed. Eventually the drinker becomes drowsy and falls asleep. With extreme intoxication, a person may lapse into a coma and die. Each of these effects varies with the way the person's body metabolizes alcohol, body weight, the amount of alcohol consumed, and whether previous drinking has led to tolerance (Gotz & others, 2001).

How does alcohol affect the brain? Like other psychoactive drugs, alcohol goes to the ventral tegmental area (VTA) and the nucleus accumbens (U. S. National Institute on Drug Abuse, 2001). Alcohol also increases the concentration of the neurotransmitter gamma aminobutyric acid (GABA), which is widely distributed in many areas of the brain, including the cerebral cortex, cerebellum, hippocampus, amygdala, and nucleus accumbens (Melis & others, 2002). Researchers believe that the frontal cortex, which is involved in decision-making and memory, holds a memory of the pleasure involved in prior alcohol use (relaxation, lowered stress, less inhibition) and contributes to continued drinking. Alcohol use also may affect the areas of the frontal cortex involved in judgment and impulse control (Mantere & others, 2002). It is further believed that the

depressants Psychoactive drugs that slow down mental and physical activity.

The Troubles Frequent Binge Drinkers Create for . . .

Themselves[1]		and Others[2]	
(% of those surveyed who admitted having had the problem)		(% of those surveyed who had been affected)	
Missed class	61	Had study or sleep interrupted	68
Forgot where they were or what they did	54	Had to care for drunken student	54
Engaged in unplanned sex	41	Were insulted or humiliated	34
Got hurt	23	Experienced unwanted sexual advances	26
Had unprotected sex	22	Had serious argument	20
Damaged property	22	Had property damaged	15
Got into trouble with campus or local police	11	Were pushed or assaulted	13
Had five or more alcohol-related problems in school year	47	Had at least one of the above problems	87

[1] Frequent binge drinkers were defined as those who had at least four or five drinks at one time on at least three occasions in the previous two weeks.
[2] These figures are from colleges or universities where at least 50% of students are binge drinkers.

FIGURE 6.12 Consequences of Binge Drinking

basal ganglia, which are involved in compulsive behaviours, may lead to a greater demand for alcohol, regardless of reason and consequences. Finally, alcohol may also lead to difficulties in the processing of emotional stimuli. In one study, alcoholics showed deficits in their ability to process the emotional dimension of language, hindering their ability to solve interpersonal problems (Uekermann & others, 2005).

After caffeine, alcohol is the most widely used drug in North America. According to Tjepkema (2004), in 2002, 77 percent of all Canadians 15 or older used alcohol, and 47 percent of men and 24 percent of women could be categorized as heavy drinkers (although such operational definitions are open to question; Chaikelson & others, 1994; DeCourville & Sadava, 1997). In a pan-Canadian analysis of the effects of alcohol consumption from 1950 to 1998, alcohol consumption played a significant role in fatal accidents, including traffic accidents, drownings, and fatal falls (Skog, 2003). Each year over 1400 Canadians are killed, and 92,000 injured, by drunk drivers (Health Canada, 1999). More than 60 percent of homicides involve the use of alcohol by either the offender or the victim, while 65 percent of aggressive sexual acts against women involve the use of alcohol by the offender.

A special concern is the high rate of alcohol use by adolescents in Canada. According to the 2003 round of the OSDUS survey, alcohol was the most commonly used drug with about 65 percent of all students reporting drinking during the past year, 18 percent reporting drinking at least once a week and about 25 percent reporting binge drinking, defined as having five or more drinks on one occasion (Adlaf & Paglia, 2003).

Heavy binge drinking often increases during the first two years of college or university, and it can take its toll on students (B. T. Jones, 2003). Chronic binge drinking is more common among male students than among females, and more common among students living away from home, especially males living in fraternity houses (Schulenberg & others, 2000). In one recent national survey of drinking patterns on campus, almost half the binge drinkers reported problems that included missed classes, injuries, trouble with police, and unprotected sex (see figure 6.12; Wechsler & others, 2000). Binge-drinking students were 11 times more likely to fall behind in school, 10 times more likely to drive after drinking, and twice as likely to have unprotected sex as students who did not binge drink. Many young people decrease their use of alcohol as they move into adult roles, such as a permanent job, marriage or cohabitation, and parenthood.

Around the world, there are differences in alcohol use by religion and gender (Koenig, 2001; Lieber, 1997; Melinder & Anderson, 2001). Catholics, Reform Jews, and liberal Protestants all consume alcohol at a fairly high level. Males drink alcohol more than females.

Europeans, especially the French, drink alcohol at high rates. Estimates are that about 30 percent of French adults have health problems related to high alcohol consumption. Alcohol use is also high in Russia, but its use in China is low. In some religions, such as Islam, use of alcohol is forbidden.

Alcoholism is a disorder that involves long-term, repeated, uncontrolled, compulsive, and excessive use of alcoholic beverages and that impairs the drinker's health and social relationships. One in nine individuals who drink continues the path to alcoholism. Those who do are disproportionately related to alcoholics. Family studies consistently find a high frequency of alcoholism in the first-degree relatives of alcoholics (Hannigan & others, 1999). Indeed, researchers have found that heredity likely plays a role in alcoholism, although the precise hereditary mechanism has not been found (Crabbe, 2002; Wall & others, 2001). An estimated 50 to 60 percent of those who become alcoholics are believed to have a genetic predisposition for it.

One possible explanation is that the brains of people genetically predisposed to alcoholism may be unable to produce adequate dopamine, a neurotransmitter that can make us feel pleasure. For these individuals, alcohol may increase dopamine concentrations and resulting pleasure to the point at which it leads to addiction.

Although studies reveal a genetic influence on alcoholism, they also show that environmental factors play a role (Heath & others, 2002). For example, family studies indicate that many alcoholics do not have close relatives who are alcoholics (Sher, 1993). The large cultural variations in alcohol use mentioned earlier also underscore the environment's role in alcoholism. Interaction theory sees alcoholism as rooted in an interaction between person variables, like the tendency to experience anxiety, and situational variables, like the availability of alcohol (Sadava, 1987).

About one-third of alcoholics recover, whether they are in a treatment program or not. This finding came from a classic long-term study of 700 individuals over 50 years (Vaillant, 1983, 1992) and has consistently been found by other researchers as well. George Vaillant formulated the one-third rule for alcoholism: By age 65, one-third are dead or in terrible shape; one-third are still trying to beat their addiction; and one-third are abstinent or drinking only socially. In his extensive research, Vaillant found that a positive outcome and recovery from alcoholism was predicted by (1) a strong negative experience with drinking, such as a serious medical emergency or condition, (2) finding a substitute dependency to compete with alcohol abuse, such as meditation, exercise, or overeating (which has its own adverse health effects), (3) developing new, positive relationships (such as a concerned, helpful employer or a new marriage), and (4) joining a support group, such as a religious organization, Alcoholics Anonymous, or Rational Recovery.

We have presented an extensive discussion of alcohol use and its effects because it is so widely used and abused. Now we consider several other depressant drugs, beginning with barbiturates.

Barbiturates **Barbiturates**, such as Nembutal and Seconal, are depressant drugs that are used to decrease central nervous system activity. They were once widely prescribed as sleep aids. In heavy dosages, they can lead to impaired memory and decision-making. When combined with alcohol (for example, sleeping pills taken after a night of binge drinking), barbiturates can be lethal. Heavy doses of barbiturates by themselves can cause death. For this reason, barbiturates are the drug most often used in suicide attempts. Abrupt withdrawal from barbiturates can produce seizures. Because of the addictive potential and relative ease of toxic overdose, barbiturates have been largely replaced by tranquilizers in the treatment of insomnia.

Tranquilizers **Tranquilizers**, such as Valium and Xanax, are depressant drugs that reduce anxiety and induce relaxation. Unlike barbiturates, which are often given to induce sleep, tranquilizers are usually given to calm an anxious, nervous individual (Rosenbloom, 2002). Tranquilizers are among the most widely prescribed drugs in North America. They can produce withdrawal symptoms when use is stopped.

alcoholism A disorder that involves long-term, repeated, uncontrolled, compulsive, and excessive use of alcoholic beverages and that impairs the drinker's health and work and social relationships.

barbiturates Depressant drugs that decrease the activity of the central nervous system.

tranquilizers Depressant drugs that reduce anxiety and induce relaxation.

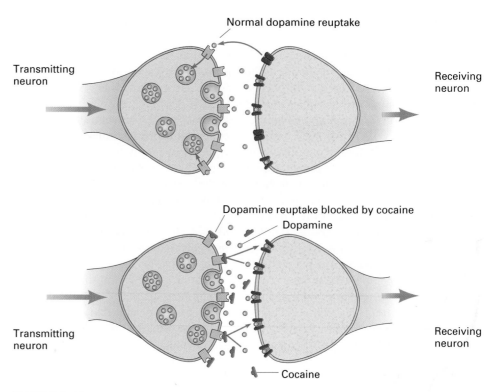

FIGURE 6.13 **Cocaine and Neurotransmitters**
Cocaine concentrates in areas of the brain that are rich in dopamine synapses, such as the VTA and the nucleus accumbens. (*Top*) What happens in normal reuptake. The transmitting neuron releases dopamine that stimulates the receiving neuron by binding to its receptor sites. After binding occurs, dopamine is carried back into the transmitting neuron for later release. (*Bottom*) What happens when cocaine is present in the synapse. Cocaine binds to the uptake pumps and prevents them from removing dopamine from the synapse. This results in more dopamine in the synapse, and more dopamine receptors are activated.

Opiates Narcotics, or **opiates**, consist of opium and its derivatives and depress the central nervous system's activity. The most common opiate drugs—morphine and heroin—affect synapses in the brain that use endorphins as their neurotransmitter. When these drugs leave the brain, the affected synapses become understimulated. For several hours after taking an opiate, the person feels euphoric and pain free and has an increased appetite for food and sex. The opiates are highly addictive drugs, leading to craving and painful withdrawal when the drug becomes unavailable.

Another hazardous consequence of opiate addiction is the risk of exposure to the virus that causes acquired immunodeficiency syndrome (AIDS). Most heroin addicts inject the drug intravenously. When they share needles without sterilizing them, one infected addict can transmit the virus to others. In Canada in 2002, 34 percent of new HIV infections occurred among intravenous drug users (Health Canada, 2004).

Stimulants **Stimulants** are psychoactive drugs that increase the central nervous system's activity. The most widely used stimulants are amphetamines, cocaine, MDMA (ecstasy), caffeine, and nicotine.

Amphetamines *Amphetamines* are stimulant drugs that are used to boost energy, stay awake, or lose weight. They are sometimes called "pep pills" or "uppers." Amphetamines are often prescribed in the form of diet pills. These drugs increase the release of dopamine, which enhances the user's activity level and pleasurable feelings.

Cocaine Cocaine is an illegal drug that comes from the coca plant, native to Bolivia and Peru. For centuries, Bolivians and Peruvians have chewed the leaves of the plant to increase their stamina. Generally, however, cocaine is either snorted or injected in the form of crystals or powder. Used this way, cocaine can trigger a heart attack, stroke, or brain seizure.

opiates Opium and its derivatives; they depress the central nervous system's activity.

stimulants Psychoactive drugs that increase the central nervous system's activity.

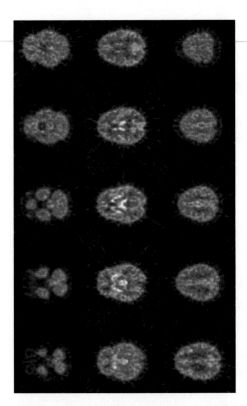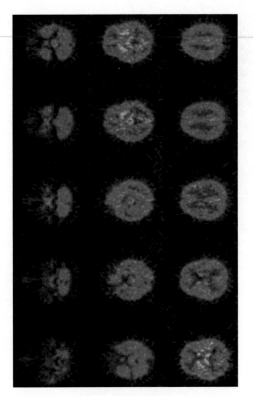

FIGURE 6.14 **MDMA (Ecstasy) and the Brain**

(*Left*) Brain scans from individuals who have never taken MDMA. (*Right*) Brain scans from individuals who have taken MDMA regularly. Notice the prevalence of yellow in the brain scans on the left, which is indicative of healthy brain neuron connections, and its absence in the brain scans of the MDMA users on the right.

When animals and humans chew coca leaves, small amounts of cocaine gradually enter the bloodstream, without any apparent adverse effects. However, when extracted cocaine is sniffed or injected, it enters the bloodstream very rapidly, producing a rush of euphoric feelings that last for about 15 to 30 minutes. Cocaine also depresses prefrontal cortical activity (Trantham-Davidson & Lavin, 2004). Because the rush depletes the supply of the neurotransmitters dopamine, serotonin, and norepinephrine in the brain, an agitated, depressed mood usually follows as the drug's effects decline. Figure 6.13 shows how cocaine affects dopamine levels in the brain.

Crack is a potent form of cocaine, consisting of chips of pure cocaine that are usually smoked. Crack is believed to be one of the most addictive substances known— it is more addictive than heroin, barbiturates, or alcohol.

In the 2003 round of the OSDUS survey, 4.8 percent of Ontario adolescents reported using cocaine during the past year, and 2.7 percent reported using crack (Adlaf & Paglia, 2003). Cocaine's addictive properties are so strong that six months after treatment more than 50 percent of cocaine abusers return to the drug. Experts on drug abuse argue that prevention is the best approach to reducing cocaine use.

MDMA (Ecstasy) MDMA is an illegal synthetic drug with both stimulant and hallucinogenic properties. Street names for MDMA include ecstasy, XTC, hug, beans, and love drug. A special concern is the use of MDMA by adolescents. According to the OSDUS survey, since monitoring began in 1991, MDMA use among Ontario students in grades 7–12 has risen from less than 1 percent to 5.8 percent in 2001 and back down to 4.1 percent in 2003 (Adlaf & Paglia, 2003).

Brain imaging studies show that MDMA can cause brain damage, especially to neurons that use serotonin to communicate with other neurons (see figure 6.14). Just four days of use can cause brain damage that is still evident six to seven years later (U. S. National Institute on Drug Abuse, 2001).

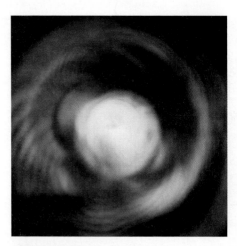

FIGURE 6.15
LSD-Induced Hallucination
Under the influence of hallucinogenic drugs, such as LSD, several users have reported seeing tunnel-like images.

Caffeine   Often overlooked as a drug, caffeine is the most widely used psychoactive drug in the world. Caffeine is a stimulant and a natural component of the plants that are the sources of coffee, tea, and cola drinks (Nehlig, 2004). Caffeine is also present in chocolate and in many nonprescribed medications. The stimulating effects of caffeine are often perceived to be beneficial for boosting energy and alertness, but some people experience unpleasant side effects.

Caffeinism is the term given to overindulgence of caffeine. It is characterized by mood changes, anxiety, and sleep disruption. Caffeinism often develops in people who drink five or more cups of coffee (at least 500 milligrams) each day. Common symptoms of caffeinism are insomnia, irritability, headaches, ringing in the ears, dry mouth, increased blood pressure, and digestive problems (Hogan, Hornick, & Bouchoux, 2002).

Caffeine affects the brain's pleasure centres, so it is not surprising that it is difficult to kick the caffeine habit. When individuals who regularly consume caffeinated beverages remove caffeine from their diet, they typically experience headaches, lethargy, apathy, and concentration difficulties. These symptoms of withdrawal are usually mild and subside after several days.

Nicotine   *Nicotine* is the main psychoactive ingredient in all forms of smoking and smokeless tobacco. Even with all the publicity given to the enormous health risks posed by tobacco, we sometimes overlook the highly addictive nature of nicotine.

In the brain, nicotine stimulates the reward centres by raising dopamine levels. Behavioural effects of nicotine include improved attention and alertness, reduced anger and anxiety, and pain relief (Rezvani & Levin, 2001). Recently, however, prolonged tobacco use has been linked to adverse moods such as anxiety (Spinella, 2005). Tolerance develops for nicotine both in the long run and on a daily basis, so that cigarettes smoked later in the day have less effect than those smoked earlier in the day. Withdrawal from nicotine often quickly produces strong, unpleasant symptoms such as irritability, craving, inability to focus, sleep disturbance, and increased appetite. Withdrawal symptoms can persist for months or longer.

Despite the positive short-term effects of nicotine (such as increased energy and alertness), most smokers recognize the serious health risks of smoking and wish they could quit. Chapter 15 further explores the difficulty in quitting smoking and strategies that can be used to quit.

Hallucinogens   **Hallucinogens** are psychoactive drugs that modify a person's perceptual experiences and produce visual images that are not real. Hallucinogens are also called *psychedelic* (meaning "mind-altering") drugs. Marijuana has a mild hallucinogenic effect, LSD a stronger one (see figure 6.15).

Marijuana   Marijuana is the dried leaves and flowers of the hemp plant *Cannabis sativa*, which originated in central Asia but is now grown in most parts of the world. The plant's dried resin is known as hashish. The active ingredient in marijuana is THC (delta-9-tetrahydrocannabinol). Unlike other psychoactive drugs, THC does not affect a specific neurotransmitter, but, rather, interacts with the membranes of neurons and affects the functioning of a variety of neurotransmitters and hormones.

The physical effects of marijuana include increases in pulse rate and blood pressure, reddening of the eyes, coughing, and dryness of the mouth. Psychological effects include a mixture of excitatory, depressive, and mildly hallucinatory characteristics that make it difficult to classify the drug. Marijuana can trigger spontaneous unrelated ideas; distorted perceptions of time and place; increased sensitivity to sounds, tastes, smells, and colours; and erratic verbal behaviour. Marijuana can also impair attention and memory. When used daily in large amounts, marijuana can also produce alterations in brain structure (Matochik & others, 2005) as well as alter sperm count and change hormonal cycles (Close, Roberts, & Berger, 1990). It may be involved in some birth defects. On a positive note, researchers have found some medical uses for marijuana, such as treating glaucoma, chemotherapy-caused vomiting, and AIDS-related weight loss.

hallucinogens Psychoactive drugs that modify a person's perceptual experiences and produce visual images that are not real.

After alcohol, marijuana is the illegal drug most widely used by high school students. According to the 2003 round of the OSDUS survey, marijuana was used by 30 percent of Ontario adolescents during the past year (Adlaf & Paglia, 2003). The American figures are comparable (Centre for Addiction and Mental Health, 2004).

LSD LSD (lysergic acid diethylamide) is a hallucinogen that even in low doses produces striking perceptual changes. Objects change their shapes and glow. Colours become kaleidoscopic, and fabulous images unfold. Designs swirl, colours shimmer, and bizarre scenes appear. LSD-induced images are sometimes pleasurable and sometimes grotesque. Figure 6.16 shows one kind of perceptual experience that a number of LSD users have reported. LSD can also influence a user's sense of time. Time seems to slow down dramatically, so that brief glances at objects are experienced as deep, penetrating, and lengthy examinations, and minutes seem to be hours or even days. A bad LSD trip can trigger extreme anxiety, paranoia, and suicidal or homicidal impulses.

LSD's effects on the body can include dizziness, nausea, and tremors. LSD acts primarily on the neurotransmitter serotonin in the brain, though it can also affect dopamine (Nichols & Sanders-Bush, 2002). Emotional and cognitive effects may include rapid mood swings or impaired attention and memory. LSD is one psychoactive drug that has no beneficial effects. Its effects are summarized in figure 6.16, along with the characteristics of the other types of drugs that have been discussed.

The use of LSD reached a peak in the 1960s and 1970s but its popularity declined after its unpredictable effects became publicized. According to the OSDUS survey, the use of LSD by Ontario adolescents decreased during the 1980s, increased in the 1990's and is currently decreasing again. In 2001, 4.8 percent reported using LSD during the past year, dropping to 2.9 percent in 2003, (Adlaf & Paglia, 2003),

Robert Chapman is coordinator of the alcohol and other drug program at La Salle University in Philadelphia. He coordinates the addictions counselling concentration in the master's degree program in clinical-counselling psychology. Robert recommends that students interested in becoming drug counsellors should go to some open recovery-group sessions, such as Alcoholic Anonymous meetings. In his words, "You can read and study and learn all about addictions, but there is something about listening to recovering people talk about life that provides a perspective that can't be captured in books or films."

Addiction

Addiction is a pattern of behaviour characterized by an overwhelming need to use the drug and to secure its supply. Addiction can occur despite the adverse consequences of drug use. There is a strong tendency to relapse after quitting or withdrawal. Withdrawal symptoms consist of significant changes in physical functioning and behaviour. Depending on the drug, these symptoms might include insomnia, tremors, nausea, vomiting, cramps, elevation of heart rate and blood pressure, convulsions, anxiety, and depression.

Controversy continues about whether addictions are diseases (Davidson & Neale, 2001). The **disease model of addiction** describes addictions as biologically based, lifelong diseases that involve a loss of control over behaviour and require medical and/or spiritual treatment for recovery. In the disease model, addiction is believed to be either inherited or bred into a person early in life (Enoch & Goldman, 2002). In this view, current or recent problems or relationships are not thought to be causes of the disease. It is believed that an addict can never fully overcome the disease. This model has been strongly promoted and supported by the medical profession and Alcoholics Anonymous.

Critics of the disease model argue that the biological origins of addiction have not been adequately identified, that treating addiction like a disease keeps people from pursuing and developing self-control, and that addiction is not necessarily lifelong (Grabowski, 1999; Sadava, 1987). Many critics prefer to characterize addiction not as a disease but rather as a habitual response and source of gratification or security that has developed in the context of social relationships and experiences.

addiction A pattern of behaviour characterized by an overwhelming need to use the drug and to secure its supply.

disease model of addiction Describes addictions as biologically based, lifelong diseases that involve a loss of control over behaviour and require medical and/or spiritual treatment for recovery.

Drug Classification	Medical Uses	Short-Term Effects	Overdose Effects	Health Risks	Risk of Physical/ Psychological Dependence
Depressants					
Alcohol	Pain relief	Relaxation, depressed brain activity, slowed behaviour, reduced inhibitions	Disorientation, loss of consciousness, even death at high blood-alcohol levels	Accidents, brain damage, liver disease, heart disease, ulcers, birth defects	Physical: moderate Psychological: moderate
Barbiturates	Sleeping pill	Relaxation, sleep	Breathing difficulty, coma, possible death	Accidents, coma, possible death	Physical and psychological: moderate to high
Tranquilizers	Anxiety reduction	Relaxation, slowed behaviour	Breathing difficulty, coma, possible death	Accidents, coma, possible death	Physical: low to moderate Psychological: moderate to high
Opiates (narcotics)	Pain relief	Euphoric feelings, drowsiness, nausea	Convulsions, coma, possible death	Accidents, infectious diseases such as AIDS	Physical: high Psychological: moderate to high
Stimulants					
Amphetamines	Weight control	Increased alertness, excitability; decreased fatigue, irritability	Extreme irritability, feelings of persecution, convulsions	Insomnia, hypertension, malnutrition, possible death	Physical: possible Psychological: moderate to high
Cocaine	Local anaesthetic	Increased alertness, excitability, euphoric feelings; decreased fatigue, irritability	Extreme irritability, feelings of persecution, convulsions, cardiac arrest, possible death	Insomnia, hypertension, malnutrition, possible death	Physical: possible Psychological: moderate (oral) to very high (injected or smoked)
MDMA (Ecstasy)	None	Mild amphetamine and hallucinogenic effects; high body temperature and dehydration; sense of well-being and social connectedness	Brain damage, especially memory and thinking	Cardiovascular problems; death	Physical: possible Psychological: moderate
Caffeine	None	Alertness and sense of well-being followed by fatigue	Nervousness, anxiety, disturbed sleep	Possible cardio-vascular problems	Physical: moderate Psychological: moderate
Nicotine	None	Stimulation, stress reduction, followed by fatigue, anger	Nervousness, disturbed sleep	Cancer and cardio-vascular disease	Physical: high Psychological: high
Hallucinogens					
LSD	None	Strong hallucinations, distorted time perception	Severe mental disturbance, loss of contact with reality	Accidents	Physical: none Psychological: low
Marijuana	Treatment of the eye disorder glaucoma	Euphoric feelings, relaxation, mild hallucinations, time distortion, attention and memory impairment	Fatigue, disoriented behaviour	Accidents, respiratory disease	Physical: very low Psychological: moderate

FIGURE 6.16 Categories of Psychoactive Drugs: Depressants, Stimulants, and Hallucinogens

Recent work points to addiction as having both biological and social/psychological underpinnings (Kolb, Gibb & Robinson, 2004; Chao & Nestler, 2004). Although drug abuse might begin as a habitual response, when it becomes chronic the synaptic effects of the drug eventually change the structure of the brain. The resulting changes can persist for years.

The Canadian government has recently revised a national drug strategy (Health Canada, 2005) to oversee provincial and community initiatives. Several components provide a framework for this strategy: research and knowledge dissemination; prevention programming; treatment and rehabilitation; legislation; enforcement and control; and international cooperation. The basic philosophy of community-based initiatives is that they should address a variety of issues including prevention, health promotion, treatment, and harm reduction issues. Any national strategy must also address the special issues facing various groups, including seniors, youth, women (Blackwell, Thurston, & Graham, 1996) as well as men, and Aboriginal peoples (McCormick, 2000; Health Canada, 2002b).

> ## > reflect and review

 Evaluate the uses and types of psychoactive drugs.

- Describe the effects of psychoactive drugs.
- List the characteristics of the three main types of psychoactive drugs: depressants, stimulants, and hallucinogens.
- Explain what addiction is and evaluate the disease model of addiction.

Do you know someone who has a drug problem? If so, describe the nature of the problem. Is he or she willing to admit to having a problem?

States of Consciousness

1 THE NATURE OF CONSCIOUSNESS

— Levels of
Awareness

— Consciousness
and the Brain

2 SLEEP AND DREAMS

— Biological
Rhythms
and Sleep

— Why Do
We Need
Sleep?

— Sleep
Stages

— Sleep and
Disease

— Sleep
Disorders

— Dreams

3 HYPNOSIS

— The Nature
of Hypnosis

— Explaining
Hypnosis

— Applications
of Hypnosis

4 PSYCHOACTIVE DRUGS

— Uses of
Psychoactive
Drugs

— Types of
Psychoactive
Drugs

— Addiction

At the beginning of the chapter, we posed four chapter questions and encouraged you to review material related to these questions at the end of each major section (see pages 233, 247, 251, and 261). Use the following reflection and review features to further your understanding of the chapter material.

CHAPTER REFLECTIONS

1. Do you think that being Canadian or living in Canada has any effect on your consciousness? If your answer is "yes," in what way? If your answer is "no," why not?

2. As noted in the chapter, we process information at many levels of consciousness. Try to bring as much sensory information into the controlled process level of consciousness as you can; pay attention to every sensation available to you (Are your socks touching your ankles? How many sounds can you hear? What is available to your visual system? Is your stomach growling?) How long can you keep track of all this sensory information, and what would happen if something important abruptly required all your attention? What does this tell you about which levels of consciousness normally process all this information?

3. Keep a sleep journal for several nights. Compare your sleep patterns with those described in the text. Do you have a sleep debt? If so, which stages of sleep are you likely missing most? Does a good night's sleep affect your behaviour? Keep a record of your mood and energy levels after a short night's sleep and then after you've had at least eight hours sleep in one night. What changes do you notice, and how do they compare with the changes predicted by research on sleep deprivation described in the chapter?

4. A quick Web search reveals sites that offer "subliminal tapes for self-hypnosis" to help you do anything from losing weight to getting a great new job. Based on the discussion of subliminal perception in chapter 5 and on hypnosis in this chapter, explain how a scientist would regard these tapes.

5. The Web site of the U.S. National Institute on Drug Abuse maintains a series of reports on current scientific knowledge about many commonly abused drugs. Visit the site (www.nida.nih.gov/Research Reports/ResearchIndex.html) and pick one of the listed reports. Using the report's information, compare the psychological effects and the risks associ-

ated with use of this drug with the psychological effects and risks of one of the psychoactive compounds described in the chapter.

CHAPTER REVIEW

Discuss the nature of consciousness.

- Consciousness is the awareness of external events and internal sensations, including awareness of the self and thoughts about experiences. William James described the mind as a stream of consciousness. Consciousness occurs at different levels of awareness that include no awareness (both low basic arousal and Freud's concept of unconscious thought), subconscious awareness (sleep and dreams, waking subconscious awareness), primary awareness (uncontrolled awareness, including automatic processes and daydreams, as well as controlled awareness), self-awareness (including metacognition), and altered states of awareness (produced by drugs, trauma, fatigue, and other factors).

- One of the great unanswered questions about consciousness is its location—in the mind or in the brain—and, if in the brain, whether there is a seat of consciousness or a distribution across different areas of the brain. Most experts agree that consciousness is likely distributed across the brain, although the association areas and prefrontal lobes are believed to play important roles in higher awareness.

Explain the nature of sleep and dreams.

- Biological rhythms are periodic physiological fluctuations. The biological rhythm that regulates the daily sleep/wake cycle is a circadian rhythm. The part of the brain that keeps our biological clocks synchronized is the suprachiasmatic nucleus, a small structure in the hypothalamus that registers light. Biological clocks can become desynchronized by such things as jet travel and work shifts. Some strategies are available for resetting the biological clock.

- We need sleep for physical restoration, adaptation, growth, and memory. An increasing number of research studies reveal that people do not function optimally when they are sleep deprived. There is currently a great deal of concern that North Americans generally, and adolescents and aging adults in particular, are not getting enough sleep.

- Stages of sleep correspond to massive electrophysiological changes that occur in the brain and that can be assessed by an EEG. Humans go through four stages of non-REM sleep and one stage of REM sleep, or rapid-eye-movement sleep. Most dreaming occurs during REM sleep. The amount of REM sleep changes over the life span. A sleep cycle of five stages lasts about 90 to 100 minutes and recurs several times during the night. The REM stage lasts longer toward the end of a night's sleep. The sleep stages are associated with distinct patterns of neurotransmitter activity. Levels of the neurotransmitters serotonin, norepinephrine, and acetylcholine decrease as the sleep cycle progresses from stage 1 through stage 4. Stage 5, REM sleep, begins when the reticular formation raises the level of acetylcholine.

- Sleep plays a role in a large number of diseases and disorders. Neurons that control sleep interact closely with the immune system, and when our bodies are fighting infection our cells produce a substance that makes us sleepy. Individuals with depression often have sleep problems.

- Many North Americans suffer from chronic, long-term sleep disorders, which can impair normal daily functioning. These disorders include insomnia, sleepwalking and sleep talking, nightmares and night terrors, narcolepsy, and sleep apnea.

- There are cultural and gender variations in dreaming. People in some cultures more often tie dreaming to reality or to the spiritual than people in modern cultures do. Males dream more about aggression, females more about friends. In Freud's view, the reason people dream is wish fulfillment. He distinguished between a dream's manifest (symbolic) and latent (unconscious) content. The cognitive theory of dreaming attempts to explain dreaming in terms of the same cognitive concepts that are used in studying the waking mind. In this view, dreams might be an arena for solving problems and thinking creatively. According to activation-synthesis theory, dreaming occurs when the cerebral cortex synthesizes neural signals emanating from activity in the lower part of the brain. In this view, the rising level of acetylcholine during REM sleep plays a role in neural activity in the reticular formation of the limbic system that the cerebral cortex tries to make sense of.

Describe hypnosis.

- Hypnosis can be defined as a psychological state or possibly altered attention and awareness in which the individual is unusually receptive to suggestions. The hypnotic state is different from a sleep state, as confirmed by EEG recordings. Inducing hypnosis involves four basic steps, beginning with minimizing distractions and making the person feel comfortable and ending with the hypnotist suggesting certain events or feelings that he or she knows will occur or observes occurring. There are substantial individual variations in people's susceptibility to hypnosis. People in a hypnotic state are unlikely to do anything that violates their morals or that involves a real danger.

- Two theories have been proposed to explain hypnosis. In Hilgard's divided consciousness view, hypnosis involves a divided state of consciousness, a splitting of consciousness into separate components. One component follows the hypnotist's commands, the other acts as a "hidden observer." In Spanos's social cognitive behaviour view, the hypnotized individual behaves the way he or she believes a hypnotized individual is expected to behave.

- Hypnosis is widely used in psychotherapy, medicine, and dentistry, in criminal investigations, and in sports.

Evaluate the uses and types of psychoactive drugs.

- Psychoactive drugs act on the nervous system to alter states of consciousness, modify perceptions, and change moods. Humans are attracted to these types of drugs because they help them adapt to change. Continued use of psychoactive drugs can lead to tolerance and physical or psychological addiction. Most addictive drugs activate the reward system of the brain by increasing dopamine concentration. The reward pathway involves the ventral tegmental area (VTA) and nucleus accumbens.

- Depressants, including alcohol, barbiturates, tranquilizers, and opiates, slow down mental and physical activity. Among the most widely used depressants are alcohol, barbiturates, tranquilizers, and opiates. After caffeine, alcohol is the most widely used drug in North America. The high rate of alcohol abuse by high school and college and university students is especially alarming. Alcoholism is a disorder that involves long-term, repeated, uncontrolled, compulsive, and excessive use of alcoholic beverages that impairs the drinker's health and work and social relationships. Stimulants increase the central nervous system's activity and include caffeine, nicotine, amphetamines, cocaine, and MDMA (ecstasy). Hallucinogens modify a person's perceptual experiences and produce visual images that are not real. Marijuana has a mild hallucinogenic effect. LSD has a strong one.

- Addiction is a pattern of behaviour characterized by a preoccupation with using a drug and with securing its supply. In the disease model of addiction, addictions are lifelong diseases that involve a loss of control over behaviour and that require medical and/or spiritual treatment for recovery. Critics of the disease approach argue that it places too much emphasis on biology and not enough on social and cognitive factors.

CONNECTIONS

For extra help in mastering the material in this chapter, see the integrator, review sections, practice quizzes, and other resources in the Student Study Guide and at the Online Learning Centre (www.mcgrawhill.ca/college/santrock).

CORE TERMS

consciousness, p. 228
stream of consciousness p. 228
controlled processes, p. 228
automatic processes, p. 230
unconscious thought, p. 231
biological rhythms, p. 233
circadian rhythms, p. 234
suprachiasmatic nucleus (SCN), p. 234
REM sleep, p. 237
wish fulfillment, p. 245

manifest content, p. 245
latent content, p. 245
cognitive theory of dreaming, p. 245
activation-synthesis theory, p. 246
hypnosis, p. 247
social cognitive behaviour view of
    hypnosis, p. 249
psychoactive drugs, p. 251
tolerance, p. 252
physical dependence, p. 252

psychological dependence, p. 252
depressants, p. 253
alcoholism, p. 255
barbiturates, p. 255
tranquilizers, p. 255
opiates, p. 256
stimulants, p. 256
hallucinogens, p. 258
addiction, p. 259
disease model of addiction, p. 259

7 Learning

CHAPTER QUESTIONS

1. What is learning?

2. What is classical conditioning?

3. What is operant conditioning?

4. What is observational learning?

5. What is the role of cognition in learning?

6. What are some biological and cultural factors in learning?

Much of what we do results from what we have *learned*. If you had grown up in another part of the world, you would speak a different language, like different foods, and behave in ways characteristic of that culture. Most of the time learning is a positive experience. But that is not always the case. As we shall see in this chapter, we may also learn our fears, our phobias, and our addictions through the same mechanisms. In extreme cases, we can learn enough to literally kill us.

For years, many deaths due to overdoses of drugs such as heroin were a mystery. Addicts recovering from near-fatal drug overdoses commonly reported that they had not taken higher-than-normal dosages and that drug impurity was not a factor (Siegel, 2001; Siegel & Ramos, 2002). So what could it be? The puzzle was solved by Shepard Siegel, of McMaster University, when it turned out that the common thread in these mysterious deaths was that the addicts had "shot up" in unfamiliar circumstances.

It has long been known that injecting a drug like heroin triggers a powerful physiological process that the body counters with an *opponent process* in a compensatory attempt to return to a normal state. With repeated drug use, the body fights back harder. The opponent process becomes stronger and the body's drug *tolerance* grows. The addict, in turn, must respond by taking ever-increasing dosages to get the same effect. Siegel's contribution was to use classical conditioning principles, which we will discuss later on in this chapter, to explain how the environmental circumstances of drug use contribute to the dynamics of drug tolerance and overdoses (Siegel, 1979, 1983).

In classical conditioning terms, according to Siegel (1983, 1999), the physiological effect of a drug injection is an unconditioned stimulus resulting in tolerance, a compensatory, unconditioned physiological response. If an addict has a history of shooting up in the same place, the setting of the drug use becomes a conditioned stimulus associated with the drug injection (Siegel, 1998). In classical conditioning, with repeated conditioning trials a conditioned stimulus becomes able, on its own, to elicit the unconditioned response, which we now call a conditioned response. In other words, as the addict prepares to shoot up, the familiar environment signals the coming drug injection and begins to trigger the compensatory tolerance response.

Suppose an addict has a long history of shooting up in the same place—say, his room. He has built up considerable drug tolerance, due to the opponent process triggered by familiar cues in his room. Now suppose the addict shoots up with his usual high dosage in an unfamiliar room. There are no familiar surroundings to act as a conditioned stimulus to trigger the usual compensatory response, and so the drug acts more strongly than usual. The result can easily be an overdose, sometimes ending in the death of the addict (Siegel & others, 1982).

As we will see in this chapter, learning applies to many areas of acquiring new behaviours, skills, and knowledge. Our focus will be on three types of learning: classical conditioning, operant conditioning, and observational learning. We will also discuss the role of cognitive or mental processes in learning, as well as biological and cultural factors.

In August 1996, 35-year-old Steven Chuvalo was found dead of a drug overdose at his Toronto home. Ever since, his father, former Canadian boxing champion George Chuvalo, has been fighting back the only way he knows how. He's been travelling across Canada, visiting every high school that he can and warning kids about the danger of drugs. *Did Steven Chuvalo mean to kill himself or was it an accident? Could classical conditioning have contributed? How is classical conditioning involved in some cases of drug overdose?*

① TYPES OF LEARNING

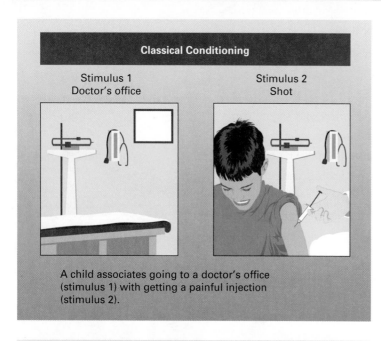

Classical Conditioning

Stimulus 1
Doctor's office

Stimulus 2
Shot

A child associates going to a doctor's office
(stimulus 1) with getting a painful injection
(stimulus 2).

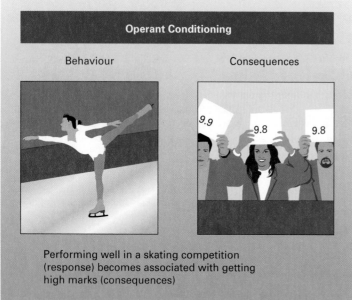

Operant Conditioning

Behaviour

Consequences

9.9   9.8   9.8

Performing well in a skating competition
(response) becomes associated with getting
high marks (consequences)

FIGURE 7.1

Associative Learning: Comparing Classical and Operant Conditioning

learning A relatively permanent change
in behaviour that occurs through experience.

associative learning Learning in which a
connection is made between two events.

What is learning?

In learning the alphabet, you made some mistakes along
the way, but at some point you learned all your letters.
Once you learned the alphabet, you didn't forget. Once
you learn how to drive a car, you do not have to go
through the process again at a later time. Through experience, you also learned that you have to study to do well
on a test, that it is more likely to snow in the winter, and
that a hat trick in hockey is scoring three goals in a game.
Putting these pieces together, we arrive at a definition of
learning: a relatively permanent change in behaviour
that occurs through experience. Psychologists explain our
many experiences with a few basic learning processes.

One common way we learn is through **associative
learning**, in which we make a connection or association
between two events (Domjan, 2006; Pearce & Bouton,
2001). *Conditioning* is the process of learning associations.
There are two types of conditioning: classical and operant
(Powell, Symbaluk, & MacDonald, 2005). In our opening
story about drug addiction, we focused on the type of
learning called *classical conditioning*, in which organisms
learn an association between two stimuli. As a result of
this association, organisms learn to anticipate events. Drug
addicts learn an association between "shooting up" and
the setting of their drug use. As another example, lightning is associated with thunder and regularly precedes it.
Thus, when you see lightning you anticipate that you will
hear thunder soon afterward.

In *operant conditioning*, organisms learn the association
between a behaviour and a consequence. As a result of
this association, organisms learn to increase behaviours
that are followed by rewards and decrease behaviours that
are followed by punishment. For example, children are
likely to repeat their good manners if their parents reward
them with praise after they have shown good manners.
Also, if children show bad manners that are followed by a
few nasty words and glances by parents, the children are
less likely to repeat the bad manners. Figure 7.1 compares
classical and operant conditioning.

A second type of learning is *observational learning*,
watching what other people do and say. Like it or not,
children learn many things by watching television. While
we often worry about what our children are watching on
television, over 1000 studies have documented the positive effects of *Sesame Street*,
which was specifically designed to improve children's cognitive and social skills (Fisch
& Truglio, 2001; Wright & others, 2001; Koolstra & others, 2004). Sesame Street continues to reach millions of households daily and has been broadcast in over 100 countries. Researchers have found that when regular Sesame Street viewers from low-
income families enter grade 1, they are rated as better prepared to learn in school than
their counterparts who don't watch the program regularly (Cole, Richman, & Brown,
2001; Wright & others, 2001).

Learning is not only extremely important in the lives of humans, but it is also vital
to lower animals. To survive and function in their world, animals such as rats and rabbits have to learn and adapt just as humans do. Much learning research has been done

with lower animals, largely because of the extensive control that researchers can exercise in studies on lower animals (e.g., Fanselow & Poulos, 2005). A century of research on learning in lower animals and in humans suggests that many of the principles generated initially in research on lower animals also apply to humans (Malott & Trojan Suarez, 2004; Mazur, 2006).

> **reflect and review**

 Explain what learning is.

- Define learning and distinguish between associative and observational and associative learning.

Think of a behaviour you engage in and describe how you learned it. Can you think of another example, in which you learned in a different way?

2 CLASSICAL CONDITIONING

— Definition of Classical Conditioning   — Applications of Classical Conditioning

What is classical conditioning?

It is a nice spring day. A father takes his baby out for a walk along the Bay of Fundy. The baby reaches over to touch a pink flower and is stung by a bumblebee sitting on the petals. The next day, the baby's mother brings home some pink flowers. She removes a flower from the arrangement and takes it over for her baby to smell. The baby cries loudly as soon as she sees the pink flower. The baby's panic at the sight of the pink flower illustrates the learning process of **classical conditioning**, in which a neutral stimulus (the flower) becomes associated with a meaningful stimulus (the pain of a bee sting) and acquires the capacity to elicit a similar response (fear).

Definition of Classical Conditioning

In the early 1900s, the Russian physiologist Ivan Pavlov was interested in the way the body digests food. In particular, he was interested in the role of salivation, which was then widely assumed to be an unchanging innate reflex. To study salivation, he routinely placed meat powder in a dog's mouth and measured how much the dog would salivate in response. Pavlov was surprised to find that the meat powder was not the only stimulus that caused the dog to salivate. As a dog was repeatedly studied, it would begin to salivate in response to a number of stimuli associated with the food, such as the sight of the food dish, the sight of the individual who brought the food into the room, and the sound of the door closing when the food arrived. Pavlov recognized that the dog's association of these sights and sounds with the food was an important type of learning, which came to be called classical conditioning.

Pavlov wanted to know how the dog learned to salivate to various sights and sounds before eating the meat powder. He observed that the dog's behaviour included both unlearned and learned components. The unlearned part of classical conditioning is based on the fact that some stimuli automatically produce certain responses apart from any prior learning; in other words, they are inborn or innate. *Reflexes* are automatic stimulus-response connections. They include salivation in response to food, nausea in response to spoiled food, shivering in response to low temperature, coughing in response to the throat being clogged, pupil constriction in response to light, and withdrawal in response to blows or burns. An **unconditioned stimulus (UCS)** is a

classical conditioning Learning by which a neutral stimulus becomes associated with a meaningful stimulus and acquires the capacity to elicit a similar response.

unconditioned stimulus (UCS) A stimulus that produces a response without prior learning.

Pavlov (the white-bearded gentleman in the centre) is shown demonstrating the nature of classical conditioning to students at the Military Medical Academy in Russia.

stimulus that produces a response without prior learning; food was the UCS in Pavlov's experiments. An **unconditioned response** (**UCR**) is an unlearned response that is automatically elicited by the UCS. In Pavlov's experiment, the saliva that flowed from the dog's mouth in response to food was the UCR.

In studying the salivary response, Pavlov rang a bell before giving meat powder to a dog. Until then, ringing the bell did not affect the dog much, except perhaps to wake it from a nap. The bell was a neutral stimulus with respect to salivation. But when the dog began to associate the bell's sound with the food and salivated when it heard the bell, the bell became a conditioned (learned) stimulus (CS) and the salivation a conditioned response (CR). During *acquisition*, then, repeated CS-UCS pairings have the effect of strengthening the conditioned association. Before conditioning, the bell and the food were unrelated. After their association, the bell (now a CS) produced a CR (salivation).

In classical conditioning, the **conditioned stimulus** (**CS**) is a previously neutral stimulus that eventually elicits the conditioned response after being associated with the unconditioned stimulus. The **conditioned response** (**CR**) is the learned response to the conditioned stimulus that occurs after CS-UCS pairing (Pavlov, 1927). In the case of the baby and the flower, the baby's learning and experience did not cause her to cry when the bee stung her. Her crying was unlearned and occurred automatically. The bee's sting was the UCS and the crying was the UCR. For the unhappy baby, the flower was the baby's bell, or CS, and crying was the CR after the sting (UCS) and the flower (CS) were paired. In the case of drug addiction, the drug addict's learning and experience do not cause any compensatory response by itself. The compensatory tolerance response is unlearned and automatically occurs in response to drug use. The drug use is the UCS and the tolerance response is the UCR. For the drug addict, the setting of drug use is the addict's bell, or CS, and a compensatory response is the CR after the drug itself (UCS) and the setting of drug use (CS) are paired. A summary of how classical conditioning works is shown in figure 7.2.

Acquisition Acquisition in classical conditioning is the initial learning of the stimulus-response link. This involves a neutral stimulus being associated with the UCS and becoming the conditioned stimulus (CS) that elicits the CR. Two important aspects of acquisition are timing and contingency/predictability.

The time interval between the CS and the UCS is one of the most important aspects of classical conditioning (Weidemann, Georgilas, & Kehoe, 1999). Conditioned responses develop when the CS and UCS are contiguous, occurring close together. *Contiguity* refers to the connectedness in time and space of the stimuli. Often, optimal spacing is a second or two (Domjan. 2005). In Pavlov's work, if the bell had rung 20 minutes before or after the presentation of the food, the dog would not have associated the bell with the food.

unconditioned response (UCR) An unlearned response that is automatically elicited by the UCS.

conditioned stimulus (CS) A previously neutral stimulus that eventually elicits the conditioned response after being associated with the unconditioned stimulus.

conditioned response (CR) The learned response to the conditioned stimulus that occurs after the CS-UCS pairing.

acquisition (in classical conditioning) The initial learning of the stimulus-response link, which involves a neutral stimulus being associated with a UCS and becoming a conditioned stimulus (CS) that elicits the CR.

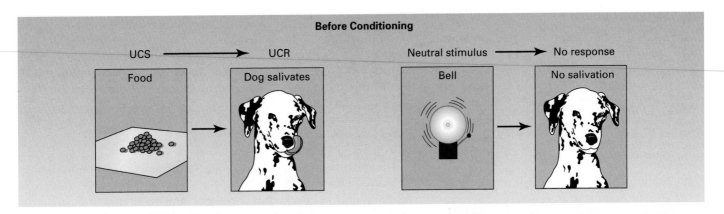

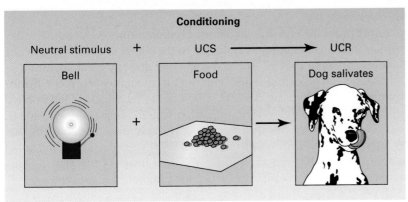
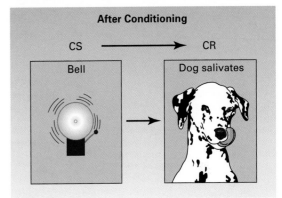

FIGURE 7.2 Pavlov's Classical Conditioning
In one experiment, Pavlov presented a neutral stimulus (bell) just before an unconditioned stimulus (food). The neutral stimulus became a conditioned stimulus by being paired with the unconditioned stimulus. Subsequently, the conditioned stimulus (bell) by itself was able to elicit the dog's salivation.

Robert Rescorla (1988, 2003) believes that, for classical conditioning to take place, it is important to have not only contiguity in the CS-UCS connection but also *contingency*. Contingency in classical conditioning means the predictability of the occurrence of one stimulus from the presence of another. If one stimulus is only occasionally followed closely by another, the occasional co-occurrences may be contiguous but the overall relationship is not terribly contingent. For example, we mentioned lightning and thunder earlier. Not only is lightning followed fairly soon by thunder (contiguity), lightning is often followed by thunder (contingency). Thus, if you see lightning, you might put your hands over your ears or lean away in anticipation of the thunder.

Generalization and Discrimination Pavlov found that the dog salivated in response not only to the tone of the bell but also to other sounds, such as a whistle. Pavlov did not pair these sounds with the unconditioned stimulus of the food. He discovered that the more similar the noise was to the original sound of the bell, the stronger was the dog's salivary flow. **Generalization** in classical conditioning is the tendency of a new stimulus that is similar to the original conditioned stimulus to elicit a response that is similar to the conditioned response (Jones, Kemenes, & Benjamin, 2001). The value of generalization is that it prevents learning from being tied to specific stimuli. For example, we do not have to learn to drive all over again when we change cars or drive down a different road.

Stimulus generalization is not always beneficial. For example, the cat that generalizes from a minnow to a piranha has a major problem; therefore it is also important to discriminate between stimuli. **Discrimination** in classical conditioning is the process of learning to respond to certain stimuli and not to respond to others (Murphy, Baker, & Fouquet, 2001). To produce discrimination, Pavlov gave food to the dog only

generalization (in classical conditioning) The tendency of a new stimulus that is similar to the original stimulus to elicit a response that is similar to the conditioned response.

discrimination (in classical conditioning) The process of learning to respond to certain stimuli and not to others.

after ringing the bell and not after any other sounds. In this way, the dog learned to distinguish between the bell and other sounds.

Many multiple-choice tests place a premium on carefully discriminating among items. Professors often deliberately include very similar items that require you to make fine discriminations in selecting the one correct answer from three or four possibilities.

Extinction and Spontaneous Recovery After conditioning the dog to salivate at the sound of a bell, Pavlov rang the bell repeatedly in a single session and did not give the dog any food. Eventually the dog stopped salivating. This result is **extinction**, which, in classical conditioning, is the weakening of the conditioned response in the absence of the unconditioned stimulus (Bouton, 2004). Without continued association with the unconditioned stimulus (UCS), the conditioned stimulus (CS) loses its power to elicit the conditioned response (CR).

Extinction is not always the end of a conditioned response (Brooks, 2000). The day after Pavlov extinguished the conditioned salivation to the sound of a bell, he took the dog to the laboratory and rang the bell, still not giving the dog any meat powder. The dog salivated, indicating that an extinguished response can spontaneously recur. **Spontaneous recovery** is the process in classical conditioning by which a conditioned response can recur after a time delay without further conditioning (Rescorla, 2004). Consider an example of spontaneous recovery you may have had: You thought that you had totally forgotten about (extinguished) an old "love" you once had. Then, all of a sudden, you are in a particular context and get a mental image of the person along with an emotional reaction to him or her from the past (spontaneous recovery).

Figure 7.3 shows the sequence of acquisition, extinction, and spontaneous recovery. Spontaneous recovery can occur several times, but as long as the conditioned stimulus is presented alone, spontaneous recovery becomes weaker and eventually stops occurring (Goddard, 1997; Mazur, 2006).

Here is one more example to help you understand acquisition, generalization, discrimination, and extinction in classical conditioning.

- *Acquisition.* A young child learns to fear (CR) going to a dentist's office by associating it with the unlearned emotional response (UCR) to the pain of having a tooth cavity filled (UCS).
- *Generalization.* The child fears all dentists' offices and similar places, including doctors' offices and the adults in them who wear white medical clothing, as well as the smells and sounds in them.
- *Discrimination.* The child goes with his mother to her doctor's office and learns that it is not associated with the pain of the UCS.
- *Extinction.* The child subsequently goes to the dentist on a number of occasions and does not have a painful experience, so his fear of dentists' offices goes away, at least for a while, until he has another painful experience with a cavity being filled.

While negative dental experiences at any age can lead to dental fears (Liddell & Locker, 2000), researchers have found that the majority of dental fears originate in childhood, likely through classical conditioning, and that these fears can keep individuals from obtaining future dental treatment as adults (Ost, 1991).

Interestingly, there are cultural variations in children's dental fear (Folayan, Idehen, & Ojo, 2004). Some reports suggests that children in the United States have the most fear (20 percent have a high level of fear), and children in Norway and Sweden have the least fear (only 3 to 4 percent have a high level of fear; Milgram, Vigehesa, & Weinstein, 1992; Neverlien & Johnsen, 1991). This cultural difference may be due to dental care being part of a free, universal health care system in Norway and Sweden. Consequently, children there go to the dentist on a regular basis, regardless of whether they have a dental problem or not. It is possible that for these children, the link between the dentist and pain is not highly contingent (Rescorla, 2003). By contrast, the United States does not have a universal health care system, and children often go to the

extinction (in classical conditioning) The weakening of the conditioned response in the absence of the unconditioned stimulus.

spontaneous recovery The process in classical conditioning by which a conditioned response can recur after a time delay without further conditioning.

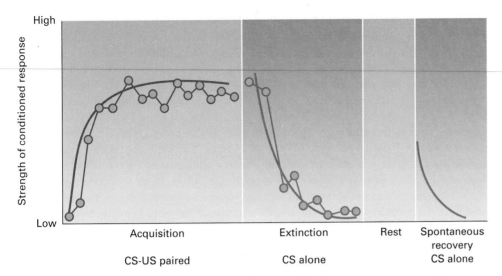

FIGURE 7.3 **The Strength of a Classically Conditioned Response During Acquisition, Extinction, and Spontaneous Recovery** During acquisition the conditioned stimulus (CS) and unconditioned stimulus (UCS) are associated. The dots are actual data points and the curve represents the ideal. As can be seen, when this occurs, the strength of the conditioned response (CR) increases. During extinction the CS is presented alone and, as can be seen, this results in a decrease of the CR. After a rest period, spontaneous recovery appears, although the strength of the CR is not nearly as great at this point as it was after a number of CS-UCS pairings. When the CS is presented alone again after spontaneous recovery, the response is extinguished rapidly.

dentist only when they have a problem, thus experiencing dental treatment as painful and something to be avoided. For American children, the link between the dentist and pain may be much more contingent and thus likely to condition a fearful association.

Applications of Classical Conditioning

Since Pavlov conducted his experiments, humans have been conditioned to respond to the sound of a buzzer, a glimpse of light, a puff of air, or the touch of a hand (Wills, 2005). Classical conditioning has a great deal of survival value for the individual. Because of classical conditioning, we jerk our hands away before they are burned by fire. Classical conditioning is also at work when a description of a tranquil scene, such as an empty beach with waves lapping the sand, causes a harried executive to relax as if she were actually lying on that beach.

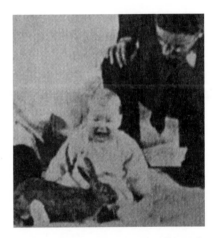

In 1920, Watson and Rayner conditioned 11-month-old Albert to fear a white rat by pairing the rat with a loud noise. When little Albert was subsequently presented with other stimuli similar to the white rat, such as the rabbit shown here with little Albert, he was afraid of them, too. This illustrates the principle of stimulus generalization in classical conditioning. *What are some other examples of generalization in classical conditioning?*

Explaining and Eliminating Fears A *phobia* is an irrational fear. Classical conditioning provides an explanation of these and other fears. John Watson and Rosalie Rayner (1920) demonstrated classical conditioning's role in phobias with an infant named Albert. They showed Albert a white laboratory rat, to see if he was afraid of it. He was not. As Albert played with the rat, a loud noise was sounded behind his head. As you might imagine, the noise caused little Albert to cry. After only seven pairings of the loud noise with the white rat, Albert began to fear the rat even when the noise was not sounded. Albert's fear was generalized to a rabbit, a dog, and a sealskin coat.

Today, Watson and Rayner's (1920) study would violate Canadian ethical guidelines. Especially noteworthy is the fact that the experimenters did not reverse Albert's fear of furry objects, so presumably this phobia remained with him after the experiment. In the early part of the twentieth century, when the experiment with little Albert was conducted, there was less concern about the ethical aspects of research. As we saw in chapter 2, today research psychologists must adhere to strict ethical guidelines.

Watson was right in concluding that many of our fears can be learned through classical conditioning. We might develop a fear of the dentist because of a painful experience, fear of driving after having been in an automobile accident, and fear of dogs after having been bitten by one.

If we can produce fears through classical conditioning, then we should be able to eliminate them using conditioning procedures (e.g., Paunovic, 2002). **Counterconditioning** is a classical conditioning procedure for weakening a CR by associating the fear-provoking stimulus with a new response that is incompatible with the fear. Though Watson was never given the opportunity to eliminate little Albert's fear of white rats, an associate of Watson's, Mary Cover Jones (1924), did eliminate the fears of a three-year-old boy named Peter. Peter had many of the same fears as Albert; however, Peter's fears were not produced by Jones. Among Peter's fears were white rats, fur coats, frogs, fish, and mechanical toys. To eliminate these fears, Jones brought a rabbit into Peter's view but kept it far enough away that it would not upset him. At the same time the rabbit was brought into view, Peter was fed crackers and milk. On each successive day the rabbit was moved closer to Peter as he ate crackers and milk. Eventually Peter reached a point at which he would eat the food with one hand and pet the rabbit with the other. The feeling of pleasure produced by the crackers and milk was incompatible with the fear produced by the rabbit, and Peter's fear was extinguished through counterconditioning. Two types of counterconditioning, systematic desensitization and aversive conditioning, are discussed in more detail in chapter 14.

Explaining Pleasant Emotions   Classical conditioning is not restricted to unpleasant emotions, such as fear. Among the things in our lives that produce pleasure because they have become conditioned might be the sight of a rainbow, a sunny day, or a favourite song. If you have a positive romantic experience, the location in which that experience took place can become a conditioned stimulus. This is the result of the pairing of a place (CS) with the event (UCS). Stimuli that are often associated with sex, such as mood music, seductive clothing, a romantic restaurant, and so on, likely become conditioned stimuli that produce sexual arousal.

Sometimes, though, classical conditioning involves an experience that is both pleasant and deviant from the norm. Consider a fetishist who becomes sexually aroused by the sight and touch of certain clothing, such as undergarments or shoes. The fetish may have developed when the fetish object (undergarment, shoe) was associated with sexual arousal, especially when the individual was young. The fetish object becomes a conditioned stimulus that can produce sexual arousal by itself (Chance, 2006).

Explaining Health Problems   Some of the behaviours we associate with health problems or mental disorders can be attributed to classical conditioning. Certain physical complaints—asthma, headaches, ulcers, and high blood pressure, for example—can be partly the products of classical conditioning. We usually say that such health problems are caused by stress, but often what happens is that certain stimuli, such as a boss's critical attitude or a wife's threat of divorce, are conditioned stimuli for physiological responses. Over time, the frequent presence of the physiological responses may produce a health problem or disorder. A boss's persistent criticism may cause an employee to develop muscle tension, headaches, or high blood pressure. Anything associated with the boss, such as work itself, can then trigger stress in the employee (see figure 7.4).

Classical conditioning can also be involved in certain aspects of drug use. Pavlov realized that conditioned reflexes are important in digestion. The digestive process begins before the food is eaten, as soon as food is seen or smelled. This reaction is similar to the response that occurs in the body before a drug arrives. When drugs are administered in particular circumstances—at a particular time of day, in a particular location, or in a particular ritual—the body reacts in anticipation of receiving the drug. As we saw at the beginning of the chapter, the conditioning aspect of drug use can even play a role in deaths caused by drug overdoses.

Classical conditioning also plays a role in withdrawal from addictive drugs like morphine. Morphine withdrawal can be precipitated by no longer using morphine or by administering Naloxone, a drug that counteracts the effects of morphine. Linda Parker, of Wilfred Laurier University, has shown that the administration of opiate *agonists*, like

counterconditioning A classical conditioning procedure for weakening a CR by associating the fear-provoking stimulus with a new response that is incompatible with the fear.

Naloxone, to rats who are addicted to morphine not only produces withdrawal, it also produces place aversion (Parker & Joshi, 1998). The very unpleasant feeling of withdrawal that is precipitated by Naloxone rapidly becomes associated with the place where the withdrawal was experienced. The result is a tendency for the rats to avoid that place in the future. Curiously, morphine itself produces taste aversion (Siegel, Parker, & Moroz, 1995). Rats avoid eating food with tastes that they have previously associated with consuming morphine. These results indicate that classical conditioning principles should be taken into account in the design of programs to help drug addicts overcome their addictions.

One surprising result is that classical conditioning can influence immune system functioning, which is important for producing antibodies to ward off disease and illness, such as AIDS and the flu (e.g., Pacheco-Lopez & others, 2005). In a classic study, Robert Ader, of the University of Rochester was examining how long a conditioned response would last in some laboratory rats (Ader, 1974). A conditioned stimulus (a saccharin solution) was paired with an unconditioned stimulus, a drug called Cytoxan, which induces nausea. Afterward, while giving the rats saccharin-laced water without the accompanying Cytoxan, Ader watched to see how long it would take the rats to extinguish the association between the two.

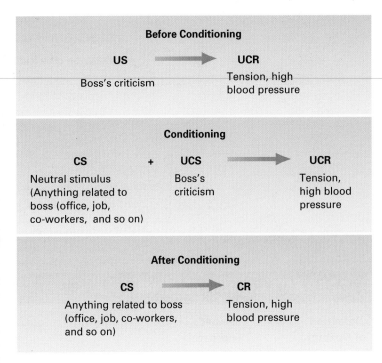

FIGURE 7.4

Classical Conditioning: Boss's Criticism and High Blood Pressure

Unexpectedly, in the second month of the study, the rats developed a disease and began to die off. In analyzing the unforeseen result, Ader investigated the properties of the nausea-inducing drug he had used. He discovered that one of its side effects was *immunosuppression* (a decrease in the production of antibodies). Thus it turned out that the rats had been classically conditioned to associate a saccharin solution not only with nausea but also with the shutdown of the immune system. The saccharin solution apparently had become a CS for immunosuppression (Ader, 1974, 2003; Ader & Cohen, 1975, 2000). Researchers have found that conditioned immune responses also may occur in humans (Ader, 2000; 2003).

Studying Consumer Psychology *Consumer psychology* is the study of how consumers think, feel, reason, and select between different alternatives, such as brands and products. Many contemporary advertisers use classical conditioning in some way (Priluck & Till, 2004). Consider this sequence:

- Beautiful woman (UCS) → emotional arousal (UCR) in heterosexual males
- Beautiful woman (UCS) paired with a particular make of automobile (not yet a CS) many times
- Automobile (CS) → emotional arousal (CR)

Fortunately, advertisers cannot automatically program television viewers. Research has shown that the viewer must be aware that the CS is preceding the UCS for conditioning to be effective (Priluck & Till, 2004). In other words, if the viewer notices only the beautiful woman or the car, conditioning will not occur (Priluck & Till, 2004). If the conditioned stimulus is encountered outside of ads, it doesn't predict the UCS (Bettman, 2001). Further, classical conditioning may work best for infrequently encountered products and cases in which the UCS is associated with only one brand.

Not all commercials involve classical conditioning. Some just give information about the product. The next time you watch TV, observe which ads are relying on classical conditioning to get their message across. Note what the UCS, UCR, CS, and CR are in the ads.

> **reflect and review**

2 **Describe classical conditioning.**

- Summarize the classical conditioning process. Include in your description the following terms: unconditioned stimulus (UCS), conditioned stimulus (CS), unconditioned response (UCR), and conditioned response (CR), as well as acquisition, generalization, discrimination, and extinction/spontaneous recovery.
- Discuss the role of classical conditioning in human phobias and specify other types of behaviour that involve classical conditioning.

Think about an attachment that you or someone you know has for a certain object or environment. Explain how classical conditioning might account for the pleasant association.

3 OPERANT CONDITIONING

| Definition of Operant Conditioning | Skinner's Approach to Operant Conditioning | Shaping | Generalization, Discrimination, and Extinction | Principles of Reinforcement and Punishment | Applications of Operant Conditioning |

What is operant conditioning?

Classical conditioning helps us to learn about our environment, but we learn about our world in other ways, too. Classical conditioning describes an organism's *response* to the environment, a view that fails to capture the active nature of the organism and its influence on the environment. Another major form of learning—instrumental conditioning, more commonly referred to by B. F. Skinner's term, operant conditioning—places more emphasis on the organism's activity in the environment (Benjafield, 2004).

Definition of Operant Conditioning

Recall from the beginning of the chapter that classical conditioning and operant conditioning are forms of associative learning, which involves learning that two events are connected. In classical conditioning, organisms learn the association between two stimuli (UCS and CS). Classical conditioning is a form of *respondent behaviour*, behaviour that occurs in automatic response to a stimulus, such as a nausea-producing drug, and later to a conditioned stimulus, such as saccharin-laced water, that was paired with the drug. Classical conditioning excels at explaining how neutral stimuli become associated with unlearned, *involuntary* responses, but it is not as effective in explaining *voluntary* behaviours, such as studying hard for a test, playing slot machines at Casino Niagara, or a pigeon playing ping-pong. Operant conditioning is usually much better at explaining such voluntary behaviours.

Although Skinner emerged as the primary figure in operant conditioning, the experiments of E. L. Thorndike established the power of consequences in determining voluntary behaviour (Mook, 2004). At about the same time that Pavlov was conducting classical conditioning experiments with salivating dogs, Thorndike, an American psychologist, was studying cats in puzzle boxes. Thorndike put a hungry cat inside a box and a piece of fish outside. To escape from the box and obtain the food, the cat had to learn how to open the latch inside the box. At first the cat made a number of ineffective responses. It clawed or bit at the bars and thrust its paw through the openings. Eventually the cat accidentally stepped on the treadle that released the door bolt. When the cat was returned to the box, it went through the same random activity until it stepped on the treadle once more. On subsequent trials, the cat made fewer and fewer random movements, until finally it immediately stepped on the treadle to open the door (see figure 7.5). The **law of effect**,

law of effect Thorndike's concept that behaviours followed by positive outcomes are strengthened, whereas behaviours followed by negative outcomes are weakened.

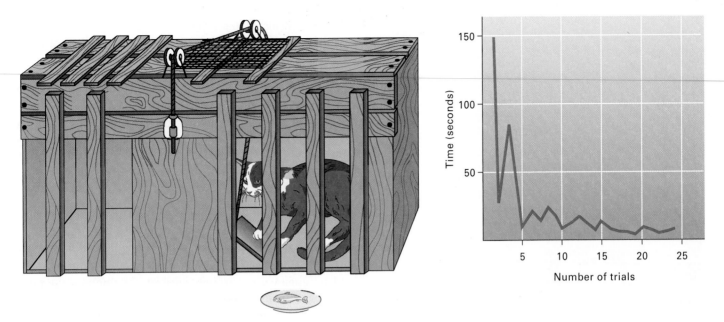

FIGURE 7.5   **Thorndike's Puzzle Box and the Law of Effect**

(*Left*) A box typical of the puzzle boxes Thorndike used in his experiments with cats to study the law of effect. Stepping on the treadle released the door bolt; a weight attached to the door then pulled the door open and allowed the cat to escape. After accidentally pressing the treadle as it tried to get to the food, the cat learned to press the treadle when it wanted to escape the box. (*Right*) One cat's learning curve over 24 separate trials. Notice that the cat escaped much more quickly after about 5 trials. It had learned the consequences of its behaviour.

developed by Thorndike, states that behaviours followed by positive outcomes are strengthened, whereas behaviours followed by negative outcomes are weakened.

The key question for Thorndike was how the correct stimulus-response bond strengthens and eventually dominates incorrect stimulus-response bonds. According to Thorndike, the correct stimulus-response (S-R) association strengthens and the incorrect association weakens because of the *consequences* of the organism's actions. Thorndike's view is called *S-R theory* because the organism's behaviour is due to a connection between a stimulus and a response.

As American psychologist B.F. Skinner expanded Thorndike's basic ideas, he developed the concept of operant conditioning (Skinner, 1938). **Operant conditioning** (or instrumental conditioning) is a form of associative learning in which the consequences of behaviour produce changes in the probability of a behaviour's occurrence. Skinner chose the term *operant* to describe the behaviour of the organism—the behaviour operates on the environment, and the environment in turn operates on the behaviour. As an example, in operant conditioning performing a great skateboarding routine in competition (behaviour) is likely to result in a high score from the judges (consequences), which in turn encourages the skateboarder to continue training and competing. Thus, whereas classical conditioning involves respondent behaviour, operant conditioning consists of *operant behaviour*, voluntary behaviour that acts or operates on the environment and may result in rewarding or punishing stimuli.

Recall that earlier we said *contingency* is an important aspect of classical conditioning in which the occurrence of one stimulus can be predicted from the presence of another one. Contingency is also important in operant conditioning. For example, when a rat pushes a lever (behaviour) that delivers food, the delivery of food (consequence) is *contingent* on that behaviour.

Skinner's Approach to Operant Conditioning

Skinner strongly believed that the mechanisms of learning are the same for all species. This conviction led him to study animals in the hope that he could discover

operant conditioning Also called instrumental conditioning; a form of learning in which the consequences of behaviour change the probability of the behaviour's occurrence.

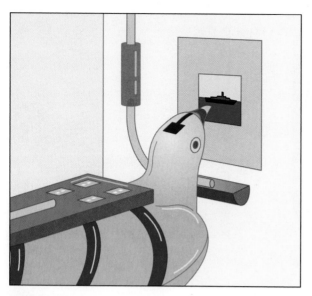

FIGURE 7.6

Skinner's Pigeon-Guided Missile
Skinner wanted to help the military during World War II by using pigeons' tracking behaviour. A gold electrode covered the tip of the pigeons' beaks. Contact with the screen on which the image of the target was projected sent a signal informing the missile's control mechanism of the target's location. A few grains of food occasionally given to the pigeons maintained their tracking behaviour.

FIGURE 7.7

The Skinner Box
B. F. Skinner conducting an operant conditioning study in his behavioural laboratory. The rat being studied is in a Skinner box.

shaping The process of rewarding approximations of desired behaviour.

the basic mechanisms of learning with organisms simpler than humans. During World War II, Skinner carried out an unusual study that involved a pigeon-guided missile. A pigeon in the warhead of the missile operated the flaps on the missile and guided it home by pecking at an image of a target. How could this possibly work? When the missile was in flight, the pigeon pecked the moving image on a screen, being rewarded with food to keep the designated target in the centre of the screen. This produced corrective signals to keep the missile on its course. The pigeons did their job well in trial runs, but top Navy officials just could not accept pigeons piloting their missiles in a war. Skinner, however, congratulated himself on the degree of control he was able to exercise over the pigeons (see figure 7.6).

Following up on his research with pigeons, Skinner (1948) wrote *Walden Two*, a novel in which he presented his ideas about building a scientifically managed society. Skinner envisioned a utopian society that could be engineered through operant conditioning. Skinner viewed existing societies as poorly managed because people believe in the myth of free will. He pointed out that humans are no freer than pigeons are and that denying that environmental forces control our behaviour is to ignore science and reality. Skinner believed that in the long run we would be much happier when we recognized such truths, especially his concept that operant conditioning would provide us with prosperous lives.

Skinner, and other behaviourists, made every effort to study organisms under precisely controlled conditions so that the connection between the operant and the specific consequences could be examined in minute detail (Mazur, 2006). One of his creations in the 1930s to control experimental conditions was the operant chamber, or Skinner box (see figure 7.7). A device in the box would deliver food pellets into a tray at random. After a rat became accustomed to the box, Skinner installed a lever and observed the rat's behaviour. As the hungry rat explored the box, it occasionally pressed the lever, and a food pellet would be dispensed. Soon the rat learned that the consequences of pressing the lever were positive: It would be fed. Further control was achieved by soundproofing the box to ensure that the experimenter was the only influence on the organism. In many of the experiments, the responses were mechanically recorded, and the food (the stimulus) was dispensed automatically. Such precautions were designed to avoid human error.

Shaping

Just as in classical conditioning, operant conditioning must be acquired. In Thorndike's version, cats were allowed to take as much time as they required in order to learn to escape from the puzzle boxes. Skinner discovered that when a behaviour takes time to occur, the learning process in operant conditioning can be shortened by rewarding an approximation of the desired behaviour (Peterson, 2004; Silverstein, Menditto, & Stuve, 2001). **Shaping** is the process of rewarding approximations of desired behaviour. In one situation, parents used shaping to toilet train their two-year-old son. The parents knew all too well that the grunting sound the child made signalled he was about to fill his diaper. In the first week they gave him candy if they heard the sound within about 6 metres of the bathroom. The second week he was given candy only if he grunted within about 3 metres of the bathroom, the third week only if he was in the bathroom, and the fourth week, he had to use the toilet to get the candy (Fischer & Gochros, 1975). It worked!

Shaping is extensively used in training animals. For example, shaping can be used to train a rat to press a bar to obtain food. When a rat is first placed in a Skinner box, it rarely presses the bar. Thus the experimenter may start off by giving the rat a food pellet

Animal trainers coax some amazing behaviours from their star performers. *What type of special conditioning is often used by animal trainers?*

if it is in the same half of the cage as the bar. Then the rat's behaviour might be rewarded only when it is within 5 centimetres of the bar, then only when it touches the bar, and finally only when it presses the bar.

Shaping is also used to train animals to perform tricks. A dolphin that jumps through a hoop held high above the water has been trained to perform this behaviour through shaping. Similarly, you can also use shaping to teach a dog tricks. For example, say that you want to teach a dog to "shake a paw" with you. You first speak the command to "shake a paw" and then wait until the dog moves one of its forepaws a little bit (operant behaviour). Following this behaviour, you give your dog a food treat (consequence). After requiring increasingly closer approximations to shaking your hand, the dog finally performs the desired behaviour to the verbal command "shake a paw."

Shaping can be used effectively in educational classrooms (Santrock & others, 2004). Suppose a teacher has a student who has never completed more than 50 percent of her math assignments. The teacher sets the target behaviour at 100 percent but rewards her for successive approximations to the target. The teacher might initially provide a reward (some type of privilege, for example) when she completes 70 percent, then 80, then 90, and finally 100 percent. Shaping can be especially helpful for learning tasks that require time and persistence to complete.

Generalization, Discrimination, and Extinction

Remember that generalization, discrimination, and extinction are important classical conditioning principles. They are also important principles in operant conditioning, but they are defined somewhat differently.

Generalization   In operant conditioning, **generalization** means giving the same response to similar stimuli (Powell, Symbaluk, & MacDonald, 2005). For example, in one classic study pigeons were reinforced for pecking at a disk of a particular colour (Guttman & Kalish, 1956). To assess stimulus generalization, researchers presented the pigeons with discs of varying colours. As shown in figure 7.8, the pigeons were most likely to peck at the disc closest in colour to the original. An example from everyday life involves a student who has great success in dating people who dress neatly and not such good results with people who dress sloppily. The student subsequently seeks dates with people who dress neatly, the neater the better, and avoids dating sloppy dressers, especially the sloppiest.

Discrimination   In operant conditioning, **discrimination** means responding to stimuli that signal that a behaviour will or will not be reinforced (Malott, & Trojan Suarez,

generalization (in operant conditioning) Giving the same response to similar stimuli.

discrimination (in operant conditioning) The tendency to only respond to stimuli that signal whether a behaviour will or will not be reinforced.

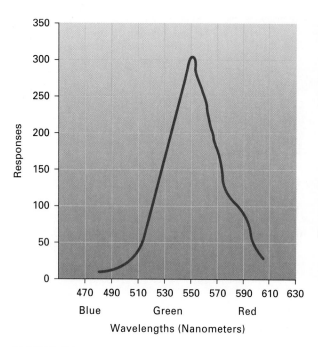

FIGURE 7.8

Stimulus Generalization

In the experiment by Guttman and Kalish (1956), pigeons initially pecked a disc of a particular colour (in this graph, a green disc with a wavelength of 550 nanometres) after they had been reinforced for this wavelength. Subsequently, when the pigeons were presented discs of colours with varying wavelengths, they were more likely to peck discs that were similar to the original disc.

"Once it became clear to me that, by responding correctly to certain stimuli, I could get all the bananas I wanted, getting this job was a pushover."

©1999 Jack Ziegler from cartoonbank.com. All Rights Reserved.

2004; Spector & Kopka, 2002). For example, you might look at two street signs, both made of metal, both the same colour, and both with words on them. However, one sign says "Enter at your own risk" and the other says, "Please walk this way." The words serve as discriminative stimuli because the sign that says, "Please walk this way" indicates that you will be rewarded for doing so. However, the sign that says, "Enter at your own risk" suggests that the consequences may not be positive. As another example, consider that football players are far likelier to tackle people in a football stadium than in a church. Furthermore, they tackle people in a uniform with certain colours (the opposing team's rather than their own). They also don't tackle certain other people in uniforms, such as cheerleaders and referees.

Extinction In operant conditioning, **extinction** occurs when a previously reinforced behaviour is no longer reinforced and there is a decreased tendency to perform the behaviour (Domjan, 2006; Conklin & Tiffany, 2002). For example, a factory worker gets a monthly bonus for producing more than her quota. Then, as a part of economic tightening, the company decides that it can no longer afford the bonuses. When bonuses were given, the worker's productivity was above quota every month; once the bonus was removed, her performance decreased. Spontaneous recovery also characterizes the operant form of extinction.

Principles of Reinforcement and Punishment

Operant behaviours are shaped by their consequences. When followed by reinforcement, operant behaviours are more likely to occur again. When followed by punishment, operant behaviours are less likely to occur again.

Positive and Negative Reinforcement **Reinforcement** is the process by which a stimulus or event strengthens or increases the probability of a behaviour or an event that it follows. Behavioural psychologists have developed a number of principles of reinforcement, including a distinction between positive and negative reinforcement. In **positive reinforcement**, the frequency of a behaviour increases because it is followed by a rewarding stimulus. For example, if someone you meet smiles at you after you say, "Hello, how are you?" and you keep talking, the smile has reinforced your talking. The same principle of positive reinforcement is at work when you teach a dog to "shake a paw" by giving it a piece of food when it lifts its paw (Watling & Schwartz, 2004).

Conversely, in **negative reinforcement**, the frequency of a behaviour increases because it is followed by the removal of an aversive (unpleasant) stimulus. For example, if your father nagged you to clean out the garage and kept nagging until you cleaned it, your response (cleaning out the garage) removed the unpleasant stimulus (nagging). Taking an aspirin when you have a headache works the same way. A reduction of pain reinforces the act of taking an aspirin.

To understand the distinction between positive and negative reinforcement, remember that "positive" and "negative" do not have anything to do with "good" and "bad." Just remember that they are processes in which something is given (positive reinforcement) or something is removed (negative reinforcement). Figure 7.9 provides some other examples to further help you understand the distinction between positive and negative reinforcement.

Positive Reinforcement

Behaviour	Rewarding Stimulus Provided	Future Behaviour
You turn in homework on time	Teacher praises your performance	You increasingly turn in homework on time
You wax your skis	The skis go faster	You wax your skis the next time you go skiing
You randomly press a button on the dashboard of a friend's car	Great music begins to play	You deliberately press the button again the next time you get into the car

Negative Reinforcement

Behaviour	Unpleasant Stimulus Removed	Future Behaviour
You turn in homework on time	Teacher stops criticizing late homework	You increasingly turn in homework on time
You wax your skis	People stop zooming by you on the slope	You wax your skis the next time
You randomly press a button on the dashboard of a friend's car	An annoying song shuts off	You deliberately press the button again the next time the annoying song is on

FIGURE 7.9 Positive and Negative Reinforcement

Primary and Secondary Reinforcement Positive reinforcement can be classified as primary or secondary reinforcement, based on whether the behaviour is inborn and unlearned or learned. **Primary reinforcement** involves the use of reinforcers that are innately satisfying; that is, they do not take any learning on the organism's part to make them pleasurable. Food, water, and sexual satisfaction are primary reinforcers.

Secondary reinforcement acquires its positive value through experience; secondary reinforcers are learned or conditioned reinforcers. We encounter hundreds of secondary reinforcers in our lives, such as getting a pat on the back, praise, and eye contact. One popular story in psychology focuses on the use of eye contact as a secondary reinforcer to shape the behaviour of a famous university professor, an expert on operant conditioning. Some students decided to train the professor to lecture from one corner of the classroom. They used eye contact as a reinforcer and began reinforcing successive approximations to the desired response. Each time the professor moved toward the appropriate corner, the students would look at him. If he moved in another direction, they looked away. By gradually rewarding successive approximations to the desired response, the students were able to get the professor to deliver his lecture from just one corner of the classroom. The professor denies that this shaping ever took place. Whether it did or not, the story provides an excellent example of how secondary reinforcers can be used to shape behaviour in real life (Chance, 2006).

Another example helps to illustrate the importance of secondary reinforcement in our everyday lives. When a student is given $25 for an A on her report card, the $25 is a secondary reinforcer. It is not innate, and it increases the likelihood that the student will work to get another A in the future. When an object can be exchanged for some other reinforcer, the object may have reinforcing value itself, so it is called a *token reinforcer*. Money, gift certificates, and poker chips are often referred to as token reinforcers.

Schedules of Reinforcement Most of the examples of reinforcement we have discussed so far have involved *continuous reinforcement*, in which a behaviour is reinforced every time it occurs. When continuous reinforcement occurs, organisms learn rapidly. However, when reinforcement stops, extinction also takes place quickly. If a pay telephone we often use starts "eating" our coins and not giving us a dial tone, we quickly stop putting in more coins. However, several weeks later, we might try it again, hoping it now works properly (this behaviour illustrates spontaneous recovery).

extinction (in operant conditioning)
A previously reinforced behaviour is no longer reinforced, and there is a decreased tendency to perform the behaviour.

reinforcement The process by which a stimulus or event strengthens or increases the probability of an event that it follows.

positive reinforcement The frequency of a behaviour increases because it is followed by a rewarding stimulus.

negative reinforcement The frequency of a behaviour increases because it is followed by the removal of an aversive (unpleasant) stimulus.

primary reinforcement The use of reinforcers that are innately satisfying.

secondary reinforcement Acquires its positive value through experience.

Slot machines are on a variable-ratio schedule of reinforcement. *Why?*

Partial reinforcement follows a behaviour only a portion of the time (Sangha & others, 2002). Most of life's experiences involve partial reinforcement. A golfer does not win every tournament she enters; a chess whiz does not win every match he plays; a student is not patted on the back each time she solves a problem. **Schedules of reinforcement** are "timetables" that determine when a behaviour will be reinforced. The four main schedules of reinforcement are fixed ratio, variable ratio, fixed interval, and variable interval.

A *fixed-ratio schedule* reinforces a behaviour after a set number of behaviours. Fixed-ratio schedules are often used to increase production. For example, a salesperson might have to sell a specific number of items to get a commission. Also referred to as "piece work," such schedules are commonly used in Canada's fruit growing regions, where a picker might be paid for every 5 or 10 pints of fruit picked. One characteristic of fixed-ratio schedules is that performance often drops off just after reinforcement.

In contrast, slot machines are on a *variable-ratio schedule*, a timetable in which behaviours are rewarded an average number of times but on an unpredictable basis. For example, a slot machine might pay off at an average of every 20 times, but unlike a fixed-ratio schedule, the gambler cannot tell when this payoff will be. The slot machine might pay off twice in a row and then not again until after 58 coins have been inserted. This averages out to a reward every 20 responses, but when the reward will be given is unpredictable. Variable-ratio schedules produce high, steady rates of responding and greater resistance to extinction than the other three schedules. These properties are partly responsible for the appeal of gambling. As a result, pathological gambling is on the rise in Canada (Ladouceur, 1996, 2000) along with its associated social costs (Ladouceur & others, 1994). The recent easy accessibility of Internet gambling may well make it the crack cocaine of gambling in Canada (Sevigny & others, 2005). Fortunately, an understanding of the contingencies that produce gambling addiction can also help in treatment (Sylvain, Ladouceur, & Boisvert, 1997; Ladouceur & others, 2002; Ladouceur & Shaffer, 2005).

The interval reinforcement schedules are determined by *time elapsed* since the last behaviour was rewarded. A *fixed-interval schedule* reinforces the first appropriate behaviour after a fixed amount of time has elapsed. For example, mail delivery usually comes once a day. You would tend to get rewarded for looking for mail after each 24-hour period has passed. The behaviour of politicians campaigning for reelection often reflects a fixed-interval schedule of reinforcement. After they have been elected, they reduce their campaigning and then do not pick it up again heavily until just before the next election (which can be two to four years later). On a fixed-interval schedule, few behaviours are enacted until the time approaches when the behaviour (such as getting reelected) will likely be reinforced. At that time the rate of behaviour picks up rapidly.

A *variable-interval schedule* is a timetable in which a behaviour is reinforced after a variable amount of time has elapsed (Staddon, Chelaru, & Higa, 2002). On this schedule, redialing a busy telephone number might reward you the first time after 10 minutes, the next after 2 minutes, the next after 18 minutes, and so on. Pop quizzes are on a variable-interval schedule. So is fishing—you don't know if the fish will bite in the next minute, in a half hour, in an hour, or at all. Because it is difficult to predict when a reward will come, behaviour is slow and consistent on a variable-interval schedule (Staddon, Chelaru, & Higa, 2002).

Figure 7.10 shows how the different schedules of reinforcement result in different rates of responding.

Punishment   From the discussion of positive and negative reinforcement, we saw that both types of reinforcement strengthen a behaviour. In contrast, the effect of punishment is usually to weaken a behaviour. Let's explore the concept of punishment in the operant conditioning context and learn why psychologists generally disapprove of punishment.

schedules of reinforcement "Timetables" that determine when a behaviour will be reinforced.

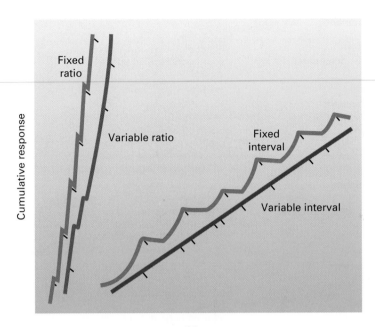

FIGURE 7.10

Schedules of Reinforcement and Different Patterns of Responding
In this figure, each hash mark indicates the delivery of reinforcement. Notice on the fixed-ratio schedule the dropoff in responding after each response; on the variable-ratio schedule the high, steady rate of responding; on the fixed-interval schedule the immediate dropoff in responding after reinforcement and the increase in responding just before reinforcement (resulting in a scalloped curve); and on the variable-interval schedule the slow, steady rate of responding.

Punishment

Behaviour	Aversive Stimulus Presented	Future Behaviour
You take medication to cure a headache	You have a bad allergic reaction	You avoid that medication in the future
You show off to a friend by speeding past a police car	You get a $200 ticket	You stop speeding

Negative Reinforcement

Behaviour	Aversive Stimulus Removed	Future Behaviour
You take medication to cure a headache	The headache goes away	You take more medication in the future
You show off to a friend by speeding past a police car	The officer pays no attention to you although officers have ticketed you in the past	You continue to show off by speeding past police cars

FIGURE 7.11 Punishment versus Negative Reinforcement

What Is Punishment? **Punishment** refers to a consequence that decreases the likelihood that a behaviour will occur. For example, a child plays with an attractive matchbox and gets burned when one of the matches is lit. In the future, the child is less likely to play with matches. Or if a student interrupts the teacher and the teacher verbally reprimands the student, the student stops interrupting the teacher.

Punishment differs from reinforcement in that, in punishment, a behaviour is weakened; in reinforcement, a behaviour is strengthened. So punishment is not the same as negative reinforcement. Also, in punishment, a response decreases because of its consequences; in negative reinforcement, a response increases because of its consequences. Figure 7.11 provides additional examples of the distinction between negative reinforcement and punishment.

Here's another example to help you distinguish between negative reinforcement and punishment. When an alcoholic consumes liquor to alleviate uncomfortable withdrawal symptoms, the probability that that person will use alcohol in the future

punishment A consequence that decreases the likelihood a behaviour will occur.

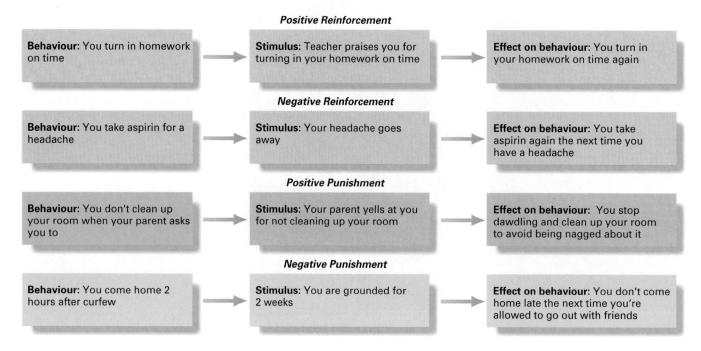

FIGURE 7.12 Positive Reinforcement, Negative Reinforcement, Positive Punishment, and Negative Punishment

increases. The reduction of the withdrawal symptoms was a negative reinforcer for drinking. But if an inebriated alcoholic is seriously injured in a car wreck and subsequently drinks less, the incident served as punishment because a behaviour (drinking) was subsequently decreased.

The positive–negative distinction also can be applied to punishment, although it is not used as widely as in reinforcement. In **positive punishment**, a behaviour decreases when it is followed by an unpleasant stimulus. In **negative punishment**, a behaviour decreases when a positive stimulus is removed from it.

Time out is a form of negative punishment in which a child is removed from a positive reinforcement. It is generally recommended over presenting an aversive stimulus (positive reinforcement), as is typically done when punishment is administered. If a child is behaving in disruptive ways in the classroom, the teacher might put the child in a chair in the corner of the room facing away from the class or take the child to a time-out room. Figure 7.12 compares positive reinforcement, negative reinforcement, positive punishment, and negative punishment.

Evaluating the Use of Punishment with Children Many people associate punishment with yelling at children or spanking them. All too often, though, aversive stimuli do not do what they are intended to do—namely, decrease an unwanted behaviour (Edwards, 1999). Some people turn too quickly to aversive stimuli when trying to change a child's behaviour. They might do this for several reasons: because they were harshly disciplined when they were growing up and they are just repeating how their parents dealt with them; because they have developed a style of handling stress by yelling or screaming; because they feel they can effectively exercise power over their smaller charges; or because they are unaware of how positive reinforcement or other techniques, such as a time out, can be used to improve children's behaviour.

To read further about whether punishing children is an effective strategy, see the Critical Reflections box.

positive punishment A behaviour decreases when it is followed by an unpleasant stimulus.

negative punishment A behaviour decreases when a positive stimulus is removed from it.

Will Sparing the Rod Spoil the Child?

Is the corporal (physical) punishment of children a defensible practice? Despite the fact that the use of physical force against another person is defined as assault, and is illegal under the Canadian Criminal Code, parents' use of physical punishment with their children has long been exempted. In recent years, however, there has been considerable debate in Canada concerning the use of physical punishment with children (Durrant & others, 2004).

On the one hand, the use of physical punishment is widespread. In one recent national survey, 50 percent of Canadian parents reported using light physical punishment and 6 percent reported using heavy physical punishment on their children (Canadian Press & Leger Marketing, 2002). Of Canadian mothers who have spanked their children, one-third report doing so at least once or twice per week (Durrant, Broberg, & Rose-Krasnor, 1999). In one Ontario sample, 85 percent of parents reported using light physical punishment and 20 percent reported hitting their children with objects (Durrant, Rose-Krasnor, & Broberg, 2003). In a 1992 Canadian sample, 75 percent of respondents believed that spanking is sometimes acceptable (Durrant, 1996).

When asked why they use corporal punishment with their children, parents often respond that their children need such strong discipline to learn how to behave. They also sometimes say that their parents punished them and they turned out okay, so there must not be that much wrong with it. Canadian researchers Joan Durrant and Linda Rose-Krasnor, along with Swede Anders Broberg, studied the use of physical punishment during mother-child conflicts in Canada and Sweden. They found that Canadian mothers suffered more physical punishment in their childhoods and, in turn, used it more frequently with their children than Swedish mothers did—a good example of observational learning in action. The mothers most likely to prescribe physical punishment were those with more positive attitudes toward spanking and a stronger belief that the target behaviours were unstable and, therefore, changeable. This was true regardless of maternal age, education, and marital status, suggesting that its use is less a matter of personal characteristics than of cultural context (Durrant, Broberg, & Rose-Krasnor, 1999; Durrant, Rose-Krasnor, & Broberg, 2003).

On the other hand, the acceptability of using any physical punishment on children has been called into question. Most recently, Joan Durrant, of the University of Manitoba, spearheaded the 2004 publication of a report opposing the physical punishment of children under any circumstances. Published by the Coalition on Physical Punishment of Children and Youth, this report has been endorsed by over 140 professional organizations in Canada, including the Canadian Psychological Association (Durrant & others, 2004).

In 2004, the Supreme Court of Canada reflected this debate in a ruling that upheld the right of Canadian parents to use physical punishment with their children while narrowing the circumstances under which it is legal (Durrant & others, 2004). For example, it is now no longer legal to physically discipline a child with an object (e.g., belt) or to strike a child's head. Similarly, it is no longer legal to physically discipline children under two years of age or teenagers.

This grade 2 student has been placed in "time out" for misbehaving. *What is the nature of time out? Why might this be better than physical punishment?*

Remember that research on the physical punishment of children is necessarily correlational, since it would be unethical to randomly assign parents to either spank or not spank their children in an experimental study. (Recall from chapter 2 that cause and effect cannot be determined in a correlational study.) With this in mind, whereas positive punishment may be effective in obtaining short-term compliance (Day & Roberts, 1993; Dinsmoor, 1998), expert consensus is that spanking and other forms of intense punishment of children should be avoided. The reasons include:

- Punishment can be abusive. When parents discipline their children, they might unintentionally become so aroused when they are punishing the child that they become abusive (Gershoff, 2002). According to Trocmé & others, (2001), around two-thirds of the 10,000 cases of child abuse in Canada in 1998 began as attempts at physical punishment.
- When intense punishment like yelling, screaming, or spanking is used, the adult is presenting children with an out-of-control model for handling stressful situations. The children might imitate this model. A recent Canadian correlational study found that children raised in a punitive style were more likely to themselves display aggressive behaviours (Thomas, 2004).
- Punishment often leads to more problems than it solves. In one correlational study, spanking by parents was linked with children's antisocial behaviour, such as cheating, telling lies, being mean to others, bullying, getting into fights, and being disobedient (Straus, Sugarman, & Giles-Sims, 1997).
- Punishment can instill fear, rage, or avoidance in children. For example, spanking a child might cause the child to avoid being around the parent and fear the parent.
- Punishment tells people what not to do rather than what to do. When an adult makes a punishing statement such as, "No, that's not right," they should always accompany it with positive feedback, such as, "But why don't you try this." According to

continued

Thomas (2004), children raised in a non-punitive way were themselves much less likely to show aggressive behaviour. Further, when punitive parents shift to a less punitive parenting style, their children's aggressiveness is also reduced.

- What is intended as punishing can turn out to be reinforcing. In school, a child might learn that misbehaving will attract the attention of the teacher and classmates.

For reasons such as these, Sweden passed a 1979 law forbidding physical punishment (spanking or slapping, for example) of children by parents. Since then, youth rates of juvenile delinquency, alcohol abuse, rape, and suicide have dropped (Durrant, 2000; Durrant & Janson, in press). The improved picture for Swedish youth could have occurred for other reasons, such as changing societal attitudes and opportunities for youth. Nonetheless, the Swedish experience suggests that physical punishment of children may be unnecessary to improve the well being of youth. As of 2004, several other countries have since passed anti-spanking laws, including Finland, Denmark, Norway, Austria, Cyprus, Latvia, Croatia, Germany, Israel, Bulgaria, Iceland, Ukraine, and Romania. In 2003, the United Nations International Committee on the Rights of the Child urged Canada to ban all forms of the physical punishment of children (Committee on the Rights of the Child, 2003).

What do you think?

- Should physical punishment of children be outlawed in Canada?
- Did your parents spank you when you were a child? What effect do you think it had on your behaviour?
- Might negative reinforcement, such as using time outs, be more effective than positive punishment, such as spanking? Explain.

Timing, Reinforcement, and Punishment How does the timing of reinforcement and punishment influence behaviour? And does it matter whether the reinforcement is small or large?

Immediate Reinforcement and Delayed Reinforcement As is the case with classical conditioning, learning is more efficient in operant conditioning when the interval between a behaviour and its reinforcement is a few seconds rather than minutes or hours, especially in lower animals (Church & Kirkpatrick, 2001). If a food reward is delayed for more than 30 seconds after a rat presses a bar, it is virtually ineffective as reinforcement. However, humans have the ability to respond to delayed reinforcers (Pierce & Cheney, 2004).

Sometimes important life decisions involve whether to obtain a small immediate reinforcer or to wait for a delayed but more highly valued reinforcer (Martin & Pear, 2003). For example, you can spend your money now on clothes, trinkets, parties, and the like, or save your money and buy a house and car later. Or, you might play around now and enjoy yourself in return for immediate small reinforcers, or you can study hard over the long haul for delayed stronger reinforcers, such as good grades, a scholarship to graduate school, and a better job.

Immediate Punishment and Delayed Punishment As with reinforcement, in most instances of research with lower animals, immediate punishment is more effective than delayed punishment in decreasing the occurrence of a behaviour. However, also as with reinforcement, delayed punishment can have an effect on human behaviour (Pierce & Cheney, 2004).

Why do so many of us postpone such activities as going to the dentist, scheduling minor surgery, or paying campus parking fines (Martin & Pear, 2003)? If we act immediately, we experience a weak punisher—it hurts to have our teeth drilled, it is painful

How might timing, reinforcement, and punishment be involved in overeating, drinking excessively, and smoking?
How might behaviour modification be able to help people change these behaviours?

to have minor surgery, and it is not pleasurable to pay a campus parking fine. However, the delayed consequences can be more punishing—our teeth might fall out, we may need major surgery, and our car might be towed away or we might be thrown in jail if we delay paying the fine.

Immediate and Delayed Reinforcement and Punishment How does receiving immediate small reinforcement versus delayed strong punishment affect human behaviour (Martin & Pear, 2003)? One reason that obesity is such a major health problem is that eating is a behaviour with immediate positive consequences—food tastes great and quickly provides a pleasurable feeling. Although the potential delayed consequences of overeating are negative (obesity and other possible health risks), immediate consequences are difficult to override. When the delayed consequences of behaviour are punishing and the immediate consequences are reinforcing, the immediate consequences usually win, even when the immediate consequences are minor reinforcers and the delayed consequences are major punishers. Smoking and drinking follow a similar pattern. The immediate consequences of smoking are reinforcing for most smokers—the powerful combination of positive reinforcement (tension relief, energy boost) and negative reinforcement (removal of craving). The punishing aspects of smoking are primarily long term, such as shortness of breath, a sore throat, coughing, emphysema, heart disease, and cancer. Likewise, the immediate pleasurable consequences of drinking override the delayed consequences of a hangover or even alcoholism.

Now think about the following situations. Why are some us so reluctant to take up a new sport, try a new dance step, go to a social gathering, or do almost anything different? One reason is that learning new skills often involves minor punishing consequences, such as initially looking and feeling stupid, not knowing what to do, having to put up with sarcastic comments from onlookers, and so on. In these circumstances, reinforcing consequences are often delayed. For example, it may take a long time to become a good enough golfer or a good enough dancer to enjoy these activities.

Applications of Operant Conditioning

A preschool child repeatedly throws his glasses and breaks them. A high school student and her parents have intense arguments. A university student is depressed. An elderly woman is incontinent. Operant conditioning procedures have helped such people to adapt more successfully and cope more effectively with their problems (Sussman, 2001).

Applied behaviour analysis, or **behaviour modification**, is the application of operant conditioning principles to change human behaviour. Consequences for behaviour are established to ensure that more adaptive actions are reinforced and less adaptive ones are not (Miltenberger, 2004; Powell, Symbaluk, & MacDonald, 2005). Advocates of behaviour modification believe that many emotional and behaviour problems are caused by inadequate, or inappropriate, response consequences (Alberto & Troutman, 2003; Petry & others, 2001). The child who acts out by throwing down his glasses and breaking them may be receiving too much attention from his teacher and peers for his behaviour; they unwittingly reinforce an unacceptable behaviour. In this instance, the parents and teachers would be instructed to divert attention from the destructive behaviour and transfer it to a more constructive behaviour, such as working quietly or playing cooperatively with peers.

Mental and Physical Health Consider the following situation. Barbara and her parents were on a collision course. Things got so bad that her parents decided to see a clinical psychologist. The psychologist, who had a behavioural orientation, talked with each family member, trying to get them to pinpoint the problem. The psychologist got the family to sign a behavioural contract that spelled out what everyone needed to do to reduce the conflict. Barbara agreed to (1) be home before 11 p.m. on weeknights; (2) look for a part-time job so she could begin to pay for some of her activities; and (3) refrain from calling her parents insulting names. Her parents agreed to (1) talk to Barbara in a low tone of voice rather than yell if they were angry; (2)

applied behaviour analysis (behaviour modification) The application of operant conditioning principles to change human behaviour.

1. Define the problem

2. Commit to change

3. Collect data about yourself

4. Design a self-control program

5. Make the program last—
   maintenance

FIGURE 7.13
**Five Steps in Developing a
Self-Control Program**

refrain from criticizing teenagers, especially Barbara's friends; and (3) give Barbara a small sum of money each week for gas, makeup, and socializing, but only until she found a job.

Also consider Raffi, a 19-year-old university student, who has been deeply depressed lately. His girlfriend broke off their relationship of two years, and his grades have been dropping. He decides to go to a psychologist who has a behavioural orientation. The psychologist enrols him in the Coping with Depression course developed by Peter Lewinsohn (1987; Rohde & others, 2005). Raffi learns to monitor his daily moods and increase his ratio of positive to negative life events. The psychologist trains Raffi to develop more efficient coping skills and gets Raffi to agree to a behavioural contract, just as the psychologist did with Barbara and her parents.

Angela is an elderly woman who lives in a nursing home. In recent months she has become incontinent and is increasingly dependent on the staff for help with her daily activities. The behavioural treatment designed for Angela's problem involves teaching her to monitor her behaviour and schedule going to the toilet. She is also required to do pelvic exercises. The program for decreasing Angela's dependence requires that the staff attend more to her independent behaviour when it occurs and remove attention from dependent behaviour whenever possible. Such strategies have been effective in reducing incontinence and dependence in older adults.

Behaviour modification can be used to help people improve their self-control in many aspects of mental and physical health (Miltenberger, 2004; Watson & Tharp, 2003). Following are five steps to better self-control (see figure 7.13; Martin & Pear, 2003):

- *Step 1. Define the behaviour to be changed in specific, concrete terms.* For Al, this is easy—he is overweight and wants to lose 14 kilograms. Stated even more precisely, he wants to consume about 1000 fewer calories per day to achieve a weight loss of about 1 kilogram per week. Some problems are more difficult to specify, such as "wasting time," "having a bad attitude toward school," "having a poor relationship with ——," or "being too nervous and worrying a lot." These types of problems have been called "fuzzies" because of their abstract nature (Mager, 1997). It is important to "unfuzzify" abstract problems and make them specific and concrete. Problems can be made precise by writing out a goal and listing the things that would give clear evidence of having reached the goal.

- *Step 2. Make a commitment to change.* Both a commitment to change and a knowledge of change techniques have been shown to help college and university students become more effective self-managers of their smoking, eating, studying, and relationship problems (Alterman, Gariti, & Mulvaney, 2001; Perkins & others, 2001). Building a commitment to change requires doing things that increase the likelihood that you will stick to your project. First, tell others about your commitment to change—they will remind you to stick to your program. Second, rearrange your environment to provide frequent reminders of your goal, making sure the reminders are associated with the positive benefits of reaching your goal. Third, put a lot of time and energy into planning your project. Make a list of statements about your project, such as "I've put a lot of time into this project; I am certainly not going to waste all this effort now." Fourth, because you will invariably face temptations to backslide or quit your project, plan ahead for ways you can deal with temptation, tailoring these plans to your problem.

- *Step 3. Collect data about your behaviour.* This is especially important in decreasing excessive behaviours such as overeating and frequent smoking. One of the reasons for tracking your behaviour is that it provides a reference point for evaluating your progress. When recording the frequency of a behaviour during initial observations, you should examine the immediate circumstances that could be maintaining the problem (Martin & Pear, 2003).

- *Step 4. Design a self-control program.* Many good self-control programs involve setting long-term and short-term goals and developing a plan for reaching the goals. Good self-control programs also usually include some type of self-talk, self-instruction, or self-reinforcement. For example, a person whose goal is to jog 30 minutes a day five days a week might say, "I'll never make it. It just won't work." This person can benefit by saying something like, "I know it's going to be tough, but I can make it." Also, individuals can engage in self-reinforcing statements or treat themselves. This might involve saying something like "Way to go. You are up to 30 minutes three times a week. You are on your way." Or they might treat themselves to something, such as a movie, some new clothes, or a new CD.

- *Step 5. Make the program last—maintenance.* One strategy is to establish specific dates for postchecks and to plan a course of action if your postchecks are not favourable. For instance, if your self-control program involves weight reduction, you might want to weigh yourself once a week. If your weight increases to a certain level, then you immediately go back on your self-control program. Another strategy is to establish a buddy system by finding a friend or someone with a similar problem. The two of you set mutual maintenance goals. Once a month, get together and check each other's behaviour. If your goals have been maintained, get together and celebrate in an agreed-on way.

For other ideas on how to establish an effective self-control program tailored to your needs, you might want to contact the counselling centre at your college or university. You might also consider consulting a good book on behaviour modification or self-control, such as *Behavior Modification* (Martin & Pear, 2003).

Education   Not only is behaviour modification effective in improving mental and physical health, but it has also been applied in classrooms to improve the education of children (Charles & Senter, 2004; Evertson, Emmer, & Worsham, 2003). Many of the concepts already discussed, including positive reinforcement, shaping, time out, contracting, and developing self-control, have been applied to learning in the classroom (e.g., Dihoff & others, 2004). Here are some other educational applications.

Teaching Machines and Computer Instruction   Before computers were common, Skinner developed a machine to help teachers instruct students (Benjafield, 2004). The teaching machine engaged the student in a learning activity, paced the material at the student's rate, tested the student's knowledge of the material, and provided immediate feedback about correct and incorrect answers. Skinner hoped that the machine would revolutionize learning in schools, but the revolution never took place.

Today the idea behind Skinner's teaching machine has been almost universally applied to computers, although the term feedback is used more commonly than Skinner's own terms, reinforcement and punishment. Research comparisons of computer-assisted instruction with traditional teacher-based instruction suggest that in many areas, such as on computer programming problems, computer-assisted practice with feedback can produce excellent results (Emurian, 2004).

Choosing Effective Reinforcers   Not all reinforcers are the same for every child. Teachers can explore what reinforcers work best with which children—that is, individualize the use of particular reinforcers. For one child, it might be praise, for another it might be getting to spend more time participating in a favourite activity, for another it might be getting to be hall monitor for a week, and for another it might be getting to surf the Internet. Natural reinforcers such as praise and privileges are generally recommended over material reinforcers such as stars and candy (Hall & Hall, 1998).

The *Premack principle* offers a useful tool to identify effective reinforcers (e.g., Brown, Spencer, & Swift, 2002). Named after psychologist David Premack, the Premack principle states that more desirable behaviours can be used to reinforce less desirable ones. For many children, playing a video game is more desirable than doing a writing assignment. Thus, a teacher might tell a child, "When you complete your writing assignment, you can play a game on the computer." The Premack principle can also be used with an entire classroom of children. For example, a teacher might say, "If of the whole class gets their homework done by Friday, we will take a field trip next week."

> **> reflect and review**

> **③ Discuss operant conditioning.**

> - Define operant conditioning and distinguish it from classical conditioning.
> - Describe Thorndike's law of effect.
> - Describe Skinner's operant conditioning.
> - Discuss shaping.
> - Identify the principles of reinforcement and explain how they affect behaviour.
> - Explain how behaviour modification works.
>
> *Describe a behaviour (yours or someone else's) that you would like to change through behaviour modification. Outline the plan. If you enacted this plan, do you think it would work? Why or why not? Would you consider the enactment of this plan to be too manipulative? Why or why not?*

④ OBSERVATIONAL LEARNING

How does observational learning occur?

Albert Bandura (2000a, 2001, 2004) believes that if we learned using only classical and operant conditioning, through trial-and-error, it would be very tedious and at times hazardous. Imagine, for example, teaching a 15-year-old to drive only by rewarding positive behaviour (and not by explaining or demonstrating). Instead, many of our complex behaviours are the result of observing and imitating competent models who display appropriate behaviour in solving problems and coping with their world (Striefel, 1998). By observing other people, we can acquire knowledge, skills, rules, strategies, beliefs, and attitudes (Schunk, 2004a). Even animals use observational (or social) learning (Galef, Jr., 2005; Galef, Jr. & Whiskin, 2004; Heyes & Galef Jr., 1996), probably because it is an adaptive specialization (Lefebvre & Giraldeau, 1996). The capacity to imitate has been attributed to many birds and mammals (e.g., Baker, 2004).

You initially encountered Bandura's ideas in chapter 1, in which his social cognitive theory was introduced. This section discusses his view of observational learning further. **Observational learning**, also called *imitation* or *modelling*, is learning that occurs when a person observes and imitates someone's behaviour. The capacity to learn behaviour patterns by observation eliminates trial-and-error learning. In many instances observational learning takes less time than operant conditioning. Bandura's ideas have been generalized into the *entertainment-education strategy*, the use of observational learning theory to guide the creation of television and radio soap operas for the express purpose of helping people learn valuable information, such as how to prevent HIV/AIDS (Arvind & Rogers, 2003) and improve cardiovascular health (Bouman, Maas, & Kok, 1998).

Bandura (1986) described four main processes that are involved in observational learning: attention, retention, motor reproduction, and reinforcement. For observational learning to take place, the first process that has to occur is *attention* (which was initially discussed in chapter 5 due to its important role in perception). In order to reproduce a model's actions, you must attend to what the model is saying or doing. You might not hear what a friend says if the television is blaring, or you might miss the teacher's analysis of a problem if you are admiring someone sitting in the next row. Imagine that you decide to take a class to improve your artistic skills. You need to attend to the instructor's words and hand movements. Attention to the model is influenced by a host of characteristics. For example, warm, powerful, atypical people command more attention than cold, weak, typical people do.

observational learning Also called imitation or modelling; learning that occurs when a person observes and imitates another's behaviour.

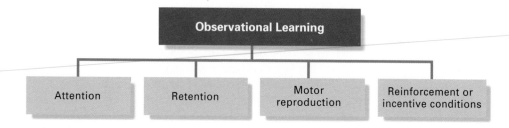

FIGURE 7.14

Bandura's Model of Observational Learning
In terms of Bandura's model, if you are learning to ski, you need to attend to the instructor's words and demonstrations. You need to remember what the instructor did and her tips for avoiding disasters. You also need the motor abilities to reproduce what the instructor has shown you. And praise from the instructor after you have completed a few moves on the slopes should improve your motivation to continue skiing.

Retention is the second process needed for observational learning to occur. To reproduce a model's actions, you must code the information and keep it in memory so that it can be retrieved. A simple verbal description or a vivid image of what the model did assists retention. (Memory is such an important cognitive process that chapter 8 is exclusively devoted to it.) In the example of taking a class to improve your art skills, you will need to remember what the instructor said and did so you can model good drawing skills.

Production is the process of imitating the model's actions. People might attend to a model and code in memory what they have seen, but limitations in motor development might make it difficult for them to reproduce the model's action. Thirteen-year-olds might admire Avril Lavigne's unmistakable and wide-ranging singing style but be unable to reproduce it. In an art class too, you will need good motor reproduction skills to follow the instructor's example.

Reinforcement, or incentive conditions, is the final component of observational learning. On many occasions we may attend to what a model says or does, retain the information in memory, and possess the motor capabilities to perform the action, but, because we don't adequately reinforce the behaviour, we might fail to repeat it. The importance of this step was demonstrated in one of Bandura's (1965) classic studies in which children who had seen a model punished for aggression reproduced the model's aggression only when they were offered an incentive to do so. In art class, if the instructor chooses one of your drawings for display, that reinforcement encourages you to keep drawing and to take another art class.

A summary of Bandura's model of observational learning is shown in figure 7.14. To think about the models and mentors in your life, see the Personal Reflections box.

Mentors and Mentees

A mentor is someone you look up to and respect, who serves as a competent model and who is willing to work with you to help you achieve your goals. Having mentors to observe as role models to learn from can make important contributions to whether individuals develop optimally and reach their full potential. At the same time, being a mentor and serving as a positive model in observational learning can be an extremely rewarding experience. In addition, being a mentor enhances your teaching and interpersonal skills.

Big Brothers Big Sisters is the most popular mentoring program in North America. Children who have been mentored in this program become more involved in school, less likely to use illegal drugs, and better able to get along with their families (Tierney & others, 1995; DeJong, 2004). Have you ever been involved in the Big Brothers Big Sisters program as either a mentee or as a mentor? Think of volunteering to "Be a Big;" there are lots of "Littles" who would benefit from sharing time with you, and you would have much to learn from them.

Mentors can be parents, teachers, an older peer, or someone in the community. Spend a few minutes and think about the mentors you have had in your life, including now. Do you remember any specific instances in which you watched them do or say something that had a lasting impact on you, behaviour you later modelled? List the most important mentors in your life and then describe what you learned from them and how they helped your learning. What did they learn from you?

Mentors	What I Learned from Them and What They Learned From Me
1. _____	_____
	_____
2. _____	_____
	_____

Have you ever been a mentor? Who did you mentor? You might have mentored a classmate at school or a younger sibling or peer. Spend a few moments and think about the mentees you have had in your life, including now. Do you remember any specific instances in which they watched you do or say something that had a lasting impact on them that they later modelled? List the most important mentees in your life and then describe what they learned from you and how you helped their learning. What did you learn from them?

Mentees	What I Learned from Me and What They Learned From Them
1. _____	_____
	_____
2. _____	_____
	_____

A mentor can be very beneficial to students. Many schools now have active mentoring programs. If you currently don't have a mentor, consider looking into whether such a program exists at your school and consider connecting with a mentor. Or you might want to become a mentor yourself. Do you have a particular skill or knowledge that you might be able to teach share with your peers at school?

> ## reflect and review

4 **Describe observational learning.**

- Define observational learning and outline the four steps in Bandura's model.

Who have been the most important models in your life? What have you learned from them?

5 COGNITIVE FACTORS IN LEARNING

— Purposive Behaviour
— Insight Learning

What role does cognition play in learning?

In discussing learning, we have said little about cognitive processes, except as they apply in observational learning. The operant and classical conditioning approaches historically ignored the role of cognitive factors such as memory, thinking, planning, or expectations in learning (Kirsch & others, 2004). Many contemporary psychologists, including behavioural revisionists who recognize that cognition should not have been ignored in classical and operant conditioning, believe that learning involves much more than environment–behaviour connections (Roberts, 1998; Bandura, 2000a).

In fact, the study of animal cognition has included research on animal counting (Olthof & Roberts, 2000; Roberts, Roberts, & Kit (2002), memory (Shettleworth, 2003) and spatial cognition (Wall & others, 2004; Shettleworth & Hampton, 1998) and sense of time (Roberts & Roberts, (2002).

Let's look at E. C. Tolman's contributions to the role of cognition in learning.

"You will note that their ability to comprehend, assess and process information increases dramatically when Professor Podhertz throws in the cat."

© Leo Cullum

Purposive Behaviour

E. C. Tolman (1932) emphasized the *purposiveness* of behaviour. In other words, he believed that much of behaviour is goal directed. Tolman believed that it is necessary to study entire behavioural sequences in order to understand why people engage in particular actions. For example, high school students whose goal is to attend a good college or university study hard in their classes. If we focus only on their studying, we would miss the purpose of their behaviour. The students don't study hard simply because they have been reinforced for studying in the past. Rather, they study as a means to intermediate goals (learning, high grades), which, in turn, improve their likelihood of getting into the college or university of their choice (Schunk, 2004b).

Tolman's legacy can be seen today in the extensive interest in the role of goal setting in human behaviour (Bagozzi & Dholakia, 2005). Researchers are especially interested in how people engage in self-regulating and self-monitoring their behaviour to reach a goal (de Jong & others, 2005; Boekaerts, Pintrich, & Zeidner, 2000). In every chapter of this book, we have set learning goals and asked you to monitor your studying so you can reach these goals.

Expectancy Learning and Information In studying the purposiveness of behaviour, Tolman went beyond the stimuli and responses of Pavlov and Skinner to focus on cognitive mechanisms. He said that when classical and operant conditioning occur, the organism acquires certain expectations. In classical conditioning, the young boy fears the rabbit because he expects it will hurt him. In operant conditioning, a woman works hard all week because she expects to be paid on Friday. People acquire expectations from their experiences with their environment.

Tolman (1932) emphasized that the information value of the CS is important as a signal or expectation that a UCS will follow. Tolman's belief that the information the CS provides is the key to understanding classical conditioning anticipated contemporary thinking.

One contemporary view of classical conditioning describes an organism as an information seeker, using logical and perceptual relations among events, along with preconceptions, to form a representation of the world (Rescorla, 1988, 1996, 2003). A classic experiment conducted by Leon Kamin (1968), who was then at McMaster University, illustrates the importance of an organism's history and the information provided by a conditioned stimulus in classical conditioning. A rat was conditioned by repeatedly pairing a tone (CS) and a shock (UCS), until the tone alone produced fear (CR). Then, the tone continued to be paired with the shock, but a light (a second CS) was turned on each time the tone was sounded. Even though the light (CS) and the shock (UCS) were repeatedly paired, the rat showed no conditioning to the light (the light by itself produced no CR). Conditioning to the light was blocked, almost as if the rat had not paid attention. The rat apparently used the tone as a signal to predict that a shock would be forthcoming; information about the light's pairing with the shock was redundant with the information already learned about the tone's pairing with the shock. In this experiment, conditioning was governed not by the contiguity of the CS and UCS but, rather, by the rat's history and the information it received. Contemporary classical conditioning researchers are exploring further the role of information in an organism's learning (Domjan, 2006).

FIGURE 7.15

Insight Learning
Sultan, one of Köhler's brightest chimps, is faced with the problem of reaching a cluster of bananas overhead. He solves the problem by stacking boxes on top of one another to reach the bananas. Köhler called this type of problem solving insight learning.

latent learning Unreinforced learning that is not immediately reflected in behaviour.

One type of expectancy involves cognitive maps (Bird & others, 2003; Olthof & others, 1999). Tolman (1948) believed that organisms form cognitive maps that are made up of expectancies about which actions are needed to attain a goal. A *cognitive map* is an organism's mental representation of the structure of physical space. His experiments with rats in a maze led Tolman to conclude that the rats developed mental awareness of physical space and the elements in it. They used these cognitive maps to find the food at the end of the maze, their goal.

Tolman's idea of cognitive maps is alive and well today. William Roberts, of the University of Western Ontario, and his colleagues have shown that many species develop cognitive maps of their surroundings, also referred to as *spatial cognition* (Bird & others, 2003; Hogarth and others, 2000; Sutton, Olthof, & Roberts, 2000). Sara Shettleworth, of the University of Toronto, has studied a common Canadian bird, the black-capped chickadee. Black-capped chickadees store food in scattered locations and find it later using memory (Shettleworth, 2003). According to Hampton & Shettleworth (1996), like other birds and animals that rely on excellent spatial memory in the wild, black-capped chickadees have a relatively enlarged hippocampus. When we move around in our environment, we humans also develop a cognitive map of where things are located, on both small and large scales. For example, we have a cognitive map of where rooms are located in our house or apartment, and we have a cognitive map of where we are located in Canada.

Latent Learning Other evidence to support the role of cognitive maps in learning was obtained in experiments on latent learning. **Latent learning** is unreinforced learning that is not immediately reflected in behaviour. In one study, two groups of hungry rats were placed in a maze and required to find their way from a starting point to an end point (Tolman & Honzik, 1930). The first group found food (a reinforcer) at the end point; the second group found nothing there. In the operant conditioning view, the first group should learn the maze better than the second group, which is exactly what happened. However, when Tolman subsequently took some of the rats from the nonreinforced group and gave them food at the end point of the maze, they began to run the maze as effectively as the reinforced group. Apparently, the nonreinforced rats had learned a great deal about the maze as they roamed around and explored it. But their learning was *latent*, stored cognitively in their memories but not yet expressed behaviourally. When these rats were given a good reason (reinforcement with food) to run the maze speedily, they called on their latent learning to help them reach the end of the maze more quickly.

Outside of a laboratory, latent learning is evident in an animal's exploration of its surroundings. Learning the layout of its environment may bring the animal no immediate benefits, but it can prove critical in the future when fleeing a predator or searching for food.

Insight Learning

Tolman was not the only psychologist in the first half of the twentieth century who believed that cognitive factors play an important role in learning. So did gestalt psychologist Wolfgang Köhler. Köhler, a German psychologist, spent four months in the Canary Islands during World War I observing the behaviour of apes. There he conducted two fascinating experiments. One is called the "stick problem," the other the "box problem." Though these two experiments are the same, the solutions to the problems are different. In both situations, the ape discovers that it cannot reach an alluring piece of fruit, either because the fruit is too high or because it is outside the ape's cage and beyond reach. To solve the stick problem, the ape has to insert a small stick inside a larger stick to reach the fruit. To master the box problem, the ape must stack several boxes to reach the fruit (see figure 7.15). According to Köhler (1925), solving these problems does not involve trial and error or simple connections between stimuli and responses. Rather, when the ape realizes that his customary actions are not going to help him get the fruit, he often sits for a period of time and appears to ponder how to solve the problem. Then he quickly gets up, as if he had a sudden flash of insight, piles the boxes on top of one another, and gets the fruit. **Insight learning** is a form of problem solving in which the organism develops a sudden insight or understanding of a problem's solution.

> **> reflect and review**
>
> **5** **Discuss the role of cognition in learning.**
>
> - Discuss the role of expectations, latent learning, and cognitive maps in learning.
> - Explain insight learning.
>
> *What are your career expectations? How might these expectations influence your behaviour this term?*

6 BIOLOGICAL AND CULTURAL FACTORS IN LEARNING

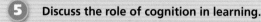

— Biological   — Cultural
Constraints   Constraints

How do biology and culture affect learning?

Albert Einstein had many special talents. He combined enormous creativity with great analytic ability to develop some of the twentieth century's most important insights about the nature of matter and the universe. On the one hand, his biology was on his side; his genes obviously endowed Einstein with extraordinary intellectual skills that enabled him to think and reason on a very high plane. On the other hand, cultural factors also undoubtedly contributed to Einstein's genius. Einstein received an excellent, rigorous European education, and later in the United States he experienced the freedom and support believed to be important in creative exploration. Would Einstein have been able to fully develop his intellectual skills and make such brilliant insights if he had grown up in a poor developing country, such as Haiti? Unlikely. Quite clearly, both biological and cultural factors contribute to learning.

Biological Constraints

We can't breathe under water, fish can't play table tennis, and cows can't solve math problems. The structure of an organism's body permits certain kinds of learning and inhibits others (Chance, 2003; D. L. Morgan, 2002). For example, chimpanzees cannot learn to speak English because they lack the necessary vocal equipment. Some of us cannot solve difficult calculus problems and others of us can—not all the differences seem to be the result of experiences.

Instinctive Drift An example of biological influences on learning is **instinctive drift**, the tendency of animals to revert to instinctive behaviour that interferes with learning. Consider the situation of Keller and Marion Breland (1961), students of B. F. Skinner, who used operant conditioning to train animals to perform at fairs, conventions, and in television advertisements. They used Skinner's techniques to teach pigs to cart large wooden nickels to a piggy bank and deposit them. They also trained raccoons to pick up a coin and place it in a metal tray. Although the pigs and raccoons, as well as chickens and other animals, performed well at most of the tasks (raccoons became adept basketball players, for example—see figure 7.16), some of the animals began acting strangely. Instead of picking up the large wooden nickels and carrying them to the piggy bank, the pigs would drop the nickels on the ground, shove them with their snouts, toss them in

insight learning A form of problem solving in which the organism develops a sudden insight or understanding of the problem's solution.

instinctive drift The tendency of animals to revert to instinctive behaviour that interferes with learning.

FIGURE 7.16
Instinctive Drift
This raccoon's skill in using its hands made it an excellent basketball player, but because of instinctive drift, the raccoon had a much more difficult time dropping coins in a tray.

the air, and then repeat these actions. The raccoons began to hold on to their coins rather than dropping them into the metal tray. When two coins were introduced, the raccoons rubbed them together. Somehow these behaviours overwhelmed the strength of the reinforcement. Why were the pigs and the raccoons misbehaving? The pigs were rooting, an instinct which is used to uncover edible roots. The raccoons were engaging in an instinctive food-washing response. Their instinctive drift interfered with learning.

Preparedness and Taste Aversion   Some animals learn readily in one situation but have difficulty learning in slightly different circumstances. The difficulty might result not from some aspect of the learning situation but from the organism's biological predisposition (Seligman, 1970). **Preparedness** is the species-specific biological predisposition to learn in certain ways but not others.

Much of the evidence for preparedness comes from research on taste aversion (Garcia, 1989). Consider this situation: A psychologist went to dinner with his wife and ordered filet mignon with béarnaise sauce, his favourite dish. Afterward they went to the opera. Several hours later, he became very ill with stomach pains and nausea. Several weeks later, he tried to eat béarnaise sauce but couldn't bear it. The psychologist's experience involves *taste aversion*, another biological constraint on learning (Yamamoto, Frequet, & Sandner, 2002). Notice that the taste aversion developed despite happening only once and despite a long delay between the eating of the béarnaise sauce and the resulting stomach pains and nausea. We humans are biologically prepared to readily associate stomach disorders with tastes.

Because of biological preparedness, if an organism ingests a substance that poisons but does not kill it, the organism often readily develops considerable distaste for that substance. Rats that experience low levels of radiation after eating show a strong aversion to the food they were eating when the radiation made them ill. This aversion has been shown to last for as long as 32 days. Such long-term effects cannot be accounted for by classical conditioning, which would argue that a single pairing of the conditioned and unconditioned stimuli would not last that long (Garcia, Ervin, & Koelling, 1966). Radiation and chemical treatment of cancer often produce nausea in patients. The resulting pattern of aversions often resembles those shown by laboratory animals.

Knowledge about taste aversion has been used to discourage animals and birds from preying on other species. For example, crows prey on the eggs of other, sometimes endangered, bird species. The culling of crows is a cruel and inefficient aproach to the conservation of the endangered species. As an alternative, Cox and her colleagues (2004) have shown that carrion crows develop a conditioned taste aversion if the eggs of endangered species are painted with an emetic. The crow eats a treated egg and throws up. Thereafter, the crow is less likely to eat similar eggs. This approach opens up the possibility that crows and endangered birds may be able to live together in a semblance of ecological balance.

Cultural Constraints

Traditionally, the influence of culture on learning has received little or no attention. The behavioural orientation that dominated North American psychology for much of the twentieth century does focus on the cultural contexts of learning, but the organisms in those contexts have often been animals. Within the behavioural tradition there has been limited interest in the cultural context of human learning.

How does culture influence learning? Most psychologists agree that the principles of classical conditioning, operant conditioning, and observational learning are universal and are powerful learning processes in every culture. However, culture can influence the degree to which these learning processes are used, and it often determines the content of learning. For example, punishment is a universal learning process, but as we saw earlier, in our discussion of the Swedish ban on spanking children, its use and type show considerable sociocultural variation.

When behaviourism began its influential reign in North America between 1910 and 1930, child-rearing experts regarded the infant as capable of being shaped into

preparedness The species-specific biological predisposition to learn in certain ways.

almost any type of child. Desirable social behaviour could be achieved if the child's antisocial behaviours were always punished and never indulged and if positive behaviours were carefully conditioned and rewarded in a highly controlled and structured child-rearing regimen. John Watson (1928) wrote a publication, *Psychological Care of the Infant and Child*, that was the official U.S. government booklet for parents. This booklet advocated never letting children suck their thumbs and, if necessary, restraining the child by tying her hands to the crib at night and painting her fingers with foul-tasting liquids. Parents were advised to let infants "cry themselves out" rather than reinforce this unacceptable behaviour by picking them up to rock and soothe them.

In Balinese culture many children are taught to be skilled dancers by the age of six, whereas other cultures value learning in other areas.

From the 1930s to the 1960s, a more permissive attitude prevailed in North America, and parents were advised to be concerned with the feelings and capacities of the child. Since the 1960s there has been a continued emphasis on the role of parental love in children's socialization, but as we saw in chapter 4, experts now advise parents to play a less permissive and more active, authoritative, role in shaping children's behaviour. Experts stress that parents should set limits and make authoritative decisions in areas in which the child is not capable of reasonable judgment. However, they should listen and adapt to the child's point of view, should explain their restrictions and discipline, and should not discipline the child in a hostile, punitive manner.

The content of learning is also influenced by culture (Cole, Cole, & Lightfoot, 2005). We cannot learn about something we do not experience. The four-year-old who grows up among the Bushmen of the Kalahari Desert is unlikely to learn about taking baths or pouring water from one glass into another. Similarly, a child growing up in downtown Toronto is unlikely to become skilled at tracking animals or finding water-bearing roots in the desert. Learning often requires practice, and certain behaviours are practised more often in some cultures than in others. In Bali many children are skilled dancers by the age of six, whereas Norwegian children are much likelier to be good skiers and skaters by that age. Children growing up in a Mexican village famous for its pottery may work with clay day after day, whereas children in a nearby village famous for woven rugs and sweaters rarely become experts at making clay pots.

> ## > reflect and review

6 **Identify biological and cultural factors in learning.**

- Discuss these biological constraints on learning: instinctive drift, preparedness, and taste aversion.
- Explain how culture can influence learning.

Think about the various types of dogs, cats, or another species of domesticated animal with which you are familiar. What evidence do they present that every organism is biologically influenced to permit certain kinds of learning and inhibit others?

Learning

1 TYPES OF LEARNING

2 CLASSICAL CONDITIONING

- Definition of Classical Conditioning
- Applications of Classical Conditioning

3 OPERANT CONDITIONING

- Definition of Operant Conditioning
- Skinner's Approach to Operant Conditioning
- Shaping
- Generalization, Discrimination, and Extinction
- Principles of Reinforcement and Punishment
- Applications of Operant Conditioning

4 OBSERVATIONAL LEARNING

5 COGNITIVE FACTORS IN LEARNING

- Purposive Behaviour
- Insight Learning

6 BIOLOGICAL AND CULTURAL FACTORS IN LEARNING

- Biological Constraints
- Cultural Constraints

At the beginning of the chapter, we posed six chapter questions and encouraged you to review material related to these questions at the end of each major section (see pages 269, 276, 290, 292, 295, and 297). Use the following reflection and review features for further your understanding of the chapter material.

CHAPTER REFLECTIONS

1. One common association that people have is called a conditioned taste aversion, which occurs when you eat or drink something and then get sick. A conditioned taste aversion is most likely to occur when the food or drink is something that is relatively unfamiliar. Suppose you have acquired a conditioned taste aversion to tequila. Identify what the unconditioned stimulus, unconditioned response, conditioned stimulus, and conditioned response are in this example.

2. Positive and negative reinforcement are often difficult concepts to understand. The psychology Web site of Athabasca University, in northern Alberta, includes examples and a practice exercise that may help you figure out the distinction more easily: http://psych.athabascau.ca/html/prtut/reinpair.htm

3. Think of all the things you have learned in the past several days. Write down an example involving each of the following types of learning: classical conditioning, operant conditioning, observational learning, latent learning, and insight learning. Which kind of learning do you use most frequently? Which seems to be the least common for you? Are there types of learning you've done that don't seem to fit any category? If so, what aspects of those types exclude them from these categories?

4. Visit Mentoring Canada (http://www.mentoring canada.ca/), a resource for Big Brothers Big Sisters of Canada. Read more about the benefits of mentoring. Did you add anything to your current understanding of the reciprocal benefits of mentoring?

5. Visit Statistics Canada and download the Eleanor Thomas Statistics Canada report entitled *Aggressive behaviour outcomes for young children: Change in parenting environment predicts change in behaviour* from http://www.statcan.ca/cgi-bin/downpub/listpub.cgi? catno=89-599-MIE2004001. Are Thomas' approach and conclusions solid?

CHAPTER REVIEW

Explain what learning is.

- Learning is a relatively permanent change in behaviour that occurs through experience. In associative learning, a connection is made between two events. Conditioning is the process by which associative learning occurs. In classical conditioning, organisms learn the association between two stimuli and, in operant conditioning, they learn the association between behaviour and a consequence. Observational learning is learning by watching what other people do.

Describe classical conditioning.

- Classical conditioning occurs when a neutral stimulus becomes associated with a meaningful stimulus and comes to elicit a similar response. Pavlov discovered that an organism learns the association between an unconditioned stimulus (UCS) and a conditioned stimulus (CS). The UCS automatically produces the unconditioned response (UCR). After conditioning (CS-UCS pairing), the CS elicits the conditioned response (CR) by itself. In classical conditioning, acquisition is the initial linking of stimuli and responses, which involves a neutral stimulus being associated with the UCS so that the CS comes to elicit the CR. Two important aspects of acquisition are contiguity and contingency/predictability. Generalization in classical conditioning is the tendency of a new stimulus that is similar to the original conditioned stimulus to elicit a response that is similar to the conditioned response. Discrimination in classical conditioning is the process of learning to respond to certain stimuli and not to others. Extinction in classical conditioning is the weakening of the CR in the absence of the UCS. Spontaneous recovery is the recurrence of a CR after a time delay without further conditioning.

- Classical conditioning has been applied to explaining and eliminating fears in humans. Counterconditioning, a classical conditioning procedure for weakening the CR by associating the fear-provoking stimulus with a new response that is incompatible with the fear, has been successful in eliminating fears. Classical conditioning can also explain pleasant emotions. Some of the behaviours we associate with health problems and mental disorders, including certain aspects of drug use and immune system functioning, can involve classical conditioning. Classical conditioninghas also been applied to consumer behaviour.

Discuss operant conditioning.

- Operant conditioning is a form of learning in which the consequences of behaviour produce changes in the probability of the behaviour's occurrence. Thorndike's law of effect states that behaviours followed by positive outcomes are strengthened, whereas behaviours followed by negative outcomes are weakened. Thorndike's view that the organism's behaviour is due to a connection between a stimulus and a response was called S-R theory. B. F. Skinner described the behaviour of the organism as operant: the behaviour operates on the environment, and the environment in turn operates on the organism. Whereas classical conditioning involves respondent behaviour, operant conditioning involves operant behaviour. In most instances, operant conditioning is better at explaining voluntary behaviour than classical conditioning is.

- Skinner believed that the mechanisms of learning are the same for all species. This led him to study lower animals extensively in the hope that the basic mechanisms of learning could be more easily understood in organisms simpler than humans. Like Skinner, contemporary behaviourists study organisms under precisely controlled conditions so that the connection between the operant behaviour and the specific consequences can be examined in minute detail.

- Shaping is the process of rewarding approximations of desired behaviour in order to shorten the learning process.

- Operant conditioning involves generalization (giving the same response to similar stimuli), discrimination (responding to stimuli that signal that a behaviour will or will not be reinforced), and extinction (a decreasing tendency to perform a previously reinforced behaviour when reinforcement is stopped).

- Principles of reinforcement include the distinction between positive reinforcement (the frequency of a behaviour increases because it is followed by a rewarding stimulus) and negative reinforcement (the frequency of behaviour increases because it is followed by the removal of an aversive, or unpleasant, stimulus). Positive reinforcement can be classified as primary reinforcement (using reinforcers that

are innately satisfying) and secondary reinforcement (using reinforcers that acquire positive value through experience). Reinforcement can also be continuous (a behaviour is reinforced every time) or partial (a behaviour is reinforced only a portion of the time). Schedules of reinforcement—fixed ratio, variable ratio, fixed interval, and variable interval— are timetables that determine when a behaviour will be reinforced. Punishment refers to a consequence that decreases the likelihood a behaviour will occur. Punishment, through which a behaviour is weakened, is different from negative reinforcement, through which a behaviour is strengthened. In positive punishment, a behaviour decreases when it is followed by an unpleasant stimulus. In negative punishment, a behaviour decreases when a positive stimulus is removed from it. Time out is a form of negative punishment. Most psychologists recommend not using positive punishment with children. Operant conditioning is more efficient, especially in lower animals, when the interval between behaviour and its reinforcement or punishment is very brief. However, in humans, delayed reinforcement and punishment can have significant effects on behaviour. Connections between the timing of reinforcement and punishment (whether they are immediate or delayed) have implications for understanding health problems, such as obesity and substance abuse.

- Behaviour modification is the application of operant conditioning principles to change human behaviour. It involves establishing consequences for behaviour to reinforce more adaptive actions. Operant conditioning has been applied to mental and physical health, as well as to education.

Understand observational learning.

- Observational learning occurs when a person observes and imitates someone's behaviour. Bandura said that observational learning includes attention, retention, production, and reinforcement.

Know about the role of cognitive factors in learning.

- E. C. Tolman emphasized the purposiveness of behaviour, Tolman's belief that much of behaviour is goal directed. There is considerable interest in goal-directed behaviour today. In studying the purposiveness of behaviour, Tolman went beyond stimuli and responses to discuss cognitive mechanisms. Tolman believed that expectancies, acquired through experiences with the environment, are an important cognitive mechanism in learning. Cognitive maps, an organism's mental representations of physical space, involve expectancies about which actions are needed to reach a goal.

- Evidence to support the role of cognitive maps was obtained in experiments on latent learning, unreinforced learning that is not immediately reflected in behaviour.
- Köhler developed the concept of insight learning, a form of problem solving in which the organism develops a sudden insight or understanding of a problem's solution.

Identify biological and cognitive factors in learning.

- Biological constraints restrict what an organism can learn from experience. These constraints include instinctive drift (the tendency of animals to revert to instinctive behaviour that interferes with learned behaviour), preparedness (the species-specific biological predisposition to learn in certain ways but not in others), and taste aversion (the biological predisposition to avoid foods that have caused sickness in the past).
- Although most psychologists agree that the principles of classical conditioning, operant conditioning, and observational learning are universal, cultural customs can influence the degree to which these learning processes are used. Culture also often determines the content of learning.

CONNECTIONS

For extra help in mastering the material in this chapter, see the integrator, review sections, practice quizzes, and other resources in the Student Study Guide and at the Online Learning Centre (www.mcgrawhill.ca/college/santrock).

CORE TERMS

learning, p. 268
associative learning, p. 268
classical conditioning, p. 269
unconditioned stimulus (UCS), p. 269
unconditioned response (UCR), p. 270
conditioned stimulus (CS), p. 270
conditioned response (CR), p. 270
acquisition (classical conditioning), p. 270
generalization (classical conditioning), p. 271
discrimination (classical conditioning), p. 271
extinction (classical conditioning), p. 272

spontaneous recovery, p. 272
counterconditioning, p. 274
law of effect, p. 276
operant conditioning, p. 277
shaping, p. 278
generalization (operant conditioning), p. 279
discrimination (operant conditioning), p. 279
extinction (operant conditioning), p. 281
reinforcement, p. 281
positive reinforcement, p. 281
negative reinforcement, p. 281
primary reinforcement, p. 281

secondary reinforcement, p. 281
schedules of reinforcement, p. 282
punishment, p. 283
positive punishment, p. 284
negative punishment, p. 284
applied behaviour analysis (behaviour modification) p. 287
observational learning, p. 290
latent learning, p. 294
insight learning, p. 295
instinctive drift, p. 295
preparedness, p. 296

8 Memory

CHAPTER QUESTIONS

1 What are the three fundamental memory processes?

2 How are memories encoded?

3 How are memories stored?

4 How are memories retrieved?

5 How are encoding, storage, and retrieval failure involved in long-term memory forgetting?

6 How are study strategies based on an understanding of memory?

In February, 2002, he was ranked the number one equities analyst in Canada by *Canadian Business Magazine*. But Doron Daniels couldn't tell you that, even though he read the article for himself while he was recovering from brain surgery to remove a life-threatening cyst. The same surgery that gave him a future stole it from him as well. Today he is reduced to finding pride in not getting lost on his walks to the Toronto Baycrest Centre for Geriatric Care. Now he cannot remember what day yesterday was, much less what he did yesterday. According to an article by Carolyn Abraham (*The Globe and Mail*, December 4, 2004), he can't even remember what he had for lunch today unless he reads a chart he updates and keeps on the fridge, to prevent him from always eating a turkey sandwich. Doron's wife Debbie explains that on a simple 5-minute drive to go shopping Doron might ask a dozen times, "Where are we going"?

You might think that amnesia arises from a bump to the head and results in forgetting your past. This is the more common *retrograde* amnesia (Guillery-Girard & others, 2004); *retro*—referring to an amnesia that extends back in time from the onset of the amnesia. But Doron remembers his past, at least before his surgery, quite well. His amnesia is *anterograde; antero*—referring to an amnesia that extends forward in time from the onset of the amnesia (Corkin, 2002). If you met Doron today, you could have a meaningful conversation with him, which indicates that his short-term memory is functional. But if you saw him again tomorrow, he would have no memory of ever meeting you, indicating that he can no longer consolidate short-term memories into his long-term memory. Amazingly, even though Doron cannot accumulate his short-term memories over successive moments in time, he is still capable of unconsciously learning new skills, indicating that consolidating skills is yet another form of memory entirely.

Marty Sheiner, another amnesiac in the Memory-Link program at the Baycrest Centre for Geriatric Care, will follow the instructions posted on his bed when he wakes up.

Although Doron is one of thousands of Canadians who suffers from anterograde amnesia, he is one of the few who benefits from Baycrest's Memory-Link Program. Baycrest psychologist Dr. Brian Richards and his colleagues have painstakingly taught amnesiacs like Doron to use a Palm Pilot to keep track of his life. Imagine having to remind Doron at the start of every one of 30 or more training sessions that he is indeed familiar with the Palm Pilot and that he already knows something about how to use it to keep track of his life. Like Leonard, the amnesiac protagonist of the 2001 film, *Memento*, who keeps track by writing all over his body, Doron now uses the Palm Pilot to gain some measure of control over a life lived completely in the here and now. Doron Daniel's extraordinary memory loss helps us to understand that ordinary memory, the theme of this chapter, is not a simple capability. As you will see, memory is a complex interaction of brain function, emotion, and individual circumstances. As psychologists learn more about this complex system and develop models to explain it, we benefit: The practical implications of psychology research are helping people overcome memory problems, and they are helping students study more effectively.

① THE NATURE OF MEMORY

What are the three fundamental memory processes?

Suppose you are trying to remember the name of that interesting person you met after class last week. You will be successful only if you had already taken that information into your memory, stored it there over the last week and now that you need it, can take it back out of storage. That is, **memory** is the retention of information over time through encoding, storage, and retrieval. The next three sections of this chapter focus on the fundamental processes of memory: encoding, storage, and retrieval. Although memory is very complex, thinking about it in terms of these three fundamental processes should help you to understand it better (see figure 8.1).

Except for annoying moments when memory fails or when someone we know is afflicted with memory loss, most of us don't think about how much everything we do or say depends on how smoothly our memory systems operate (Schacter, 2001; Buckner & Schacter, 2004). Think about how important memory is in carrying out the simple task of inviting that interesting person out for coffee. To begin with, you have to remember how to look up a phone number using the name you just remembered. You have to bring to mind all the information needed to execute the phone call. You have to use your memory of voices to determine whether the person answering the phone is the person you intended to call. To carry on the phone conversation with your new friend, you have to access a vast dictionary of words, sounds, meanings, and syntax stored in your memory. At some point, you will have to sort through your memory of visits to coffee shops or recommendations of new ones to decide where to meet. You have to recall details of how to get to the coffee shop. You also have to remember what else is going on in your life so that you don't plan to meet your new friend when you have something else scheduled.

We rely on our memory systems to carry out similar plans every day of our lives. Human memory systems are truly remarkable when you think of how much information we encode in our memories and how much we must retrieve to perform all of life's activities.

Human memory also has its imperfections, as we have all experienced. It is not unusual for two people to argue about whether something did or didn't happen, each intensely confident that his or her memory is accurate and the other person's is inaccurate. Each of us has also had the frustrating experience of trying to remember the name of someone or some place but not quite being able to retrieve it.

Other imperfections of memory surface in ongoing debates about the accuracy of memory in eyewitness testimony and the recovery of repressed experiences, both discussed later in this chapter. One dramatic example comes from a court case involving a

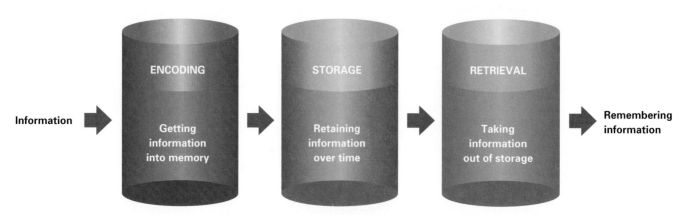

memory The retention of information over time through encoding, storage, and retrieval.

FIGURE 8.1 Processing Information in Memory

As you read about the many aspects of memory, keep in mind that we cannot successfully remember information without successfully encoding, storing, and retrieving that information.

father accused of the sexual abuse of his two daughters (Loftus, 1979). Under repeated questioning, the father began to "remember" episodes of abuse. In fact, a psychologist constructed a completely false story, which was repeatedly presented to the father, who responded by "remembering" that those events had happened as well.

This underscores an important point about memory: We don't just coldly encode, store, and retrieve bits of data in computer-like fashion (Schacter, 2000; Buckner & Schacter, 2004). In the early study of memory, subjective experience was considered inappropriate subject matter. Today, however, scientists who study memory recognize its subjective nature and investigate how people reconstruct their own versions of the past. They recognize that the mind can distort, invent, and forget. And they know that emotions colour memories. Clearly, we don't store judgment-free memories of reality.

> **reflect and review**

1 **Identify the three fundamental processes of memory.**

- Define memory and briefly profile the three fundamental processes of memory.

How important is memory in your life? What would your life be like without memory?

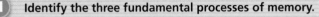

2 **MEMORY ENCODING**

— **Attention** — **Levels of Processing** — **Elaboration** — **Imagery**

How are memories encoded?

Encoding is the way in which information is processed for storage in memory. When you are listening to a lecture, watching a movie, listening to music, or talking with a friend, you are encoding information into memory. In everyday experiences, encoding has much in common with learning.

Some information gets into memory virtually automatically, whereas getting other information in takes effort. Let's examine some encoding processes that require effort. The issues that interest psychologists include how effectively we attend to information, how deeply we process it, how extensively we elaborate it with details, and how much we use mental imagery to encode it.

Attention

Look at the pictures of the three individuals in figure 8.2 for a few seconds. Then, before reading further, look away from them and state what you remember about the pictures.

FIGURE 8.2 Encoding Memories
Look at these three pictures for a few seconds; then look away and state what you remember about them.

encoding The way in which information gets into memory storage.

These are actually famous faces—George Washington, the Mona Lisa, and former U.S. president George H. W. Bush—with Elvis Presley's hair grafted onto their images. You likely did not recognize these famous individuals because of the prominent hair. When we remember a face, we usually attend to only a few key features and ignore the others. Therefore, in these pictures, you may have focused more on the hair than on the facial features.

To begin the process of memory encoding, we have to attend to information (Mangels, Picton, & Craik, 2001). Recall that in chapter 5 we discussed the role of attention in perception. Specifically, we highlighted the importance of selective attention, which involves focusing on a specific aspect of experience while ignoring others. Attention is selective by nature because the brain's resources are limited. Although our brains are remarkably efficient, they cannot attend to everything. Limitations mean that we have to selectively attend to some things in our environment and ignore others (Huang & Pashler, 2005; Macaluso, Frith, & Driver, 2002).

Divided attention also affects memory encoding. It occurs when a person must attend to several things simultaneously, as when driving a car (Brouwer & others, 2002). In studies of divided attention, researchers often have participants remember a set of materials, such as a list of words or a story (Cowan, 2005). At the same time they are trying to encode this information, participants are required to perform an additional task that draws their attention away from the initial task. In one study, pilots were asked to listen to air-traffic controller messages while carrying them out in flight simulator (Taylor & others, 2005). In a number of such studies, individuals who are allowed to give their full attention to information they are asked to remember do much better on subsequent memory tests of the information than do their counterparts who experienced divided attention (Pomplum, Reingold, & Shen, 2001; Cowan, 2005).

Levels of Processing

Simple attention to a stimulus does not completely explain the encoding process. For example, if you paid attention to the word *boat*, you might process the word at three different levels. At the shallowest level, you might notice the shapes of the letters. At an intermediate level, you might think of characteristics of the word (such as that it rhymes with *coat*). At the deepest level, you might think about the kind of boat you would like to own and the last time you went fishing.

University of Toronto psychologists Fergus Craik and Robert Lockhart (1972) proposed this influential model of the encoding process. Their **levels of processing theory** states that encoding is on a continuum from shallow to deep, with deeper processing producing better memory (see figure 8.3):

- *Shallow level.* The sensory or physical features of stimuli are analyzed. For instance, we might detect the lines, angles, and contours of a printed word's letters or detect a sound's frequency, duration, and loudness (recall the discussion of feature detection in chapter 5).
- *Intermediate level.* The stimulus is recognized and given a label. For example, we identify a four-legged, barking object as a dog.
- *Deepest level.* Information is processed semantically, in terms of its meaning. At this deepest level, we make associations. For example, we might associate the barking dog with a warning of danger or with good times such as playing fetch with a pet. The more associations, the deeper the processing (Lee, Cheung, & Wurm, 2000; Otten, Henson, & Rugg, 2001).

levels of processing theory States that memory is on a continuum from shallow to deep, with deeper processing producing better memory.

A number of studies have shown that people's memories improve when they use deep processing, as opposed to shallower processing (Craik & Lockhart, 1972; Conway, 2002). This has recently been shown to be true even for schizophrenics (Paul & others, 2005). For example, if you encode something meaningful about a face and make associations with it, you are more likely to remember it. You might attach meaning to the face of a person in your introductory psychology class by noting that she reminds you of someone you have seen on TV, or by associating her face with your psychology class.

Shallow Processing	Physical and perceptual features are analyzed.	The lines, angles, and contour that make up the physical appearance of an object, such as a car, are detected.
Intermediate Processing	Stimulus is recognized and labelled.	The object is recognized as a car.
Deep Processing	Semantic, meaningful, symbolic characteristics are used.	Associations connected with *car* are brought to mind—you think about the Porsche or Ferrari you hope to buy or the fun you and friends had on spring break when you drove a car to the beach.

Depth of Processing (vertical axis label)

FIGURE 8.3

Depth of Processing
According to the levels of processing theory of memory, deeper processing of stimuli produces better memory of them.

In fact, even meaningless stimuli can be remembered well if they are processed meaningfully. In one study, participants were asked to remember lists of nonsense syllables like *NGR* or *PFQ*. If participants imagined that the nonsense syllables were actually acronyms (one participant imagined that *NGR* stood for *National Government Review*), they remembered the nonsense syllables just as well as if they were real acronyms, such as *FBI* or *IBM* (Mitterer & Begg, 1979).

Elaboration

Psychologists soon recognized that there is more to good memory than depth of processing. Within deep processing, the more extensive the processing, the better the memory (Craik & Tulving, 1975). **Elaboration** is the extensiveness of processing at any given level. For example, rather than memorizing the definition of *memory*, you would do better to come up with some examples of how information enters your mind, how it is stored, and how you can retrieve it. Thinking of examples of a concept is a good way to understand it. Self-reference is another effective way to elaborate information (Fujita & Horiuchi, 2004; Czienskowski & Giljohann, 2002; see figure 8.4). For example, if the word *win* is on a list of words to remember, you might think of the last time you won a draw, or if the word *cook* appears, you might imagine the last time you cooked dinner. In general, elaborate processing of meaningful information, also referred to as *elaborative rehearsal* (Craik & Lockhart, 1972), is a good way to remember.

One reason elaboration produces good memory is that it adds to the *distinctiveness* of the "memory codes" (Hege & Dodson, 2004). Distinctiveness describes the extent to which one memory differs from another in our memory. To remember some information, such as a name or a fact about geography, you need to search for the code that contains this information among the mass of codes contained in long-term memory. The search process is easier if the memory code is somehow highly distinctive (Dodson,

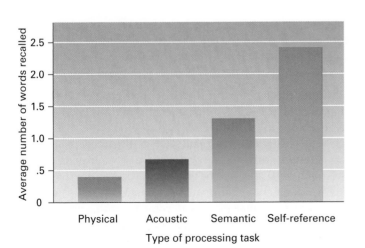

FIGURE 8.4

Memory Improves when Self-Referencing Is Used
In one study, researchers asked participants to remember lists of words according to the words' physical, acoustic (sound), semantic (meaning), or self-referent characteristics. As can be seen, when individuals generated self-references for the words, they remembered them better.

elaboration The extensiveness of processing at any given level of memory.

The more that you elaborate about an event, the better your memory of the event will be. For example, if you were at an open-air rock concert and you encoded information about how large the crowd was, who accompanied you, which songs you heard, how powerful the performances were, what the weather was like, and other vivid sights, sounds, and smells, you probably will remember the concert clearly.

& Schacter, 2002). This is not unlike searching for a friend at a busy airport. If your friend is two metres tall and has flaming red hair and a nose ring, it will be easier to find him or her in the crowd.

As encoding becomes more elaborate, more information is stored. And as more information is stored, the more likely it is that this code will become more distinctive, and thus easier to differentiate from other memory codes. For example, if you witnessed a bank robbery and observed that the getaway car was a jet black 2005 Ford Mustang with tinted windows and spinners on the wheels, your memory of the car would be more distinctive than if you had noticed only that the getaway car was black. Neuroscience research has shown a link between elaboration during encoding and brain activity. In one study, individuals were placed in magnetic resonance imaging (MRI) machines (which were discussed in chapter 3), and pictures were flashed on a screen inside (Mandzia & others, 2004). Sometimes individuals judged whether the pictures were in colour or black-and-white (shallow processing) and sometimes they judged whether the photos were of natural or man-made objects (deeper, more elaborated processing). In this study, the participants showed more neural activity and better memory during the deeper task than they did when they were asked merely to state whether the pictures were colour or black-and-white. The researchers' conclusions: Deeper processing and greater elaboration of information is linked with neural activity, including in the brain's left frontal lobe, and with improved memory.

As we explained in the preface, if you are following the PQ4R method around which this textbook is organized, you are spending a fair amount of effort elaborating your encoding of the material in the textbook. Your efforts should result in deeper, more elaborated encodings of the textbook content and, rthus, better recall for that material when you need to remember it, such as on exams.

Imagery

Psychologist Alexander Luria (1968) chronicled the life of S., whose unique visual imagination allowed him to remember an extraordinary amount of detail. Imagery helped S. remember complicated lists of items and information. For example, S. once was asked to remember the following formula:

$$N \cdot \sqrt{d^2 \cdot \frac{85}{VX} \cdot 3\sqrt{\frac{276^2 \cdot 86x}{n^2 V \cdot \pi 264}}} \, n^2 b$$
$$= sv \, \frac{1624}{32^2} \cdot r^2 s$$

S. studied the formula for seven minutes and then reported how he memorized it. Notice in his account of this process, which follows, how he used imagery:

> Neiman (N) came out and jabbed at the ground with his cane (·). He looked up at a tall tree, which resembled the square-root sign (√), and thought to himself: "No wonder this tree has withered and begun to expose its roots. After all, it was here when I built these two houses" (d^2). Once again he poked his cane (·). Then he said: "The houses are old, I'll have to get rid of them; the sale will bring in far more money." He had originally invested 85,000 in them (85) . . . (Luria, 1968)

S.'s complete story was four times this length. But the elaborated imagery in the story he created must have been powerful, because S. remembered the formula perfectly 15 years later without any advance notice!

You may not be capable of this feat, but you are still likely to use imagery to encode information. Here's a demonstration: How many windows are in your apartment or house? If you live in a dorm room with only one or two windows, this question might be too easy. If so, how many windows are in your parents' home? Few of us have ever set out to memorize this information, but many of us can come up with a good answer, especially if we use imagery to "reconstruct" each room. We take a mental walk through the house, counting windows as we go.

For years psychologists ignored the role of imagery in memory, but the studies of University of Western Ontario psychologist Allan Paivio (1971, 1986; Sadowski & Paivio, 2001) documented just how much imagery can improve memory. Paivio argued that memory is stored in one of two ways: as a verbal code or as an image code. For example, a picture can be remembered by a label (verbal code) or by a mental image. Paivio thinks that the image code, which is highly detailed and distinctive, produces better memory through deeper, more elaborated processing. The *dual-code hypothesis* claims that memory for images is better because the memory for the concept (image) is stored both as an imaginal code *and* as a verbal code, thus providing two potential avenues by which information can be retrieved.

Imagery is now accepted as an important aspect of memory (Roeckelein, 2004). Paivio's dual-code hypothesis is even commonly used to help design web pages (Hong, Thong, & Tam, 2004). However, there is still controversy over whether the brain actually has separate codes for words and images, as opposed to two different ways to treat the same code (Pylyshyn, 1981, 2003). More about imagery appears later in the chapter when we discuss strategies for improving memory. For now, keep in mind that if you need to remember a list of things, forming mental images will help. It will be especially helpful if you imagine items interacting with each other (Begg, 1983) or can animate your images (Lowe, 2004).

> ## > reflect and review
>
> **(2)** **Explain how memories are encoded.**
>
> - Summarize how attention is involved in memory.
> - Describe the levels of processing involved in memory.
> - Discuss elaboration.
> - Describe the role of imagery in memory.
>
> *Think of a common object or location that you see every day (for example, your alarm clock or the place where you live) but that is not currently in your sight. Draw the object or location, or write a detailed description of it. Then compare your results with the real thing. What differences do you notice? Does what you learned about encoding help to explain the differences?*

(3) MEMORY STORAGE

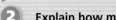

Sensory Memory — Short-Term Memory — Long-Term Memory

What are the main features of the three systems of memory storage?

The quality of encoding is not the only thing that determines the quality of memory. The memory also needs to be stored properly after it is encoded. **Storage** encompasses how information is retained over time and how it is represented in memory.

We remember some information for less than a second, some for half a minute, and some for minutes, hours, years, even a lifetime. Richard Atkinson and Richard Shiffrin (1968) formulated a very influential theory of memory (e.g., Chizuko, 1999) that acknowledged the varying life span of memories. The **Atkinson-Shiffrin theory** states that memory storage involves a system characterized by time frames (see figure 8.5):

- *Sensory memory*: time frames of a fraction of a second to several seconds
- *Short-term memory*: time frames up to 30 seconds
- *Long-term memory*: time frames up to a lifetime

storage Ways in which information is retained over time and how it is represented in memory.

Atkinson-Shiffrin theory The view that memory involves a sequence of three stages: sensory memory, short-term memory, and long-term memory.

FIGURE 8.5
Atkinson and Shiffrin's Theory of Memory
In this model, sensory input goes into sensory memory. Through the process of attention, information moves into short-term memory, where it remains for 30 seconds or less, unless it is rehearsed. When the information goes into long-term memory storage, it can be retrieved over the lifetime.

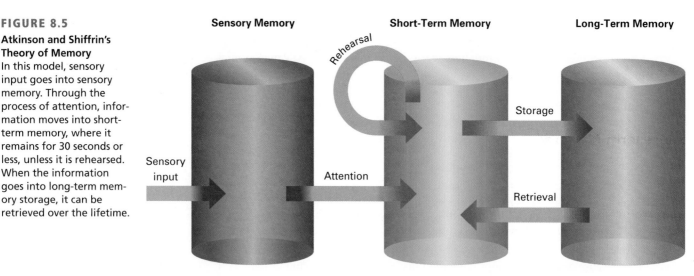

FIGURE 8.5

Type of sensory memory	
Echoic	Iconic
Up to several seconds	About ¼ second

FIGURE 8.6

Auditory and Visual Sensory Memory
If you hear this bird's call while walking in a nearby provincial park, your auditory sensory memory holds the information for several seconds. If you see the bird, your visual sensory memory holds the information for only about ¼ of a second.

sensory memory Holds information from the world in its original form only for an instant, not much longer than the brief time it is exposed to the visual, auditory, and other senses.

As you read about these three memory storage systems, you will find that time frame is not the only thing that makes them different from one another. Each type of memory operates in a unique way and has a special purpose.

Sensory Memory

Sensory memory holds information from the world in its original sensory form for only an instant, not much longer than the brief time it is exposed to the visual, auditory, and other senses (Lu & Sperling, 2003). Sensory memory is very rich and detailed, but the information in it is very quickly lost unless certain processes are engaged in that transfer it into short-term or long-term memory.

Think about all the sights and sounds you encounter as you walk to class on a typical morning. Literally thousands of stimuli come into your fields of vision and hearing—cracks in the sidewalk, chirping birds, a noisy motorcycle, the blue sky, faces of hundreds of people. We do not process all these stimuli, but we do process a number of them. In general, you process many more stimuli at the sensory level than you consciously notice. Sensory memory retains this information from your senses, including a large portion of what you think you ignore.

But sensory memory does not retain the information very long (Grau & others, 2002). *Echoic memory* (from the word *echo*) is the name given to auditory sensory memory, which is retained for up to several seconds. *Iconic memory* (from the word *icon*, which means "image") is the name given to visual sensory memory, which is retained only for about one-quarter of a second (see figure 8.6). The sensory memory for other senses, such as smell and touch, has received little attention.

The first scientific research on sensory memory focused on iconic memory. In George Sperling's (1960) classic study, participants were presented with patterns of stimuli such as those in figure 8.7. As you look at the letters, you have no trouble recognizing them. But Sperling flashed the letters on a screen for very brief intervals, about one-twentieth of a second. After a pattern was flashed on the screen, the participants could report only four or five letters. With such short exposure, reporting all nine letters was impossible.

Some of the participants in Sperling's study reported feeling that, for an instant, they could *see* all nine letters within a briefly flashed pattern. But they ran into trouble when they tried to *name* all the letters they had initially seen. One hypothesis to explain this experience is that all nine letters were initially processed as far as the iconic sensory memory level. This is why all nine letters were *seen*. However, forgetting was so rapid that the participants could *name* only a handful of letters before the others were lost from sensory memory.

Sperling reasoned that if all nine letters were actually processed in sensory memory, they must all be available for a brief time. To test this possibility, Sperling sounded a low, medium, or high tone just after a pattern of letters was shown. The participants were told that the tone was a signal to report only the letters from the bottom, middle, or top row. Under these conditions, the participants performed much better, suggesting a brief memory for most or all of the letters in the display.

FIGURE 8.7

Sperling's Sensory Memory Experiment This array of stimuli is similar to those flashed for about ½₀ of a second to the participants in Sperling's study.

Short-Term Memory

Much information goes no further than the stage of sensory memory of sounds and sights. This information is retained for only a brief instant. However, some of the information, especially that to which we pay attention, is transferred to short-term memory. **Short-term memory** is a limited-capacity memory system in which information is usually retained only for as long as 30 seconds unless strategies are used to retain it longer. Compared with sensory memory, short-term memory is limited in capacity, but it can store information for a longer time.

The limited capacity of short-term memory was examined by George Miller (1956) in a classic paper with a catchy title, *The Magical Number Seven, Plus or Minus Two*. Miller pointed out that on many tasks individuals are limited in how much information they can keep track of without external aids. Usually the limit is in the range of 7 ± 2 items. The most widely cited example of the 7 ± 2 phenomenon involves *memory span*, which is the number of digits an individual can report back in order after a single presentation of them. Most college or university students can remember lists of eight or nine digits without making errors. Longer lists, however, pose problems because they exceed short-term memory capacity. If you rely on simple short-term memory to retain longer lists of items, you will probably make errors.

Chunking and Rehearsal   Two ways to improve short-term memory are chunking and rehearsal. *Chunking* involves grouping or "packing" information that exceeds the 7 ± 2 memory span into higher order units that can be remembered as single units. In essence, chunking is a form of memory encoding: specifically, elaboration. It works by making large amounts of information more manageable.

For an example of how chunking works, consider this simple list of words: *hot, city, book, forget, tomorrow,* and *smile*. Try to hold these words in memory for a moment, then write them down. If you recalled the words, you succeeded in holding 34 letters, grouped into seven chunks, in your memory. Now try another example of how chunking works. Hold the following in memory and then write it down:

O LDH ARO LDAN DYO UNGB EN

How did you do? Don't feel bad if you did poorly. This string of letters is very difficult to remember, even though it is arranged in chunks. However, if you shift the spaces so that the chunks form the meaningful words *Old Harold and Young Ben*, they become much easier to remember. Recall that this sort of deep, semantic processing during encoding helps with memory tasks.

Another way to improve short-term memory involves *rehearsal*, the conscious repetition of information. Information stored in short-term memory lasts half a minute or less without rehearsal. However, if rehearsal is not interrupted, information can be retained indefinitely. Rehearsal is often verbal, giving the impression of an inner voice, but it can also be visual or spatial, giving the impression of a private inner eye. One way to use your visualization skills is to maintain the appearance of an object or scene for a period of time after you have viewed it. People who are unusually good at this task are said to have *eidetic imagery*, or a *photographic memory*. All of us can do this to some degree, but a small number of individuals may be so good at maintaining an image that they literally "see" the page of a textbook as they try to remember information during a test. Luria's case study, S., mentioned earlier, had a photographic memory. However, eidetic imagery is so rare it has been difficult to study.

short-term memory A limited-capacity memory system in which information is retained for only as long as 30 seconds unless strategies are used to retain it longer.

Working Memory

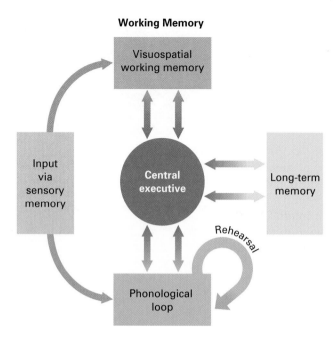

FIGURE 8.8 Working Memory
In Baddeley's working memory model, working memory is like a mental workbench where a great deal of information processing is carried out. Working memory consists of three main components: The phonological loop and visuospatial working memory serve as assistants, helping the central executive do its work. Input from sensory memory goes to the phonological loop, where information about speech is stored and rehearsal takes place, and visuospatial working memory, where visual and spatial information, including imagery, are stored. Working memory is a limited-capacity system, and information is stored there for only a brief time. Working memory interacts with long-term memory, using information from long-term memory in its work and transmitting information to long-term memory for longer storage.

working memory A three-part system that temporarily holds information. Working memory is a kind of mental workbench on which information is manipulated and assembled to perform other cognitive tasks.

Rehearsal works best when we need to briefly remember a list of numbers or items. When we have to remember information for longer periods of time, as when we are studying for a test coming up next week, tomorrow, or even an hour from now, other strategies usually work better. The main reason rehearsal does not work well for retaining information over the long term is that rehearsal often involves just rote repetition of information without imparting any meaning to it. Remembering information over the long term works better when we add meaning to it, which, again, is an example of the importance of deep, semantic processing.

Working Memory Some contemporary experts on memory believe that Atkinson and Shiffrin's theory of the three time-linked memory systems is too simplistic (Baddeley, 2000, 2001, 2003; Neath & others, 2005) They believe that memory does not always work in a neatly packaged three-stage sequence such as Atkinson and Shiffrin proposed; and they think that both short-term and long-term memory are far more complex and dynamic. For example, some experts believe that short-term memory uses long-term memory's contents in more flexible ways than simply retrieving information from it (Murdock, 1999). And they believe that short-term memory involves far more than rehearsal and passive storage of information. We now examine the working-memory view of short-term memory.

British psychologist Alan Baddeley (Baddeley & Hitch, 1974; Baddeley, 2000, 2001) proposed that short-term memory is better thought of as **working memory**, a three-part system that temporarily holds information as people perform cognitive tasks. Working memory is a kind of mental "workbench" on which information is manipulated and assembled to help us comprehend written and spoken language, make decisions, and solve problems. Notice that working memory is not like a passive storehouse with shelves to store information until it moves to long-term memory, but rather an active memory system (Jonides, Lacey, & Nee, 2005; Nyberg & others, 2002).

Figure 8.8 shows Baddeley's view of the three components of working memory. Think of them as a boss (the central executive) who has two assistants (the phonological loop and visuospatial working memory) to help do the work.

1. The *phonological loop* is specialized to briefly store speech-based information about the sounds of language. The phonological loop contains two separate components: an acoustic code, which decays in a few seconds, and rehearsal, which allows individuals to repeat the words in the phonological store.

2. *Visuospatial working memory* stores visual and spatial information, including visual imagery (Finke & others, 2005). Visuospatial working memory has also been called the *visuospatial scratch pad*. As in the case of the phonological loop, the capacity of visuospatial working memory is limited. For example, if you try to put too many items in visuospatial working memory, you can't represent them accurately enough to successfully retrieve them. The phonological loop and visuospatial memory function independently (Reed, 2004; Baddeley, 2003). You could rehearse numbers in the phonological loop while making spatial arrangements of letters in visuospatial working memory (Baddeley & Hitch, 1974; Cornoldi & Vecchi, 2003).

3. The *central executive* integrates information not only from the phonological loop and visuospatial working memory but also from long-term memory. In Baddeley's (2000, 2001, 2003) view, the central executive plays important roles in attention, planning, and organizing. The central executive acts much like a supervisor who

monitors which issues and information deserve attention and which should be ignored. It also selects which strategies to use to process information and solve problems. As with the other two components of working memory—the phonological loop and visuospatial working memory—the central executive has a limited capacity.

The idea of working memory has proven useful. Individual differences in working memory are related to performance in other cognitive domains (e.g., reading; Daneman & Merikle, 1996; verbal fluency; Daneman, 1991). The working memory concept also allows us to better understand how brain damage influences cognitive skills. For example, some amnesiacs perform well on working memory tasks, but show deficits in learning new information in long-term memory tasks. Another group shows the reverse pattern. One patient had good long-term memory despite having a two-digit memory span (Baddeley, 1992)! The phonological loop was the source of this patient's memory problem. Because he could not maintain verbal codes in the loop, his memory span suffered. He also had difficulty learning new associations between words and nonsense sounds. Working memory deficits are also involved in Alzheimer's disease—a progressive, irreversible brain disorder in older adults that was discussed in chapter 4. Baddeley believes the central executive of the working memory model is the culprit—Alzheimer's patients have great difficulty coordinating different mental activities, one of the central executive's functions (Baddeley, 2003; Logie & others, 2004).

Let's examine another aspect of life in which working memory is involved. In one recent study, verbal working memory was impaired by negative emotion (Gray, 2001; Kensinger & Corkin, 2003). Recall from chapter 2 that writing about emotionally traumatic experiences was linked with improvement in college students' health (Pennebaker, 2001, 2004). Might writing about negative events also produce improvement in working memory? In one study, college students who wrote about a negative emotional event showed sizable improvement in working memory compared with students who wrote about a positive event and those in a control group who wrote about their daily schedule (Klein & Boals, 2001). The expressive-writing effect on working memory occurred only when students had fewer intrusive and avoidant thoughts. In the study, improvement in working memory was associated with higher grade point averages. An important implication of this study is its demonstration that working memory is malleable and can be affected by an experience, such as expressive writing. For example, students with math anxiety often experience working memory deficits when doing math problems because of intrusive thoughts and their worry about performance (Ashcraft & Kirk, 2001; Beilock & others, 2004). Such students might benefit from writing about their math anxiety.

Long-Term Memory

Long-term memory is a relatively permanent type of memory that stores huge amounts of information for a long time. The capacity of long-term memory is indeed staggering. John von Neumann, a distinguished computer scientist, put the size at 2.8×10^{20} (280 quintillion) bits, which in practical terms means that our storage capacity is virtually unlimited. Von Neumann assumed that we never forget anything, but even considering that we do forget things, we can hold several billion times more information than a large computer.

Long-term memory is complex, as figure 8.9 shows. At the top level, it is divided into substructures of explicit memory and implicit memory. Explicit memory can be further subdivided into episodic and semantic memory. Implicit memory includes the systems involved in procedural memory, priming, and classical conditioning (Squire, 2004).

In simple terms, explicit memory has to do with remembering who, what, where, when, and why; implicit memory has to do with remembering how. At the beginning of this chapter, we met Doron Daniels, who developed anterograde amnesia as a result of brain surgery. To explore the distinction between explicit and implicit memory, let's

long-term memory A relatively permanent type of memory that holds huge amounts of information for a long period of time.

FIGURE 8.9

Systems of Long-Term Memory

```
                        ┌─────────────────────────┐
                        │  Long-Term Memory Systems │
                        └─────────────────────────┘
                  ┌──────────────┴──────────────────┐
      ┌───────────────────────┐          ┌─────────────────────────┐
      │   Explicit Memory      │          │    Implicit Memory       │
      │ (Declarative Memory)   │          │ (Nondeclarative Memory)  │
      └───────────────────────┘          └─────────────────────────┘
        ┌──────────┴─────────┐      ┌───────────────┼────────────────┐
  ┌──────────┐  ┌──────────┐  ┌──────────────┐ ┌──────────┐ ┌──────────────┐
  │ Episodic │  │ Semantic │  │  Procedural  │ │ Priming  │ │  Classical   │
  │ Memory   │  │ Memory   │  │Memory (Skills)│ │          │ │ Conditioning │
  └──────────┘  └──────────┘  └──────────────┘ └──────────┘ └──────────────┘
```

University of Toronto psychologist Endel Tulving says: "Remembering events is a universally familiar experience. It is also a uniquely human one. As far as we know, members of no other species possess quite the same ability to experience again now, in a different situation and perhaps in a different form, happenings from the past, and know that the experience refers to an event that occurred in another time and place."

explicit memory (declarative memory) The conscious recollection of information, such as specific facts or events and, at least in humans, information that can be verbally communicated.

episodic memory The retention of nformation about the where and when of life's happenings.

look at the first well-studied case of anterograde amnesia, a person known only as H. M. (Corkin, 2002). He had a severe case of epilepsy and underwent surgery in 1953 that involved removing the hippocampus and a portion of the temporal lobes of both hemispheres in his brain. (The location and functions of these areas of the brain were discussed in chapter 3. His epilepsy improved, but something devastating happened to his memory. Though he could still retrieve long-term memories from before his surgery and function on a moment-by-moment basis, relying on his working memory, what he could *not* do was consolidate new memories that outlive working memory. H. M.'s memory time frame is only a few minutes at most, so he lives, as he has done since 1953, in a perpetual present and cannot remember any past events since 1953 (explicit memory). In contrast, his memory of how to do things (implicit memory) was less affected. For example, he can learn new physical tasks. In one such task, H. M. was asked to trace the outline of a star-shaped figure while he was able to view the figure and his hand only through a mirror. This is a task that most people find difficult in the beginning. Over three days of training, H. M. learned this task as effectively and rapidly as normal individuals. On the second and third days, he began at the level he had achieved the previous day (a success in implicit memory), even though he was completely unaware that he had previously practised the task (a failure in explicit memory). H. M.'s situation clearly demonstrates a distinction between explicit memory, which was dramatically impaired in his case, and implicit memory, which in his case was less influenced by his surgery.

Let's now explore the long-term memory subsystems of explicit and implicit memory. After you read about these basic structures, you will learn about the theories developed to explain how they are organized. You will also read about recent discoveries in neuroscience that shed light on where in the brain memory is stored.

Explicit Memory **Explicit memory** (or **declarative memory**) is the conscious recollection of information, such as specific facts or events and, at least in humans, information that can be verbally communicated (Tulving, 1989, 2000). Examples of explicit, or declarative, memory include recounting the events of a movie you have seen and describing a basic principle of psychology to someone. However, you do not need to be talking to be using explicit memory. Simply sitting and consciously reflecting about Einstein's theory of relativity or the date you had last weekend involves explicit memory (Graf & Schacter, 1985; Badgaiyan, 2005).

Episodic and Semantic Memory University of Toronto psychologist Endel Tulving (1972, 1989, 2000) has forcefully advocated distinguishing between two subtypes of explicit memory: episodic and semantic. **Episodic memory** is the retention of information about the where and when of life's happenings (Tulving, 2002). It is autobiographical. For example, episodic memory includes the details of what it was like when your younger brother or sister was born, what happened on your first date, what you were doing when you heard of the Asian tsunami, and what you had for breakfast this morning (Tulving, 1999a).

Characteristic	Episodic Memory	Semantic Memory
Units	Events, episodes	Facts, ideas, concepts
Organization	Time	Concepts
Emotion	More important	Less important
Retrieval process	Deliberate (effortful)	Automatic
Retrieval report	"I remember"	"I know"
Education	Irrelevant	Relevant
Intelligence	Irrelevant	Relevant
Legal testimony	Admissible in court	Inadmissible in court

FIGURE 8.10

Some Differences Between Episodic and Semantic Memory
The above characteristics have been proposed as the main ways to differentiate episodic and semantic memory.

Semantic memory, on the other hand is a person's knowledge about the world. It includes your fields of expertise, general knowledge of the sort you learned in school, and everyday knowledge about meanings of words, famous individuals, important places, and common things. For example, semantic memory is involved in a person's knowledge of video games, of geography, and of who Nelson Mandela and Louis Riel are. An important aspect of semantic memory is that it appears to be independent of an individual's personal identity with the past. You can access a fact— such as that Whitehorse is the capital of the Yukon—and not have the foggiest notion of when and where you learned it.

Several examples help to clarify the distinction between episodic and semantic memory. Your memory of your first day on campus involves episodic memory. If you take a history class, your memory of the information you need to know to do well on the next test involves semantic memory.

Consider also that in a certain type of amnesiac state, a person might forget entirely who she is—her name, family, career, and all other information about herself—yet she can talk and demonstrate general knowledge about the world. Her episodic memory is impaired, but her semantic memory is functioning. Endel Tulving (1989) reported an especially dramatic case of this type, a young Ontario man named K. C. After suffering a motorcycle accident, K. C. lost virtually all use of his episodic memory. The loss was so profound that he was unable to consciously recollect a single thing that had ever happened to him. At the same time, K. C.'s semantic memory was sufficiently preserved that he could learn about his past as a set of facts, just as he would learn about another person's life. He could report, for example, that the saddest day of his life was when his brother died of drowning about 10 years before. But further questioning revealed that K. C. had no conscious memory of the event. He simply knew about the drowning because he was able to recall—apparently through use of his semantic memory—what he had been told about his brother by other members of his family.

Some aspects of the episodic/semantic distinction are summarized in figure 8.10. Although the distinctions listed have attracted considerable attention, they remain controversial. One criticism is that many cases of explicit, declarative memory are neither purely episodic nor purely semantic but fall in a grey area in between. Consider your memory for what you studied last night. You probably added knowledge to your semantic memory—that was, after all, the reason you were studying. You probably remember where you were studying, as well as about when you started and when you stopped. You can probably also remember some minor occurrences, such as a burst of loud laughter from the room next door or the coffee you spilled on the desk. Is episodic or semantic memory involved here? Tulving (1983, 2000) argues that semantic and episodic systems often work together in forming new memories. In such cases, the memory that is ultimately formed might consist of an autobiographical episode and semantic information.

Ontario resident K. C. suffered a motorcycle accident that left him with an amazing form of retrograde amnesia. While K. C. could remember most of his general knowledge of the world, he lost pretty well everything he had ever known about his own past and never recovered it. He could still play chess but could not remember ever having played. That is, he had lost his episodic memory, but not his semantic memory, thus providing strong evidence in support of this distinction, which was advanced by Tulving (1972).

semantic memory A person's knowledge about the world.

Prospective Memory One interesting area in episodic memory research is prospective memory (Smith & Bayen, 2004; Graf & Uttl, 2001; Burgess, Quayle, & Frith, 2001). The main focus of this chapter is **retrospective memory**, which is remembering the past. **Prospective memory** involves remembering information about doing something in the future; it includes memory for intentions. Many of us have somewhat embarrassing or difficult experiences when prospective memory fails. For example, we might forget to buy a food item at the store, miss an appointment, or forget that a homework assignment is due. Prospective memory includes both *timing*—when to do something—and *content*—what it is we have to do.

A distinction can be made between time-based and event-based prospective memory (Mathias & Mansfield, 2005). *Time-based* prospective memory is your intention to engage in a given behaviour after a specified amount of time has gone by (such as an intention to make a phone call to someone in one hour). In event-based prospective memory, you engage in the intended behaviour when it is elicited by some external event or cue (such as giving a message to a roommate when you see him or her). Researchers have found that the cues available in *event-based* prospective memory make it more effective than time-based prospective memory (Einstein & McDaniel, 1996).

Some failures in prospective memory are referred to as *absentmindedness*. We become more absentminded when we become preoccupied with something else, are distracted by something, or are under a lot of time pressures (Mäntylä, 2003). Absentmindedness often involves a breakdown between attention and memory storage (Schacter, 2001). Absentmindedness may especially be a problem when we have too little time or are too distracted to elaboratively encode something we need to remember. We spend a great deal of our lives on autopilot, which helps us to perform routine tasks effectively but also makes us vulnerable to absentminded errors.

Continuing research on prospective memory is providing new clues that will help people improve their memories (d'Ydewalle, Bouckaert, & Brunfaut, 2001). In one study, individuals were given four minutes to recall what they did yesterday, last week, or last year (retrospective memories) and four minutes to recall what they intended to do tomorrow, next week, or next year (prospective memories; Maylor, Chater, & Brown, 2001). More prospective memories were recalled than retrospective memories. Researchers have also found that older adults perform worse on prospective memory tasks than younger adults do (Mäntylä, 2003; Einstein & others, 2000; West & Craik, 2001).

Implicit (Nondeclarative Memory) In addition to explicit memory, there is a type of long-term memory, which is related to nonconsciously remembering skills and sensory perceptions rather than consciously remembering facts. **Implicit memory** (or **nondeclarative memory**) is memory in which behaviour is affected by prior experience without that experience being consciously recollected (Graf & Schacter, 1985). Examples of implicit memory include the skills of playing tennis, riding a bicycle, and typing. Another example of implicit memory is the repetition in your mind of a song you heard playing in the supermarket, even though you did not consciously attend to what music was playing.

The distinction between explicit and implicit memory has also illuminated forgetting in amnesiacs and the elderly. Amazingly, amnesiacs who perform poorly when given an explicit memory test such as cued recall perform just fine when an implicit memory task is used (Graf & Schacter, 1985). How can amnesiacs, who are supposed to be unable to remember, show a *dissociation* between explicit and implicit memory performance (Cavaco & others, 2004)? Incidentally, Fleischman and her colleagues (2004) have shown that older people show the same dissociation. While we do know that the memory deficits of amnesiacs and the elderly are relatively restricted to explicit memory, we do not yet know why.

Three subsystems of implicit memory are procedural memory, priming, and classical conditioning. These subsystems all consist of memories that you are not aware of, although they predispose you to behave in certain ways (Schacter, 2000).

retrospective memory Remembering the past.

prospective memory Remembering information about doing something in the future.

implicit memory (nondeclarative memory) Memory in which behaviour is affected by prior experience without that experience being consciously recollected.

FRANK AND ERNEST   by Bob Thaves

CITY STREET DEPT. - Planning Section

FIFTH ST.
FIRST ST.
FOURTH ST.
SECOND ST.
SIXTH ST.
THIRD ST.

TO AVOID CONFUSION, WE DECIDED TO REARRANGE THE STREETS ALPHABETICALLY.

FRANK & ERNEST reprinted by permission of Newspaper Enterprise Association, Inc.

Procedural memory involves memory for skills (Lieberman, 2004; Tulving, 1985). For example, as you surf the Internet, you may not be conscious of where the function keys are for going back or for bookmarking a Web site, yet your automatized, nonconscious skill of surfing allows you to hit the right keys. Once you have learned to drive a car, you don't even notice remembering how to do it: You do not have to consciously remember how to drive the car as you put the key in the ignition, turn the steering wheel, press on the gas pedal, hit the brakes, and so on.

Priming is the activation of information that people already have in storage to help them remember new information better and faster (Rueckl & Galantucci, 2005; Badgaiyan, Schacter, & Alpert, 2001). In a common demonstration of priming, individuals study a list of words (such as *hope*, *walk*, and *cake*). Then they are given a standard recognition task to assess explicit memory. They must select all the words that appeared on the first list—for example, "Did you see the word *hope*? Did you see the word *truck*?" Then participants are given a *stem-completion* task, which assesses implicit memory since it does not require deliberate memory retrieval. In this task, they are shown a list of incomplete words (for example, *ho__, wa__, ca__*), called word stems, and are told to fill in the blanks with whatever word comes to mind. The results show that individuals fill in the blanks with words they had previously studied more often than would be expected if they were filling them in randomly. For example, they are more likely to complete the stem *ho__* with *hope* than with *hole*. This is so even when individuals did not recognize the words on the earlier recognition task. Because priming occurs even when explicit memory for previous information is not required, it is assumed to be an involuntary and nonconscious process (Hauptmann & Karni, 2002).

Another type of implicit memory is found in *classical conditioning*, a form of learning discussed in chapter 7. Recall that classical conditioning involves the automatic learning of associations between stimuli. For instance, a person who is constantly criticized may develop high blood pressure or other physical problems. Classically conditioned associations such as this involve nonconscious, implicit memory.

How Memory Is Organized Cognitive psychologists have been successful in classifying the types of long-term memory. But classifying the components of long-term memory does not address the question of how the different types of memory are organized for storage. The word *organized* is important: Memories are not haphazardly stored but are instead carefully sorted.

Here's a demonstration. Recall the 12 months of the year as quickly as you can. How long did it take you? What was the order of your recall? Chances are you listed them within a few seconds in "natural," chronological order (January, February, March, and so on). Now try to remember the months in alphabetical order. Did you make any errors? How long did it take you? It should be obvious that your memory for the months of the year is organized in a particular way. Indeed, one of memory's most distinctive features is its organization. Researchers have found that if people are encouraged to simply organize material, their memories of the material improve, even if no warning is given that their memories will be tested (Mandler, 1980). Psychologists have developed four main theories of how long-term memory is organized: hierarchies, semantic networks, schemas, and connectionist networks.

procedural memory Memory for skills.

priming A type of implicit memory; information that people already have in storage is activated to help them remember new information better and faster.

FIGURE 8.11
Semantic Networks in the Organization of Long-Term Memory
Originally, the theory of semantic networks envisioned long-term memory as a hierarchy of concepts with nodes (branching points) at different levels of abstraction. Notice how the information becomes more detailed and specific as you move through the levels of the hierarchy in this model. Some psychologists have challenged this representation as too "clean" to portray the true complexity of our representation processes.

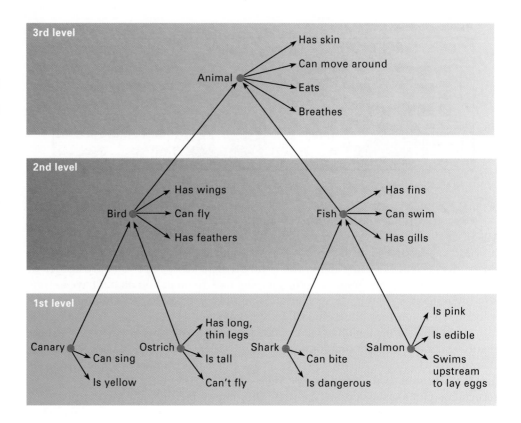

Hierarchies In many instances we remember facts better when we organize them hierarchically (Bruning & others, 2004). A *hierarchy* is a system in which items are organized from general to specific classes. One common example is the organization chart showing the relationship of units in a business or a school, with the CEO or president at the top, the vice presidents or deans at the next level, and the managers or professors at a third level. This textbook is also organized hierarchically—with four levels of headings—to help you understand how the various bits of information in the book are related; the table of contents provides a visual representation of the hierarchy of the top two levels of headings.

In an early research study, Gordon Bower and his colleagues (1969) showed the importance of hierarchical organization in memory. Participants who were given the words in hierarchies remembered them better than those who were given the words in random groupings.

Semantic Networks Early theories of the organization of explicit memory held that memory is organized into *semantic networks*, complex interconnected webs of nodes that stand for labels or concepts (see figure 8.11). The networks were assumed to be hierarchically arranged, with more concrete concepts (*canary*, for example) nested under more abstract concepts (*bird*).

More recently, cognitive psychologists realized that such hierarchical networks are too simple to describe the way human cognition actually works (Shanks, 1991). For example, people take longer to answer the true-or-false statement "An ostrich is a bird" than they do to answer the statement "A canary is a bird." Yet, according to the hierarchically organized semantic network in figure 8.11, both the canary and ostrich nodes are equally closely linked to the bird node.

Memory researchers now see human semantic networks as much more irregular and distorted: a typical bird, such as a *canary*, is closer to the node or centre of the category *bird* than is the atypical *ostrich*. Figure 8.12 shows an example of a revised model. Here we see that the link between the *bird* and *ostrich* nodes is "longer" than that between the *bird* and *canary* nodes. If it seems to you that the semantic network pictured in this figure is like the organization of Web pages in the World Wide Web

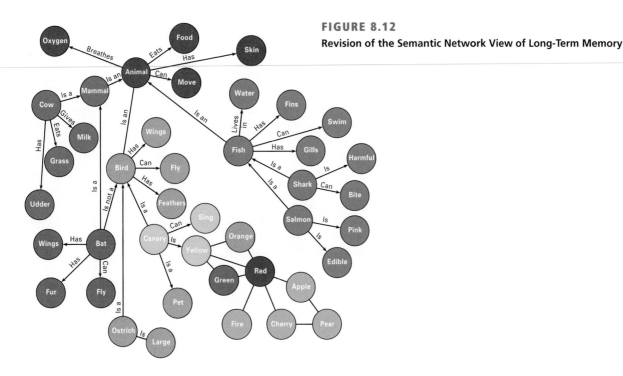

FIGURE 8.12
Revision of the Semantic Network View of Long-Term Memory

(WWW), you are right; the links and nodes which make up the WWW are also not simple hierarchical networks (Micarelli & Sciarrone, 2004). Instead they form richly interconnected webs, just like human memory.

We add new material to a semantic network by placing it in the middle of the appropriate region of memory. The new material is gradually tied in to related nodes in the surrounding network. This model reveals why, if you cram for a test, you will not remember the information over the long term. The new material is not woven into the long-term web. In contrast, discussing the material or incorporating it into a research paper interweaves it and connects it to other knowledge you have. These multiple connections increase the probability that you will be able to retrieve the information many months or even years later. The concept of multiple connections fits with the description of the importance of elaboration in memory given earlier in the chapter.

Schemas Imagine overhearing the following conversation between two university students living in a dorm:

Rahul: Did you order it?
Kayleigh: Yeah, it will be here in about 45 minutes.
Rahul: Well, I have to leave before then but save me a couple of slices, okay?

Do you know what these two students are talking about? You likely guessed that they were talking about *pizza*, but how did you know this? The word *pizza* was never mentioned. But you knew what they were talking about because you activated your concept of "pizza" or "ordering pizza for delivery" and used that concept to comprehend the situation.

When we store information in memory, we often fit it into the collection of information that already exists, as you did in comprehending the pizza delivery situation. Piaget, whose theory of cognitive development we encountered in chapter 4, described this as assimilating new information into an existing schema. As we saw in chapter 4, a **schema** is a preexisting mental concept or framework that helps people to organize and interpret information. Schemas from prior encounters with the environment influence the way we encode, make inferences about, and retrieve information.

Semantic network theories assume that memory involves specific facts with clear links from one to another. In contrast, schema theory claims that long-term memory is not very exact. We seldom find precisely the memory that we want, or at least not all of

schema A preexisting mental concept or framework that helps people to organize and interpret information.

One night two young men from Egulac went down to the river to hunt seals, and while they were there it became foggy and calm. Then they heard war cries, and they thought: "Maybe this is a war party." They escaped to the shore, and hid behind a log. Now canoes came up, and they heard the noise of paddles, and they saw one canoe coming up to them. There were five men in the canoe and they said:

"What do you think? We wish to take you along. We are going up the river to make war on the people."

One of the young men said: "I have no arrows."

"Arrows are in the canoe," they said.

"I will not go along, I might be killed. My relatives do not know where I have gone. But you," he said, turning to the other, "may go with them."

So one of the young men went, but the other returned home.

And the warriors went up the river to a town on the other side of Kalama. The people came down to the water, and they began to fight, and many were killed. But presently the young man heard one of the warriors say: "Quick, let us go home: that Indian has been hit." Now he thought: "Oh, they are ghosts." He did not feel sick, but they said he had been shot.

So the canoes went back to Egulac and the young man went ashore to his house, and made a fire. And he told everybody and said: "Behold I accompanied the ghosts, and we went to fight. Many of our fellows were killed, and many of those who attacked us were killed. They said I was hit, and I did not feel sick."

He told it all, and then he became quiet. When the sun rose he fell down. Something black came out of his mouth. His face became contorted. The people jumped up and cried.

He was dead.

FIGURE 8.13 **The War of the Ghosts**
When Sir Frederick Bartlett (1932) asked individuals to recall this story, they tended to change details.

"Why? You cross the road because it's in the script—that's why!"

© The New Yorker Collection 1986 Edward Koren from cartoonbank.com. All Rights Reserved.

script A schema for an event, often containing information about physical features, people, and typical occurrences.

connectionism (parallel distributed processing, PDP) The theory that memory is stored throughout the brain in connections between neurons, several of which may work together to process a single memory.

what we want; hence, we have to reconstruct the rest. Our schemas support the reconstruction process, helping us fill in gaps between our fragmented memories.

The schema theory of memory began with Sir Frederick Bartlett's (1932) studies of how people remember stories. Bartlett was concerned with how people's backgrounds determine what they encode, store, and recall. Bartlett chose stories that sounded strange and were difficult to understand. He reasoned that a person's background, which is encoded in schemas, would reveal itself in the person's reconstruction (modification and distortion) of the story's content. One of Bartlett's stories was called *War of the Ghosts*, an English translation of an Aboriginal folktale (see figure 8.13). The story tells of events that were completely foreign to the experiences of Bartlett's middle- and upper-income British research participants. They read the story twice and then, after 15 minutes, wrote down the tale the best they could remember it.

What interested Bartlett was how differently the participants might reconstruct this and other stories from the original versions. The British participants used both their general schemas for daily experiences and their specific schemas for adventurous ghost stories to reconstruct *War of the Ghosts*. Familiar details from the story that fit into the participants' schemas were successfully recalled. But details that departed from the person's schemas were often extensively distorted. For example, the "something black" that came out of the dying man's mouth became blood in one reconstruction and condensed air in another. For one individual the two young men were hunting beavers rather than seals. Another person said the death at the end was due to a fever (this wasn't in the story).

We have schemas not only for stories but also for scenes or spatial layouts (a beach, a bathroom), as well as for common events (going to a restaurant, playing football, writing a term paper). A **script** is a schema for an event (Schank & Abelson, 1977; Godbout & others, 2004). Scripts often have information about physical features, people, and typical occurrences. This kind of information is helpful when people need to figure out what is happening around them. For example, if you are enjoying your after-dinner coffee in a restaurant and a man in a tuxedo comes over and puts a piece of paper on the table, your script tells you that the man is probably a waiter who has just given you the cheque. Thus scripts help to organize our storage of memories about events.

Connectionist Networks Theories of semantic networks, hierarchical or otherwise, and schemas have little or nothing to say about the role of the physical brain in memory. Thus, a newer theory based on brain research has generated a wave of excitement among psychologists (e.g., Kinder & Shanks, 2003). **Connectionism**, or **parallel distributed processing** (**PDP**), is the theory that memory is stored throughout the brain in connections between neurons, several of which may work together to process a single memory (Berthier, Rosenstein, & Barto, 2005; Dehaene & Naccache, 2001). Recall that the concept of neural networks was initially discussed in chapter 3 and the concept of parallel processing pathways in chapter 5. This section expands on those discussions and applies these concepts to memory.

In the connectionist view, memories are neither abstract concepts (as in semantic network theories) nor large knowledge structures (as in schema theories). Instead, memories are more like electrical impulses, organized only to the extent that neurons, the connections between them, and their activity are organized. Any piece of knowledge—such as the name of your dog, Coco—is embedded in the strengths of hundreds

Shown here are representative scripts from a Japanese tea ceremony, a Western dinner, and an Ethiopian meal. *With which script do you feel most comfortable? least comfortable?*

or thousands of connections between neurons and is not limited to a single location. Figure 8.14 compares the semantic-network, schema, and connectionist-network theories of memories.

How does the connectionist process work? A neural activity involving memory, such as remembering the name of your dog, Coco, is distributed across a number of areas of the cerebral cortex. The locations of neural activity, called nodes, are interconnected. When a node reaches a critical level of activation, it can affect another node, either by exciting it or inhibiting it, across synapses. We know that the human cerebral cortex contains millions of neurons that are richly interconnected through hundreds of millions of synapses. Because of these synaptic connections, the activity of one neuron can be influenced by many other neurons. For example, if there is an excitatory connection between neurons A and B, activity in neuron A will tend to increase activity in neuron B. If the connection is inhibitory, activity in neuron A will tend to reduce the activity in neuron B. Because of these simple reactions, the connectionist view argues that changes in the strength of synaptic connections are the fundamental bases of memory (O'Brien & Opie, 1999).

Part of the appeal of the connectionist view is that it is consistent with what we know about the way the brain functions. Another part of its appeal is that when programmed on a computer, the connectionist view has been successful in predicting the

FIGURE 8.14

Key Features of Semantic-Network, Schema, and Connectionist Theories

	Theory		
	Semantic Network	**Schema**	**Connectionist**
Nature of memory units	Abstract concepts ("bird")	Large knowledge structures ("going to a restaurant")	Small units, connections among neurons
Number of units	Tens of thousands	Unknown	Tens of millions
Formation of new memories	Form new nodes	Form new schemas or modify old ones	Increased strength of excitatory connections among neurons
Attention to brain structure	Little	Little	Extensive

results of some memory experiments (Berthier, Rosenstein, & Barto, 2005). One connectionist network simulated by a digital computer has even shown amnesia during explicit memory tasks while performing well on implicit memory tasks (Kinder & Shanks, 2003). This is the same dissociation between tests of explicit and implicit memory which human amnesiacs show, as we just discussed above. The insights of connectionism into the organization of memory also support brain research undertaken to determine where memories are stored in the brain.

So far we have discussed the time frames of storage, the differentiated systems for storage, and how information is represented in storage. The brain is a key aspect of the connectionist, PDP view of how memory is represented in storage. The next section further examines where memories are stored.

Where Memories Are Stored Karl Lashley (1950) spent a lifetime looking for a location in the brain in which memories are stored. He trained rats to discover the correct pathway in a maze and then cut out various portions of the animals' brains and retested their memory of the maze pathway. After experimenting with thousands of rats, Lashley found that the loss of various cortical areas did not affect rats' ability to remember the pathway. Lashley concluded that memories, which he called *engrams*, are not stored in a specific location in the brain. Other researchers, continuing Lashley's quest, would agree that memory storage is diffuse but have developed some new insights. McGill psychologist Donald Hebb (1949, 1980) suggested that assemblies of cells, distributed over large areas of the cerebral cortex, work together to represent information. Hebb's idea of distributed memory was farsighted.

Neurons and Memory Today, many neuroscientists believe that memory is located in specific sets or circuits of neurons. Brain researcher Larry Squire (1990), for example, says that most memories are probably clustered in groups of about 1000 neurons. Single neurons, of course, are at work in memory. Researchers who measure the electrical activity of single cells have found that some respond to faces, others to eye or hair colour, for example. But, for you to recognize your Uncle Albert, individual neurons that provide information about hair colour, size, and other characteristics act together.

Researchers also believe that brain neurotransmitters may be the ink with which memories are written. Ironically, some of the answers to the complex questions about the neural mechanics of memory come from studies on very simple animals—the sea slug (Kandel & Schwartz, 1982) and the nematode (Wicks & Rankin, 1997). Eric Kandel and James Schwartz (1982) chose the sea slug, a large snail-without-a-shell, because of the simple architecture of its nervous system, which consists of only about 10,000 neurons. The sea slug can hardly be called a quick learner or an animal with a good memory, but it is equipped with a reliable reflex. When anything touches the gill on its back, it quickly withdraws it. First, the researchers accustomed the sea slug to having its gill prodded. After a while, the animal ignored the prod and stopped withdrawing its gill. Next, the researchers applied an electric shock to its tail when they touched the gill. After many rounds of the shock-accompanied prod, the sea slug violently withdrew its gill at the slightest touch. The researchers found that the sea slug remembered this message for hours or even weeks. They also found that shocking the sea slug's gill releases the neurotransmitter serotonin at the synapses of its nervous system, and this chemical release provides a reminder that the gill was shocked. This "memory" informs the nerve cell to send out chemical commands to retract the gill the next time it is touched. If nature builds complexity out of simplicity, then the mechanism used by the sea slug may work in the human brain as well.

One concept that has been proposed to understand how memory functions at the neuronal level is *long-term potentiation*. In line with connectionist theory, this concept states that if two neurons are activated at the same time, the connection between them—and thus the memory—may be strengthened (Squire & Kandel, 2000; García-Junco-Clemente & colleagues, 2005). Long-term potentiation has been demonstrated experimentally by administering a drug that increases the flow of information from one neuron to another across the synapse (Shakesby, Anwyl, & Rowan, 2002). In one study,

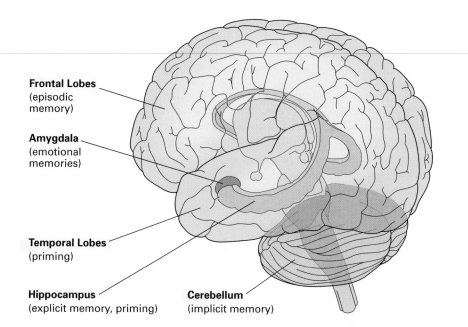

Frontal Lobes
(episodic memory)

Amygdala
(emotional memories)

Temporal Lobes
(priming)

Hippocampus
(explicit memory, priming)

Cerebellum
(implicit memory)

rats given the drug learned a maze with far fewer mistakes along the way than those not given the drug (Service, 1994). In another study, the genes of mice were altered to increase long-term potentiation in the hippocampus and other areas of the brain (Tang & others, 1999; Tsien, 2000). The mice with the enhanced genes were able to remember information better than mice whose genes had not been altered. These studies raise the possibility of some day improving memory through drugs or even gene enhancement to increase neural connections (Schacter, 2000). Long-term potentiation has also been demonstrated experimentally by electrically stimulating brain structures involved in memory (Ivanco & Racine, 2000; Trepel & Racine, 1998). Overstimulating those areas using electroconvulsive shock results in a disruption of long-term potentiation (Trepel & Racine, 1999). Interestingly, one side-effect of the use of electroconvulsive shock to treat depression in humans is some degree of memory loss.

Brain Structures and Memory Functions While some neuroscientists are unveiling the cellular basis of memory, others are examining its broadscale architecture in the brain. Larry Squire, of the University of California at San Diego, believes that memory is distributed throughout the brain and that no specific memory centre exists (Squire, 2004). Instead, many parts of the brain and nervous system participate in the memory of a particular event. Yet memory is localized in the sense that a limited number of brain systems and pathways are involved, and each probably contributes in different ways (Squire & Schacter, 2002). Psychologists and neuroscientists work together to relate different memory systems identified through research to different areas of the brain.

Figure 8.15 shows the location of some of the brain structures involved in different types of long-term memory. For instance, explicit and implicit memory take place in separate areas of the brain.

- *Explicit memory.* Neuroscientists have found that the hippocampus, the temporal lobes in the cerebral cortex, and other areas of the limbic system are involved in explicit memory (Gomez Beldarrain & others, 2002; Zola & Squire, 2001), especially episodic memory (Tulving & Markowitsch, 1998; Tulving, 2002). In many aspects of explicit memory, information is transmitted from the hippocampus to the frontal lobes, which are involved in both retrospective and prospective memory (Burgess & others, 2001). The left frontal lobe is especially active when we encode new information into memory; the right frontal lobe is more active when we subsequently retrieve it (Otten, Henson, & Rugg, 2001; Badgaiyan, (2005). Temporal lobe atrophy is related to dementia (Murtha & others, 1998). The amygdala, part of the limbic system, is involved in emotional memories (Siegle & others, 2002).

- *Implicit memory.* The cerebellum is involved in the implicit memory required to perform skills (Thompson, 2005). Various areas of the cerebral cortex, such as the temporal lobes and hippocampus, function in priming (Marshall & others, 2004; Jernigan, Ostergaard, & Fennema-Notestine, 2001).

Neuroscientists have benefited from the use of MRI to track neural activity during cognitive tasks (Cabeza, Nyberg & Park, 2005). In one study, participants were shown colour photographs of indoor and outdoor scenes while in an MRI machine (Brewer & others, 1998). They were not told that they would be given a memory test. After the MRI scans, they were asked which pictures they remembered well, vaguely, or not at all. Their memories were compared with the brain scans. The longer that both prefrontal lobes and a particular region of the hippocampus remained lit up on the MRI scans, the better the participants remembered the scenes. Pictures paired with weak brain activity in these areas were forgotten. MRI has also helped in the study of amnesia. For example, Levine and others (1997) have used MRI scans to identify malfunctioning areas of the brain in selective retrograde amnesia. Similarly, a recent edited volume reports on work using new imaging technologies to relate cognitive aging to changes in the brain (Cabeza, Nyberg & Park, 2005). This new cognitive neuroscience research is helping scientists pinpoint the specific aspects of the brain involved in memory.

As neuroscientists identify memory circuits in the brain, might the psychological study of memory become unimportant? That's unlikely. We will likely always rely on the functional specifications of memory supplied by psychologists using experimental methods to confirm the broad outlines of new neurochemical theories and to provide new hypotheses for future neuroscientific exploration. We are far from working out all the complexities of the neurochemical activity underpinning human memory.

> **reflect and review**

③ Discuss how memories are stored.

- Explain sensory memory.
- Summarize how short-term memory works.
- Describe how long-term memory functions and the role of the brain in memory storage.

How might semantic network theory explain why cramming for a test is not a good way to acquire long-term memory?

---

④ MEMORY RETRIEVAL

Serial Position Effect — Retrieval Cues and the Retrieval Task — Retrieval of Autobiographical Memories — Retrieval of Emotional Memories — Eyewitness Testimony

How are memories retrieved?

Long-term memory has been compared to a library. Your memory stores information like a library stores books and you retrieve information in a fashion similar to the process you use to locate and check out a book. To retrieve something from your mental data banks, you search your store of memory to find the relevant information. Memory **retrieval** takes place when information is taken out of storage.

The efficiency with which we retrieve information from memory is often impressive. It usually takes only a moment to search through a vast storehouse to find the information we want. When were you born? Who is the Prime Minister of Canada? What was the name of your first date? Who developed the first psychology laboratory? You can, of course, answer these questions instantly ;).

retrieval The memory process of taking information out of storage.

But the process of retrieving information from long-term memory is not as precise as the library analogy suggests. When we search through our long-term memory storehouse we don't always find the exact "book" we want. Our retrieval of memories is affected by a number of things, including the pattern of facts we remember, the situations we associate with memories, and the personal or emotional context. Or we might find the book we want but discover that only a few pages are intact. We have to reconstruct the rest. Since Bartlett's (1932) pioneering work on the schema theory of memory, psychologists have been interested in *reconstructive memory*, especially in the way people recall stories, remember their past, recall conversations, and give eyewitness testimony (see e.g., Levine & Bluck, 2004). Now let's take a closer look at some of these memory quirks and glitches.

Serial Position Effect

Understanding how retrieval works also requires knowledge of the **serial position effect**—the tendency for items at the beginning and at the end of a list to be recalled more readily. If someone gave you the directions "left on Mockingbird, right on Central, right on Stemmons, left on Balboa, and right on Parkside" you would probably remember "left on Mockingbird" and "right on Parkside" more easily than the turns and streets in the middle. The *primacy effect* refers to better recall for items at the beginning of a list. The *recency effect* refers to better recall for items at the end of the list. Together with the relatively low recall of items from the middle of the list, this pattern makes up the *serial position effect* (Addis & Kahana, 2004; Stewart & others, 2004). See figure 8.16 for a typical serial position effect that shows a weaker primacy effect and a stronger recency effect. One application of primacy and recency effects is the advice to job candidates to try to be the first or last candidate interviewed. Another is for suspects in police lineups to try to avoid being at either end of the lineup, a practice understandably frowned upon by police departments (Wogalter, Malpass, & Mcquiston, 2004).

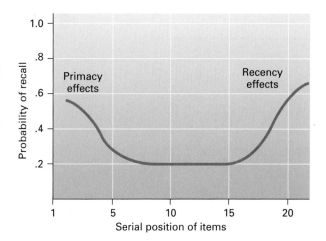

FIGURE 8.16 The Serial Position Effect
When a person is asked to memorize a list of words, the words memorized last usually are recalled best, those at the beginning next best, and those in the middle least efficiently.

How can primacy and recency effects be explained? As for the primacy effect, the first few items in the list are easily remembered because they are rehearsed more often than later items (Atkinson & Shiffrin, 1968). Working memory is relatively empty when they enter, so there is little competition for rehearsal time. And, because they get more rehearsal, they stay in working memory longer and are more likely to be successfully encoded into long-term memory. In contrast, many items from the middle of the list drop out of working memory before being encoded into long-term memory.

As for the recency effect, the last several items are remembered for different reasons. First, at the time these items are recalled, they might still be in working memory. Second, even if these items are not in working memory, their relative recency, compared with other list items, makes them easier to recall. For example, if you are a music fan, try remembering concerts you saw over the last few years, or if you like the movies, try remembering the last 10 movies you saw. You will probably find that the more recent concerts or movies are easier to remember than less recent ones. This example of the recency effect extends far beyond the time span of working memory.

Retrieval Cues and the Retrieval Task

Two other factors involved in retrieval are (1) the nature of the cues that can prompt your memory and (2) the retrieval task that you set for yourself. If effective cues for what you are trying to remember do not seem to be available, you need to create them—a process that takes place in working memory. For example, if you have a block about remembering a new friend's name, you might go through the alphabet, generating names that begin with each letter. If you manage to stumble across the right name, or one close to it, you'll probably recognize it.

serial position effect The tendency for items at the beginning and at the end of a list to be recalled more readily.

FIGURE 8.17
Remembering Faces
(*Left*) The FBI artist's sketch of Ted Kaczynski. (*Right*) A photograph of Kaczynski. The FBI widely circulated the artist's sketch, which was based on bits and pieces of observations people had made of the infamous Unabomber, in the hope that someone would recognize him. Would you have been able to recognize Kaczynski from the artist's sketch? Probably not. Although most people say they are good at remembering faces, they are usually not as good as they think they are.

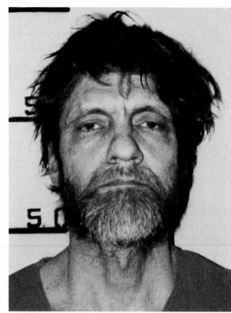

We can learn to generate retrieval cues (Allan & others, 2001; Carlin, Soraci, & Strawbridge, 2005). One good strategy is to use different subcategories as retrieval cues. For example, write down the names of as many of your classmates from grade 10 as you can remember. When you run out of names, think about the activities you were involved in during those school years, such as math class, student council, eating lunch, team sports, and so on. Did this set of cues help you to remember more of your classmates?

Although cues help, your success in retrieving information also depends on the task you set for yourself. For instance, if you're simply trying to decide if something seems familiar, retrieval is probably a snap. Let's say you see a short, dark-haired woman walking toward you. You quickly decide she's someone who lives in the next dorm. But remembering her name or a precise detail, such as when you met her, can be harder. Such distinctions have implications for police investigations: A witness might be certain she has previously seen a face, yet she might have a hard time deciding if it was at the scene of the crime or in a mug shot.

Recall and Recognition   The presence or absence of good cues and the retrieval task required are factors in an important memory distinction: recall versus recognition (Nobel & Shiffrin, 2001; Brébion & others, 2005). *Recall* is a memory task in which the individual has to retrieve previously learned information, as on essay tests. *Recognition* is a memory task in which the individual only has to identify (recognize) learned items, as on multiple-choice tests. Wouldn't you agree that multiple-choice tests are easier than essay tests or fill-in-the-blank tests? Recall tests, such as essay tests, have poor retrieval cues. You are told to try to recall a certain class of information ("Discuss the factors that caused Canada's entry into World War II"). In recognition tests, such as multiple-choice tests, you merely judge whether any of the stimuli are familiar (whether they match something you experienced in the past).

You have probably heard some people say that they are terrible at remembering names but that they never forget a face. What they are likely really saying is that they are better at recognition (realizing that they have seen a face before) than at recall (mentally reconstructing a person's facial features). If you have made that claim yourself, try to actually recall a face. It's not easy, as law enforcement officers know. In some cases the police bring in an artist to draw the suspect's face from witnesses' descriptions (see figure 8.17). But recalling faces is difficult, and artists' sketches of suspects are frequently not detailed or accurate enough to result in apprehension.

Encoding Specificity Another consideration in understanding retrieval is the *encoding specificity principle*, which states that information present at the time of encoding or learning tends to be effective as a retrieval cue (Tulving & Thomson, 1973; Hannon & Craik, 2001; Mitchell, Macrae, & Banaji, 2004). For example, imagine that you have met someone who is a Mountie. If you encode that information, along with observations such as "the person looks fit and alert," this might help you to remember the person's occupation when you encounter her again.

Encoding specificity is compatible with our earlier discussion of elaboration. Recall that the more elaboration you use in encoding information, the better your memory of the information will be, and the better your ability to retrieve it will be. Encoding specificity and elaboration reveal how interdependent encoding and retrieval are.

Priming Retrieval also benefits from *priming*, which was discussed earlier in the chapter. Recall that priming means that people remember information better and faster when it is preceded by similar information. Priming is a form of implicit memory that is nonconscious (Rueckl & Galantucci, 2005).

A practical everyday example of priming involves those times when you are wandering the grocery store unable to remember one of the items you were supposed to buy. As you walk down an aisle you hear two people talking about fruit, which triggers your memory that you were supposed to buy raspberries. That is, hearing *fruit* primes your memory for raspberries.

Also, priming is likely involved in unintentional acts of plagiarism. For example, you propose an idea to a friend, who seems unimpressed by it or even rejects it outright. Weeks or months later, the friend excitedly describes your idea as if she had just come up with it herself. Her memory of having the idea has been primed by your explanation of the idea. When you call your friend's attention to the fact that her idea is really your idea, you may well face either heated denial or a sheepish apology born of a sudden dose of explicit memory.

Tip-of-the-Tongue Phenomenon Brown & McNeill (1966) were among the first psychologists to study the *tip-of-the-tongue phenomenon*, or *TOT state*, one glitch in retrieving information that we're all familiar with. It is a type of *effortful retrieval* that occurs when people are confident that they know something but they can't quite pull it out of memory (Kikyo, Ohki, & Sekihara, 2001; Schwartz, 2002).

The TOT state arises because a person can retrieve some of the desired information but not all of it (Maril, Wagner, & Schacter, 2001). For example, imagine that you are at a university social event and spot two people standing together. You easily recall that one of them is Barbara. You know that you've seen the other person before and are sure his name begins with a J (a good retrieval cue) although you can't remember it at the moment. But maybe when you were introduced you didn't pay enough attention to his name to remember more than the first letter. Your confidence in the retrieval cue can induce a strong—sometimes spurious—feeling of knowing other information (in this case the name) that you actually haven't stored in memory.

People in a TOT state can usually successfully retrieve characteristics of the word, such as the first letter and the number of syllables, but not retrieve the word itself. In one classic study of the TOT state, participants were shown photographs of famous people and asked to say their names (Yarmey, 1973). The researcher found that people tended to use two strategies to try to retrieve the name of a person they thought they knew. One strategy was to pinpoint the person's profession. For example, one participant correctly identified the famous person as an artist, but the artist's name, Picasso, remained elusive. Another retrieval strategy was to repeat initial letters or syllables—such as *Monetti, Mona, Magett, Spaghetti,* and *Bogette* in the attempt to identify Liza Minnelli.

Context and State at Encoding and Retrieval In many instances, people remember better when they attempt to recall information in the same context in which they learned it, a process referred to as *context-dependent memory*. This is believed to occur because they have encoded features of the context in which they learned the information along with the information. Such features can later act as retrieval cues (Smith & Vela, 2001; Chu, Handley, & Cooper, 2003).

In a famous study, scuba divers learned information on land and under water (Godden & Baddeley, 1975). Later they were asked to recall the information when they were either on land or under water. The divers' recall was much better when the encoding and retrieval contexts were the same (both on land or both under water).

Just as external contexts can influence memory, so can internal states (Duka, Weissenborn, & Dienes, 2001). People tend to remember information better when their psychological state or mood is similar at encoding and retrieval, a process referred to as *state-dependent memory*. For example, when people are in sad moods, they are more likely to remember negative experiences, such as failure and rejection. When they are in happy moods, they are inclined to remember positive experiences, such as success and acceptance (Mineka & Nugent, 1995). Unfortunately, when people who are depressed recall negative experiences, it tends to perpetuate their depression.

Drug use also produces state-dependent memory (Duka, Weissenborn, & Dienes, 2001). For example, Iraqi neuropharmacologist Mohammad-Reza Zarrindast, and his colleagues, have shown that morphine use is associated with state-dependent memory (Jafari, Zarrindast, & Djahanguiri, 2004).

Retrieval of Autobiographical Memories

The various quirks of memory related to retrieval cues and tasks are at play in many different facets of memory. Consider personal memories. *Autobiographical memory*, a form of episodic memory (discussed earlier in the chapter), is a person's recollections of his or her life experiences.

Autobiographical memories are complex and seem to contain unending strings of stories and snapshots, but researchers have found that they can be categorized. For example, based on his research, English psychologist Martin Conway (Conway & Rubin, 1993; Wang & Conway, 2004) sketches a structure of autobiographical memory that has three levels (see figure 8.18). The most abstract level consists of *life time periods*; for example, you might remember something about your life in high school. The middle level in the hierarchy is made up of *general events*, such as a trip you took with your friends when you graduated from high school. The most concrete level in the hierarchy is composed of *event-specific knowledge*; for example, from that postgraduation trip, you might remember the exhilarating time you had when you took your first bungee jump. When people tell their life stories, all three levels of information are usually present and intertwined.

Most autobiographical memories include some reality and some myth. Autobiographical memories are in fact less about facts and more about meanings. They provide a reconstructed, embellished telling of the past that connects the past to the present. Our autobiographical memories form the core of our personal identity (Behrend, Beike, & Lampinen, 2004; McAdams, 1993).

Level	Label	Description
Level 1	Life time periods	Long segments of time measured in years and even decades
Level 2	General events	Extended composite episodes measured in days, weeks, or months
Level 3	Event-specific knowledge	Individual episodes measured in seconds, minutes, or hours

FIGURE 8.18 The Three-Level Hierarchical Structure of Autobiographical Memory

Retrieval of Emotional Memories

When we remember our life experiences, the memories are often wrapped in emotion. Keep in mind that emotion affects the encoding and storage of memories and thus shapes the details that are retrieved (Wessel & Wright, 2004). Today, the effects of emotion on memory are of considerable interest to researchers and have echoes in public life (Reisberg & Hertel, 2004). Let's first examine flashbulb memories.

Flashbulb Memories *Flashbulb memories* are memories of emotionally significant events that people often recall with more accuracy and vivid imagery than everyday

Do you have a flashbulb memory of the terrorist attack on the World Trade Center in New York City on September 11, 2001? How about the tsunami that hit Asia on December 26, 2004?

events (Davidson & Glisky, 2002). Perhaps you can remember where you were when you first heard of the terrorist attacks on New York City and Washington, D.C., on September 11, 2001 or when the Asian tsunami struck on December 26, 2004. An intriguing dimension of flashbulb memories is that several decades later people often remember where they were and what was going on in their lives at the time of such an event. These memories seem to be part of an adaptive system that fixes in memory the details that accompany important events so that they can be interpreted at a later time.

The vast majority of flashbulb memories are of a personal nature rather than of nationally prominent events or circumstances. In one classic study, university students were asked to report the three most vivid memories in their lives (Rubin & Kozin, 1984). Virtually all of these memories were of a personal nature. They tended to centre on an injury or accident, sports, members of the opposite sex, animals, deaths, the first week of university, and vacations. Students also answered questions about the types of events that were most likely to produce flashbulb memories. Figure 8.19 shows which types of events more than 50 percent of the students said were of flashbulb quality.

Most people are confident about the accuracy of their flashbulb memories. However, most flashbulb memories probably are not as accurately etched in our brains as we think. For example, many flashbulb memories deteriorate over time (Schmolck, Buffalo, & Squire, 2000). Still, flashbulb memories are far more durable and accurate than memories of day-to-day happenings (Niedzwienska, 2004). One reason is that flashbulb memories are often discussed and thought about in the days, weeks, and even years following an event. That has certainly been the case with the 9/11 terrorist attacks. However, it is not just the discussion and rehearsal of information that make flashbulb memories so long-lasting. The emotions triggered by flashbulb events are also involved in their durability. The emotional arousal you experienced when you heard about the terrorist attacks also likely contributed to the vividness of your memory.

Some flashbulb memories involve emotionally uplifting experiences, such as the positive experience of high school graduation night. Other flashbulb memories are at the opposite end of the emotional spectrum and involve personal trauma.

Event	Percent
A car accident you were in or witnessed	85
When you first met your first college roommate	82
The night of your high school graduation	81
The night of your senior prom (if you went or not)	78
An early romantic experience	77
A time you had to speak in front of an audience	72
When you got your admissions letter	65
Your first date—the moment you met him/her	57

FIGURE 8.19 **University Students' Flashbulb Memories**
The numbers refer to the percentages of university students who said these events triggered memories of flashbulb quality.

Personal Trauma   In 1890, William James said that an experience could be so arousing emotionally as to almost leave a scar on the brain's tissue. Personal traumas are candidates for the type of emotionally arousing experience James was referring to.

Some psychologists argue that memories of emotionally traumatic events are accurately retained, possibly forever, in considerable detail (Langer, 1991). There is good evidence that memory for traumatic events is usually more accurate than memory for ordinary events (Paradis & others, 2004). For example, a sample of New York City college students were repeatedly asked to describe their experiences on both 9/11 and the day after. Their recollections one year afterwards were vivid and consistent as compared to their recollections one week afterwards.

However, when President George W. Bush was asked what went through his head when he first learned of the terrorist attacks, he mentioned seeing a plane fly into the first building and thinking it had to be pilot error. But there was no footage of the first plane available when Bush was notified. Although conspiracy theorists immediately seized upon Bush's comments as evidence that some factions in the American government had foreknowledge of the attacks, Greenberg (2004) noted that Bush has provided a good example of a false flashbulb memory. Of course, during the course of September 11th, 2001, Bush, like most of the rest of us, repeatedly watched footage of the events as it became available. When he was later asked to describe his first thoughts, he likely misretrieved information from later on in the day and inadvertently wove it into his description (Greenberg, 2004).

How can a traumatic memory be so vivid and detailed, yet at the same time have inaccuracies? A number of factors can be involved. Sometimes people make perceptual errors while encoding information because the episode was so shocking. Or they might distort the information and recall the episode as being less traumatic than it actually was in order to reduce their anxiety about what happened. Alternately, in discussing the traumatic event with other people, they might have incorporated bits and pieces of these persons' recollections of what happened into their own version of the event.

Usually, memories of real-life traumas are more accurate and longer lasting than those of everyday events. Although memories of traumas are subject to some deterioration and distortion, the central part of the memory is almost always effectively remembered. Where distortion often arises is in the details of the traumatic episode.

Some cases of memory of personal trauma involve a mental disorder called *post-traumatic stress disorder*, which includes severe anxiety symptoms that can immediately follow the trauma or can be delayed by months or even years (Wiederhold & Wiederhold, 2005). The symptoms can include flashbacks in which the individual relives the traumatic event in nightmares or in an awake but distracted state. Individuals can also have difficulties with memory and concentration. Post-traumatic stress disorder can emerge after exposure to several kinds of traumatic events, such as war, severe abuse (such as rape), and accidental disasters (such as a plane crash). Post-traumatic stress disorder is discussed further in chapter 13.

Stress-related hormones likely play a role in memories that involve personal trauma. The release of stress-related hormones, signalled by the amygdala (see figure 8.15), likely accounts for some of the extraordinary durability and vividness of traumatic memories (Pelletier & Paré, 2004).

Repressed Memories   The emotional blows of personal trauma can produce distortions of memory or vivid reenactments of the event in memory. Personal trauma can also result in *repression*, in which all memory of the occurrence is pushed into some inaccessible part of the unconscious mind. At some later point, the memory might emerge in consciousness, as in the case of post-traumatic stress disorder.

Psychodynamic theory, which was initially discussed in chapter 1, contends that repression's main function is to protect the individual from threatening information. Repression does not erase a memory, but it makes conscious remembering extremely difficult (Anderson & Green, 2001; Anderson & others, 2004). Just how extensively repression occurs is a controversial issue.

Repressed memories are further discussed in chapters 12 and 14. To think about the accuracy of reconstructed memories of childhood abuse, see the Critical Reflections box.

Recovered Memories or False Memories?

George Franklin, a California man, spent six years in prison for the 1969 murder of a young woman. His own daughter's testimony, based on her memory of the attack, was at the heart of the prosecution's case against him. What made this case unusual is that the daughter's memories were allegedly recovered in adulthood as a part of her own ongoing therapy (Loftus & Ketcham, 1994). In fact, Franklin became the first person in the United States to be convicted on the basis of repressed memory evidence. During the 1990s, memories allegedly recovered during therapy also served as the basis for many charges of physical and sexual abuse. George Franklin's conviction was eventually overturned when it came out that his daughter might have lied about having been hypnotized before the trial.

The idea that childhood abuse, and in particular sexual abuse, could be completely repressed yet nevertheless lead to psychological disorders in adulthood was first expressed in Sigmund Freud's seduction theory. In this vein, some therapists today continue to believe that adult disorders such as depression, thoughts of suicide, eating disorders, low self-esteem, sexual dysfunction, and trouble maintaining relationships may stem from sexual abuse in childhood. Treatment usually involves bringing these long-repressed childhood traumas back into consciousness, thus freeing the client from their unconscious effects.

Methods used to recover repressed childhood memories have included hypnotic age regression, guided imagery, keeping a journal of fragments of childhood memories, and even the administration of truth drugs. In cases in which memories have been recovered, clients have often been encouraged to confront the alleged perpetrator, usually a parent. In many cases, charges were filed as a part of the therapeutic process (Pezdek & Banks, 1996).

Almost all accused parents vehemently deny having ever abused their offspring in childhood. In 1992, the False Memory Syndrome (FMS) Foundation was formed as a parents' support group. The very name of this group expresses the conviction that their children's memories were not recovered but were somehow falsely implanted, perhaps as a result of the therapeutic process itself (Olio, 2004). Interestingly, almost 100 years earlier, Sigmund Freud himself had rejected his seduction theory in favour of the view that his patient's "memories" of childhood abuse were based on their own repressed sexual desires. What has complicated matters is the growing awareness that childhood sexual abuse is much more common than Freud was aware of and continues to be a serious problem today. Many therapists have wondered if Freud was afraid to face the implications of his seduction theory and instead ended up betraying his patients by claiming that their memories were just fantasies.

It was against this bitter backdrop that experimental psychology entered the fray. Led by the research of University of California at Irvine's Elizabeth Loftus (Loftus & Ketcham, 1994; Loftus & Bernstein, 2005), study after study found that it is easy to create false memories, especially by using hypnosis. All that is required is to repeatedly suggest to someone that he or she has had an experience. Afterwards, that person may well "remember" the experience as vividly real. Loftus (2003) recounts a practical joke played on actor Alan Alda when, as the host of the television program *Scientific American Frontiers*, he and his crew came to do a program on her. Before arriving, Alda had been asked to fill out a questionnaire on his eating preferences. Upon his arrival, Loftus and her students explained to Alda that they analyzed his answers and discovered that when he was a child he must have gotten sick eating too many hard-boiled eggs (which was not true). An hour later, at a picnic, Alda refused to eat hard-boiled eggs. Loftus had whimsically demonstrated how easy it is to implant false memories.

In a more serious vein, Loftus (2003; Loftus & Bernstein, 2005) reviews numerous studies in which people have been led to believe, for example, that they were once lost in a mall, attacked by a vicious animal, nearly drowned, been hospitalized overnight, or had an accident at a family wedding. Research such as this has led to the concern that therapists who are convinced that their patients suffered sexual abuse as children may inadvertently implant false memories that are later "recovered" by the client. The end result may be false memories, which tear families apart and cause more harm than good.

This research has led courts to be skeptical of recovered-memory testimony—and directly resulted in the reversal of George Franklin's murder conviction. Unfortunately, nothing can compensate him for the loss of six years of his life and the destruction of his family life. At the same time, rejecting all claims by adults that they were victims of childhood sexual abuse is also inappropriate (Olio, 2004; Lanham, 2003). Instead, looking for corroborative evidence such as the testimony of other family members, and hard evidence like photos and other records should be considered. One promising approach, according to Kathy Belicki, of Brock University, is to corroborate such claims through the use of other psychological methods such as analyzing the sleep patterns (Chambers & Belicki, 1998) and dreams (Belicki & Cuddy, 1996) of those who may have been sexually traumatized.

Current consensus is still well represented by the American Psychological Association's (1994) interim report of the working group investigating memories of childhood abuse, which offers these tentative conclusions: (1) Controversies regarding adult recollections should not be allowed to obscure the fact that child sexual abuse is a complex and pervasive problem in America that has historically gone unacknowledged; (2) most people who were sexually abused as children remember all or part of what happened to them; (3) it is possible for memories of abuse that have been forgotten for a long time to be remembered, although the mechanism by which such delayed recall occurs is not currently well understood; (4) it is also possible to construct convincing false memories for events that never occurred, although the mechanism by which these false memories occur is not currently well understood; (5) there are gaps in our knowledge about the processes that lead to accurate and inaccurate recollections of childhood abuse.

What do you think?

- How should courts of law deal with the recovered memory versus false memory problem?
- Suppose that you meet someone who reports recovered memories of childhood abuse. How can you tell whether you should believe him or her? What should your attitude be toward that person?
- Does the likelihood that some reports of childhood sexual abuse are in fact false memories entitle us to conclude that childhood sexual abuse rarely, if ever, occurs? If we cannot trust the testimony of adult survivors of childhood sexual abuse, how can we determine the likelihood of its occurrence today?

Eyewitness Testimony

By now you should realize that memory is not a perfect reflection of reality. Understanding the distortions of memory is especially important when people are called on to report what they saw or heard in relation to a crime. Eyewitness testimonies, like other sorts of memories, may contain errors (Yarmey, 2003; S. Porter & others, 2003; Loftus, 2003). But faulty memory in criminal matters has especially serious consequences. When eyewitness testimony is inaccurate, the wrong person may go to jail or even be put to death, or the person who committed the crime might not be prosecuted. In a 1981 Canadian case, four eye-witnesses testified that Thomas Sophonow murdered 16-year-old Barbara Stoppel, of Winnipeg. He spent four years in prison while his case was repeatedly tried and was finally definitively cleared 15 years later by DNA evidence (Manitoba Justice, 2001). Justice Canada has recently acknowledged that wrongful conviction remains a serious problem in the Canadian legal system (FPT Heads of Prosecutions Committee Working Group, 2005).

There are a variety of reasons for false eyewitness testimony. One possibility, discussed in the Critical Reflections box, is that false memories may have been implanted in the eyewitness. An enquiry into the Sophonow case identified faulty police procedures as contributing to the false memories of the eyewitnesses in this case (Manitoba, 2001). A variety of suggestions for improving eyewitness identification procedures in Canada have been offered (Yarmey, 2003; Loftus, 2003) and are currently under consideration (FPT Heads of Prosecutions Committee Working Group, 2005).

Much of the interest in eyewitness testimony focuses on inherent distortion, bias, and inaccuracy in memory (S. Porter & others, 2003). One reason for distortion is that memory fades over time. For that reason the amount of time that has passed between an incident and a person's recollection of it is a critical factor in eyewitness testimony. In one classic study, people were able to identify pictures with 100 percent accuracy after a two-hour time lapse. However, four months later they achieved an accuracy of only 57 percent; chance alone accounts for 50 percent accuracy (Shepard, 1967).

Daniel Yarmey, of the University of Guelph, has shown that "earwitness" testimony, based on what a witness thought was heard, rather than seen, is vulnerable to the same distortions as eyewitness testimony (Memon & Yarmey, 1999; Yarmey, 2001). Like other memories, eyewitness and earwitness memories are constructions that don't always match what really happened.

Unlike a videotape, memory can be altered by new information. In one study, students were shown a film of an automobile accident (Loftus, 1975). Students were asked how fast the white sports car was going when it passed a barn. In fact, there was no barn in the film. However, 17 percent of the students who were asked the question mentioned the barn in their answer.

Bias is also a factor in faulty memory. Studies have shown that people of one ethnic group are less likely to recognize individual differences among people of another ethnic group (Smith, Stinson, & Prosser, 2004). In one U.S. study, a mugging was shown on a television news program (Loftus, 1993). Immediately afterward, a lineup of six suspects was broadcast, and viewers were asked to phone in and identify which of the six individuals they thought committed the robbery. Of the 2000 callers, more than 1800 identified the wrong person. In addition, even though the robber was white, one-third of the viewers identified an African American or Latino suspect as the criminal.

To get an idea of just how much eyewitness testimony should be trusted, researchers asked 64 psychologists who had either conducted eyewitness research or testified as expert witnesses to evaluate the accuracy of 30 statements regarding eyewitness testimony (Kassin & others, 2001). Figure 8.20 lists the statements that 90 percent or more of the experts agreed with and the statements that 50 percent or fewer agreed with. As you can see, the experts had the most confidence in the statements related to the wording of questions and lineup instructions and the least confidence in statements related to long-term repression of memories.

Statements Rated as Reliable by 90 Percent or More of the Experts

Category	Statement	Percent
Wording of questions	An eyewitness's testimony about an event can be affected by how the questions put to the witness are worded.	98
Lineup instructions	Police instructions can affect an eyewitness's willingness to make an identification.	98
Confidence malleability	An eyewitness's confidence can be influenced by factors that are unrelated to identification accuracy.	95
Mug-shot induced bias	Exposure to mug shots of a suspect increases the likelihood that the witness will later select that suspect in the lineup.	95
Postevent information	Eyewitness testimony about an event often reflects not only what the witness saw but also information the witness obtained later on.	94
Child suggestibility	Young children are more vulnerable than adults to interviewer suggestion, peer pressures, and other social influences.	94
Attitudes and expectations	An eyewitness's perception of and memory for an event can be affected by his or her attitudes and expectations.	92
Hypnotic suggestibility	Hypnosis increases suggestibility to leading and misleading questions.	91
Alcoholic intoxication	Alcoholic intoxication impairs an eyewitness's later ability to recall persons and events.	91
Cross-race bias	Eyewitnesses are more accurate when identifying members of their own race than members of other races.	90

Statements Rated as Reliable by 50 Percent or Less of the Experts

Category	Statement	Percent
Elderly witness	Elderly witnesses are less accurate than are younger adults.	50
Hypnotic accuracy	Hypnosis increases the accuracy of the eyewitness's reported memory.	45
Identification speed	The more quickly a witness makes an identification upon seeing the lineup, the more accurate he or she is likely to be.	40
Trained observers	Police officers and other trained observers are no more accurate as eyewitnesses than the average person.	39
Event violence	Eyewitnesses have more difficulty remembering violent than nonviolent events.	37
Discriminability	It is possible to reliably differentiate between true and false memories.	32
Long-term repression	Traumatic experiences can be repressed for many years and then be recovered.	22

FIGURE 8.20 Experts' Judgments of Statements Regarding Eyewitness Testimony

During 2005, the child molestation trial of Michael Jackson dramatically demonstrated that problems with eyewitness testimony are exacerbated when the eyewitnesses are children (Rooy, Pipe, & Murray, 2005). According to John Yuille, of the University of British Columbia, one difficulty centres on the extreme suggestibility of children, making interviewing them a daunting task (Yuille, 1997). The other difficulty is that children who must testify in court are vulnerable to emotional trauma, especially when the case is one of sexual abuse (Raskin & Yuille, 1989). Pressures on children testifying in court may include the laying of criminal charges against a family member, a family member going to jail, the breakup of the family and/or the placing of the child under foster care. Coupled with children's natural suggestibility, these pressures mean that such cases must be handled with special care (Raskin & Yuille, 1989). In recognition of these challenges, Yuille and his colleagues (1993) have developed a method for conducting forensic interviews with children that can stand up in court and yet minimize the traumatic impact on the child. Their Step-Wise Interview is now in wide use throughout Canada (Hardy & van Leeuwen, 2004).

The pressures on vulnerable children when they are called to testify, especially against family members, combined with their natural suggestibility, makes the validity of their testimony especially difficult to determine.

> **reflect and review**

④ Summarize how memories are retrieved.

- Describe the serial position effect.
- Explain the role of retrieval cues and the retrieval task.
- Define autobiographical memory.
- Discuss three types of emotional memories and complications in their retrieval.
- Evaluate eyewitness testimony.

Do you think that, on the whole, negative emotional events are likely to be more memorable than positive ones? How would you go about studying whether negative events are more memorable than positive ones?

⑤ FORGETTING FROM LONG-TERM MEMORY

Encoding → Storage → Retrieval
Failure   Failure   Failure

HERMANN EBBINGHAUS (1850–1909)

The first psychologist to conduct scientific research on forgetting. *What was the nature of this research?*

How does forgetting involve encoding, storage, and retrieval failures?

Missed appointments, misplaced eyeglasses, failures to recall the names of familiar faces, and not being able to remember your password for Internet access are common examples of forgetting. Why do we forget?

One of psychology's pioneers, Hermann Ebbinghaus (1850–1909), was the first person to conduct scientific research on forgetting. In 1885, he made up and memorized a list of 13 nonsense syllables and then assessed how many of them he could remember as time passed. (*Nonsense syllables* are meaningless combinations of letters that are unlikely to have been learned already, such as *zeq, xid, lek, vut,* and *riy*.) Even just an hour later, Ebbinghaus could recall only a few of the nonsense syllables he had memorized. Figure 8.21 shows Ebbinghaus's learning curve for nonsense syllables. Based on his research, Ebbinghaus concluded that the most forgetting takes place soon after we learn something.

If we forget so quickly, why put effort into learning something? Fortunately, researchers have demonstrated that forgetting is not as extensive as Ebbinghaus envisioned (Baddeley, 1992; Lieberman, (2004). Ebbinghaus studied meaningless nonsense syllables. When we memorize more meaningful material, such as poetry, history, or the type of material in this text, forgetting is neither so rapid nor so extensive. Following are some of the factors that influence how well we can retrieve information from long-term memory.

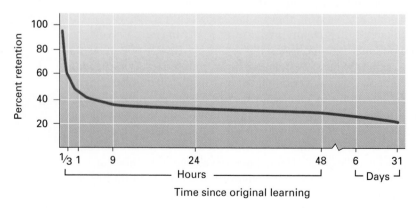

FIGURE 8.21 Ebbinghaus's Forgetting Curve

(a)   (b)   (c)   (d)   (e)   (f)   (g)

FIGURE 8.22 **Which Is a Real U.S. Penny?**
In the original experiment, 15 versions of pennies were shown to participants; only 1 was an actual U.S. penny. We have included only 7 of the 15 versions, and, as you likely can tell, this is still a very difficult task. *Why*? By the way, the actual U.S. penny is (c).

Encoding Failure

Before going on, first look at the pennies in figure 8.22 on the next page. Sometimes when people say they have forgotten something, they have not really forgotten it; they never encoded the information in the first place. *Encoding failure* is when the information was never entered into long-term memory.

As an example of encoding failure, could you pick out the real U.S. penny in figure 8.22? (By the way, (c) is the actual U.S. penny.) In the original classic study, researchers showed 15 versions of the penny to participants (we only showed you 7) and asked them which was correct (Nickerson & Adams, 1979). Most people, even Americans, do not do well on this task. Unless you are a coin collector, you likely have not encoded a lot of specific details about pennies. You may have encoded just enough information to distinguish them from other coins (pennies are copper coloured, dimes and nickels are silver coloured; pennies fall between the sizes of dimes and quarters).

The penny exercise illustrates that we encode and enter into long-term memory only a small portion of the experiences we have in life. In a sense, then, encoding failures really are not cases of forgetting; they are cases of not noticing.

Storage Failure

Another possible reason for forgetting is *storage failure*, in which the storage medium of long-term memory is imperfect and tends to deteriorate with the passage of time. **Decay theory** states that when something new is learned, a neurochemical "memory trace" is formed, but over time this trace tends to disintegrate. Decay theory suggests that the passage of time always increases forgetting. While memories do decay from sensory memory, within a second or so, and short-term memory, within about 30 seconds, there is little evidence that memories actually decay in long-term memory.

Of course memories become less vivid and less accessible with the passage of time. Memory researcher Daniel Schacter (2001) refers to the forgetting that occurs with the passage of time as *transience*. As an example of transience, recall that on October 3, 1995, a sensational criminal trial reached a dramatic conclusion: A jury acquitted O. J. Simpson of murder. The Simpson verdict seemed like just the kind of "flashbulb" memory that most of us would remember vividly for years to come. How well can you remember finding out about the Simpson verdict? In one research study, undergraduate students provided detailed accounts of how they learned about the Simpson verdict (Schmolck, Buffalo, & Squire, 2000). However, 15 months later, only half remembered the details, and nearly 3 years after the verdict, less than 30 percent of the students' memories were accurate.

But was this observed transience due to long-term memory decay? The single largest factor was an increase in the proportion of memory distortions reported (Schmolck, Buffalo, & Squire, 2000). It is quite possible that the original, more accurate, information still remained in long-term memory but that retrieval failures became more pronounced with the passage of time. For example, under the right retrieval conditions, memories that seem to have been forgotten can be accurately retrieved. You

decay theory States that when something new is learned, a neurochemical memory trace is formed, but over time this trace tends to disintegrate.

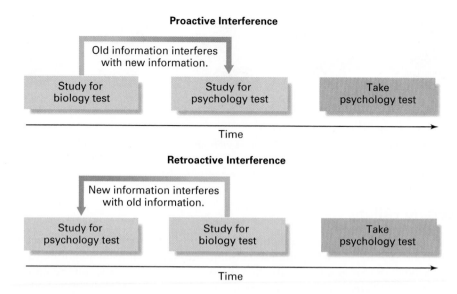

FIGURE 8.23 Proactive and Retroactive Interference

Pro- means "forward"; in proactive interference, old information has a forward influence by getting in the way of new material learned. *Retro-* means "backward"; in retroactive interference, new information has a backward influence by getting in the way of material learned earlier.

might have forgotten the face or name of someone in your high school class, but when you return to the setting in which you knew the person, you may remember. In general, there is no way to establish that a long-term memory that has faded over time has, in fact, decayed, rather than simply being inaccessible due to retrieval failure, or possibly being retrieved at some time in the future.

Retrieval Failure

Problems in retrieving information from memory are clearly examples of forgetting (Williams & Zacks, 2001). Psychologists have theorized that the causes of retrieval failure include problems with the information in storage, the effects of time, personal reasons for remembering or forgetting, and the brain's health.

Interference Interference has been proposed as one reason that people forget (Wixted, 2005). **Interference theory** states that people forget not because memories are actually lost from storage but because other information gets in the way of what they want to remember (Anderson, 2003).

There are two kinds of interference: proactive and retroactive. **Proactive interference** occurs when material that was learned earlier disrupts the recall of material learned later (Postle & Brush, 2004). Remember that pro- means "forward in time." For example, suppose you had a good friend 10 years ago named Kayleigh and that last night you met someone named Kylie. You might find yourself calling your new friend Kayleigh because the old information (*Kayleigh*) interferes with retrieval of new information (*Kylie*). **Retroactive interference** occurs when material learned later disrupts the retrieval of information learned earlier. Remember that retro- means "backward in time." Suppose you have lately become friends with Ewan. In sending a note to your old friend Ethan, you might mistakenly address it to Ewan because the new information (*Ewan*) interferes with the old information (*Ethan*). Figure 8.23 depicts another example of proactive and retroactive interference.

Proactive and retroactive interference might both be explained as problems with retrieval cues. The reason *Kayleigh* interferes with *Kylie* and *Ewan* interferes with *Ethan* might be that the cue you are using to remember the one name does not distinguish between the two memories. For example, if the cue you were using was "my good friend," it might evoke both names. The result could be retrieving the wrong name or a

interference theory States that people forget not because memories are actually lost from storage but because other information gets in the way of what we want to remember.

proactive interference Occurs when material that was learned earlier disrupts the recall of material learned later.

retroactive interference Occurs when material learned later disrupts the retrieval of information learned earlier.

kind of blocking in which each name interferes with the other and neither comes to mind. Retrieval cues (like "friend" in our example) can become overloaded, and when that happens we are likely to forget or to retrieve incorrectly.

Motivated Forgetting *Motivated forgetting* occurs when people deliberately forget something. In more extreme cases motivated forgetting is also referred to as *repression*, which was described earlier in discussing the difficulties that some people have in retrieving emotional memories. A past experience might be repressed because it is so painful or anxiety-laden that remembering is intolerable. In the psychodynamic view, unpleasant memories are repressed into our unconscious minds, and we are no longer aware of them. Such extreme motivated forgetting may be a consequence of the emotional blows of personal trauma that occur in victims of rape or physical abuse, in war veterans, or in survivors of earthquakes, plane crashes, and other terrifying events. These emotional traumas may haunt people for many years unless they can put the details out of their minds. Even when people have not experienced trauma, they may use motivated forgetting to protect themselves from memories of painful, stressful, unpleasant circumstances.

Amnesia Recall the cases of Doron Daniels, at the beginning of this chapter, and H. M. in the discussion of explicit and implicit memory. In their surgery, the part of their brain that was responsible for laying down new memories was damaged beyond repair, which resulted in **amnesia**, the loss of memory. Although some types of amnesia clear up over time, Doron Daniels and H. M.'s amnesia endured (Milner, Corkin, & Teuber, 1968; Corkin, 2002).

The type of amnesia that they suffer from is **anterograde amnesia**, a memory disorder that affects the retention of new information and events (*antero-* indicates amnesia that extends forward in time from the onset of the amnesia). What they learned before the surgery and the resulting onset of amnesia was not affected. For example, H. M. could identify his friends, recall their names, and even tell stories about them—but only if he had known them before surgery. People who met H. M. after surgery remained strangers, even if they spent thousands of hours with him. H. M.'s post-surgical experiences were rarely encoded in his long-term memory.

Amnesia also occurs in a form known as **retrograde amnesia**, which involves memory loss for a segment of the past but not for new events (*retro-* indicates amnesia that extends back in time from the onset of the amnesia) (Dutton & others, 2002; Guillery-Girard & others, 2004). Retrograde amnesia is much more common than anterograde amnesia and frequently occurs when the brain is assaulted by an electrical shock or a physical blow—such as a head injury suffered during an automobile accident. In contrast to anterograde amnesia, in retrograde amnesia the forgotten information is *old*—prior to the event that caused the amnesia—and the ability to acquire new memories is not affected. Sometimes, individuals have both anterograde and retrograde amnesia.

> ## reflect and review

5 **Describe how encoding, storage, and retrieval failure are involved in forgetting.**

- Define encoding failure.
- Explain why storage failure is not a compelling explanation for long-term memory forgetting.
- Discuss three reasons for retrieval failure.

Think about three or four recent instances in which you were unable to remember something. What principle of forgetting do you think best explains your failure to remember in each case?

amnesia The loss of memory.

anterograde amnesia A memory disorder that affects the retention of new information or events.

retrograde amnesia A memory disorder that involves memory loss for a segment of the past but not for new events.

6 MEMORY AND STUDY STRATEGIES

Encoding
Strategies — Storage
Strategies — Retrieval
Strategies

How can you apply what you have learned about memory to your academic studies?

Most of us face memory problems far less serious than amnesia or repression. The simple memory strategies that follow can help you to encode, store, and retrieve information more effectively. In fact, using the right memory strategies to study can help you improve your academic performance.

Keep in mind that even under the best circumstances memory is not perfect. And students who engage in ill-advised habits, such as not getting enough sleep, taking drugs, and not going to class regularly, may further impair the remembering that is necessary to do well on an exam.

Encoding Strategies

The first step in improving your academic performance is to make sure the information you're studying is processed effectively so it will be stored in long-term memory. Although some types of information are encoded automatically, the academic learning process usually requires considerable effort. Recall that encoding involves paying attention, processing information at an appropriate level, elaborating, and using imagery.

Be a Good Time Manager and Planner Managing your time effectively and planning to allow the necessary time to study will give you the hours you need to do well academically. As suggested in the discussion of study habits in chapter 1, to-do lists are an effective way of planning and managing time (see figure 1.5). To make high grades, you need to set aside at least two or three study hours for each hour you spend in class (Santrock & Halonen, 2006). Thus, if you are in class 15 hours, you should be studying 30 to 45 hours outside of class each week.

Another aspect of good planning is having the right resources to draw on and allowing enough time for the task. When you're studying for a test, make sure you have your textbook and class notes on hand. If you are writing a paper, plan enough time to write a first draft and revise it one or more times. And don't forget Doron Daniels and the Baycrest Memory-Link program. Consider using personal digital assistants and other tools, like calendars, daytimers, and diaries, to help you keep track of your academic life.

Pay Attention and Minimize Distraction Once you have made a commitment to spending the time needed on your studies, you have to make sure other things don't distract you during that time. If you want to encode information effectively, you have to give it your undivided attention.

Monitor how well you are paying attention. If you find yourself getting distracted, say to yourself a cue word or phrase such as "focus" or "zero in" to increase your attention.

Process More Deeply and Avoid Rote Memorization You are more likely to remember information over the long term if you process it to deeper levels (i.e. understand it) rather than process it to more shallow levels (i.e. rely on rote rehearsal and memorization). Rote rehearsal works well for information in short-term memory, but when you need to encode, store, and then retrieve information from long-term memory, it is much less efficient. So, for most information, understand it, give it meaning, elaborate on it, and personalize it.

One technique you can use to make sure you understand the material is *cognitive monitoring*, which involves taking stock of your progress in an activity such as reading or studying. For example, you might make sure that you understand the material by summarizing what you have read and restudying those parts of the material that were unclear.

Ask Yourself Questions   A self-questioning strategy can help you to remember. As you read, periodically stop and ask yourself questions, such as "What is the meaning of what I just read?", "Why is this important?", and "What is an example of the concept I just read about?" Take advantage of the numerous questions posed throughout this textbook. When you have made a concerted effort to ask yourself questions about what you have read or about an activity in class, you will elaborate the number of associations you make with the information you will need to retrieve later.

Take Good Notes   Taking good notes while listening to a lecture or reading a textbook also benefits your memory (Austin, Lee, & Carr, 2004). But don't try to write down everything: It is distracting, and it can prevent you from getting the big picture of what the instructor or textbook author is communicating.

Some good note-taking strategies include the following:

- *Summarizing.* Listen or read for a few minutes and then write down the main idea that the instructor or author is trying to get across in that time frame. Then listen or read for several more minutes and write down another idea, and so on.
- *Outlining.* Create an outline of what the instructor is saying, using a hierarchy to show which ideas are related and how general or specific they are. Model your system after the one used to organize textbook chapters, with "A"-level heads being the main topics, "B"-level heads the subtopics under the "A" heads, and "C"-level heads the subtopics under the "B" heads.
- *Concept maps.* If outlines don't seem to capture your thought processes, try drawing concept maps of what the instructor is saying or what you are reading. Concept maps are similar to outlines, but they visually display information in a chart or diagram format.
- *The Cornell method.* Divide a sheet of paper into two columns by drawing a line down the page about one-quarter to one-third of the way from the left edge. Write your notes on the right two-thirds to three-quarters of the page. When you review your notes, you can then add comments about the notes on the left side, which personalizes them for better understanding and later retrieval.
- *Note reviews.* Get into the habit of reviewing your notes periodically rather than waiting to study them at the last minute before a test. If possible, take a few minutes to review your notes just after a lecture or a reading section. You will be able to fill in information you might have missed that is still in your memory. This strategy also helps you to consolidate your learning.

Use Mnemonic Strategies   *Mnemonics* are specific visual and/or verbal memory aids. Following are three types of mnemonic devices:

- *Method of loci.* You develop an image of items to be remembered and then store them mentally in familiar locations (which is what "loci," the plural of "locus," means). Rooms of houses or stores on a street are common locations used in this memory strategy. For example, if you need to remember a list of brain structures, you can mentally place them in the rooms of a house you are familiar with, such as the entry hall, the living room, the dining room, the kitchen, and so on. Then, when you need to retrieve the information, you imagine the house, mentally go through the rooms, and retrieve the concepts.

"You simply associate each number with a word, such as 'lipoprotein' and 3,467,009."

© Sidney Harris

FIGURE 8.24

The Keyword Method
The keyword method can be used to help you learn foreign vocabulary. To learn an association between the English *truck* and the French *camion*, you might notice that *camion* starts with the same sound as *camel*, and associate the key word *camel* with a truck in an image, say, of a *camel* pulling a truck. Later, *camel* would provide a cue to retrieve *camion*.

- *Keyword method.* (see figure 8.24) You attach vivid imagery to important words. For example, recall from chapter 3 that the limbic system consists of two main regions: amygdala and hippocampus. To remember these three brain areas, you might imagine two legs (limbs) (limbic system) → ambling (amygdala) like a hippo (hippocampus).
- *Acronyms.* Create a word from the first letters of items to be remembered. For example, *HOMES* can be used to remember the Great Lakes: *H*uron, *O*ntario, *M*ichigan, *E*rie, and *S*uperior. An acronym commonly used to remember the sequence of colours in the light spectrum is the name of an imaginary man named *ROY G. BIV*: *R*ed, *O*range, *Y*ellow, *G*reen, *B*lue, *I*ndigo, and *V*iolet.

Many experts on memory and study skills recommend that mnemonics be used mainly when you need to memorize a list of items or specific facts. However, in most cases, techniques that promote memory by understanding the material are better than rote memorization.

Storage Strategies

Perhaps the best way to promote effective memory storage is to make sure that your brain is able to function at maximum capacity. For most of us, that means being well rested, well nourished, and free of mind-altering substances. In addition, you can try the following strategies.

Organize Your Memory You will remember information better if you consciously organize it while trying to absorb it. Arrange information, rework material, and give it a structure that will help you to remember it. One organizational technique is a hierarchy, like an outline. You might use a concept map, which draws on semantic-network theory, or create analogies (such as the earlier comparison of retrieval from long-term memory to finding a book in the library) that take advantage of your preexisting schemas.

Spread Out and Consolidate Your Learning To help move information from working memory to long-term memory, regularly review what you learn. You will also benefit by distributing your learning over a longer period rather than cramming for a test at the last minute. Cramming tends to produce short-term memory that is processed in a shallow rather than a deep manner. Then you can do a final, concentrated tune-up before the test instead of struggling to learn everything at the last minute (Santrock & Halonen, 2006).

Retrieval Strategies

Assuming you have encoded and stored the desired information effectively, you should have a relatively easy time retrieving it when you participate in a class discussion, take a test, or write a paper. Following are several good strategies for retrieving information more easily and making sure it is as accurate as possible.

Use Good Retrieval Cues Tatiana Cooley was the U.S. National Memory Champion in 1999, beating out many other contestants in memorizing thousands of numbers and words, pages of faces and names, and lengthy poems (Schacter, 2001). Tatiana relied on elaborative encoding strategies, creating visual images, stories, and associations that linked new information with what she already knew.

The reason Tatiana is mentioned here, though, is that she said in her everyday life she is incredibly absentminded. Fearing that she will forget to do many daily tasks (running errands, keeping appointments, and so on), she relies on to-do lists and notes scribbled on sticky pads as reminders. As Tatiana said, "I live by Post-Its." Like Tatiana, you can help your prospective memory by using good retrieval cues, as well as focused attention and elaboration at encoding. In this context it is again worth mentioning the Memory-Link project at the Baycrest Centre for Geriatric Care. One way to think about personal digital assistants like the Palm Pilot is that they function as very sophisticated retrieval cues.

Personal Reflections: Memory and Study Strategies

Candidly respond to the following items about your own memory and study strategies. Rate yourself 1 = never, 2 = some, 3 = moderate, 4 = almost always, and = 5 always. Then total your points.

1. I'm a good time manager and planner.
2. I'm good at focusing my attention and minimizing distractions.
3. I try to understand material rather than memorizing it by rote.
4. I ask myself questions about what I have read or about class activities.
5. I take good notes in class and from textbooks.
6. I regularly review my notes.
7. I use mnemonic strategies.
8. I'm very organized in the way I encode information.
9. I spread out my studying and consolidate my learning.
10. I use good retrieval cues.
11. I use the PQ4R or a similar study system.

If you scored 50 to 55 points, you likely use good memory and study strategies. If you scored 45 to 49 points, you likely have some reasonably good memory and study strategies. If you scored below 45, spend some time working on improving your memory and study strategies. Most colleges and universities have a study skills centre where specialists can help you.

Use the PQ4R Method Various systems have been developed to help students remember information that they are studying. The one used in this book, described in greater detail in the preface, is called *PQ4R*, which is an acronym for a six-step process (*P*, *Q*, and four *R*s):

1. Preview
2. Question
3. Read
4. Reflect
5. Recite
6. Review

This system can benefit you by getting you to meaningfully organize information, ask questions about it, reflect on and think about it, and review it. All these steps together make it easier to retrieve information when you need it, as well as to encode the information effectively.

To think further about your study strategies, see the Personal Reflections box.

> **> reflect and review**

6 **Evaluate study strategies based on an understanding of memory.**

- Describe some effective encoding strategies.
- Summarize some good storage strategies.
- Discuss some efficient retrieval strategies.

Get together with three or four students in this class and compare your note-taking and study strategies for the class. How are your strategies similar to or different from those of the other students? What did you learn from the comparison and this chapter about how to study more effectively?

Memory

1 THE NATURE OF MEMORY

2 MEMORY ENCODING

— Attention — Levels of Processing — Elaboration — Imagery

3 MEMORY STORAGE

— Sensory Memory — Short-Term Memory — Long-Term Memory

4 MEMORY RETRIEVAL

— Serial Position Effect — Retrieval Cues and the Retrieval Task — Retrieval of Autobiographical Memories — Retrieval of Emotional Memories — Eyewitness Testimony

5 FORGETTING FROM LONG-TERM MEMORY

— Encoding Failure — Storage Failure — Retrieval Failure

6 MEMORY AND STUDY STRATEGIES

— Encoding Strategies — Storage Strategies — Retrieval Strategies

At the beginning of the chapter, we posed four chapter questions and encouraged you to review material related to these questions at the end of each major section (see pages 305, 309, 324, 334, 337, and 341). Use the following reflection and review features for further your understanding of the chapter material.

CHAPTER REFLECTIONS

1. Try the following exercise: Take the key terms in a chapter of this text that you have not yet read. Spend 20–30 minutes trying to learn half of the words in an environment filled with distractions (such as the cafeteria at lunchtime or a crowded coffeehouse). Then spend the same amount of time trying to learn the other half of the words in a distraction-free environment. Test yourself later on your memory for the words. Which list was easier to remember? Are there distractions in your current study environment, and how do you think eliminating them would affect your memory?

2. Some people believe that they have memories from past lives stored in their brains. Consider each of the ways the brain may store memory. Are any of these compatible with memories from past lives?

3. It is sometimes difficult to believe that our memories are not as accurate as we think they are. To test your ability to be a good eyewitness, visit http://www.pbs.org/wgbh/pages/frontline/shows/dna/. To read more about the Thomas Sophonow case, visit http://www.gov.mb.ca/justice/publications/sophonow/toc.html. Did these Web sites change your opinion of the accuracy of eyewitness testimony? What about eyewitness accounts of UFO sightings or other paranormal events? Are these likely to be more accurate than memories for other events?

4. Think about the serial position effect. What does it suggest about how you should organize your study time? When should you study information you think is most important?

5. For several days, keep a list of times when you failed to remember something. Take a look at the list and identify whether they were instances of encoding failure or one of the types of retrieval failure. Is there one kind of forgetting that seems to be most problematic for you? Can you think of any strategies to help you with this kind of forgetting?

CHAPTER REVIEW

Identify three fundamental memory processes.

- Memory is the retention of information over time through encoding, storage, and retrieval—which are the three fundamental processes of memory. Encoding involves getting information into storage, storage consists of retaining information over time, and retrieval involves taking information out of storage.

Explain how memories are encoded.

- To begin the process of memory encoding, we have to attend to information. Selective attention is a necessary part of encoding. Memory is often negatively influenced by divided attention.

- Levels of processing theory states that information is processed on a continuum from shallow (sensory or physical features are encoded) to intermediate (labels are attached to stimuli) to deep (the meanings of stimuli and their associations with other stimuli are processed). Deeper processing produces better memory.

- Elaboration, the extensiveness of processing at any given level of memory, improves memory.

- Using imagery, or mental pictures, as a context for information can improve memory.

Discuss how memories are stored.

- The Atkinson-Shiffrin theory describes memory as a three-stage process: sensory memory, short-term memory, and long-term memory. Sensory memory holds perceptions of the world for only an instant, not much longer than the brief time the person is exposed to visual, auditory, and other sensory input. Visual sensory memory (iconic memory) retains information about one-quarter of a second, auditory sensory memory (echoic memory) for several seconds.

- Short-term memory is a limited-capacity memory system in which information is usually retained for as long as 30 seconds. Short-term memory's limitation is 7 ± 2 bits of information. Chunking and rehearsal can benefit short-term memory. Baddeley's concept of working memory characterizes short-term memory as more active and complex than Atkinson and Shiffrin proposed. Baddeley's model of working memory has three components: a central executive and two assistants (phonological loop and visuospatial working memory).

- Long-term memory is a relatively permanent type of memory that holds huge amounts of information for a long period of time. Long-term memory can be divided into two main subtypes. Explicit memory is the conscious recollection of information, such as specific facts or events. Implicit memory affects behaviour through prior experiences that are not consciously recollected. Explicit memory has two dimensions. One dimension includes episodic memory and semantic memory. The other dimension includes retrospective memory and prospective memory. Implicit memory is multidimensional, too. It includes systems for procedural memory, priming, and classical conditioning.

    Several models have been developed to describe how long-term memory is organized. The simplest theory recognizes that we store information better when we represent it in an organized, hierarchical manner. Another theory recognizes that we often use semantic networks (based on labels and meaning) to organize material. Schema theory claims that long-term memory is not exact; we construct our past by fitting new information into a preexisting mental framework. Scripts are schemas for events. Connectionist theory states that memory is organized as a wide range of connections between neurons, many of which operate simultaneously to store memory. Single neurons are involved in memory, but some neuroscientists believe that many memories are stored in circuits of about 1000 neurons. There is no specific memory centre in the brain, but some brain structures are more involved in certain aspects of memory than others. The hippocampus and nearby areas of the temporal lobes in the cerebral cortex, along with other areas of the limbic system, are involved in explicit memory. In many aspects of memory, information is transmitted from the hippocampus to the frontal lobes. The cerebellum is involved in implicit memory. Various areas of the cerebral cortex, such as the temporal lobes and the hippocampus, are involved in priming. The amygdala is at work in emotional memories.

Summarize how memories are retrieved.

- The serial position effect is the tendency for items at the beginning and the end of a list to be remembered better than items in the middle of a list. The primacy effect refers to better recall for items at the beginning of the list. The recency effect refers to better remembering items at the end of a list.

- Memory retrieval is easier when effective cues are present. Another factor in effective retrieval is the nature of the retrieval task. Simple recognition of previously remembered information in the presence of cues is generally easier than recalling the information. The encoding specificity principle states that information present at the time of encoding or learning tends to be effective as a retrieval cue. Retrieval also benefits from priming, which activates particular connections or associations in memory. The tip-of-the-tongue phenomenon occurs when we cannot quite pull something out of memory. In many instances, people recall information better when they attempt to recall information in the same context or internal state in which they learned the information. These processes are referred to as context-dependent and state-dependent memory, respectively.

- Autobiographical memory is a person's recollections of his or her life experiences. Autobiographical memory has three levels: (1) life time periods, (2) general events, and (3) event-specific knowledge. Biographies of the self connect the past and the present to form our identity.

- Flashbulb memories are memories of emotionally significant events that people often recall with more accuracy and vivid imagery than they recall everyday events. Although flashbulb memories are typically more vivid and durable than everyday memories, they are subject to some deterioration and change. Memory for personal trauma is also usually more accurate than memory for ordinary events, but it too is subject to some distortion and inaccuracy. People tend to remember the core information about a personal trauma but might distort some of the details. Some cases of personal trauma result in post-traumatic stress disorder. The release of stress hormones, which is signalled by the amygdala, likely accounts for some of the extraordinary longevity and vividness of memories of emotional or traumatic experiences. Personal trauma can cause individuals to repress emotionally laden information so that it is not accessible to consciousness. Repression does not erase a memory; it just makes it far more difficult to retrieve.

- Eyewitness testimony may contain errors due to memory decay or bias. Wording of questions and lineup instructions are examples of circumstances that influence eyewitness testimony.

Describe how encoding, storage, and retrieval failure are involved in forgetting from long-term memory.

- Encoding failure is forgetting information that was never entered into long-term memory.

- Storage failure, termed decay, is unlikely to be the cause of much long-term forgetting. Decay theory states that when something new is learned, a neuro-chemical memory trace is formed, but over time this chemical trail tends to disintegrate; the term for the phenomenon of memories fading with the passage of time is also called transience. However, information does decay from sensory memory and short-term memory.

- Retrieval failure can occur for at least three reasons: Interference theory states that we forget not because memories are lost from storage but because other information gets in the way of what we want to remember. Interference can be proactive or retroactive. Motivated forgetting, which occurs when people want to forget something, is common when a memory becomes painful or anxiety laden, as in the case of emotional traumas such as rape or physical abuse. Amnesia, the physiologically based loss of memory, can be anterograde, affecting the retention of new information or events; retrograde, affecting memories of the past but not new events; or both.

Evaluate study strategies based on an understanding of memory.

- Effective encoding strategies when studying include being a good time manager and planner, paying attention and minimizing distraction, understanding the material rather than memorizing it by rote, asking yourself questions, taking good notes, and using mnemonic strategies.

- Effective storage strategies when studying include organizing your memory and spreading out and consolidating your learning.

- Effective retrieval strategies when studying include using good retrieval cues and using the PQ4R method.

CONNECTIONS

For extra help in mastering the material in this chapter, see the integrator, review sections, practice quizzes, and other resources in the Student Study Guide and at the Online Learning Centre (www.mcgrawhill.ca/college/santrock).

CORE TERMS

memory, p. 304
encoding, p. 305
levels of processing theory, p. 306
elaboration, p. 307
storage, p. 309
Atkinson-Shiffrin theory, p. 309
sensory memory, p. 310
short-term memory, p. 311
working memory, p. 312
long-term memory, p. 313
explicit memory (declarative memory), p. 314

episodic memory, p. 314
semantic memory, p. 315
retrospective memory, p. 316
prospective memory, p. 316
implicit memory (nondeclarative memory), p. 316
procedural memory, p. 317
priming, p. 317
schema, p. 319
script, p. 320
connectionism (parallel distributed processing), p. 320

retrieval, p. 324
serial position effect, p. 325
decay theory, p. 335
interference theory, p. 336
proactive interference, p. 336
retroactive interference, p. 336
amnesia, p. 337
anterograde amnesia, p. 337
retrograde amnesia, p. 337

9 Thinking and Language

CHAPTER QUESTIONS

1. How would you characterize the "cognitive revolution" in psychology?

2. What is concept formation?

3. What are the requirements for solving problems?

4. What are the main factors in thinking critically, reasoning, and making decisions?

5. Can you identify the possible connections between language and thought?

6. How is language acquired and how does it develop?

When she was 18 years old, Wendy Verougstraete felt that she was on the road to becoming a writer. "You are looking at a professional author," she said. "My books will be filled with drama, action, and excitement. And everyone will want to read them. I am going to write books, page after page, stack after stack."

Overhearing her remarks, you might have been impressed not only by Wendy's optimism and determination but also by her expressive verbal skills. In fact, at a young age, Wendy showed a flair for writing and telling stories. And now, years later, Wendy has a rich vocabulary, creates lyrics for love songs, and enjoys telling stories. You would probably not be able to immediately guess that she has an IQ of only 49 and cannot tie her shoes, cross the street by herself, read or print words beyond the grade 1 level, or do even simple arithmetic.

Wendy Verougstraete has *Williams Syndrome*, a genetic birth disorder that was first described in 1961 and that affects about 1 in 20,000 births (Morris, 2005). The syndrome includes a number of physical characteristics such as heart defects, a pixie-like facial appearance, and brain abnormalities (Jackowski & Schultz, 2005). The most noticeable psychological features of the syndrome include a unique combination of expressive verbal skills, extremely low IQ, and limited spatial and motor control (Semel & Rosner, 2003; Osborne & Pober, 2001). Figure 9.1 shows the great disparity in the verbal and motor skills of one person with Williams Syndrome. Individuals with Williams Syndrome often have good musical skills and interpersonal skills. Despite having excellent verbal skills and competent interpersonal skills, most individuals with Williams Syndrome cannot live independent lives (American Academy of Pediatrics, 2001). For example, Wendy Verougstraete lives in a group home for adults who are mentally retarded.

The verbal abilities of individuals with Williams Syndrome are very distinct from those shown by individuals with Down Syndrome, a type of mental retardation that is discussed in chapter 10 (Laing & others, 2005). On vocabulary tests, children with Williams Syndrome show a liking for unusual words. When asked to name as many animals as they can think of in one minute, Williams children come up with creatures such as ibex, chihuahua, sabre-toothed tiger, weasel, crane, and newt. Children with Down Syndrome give simple examples such as dog, cat, and mouse. When children with Williams Syndrome tell stories, their voices come alive with drama and emotion, punctuating the dialogue with attention grabbers such as "gadzooks" or "lo and behold!" In contrast, children with Down Syndrome tell very simple stories with little emotion.

Aside from being an interesting genetic disorder, Williams Syndrome offers insights into the normal development of thinking and language. In our society, verbal ability is generally associated with high intelligence. But Williams Syndrome raises the possibility that thinking and language might not be so closely related. Williams disorder is due to a defective gene that seems to protect expressive verbal ability but not reading and many other cognitive skills (Ypsilanti & others, 2005). Thus, cases such as Wendy Verougstraete's cast some doubt on the general categorization of intelligence as verbal ability and prompts the question, What is the relation between thinking and language? This question is addressed later in the chapter.

Wendy Verougstraete was born with Williams Syndrome, characterized by a unique combination of expressive verbal skills, extremely low IQ, and limited spatial and motor control.

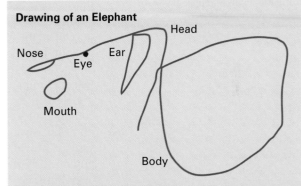

Drawing of an Elephant

Verbal Description of an Elephant

And what an elephant is, it is one of the animals. And what the elephant does, it lives in the jungle. It can also live in the zoo. And what it has, it has long grey ears, fan ears, ears that can blow in the wind. It has a long trunk that can pick up grass, or pick up hay. . . . If they're in a bad mood it can be terrible. . . . If the elephant gets mad it could stomp; it could charge. Sometimes elephants can charge. They have big long tusks. They can damage a car. . . . It could be dangerous. When they're in a pinch, when they're in a bad mood it can be terrible. You don't want an elephant as a pet. You want a cat or a dog or a bird. . . .

FIGURE 9.1

Disparity in the Verbal and Motor Skills of an Individual with Williams Syndrome

① THE COGNITIVE REVOLUTION IN PSYCHOLOGY

What is the "cognitive revolution" in psychology?

Behaviourism was a dominant force in psychology until the late 1950s and 1960s, when many psychologists began to realize that they could not understand or explain human behaviour without referring to mental processes (Reed, 2004; Gardner, 1985). The term *cognitive psychology* became a label for approaches that sought to explain observable behaviour by investigating mental processes and structures that cannot be directly observed (Solso, MacLin, & MacLin, 2005; Sternberg, 2003a; Spellman & Willingham, 2004). Cognitive psychologists are fascinated by cases such as Wendy Verougstraete's because of their interest in language, problem solving, reasoning, and decision making. Cognitive psychologists also are interested in how people process memories in adapting to their world. Cognitive psychologists study **cognition**—how information is processed and manipulated in remembering, thinking, and knowing.

Raymond Klein of Dalhousie University, a leading cognitive psychologist, provides one example of what cognitive psychologists do. He conducts research on the basic mechanism of attention, often with the use of sophisticated computer technologies, such as eye-movement trackers (Klein, 2004, 2005). He has also worked on various applications of cognitive psychology, including problem gambling (S. Stewart & others, 2002) and the design of advanced consumer telecommunications devices (Christie & Klein, 1998).

It is no surprise that Klein, with his educational and research background, makes extensive use of computer technology in his research and applied work. Of all the factors that stimulated the growth of cognitive psychology, probably none was more important than the development of computers. Computers rapidly became the tool of choice for collecting data as cognitive psychology developed ever more sophisticated experimental methods (Healy, 2005). Cognitive psychologists have long seen an analogy between the computer and the human brain and used the analogy to help explain the relation between cognition and the brain (Russell & Norvig, 2003). This analogy was first noted in the late 1940s by John von Neumann (but see Green, 2005), who developed the first modern computer in the late 1940s and showed that machines could perform logical operations. By the 1950s, researchers often speculated that some mental operations might be modelled by computers, possibly telling us something about the way the human mind works (Hirstein & others, 2006).

Herbert Simon (1969) was among the pioneers in comparing the human mind to computer processing systems. In his analogy, the physical brain is described as the computer's hardware, cognition as its software. In this analogy, the sensory and perceptual systems provide an "input channel," similar to the way data are entered into a computer (see figure 9.2). As input (information) comes into the mind, mental processes, or operations, act on it, just as the computer's software acts on the data. The transformed input generates information that remains in memory in much the same way as a computer stores what it has worked on. Finally, the information is retrieved from memory and "printed out" or "displayed" (so to speak) as an overt, observable response.

Although computers continue to play an important role in psychology's cognitive revolution, recent work in neuroscience has shown that digital computers and human brains function quite differently in some respects (Goel, 2005a; Houghton, 2005). Because of this, Simon's (1969) early analogy, which relies on computers to provide a logical and concrete model of how information is processed in the mind, has been criticized as oversimplified. As we saw in Chapter 3, our emerging understanding of the plasticity of the human brain has shown that relatively permanent changes in human cognition and behaviour probably always result in changes in the structure of the brain (Kolb, Gibb, & Robinson, 2003; Neville, 2005). Thus, while you can load new software into your computer without changing the hardware, when you learn new ways of thinking or acting, your brain probably always changes as a result. And because computers and brains function differently, they have different patterns of strengths and weaknesses.

Raymond Klein balances his basic research on attention with his applied work in cognitive psychology.

cognition The way in which information is processed and manipulated in remembering, thinking, and knowing.

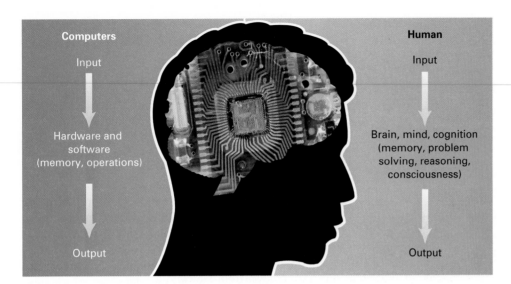

Computers

Input

Hardware and software (memory, operations)

Output

Human

Input

Brain, mind, cognition (memory, problem solving, reasoning, consciousness)

Output

FIGURE 9.2

Computers and Human Cognition
An analogy is commonly drawn between human cognition and the way computers work. The physical brain is analogous to a computer's hardware, and cognition is analogous to a computer's software.

Most computers rely on one or two central processing units (CPUs) that can precisely process billions of calculations per second. No matter how fast the CPU, the information processing is always *serial*, carried out one calculation at a time. Because of this form of *architecture*, computers can perform repetitive complex numerical calculations much faster and more accurately than humans could ever hope to (Russell & Norvig, 2003). Computers can also apply and follow rules more consistently and with fewer errors than humans and represent complex mathematical patterns better than humans can. However, these calculations must be precisely specified.

In contrast, each brain cell, or neuron, is a living information processor. It accepts inputs from neurons synapsing with it, integrates that information and sends its own signal onward as it synapses with other neurons. At any instant in time, then, billions of neurons may be simultaneously active. Thus the brain is a massively *parallel* information processor. Even though any single neuron is incredibly simple as compared with any computer CPU, the computing power of even an infant human brain far outstrips that of most computers. Further, neurons, and thus the brain, can respond to information, often ambiguous, transmitted through the sensory receptors described in chapter 5, such as the eyes and ears. By comparison, most computers receive information from a human who has already coded the information and removed much of the ambiguity.

This capacity of the human brain to deal with ambiguity means that the brain's extraordinary capabilities will probably not be mimicked completely by computers any time in the near future. Attempts to use computers to process visual information or spoken language have achieved only limited success in highly specific situations. The human brain also has an incredible ability to learn new rules, relationships, concepts, and patterns that it can generalize to novel situations. In comparison, computers are quite limited in their ability to learn and generalize. Although a computer can improve its ability to recognize patterns or use rules of thumb to make decisions, it does not have the means to develop new learning goals. Furthermore, the human mind is aware of itself; the computer is not. Indeed, no computer is likely to approach the richness of human consciousness (Fauconnier & Turner, 2002).

Nonetheless, the computer's role in cognitive psychology continues to increase, and has given rise in recent years to a field called **artificial intelligence (AI)**, the science of creating machines capable of performing activities that require intelligence when they are done by people. There are currently two different approaches to AI. One relies on the serial architecture of traditional computers to create software that produces intelligent outputs and sometimes mimics human functioning. The other seeks to combine large numbers of simpler processing units to create a parallel computer that can also produce intelligent outputs, but do so by mimicking the architecture of the human brain.

artificial intelligence (AI) The science of creating machines capable of performing activities that require intelligence when they are done by people.

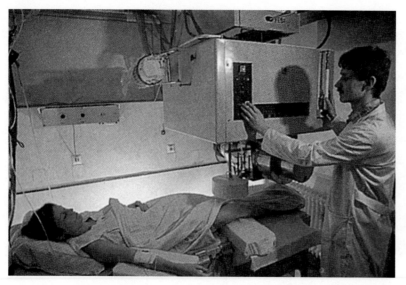

Artificial intelligence systems have been used to assist in medical diagnosis and treatment. *What are some other ways they can be used?*

AI is especially helpful in tasks requiring speed, persistence, and a vast memory (Russell & Norvig, 2003; Simon, 2000). AI systems have also been designed to assist in diagnosing medical illnesses and prescribing treatment, examining equipment failures, evaluating loan applicants, and advising students about which courses to take (Houghton, 2005; Hatzakis & Tsoukas, 2002).

Artificial intelligence systems attempt to mimic the way humans think. But are their capabilities the same as thinking? What exactly is thinking? The next three sections explore this question. **Thinking** involves manipulating information, as when we form concepts, solve problems, think critically, reason, and make decisions. You will see that some of the processes you learned about in previous chapters, such as how people perceive information (chapter 5) and how information is encoded, stored, and retrieved (chapter 8) play a part in thinking.

> **reflect and review**

1 **Characterize the "cognitive revolution" in psychology.**

- Define cognition and discuss the cognitive revolution in psychology.
- Compare and contrast the architecture of computers and the human brain.

What can your mind do that a computer cannot do? What can a computer do that your mind cannot? Do you think you might have to answer these questions differently 40 to 50 years from now? Explain.

2 CONCEPT FORMATION

— **Functions** — **Structure**
of Concepts **of Concepts**

© The New Yorker Collection 1986 Edward Koren from cartoonbank.com. All Rights Reserved.

thinking Manipulating information, as when we form concepts, solve problems, think critically, reason, and make decisions.

concepts Mental categories that are used to group objects, events, and characteristics.

How are concepts formed?

Regardless of the kind of thinking we engage in, our thinking is fuelled by concepts. **Concepts** are mental categories that are used to group objects, events, and characteristics. Humans have a special ability for creating categories to help us make sense of information in our world (Woo-kyoung & others, 2005; Ashby & Maddox, 2005). We know that kiwis and strawberries are both fruits, although they have different tastes and colours. We know that Smart cars and Hummers are both automobiles, although they differ in environmental impact, speed, and prestige. How do we know these things? The answer lies in our ability to group them on the basis of their features. For example, Smart cars and Hummers, although quite different, still both have an engine, four wheels, and a steering wheel, and both provide transportation. By such features we know that they are both automobiles. In other words, we have a concept of what an automobile is.

Functions of Concepts

Concepts are important for several reasons:

1. Concepts allow us to generalize. If we did not have concepts, each object and event in our world would be unique to us.

Monet's *Palazzo Da Mula, Venice*

FIGURE 9.3
The Concept of Schools of Art
The concept of schools of art lets us compare paintings by different artists. How do other Neoclassicist paintings compare to the one by Michelangelo? How do other Impressionist paintings compare to the one by Monet? How do other Expressionist paintings compare to the one by Klee?

Michelangelo's *Libyan Sibyl,* Sistine Chapel

Klee's *Dance You Monster to My Soft Song*

2. Concepts allow us to associate experiences and objects. Basketball, hockey, and track are sports. The concept of *sport* gives us a way to compare these activities. Neoclassicism, Impressionism, and Expressionism are all *schools of art*. The concept *schools of art* lets us compare paintings by artists from these different schools (see figure 9.3).
3. Concepts grease the wheels of memory, making it more efficient so that we don't have to "reinvent the wheel" each time we come across a piece of information. For example, we don't have to relearn what the Parliament buildings in Ottawa are each time we pick up a newspaper. We already have the concept.
4. Concepts also provide clues about how to react to a particular object or experience. For example, if we see a bowl of natchos, our concept of food lets us know it is okay to eat them.

Structure of Concepts

Two models of how people structure concepts have been proposed: the classical model and the prototype model (Medin, Profitt, & Schwartz, 2000; Burnett & others, 2005). In the **classical model**, all instances of a concept share defining properties. For example, to be an instance of the concept *triangle*, a geometric form must have three sides and interior angles that equal 180 degrees.

Although the classical model describes concepts that involve geometric forms reasonably well, it does not fare so well for many concepts. If the definition of a concept depends on its defining characteristics, then specifying these characteristics should be straightforward. However, it can be difficult to define the characteristics of even frequently used concepts. For example, "can fly" might seem to be an appropriate defining characteristic of the concept *bird*. However, ostriches and penguins are birds that do not fly. Another criticism of the classical model is that it cannot explain how people are able to judge some instances of a concept as being more typical than others. For example, robins are considered to be more typical of the concept of bird than penguins are.

The **prototype model** emphasizes that people decide whether an item reflects a concept by comparing it with the most typical item(s) in that category. To continue with the concept of bird, birds generally fly, sing, and build nests, but there are exceptions to these properties. Thus, Eleanor Rosch (1973; 2002) argues that membership in a concept can be graded, rather than all or none. In her view, the better members of the concept (such as robins for the concept of bird) have more characteristics than the poorer members of the category (such as penguins). The prototype model maintains that characteristic properties are used to create a representation of the average or ideal member, or prototype, for each concept. Potential members of the concept are then compared to this prototype. Thus the prototype model is able to explain typicality effects (Minda & Smith, 2001; Burnett & others, 2005). Recently, for example, Von Lengerke (2005) has shown that lay people understand medical illnesses in terms of typical symptoms clustered together into prototypes.

Each of these models accounts for some but not all of the findings regarding the structure of concepts, and thus each has its proponents (Medin, Lynch, & Solomon, 2000; Ashby & Maddox, 2005). Although research continues to be carried out on the categorization aspects of concepts, current research also focuses on other aspects of concepts. For example, some researchers have found that the way we use concepts affects a concept's structure and organization (Ross, 2000). Other researchers are studying people's concepts of events (Zacks & Tversky, 2001). And yet others are focusing on how people combine concepts to express new ideas or to refer to new situations (Wisniewski, 2000). Interest in the combination of concepts includes language use. For example, most of the sentences you have ever read or heard, including this one, correspond to a novel combination of concepts. One contemporary research interest is on novel noun-noun and adjective-noun combinations, such as "ostrich steak" and "space shuttle." The creation of such combinations is an important mechanism that speakers use to expand their language.

Concept Formation Different models of how concepts are learned in the first place have also been proposed. Lee Brooks (1978, 2005) of McMaster University has argued that concept learning may occur both implicitly and explicitly. This distinction parallels the distinction between explicit and implicit memory, discussed in the previous chapter. Recently, Ashby & Maddox (2005) have distinguished between the explicit, conscious rule-based learning of abstract *concepts* and the implicit, unconscious learning of perceptual *categories*.

For example, suppose you are an avid tennis player but think your serve is weak, especially as compared with the serves of professional tennis players. Even though you can clearly tell the difference, you may not have an explicit concept of "your serve" or of what makes a "killer" serve. You may not be able to articulate the rules of good serving. In this case, you have implicitly, unconsciously, formed two categories (your serve vs. killer serve) based on global perceptions. We are capable of this type of unconscious,

classical model States that all instances of a concept share defining properties.

prototype model People decide whether an item reflects a concept by comparing it with the most typical item(s) of that concept that they know about.

perceptual concept formation, sometimes called *category formation*, even when we are infants (Horst, Oakes, & Madole, 2005).

With a difficult concept (such as the mechanics of a good serve), you might need an expert—a professional tennis coach—to help you. The pro's concept is likely to be conscious rather then unconscious and more conceptual rather than perceptual. The pro's concept is likely to include some explicit features as well as complex rules related to those features. In general, concepts with more features and more complicated rules are more difficult to learn. For example, the pro might tell you that tossing the ball higher helps, but that it works much better if you rotate the grip on your racket slightly counterclockwise. It is worth noting that someone may become an expert at, say, tennis, and yet be unable to explicitly describe how he or she does it. This explains why some experts are, nevertheless, poor coaches. The best coaches are those who can explicitly describe the complex rules underlying their expert knowledge of the field that they are in (Brooks, 1978).

Working with your coach and watching good players serve, you may develop an explicit hypothesis about the mechanics of an excellent serve. For example, you may decide that the ball must be tossed high and that the server needs to swing the racket like a baseball pitcher throws an overhead pitch. You'll want to test the hypothesis in your own game to see if tossing the ball high and swinging the racket like a baseball pitcher's overhead throw improves your serve.

The distinction between the explicit learning of more abstract concepts and the perceptual learning of more perceptual concepts, or categories, has been supported by neuropsychological investigations. For example, explicit rule-based concept formation involves activating the prefrontal cortex (Rogers & others, 2000). In contrast, implicit perceptual concept formation does not involve prefrontal cortex activation (Ashby & Maddox, 2005) but does involve the activation of the occipital cortex (Aizenstein & others, 2000).

> **reflect and review**

 Explain concept formation.

- Discuss the functions of concepts.
- Describe two models of concept structure.
- Describe two models of concept formation.

Write down seven concepts that come to mind. Make sure some are more perceptual and some are more conceptual. Note how hard it is to define the concepts in terms of features and/or rules. Then create a diagram to show meaningful connections among them. Add more categories if you need them to link everything together. Compare your diagram with someone else's in the class. What does this exercise suggest about the simplicity or complexity of concepts?

---

③ PROBLEM SOLVING

| Steps in Problem Solving | — | Obstacles to Solving Problems | — | Expertise |

What are the requirements for solving problems?

Concepts are basic to another cognitive skill: problem solving (Stanovich, 1999, 2004). It is impossible to solve problems without concepts. Think about driving. Signs and traffic signals tell us to stop, yield, proceed, or not to pass or park. Most of the symbols that keep traffic moving so smoothly are the brainchild of William Eno, the "father of traffic

In the nineteenth century, New York City began to experience traffic jams. The horse-drawn vehicles were making street traffic dangerous. *How did William Eno solve this problem?*

safety." Eno, born in New York City in 1858, became concerned about the city's horrendous traffic jams. Horse-drawn vehicles were making street traffic dangerous. Eno published a paper about the urgency of street traffic reform. His proposed solutions to the problem created new concepts, such as the concepts "stop signs," "one-way streets," and "pedestrian islands," which continue to be important to traffic safety today (Bransford & Stein, 1993).

Like William Eno, we face many problems in the course of our everyday lives. These include trying to figure out the fastest way to get across town, planning how to get enough money to buy a computer system, working out a jigsaw puzzle, or estimating how much financial aid we need for school. **Problem solving** is an attempt to find an appropriate way of attaining a goal when the goal is not readily available. Among the methods for doing so are following the steps required for problem solving, overcoming mental obstacles, and developing expertise.

Steps in Problem Solving

Given the importance of solving problems in our everyday lives—and the importance of solving some extraordinarily difficult problems—psychologists have gone to great efforts to specify the thinking process that individuals go through to effectively solve problems (Wenke, Frensch, & Funke, 2005). Psychological research points to four steps in the process: (1) find and frame problems, (2) develop good problem-solving strategies, (3) evaluate solutions, and (4) rethink and redefine problems and solutions over time.

Find and Frame the Problem Before a problem can be solved, it has to be recognized (Lovett, 2002; Mayer, 2000). Finding and framing problems often involves asking questions in creative ways (Goleman, Kaufman, & Ray, 1993). Bill Bowerman (inventor of Nike shoes) asked, "What happens if I pour rubber over a waffle iron?" Fred Smith (founder of Federal Express) asked, "Why can't there be reliable overnight mail service?" Godfrey Hounsfield (inventor of the CAT scan) asked, "Why can't we see in three dimensions what is inside the human body without cutting it open?" Masaru Ibuka (honorary chairman of Sony) asked, "Why don't we remove the recording function and speaker from the portable music player and put the headphones directly on the player?"

Many of these questions were ridiculed at first. Other shoe companies thought Bowerman's waffle shoe was a "really stupid idea." Fred Smith proposed the idea of Federal Express during his days as a student at Yale and got a C on the paper. Godfrey Hounsfield was told that the CAT scan was impractical. And Masaru Ibuka was told that the Walkman would never sell: "A player without speakers—you must be crazy!"

In the past, students were taught to solve problems through exercises involving well-defined problems with well-defined steps for solving them (Anderson, Douglass, & Qin, 2005). However, many of life's real-world problems are ill-defined or vague, and don't have clearly defined ways of being solved. According to University of Western Ontario psychologist Richard Sorrentino, the ability to deal with vague situations, what he refers to as *uncertainty orientation*, is an important and unexplored personality characteristic (Sorrentino & Roney, 2000; Sorrentino & others, 2005). Consider the ill-defined problem of writing a paper for a psychology course. You have to proceed by narrowing down to a more specific problem such as deciding on the area of psychology (neuroscience, cognitive psychology, abnormal psychology, and so on) you will write about. You will then need to narrow your focus even further to find a specific problem within that area to write about, and so on. A good strategy is to weigh several specific alternatives before selecting one to write about. This type of exercise in finding and framing problems is an important aspect of problem solving.

Unfortunately, our society all too often discourages people from identifying problems. Many businesses, government agencies, and schools reprimand or fire employees who identify problems in the workplace. For example, increased incidences of cancer

problem solving An attempt to find an appropriate way of attaining a goal when the goal is not readily available.

from asbestos might have been avoided if problems identified by employees had been acknowledged and acted on by people in authority. The pressure to ignore problems is so strong that the U.S. Congress finally passed a bill that provides protection for employees who are brave enough to persist in their fight to have the problems they identify recognized. It became known as the Whistle-Blower Protection Act. In Canada, only New Brunswick currently protects Canadians who come forward to identify problems in their company or branch of government.

Develop Good Problem-Solving Strategies Once you find a problem and clearly define it, you need to develop strategies for solving it. Among the effective strategies are subgoals, algorithms, and heuristics.

Subgoaling involves setting intermediate goals or defining intermediate problems that put you in a better position for reaching the final goal or solution. Let's return to the problem of writing a paper for a psychology course. What might be some subgoaling strategies? One might be locating the right books and research journals on the problem you have decided to study. At the same time that you are searching for the right books and journals, you will likely benefit from establishing some subgoals within the time frame you have for completing the project. If the paper is due in two months, you might set a subgoal of a first draft of the paper two weeks before it is due, another subgoal of completing reading for the paper one month before it is due, and yet another subgoal of starting library research tomorrow.

Notice that in establishing the subgoals for meeting the deadline, we worked backward. Working backward in establishing subgoals is a good strategy. You first create the subgoal that is closest to the final goal and then work backward to the subgoal that is closest to the beginning of the problem-solving effort.

Algorithms are strategies that guarantee a solution to a problem. Algorithms come in different forms, such as equations, computer programs, formulas, instructions, or trying out all possible solutions (Lovett, 2002). We often use algorithms, in mathematics (when we solve an equation), in cooking (by following a recipe) and driving (by following directions to an address).

In some cases an algorithmic strategy might take a long time. Consider a person who is working on a crossword puzzle. She comes across c_nt_ _ker_ _ _ and looks to see what hint is given. It says, "Ill-tempered and quarrelsome." An algorithm that guarantees finding the correct word exists. She could try every possible alphabet combination in the six blank spaces and then check through a dictionary to see which one is correct. However, not many people would want to go through the more than one million steps in this algorithmic effort. Clearly, the algorithmic strategy of trying out all possible solutions should be applied to problems with a small number of possible solutions or executed with a suitably programmed computer.

So, instead of using an algorithm to solve this type of problem, most crossword-puzzle enthusiasts use **heuristics**, which are strategies or guidelines that suggest a solution to a problem but do not guarantee an answer (Stolarz-Fantino & Fantino, 2005; Oaksford, Roberts, & Chater, 2002). Crossword enthusiasts know that certain combinations of letters are likelier to work than others. For example, c_nt_ _ker_ _ _ is almost certain to require a vowel between c and n, so b, q, and a lot of other letters won't work. We also know that combinations of letters such as *an* are acceptable between t and k. We also know that it helps to sound out some words at this point. We come up with "contank" and "cantank." Then we get it: *cantankerous*.

In the real world, the types of problems we face are likelier to be solved by heuristics than by algorithms (Sorrentino & Roney, 2000; Hall, 2002). Heuristics help us narrow down the possible solutions to find the one that works (Snook, Canter, & Bennell, 2002; Stanovich & West, 2000; Todd & Gigerenzer, 2001).

Evaluate Solutions Once we think we have solved a problem, we really won't know how effective our solution is until we find out if it actually works. It helps to have in mind a clear criterion for the effectiveness of the solution.

For example, what will your criterion be for judging the effectiveness of your solution to the psychology assignment? Will you judge your solution effective if you simply

subgoaling Involves setting intermediate goals or defining intermediate problems that put you in a better position to reach the final goal or solution.

algorithms Strategies that guarantee a solution to a problem.

heuristics Strategies or guidelines that suggest, but do not guarantee, a solution to a problem.

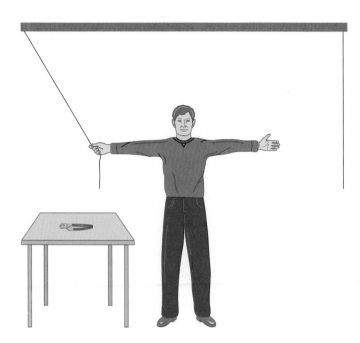

FIGURE 9.4 **Maier String Problem**
How can you tie the two strings together if you cannot reach them both at the same time?

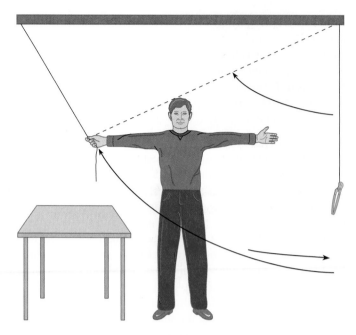

FIGURE 9.5 **Solution to the Maier String Problem**
Use the pliers as a weight to create a pendulum motion that brings the second string closer.

get it completed? If you receive positive feedback on the paper? If you get an A? If the instructor says that it is one of the best papers ever turned in on the topic?

Rethink and Redefine Problems and Solutions Over Time An important final step in problem solving is to continually rethink and redefine problems (Bereiter, 2002). People who are good at problem solving tend to be more motivated than the average person to improve on their past performances and to make original contributions.

Thus, you can examine your psychology paper after your instructor returns it and use the feedback to think about ways to improve it. Although Apple Computer is widely regarded as the most innovative company in the personal computer business, it continues to seek ways to improve its product lines, from releasing new versions of its operating system and computer hardware, to pioneering new products like the iPod.

Obstacles to Solving Problems

Psychologists have not only sought to understand how problems can be solved; they have also studied the obstacles that often prevent people from solving problems effectively. The obstacles include becoming fixated, not being adequately motivated, and not controlling emotions.

Becoming Fixated It is easy to fall into the trap of becoming fixated on a particular strategy for solving a problem. **Fixation** involves automatically using a prior strategy without looking at a problem from a fresh, new perspective. Psychologists have identified several kinds of fixation.

One type is **functional fixedness**, in which individuals fail to solve a problem because they are fixated on a thing's usual functions (German & Barrett, 2005). If you have ever used a shoe to hammer a nail, you have overcome functional fixedness to solve a problem.

A classic example of a problem that requires overcoming functional fixedness is the Maier String Problem, which is depicted in figure 9.4 (Maier, 1931). The problem is to figure out how to tie two strings together when you must stand in one spot and cannot reach both at the same time. It seems as though you are stuck, but there is a pair of pliers on a table. Can you solve the problem?

fixation Involves using a prior problem-solving strategy and failing to look at a problem from a new perspective.

functional fixedness A type of fixation in which individuals fail to solve a problem because they are fixated on a thing's usual functions.

The Candle Problem
How would you mount a candle on a wall so that it won't drip wax on a table or a floor while it is burning?

The Nine-Dot Problem
Take out a piece of paper and copy the arrangement of dots shown below. Without lifting your pencil, connect the dots using only four straight lines.

The Six-Matchstick Problem
Arrange six matchsticks of equal length to make four equilateral triangles, the sides of which are one matchstick long.

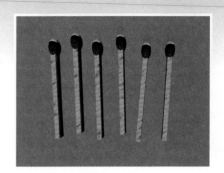

Solutions to the problems are presented at the end of the chapter on page 379.

The solution is to use the pliers as a weight, tying them to the end of one string (see figure 9.5). Swing this string back and forth like a pendulum and grasp the stationary string. Your past experience with pliers and fixation on their usual function makes this a difficult problem to solve. To solve the problem, you need to find an unusual use for the pliers, in this case as a weight to create a pendulum.

Effective problem solving may also be blocked by a **mental set**, a type of fixation in which an individual tries to solve a problem in a particular way that has worked in the past (Mai & others, 2004). Each of us occasionally gets in the mental rut of trying to solve problems with a well-worn strategy.

The authors of this text had to overcome mental sets about using CDs rather than MP3s for listening to our favourite music. It took time to break out of the mental set of collecting stacks of CDs. It also took time to become more familiar with computer-based tools for encoding CDs as well as playing the MP3s on iPods. Once we did so, the problem goal of having our music to listen to whenever we wanted became much easier. You might feel the same about some aspects of technology. A good strategy is to keep an open mind and monitor whether your mental set is keeping you from trying something new.

Figure 9.6 invites you to explore how fixation might be involved in your own problem-solving efforts.

Motivation and Emotion Individuals might have great problem-solving skills and know all the steps for solving problems, but it hardly matters what talents they have if they are not motivated to use them (Sternberg & Spear-Swerling, 1996). Martens & Witt (2004) have demonstrated that children become more effective problem solvers when their motivation levels have been increased by rewarding their success. It is especially important to be internally motivated to solve a problem and to persist with the effort at finding a solution. Some people give up too easily.

Emotion can also facilitate or inhibit problem solving. As well as being highly motivated, good problem solvers are often able to control their emotions and concentrate on a solution to a problem (Barron & Harackiewicz, 2001). Individuals who are competent at solving problems are also usually not afraid of making mistakes (Bless & Igou, 2005; Slavin, 2006).

Expertise

Researchers are very interested in how experts and novices differ in the way they think and solve problems (Ericsson, 2005). Researchers have studied experts and novices in such diverse areas as chess, physics, mathematics, electronics, squash, and history (Abernethy & others, 2001; Wenke, Frensch, & Funke, 2005). They have found that experts have acquired extensive knowledge that affects what they pay attention

FIGURE 9.6
Examples of How Fixation Impedes Problem Solving

mental set A type of fixation in which an individual tries to solve a problem in a particular way that has worked in the past.

Stephen J. Hawking is a world-renowned expert in physics. Hawking authored the best-selling books *A Brief History of Time* and *The Universe in a Nutshell*. Hawking has a neurological disorder that prevents him from walking or talking. He communicates with the aid of a voice-equipped computer. *What might be some differences in the ways Hawking solves physics problems and the ways novices solve them?*

to and how they organize, represent, and interpret information. The way they encode and store information, in turn, influences their ability to remember, reason, and solve problems.

Experts solve problems differently from the way novices do because they are better than novices in four specific ways:

- *Knowledge base*. Experts have broad and highly organized knowledge about their fields, which often allows them to solve a problem from memory without going through a tedious problem-solving effort (Kellogg & others, 2005). In the expert's mind, knowledge is organized hierarchically. Specific details are grouped into chunks, which in turn are grouped into more general topics, which in turn come under the heading of more general topics, and so on as described in chapter 8. Figure 9.7a shows the hierarchical arrangement one physicist used to organize the knowledge that was needed to solve a physics problem. The dotted lines connecting the smaller branches of the "concept tree" are *pointers*, associations made by experience that possibly produce shortcuts in solving the problem. An example of how a novice might try to solve the same problem is shown in Figure 9.7b. Notice the absence of pointers and the smaller number of levels and interconnections. Experts usually have far more interconnections in their storehouse of knowledge, and these interconnections are organized in ways that reflect a deep understanding of their subject matter.
- *Domain memory*. Experts are usually better than novices at remembering information in their domain of expertise (Chase & Simon, 1973). It is not that their general memory skills are better; it is just that they use their vast storehouse of knowledge to organize and chunk information in ways that make it more memorable (Hambrick & Oswald, 2005). Good memory for relevant information in a problem can often improve your ability to solve it.
- *Strategies*. Experts often have more effective strategies to solve a problem than novices (Ericsson, 2005). Experts are more likely to have effective strategies at their command before they start to solve the problem and are more flexible in reorganizing or modifying them as the problem solving progresses.
- *Deliberate practice*. Becoming an expert in a particular field is not accomplished overnight. It usually takes years of experience and a conscious effort to practise, whether the field is commodities trading, chemical engineering, law, gardening, or medicine (Norman, 2005). In deliberate practice, individuals expend extensive effort and time motivated by the goal of improving their skill.

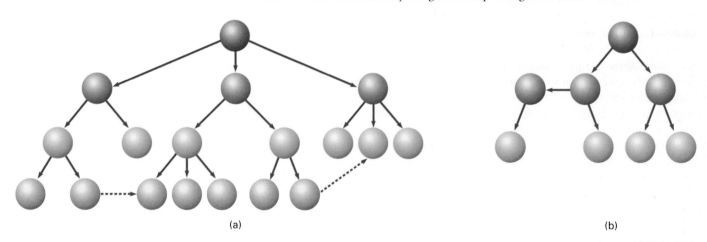

(a)   (b)

FIGURE 9.7 An Example of How Information Is Organized in the Minds of an Expert and a Novice
(*a*) An expert's knowledge is based on years of experience in which small bits of information have been linked with many others, which together are placed in a general category. This category is in turn placed in a more general category of knowledge. The dotted lines, *pointers*, show associations between specific elements of knowledge that connect the lower branches and provide mental shortcuts in the expert's mind. (*b*) A novice's knowledge shows far fewer connections, levels, and shortcuts than an expert's knowledge.

We can all appreciate and admire expertise but need to remember that the ability to solve specific kinds of problems effectively is often limited to a particular field. For example, being an expert at chess does not make you an expert at gardening or chemical engineering. Being an expert at playing sports or music or acting does not make you an expert at policy making or running a business—just as being an expert politician or entrepreneur does not make you an expert athlete or entertainer.

> ## > reflect and review

3 **Describe the requirements for solving problems.**

- Define problem solving and identify four steps in solving problems.
- Describe some obstacles to solving problems.
- Discuss the role of expertise in solving problems.

Think of a problem that you have not been able to solve or would like to solve. How might following the steps in problem solving and avoiding obstacles in problem solving help you solve this problem? Explain.

4 CRITICAL THINKING, REASONING, AND DECISION MAKING

— **Critical** — **Reasoning** — **Decision**
Thinking   **Making**

What are the main factors in thinking critically, reasoning, and making decisions?
In addition to forming concepts and solving problems, thinking includes three types of higher-order mental processing: critical thinking, reasoning, and decision making. All involve the prefrontal cortex (Duncan, 2005) and the ability to apply judgment. The end result of this type of thinking is an evaluation, conclusion, or decision.

Critical Thinking

In chapter 1, we defined *critical thinking* as thinking reflectively and productively and evaluating the evidence. People who think critically grasp the deeper meaning of ideas, keep an open mind about different approaches and perspectives, and decide for themselves what to believe or do (Halpern, 2002; Kamin & others, 2001).

Critical thinking is currently of considerable interest to both psychologists and educators (Howe, 2004). However, critical thinking is not an entirely new idea. Educator John Dewey (1933) was working with a similar idea when he advocated teaching students to "think reflectively." Today, educators at all levels embrace the idea that an important outcome of education is to develop students' ability to think critically.

"For God's sake, think! Why is he being so nice to you?"

© 1998 Sam Gross from cartoonbank.com. All Rights Reserved.

Yet not enough schools teach students to think critically and to develop a deep understanding of concepts (Brooks & Brooks, 2001; but see Burbach, Matkin, & Fritz, 2004; Weigel, 2001). For example, many high school students read *Hamlet* but are not asked to think about how its notions of power, greed, and conflicting relationships apply to their lives or the wider world. They are rarely stimulated to rethink their prior ideas about these matters. Instead, schools spend too much time on getting students to give a single correct answer in an imitative way rather than encouraging students to come up with new ideas. Too often teachers ask students to recite, define, describe,

The centre panel of this collage of photos shows a student-generated view in CSILE/Knowledge Forum. Surrounding pictures suggest the integrated classroom activities (experiments, writing, reading, and conversations) that support and are enhanced by work in Knowledge Forum.

state, and list rather than to analyze, infer, connect, synthesize, criticize, create, evaluate, think, and rethink. Too often we are inclined to stay on the surface of problems rather than to stretch our minds.

Marlene Scardamalia and Carl Bereiter, of the Ontario Institute for Studies in Education, have developed an influential Canadian effort to foster critical thinking in schools (Bereiter, 2002; Bereiter & Scardamalia, 1996, 2000; Scardamalia & Bereiter, 1999, 2003). Knowledge Forum, previously known as CSILE (Computer Supported Intentional Learning Environments), is a knowledge-building environment used worldwide by students from grade 1 to graduate level, in a wide range of educational contexts. A coordinated system of face-to-face and online work encourages collective responsibility for knowledge advances, engagement in higher levels of critical thinking and reflection, theory improvement, and reflective writing and text composition (Bryson & Scardamalia, 1996; Oshima, Scardamalia, & Bereiter, 1999). For example, a web-based version (Web Knowledge Forum) was recently used to support the online collaboration of teachers as they learned to educate students with special learning needs (Winter & McGhie-Richmond, 2005).

Mindfulness Mindfulness is a characteristic of critical thinkers, according to Ellen Langer, of Harvard University (1989, 1997, 2000; Grant & others, 2004). She studies mindless behaviour and encourages people to be more mindful. One of her favourite examples of mindless behaviour involves the time she used a new credit card in a department store. The clerk noticed that she had not signed the card and handed it to her to sign on the back. After passing the credit card through the machine, the clerk handed her a receipt to sign. Then the clerk held up the receipt Langer had signed and compared the signatures.

Langer's concept of mindfulness is similar to the description of critical thinking. She says that a mindful person continues to create new ideas, is open to new information, and is aware of more than one perspective. In contrast, a mindless person is trapped in old ideas, engages in automatic behaviour, and operates from a single perspective. Langer believes that asking good questions is an important ingredient of mindful thinking. If mindfulness is important to critical thinking and cognition in general, where does intuition fit in? To think about the role of intuition in cognition, see the Critical Reflections box.

Is *Mindful* the Opposite of *Intuitive*?

Thinking seems like it should take time. When we are engaged in the cognitive processes of problem solving, critical thinking, reasoning, or decision making we should be thoughtfully reflective and, well, mindful, shouldn't we? In this sense of the words, *thoughtful* and *mindful* seem to be the opposite of *intuitive*, which refers to a spontaneous and unreflective process. In fact, as we saw in Chapter 4, Piaget described the thought of preoperational children as intuitive, by which he meant lacking in any deliberate logic and instead relying on personal insights or guessing.

In his recent book, *Blink*, Malcolm Gladwell (2005) argues that just the opposite is often true. He calls it "thin-slicing," the human ability to make sense out of situations based on the tiniest bits of experience. In Gladwell's view, our immediate, intuitive reactions to situations can be as good as, and even better than, our deliberate thoughtfulness. He offers many examples, including some drawn from the work of Harvard social psychologist Nalini Ambady (Ambady & Rosenthal, 1992, 1993; Ambady, LaPlante, & Johnson, 2001).

In what is perhaps her most infamous study (Ambady & Rosenthal, 1993), Ambady presented three ten-second video clips of university instructors to research participants who had never met these instructors. The participants were asked to rate both the nonverbal behaviours and physical attractiveness of the instructors. Amazingly, the participant's ratings were highly correlated with the end-of-year course evaluations of those instructors, as supplied by their actual students. Even more amazingly, when Ambady further "thinned out" the slices by cutting each video clip to a mere two seconds and repeated her study, she obtained a similar result. Apparently, a six-second glimpse of an instructor teaching is all that is needed to form a highly accurate intuitive judgment of that instructor's teaching performance.

As you can imagine, Ambady's finding has been controversial. Despite finding no evidence that differences in physical attractiveness were responsible for her results, other researchers have proposed that differences in physical attractiveness may actually bias students' end-of-year course evaluations (Hamermesh & Parker, 2005). In other words, according to Hamermesh & Parker, in this situation thin-slicing teaching may not produce accurate snap judgments of teaching quality as much as it results in judgments of physical attractiveness which, in turn, misleadingly determine students course evaluations.

In Chapter 6 we saw that consciousness is associated with the frontal cortex and with *controlled processing* (Striedter, 2005). We also encountered the notion of *automatic processing*, which occurs, unconsciously. Perhaps much of our thinking is automatic rather than controlled. According to T. D. Wilson (2002), Ambady's results are just one example of the power of what he calls the *cognitive unconscious*. From Wilson's point of view, the phenomenon of thin-slicing reveals that automatic processing may be very fast as well as accurate.

A less controversial example of thin-slicing involves the Iowa Gambling Task (Bechara & others, 1997, 2005). In this task, participants must turn over cards from decks of red and blue cards. Some cards win "money" and some lose it and the participant's job is to begin to turn over cards and figure out what the rule is. As it turns out, the rule is simple: you do best if you always choose blue cards. According to Bechara & others (1997), after turning over about 50 cards, most participants are pretty sure the rule has to do with blue cards and by about 80 cards they can describe the exact rule. At the same time, the participants' skin conductance, a measure of physiological stress, was also measured. Remarkably, the skin conductance measure began to show a stress response when red cards were turned over after as few as 10 cards. In other words, participants were displaying evidence of unconscious automatic processing long before they experienced any controlled processing in the form of consciously expressed hunches.

To explain these results, Bechara & colleagues (1997, 2005), advanced the *somatic marker hypothesis*, that faster automatic unconscious emotional processing can assist slower conscious controlled processing. They also proposed that clinical patients with damage to the ventromedial prefrontal cortex fail to show this effect and also do more poorly on the Iowa Gambling Task. The intriguing possibility is that thin-slicing is partially carried out by parts of the brain engaged in more unconscious automatic processing. Further, thin-slicing may be an important part of our cognitive capacity. Rather than being the opposite of thoughfulness, intuition may be a vital component of effective cognition (T. D. Wilson, 2002).

What do you think?

- Can you think of examples of your own thin-slicing that were successful? Do you think of yourself as an intuitive person? Does Gladwell give us a way to think about intuition?
- Can you think of any rapid judgments you have made that turned out to be wrong? What went wrong?
- According to the somatic marker hypothesis, your emotional reaction is a component of your cognition. Do you trust your emotional reactions? If so, why? If not, why not?

Open-Mindedness Note that, in Langer's view, mindful people are aware of more than one perspective. Too often, we take one side of an issue without really evaluating the issue or examining it from different perspectives. However, critical thinking means being open to the possibility of other ways of looking at things (Peterson & Seligman, 2004).

People often don't know that there even is another side to an issue or evidence contrary to what they believe (Slife & Yanchar, 2000). Simple openness to other viewpoints can help to keep people from jumping to conclusions. As Socrates once said, such caution in thinking—that is, knowing what it is you don't know—is sometimes the first step to true wisdom.

Sharpening the Saw

Critical thinkers ask good questions (Santrock & Halonen, 2006). Some college and university students feel discouraged about asking questions, possibly because they acquired passive learning habits in elementary and secondary school. They may also fear being embarrassed by asking a question. However, critical thinkers get their curiosity out in the open, and developing an enthusiasm for asking questions can make college or university more interesting and enjoyable. Are you a critical thinker?

Sometimes you can spot people who have studied psychology just by the questions they ask about behaviour. Just as carpenters keep their tools well honed, psychological thinkers use questions as tools to help them make good judgments about behaviour. Have you begun to use the following questions as critical thinking tools?

- *What exactly do you mean by that?*

Once you have examined behaviour carefully, you recognize that it is important to precisely *describe* it. Starting with precise descriptions can help you interpret behaviour or make good predictions about behaviour. For example, a fuzzy description is "He is a nervous person." A more precise description might be "His anxious behaviour is characterized by feelings of helplessness, trembling, and sweating, which intensify when he takes tests."

- *Why does that happen?*

Thinking like a psychologist involves trying to *explain* behaviour. Showing curiosity about what motivates people to do what they do is a hallmark of people interested in psychology. For example, you might wonder why some people ask good questions and others don't.

- *What is the evidence to back up your claims?*

When an explanation about the causes of behaviour is at issue, personal testimony is not sufficient. When you think like a psychologist, you need to see the data that back up claims before you believe them. For example, if someone claims that the vast majority of Canadians believe in maintaining our current universal-access national public health care system as is, ask to see the evidence. For example, in 1998, a survey found that 79 percent of Canadians favoured a fundamental reworking of Canada's health system. Of course, you would likely also want to see if there is a more recent survey and if it yielded the same results.

- *Is there another way to explain the behaviour?*

When you don't have data to support an explanation, you may be able to generate other ideas. Coming up with alternative explanations for the cause of a behaviour is a skill that psychologists value highly. For example, you might originally hypothesize that the reason someone is behaving in a particular way is because he or she is a first-born child. However, further inquiry might suggest other possible explanations, such as current stressful circumstances and growing up in impoverished conditions.

- *Is that a label or an explanation of behaviour?*

If Trudy has problems sleeping through the night, her behaviour is labelled "insomnia." When asked why she has trouble sleeping, she says, "Because I have insomnia." However, insomnia is not an explanation; it is not the *cause* of her inability to sleep, it simply *describes the fact* that she is unable to sleep. In fact, the term insomnia comes from the Latin "in," meaning *not* and "somnus" meaning *sleep*. The *cause* of her insomnia might be drinking too much coffee at night, stress in her life, or sleeping too much during the day.

In chapter 1, we urged you to think critically about controversies in psychology. Psychology has advanced as a field because psychologists have thought deeply about controversial issues, conducted extensive research on them, examined the evidence, and kept open minds about interpreting the results. We hope the Critical Reflections boxes that appear in each chapter challenge you to think about issues in less biased, more flexible, more reflective ways. In doing so, you will become a better critical thinker. To evaluate the extent to which you use critical thinking strategies, see the Personal Reflections box.

Reasoning

Reasoning is the mental activity of transforming information to reach conclusions. It is a skill closely tied to critical thinking (Hunt, 2002; Markman & Gentner, 2001). Reasoning can be either inductive or deductive (see figure 9.8).

Inductive Reasoning **Inductive reasoning** involves reasoning from the specific to the general (Rips, 2002). That is, it involves drawing conclusions about all members of a category based on observing some members (Coley & others, 2005; Bisanz, Bisanz, & Korpan, 1994). For example, suppose that in a literature class you read some of Shakespeare's plays and try to describe his idea of romantic love. Here, your inductive reasoning is being tapped as you draw together your insights from specific plays to support a general conclusion. Applying concepts also challenges inductive reasoning, as when

reasoning The mental activity of transforming information to reach conclusions.

inductive reasoning Reasoning from the specific to the general.

students use knowledge about research methods to evaluate science news (Lohman, 2005; Zimmerman, Bisanz, & Bisanz, 1998).

Notice that an inductive conclusion is never entirely certain—that is, it may be inconclusive. And, although an inductive conclusion may be right, there is always a chance that it is wrong, perhaps because the sample does not perfectly represent its population (Johnson-Laird, 2000).

Inductive reasoning is basic to analogies (Chen, 2002). An *analogy* is a type of formal reasoning that involves four parts, with the relation between the first two parts being the same as the relation between the last two. For example, solve this analogy: Beethoven is to music as Picasso is to _____. To answer correctly ("art"), you had to induce the relation between Beethoven and music (the former created the latter) and apply this relationship to Picasso (what did he create?).

Analogies can be helpful in solving problems (Vishton, 2005), especially when they are presented in the form of stories (Blenkiron, 2005) or are visually represented (Mumford & Porter, 1999). Benjamin Franklin noticed that a pointed object drew a stronger spark than a blunt object when both were in the vicinity of an electrified body. Originally he believed this was an unimportant observation, but then he realized that a pointed rod could be used to attract lightning (analogous to the spark), thus deflecting it from buildings and ships.

Deductive Reasoning   In contrast to inductive reasoning, **deductive reasoning** is reasoning from the general to the specific (Newstead & others, 2004; Knauff & others, 2002). The fictional British detective Sherlock Holmes was a master at deductive reasoning. When solving a case, he sorted through a number of clues to zero in on the one correct solution to a crime.

When you solve puzzles or riddles, you are engaging in deductive reasoning. When you learn a general rule and then understand how it applies in some situations but not in others, you are engaging in deductive reasoning. When psychologists and other scientists use theories and intuitions to make predictions and then evaluate their predictions by making further observations, deductive reasoning is at work.

Deductive reasoning is always certain in the sense that if the initial rules or assumptions are true, then the conclusion will follow directly as a matter of logic. When psychologists develop a hypothesis from a theory, they are using a form of deductive reasoning, because the hypothesis is a specific, logical extension of the general theory. And if the theory is true, then the hypothesis will be true as well. As with other forms of higher cognition, induction and deduction are carried out in the frontal lobes (Goel & Dolan, 2004; Goel, 2005b).

Decision Making

Think of all the decisions you have to make in your life. Should I major in biology, psychology, or business? Should I go to graduate school right after university or get a job first? Should I establish myself in a career before settling down to have a family? Should I buy a house or rent? **Decision making** involves evaluating alternatives and making choices among them (Montgomery, Lipshitz, & Brehmer, 2005; Galotti, 2002).

In inductive reasoning, people use established rules to draw conclusions. In contrast, when we make decisions, such rules are not established, and we don't know the consequences of the decisions (Gigerenzer & Selton, 2001; Tversky & Fox, 1995). Some of the information might be missing, and we might not trust all the information we have (Matlin, 2004).

In one type of decision-making research, investigators study how people weigh the costs and benefits of various outcomes. They have found that people choose the outcome with the highest expected value (Hastie & Dawes, 2001). For example, in choosing a college or university, you might have listed the pluses and minuses of going to different colleges or universities (related to such factors as cost, quality of education, social

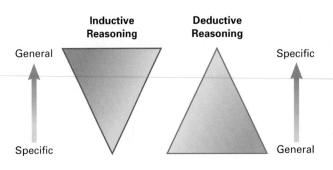

FIGURE 9.8

Inductive and Deductive Reasoning (*Left*) The upside-down pyramid represents inductive reasoning— going from specific to general. (*Right*) The right-side-up pyramid represents deductive reasoning—going from general to specific.

deductive reasoning Reasoning from the general to the specific.

decision making Involves evaluating alternatives and making choices among them.

"You take all the time you need, Larry—this certainly is a big decision."

© The New Yorker Collection 1990, Eric Teitelbaum, from cartoonbank.com.
All rights reserved.

life, and so on) and then made a decision based on how the colleges or universities rated on these criteria. In making your decision, you might have weighed some of these factors more heavily than others (e.g., giving cost three points, quality of education two points, and social life one point).

Another fruitful subject of decision-making research is the biases and flawed heuristics (rules of thumb) that affect the quality of decisions. In many cases, our decision-making strategies are well adapted to deal with a variety of problems (Betsch & Haberstroh, 2005). However, we are prone to make a number of mistakes in our thinking (Stanovich, 1999, 2004).

Confirmation Bias **Confirmation bias** is the tendency to search for and use information that supports our ideas rather than refutes them (Betsch & others, 2001; Fugelsang & others, 2004). Let's say that I have an initial hypothesis that something is going to work to solve a problem. I test the hypothesis and find that it is right some of the time. I conclude that my hypothesis was right, rather than exploring possible reasons it did not work all the time. Our decisions can also become further biased because we tend to seek out and listen to people whose views confirm our own and tend to avoid those who have dissenting views.

It is easy to detect the confirmation bias in the way that many people think. Consider politicians. They often accept news that supports their views and dismiss evidence that runs counter to their views. Consider also physicians who misdiagnose a patient because one or two symptoms fit with previous successful diagnoses they have made. In their desire to confirm their diagnosis, they ignore symptoms that do not fit their diagnosis.

In a classic study, Deanna Kuhn and her colleagues (Kuhn, Weinstock, & Flaton, 1994) had participants listen to an audiotaped reenactment of an actual murder trial. The participants were then asked what their verdict would be and why. Rather than considering and weighing the possibilities drawing on all the evidence, many participants hurriedly composed a story that drew only from evidence that supported their views of what happened. These participants showed a confirmation bias by ignoring evidence that ran counter to their version of events.

Belief Perseverance Closely related to confirmation bias, **belief perseverance** is the tendency to hold on to a belief in the face of contradictory evidence. People have a difficult time letting go of an idea or strategy once they have embraced it. Consider the Canadian comedian Jim Carrey (see figure 9.9). We have a hard time thinking of him in a dramatic role because of the belief perseverance that he is a wild and over-the-top comic actor.

Another example of belief perseverance gives some students trouble in the first year of college or university. They may have gotten good grades in high school by using the strategy of cramming for tests the night before. The ones who don't adopt a new strategy—spacing their study sessions more evenly through the term—often do poorly in college or university.

Overconfidence Bias **Overconfidence bias** is the tendency to have more confidence in judgments and decisions than we should based on probability or past experience. People are overconfident about how long people with a fatal disease will live, which businesses will go bankrupt, which psychiatric inpatients have serious mental disorders, whether a defendant is guilty in a court trial, and which students will do well in graduate school (Kahneman & Tversky, 1995). People consistently have more faith in their judgments than predictions based on statistically objective measures indicate they should.

confirmation bias The tendency to search for and use information that supports, rather than refutes, our ideas.

belief perseverance The tendency to hold on to a belief in the face of contradictory evidence.

overconfidence bias The tendency to have more confidence in judgments and decisions than we should based on probability or past occurrence.

In one study, university students were asked to make predictions about themselves in the coming academic year (Vallone & others, 1990). They were asked to predict whether they would drop any courses, vote in an election, and break up with their girlfriend or boyfriend. Then they were asked to rate how confident they were in their predictions. At the end of the year, the accuracy of their predictions was examined. The results: They were more likely to drop a class, not vote in an election, and break up with a girlfriend or a boyfriend than they had predicted.

Overconfidence can have serious consequences for people's lives (Matlin, 2004). For instance, on April 17, 2002, four Canadian soldiers were killed in Afghanistan by "friendly fire" when an American pilot bombed them, mistaking their night live-fire exercise as enemy fire. A subsequent U.S. military inquiry blamed the pilot for being too quick to react. A similar event occurred in 1988 when the *USS Vincennes*, a warship in the Persian Gulf, detected an unknown aircraft and decided to launch two missiles in self-defence. Tragically, all 290 passengers on board the misidentified civilian aircraft were killed when it was shot down. A panel of decision-making experts concluded that the captain of the *Vincennes* had been overconfident about his original decision and had failed to verify critical factors in the situation (Bales, 1988).

Hindsight Bias People are not only overconfident about what they predict will happen in the future, but they also tend to be overconfident about circumstances that have already happened (Guilbault & others, 2004; Bonds-Raacke & others, 2001). **Hindsight bias** is our tendency to falsely report, after the fact, that we accurately predicted an event.

As we write this chapter, hockey season is just beginning. Lots of people in different cities are predicting that their teams are going to make it to the Stanley Cup. Come May, after almost all of the teams have fallen by the wayside, many of the same people will say, "I told you our team wasn't going to have a good season."

In one study of introductory psychology students, a professor had students make either preverdict predictions regarding the outcome of the O. J. Simpson trial or postverdict predictions about what they would have predicted the outcome to be (Demakis, 1997). Students who estimated their prediction of the trial postverdict were more accurate than students who predicted the outcome preverdict, illustrating the principle of hindsight bias.

Availability Heuristic Earlier in the chapter we described heuristics as rules of thumb that suggest a solution but do not ensure that it will work. One heuristic that can produce flawed thinking is the **availability heuristic**, a prediction about the probability of an event based on the frequency of the event's past occurrences. When an event has recently occurred, we especially tend to overestimate its future occurrence (McKelvie & Drumheller, 2001).

How likely do you think you are to be a victim of a crime, for instance? The fear of crime tends to go up when the media go through a phase of highlighting murder or covering a sensational murder story. Because of the excess of information about crime, we are likely to estimate that crime is more prevalent than it really is. The media contribute to this prediction error every time they expose us to a rash of vivid stories about tornadoes, murders, diseases, accidents, or terrorist attacks.

Representativeness Heuristic The **representativeness heuristic** suggests that we sometimes make faulty decisions based on how well something matches a prototype—that is, the most common or representative example—rather than its relevance to a particular situation. Consider the following description of an individual's dinner companion: skilled at carpentry, proficient at wrestling, owns a pet snake, knows how to repair motorcycles, and has a police record. What is the probability that this person is a male?

FIGURE 9.9

Belief Perseverance
Belief perseverance is a common bias that infiltrates our judgments. *How is belief perseverance involved in thinking it improbable that Jim Carrey could be a dramatic actor (Eternal Sunshine of the Spotless Mind) rather than a comic actor (Lemony Snicket's A Series of Unfortunate Events)?*

hindsight bias The tendency to falsely report, after the fact, that we accurately predicted an event.

availability heuristic A prediction about the probability of an event based on the frequency of the event's past occurrences.

representativeness heuristic Making faulty decisions based on how well something matches a prototype—the common or representative example—rather than on its relevance to the particular situation.

Most likely the description fits your prototype of a male more than a female, so you might estimate that there is a 9 in 10 chance that the dinner companion is a male.

In this example, your prototype served you well, because there are far more men than women in the population who fit the description. Sometimes, however, our prototypes do not take into account the frequency of events in the entire population. For example, would you say that the dinner companion is more likely to be a member of a motorcycle gang or a salesman? You would probably say there is a much greater chance that he is a member of a motorcycle gang, in which case you would be wrong. Why? Although only a small percentage of the millions of salesmen fit the description of this dinner companion, the total number is greater than the total number of motorcycle gang members who fit the description. Let's assume that there are 10,000 members of motorcycle gangs in the world versus 100 million salesmen. Even if 1 of every 100 motorcycle gang members (1 percent) fits our description, there would be only 100 of them. If just 1 of every 100,000 salesmen fits our description (.01 percent), their number would total 1000. So the probability is 10 times greater that the dinner companion is a salesman than a member of a motorcycle gang.

Our lives involve many such instances in which we judge probabilities based on representativeness and fail to consider the population from which a sample is drawn (Nickerson, 2004). If we are to make better decisions, we have to try to avoid this logical error, along with the others mentioned here.

> ## reflect and review

 Discuss the main factors in thinking critically, reasoning, and making decisions.

- Describe what critical thinking is and discuss its role in schools, along with mindfulness and open-mindedness.
- Define reasoning and explain the distinction between inductive and deductive reasoning.
- Summarize how people make decisions and the biases and flawed heuristics that can develop.

Do you ever rely on the availability heuristic or the representativeness heuristic? Give examples.

5 LANGUAGE AND THOUGHT

— The Structure — The Link — Animal
   of Language   Between   Language
                  Language
                  and Cognition

How are language and thought connected?

Language is a form of communication, whether spoken, written, or signed, that is based on a system of symbols. Think about how important language is in our everyday lives. We need language to speak with others, listen to others, read, and write (Jay, 2003). Our language enables us to describe past events in detail and to plan for the future. Without language, much of our thinking would be focused on the here and now. Language also lets us pass down information from one generation to the next and create a rich cultural heritage, which in turn affects not only the language we use but the way we think about the world. Before exploring the links between language and cognition more closely, let's examine the way language is structured.

language A form of communication, whether spoken, written, or signed, that is based on a system of symbols.

The Structure of Language

All human languages possess **infinite generativity**, the ability to produce an endless number of meaningful sentences, making language a highly creative enterprise. The beauty of language is that this superb flexibility comes from a relatively limited set of rules. In fact, all human languages are characterized by four main rule systems:

- **Phonology**: a language's sound system. Language is made up of basic sounds, or phonemes. Phonological rules ensure that certain sound sequences occur (for example, *sp*, *ba*, or *ar*) and others do not (for example, *zx* or *qp*; Mattys & Jusczyk, 2001). A good example of a phoneme in the English language is /k/, the sound represented by the letter *k* in the word *ski* and the letter *c* in the word *cat*. Although the /k/ sound is slightly different in these two words, the /k/ sound is described as a single phoneme in English. In some languages, though, such as Arabic, this kind of variation is represented by separate phonemes.

- **Morphology**: a language's rules for word formation. Every word in the English language is made up of one or more morphemes. A morpheme is the smallest unit of language that carries meaning. Some words consist of a single morpheme: for example, *help*. Others are made up of more than one: for example, *helper* has two morphemes, *help + er*. The morpheme *-er* means "one who," in this case "one who helps." As you can see, not all morphemes are words: some are suffixes and prefixes, for example, *pre-*, *-tion*, and *-ing*. Just as the rules that govern phonemes ensure that certain sound sequences occur, the rules that govern morphemes ensure that certain strings of sounds occur in particular sequences.

- **Syntax**: a language's rules for combining words to form acceptable phrases and sentences. If someone says to you, "Bob slugged Tom" or "Bob was slugged by Tom," you know who did the slugging and who was slugged in each case because you share that person's same syntactic understanding of sentence structure. You also understand that the sentence, "You didn't stay, did you?" is a grammatical sentence but that "You didn't stay, didn't you?" is unacceptable and ambiguous. Recall the opening story about individuals with Williams Syndrome. Their language is syntactically impeccable and grammatically complex.

- **Semantics**: the meaning of words and sentences in a particular language. Every word has a unique set of semantic features (Cicourel, 2005; Bloom, 2000; Field, 2004). *Girl* and *woman*, for example, share many of the same semantic features (for example, both signify female human beings), but they differ semantically in regard to age. Words have semantic restrictions on how they can be used in sentences. The sentence *The bicycle talked the boy into buying a candy bar* is syntactically correct but semantically incorrect. The sentence violates our semantic knowledge that bicycles do not talk. Recall from the chapter opening story that the semantic quality of the language of individuals with Williams Syndrome is rich but unusual.

Now that you have a basic understanding of what language is and how it is structured, you can examine some connections between language and cognition.

Frank & Ernest reprinted by permission of Newspaper Enterprize Association, Inc.

infinite generativity The ability to produce an infinite number of sentences using a finite set of words and rules.

phonology A language's sound system.

morphology A language's rules for word formation.

syntax A language's rules for the way words are combined to form acceptable phrases and sentences.

semantics The meaning of words and sentences in a particular language.

Whorf's view is that our cultural experiences with a particular concept shape a catalogue of names that can be either rich or poor. Consider how rich your mental library of names for camel might be if you had extensive experience with camels in a desert world and how poor your mental library of names for snow might be if you lived in a tropical world of palm trees and parrots. Despite its intriguing appeal, Whorf's view is controversial, and many psychologists do not believe it plays a pivotal role in shaping thought.

The Link Between Language and Cognition

Because language is virtually an unbounded symbol system, it is capable of expressing most thoughts. At the same time, language is the way we humans communicate most of our thoughts to each other. We do not always think in words, but our thinking would be greatly impoverished without words. This connection between language and thought has been a topic of considerable interest to psychologists. Some psychologists have argued that we cannot think without language, a proposition that has produced heated controversy (Field, 2004). Is thought dependent on language, or is language dependent on thought?

Language's Role in Cognition What role does language play in important cognitive activities? For one thing, memory is stored not only in the form of sounds and images but also in words. Language helps us think, make inferences, tackle difficult decisions, and solve problems (Amsel & Byrnes, 2001). Language can be thought of as a tool for representing ideas (Gentner & Lowenstein, 2001).

Today, most psychologists would accept these points. However, linguist Benjamin Whorf (1956) went a step further. He argued that language actually determines the way we think, a view often refered to as *linguistic relativity*. Whorf and his teacher Edward Sapir were specialists in Native American languages, and they were fascinated by the possibility that people might view the world differently as the result of the different languages they speak. For instance, Whorf famously claimed that the Inuit of the Arctic have a dozen or more words to describe the various textures, colours, and physical states of snow compared to English, which has relatively few words to describe snow. According to Whorf, this means that English speakers cannot as easily talk or even think about snow as the Inuit can . However, further analysis has revealed that Whorf was wrong in his assertions about the relative frequency of words for snow in Inuit and English (Martin, 1986).

Critics of Whorf's view say that words merely reflect, rather than cause, the way we think. The Inuits' adaptability and livelihood in the Arctic depends on their capacity to recognize various conditions of snow and ice. A skier or snowboarder who is not Inuit might also know numerous words for snow, far more than the average person; and a person who doesn't know the words for the different types of snow might still be able to perceive these differences.

A classic study by Eleanor Rosch (1973) found that a lack of words for a concept does not reflect a lack of ability to perceive and think about it. She studied the effect of language on colour perception among the Dani in New Guinea. The Dani have only two words for colour—one that approximately means "white" and one that approximately means "black." If the linguistic relativity hypothesis were correct, the Dani would lack the ability to tell the difference between colours such as green, blue, red, yellow, and purple. But Rosch found that the Dani perceived colours just as we perceive them. As we know, colour perception is biologically determined by receptors in the retinas in the eyes.

Even though Whorf's view appears to have missed the mark—language does not *determine* thought—researchers agree on the weaker view that language can *influence* thought (Slobin, 2003; Niraula, Mishra, & Dasen, 2004). Thus, our cultural experiences for a particular concept shape a catalogue of names that can be either rich or poor. An example of a name-rich concept in Canada is "automobile" (we use terms such as *coupe, convertible, minivan, station wagon*, and many others, not to mention various makes and models). The automobile part of your mental library of names is the product of many years of experience with automobiles. You will probably see and think about them in finer gradations than people who live in the rain forest in South America or on an isolated island in the Pacific Ocean. In this way, language acts as a window that helps to filter the amount and nature of information that is passed on for further processing.

Cognition's Role in Language Researchers are also studying the possibility that cognition is an important foundation for language (Gupta & Dell, 1999; Zwaan, Stanfield, & Yaxley, 2002). If language is a reflection of cognition in general, we would expect to find a close link between language ability and general intellectual ability. In particular, we would expect to find that problems in one domain (cognition) are paralleled by problems in the other domain (language). For example, we would anticipate that general mental retardation is accompanied by lowered language abilities.

Researchers have found that mental retardation is not always accompanied by poor language skills. Consider the discussion of Williams Syndrome earlier in the chapter. Individuals with Williams Syndrome have a general intelligence that places them in the category of mentally retarded. However, their language abilities, especially syntax and semantics, are well within the normal range, as is their ability to use language for communicative purposes. The nature of Williams Syndrome suggests a mind composed of separate, biologically prepared thinking and language abilities rather than a single, all-purpose cognitive ability that includes language (Flavell, Miller, & Miller, 2002; Bennardo, 2003; Pinker & Jackendoff, 2005).

Other evidence that cognition is separate from language comes from studies of deaf children. On a variety of thinking and problem-solving tasks, deaf children perform at the same level as children of the same age who have no hearing problems (Marschark, 2003a, b). Some of the deaf children in these studies do not even have command of written or sign language (Furth, 1971).

In sum, although it is likely thought can influence language, and language likely can influence thought, there is increasing evidence that language and thought are not part of a single, automated cognitive system. Instead, they seem to be functionally distinct. Some researchers even argue that cognition and language have evolved as separate, modular, biologically prepared components of the mind (Smith, 2003).

"Remember, don't talk sex, politics, or religion."

Reprinted courtesy of Omni Magazine © 1982.

Animal Language

The desire to figure out the link between language and thought has generated a great deal of research interest in animal communication (Fouts & Waters, 2001; Rilling & Seligman, 2002). Do animals communicate in the same way that humans do? What cognitive abilities are linked to their ability to communicate?

Many animal species do have complex and ingenious ways to signal danger and to communicate about basic needs such as food and sex. For example, in one species of firefly, the female evolved the ability to imitate the flashing signal of another species to lure them into her territory. Then she eats them. But is this language in the human sense? Most psychologists agree that it is not.

But what about the language abilities of animals with more brain power—specifically, our closest relatives, the great apes? Chimpanzees and *Homo sapiens* have 98 percent of their genetic material in common. Chimpanzee behaviour includes many things that human beings do, such as hunting, toolmaking, embracing, back patting, kissing, and holding hands.

Some researchers believe apes can learn human language. One classic celebrity in this field is a chimp named Washoe, who was adopted when she was about 10 months old (Gardner & Gardner, 1971). Because apes do not have the vocal apparatus to speak, the researchers taught Washoe American Sign Language, which is one of the sign languages of the deaf. Washoe used sign language during everyday activities, such as meals, play, and car rides. In two years, Washoe learned 38 different signs, and by the age of five she had a vocabulary of 160 signs. Washoe learned how to put signs together in novel ways, such as *You drink* and *You me tickle*. A number of other efforts to teach language to chimps have had similar results (Premack, 1986).

The debate about chimpanzees' ability to use language focuses on two key issues: Can apes understand the meaning of symbols—that is, can they comprehend that one thing stands for another? And can apes

In the wild, chimps communicate through calls, gestures, and expressions, which evolutionary psychologists believe might be the roots of true language.

FIGURE 9.10

Chimps and Symbols
Sue Savage-Rumbaugh and her colleagues at the Yerkes Primate Center and Georgia State University have studied the basic question of whether chimps understand symbols. Their research suggests that the answer is yes.

learn syntax—that is, can they learn the kinds of mechanics and rules that give human language its creative productivity? Sue Savage-Rumbaugh and her colleagues (1993) may have settled the first of these issues. These researchers found strong evidence that the chimps Sherman and Austin can understand symbols. For example, if either Sherman or Austin is sitting in a room, and a symbol for an object is displayed on a screen, he will go into another room, find the object, and bring it back. If the object is not there, he will come back empty-handed (Cowley, 1988). Austin and Sherman play a game in which one chimp points to a symbol for food (such as M&Ms), the other chimp selects the food from a tray, and then they both eat it. These observations are clear evidence that chimps can understand symbols (see figure 9.10).

Evidence concerning chimps' syntactic ability has come from study of rare pygmy chimpanzees (*Pan paniscus*), also known as bonobos (Benson, & others, 2002). These chimps are friendlier and brighter than their cousins, and show some remarkable language abilities. For example, star pupil Kanzi is very good at understanding spoken English and has been shown to comprehend over 600 sentences, such as *Can you make the bunny eat the sweet potato*? (Savage-Rumbaugh, Shanker, & Taylor, 1998). Kanzi also produces fairly complex sentences using a response board hooked to a speech synthesizer.

The debate over whether animals can use language to express thoughts is far from resolved. Researchers agree that animals can communicate with each other and that some can manipulate language-like symbols with syntax that resembles that of young children. At the same time, research has not yet proved that any animals can use language to express as many ideas as adult humans can or can use language as complexly as adult humans do. According to York University's Stuart Shanker and his colleagues, however, it may be more fruitful to focus on what language capacities animals like Kanzi do have (Shanker, Savage-Rumbaugh, & Taylor, 1999; Shanker & Taylor, 2005).

> reflect and review

5   **Identify the possible connections between language and thought.**

- Define language and describe the structure of language.
- Summarize the possible links between language and thought.
- Discuss whether animals have language.

When a pet, such as your dog or cat, barks or meows, is that language in the human sense? Explain.

---

6   LANGUAGE ACQUISITION AND DEVELOPMENT

Biological Influences — Environmental Influences — Early Development of Language — Language and Education

How is language acquired and how does it develop?

In 1970, a California social worker made a routine visit to the home of a partially blind woman who had applied for public assistance. The social worker discovered that the woman and her husband had kept their 13-year-old daughter, Genie, locked away from the world. Kept in almost total isolation during her childhood, Genie could not speak or stand erect. She was forced to sit naked all day on a child's potty seat, restrained by a harness her father had made—she could move only her hands and feet. At night she was placed in a kind of straitjacket and caged in a crib with wire mesh sides and a cover. Whenever Genie made a noise, her father beat her. He never communicated with her in words but growled and barked at her.

Genie spent a number of years in extensive rehabilitation programs, such as speech and physical therapy (Curtiss, 1977; Rymer, 1993). She eventually learned to walk upright with a jerky motion and to use the toilet. Genie also learned to recognize many words and to speak in rudimentary sentences. At first she spoke in one-word utterances. Later she was able to string together two-word combinations such as "big teeth," "little marble," and "two hand." Consistent with the language development of most children, three-word combinations followed—for example, "small two cup." Unlike normal children, however, Genie did not learn how to ask questions, and she does not understand grammar. Genie is not able to distinguish between pronouns or between passive and active verbs. Four years after she began stringing words together, her speech still sounded like a garbled telegram. And as an adult she speaks in short, mangled sentences, such as "Father hit leg," "Big wood," and "Genie hurt." Her unfortunate story is consistent with the idea that people have to learn language rules during childhood or miss the chance to become fully proficient.

The case of Genie raises questions about how people acquire language. Is the ability to generate rules for language and then use them to create an infinite number of words the product of biological factors and evolution? Or is language learned and influenced by the environment? Precisely when and how does language ability develop? As you will see, the answers to these questions are complex and are still a focus of research inquiry (Tomasello, 2003; Gleason, 2005).

GENIE

What were Genie's experiences like? What implications do they have for language acquisition?

Biological Influences

Estimates vary, but scientists believe that humans acquired language about 100,000 years ago. In evolutionary time, then, language is a very recent human ability. However, a number of experts believe biological evolution that took place long before language emerged undeniably shaped humans into linguistic creatures (Chomsky, 1975; MacWhinney, 2005). The brain, nervous system, and vocal apparatus of our predecessors changed over hundreds of thousands of years. Physically equipped to do so, *Homo sapiens* went beyond grunting and shrieking to develop abstract speech. This sophisticated language ability gave humans an enormous edge over other animals and increased their chances of survival (Lieberman, 2002; Pinker & Jackendoff, 2005).

MIT linguist Noam Chomsky was one of the early architects of the view that children's language development cannot be explained by environmental input. In Chomsky's view, language has strong biological underpinnings, with children biologically prewired to learn language at a certain time and in a certain way.

Language Universals   The famous linguist Noam Chomsky is one of those who argues that humans are biologically prewired to learn language at a certain time and in a certain way (Chomsky, 1975). According to Chomsky and many other language experts, the strongest evidence for language's biological basis is the fact that children all over the world reach language milestones at about the same time developmentally and in about the same order, despite vast variations in the language input they receive from their environments. For example, in some cultures adults never talk to infants under one year of age, yet these infants still acquire language. Also, according to this line of reasoning, there is no convincing way other than biological factors to explain how quickly children learn language (Toppelberg & Collins, 2004; Maratsos, 1999).

In Chomsky's view, children cannot possibly learn the full rules and structure of languages only by imitating what they hear. Rather, he argues, nature must provide children with a biological prewired universal grammar, allowing them to understand the basic rules of all languages and to apply these rules to the speech they hear. They learn language without being aware of the underlying logic involved.

Language and the Brain   There is strong evidence to back up those who believe language has a biological foundation. Neuroscience research has shown that the brain contains particular regions that are predisposed to be used for language (Grodzinsky, 2001; Gernsbacher & Robertson, 2005). As discussed in chapter 3, accumulating evidence further suggests that language processing occurs mainly in the brain's left hemisphere (Wood & others, 2004). Also recall from chapter 3 the importance of these two areas of the brain in language: *Broca's area*, which contributes to speech production, and *Wernicke's area*, which is involved in language comprehension. Neuroscience research has also shown that the left hemisphere comprehends syntax and grammar, which the right hemisphere does not.

Using brain imaging techniques, such as PET scans, researchers have found that when an infant is about nine months old, the part of the brain that stores and indexes many kinds of memory becomes fully functional (Bloom, Nelson, & Lazerson, 2001). This is also the time at which infants appear to be able to attach meaning to words, suggesting a link between language, cognition, and the early development of the brain.

Environmental Influences

Contradicting those who believe that language is biologically determined, behaviourists have advocated the view that language is primarily determined by environmental influences. For example, the famous behaviourist B. F. Skinner (1957) said that language is just another behaviour, like sitting, walking, or running. He argued that all behaviours, including language, are learned through reinforcement. Albert Bandura (1977) later emphasized that language is learned through imitation.

However, virtually all language experts today agree that reinforcement and imitation alone cannot explain children's language development. Many children's sentences are novel in the sense that the children have not previously heard them. A child might hear the sentence, "The plate fell on the floor," but then be able to say, "My mirror fell on the blanket." Simple reinforcement and/or imitation (modelling of words and syntax) cannot explain this utterance.

Roger Brown (1973) spent long hours observing parents and their young children, searching for evidence that children learn the rules of language through their parents' reinforcement (smiles, hugs, pats on the back, corrective feedback). He found that parents sometimes smiled and praised their children for sentences they liked but that they reinforced ungrammatical sentences as well. Brown concluded that no evidence exists that reinforcement alone is responsible for the development of children's language rule systems.

Although reinforcement and imitation alone are likely not responsible for children's development of language rule systems, it is nevertheless important that children interact with language-skilled people (Tomasello, 2003; Hoff & Tian, 2005). Genie was not around such people when she was a young child, and that likely played a role in harming her language development.

In one study of more typical language learning, researchers observed the language environments of children from two different backgrounds: middle-income professional families and families who received welfare (Hart & Risley, 1995). Then they examined the children's language development. All the children developed normally in terms of learning to talk and acquiring all of the basic rules of English and a basic vocabulary. However, the researchers found enormous differences in the sheer amount of language the children were exposed to and the level of the children's language development. For example, in a typical hour, the middle-income professional parents spent almost twice as much time communicating with their children as the parents receiving welfare did. The children from the middle-income professional families heard about 2100 words an hour, whereas their child counterparts in families receiving welfare only 600 words an hour. The researchers estimated that by four years of age, the average child from a family receiving welfare would have 13 million fewer words of cumulative language experience than the child in the average middle-income professional family. Amazingly, some of the three-year-old children from middle-class professional families had a recorded vocabulary that exceeded the recorded vocabulary of some of the parents on welfare.

Michael Tomasello has proposed that that infants use their abilities of intention-reading and pattern-finding to learn language from language-skilled people. *Intention-reading* refers to infants' abilities to understand the intentions of the adults around them and *pattern-finding* refers to infants' abilities to construct complex categories. According to Tomasello (2003), infants use these sophisticated sources of information to sort out the details of the spoken language that they hear every day, resulting in rapid language learning.

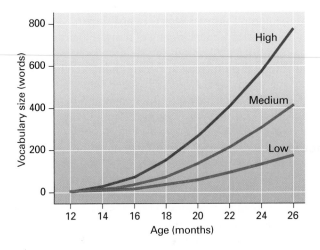

FIGURE 9.11 **Level of Maternal Speech and Infant Vocabulary**

It is unquestionably good for parents to begin talking to their babies right at the start. The best language teaching occurs when talking is begun before the infant becomes capable of its first intelligible speech.

Janellen Huttenlocher, of the University of Chicago, has also studied the language experience of infants (Huttenlocher & others, 1991; Huttenlocher & others, 2002). In one study, she carefully assessed the level of maternal speech to infants (Huttenlocher & others, 1991). As indicated in figure 9.11, mothers who regularly used a higher level of language when interacting with their infants had infants with markedly higher vocabularies. By the second birthday, vocabulary differences were substantial.

What are some good strategies for parents in talking to their babies? They include (Baron, 1992)

- Be an active conversational partner. Initiate conversation with the infant. If the infant is in a day-long child-care program, ensure that he or she gets adequate language stimulation from adults.
- Talk as if the infant understands what you are saying. Adults can generate positive self-fulfilling prophecies by addressing their young children as if they understand what is being said. The process may take four to five years, but children gradually rise to match the language model presented them.
- Use a language style with which you feel comfortable. Don't worry about how you sound to other adults when you talk with an infant. The mood and feeling you convey, not the content, is more important when talking with an infant. Use whatever type of baby talk you feel comfortable with in the first years of the child's life.

Research findings about environmental influences on language learning complicate the understanding of its foundations. In the real world of language learning, children appear to be neither exclusively biologically programmed linguists nor exclusively socially driven language experts (Kovas & others, 2005). As with all areas of psychology we have studied, we have to look at how biology and environment interact when children learn language. That is, children are biologically prepared to learn language but benefit enormously from being bathed in a competent language environment from an early age (Bochner & Jones, 2003).

Early Development of Language

One of the most interesting things about the development of language is that the child's linguistic interactions with parents and others obey certain rules (MacWhinney, 1999). Although children are learning vocabulary and concepts from an early age, they are also learning how their language is stitched together. In a classic study of this aspect of language learning, Jean Berko (1958) presented preschool and grade 1 children with cards like the one shown in figure 9.12. The children were asked to look at the card while the experimenter read the words on it aloud. Then the children were asked to

FIGURE 9.12
Stimuli in Berko's Classic Study of Children's Understanding of Morphological Rules
In Jean Berko's study, young children were presented cards such as this one with a "wug" on it. Then the children were asked to supply the missing word and say it correctly.

supply the missing word. *Wugs* is the correct response for the card shown. Coming up with wugs might seem easy, but it requires an understanding of morphological rules (in this case, the proper word ending for plurals). Although the children's responses were not always completely accurate, they were much better than chance. What makes Berko's study so impressive is that the words were fictional, created solely for the purpose of the study. Thus, the children could not have based their answers on remembering past instances of hearing the words. Instead, they were forced to rely on rules.

The "Critical Period" Some language researchers have focused on the question of whether language must be learned by a certain time in development. A *critical period* is a span of time when the individual is ready to learn; beyond this period learning is difficult or impossible. This is basically a biological view of language acquisition, which is controversial.

In the 1960s, Eric Lenneberg (1967) proposed that there is a critical period between about 18 months of age and puberty during which a first language must be acquired. Lenneberg provided support for his critical period concept from studies of children and adults with damage in the left hemisphere of the brain, deaf children, children with mental retardation, and other people who had not been able to learn language in the typical way (Tager-Flusberg, 1999; Grimshaw & others, 1998). Lenneberg found that the children he studied were able to recover their language skills, but the adults were not. Lenneberg believed that the difference was that the children's brains had plasticity. Once the brain structures matured and became more rigid, the brain could reassign language skills to undamaged areas. However, because the adults had already passed the critical period, they did not have the neurological capability to relearn language skills.

Lenneberg's (1967) conclusions are almost certainly too strong since many adults do, in fact, learn a second language. For example, Israeli psychologists Salim Abu-Rabia and Simona Kehat (2004) have presented evidence that normal adults can become fluent in a second language (Hebrew). In general, while adults tend to be less able than children to learn a second language, recent data have been interpreted as showing that the decline in second language learning ability is gradual rather than showing an abrupt shift at a critical age (Hakuta, Bialystok, & Wiley, 2003; Wiley, Bialystok, & Hakuta, 2005).

Language Milestones Most people do develop a clear understanding of their language's structure during childhood, as well as a large vocabulary. Most adults in North America have acquired a vocabulary of nearly 50,000 words. Researchers have taken a great interest in the process by which these aspects of language develop. Through many studies, we now have an understanding of the important milestones of language development (see figure 9.13).

Before babies ever say their first words, they babble. Babbling—endlessly repeating sounds and syllables such as *bababa* or *dadada*—begins at the age of three to six months and is determined by biological readiness, not by the amount of reinforcement or the ability to hear (Locke, 1993). Even deaf babies babble for a time (Lenneberg, Rebelsky, & Nichols, 1965). Babbling probably allows the baby to exercise its vocal cords and helps develop the ability to articulate different sounds.

Patricia Kuhl's research (Kuhl, 2004; Rivera-Gaxiola, Silva-Pereyra, & Kuhl, 2005) reveals that long before they actually begin to learn words, infants can sort through a number of spoken sounds in search of the ones that have meaning. Kuhl argues that from birth to about six months of age, children are "universal linguists" who are capable of distinguishing each of the sounds that make up human speech. But, by about six months of age, they have started to specialize in the speech sounds of their native language. In addition, Kuhl has shown that six-month olds who are better at speech discrimination remain advanced in their language development at the age of two (Tsao, Liu, & Kuhl, 2004).

An important language task for infants is to fish out individual words from the non-stop stream of sound that makes up ordinary speech (Field, 2004). But, to do so, they

FIGURE 9.13
Language Milestones

Age	Milestone
0–6 Months	Cooing Discrimination of vowels Babbling present by 6 months
6–12 Months	Babbling expands to include sounds of spoken language Gestures used to communicate about objects First words spoken 10–13 months
12–18 Months	Understands 50+ words on average
18–24 Months	Vocabulary increases to an average of 200 words Two-word combinations
2 Years	Vocabulary rapidly increases Correct use of plurals Use of past tense Use of some prepositions
3–4 Years	Mean length of utterances increases to 3–4 morphemes in a sentence Use of "yes" and "no" questions, wh- questions Use of negatives and imperatives Increased awareness of pragmatics
5–6 Years	Vocabulary reaches an average of about 10,000 words Coordination of simple sentences
6–8 Years	Vocabulary continues to increases rapidly More skilled use of syntactical rules Conversational skills improve
9–11 Years	Word definitions include synonyms Conversational strategies continue to improve
11–14 Years	Vocabulary increases with addition of more abstract words Understanding of complex grammar forms Increased understanding of function a word plays in a sentence Understands metaphor and satire
15–20 Years	Understands adult literary works

Note: This list is meant not to be exhaustive but rather to highlight some of the main language milestones. Also keep in mind that there is a great deal of variation in the ages at which children can reach these milestones and still be considered within the normal range of language development.

have to find the boundaries between words, which is very difficult for infants because adults don't pause between words when they speak. Still, researchers have found that infants begin to detect word boundaries by eight months of age. For example, in one study, eight-month-old infants listened at home to recorded stories that contained unusual words, such as *hornbill* and *python* (Jusczyk & Hohne, 1997). Two weeks later, the researchers tested the infants with two lists of words, one made up of words they had already heard in the stories and the other of new, unusual words that had not appeared in the stories. The infants listened to the familiar words for a second longer, on average, than to new words.

An English-speaking child's first words, uttered at the age of 10 to 13 months, tend to be nouns, naming important people (*dada*), familiar animals (*kitty*), vehicles (*car*), toys (*ball*), food (*milk*), body parts (*eye*), clothes (*hat*), household items (*clock*), and also include greetings (*bye*). (Clark, 1983). According to Tardif, Gelman, & Xu (1999). Mandarin-speaking children utter relatively more verbs.

By the time children reach the age of 18 to 24 months, they usually utter two-word statements. They quickly grasp the importance of expressing concepts and the role that language plays in communicating with others. To convey meaning in two-word statements,

Around the world, young children learn to speak in two-word utterances at 18 to 24 months of age. *What implications does this have for the biological basis of language?*

the child relies heavily on gesture, tone, and context (Behrens & Gut, 2005). Still, children can communicate a wealth of meaning with two words: for instance,

Identification: See doggie.	*Attribution*: Big car.
Location: Book there.	*Agent-action*: Mama walk.
Repetition: More milk.	*Action-direct-object*: Hit you.
Nonexistence: Allgone thing.	*Action-indirect-object*: Give papa.
Negation: Not wolf.	*Action-instrument*: Cut knife.
Possession: My candy.	*Question*: Where ball? (Slobin, 1972)

These examples are from children whose first languages were English, German, Russian, Finnish, Turkish, and Samoan. Although these two-word sentences omit many parts of speech, they are remarkably succinct in conveying many messages. When we send a telegram, we try to be short and precise, excluding any unnecessary words. As a result, we usually omit articles, auxiliary verbs, and other connectives. In every language, a child's first combination of words has this economical quality. *Telegraphic speech*—the use of short and precise words to communicate—characterizes young children's two- and three-word combinations.

Of course, telegraphic speech is not limited to two-word phrases. "Mommy give ice cream" or "Mommy give Tommy ice cream" are also examples of telegraphic speech. As children leave the two-word stage, they move rather quickly into three-, four-, and five-word combinations (Huttenlocher & others, 2002).

Language and Education

The early development of language skills through informal interaction with parents and other people in the family's social circle is an essential part of language acquisition. However, formal education in schools is also important. There, children learn more sophisticated rules of language structure, increase their vocabularies, and apply language skills to learn about a wide variety of concepts. In fact, one of the main purposes of schooling is to increase language skills. The ways that schools go about this is controversial, however. One of the controversies is whether and how to approach second language education in Canada, a country with two official languages, French and English. Another controversy is how children best learn to read.

Bilingualism Because Canada was founded by two peoples, the English and the French, and because we have always opened our borders to peoples from other countries, many Canadians are bilingual. Partly as a consequence of the official Canadian government policy favouring bilingualism, by 2001 5.2 million Canadians were able to carry out a conversation in both English and French (Statistics Canada, 2004b). At the same time, many other Canadians are conversant in *either* English *or* French and another language. So no matter which way you look at it, Canada is a more or less bilingual country.

Many Canadians worry that we sacrifice the education of our children to the demands of official bilingualism, spending so much effort teaching a second language and consequently hurting children's learning of their first language and their learning of other subjects. As a consequence, considerable research effort has been focused on bilingual education, with the general conclusion that bilingualism seems to be beneficial to students (Hinkel, 2005; Lessow-Hurley, 2005; Peregoy & Boyle, 2005). For example, the research has been interpreted as consistently revealing that bilingualism does not interfere with performance in either language (Hakuta, 1999; Hakuta & Garcia, 1989). Children's use of their native language need not be restricted because it might interfere with learning a second language.

Further, a groundbreaking Canadian research program, initiated by Wallace Lambert of McGill University, found that bilingual Canadian children actually perform better than unilingual children on both verbal and nonverbal measures of intelligence (Lambert & Anisfeld, 1969). More recently, Lambert and his colleagues (1993) replicated and extended this work across a number of countries such as Israel, Singapore, and Switzerland.

Based on these findings, a Canadian program was developed to immerse English-speaking children in French for much of their early elementary school education in Quebec (Lambert & Tucker, 1972). Their English did not appear to have been harmed and their math scores, aptitude scores, and appreciation of French culture benefited. Results such as these have influenced official Canadian government policy in favour of bilingual education (Noels & Clément, 1998).

Ellen Bialystok of York University has clarified the contribution bilingualism can make to the development of intelligence and skills such as mathematics and reading (Bialystok, 1991, 2001; Craik & Bialystok, 2005). According to Bialystok, the link is via *metalinguistic awareness*, or a knowledge of the properties and structures of language (Bialystok, 1995). Bilingualism is beneficial because of the perspective gained from knowing and using a whole new set of linguistic signs and categories (Segalowitz, 1997). That is, the bilingual child learns early on, among other things, that the relationship between words and their referents is arbitrary. A child learning both English and French, for example, would learn that the family pet is referred to as a "dog" in one language but as a "chien" in the other. This makes it easier for the child to appreciate the distinction between his or her language and the world to which that language refers.

Children with more developed metalinguistic awareness can appreciate literacy earlier (Bialystok, 1997; Bialystok, Luk, & Kwan, 2005), likely because they more easily understand the symbolic relation between letters and sounds. Conversely, poor readers also have poor metalinguistic skills (Bialystok & Mitterer, 1987). Arguably, then, the advanced metalinguistic ability of bilingual children enables them to develop literacy more easily than unilingual children (Bialystok & Herman, 1999; Bialystok, Luk, & Kwan, 2005).

Canadian research has indicated that *willingness to communicate* may be a more important outcome of immersion education than language proficiency per se (Macintyre & others, 1998; Clément, Baker, & MacIntyre, 2003). That is, it is better to produce students who want to speak French outside their classrooms than students who choose to speak French only in class. Willingness to communicate increases when teachers foster intrinsic motivation in their students (Noels, Clément, & Pelletier, 1999; Noels and others, 2000). Willingness to communicate is also higher when immersion extends beyond the classroom. For example, MacIntyre and his colleagues (2001) have shown that the willingness of French immersion students to speak French outside their classrooms was related to the social support of their friends. Similarly, Dagenais & Berron (2001) stressed parental support and saw immersion proceeding best when it is part of a family project aimed at developing multilingualism in children.

One important question regarding bilingual education is when to offer second-language classes. Although adolescents and adults can learn a second language, it is easier for children. Adults make faster initial progress in learning a second language, but their eventual success is not usually as great as children's. According to one classic study, children's ability to pronounce a second language with the correct accent also decreases with age, with an especially sharp decline occurring after the age of about 10 to 12 (Asher & Garcia, 1969). This result has been interpreted as evidence in support of the critical period hypothesis (Birdsong & Molis, 2001), which we discussed earlier. As discussed previously, recent data have been interpreted as showing that the decline in second language learning ability is gradual rather than showing an abrupt shift at a critical age (Hakuta, Bialystok, & Wiley, 2003; Wiley, Bialystok, & Hakuta, 2005).

Nevertheless, it is clear that young children are the best at second language learning regardless of whether the decline in second language learning ability is abrupt or gradual. In this light, French immersion education has been a Canadian response to a uniquely Canadian language situation. French immersion involves teaching younger English-speaking children regular school subjects mainly in French.

Another important question regarding bilingual education is how long it takes language-minority students to learn a second language. Kenji Hakuta and his colleagues (2000) collected data on children in four different U.S. school districts to determine how long it takes language minority students to speak and read English effectively.

Ellen Bialystok is a professor of psychology at York University. Her research focuses on the effects of bilingualism on metalinguistic awareness. According to Dr. Bialystok, "It is because metalinguistic awareness is consequential for other aspects of cognition, both linguistic and non-linguistic, that its study is important."

Speaking proficiency took three to five years, while reading proficiency took four to seven years. However, many schools assume that language-minority students will learn a second language effectively in one year or less, which may be unrealistic, even when those students are immersed in the second language.

Regardless of when and how children learn English or French as a second language, we need to be sensitive to the implications of asking them to communicate in some language other than the one they learned at home. Following are some recommendations for working with linguistically and culturally diverse children (U. S. National Association for the Education of Young Children, 1996):

- Recognize that all children are cognitively, linguistically, and emotionally connected to the language and culture of their homes.
- Understand that second-language learning can be difficult. It takes time to become linguistically competent in any language. Although verbal proficiency in a second language can be attained in two to three years, the skills needed to understand academic content through reading and writing can take four or more years. Children who do not become proficient in their second language after two or three years are usually not proficient in their first language, either.
- Recognize that children can and will acquire the use of a second language even when their home language is respected.

Reading Another important school-related aspect of language involves how we read (Risko, Stolz, & Besner, 2005) and, therefore, the best way to teach children to read (Farris, 2004). The reading debate focuses on the basic-skills-and-phonetics approach versus the whole-language approach.

The **basic-skills-and-phonetics approach** is the method for teaching reading that stresses the basic rules for translating written patterns into sounds. In order for children to use this approach, they must already have developed *phonological awareness*, the ability to identify and manipulate phonemes, the basic language sounds (Stuart, 2005) and must also be capable of paying attention to the written patterns of letters as well (Besner, Risko, & Sklair, 2005). Also, the basic-skills-and-phonetics approach emphasizes that early reading instruction should involve simplified materials designed to make correspondences between letters and phonemes more obvious. Only after they have learned phonological rules (how letters represent sounds) should children be given complex reading materials such as books and poems. This approach rests upon research showing that good readers can use phonetics to decipher unfamiliar words as required (Barron, 1994).

In contrast, the **whole language approach** stresses that reading instruction should parallel children's natural language learning (Shaw, 2003). In early reading instruction, children should be presented with materials in their complete form, such as stories and poems. Reading is also integrated with other skills (such as listening and writing), subjects (such as science and social studies), and real-world activities. A class might read newspapers, magazines, or books, then write about them and discuss them. In this way, say the whole language advocates, children learn to understand language's communicative function. This approach rests upon research showing that good readers can use their broader experience to treat texts as meaningful wholes (Masson & MacLeod, 1997), recognize familiar words as visual wholes (Perea & Rosa, 2002; Buchanan & Besner, 1993), and fill in missing meanings when they cannot read a word.

basic-skills-and-phonetics approach Stresses that reading instruction should emphasize the basic rules for translating written patterns into sounds.

whole language approach Stresses that reading instruction should parallel a child's natural language learning; so reading materials should be whole and meaningful.

Which approach is best? Popular press reports often imply that "phonics first" approaches are preferable but many researchers disagree (Meyer, 2002; Yatvin, 2005). Mitterer (1982) showed that different types of poor readers rely exclusively upon one or the other approach while good readers use both. Several U. S. national panels have concluded that a combination of the two approaches is the best strategy (Snow, 1998; U. S. National Reading Panel, 2000). The panels recommended that beginning readers be taught to sound out letters as the main way to identify unfamiliar words, the cornerstone of the basic-skills-and-phonetics approach. But the panels also endorsed several aspects of the whole language approach: encourage children, as they begin to recognize words, to predict what might happen in a story, draw inferences about stories, and write their own stories. The combination approach helps children learn the full range of language rules: phonology, morphology, syntax, and semantics (Rasinski & Padak, 2004).

> **reflect and review**

 Summarize how language is acquired and develops.

- Discuss the biological foundations of language.
- Identify the environmental influences on language.
- Describe the relevance of a critical period in learning language and the major milestones in early language development.
- Explain the opposing views of how schools should approach teaching a second language and reading.

How did you learn to read? Was it an effective approach? Explain.

The Candle Problem

The solution requires a unique perception of the function of the box in which the matches came. It can become a candleholder when tacked to the wall.

The Nine-Dot Problem

Most people have difficulty with this problem because they try to draw the lines within the boundaries of the dots. Notice that by extending the lines beyond the dots, the problem can be solved.

The Six-Matchstick Problem

Nothing in the instructions said that the solution had to be two-dimensional.

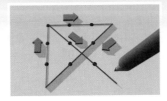

Solutions to problems from figure 9.6.

Thinking and Language

1 THE COGNITIVE REVOLUTION IN PSYCHOLOGY

2 CONCEPT FORMATION

— Functions of Concepts — Structure of Concepts

3 PROBLEM SOLVING

— Steps in Problem Solving — Obstacles to Solving Problems — Expertise

4 CRITICAL THINKING, REASONING, AND DECISION MAKING

— Critical Thinking — Reasoning — Decision Making

5 LANGUAGE AND THOUGHT

— The Structure of Language — The Link Between Language and Cognition — Animal Language

6 LANGUAGE ACQUISITION AND DEVELOPMENT

— Biological Influences — Environmental Influences — Early Development of Language — Language and Education

At the beginning of the chapter, we posed four chapter questions and encouraged you to review material related to these questions at the end of each major section (see pages 350, 353, 359, 366, 370, and 379). Use the following reflection and review features for further your understanding of the chapter material.

Are these sounds language? How would we know? Web sites offering to some such sounds include

http://www.findsounds.com/types.html
http://ars.usda.gov/pandp/docs.htm?docid=10919
http://www.ent.iastate.edu/list/insect_sounds.html
http://buzz.ifas.ufl.edu/index.htm

CHAPTER REFLECTIONS

Apply Your Knowledge

1. Due to the cognitive revolution, the computer is currently the dominant model psychologists use to think about how our brains process information. Could this model contribute to functional fixedness among psychologists? How? Can you think of a model other than the computer to describe how the brain works? Think back to how the brain actually works—in what ways might it be similar to a computer, and in what ways does it differ?

2. Currently, you should be trying to form a concept that we could call "cognitive psychology." What kinds of things would fit into this concept? What would make it easier to define your "cognitive psychology" concept? Compare this to a concept that you're already familiar with. What are the differences between the familiar concept and the new concept? How do you think your "cognitive psychology" concept differs from your instructor's "cognitive psychology" concept?

3. Think about two or three courses you are currently taking or have taken recently. Based on the definitions of critical thinking, mindfulness, and open-mindedness discussed in this chapter, which courses most required or best encouraged these practices? How did they do this? Which was the worst course from this perspective? How might this course be improved? Should all courses encourage critical thinking, or are there some for which this should not be a goal?

4. Think critically about the characteristics of language that have been applied to determining whether animals other than humans are capable of language. Now, listen to communication sounds that have been recorded from species not described in the text.

CHAPTER REVIEW

Characterize the "cognitive revolution" in psychology.

- Cognition is the way in which information is processed and manipulated in remembering, thinking, and knowing. The cognitive revolution, which has occurred over the past 50 years, is an interest in the way the mind works to process and to manipulate information. The computer has played an important role in this revolution, stimulating the model of the mind as an information-processing system. A parallel was originally drawn between computer software and human information processing but more recently the architectures of computers (linear) and the brain (parallel) have been shown to dramatically differ, A by-product of the cognitive revolution, artificial intelligence (AI) is the science of creating machines capable of performing activities that require intelligence when they are done by people.

Explain concept formation.

- Concepts are mental categories that are used to group objects, events, and characteristics. Concepts are important because they help us to generalize, improve our memories, and keep us from constantly having to learn.

- Two models of concept structure are classical (all instances of a concept share defining properties) and prototypical (people decide whether an item reflects a concept by comparing it with the most typical item(s) of the concept).

- Concept formation may be either consciously explicit (usually for more abstract concepts) or implicit and unconscious (usually for more perceptual categories). Different areas of the brain are involved in these two forms of concept formation.

Describe the requirements for solving problems.

- Problem solving is an attempt to find an appropriate way of attaining a goal when the goal is not readily available. Four main steps in problem solving are (1) find and frame the problem, (2) develop good problem-solving strategies, (3) evaluate solutions, and (4) rethink and redefine problems and solutions over time. Finding and framing problems is an often-overlooked dimension of problem solving. Among effective strategies for solving problems are subgoaling (setting intermediate goals that put you in a better position to reach your goal), using algorithms (strategies that guarantee a solution), and using heuristics (strategies or guidelines that suggest, but do not guarantee, a solution to a problem).

- Obstacles to problem solving include being fixated, as well as not being adequately motivated and not controlling emotions. Being fixated means focusing on prior strategies and failing to look at a problem from a new perspective. Functional fixedness is being fixated on the usual functions of a thing. A mental set is a type of fixation in which an individual tries to solve a problem in a particular way that has worked in the past.

- There is considerable interest in the role of expertise in problem solving. Compared with novices, experts have a superior knowledge base, are better at remembering information in the domain in which they are experts, use better problem-solving strategies, and engage in deliberate practice to a far greater extent.

Discuss the main factors in critical thinking, reasoning, and making decisions.

- Critical thinking involves thinking reflectively and productively and evaluating the evidence. Some critics argue that schools do not do a good job of guiding students to think critically, especially in coming up with new ideas and revising earlier conclusions. One obstacle to critical thinking is engaging in mindless behaviour. Sometimes, however, quick, intuitive judgments can be very accurate. People can become more mindful by creating new ideas, being open to new information, and being aware of more than one perspective. Open-mindedness is another good strategy for improving critical thinking. Too often we take one side of the issue without thinking in depth about the issue and evaluating it from different perspectives.

- Reasoning is the mental activity of transforming information to reach conclusions. It is closely tied to critical thinking. Inductive reasoning is reasoning from the specific to the general. Analogies draw on inductive reasoning. Deductive reasoning is reasoning from the general to the specific.

- Decision making involves evaluating alternatives and making choices among them. One type of decision making research studies how people weigh costs and benefits of various outcomes. Another type studies people's biases and the flawed heuristics they use in making decisions. These biases and flaws include confirmation bias, belief perseverance, overconfidence bias, hindsight bias, availability heuristics, and representativeness heuristics.

Identify the possible connections between language and thought.

- Language is a form of communication, whether spoken, written, or signed, that is based on a system of symbols. All human languages have some common characteristics, including infinite generativity and organizational rules about structure. Language has four sets of structural rules: phonology, the sound system of a language; morphology, the rules for combining morphemes, meaningful strings of sounds that contain no smaller meaningful parts; syntax, the ways words are combined to form acceptable phrases and sentences; and semantics, the meaning of words and sentences.

- Thoughts and ideas are associated with words. Language does not completely determine thought but does influence it. For instance, different languages promote different ways of thinking. Language is also important in the cognitive activities, such as memory. Cognitive activities can also influence language. Although language and thought influence each other, there is increasing evidence that they are not part of a single, automated cognitive system but rather evolved as separate, modular, biologically prepared components of the mind.

- Animals clearly can communicate but few have language skills that approach those of adult humans. Chimps have been taught to use symbols, and some pygmy chimps demonstrate an understanding of syntax. Whether animals have the same language abilities as humans continues to be debated.

Summarize how language is acquired and develops.

- Evolution shaped humans into linguistic creatures. Linguist Noam Chomsky said that humans are biologically prewired to learn language at a certain time and in a certain way. Chomsky and other experts believe that the strongest evidence for the biological foundations of language lies in the fact that children all over the world reach language milestones at about the same age and in the same order, despite vast variations in the language input they receive from the environment. In addition, there is strong evidence that particular regions in the brain, such as Broca's area and Wernicke's area, are predisposed to be used for language.

- Behaviourists, such as B. F. Skinner and Albert Bandura, have advocated that language is primarily determined by environmental influences, especially reinforcement and imitation. However, evidence suggests that reinforcement and imitation are not responsible for children's acquisition of language's rule systems. Nonetheless, it is important for children to interact with language-skilled people. Evidence for the influence of the environment on language acquisition comes from studies comparing children in language-impoverished and language-enriched environments. Children are biologically prepared to learn language but benefit enormously from being in a competent language environment from early in their development.

- Language learning, especially learning a language's structure, may be linked to a critical period, which is a time span in which there is learning readiness. Beyond this period, learning is difficult or impossible. The stunted language development of wild children such as Genie supports the notion that a critical period exists. However, this concept is still controversial. Far less controversial is the understanding of the milestones in early language development. Before babies say their first words, they babble. At about eight months, they discover boundaries between words. At 10 to 13 months, they utter their first word. Infants' early speech is telegraphic.

- Bilingualism is associated with greater metalinguistic awareness and may also be associated with higher intelligence. The reading debate focuses on the basic-skills-and-phonetics approach and the whole-language approach. The best reading instruction consists of a combination of these two approaches.

CONNECTIONS

For extra help in mastering the material in this chapter, see the integrator, review sections, practice quizzes, and other resources in the Student Study Guide and at the Online Learning Centre (www.mcgrawhill.ca/college/santrock).

CORE TERMS

cognition, p. 348
artificial intelligence (AI), p. 349
thinking, p. 350
concepts, p. 350
classical model, p. 352
prototype model, p. 352
problem solving, p. 353
subgoaling, p. 355
algorithms, p. 355
heuristics, p. 355
fixation, p. 356

functional fixedness, p. 356
mental set, p. 357
reasoning, p. 362
inductive reasoning, p. 362
deductive reasoning, p. 363
decision making, p. 363
confirmation bias, p. 364
belief perseverance, p. 364
overconfidence bias, p. 364
hindsight bias, p. 365
availability heuristic, p. 365

representativeness heuristic, p. 365
language, p. 366
infinite generativity, p. 367
phonology, p. 367
morphology, p. 367
syntax, p. 367
semantics, p. 367
basic-skills-and-phonetics approach, p. 378
whole language approach, p. 378

10 Intelligence

CHAPTER QUESTIONS

1. What is intelligence?

2. How is intelligence measured and what are the limitations of intelligence tests?

3. What are four neuroscience approaches to intelligence?

4. What are the theories of multiple intelligences?

5. What are some characteristics of mental retardation, giftedness, and creativity?

6. What are the contributions of heredity and environment to intelligence?

His cartoons include cows, aliens, nerds, nature, and improbable science. Although he retired in the mid-1990s you still see his cartoons everywhere. The artist is Gary Larson, who finished university though not in any blaze of glory. His most impressive job before his cartoons began to support him was as an investigator for the local Humane Society (Larson claims that on his way to the job interview, he actually ran over a dog).

Look at Larson's cartoons themselves. Is this cartoonist just totally wacko? The success of *The Far Side* cartoons and books suggests that Larson is anything but. Many people, including scientists all over the world, consider his work creative and intelligent. Larson has even had a louse and a butterfly named after him.

Should Larson's highly creative talents be considered a part of intelligence? How about the short-story writing talents of Alice Munro and the song writing talents of Leonard Cohen? Traditionally, they have not been. However, an increasing number of psychologists believe that creativity is a component of intelligence. In this chapter, the discussion of cognition continues with an examination of the nature of intelligence. Controversy exists over both how intelligence should be conceptualized and how it should be measured. Creativity is discussed both as a component of intelligence and as a separate process (Runco, 2004). Other topics covered are the extremes of intelligence—mental retardation and giftedness—as well as the contributions of heredity and environment to intelligence.

THE FAR SIDE   By GARY LARSON

"The picture's pretty bleak, gentlemen. ... The world's climates are changing, the mammals are taking over, and we all have a brain about the size of a walnut."

Gary Larson in front of some of his *The Far Side* cartoons.

Source: © 1985 Far Works, Universal Press Syndicate.

1 THE NATURE OF INTELLIGENCE

What is intelligence?

What does the term **intelligence** mean to psychologists? Some experts describe intelligence as the ability to solve problems. Others describe it as the capacity to adapt and learn from experience. Still others argue that defining intelligence in these cognitive terms ignores other dimensions of intelligence, such as creativity and practical and interpersonal intelligence. In fact, many psychologists argue that we do not as yet know what intelligence actually is (Sternberg, Grigorenko, & Kidd, 2005). Perhaps all that the existing expert definitions of intelligence share in common is a recognition that intelligence is an incredibly complex human trait.

The problem with intelligence is that, unlike height, weight, and age, intelligence cannot be directly seen or measured. We can't peel back a person's scalp and see how much intelligence he or she has. We can evaluate intelligence only *indirectly* by studying and comparing the intelligent acts that people perform.

The primary components of intelligence are similar to those of the cognitive processes—problem solving, thinking, and memory—that were discussed in chapter 9. The differences in how these cognitive processes were described there and how intelligence is discussed here lie in the concepts of individual differences and assessment. *Individual differences* are the stable, consistent ways in which people are different from one another. Intelligence and personality, the subject of chapter 12, are the two areas of psychology in which individual differences have mainly been emphasized. Individual differences in intelligence have generally been measured by tests designed to tell us whether a person can reason better than others who have taken the test. As you will see later in the chapter, though, the use of conventional intelligence tests to assess intelligence is controversial. However, we will temporarily set aside the contentions of psychologists over how intelligence is measured and fall back on the definition of **intelligence** as the ability to solve problems and to adapt and learn from experience.

> ### > reflect and review
>
> **Describe what intelligence is.**
>
> • Define intelligence and explain how it is linked to the concepts of individual differences and assessment.
>
> *Given the definition of intelligence proposed here, do you think that humans are the only intelligent species on earth? Explain.*

2 INTELLIGENCE TESTING

| Approaches to Testing | Criteria of a Good Test of Intelligence | Cultural Bias in Testing | The Use and Misuse of Intelligence Tests |

How is intelligence measured?

If you have ever taken an intelligence test, you might understand psychologist Robert Sternberg's (1997b) childhood anxieties. Because he got so stressed out about taking the tests, he did very poorly on them. Fortunately, a grade 4 teacher worked with Robert and helped instill the confidence he needed to overcome his anxieties. Robert not only began performing better on the tests but also, when he was 13, devised his own intelligence test and began using it to assess classmates—until the school principal found out and scolded

intelligence Problem-solving skills and the ability to adapt to and learn from life's everyday experiences.

him. Sternberg became so fascinated by intelligence that he made its study a lifelong pursuit. His approach to intelligence is discussed later in the chapter.

Approaches to Testing

Early psychologists completely ignored the "higher mental processes," such as thinking and problem solving, that we equate with intelligence today. They believed that simple sensory, perceptual, and motor processes were the key dimensions of intelligence. Sir Francis Galton, an English psychologist who is considered the father of mental tests, shared this point of view. In the late nineteenth century, he set out to demonstrate that there are systematic individual differences in these processes (Bulmer, 2003). Galton's focus on assessing sensory, perceptual, and motor processes was later overshadowed. Regardless, research continues on the relationship between intelligence and the speed of information processing (Deary & Der, 2005; Miller & Vernon, 1996) and intelligence and the speed of neural conduction (Budak & others, 2005; Rijsdijk, Boomsma, & Vernon, 1995).

The Binet Tests   In 1904 the French Ministry of Education asked psychologist Alfred Binet to devise a method that would determine which students did not benefit from regular classroom instruction (Fancher, 1998; Jarvin & Sternberg, 2003). School officials wanted to reduce overcrowding by placing those who did not benefit in special schools. Binet and his student, Theophile Simon, developed an intelligence test to meet this request. The test consisted of 30 items ranging from the ability to touch one's nose or ear when asked, to the ability to draw designs from memory and to define abstract concepts.

Binet developed the concept of **mental age (MA)**, which is an individual's level of mental development relative to that of others. Binet reasoned that a mentally retarded child would perform like a normal child of a younger age. He developed norms for intelligence by testing 50 nonretarded children from the ages of 3 to 11. Children suspected of mental retardation were given the test, and their performances were compared with those of children of the same chronological age in the normal sample. Average mental age (MA) corresponds to chronological age (CA), which is age from birth. A bright child has an MA considerably above CA; a dull child has an MA considerably below CA.

William Stern devised the term **intelligence quotient (IQ)** in 1912. IQ consists of an individual's mental age divided by chronological age multiplied by 100:

$$IQ = \frac{MA}{CA} \times 100$$

If mental age is the same as chronological age, then the individual's IQ is 100 (average); if mental age is above chronological age, the IQ is more than 100 (above average); if mental age is below chronological age, the IQ is less than 100 (below average). For example, a six-year-old child with a mental age of eight would have an IQ of 133, whereas a six-year-old child with a mental age of five would have an IQ of 83.

The Binet scales represented a major advance over earlier efforts to measure intelligence. Binet stressed that the core of intelligence consists of complex cognitive processes, such as memory, imagery, comprehension, and judgment. In addition, he believed that a developmental approach was crucial for understanding the concept of intelligence. His developmental interest was underscored by the emphasis on the child's mental age compared with chronological age.

The Binet test has been revised many times to incorporate advances in the understanding of intelligence and intelligence testing. It is currently in its fifth edition (Roid, 2003; Bain & Allin, 2005). Many of the revisions were carried out in 1915 by American psychologist Lewis Terman, who applied Stern's IQ concept to the test, developed extensive norms, and provided detailed, clear instructions for each problem on the test. In This revision was named the Stanford-Binet since the revisions were done at Stanford University. In 1985, the test) was revised to analyze an individual's responses in four content areas: verbal reasoning, quantitative reasoning, abstract/visual reasoning, and short-term memory. A composite score is also obtained

ALFRED BINET (1857–1911)
Alfred Binet constructed the first intelligence test after being asked to create a measure to determine which children would benefit from instruction in France's schools.

mental age (MA) An individual's level of mental development relative to that of others.

intelligent quotient (IQ) Consists of an individual's mental age divided by chronological age multiplied by 100.

FIGURE 10.1

The Normal Curve and Stanford-Binet IQ Scores
The distribution of IQ scores approximates a normal curve. Most of the population falls in the middle range of scores, between 84 and 116. Notice that extremely high and extremely low scores are rare. Only about 1 in 50 individuals has an IQ of more than 132 or less than 68.

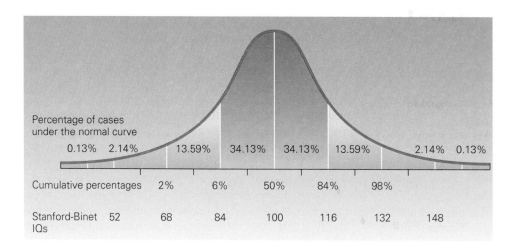

to reflect overall intelligence. The Stanford-Binet is currently in its fifth edition (Roid, 2003; Bain & Allin, 2005).

The current Stanford-Binet is given to individuals from the age of two through adulthood. It includes a wide variety of items, some requiring verbal responses, others nonverbal responses. For example, items that characterize a six-year-old's performance on the test include the verbal ability to define at least six words, such as *orange* and *envelope*, and the nonverbal ability to trace a path through a maze. Items that reflect the average adult's intelligence include defining such words as *disproportionate* and *regard*, explaining a proverb, and comparing idleness and laziness.

Over the years, the Binet test has been given to thousands of children and adults of different ages selected at random from different parts of the world. By administering the test to large numbers of individuals and recording the results, it has been found that intelligence measured by the Binet approximates a **normal distribution** (see figure 10.1). A normal distribution is a symmetrical, bell-shaped curve with a majority of the scores falling in the middle of the possible range and few scores appearing toward the extremes of the range. The Stanford-Binet continues to be one of the most widely used individual tests of intelligence.

The Wechsler Scales Besides the Stanford-Binet, the most widely used intelligence tests are the three Wechsler scales, developed by David Wechsler. In 1939, Wechsler introduced the first of his scales, designed for use with adults (Wechsler, 1939). Now in its third edition, the Wechsler Adult Intelligence Scale—III (WAIS-III) was followed by the Wechsler Intelligence Scale for Children (WISC) (Saklofske, Tulsky & others, 2003; Saklofske, Weiss & others, 2003). Meant for use with children between the ages of 6 and 16, the WISC is now in its fourth edition (WISC-IV). Finally, the Wechsler Preschool and Primary Scale of Intelligence (WPPSI) is meant for use with children from the ages of 4 to 6 and is also now in its third edition (WPPSI-III).

The Wechsler scales not only provide an overall IQ score but also yield scores on a number of verbal and nonverbal measures. This allows the examiner to separate verbal and nonverbal IQ scores and to quickly see the areas of mental performance in which the individual is below average, average, or above average. The inclusion of a number of nonverbal subscales makes the Wechsler test more representative of verbal and nonverbal intelligence; the Binet test includes some nonverbal items, but not as many as the Wechsler scales. Several of the WAIS-III subscales are shown in figure 10.2.

Group Tests of Intelligence The Stanford-Binet and Wechsler tests are individually administered intelligence tests. A psychologist approaches the testing situation as a structured interaction between the psychologist and the individual being tested. This provides an opportunity to sample the individual's behaviour. During testing the psychologist observes the ease with which rapport is established, the level of energy and enthusiasm the individual expresses, and the degree of frustration tolerance and

normal distribution A symmetrical, bell-shaped curve with a majority of the scores falling in the middle of the possible range and few scores appearing toward the extremes of the range.

VERBAL SUBSCALES

Similarities

An individual must think logically and abstractly to answer a number of questions about how things might be similar.

Example: "In what ways are boats and trains the same?"

Comprehension

This subscale is designed to measure an individual's judgment and common sense.

Example: "Why do individuals buy automobile insurance?"

NONVERBAL SUBSCALES

Picture Arrangement

A series of pictures out of sequence is shown to an individual, who is asked to place them in their proper order to tell an appropriate story. This subscale evaluates how individuals integrate information to make it logical and meaningful.

Example: "The pictures below need to be placed in an appropriate order to tell a story."

Block Design

An individual must assemble a set of multicoloured blocks to match designs that the examiner shows. Visual-motor coordination, perceptual organization, and the ability to visualize spatially are assessed.

Example: "Use the four blocks on the left to make the pattern at the right."

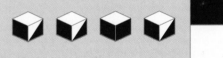

persistence the individual shows in performing difficult tasks. Each of these observations helps the psychologist understand the individual.

On some occasions, though, it is more convenient and economical to administer group intelligence tests than individual tests. For example, when World War I began, Binet's test was already popular, and the idea of using tests to measure intelligence was generally accepted. The U.S. armed services thought it would be beneficial to know the intellectual abilities of its thousands of recruits; but, clearly, not all of them could be tested individually. The result was the publication of the Army Alpha Test in 1917 to measure the intelligence of this large number of individuals on a group basis. In the same year, the Army Beta Test, mainly a performance test given orally, was designed for individuals who could not read the Army Alpha Test.

Though economical and convenient, group tests have some significant disadvantages. When a test is given to a large group, the examiner cannot establish rapport, determine the level of anxiety, and so on. Most testing experts recommend that, when important decisions are to be made about an individual, a group intelligence test should be supplemented by other information about the individual's abilities. For example, many children take ability tests at school in a large group. If a decision is to be made about placing a child in a special education class, it is a legal requirement that the decision not be based on a group intelligence test. A psychologist must administer an individual intelligence test,

FIGURE 10.2

Sample Subscales of the Wechsler Adult Intelligence Scale-III
The Wechsler includes 14 subscales, 7 verbal and 7 nonverbal. Examples from four of the subscales are shown here.

Wechsler Adult Intelligence Scale, Third Edition, Copyright © 1997 by the Psychological Corporation, a Harcourt Assessment Company. Reproduced by permission. All rights reserved. "Wechsler Adult Intelligence Scale" and "WAIS" are trademarks of the Psychological Corporation, a Harcourt Assessment Company, registered in the United States of America and/or other jurisdictions.

Donald Saklofske, of the University of Saskatchewan, has long been concerned with the psychometric properties of intelligence tests, especially the Wechsler scales.

such as the Stanford-Binet or Wechsler, and obtain extensive additional information about the child's abilities outside the testing situation.

Have you taken the Canadian Achievement Tests (CAT) or the Canadian Test of Cognitive Skills (CTCS)? Many Canadian students take group tests like these annually (Saklofske, Caravan, & Schwartz, 2000). Or perhaps you have taken the Scholastic Aptitude Test (SAT)? More common in the U.S. than Canada, this test, like the CTCS, measures some of the same abilities as intelligence tests. However, the SAT and CTCS do not yield an overall IQ score; rather, these tests provide separate scores for skills such as verbal and mathematical ability.

Tests like the CTCS and SAT may be used to predict success in university, but they are only one of many pieces of information that determine whether a university admits a student. High school grades, the quality of the student's high school, letters of recommendation, individual interviews with the student, and special circumstances in the student's life are also taken into account.

Aptitude and Achievement Tests Psychologists distinguish between aptitude tests and achievement tests. **Aptitude tests** predict an individual's ability to learn a skill or what the individual can accomplish with training. **Achievement tests** measure what a person has learned or the skills the person has mastered. Aptitude tests measure future performance; achievement tests measure current performance. The CTCS is an aptitude test. The tests you take in university that assess what you have learned are achievement tests. So is the CAT, which is used by Statistics Canada to track achievement of Canadian students.

The distinction between aptitude and achievement tests can be unclear. When someone gives a correct answer to a test item, it can be difficult to tell if the answer is correct because that person is naturally good at figuring out such answers (aptitude), or because he or she knew the answer through previous learning (achievement). Regardless, the CTCS and CAT can be used together to compare aptitude and achievement. A student would be underachieving if he or she received a higher CTCS than CAT score.

Criteria of a Good Test of Intelligence

Measurement and testing have been components of human decision making for centuries. The Chinese first developed formal oral tests of knowledge as early as 2200 B.C., when the Chinese emperor Ta Yü conducted a three-year cycle of "competency testing" of government officials. After three examinations, the officials were either promoted or fired (Sax, 1997). In today's world, tests have become commonplace as psychologists have sought more precise measurement of psychology's concepts (Aiken, 2006; Haladyna, 2002).

Psychometrists specialize in psychological testing, possibly creating tests, administering them, or interpreting them. Most psychometrists have at least a minimum of a master's degree in psychology and have completed extensive coursework in psychological testing. Psychometrists work in education, business, and clinical fields. A school psychometrist might test children who are having difficulties in school to determine their weaknesses, as well as their strengths. A psychometrist who works for a corporation might test job candidates to determine which are most likely to succeed in a job. Yet another psychometrist might work in a mental health clinic or hospital giving psychological tests to determine an individual's mental health profile. In any of these settings, psychometrists might use a test of intelligence to determine an individual's intellectual strengths and weaknesses.

Psychometrists are generally quite knowledgeable about the tests they administer. They know that a good test must meet three criteria: validity, reliability, and standardization.

aptitude tests Tests that predict an individual's ability to learn.

achievement tests Tests that measure what a person has learned or the skills that a person has mastered.

validity The extent to which a test measures what it is intended to measure.

Validity **Validity** is the extent to which a test measures what it is intended to measure. If a test is supposed to measure intelligence, then it should measure intelligence, not some other characteristic of the person, such as anxiety.

A test's validity can be established in a number of ways (Cohen & Swerdlik, 2005). One is making sure that the test samples a broad range of the content that is to be measured. For example, a final exam in this class, if it is to cover the entire book, should sample items from each of the chapters rather than just two or three chapters. If an intelligence test purports to measure both verbal ability and problem-solving ability, the items should include a liberal sampling of items that reflect both these domains; it should not test mostly vocabulary items with few items that require logical reasoning to solve problems.

One of the most important measures of validity is the degree to which a test predicts an individual's performance when assessed by other measures, or criteria, of the attribute. For example, a psychologist might validate an intelligence test by asking the employers of the individuals who took the intelligence test how intelligent they are at work. The employers' perceptions would be another criterion for measuring intelligence. It is not unusual for the validation of an intelligence test to be another intelligence test. When the scores on the two measures overlap substantially, we say the test has high *criterion validity*. Of course, we may use more than one other measure to establish criterion validity. We might give the individuals a second intelligence test, get their employers' perceptions of their intelligence, and observe their behaviour in real-life, problem-solving situations.

Reliability   A test that is stable and consistent should not fluctuate significantly because of chance factors, such as how much sleep the test taker gets the night before the test, who the examiner is, the temperature in the room where the test is given, and so on. **Reliability** is the extent to which a test yields a consistent, reproducible measure of performance (Cohen & Swerdlik, 2005). Ideally, a test should yield the same measure of performance when an individual is given the test on two different occasions. Thus, if we gave an intelligence test to a group of high school students today and then gave them the same test in six months, the test would be considered reliable if those who scored high on the test today generally score high on the test in six months. However, individuals sometimes do better the second time they take the test because they are familiar with it (McMillan, 2004b). Giving alternate forms of the same test on two different occasions is a way of dealing with this problem. The test items on the two forms of the test are similar but not identical. This strategy eliminates the chance of individuals performing better due to familiarity with the items, but it does not eliminate an individual's familiarity with the procedures and strategies involved in the testing. Also, it is difficult to create two truly parallel alternate forms of the test in which the items are similar but not identical.

In considering reliability and validity, a test that is valid is reliable, but a test that is reliable is not necessarily valid. People can respond consistently on a test, but the test might not be measuring what it purports to measure (Reynolds, Livingston, & Willson, 2006.

Standardization   Good tests are not only reliable and valid, they are also standardized (Cohen & Swerdlik, 2005; Impara & Plake, 2001). **Standardization** involves developing uniform procedures for administering and scoring a test, as well as creating *norms* or performance standards for the test. Uniform testing procedures require that the testing environment be as similar as possible for all individuals. The test directions and the amount of time allowed to complete the test should be the same, for example. Without standardization, it is difficult to compare scores across individuals. If some individuals take a test in a room in which loud music is playing, they are at a disadvantage compared with others who take the test in a quiet room.

Norms are created by giving the test to a large group of individuals representative of the population for whom the test is intended. This allows the test constructor to determine the distribution of test scores. Norms inform us which scores are considered high, low, or average. For example, suppose you receive a score of 120 on an intelligence test; that number alone has little meaning. The score takes on meaning when we compare it with the other scores. If only 20 percent of the standardized group scored above 120, then we can interpret your score as high rather than low or average. Many tests of intelligence are designed for individuals from diverse groups. So that the tests

reliability The extent to which a test yields a consistent, reproducible measure of performance.

standardization Involves developing uniform procedures for administering and scoring a test, as well as creating norms for the test.

Validity

Does the test measure what it purports to measure?

Reliability

Is test performance consistent?

Standardization

Are uniform procedures for administering and scoring the test used?

FIGURE 10.3
Test Construction and Evaluation

are applicable to such different groups, many of them have norms for individuals of different ages, socioeconomic statuses, and ethnic groups (Popham, 2005). Figure 10.3 summarizes the criteria for test construction and evaluation.

Cultural Bias in Testing

Many early IQ tests were culturally biased, favouring people who were urban, middle class, and white, rather than rural, lower class, and/or from a visible minority (Provenzo, 2002; Watras, 2002). For example, one question asked what should be done if you find a three-year-old child in the street. The correct answer was "call the police." But visible minority inner-city children who perceive police as adversaries are unlikely to choose this answer. Similarly, children from rural areas might not choose this answer if there is no police force nearby. Such questions clearly do not measure the knowledge necessary to be "intelligent" in an inner-city neighbourhood or in a rural area. Another infamous example comes from Darou (1992) who gave what he thought was an unbiased IQ test question to an Aboriginal Canadian: "*Saw* is to *whine* as *snake* is to …?" The Aboriginal Canadian did not "correctly" answer "*hiss*." He was from the far north and had never seen a snake. Besides, the saws he had used in the bush did not whine. Also, minority group members who do not speak English or speak nonstandard English may have difficulty understanding verbal questions framed in standard English, even if the test content is appropriate (Banks, 2006; Darou, 1992).

Even white Canadians do not perform identically to white Americans on IQ tests (Beal & others, 1996; Saklofske, 1996). Saklofske and his colleagues (1998) reported that Canadian children score higher than American children on some WISC-III scales. The WAIS-R is also biased (Peckford, Templer, & Ruff, 1975), especially the Information subtest (Pugh & Boer, 1989). Pugh & Boer (1991) studied problematic WAIS-R questions (e.g., about U.S. senators) and suggested Canadian replacements (e.g., about prime ministers). Interestingly, even within a cultural group, an easy question in 1991 (when this research was published) might be harder to answer over a decade later (e.g., "Who is Gordon Lightfoot?").

As a result of problems such as these, researchers have tried to develop tests that accurately reflect a person's intelligence. **Culture-fair tests** are intelligence tests that are intended to be culturally unbiased. Two types of culture-fair tests have been developed. The first includes questions that are familiar to people from all socioeconomic and ethnic backgrounds. For example, a child might be asked how a bird and a dog are different, on the assumption that virtually all children are familiar with birds and dogs. The second type of culture-fair test contains no verbal questions (R. N. Jones, 2003; Mawhinney, 1983). Figure 10.4 shows a sample question from the Raven Progressive Matrices Test. Even though tests such as the Raven Progressive Matrices are designed to be culture-fair, people with more education still score higher than those with less education.

Why is it so hard to create culture-fair tests? Most tests tend to reflect what is important to the dominant culture. If tests have time limits, the test will be biased against groups not concerned with time. If languages differ, the same words might have different meanings for different language groups. Even pictures can produce bias, because some cultures have less experience with drawings and photographs (Anastasi & Urbina, 1996). Within the same culture, different groups can have different attitudes, values, and motivation, and this could affect their performance on intelligence tests. Items that ask why buildings should be made of brick are biased against children who have little or no experience with brick houses. Questions about railroads, furnaces, seasons of the year, distances between cities, and so on can be biased against groups who have less experience than others with these contexts.

The Use and Misuse of Intelligence Tests

Psychological tests are tools. Like all tools, their effectiveness depends on the knowledge, skill, and integrity of the user. A hammer can be used to build a beautiful kitchen cabinet, or it can be used as a weapon of assault. Like a hammer, psychological tests can

culture-fair tests Intelligence tests that are intended to be culturally unbiased.

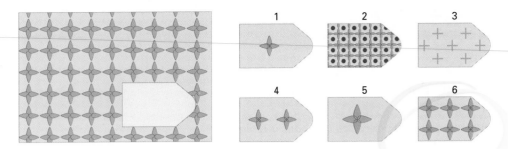

FIGURE 10.4

Sample Item from the Raven Progressive Matrices Test
Individuals are presented with a matrix arrangement of symbols, such as the one at the left of this figure, and must then complete the matrix by selecting the appropriate missing symbol from a group of symbols.

be used for positive purposes, or they can be abused. It is important for both the test constructor and the test examiner to be familiar with the current state of scientific knowledge about intelligence and intelligence tests. Even though they have limitations, tests of intelligence are among psychology's most widely used tools. To be effective, they should be used in conjunction with other information about an individual, not relied on as the sole indicator of intelligence. For example, an intelligence test alone should not determine whether a child is placed in a special education or gifted class. The child's developmental history, medical background, performance in school, social competencies, and family experiences should also be taken into account.

The single number provided by many IQ tests can easily lead to stereotypes and expectations about an individual (Rosnow & Rosenthal, 2002). Many people do not know how to interpret the results of intelligence tests, and sweeping generalizations are too often made on the basis of an IQ score. For example, imagine that you are a teacher in the teacher's lounge the day after school has started in the fall. You mention a student—Johnny—and a fellow teacher remarks that she had Johnny in class last year; she comments that he was a real dunce and points out that his IQ is 78. You cannot help but remember this information, and it might lead to thoughts that since Johnny is not very bright, it is useless to spend much time teaching him. In this way, IQ scores are misused, and stereotypes are formed (Rosenthal & Jacobsen, 1968).

Ability tests can help a teacher group children who function at roughly the same level in math or reading so they can be taught the same concepts together. However, extreme caution is necessary when test scores are used to place children in tracks such as "advanced," "intermediate," and "low." Periodic assessment of the groups, especially the "low" group, is required. Ability tests measure *current* performance, and maturational changes or enriched environmental experiences may advance a child's intelligence, indicating that she should be moved to a higher level group.

Despite their limitations, when used judiciously by a competent examiner, intelligence tests provide valuable information about individuals (Kaufman & Lichtenberger, 2006). There are not many alternatives to these tests. Subjective judgments about individuals simply reintroduce the bias that the tests were designed to eliminate.

"How are her scores?"

The New Yorker Collection 1987
Edward Koren from cartoonbank.com.
All Rights Reserved.

> **reflect and review**

2 **Explain how intelligence is measured and what the limitations of intelligence tests are.**

- Distinguish among these aspects of testing: early approaches, the Stanford-Binet tests, the Wechsler scales, group tests, and aptitude and achievement tests.
- Identify the criteria for a good test of intelligence.
- Discuss cultural bias in testing.
- Describe the use and misuse of intelligence tests.

A CD-ROM is being sold to parents for testing their child's IQ and how the child is performing in relation to his or her grade in school. The company that makes the CD-ROM says that it helps to get parents involved in their child's education. What might be some problems with parents giving their children an IQ test and interpreting the results?

③ NEUROSCIENCE AND INTELLIGENCE

| Head and Brain Size | Information Processing Speed | Electrical Activity in the Brain | Energy Consumption in the Brain |

HERMAN®
by Jim Unger

"You did very well on your IQ test!"

Copyright 1980 Universal Press Syndicate. Reprinted with permission. All rights reserved.

What can neuroscience tell us about intelligence?

The use of intelligence tests such as the Stanford-Binet and the Wechsler scales is one way to examine individual differences in intelligence. Neuroscience offers another. For example, Tony Vernon, of the University of Western Ontario, has asked if it might be possible to examine people's brains to reveal individual variations in their intelligence. For neuroscientists, intelligence is a research area that has opened up only recently, as advances in technology have made it possible to study the living brain at work. Many neuroscience studies have focused on the correlation of head and brain size with intelligence or on individual differences in brain activity, such as information-processing speed, brain electrical activity, and brain energy consumption (Reed, Vernon & Johnson 2004; Vernon, 2000). While the neuroscientific study of intelligence is making tremendous strides, results to date have not yet made it possible to use physical characteristics or measures of brain activity to provide an assessment alternative to the standard type of intelligence tests (Sternberg, 2005).

Head and Brain Size

Does having a big head or brain have anything to do with intelligence? Early studies used external measures such as head size as a substitute for brain size or measured the brain sizes of deceased individuals. Modern brain imaging technology such as magnetic resonance imaging (MRI) now enables neuroscientists to routinely estimate brain size in living persons.

In general, researchers have found that a larger head size and a larger brain size are associated with higher intelligence, brain size more so than head size (Walhovd & others, 2005; Tisserand & others, 2001; Wickett & others, 2000). In one recent study (Haier & others, 2004), differences in brain size were estimated to account for only 16 percent of the variance in intelligence, a small correlation. Further, Haier and his colleagues (2004) demonstrated that higher intelligence was associated with more grey matter (neuron cell bodies) in some regions of the frontal lobes as well as with areas in the other three lobes. In addition, they found that higher intelligence was associated with more white matter (neuron axons) in one parietal lobe region and that white matter differences might be more highly correlated with overall intelligence than grey matter differences.

It appears that both the density of neurons in particular brain regions and the richness of interconnections between them are both related to differences in intelligence. Exactly how many interconnected brain areas cooperate to produce intelligent behaviour remains to be worked out. Also, because these studies are correlational, it's not certain whether a larger brain size, or particular pattern of interconnectedness, causes greater intelligence or whether behaving intelligently causes a larger brain size or particular pattern of interconnectedness.

Information Processing Speed

A number of studies have identified a possible connection between intelligence and the speed with which individuals can process information (Bates, 2005; Fry & Hale, 2000). The main focus of these studies has been on reaction time. One measure of reaction time is the speed with which individuals press a button on a console when they see a light appear. Using such measures, researchers have found significant correlations of reaction time with scores on traditional intelligence tests such as the Stanford-Binet, with higher IQ scores being associated with faster, or shorter, reaction times (Rijsdijk,

Vernon, & Boomsma, 1998; Schretlen & others, 2000). Based on these studies, some experts on intelligence have concluded that the speed with which individuals can process information is an important aspect of intelligence (Vernon, 2000).

Others, however, say that the link between intelligence and processing speed is more complex. Some researchers have found that individuals who do well on intelligence tests actually take more time to decide on the type of reasoning needed to solve a problem, which enables them to respond more quickly with the correct answer (Sternberg, 1997a). Thus, speed of processing by itself does not determine intelligence. Regardless, the WISC-III now includes a Processing Speed Index subscale that has recently been shown to be useful for differentiating various clinical disorders in children (Calhoun & Dickerson Mayes, 2005).

Electrical Activity in the Brain

Given the association of information processing speed and intelligence found in some studies, researchers began to explore the possibility that actual neural transmission might be linked with intelligence (Reed, Vernon, & Johnson, 2004; Jausovec & Jausovec, 2001; Rijsdijk & Boomsma, 1997). Neuroscientists have sought to discover a link between brain activity and intelligence by measuring nerve conduction velocity and evoked potential.

Nerve conduction velocity (NCV) is the speed with which electrical impulses are transmitted along nerve fibres and across synapses. Research on NCV has focused on peripheral nerves. There has been less consistency in the results involving a relation between NCV and intelligence (Vernon, 2000).

Evoked potential refers to an electrical activity in the sensory areas of the brain that is caused by some external stimulus, such as a visual stimulus (a flash of light) or an auditory stimulus (a beep or a click). Researchers have found that individuals who register such stimuli more quickly score higher on intelligence tests than perceptually slower counterparts (Jausovec & Jausovec, 2000). Remember, though, that these are correlational studies, so we cannot conclude that faster brain activity in the evoked potential studies causes higher intelligence—it is just related to it. In this regard, Walhovd & colleagues (2005) have shown that the correlation between evoked potentials and intelligence is distinct from that between brain size and intelligence.

Energy Consumption in the Brain

Like any physical organ, the brain consumes energy. Thus, when people engage in a task that requires cognitive activity, one index of the extent to which their brain is "working" is the rate at which it breaks down glucose to compensate for the energy it uses (Haier, 2003; Vernon, 2000). The rate at which the brain uses glucose can be measured by positron emission tomography (PET) scans.

The results of a number of PET scan studies reveal that when individuals are at rest and can engage in any cognitive activity they choose, those with higher intelligence demonstrate increased brain activity and their brains use more glucose (Hu & others, 2000; Wu & others, 2000). However, when individuals perform an assigned cognitive task, those with higher intelligence successfully complete the task using less energy. This possibly means that individuals with higher intelligence have higher levels of brain activity at their disposal and can use it more efficiently than less intelligent individuals (Haier, White, & Alkire, 2003; Vernon, 2000).

people who are intelligent use less energy.

In sum, the use of biological measures to assess intelligence has been progressing rapidly. As technology progresses, our neuroscientific understanding of intelligence may allow it to develop direct, biological measures of intelligence to supplement traditional intelligence tests (Sternberg, 2005).

> ### > reflect and review

 Identify four neuroscience approaches to the study of intelligence.

- Describe the relation of head size and brain size to intelligence.
- Discuss the possibility of a connection between information processing speed and intelligence.
- Explain what the brain's electrical activity reveals about intelligence.
- Relate the brain's energy consumption to intelligence.

Nonhuman primates often have faster reaction times than humans. Does that make them more intelligent than humans? Explain.

④ THEORIES OF MULTIPLE INTELLIGENCES

Factor Analysis, Two-Factor Theory, and Multiple-Factor Theory	Gardner's Theory of Eight Intelligences	Sternberg's Triarchic Theory	Emotional Intelligence	Evaluating the Multiple-Intelligences Approach

Do we have a single intelligence or multiple intelligences?

The concept of mental age and IQ is based on the idea that intelligence is a general ability. Both the Binet and Wechsler tests yield a single score that is commonly taken as an indication of a person's general intelligence, or g (Charles Spearman, 1904). However, as we discussed previously, both the Binet and Wechsler tests also comprise a number of subtests that assess different intellectual skills. In fact, most psychologists break down intelligence into a number of abilities. A number of contemporary psychologists continue to search for the specific components that make up intelligence. Unlike Wechsler and other intelligence theorists, however, they do not rely on traditional intelligence tests in their conceptualization of intelligence (e.g., Das, 2002; Sarouphim, 2004). Following are several key alternative conceptions of intelligence, beginning with Charles Spearman's.

Factor Analysis, Two-Factor Theory, and Multiple-Factor Theory

For a hundred years now, psychologists have rejected any simplistic view that intelligence is no more than a general ability. It was Charles Spearman (1904) who first proposed that intelligence is made up of two factors. His **two-factor theory** states that individuals have both general intelligence, which he called g, and a number of specific abilities, or s. Spearman believed that these two factors accounted for a person's performance on an intelligence test. Spearman developed his theory by applying a technique called **factor analysis** to a number of intelligence tests. Factor analysis is a statistical procedure that correlates test scores to identify clusters, or factors, that measure a specific ability, such as verbal or mathematical reasoning.

Using factor analysis, Spearman found that most measures of specific abilities were partially correlated; it was this mathematical result that led him to propose the idea of g. The fact that the correlations were only partial led him to propose that each of the specific abilities was also somewhat independent of g, which led him to propose the idea of s. Spearman conceived of g as a form of overall mental energy that fueled all the specific abilities. He also conceived of each specific ability as having its own allotment of mental energy. Thus, a person's performance on a test of any specific intellectual skill would be determined by both that person's general intelligence and his or her ability at that specific skill.

Like Spearman, many experts on intelligence believe that people have both general intelligence and specific intelligences. Both Binet and Wechsler followed Spearman's

two-factor theory Spearman's theory that individuals have both general intelligence (g) and a number of specific abilities (s).

factor analysis A statistical procedure that examines various items or measures and identifies factors that are correlated with each other.

lead in this regard. For example, in one study, John Carroll (1993) extensively assessed intellectual abilities and concluded that, although all intellectual abilities are related to each other (which supports the concept of general intelligence), there are many specialized abilities as well. Beyond general intelligence, Carroll found an intermediate level of intellectual abilities, reflected in such abilities as memory and speed of processing information to make decisions, and a narrower level, reflected in such abilities as the skill to code sounds.

L. L. Thurstone (1938) also used factor analysis in analyzing a number of intelligence tests, but differed from Spearman in concluding that the tests measure only specific factors, not general intelligence. Thurstone's **multiple-factor theory** states that intelligence consists of seven primary mental abilities: verbal comprehension, number ability, word fluency, spatial visualization, associative memory, reasoning, and perceptual speed.

Gardner's Theory of Eight Intelligences

Imagine someone who has great musical skills but does not do well in math or English. Just such a person was the famous composer Ludwig van Beethoven. Would you call Beethoven "unintelligent?" Unlikely! Recently, Howard Gardner has considerably expanded the components of intelligence to include even musical skills. Following Thurstone, Gardner has argued that his "intelligences" are true multiple factors, so that individuals might be quite talented in one intelligence but not necessarily (as the concept of *g* might predict) in any of the others.

Ludwig van Beethoven, a musical genius, did not do well in math or English. *What are the implications of such inconsistencies for the concept of intelligence?*

From Verbal Intelligence to Naturalist Intelligence Gardner (1983, 1993) believes there are eight types of intelligence. He has evaluated proposals to add more intelligences to his list, including emotional intelligence, existential/spiritual intelligence, sexual intelligence, and digital intelligence, but has not yet done so (Gardner, 2003). His eight intelligences are described below, along with examples of the occupations in which they are reflected as strengths (Campbell, Campbell, & Dickinson, 2003):

- *Verbal skills:* The ability to think in words and to use language to express meaning. Occupations: Authors, journalists, speakers.
- *Mathematical skills:* The ability to carry out mathematical operations. Occupations: Scientists, engineers, accountants.
- *Spatial skills:* The ability to think three-dimensionally. Occupations: Architects, artists, sailors.
- *Bodily-kinesthetic skills:* The ability to manipulate objects and be physically adept. Occupations: Surgeons, craftspeople, dancers, athletes.
- *Musical skills:* A sensitivity to pitch, melody, rhythm, and tone. Occupations: Composers, musicians, and any career involving sensitive listening.
- *Interpersonal skills:* The ability to understand and effectively interact with others. Occupations: Teachers, mental health professionals.
- *Intrapersonal skills:* The ability to understand oneself. Occupations: Theologians, psychologists.
- *Naturalist skills:* The ability to observe patterns in nature and understand natural and human-made systems. Occupations: Farmers, botanists, ecologists, landscapers.

Naturalist skills are Gardner's (1999) latest addition to his multiple-intelligences list. Scientist David Suzuki excels in naturalist skills, as does cartoonist Gary Larson. Both have had a strong interest in science and nature since they were young boys, though rather than pursuing a career in these areas, Larson incorporated them as themes in many of his cartoons.

Gardner believes that each of the eight intelligences can be selectively destroyed by brain damage, that each involves unique cognitive skills, and that each shows up in exaggerated fashion in both the gifted and individuals who have mental retardation or

multiple-factor theory Thurstone's theory that intelligence consists of seven primary mental abilities: verbal comprehension, number ability, word fluency, spatial visualization, associative memory, reasoning, and perceptual speed.

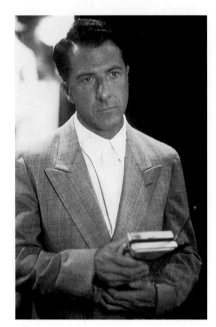

In *Rain Man,* Dustin Hoffman portrayed a man with autism and cognitive deficits who accomplished remarkable feats of counting and mathematics. Such skills are described as *savant skills.* They support the idea that intelligence can be expressed in multiple abilities.

extreme gift in one area.

autism (a psychological disorder marked by deficits in social interaction and interests). Dustin Hoffman portrayed an individual with autism who had a remarkable computing ability in the movie *Rain Man.* In one scene, Hoffman's character helped his brother successfully gamble in Las Vegas by keeping track of all the cards that had been played.

Multiple Intelligences in the Classroom   There has been considerable interest in applying Gardner's theory of multiple intelligences to children's education (Campbell, Campbell, & Dickinson, 2003). One experimental program, Project Spectrum, begins with the idea that every student has the potential to develop strengths in one or more areas (Gardner, 1993, 2002).

What is a Spectrum classroom like? The classroom has rich and engaging materials that can stimulate a range of intelligences. Teachers do not try to evoke intelligences directly by using materials that are labelled *spatial* or *verbal.* Rather, materials that relate to a combination of intelligence domains are used. For example, a naturalist corner has biological specimens that students can explore and compare. This area stimulates students' sensory capacities and logical thinking skills. In a storytelling area, students create imaginative tales with stimulating props and design their own storyboards. This area encourages children to use their linguistic, dramatic, and imaginative skills. In a building corner, students can construct a model of their classroom and arrange small-scale photographs of the students and the teachers in their class using spatial and personal skills. The Spectrum classroom has 12 areas in all that are designed to bring out students' multiple intelligences.

The Spectrum classroom can identify skills that are not typically tapped in a regular classroom. In one grade 1 class, a boy who was a product of a highly conflicted broken home was at risk for school failure. However, when Project Spectrum was introduced, the boy was identified as especially skilled in one area: He was the best student in the class at taking apart and putting together common objects, such as a doorknob and a food grinder. His teacher became encouraged when she found that he possessed this skill, and his overall school performance began to improve.

In addition to identifying unexpected strengths in students, Project Spectrum can also pinpoint undetected weaknesses. Gregory, who was especially skilled in math computation and conceptual knowledge, was doing very well in grade 1. However, he performed poorly in a number of Spectrum areas. Gregory did well only in the areas in which he needed to give the correct answer and when a person in authority gave it to him. As a result of Project Spectrum, Gregory's teacher began to search for ways to encourage him to take risks on more open-ended tasks, to try different ways of doing things, and to realize that it is okay to make mistakes.

A student in the naturalist corner of a Spectrum classroom. *What combinations of materials might you expect to find in other corners of a Spectrum classroom?*

Sternberg's Triarchic Theory

At the beginning of the chapter, we profiled cartoonist Gary Larson's creative talents and asked whether his creativity should be considered a part of the concept of intelligence. Gardner does not have a category for creativity in his intelligence theory, but Robert J. Sternberg does. In his **triarchic theory**, Sternberg (1986, 2002) proposes that there are three main types of intelligence: analytical, creative, and practical. Recall from earlier in the chapter that Sternberg had some very stressful experiences when he had to take traditional intelligence tests as a child. As an adult, he concluded that those intelligence tests did not adequately assess several important dimensions of intelligence.

Analytical, Creative, and Practical Intelligence Let's further explore what analytical, creative, and practical intelligence mean and look at examples of people who reflect these types of intelligence.

Analytical Intelligence Consider Latisha, who scores high on traditional intelligence tests such as the Stanford-Binet and is a star analytical thinker. Sternberg calls Latisha's analytical thinking and abstract reasoning *analytical intelligence*. It is the closest to what has traditionally been called intelligence and what is commonly assessed by intelligence tests.

In Sternberg's view of analytical intelligence, the fundamental unit in intelligence is a component simply defined as a basic unit of information processing. Sternberg believes such components include the ability to acquire or store information; to retain or retrieve information; to transfer information; to plan, make decisions, and solve problems; and to translate thoughts into performance.

Creative Intelligence Jacques does not have the best test scores but he does have an insightful and creative mind. Sternberg called the type of thinking at which Jacques excels *creative intelligence*. According to Sternberg, creative people such as Jacques have the ability to solve new problems quickly, but they also learn how to solve familiar problems in an automatic, rote way so that their minds are free to handle other problems that require insight and creativity.

Practical Intelligence Consider Emanuel, a street-smart person who learned to deal in practical ways with his world, although his scores on traditional IQ tests are low. Emanuel's street smarts and practical know-how indicate that he has what Sternberg calls *practical intelligence*, which includes the ability to get out of trouble, an aptitude for replacing a fuse, and a knack for getting along with people. Sternberg describes practical intelligence as all the important information about getting along in the world that you are not taught in school. He believes practical intelligence is sometimes more important than analytical intelligence, the book knowledge that is taught in school.

Triarchic Intelligence in the Classroom Sternberg (1997d, 2002, 2003b) says that students with different triarchic patterns look different in school. Students with high analytic ability tend to be favoured in conventional schools. They often do well in direct instruction classes in which the teacher lectures and gives objective tests. They are often considered smart students, typically get good grades, do well on traditional IQ tests, and later gain admission to competitive universities. Students who are high in creative intelligence are often not in the top rung of their class. Sternberg says that many teachers have expectations about how assignments should be done, which creatively intelligent students might not conform to. Instead of giving expected answers, they give unconventional, although correct, answers—for which they might get reprimanded or marked down. Like students high in creative intelligence, students who are practically intelligent often do not relate well to the demands of school. However, these students frequently do well outside classroom walls. They often have excellent social skills and good common sense. As adults,

"You're wise, but you lack tree smarts."

Donald Reilly ©1988 from The New Yorker Collection. All Rights Reserved.

triarchic theory Sternberg's theory that there are three main types of intelligence: analytical, creative, and practical.

they may become successful managers, entrepreneurs, or politicians, despite undistinguished school records.

Sternberg (1999; 2002) believes that few tasks are purely analytic, creative, or practical. Most tasks require some combination of these skills. For example, when students write a book report, they might (1) analyze the book's main themes, (2) generate new ideas about how the book could have been written better, and (3) think about how the book's themes can be applied to people's lives. Sternberg argues that it is important to balance classroom instruction with respect to all three types of intelligence. That is, students should be given opportunities to learn through analytical, creative, and practical thinking, in addition to conventional memorization.

Emotional Intelligence

Both Gardner's and Sternberg's theories include one or more categories of social intelligence. In Gardner's theory, the categories are interpersonal intelligence and intrapersonal intelligence. In Sternberg's theory, the category is practical intelligence. Another theory that captures the importance of the interpersonal, intrapersonal, and practical aspects of intelligence has generated a great deal of interest (Parker & others, 2005; Bar-On & Parker, 2000; Saklofske, Austin, & Minski, 2003). It is **emotional intelligence**, defined by Peter Salovey and John Mayer (1990) as the ability to monitor one's own and others' feelings and emotions, to discriminate among them, and to use this information to guide one's thinking and actions.

Daniel Goleman (1995) popularized the concept of emotional intelligence. Goleman believes that when it comes to predicting a person's competence, IQ as measured by traditional intelligence tests matters less than emotional intelligence. In Goleman's view, emotional intelligence involves these four areas:

- *Developing emotional awareness* (such as the ability to separate feelings from actions)
- *Managing emotions* (such as being able to control anger)
- *Reading emotions* (such as taking the perspective of others)
- *Handling relationships* (such as the ability to solve relationship problems)

Evaluating the Multiple-Intelligences Approach

The multiple-intelligence theories have much to offer. They stimulate us to think more broadly about what makes up people's intelligence and competence. And they have motivated educators to develop programs that instruct students in different domains.

Figure 10.5 provides a comparison of Gardner's, Sternberg's, and Salovy/Mayer/Goleman's views. Notice that Gardner includes a number of types of intelligence that are not addressed by the other views and that Sternberg is unique in emphasizing creative intelligence.

Some critics say that Gardner's classification of such domains as musical skills as a type of intelligence is off base. They ask whether there might not be other skills domains that Gardner has left out. For example, there are outstanding chess players, prizefighters, writers, politicians, lawyers, ministers, and poets. Yet we don't refer to chess intelligence, prizefighter intelligence, and so on. Other critics say that the research base to support either the eight intelligences of Gardner, the three intelligences of Sternberg, or the emotional intelligence of Salovy/Mayer/Goleman as the best way to characterize intelligence has not yet been developed.

Gardner (1999)—the ultimate multiple-intelligences advocate—has even criticized the emotional-intelligence advocates as going too far in including emotions in the concept of intelligence. He also believes that creativity should not be included. Although he believes that understanding emotions and being creative are important aspects of human competence and functioning, Gardner thinks that emotional understanding and creativity are not factors of intelligence.

There are also a number of psychologists who still support Spearman's concept of g (general intelligence), and many of them believe that the multiple-intelligences views have taken the concept of s (specific intelligences) too far (M. Anderson, 2005). For

emotional intelligence The ability to monitor one's own and others' emotions and feelings, to discriminate among them, and to use this information to guide one's thinking and actions.

Gardner	Sternberg	Salovy/Mayer/Goleman
Verbal Mathematical	Analytical	
Spatial Movement Musical	Creative	
Interpersonal Intrapersonal	Practical	Emotional
Naturalistic		

FIGURE 10.5

Comparing Gardner's, Sternberg's, and Salovy/Mayer/Goleman's Intelligences

example, one expert on intelligence, Nathan Brody (2000, 2004), argues that people who excel at one type of intellectual task are likely to excel at other intellectual tasks. Thus, individuals who do well at memorizing lists of digits are also likely to be good at solving verbal and spatial layout problems. Brody (2000) further argues that individuals do have a general intelligence and that it includes abstract reasoning or thinking, the capacity to acquire knowledge, and problem-solving ability. In addition, he maintains, it has real-world applications as a predictor of school and job success (Brody, 2000, 2004). For example, scores on tests of general intelligence are substantially correlated with academic achievement and moderately correlated with work performance (Lubinski, 2000). Individuals with higher scores on tests of general intelligence tend to get higher-paying, more prestigious jobs (Wagner, 1997).

However, general IQ tests predict only about one-quarter of the variation in job success, with the majority of job success linked to such other factors as motivation and education (Wagner & Sternberg, 1986). Further, the correlations between IQ and achievement decrease the longer people work at a job, presumably because as they gain more experience they perform better (E. B. Hunt, 1995).

There is a further wrinkle in the general intelligence issue. Researchers have found that the higher individuals' general IQ scores are, the more their scores on subtests of intellectual abilities vary (E. B. Hunt, 1995). For example, some bright individuals might score high on vocabulary and low on perceiving geometric patterns, and the reverse might be true for other bright individuals. However, researchers have found that individuals who score low on intelligence tests tend not to do well on any of the subtests (E. B. Hunt, 1995). These findings suggest that general intelligence might be a more appropriate concept for individuals with low intellectual ability than for individuals with high intellectual ability.

In sum, there continues to be controversy about whether people have a general intelligence. There also continues to be controversy about what the specific intelligences are.

> **reflect and review**

 Evaluate theories of multiple intelligence.

- Explain the role of factor analysis in the development of two-factor theory and multiple-factor theory.
- Discuss Gardner's theory of eight intelligences.
- Describe Sternberg's triarchic theory.
- Summarize what emotional intelligence is.
- Discuss the multiple-intelligences approach.

Apply Gardner's and Sternberg's multiple intelligences to yourself (or someone else you know well). Write a narrative description of yourself based on each of these theorists' views.

⑤ THE EXTREMES OF INTELLIGENCE AND CREATIVITY

— Mental Retardation   — Giftedness   — Creativity

What are the characteristics of mental retardation, giftedness, and creativity?

Mental retardation and intellectual giftedness are the extremes of intelligence. Often, intelligence tests are used to identify exceptional individuals. Keeping in mind that an intelligence test should not be used as the sole basis for decisions about intelligence, let's first consider the nature of mental retardation and giftedness, then discuss how creativity differs from intelligence.

Mental Retardation

The original defining feature of mental retardation is inadequate intellectual functioning (Hallahan & Kaufmann, 2006; Das, 1998). Long before formal tests were developed to assess intelligence, individuals with mental retardation were identified by a lack of age-appropriate skills in learning and caring for themselves. Once intelligence tests were developed, numbers were assigned to indicate degrees of mental retardation. It is not unusual to find that, of two individuals with mental retardation who have the same low IQ, one is married, employed, and involved in the community and the other requires constant supervision in an institution. Such differences in social competence led psychologists to include deficits in adaptive behaviour in their definition of mental retardation (American Association on Mental Retardation, 2002; Hallahan & Kauffman, 2006; Das, 1998).

Mental retardation is a condition of limited mental ability in which an individual has a low IQ, usually below 70 on a traditional intelligence test, and has difficulty adapting to everyday life; he or she first exhibited these characteristics during the so-called developmental period—by age 18. The reason for including developmental period in the definition of mental retardation is that we do not usually think of a university student who suffers massive brain damage in a car accident, resulting in an IQ of 60, as "mentally retarded." Low IQ and low adaptiveness are evident in childhood, not following a long period of normal functioning that is interrupted by an insult of some form. Over 7.5 million North Americans fit this definition of mental retardation.

Type of Mental Retardation	IQ Range	Percentage
Mild	55–70	89
Moderate	40–54	6
Severe	25–39	4
Profound	Below 25	1

FIGURE 10.6

Classification of Mental Retardation Based on IQ

mental retardation A condition of limited mental ability in which the individual has a low IQ, usually below 70, has difficulty adapting to everyday life, and has an onset of these characteristics in the so-called developmental period.

There are several classifications of mental retardation (Hallahan & Kaufmann, 2006). As indicated in figure 10.6, mental retardation may be mild, moderate, severe, or profound. Note that a large majority of individuals diagnosed with mental retardation fit into the mild category. While less than 1 percent are classified as profoundly retarded, those individuals are in need of constant supervision (Minnes, 1998; Nachshen, Woodford, & Minnes, 2003). Most school systems still use these classifications. However, because these categories are based on IQ ranges, they are not perfect predictors of functioning. The American Association on Mental Retardation (2002) developed a different classification based on the degree of support required for a person with mental retardation to function at the highest level. As shown in figure 10.7, these categories of support are intermittent, limited, extensive, and pervasive.

Mental retardation may have an organic cause, or it may be social and cultural in origin. *Organic retardation* is mental retardation caused by a genetic disorder or by brain damage; "organic" refers to the tissues or organs of the body, so there is some physical damage in organic retardation. Down syndrome, one form of organic mental retardation, occurs when an extra chromosome is present in the individual's genetic makeup. It is not known why the extra chromosome is present, but it may involve the health or age of the female ovum or male sperm.

Intermittent	Supports are provided "as needed." The individual may need episodic or short-term support during life-span transitions (such as job loss or acute medical crisis). Intermittent supports may be low or high intensity when provided.
Limited	Supports are intense and relatively consistent over time. They are time-limited but not intermittent. Require fewer staff members and cost less than more intense supports. These supports likely will be needed for adaptation to the changes involved in the school-to-adult period.
Extensive	Supports are characterized by regular involvement (e.g., daily) in at least some setting (such as home or work) and are not time-limited (for example, extended home-living support).
Pervasive	Supports are constant, very intense, and are provided across settings. They may be of a life-sustaining nature. These supports typically involve more staff members and intrusiveness than the other support categories.

FIGURE 10.7 **Classification of Mental Retardation Based on Levels of Support Needed**

A child with Down syndrome. *What causes Down syndrome?*

Other types of organic retardation include Williams Syndrome, which was discussed in chapter 9; fragile X syndrome, caused by an abnormality in the X chromosome that is more common in males than females; prenatal malformation; metabolic disorders; and diseases that affect the brain (Hallahan & Kaufmann, 2006; Das, 2000). Most people who suffer from organic retardation have IQs between 0 and 50.

Cultural-familial retardation is a mental deficit in which no evidence of organic brain damage can be found. Individuals with this type of retardation have IQs between 55 and 70. Psychologists suspect that such mental deficits result at least in part from growing up in a below-average intellectual environment. As children, those who are familially retarded can be identified in school, where they often fail, need tangible rewards (candy rather than praise), and are highly sensitive to what others—both peers and adults—expect of them (Vaughn, Bos, & Schumm, 2006). However, familially retarded adults are usually invisible, perhaps because adult settings don't tax their cognitive skills as sorely and they can benefit from training (e.g., Feldman & Case, 1997). It may also be that the familially retarded increase their intelligence as they move toward adulthood.

Giftedness

There have always been people whose abilities and accomplishments outshine those of others—the whiz kid in class, the star athlete, the natural musician. People who are **gifted** have high intelligence (an IQ of 120 or higher) and/or superior talent for something. When it comes to programs for the gifted, most school systems select children who have intellectual superiority and academic aptitude. Children who are talented in the visual and performing arts (arts, drama, dance) or in athletics or who have other special aptitudes tend to be overlooked.

Until recently, giftedness and emotional distress were thought to go hand in hand. English novelist Virginia Woolf suffered from severe depression, for example, and eventually committed suicide. And Sir Isaac Newton, Vincent van Gogh, Anne Sexton, Socrates, and Sylvia Plath all had emotional problems. However, these individuals are the exception rather than the rule; in general, no relation between giftedness and mental disorder has been found. Recent studies support the conclusion that gifted people tend to be more mature and have fewer emotional problems than others and to have grown up in a positive family climate (Feldhusen & Westby, 2003; Feldhusen, 1999).

Lewis Terman (1925) conducted a study of 1500 children whose Stanford-Binet IQs averaged 150. A popular myth is that gifted children are maladjusted, but Terman found in his study that they were not only academically gifted, but also socially well adjusted. Many of these gifted children went on to become successful doctors, lawyers, professors, and scientists.

gifted Individuals who have an IQ of 120 or higher and/or superior talent in a particular domain.

Art prodigy Alexandra Nechita. *What are some characteristics of gifted children?*

Ellen Winner (1996, 2003) recently described three criteria that characterize gifted children, whether in art, music, or academic domains:

1. *Precocity*. In most instances, gifted children are precocious because they have an inborn high ability in a particular domain or domains. They begin to master an area earlier than their peers. Learning in their domain is more effortless for them than for ordinary children.

2. *Marching to their own drummer*. Gifted children learn in a qualitatively different way than ordinary children do. For one thing, they need minimal help, or scaffolding, from adults to learn. In many cases, they resist any kind of explicit instruction. They also often make discoveries on their own and solve problems in unusual ways.

3. *A passion to master*. Gifted children are driven to understand the domain in which they have high ability. They display an intense, obsessive interest and an ability to focus. They are not children who need to be pushed by their parents. They motivate themselves.

As a 10-year-old, Alexandra Nechita was described as a child prodigy. Now twenty, she paints quickly and impulsively on large canvases, some as large as 1.5 metres by 2.5 metres. It is not unusual for her to complete several of these large paintings in a week. Her paintings—in the modernist tradition—sell for up to $200,000 apiece. When she was only two years old, Alexandra coloured in colouring books for hours. She had no interest in dolls or friends. Once she started school, she would start painting as soon as she got home. And she continues to paint—relentlessly and passionately. It is, she says, what she loves to do.

Is giftedness such as Alexandra Nechita's artistic talent a product of heredity or environment? Likely both. Experts who study giftedness point out that gifted individuals recall that they had signs of high ability in a particular area at a very young age, prior to or at the beginning of formal training (Winner, 2003). This suggests the importance of innate ability in giftedness. However, researchers have also found that the individuals who enjoy world-class status in the arts, mathematics, science, and sports all report strong family support and years of training and practice (Bloom, 1985). Recall the distinction between experts and novices made in chapter 9, that deliberate practice is an important characteristic of individuals who become experts in a particular domain. For example, in one study, the best musicians engaged in twice as much deliberate practice over their lives as the least successful ones did (Ericsson, Krampe, & Tesch-Roemer, 1993).

Do gifted children become gifted and highly creative adults? In Terman's research, gifted children typically did become experts in a well-established domain, such as medicine, law, or business. However, although they may have been creative in coming up with innovative ideas in these well-established domains, Ellen Winner (2000) points out that they did not become major creators.

"What do you mean 'What is it?' It's the spontaneous, unfettered expression of a young mind not yet bound by the restraints of narrative or pictorial representation."

© Sidney Harris

Thus, although giftedness in childhood and in adulthood are linked, only a fraction of gifted children eventually become revolutionary adult creators. Those who do must make a difficult transition from child prodigy (learning rapidly and effortlessly in an established domain) to adult creator (disrupting and ultimately remaking a domain or creating a new one).

One reason that some gifted children do not become gifted adults or even adult creators is that they have been pushed so hard by overzealous parents and teachers that they lose their intrinsic (internal) motivation (Winner, 1996, 2003). As adolescents, they may ask themselves, "Who am I doing this for?" If the answer is not for themselves, they may not want to do it anymore.

We have brought up the term *creative* on several occasions in discussing giftedness. The next section explores the topic of creativity in greater depth.

Paul MacCready is one of North America's most prolific inventors. His best-known invention is the Gossamer Condor, the first human-powered plane to travel a mile. MacCready's task was to design something stable and very light that would fly. It had to be different from any other airplane. MacCready's accomplishment won him $100,000 and a place in the Smithsonian Institution next to the Wright brothers' plane. MacCready says that asking the right questions and seeing things in a fresh way are critical for creativity.

Creativity

What does it mean to be creative? **Creativity** is the ability to think about something in novel and unusual ways and to come up with unconventional solutions to problems. Good scientists like David Suzuki often possess a very creative streak (Saunders & Thagard, 2005; Culross, 2004). And Gary Larson's bizarre cartoons certainly reflect the ability to think about science and nature in novel and unusual ways.

Intelligence and creativity are not the same thing (Kaufmann, 2003). Sternberg, 2001, 2003a), who included creativity in his triarchic theory of intelligence, says that many highly intelligent people produce large numbers of products, but the products are not necessarily novel. He also believes that highly creative people defy the crowd, whereas people who are highly intelligent but not creative often try to simply please the crowd.

Creative people tend to be divergent thinkers (Runco, 2003; Guilford, 1967). **Divergent thinking** produces many answers to the same question. In contrast, the kind of thinking required on conventional intelligence tests is **convergent thinking**. For example, a typical item on an intelligence test is "How many quarters will you get in return for 60 dimes?" There is only one correct answer to this question. However, the following question has many possible answers: What image comes to mind when you hear the phrase "sitting alone in a dark room"?

Thinking further about intelligence and creativity, most creative people are quite intelligent, but the reverse is not necessarily true. Many highly intelligent people (as measured by high scores on conventional tests of intelligence) are not very creative (Sternberg & O'Hara, 2000).

Steps in the Creative Process The creative process has often been described as a five-step sequence:

1. *Preparation.* You become immersed in a problem or an issue that interests you and arouses your curiosity.
2. *Incubation.* You churn ideas around in your head. This is the point at which you are likely to make some unusual connections in your thinking.
3. *Insight.* At this point, you experience the "Aha!" moment when all the pieces of the puzzle seem to fit together (Schilling, 2005).
4. *Evaluation.* Now you must decide whether the idea is valuable and worth pursuing. Is the idea really novel, or is it just obvious?
5. *Elaboration.* This final step often covers the longest span of time and the hardest work. This is what the famous twentieth-century American inventor Thomas Edison was talking about when he said that creativity is 1 percent inspiration and 99 percent perspiration. Elaboration may require a great deal of perspiration.

Mihaly Csikszentmihalyi (1996) believes that this five-step sequence provides a helpful framework for thinking about how creative ideas are formed and developed.

creativity The ability to think about something in novel and unusual ways and come up with unconventional solutions to problems.

divergent thinking Thinking that produces many answers to the same question; characteristic of creativity.

convergent thinking Thinking that produces one correct answer; characteristic of the type of thinking required on traditional intelligence tests.

Canadian short-story writer Alice Munro's stories reflect the intricate tapestry of her Ontario childhood. She says that she is "not an intellectual writer" but rather focuses on people, "The way they look, the way they sound, the way things smell, the way everything is that you go through every day." Relying on her intuition and rich language skills, she carefully crafts deeply creative stories that are richly associative and subtly connected, without being directly conscious of their underlying symbolic significance.

Leonard Cohen, Montreal-born singer-songwriter, poet, novelist and even filmmaker, writes songs that eloquently express the darker side of the human soul. He experiences his creativity as coming from a place beyond his personal control. Regardless, Cohen stresses that, for him, creating these songs is hard work: "I usually rewrite songs for a long time, sometimes for years. I keep trying to uncover what it is I am trying to say. I know that if I stop too soon I'll end up with slogans."

Jonas Salk, who invented the polio vaccine, says his best ideas come to him when he suddenly wakes up. After a few minutes of visualizing problems he had thought about the day before, he begins to see an unfolding, as if a painting or story is taking form. Salk also believes that many creative ideas are generated in conversations with others who have open, curious minds and positive attitudes. Salk's penchant for seeing emergent possibilities often brought him in conflict with people who had orthodox opinions.

However, he argues that creative people don't always go through the steps in a linear sequence. For example, elaboration is often interrupted by periods of incubation. Fresh insights may also appear during incubation, evaluation, and elaboration. And, in terms of a time frame, insight might last for years or it might take only a few hours. Sometimes the creative idea consists of one deep insight and other times a series of small ones.

Characteristics of Creative Thinkers   Creative thinkers tend to have the following characteristics (Perkins, 1994):

- *Flexibility and playful thinking.* Creative thinkers are flexible and play with problems, which gives rise to a paradox. Although creativity takes hard work, the work goes more smoothly if it is taken lightly. In a way, humour greases the wheels of creativity (Goleman, Kaufman, & Ray, 1993). When you are joking around, you are more likely to consider any possibility. Having fun helps to disarm the inner censor that can condemn your ideas as off base. Brainstorming is a technique in which members of a group are encouraged to come up with as many ideas as possible, play off each other's ideas, and say practically anything that comes to mind. Individuals usually avoid criticizing others' ideas until the end of the session.
- *Inner motivation.* Creative people are often motivated by the joy of creating. They tend to be less inspired by grades, money, or favourable feedback from others. Thus creative people are motivated more internally than externally. (Motivation is discussed more thoroughly in chapter 11.)
- *Willingness to risk.* Creative people make more mistakes than their less imaginative counterparts. It's not that they are less proficient but that they come up with more ideas, more possibilities. They win some, they lose some. For example, the twentieth-century Spanish artist Pablo Picasso created more than 20,000 paintings. Not all of them were masterpieces. Creative thinkers learn to cope with unsuccessful projects and see failure as an opportunity to learn.

- *Objective evaluation of work.* Despite the stereotype that creative people are eccentric and highly subjective, most creative thinkers strive to evaluate their work objectively. They may use an established set of criteria to make judgments or rely on the judgments of respected, trusted others. In this manner, they can determine whether further creative thinking will improve their work.

Living a More Creative Life Csikszentmihalyi (1996) interviewed 90 leading figures in art, business, government, education, and science to learn how creativity works. He discovered that creative people regularly engage in challenges that absorb them. Based on his interviews with some of the most creative people in the world, he concluded that the first step toward a more creative life is to cultivate your curiosity and interest, two important ideas from positive psychology (Nakamura & Csikszentmihalyi, 2003). Here are his recommendations for doing this:

- Try to be surprised by something every day. Maybe it is something you see, hear, or read about. Become absorbed in a lecture or a book. Be open to what the world is telling you. Life is a stream of experiences. Swim widely and deeply in it, and your life will be richer.
- Try to surprise at least one person every day. In a lot of things you do, you have to be predictable and patterned. Do something different. Ask a question you normally would not ask. Invite someone to go to a show or a museum you have never visited.
- Each day, write down what surprised you and how you surprised others. Most creative people keep a diary, notes, or lab records to ensure that experiences are not fleeting or forgotten. Start with a specific task. Each evening record the most surprising event that occurred that day and your most surprising action. After a few days, reread your notes and reflect on your past experiences. After a few weeks, you might see a pattern of interest emerging in your notes, one that might suggest an area you can explore in greater depth.
- When something sparks your interest, follow it. Usually when something captures your attention, it is short-lived—an idea, a song, a flower. Too often we don't explore the idea, song, or flower further. Or we think these areas are not our business because we are not experts about them. Yet the world is our business. We can't know which parts are most interesting until we make a serious effort to learn as much about as many aspects of it as possible.
- Wake up in the morning with a specific goal to look forward to. Creative people wake up eager to start the day. Why? Not necessarily because they are cheerful, enthusiastic types but because they know that there is something meaningful to accomplish each day, and they can't wait to get started.
- Take charge of your schedule. Figure out which time of the day is your most creative time. Some of us are more creative late at night, others early in the morning. Carve out time for yourself when your creative energy is at its best.
- Spend time in settings that stimulate your creativity. In Csikszentmihalyi's (1996) research, he gave people an electronic pager and beeped them randomly at different times of the day. When he asked them how they felt, they reported the highest levels of creativity when walking, driving, or swimming. These activities are semiautomatic in that they take only a certain amount of attention while leaving some free to make connections among ideas. Highly creative people also report coming up with novel ideas in the deeply relaxed state we are in when we are half-asleep, half-awake.

To evaluate the extent to which you engage in creative thinking, see the Personal Reflections box.

How Creative Is Your Thinking?

Rate each of the following items as they apply to you on a scale from
1 5 not like me at all, 2 5 somewhat unlike me, 3 5 somewhat like me,
to 4 5 very much like me.

1. I am good at coming up with lots of new and unique ideas.
2. I like to brainstorm with others to creatively find solutions to problems.
3. I tend to be internally motivated.
4. I'm a flexible person and like to play with my thinking.
5. I like to be around creative people and I learn from how they think.
6. I like to be surprised by something every day and to surprise others.
7. I wake up in the morning with a mission.
8. I search for alternative solutions to problems rather than giving a pat answer.
9. I know which settings stimulate me to be creative and I try to spend time in those settings.

1	2	3	4	5

Total your scores for all nine items. Your creativity score is _____. If you scored 32–36 points, you likely are a creative thinker. If you scored 27–31 points, you are inclined to be creative but could benefit from thinking about some ways to get more creativity in your life. If you scored 26 or below, seriously think about ways to become more creative. Read again the suggestions in the text for becoming a more creative person.

> ## reflect and review

5 **Describe the characteristics of mental retardation, giftedness, and creativity.**

- Define mental retardation and discuss its causes.
- Explain what makes people gifted.
- Identify the characteristics associated with creativity.

How many of the tips in the section on "Living a More Creative Life" do you currently practise? How might you benefit from these suggestions, in addition to becoming more creative?

6 THE INFLUENCE OF HEREDITY AND ENVIRONMENT

— Genetic Influences — Environmental Influences — Genetics-Environment Interactions — Group Influences

What do heredity and environment contribute to intelligence?

One important debate centres on the extent to which intelligence is influenced by genetics as opposed to environment. In chapter 3, we saw that, in 2003, the Human Genome Project completed sequencing the 3 billion chemical base pairs that make up the *human genome* and identifying all of the genes in human DNA (U. S. Department of Energy Human Genome Project, 2003). The result has been an explosion of work on the genetic underpinnings of every facet of the human condition, including, of course, intelligence. As we saw in our earlier discussion of theories of intelligence, intelligence is a complex human quality around which there is still considerable controversy. In this section we explore three further issues: the complexity of the genetics of intelligence, the complexity of environmental influences on intelligence, and the interaction of genetics and environmental factors in determining intelligence.

Genetic Influences

Although it may be a truism to assert that genes influence intelligence, the relationship is undoubtedly a complex one. Researchers found genetic markers (unique genetic locations) for intelligence on chromosomes 4, 6, and 22 (Plomin, 1999; Plomin & Craig, 2001). The genetic marker on chromosome 6 was shown to be carried by one-third of children with high IQs but only one-sixth of children with average IQs (Chorney & others, 1998). By 2001, 150 genes related to individual differences in human cognition had already been identified (Morley & Montgomery, 2001). Despite this complexity, researchers have long attempted to specify the degree to which our genes make us smart.

At one end of the debate, Jensen (1969) claimed that intelligence is primarily inherited. Jensen reviewed research involving comparisons of identical and fraternal twins. Identical twins have exactly the same genetic makeup. If intelligence is genetically determined, identical twins' IQs should be similar. Fraternal twins and ordinary siblings are less similar genetically, so their IQs should be less similar.

The studies on intelligence in identical twins that Jensen examined showed an average correlation of .82, a very high positive association. Investigations of fraternal twins, however, produced an average correlation of .50, a moderately high positive correlation. This difference of .32 is substantial. However, in one research review, the difference in intelligence between identical and fraternal twins was only .15, substantially less than what Jensen found (Grigorenko, 2000, 2005). To demonstrate that genetic factors are more important than environmental factors, Jensen compared identical twins reared together with those reared apart. The correlation for those reared together was .89, and for those reared apart it was .78, a difference of .11. Jensen argued that if environmental factors were more important than genetic factors, siblings reared apart, in different environments, should have IQs that differed more than .11.

Adoption studies have been inconclusive. In one study, the educational levels attained by biological parents were better predictors of children's IQ scores than the IQs of the children's adoptive parents were (Scarr & Weinberg, 1983). Because of the genetic link between adopted children and their biological parents, the implication is that heredity is more important than environment. But environmental effects have also been found. For example, in one study, moving black children into white adoptive families increased the children's IQs by an average of 13 points (Nisbett, 2005).

The concept of **heritability** seeks to tease apart the effects of heredity and environment in a population. Heritability refers to the fraction of the variance in IQ that is attributed to genetics. An important point to keep in mind about heritability is that it refers to groups (populations), not to individuals (Okagaki, 2000; Sternberg, Grigorenko, & Kidd, 2005). The *heritability index* is computed using correlational techniques. Thus, the highest degree of heritability is 1.00. Correlations of .70 and above suggest a strong genetic influence. By one estimate, the heritability of intelligence is about .75, which reflects a strong genetic influence (Neisser & others, 1996; Dickens & Flynn, 2001).

Interestingly, researchers have found that the heritability of intelligence increases from childhood (about 35 percent) to adulthood (about 75 percent; McGue & others, 1993). Possibly, as we grow older, our interactions with the environment are shaped less by the influence of others and the environment on us, and more by our ability to choose our environments to allow the expression of genetic tendencies we have inherited (Neisser & others, 1996; Dickens & Flynn, 2001).

Environmental Influences

Today, most researchers agree that heredity does not determine intelligence to the extent that Jensen claimed (Schooler, 1998; Grigorenko, 2000). To what extent, then, do environmental influences play a role in determining intelligence? Just as in the case of the role of genetic factors, the role of environmental influences in determining intelligence is complex.

heritability The fraction of the variance in IQ in a population that is attributed to genetics.

Consider, for example, the *Flynn effect*, named after the researcher who discovered it, James Flynn (Flynn, 1999; Dickens & Flynn, 2001). Flynn found that a worldwide increase in intelligence test scores has occurred over a short time frame. Scores on these tests have been increasing so fast that a high percentage of people regarded as having average intelligence at the turn of century would be regarded as having below average intelligence today (see figure 10.8; Howard, 2001). If a representative sample of people today took the Stanford-Binet test used in 1932, about one-quarter would be defined as having very superior intelligence, a label usually accorded to fewer than 3 percent of the population (Horton, 2001). Because the increase has taken place in a relatively short period of time, it cannot be due to heredity, but rather may be due to increasing levels of education attained by a much greater percentage of the world's population, or to other environmental factors, such as the explosion of information to which people are exposed.

More focused investigations have also shown that, for most people, modifications in environment can change their IQ scores considerably (Schooler, 1998). It also means that programs designed to enrich an environment can have considerable effects, improving school achievement and fostering the acquisition of skills needed for employment. Although genetic endowment may always influence a person's intellectual ability, the environmental influences and opportunities that children and adults experience do make a difference.

In one study (described in the discussion of environmental influences on language in chapter 9), researchers went into homes and observed how extensively parents from welfare-recipient and middle-income professional families talked and communicated with their young children (Hart & Risley, 1995). They found that middle-income professional parents were much likelier to talk and communicate with their young children than the parents on welfare were. And how much the parents talked and communicated with their children in the first three years of their lives was correlated with the children's Stanford-Binet IQ scores at age three: The more parents talked and communicated with their children, the higher the children's IQs were. Other studies have also found substantial socioeconomic status differences in intelligence (Turkheimer & others, 2003).

Researchers are increasingly interested in manipulating the early environment of children who are at risk for impoverished intelligence (Blair & Ramey, 1996; Ramey, Ramey, & Lanzi, 2001; Sternberg & Grigorenko, 2001). The emphasis is on prevention rather than remediation. Many low-income parents have difficulty providing an intellectually stimulating environment for their children. Programs that educate parents to be more sensitive caregivers and that train them to be better teachers can make a difference in a child's intellectual development, as can support services, such as high quality child-care programs.

In one study, Craig Ramey and his colleagues (Ramey & Campbell, 1984; Ramey & Ramey, 2004) randomly assigned 111 young children from low-income, poorly educated families to either an intervention group, which received full-time, year-round daycare along with medical and social work services, or a control group, which received medical and social benefits but no daycare. The daycare program included gamelike learning activities aimed at improving language, motor, social, and cognitive skills. The success of the program in improving IQ was evident by the time the children were three years of age. At that age, the experimental group showed IQs averaging 101, a 17-point advantage over the control group. Recent follow-up results suggest that the effects are long-lasting. More than a decade later, at age 15, children from the intervention group still maintained an IQ advantage of 5 points (97.7 to 92.6) over the control-group children (Campbell & others, 2001; Ramey & others, 2001). They also did better

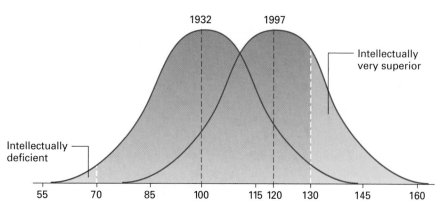

FIGURE 10.8 **The Increase in IQ Scores from 1932 to 1997**
As measured by the Stanford-Binet intelligence test, American children seem to be getting smarter. Scores of a group tested in 1932 fell along a bell-shaped curve with half below 100 and half above. Studies show that if children took that same test today, using the 1932 scale, half would score above 120. Few of them would score in the "intellectually deficient" range and about one-quarter would rank in the "very superior" range.

Are Television and Computer Games Making Us Smarter?

The Flynn effect has been widely interpreted as indicating that environmental factors play a significant role in determining intelligence. But which factors? The common assumption is that improvements in health and nutrition (Colom, Lluis-Font, & Andrés-Pueyo, 2005) or formal education (Ceci & Gilstrap, 2000) are the most likely candidates. Recently, however, Johnson (2005) has creatively proposed an alternative factor: popular culture. Turning the usual assumption that popular culture "dumbs us down" on its head, Johnson argues that changes in popular culture underlie the Flynn effect. While he admits that the *content* of much popular culture is open to criticism as being too violent or preoccupied with sex, he argues that, over the years, television, computer games and the Internet have become more and more complex, demanding more and more concerted cognitive effort. In other words, it is not *what* we experience in popular culture that is important, it is *how* we experience it. Schooler (1998) has similarly argued that the growth of environmental complexity underlies the Flynn effect.

When it comes to television, Johnson compares television programs of today with older programs. He suggests that following a television program from thirty years ago, such as the incredibly popular soap opera, *Dallas*, was relatively simple, with few characters to keep track of, simple, linear plots, and stories that were completely played out in a single episode. In contrast, today's award-winning dramas, such as the *Sopranos* or the *West Wing*, follow many more characters, both minor and major, through several intertwined plot lines that play out over an entire season. The net result is that while early television insisted on clarity and simplicity, modern television has become more and more challenging as we work to keep characters separate and puzzle through the interrelationship of different plot lines

Johnson also argues that videogames have undergone a similar development. Early videogames such as PacMan or Tetris offered simple, repetitive perceptual experiences. Today's popular video games, such as the *Sims* or even the much-reviled *Grand Theft Auto*, instead offer complicated environments within which the player must figure out the rules for herself. The successful completion of a modern computer game may take forty or more hours of intense cognitive problem-solving effort. As a telling bit of evidence, Johnson points out that it is possible to search the Internet for walk-throughs —fan-generated detailed instructions for how to successfully complete popular computer games. Johnson notes that one walk-through for *Grand Theft Auto* is about 53,000 words long, as long as his own book. Only a complex and engaging game would prompt fans to devote their effort to either compiling such walk-throughs or following them to improve their gaming experience.

Finally, Johnson argues that the rise of the Internet has again raised the cognitive complexity of popular culture. Not only are we forced to grapple with ever more complex computer interfaces and ever more computer applications, we are exposed to an ever-growing flood of networked media from Web sites and emails to blogs and chat.

But what about the cost to reading, the traditional route to literacy and the improvement of intelligence? Johnson points out that, while fewer books are being read, reading is nevertheless required while playing many computer games and is certainly a major skill exercised while using the Internet. Besides, he argues, the net result of spending more and more of our free time immersed in the rapidly evolving world of television, computer games, and the Internet is practice at all the steps of problem solving, another component of intelligence.

What do you think?

- Is modern television more challenging than ever before?
- Johnson (2005) claims that only people who don't play computer games would think they dumb you down. Are you a gamer? Do you agree with Johnson? Why or why not?
- What do you think is the major reason why IQ scores have risen so dramatically over the last fifty years?

on standardized tests of reading and math and were less likely to be held back a year in school. Also, the greatest IQ gains were by the children whose mothers had especially low IQs—below 70. At age 15, these children showed a 10-point IQ advantage over children whose mothers had IQs below 70 but who did not experience the daycare intervention.

Studies of schooling also reveal effects on intelligence (Ceci & Gilstrap, 2000; Ceci, 2003; Christian, Bachnan, & Morrison, 2001). The biggest effects have been found in cases in which large groups of children have been deprived of formal education for an extended period of time, resulting in lower intelligence. One classic study investigated the intellectual functioning of Indian children in South Africa whose schooling was delayed for four years because of the unavailability of teachers (Ramphal, 1962). Compared with children in nearby villages who had teachers, the Indian children whose schooling was delayed experienced a decrement of five IQ points for every year of delay.

Keep in mind that environmental influences are complex (Neisser & others, 1996; Sternberg, 2001). Growing up with all the advantages, for example, does not necessarily guarantee success. Children from wealthy families living in Western countries may have easy access to excellent schools, books, travel, and tutoring, but they may take such opportunities for granted and not be motivated to learn and to achieve. And, alternatively, poor or disadvantaged children may be highly motivated and successful. To read about a creative recent explanation of the causes of the Flynn effect, see the Critical Reflections box.

University of Alberta professor Douglas Wahlsten argues that it is not possible to sort out the relative effects of heredity and environment in determining the IQ of human individuals or groups. *What are the details of his argument?*

Genetics–Environment Interactions

The so-called "nature-nurture" debate between those proposing genetic and environmental explanations for individual differences in intelligence often degenerates into an either/or form: either intelligence is determined by genetics or it is determined by environmental factors. But in chapter 3, and above, we saw that it may be difficult to tease apart the relative contributions of genetics and environment when it comes to understanding human qualities like intelligence (Grigorenko, 2005). Psychologists now commonly reject this debate in its either/or form in favour of the view that both genetic and environmental factors contribute to intelligence. Even the heritability index, which attempts to separate out genetic and environmental effects has been criticized (Dickens & Flynn, 2001). One problem with the data is that they are virtually all from traditional IQ tests, which may not be the best indicators of intelligence (Sternberg, 2000).

Perhaps the most serious criticism has been championed by Douglas Wahlsten, of the University of Alberta (Wahlsten, 1994, 1996). Recall the earlier suggestion that the heritability of IQ in adults is about 75 percent. Wahlsten claims that it makes no sense to treat heredity and environment as two separate, or *additive*, factors, contributing together like two friends giving $75 and $25 to buy a gift for another friend. Instead, Wahlsten argues, heredity and environment are interactive, or *multiplicative*, in their action. Recall that in chapter 3 we noted Donald Hebb's argument that the relationship of heredity and environment is like that of height and width of a rectangle—it doesn't make sense to ask which is more important to the rectangle (Gottlieb, Wahlsten, & Lickliter, 1998).

Thus, according to Wahlsten (see also Dickens & Flynn, 2001), the interaction of heredity and environment is bi-directional. In one direction, each child's heredity helps determine its environment. For example, those nurturing a "naturally" less intelligent child may end up posing fewer intellectual challenges for that child and hence not stimulating that child's growth as much as they might a "naturally" brighter child. Conversely, each child's environment helps to determine how his or her heredity is expressed. For example, malnourishment stunts development, including that of intelligence. The two effects, then, are so intertwined that the study of the distribution of IQ scores in human populations or the study of the IQs of identical and fraternal twins cannot cleanly separate them. Thus, any measure of the effect of heredity cannot be accurate and does not indicate any constraint on the modifiabilty of intelligence (Wahlsten, 1997).

This does not mean it is worthless to examine the role of heredity and environment in development. Wahlsten (Wahlsten & Gottlieb, 1997) makes it clear that carefully controlled animal studies, where it is possible to exert near-perfect control over the genetic make-up and environmental experiences of the animals, can teach us much about the relationship between nature and nurture. It is just that human studies cannot use such control and thus cannot clearly separate the effects of heredity and environment.

Group Influences

Among the ways that group influences can be linked to intelligence are comparisons of cultures, ethnic groups, and males and females.

Cross-Cultural Comparisons Cultures vary in the way they define intelligence (Correa-Chávez, Rogoff, & Arauz, 2005; Rogoff, 2003; Serpell, 2000). Most European-heritage North Americans think of intelligence in terms of reasoning and thinking skills, but people in Kenya consider responsible participation in family and social life an integral part of intelligence. An intelligent person in Uganda is someone who knows what to do and then follows through with appropriate action. James Bay Cree value the visual pattern recognition skills necessary to find food (Darou, 1992). Intelligence to the Iatmul people of Papua New Guinea involves remembering the names of up to 20,000 clans, and the islanders in the Caroline Islands value the talent of navigating by the stars (see figure 10.9). In a cross-cultural context, then, intelligence depends a great deal on environment.

The intelligence of the Iatmul people of Papua New Guinea involves the ability to remember the names of many clans.

On the 680 Caroline Islands in the Pacific Ocean east of the Philippines, the intelligence of their inhabitants includes the ability to navigate by the stars.

FIGURE 10.9

Iatmul and Caroline Islander Intelligence

Ethnic Comparisons The most contentious area of research involving intelligence remains the research into the relationship between race and ethnicity on the one hand and heredity and intelligence on the other. In one of his most provocative statements, Arthur Jensen (1969; Rushton & Jensen, 2005). claimed that genetics accounts for clear-cut differences in the average intelligence between races, nationalities, and socioeconomic groups. Similarly, Herrnstein & Murray (1994) argued that America is rapidly evolving a huge underclass that consists of intellectually deprived individuals whose cognitive abilities will never match the future needs of most employers. They believe that this underclass, a large proportion of which is African American, may be doomed by their shortcomings to welfare dependency, poverty, crime, and lives devoid of any hope of ever reaching the American dream.

How extensively are ethnic differences in intelligence influenced by heredity and environment? Historically, Aboriginal students have tended to score 20 points lower on verbal scales and 5 points higher on performance scales of standardized intelligence tests when compared against white norms (McShane & Plas, 1984). Signalling a deep sociocultural problem in the United States, children from African American and Latino families score below children from white families on standardized intelligence tests. On average, African American schoolchildren score 10 to 15 points lower on standardized intelligence tests than white American schoolchildren do (Brody, 2000; Lynn, 1996). We are talking about average scores, though. Estimates also indicate that 15 to 25 percent of all African American schoolchildren score higher than half of all white school-children do, and many whites score lower than most African Americans. The reason is that the distribution of scores for African Americans and whites overlap. At the same time, Asians tend to score higher than African Americans or whites and to be dispro-portionately represented in more demanding academic fields (Templer & others, 2003).

Significant criticisms have been levelled at Herrnstein and Murray's as well as at Jensen's work (Sternberg, Grigorenko, & Kidd, 2005). The variety of forms these criti-cisms take underscores the complexity of the construct of intelligence. In the first place, while many experts on intelligence generally agree that, for example, African Americans score lower than whites on IQ tests, they raise serious questions about the ability of IQ tests to accurately measure a person's intelligence.

For instance, we saw earlier in this chapter that the tests are culturally biased toward European Americans. John Berry, of Queen's University, has argued forcefully that comparing intelligence across cultures must take into account cultural differences in the notion of intelligence. For example, working with Cree adults in Northern Ontario, Berry & Bennett (1992) showed that Cree conceptions of intelligence differed significantly from those of mainstream Canadians. Interestingly, Aboriginal people liv-ing further from large urban centres tend to have higher IQ scores than those living closer (Berry, 1976). Berry (1996) argues that human cognitive abilities develop in

"You can't build a hut, you don't know how to find edible roots and you know nothing about predicting the weather. In other words, you do *terribly* on our I.Q. test."

© by Sidney Harris.

414 Chapter 10 Intelligence

ecological and cultural contexts. The development of intelligence is inextricably linked to the circumstances of the culture in which it develops. Any attempts to assess intelligence without understanding the relevant cultural factors will produce uninterpretable results (Berry, 2001; Berry & Triandis, 2004). When it comes to the academic performance of African Americans, University of California anthropologist John Ogbu has argued that a cultural bias against "acting white" leads many African American students to perform poorly in intellectual environments (Ogbu, 2004).

In the end, the question is whether we are ever entitled to use the IQ scores of individuals or groups to justify failing to provide them with the best possible work or educational environments. Today, courts in Canada and the U.S. generally refuse to accept IQ scores as a reason for providing a substandard educational experience to any individual or group. Further, tests of general intelligence, in contrast to tests that solely measure fitness for a particular job, are generally viewed as discriminatory and cannot be administered as a condition of employment. Cognitive psychologist Robert J. Sternberg (1994) said that using one index—IQ—as a basis of policy judgment is not only irresponsible, but also dangerous. In the end, we are obliged to provide all individuals and all groups with the best environments possible so that they can develop to the fullest possible extent.

A further criticism of research on ethnic and racial differences in the heredity of intelligence centres on how to appropriately define ethnicity and race in the first place (Bonham, Warshauer-Baker, & Collins, 2005; Sternberg, Grigorenko, & Kidd, 2005). Race is often oversimplified with, for example, skin colour used as a dichotomous variable to split "blacks" and "whites" into two groups whose IQ scores are then compared. This is one more example of ethnic gloss, which we discussed in chapter 2, the tendency to portray an ethnic group as being more homogeneous than it really is. According to Fish (2002), the "black-white" distinction amounts to no more than a popular American myth. Sternberg, Grigorenko, & Kidd (2005) argue that skin colour is not helpful in constructing scientifically valid distinctions between races and suggest that "race" is a socially constructed category, not a biological or genetic one. Similarly, Bonham, Warshauer-Baker, & Collins (2005) argue that currently available genetic data do not provide any support for the notion that the races form populations that are genetically distinct.

A third type of criticism centres on the relationship between environment and heredity in determining intelligence, a topic we explored earlier in this chapter. For example, one criticism is that most research on heredity and environment does not include environments that vary widely. Thus, it is not surprising that many genetic studies show environment to be a fairly weak influence on intelligence (Fraser, 1995). As African Americans have gained social, economic, and educational opportunities, the gap between African Americans and whites on standardized intelligence tests has begun to narrow (Ogbu & Stern, 2001; Ogbu, 2004; Onwuegbuzi & Daley, 2001). This gap especially narrows in college and university, where African American and white students often experience more similar educational environments than in the elementary and high school years (Myerson & others, 1998). Also, when children from disadvantaged African American families are adopted into more-advantaged middle–socioeconomic status families, their scores on intelligence tests more closely resemble national averages for middle–socioeconomic status children than for lower–socioeconomic status children (Scarr & Weinberg, 1983).

Gender Comparisons The average scores of males and females do not differ on intelligence tests, but their scores' variability does differ (Brody, 2000). For example, males are more likely than females to have extremely high or extremely low scores. There are also gender differences in specific intellectual abilities (Brody, 2000). Males score better than females in some nonverbal areas, such as spatial reasoning, and females score better than males in some verbal areas, such as the ability to find synonyms for words. However, as discussed in chapter 4, there is often extensive overlap in the scores of females and males in these areas, and debate continues about how strong such differences are (Eagly, 2001; Eagly, Beall, & Sternberg, 2004; Hyde & Mezulis, 2002).

According to a feminist perspective, the similarities between females and males far out-weigh minor differences (Hyde, 2005).

Haier and his colleagues (2005) have shown that the brains of men and women who perform identically on IQ tests nevertheless differ. Specifically, women show a greater correlation between white matter (neuron axons) and general intelligence, while men show a greater correlation between grey matter (neuron cell bodies) and general intelligence. Further, men show the largest correlations between grey matter and intelligence in the frontal and parietal lobes while women show the largest correlations between white matter and intelligence in the frontal lobes and Broca's area. Haier and his colleagues (2005) conclude that men and women achieve similar levels of general intelligence with different brain organizations.

> **reflect and review**

 Analyze the contributions of heredity and environment to intelligence.

- Discuss the ways in which heredity influences intelligence.
- Identify several ways in which changes in environment can produce gains in intelligence.
- Explain why the interaction of genetics and environment may make it impossible to separate out their relative contributions to intelligence in humans.
- Explain how cultural, ethnic, and gender differences are linked with intelligence.

Someone tells you that he or she has analyzed his or her genetic background and environmental experiences and has reached the conclusion that environment definitely has had little influence on his or her intelligence. What would you say to this person about his or her ability to come to this self-diagnosed conclusion?

Intelligence

1 THE NATURE OF INTELLIGENCE

2 INTELLIGENCE TESTING

— Approaches to Testing — Criteria of a Good Test of Intelligence — Cultural Bias in Testing — The Use and Misuse of Intelligence Tests

3 NEUROSCIENCE AND INTELLIGENCE

— Head and Brain Size — Information Processing Speed — Electrical Activity in the Brain — Energy Consumption in the Brain

4 THEORIES OF MULTIPLE INTELLIGENCES

— Factor Analysis, Two-Factor Theory, and Multiple-Factor Theory — Gardner's Theory of Eight Intelligences — Sternberg's Triarchic Theory — Emotional Intelligence — Evaluating the Multiple-Intelligences Approach

5 THE EXTREMES OF INTELLIGENCE AND CREATIVITY

— Mental Retardation — Giftedness — Creativity

6 THE INFLUENCE OF HEREDITY AND ENVIRONMENT

— Genetic Influences — Environmental Influences — Genetics-Environment Interactions — Group Influences

At the beginning of the chapter, we posed six chapter questions and encouraged you to review material related to these questions at the end of each major section (see pages 386, 393, 396, 401, 408, and 415). Use the following reflection and review features for furthering your understanding of the chapter material.

CHAPTER REFLECTIONS

Apply Your Knowledge

1. There are many different intelligence tests available online. Do a Web search for intelligence tests, and take one. How reliable is the test you took, and how do you know if it's reliable? How well standardized is the test, and on what evidence did you base your answer? How valid is the test, and how do you know what its validity is?

2. Think about the tests used to assess intelligence. Now consider the ways in which neuroscientists have tried to determine the neural basis of intelligence. Do the tasks that have been assessed by neuroscientists match those used in other intelligence tests? How might this contribute to the kinds of answers neuroscientists have gotten?

3. What is, or should be, the purpose of intelligence testing? To determine who will do well in school? To determine what career someone should pursue? To keep psychologists occupied? Given what you think the purpose should be, which definition of intelligence is most useful?

4. Consider the characteristics of gifted people and creative people. Which would you rather be? Why? If you had children, which would you rather have, gifted children or creative children? Why?

5. One controversial theory about intelligence suggests a relationship between birth order and intelligence: The IQs of children born first are higher than those of children born second, and so on. Imagine this is true. What would this tell you about the role of environment and heredity on intelligence? What does it say about large families? Now imagine it's not true. What factors might have influenced researchers to make this conclusion erroneously?

CHAPTER REVIEW

Describe what intelligence is.

• Intelligence consists of the ability to solve problems and to adapt and learn from everyday experiences. A key aspect of intelligence involves individual variations. Traditionally, intelligence has been measured by tests designed to compare people's performance on cognitive tasks.

Explain how intelligence is measured and what the limitations of intelligence tests are.

• Sir Frances Galton is the father of mental tests. Alfred Binet developed the first intelligence test and created the concept of mental age. William Stern developed the concept of IQ for use with the Binet test. Revisions of the Binet test are called the Stanford-Binet. The test scores on the Stanford-Binet approximate a normal distribution. The Wechsler scales, created by David Wechsler, are the other main intelligence-assessment tool. These tests provide an overall IQ, verbal and performance IQs, and information from 14 subtests. Group intelligence tests are convenient and economical, but they do not allow an examiner to closely monitor the testing. Aptitude tests like the CTCS (Canadian Test of Cognitive Skills) predict an individual's ability to learn a skill or future performance. Achievement tests like the CAT (Canadian Achievement Tests) assess what a person already knows. The distinction between these two types of tests is sometimes blurred.

• A good test of intelligence meets three criteria: validity, reliability, and standardization. Validity is the extent to which a test measures what it is intended to measure. Validity can be assessed in terms of criterion validity, the degree to which a test correlates with another measure, or criterion, of what the test purports to measure. Reliability means how consistently an individual performs on a test. Standardization focuses on uniform procedures for administering and scoring a test; it also involves norms.

• Early intelligence tests favoured white, middle-class–socioeconomic status, urban individuals. Culture-fair tests are intelligence tests that are intended to be culturally unbiased. Many psychologists believe that such culture-fair tests cannot replace traditional intelligence tests.

When used by a judicious examiner, tests can be valuable tools for determining individual differences in intelligence. Test scores should be used with other types of information to evaluate an individual. IQ scores can produce unfortunate stereotypes and expectations. Ability tests can help divide children into homogeneous groups, but periodic testing should be done to ensure that the groupings are appropriate.

Identify four neuroscience approaches to intelligence.

- In general, researchers have found that a larger head size and a larger brain size, especially larger brain size, are associated with higher intelligence. However, because these findings are correlational, it's not certain whether a large head or brain size causes greater intelligence or vice versa.

- There is a correlation between information processing speed, often measured as reaction time, and IQ scores. Higher scores are linked with faster, or shorter, reaction times. However, the relation of processing speed to intelligence is complex, and processing speed by itself does not determine intelligence.

- Efforts to link electrical activity in the brain and intelligence have focused on measures of nerve conduction velocity and evoked potential. Studies of nerve conduction velocity have yielded inconsistent results, but studies of evoked potential show more robust correlation with intelligence.

- Individuals with higher intelligence test scores demonstrate increased brain activity (increased use of glucose) when they are engaged in a cognitive activity of their own choosing. However, individuals with higher intelligence successfully complete an assigned task using less energy. This finding may mean that individuals with high intelligence have more active brains than those with less intelligence and use them more efficiently.

Evaluate theories of multiple intelligence.

- Factor analysis is a statistical procedure that compares various items or measures and identifies factors that are correlated with each other. Spearman (two-factor theory of *g* and *s*) and Thurstone (multiple-factor theory) used factor analysis in developing their views of intelligence.

- Gardner believes there are eight types of intelligence: verbal skills, mathematical skills, spatial skills, bodily-kinesthetic skills, musical skills, interpersonal skills, intrapersonal skills, and naturalist skills. Project Spectrum applies Gardner's view to educating children.

- Sternberg's triarchic theory states there are three main types of intelligence: analytical, creative, and practical.

- Emotional intelligence is the ability to monitor one's own and others' feelings and emotions, to discriminate among them, and to use this information to guide one's thinking and actions. Goleman popularized emotional intelligence.

- The multiple-intelligences approaches have broadened the definition of intelligence and motivated educators to develop programs that instruct students in different domains. Critics maintain that the multiple-intelligences theories include factors that are not really part of intelligence, such as musical skills and creativity. Critics also say that there is not enough research to support the concept of multiple intelligences.

Discuss characteristics of mental retardation, giftedness, and creativity.

- Mental retardation is a condition of limited mental ability in which the individual has a low IQ, usually below 70, has difficulty adapting to everyday life; and has an onset of these characteristics during the so-called developmental period. Most affected individuals have IQs in the 55 to 70 range (mild retardation). Mental retardation can have an organic cause (called organic retardation) or can be social and cultural in origin (called cultural-familial retardation).

- People who are gifted have high intelligence (IQs of 120 or higher) and/or superior talent for a particular domain. Three characteristics of gifted children are precocity, marching to one's own drummer, and a passion to master. Giftedness is likely a consequence of both heredity and environment.

- Creativity is the ability to think about something in novel and unusual ways and come up with unconventional solutions to problems. The difference between intelligence and creativity is the ability to produce something original or unique. Creative people tend to be divergent thinkers who can see more than one possible answer to a question. Traditional intelligence test questions have only one correct answer and thus measure convergent thinking. Creativity has often been described as occurring in a five-step process: preparation, incubation, insight, evaluation, and elaboration. Characteristics of creative thinkers include flexibility and playful thinking, inner motivation, willingness to risk, and objective evaluation of work. Csikszentmihalyi believes that cultivating curiosity and interest is the first step toward a more creative life.

Analyze the contributions of heredity and environment to intelligence.

- At least 150 genes have already been linked to intelligence. Genetic similarity might explain why identical twins show stronger correlations on intelligence tests than fraternal twins do. Some studies indicate that the IQs of adopted children are more similar to the IQs of their biological parents than to those of their adoptive parents. Many studies show that intelligence has a reasonably strong heritability component, although criticisms of the heritability concept have been made.

- Intelligence test scores have risen considerably around the world in recent decades—called the Flynn effect—which supports the role of environment in intelligence. Environmental influences on intelligence have been demonstrated in studies of the effects of parenting, intervention programs for children at risk for having low IQs and dropping out of school, and sociohistorical changes. Researchers have found that how much parents talk with their children in the first three years of life is correlated with the children's IQs. Ramey's research revealed the positive effects of educational child care on intelligence. The increasing complexity of popular culture may also exert a positive effect in intelligence.

- The likelihood that genetics and environment interact may make it impossible to separate out their relative contributions to intelligence in humans.

- Among the ways that group influences can be linked with intelligence are comparisons of cultures, ethnic groups, and males and females. Cultures vary in the way they define intelligence. In the United States, children from African American and Latino families score below children from white families on standardized intelligence tests; the extent to which such differences are caused by heredity or environment is controversial. The average scores of males and females do not differ on intelligence tests, but variability in their scores does differ. For example, males are more likely than females to have extremely high or extremely low scores. There are also gender differences in specific intellectual abilities.

CONNECTIONS

For extra help in mastering the material in the chapter, see the review questions and practice quizzes in the Student Study Guide and the Online Learning Centre.

CORE TERMS

Motivation and Emotion

CHAPTER QUESTIONS

1 What are some psychological approaches to motivation?

2 What is the physiological basis of hunger and the nature of eating behaviour?

3 What is the motivation for sex?

4 What are the social cognitive motives and how do they influence behaviour?

5 What is emotion and what factors underlie it?

Perhaps it is no accident that Douglas Coupland, who became famous writing about the lack of motivation of Gen X, has recently written a book about Terry Fox, whose achievements stand as a testament to what motivation can accomplish in the face of adversity (Coupland, 2005).

In 1980, Terry died of cancer attempting to run across Canada. During his Marathon of Hope he averaged 42.2 km a day for five months as he ran 5372 km across six Canadian provinces. That's a marathon every day for 143 days. He had already lost his leg to cancer and completed his gruelling run with the aid of a prosthetic limb. What motivated Terry to undertake his run? When he was hospitalized with cancer, he decided that if he survived he would do something to generate funds for cancer research. Terry raised $24,000,000 for cancer research before he died. Terry's accomplishments are all the more impressive when we consider that he was only an average athlete and had a shy, introverted personality. Once his motivation had kicked in, however, he completed one of the most meaningful runs in history.

Terry Fox's feat has, in turn, motivated generations of Canadians. His friend, Rick Hansen, left a paraplegic at 15 by an automobile accident, was already on his way to winning 19 wheelchair marathons around the world. But in 1985, he followed Terry's lead and launched Wheels in Motion, his own fundraising effort. When he was done, Rick had wheeled 40,000 kilometres through 34 countries on four continents, the equivalent of an around-the-world tour. Rick raised $26,000,000 for spinal cord injury research. Every year, Terry's and Rick's stories motivate tens of thousands of Canadians to walk, cycle, skate, or run to raise money, and countless others to donate millions of dollars for medical research.

When you are motivated, you do something. The way you feel—your emotions—can either strengthen or weaken your motivation. For Terry Fox, and his friend Rick Hansen, motivation and emotion played a significant role in their accomplishments:

- *Motivation*: The intense motivation required to make it through the gruelling day-after-day struggles; the motivation to battle severe disabilities; the motivation to continue to make a difference in the lives of others.

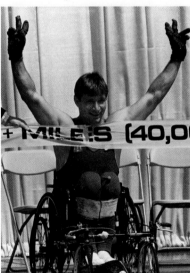

- *Emotion*: The anger that emerged when Terry found out he had cancer and when Rick suffered his injuries; their fear that they would die; the happiness of raising millions for medical research, and the joy of affecting the lives of millions of Canadians.

Hunger, sex, achievement, affiliation, and well-being are five important motives in our lives. Hunger is usually described as a biological motive; sex is categorized as a bridge between biological and social cognitive motives; and achievement, affiliation, and well-being are portrayed as social cognitive motives. Each of these areas of motivation is examined in greater depth in the chapter.

Terry Fox and Rick Hansen in moments of personal triumph exemplify the power of motivation.

Motivations differ not only in kind, such as an individual being motivated to eat rather than have sex, but also in intensity. We can speak of an individual as being more or less hungry or more or less motivated to have sex. The first section looks at different approaches to motivation.

① APPROACHES TO MOTIVATION

The Evolutionary Approach	Drive Reduction Theory	Optimum Arousal Theory	The Cognitive Approach	Issues in Motivation

How do psychologists think about motivation?

Motivation and emotion are closely linked. The terms *motivation* and *emotion* both come from the Latin word *movere*, which means "to move." Both motivation and emotion spur us into action. We will begin with an examination of motivation. We are all motivated, but some of us are motivated to do different things. Thus, some students are motivated to watch television, others to study for an exam. **Motivation** moves people to behave, think, and feel the way they do. Motivated behaviour is energized, directed, and sustained.

There is no shortage of theories about why organisms are motivated to do what they do (Gardner & Tremblay, 1995; R. C. Beck, 2004). Let's explore the main approaches to motivation, beginning with the evolutionary approach, which emphasizes the biological basis of motivation.

The Evolutionary Approach

Early in psychology's history, the evolutionary approach emphasized the role of instincts in motivation. Ethology also has described motivation from an evolutionary perspective.

An **instinct** is an innate (unlearned), biological pattern of behaviour that is assumed to be universal throughout a species. A student of Darwin's evolutionary theory, American psychologist William McDougall (1908) argued that all behaviour involves instincts. In particular, he said that we have instincts for acquisitiveness, curiosity, pugnacity, gregariousness, and self-assertion. At about the same time, Sigmund Freud (1917) argued that behaviour is based on instinct. Freud believed that sex and aggression were especially powerful instincts.

It was not long before a number of psychologists had crafted laundry lists of instincts, some of them running to thousands of items. However, it soon became apparent that what the early instinct theorists were doing was naming a behaviour rather than explaining it. If we say that people have an instinct for sex or for curiosity or for acquisitiveness, we are merely naming these behaviours, not explaining them.

Although the approach of merely labelling behaviours as instincts landed in psychology's trash heap many years ago, the idea that some motivation is unlearned is still alive and well today. It is widely accepted that instinctive behaviour is common in non-human species. In chapter 4 you learned that human infants come into the world equipped with some unlearned instincts such as sucking. Most attachment theorists also believe that infants have an unlearned instinct for orienting toward a caregiver.

Recently, evolutionary psychology, which was discussed in chapters 1 and 3, has rekindled interest in the evolutionary basis of motivation. According to evolutionary psychologists such as David Buss (Buss, 2004) and McMaster's Denys deCatanzaro (1999), to understand motivation it is necessary to examine its evolutionary ties. They argue that the motivation for sex, aggression, achievement, and other behaviours is rooted in our evolutionary past. Thus, a species may be highly competitive because competitiveness provided an advantage and was passed down through the genes from generation to generation.

Drive Reduction Theory

If you do not have an instinct for sex, maybe you have a drive or a need for it. A **drive** is an aroused state that occurs because of a physiological need. A **need** is a deprivation that energizes the drive to eliminate or reduce the deprivation. You might have a

motivation Why people behave, think, and feel the way they do. Motivated behaviour is energized, directed, and sustained.

instinct An innate (unlearned), biological pattern of behaviour that is assumed to be universal throughout a species.

drive An aroused state that occurs because of a physiological need.

need A deprivation that energizes the drive to eliminate or reduce the deprivation.

need for water, for food, or for sex. The body's need for food, for example, arouses your hunger drive. Hunger motivates you to do something—to go out for a hamburger, for example—to reduce the drive and satisfy the need. Drive reduction theory explains that, as a drive becomes stronger, we are motivated to reduce it (Deckers, 2005).

Usually, but not always, needs and drives are closely associated in time. For example, when your body needs food, your hunger drive will probably be aroused. An hour after you have eaten a hamburger, you might still be hungry (thus you need food), but your hunger drive might have subsided. From this example you can sense that drive pertains to a psychological state; need involves a physiological state.

The goal of drive reduction is **homeostasis**, the body's tendency to maintain an equilibrium, or steady state. Literally hundreds of biological states in our bodies must be maintained within a certain range: temperature, blood sugar level, potassium and sodium levels, oxygen, and so on. When you walk out into the cold of a winter day, your body may shiver, thus using energy to maintain its normal temperature. When you walk out of an air-conditioned room into the heat of a summer day, your body may release excess heat by sweating. These physiological changes occur automatically to keep your body in an optimal state of functioning.

An analogy for homeostasis is the thermostat that keeps the temperature constant in a house. For example, assume that the thermostat in your house is set at 20° during the winter. The furnace heats the house to 20°, and then it shuts off. Without a source of heat, the temperature in the house eventually falls below 20°—if the outside temperature is below 20°. The thermostat detects this change and turns the furnace back on again. The cycle is repeated so that the temperature is maintained within narrow limits. Today, homeostasis is used to explain both physiological and psychological balances and imbalances (Berridge, 2004).

Most psychologists believe that drive reduction theory does not provide a comprehensive framework for understanding motivation because people often behave in ways that increase rather than reduce a drive. For example, they might skip meals in an effort to lose weight, which can increase their hunger drive rather than reduce it. Consider also people who seek stimulation and thrills, say, by bungee jumping or riding a roller coaster. Instead of reducing a drive, they appear to be increasing their level of stimulation.

Optimum Arousal Theory

The circumstance just described—seeking stimulation and thrills—suggests that individuals seek arousal (a state of alertness or activation) in their lives. Is there an optimum level of arousal that motivates behaviour? Early in this century, two psychologists, Robert Yerkes and John Dodson, described what optimum arousal might be (Hancock & Ganey, 2003). Their formulation, now known as the **Yerkes-Dodson law**, states that performance is best under conditions of moderate arousal than either low or high arousal. At the low end of arousal, you might be too lethargic to perform tasks well; at the high end, you may not be able to concentrate. Think about how aroused you were the last time you took a test. If your arousal was too high, your performance probably suffered. If it was too low, you may not have worked fast enough to finish the test. Also, think about performance in sports. Being too aroused usually harms athletes' performance. For example, a thumping heart and rapid breathing have accompanied many golfers' missed putts and curlers' failed draw attempts. However, if athletes' arousal is too low, they may not concentrate well on the task at hand.

Moderate arousal often serves us best in tackling life's tasks, but there are times when low or high arousal produces optimal performance. For well-learned or simple tasks (signing your name, pushing a button on request), optimal arousal may be quite high. In contrast, when learning a task or doing something complex (solving an algebraic equation), much lower arousal is preferred. Figure 11.1 projects how arousal might influence easy, moderate, and difficult tasks. As tasks become more difficult, the ability to be alert and attentive but relaxed is critical to optimal performance.

homeostasis The body's tendency to maintain an equilibrium, or steady state.

Yerkes-Dodson law States that performance is best under conditions of moderate arousal than under those of low or high arousal.

FIGURE 11.1

Arousal and Performance
The Yerkes-Dodson law states that optimal performance occurs under moderate arousal. However, for new or difficult tasks, low arousal may be best; for well-learned, easy tasks, high arousal may be best.

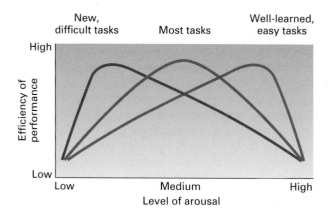

As mentioned earlier, some people seek a great deal of stimulation in their lives and enjoy the thrill of engaging in risky behaviour (Roberti, 2004). *Sensation seeking* is the motivation to experience varied, novel, complex, and intense sensations and experiences. It also involves the willingness to take risks just for the sake of such an experience.

Marvin Zuckerman (2000, 2002) has found that high sensation seekers are more likely than low sensation seekers to

- Be motivated to engage in sports such as mountain climbing, parachuting, hang gliding, scuba diving, car and motorcycle racing, and downhill skiing
- Be attracted to vocations involving exciting experiences, such as firefighting, emergency-room work, and air traffic control (when confined to monotonous desk jobs, they report high job dissatisfaction)
- Drink heavily, smoke, and use illicit drugs
- Have a short-term hedonistic attitude toward intimate relationships (high sensation seekers also tend to engage in more varied sexual activities with more partners)

The Cognitive Approach

The contemporary view of motivation emphasizes cognitive factors (Zimmerman & Campillo, 2003). Consider your motivation to do well in this class. Your confidence in your ability to do well and your expectation for success may help you to relax, concentrate better, and study more effectively. If you think too much about not doing well in the class and fear that you will fail, you can become too anxious and not perform as well. Your ability to consciously control your behaviour and resist the temptation to party too much and avoid studying will improve your achievement, as will your ability to use your information processing abilities of attention, memory, and problem solving as you study for and take tests.

Psychologists continue to debate the role of conscious versus unconscious thought in understanding motivation. Freud's legacy to contemporary psychodynamic theory is the belief that we are largely unaware of why we behave the way we do (Mills, 2004). Psychodynamic theorists argue that few of us know why we love someone, why we eat so much, why we are so aggressive, or why we are so shy. Although some cognitive psychologists have begun to study the role of the unconscious mind, for the most part they emphasize that human beings are rational and aware of their motivation. Humanistic theorists also stress our ability to examine our lives and become aware of what motivates us.

intrinsic motivation Based on internal factors, such as self-determination, curiosity, challenge, and effort.

extrinsic motivation Involves external incentives, such as rewards and punishments.

Intrinsic and Extrinsic Motivation Intrinsic motivation is a key aspect of the cognitive approach to motivation. **Intrinsic motivation** is based on internal factors such as self-determination, curiosity, challenge, and effort. **Extrinsic motivation** involves external incentives such as rewards and punishments. Some students study hard because they are internally motivated to put forth considerable effort and achieve high quality in their work (intrinsic motivation). Other students study hard because they want to make good grades or avoid parental disapproval (extrinsic motivation).

Some psychologists stress that many highly successful individuals are both intrinsically motivated (have a high personal standard of achievement and emphasize personal effort) and extrinsically motivated (are highly competitive). Terry Fox is a good example. Fox had an incredible amount of intrinsic motivation to come back from losing a leg to cancer to mount his Marathon of Hope. However, the extrinsic motivation of raising millions for cancer research likely also played a role.

In general, most psychologists believe intrinsic motivation leads to greater achievement than extrinsic motivation does (Deci, Koestner, & Ryan, 2001; Baard, Deci, & Ryan, 2004). They argue that intrinsic motivation is more likely to produce improved performance, mastery, persistence, creativity, and self-esteem (Deci & Ryan, 2002). Especially important is the view that self-determination (which is intrinsic) produces a sense of personal control (Gagné & Deci, 2005). Feehan & Enzle (1991) have shown that subjective control (even when it is illusory) acts to protect intrinsic motivation. The problem, then, with using a reward as an incentive is that individuals may perceive that the reward is what caused their achievement behaviour rather than their own motivation to be competent. Researchers have found, for instance, that students' internal motivation and intrinsic interest in school tasks increases when they have some choice and some opportunities to take responsibility for their learning (Stipek, 2001).

Almost every boss, parent, or teacher has wondered whether to offer a reward to someone who does well (extrinsic motivation) or whether to let the results of the individual's self-determined efforts be the reward (intrinsic motivation). If someone is producing shoddy work, seems bored, or has a negative attitude, offering incentives may improve motivation. But there are times when external rewards can diminish achievement motivation. One classic study showed that, among students who already had a strong interest in art, those who did not expect a reward spent more time drawing than their counterparts who knew they would be rewarded for drawing (Lepper, Greene, & Nisbett, 1973). According to University of Alberta psychologist Michael Enzle, a wide variety of events, such as deadlines, surveillance (Enzle & Anderson, 1993), and coercive rewards (Enzle, Roggeveen, & Look, 1991) can reduce the enjoyment of work, play, and study. These ideas have exerted a broad influence in educational and occupational settings, where teachers and employers seek to increase the intrinsic motivation of their students and employees, respectively (Stipek, 2001; Wigfield & Eccles, 2002).

According to University of Alberta educational psychologist Judy Cameron and her colleagues (Cameron, Banko, & Pierce, 2001; Cameron & Pierce, 2002), however, the effects of extrinsic motivation are not always negative. For example, people often do things that are not intrinsically motivating (such as mowing the lawn or, for them, studying mathematics). Without external rewards, they may simply lose interest in doing them (Cameron, Banko, & Pierce, 2001; Cameron & Pierce, 2002). In such cases, extrinsic motivation may help foster intrinsic motivation in an activity. For example, a creative mathematics teacher might use rewards, such as extra credit, math games, and verbal praise, as a way to instill a life-long love of mathematics.

Even when intrinsic motivation is high, the effects of extrinsic motivation need not always be negative. For example, while tangible reinforcers, such as money or prizes, can undermine intrinsic motivation, verbal reinforcers, such as praise, can actually enhance intrinsic motivation (Gear, Wizniak, & Cameron, 2004). Thus, paying a beginning reader money to read books may undermine that child's interest in reading, but praising that child for good reading may increase the same child's interest. Similarly, Cameron believes that extrinsic motivation undermines intrinsic motivation when intrinsic motivation is high but can be very helpful when intrinsic motivation is low (Cameron, Banko, & Pierce, 2001). Thus, many beginning readers who are motivated to read may actually lose interest if they are reinforced for reading. In contrast, children who are not internally motivated to read may benefit from reinforcement and encouragement until their intrinsic motivation increases.

FIGURE 11.2
Maslow's Hierarchy of Needs
Abraham Maslow developed the hierarchy of human needs to show that we have to satisfy basic physiological needs before we can satisfy other, higher needs.

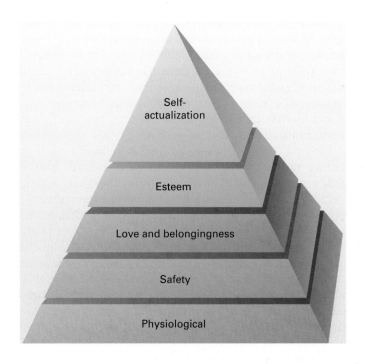

The Importance of Self-Generated Goals Currently, there is considerable interest in studying people's self-generated goals (Eccles & Wigfield, 2002). Our intrinsic motivation is highest when we are pursuing goals we have set for ourselves. Some examples of these goals are personal projects, life tasks, and personal strivings. Personal projects can range from trivial pursuits (such as letting a bad haircut grow out) to life goals (such as becoming a good parent). Life tasks are problems individuals are currently working on. They usually focus on normal life transitions such as going to university, getting married, and entering an occupation. Many university students say that their life tasks revolve around academic achievement and social concerns. Personal strivings represent what a person is typically trying to do. For example, someone might say that she typically tries to do well in school. We explore goal setting in greater detail later, when we discuss achievement.

Maslow's Hierarchy of Human Needs Is getting an A in this class more important than eating? If the person of your dreams told you that you were marvellous, would that motivate you to throw yourself in front of a car for that person's safety? According to the humanistic theorist Abraham Maslow (1954, 1971), our basic needs must be satisfied before our higher needs. Maslow's **hierarchy of needs** states that individuals' main needs are satisfied in the following sequence: physiological, safety, love and belongingness, esteem, and self-actualization (see figure 11.2). According to this hierarchy, people are motivated to satisfy their need for food first. Their need for safety must be satisfied before their need for love.

Self-actualization, the highest and most elusive of Maslow's needs, is the motivation to develop one's full potential as a human being (Reiss & Havercamp, 2005). According to Maslow, self-actualization is possible only after the other needs in the hierarchy are met. Maslow cautions that most people stop maturing after they have developed a high level of esteem and thus do not become self-actualized. Many of Maslow's writings focus on how people can reach this elusive motivational state. Self-actualization is discussed further in chapter 12.

The idea that human motives are hierarchically arranged is an appealing one. Maslow's theory stimulates us to think about how we order motives in our own lives. However, how we order our needs is somewhat subjective. Some people might seek greatness in a career to achieve self-esteem, while putting on hold their needs for love and belongingness.

hierarchy of needs Maslow's view that individuals' main needs are satisfied in the following sequence: physiological, safety, love and belongingness, esteem, and self-actualization.

self-actualization The highest and most elusive of Maslow's needs; the motivation to develop one's full potential as a human being.

Issues in Motivation

In the discussion of dimensions of motivation, three important issues were discussed: (1) To what degree are we motivated by innate, unlearned, biological factors as opposed to learned, experientially based factors? (2) To what degree are we aware of what motivates us—that is, to what extent is our motivation conscious? (3) To what degree are we internally or externally motivated? These are issues that researchers continue to wrangle with and debate.

Keep in mind that, although we separated the biological, cognitive, and behavioural/social/cultural underpinnings of motivation for the purpose of organization and clarification, in reality they are often interrelated. For example, in the study of social cognition, psychologists call attention to how contextual/social factors interact with thinking to determine our motivation. Thus a person's achievement motivation might be influenced by both the person's optimistic outlook (cognitive) and his or her relationship with an outstanding mentor (social).

> **> reflect and review**

 Describe psychological approaches to motivation.

- Define motivation and instinct and explain the evolutionary approach to motivation.
- Summarize drive reduction theory.
- Discuss optimum arousal theory.
- Identify the cognitive factors involved in emotion.
- Characterize Maslow's hierarchy of human needs.
- List three main issues in motivation research.

Advertisers often draw on Maslow's hierarchy of human needs to sell their products. Look through some magazine advertisements for evidence of Maslow's hierarchy.

---

2 HUNGER

| The Biology of Hunger | Obesity and Eating | Dieting | Eating Disorders |

What is the physiological basis of hunger and the nature of eating behaviour?
As Maslow's hierarchy indicates, hunger is a very basic human need and a powerful motivator. Food is an important aspect of life in all cultures. Whether we have very small or large amounts of food available to us, hunger influences our behaviour. We have to eat to stay alive. What mechanisms cause us to feel hungry?

The Biology of Hunger

You are sitting in class and it is 2 p.m. You were so busy today that you skipped lunch. As the professor lectures, your stomach starts to growl. What role, if any, do such gastric signals play in hunger?

Gastric Signals In 1912, Walter Cannon and A. L. Washburn conducted an experiment that revealed a close association between stomach contractions and hunger (see figure 11.3). As part of the procedure, a partially inflated balloon was passed through a tube inserted in Washburn's mouth and pushed down into his stomach. A machine that measures air pressure was connected to the balloon to monitor Washburn's stomach contractions. Every time Washburn reported hunger pangs, his stomach was also contracting.

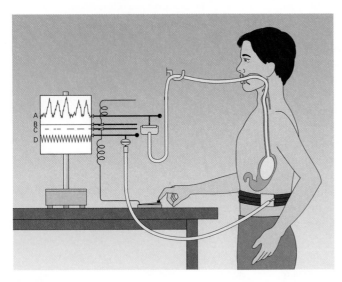

FIGURE 11.3 Cannon and Washburn's Classic Experiment on Hunger

In this experiment, the researchers demonstrated that stomach contractions, which were detected by the stomach balloon, accompany a person's hunger feelings, which were indicated by pressing the key. Line A in the chart records increases and decreases in the volume of the balloon in the participant's stomach. Line B records the passage of time. Line C records the participant's manual signals of feelings of hunger. Line D records a reading from the belt around the participant's waist to detect movements of the abdominal wall and ensure that such movements are not the cause of changes in stomach volume.

This finding, which was confirmed in subsequent experiments with other volunteers, led the two researchers to believe that gastric activity was *the* basis for hunger.

Stomach signals are not the only factors that affect hunger, however. People whose stomachs have been surgically removed still get hunger pangs. And, the stomach may contract to signal hunger, but the stomach can also send signals that stop hunger. We all know that a full stomach can decrease our appetite. In fact, the stomach actually tells the brain not only how full it is but also how much nutrient is present. That is why rich food stops your hunger faster than the same amount of water. The hormone *cholecystokinin* (*CCK*) helps start the digestion of food, travels to the brain through the bloodstream, and signals you to stop eating (Naslund, Hellstrom, and Kral, 2001; Geary, 2004). As explained in the following sections, there is a lot more involved in hunger than an empty stomach.

Blood Chemistry Four important chemical substances are involved in hunger, eating, and satiety (the sense of being filled and not wanting to eat more): glucose, insulin, leptin, and ghrelin.

Glucose (blood sugar) is an important factor in hunger, probably because the brain is critically dependent on sugar for energy. One set of sugar receptors, located in the brain itself, triggers hunger when sugar levels fall too low. Another set of sugar receptors is in the liver, which stores excess sugar and releases it into the blood when needed. The sugar receptors in the liver signal the brain when its sugar supply falls, and this signal can also make you hungry. When we eat complex carbohydrates such as cereals, bread, and pasta, blood sugar levels go up but then fall off gradually. When we consume simple sugars such as candy bars and Cokes, blood sugar levels rise and then fall off sharply—the all-too-familiar "sugar low."

The consequence is that we are more likely to eat within the next several hours after eating simple sugars than after eating complex carbohydrates. And the food we eat at one meal often influences how much we will eat at our next meal. So consuming doughnuts and candy bars, which provide no nutritional value, sets up an ongoing sequence of what and how much we will probably crave the next time we eat.

Another important factor in blood sugar control is insulin, the hormone that is released into the blood from the pancreas as blood sugar rises. Insulin helps to metabolize blood sugar into the body and brain and causes excess blood sugar in the blood to be stored in cells as fats and carbohydrates (Williams & others, 2004). Insulin injections cause profound hunger because they lower blood sugar drastically. A lack of insulin results in *diabetes*, the build up of excess sugar in the bloodstream, damaging small blood vessels and, in turn, damaging the heart, the kidneys, the eyes and the extremities.

Another pair of chemical substances, *ghrelin* and *leptin* are directly involved in controlling our feelings of hunger and of satiety. Ghrelin, a hormone that is released by the stomach lining, increases feelings of hunger via the hypothalamus (Olszewski & others, 2003). Ghrelin levels are elevated before meals and drop afterwards. According to Schmid & colleagues (2005), when our ghrelin levels are elevated we are not only hungry, we find ourselves imagining food. Leptin (from the Greek word *leptos,* which means "thin"), a protein that is released by fat cells, decreases food intake and increases energy expenditure (Oberbauer & others, 2001; Williams & others, 2004).

The role of leptin in long-term satiety was discovered in a strain of *ob mice,* genetically obese mice (Campfield & others, 1995; Carlson, 2005). The ob mouse has a low metabolism, overeats, and gets extremely fat. A particular gene called *ob* normally produces leptin. However, because of a genetic mutation, the fat cells of ob mice cannot

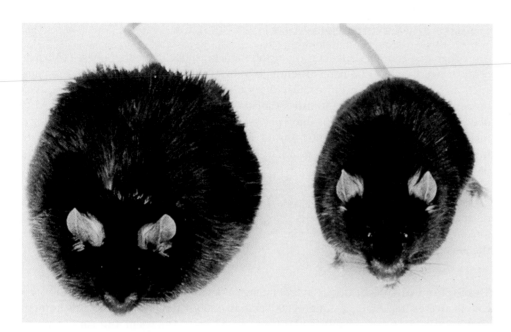

FIGURE 11.4
Leptin and Obesity
The ob mouse on the left is untreated; the one on the right has been given injections of leptin.

produce leptin. Leptin strongly affects metabolism and eating, acting as an antiobesity hormone (Misra & others, 2001). If ob mice are given daily injections of leptin, their metabolic rate increases, they become more active, and they eat less. Consequently, their weight falls to a normal level. Figure 11.4 shows an untreated ob mouse and an ob mouse that has received injections of leptin.

In humans, leptin concentrations have been linked with weight, percentage of body fat, weight loss in a single diet episode, and cumulative percentage of weight loss in all diet episodes (Benini & others, 2001; Van Dielen & others, 2002). Today, scientists are interested in the possibility that leptin might help obese individuals lose weight (Wauters & others, 2001).

Brain Processes   Chapter 3 described the central role of the hypothalamus in regulating important body functions, including hunger. More specifically, activity in two areas of the hypothalamus contributes to our understanding of hunger. The *lateral hypothalamus* is involved in stimulating eating. When it is electrically stimulated in a well-fed animal, the animal begins to eat. And if this area of the hypothalamus is destroyed, even a starving animal will show no interest in food. Ghrelin influences eating by stimulating the lateral hypothalamus (Olszewski & others, 2003).

The *ventromedial hypothalamus* is involved in reducing hunger and restricting eating. When this area of an animal's brain is stimulated, the animal stops eating. When the area is destroyed, the animal eats profusely and quickly becomes obese. Leptin influences eating by inhibiting the production of a neuropeptide neurotransmitter in the ventromedial hypothalamus that induces eating (Cowley & others, 2001; A. Sorensen & others, 2002).

Today, neuroscientists believe that, although the lateral and ventromedial hypothalamus play roles in hunger, there is much more to the brain's role in determining hunger than these on/off centres in the hypothalamus. They are exploring how neurotransmitters (the chemical messengers that convey information from neuron to neuron) and neural circuits (clusters of neurons that often involve different parts of the brain) function in hunger.

The neurotransmitter serotonin is partly responsible for the satiating effect of CCK, and serotonin antagonists have been used to treat obesity in humans (Bray, 2005; Thrybom, Rooth, & Lindstrom, 2001). Neural circuits involved in the action of such drugs may be in the brain stem, as well as the hypothalamus (Carlson, 2005). The neural circuitry also extends to the cerebral cortex, where humans make decisions about whether to eat or not to eat.

Obesity and Eating Behaviour

More than one-third of Canadians (Statistics Canada, 2004c) are either obese (14.9 percent) or overweight (33.3 percent) enough to be at increased risk for health problems such as hypertension, cardiovascular disease, and diabetes. Obesity rates are even higher in the United States (Statistics Canada, 2003). The health-care costs linked to obesity are estimated to be $50 billion per year in North America. The rate of obesity is increasing (Statistics Canada, 2004c). And, obesity often becomes more common with increased age, especially among women. Thus, as baby boomers age, the number of obese individuals is likely to continue to increase.

Why do so many North Americans overeat to the point of being obese? As is the case with much behaviour, biological, cognitive, and sociocultural factors interact in diverse ways in different individuals, making it difficult to point to a specific cause. Let's look at some of the factors that are known to contribute to overeating, beginning with the biological causes.

The Biology of Overeating Several biological factors have been proposed to play a role in overeating. Pinel, Assanand, & Lehman (2000) have suggested that humans evolved at a time when reliable food sources were scarce. As a result, our earliest ancestors probably evolved a tendency to eat as much as possible when food was freely available. In the past, this mechanism was adaptive because it resulted in excess fat serving as a buffer against the unpredictability of food supplies and the inevitable food shortages. However, when plentiful food is always available, the result is obesity. Similarly, our ancestors probably also developed a preference for sweets, because ripe fruit, which is a concentrated source of sugar (and calories), was so accessible. Today many people still have a "sweet tooth," but, unlike our ancestors' ripe fruit that contained sugar plus vitamins and minerals, the soft drinks and candy bars we snack on today often fill us with nutrient-free calories.

Until recently, the genetic component of obesity was underestimated. As discussed earlier, scientists discovered an ob gene in mice that controls the production of leptin. In the 1990s, a similar gene was found in humans. Some individuals do inherit a tendency to be overweight (Kowalski, 2004; Yanovski & Yanovski, 2002). Only 10 percent of children who do not have obese parents become obese themselves, whereas 40 percent of children who have one obese parent become obese, and 70 percent of children who have two obese parents become obese. Further, identical human twins have similar weights, even when they are reared apart. Estimates of the degree to which heredity can explain obesity range from 25 to 70 percent.

Another factor in weight is **basal metabolism rate (BMR)**, the minimal amount of energy an individual uses in a resting state (Marra & others, 2002). BMR varies with age and sex. It declines precipitously during adolescence and then more gradually in adulthood; it is slightly higher for males than for females (see figure 11.5). Many people gradually increase their weight over many years. To some degree, this weight gain can be due to a declining basal metabolism rate.

Set point, the weight maintained when no effort is made to gain or lose weight, is determined in part by the amount of stored fat in the body. Fat is stored in *adipose cells*, or fat cells. When these cells are filled, you do not get hungry. When people gain weight—because of genetic predisposition, childhood eating patterns, or adult overeating—the number and size of their fat cells increases, and they might not be able to get rid of extra ones. A normal-weight individual has 30 to 40 billion fat cells. An obese individual has 80 to 120 billion fat cells. Consequently, an obese individual has to eat more to feel satisfied. Some scientists have proposed that fat cells may shrink but might not go away.

Researchers have found that a high-fat diet may raise a person's set point for body weight (Frederich & others, 1995; Harris, Bowen, & Mitchell, 2003). They have also found that exercise can lower the body's set point for weight and contribute to weight loss (Rosenbaum, Leibel, & Hirsch, 1997).

basal metabolism rate (BMR) The minimal amount of energy an individual uses in a resting state.

set point The weight maintained when no effort is made to gain or lose weight.

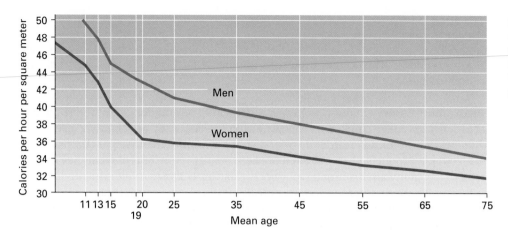

FIGURE 11.5

Changes in Basal Metabolism Rate with Age
BMR varies with age and sex. Rates are usually higher for males and decline proportionately with age for both sexes.

Cognitive and Sociocultural Factors in Hunger and Obesity Biological factors, such as evolution, heredity, chemical substances, and brain processes, cannot give a complete explanation of hunger or obesity because cognitive and sociocultural factors are also important. As an example of a cognitive factor, the presence of others can affect whether people over- or undereat, depending on how much everyone else is eating and how important it is to impress them (Pliner & Mann, 2004; Herman, Roth, & Polivy, 2003).

Similarly, time and place can affect our eating. Learned associations of food with a particular place and time are characteristic of organisms (Bloom, Nelson, & Lazerson, 2001). For example, when it is noon we are likely to feel hungry even if we have had a big breakfast and snacked at midmorning. We also associate eating with certain places. Many people link watching television with eating and feel uncomfortable if they aren't eating something while they are watching TV.

Strong evidence of the environment's influence on weight is the rapidly rising rates of obesity. In Canada, between 1985 and 1997 alone, the percentage of men who reported themselves as overweight increased from 22 percent to 35 percent (the comparable figures for Canadian women are 14 percent and 24 percent; Health Canada, 1999). Also, as shown in figure 11.6, obesity among adolescents in the United States has increased significantly since the late 1960s (U. S. National Center for Health Statistics, 2000b). This dramatic increase is likely due to greater availability of food (especially food high in fat), energy-saving devices, and declining physical activity. Obesity is six times more prevalent among women with low incomes than among women with high incomes. Also, North Americans are more obese than Europeans and people in many other areas of the world.

North American culture provides substantial opportunities and encouragement for overeating. Food is everywhere you go, and it is easily accessed—in vending machines, fast-food restaurants, at work. Nowhere else in the world will you find as many fast-food restaurants as in Canada and the United States. Also, both portion size and the quantity of food that North Americans eat at mealtime have grown. Fast-food restaurants capitalize on this by giving you the opportunity to "super-size" your meal at a relatively low additional cost. Also, a higher percentage of our food is made up of fat content than in the past. And, although we hear a lot about exercise in the media and although people talk about exercising, there is good evidence that, overall, North Americans are getting less exercise than they did in the past (U. S. National Center for Health Statistics, 2000b).

In sum, an abundance of food in a culture that encourages food consumption, an increase in the amount of food eaten, a higher percentage of fat content in the food we eat, and a decrease in exercise add up to a population that has a serious number of overweight and obese individuals.

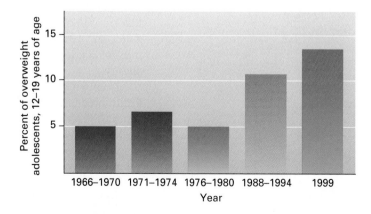

FIGURE 11.6 The Increase in Adolescent Obesity from 1966 to 1999 in the United States

Janet Polivy, of the University of Toronto, often in collaboration with her University of Toronto colleague Peter Herman, has focused her research career on dieting and eating behaviour. Recently, she has become interested in what she labels "false hope syndrome," a common outcome of making unrealistic resolutions to change. Of dieting, she has said, "Our reach tends to exceed our grasp where weight loss is concerned. Frustration and dissatisfaction are the understandable consequences."

Dieting

Ironically, even as obesity is on the rise, dieting has become an obsession with many North Americans. This section explores a number of factors in dieting, beginning with restrained eating.

Restrained Eaters   Many people spend their lives on one long diet, interrupted by occasional hot fudge sundaes or chocolate chip cookies. They are *restrained eaters*, individuals who chronically restrict their food intake to control their weight (Drobes & others, 2001). Restrained eaters are often on diets, are very conscious of what they eat, and tend to feel guilty after splurging on sweets (Martins & Pliner, 1999; Mulvihill, Davies, & Rogers, 2002). An interesting characteristic of restrained eaters is that when they stop dieting, they tend to binge eat—that is, to eat large quantities of food in a short time (Freeman & Gil, 2004; McFarlane, Polivy, & Herman, 1998).

The Use and Misuse of Diets   Many interests are involved in the topic of dieting. These include the public, health professionals, policy makers, the media, and the powerful diet and food industries. On one side are the societal norms that promote a very lean body. This ideal is supported by the billions of dollars a year spent on diet books, programs, videos, foods, and pills. On the other side are health professionals, feminist psychologists, and some members of the press. Although they recognize the high rate of obesity, they are frustrated by high relapse rates and the obsession with excessive thinness that can lead to self-esteem problems, chronic dieting, and serious health risks (Pipher, 1995; Wang & Brownell, 2005; McFarlane, Polivy, & McCabe, 1999).

Although many North Americans regularly embark on diets, few are successful in keeping weight off long-term. Janet Polivy and Peter Herman, of the University of Toronto, argue that many dieters are vulnerable to false hope syndrome (Polivy & Herman, 1999, 2000; Trottier, Polivy, & Herman, 2005): They begin their diets with unrealistic expectations, which lead to overconfidence, false hope, inflated expectations of success, and, eventually, the failure of the diet.

However, some individuals do lose weight and maintain the loss (Herman & Polivy, 2004). How often this occurs and whether some diet programs work better than others are still open questions. What we do know about losing weight is that the most effective programs include an exercise component (Abdel-Hamid, 2003). Exercise not only burns up calories, but also continues to elevate the person's metabolic rate for several hours after the exercise. Also, as we said earlier in the chapter, exercise lowers a person's set point for weight, which makes it easier to maintain a lower weight.

Dieting is a pervasive concern of many North Americans, but the population is not uniform, and many people who are on diets should not be. A 10 percent reduction in body weight might produce striking benefits for an older, obese, hypertensive man yet be unhealthy for a younger girl who is not overweight. McVey, Tweed, & Blackmore (2004) found that 30 percent of adolescent and preadolescent girls are on a diet and 10 percent show signs of disordered eating. The pressure to be thin, and thus to diet, is greatest among young women, yet they do not have the highest risk of obesity.

Even when diets produce healthy weight loss, they can place the dieter at risk for health problems. One main concern focuses on *weight cycling* (commonly called "yo-yo dieting"), in which the person is in a recurring cycle of dieting and weight gain (Noël, & Pugh, 2002; Wadden & others, 1996). Researchers have found a link between frequent changes in weight and chronic disease (Berg, 1998). Also, liquid diets and other very low calorie strategies are related to gall bladder damage.

With these problems in mind, when overweight people diet and maintain their weight loss, they do become less depressed and reduce their risk for a number of health-impairing disorders (Fontaine & others, 2004). The next section explores problems that occur at the other end of the weight spectrum—people who become so thin that it impairs their health.

Eating Disorders

This section examines two major eating problems, anorexia nervosa and bulimia nervosa, both of which are more common in young women than in any other gender/age segment of the population (Polivy & Herman, 2002; Health Canada, 2002a; Cooper, 2005). According to Kaye & colleagues (2004), anorexia and bulimia are both accompanied by abnormal cortical activity and abnormalities in the function of the neurotransmitter serotonin.

Anorexia Nervosa **Anorexia nervosa** is an eating disorder that involves the relentless pursuit of thinness through starvation. Anorexia nervosa can eventually lead to death. The main characteristics of anorexia nervosa are (Davison & Neale, 2006)

- Weighing less than 85 percent of what is considered normal for age and height
- Having an intense fear of gaining weight that does not decrease with weight loss
- Having a distorted body image (Kaye, Strober, & Rhodes, 2002) but an accurate conception of body weight (McCabe & others, 2001). Even when individuals with anorexia nervosa are extremely thin, they see themselves as fat, especially in the abdomen, buttocks, and thighs. They never think they are thin enough: They weigh themselves frequently, often take their body measurements, and gaze critically at themselves in mirrors.

Anorexia nervosa typically begins in the teenage years, often following an episode of dieting and the occurrence of some type of life stress (Lewinsohn, Striegel-Moore, & Seeley, 2000). About 10 times more females than males develop anorexia nervosa. When anorexia does occur in males, its symptoms and other characteristics (including family conflict) are usually similar to those reported by females who have the eating disorder, with the exception that the distorted body image of males involves overestimating their shoulders and thighs (Gila & others, 2005).

Most anorexics are white adolescent or young adult females from well-educated, middle- and upper-income families that are competitive and high achieving. Unable to meet their own high expectations, they turn to something they can control: their weight. Females who become anorexic often set high standards, become stressed about not being able to reach those standards, and are intensely concerned about how others perceive them (Striegel-Moore, Silberstein, & Rodin, 1993). The resulting anxiety (Buree, Papageorgis, & Hare, 1990) can even lead to suicide (Coren & Hewitt, 1998).

According to Health Canada (2002a), .5–4 percent of women in Canada will develop anorexia in their lifetime. Recent evidence suggests that the situation may be worsening. In a recent survey of Ontario schoolgirls, Jones and his colleagues (2001) found that over one-quarter of those surveyed displayed disordered eating attitudes and behaviours, precursors to severe eating disorders. So, for example, in a sample of 1739 12–18 year-olds, 23 percent reported currently dieting to lose weight, 15 percent reported binge eating and 8.2 percent reported self-induced vomiting.

According to feminist psychology, the fashion image in North American culture that emphasizes "thin and buff is beautiful" contributes to the incidence of anorexia nervosa (Simpson, 2002). The media portrays being thin and buff as beautiful in their choice of models, who many females want to emulate.

About 70 percent of individuals with anorexia nervosa eventually recover. Recovery often takes six to seven years, and relapses are common before a stable pattern of eating and weight maintenance are achieved (Strober, 2005).

Bulimia Nervosa **Bulimia nervosa** is an eating disorder in which the individual consistently follows a binge-and-purge eating pattern. The bulimic goes on an eating binge and then purges by self-induced vomiting or using a laxative. As with anorexics, most bulimics are preoccupied with food, have a strong fear of becoming overweight, and are depressed or anxious (Byrne & Mclean, 2002). Unlike anorexia nervosa, the binge-and-purge pattern in bulimia nervosa occurs within a normal weight range, which means that it is often difficult to detect (Mizes & Miller, 2000).

Might the current fashion image of "thin and buff is beautiful" contribute to anorexia nervosa?

anorexia nervosa An eating disorder that involves the relentless pursuit of thinness through starvation.

bulimia nervosa An eating disorder in which the individual consistently follows a binge-and-purge eating pattern.

Bulimia nervosa typically begins in late adolescence or early adulthood. About 90 percent of the cases are females. According to Health Canada (2002a), 1–4 percent of women in Canada will develop bulimia. Polivy & Herman (1985) first proposed that chronic dieting may actually cause bingeing and Heatherton & Polivy (1992) have extended this line of reasoning to other eating disorders. As with anorexia nervosa, about 60—70 percent of individuals with bulimia nervosa eventually recover from it (Jäger & others, 2004). Chapter 15 further explores eating patterns and proper nutrition.

> **> reflect and review**

2 **Explain the physiological basis of hunger and the nature of eating behaviour.**

- Discuss the biology of hunger.
- Describe the biological, cognitive, and sociocultural factors involved in overeating and obesity.
- Discuss the benefits and risks of dieting.
- Distinguish between anorexia nervosa and bulimia nervosa.

Many first-year students just out of high school gain as much as 7 kilos in their first year of university or college. This is sometimes referred to as "Frosh 15" (as in 15 pounds). What factors might explain this weight increase? If you are experiencing body image dissatisfaction or disordered eating, please consider a visit to your university or college counselling services.

3 SEXUALITY

| The Biology of Sex | Cognitive and Sensory/Perceptual Factors | Cultural Factors | Psychosexual Dysfunctions | Sexual Behaviour and Orientation |

What factors motivate our sexual behaviour?

We do not need sex for everyday survival, the way we need food and water, but we do need it for the survival of the species. Like hunger, sex has a strong physiological basis, as well as cognitive and sociocultural components.

The Biology of Sex

What brain areas are involved in sex? What role do hormones play in sexual motivation? What is the nature of the human sexual response pattern?

The Hypothalamus, Cerebral Cortex, and Limbic System Motivation for sexual behaviour is centred in the hypothalamus (Gorman, 2003). However, like many other areas of motivation, brain functioning related to sex radiates outward to connect with a wide range of other brain areas in both the limbic system and the cerebral cortex.

The importance of the hypothalamus in sexual activity has been shown by electrically stimulating or surgically removing it. Electrical stimulation of certain hypothalamic areas increases sexual behaviour; surgical removal of some hypothalamic areas produces sexual inhibition. Electrical stimulation of the hypothalamus in a male can lead to as many as 20 ejaculations in one hour. The limbic system, which runs through the hypothalamus, also seems to be involved in sexual behaviour. Its electrical stimulation can produce penile erection in males and orgasm in females.

In humans, the temporal lobes of the neocortex play an important role in moderating sexual arousal and directing it to an appropriate goal object (Cheasty, Condren, & Cooney,

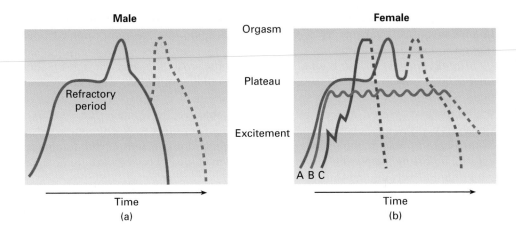

FIGURE 11.7

Male and Female Sexual Response Patterns Identified by Masters and Johnson
(*a*) The excitement, plateau, orgasm, and resolution phases of the human male sexual response pattern. Notice that males enter a refractory period, which lasts from several minutes up to a day, in which they cannot have another orgasm. (*b*) The excitement, plateau, orgasm, and resolution phases of the human female sexual response pattern. Notice that female sexual responses follow one of three basic patterns: Pattern A somewhat resembles the male pattern, except it includes the possibility of multiple orgasm (the second peak in pattern A) without falling below the plateau level. Pattern B represents nonorgasmic arousal. Pattern C represents intense female orgasm, which resembles the male pattern in its intensity and rapid resolution.

2002). Temporal lobe damage in male cats has been shown to impair the animals' ability to select an appropriate partner. Male cats with temporal lobe damage try to copulate with everything in sight: teddy bears, chairs, even researchers. Temporal lobe damage in humans also has been associated with changes in sexual activity (Mendez & others, 2000).

The brain tissues that produce sexual feelings and behaviours are activated by various neurotransmitters in conjunction with various sex hormones. Sexual motivation is also characterized by a basic urge–reward–relief neural circuit. The motivation for sex is generated by excitatory neurotransmitters. The intense reward of orgasm is caused by a massive rush of dopamine, and the deep feeling of relaxation that follows is linked with a hormone called *oxytocin* (Hiller, 2004).

Sex Hormones Sex hormones are powerful chemicals that are controlled by the master gland in the brain, the pituitary. The two main classes of sex hormones are estrogens and androgens. **Estrogens**, the class of sex hormones that predominate in females, are produced mainly by the ovaries. **Androgens**, the class of sex hormones that predominate in males, are produced by the testes in males and by the adrenal glands in both males and females. Testosterone is an androgen. Estrogens and androgens can influence sexual motivation in both sexes.

The secretion of sex hormones is regulated by a feedback system. The pituitary gland, regulated by the hypothalamus, monitors hormone levels. The pituitary gland signals the testes or ovaries to manufacture the hormone. Then the pituitary gland, through interaction with the hypothalamus, detects the point at which an optimal hormone level is reached and stops production of the hormone.

The role of hormones in motivating human sexual behaviour, especially for females, is not clear (Crooks & Bauer, 2005). For human males, higher androgen levels are associated with sexual motivation and orgasm frequency (Goldstein, 2004; Thijssen, 2002). Nonetheless, sexual behaviour is so individualized in humans that it is difficult to specify the effects of hormones.

The Human Sexual Response Pattern What physiological changes do humans experience during sexual activity? To answer this question, gynecologist William Masters and his colleague Virginia Johnson (1966) carefully observed and measured the physiological responses of 382 female and 312 male volunteers as they masturbated or had sexual intercourse. The **human sexual response pattern** consists of four phases—excitement, plateau, orgasm, and resolution—as identified by Masters and Johnson (see figure 11.7).

The *excitement phase* begins erotic responsiveness; it lasts from several minutes to several hours depending on the nature of the sex play involved. Engorgement of blood vessels and increased blood flow in genital areas and muscle tension characterize the excitement phase. The most obvious signs of response in this phase are lubrication of the vagina and partial erection of the penis.

The second phase of the human sexual response, called the *plateau phase*, is a continuation and heightening of the arousal begun in the excitement phase. The increases

estrogens The class of sex hormones that predominate in females.

androgens The class of sex hormones that predominate in males.

human sexual response pattern Identified by Masters and Johnson; consists of four phases—excitement, plateau, orgasm, and resolution

in breathing, pulse rate, and blood pressure that occurred during the excitement phase become more intense, penile erection and vaginal lubrication are more complete, and orgasm is closer.

The third phase of the human sexual response cycle is *orgasm*. How long does orgasm last? Some individuals sense that time is standing still when it takes place, but orgasm lasts for only about 3 to 15 seconds. Orgasm involves an explosive discharge of neuromuscular tension and an intense pleasurable feeling (Mah & Binik, 2001). However, orgasms are not all alike. For example, females show three different patterns in the orgasm phase: multiple orgasms; no orgasm; and excitement rapidly leading to orgasm, bypassing the plateau phase (this pattern most clearly corresponds to the male pattern in intensity and resolution; see figure 11.7).

Following orgasm, the individual enters the *resolution phase*, in which blood vessels return to their normal state. One difference between males and females in this phase is that females may be stimulated to orgasm again without delay. Males enter a refractory period, lasting anywhere from several minutes to a day, in which they cannot have another orgasm. The length of the refractory period increases as men age.

Cognitive and Sensory/Perceptual Factors

From experience, we know that our cognitive world plays an important role in our sexuality (Crooks & Bauer, 2005). We might be sexually attracted to someone but understand that it is important to inhibit our sexual urges until the relationship has time to develop and we get to know the person better. We have the cognitive capacity to think about the importance of not raping or inflicting sexual harm on others. We also have the cognitive capacity to generate sexual images. For example, some individuals become sexually aroused by generating erotic images and even reach orgasm while they are having fantasy images of sex (Whipple, Ogden, & Komisaruk, 1992).

Sexual motivation is influenced by sexual scripts, stereotyped patterns of expectancies for how people should behave sexually (Schleicher & Gilbert, 2005). Recall from the discussion of memory in chapter 9 that scripts are schemas for events. We carry these scripts with us in our memories. Two well-known sexual scripts are the traditional religious script and the romantic script. In the *traditional religious script*, sex is accepted only within marriage. Extramarital sex is taboo, especially for women. Sex means reproduction and sometimes affection. In the *romantic script*, sex is equated with love. In this script, if we develop a relationship with someone and fall in love, it is acceptable to have sex with the person whether we are married or not.

Traditionally, men and women have had different sexual scripts. Females tended to link sexual intercourse with love more than males did, and males were more likely to emphasize sexual conquest (Byers, 2001). Some sexual scripts involve a double standard: For example, it is okay for male adolescents to have sex, but not for females; and women are held solely to blame if they become pregnant. However, the double standard is not as strongly held now as it was in previous generations (Schleicher & Gilbert, 2005).

Cognitive interpretation of sexual activity also involves our perception of the individual with whom we are having sex and his or her perception of us. We imbue our sexual acts with such perceptual questions as: Is he loyal to me? What is our future relationship going to be like? How important is sex to her? What if she gets pregnant? Amid the wash of hormones in sexual activity is the cognitive ability to control, reason about, and try to make sense of the activity.

Along with cognitive factors, sensory/perceptual factors are involved in sexual behaviour. The sensory system of touch usually predominates during sexual intimacy, but vision also plays an important role for some individuals (Brown, Steele, & Walsh-Childers, 2002).

Men and women differ in how much touch and visual stimulation motivate them sexually. In general, women are more aroused by touch, men by what they see. This might explain why erotic magazines and movies are directed more toward males than toward females (Pease & Pease, 1998). Women are more aroused by tender, loving touches that are coupled with verbal expressions of love than men are. Men are likely to become sexually aroused quickly, whereas women's sexual arousal tends to build gradually.

Might smell also be involved in sexual interest between women and men? **Pheromones** are scented substances that are powerful attractants in some animals (Brennan & Keverne, 2004; Savic, 2002). Pheromones in the urine of ovulating female guinea pigs attract male guinea pigs. All the male cats in a neighbourhood know that a female cat is in heat when they pick up the scent of pheromones. Several years ago, Jovan developed a fragrance the company claimed would attract men to women who wore it. The company advertised that the perfume contained a pheromone derived from human sweat. It was designed to lure human males, just as pheromones attract male guinea pigs and cats (Winman, 2004). The fragrance was not the smashing success the perfumery anticipated, indicating that there is far more to sexual attraction in humans than smell.

Various foods and other substances have also been proposed as dramatically increasing sexual arousal. *Aphrodisiacs* are substances that supposedly arouse a person's sexual desire and increase his or her capacity for sexual activity. Recall from chapter 1 that we urged you to be skeptical about claims that eating ground-up tiger's penis will increase male sexual potency. Some foods, such as oysters, bananas, celery, tomatoes, and potatoes, are touted as aphrodisiacs. Be wary of such claims. These foods do not influence sexual behaviour. A substance referred to as "Spanish fly" has also been promoted as a powerful aphrodisiac. Not only is Spanish fly ineffective as a sexual stimulant, but it can cause genital inflammation, tissue damage, and even death.

Cultural Factors

Sexual motivation is also influenced by cultural factors. The range of sexual values across cultures is substantial. Some cultures consider sexual pleasures to be "normal" or "desirable," while other cultures view sexual pleasures as "weird" or "abnormal." We would consider the people who live on the small island of Ines Beag off the coast of Ireland to be among the most sexually repressed people in the world. They know nothing about tongue kissing or hand stimulation of the penis, and they detest nudity. For both females and males, premarital sex is out of the question. Men avoid most sexual experiences because they believe that sexual intercourse reduces their energy level and is bad for their health. Under these repressive conditions, sexual intercourse occurs only at night and takes place as quickly as possible as the husband opens his nightclothes under the covers and the wife raises her nightgown. As you might suspect, female orgasm is rare in this culture (Messinger, 1971).

In contrast, the Mangaian culture in the South Pacific seems promiscuous to us. In Mangaia, young boys are taught about masturbation and are encouraged to engage in it as much as they like. At age 13, the boys undergo a ritual that initiates them into sexual manhood. First, their elders instruct them about sexual strategies, including how to aid their female partner in having orgasms. Then, two weeks later, the boy has intercourse with an experienced woman who helps him hold back ejaculation until she can achieve orgasm with him. By the end of adolescence, Mangaians have sex pretty much every day. Mangaian women report a high frequency of orgasm.

Psychosexual Dysfunctions

Myths about females and males would have us believe that many women are uninterested in sexual pleasure and that most men can hardly get enough. Although men do think about sex more than women do, most men and women have desires for sexual pleasure, and both sexes can experience psychological problems that interfere with the attainment of sexual pleasure. *Psychosexual dysfunctions* are disorders that involve impairments in the sexual response pattern, either in the desire for gratification or in the inability to achieve it.

In disorders associated with the desire phase, both men and women may show little or no sexual drive or interest. In disorders associated with the excitement phase, men may not be able to maintain an erection (Baldo & Eardley, 2005; Becker & others, 2002). In disorders associated with the orgasmic phase, both women and men may reach orgasm either too quickly or not at all. Premature ejaculation in men occurs when

pheromones Odorous substances released by animals that are powerful attractants.

Sexual behaviour has its magnificent moments throughout the animal kingdom. Insects mate in midair, peacocks display their plumage, and male elephant seals have prolific sex lives. Experience plays a more important role in human sexual behaviour. We can talk about sex with each other, read about it in magazines, and watch it on television and the movie screen.

the time between the beginning of sexual stimulation and ejaculation is unsatisfactorily brief. Many women do not routinely experience orgasm in sexual intercourse. Inhibited male orgasm does occur, but it is much less common than inhibited female orgasm.

The treatment of psychosexual dysfunctions has undergone nothing short of a revolution in recent years. Attempts to treat psychosexual dysfunctions through traditional forms of psychotherapy, as if the dysfunctions were personality disorders, have not been very successful. However, new treatments that focus directly on each sexual dysfunction have reached high success rates (McConaghy, 1993; Heiman, 2002; Crooks & Bauer, 2005). For example, the success rate of a treatment that encourages women to enjoy their bodies and engage in self-stimulation to orgasm, with a vibrator if necessary, approaches 100 percent (Segraves & Althof, 2002). Some of these women subsequently transfer their newly developed sexual responsiveness to interactions with partners.

Recently, attention in helping males with sexual dysfunction has focused on Viagra, a drug designed to conquer impotence (McAnulty & Burnette, 2004; Nehra & others, 2002). Its success rate is in the range of 60 to 80 percent, and it rapidly became one of the most prescribed drugs in North America. Viagra is also being taken by some women to improve their sexual satisfaction. However, Viagra is not an aphrodisiac; it won't work in the absence of desire. The downsides of Viagra include headaches in 1 of 10 men, seeing blue (because the eyes contain an enzyme similar to the one on which Viagra works in the penis, about 3 percent of users develop temporary vision problems ranging from blurred vision to a blue or green halo effect), and blackouts (Viagra can trigger a sudden drop in blood pressure; Steers & others, 2001). Also, scientists do not yet know the long-term effects of taking the drug, although in short-term trials it appears to be relatively safe. Further, treating a male partner with Viagra, while leaving his female partner untreated and largely uninterested, may lead to problems other than impotence (Potts & others, 2003).

Sexual Behaviour and Orientation

Earlier we contrasted the sexual values and behaviours of two remote cultures—Ines Beag and Mangaia. Few cultures are as isolated and homogeneous as these two. In Canada and the United States, sexual behaviours and attitudes reflect their diverse, multicultural populations, placing North Americans somewhere in the middle of a continuum going from repressive to liberal. We are more conservative in our sexual habits than we once thought but somewhat more open-minded regarding sexual orientation than a century ago.

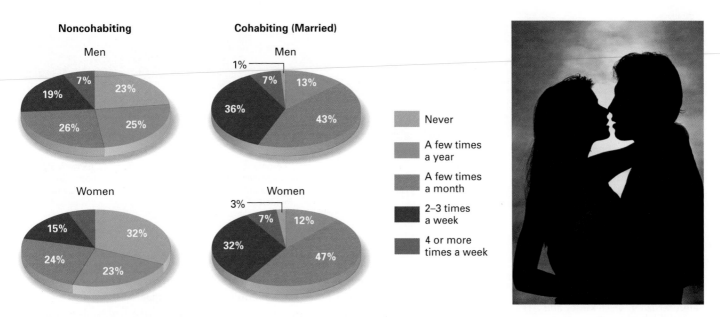

FIGURE 11.8 **Sex and Cohabitation**
Percentages show noncohabiting and cohabiting (married) males' and females' responses to the
question "How often have you had sex in the past year?"

Source: Michael and others, 1994.

Sexual Attitudes and Practices It is hard to accurately describe the sexual practices
of diverse countries like Canada and the United States (Fraser, Maticka-Tyndale, &
Smylie, 2004; Wiederman & Whitley, 2002). The Kinsey report (1948) on Americans'
sexual practices shocked the continent by reporting, among other observations, that
half of American men had engaged in extramarital affairs. However, Kinsey's results
were not representative, because he recruited volunteers, including drifters and mental
patients. Nevertheless, the Kinsey data were widely circulated and many people felt
that they must be leading a more conservative sexual life than others.

Subsequent large-scale magazine surveys confirmed the trend toward permissive
sexuality (Hunt, 1974). However, most magazine polls are also flawed. For example,
surveys in *Playboy* and *Cosmopolitan* might appeal to subscribers who want to use the
survey to brag about their sexual exploits.

Fortunately, some more accurate data have been obtained using large random samples of men and women from all age groups in both Canada (Barrett & others, 1997)
and the U.S. (Michael & others, 1994). Some of the key findings from these studies are:

- Compared with singles, married couples have sex the most and are also the most
  likely to have orgasms when they do. Figure 11.8 portrays the frequency of sex
  for married and noncohabitating U.S. individuals in the year before the survey
  was taken.
- Adultery is the exception, not the rule. Between 75 percent (U.S.) and 86 percent
  (Canada) of married men and between 85 percent (U.S.) and 93 percent (Canada)
  of married women indicated that they have never been unfaithful.
- One Canadian poll asked if the respondent had had two or more sexual partners
  in the previous year. The results ranged from a high of 32 percent for males aged
  between 18 and 24 down to 0 percent for females between 55 and 64. In the U.S.
  survey, only 17 percent of men and 3 percent of women said they had had sex
  with at least 21 partners.
- Men think about sex far more than women do—in the U.S. study, 54 percent of
  men said they think about it every day or several times a day, whereas 67 percent
  of women said they think about it only a few times a week or a few times a month.

In sum, North Americans' sexual lives are more conservative than previously
believed. The overall impression is that sexual behaviour is ruled by marriage and

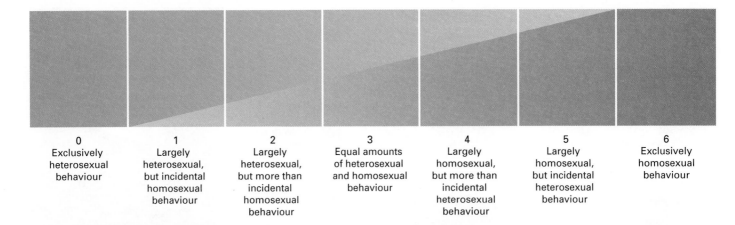

0	1	2	3	4	5	6
Exclusively heterosexual behaviour	Largely heterosexual, but incidental homosexual behaviour	Largely heterosexual, but more than incidental homosexual behaviour	Equal amounts of heterosexual and homosexual behaviour	Largely homosexual, but more than incidental heterosexual behaviour	Largely homosexual, but incidental heterosexual behaviour	Exclusively homosexual behaviour

FIGURE 11.9

The Continuum of Sexual Orientation
The continuum ranges from exclusive heterosexuality, which Kinsey and associates (1948) labelled 0, to exclusive homosexuality, 6. People who are about equally attracted to both sexes, 2 to 4, are bisexual.

monogamy for most North Americans. Within monogamous, married relationships, however, there is some evidence that sexual scripts are changing. In Quebec, for example, 80 percent of cohabiting heterosexual adults reported engaging in oral-genital sex (Samson and others, 1993). Further, the frequency of intercourse and oral-genital sex is correlated with both sexual satisfaction and general relationship satisfaction, suggesting that higher frequencies of these behaviours are becoming a more accepted part of the sexual script for mature adults.

According to sexuality expert Bernie Zilbergeld, dramatic changes in the sexual landscape have taken place in the past several decades—from changing expectations of sexuality in older people to new definitions of masculinity, from the fear of disease to the renewed focus on long-term relationships (Zilbergeld, 1992; Zilbergeld & Zilbergeld, 2004). For example, Eleanor Maticka-Tyndale, of the University of Windsor, and her colleagues have studied several aspects of the changing sexual habits of young Canadians (Maticka-Tyndale and others, 2000; Maticka-Tyndale, 2001). While the teen birth rate has dropped over the last 25 years, young people, especially women, have higher rates of sexually transmitted diseases than other age groups in Canada. Age of first intercourse has also declined more for women than for men, while both men and women have more casual short-term partnerships and more sexual partners.

In general, young Canadians have more casual attitudes toward sex (Herold and others, 1998). These attitudes are reflected in, for example, casual sex on spring break in Florida (Maticka-Tyndale and others, 1998) and the attendant issues of condom use (Maticka-Tyndale & Herold, 1999). They are also reflected in the increased participation of young women in the sex trade in Canada, and the attendant need for government control (Lewis, 2000; Lewis & Maticka-Tyndale, 2000) and concern for the sexual health of those in the sex trade (Maticka-Tyndale, Lewis, & Street, 2005; Maticka-Tyndale & others 2000).

Myths about sexuality have also led to unrealistic expectations for our sexual lives. Among the sexual myths, according to Zilbergeld (1992), are the myths that men need a large penis to satisfy a woman; that male and female orgasm are absolutely necessary for sexual satisfaction; that intercourse is the only real sexual act; that good sex has to be spontaneous (without planning or talking); and that for men to have questions, doubts, or problems in sex is virtually a crime.

Although the majority of us manage to develop a mature sexuality, most individuals experience some periods of vulnerability and confusion along the way. Many individuals have an almost insatiable curiosity about sexuality. Some wonder and worry about their sexual attractiveness, their ability to satisfy their sexual partner, and whether they will experience the ultimate sexual fantasy.

Sexual Orientation Until the end of the nineteenth century, it was generally believed that people were either heterosexual or homosexual. Today, it is more accepted to view sexual orientation along a continuum, from exclusive heterosexuality to exclusive homosexuality, rather than as an either/or proposition (Rathus, Nevid, & Fichner-Rathus,

An individual's sexual preference is most likely determined by a combination of genetic, hormonal, cognitive, and environmental factors.

2005). Kinsey, Pomeroy, and Martin (1948) first described this continuum on a scale ranging from 0 (exclusive heterosexuality) to 6 (exclusive homosexuality; see figure 11.9). Also, some individuals are bisexual, being sexually attracted to people of both sexes. As of 2003, about 1 percent of Canadians reported that they are homosexual (1.3 percent for men and .7 percent for women) and .7 percent reported that they are bisexual (.6 percent for men and .9 percent for women) (Statistics Canada, 2004b).

Why are some individuals homosexual and others heterosexual? Speculation about this question has been extensive, but no firm answers are available. Homosexuals and heterosexuals have similar physiological responses during sexual arousal and seem to be aroused by the same types of tactile stimulation. Investigators find no differences between homosexuals and heterosexuals in a wide range of attitudes, behaviours, and adjustments (Bell, Weinberg, & Mammersmith, 1981). Homosexuality was once classified as a mental disorder, but the Canadian Psychological Association, along with the American Psychiatric Association and the American Psychological Association, discontinued this classification in the 1970s.

An individual's sexual orientation—homosexual, heterosexual, or bisexual—is most likely determined by a combination of genetic, hormonal, cognitive, and environmental factors (Baldwin & Baldwin, 1998; Garnets, 2002). Most experts on homosexuality believe that no one factor alone causes homosexuality and that the relative weight of each factor can vary from one individual to the next. In effect, no one knows exactly why some individuals are homosexual.

Recently, researchers have explored the possible biological basis of homosexuality (Rahman & Wilson, 2003). The results of hormone studies have been inconsistent. If male homosexuals are given male sex hormones (androgens), their sexual orientation doesn't change. Their sexual desire merely increases. However, in the second to fifth months after conception, exposure of the fetus to hormone levels characteristic of females might cause the individual (male or female) to become attracted to males (Hines, 2004).

Sandra Witelson of McMaster University, and her colleagues, have also provided evidence that a biological factor is involved in the origins of sexual orientation. This includes finding different patterns of functional cerebral asymmetry (McCormick & Witelson, 1994) and an increased incidence of left-hand preference (Lalumière, Blanchard, & Zucker, 2000) in gay men and lesbians compared with heterosexuals. With regard to anatomical structures, an area of the hypothalamus that governs sexual behaviour is twice as large (about the size of a grain of sand) in heterosexual males as in homosexual males. This area was found to be about the same size in homosexual males and heterosexual females (LeVay, 1991; Matsumoto, 2000).

While social environmental factors seem like they should play a role in determining sexual orientation, little strong evidence is currently available. For example, children raised by gay or lesbian parents or couples are no more likely to be homosexual than children raised by heterosexual parents (Patterson, 2000, 2003). There is some evidence that male homosexuality is related to a weak or emotionally absent father (Seutter & Rovers, 2004) but not that it is related to a dominant mother, or that female homosexuality is caused by girls choosing male role models.

One intriguing finding is that homosexual men often have more older brothers than heterosexual men (Bogaert, 2005a,b). It has been hypothesized that in the presence of their more masculine older brothers, slightly more feminine younger brothers may experience an exaggerated sense of being different, which may influence sexual orientation. However, recent data have failed to support this hypothesis (Bogaert, 2005a,b).

How do gays and lesbians adapt to a world in which they are a minority? According to psychologist Laura Brown (1989), gays and lesbians experience life as a minority in a dominant, majority culture. For lesbian women and gay men, developing a bicultural identity creates new ways of defining themselves. Brown believes that gays and lesbians adapt best when they do not define themselves in polarities—for instance, either by trying to live in a completely gay or lesbian world divorced from the majority culture or by completely accepting the dictates and biases of the majority culture. Balancing the demands and seeking the benefits of the two cultures—the minority gay/lesbian culture and the majority heterosexual culture—can often lead to more effective coping for homosexuals, says Brown.

> ## > reflect and review

 Discuss the motivations for sexual behaviour.

- Describe the biology of sex.
- Identify cognitive and sensory/perceptual factors that affect sexual behaviour.
- Summarize the importance of culture in sexual motivation.
- Explain the nature and treatment of psychosexual dysfunctions.
- Characterize sexual behaviour and orientation in North America.

A substance called "Spanish fly" has been promoted as a powerful aphrodisiac. As mentioned, it is not an effective sexual stimulant and can cause severe side effects. Could the placebo effect (discussed in chapter 2) explain people's faith in this and other aphrodisiacs? How?

④ SOCIAL COGNITIVE MOTIVES

—— Achievement —— Affiliation —— Well-Being

What are some important social cognitive motives and how do they influence behaviour?

The previous discussions of hunger and sexual motivation focused to a large degree on physiological factors and on the involvement of the hypothalamus and other brain structures. Although there is a significant cognitive component to sexual behaviour, it does not always predominate. This section presents three motives that have strong social cognitive foundations: achievement, affiliation, and well-being.

Achievement

Some people are highly motivated to succeed and spend considerable effort striving to excel—like Terry Fox and Rick Hansen, who did not allow themselves to be overwhelmed

Calvin and Hobbes   **by Bill Watterson**

Calvin and Hobbes © 1991 Watterson. Reprinted with permission of Universal Press Syndicate. All rights reserved.

by their medical conditions and resign themselves to a lesser quality of life. But individuals differ in their achievement motivation. Others are not as motivated to succeed and don't work as hard to achieve.

Need for Achievement **Need for achievement** is the desire to accomplish something, to reach a standard of excellence, and to expend effort to excel (Deckers, 2005). Borrowing from Henry Murray's (1938) theory and measurement of personality, psychologist David McClelland (1955) assessed achievement by showing individuals ambiguous pictures that were likely to stimulate achievement-related responses. The individuals were asked to tell stories about the pictures, and their comments were scored according to how strongly they reflected achievement. Researchers have found that individuals whose stories reflect high achievement motivation have a stronger hope for success than fear of failure, are moderate rather than high or low risk takers, and persist with effort when tasks become difficult (Atkinson & Raynor, 1974).

McClelland (1978) also wondered if achievement behaviour could be increased by increasing achievement motivation. To find out, he trained the businessmen in a village in India to be more achievement oriented, encouraging them to increase their hope for success, reduce their fear of failure, take moderate risks, and try harder in the face of difficulty. Compared with businessmen in a nearby village, the businessmen that McClelland trained started more new businesses and employed more new people in the two years after the training.

Cognitive Factors Chapter 1 discussed Albert Bandura's social cognitive theory. You might recall that Bandura (1997, 2000a, 2001) believes that cognitive factors are an important aspect of understanding behaviour. Earlier in this chapter, we highlighted a key cognitive factor in motivation: intrinsic motivation. Intrinsic motivation, which is based on such internal factors as self-determination, curiosity, challenge, and effort, contrasts with extrinsic motivation, which involves external incentives such as rewards and punishments. The following section on attribution shows that intrinsic and extrinsic motivation are often one set of causes that individuals look at as they attempt to explain their behaviour.

Attribution **Attribution theory** states that individuals are motivated to discover the underlying causes of behaviour in an effort to make sense of the behaviour (R. C. Beck, 2004). In this way, say attribution theorists, people are like intuitive scientists, seeking the cause behind what happens. Attribution is also discussed in the context of social thinking in chapter 16.

The reasons individuals behave the way they do can be classified in a number of ways, but one basic distinction stands out above all others—the distinction between

need for achievement The desire to accomplish something, to reach a standard of excellence, and to expend effort to excel.

attribution theory States that individuals are motivated to discover the underlying causes of behaviour as part of their effort to make sense of it.

internal causes, such as personality traits or motives, and external causes, which are environmental, situational factors, such as rewards or task difficulty (Heider, 1958). If university students do not do well on a test, do they attribute it to the teacher's plotting against them and making the test too difficult (external cause) or to not studying hard enough (internal cause)? The answer to such a question influences how people feel about themselves. If students believe that their performance is the teacher's fault, they will not feel as badly when they do poorly as they will if they believe they did not spend enough time studying.

Individuals differ in attributional style; they habitually make either internal or external attributions. In one study, women with different attributional styles watched a peer model exhibit restraint in food consumption. Afterwards, the women with an internal attributional style themselves ate less than the women with an external attributional style did (Rotenberg, Carte, & Speirs, 2005).

Goal Setting, Planning, and Monitoring In the discussion of cognitive factors earlier in the chapter, the importance of self-generated goals was emphasized. Goal setting, planning, and self-monitoring are critical aspects of achievement (Pintrich & Schunk, 2002). Goals help individuals reach their dreams, increase their self-discipline, and maintain interest. Goal setting and planning often work in concert, and are usually grounded in past experience (Bagozzi & Dholakia, 2005).

Researchers have found that individuals' achievement improves when they set goals that are specific, short term, and challenging (Bandura, 1997; Schunk, 2004b). A fuzzy, nonspecific goal is "I want to be successful." A concrete, specific goal is "I want to have a B+ average at the end of the semester." You can set both long-term (distal) and short-term (proximal) goals. It is okay to set long-term goals, such as "I want to be a clinical psychologist," but, if you do, make sure that you also create short-term goals as steps along the way, such as "I want to get an A on the next psychology test" or "I will do all of my studying for this class by 4 p.m. Sunday."

Another good strategy is to set challenging goals (Zetik & Stuhlmacher, 2002). A challenging goal is a commitment to self-improvement. Strong interest and involvement in activities are sparked by challenges. Goals that are easy to reach generate little interest or effort. However, unrealistically high goals can bring failure and diminish self-confidence.

Achievement motivation researcher John Nicholls and his colleagues (Nicholls & others, 1990; Lau & others, 2000) distinguish among ego-involved goals, task-involved goals, and work-avoidant goals. Individuals with ego-involved goals strive to maximize favourable evaluations and minimize unfavourable ones. Thus ego-involved individuals focus on how smart they will look and on their ability to outperform others. In contrast, individuals with task-involved goals focus more on mastering tasks. They concentrate on how well they can do the task and what they can learn. Individuals with work-avoidant goals try to exert as little effort as possible on a task. A good achievement strategy is to develop task-involved mastery goals rather than ego-involved or work-avoidant goals.

Planning how to reach a goal and monitoring progress toward the goal are critical aspects of achievement (Eccles, Wigfield, & Schiefele, 1998). Researchers have found that high-achieving individuals monitor their own learning and systematically evaluate their progress toward their goals more than low-achieving individuals do (Zimmerman, 2001). As a result, training programs have been developed to help students more effectively reach their educational goals (Cleary & Zimmerman, 2004). To evaluate how goal directed you are, see the Personal Reflections box.

Sociocultural Factors In addition to cognitive factors such as attribution, intrinsic motivation, and self-generation of goals, the sociocultural contexts in which we live contribute to our motivation to achieve (Wigfield & Eccles, 2002; Sameroff, Peck, & Eccles, 2004). This section focuses on comparisons across cultures and ethnicities.

Cross-Cultural Comparisons People in North America tend to be more achievement oriented than people in many other parts of the world. One classic study of 104 societies

How Goal Directed Are You?

To evaluate how goal directed you are, consider how much each of the following statements is like you or not like you.

- I set long-term and short-term goals.
- I set challenging goals that are neither too easy nor beyond my reach.
- I am good at managing my time and setting priorities to make sure I get the most important things done.
- I regularly make "to do" lists and successfully get most items done.
- I set deadlines and consistently meet them.

- I regularly monitor how well I'm progressing toward my goals and make changes in my behaviour if necessary.
- When I am under pressure, I still plan my days and weeks in a clear, logical manner.
- I set task-involved, mastery goals rather than ego-involved or work-avoidant goals.

If most of these descriptions characterize you, then you are likely a goal-directed individual. If these statements do not characterize you, then consider ways that you can become more goal-directed.

revealed that parents in nonindustrialized countries placed a lower value on their children's achievement and independence and a higher value on obedience and cooperation than the parents in industrialized countries did (Barry, Child, & Bacon, 1959). In comparisons of white American children with children of Mexican and Latino heritage, the white children were more competitive and less cooperative. For example, one study found that white children were likelier to keep other children from achieving a goal when they could not achieve the goal themselves (Kagan & Madsen, 1972). Another study showed that Mexican children were more family-oriented than white children, who tended to be more concerned about themselves (Holtzmann, 1982).

Other studies focus on the poor performance of North American students on tests of mathematics and science in comparison with students in other countries. The Trends in International Mathematics and Science Study (TIMSS) was conducted in 1995, 1999 and 2003 at five grade levels in more than 40 countries (Gonzales & others, 2004). Mathematics achievement data for 1999 are available for grades 3 (24 countries), 4 (25 countries), 7 (41 countries) and 8 (43 countries), and the final year of secondary school (21 countries). The four top-ranked countries in grades 3, 4, 7, and 8 were Singapore, Korea, Japan, and Hong Kong. Canada's ranking was 13, 12, 18, and 19 respectively while that of the U.S. was 11, 10, 28, and 26. In the final year of secondary school, Canada was 9th while the U.S. was 19th—though with the inclusion of data for the Asian countries (which were not available), these rankings would undoubtedly be considerably lower. Go to the Apply Your Knowledge section at the end of the chapter to find a Web address for the TIMSS.

Reasons for the superior performance of Asian students have emerged from studies by Harold Stevenson (Stevenson and others, 1992, 2000). The longer they are in school, the wider the gap between Asian and North American students becomes—the smallest difference is in grade 1, the largest in grade 11. Asian teachers spent more of their time teaching math than North American teachers did. One-quarter of total classroom time in grade 1 was spent on math instruction in Japan, compared with only one-tenth of the time in U.S. grade 1 classrooms. Also, Asian students were in school an average of 240 days a year compared to 178 days in North America.

In addition, North American parents had much lower expectations for their children's education and achievement than the Asian parents. North American parents were also more likely to believe that their children's math achievement is due to innate ability, whereas Asian parents were more likely to say that their children's math achievement is the consequence of effort and training (see figure 11.10). Asian students were more likely than North American students to do math homework, and Asian parents were far more likely to help their children with their math homework than North American parents were (Chen & Stevenson, 1989).

A study of grade 8 teachers' instruction in the United States, Japan, and Germany (Stigler & Hiebert, 1997) found: (1) Japanese students spent less time solving routine

Asian students score considerably higher than North American students on math achievement tests. *What are some possible explanations for these findings?*

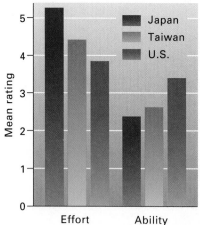

FIGURE 11.10

Mothers' Beliefs About the Factors Responsible for Children's Math Achievement in Three Countries
In one study, mothers in Japan and Taiwan were likelier to believe that their children's math achievement was due to effort rather than to innate ability, whereas U.S. mothers were likelier to believe their children's math achievement was due to innate ability (Stevenson, Lee, & Stigler, 1986).

math problems and more time inventing, analyzing, and proving than U.S. or German students; (2) Japanese teachers engaged in more direct lecturing than U.S. or German teachers; and (3) Japanese teachers were more likely to emphasize math thinking, whereas U.S. and German teachers were more likely to stress math skills (solving a specific problem or using a specific formula).

An important conclusion from these cross-cultural studies is that learning and achievement take time. The more time students spend learning, the more likely they are to learn the material and achieve high standards.

Ethnic Comparisons Until recently, researchers studying achievement focused mainly on white males, and when achievement in ethnic minority groups has been studied, the cultural differences have too often been viewed against standards of achievements for white males. As a result, many early researchers unfortunately concluded that ethnic minorities were somehow deficient in achievement motivation (Gibbs & Huang, 1989). In reaching these conclusions, however, alternative explanations were often not considered. In the case of Canada's Aboriginal peoples, for example, poor achievement may be the result of negative attitudes toward mainstream notions of achievement and schooling that can be traced directly to the disastrous early attempts to assimilate Canadian Aboriginal populations through the residential school system (Barman, 1996).

Negative attitudes toward ethnic minorities can even influence their own attitudes toward achievement. Steele & Aronson (1995) administered some questions from the Graduate Record Examination (GRE) to African American American college students. Before beginning, half were asked to list their race on a questionnaire while the other half were not. The students who were asked to list their race performed much worse on the GRE questions. Steele & Aronson (1995) explained this result in terms of *stereotype threat*, the tendency of members of stereotyped groups to worry that their behaviour will confirm a negative group stereotype. Stereotype threat generates extra stress, which results in poorer achievement. Thus, when the African American students in the Steele & Aronson (1995) study were confronted with the question about their race, the resulting stereotype threat actually hurt their performance on the GRE questions. According to Suzuki & Aronson (2005), stereotype threat even underlies ethnic differences in measured intelligence.

Achievement Applications   Findings about achievement can be applied to many different aspects of life. On a personal level, attribution, intrinsic motivation, goal setting, planning, and monitoring can be used to reach educational, career, and financial goals, even to find fulfillment. In the workplace, managers apply techniques based on achievement research to motivate employees.

The Workplace   Work is what most of us will do at least half of our waking hours for more than 40 years of our lives. *Industrial/organizational (I/O) psychology* is the branch of psychology that focuses on the workplace—both the workers and the organization that employs them—to make work more enjoyable and productive (Latham & Pinder, 2005; Borman & others, 2003).

The workplace is characterized by both intrinsic and extrinsic motivation. An important I/O task is to select employees who will be intrinsically motivated to do the job required (Baard, Deci, & Ryan, 2004; Catano & others, 1997). Another important task is to figure out how to extrinsically motivate employees to do their best work possible (Gagné & Deci, 2005). Among possible reinforcements or incentives are bonuses, awards, time off, promotions, and praise. For example, an I/O psychologist might recommend that the company initiate an "Employee of the Month" program.

Good leaders know how to motivate employees. The contemporary view of effective workplace leadership involves creating a vision for others to follow, establishing values and ethics, and transforming the way an organization does business to improve its effectiveness and efficiency (Nickels, McHugh, & McHugh, 2005). Ramona Bobocel, an industrial/organizational psychologist at the University of Waterloo, and her colleagues, have focused on the importance of leaders stressing justice and fairness in motivating their employees (Bobocel & Zdaniuk, 2005; Bobocel & others, 2002). For example, Bobocel and her colleagues (1998) showed that managers who offer justifications for resolving disputes between employees are perceived to be fairer than managers who offer no justification. Similarly, companies that explain why and how decisions are made are perceived to be more fair than companies that do not (Bobocel & Debeyer, 1998).

The workplace is changing from a context in which a few people dictate what others do to a context in which all employees work together to reach common goals. Participating in an organization's decision making gives employees a sense of intrinsic motivation and self-determination that is lacking when they are simply told what to do by superiors. Goal setting, planning, and monitoring are also seen as important aspects of motivation in the workplace (Ilgen, 2000). I/O psychologists advise companies to guide employees in setting goals, planning how to achieve them, and monitoring their progress toward goals.

I/O psychologists attempt to influence the motivation of employees through *job design* (Fine & Cronshaw, 1999). In this case, the goal is to design jobs so that employees believe that their needs are met in a way that meets the organization's goals. Recent emphasis in job design has focused on modifying jobs so that they will allow employees to have more control, autonomy, feedback, and opportunity for involvement in their work (Ilgen, 2001).

Sports   Athletes tend to be achievement-oriented individuals, at least in their sports domain. Some athletes turn to sport psychologists for help in achieving their full potential (Durand-Bush & Salmela, 2001; Smith & others, 2005; Fournier & others, 2005). For example, in his amazing rise to become the world's best golfer, Tiger Woods benefitted from the advice of a team of advisors and coaches, including sport psychologist

Natalie Durand-Bush, of the University of Ottawa, has been working as a performance enhancement consultant with many athletes of different levels for the past eight years, including athletes from two Canadian national teams. Her work as a performance enhancement consultant mainly focuses on helping athletes develop and maintain confidence, focus, resonance, commitment, and a positive perspective. She teaches skills that allow them to set meaningful goals, plan for competitions, train with quality, regulate their intensity, deal with stress, engage in mental imagery, and communicate effectively with others.

Jay Brunza. *Sport psychology* is a relatively new field that applies psychological principles to improving sports performance and the enjoyment of sports.

Many sport psychology techniques come from the cognitive and behavioural perspectives (Porter, 2003). Five techniques that many sport psychologists use to improve the motivation and performance of athletes are:

- *Emphasize the process rather than the outcome.* Legendary Green Bay Packers football coach Vince Lombardi once said, "Winning isn't everything; it is the only thing." Today, however, sport psychologists advise against this type of thinking because it can actually take the athlete's focus away from immediate performance. Sport psychologists encourage athletes to immerse themselves in what they are doing and to not worry about the outcome. Focusing on the achievement process and the task at hand has been described as *mastery motivation,* in contrast with focusing on achievement outcome and winning, described as *performance motivation* (Henderson & Dweck, 1990; Treasure & Roberts, 2001).
- *Use cognitive restructuring and positive self-talk.* Often athletes in a slump think and say negative things about themselves. A sport psychologist might get them to cognitively restructure their thoughts and words more positively. For example, if a baseball player has been in a hitting slump for three weeks, a sport psychologist would encourage the player to think more about his overall successful batting average for the entire year to help rebuild his confidence.
- *Overcome adversity.* Adverse, difficult circumstances crop up for athletes, not just in sports but in life as well. Consider Terry Fox's tremendous struggle with life-threatening cancer. His desire to cope and this adversity strengthened his motivation. Terry Fox said, about the return of his cancer, "This just intensifies what I did—it gives it more meaning. It will inspire more people." Setbacks become an opportunity for learning, opening the way for growth and improvement.
- *Use deep breathing and muscle relaxation.* Some athletes get nervous as the competition is about to begin. Deep breathing and muscle relaxation can help them calm down and concentrate better. Deep breathing and muscle relaxation are discussed further in chapter 15.
- *Use visualization.* In visualization, athletes imagine how they will perform. The sport psychologist might work with a golfer to visualize the golf ball going in the hole after it is putted or with a tennis player to visualize clean, fluid strokes. Sport psychologists sometimes review video clips of the athlete's performance, select the best performances, and have the athlete watch those clips as part of developing positive imagery. Psychologist Richard Suinn caught the interest of athletes when he worked with the U.S. Olympic ski team. He divided the team into two groups of equally matched ability, one group using visual imagery, the other group not using it. The group using visual imagery improved so much that the coach called off the experiment and insisted that all the skiers use visual imagery (Suinn, 1976).

Achievement is an important social cognitive motive. But people not only have varying degrees of need for achievement, they also vary in the extent to which they are motivated to be with other people.

Affiliation

Are you the kind of person who likes to be around people a lot? Or would you rather stay home and read a book? The **need for affiliation** is the motive to be with other people. This involves establishing, maintaining, and restoring warm, close, personal relationships. Our need for affiliation is reflected in the importance of parents' nurturance in children's development, the intimate moments of sharing private thoughts in friendship, the uncomfortable feelings we have when we are lonely, and the powerful attraction we have for someone else when we are in love.

Although each of us has a need for affiliation or relatedness, some people have a stronger need than others. Some of us are motivated to be surrounded by lots of friends and feel as if something is drastically missing from our lives if we are not in love with

need for affiliation The motive to be with other people.

someone and they with us. Others of us don't have such a strong need for relatedness. We don't fall apart if we don't have friends around us all of the time, and we don't sit around all day in an anxious state because we don't have someone in love with us.

Cultures vary in how strongly they promote the need for relatedness. Many Western cultures—such as Canada, the United States, and Western European countries—emphasize individual achievement, independence, and self-reliance. Many Eastern cultures—such as China, Japan, and Korea—emphasize affiliation, cooperation, and interdependence (Triandis, 2001, 2005). Affiliation and relatedness are believed to be an important dimension of well-being.

Well-Being

Are you motivated to live the good life? What constitutes living the good life and well-being? What do you think? What would your list of items be for living the good life and experiencing well-being? Might it include happiness? Being able to spend time with the people you love? And what about intelligence and wisdom? Might they be important dimensions of the good life and well-being? Some people might value happiness more than intelligence and wisdom; others might value intelligence and wisdom more than happiness.

Well-being is subjective. Indeed, when researchers study well-being, they often refer to it as *subjective well-being*. Richard Ryan and Edward Deci (2000) have proposed that three factors need to be present for well-being:

- *Competence*. This sense of mastery entails the motivation to do whatever you attempt well. It involves using your intelligence and skills effectively.
- *Autonomy*. This consists of doing things independently. It involves intrinsic motivation, self-initiation, and self-determination.
- *Affiliation*. As we have seen, affiliation has to do with the need to be with other people.

In Ryan and Deci's view, when the needs for competence, autonomy, and affiliation are satisfied, the result is enhanced well-being. When these needs are thwarted, the result is diminished well-being. They believe that excessive control by others, nonoptimal challenges, and lack of connectedness result in a lack of initiative and responsibility and, in some cases, produce distress and psychological problems.

Some critics argue, though, that you can have too much autonomy (Schwartz, 2000; Schwartz & Ward, 2004). In this view, autonomy, freedom, and self-determination can become excessive, and when that happens people have an imbalance in their lives that may undermine their competence and affiliation. Thus, living the good life and attaining well-being may involve a balance of the three components of competence, autonomy, and affiliation.

As was mentioned previously, cultures often vary in the extent to which they emphasize autonomy or affiliation. Thus, what individuals believe constitutes the good life and well-being in some cultures might include a stronger emphasis on autonomy (for example, Canada), in others a stronger emphasis on affiliation (for example, Japan).

Carol Ryff and Burton Singer have conducted research on well-being for a number of decades (Ryff, 2001; Ryff & Singer, 1998, 2005). Based on their research, they concluded that living the good life and experiencing well-being involves both positive physical health and positive psychological health. Furthermore, they argued that positive psychological health is most likely to be achieved by leading a life of purpose (a sense of doing something meaningful), having quality connections with others (affiliation and relatedness), having positive self-regard (self-esteem), and having mastery (a sense of competence and doing things effectively).

Let's examine wheelchair athlete Rick Hansen's well-being and see how these dimensions are involved.

- *Physical well-being*. Rick Hansen's automobile accident threatened his physical well-being. Rather than dwelling on this major physical setback, he turned the situation into a positive life experience by challenging himself to become physically stronger than he was before the cancer and to focus on his psychological well-being as well.

- *Psychological well-being.* Rick Hansen was extremely competent in his sport; indeed, the very best in the world. He competed in the 1984 Olympic Games for Canada. Becoming a great wheelchair athlete required considerable autonomy, self-determination, and intrinsic motivation. He may have focused too much on developing those attributes, though. Through his friendship with Terry Fox, he realized that he also wanted to contribute to the well-being of others. After his Man in Motion tour he founded the Man in Motion Foundation through which he continues to organize fund-raising events and fund research into spinal cord injury. Today Rick lives in Richmond, BC with his wife, Amanda, and their three daughters.

> **reflect and review**

4 **Characterize the social cognitive motives and how they influence behaviour.**

- Discuss the need for achievement and the factors that motivate people to excel.
- Describe the concept of affiliation.
- Identify the components of well-being.

Make a list of five factors that you believe are the most important aspects of your well-being. How well do they match up with the factors discussed in the chapter?

5 EMOTION

The Biology of Emotion — Cognitive Factors — Behavioural Factors — Sociocultural Factors — Classifying Emotions

What are some views of emotion?

With his good leg, Terry Fox kicked the opening football of a CFL exhibition game between Saskatchewan and Ottawa. It was in Ottawa, on July 1, 1980, and he had already run 3123 kilometres. He felt a swell of emotion as he received a standing ovation from the crowd of over 16,000.

As was mentioned at the beginning of the chapter, motivation and emotion are closely linked. Think about sexual motivation, which is often associated with joy; about aggression, which is usually associated with anger; and about achievement, which is associated with pride, joy, and anxiety.

Just as there are different kinds and intensities of motivation, so it is with emotions. A person can be more motivated to eat than to have sex, and at different times can be more or less hungry or more or less interested in having sex. Similarly, a person can be happy (from fairly happy to ecstatic) or angry (from mildly annoyed to fuming).

Defining emotion is difficult because it is not easy to tell when a person is in an emotional state. Are you in an emotional state when your heart beats fast, your palms sweat, and your stomach churns? Or are you in an emotional state when you think about how much you are in love with someone? Or when you smile or grimace? The body, the mind, and the face play important roles in emotion, although psychologists debate which of these components is the most important aspect of emotion and how they mix to produce emotional experiences (Davidson, Scherer, & Goldsmith, 2002). For our purposes, **emotion** is defined as feeling, or affect, that can involve physiological arousal (a fast heartbeat, for example), conscious experience (thinking about being in love with someone, for example), and behavioural expression (a smile or grimace, for example).

emotion Feeling, or affect, that can involve physiological arousal, conscious experience, and behavioural expression.

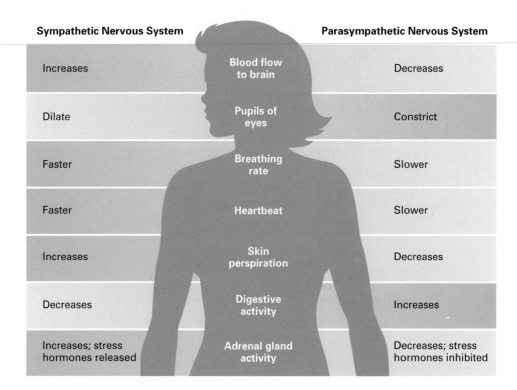

Sympathetic Nervous System		Parasympathetic Nervous System
Increases	Blood flow to brain	Decreases
Dilate	Pupils of eyes	Constrict
Faster	Breathing rate	Slower
Faster	Heartbeat	Slower
Increases	Skin perspiration	Decreases
Decreases	Digestive activity	Increases
Increases; stress hormones released	Adrenal gland activity	Decreases; stress hormones inhibited

The Biology of Emotion

As you drive down the highway, the fog thickens. Suddenly you see a pile of cars in front of you. Your mind temporarily freezes, your muscles tighten, your stomach becomes queasy, and your heart feels like it is going to pound out of your chest. You immediately slam on the brakes and try to veer away from the pile of cars. Tires screech, windshield glass flies, and metal smashes. Then all is quiet. After a few short seconds, you realize that you are alive. You find that you can climb out of the car. Your fear turns to joy, as you sense your luck in not being hurt. In a couple of seconds, the joy turns to anger. You loudly ask, "Who caused this accident?" As you moved through the emotions of fear, joy, and anger, your body changed.

Arousal   Recall from chapter 3 that the *autonomic nervous system (ANS)* takes messages to and from the body's internal organs, monitoring such processes as breathing, heart rate, and digestion. The ANS is divided into the sympathetic and the parasympathetic nervous systems (see figure 11.11). The *sympathetic nervous system (SNS)* is involved in the body's arousal; it is responsible for a rapid reaction to a stressor, sometimes it is referred to as the fight-or-flight response. The SNS immediately causes an increase in blood pressure, a faster heart rate, more rapid breathing for greater oxygen intake, and more efficient blood flow to the brain and major muscle groups. All these changes prepare us for action. At the same time the body stops digesting food, because it is not necessary for immediate action (which could explain why just before an exam, students are usually not hungry).

The *parasympathetic nervous system (PNS)* calms the body. Whereas the sympathetic nervous system prepares the individual for fighting or running away, the parasympathetic nervous system promotes relaxation and healing. When the PNS is activated, heart rate and blood pressure drop, stomach activity and food digestion increase, and breathing slows (Kalat, 2004).

The sympathetic and parasympathetic nervous systems evolved to improve the mammalian species' likelihood of survival, but it does not take a life-threatening situation to activate them (Clark, Boutros, & Mendez, 2005). Emotions such as anger are associated with elevated SNS activity, as exemplified in heightened blood pressure and heart rate. But states of happiness and contentment also activate the SNS to a lesser extent.

Examiners use a polygraph to tell if someone is lying. A polygraph monitors changes in the body believed to be influenced by emotional states. Controversy has swirled about the polygraph's use because it is unreliable.

Measuring Arousal Because arousal includes a physiological response, researchers have been intrigued by how to accurately measure it. One aspect of emotional arousal is *galvanic skin response (GSR)*, which involves an increase in the skin's electrical conductivity when sweat gland activity increases. Measurement of this electrical activity provides an index of arousal that has been used in a number of studies of emotion.

Another measure of arousal is the **polygraph**, a machine used by examiners to try to determine if someone is lying; it monitors changes in the body—heart rate, breathing, and electrodermal response (an index detecting skin resistance to passage of a weak electric current)—thought to be influenced by emotional states (Grubin & Madsen, 2005; Kircher & Raskin, 2002).

In a typical polygraph test, an individual is asked a number of neutral questions and several nonneutral, key questions. If the individual's heart rate, breathing, and electrodermal responses increase substantially when the key questions are asked, the individual is assumed to be lying.

How accurate is the lie detector? No one has found a unique physiological response to deception (Lykken, 2001). Heart rate and breathing can increase for reasons other than lying, making it difficult to interpret the physiological indicators of arousal. Experts argue that the polygraph errs just under 50 percent of the time (Vrij, 2000). However, some psychologists defend the polygraph's use, saying that polygraph results are as sound as other forms of evidence, such as hair fibre analysis (Honts, 1998). The majority of psychologists, though, argue against the polygraph's use because of its inability to tell who is lying and who is not (Lykken, 2001). As a result, polygraph tests are not usually admissible in courts of law in Canada, the United States, and many other countries (Ben-Shakhar, Bar-Hillel, & Kremnitzer, 2002).

To address these concerns, researchers from the University of New Brunswick have explored improved polygraph methodologies (Cullen & Bradley, 2004; Bradley & Rettinger, 1992). One such method is the *Guilty Knowledge Test* (MacLaren, 2001; Verschuere, Crombez, & Koster, 2004). The test is premised on the fact that some crime details may be known only to investigators and the criminal. The investigators create questions that take advantage of this fact. For example, if the criminal had stolen $500 in a yellow envelope from the bottom drawer of a desk, the following questions could be created:

1: You stole: $700, $400, $800, $500, or $200?
2: The envelope containing the money was: blue, red, yellow, brown, or white?
3: The envelope containing the money was in: a safe, a filing cabinet, a cupboard, a desk, or a briefcase?

The first item in each set typically generates a large physiological response from both guilty and innocent suspects, so it is always a dummy item, and never the "correct," crime-relevant answer. The responses to the other four items are compared. The criminal, who knows the details of the crime, should have a large response to each of the correct details. By contrast, innocent suspects, unaware of the relevant details, will have large responses only at random. In probability terms, respondents have a one-in-four, or 25 percent, chance of showing their largest response to the correct detail in any one set. However, the probability of having the largest response on all three sets is the multiple of the individual set probabilities, that is, 0.25 x 3. This means that an innocent suspect has only a 1.5 percent chance of being falsely considered guilty. If more items are used in the test or the sets are repeated, the probability of mistakenly identifying innocent suspects becomes even less likely.

James-Lange and Cannon-Bard Theories Imagine that you and your date are enjoying a picnic in the country. Suddenly, a bull runs across the field toward you. Why are you afraid? Two well-known theories of emotion that involve physiological processes provide answers to this question.

Common sense tells you that you are trembling and running away from the bull because you are afraid. But William James (1890/1950) and Carl Lange (1922) said emotion works in the opposite way. The **James-Lange theory** states that emotion results from physiological states triggered by stimuli in the environment: Emotion

polygraph A machine that monitors physiological changes thought to be influenced by emotional states; it is used by examiners to try to determine if someone is lying.

James-Lange theory States that emotion results from physiological states triggered by stimuli in the environment.

James–Lange Theory

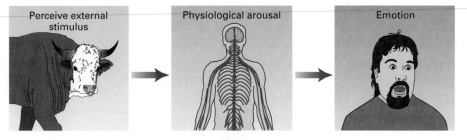

Perceive external stimulus → Physiological arousal → Emotion

Cannon–Bard Theory

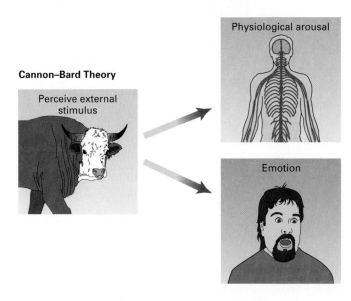

Perceive external stimulus → Physiological arousal / Emotion

FIGURE 11.12
James-Lange and Cannon-Bard Theories

occurs after physiological reactions. Moreover, each emotion, from anger to rapture, has a distinct set of physiological changes, evident in changes in heart rate, breathing patterns, sweating, and other responses. Essentially, the James-Lange theory proposes that after the initial perception, the experience of the emotion results from the perception of one's own physiological changes.

Let's see how the James-Lange theory would explain fear in the situation with the bull. You see the bull scratching his hoof on the ground, and you begin to run away. Your aroused body then sends sensory messages to your brain, at which point emotion is perceived. According to this theory, you do not run away because you are afraid; rather, you are afraid because you are running away. In other words, you perceive a stimulus in the environment, your body responds, and you interpret the body's reaction as emotion. In one of James' own examples, you perceive you have lost your fortune, you cry, and then interpret the crying as feeling sad. This goes against the common sense sequence of losing your fortune, feeling sorry, and then crying.

Walter Cannon (1927) objected to the assumption in the James-Lange theory that each emotional experience has its own particular set of physiological changes. He argued that different emotions could not be associated with specific physiological changes because autonomic nervous system responses are too diffuse and slow to account for rapid and differentiated emotional responses.

To understand Cannon's view, imagine the bull and the picnic once again. Seeing the bull scratching its hoof causes the thalamus of your brain to do two things simultaneously: First, it stimulates your autonomic nervous system to produce the physiological changes involved in emotion (increased heart rate, rapid breathing); second, it sends messages to your cerebral cortex, where the experience of emotion is perceived. Philip Bard (1934) supported this theory, and so the theory became known as the **Cannon-Bard theory**, the theory that emotion and physiological reactions occur simultaneously. In the Cannon-Bard theory, the body plays a less important role than in the James-Lange theory. Figure 11.12 shows how the James-Lange and Cannon-Bard theories differ.

Cannon-Bard theory States that emotion and physiological states occur simultaneously.

FIGURE 11.13

Direct and Indirect Brain Pathways in the Emotion of Fear
Information about fear can follow two pathways in the brain when an individual sees a snake. The direct pathway (*broken arrow*) conveys information rapidly from the thalamus to the amygdala. The indirect pathway (*solid arrows*) transmits information more slowly from the thalamus to the sensory cortex (here, the visual cortex), then to the amygdala.

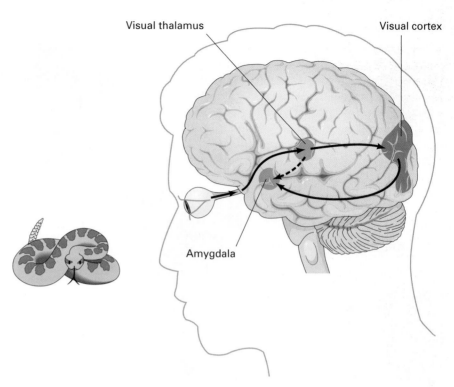

The question of whether or not emotions involve discrete autonomic nervous system responses continues to be debated (Keltner & Ekman, 2000). Recent studies have documented some emotion-specific autonomic nervous system responses (Christie & Friedman, 2004; Lang, Davis, & Ohman, 2000). For example, fear, anger, and sadness are associated with increased heart rate, but disgust is not. Also, anger is linked with increased blood flow to the hands, an effect that is not triggered by fear.

Neural Circuits and Neurotransmitters   Contemporary researchers are more interested in charting the neural circuitry of emotions and discovering the role of neurotransmitters in emotion than was the case in the early twentieth century (Phan & others, 2004). The focus of much of their work has been on the amygdala, the almond-shaped structure in the limbic system discussed in chapter 3. The amygdala houses circuits that are activated when we experience negative emotions.

Joseph LeDoux (2000, 2002; LaBar & LeDoux, 2002; Fellous & Ledoux, 2005) has conducted a number of research studies that focus on the neural circuitry of one emotion: fear. The amygdala plays a central role in fear. When the amygdala determines that danger is present, it shifts into high gear, marshalling the resources of the brain in an effort to protect the organism from harm. This fear system was designed by evolution to detect and respond to predators and other types of natural dangers that threaten survival or territory.

The amygdala receives neurons from all the senses: sight, hearing, smell, touch. If a danger is communicated by any of these neurons, the amygdala is activated and immediately sends out messages to bodily organs that respond in ways to prevent harm to the organism.

The brain circuitry that involves the emotion of fear can follow two pathways: a direct pathway from the thalamus to the amygdala or an indirect pathway from the thalamus through the sensory cortex to the amygdala (see figure 11.13). The direct pathway does not convey detailed information about the stimulus, but it has the advantage of speed. And speed clearly is an important characteristic of information available to an organism facing a threat to its survival. The indirect pathway carries nerve impulses from the sensory organs (eye, ear, for example) to the thalamus (recall that the thalamus is a relay station for incoming sensory stimuli); from the thalamus, the nerve impulses travel to the sensory cortex, which then sends appropriate signals to the amygdala.

Recall from chapter 9 that the amygdala is linked with emotional memories. LeDoux (2000) says that the amygdala hardly ever forgets. This quality is useful because, once we learn that something is dangerous, we don't have to relearn it. However, we pay a penalty for this ability. Many people carry fears and anxieties around with them that they would like to get rid of but cannot seem to shake. Part of the reason for this dilemma is that the amygdala is well connected to the cerebral cortex, in which thinking and decision making primarily occur (McGaugh & Cahill, 2002). The amygdala is in a much better position to influence the cerebral cortex than the other way around, because it sends more connections to the cerebral cortex than it gets back. This may explain why it is so hard to control our emotions, and why, once fear is learned, it is so hard to erase.

LeDoux (2002) says that it is unlikely that the amygdala mediates all emotions. There is some evidence that the amygdala participates in positive emotions, but that role is not yet well understood (Hamann & others; 2002; Park & others, 2001; Zalla & others, 2000).

Researchers are also finding that the brain's cerebral hemispheres may be involved in understanding emotion. Several studies have shown that the cerebral hemispheres work differently in approach- and withdrawal-related emotions (Demaree & others, 2005; Lee & others, 2004; Davidson, Shackman, & Pizzagalli, 2002). Approach-related emotions, such as happiness, are linked more strongly with left hemisphere brain activity, whereas withdrawal-related emotions, such as disgust, show stronger activity in the brain's right hemisphere.

In addition to charting the main brain structures involved in neural pathways of emotions, researchers are intrigued by the roles that neurotransmitters play in these pathways. Endorphins and dopamine might be involved in positive emotions such as happiness, and norepinephrine might function in regulating arousal (Verhoeff & others, 2003; Berridge & O'Neil, 2001; Robbins, 2000).

Cognitive Factors

Does emotion depend on the tides of the mind? Are we happy only when we think we are happy? Cognitive theories of emotion centre on the premise that emotion always has a cognitive component (Derryberry & Reed, 2002; Ellsworth, 2002). Thinking is said to be responsible for feelings of love and hate, joy and sadness. Cognitive theorists also recognize the role of the brain and body in emotion, but they give cognitive processes the main credit for emotion.

The Two-Factor Theory of Emotion   In the **two-factor theory of emotion** developed by Stanley Schachter and Jerome Singer (1962), emotion is determined by two factors: physiological arousal and cognitive labelling (see figure 11.14). They argued that we look to the external world for an explanation of why we are aroused. We interpret external cues and label the emotion. For example, if you feel good after someone has made a pleasant comment to you, you might label the emotion "happy." If you feel badly after you have done something wrong, you may label the feeling "guilty."

To test their theory of emotion, Schachter and Singer (1962) injected volunteer participants with epinephrine, a drug that produces high arousal. After participants were given the drug, they observed someone else behave in either a euphoric way (shooting papers at a wastebasket) or an angry way (stomping out of the room). As predicted, the euphoric and angry behaviour influenced the participants' cognitive interpretation of their own arousal. When they were with a happy person, they rated themselves as happy; when they were with an angry person, they said they were angry. But this effect occurred only when the participants were not told about the true effects of the injection. When they were told that the drug would increase their heart rate and make them jittery, they said the reason for their own arousal was the drug, not the other person's behaviour.

Psychologists have had difficulty replicating the Schachter and Singer experiment, but, in general, research supports the belief that misinterpreted arousal intensifies emotional experiences (Leventhal & Tomarken, 1986). An intriguing study by Dutton and Aron (1974) illustrates this conclusion. In this classic study, an attractive woman approached men while they were walking across the Capilano River Bridge in British Columbia. Only those without a female companion were approached. The woman asked the men to make up a brief story for a project she was doing on creativity. The

two-factor theory of emotion Schachter and Singer's theory that emotion is determined by two main factors: physiological arousal and cognitive labelling.

FIGURE 11.15

Capilano River Bridge Experiment: Misinterpreted Arousal Intensifies Emotional Experiences

(*Top*) The precarious Capilano River Bridge in British Columbia. (*Bottom*) The experiment in progress. An attractive woman approached men while they were crossing the bridge; she asked them to make up a story to help her with a creativity project. She also made the same request on a lower, much safer bridge. The men on the Capilano River Bridge told sexier stories, probably because they were aroused by the fear or excitement of being up so high on a swaying bridge and interpreted their arousal as sexual attraction for the female interviewer.

FIGURE 11.14

Schachter and Singer's Two-Factor Theory of Emotion

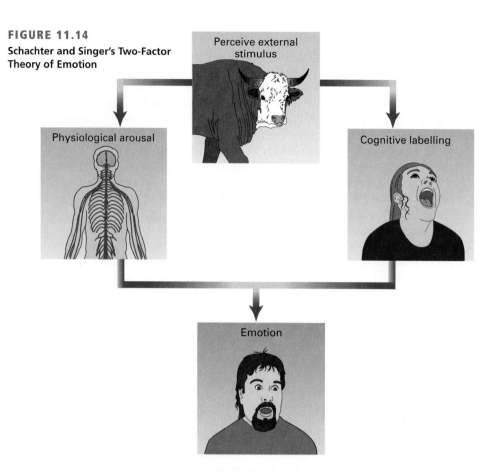

Capilano River Bridge sways precariously more than 60 metres above rapids and rocks (see figure 11.15). The female interviewer made the same request of other men crossing a much safer, lower bridge. The men on the Capilano River Bridge told more sexually oriented stories and rated the female interviewer more attractive than men on the lower, less frightening bridge did .

The Primacy Debate: Cognition or Emotion? Richard Lazarus (1991, 1999) believes cognitive activity is a precondition for emotion. He says that we cognitively appraise ourselves and our social circumstances. These appraisals, which include values, goals, commitments, beliefs, and expectations, determine our emotions. People may feel happy because they have a deep religious commitment, angry because they did not get the raise they anticipated, or fearful because they expect to fail an exam.

Robert Zajonc (1984) disagrees with Lazarus. Emotions are primary, he says, and our thoughts are a result of them. Who is right? Likely, both are correct. Lazarus refers mainly to a cluster of related events that occur over a period of time, whereas Zajonc describes single events or a simple preference for one stimulus over another. Lazarus speaks about love over the course of months and years, a sense of value to the community, and plans for retirement; Zajonc talks about a car accident, an encounter with a snake, and liking ice cream better than spinach.

Some of our emotional reactions are virtually instantaneous and probably do not involve cognitive appraisal, such as shrieking on detecting a snake. They may even constitute a different form of consciousness (Panskepp, 2003, 2005). Other emotional circumstances, especially those that occur over a long period of time, such as a depressed mood or anger toward a friend, are likelier to involve cognitive appraisal. Indeed, the direct and indirect brain pathways described earlier support the idea that some of our emotional reactions do not involve deliberate thinking, whereas others do (LeDoux, 2000).

Regardless of whether our emotions arise directly or involve cognitive appraisal, we are used to being able to label them. But not everyone can say the same. To learn more about *alexithymia*, the inability to verbally describe emotions see the Critical Reflections box.

What Difference Does It Make If You Can't Name Your Emotions?

Clinical psychologist Mark Lumley describes the case of a 40-year-old man who came to him for psychotherapy. The man had suffered a number of "strange attacks" in which he stated that "the atmosphere changed, the walls seemed to close in, and the voices of the other patients became a buzz" (Lumley, 2004). According to Lumley, the man used no subjective terms to describe his experience. He did not speak of apprehension or fear, offered no mental imagery, and did not describe any psychological factors involved in triggering these experiences. Throughout therapy, the man was consistently unable to recognize his own psychological states or those of others. He consistently made external, rather than internal attributions about his behaviour. His attacks, for example, he believed, might be triggered by his wife, his job, his diet, the season of the year or changing light levels. Yet this man was conscientious and well-educated and attended therapy regularly. Lumley diagnosed him as alexithymic.

Alexithymia, the inability to name emotions, was derived from the Greek words a meaning "lack," *lexis* meaning "word," and *thymos* meaning "emotions." First described by Peter Sifneos in 1972 (Sifneos, 1972), alexithymia raises questions about the relationship between our emotions and our cognitions (Kreitler, 2005). For example, does the inability to name emotions mean they are not felt at all?

According to Lumley (2004), alexithymics cannot describe their feelings because they have little insight into them in the first place. Consequently, they typically engage in externally oriented thinking (Parker, Prkachin, & Prkachin, 2005). In one experiment, Roedema & Simons (1999) used the Toronto Alexithymia Scale (Taylor. Ryan, & Bagby, 1985) to identify groups of alexithymic and normal students who were then shown a series of emotional images. Not only were the alexithymic students poorer at providing emotion-related words in response to the slides, they also showed lessened skin conductance and heart rate changes to the slides, indicating a reduced arousal response in the first place.

Despite being conscientious, Lumley's male patient was unsuccessful in therapy because he was unable to develop insight into the underlying psychological causes of, and emotional consequences of, his panic attacks. Similarly, despite being well educated, he was underemployed and few intimate friends. (Lumley, 2004).

"Hot cognition," the integration of our emotions into our cognition, may sometimes be a problem, as when we let anxiety get the better of us on an exam or when we let our emotional reactions to a political candidate overly influence our judgments of that candidate's suitability for public office (Lodge & Taber, 2005). But the difficulties suffered by alexithymics points out the importance of emotion to many forms of cognition. A popular stereotype of the relationship of emotions to cognition is that emotions only get in the way. One folk saying holds that "Revenge is a dish best eaten cold." Mark Twain's commented, "When angry, count four." Yet our best thinking about the social world around us requires that we factor in our emotions and the emotions of the people around us. Without a clear understanding of these internal factors, our ability to make informed social judgments suffers.

Lumley's (2004) client faces a difficult future. He remains vulnerable to negative psychological health outcomes and continued difficulties in his work and personal relationships. And perhaps his maleness was no accident. The master stereotype we alluded to earlier, that women are emotional and men are not, may turn out to be a folk psychology acknowledgement of the prevalence of alexithymia among males. According to Levant (2003), this problem is so much more common among men that he has labelled it "normative male alexithymia." Gaining more insight into alexithymia may hold the key to understanding not only the relationship between emotion and cognition but the relationship between men and women as well.

What do you think?

- Have you ever met anyone that you think might be alexithymic? What symptoms did they show? Do you have a better understanding of that person now?
- When do you emotions get in the way of your thinking? When are they helpful?
- Do you think men are more prone to alexithymia than women? Do you think this is a biological difference or might it arise through the differential socialization of men and women?

Behavioural Factors

Remember that our definition of emotion includes not only physiological and cognitive components but also a behavioural component. The behavioural component can be verbal or nonverbal. Verbally, a person might show love for someone by professing it verbally or might display anger by saying some nasty things. Nonverbally, a person might smile, frown, show a fearful expression, look down, or slouch.

Most interest in the behavioural dimension of emotion has focused on the nonverbal behaviour of facial expressions (Russell & Fernandez-Dols, 1997). Emotion researchers have been intrigued by people's ability to detect emotion from a person's facial expression. In a typical research study, participants, shown photographs like those in figure 11.16, are usually able to identify these six emotions: happiness, anger, sadness, surprise, disgust, and fear (Ekman & O'Sullivan, 1991). Recently, Montagne & colleagues (2005) reported that men are not as accurate as women at processing emotional expressions in faces.

FIGURE 11.16 Recognizing Emotions in Facial Expressions

Look at the six photographs and determine the emotion reflected in each of the six faces. (*Top*) happiness, anger, sadness (*Bottom*) surprise, disgust, fear

Might our facial expressions not only reflect our emotions but also influence them? The **facial feedback hypothesis** states that facial expressions can influence emotions, as well as reflect them. In this view, facial muscles send signals to the brain, which help individuals recognize the emotion they are experiencing (Keillor & others, 2002; Soussignan, 2002). For example, we feel happier when we smile and sadder when we frown. Recently, however, Prkachin (2005) has shown that facial feedback does not modulate the experience of pain.

Support for the facial feedback hypothesis comes from a classic experiment by Ekman, Levenson, & Friesen (1983). In this study, professional actors moved their facial muscles in very precise ways, such as raising their eyebrows and pulling them together, raising their upper eyelids, and stretching their lips horizontally back to their ears (you might want to try this out yourself). They were asked to hold their expression for 10 seconds, during which time the researchers measured their heart rate and body temperature. When they moved facial muscles in the ways described, they showed a rise in heart rate and a steady body temperature, physiological reactions that characterize fear. When the actors made an angry expression with their faces (eyes have a penetrating stare, brows are drawn together and downward, and lips are pressed together or opened and pushed forward), their heart rate and body temperature both increased. The concept involved in the facial feedback hypothesis might sound familiar. It provides support for the James-Lange theory of emotion discussed earlier—namely, that emotional experiences can be generated by changes in and awareness of our own bodily states.

Sociocultural Factors

Are the facial expressions that are associated with different emotions largely innate, or do they vary across cultures? Are there gender variations in emotion?

facial feedback hypothesis States that facial expressions can influence emotions, as well as reflect them.

Culture and the Expression of Emotion In *The Expression of the Emotions in Man and Animals,* Charles Darwin (1872/1965) stated that the facial expressions of human beings are innate, not learned; are the same in all cultures around the world; and evolved from the emotions of animals. Darwin compared the similarity of human snarls of anger with the growls of dogs and the hisses of cats. He compared the giggling of chimpanzees when they are tickled under their arms with human laughter.

Today psychologists still believe that emotions, especially facial expressions of emotion, have strong biological ties (Goldsmith, 2002). For example, children who are blind from birth and have never observed the smile or frown on another person's face smile or frown in the same way that children with normal vision do. If emotions and facial expressions that go with them are unlearned, then they should be the same the world over.

The universality of facial expressions and the ability of people from different cultures to accurately label the emotion that lies behind the facial expression has been researched extensively (Beaupré & Hess, 2005). Psychologist Paul Ekman's (1980, 1996, 2003) careful observations reveal that the many facial expressions of emotion do not differ significantly from one culture to another. For example, Ekman and his colleague photographed people expressing emotions such as happiness, fear, surprise, disgust, and grief. They found that when they showed the photographs to other people from the United States, Chile, Japan, Brazil, and Borneo (an Indonesian island in the western Pacific Ocean), all tended to label the same faces with the same emotions (Ekman & Friesen, 1968). Another study focused on the way the Fore tribe, an isolated Stone Age culture in New Guinea, matched descriptions of emotions with facial expressions (Ekman & Friesen, 1971). Before Ekman's visit, most of the Fore had never seen a Caucasian face. Ekman showed them photographs of North American faces expressing emotions such as fear, happiness, anger, and surprise. Then he read stories about people in emotional situations. The Fore were able to match the descriptions of emotions with the facial expressions in the photographs. The similarity of facial expressions of emotions by persons in New Guinea and North America is shown in figure 11.17.

Whereas facial expressions of basic emotions appear to be universal across cultures, display rules for emotion are not culturally universal. **Display rules** are sociocultural standards that determine when, where, and how emotions should be expressed (Matsumoto & others, 2005). For example, although happiness is a universally expressed emotion, when, where, and how it is displayed may vary from one culture to another. The same is true for other emotions, such as fear, sadness, and anger. For example, members of the Utku culture in Alaska discourage anger by cultivating acceptance and by dissociating themselves from any display of anger. If a trip is hampered by an unexpected snowstorm, the Utku do not become frustrated but accept the presence of the snowstorm and build an igloo. Most of us would not act as mildly in the face of subzero weather and barriers to our travel.

Just like facial expressions, some other nonverbal signals appear to be universal indicators of certain emotions. For example, when people are depressed, it shows not

FIGURE 11.17

Emotional Expressions in North America and New Guinea
(*Left*) Two women from North America. (*Right*) Two men from the Fore tribe in New Guinea. Notice the similarity in their expressions of disgust and happiness. Psychologists believe that the facial expression of emotion is virtually the same in all cultures.

display rules Sociocultural standards that determine when, where, and how emotions should be expressed.

In the Middle Eastern country of Yemen, male-to-male kissing is commonplace, but in North America it is uncommon.

only in their sad facial expressions but also in their slow body movements, downturned heads, and slumped posture.

Many nonverbal signals of emotion, though, vary from one culture to another (Cohen & Borsoi, 1996; Mesquita, 2002). For example, male-to-male kissing is commonplace in Yemen but uncommon in North America, with the exception of Quebec. And the "thumbs up" sign, which in most cultures means either everything is okay or the desire to hitch a ride, is an insult in Greece, similar to a raised third finger in North America.

Gender Influences Unless you've been isolated on a mountaintop, away from people, television, magazines, and newspapers, you probably know the stereotype about gender and emotion: She is emotional, he is not. This stereotype is a powerful and pervasive image in our culture (Shields, 1991).

Is this stereotype supported by research on the nature of emotional experiences in females and males? Researchers have found that females and males are often more alike in the way they experience emotion than the stereotype would lead us to believe. Females and males often use the same facial expressions, adopt the same language, and describe their emotional experiences similarly when they keep diaries about their life experiences. For many emotional experiences, researchers do not find differences between females and males—both sexes are equally likely to experience love, jealousy, anxiety in new social situations, anger when they are insulted, grief when close relationships end, and embarrassment when they make mistakes in public (Tavris & Wade, 1984). Thus, the master stereotype that females are emotional and males are not is simply that—a stereotype.

When we go beyond stereotype and consider some specific emotional experiences, contexts in which emotion is displayed, and certain beliefs about emotion, gender does matter in understanding emotion (Brannon, 2005; Shields, 1991). Consider anger. Men are more likely to show anger toward strangers, especially other men, when they feel they have been challenged, and men are more likely to turn their anger into aggressive action than women are. This difference may be due to socialization. According to Chaplin, Cole, & Zahn-Waxler (2005), parents, especially fathers, are more likely to attend to submissive emotions in girls and disharmonious emotions in boys.

Differences between females and males regarding emotion are more likely to occur in contexts that highlight social roles and relationships. For example, females are more likely than males to give accounts of emotion that include interpersonal relationships. And females are more likely to express fear and sadness than males are, especially when communicating with their friends and family.

Classifying Emotions

There are more than 200 words for emotions in the English language, indicating the complexity and variety of emotions. Not surprisingly, psychologists have created ways to classify emotions. One of these schemes is the wheel model. Another is a two-dimensional model.

The Wheel Model A number of psychologists have classified the emotions we experience by placing them on a wheel. One such model was proposed by Robert Plutchik (1980, 2003; see figure 11.18). He believes emotions have four dimensions: (1) They are positive or negative, (2) they are primary or mixed, (3) many are polar opposites, and (4) they vary in intensity. Ecstasy and enthusiasm are positive emotions; grief and anger are negative emotions. For example, think about your ecstasy when you get an unexpected A on a test or your enthusiasm about the ski trip this weekend—these are positive emotions. In contrast, think about negative emotions, such as grief when someone close to you dies or anger when someone verbally attacks you. Positive emotions enhance our self-esteem; negative emotions lower our self-esteem. Positive emotions improve our relationships with others; negative emotions depress the quality of those relationships.

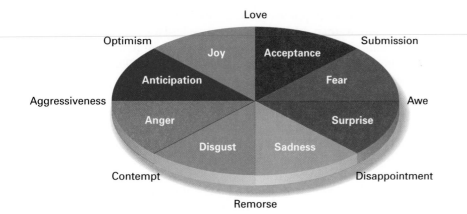

FIGURE 11.18
Plutchik's Classification of Emotions
Plutchik theorized that people experience the eight basic emotions represented in the coloured sections of the drawing as well as combinations of these emotions, shown outside the wheel.

Plutchik believes that emotions are like colours. Every colour of the spectrum can be produced by mixing the primary colours. Possibly some emotions are primary, and, if mixed together, they combine to form all other emotions. Happiness, disgust, surprise, sadness, anger, and fear are candidates for primary emotions. For example, combining sadness and surprise gives disappointment. Jealousy is composed of love and anger. Plutchik developed the emotion wheel to show how primary emotions work. Mixtures of primary emotions adjacent to each other produce other emotions. Some emotions are opposites—love and remorse, optimism and disappointment.

Another wheel-like model of emotion was proposed by Sylvan Tomkins (1962, 1981). He believes that the basic emotions are fear, anger, joy, distress, disgust, interest, surprise, contempt, and shame. Figure 11.19 shows that there is some consensus between Plutchik and Tomkins.

Theorists such as Plutchik and Tomkins view emotions as essentially innate reactions that require little cognitive interpretation. As such, their views reflect an evolutionary perspective on emotion. In this perspective, the basic emotions evolved and were retained because of their adaptive survival value.

The Two-Dimensional Approach The two-dimensional approach to classifying emotions argues that there are two broad dimensions of emotional experiences: positive affectivity and negative affectivity. *Positive affectivity (PA)* refers to positive emotions, such as love, joy, happiness, and interest. *Negative affectivity (NA)* refers to negative emotions, such as fear, anxiety, anger, guilt, and sadness.

Positive emotions facilitate approach behaviour (Cacioppo & Gardner, 1999; Watson, 2001; Watson & others, 1999). In other words, positive affect increases the likelihood that individuals will interact with their environment and engage in activities, many of which are adaptive for the individual, its species, or both. Positive emotions can also broaden people's horizons and build their personal resources. For example, joy broadens by creating the urge to play, push the limits, and be creative. Interest broadens by creating the motivation to explore, absorb new information and experiences, and expand the self (Csikszentmihalyi, 1990; Ryan & Deci, 2000).

Negative emotions, such as fear, carry direct and immediate adaptive benefits in situations that threaten survival. However, whereas positive emotions tend to broaden a person's attention, negative emotions—such as anxiety and depression—often narrow attention (Basso & others, 1996). Negative emotions may, so to speak, cause a person to miss the forest (or the suspect's style of dress or gun) for the trees.

There is increasing interest in the role that positive affectivity might play in well-being (Diener, Oishi, & Lucas, 2003). For example, positive emotions can serve as markers of well-being (Frederickson, 2001). When people's lives are characterized by joy, happiness, love, and interest, it is likely that these override negative emotions such as sadness, anger, and despair (Diener, 1999). Positive emotions can also broaden the scope of action and attention (Fredrickson & Branigan, 2005).

Plutchik	Tomkins
Fear	Fear
Anger	Anger
Joy	Joy
Sadness	Distress
Acceptance	Interest
Surprise	Surprise
Disgust	Contempt
Anticipation	Shame

FIGURE 11.19
Comparison of Plutchik's and Tomkins's Classifications of Basic Emotions

Positive emotions can improve coping. In one study, individuals who experienced more positive emotions than others developed broader-based coping strategies, such as thinking about different ways of dealing with a problem and stepping back from the situation and being more objective (Frederickson & Joiner, Jr., 2002).

In some cases, positive emotions can undo lingering negative emotions (Frederickson, 2001). For example, mild joy and contentment have been found to undo the lingering cardiovascular effects of negative emotions, such as sadness (Frederickson & Levenson, 1998). In sum, positive emotions likely serve important functions in an individual's adaptation, growth, and social connection. By building personal and social resources, positive emotions improve people's well-being.

A Negative Emotion: Anger Anger is a powerful emotion. It has strong effects not only on social relationships but also on the person experiencing the emotion. We can easily recount obvious examples of anger that often harm not only others but the angry individual as well—unrestrained and recurrent violence toward others, verbal and physical abuse of children, perpetual bitterness, the tendency to carry a "chip on the shoulder" in which a person overinterprets others' actions as demeaning, and the inability to inhibit the expression of anger.

What makes people angry? People often get angry when they feel they are not being treated fairly or when their expectations are violated. One researcher asked people to remember or keep records of their anger experiences (Averill, 1983). Most of the people said they became at least mildly angry several times a week; some said they became mildly angry several times a day. In many instances, people said they got angry because they perceived that a friend or a loved one had performed a misdeed. They especially got angry when they perceived the other person's behaviour as unjustified, avoidable, and willful (Zillman, 1998).

Catharsis is the release of anger or aggressive energy by directly or vicariously engaging in anger or aggression; the *catharsis hypothesis* states that behaving angrily or watching others behave angrily reduces subsequent anger. Psychodynamic theory promotes catharsis as an important way to reduce anger, arguing that people have a natural, biological tendency to display anger. From this perspective, taking out your anger on a friend or a loved one should reduce your subsequent tendency to display anger; so should heavy doses of anger on television and the anger we see in professional sports and other aspects of our culture. Why? Because such experiences release pent-up anger.

Social cognitive theory argues strongly against this view. This theory states that by acting angrily, people are often rewarded for their anger, and that by watching others display anger, people learn how to be angry themselves. Which view is right? Research on catharsis suggests that acting angrily does not have any long-term power to reduce anger (Bushman, 2002). If the catharsis hypothesis were correct, war should have a cathartic effect in reducing anger and aggression, but a study of wars in 110 countries since 1900 showed that warfare actually stimulated domestic violence (Archer & McDaniel, 1995; Archer & Gartner, 1976). Compared with nations that remained at peace, postwar nations saw an increase in homicide rates. As psychologist Carol Tavris (1989) says in her book *Anger: The Misunderstood Emotion*, one of the main results of the ventilation approach to anger is to raise the noise level of our society, not to reduce anger or solve our problems. Individuals who are the most prone to anger get angrier, not less angry. Ventilating anger often follows a cycle of a precipitating event, an angry outburst, shouted recriminations, screaming or crying, a furious peak (sometimes accompanied by physical assault), exhaustion, and a sullen apology or just sullenness.

Every person gets angry at one time or another. How can we control our anger so it does not become destructive (Glancy & Saini, 2005)? As we mentioned earlier, Mark Twain once remarked, "When angry, count four; when very angry, swear." Tavris (1989) would agree with Twain's first rule, if not the second. She makes the following recommendations:

catharsis The release of anger or aggressive energy by directly or vicariously engaging in anger or aggression; the catharsis hypothesis states that behaving angrily or watching others behave angrily reduces subsequent anger.

1. When your anger starts to boil and your body is getting aroused, work on lowering the arousal by waiting. Emotional arousal will usually decrease if you just wait long enough.

2. Cope with the anger in ways that involve being neither chronically angry over every little annoyance nor passively sulking, which simply rehearses your reasons for being angry.

3. Form a self-help group with others who have been through similar experiences with anger. The other people will likely know what you are feeling, and together you might come up with some good solutions to anger problems.

4. Take action to help others, which can put your own miseries in perspective, as exemplified by the actions of the women who organized Mothers Against Drunk Driving or any number of people who work to change conditions so that others will not suffer as they did.

5. Seek ways of breaking out of your usual perspective. Some people have been rehearsing their "story" for years, repeating over and over the reasons for their anger. Retelling the story from other participants' points of view often helps people to find routes to empathy.

A Positive Emotion: Happiness   Earlier in the chapter we discussed well-being and raised the question of whether happiness is an important aspect of well-being. Indeed, some psychologists equate happiness with subjective well-being, although it was not until 1973 that *Psychological Abstracts*, the major source of psychological research summaries, included *happiness* as an index term.

Psychologists' interest in happiness focuses on positive ways we experience life, including cognitive judgments of our well-being (Diener, Oshi, & Lucas, 2003; Locke, 2002). That is, psychologists want to know what makes you happy and how you perceive your happiness (Lyubomirsky, Sheldon, & Schkade, 2005).

Many years ago, the French philosopher Jean-Jacques Rousseau described the subjective nature of happiness this way: "Happiness is a good bank account, a good cook, and a good digestion." In a review of research on happiness, having a good cook and a good digestion were not on the list of factors that contribute to our happiness, but the following were (Diener & Seligman, 2002; Diener, Oishi, & Lucas, 2003; Diener & others, 1999; Post, 2005):

- Psychological and personality characteristics: high levels of self-esteem, optimism, extroversion, and personal control
- A supportive network of close relationships
- A culture that offers positive interpretations of most daily events
- Being engaged by work and leisure
- Being engaged in altruistic emotions and behaviours
- A faith that embodies social support, purpose, hope, and religious attendance (see figure 11.20)

Some factors that many people believe are involved in happiness, such as age and gender, are not.

But what about Rousseau's "good bank account"? Can we buy happiness? One study tried to find out if lottery winners are happier than other people (Brickman, Coates, & Janoff-Bulman, 1978). Major lottery winners were not happier than people who hadn't won, when they were asked about the past, present, and the future. The people who hadn't won a lottery were actually happier doing life's mundane things such as watching television, buying clothes, and talking with a friend. Winning a lottery does not appear to be the key to happiness. Extremely wealthy people are not happier than people who can purchase the necessities. People in wealthy countries are not happier than people in poor countries. What is important, though, is having enough money to buy life's necessities.

"My life is O.K., but it's no jeans ad."

Richard Cline © 1988 from The New Yorker Collection.
All Rights Reserved.

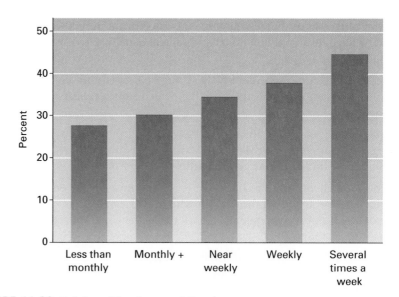

FIGURE 11.20 **Religious Attendance and Happiness**
In surveys of more than 34,000 Americans from 1972 to 1996, the more often American adults attended religious services the more likely they were to say that they were "very happy."

Intense positive emotions—such as winning a lottery or getting a date with the person of your dreams—do not add much to a person's general sense of well-being because they are rare, and because they can decrease the positive emotion and increase the negative emotion we feel in other circumstances. For example, if you get a perfect grade on an essay, you may be overwhelmed with happiness at the time, but if your next essay gets a good but not perfect grade, the previous emotional high can diminish your positive emotion the next time. It is the rare, if nonexistent, human being who experiences intense positive emotions and infrequent negative emotions week after week after week. According to Diener (1984), happiness boils down to the frequency of positive emotions and the infrequency of negative emotions.

You might wonder just how you objectively measure a subjective state such as happiness. Albert Kozma & Michael Stones (1980) developed the Memorial University of Newfoundland Scale of Happiness (MUNSH) for precisely this purpose. The MUNSH relies upon responses to 24 statements like "Most of the things I do are boring or monotonous" to produce a reliable and valid measure of happiness. The MUNSH has been widely used in research on happiness. For example, Kozma, Stones, & McNeil (1991) applied it to the study of happiness in older people. A Chinese version of the MUNSH was recently developed (Liu & Gong, 1999; Dahua & others, 2004).

How might winning the lottery affect your happiness?

Albert Kozma, of Memorial University, and Michael Stones, now at Lakehead University, have been interested in the measurement of happiness and subjective well-being. They are the developers of the widely used Memorial University of Newfoundland Scale of Happiness (MUNSH). Kozma & Stones have commented that "Because the subjective happiness of another person cannot be gauged directly, any form of objective measurement must be indirect."

Evolutionary psychologist David Buss (2000) believes that humans possess evolved mechanisms that can produce a deep sense of happiness. These include mating bonds, friendship, close kinship, and cooperative relationships. However, he cautions that some evolved mechanisms impede happiness. These include the distress created by jealousy and anger and the competition that benefits one person at the expense of another.

> ## reflect and review

 Summarize views of emotion.

- Define emotion and explain the biology of emotion in terms of arousal and neural activity.
- Discuss the two-factor theory and the primacy debate over cognition and emotion.
- Describe behavioural expressions of emotion.
- Identify sociocultural similarities and differences in the expression of emotion.
- Compare the wheel model and the two-dimensional model of classifying emotions, and discuss the role of emotions in well-being.

Think about the last time you became angry. Compare how you handled your anger with the strategies recommended in the chapter. What strategies can you use to better control your anger? Is catharsis a good way to handle your anger? Explain.

Motivation and Emotion

1 APPROACHES TO MOTIVATION

- The Evolutionary Approach
- Drive Reduction Theory
- Optimum Arousal Theory
- The Cognitive Approach
- Issues in Motivation

2 HUNGER

- The Biology of Hunger
- Obesity and Eating
- Dieting
- Eating Disorders

3 SEXUALITY

- The Biology of Sex
- Cognitive and Sensory/Perceptual Factors
- Cultural Factors
- Psychosexual Dysfunctions
- Sexual Behaviour and Orientation

4 SOCIAL COGNITIVE MOTIVES

- Achievement
- Affiliation
- Well-Being

5 EMOTION

- The Biology of Emotion
- Cognitive Factors
- Behavioural Factors
- Sociocultural Factors
- Classifying Emotions

At the beginning of the chapter, we posed five chapter questions and encouraged you to review material related to these questions at the end of each major section (see pages 427, 434, 442, 450, and 465). Use the following reflection and review features for further your understanding of the chapter material.

CHAPTER REFLECTIONS

Apply Your Knowledge

1. Ask your friends to define the word motivation. Think about the way your friends define motivation and the way psychologists approach motivation. What are the similarities? What are the differences? Are your friends likelier to say they have too much motivation or not enough? Why might that be?

2. Do a Web search for the word hunger. What kinds of sites are listed first? How do the topics that these sites cover compare with the discussion of hunger in the text? Do the sites give you any insight into the role of environment in hunger?

3. Imagine, if you are male, that someone offered you a pill that would double the size of your lateral hypothalamus but make your androgen levels go down to half their current level. How might this pill affect your eating and sexual behaviour? Would you take the pill?

4. How much of our interpretation of emotions depends on verbal or nonverbal cues? Try the following exercise: Watch a movie that you're not familiar with and find a scene with a number of people in it. First watch the scene with the sound off and try to guess what emotions each person is experiencing. Describe the nonverbal cues that led you to your conclusions. Find a different scene, and listen to it without watching to guess what emotions are being experienced; describe the verbal cues that you used. Then, watch both scenes with the sound on. Which cues were more useful—verbal or nonverbal ones?

5. Visit the Web site of the Trends in International Mathematics and Science Study (TIMSS) at http://nces.ed.gov/timss/. Access the data from the largest and most ambitious international study of student achievement ever conducted.

CHAPTER REVIEW

Describe psychological approaches to emotion.

- Motivation gives our behaviour, thoughts, and feelings a purpose. Motivated behaviour is energized, directed, and sustained. Early evolutionary theorists considered motivation to be based on instinct, the innate biological pattern of behaviour that is assumed to be universal throughout a species. The idea that some of our motivation is unlearned and involves physiological factors is still present today. The evolutionary psychology view emphasizes that various aspects of motivation that provided evolutionary advantages were passed down through the genes from generation to generation.

- A drive is an aroused state that occurs because of a physiological need. A need is a deprivation that energizes the drive to eliminate or reduce the deprivation. Drive reduction theory was proposed as an explanation of motivation, with the goal of drive reduction being homeostasis, the body's tendency to maintain an equilibrium.

- Optimum arousal theory focuses on the Yerkes-Dodson law, which states that performance is best under conditions of moderate rather than low or high arousal. Moderate arousal often serves us best when we tackle life's tasks, but there are times when low or high arousal is linked with better performance. Sensation seeking is one aspect of the motivation for high arousal that psychologists study.

- The contemporary view of motivation emphasizes cognitive factors, including such information processing abilities as attention, memory, and problem solving. Psychologists debate how extensively motivation is influenced by conscious versus unconscious thought. Intrinsic motivation, based on internal factors such as self-determination, curiosity, challenge, and effort, is one of the most widely studied aspects of achievement motivation. Extrinsic motivation is based on external incentives such as rewards and punishments. Most psychologists believe that intrinsic motivation is more positively related to achievement than extrinsic motivation.

- According to Maslow's hierarchy of needs, our main needs are satisfied in this sequence: physiological, safety, love and belongingness, esteem, and self-actualization. Maslow gave the most attention to self-actualization, the motivation to develop to one's full potential.

- Three important issues in motivation are whether motivation is based on innate, unlearned, biological factors or learned, sociocultural, experiential factors; to what degree we are aware of what motivates us; and to what degree we are internally or externally motivated.

Explain the physiological basis of hunger and the nature of eating behaviour.

- Interest in the stomach's role was stimulated by Cannon's classic research, but stomach signals are not the only factors that affect hunger. Glucose (blood sugar) is an important factor in hunger, probably because the brain is critically dependent on sugar for energy. Rodin's work helped clarify the role of insulin and glucose in hunger. Ghrelin, a hormone that is released by the stomach lining, increases feelings of hunger via the hypothalamus. Leptin, a protein secreted by fat cells, decreases food intake and increases energy expenditure. The hypothalamus plays an important role in regulating hunger. The lateral hypothalamus is involved in stimulating eating, the ventromedial hypothalamus in restricting eating. Today, neuroscientists are exploring the roles that neurotransmitters and neural circuits play in hunger.

- Obesity is a serious and pervasive problem in North America. Heredity, basal metabolism, set point, and fat cells are biological factors involved in obesity. Obese persons are more responsive to external cues than normal-weight persons are, although there are individuals at all weight levels who respond more to external than to internal stimuli. Self-control is an important cognitive factor in eating behaviour. Time and place affect eating, as does the type of food available. Our early ancestors ate natural fruits to satisfy nutritional needs, but today we fill up on the empty calories in candy and soda. The dramatic increase in obesity in the late twentieth century underscores the significance of environmental factors in obesity as increasing numbers of people eat high-fat foods and lead sedentary lives.

- Dieting for weight loss and restrained eating for weight control are common in North American society. Most diets don't work, although some people do lose weight when they diet and maintain the loss. Exercise is an important component of a successful weight-loss program. Many people, especially in their teens and 20s, diet even if they don't need to lose weight. The pressure to be thin can be harmful for people who are not overweight. However, when overweight people diet and maintain their weight loss, they reap health benefits.

- Anorexia nervosa is an eating disorder that involves the relentless pursuit of thinness through starvation. Bulimia nervosa is an eating disorder that consists of a binge-and-purge pattern. Both disorders are most common among adolescent and young adult females.

Discuss the motivation for sex.

- Motivation for sexual behaviour involves the hypothalamus. The pituitary gland controls the secretion of two classes of sex hormones: estrogens, which predominate in females, and androgens, which have stronger concentrations in males. The role of sex hormones in human sexual behaviour, especially in women, is not clear. Masters and Johnson mapped out the human sexual response pattern, which consists of four physiological phases: excitement, plateau, orgasm, and resolution.

- Thoughts and images are central in the sexual lives of humans. Sexual scripts influence sexual behaviour, as do sensory/perceptual factors. Females tend to be more sexually aroused by touch, males by visual stimulation. Pheromones are sexual attractants for many nonhuman animals, but their role in human sexual behaviour has not been documented. Many aphrodisiacs allegedly act as sexual stimulants, but there is no clear evidence that what we eat, drink, or inject has aphrodisiac qualities.

- Sexual values vary extensively across cultures. These values exert a significant effect on sexual behaviour.

- Psychosexual dysfunctions involve impairments in the sexual response pattern. Significant advances have been made in treating these dysfunctions in recent years.

- Describing sexual practices in North America has always been challenging due to the difficulty of surveying a representative sample of the population. A 1994 U.S. survey (Michael & others, 1994) and a 1997 Canadian article (Barrett & others, 1997) were major improvements over the earlier surveys by Kinsey & Hunt. This work revealed that North Americans' sex lives are more conservative than the earlier work indicated. Sexual orientation—heterosexual, homosexual, or bisexual—is most likely determined by a combination of genetic, hormonal, cognitive, and environmental factors.

Characterize the social cognitive motives and how they influence behaviour.

- Early interest in achievement focused on need for achievement. Cognitive factors in achievement focus on intrinsic motivation, attribution, and goal setting, planning, and monitoring. Attribution theory states that people are motivated to discover the underlying causes of behaviour in an effort to make sense out of the behaviour. The main emphasis in attribution theory has focused on internal causes, especially effort, and external causes. High achievers often set specific, proximal, and challenging goals. Individuals in North America are often more achievement oriented than individuals in other countries, although recent comparisons with Asian countries reveal higher achievement in those countries. A special concern is the achievement of individuals in ethnic minority groups. Minority group members are vulnerable to stereotype threat, the tendency of members of stereotyped groups to worry that their behaviour will confirm a negative group stereotype. Strategies based on achievement research are used in the workplace and in sports to motivate individuals to do their best.

- The need for affiliation (relatedness) is the motive to be with other people. It is a powerful motive in many people's lives. Cultures vary in how strongly they promote affiliation.

- Psychologists are increasingly interested in what constitutes the good life and well-being. One proposal is that well-being involves competence, autonomy, and affiliation.

Summarize views of emotion.

- Emotion is feeling, or affect, that has three components: physiological arousal, conscious experience, and behavioural expression. The biology of emotion focuses on physiological arousal involving the autonomic nervous system and its two subsystems. The galvanic skin response and the polygraph have been used to measure emotional arousal. The polygraph is considered unreliable for use as a lie detector. The James-Lange theory states that emotion results from physiological states triggered by environmental stimuli: Emotion follows physiological reactions. The Cannon-Bard theory states that emotion and physiological reactions occur simultaneously. Contemporary biological views of emotion increasingly highlight neural circuitry and neurotransmitters. LeDoux has charted the neural circuitry of fear, which focuses on the amygdala and consists of two pathways, one direct and the other indirect. It is likely that positive and negative emotions use different neural circuitry and neurotransmitters.

- Schachter and Singer's two-factor theory states that emotion is the result of both physiological arousal and cognitive labeling. Lazarus believes that cognition always directs emotion, but Zajonc argues that emotion directs cognition. Probably both are right. Alexithymia is the inability to verbally describe emotions.

- Research on the behavioural component of emotion focuses on facial expressions. The facial feedback hypothesis states that facial expressions can influence emotions, as well as reflect them.

- Most psychologists believe that facial expressions of basic emotions are the same across cultures. However, display rules, which involve nonverbal signals of body movement, posture, and gesture, vary across cultures. The master stereotype that women are emotional and men are not is just a stereotype. However, there are many contextual influences on the expression of emotion by males and females.

- Classifications of emotions have included wheel models and the two-dimensional approach. Plutchik's wheel model portrays emotions in terms of four dimensions: positive or negative, primary or mixed, polar opposites, and intensity. Both Plutchik's and Tompkins's lists of basic emotions reflect an evolutionary perspective. The two-dimensional approach to classifying emotions argues that there are just two broad dimensions of emotional experiences: positive affectivity and negative affectivity. Positive emotions likely play an important role in well-being through adaptation, growth, social connection, and building personal and social resources.

CONNECTIONS

For extra help in mastering the material in the chapter, see the review questions and practice quizzes in the Student Study Guide and the Online Learning Centre.

CORE TERMS

motivation, p. 422
instinct, p. 422
drive, p. 422
need, p. 422
homeostasis, p. 423
Yerkes-Dodson law, p. 423
intrinsic motivation, p. 424
extrinsic motivation, p. 424
hierarchy of needs, p. 426
self-actualization, p. 426

basal metabolism rate (BMR), p. 430
set point, p. 430
anorexia nervosa, p. 433
bulimia nervosa, p. 433
estrogens, p. 435
androgens, p. 435
human sexual response pattern, p. 435
pheromones, p. 437
need for achievement, p. 443
attribution theory, p. 443

need for affiliation, p. 448
emotion, p. 450
polygraph, p. 452
James-Lange theory, p. 452
Cannon-Bard theory, p. 453
two-factor theory of emotion, p. 455
facial feedback hypothesis, p. 458
display rules, p. 459
catharsis, p. 462

12 Personality

CHAPTER QUESTIONS

1 What is personality and what are the major issues in the study of personality?

2 What are the psychodynamic perspectives?

3 What are the behavioural and social cognitive perspectives?

4 What are the humanistic perspectives?

5 What are the trait perspectives?

6 What are the main methods of personality assessment?

What makes a public figure great? One interesting approach to answering this question focused on indirectly assessing personality (Winter, 2005). For example, Rubenzer and his colleagues (2000) asked historians to rate U.S. presidents on their personality characteristics. They then correlated each president's personality traits with his degree of presidential greatness as determined by referencing generally accepted lists of America's great presidents. Abraham Lincoln, who led the fight against slavery, is rated as the greatest U.S. president.

The personality trait of openness to experience showed the highest correlation with greatness as a U.S. president, perhaps partly because individuals with higher cognitive abilities have more open minds. Great presidents were rated as attentive to their emotions, willing to question traditional values and try new ways of doing things. Successful presidents also have tended to be extraverted, assertive, and stubborn, and to stand up for their ideas.

How well does this list apply to other world leaders? Consider, for example, Nelson Mandela. Born in 1918, Nelson Rolihlahla Mandela became a lawyer and a member of the African National Congress in his quest to overturn the South African apartheid system. Imprisoned in 1962 for plotting to overthrow the South African government by violence, Mandela was finally released in 1990. Apartheid, the system that systematically denied political, social, and economic rights to South Africa's majority black population, was dismantled shortly thereafter. For their roles in bringing down apartheid, Mandela and F. W. de Klerk shared the Nobel Peace Prize for 1993. Nelson Mandela went on to become the first black president of South Africa and to win worldwide praise for his attitude of reconciliation toward South African whites.

Nelson Mandela has consistently been open to experience and has questioned traditional values as he has championed human rights, education, and health care reform. He is definitely stubborn, assertive, extraverted, and willing to stand up for his ideas, repeatedly refusing to compromise his political views in return for release from prison. Retired since 1999, he continues to travel as an advocate for social and human rights.

What about your own personality? Write down seven or eight personality traits that you think best describe you. Are any of the traits that characterize great world leaders on your own list? Do people who know you well describe you as serious or wild? Shy or outgoing? Self-confident or uncertain? Friendly or hostile?

In compiling this list, you likely chose personality characteristics that you believe are an enduring part of your makeup as a person. For example, if you said that you are an outgoing person, wouldn't you also say that you were outgoing a year ago and that you will probably be an outgoing person 1 year, 5 years, and 10 years from now? The concept of personality involves the notion that each of us has some enduring core characteristics. Each of us has a more or less persistent style of thinking and behaving. Personality theories seek to describe such patterns and their underlying causes (Pervin & John, 2001; Feist & Feist, 2006).

How might the personalities of world leaders influence the fate of their countries? Can you think of other world leaders, like Abraham Lincoln and Nelson Mandela, who possess traits like openness to experience, stubbornness, the willingness to stand up for their ideas, and extroversion? Can you think of world leaders who do not possess these traits?

① THEORIES OF PERSONALITY

What is personality? What are the major issues in the study of personality?

Personality is one of those concepts that is familiar to everyone but difficult to define (Feist & Feist, 2006). In this chapter, **personality** is defined as a pattern of enduring, distinctive thoughts, emotions, and behaviours that characterize the way an individual adapts to the world.

Personality theorists and researchers ask why individuals react to the same situation in different ways, and they come up with different answers (Pervin, Cervone, & John, 2005). For example, why is Sam so talkative and gregarious and Pierre so shy and quiet when meeting someone for the first time? Why is Kendra so confident and Marie so insecure about upcoming job interviews? Some theorists believe that biological and genetic factors are responsible; others argue that life experiences are more important factors. Some theorists claim that the way we think about ourselves is the key to understanding personality, whereas others stress that the way we behave toward each other is the key (Endler, 1993). This chapter presents four broad theoretical perspectives on personality—psychodynamic, behavioural and social cognitive, humanistic, and trait. You will see how different the answers can be.

As you read about these perspectives on personality, you will notice that they address three important questions:

1. *To what degree is personality a result of innate characteristics as opposed to learned experiences* (DiLalla, 2004; Ashton & others, 1998b)? Is personality due more to heredity and biological factors or more to learning and environmental experiences? For example, are individuals conceited and self-centred because they inherited the tendency to be conceited and self-centred from their parents, or did they learn to be that way through experiences with other conceited, self-centred individuals? Freud, the originator of the psychodynamic perspective, saw personality as strongly rooted in innate factors, although many more recent psychodynamic theorists believe that environmental experiences and culture play a role in determining personality. Behavioural and social cognitive perspectives, along with humanistic perspectives, endorse environment as a powerful determinant of personality, B. F. Skinner being the strongest advocate of the influence of the environment. However, humanistic theorists do believe that people have the innate ability to reach their full potential. Trait perspectives vary in their emphasis on heredity and environment.

2. *To what degree is personality a result of conscious as opposed to unconscious forces?* How aware are individuals that they are, say, conceited and self-centred? How aware are they of the reasons they became conceited and self-centred? Psychodynamic theorists have been the strongest advocates of the unconscious mind's role in personality (Auld, Hyman, & Rudzinski, 2005). Most argue that we are largely unaware of how our individual personalities developed. Behaviourists argue that neither unconscious nor conscious thought is important in determining personality, whereas social cognitive theorists stress that conscious thought affects the way the environment influences personality. Humanists stress the conscious aspects of personality, especially in the form of self-perception. Trait theorists pay little attention to the conscious/unconscious issue.

3. *To what degree is the expression of personality a result of internal disposition as opposed to external, or situational, forces* (Kammrath, Mendoza-Denton, & Mischel, 2005)? Is the way personality is expressed in any given situation due more to an inner disposition or to the situation itself? Are individuals conceited and self-centred because of something inside themselves, a characteristic they have and carry around with them, or are they conceited and self-centred because of the situations they are in and the way they are influenced by people around them? Psychodynamic, humanistic, and trait theorists emphasize the internal dimensions

personality A pattern of enduring, distinctive thoughts, emotions, and behaviours that characterize the way an individual adapts to the world.

of personality. By contrast, behaviourists emphasize personality's external, situational determinants. Social cognitive theorists examine both external and internal determinants.

You will learn more about how the four theoretical perspectives address these issues in the rest of the chapter. The diversity of theories makes understanding personality a challenging undertaking (Derlega, Winstead, & Jones, 2005; Schultz & Schultz, 2005). Just when you think one theory has the correct explanation of personality, another theory will crop up and make you rethink your earlier conclusion. To keep from getting frustrated, remember that personality is a complex, multifaceted topic. And remember, nobody, as yet, has a complete theory of personality, although much of the available information is complementary as well as contradictory. By approaching personality from a different perspective, each theory contributes an important piece to the personality puzzle. Together they let us better appreciate the total landscape of personality in all its richness (Funder, 2001, 2004).

> ## > reflect and review

 Define personality and identify the major issues in the study of personality.

- Define the concept of personality and summarize three issues addressed by the major personality perspectives.

Earlier we asked you to list your main personality characteristics. Go over the list and evaluate whether you think you inherited these traits or learned to be this way, how aware you are of these traits in your day-to-day life, and the extent to which they are internally or externally determined.

② PSYCHODYNAMIC PERSPECTIVES

— Freud's — Psychodynamic — Evaluating
Psychoanalytic   Dissenters and   Psychodynamic
Theory   Revisionists   Perspectives

What are the main themes of psychodynamic perspectives?
Psychodynamic perspectives view personality as being primarily unconscious (that is, beyond awareness) and as developing in stages. Most psychodynamic perspectives emphasize that early experiences with parents play an important role in shaping the individual's personality. Psychodynamic theorists believe that behaviour is merely a surface characteristic and that to truly understand someone's personality we have to explore the symbolic meanings of behaviour and the deep inner workings of the mind (Feist & Feist, 2006). These characteristics were sketched by the architect of psychoanalytic theory—Sigmund Freud. As you learned in chapter 1, the psychodynamic theorists who followed Freud took issue with his original theory and have diverged from it, but still embrace his core ideas about personality.

Freud's Psychoanalytic Theory

Sigmund Freud, one of the most influential thinkers of the twentieth century, was born in Austria in 1856 and died in London at the age of 83 (Jacobs, 2003). Freud spent most of his life in Vienna, but he left the city near the end of his career to escape the Holocaust. Freud was a medical doctor who specialized in neurology. He developed his ideas about psychoanalytic theory from his work with psychiatric patients (Freud, 1917).

SIGMUND FREUD (1856–1939)
The architect of psychoanalytic theory.

psychodynamic perspectives View personality as primarily unconscious (that is, beyond awareness) and as occurring in stages. Most psychoanalytic perspectives emphasize that early experiences with parents play a role in sculpting personality.

"Good morning beheaded—uh, I mean beloved."

© The New Yorker Collection 1979 Dana Fradon from cartoonbank.com. All Rights Reserved.

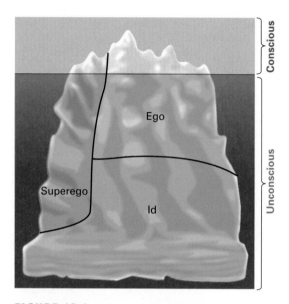

Conscious

Unconscious

Ego

Superego

Id

FIGURE 12.1

The Conscious and Unconscious Mind: The Iceberg Analogy
The analogy of the conscious and unconscious mind to an iceberg is often used to illustrate how much of the mind is unconscious in Freud's theory. The conscious mind is the part of the iceberg above water, the unconscious mind the part below water. Notice that the id is totally unconscious, while the ego and superego can operate at either the conscious or the unconscious level.

id The Freudian structure of personality that consists of instincts, which are the individual's reservoir of psychic energy.

ego The Freudian structure of personality that deals with the demands of reality.

superego The Freudian structure of personality that deals with morality.

As a child, Freud was regarded as a genius by his younger brothers and sisters and doted on by his mother. One aspect of Freud's theory emphasizes a young boy's sexual attraction for his mother; it is possible that this aspect of his theory derived from his own romantic attraction to his mother, who was beautiful and some 20 years younger than Freud's father.

For Freud, the unconscious mind holds the key to understanding behaviour. Our lives are filled with tension and conflict; to reduce the anxiety we experience as a result, we keep troubling information locked in our unconscious mind or distort it to make it personally or socially acceptable. Freud believed that even trivial behaviours have special significance when the unconscious forces behind them are revealed. A twitch, a doodle, a joke, a smile, each may have an unconscious reason for appearing. They often slip into our lives without our awareness. For example, Barbara is kissing and hugging Tom, whom she is to marry in several weeks. She says, "Oh, *Jeff*, I love you so much." Tom pushes her away and says, "Why did you call me Jeff? I thought you didn't think about him anymore. We need to have a talk!" You can probably think of times when these *Freudian slips* (misstatements that perhaps reveal unconscious thoughts) have tumbled out of your own mouth.

Freud also believed that dreams hold important clues to our behaviour, referring to them as the "royal road to the unconscious." He said dreams are unconscious representations of the conflict and tension in our everyday lives that are too painful to handle consciously. Much of the dream content is disguised in symbolism and requires extensive analysis and probing to be understood.

Remember that Freud considered the unconscious mind to be the key to understanding personality (Gedo, 2002). He likened personality to an iceberg, existing mostly below the level of awareness, just as the massive part of an iceberg is beneath the surface of the water. Figure 12.1 illustrates this analogy and how extensive the unconscious part of our mind is in Freud's view.

Personality's Structures Notice that figure 12.1 shows the iceberg divided into three segments. Freud (1917) believed that personality has three structures: the id, the ego, and the superego.

The **id** consists of instincts and is the individual's reservoir of psychic energy. In Freud's view, the id is unconscious and has no contact with reality. The id processes according to the *pleasure principle*, the Freudian concept that the id always seeks pleasure and avoids pain.

As infants mature, they learn that they cannot simply do as they please; they must take into account the real world, as well as the values of the society around them. In response to the demands and constraints of reality, a new structure of personality is formed—the **ego**, the Freudian structure of personality that deals with the demands of reality. According to Freud, the ego processes according to the *reality principle*. While the id is completely unconscious, the ego is partly conscious. It houses our higher mental functions—reasoning, problem solving, and decision making, for example. For this reason, the ego is referred to as the executive branch of the personality; like an executive in a company, it makes the rational decisions that help the company succeed. The ego helps us to test reality, to see how far we can go without getting into trouble and hurting ourselves.

The id and ego have no morality. They do not consider whether something is right or wrong. The **superego** is the Freudian structure that is the moral branch of personality. It is what we often refer to as our "conscience"—those actions the child is reproved for doing—and our "ego ideal"—those actions the child is praised for doing. Like the id, the superego does not consider reality; it only processes whether the id's impulses—sexual, aggressive, and otherwise—can be satisfied in moral terms.

Defence Mechanism	How It Works	Example
Repression	The master defence mechanism; the ego pushes painful or conflictual thoughts, impulses, or memories out of awareness, back into the unconscious mind.	A young girl was sexually abused by her uncle. As an adult, she can't remember anything about the traumatic experience.
Rationalization	The ego replaces a less acceptable unconscious thought or impulse with a more acceptable conscious one.	A university student who does not get into the university of his choice is unconsciously afraid he is not smart enough to go to university. He says that if he had tried harder he could have gotten in.
Displacement	The ego shifts feelings toward an unacceptable object to another, more acceptable object.	A woman can't take her anger out on her boss so she goes home and takes it out on her husband.
Sublimation	The ego replaces an unacceptable impulse with a socially acceptable one.	A man with strong sexual urges becomes an artist who paints nudes.
Projection	The ego attributes personal shortcomings, problems, and faults to others.	A man who has a strong desire to have an extramarital affair accuses his wife of flirting with other men.
Reaction Formation	The ego transforms an unacceptable motive into its opposite.	A woman who fears her sexual urges becomes a religious zealot.
Denial	The ego refuses to acknowledge anxiety-producing realities.	A man won't acknowledge that he has cancer even though a team of doctors has diagnosed his cancer.
Regression	The ego seeks the security of an earlier developmental period in the face of stress.	A woman returns home to mother every time she and her husband have a big argument.

It would be a dangerous and scary world if our personalities were dominated by the id. The superego tries to bring the individual's pleasure within the norms of society. Young children must realize that they cannot merely slug other children in the face. As adults, few of us are cold-blooded killers or wild wheeler-dealers; we accept the obstacles to satisfaction that exist in our world. We recognize that we need to restrain our sexual and aggressive impulses.

Both the id and the superego make life rough for the ego, which must strive to find a balance between their often contradictory demands, all the while accommodating to the demands of the real world. Your ego might say, "I will have sex only occasionally and be sure to use an effective form of birth control." But your id is saying, "I want to be satisfied; sex feels so good." And your superego is at work too, saying, "I feel guilty about having sex at all."

Defence Mechanisms The ego calls on a number of strategies to resolve the conflict between its demands for reality, the wishes of the id, and the constraints of the super-ego. These **defence mechanisms** reduce anxiety by unconsciously distorting reality. For example, when unacceptable sexual feelings threaten to become conscious, a person feels anxiety, which the ego resolves by means of defence mechanisms. The functioning of defence mechanisms was definitively highlighted by Freud's daughter, Anna Freud, herself an accomplished psychoanalyst. Figure 12.2 describes several of Freud's defence mechanisms and gives an example of each. All of them work to protect the personality and reduce anxiety (Kreitler & Kreitler, 2004).

Repression is the most powerful and pervasive defence mechanism, according to Freud; it pushes unacceptable id impulses out of awareness and back into the unconscious mind. Repression is the foundation for all psychological defence mechanisms, the

FIGURE 12.2

Defence Mechanisms
Defence mechanisms reduce anxiety in various ways, in all instances by distorting reality.

defence mechanisms The ego's protective methods for reducing anxiety by unconsciously distorting reality.

goal of which is to push, or *repress*, threatening impulses out of awareness. Freud said that our early childhood experiences, many of which he believed were sexually laden, are too threatening and stressful for us to deal with consciously; so we reduce the anxiety of childhood conflict through repression.

Two final points about defence mechanisms need to be understood. First, they are unconscious; we are not aware that we are calling on them. Second, using defence mechanisms is not, in itself, unhealthy. Healthy people often use them and they may yield desirable consequences depending on the manner and extent of their use (Cramer & Tracy, 2005). For example, when used in moderation or on a temporary basis, the defence mechanism called denial can help a person cope with impending death. For the most part, though, we should not let defence mechanisms dominate our behaviour and prevent us from facing the demands of life.

Personality Development As Freud listened to, probed, and analyzed his patients, he became convinced that their personalities were the result of experiences early in life. Freud believed that we go through five stages of personality development, which result from biological shifts in the primary focus of erogenous pleasure. At each stage of development we experience pleasure in one part of the body more than in others. *Erogenous zones*, according to Freud, are parts of the body that have especially strong pleasure-giving qualities at particular stages of development. Freud thought that our adult personality is determined by the way we resolve conflicts between how we secure pleasure from these erogenous zones—the mouth, the anus, and then the genitals—and the demands of reality.

- *Oral stage* (first 18 months). The infant's pleasure centres on the mouth. Chewing, sucking, and biting are the chief sources of pleasure that reduce tension in the infant.
- *Anal stage* (18 to 36 months of age). The child's greatest pleasure involves the anus or the eliminative functions associated with it. In Freud's view, the exercise of anal muscles reduces tension.
- *Phallic stage* (three to six years of age). The name of Freud's third stage comes from the Latin word *phallus*, which means "penis." Pleasure focuses on the genitals as the child discovers that self-stimulation is enjoyable. In Freud's view the phallic stage has a special importance in personality development because it triggers the Oedipus complex. This name comes from the Greek myth in which Oedipus unwittingly killed his father and married his mother. The **Oedipus complex** is the young boy's development of an intense desire to replace the parent of the same sex and enjoy the affections of the opposite-sex parent. The female version of the Oedipus complex is referred to as the Electra complex. At about five to six years of age, children recognize that their same-sex parent might punish them for their incestuous wishes. To reduce this conflict, the child identifies with the same-sex parent, striving to be like him or her. If the conflict is not resolved, though, the individual may become fixated at the phallic stage.
- *Latency stage* (six years of age to puberty). The child represses all interest in sexuality and develops social and intellectual skills. This activity channels much of the child's energy into emotionally safe areas and aids the child in forgetting the highly stressful conflicts of the phallic stage.
- *Genital stage* (adolescence and adulthood). The genital stage is the time of sexual reawakening; the source of sexual pleasure now becomes someone outside the family. Freud believed that unresolved conflicts with parents reemerge during adolescence. But once resolved, the individual becomes capable of developing a mature love relationship and functioning independently as an adult.

While one individual may develop through these stages normally, another may experience difficulties at one stage or another because his or her needs are under- or overgratified. For example, a parent might wean a child too early, be too casual in toilet training, punish the child for masturbation, or "smother" the child with too much attention. *Fixation* is the psychoanalytic mechanism that occurs when the individual remains focused on the method of obtaining the satisfaction that characterized that

Oedipus complex In Freud's theory, the young child's development of an intense desire to replace the same-sex parent and enjoy the affections of the opposite-sex parent.

Stage	Adult Extensions (Fixations)	Sublimations	Reaction Formations
Oral	Smoking, eating, kissing, oral hygiene, drinking, chewing gum	Seeking knowledge, humour, wit, sarcasm, being a food or wine expert	Speech purist, food faddist, prohibitionist, dislike of milk
Anal	Notable interest in one's bowel movements, love of bathroom humour, extreme messiness	Interest in painting or sculpture, being overly giving, great interest in statistics	Extreme disgust with feces, fear of dirt, prudishness, irritability
Phallic	Heavy reliance on masturbation, flirtatiousness, expressions of virility	Interest in poetry, love of love, interest in acting, striving for success	Puritanical attitude toward sex, excessive modesty

stage, even though he or she continues to develop through the remaining psychosexual stages. The result is an adult personality that is unduly reliant on immature means of obtaining satisfaction. Figure 12.3 illustrates some possible links between adult personality characteristics and fixation at oral, anal, and phallic stages.

FIGURE 12.3
Defence Mechanisms and Freudian Stages

Psychodynamic Dissenters and Revisionists

Because Freud was among the first theorists to explore personality, over time some of his ideas have needed to be updated, others revised, and some tossed out altogether. Freud's critics have said that his ideas about sexuality, early experience, social factors, and the unconscious mind were misguided (Adler, 1927; Erikson, 1968; Fromm, 1947; Horney, 1945; Jung, 1917; Kohut, 1977; Rapaport, 1967; Sullivan, 1953). His critics stress the following points:

- Sexuality is not the pervasive force behind personality that Freud believed it to be. Nor is the Oedipus or Electra complex as universal as Freud believed. Freud's concepts were heavily influenced by the setting in which he lived and worked—turn-of-the-century Vienna, a society that was, compared with contemporary society, sexually repressed and paternalistic.
- The first five years of life are not as powerful in shaping adult personality as Freud thought; later experiences deserve more attention.
- The ego and conscious thought processes play more dominant roles in our personality than Freud gave them credit for; we are not forever in thrall to the instinctual, unconscious clutches of the id. Also, the ego has a separate line of development from the id, so achievement, thinking, and reasoning are not always tied to sexual impulses.
- Sociocultural factors are much more important than Freud believed. In stressing the id's dominance, Freud placed more emphasis on the biological roots of personality.

The theories of three dissenters and revisionists—Horney, Jung, and Adler—have been especially influential in the development of psychodynamic theories, the successors to Freud's psychoanalytic theory.

Horney's Sociocultural Approach In rejecting the classical psychoanalytic concept that "anatomy is destiny," Karen Horney (1885–1952) proposed her own *psychoanalystic interpersonal theory* (Eckardt, 2005). She cautioned that some of Freud's most popular ideas were only hypotheses. She insisted that these hypotheses be supported with observable data before being accepted as fact and that sociocultural influences on personality development also be considered.

Take Freud's concept of "penis envy:" He attributed some of the behaviour of his female patients to their repressed desire to have a penis. Horney pointed out that previous research about how women function was limited by the fact that those who described women, who influenced and represented the culture, and who determined the standards for suitable growth and development were men. She countered the notion of penis envy with the hypothesis that both sexes envy the attributes of the other, with men suffering "womb envy," coveting women's reproductive capacities. She

KAREN HORNEY (1885–1952)
Developed the first feminist criticism of Freud's theory. Horney's view emphasizes women's positive qualities and self-evaluation.

CARL JUNG (1875–1961)
Swiss psychoanalytic theorist Carl Jung developed the concepts of the collective unconscious and archetypes.

also argued that women who are described as feeling penis envy are desirous only of the status that men have in most societies (Gilman, 2001).

Horney also believed that the need for security, not for sex or aggression, was the prime motive in human existence. Horney reasoned that an individual whose needs for security are met should be able to develop his or her capacities to the fullest extent.

She also suggested that people usually develop one of three strategies in their effort to cope with anxiety. First, individuals might *move toward* people, seeking love and support. Second, individuals might *move away* from people, becoming more independent. And, third, individuals might *move against* people, becoming competitive and domineering. The secure individual uses these three ways of coping in moderation and balance, whereas the insecure individual often uses one or more of these strategies in an exaggerated fashion, becoming too dependent, too independent, or too aggressive.

Psychologists are still revamping psychoanalytic theory in the sociocultural direction that Horney pointed. Nancy Chodorow's (1978, 1989, 2004) feminist revision of psychoanalytic theory, for example, emphasizes that many more women than men define themselves in terms of their relationships and that emotions tend to be more important in women's lives. In short, personality is not simply a matter of biology; social experiences and culture also shape personality.

Jung's Analytical Theory Freud's contemporary Carl Jung (1875–1961) had a different complaint about psychoanalytic theory. Jung shared Freud's interest in the unconscious, but he believed that Freud underplayed the role of the unconscious mind in personality. In fact, Jung believed that the roots of personality go back to the dawn of human existence. The **collective unconscious** is the impersonal, deepest layer of the unconscious mind, shared by all human beings because of their common ancestral past. The experiences of a common past have made a deep, permanent impression on the human mind (Mayer, 2002). According to Jung, the purpose of the unconscious is to urge the individual toward wholeness, or psychological growth, by balancing the narrower one-sidedness of conscious experience.

The collective unconscious is expressed through what Jung called **archetypes**, emotionally laden ideas and images that have rich and symbolic meaning for all people. Jung believed that these archetypes emerge in art, religion, and dreams. He used archetypes to help people understand themselves (Knox, 2003; McDowell, 2001).

Two common archetypes are the *anima* (woman) and *animus* (man). The anima is the feminine archetype, all of the feminine psychological tendencies within the man's unconscious. Similarly, the animus is the masculine archetype, all of the masculine psychological tendencies within the woman's unconscious. Another archetype, the *mandala*, a figure within a circle, has been used so often in art that Jung took it to represent the self (see figure 12.4). Yet another archetype is the *shadow*, the repressed darker side of our personality. The shadow, which is evil and immoral, is represented by many fictional characters, such as Dracula, Mr. Hyde (of Jekyll and Hyde), and Darth Vader in the *Star Wars* films (see figure 12.5; Frager & Fadiman, 2005).

collective unconscious Jung's term for the impersonal, deepest layer of the unconscious mind, shared by all human beings because of their common ancestral past.

archetypes The name Jung gave to the emotionally laden ideas and images in the collective unconscious that have rich and symbolic meaning.

FIGURE 12.4

The Mandala as a Symbol of the Self Archetype
In his exploration of mythology, Carl Jung found that the self is often symbolized by a mandala, from the Sanskrit word for "circle." Jung believed that the mandala represents the self's unity.

FIGURE 12.5
***Star Wars* Characters as Archetypes of Good and Evil**
In *Star Wars*, Ben Kenobi (*left*) represented the archetype of good and Darth Vader (*right*) the archetype of evil.

Adler's Individual Psychology   Alfred Adler (1870–1937) was another of Freud's contemporaries. In Adler's **individual psychology**, people are motivated by purposes and goals. They are creators of their own lives. Unlike Freud, who believed in the overwhelming power of the unconscious mind, Adler argued that people have the ability to consciously monitor their lives. He also believed that social factors are more important than sexual motivation in shaping personality (Shulman, 2004).

Adler thought that everyone strives for superiority, seeking to adapt, improve, and master the environment. He did not mean that everyone strives to feel superior to others; rather, he meant that everyone strives to become better. Adler also referred to this as a striving for perfection. Striving for superiority is our response to the uncomfortable feelings of inferiority that we all experience as infants and young children when we interact with people who are bigger and more powerful. *Compensation* is Adler's term for the individual's attempt to overcome imagined or real inferiorities or weaknesses by developing one's own abilities. Adler believed that compensation was normal, and he said that we often make up for a weakness in one ability by excelling in a different ability. For example, one person may be a mediocre student but compensate by excelling in athletics.

Overcompensation is Adler's term for the individual's attempt to deny rather than acknowledge a real situation or for the exaggerated effort to conceal a weakness. Adler described two patterns of overcompensation: *Inferiority complex* is his term for exaggerated feelings of inadequacy; *superiority complex* is his term for exaggerated self-importance invoked to mask feelings of inferiority.

Evaluating Psychodynamic Perspectives

Although psychodynamic theories have diverged from Freud's original psychoanalytic version, they do share some core principles:

- Personality is determined both by current experiences and, as the original psychoanalytic theory proposed, by those from early in life.
- Personality can be better understood by examining it developmentally, as a series of stages that unfold with the individual's physical, cognitive, and socioemotional development.
- We mentally transform our experiences, giving them meaning that shapes our personality.
- The mind is not all consciousness; unconscious motives lie behind some of our puzzling behaviour.

individual psychology The term for Adler's approach, which views people as motivated by purposes and goals, being creators of their own lives.

- The individual's inner world often conflicts with the outer demands of reality, creating anxiety that is not easy to resolve.
- Personality and adjustment—not just the experimental laboratory topics of sensation, perception, and learning—are rightful and important topics of psychological inquiry.

One criticism of the psychodynamic perspectives is that the main concepts have been difficult to test; they are largely matters of inference and interpretation. Until recently, researchers have not, for example, successfully investigated such key concepts as repression in the laboratory. More recent work (Shevrin, 2000, 2001; Shulman & Reiser, 2004) holds forth the promise of developing neurophysiological measures of psychodynamic concepts.

Thus much of the data used to support psychodynamic perspectives have come from clinicians' subjective evaluations of clients; clinicians can easily see evidence of theories they hold. Other data come from patients' recollections of the distant past (especially those from early childhood) and are of unknown accuracy.

Others object that psychodynamic perspectives have too negative and pessimistic a view of the person. For example, these perspectives place too much weight on early experiences within the family and their influence on personality and do not acknowledge that we retain the capacity for change and adaptation throughout our lives. Some psychologists believe that Freud and Jung placed too much faith in the unconscious mind's ability to control behaviour. Others object that Freud overemphasized the importance of sexuality in understanding personality; we are not born into the world with only a bundle of sexual and aggressive instincts. The demands of reality do not always conflict with our biological needs.

Finally, some critics have noted that many psychodynamic perspectives, especially Freud's, have a male, Western bias. Although Horney's theory helped to correct this bias, psychologists studying female personality development, as well as personality development in various ethnicities and cultures continue to revise psychodynamic theory today (Callan, 2002; Chodorow, 2004).

> ## reflect and review

2 **Summarize the psychodynamic perspectives.**

- Describe the main tenets of the psychodynamic perspectives.
- Explain the key concepts in Freud's psychoanalytic theory.
- Discuss how the ideas of three psychodynamic dissenters and revisionists differed from Freud's.
- Identify the pros and cons of the psychodynamic perspectives.

What psychodynamic ideas may apply to all human beings? Which ones may not apply to everyone?

3 BEHAVIOURAL AND SOCIAL COGNITIVE PERSPECTIVES

Skinner's Behaviourism	Bandura's Social Cognitive Theory	Evaluating the Behavioural and Social Cognitive Perspectives

What are the main features of the behavioural and social cognitive perspectives?
John is married to Heather. Both have warm, friendly personalities, and they enjoy being with each other. Psychodynamic theorists would say that their personalities

derive from long-standing relationships with their parents, especially from their early childhood experiences. They would also say that the reason for their attraction is unconscious, that they are unaware of how their biological heritage and early life experiences have been carried forward to influence their adult personalities.

But behaviourists and social cognitive theorists would observe John and Heather and see something quite different. They would examine the two people's experiences, especially their most recent ones, to understand the reason for John and Heather's attraction to each another. John might be described as rewarding Heather's behaviour, and vice versa. Behaviourists and social cognitive theorists would make no reference to unconscious thoughts, the Oedipus complex, defence mechanisms, and so on.

The behavioural and social cognitive perspectives, introduced in chapter 1, emphasize the importance of environmental experiences and people's observable behaviour to understand their personalities. Within that broad framework, behaviourists focus on behaviour; social cognitive theorists also examine cognitive factors in personality.

Skinner's Behaviourism

At about the same time Freud was interpreting his patients' unconscious minds through their recollections of childhood experiences, John B. Watson and Ivan Pavlov were conducting detailed observations of behaviour under controlled laboratory conditions. Recall from chapter 7 that Pavlov believed organisms learn through classical conditioning. Chapter 7 also described B. F. Skinner's approach to learning, called operant conditioning.

Skinner believed that all overt behaviour is determined by the external environment and that personality refers to a person's relatively stable behavioural patterns. Accordingly, Skinner believed that we do not have to understand biological or cognitive processes to explain personality (behaviour). Following Skinner, behaviourists suggest that you cannot pinpoint where personality is or how it is determined; you can only observe what people do. For example, observations of Sam might reveal his relatively consistent shy, achievement-oriented, and caring behaviours. According to Skinner, these behaviours *are* his personality. Furthermore, Sam is this way because rewards and punishments in his environment shaped him into a shy, achievement-oriented, and caring person. Because of interactions with family members, friends, teachers, and others, Sam has *learned* to behave in this fashion.

Skinner stressed that our behaviour always has the capacity for change if new experiences are encountered (Monte & Soldod, 2003). Thus Sam's shy, achievement-oriented, and caring behaviour may not be unchangeable and enduring. For example, Sam may be uninhibited on Saturday night with friends at a bar, unmotivated to excel in English class, and occasionally nasty to his sister. Skinnerians believe that consistency in behaviour comes only from consistency in environmental experiences. If Sam's shy, achievement-oriented, and caring behaviour is consistently rewarded, his pattern of behaviour likely will be consistent. The issue of consistency in personality is an important one, and it will be discussed often throughout this chapter.

Because behaviourists believe that personality is learned and often changes according to environmental experiences and situations, it follows that, by rearranging experiences and situations, the individual's personality can be changed (Larsen & Buss, 2005). For the behaviourist, shy behaviour can be changed into outgoing behaviour; aggressive behaviour can be shaped into docile behaviour; and lethargic, bored behaviour can be shaped into enthusiastic, interested behaviour.

Bandura's Social Cognitive Theory

Most psychologists believe the behaviourists are right when they say that personality is learned and influenced strongly by environmental experiences. But they think Skinner went too far in declaring that a person's characteristics are irrelevant in understanding personality. **Social cognitive theory** states that behaviour, environment, and cognitive factors are important in understanding personality. Like the behavioural approach

social cognitive theory States that behaviour, environment, and cognitive factors are important in understanding personality.

Albert Bandura (*above*) and Walter Mischel are the architects of contemporary social cognitive theory.

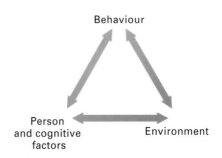

FIGURE 12.6

Bandura's Social Cognitive Theory
Bandura's social cognitive theory emphasizes reciprocal influences of behaviour, environment, and person/cognitive factors.

self-efficacy The belief that one can master a situation and produce positive outcomes.

of Skinner, the social cognitive view relies on empirical research in studying personality. But this research has focused not just on observable behaviour but also on the cognitive factors that influence what we are like as people. Albert Bandura (1997, 2000a, 2001, 2004) and Walter Mischel (1973, 2004; Idson & Mischel, 2001; Mischel & Shoda, 2001) are the main architects of social cognitive theory's contemporary version, which was initially labelled *cognitive social learning theory* by Mischel (1973).

Reciprocal Determinism Bandura coined the term *reciprocal determinism* to describe the way behaviour, environment, and person/cognitive factors interact to create personality (see figure 12.6). The environment can determine a person's behaviour (which matches up with Skinner's view), but, also, the person can act to change the environment. And, person/cognitive factors can influence behaviour and can be influenced by behaviour.

Observational Learning Remember from chapter 7 that Bandura believes observational learning is a key aspect of how we learn. Here, a cognitive factor, our powers of observation, mediates between the environment (what we are observing) and our resultant behaviour. Through observational learning, we form ideas about the behaviour of others and then, possibly, adopt this behaviour ourselves. For example, a young boy might observe his father's aggressive outbursts and hostile exchanges with people; when the boy is with his peers, he interacts in a highly aggressive way, showing the same characteristics that his father's behaviour does. Or a young executive adopts the dominant and sarcastic style of her boss. When interacting with one of her subordinates, she says, "I need this work immediately if not sooner; you are so far behind you think you are ahead!" Social cognitive theorists believe that we acquire a wide range of behaviours, thoughts, and feelings through observing others' behaviour; these observations form an important part of our personalities.

Personal Control Social cognitive theorists differ from the behavioural view of Skinner by emphasizing that we can regulate and control our own behaviour, despite our changing environment (Mischel & Shoda, 2001; Mischel, Shoda, & Mendoza-Denton, 2002; Zarit, Pearlin, & Schaie, 2002). For example, another young executive who observes her boss behave in a dominant and sarcastic manner may find the behaviour distasteful and go out of her way to be encouraging and supportive of her subordinates. Or imagine that someone tries to persuade you to join a particular social club on campus and makes you an enticing offer. You reflect on the offer, consider your interests and beliefs, and make the decision not to join. Your *cognition* (your thoughts) leads you to control your behaviour and resist environmental influence in this instance (Matthews & others, 2000).

Bandura (2001) and other social cognitive theorists and researchers emphasize that psychological health—being well-adjusted—can be measured by people's beliefs in their capacity to exercise some control over their own functioning and over environmental events. Three aspects of personal control that these theorists are exploring are delay of gratification, self-efficacy, and locus of control.

Delay of Gratification One element of personal control that Walter Mischel (Mischel & Ayduk, 2004; Metcalfe & Mischel, 1999) believes is important in understanding an individual's personality is the ability to delay gratification. Those who can defer immediate satisfaction for a desirable future outcome are demonstrating the importance of person/cognitive factors in determining their own behaviour. For example, when you are in school you resist the temptation to slack off and have a good time now so you will be rewarded with good grades later. Again, the point is that we are capable of controlling our behaviour rather than being influenced by others.

Self-Efficacy Another element of personal control is **self-efficacy**, the belief that one can master a situation and produce positive outcomes. Bandura (1997, 2000b, 2001, 2004) and others have shown that self-efficacy is related to a number of positive developments in people's lives, including solving problems, becoming more sociable, initiating a diet or exercise program and maintaining it, and quitting smoking (see figure 12.7; Warnecke & others, 2001; Fletcher & Banasik, 2001). Self-efficacy influences whether people even try to develop healthy habits, as well as how much effort they expend in coping with stress, how long they persist in the face of obstacles, and how much stress they experience (Clark & Dodge, 1999). Self-efficacy is related to whether people initiate psychotherapy to deal with their problems and whether it succeeds or not (Sandahl, Gerge, & Herlitz, 2004; Longo, Lent, & Brown, 1992). Researchers also have found that self-efficacy is linked with successful job performance (Judge & Bono, 2001).

Self-efficacy helps people in unsatisfactory situations by encouraging them to believe that they can succeed (Murray & others, 2002). Overweight individuals will likely have more success with their diets if they believe they have the self-control to restrict their eating. Smokers who believe they will not be able to break their habit probably won't even try to quit smoking, even though they know that smoking is likely to cause poor health and shorten their lives.

How can you increase your self-efficacy? The following strategies can help (Watson & Tharp, 2003):

- Select something you expect to be able to do, not something you expect to fail at accomplishing. As you develop self-efficacy, you can tackle more daunting projects.
- Distinguish between past performance and your present project. You might come to expect from past failures that you cannot do certain things. However, remind yourself that your past failures are in the past and that you now have a new sense of confidence and accomplishment.
- Pay close attention to your successes. Some individuals have a tendency to remember their failures, but not their successes.
- Keep written records so that you will be concretely aware of your successes. A student who sticks to a study schedule for four days and then fails to stick to it on the fifth day should not think, "I'm a failure. I can't do this." This statement ignores the fact that the student was successful 80 percent of the time (keeping to the schedule four out of five days).
- Make a list of the specific kinds of situations in which you expect to have the most difficulty and the least difficulty. Begin with the easier tasks and cope with the harder ones after you have experienced some success.

Locus of Control   Much of psychology's current interest in intrinsic motivation, self-determination, and self-responsibility (discussed in chapter 11) grew out of a third element of personal control, the concept of **locus of control** (Rotter, 1966). This concept refers to individuals' beliefs about whether the outcomes of their actions depend on what they do (internal control) or on events outside their personal control (external control). Internally controlled people assume that their own behaviours and actions are responsible for the consequences that happen to them. In contrast, externally controlled people believe that, regardless of how they behave, they are subject to the whims of fate, luck, or other people.

Locus of control has been studied especially in regard to physical and mental health. Individuals with internal locus of control know more about the conditions that lead to good physical and psychological health and are likelier to take positive steps to improve their health, such as quitting smoking, avoiding substance abuse, and exercising regularly (Lindqvist & Aberg, 2002; Lin & Tsay, 2005).

A wealth of research has documented that having an internal, but not external, locus of control is associated with positive functioning and adjustment. Lester (1992) found that individuals high in external locus of control often use defensive strategies in problem solving and coping instead of actively pursuing solutions; thus, they fail more often. In contrast, Hassall, Rose, & McDonald (2005) studied the parents of learning disabled children. Parents with an internal parental locus of control experienced lower stress and were more effective in coping with their children's difficulties. Croatian psychologist Gordana Kuterovac-Jagodic (2003) studied symptoms of post-traumatic stress in children from Osijek, Croatia, which suffered military attacks in 1994. She found that internal locus of control was associated with less severe symptoms.

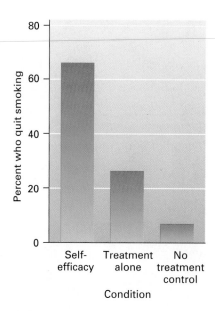

FIGURE 12.7

Self-Efficacy and Smoking Cessation
In one study, smokers were randomly assigned to one of three conditions. In the self-efficacy condition, individuals were told they had been chosen for the study because they had great potential to quit smoking. Then, they participated in a 14-week program on smoking cessation. In the treatment-alone condition, individuals participated in the 14-week smoking cessation program but were told that they had been randomly selected for it. In the no-treatment control condition, individuals did not participate in the smoking cessation program. At the conclusion of the 14-week program, individuals in the self-efficacy condition were likelier to have quit smoking than their counterparts in the other two conditions.

locus of control Individuals' beliefs about whether the outcomes of their actions depend on what they do (internal control) or on events outside of their personal control (external control).

Martin Seligman went from pessimist to optimist and believes that you can, too. Seligman (1990) provided the details in his book *Learned Optimism.* Recall Seligman's interest in changing psychology from a discipline that focuses mainly on the negative aspects of life to one that spends more time charting the positive aspects of life.

Optimism Another factor that is often related to positive functioning and adjustment is being optimistic (Kubzansky & others, 2002). Interest in the concept of optimism in the field of psychology has especially been fuelled by Martin Seligman's (1990) theory and research on optimism. Seligman views optimism as a matter of how a person explains the causes of bad events (Peterson & Seligman, 2004). Optimists explain the causes of bad events as due to external, unstable, and specific causes. Pessimists explain bad events as due to internal, stable, and global causes.

To illustrate the power of optimism, Seligman (1990) recalled the situation of 45-year-old Bob Dell, who had a wife, two children, and a mortgage. After working 25 years in a meat-packing plant, he was suddenly fired from his job. With no immediate job prospects and only a high school education, his situation looked grim. He was approached by an insurance agent who wanted to sell him a policy. Bob informed the agent that he was unemployed and could not afford anything. The agent told Bob that his insurance company was currently hiring new sales representatives and suggested that he apply for a position. Bob had never sold anything, but, being an optimist, he decided to give it a try.

Seligman was a consultant for the insurance company at the time. He had persuaded the company to hire salespeople who did not meet all their qualifications but were high in optimism. Dell was one of 130 applicants who were identified as "optimists" on a measure Seligman had developed, which was included in the measures that job applicants had to complete.

In less than one year, Bob went from sausage-stuffer to super-salesman, earning twice what he had at the meat-packing plant. When Bob learned from a magazine article about the experimental program that he had participated in, with characteristic optimism, he called Seligman, introduced himself, and sold him a retirement policy!

Seligman's interest in optimism stemmed from his work on *learned helplessness,* which initially focused on animals who learned to become helpless (passive and unresponsive) after they experienced uncontrollable negative events (Seligman, 1975). In his view, pessimism is much like learned helplessness and belief in external locus of control. Optimism is much like belief in self-efficacy and internal locus of control.

Other researchers have defined optimism as the expectancy that good things are more likely, and bad things less likely, to occur in the future (Carver & Scheier, 2001). This view focuses on how people pursue their goals and values. In the face of adversity, optimists still believe that their goals and values can be attained. Their optimism keeps them working to attain their goals, whereas pessimism results in people giving up.

Numerous research studies reveal that optimists generally function more effectively and are physically and mentally healthier than pessimists:

- *Physical health.* In one rather remarkable classic finding, people who were classified as optimistic at age 25 were healthier at ages 45 to 60 than those who had been classified as pessimistic (Peterson, Seligman, & Vaillant, 1988). In another study, pessimism was linked with less effective immune system functioning and poor health (Brennan & Charnetski, 2000). Optimists have also been found to live longer after open heart surgery and have lower blood pressure than pessimists (Ben-Zur, Rappaport, & Uretzky, 2004).
- *Mental health.* In one study, optimism was a better predictor than self-efficacy of a person's ability to avoid depression over time (Shnek & others, 2001). In another study, optimism was related to better mental health in cancer patients (Cohen, de Moor, & Amato, 2001). Another study found that optimism was linked with better mental health and lower perceptions of pain in older adults (Achat & others, 2000).

Optimism is not all good, however. It can have costs if it is too unrealistic (Clarke & others, 2000; Peterson, 2000; Schneider, 2001). But being optimistic is a good strategy when you have some chance of affecting the future through an optimistic outlook. Thinking optimistically is discussed further in chapter 15.

Evaluating the Behavioural and Social Cognitive Perspectives

The behavioural and social cognitive theories both focus on the influence of environment on personality. They have fostered a scientific climate for understanding personality that highlights the observation of behaviour. In addition, social cognitive theory emphasizes the influence of cognitive processes in explaining personality and suggests that people have the ability to control their environment.

Critics of both the behavioural and social cognitive perspectives take issue with one or more of these points:

- The behavioural view is criticized for ignoring the importance of cognition in personality and giving too much importance to the role of environmental experiences.
- Both approaches have been described as too concerned with change and situational influences on personality and not paying adequate tribute to the enduring qualities of personality.
- Both views are said to ignore the role biology plays in personality.
- Both are labelled reductionistic, which means they try to explain the complex concept of personality in terms of one or two factors.
- Both the behavioural and social cognitive views are criticized for being too mechanical, missing the most exciting and richest dimensions of personality.

This latter criticism—that the creative, spontaneous, human dimensions of personality are missing from the behavioural and social cognitive perspectives—has been made on numerous occasions by humanists, whose perspective we consider next.

> ### reflect and review

3 **Explain the behavioural and social cognitive perspectives.**

- Define the behavioural and social cognitive perspectives.
- Summarize Skinner's behaviourism.
- Discuss social cognitive theory.
- Discuss the behavioural and social cognitive perspectives.

Are you an optimist or a pessimist? Explain how your style of thinking about bad events has helped you or hindered you as a student.

4 HUMANISTIC PERSPECTIVES

— **Rogers's Approach** — **Maslow's Approach** — **Self-Esteem** — **Evaluating Humanistic Perspectives**

What are the main themes of the humanistic perspectives?

Remember the example of the married couple, John and Heather, who were described as having warm, friendly personalities? Humanistic psychologists would say that John's and Heather's warm, friendly personalities are a reflection of their inner selves. They would emphasize that a key to understanding the attraction between John and Heather is their positive perception of each other. John and Heather are not trying to control each other. Rather, they have determined their own courses of action, and each has freely chosen to marry. According to the humanistic perspectives, neither raw biological instincts nor unconscious thoughts are reasons for their attraction.

The **humanistic perspectives** stress a person's capacity for personal growth, freedom to choose one's own destiny, and positive human qualities. Humanistic psychologists

humanistic perspectives Stress the person's capacity for personal growth, freedom to choose a destiny, and positive qualities.

CARL ROGERS (1902–1987)
Carl Rogers was a pioneer in the development of the humanistic perspective.

believe that each of us has the ability to cope with stress, to control our lives, and to achieve what we desire (Cain, 2001; O'Hara & Taylor, 2000; Smith, 2001). Each of us has the ability to break through and understand ourselves and our world; we can burst the chrysalis and become a butterfly, say the humanists.

You probably sense that the humanistic perspectives provide clear contrasts to the psychodynamic perspectives, which often seem to be based on conflict, destructive drives, and a pessimistic view of human nature. The humanistic perspectives also seem to contrast with the behavioural perspective, which, at its extreme, reduces human beings to mere puppets on the strings of rewards and punishments. Humanistic perspectives do have some similarities with the social cognitive perspective, though, especially with those theories that emphasize the role of personal control and optimism in personality.

Carl Rogers and Abraham Maslow were the leading architects of the humanistic perspectives. Their work has provided the foundation for more contemporary studies of self-esteem.

Rogers's Approach

Like Freud, Carl Rogers (1902–1987) began his inquiry about human nature with people who were troubled. In the knotted, anxious, defensive verbal stream of his clients, Rogers (1961) noted the things that seemed to be keeping them from having positive self-concepts and reaching their full potential as human beings.

Rogers believed that most people have considerable difficulty accepting their own true, innately positive, feelings. As we grow up, people who are central to our lives condition us to move away from these positive feelings. Too often we hear our parents, siblings, teachers, and peers say things like "Don't do that," "You didn't do that right," and "How can you be so stupid?" When we don't do something right, we often get punished. Parents may even threaten to withhold their love unless we conform to their standards. The result is lower self-esteem.

These constraints and negative feedback continue during our adult lives. The result tends to be either that our relationships carry a dark cloud of conflict or that we conform to what others want. As we struggle to live up to society's standards, we distort and devalue our true selves. We might even completely lose our sense of self by mirroring what others want.

The Self   Through the individual's experiences with the world, a self emerges—the "I" or "me" of our existence. Rogers did not believe that all aspects of the self are conscious, but he did believe they are all accessible to consciousness. The self is a whole, consisting of one's self-perceptions (how attractive I am, how well I get along with others, how good an athlete I am) and the values we attach to these perceptions (good/bad, worthy/unworthy).

Self-concept, a central theme in Rogers's and other humanists' views, refers to individuals' overall perceptions and assessments of their abilities, behaviour, and personalities. In Rogers' view, a person who has an inaccurate self-concept is likely to be maladjusted.

In discussing self-concept, Rogers distinguished between the real self, which is the self resulting from our experiences, and the ideal self, which is the self we would like to be. The greater the discrepancy between the real self and the ideal self, said Rogers, the more maladjusted we will be. To improve our adjustment, we can develop more positive perceptions of our real self, not worry as much about what others want, and increase our positive experiences in the world.

Unconditional Positive Regard, Empathy, and Genuineness   Rogers proposed three methods to help a person develop a more positive self-concept: *unconditional positive regard*, *empathy*, and *genuineness*.

Rogers said that we need to be accepted by others, regardless of what we do. **Unconditional positive regard** is his term for accepting, valuing, and being positive toward another person regardless of the person's behaviour. When a person's behaviour is inappropriate, obnoxious, or unacceptable, the person still needs the respect, comfort, and love of others. Rogers strongly believed that unconditional positive regard elevates

self-concept A central theme in Rogers's and other humanists' views; self-concept refers to individuals' overall perceptions of their abilities, behaviour, and personalities.

unconditional positive regard Rogers's term for accepting, valuing, and being positive toward another person regardless of the person's behaviour.

the person's self-worth. However, Rogers (1974) distinguished between unconditional positive regard directed at the individual as a person of worth and dignity, and directed at the individual's behaviour. For example, a therapist who adopts Rogers's view might say, "I don't like your behaviour, but I accept you, value you, and care about you as a person."

Rogers also said that we can help other people develop a more positive self-concept if we are *empathic* and *genuine*. Being empathic means being a sensitive listener and understanding another's true feelings. Being genuine means being open with our feelings and dropping our pretences and facades.

For Rogers, unconditional positive regard, empathy, and genuineness are three key ingredients of human relations. We can use these techniques to help other people feel good about themselves and to help us get along better with others (Kirschenbaum & Jourdan, 2005; Bozarth, Zimring, & Tausch, 2001).

The Fully Functioning Person Rogers (1980) stressed the importance of becoming a fully functioning person—someone who is open to experience, is not overly defensive, is aware of and sensitive to the self and the external world, and, for the most part, has a harmonious relationship with others. Rogers believed that we are highly resilient and capable of being fully functioning persons—whether we experience a discrepancy between our real selves and our ideal selves, whether we encounter others who may try to control us, or whether we receive too little unconditional positive regard.

Humans' self-actualizing tendencies, which were discussed in chapter 11, are reflected in Rogers' comparison of a person with a plant he once observed on the northern California coastline. As Rogers looked out at the waves furiously beating against the jagged rocks and shooting mountains of ocean spray into the air, he noticed the waves were also pounding against a palm tree two or three feet tall. The waves bent its slender trunk and whipped its leaves in a torrent of spray. Yet the moment each wave passed, the tree stood erect once again. The tree took this incessant pounding hour after hour, week after week, year after year, all the time nourishing itself, maintaining its position, and growing. In this persevering tree, Rogers saw the tenacity of the human spirit and the ability of a living thing to push into a hostile environment and not only hold its own, but adapt, develop, and become itself.

Rogers believed that a person's basic tendencies are to actualize, maintain, and enhance their life. He thought that the tendency for fulfillment—toward actualizing one's essential nature and attaining potential—is inborn in every person.

Maslow's Approach

Recall from chapter 11 that another psychologist, Abraham Maslow (1908–1970), believed that human needs can be arranged into a hierarchy and that self-actualization is the highest form of need and therefore of motivation. He also believed that it is an important aspect of personality. Maslow was one of the most powerful figures in psychology's humanistic movement. He called the humanistic approach the "third force" in psychology—that is, an important alternative to the psychodynamic and behavioural forces. Maslow argued that psychodynamic theories place too much emphasis on disturbed individuals and their conflicts and behaviourists ignore the person altogether.

According to Maslow's (1954, 1971) hierarchy of needs, self-actualization is the highest-level human need. The motivation to develop one's full potential as a human being is what Maslow primarily focused on (Reiss & Havercamp, 2005). Figure 12.8 describes the main characteristics that Maslow attributes to a self-actualizing individual.

Although Maslow believed that most people have difficulty reaching this level, he identified the following individuals as among the self-actualized: Pablo Casals (cellist), Albert Einstein (physicist), Ralph Waldo Emerson (writer), William James (psychologist), Thomas Jefferson (politician), Abraham Lincoln (politician), Eleanor Roosevelt (humanitarian, diplomat), and Albert Schweitzer (humanitarian).

Maslow made his list over three decades ago. Not all his examples of self-actualizing individuals were included here, but he did name considerably more men than women on the complete list. Also, most of the individuals were from Western cultures.

Maslow's Characteristics of Self-Actualizing Individuals

Realistic orientation

Self-acceptance and acceptance of others and the natural world as they are

Spontaneity

Tendency to have strong intimate relationships with a few special, loved people rather than superficial relationships with many people

Democratic values and attitudes

No confusion of means with ends

Philosophical rather than hostile sense of humour

Problem-centred rather than self-centred

Air of detachment and need for privacy

Autonomous and independent

Fresh rather than stereotyped appreciation of people and things

Generally have had profound mystical or spiritual, although not necessarily religious, experiences

Identification with humankind and a strong social interest

High degree of creativity

Resistance to cultural conformity

Transcendence of environment rather than always coping with it

FIGURE 12.8 Maslow's Characteristics of Self-Actualizing
Former South African president Nelson Mandela smiles to the crowd during the November 2001 ceremony in Hull, Quebec, where he was made an Honourary Canadian Citizen.

With Maslow's description of self-actualization in mind (including the characteristics listed in figure 12.8), think of others you would add to Maslow's list of self-actualizing persons. For starters, consider Nelson Mandela (statesman), Mother Teresa (spiritual leader) and Martin Luther King (clergyman, civil rights activist; Pervin, 2003). More recent additions to the list might include Terry Fox, Bono, the social activist lead singer of the Irish rock group U2 or Bob Geldof, the Irish musician known for his charity work, from Band Aid and Live Aid to the more recent Live 8 concerts.

Self-Esteem

Rogers's and Maslow's interest in the self led to their belief that self-esteem is an important aspect of personality. **Self-esteem** is a person's overall evaluation of his or her self-worth or self-image.

Psychologists have shown considerable interest in self-esteem and how it is developed and maintained (Tesser, Stapel, & Wood, 2002; Scarpa & Luscher, 2002). Following are some of the research issues and findings on self-esteem (Baumeister, 1997; Baumeister & others, 2003):

● *Does self-esteem fluctuate from day to day or remain stable?* Most research studies have found it to be stable across a month or so at least (Baumeister, 1991). Self-esteem can change, however, especially in response to transitions in life (such as graduating from high school or going to university) and to life events (such as getting or losing a job). One study found that self-esteem is high in childhood, declines in adolescence, and increases through adulthood until late adulthood, at which time it declines again (see figure 12.9; Robins & others, 2002). In this study, the self-esteem of males was higher than that of females through most of the lifespan. During adolescence, girls' self-esteem of declined more than boys'.

self-esteem The person's overall evaluation of self-worth or self-image.

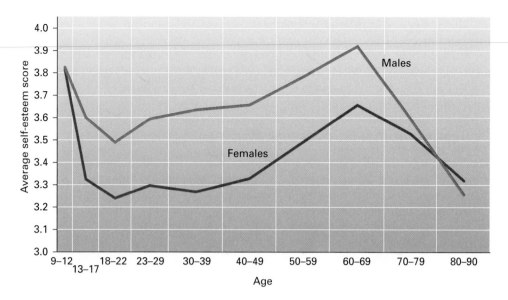

FIGURE 12.9

Self-Esteem Across the Life Span
One large-scale study asked more than 300,000 individuals to rate the extent to which they have high self-esteem on a 5-point scale, 5 being "Strongly Agree" and 1 being "Strongly Disagree." Self-esteem dropped in adolescence and late adulthood. Self-esteem of females was lower than self-esteem of males through most of the life span and was especially low for females during adolescence.

- *Is self-esteem something very general or does it consist of a number of independent self-evalu-ations in different areas?* That is, is it more appropriate to think of people having high or low self-esteem overall or as having high or low self-esteem in specific areas of their lives, such as being high in social self-esteem and low in cognitive (academic) self-esteem? Current thinking about this issue has evolved toward the conclusion that people do have a general level of self-esteem but can still have fluctuating lev-els of self-esteem in particular areas of their lives (Fleming & Courtney, 1984).

- *How does the lack of self-esteem affect an individual's ability to cope with the demands of life?* Researchers from the University of Waterloo have found that people with low self-esteem are not as motivated to improve their negative moods and are more likely to dampen their positive moods than people with high self-esteem are (Heimpel & others, 2002; Wood, Heimpel, & Michela, 2003). The failure to live up to one's own standards is especially implicated in the connection between low self-esteem and depression (Harter, 1998).

- *Are there sometimes costs associated with seeking high self-esteem?* The pursuit of self-esteem has become a preoccupation in North America. Self-help books advise how to achieve high self-esteem, child-rearing guides tell parents how to raise children with high self-esteem, and many people avoid certain activities, situations, and people so they can protect and enhance their self-esteem. Might there be some costs to this pursuit (Crocker & Park, 2004)? In one study of more than 600 first-year university students, the costs occurred when individuals sought high self-esteem for external reasons, especially appearance, to get positive feedback from others (Crocker, 2001). In this study, seeking high self-esteem because of a motivation to look physically attractive to others was linked with stress, drug and alcohol use, and disordered eating.

An important point needs to be made about much of the research on self-esteem: It is correlational rather than experimental. Remember from the discussion in chapter 2 that correlation does not equal causation. Thus, if a correlational study finds an associ-ation between low self-esteem and depression, depression could cause low self-esteem as much as low self-esteem causes depression.

A topic of considerable interest among clinical and educational psychologists is what can be done to increase the self-esteem of individuals with low self-esteem. Researchers have found that four main strategies help to improve self-esteem (Bednar, Wells, & Peterson, 1995; Harter, 1998):

- Identifying the causes of low self-esteem
- Experiencing emotional support and approval
- Achieving
- Coping

The strategy of experiencing emotional support and approval meshes with Carl Rogers's concept of unconditional positive regard. But some psychologists argue that the most effective ways to improve self-esteem are by improving the person's achievement and coping skills. Rogers himself believed that when a person's achievement and coping skills improve, the individual's self-esteem is likely to follow suit. Coping skills are further discussed in chapter 15.

Evaluating Humanistic Perspectives

The humanistic perspectives made psychologists aware that the way we perceive ourselves and the world around us are key elements of personality. Humanistic psychologists also reminded us that we need to consider the whole person and the positive bent of human nature (Bohart & Greening, 2001). Their emphasis on conscious experience has given us the view that personality contains a well of potential that can be developed to its fullest (Giorgi, 2005).

A weakness of the humanistic perspective is that it is difficult to test. Self-actualization, for example, is difficult to define, much less observe (Crandall & Jones, 1991). Although attempts have been made to measure it (Jones & Crandall, 1986; Reiss & Havercamp, 2005), psychologists are not certain how to study this concept empirically. Complicating matters is the fact that some humanists scorn the experimental approach, preferring clinical interpretation as a database. Indeed, verification of humanistic concepts has come mainly from clinical experiences rather than from controlled, experimental studies.

Some critics also believe that humanistic psychologists are too optimistic about human nature, overestimating human freedom and rationality. And some critics say humanists may encourage excessive self-love and narcissism by encouraging people to think so positively about themselves.

> **> reflect and review**
>
> **4** **Describe the humanistic perspectives.**
>
> - Define the main themes of the humanistic perspectives.
> - Explain the key elements in Rogers's theory.
> - Summarize Maslow's theory.
> - Discuss the importance of self-esteem to individuals.
> - Discuss the humanistic perspectives.
>
> *What is the level of your self-esteem? That is, on the whole, are you satisfied with yourself? Or do you wish that you could have a more positive attitude toward yourself? Is your self-esteem higher in some areas of your life than others? If so, which ones? If your self-esteem is low, what do you think it would take to increase it?*

5 TRAIT PERSPECTIVES

Trait Theories	The Big Five Personality Factors	Trait-Situation Interaction	Evaluating Trait Perspectives

What are the main ideas of the trait perspectives?

Through the ages we have described ourselves and one another in terms of basic traits. A **trait** is an enduring personality characteristic that tends to lead to certain behaviours. Around 400 b.c., Hippocrates, the "father of medicine," described human beings as having one of four basic "humours," or personalities, that were determined by a person's physical makeup: choleric (quick-tempered), phlegmatic (placid), sanguine (optimistic),

trait An enduring personality characteristic that tends to lead to certain behaviours.

or melancholic (pessimistic). Others have proposed different sets of traits, but these descriptions of personality have remained remarkably relevant. Hans Eysenck's (1952, 1967) personality theory incorporated elements of Hippocrates' millennia-old approach.

Think about yourself and your friends. How would you describe yourself? You might say that you're outgoing and sociable and that, in contrast, one of your friends is shy and quiet. You might refer to yourself as emotionally stable and describe one of your other friends as a bit skittish. Part of our everyday existence involves describing ourselves and others in terms of traits.

According to Michael Ashton, traits have a deeper application as well (Ashton & Lee, 2005). They have long been used in both the construction of theories of personality and their measurement (Ashton, Lee, & Goldberg, 2004; Matthews, Deary, & Whiteman, 2003; Wiggins, 1997; Wiggins & Pincus, 1992).

Trait Theories

Trait theories state that personality consists of broad, enduring dispositions that tend to lead to characteristic responses. In other words, people can be described in terms of the basic ways they behave, such as whether they are outgoing and friendly or whether they are dominant and assertive. People who have a strong tendency to behave in certain ways are described as high on the traits; those who have a weak tendency to behave in these ways are described as low on the traits. Although trait theorists sometimes differ on which traits make up personality, they all agree that traits are the fundamental building blocks of personality (Larsen & Buss, 2005; Ashton & Lee, 2005).

Allport's View of Traits   Gordon Allport (1897–1967) believed that each individual has a unique set of personality traits According to Ian Nicholson, of St. Thomas University in Fredericton, Allport argued that if we can determine a person's traits, we can predict that individual's behaviour in various circumstances (Nicholson, 2003).

In going through an unabridged dictionary, Allport (1937) identified more than 4500 personality traits. To impose some organization on the vast number of terms that might be used to describe an individual's personality, Allport distinguished between common and individual traits. Common traits are those that characterize most mature people in a given culture. Individual traits are those that distinguish one person from another. Allport divided individual traits into three main categories (Nicholson, 2003):

- *Cardinal traits* are the most powerful and pervasive. When they are present, they dominate an individual's personality. However, according to Allport, few people actually possess cardinal traits. We might think of some famous individuals as having these (Hitler's hunger for power, Mother Teresa's altruism). But most people aren't characterized by just one or two traits (unlike the way we think about Hitler or Mother Teresa).
- *Central traits* are the building blocks of personality. When you describe someone, or are asked to write a letter of reference for that person, you would likely use words that refer to these central traits. For example, you might describe a friend's personality as friendly, calm, kind, humorous, messy, and nostalgic. Allport believed that about 6 to 12 central traits are usually adequate to describe most people's personalities.
- *Secondary traits* are limited in frequency and are the least important in understanding an individual's personality. They include particular attitudes and preferences, such as the type of food or music a person likes.

Eysenck's Dimensions of Personality   Hans Eysenck (1967) also tackled the task of determining the basic traits of personality. He gave personality tests to large numbers of people and analyzed each person's responses. Eysenck said that three main dimensions were needed to explain personality:

- *Introversion-extraversion.* An introverted person is quiet, unsociable, passive, and careful; an extraverted person is active, optimistic, sociable, and outgoing (Saklofske & Eysenck, 1994; Thorne, 2001).

FIGURE 12.10
Eysenck's Dimensions of Personality
Eysenck believed that for people without a psychological disorder, personality consists of two basic dimensions: introversion-extraversion and stability-instability. He thought that a third dimension—psychoticism—was needed to describe the personality of individuals with a psychological disorder.

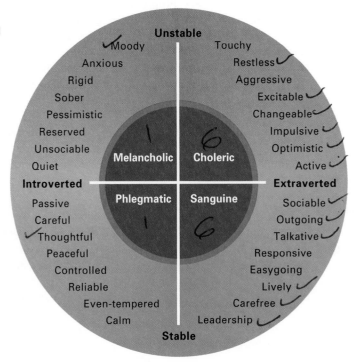

- *Stable-unstable* (known as the *neuroticism* dimension). A stable person is calm, even-tempered, carefree, and capable of leadership; an unstable person is moody, anxious, restless, and touchy.
- *Psychoticism.* This dimension reflects the degree to which people are in contact with reality, control their impulses, and are cruel or caring toward others.

Figure 12.10 shows the interaction of what Eysenck considered to be two of the basic dimensions of personality: introversion/extraversion and stable/unstable. Eysenck believed that various combinations of these dimensions result in certain personality traits. For example, a person who is extraverted and unstable is likely to be impulsive. To evaluate the extent to which you are introverted or extraverted, see the Personal Reflections box.

The Big Five Personality Factors

Psychologists still take considerable interest in determining what the key factors of personality really are. A rash of research studies point toward a handful of factors as being the most important dimensions of personality (McCrae & Terracciano, 2005; Widiger, Costa, & McCrae, 2002). The **big five factors of personality**, the "supertraits" that are thought to describe the main dimensions of personality, are openness, conscientiousness, extraversion, agreeableness, and neuroticism (emotional stability; see figure 12.11). (Notice that if you create an acronym from these trait names, you get the word OCEAN.) Recall, from the beginning of the chapter, the description of the personality traits of U2's Bono. Two traits that characterized him were openness to experience and extraversion.

Research on the big five factors includes the extent to which the factors appear in personality profiles in different cultures, how stable the factors are over time, and the role the factors might play in predicting physical and mental health (McCrae & Terracciano, 2005; Lingjaerde, Foreland, & Engvik, 2001; Wiggins, 1996). The more universal, stable, and predictive the big five factors prove to be, the more confidence we can have that they truly describe a person's fundamental traits.

Do the five factors show up in the assessment of personality in cultures around the world (McCrae & Terracciano, 2005)? University of Western Ontario psychologist Sampo Paunonen and his colleagues have found that some version of the five factors

big five factors of personality Openness to experience, conscientiousness, extraversion, agreeableness, and neuroticism (emotional stability).

Are You Extraverted or Introverted?

To determine how extraverted or introverted you are, read each of the following 20 questions and answer either yes (if it is generally true for you) or no (if it is not generally true for you).

	Yes	No
1. Do you often long for excitement?	✓	
2. Are you usually carefree?	✓	
3. Do you stop and think things over before doing anything?		✓
4. Would you do almost anything on a dare?	✓	
5. Do you often do things on the spur of the moment?	✓	
6. Generally, do you prefer reading to meeting people?		✓
7. Do you prefer to have few but special friends?		✓
8. When people shout at you, do you shout back?	✓	
9. Do other people think of you as very lively?	✓	
10. Are you mostly quiet when you are with people?		✓
11. If there is something you want to know about, would you rather look it up in a book than talk to someone about it?		✓
12. Do you like the kind of work that you need to pay close attention to?		✓
13. Do you hate being with a crowd who plays jokes on one another?		✓

	Yes	No
14. Do you like doing things in which you have to act quickly?	✓	
15. Are you slow and unhurried in the way you move?		✓
16. Do you like talking to people so much that you never miss a chance of talking to a stranger?	✓	
17. Would you be unhappy if you could not see lots of people most of the time?	✓	
18. Do you find it hard to enjoy yourself at a lively party?		✓
19. Would you say that you were fairly self-confident?	✓	
20. Do you like playing pranks on others?	✓	

To arrive at your score for extraversion, give one point for each of the following items answered yes: 1, 2, 4, 5, 8, 9, 14, 16, 17, 19, and 20. Then give yourself one point for each of the following items answered no: 3, 6, 7, 10, 11, 12, 13, 15, 18. Add up all the points to arrive at a total score.

Your total score should be between 0 and 20. If your scores are very high (15–20), you are the "life of the party." You clearly prefer being with others to being alone. If your scores are very low (0–5), you are a loner. You find greater pleasure in solitary activities. If you are somewhere in between (6–14), you are flexible in how you prefer to spend your time. You take pleasure in the company of others (especially if your score is in the higher range) but still also appreciate solitude.

Openness
- Imaginative or practical
- Interested in variety or routine
- Independent or conforming

Conscientiousness
- Organized or disorganized
- Careful or careless
- Disciplined or impulsive

Extraversion
- Sociable or retiring
- Fun-loving or sombre
- Affectionate or reserved

Agreeableness
- Softhearted or ruthless
- Trusting or suspicious
- Helpful or uncooperative

Neuroticism (emotional stability)
- Calm or anxious
- Secure or insecure
- Self-satisfied or self-pitying

FIGURE 12.11

The Big Five Factors of Personality
Each of the broad supertraits that encompasses more narrow traits and characteristics. Use the acronym OCEAN to remember the big five personality factors (Openness, Conscientiousness, and so on).

appears in people in countries as diverse as Canada, Finland, Poland, China, and Japan (Paunonen & others, 1992, 2003; Paunonen & Ashton, 1998). It may be that trait approaches to personality depend on the structure of language. One way to address this possibility is to look for the consistency of traits across cultures (Paunonen & others, 1992). Another approach is to use nonverbal assessment methods (Paunonen & Ashton & Jackson, 2001, Paunonen & Ashton, 2002).

What about the stability of these particular traits? Using a five-factor personality test that they devised, Paul Costa and Robert McCrae (1995) studied approximately 1000 university-educated men and women aged 20 to 96, assessing the same individuals over many years. Data collection began in the 1950s to the mid-1960s and is ongoing. Costa and McCrae have so far concluded that the five personality factors—openness, conscientiousness, extraversion, agreeableness, and neuroticism (emotional stability)—are reasonably stable. For instance, individuals high on agreeableness tend to remain so throughout the years.

Can the big five factors help us to understand how personality is linked to physical and mental health? The notion that personality characteristics might influence health continues to attract widespread research attention. Much of this research, though, has been conducted using a hodgepodge of traits. The big five trait structure offers the potential of a unified, coherent framework for understanding which types of people are likely to stay healthy and to recover quickly from illness.

Research has generally supported the concept of the big five "general" traits, but some personality researchers believe they might not end up being the final list of broad supertraits. Michael Ashton, of Brock University and Kibeom Lee, of the University of Calgary, have proposed a six trait model they refer to as *HEXACO*, an acronym for their six proposed traits, Honesty-Humility (H), Emotionality (E), Extraversion (X), Agreeableness (A), Conscientiousness (C), and Openness to Experience (O) (Ashton, Lee, & Goldberg, 2004; Lee & Ashton, 2005). Three of the big five traits are included (Openness, Conscientiousness, and Extraversion). The other two big five traits (Agreeableness and Neuroticism) have been differentiated into three traits in the HEXACO model. Lee and Ashton (2004) have also recently published the HEXACO-PI, a personality inventory designed to measure the six personality factors in the HEXACO.

Trait-Situation Interaction

Today, most psychologists in the field of personality are interactionists. They believe that both trait (person) and situation need to be taken into account to understand personality (Block, 2002; Edwards & Rothbard, 1999; Mischel, Shoda, & Mendoza-Denton, 2002). They also agree that consistency in personality depends on the kind of persons, situations, and behaviours sampled (Pervin, 2003; Swartz-Kulstad & Martin, 2000).

Suppose you want to assess the happiness of Bob, an introvert, and of Sasha, an extravert. According to trait-situation interaction theory, we cannot predict who will be happier unless we know something about the situations they are in. Imagine you get the opportunity to observe them in two situations, at a party and in a library. Do you think Bob or Sasha will feel more comfortable at the party? Which one will be more content at the library? The extravert, Sasha, is likelier to enjoy the party, and the introvert, Bob, is likelier to enjoy the library.

Recent research has found that (1) the narrower and more limited a trait is, the more likely it will predict behaviour; (2) some people are consistent on some traits and other people are consistent on other traits; and (3) personality traits exert a stronger influence on an individual's behaviour when situational influences are less powerful (Martin & Swartz-Kulstad, 2000).

Cross-cultural psychologists believe that considering both the immediate setting and the broader cultural context leads to a better understanding of the situation's role in the way personality is expressed (Kitayama, 2002; Oyserman, Coon, & Kemmelmeier, 2002; Triandis & Suh, 2002).

Evaluating Trait Perspectives

Studying people in terms of their personality traits has practical value. Identifying a person's traits allows us to know the person better. Our traits also influence our health, the way we think, how well we do in a career, and how well we get along with others (Larsen & Buss, 2005; McCrae & Costa, 2001).

However, viewing people only in terms of their traits may provide at best a partial view of personality. In his landmark book *Personality and Assessment*, Walter Mischel (1968) criticized the trait view of personality, which emphasizes the internal organization of personality. Rather than viewing personality as consisting of broad, internal traits that are consistent across situations and time, Mischel said that personality often changes according to a given situation, a view called situationism (Bowers, 1973). This view is consistent with Mischel's social cognitive perspective.

Mischel went beyond theoretical criticism, however. He reviewed an array of studies and concluded that trait measures by themselves often do a poor job of predicting actual behaviour. For example, let's say Anne is described as an aggressive person. But when we observe her behaviour we find that she might be aggressive if she is with her boyfriend, but if she is with her new boss, she might be quite submissive. According to Mischel (2004; Kammrath, Mendoza-Denton, & Mischel, 2005), these *if…then…personality signatures* are the basic elements of personality, not traditional cross-situational traits.

Nevertheless, many trait psychologists are unwilling to abandon altogether the idea of consistent, enduring personality characteristics (Ashton & Lee, 2005; McCrae & Terracciano, 2005; Wiggins, 1997) and prefer the idea of trait-situation interaction to Mischel's situationism.

> **reflect and review**

 Discuss the trait perspectives.

- Define traits and describe the views of Allport and Eysenck.
- Identify the big five factors in personality.
- Explain trait-situation interaction.
- Discuss the trait perspectives.

To what extent do you believe the big five factors capture your personality? Look at the characteristics of the five factors listed in figure 12.11 and decide how you line up on each one. Then choose one of the factors, such as extraversion or openness to experience, and give an example of how different situations might influence the expression of this trait in your life.

---

6 PERSONALITY ASSESSMENT

— Projective Tests   — Self-Report Tests   — Behavioural and Cognitive Assessment   — Assessment in the Selection of Employees

What are the main methods of personality assessment?

"This line running this way indicates that you are a gregarious person, someone who really enjoys being around people. This division over here suggests that you are a risk taker; I bet you like to do things that are adventurous sometimes." These are words you might hear from a palmist. Palmistry purports to "read" an individual's personality by interpreting the irregularities and folds in the skin of the palm. Each of these signs is interpreted in a precise manner. For example, a large mound of Saturn, the portion of the palm directly below the third joint of the middle finger, is said to relate to wisdom, good fortune, and prudence.

Although palmists claim to provide a complete assessment of personality through reading lines on the palm, psychological researchers debunk palmistry as quackery. They argue that palmists give no reasonable explanation for their inferences about personality and point out that the palm's characteristics can change through age and even exercise.

Even so, palmists manage to stay in business. They do so, in part, because they are keen observers—they respond to such cues as voice, general demeanour, and dress, which are more relevant signs of personality than the lines and folds on a person's palm. Palmists are also experts at offering general, trivial statements such as, "Although you are usually affectionate with others, sometimes you don't get along with people." This statement falls into the category of the *Barnum effect*: If you make your predictions broad enough, any person can fit the description. The effect was named after circus owner P. T. Barnum.

"Rorschach! What's to become of you?"
© Sidney Harris

In contrast to palmists, psychologists use scientifically developed tests and methods to evaluate personality (Thomas & Segal, 2005; Derlega, Winstead, & Jones, 2005). Further, many different tests have been constructed to assess personality for different reasons. For example, Douglas Jackson, of the University of Western Ontario, developed the widely used *Personality Research Form (PRF)*. Based on Murray's (1938) theory of needs, the PRF was developed from a theoretical, rather than an empirical perspective. Jackson also developed the *Jackson Personality Inventory (JPI)*, which provides personality profiles of managers, executives, and professionals and has been instrumental in refining test development methodologies (Jackson, 1991; Smither, London, & Richmond, 2005).

Before we describe some specific personality tests, two more important points need to be made about the nature of personality assessment. First, the kinds of tests chosen by psychologists frequently depend on the psychologist's theoretical bent. And second, most personality tests are designed to assess stable, enduring characteristics, free of situational influence (Ozer, 2001).

Projective Tests

A **projective test** presents individuals with an ambiguous stimulus and then asks them to describe it or tell a story about it—in other words, to *project* their own meaning onto the stimulus. Projective tests are based on the assumption that the ambiguity of the stimulus allows individuals to invest it with their feelings, desires, needs, and attitudes. The test is especially designed to elicit the individual's unconscious feelings and conflicts, providing an assessment that goes deeper than the surface personality (Garb & others, 2005; Blatt, 2000). Projective tests attempt to get inside your mind to discover how you really feel and think, going beyond the way you overtly present yourself. Projective tests are theoretically aligned with the psychodynamic perspectives on personality, which give more weight than the other perspectives to the unconscious.

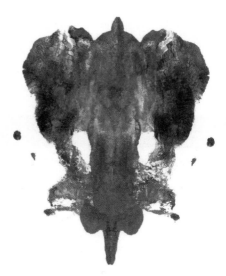

FIGURE 12.12
Type of Stimulus Used in the Rorschach Inkblot Test

Rorschach Inkblot Test The **Rorschach inkblot test**, developed in 1921 by the Swiss psychiatrist Hermann Rorschach, is a widely used projective test; it uses an individual's perception of the inkblots to determine his or her personality. The test consists of 10 cards, half in black and white and half in colour, which are shown to the individual one at a time (see figure 12.12). The person taking the Rorschach test is asked to describe what he or she sees in each of the inkblots. For example, an individual may say, "That looks like two people fighting." After the individual has responded to all 10 inkblots, the examiner presents each of the inkblots again and inquires about the individual's earlier response. For example, the examiner might ask, "*Where* did you see the two people fighting?" and "*What* about the inkblot made the two people look like they were fighting?" Besides recording the responses, the examiner notes the individual's mannerisms, gestures, and attitudes.

How useful is the Rorschach in assessing personality? The answer to this question depends on one's perspective. Many research psychologists have serious reservations about the Rorschach's use in diagnosis and clinical practice because it does not meet scientific criteria of reliability and validity (Pervin, 2003; Garb & others, 2001). If the Rorschach were reliable, two different scorers should agree on the personality characteristics of the individual. If the Rorschach were valid, the individual's personality should predict behaviour outside of the testing situation; it should predict whether an individual will attempt suicide, become severely depressed, cope successfully with stress, or get along well with others. Research evidence suggests that the Rorschach does not meet the criteria of reliability and validity (Wood & others, 2003). Yet the Rorschach enjoys widespread use in clinical practice. Some clinicians swear by the Rorschach, saying it is better than any other measure at getting at the true, underlying core of an individual's personality (Ephraim, 2000; Sloan & others, 1996). The debate between researchers and clinicians over the Rorschach is ongoing and probably will not subside in the near future (Meyer, 2001; Garb & others, 2001). For a closer look at this issue, see the Critical Reflections box.

projective test Personality assessment tool that presents individuals with an ambiguous stimulus and then asks them to describe it or tell a story about it; based on the assumption that the ambiguity of the stimulus allows individuals to project their personalities onto it.

Rorschach inkblot test A widely used projective test; it uses an individual's perception of inkblots to determine his or her personality.

Is the Rorschach Clinically Useful?

The Rorschach inkblot test has been said to be "simultaneously, the most cherished and the most reviled of all psychological assessment instruments" (Hunsley & Bailey, 1999). How can this be?

With millions of tests administered every year, the Rorschach is one of the most frequently used projective tests. According to one survey, 82 percent of clinical psychologists occasionally administer the Rorschach and 43 percent often use the test (Watkins & others, 1995). Yet the Rorschach has long been attacked as unreliable and lacking in validity (Wood & others, 2003).

A psychological assessment is judged to be reliable if it yields consistent results over repeated use. If different scorers can interpret the same individual's test differently, the test does not meet the reliability criterion. To understand how different clinicians might reach different conclusions about an individual from answers to a Rorschach series, consider whether a description should be scored as food-related if someone identifies the whole inkblot as a hamburger. What if the person identifies only one small portion of the inkblot as food? What if other, non-edible, objects are identified in the same inkblot? What if the individual sees another person eating? What if the colour of the inkblot played (or did not play) a role in the description? And what would any of this tell you about this person's state of mind?

Some psychologists believe that many of the ways in which the Rorschach is scored are not reliable enough to be clinically useful (Wood & others, 2003) while others argue the opposite (Meyer, Mihura, & Smith, 2005; McGrath & others, 2005). What would it mean, for example, if two clinical psychologists administered the Rorschach to the same person and came up with diametrically opposed interpretations? It could mean that the two clinicians are projecting their own personalities onto their patient's Rorschach responses. In other words, the test interpretation might depend more on the interpretations of the clinicians than on any characteristic of the test taker. Because the results of a clinical assessment may determine the course of treatment or even the outcome of a court case, the stakes can be very high.

A psychological assessment is considered valid if it measures what it is intended to measure. One use of the Rorschach has been to diagnose psychological disorders, such as schizophrenia and depression (Weiner, 2003). Therefore, one way to test the diagnostic validity of the Rorschach would be to administer the test to two groups: a known group of normal people and a known group of people with a disorder such as schizophrenia. If the Rorschach is valid for diagnosing schizophrenia, then the responses of the two groups should differ. Otherwise, as said above, a diagnosis might well depend on the interpretations of clinicians. And, indeed, research

evidence suggests that the Rorschach has little validity as a diagnostic tool (Wood & others, 2003).

So why would clinical psychologists continue to use a test with known problems of reliability and validity? Some clinicians swear by the Rorschach (Hilsenroth, 2000; Ephraim, 2000; Sloan & others, 1996). They are not especially bothered by the Rorschach's low reliability and validity, pointing out that the test encourages extensive freedom of response. This freedom of response is what makes the Rorschach such a rich clinical tool, say its advocates. In one survey, Rorschach-based testimony was legally challenged in only 6 of nearly 8000 court cases (Weiner, Exner, & Sciara, 1996).

Additionally, when coupled with information from structured interviews and other personality assessment tools, the results from projective tests like the Rorschach provide extra information the insightful clinician can use to better understand an individual (Meyer & Archer, 2001). Even critics caution that projective tests like the Rorschach should not be rejected as inherently unreliable and/or invalid (Wood, Nezworski, & Garb, 2003). Instead they urge continuing efforts to construct better projective tests.

Attempts have been made to improve reliability by standardizing scoring systems (Bornstein & Masling, 2005). As a result, responses are typically scored for:

Location: Does the person respond to the whole inkblot or specific parts?
Quality: Does the person respond to the colour, the shape, or perceived movement?
Content: Does the person perceive animals, humans, or objects?
Conventionality: How do the responses compare with average responses?

The goals of such systems include standardizing the test procedure itself as well as improving the reliability and validity of the test interpretation.

What do you think?

- What role should evidence based on projective tests like the Rorschach play in courts of law?
- If you took an actual Rorschach test, what would you make of the results as they were explained to you by a clinical psychologist?
- Spend some time looking at the inkblot in Fig 12.12. Write down everything you see there. Ask some friends to do the same. Discuss your interpretations of your responses. If you do not agree, how could you settle the matter?

Other Projective Tests The **Thematic Apperception Test (TAT)**, which was developed by Henry Murray and Christina Morgan in the 1930s, is designed to elicit stories that reveal something about an individual's personality (W. G. Morgan, 2002). The TAT consists of a series of pictures like the one in figure 12.13, each on an individual card. The person taking the TAT is asked to tell a story about each of the pictures, including events leading up to the situation described, the characters' thoughts and feelings, and the way the situation turns out. The tester assumes that the person projects his or her

Thematic Apperception Test (TAT) An ambiguous projective test designed to elicit stories that reveal something about an individual's personality.

FIGURE 12.13

Picture from the Thematic Apperception Test (TAT)

own unconscious feelings and thoughts into the story (Herzberg, 2000). In addition to being used as a projective test in clinical practice, the TAT is used in research on people's need for achievement (Cramer, 1999; Cramer & Brilliant, 2001). Several of the TAT cards stimulate the telling of achievement-related stories (McClelland & others, 1953).

Many other projective tests are used in clinical assessment. One test asks the individual to complete a sentence (for example, "I often feel . . . ," "I would like to . . ."); another test asks the individual to draw a person; and another test presents a word, such as *fear* or *happy*, and asks the individual to say the first thing that comes to mind. Like the Rorschach, these projective tests have their detractors and advocates; the detractors often criticize the tests' low reliability and validity, and the advocates describe the tests' abilities to reveal the underlying nature of the individual's personality better than more straightforward tests can (Holaday, Smith, & Sherry, 2000; Wood & others, 2003).

Another controversial projective measure is *graphology*, the use of handwriting analysis to determine an individual's personality. Examine the writing in figure 12.14 to see the kinds of interpretations graphologists make. At one time, many firms in North America and Europe used graphology as part of their employee-selection process. But the growing research literature on graphology is almost universally negative (Simner, & Goffin, 2003; Furnham, Chamorro-Premuzic, & Callahan, 2003; King & Koehler, 2000).

Dean and others (1992) have examined biases in the decision processes involved in graphology. One classic study typifies these negative results (Ben-Shakhar & others, 1986). Three professional graphologists were asked to assess the competence of 52 bank employees at their jobs and the nature of their relationships with co-workers. The samples consisted of brief autobiographical essays and responses to a short biographical questionnaire. The researchers also used information from the samples to make assessments about the employees' competence. The researchers' predictions and the graphologists' ratings were compared with the ratings by the employees' supervisors. The graphologists did no better than the researchers at matching the supervisors' ratings. In a second study, five graphologists did no better than chance when asked to predict the occupations of 40 successful professional men based on several pages of their handwriting. Carswell (1992) points out that because graphology lacks scientific validity, its Canadian practitioners may run the risk of civil or criminal liability to those who suffer damages as a result of its use.

If the research results are so negative, why is graphology still used and accepted? To some degree, it is because graphologists' predictions, like those of palmists and astrologers, are usually so general they're difficult to prove or disprove. However, all projective tests are difficult to validate scientifically, which has led some to suggest that projective tests do little more than show the biases of the testers.

Self-Report Tests

Unlike projective techniques, self-report tests do not attempt to assess an individual's hidden, unconscious personality. Rather, **self-report tests**, also called objective tests or inventories, directly ask people whether items describe their personality traits or not (Ryckman, 2004). For example, self-report personality tests include items such as

1. **Level of Emotional Responsiveness**

Withdrawal   Objectiveness   Intensity

The backward slant at left indicates withdrawal, the vertical slant in the middle indicates objectiveness, and the forward slant on the right indicates intensity.

2. **Social Responsiveness**

Repression   Lack of inhibition

Note the tight loops of the *m* and *n* on the left, which indicate repression, and the spread loops of the *m* and *n* on the right, which indicate a lack of inhibition.

3. **Approach to Achievement**

Lack of self-confidence   Strong willpower

Note the low t-bar on the left, which indicates a lack of self-confidence, and the high t-bar on the right, which indicates strong willpower.

FIGURE 12.14 Some Graphological Interpretations
Graphology is a highly controversial assessment technique, unsupported by empirical research.

self-report tests Also called objective tests or inventories, they directly ask people whether items (usually true/false or agree/disagree) describe their personality traits or not.

- I am easily embarrassed.
- I love to go to parties.
- I like to watch cartoons on TV.

Self-report tests include a large number of statements or questions such as these. The respondent has a limited number of answers to choose from (yes or no, true or false, agree or disagree).

Adherents of the trait perspectives on personality have strong faith in self-report tests. They point out that self-report tests have produced a better understanding of an individual's personality traits than can be derived from, for example, projective tests. However, some critics (especially psychodynamic theorists) believe that the self-report measures do not get at the underlying core of personality and its unconscious determinants. Other critics (especially behaviourists and social cognitive theorists) believe that the self-report measures do not adequately capture the situational variation in personality and the way personality changes as the individual interacts with the environment.

Supporters of self-report tests do concede, however, that they have room for improvement. Many of the early personality tests were based on *face validity*, which is an assumption that the content of the test items is a good indicator of the individual's personality. For example, if we develop a test item that asks you to respond whether or not you are introverted, and you answer positively to "I enjoy being with people," we accept your response as a straightforward indication that you are not introverted. Tests based on face validity assume that you are responding honestly and nondefensively, giving the examiner an accurate portrayal of your personality.

But not everyone is honest, especially when it concerns one's own personality. Even if the individual is basically honest, he or she may be giving socially desirable answers. When motivated by *social desirability*, individuals say what they think the interviewer wants to hear or what they think will make them look better. For example, if someone is basically a lazy person, he may try to present himself in a more positive way; therefore, he would respond negatively to the following item: "I fritter away time too much."

Because of such responses, psychologists developed **empirically keyed tests**. An empirically keyed test relies on its items to predict some criterion. Unlike tests based on face validity, in which the content of the items is, on the face of it, a good indicator of what the individual's personality is like, empirically keyed tests make no assumptions about the nature of the items (Segal & Coolidge, 2000). Imagine that we want to develop a test that will determine whether or not applicants for a position as a police officer are likely to be competent at the job. We might ask a large number of questions of police officers, some of whom have excellent job records and others who have not performed as well. We would then use the questions that differentiate between competent and incompetent police officers on our test to screen job applicants. If the item, "I enjoy reading poetry" predicts success as a police officer, then we would include it on the test even though it seems unrelated to police work.

Minnesota Multiphasic Personality Inventory (MMPI) The **Minnesota Multiphasic Personality Inventory (MMPI)** is the most widely used and researched empirically keyed self-report personality test. The MMPI was initially constructed in the 1940s to assess "abnormal" personality tendencies and to improve the diagnosis of individuals with mental disorders. One thousand statements were given to both mental patients and apparently normal people. How often individuals agreed with each item was calculated; only the items that clearly differentiated the psychiatric patients from the normal individuals were retained. A statement might be included on the Depression scale of the MMPI if patients diagnosed with a depressive disorder agreed with the statement significantly more than did normal individuals. For example, the statement, "I sometimes tease animals" seems to have little to do with depression—that is, it has little face validity—but it might still be included on the depression scale of the MMPI.

The MMPI was eventually streamlined to 550 items, each of which can be answered "true," "false," or "cannot say." The items vary widely in content and include such statements as

- I like to read magazines.
- I never have trouble falling asleep.
- People are out to get me.

A person's answers are grouped according to 10 clinical categories, or scales, that measure problems such as depression, psychopathic deviation, schizophrenia, and social introversion. Figure 12.15 shows the 10 clinical scales of the MMPI and sample items for each scale.

empirically keyed test Relies on items to predict some criterion that discriminates between groups individually.

Minnesota Multiphasic Personality Inventory (MMPI) The most widely used and researched self-report personality test.

Clinical Scales	Sample Items
Hypochondriasis (Hs). (Abnormal concern with bodily functions)	"At times I get strong cramps in my intestines."
Depression (D). (Pessimism, hopelessness, slowing of action and thought)	"I am often very tense on the job."
Conversion Hysteria (Hy). (Unconscious use of physical and mental problems to avoid conflicts or responsibility)	"Sometimes there is a feeling like something is pressing in on my head."
Psychopathic Deviate (Pd). (Disregard of social custom, shallow emotions, inability to profit from experience)	"I wish I could do over some of the things I have done."
Masculinity-Femininity (Mf). (Items differentiating stereotypical masculine and feminine interests)	"I used to like to do the dances in gym class."
Paranoia (Pa). (Abnormal suspiciousness, delusions of grandeur or persecution)	"It distresses me that people have the wrong ideas about me."
Psychasthenia (Pt). (Obsessions, compulsiveness, fears, guilt, indecisiveness)	"The things that run through my head sometimes are horrible."
Schizophrenia (Sc). (Bizarre, unusual thoughts or behaviour, withdrawal, hallucinations, delusions)	"There are those out there who want to get me."
Hypomania (Ma). (Emotional excitement, flight of ideas, overactivity)	"Sometimes I think so fast I can't keep up."
Social Introversion (Si). (Shyness, disinterest in others, insecurity)	"I give up too easily when discussing things with others."

FIGURE 12.15

Clinical Scales of the MMPI and Sample Items
The MMPI is the most widely used self-report personality test. This figure shows the 10 clinical scales and a sample item for each scale. Answering each sample item "true" would reflect the direction of the scales.

The MMPI also includes four validity scales designed to indicate whether an individual is lying, careless, defensive, or evasive when answering test items. For example, if the individual consistently responds "false" to certain types of items, such as "I get angry sometimes," it would be interpreted that she is trying to make herself look better than she really is. We all get angry at least some of the time, so the individual who responds "false" to many such items is faking her responses. Ronald Holden, of Queens University, and his colleagues, have shown that another approach to verifying a test's validity is to time how long answers take (Holden & Kroner, 1992). For example, fakers take longer to admit to negative information about themselves than honest respondents do (Holden, 1995; Holden & Hibbs, 1995).

The MMPI was revised for the first time in 1989. The revision, called the MMPI-2, has a number of new items (for a total of 567 items), but the 10 clinical scales were retained, as were several of the validity scales (such as the lie scale). New content scales were added to the MMPI-2. These include substance abuse, eating disorders, anger, self-esteem, family problems, and inability to function in a job.

The MMPI-2 continues to be widely used around the world to assess personality and predict outcomes (Butcher, 2005; Endler, Parker, & Butcher, 2003; Archer & others, 2001). It has been so popular that it has been translated into more than 20 languages. Not only is it used by clinical psychologists to assess a person's mental health, but it is also used to predict which individuals will make the best job candidates or which career an individual should pursue. Another important trend is the increased use of computers to score the MMPI-2 (Iverson & Barton, 1999). However, some critics argue that too often the availability of computer scoring has tempted untrained individuals to use the test in ways for which it has not been validated.

Assessments of the Big Five Factors Paul Costa and Robert McRae (1992) constructed a test, the *Neuroticism Extraversion Openness Personality Inventory, Revised* (or *NEO-PI-R* for short), to assess the big five factors: openness, conscientiousness, extraversion, agreeableness, and neuroticism (emotional stability). The test also evaluates six subdimensions that make up the five main factors. Costa and McRae believe that the test can improve the diagnosis of personality disorders and help therapists understand how therapy might influence different types of clients. For instance, individuals identified as extraverts might prefer group psychotherapy whereas introverts might do better in individual psychotherapy. The NEO-PI-R is used in many research studies of personality as well. McCrae, Costa, & Martin (2005) have recently released an updated version, the NEO-PI-3.

Type of Behaviour	Item
Shared activities	We sat and read together. We took a walk.
Pleasing interactive events	My spouse asked how my day was. We talked about personal feelings. My spouse showed interest in what I said by agreeing or asking relevant questions.
Displeasing interactive events	My spouse commanded me to do something. My spouse complained about something I did. My spouse interrupted me.
Pleasing affectionate behaviour	We held each other. My spouse hugged and kissed me.
Displeasing affectionate behaviour	My spouse rushed into intercourse without taking time for foreplay. My spouse rejected my sexual advances.
Pleasing events	My spouse did the dishes. My spouse picked up around the house.
Displeasing events	My spouse talked too much about work. My spouse yelled at the children.

FIGURE 12.16 Items from the Spouse Observation Checklist
Couples are instructed to complete an extensive checklist for 15 consecutive evenings. Spouses record their partner's behaviour and make daily ratings of their overall satisfaction with the spouse's behaviour. The Spouse Observation Checklist is a behavioural assessment instrument.

Another measure used to assess the big five factors is Hogan's (1986) Hogan Personality Inventory (HPI). The Jackson Personality Inventory and the Personality Research Form have also been analyzed in terms of the big five factors (Ashton & others, 1998a). One way the HPI and the NEO-PI-R are used is to attempt to predict job success. Researchers have found that the HPI effectively predicts such job performance criteria as supervisor ratings and training course success (Wiggins & Trapnell, 1997).

Behavioural and Cognitive Assessment

Unlike either projective tests or self-report tests, behavioural assessment of personality is based on observing the individual's behaviour directly. Instead of removing situational influence, as projective tests and self-report measures do, behavioural assessment assumes that personality cannot be evaluated apart from the environment.

Behavioural assessment of personality emerged from the tradition of behaviour modification, which you learned about in chapter 7. Recall that often the first step in the process of changing an individual's maladaptive behaviour is to make baseline observations of its frequency. The therapist then modifies some aspect of the environment, such as getting the parents and the child's teacher to stop giving the child attention when he or she engages in aggressive behaviour. After a specified period of time, the therapist will observe the child again to determine if the changes in the environment were effective in reducing the child's maladaptive behaviour.

What does a psychologist with a behavioural orientation do to assess personality? Direct observation may be desirable, but it is not always possible. When it is not, the psychologist might ask individuals to make their own assessments of behaviour, encouraging them to be sensitive to the circumstances that produced the behaviour and the outcomes or consequences of the behaviour. For example, a therapist might want to know the course of marital conflict in the everyday experiences of a couple. Figure 12.16 shows a Spouse Observation Checklist that couples can use to record their partner's behaviour.

Douglas Jackson, of the University of Western Ontario, is a prolific author of widely used psychological tests, personality questionnaires, and inventories of career interests. His Jackson Vocational Interest Survey has helped many university-bound young people with their career planning. He has also authored the Career Directions Inventory for use by anyone interested in finding a vocation and has co-developed the Ashland Interest Assessment for handicapped persons.

The influence of social cognitive theory has increased the use of cognitive assessment in personality evaluation. The strategy is to discover what thoughts underlie the individual's behaviour; that is, how do individuals think about their problems? What kinds of thoughts precede maladaptive behaviour, occur during its manifestation, and follow it? Cognitive processes such as expectations, planning, and memory are assessed, possibly by interviewing the individual or asking him or her to complete a questionnaire. An interview might include questions that address whether the individual exaggerates his faults and condemns himself more than is warranted. A questionnaire might ask a person what her thoughts are after an upsetting event, or it might assess the way she thinks during tension-filled moments.

Locus of control, a key concept in the social cognitive perspectives, is most often assessed with Julian Rotter's (1966) I-E Scale, in which I stands for *internal* and E for *external*. Following are examples of the types of items used on the I-E Scale:

I More Strongly Believe That	*Or*
Promotions are earned through hard work and persistence.	Making a lot of money is largely a matter of getting the right breaks.
When I am right I can convince others.	It is silly to think that one can really change another person's basic attitudes.
I believe there is a direct connection between how hard I study and the grades I get.	Many times the reactions of teachers seem haphazard to me.
I am the master of my fate.	A great deal that happens to me is probably due to chance.
The number of divorces suggests that more and more people are not trying to make their marriages work.	Marriage is largely a gamble.

If you more strongly believed that the items in the left column are like you, you likely have a stronger internal locus of control. If you more strongly believed that the items in the right column are like you, you likely have a stronger external locus of control.

The I-E Scale has been used in a wide range of research studies (Al-Mashaan, 2001; Wallston, 2001). Generally, those studies have found that individuals with internal loci of control are more perceptive and are more ready to learn about their surroundings than those who have external loci of control. People with internal loci of control ask more questions and show better problem-solving skills.

Assessment in the Selection of Employees

Personality assessments are used in clinical psychology for diagnosis and therapy and are sometimes used in educational settings. But another important use is in the workplace. Industrial psychologists use many different selection tools to pick the right person for the right job (Landy & Conte, 2004; Roberts & Hogan, 2001). Among the most widely used personnel selection tools are application forms, psychological tests, interviews, and work sample tests.

Interviews are often given special weight in hiring decisions (Gibb & Taylor, 2003), and they can be especially helpful in evaluating a candidate's interpersonal and communication skills. Interviews that are structured and specific are often the most successful at selecting employees who eventually perform well on the job. Indeed, unstructured interviews have shown little success in predicting job performance (Huffcutt & others, 2001).

Psychological tests are also useful predictors of job performance. The tests used by industrial psychologists include general aptitude tests (such as IQ tests), specific aptitude tests (such as those designed to assess mechanical ability, clerical ability, or spatial

PERSONALITY PERSPECTIVES

	Psychodynamic Perspectives	Behavioural and Social Cognitive Perspectives	Humanistic Perspectives	Trait Perspectives
Preferred Personality Assessment Techniques	Clinical interviews, unstructured personality tests, psychohistorical analysis of clients' lives	Observation, especially laboratory observation	Self-report tests, interviews. For many humanists, clinical judgment is more important than scientific measurement.	Self-report tests, such as MMPI-2
Theoretical Issues				
Is personality innate or learned?	Freud strongly favoured biological foundations. Horney, Jung, and Adler gave social experiences and culture more weight.	Skinner said personality is behaviour, which is environmentally determined. Social cognitive theorists, such as Bandura, also emphasize environmental experiences.	Rogers, Maslow, and other humanistic psychologists believe personality is influenced by experience and can be changed.	Eysenck stresses personality's biological basis. Allport and other trait theorists consider both heredity and environment.
Is personality conscious or unconscious?	Psychodynamic theorists, especially Freud and Jung, place a strong emphasis on unconscious thought.	Skinner didn't think conscious or unconscious thought was important. Bandura and Mischel emphasize the cognitive process.	Humanistic psychologists stress the conscious aspects of personality, especially self-concept and self-perception.	Trait theorists pay little attention to this issue.
Is personality determined internally or externally?	Psychodynamic theorists emphasize internal determinants and internal personality structures.	Behaviourists emphasize external, situational determinants. Social cognitive theorists emphasize both internal and external determinants but especially self-control.	Humanistic theorists emphasize internal determinants such as self-concept and self-actualization.	Trait theorists stress internal, personal variables.

relations), personality tests (such as the MMPI), and vocational inventories (such as the Strong Interest Inventory) (Varela & others, 2004; Reynolds, 2001). Currently, researchers are interested in whether psychological tests based on the big five personality factors can predict job success (Griffin & Hesketh, 2004; Timmerman, 2004).

Whether personality assessments are being used by industrial psychologists, clinical psychologists, or psychological researchers, the choice of instrument depends to a great extent on the psychologist's theoretical perspective. Figure 12.17 summarizes which methods are advocated by different types of theorists. The figure also summarizes the positions of the main personality perspectives on the three issues mentioned earlier in the chapter: whether personality is innate or learned, whether it is conscious or unconscious, and whether it is determined internally or externally. Although the diversity of perspectives—psychodynamic, behavioural and social cognitive, humanistic, and trait—may seem overwhelming, remember that together they give us a more complete picture of human complexity.

FIGURE 12.17

Comparing Perspectives on Personality

> **reflect and review**

 Characterize the main methods of personality assessment.

- Describe the reasons psychologists use personality assessment.
- Discuss projective techniques.
- Explain self-report tests.
- Summarize behavioural and cognitive assessment.
- Identify assessment in the selection of employees.

Which of the assessment tools that we discussed do you think would likely provide the most accurate picture of your personality? Explain.

Personality

1 THEORIES OF PERSONALITY

2 PSYCHODYNAMIC PERSPECTIVES

- Freud's Psychoanalytic Theory
- Psychodynamic Dissenters and Revisionists
- Evaluating Psychodynamic Perspectives

3 BEHAVIOURAL AND SOCIAL COGNITIVE PERSPECTIVES

- Skinner's Behaviourism
- Bandura's Social Cognitive Theory
- Evaluating the Behavioural and Social Cognitive Perspectives

4 HUMANISTIC PERSPECTIVES

- Rogers's Approach
- Maslow's Approach
- Self-Esteem
- Evaluating Humanistic Perspectives

5 TRAIT PERSPECTIVES

- Trait Theories
- The Big Five Personality Factors
- Trait-Situation Interaction
- Evaluating Trait Perspectives

6 PERSONALITY ASSESSMENT

- Projective Tests
- Self-Report Tests
- Behavioural and Cognitive Assessment
- Assessment in the Selection of Employees

At the beginning of the chapter, we posed six chapter questions and encouraged you to review material related to these questions at the end of each major section (see pages 473, 480, 485, 490, 495, and 503). Use the following reflection and review features for further your understanding of the chapter material.

CHAPTER REFLECTIONS

Apply Your Knowledge

1. Consider a facet of your personality that you might want to change. From the perspective of Freud's psychoanalytic theory, could you change this aspect of your personality? How? From the perspective of psychodynamic revisionists, would it be possible to make the desired change? How?

2. Try the following exercise: The next time you are in a situation in which the outcome is unknown (for example, you have a test coming up, or you're thinking about an upcoming date), pay attention to how you respond to the situation in terms of the three important concepts of social cognitive theory described in this chapter. Now try to approach the situation using the characteristic opposite to whatever you would normally do. How easy or hard is this? Did it have an effect on the outcome? How would you know?

3. Think about the big five (or big seven) factors in personality and their relationship to various situations. Which factors can be assessed in the individual, and which are measures of interactions between people? Based on your answers, which factors would you expect to vary more depending on the situation?

4. Type "personality test" into an online search engine, and take two or more of the tests available online. Now look at the results—which perspective do the results seem to reflect most? How might the structure of the test have affected the outcome?

5. Think about the three major issues in the study of psychology described in the text. In many cases, questions posed as "either/or" turn out to be best answered by "some of both." After reading about all of the theories in the chapter, how might you rephrase the personality questions if you were interested in answering them scientifically?

CHAPTER REVIEW

Define personality and identify the major issues in the study of personality.

- Personality involves the enduring thoughts, emotions, and behaviours that characterize the way we adapt to the world. A key question is why different individuals respond to the same situation in different ways.

Summarize the psychodynamic perspectives.

- The psychodynamic perspectives view personality as primarily unconscious and as occurring in stages. Most psychodynamic perspectives emphasize the importance of early experience with parents in sculpting personality.

- Freud believed that most of the mind is unconscious, and his psychoanalytic theory stated that personality has three structures: id, ego, and superego. The conflicting demands of these personality structures produce anxiety. Defence mechanisms protect the ego and reduce this anxiety. Freud was convinced that problems develop because of early childhood experiences. He said that we go through five psychosexual stages: oral, anal, phallic, latency, and genital. During the phallic stage, which occurs in early childhood, the Oedipus (for boys) or Electra (for girls) complex is a major source of conflict.

- A number of psychodynamic theorists criticized Freud for placing too much emphasis on sexuality and the first five years of life. They argued that Freud gave too little credit to the ego, conscious thought, and sociocultural factors. Horney said that the need for security, not sex or aggression, is our most important need. Jung thought Freud underplayed the role of the unconscious mind. He developed the concept of the collective unconscious and placed special emphasis on archetypes. Adler's theory, called individual psychology, stresses that people are striving toward a positive being and that they create their own goals. Adler placed more emphasis on social motivation than Freud did.

- Strengths of the psychodynamic perspectives include emphases on the individual's past experiences, on personality's developmental course, on mental representation of the environment, on the unconscious mind, and on conflict as an influence on personality. These perspectives have also had a substantial influence on psychology as a discipline. Weaknesses of the psychodynamic perspectives include overreliance on reports from the past, too much emphasis on sexuality and the unconscious mind, a negative view of human nature, too much attention to early experience, and a male, Western bias.

Explain the behavioural and social cognitive perspectives.

- The behavioural and social cognitive perspectives emphasize the importance of environmental experience in understanding the person's personality. Within that broad framework, behaviourists focus on people's observable behaviour; social cognitive theorists also examine cognitive factors in personality.
- Skinner's behaviourism emphasizes that cognition is unimportant in personality; personality is observable behaviour, which is influenced by rewards and punishments in the environment. In the behavioural view, personality often varies according to the situation.
- Social cognitive theory, created by Albert Bandura and Walter Mischel, states that behaviour, environment, and person/cognitive factors are important in understanding personality. In Bandura's view, these factors reciprocally interact. Three important concepts in social cognitive theory are self-efficacy, locus of control, and optimism. Self-efficacy is the belief that one can master a situation and produce positive outcomes. Locus of control refers to individuals' beliefs about whether the outcomes of their actions depend on what they do (internal) or on events outside their control (external). Seligman defines optimism as an individual's explanatory style, especially how a person explains the causes of bad events. Optimists explain bad events as being caused by external, unstable, and specific circumstances. Pessimists explain bad events as being caused by internal, stable, and global factors. Another view of optimism involves the expectancy that good things are more likely, and bad things less likely, to occur in the future. Numerous research studies reveal that individuals characterized by self-efficacy, internal locus of control, and optimism generally show positive functioning and adjustment.
- Strengths of the behavioural and social cognitive perspectives include their emphases on environmental determinants and on a scientific climate for investigating personality. An additional strength of social cognitive theory is its focus on cognitive processes and self-control. The behavioural view has been criticized for taking the "person" out of personality and for ignoring cognition. These approaches have also not given adequate attention to enduring individual differences, to biological factors, and to personality as a whole.

Describe the humanistic perspectives.

- The humanistic perspectives stress the person's capacity for personal growth and freedom, ability to choose a destiny, and positive qualities.
- In Rogers's approach, each of us has a need for unconditional positive regard. The result is that the real self is not valued unless it meets the standards of other people. The self is the core of personality; it includes both the real and ideal selves. Rogers said that we can help others develop more positive self-concept in three ways: unconditional positive regard, empathy, and genuineness. Rogers also stressed that each of us has the innate, inner capacity to become a fully functioning person.
- Maslow called the humanistic movement the "third force" in psychology. Maslow developed the hierarchy of needs concept, with self-actualization being the highest human need.
- Self-esteem is the person's overall evaluation of self-worth or self-image. Four main strategies for increasing a person's self-esteem are to identify the causes of low self-esteem, provide emotional support and approval, help the person achieve valued goals, and help the person learn to cope successfully with challenges.
- The humanistic perspectives sensitized us to the importance of subjective experience, of consciousness, of self-conception, of considering the whole person, and of our innate, positive nature. Its weaknesses are a tendency to avoid empirical research, a tendency to be too optimistic, and an inclination to encourage excessive self-love.

Discuss the trait perspectives.

- A trait is an enduring personality characteristic that tends to lead to certain behaviours. Trait theories emphasize that personality consists of broad, enduring dispositions that lead to characteristic responses. Trait theorists are also interested in how traits are organized within the individual. Traits are assumed to be essentially stable over time and across situations. Allport believed that each individual has a unique set of personality traits, grouped into three main categories: cardinal, central, and secondary. Eysenck's basic dimensions of personality are introversion-extraversion, stability-instability (neuroticism), and psychoticism.

- There is much current interest in the big five factors in personality, which are considered to be "super-traits:" openness to experience, conscientiousness, extraversion, agreeableness, and neuroticism (emotional stability).
- Today, most personality psychologists are interactionists. They believe that personality is determined by a combination of traits, or person factors, and the situation, or environmental factors.
- Studying people in terms of their traits has practical value. Identifying a person's traits allows us to know the person better. Understanding a person's traits may also help us better predict the person's health, thinking, job success, and interpersonal skills. Mischel's (1968) Personality and Assessment attacked trait theory, arguing that personality varies across situations more than trait theorists acknowledged.

Characterize the main methods of personality assessment.

- Psychologists use a wide variety of tests and measures to assess personality. These measures are often tied to psychologists' theoretical orientations. Personality tests were designed to measure stable, enduring aspects of personality.
- Projective tests, designed to assess the unconscious aspects of personality, present individuals with an ambiguous stimulus and then ask them to describe it or tell a story about it. Projective tests are based on the assumption that the ambiguity of the stimuli allows individuals to project their personalities onto them. The Rorschach inkblot test is a widely used projective test; its effectiveness is controversial. The Thematic Apperception Test (TAT) is another projective test.
- Self-report tests assess personality traits by asking test takers questions about their preferences and behaviours. Even though a self-report test may have face validity, it may still elicit invalid responses when people try to answer in a socially desirable way. Empirically keyed tests, which rely on items that are indirect questions about some criterion, were developed to overcome the problem of face validity. The Minnesota Multiphasic Personality Inventory (MMPI) is the most widely used and researched self-report personality test; it has 10 clinical scales to assist therapists in diagnosing psychological problems and also contains validity scales. Tests have also been created to assess the big five personality factors. Some of the most popular are the Neuroticism Extraversion Openness Personality Inventory (NEO-PI-R), the Jackson Personality Inventory (JPI), and the Hogan Personality Inventory (HPI).
- Behavioural assessment seeks to obtain objective information about personality by observing behaviour and its environmental ties. Cognitive assessment seeks to discover individual differences in processing and acting on information through interviews and questionnaires.
- Industrial psychologists use many different selection tools to pick the right person for the right job. Among the most widely used personnel selection tools are application forms, psychological tests, interviews, and work sample tests.

CONNECTIONS

For extra help in mastering the material in the chapter, see the review questions and practice quizzes in the Student Study Guide and the Online Learning Centre.

CORE TERMS

Psychological Disorders

In 2003, Canadian psychology lost a unique scholar with the passing of Norman Endler of York University (McCann & Flett, 2004). Endler's field was psychological disorders, especially depression and anxiety. He was prolific and his work was well-regarded. His edited volume on depression (McCann & Endler, 1990) and his interactional model of anxiety, stress and coping (Endler, 1997) are classics. But he was not only a scholar of depression, he knew first hand what he was talking about.

Norman Endler is a psychologist who has waged his own personal battle with bipolar disorder.

In 1977, Endler was the Chair of the Department of Psychology at York University and was already a leading expert on anxiety, stress, and coping. That summer, he descended into a bipolar mood disorder, in which moods alternate between mania (an overexcited, unrealistically optimistic state) and depression. In his book *Holiday of Darkness*, Endler (1990a) mixes his scholarly bent with his personal experience to tell of his battle with the disorder and the treatment, including antidepressant drugs and electroconvulsive therapy. He chronicles his feelings while in the full grip of his depression:

"One of the hardest things was getting up in the morning. Although I had had some sleep, I felt as though a ton of bricks was resting on me. It had become extremely difficult to get out of bed. I was lethargic and drowsy, probably because of the depression and heavy medication."

"My indecisiveness was the worst of all. I couldn't decide what to eat or what to wear. I couldn't decide whether to get out of bed or stay, I couldn't decide whether to shower or not to shower. I could never decide what I wanted to do because I didn't know myself. I was completely apathetic."

"I guess my one major reaction was one of despair—a despair of ever being human again. I honestly felt subhuman, lower than the lowest vermin. Further, I was self-deprecatory, and could not understand why anyone would want to associate with me, let alone love me. I became mistrustful and suspicious of others and was certain that they were checking up on me to prove that I was incompetent."

With help from his family, colleagues, and friends, and with good health care, Norman Endler conquered his disorder and resumed his career as one of Canada's pre-eminent psychologists.

① UNDERSTANDING PSYCHOLOGICAL DISORDERS

| Defining Abnormal Behaviour | Theoretical Approaches to Psychological Disorders | Classifying Abnormal Behaviour |

What are the characteristics of abnormal behaviour and how is it categorized?

Six million Canadians, or 20 percent of today's population, may suffer from a psychological disorder in their lifetime (Canadian Alliance on Mental Illness and Mental Health, 2003). In 1993 alone, the cost of mental illnesses to Canadians was estimated at $7.331 billion (Health Canada, 2002a). Similarly, about 44 million Americans each year suffer from some kind of psychological disorder (U.S. National Institute of Mental Health, 2001). In one study, nearly 20,000 randomly selected individuals from the United States were asked whether they had experienced any of a list of psychological disorders in their lifetime and whether they were currently suffering from one (Robins & Regier, 1991). Almost one-third (32 percent) of the respondents said that they had experienced one or more psychological disorders in their lifetime, and 20 percent said they currently had an active disorder.

You might be surprised that so many individuals acknowledge having a psychological disorder. However, the figures from the study include both individuals in institutions and in the community. They also include individuals with a substance abuse disorder (alcohol or other drugs, 17 percent). Surprisingly, only one-third of the individuals in this study who said they currently had a psychological disorder had received treatment for it in the previous six months. In Canada, psychological disorders are, nevertheless, the second most common reason for hospitalization among 20 to 44-year-olds (Canadian Psychological Association, 2001). By 2020, disabling depression will become the most expensive cause of loss of productivity in the workplace (Canadian Alliance on Mental Illness and Mental Health, 2003).

Defining Abnormal Behaviour

To understand psychological disorders, we need to examine what is meant by abnormal behaviour. In thinking about how to define abnormal behaviour, consider the following four individuals:

- At 32, Jenny seeks help for her blank spells (Ross, 1994). She does not remember her recent flight back to Winnipeg from Vancouver or getting in trouble with the law. When she is hypnotized, she vividly relives her brutal rapes at the age of 12 by her father. Later, under hypnosis, a second personality, Sally, emerges. It was Sally, not Jenny, who passed the bad cheques in Vancouver. Sally does not feel that Jenny's body is hers; she has never been raped and Jenny's father is not hers. Because Jenny was repeatedly abused, she learned to retreat out of her body to escape the humiliation and pain. Jenny became depressed and nightmare-prone, while Sally was bright and outgoing. Therapy eventually helped Jenny, but not before she lost contact with her children, spent time in jail, become a prostitute, and abused alcohol.
- Thirty-year-old Ralph has feelings of contamination that compel him to carry out numerous cleansing activities each day (Leon, 1990). Intensely uncomfortable when he notices any dirt on himself or in his immediate environment, he thoroughly washes his hands and arms. If he finds any dirt in his apartment, he feels compelled to scrub it from top to bottom, then shower in a rigidly specific manner. He washes his hands three to four times an hour, showers six to seven times a day, and scrubs his apartment at least twice a day. Ralph reports that his life is very restricted because he feels driven to carry out these cleansing activities.
- Thirty-year-old Janet is divorced and raising her three children and recently resumed part-time study at a college (Oltmanns, Neale, & Davison, 1986). Her

return to college didn't last long, because one of her children was having sleep-related problems. Janet became depressed when her husband fell in love with a younger woman and asked for a divorce. She felt sad, discouraged, and lonely. The feeling became more severe just before she withdrew from college. Nothing seems to cheer her up, she doesn't have any interest in her friends, and she sees her children as more burdensome than ever. The future looks bleak for Janet.

• Twenty-seven-year-old Jim is unemployed and single. It really bothers him that he has a special power (Gorenstein, 1997). He says he can influence other people, even endanger them, by the way he breathes. He believes he has to go to great lengths to avoid people so that he won't put them in jeopardy. Jim has currently secluded himself in a room at his parents' house and comes out only for occasional meals, bathroom visits, and church services. He doesn't want his power to fall into malevolent hands, which he sees as another reason for not appearing in public.

Would you agree that the behaviour of all four of these individuals is abnormal? If so, what would you base your judgment on?

There are a number of myths and misconceptions about abnormal behaviour. Here are some of the most common:

Myth: Abnormal behaviour is always bizarre.
Fact: Often, the behaviour of many people who are diagnosed with a mental disorder cannot be distinguished from the behaviour of normal people. In Jim's case, belief in the power of his breath is bizarre. However, Janet's behaviour would not be considered bizarre.
Myth: Normal and abnormal behaviour are different in kind.
Fact: Few, if any, types of behaviour displayed by people with a mental disorder are unique to them. Abnormal behaviour consists of a poor fit between the behaviour and the situation in which it is enacted.
Myth: Once people have a mental disorder, they will always have it.
Fact: Most people, like Norman Endler, can be successfully treated for a mental disorder.

Abnormal behaviour is one of those concepts that is not easy to define (Widiger, 2005). The definition varies across academic disciplines and across social, medical, and legal institutions. For example, The American Psychiatric Association (2001) defines *abnormal behaviour* in medical terms: a mental illness that affects or is manifested in a person's brain and can affect the way a person thinks, behaves, and interacts with people. Alternately, Canadian courts define "not criminally responsible on account of mental disorder" (the U.S. equivalent is "insanity")—a legalism, not a psychological term—as the inability to appreciate the nature and quality or wrongfulness of one's acts (Livingston & others, 2003; Pikona-Sapir & others, 2001; Gray, Shone, & Liddle, 2000). Many legal questions arise in society's response to mental illness (Roesch & others, 1999; Evans, 1997).

Keep in mind that the line between what is normal and what is abnormal is not always clear-cut. We can use three criteria to help distinguish normal from abnormal behaviour. **Abnormal behaviour** is behaviour that is deviant, maladaptive, or personally distressful. Only one of the three criteria listed needs to be met for the behaviour to be classified as abnormal, but two or all three may be present.

Let's take a closer look at what each of the three criteria of abnormal behaviour entails. First, abnormal behaviour is *deviant*. Abnormal behaviour has been described as being *atypical*. However, people like J. K. Rowling, Albert Einstein, and Shania Twain are atypical. We don't usually categorize them as abnormal because of their extraordinary storytelling ability, intellectual power, and entertaining skills, respectively. However, when atypical behaviour deviates from what is acceptable in a culture, it is often considered abnormal. Ralph's compulsive behaviour deviates from acceptable norms. People do not normally wash their hands three to four times an hour, take seven showers a day, and clean their apartments at least twice a day.

Second, abnormal behaviour is *maladaptive*. Maladaptive behaviour interferes with a person's ability to function effectively in the world. Jenny's criminal activities marginalize

In July 1995, 14-year-old Sandy Charles of La Ronge, Saskatchewan, along with an 8-year-old accomplice, brutally murdered 7-year-old Johnathan Thimpsen. Charles then cut sections of flesh from Thimsen's body and boiled them down to fat. He was mimicking a scene in the movie *Warlock*, in which the protagonist drank the rendered fat of a young male virgin in order to fly. While in detention awaiting trial, he claimed that he needed to drink blood because his teeth were becoming vampire's teeth. A Saskatoon judge ruled that Charles was aware of his actions but not criminally responsible because he suffered from schizophrenia. He was remanded for treatment and a case review every six months until he is able to return to society.

abnormal behaviour Behaviour that is deviant, maladaptive, or personally distressful.

her while Jim's belief that his breath has powerful effects on others prevents him from functioning in the everyday world.

Third, abnormal behaviour involves *personal distress*. Jenny's history of sexual abuse and her battle with alcohol abuse have caused her great personal suffering. Janet is also distressed about her life and sees her future as extremely bleak.

Theoretical Approaches to Psychological Disorders

What causes people to develop a psychological disorder? Behaving in deviant, maladaptive, and personally distressful ways? We can look to the biological, psychological, and sociocultural perspectives for theoretical explanations and also consider the possibility that a combination of factors might contribute to an individual's maladaptive behaviour (Barlow, Durand, & Stewart, 2006).

The Biological Approach The biological approach to psychological disorders attributes them to organic, internal causes. Scientists who adopt a biological approach to psychological disorders often focus on brain and genetic factors as the sources of abnormal behaviour. In the biological approach, drug therapy is frequently used to treat abnormal behaviour.

The biological approach is evident in the **medical model**, which describes psychological disorders as medical diseases with a biological origin. From the perspective of the medical model, abnormalities are called mental *illnesses*, the individuals afflicted are *patients*, and they are treated by *doctors*.

Biological views on psychological disorders fall into three main categories (Nolen-Hoeksema, 2004):

- *Structural views*. Abnormalities in the brain's structure cause mental disorders.
- *Biochemical views*. Imbalances in neurotransmitters or hormones cause mental disorders.
- *Genetic views*. Disordered genes cause mental disorders.

These biological factors are discussed later in the chapter.

The Psychological Approach Chapter 12 described the psychodynamic, behavioural and social cognitive, and humanistic perspectives on personality. These perspectives serve as a foundation for understanding the psychological factors involved in psychological disorders:

- *Psychodynamic perspectives*. Psychological disorders arise from unconscious conflicts that produce anxiety and result in maladaptive behaviour. Ineffective early relationships with parents are believed to be the origin of psychological disorders. Recall that these ideas stem from Freud's psychoanalytic theory but that some contemporary proponents of this approach place less emphasis on unconscious thought and sexuality.
- *Behavioural and social cognitive perspectives*. In the behavioural perspective, the focus is on the rewards and punishments in the environment that determine abnormal behaviour. Social cognitive theory accepts that environmental experiences are important determinants of psychological disorders but adds that a number of social cognitive factors are also involved. In this way, observational learning, expectancies, self-efficacy, self-control, beliefs about oneself and the world, and many other cognitive processes are key to psychological disorders.
- *Humanistic perspectives*. These perspectives emphasize a capacity for growth, freedom to choose one's own destiny, and positive personal qualities. A psychological disorder reflects an inability to fulfill one's potential, likely arising from pressures of society to conform to others' expectations and values. A person with a psychological disorder is likely to have a low self-concept because he or she has experienced excessive criticism and negative circumstances.

medical model A biological approach that describes psychological disorders as medical diseases with a biological origin.

The psychological perspectives focus mainly on the individual. Chapter 14 extensively examines how theories of personality—psychodynamic, behavioural and social cognitive, and humanistic—influence the treatment of psychological disorders.

FIGURE 13.1
Some Culture-Related Disorders

Disorder	Culture	Description/Characteristics
Amok	Malaysia, Philippines, Africa	This disorder involves sudden, uncontrolled outbursts of anger in which the person may injure or kill someone. Amok is often found in males who are emotionally withdrawn before the onset of the disorder. After the attack on someone, the individual feels exhausted and depressed and does not remember the rage and attack.
Anorexia Nervosa	Western cultures, especially the United States	This eating disorder involves a relentless pursuit of thinness through starvation, and can eventually lead to death.
Windigo	Algonquin hunters	This disorder involves a fear of being bewitched. The hunter becomes anxious and agitated, worrying he will be turned into a cannibal with a craving for human flesh.

The Sociocultural Approach Although the psychological approach mainly attributes psychological problems to unconscious conflicts, negative cognitions, low self-concept, and other factors within the individual, they still give environmental experiences a role in creating psychological disorders (Nolen-Hoeksema, 2004). The sociocultural approach places more emphasis on the larger social contexts in which a person lives—including the individual's marriage or family, neighbourhood, socioeconomic status, ethnicity, gender, or culture—than the other approaches do. For example, marital conflict might be the cause of mental disorder in one individual. In this view, when a member of a family has a psychological problem, it may not be due to something within the individual but rather to ineffective family functioning (Atwood, 2001). Any number of psychological problems can develop because of power struggles in a family: sibling conflicts, one child being favoured over another, marital conflict, and so on (Cuffe & others, 2005).

Individuals from low-income, minority neighbourhoods have the highest rates of mental disorders. In studies of the role of socioeconomic status and ethnicity in psychological disorders, socioeconomic status plays a much stronger role than ethnicity: The living conditions of poverty create stressful circumstances that can contribute to the development of a mental disorder (Hatton & Emerson, 2004; Weich, Lewis, & Jenkins, 2001).

Gender, another sociocultural factor, is associated with the presence of certain psychological disorders (Winstead & Sanchez, 2005; Greenglass, 1998; Nolen-Hoeksema, 2004). Women tend to be diagnosed with internalized disorders. In particular, women are likelier than men to suffer from anxiety disorders and depression, which have symptoms that are turned inward (internalized). Conversely, men are socialized to direct their energy toward the external world (to externalize their feelings) and they have externalized disorders more often that involve aggression and substance abuse. Gender differences are discussed more fully later in the chapter.

Most experts on abnormal behaviour agree that many psychological disorders are universal (Al-Issa, 1982). However, the frequency and intensity of psychological disorders varies across cultures and depends on social, economic, technological, and religious aspects of cultures (López, & Guarnaccia, 2000, 2005; Fabrega, Jr., 2004; Tanaka-Matsumi, 2001). Some disorders, though, are culture-related, as indicated in figure 13.1 (Marsella, 2000).

An Interactionist Approach: Biopsychosocial Normal and abnormal behaviour alike may involve biological, psychological, and sociocultural factors alone or in combination with other factors. Abnormal behaviour can be influenced by biological factors (such as brain processes and heredity), psychological factors (such as distorted thoughts or low self-esteem), and sociocultural factors (such as ineffective family functioning or poverty). These factors can interact to produce abnormal behaviour. Sometimes this interactionist approach is called *biopsychosocial* (Barlow & Durand, 2005). For example, problem gambling is productively viewed from the biopsychosocial perspective (Sharpe, 2002; González-Ibáñez, Rosel, & Moreno, 2005). At the biological level, a genetic predisposition to abnormal serotonin and dopamine function may make a person vulnerable to developing impulsive tendencies. At the psychological level, life stressors or family influences may lead a person to seek solace in an activity like gambling. Similarly, at the social level, the easy availability of access to casinos and other gambling venues may lead to impulsive gambling. A person with a biological predisposition to impulsiveness who is experiencing serious life stress while living near a casino, then, might be at extreme risk for developing into a problem gambler.

Classifying Abnormal Behaviour

Ever since human history began, people have suffered from diseases, sadness, and bizarre behaviour. And, for almost as long, healers have tried to treat and cure them. The classification of psychological disorders goes back to the ancient Egyptians and Greeks and has its roots in biology and medicine. To this day, the classification of psychological disorders follows a medical model.

Classifying psychological disorders is a difficult undertaking and one that provokes criticism not only from mental health professionals but also from many other segments of society. However, the benefits of a classification system far outweigh the disadvantages (Comer, 2005). For one thing, a classification system gives mental health professionals a common basis for communicating with one another. For example, if one psychologist says in a case review that her client has a panic disorder and another psychologist says that his client has schizophrenia, the two psychologists understand that the clients have exhibited certain behaviour that led to their diagnoses. A classification system can also help clinicians make predictions about disorders; it provides information about the likelihood that a disorder will occur, about which individuals are most susceptible to the disorder, about the progress of the disorder once it has appeared, and about the prognosis for effective treatment (Rogers, 2001).

The DSM-IV Classification System In 1952, the American Psychiatric Association published the first major classification of psychological disorders in the United States. **DSM-IV** (*Diagnostic and Statistical Manual of Mental Disorders*, 4th edition; American Psychiatric Association, 1994) is the current edition of the APA's guidelines. It contains 17 major classifications and describes more than 200 specific disorders. It is widely used throughout Canada.

Continuing changes in the *DSM* reflect advancements in knowledge about the classification of psychological disorders (First & Pincus, 2002). On the basis of research and clinical experience, the *DSM-IV* added, dropped, or revised categories, sometimes generating controversy among the diagnosticians who rely on the classification system.

A key feature of the *DSM-IV* is its *multiaxial system*, which classifies individuals on the basis of five dimensions, or axes, that take into account the individual's history and highest level of functioning in the previous year. This system ensures that the individual is not merely assigned to a psychological disorder category but is characterized in terms of a number of clinical factors (Sperry, 2003).

The five axes of *DSM-IV* are:

Axis I: All diagnostic categories except personality disorders and mental retardation
Axis II: Personality disorders and mental retardation
Axis III: General medical conditions
Axis IV: Psychosocial and environmental problems
Axis V: Current level of functioning

Axes I and II comprise the classification of psychological disorders (Davison & Neale, 2006). Figure 13.2 describes the major categories of these psychological disorders. Axes III through V may not be needed to diagnose a psychological disorder, but they are included so that the person's overall life situation is considered. Thus, a person might have a heart condition (Axis III), which has important implications for treatment because some antidepressant drugs can worsen heart conditions. Axis IV includes occupational problems, economic problems, and family problems. On Axis V, the clinician

DSM-IV Diagnostic and Statistical Manual of Mental Disorders, fourth edition; the APA's major classification of psychological disorders.

Major Categories of Psychological Disorders	**Description**
Axis I Disorders	
Disorders usually first diagnosed in infancy, childhood, or adolescence and communication disorders	Include disorders that appear before adolescence, such as attention-deficit hyperactivity disorder, autism, learning disorders (stuttering, for example).
Anxiety disorders	Characterized by motor tension, hyperactivity, and apprehensive expectations/thoughts. Includes generalized anxiety disorder, panic disorder, phobic disorder, obsessive-compulsive disorder, and post-traumatic stress disorder.
Somatoform disorders	Occur when psychological symptoms take a physical form even though no physical causes can be found. Includes hypochondriasis and conversion disorder.
Factitious disorders	The person deliberately fabricates symptoms of a medical or mental disorder, but not for external gain (such as a disability claim).
Dissociative disorders	Involve a sudden loss of memory or change of identity. Includes the disorders of dissociative amnesia, dissociative fugue, and dissociative identity disorder.
Delirium, dementia, amnestic, and other cognitive disorders	Consist of mental disorders involving problems in consciousness and cognition, such as substance-induced delirium or dementia involving Alzheimer's disease.
Mood disorders	Disorders in which there is a primary disturbance in mood; includes depressive disorders and bipolar disorder (which involves wide mood swings from deep depression to extreme euphoria and agitation).
Schizophrenia and other psychotic disorders	Disorders characterized by distorted thoughts and perceptions, odd communication, inappropriate emotion, and other unusual behaviours.
Substance-related disorders	Include alcohol-related disorders, cocaine-related disorders, hallucinogen-related disorders, and other drug-related disorders.
Sexual and gender identity disorders	Consist of three main types of disorders: gender-identity disorders (person is not comfortable with identity as a female or male), paraphilias (person has a preference for unusual sexual acts to stimulate sexual arousal), and sexual dysfunctions (impairments in sexual functioning; see chapter 11).
Eating disorders	Include anorexia nervosa and bulimia nervosa (see chapter 11).
Sleep disorders	Consist of primary sleep disorders, such as insomnia and narcolepsy (see chapter 6), and sleep disorder due to a general medical condition.
Impulse control disorders not elsewhere classified	Include kleptomania, pyromania, and compulsive gambling.
Adjustment disorders	Characterized by distressing emotional or behavioural symptoms in response to an identifiable stressor.
Axis II Disorders	
Mental retardation	Low intellectual functioning and an inability to adapt to everyday life (see chapter 10).
Personality disorders	Develop when personality traits become inflexible and maladaptive.
Other conditions that may be a focus of clinical attention.	Include relational problems (with a partner, sibling, and so on), problems related to abuse or neglect (physical abuse of a child, for example), or additional conditions (such as bereavement, academic problems, religious or spiritual problems).

makes a diagnosis about the highest level of adaptive functioning the person has attained in the preceding year in social, occupational, or school activities. This diagnosis ranges from a rating of 100 (superior functioning in a wide range of activities) to 10 (persistent danger of severely hurting self or others), with eight other ratings at 10-point increments. For example, a rating of 50 indicates serious symptoms or impairment in social, occupational, or school functioning.

FIGURE 13.2

Main Categories of Psychological Disorders in DSM-IV

The more than 200 mental health professionals who contributed to the development of the *DSM-IV* were a much more diverse group than their predecessors, who were mainly white male psychiatrists. More women, ethnic minorities, and nonpsychiatrists, such as clinical psychologists, were involved in constructing the *DSM-IV*, and greater attention was given to gender- and ethnicity-related diagnoses. For example, the *DSM-IV* contains an appendix titled "Guidelines for Cultural Formation and Glossary of Culture-Related Syndromes." Also, the *DSM-IV* is accompanied by a number of sourcebooks that present the empirical base of the *DSM-IV*. In previous versions of the *DSM*, the reasons for diagnostic changes were not always explicit, so the evidence that led to their formulation was never available for public evaluation.

The most controversial aspect of the *DSM-IV* is an issue that has existed since the publication of the *DSM-I* in 1952. Although more nonpsychiatrists than ever were responsible for drafting the *DSM-IV*, it still classifies individuals based on their symptoms and uses medical terminology in the psychiatric tradition of thinking about mental disorders in terms of illness and disease (Nathan & Langenbucher, 1999; Oltmanns & Emory, & Taylor, 2006). This strategy implies an internal cause that is more or less independent of external or environmental factors (Hansell & Damour, 2004). Thus, even though researchers have begun to shed light on the complex interaction of genetic, neurobiological, cognitive, and environmental factors in the *DSM* disorders, the *DSM-IV* continues to reflect the medical/disease model of psychological disorders (Goldberg & Goodyer, 2005).

The American Psychiatric Association revised the text of *DSM-IV* to include new research that had been conducted since its publication in 1994. The revision, *DSM-IV-TR* (Text Revision; American Psychiatric Association, 2000) includes changes in the criteria for several disorders. For example, paraphilias (sexual disorders such as exhibitionism and voyeurism) can now be diagnosed if they are acted on, even though they may not cause the person in question distress or impaired functioning. Consultation has begun on a new edition, the *DSM-V*, which is scheduled for publication in 2010 (Widiger & Simonsen, 2005),

The Issue of Labelling The *DSM-IV* is also controversial because it labels as psychological disorders what are often thought of as everyday problems. For example, under learning or academic skills disorders, the *DSM-IV* includes reading disorder, mathematics disorder, and disorder of written expression. Under substance-related disorders, the *DSM-IV* includes caffeine-use disorders. We don't usually think of these problems as mental disorders, but including them implies that such "normal behaviour" should be treated as a mental disorder. In a related vein, Hacking (1998) worries about the rapidity with which classifications have changed and wonders why some disorders become "currently fashionable." The developers of the *DSM* argue that mental health providers have been treating many problems not included in earlier editions and that comprehensiveness is important. One practical reason for including everyday problems is to help more individuals get their health insurance companies to pay for help. Most health insurance companies reimburse their clients only for disorders listed in the *DSM-IV* system.

Another criticism of the *DSM-IV*, and indeed of this type of classification system in general, is that the system focuses strictly on pathology and problems, with a bias toward finding something wrong with anyone who becomes the object of diagnostic study (Allen, 1998). Because labels can become self-fulfilling prophecies, emphasizing strengths as well as weaknesses might help to destigmatize labels such as *paranoid schizophrenic* or *ex-mental patient*. It would also help to provide clues to treatments that promote mental competence rather than working only to reduce mental distress.

In a classic and controversial study that illustrated the problem of labelling a person with a psychological disorder, David Rosenhan (1973) recruited eight university students, none with a psychological disorder, to see a psychiatrist at a hospital. They were instructed to act in a normal way except to complain about hearing voices that said such things as "empty" and "thud." All eight expressed an interest in leaving the hospital and behaved in a cooperative manner. Nonetheless, they were labelled with schizophrenia, a severe psychological disorder, and kept in the hospital from 3 to 52 days.

Are Psychological Disorders a Myth?

When he published *The Myth of Mental Illness* in 1961, psychiatrist Thomas Szasz set off a bitter debate, which still rages today (Szasz, 2004; Wyatt, 2004). He made the surprising claim that there is no such thing as "mental illness." Szasz begins his argument with a distinction between diseases of the brain and diseases of the mind. Although he accepts that there are diseases of the brain, such as epilepsy, he suggests that psychological disorders are not "illnesses" and are better labelled "problems of living." Imagine, for example, someone who believes that his body is already dead. That person may behave in strange ways but may exhibit no physical defects or diseases. In this case, according to Szasz, the person certainly holds some maladaptive beliefs but does not have a mental illness.

For Szasz this is not just a question of semantics. Suppose someone's "problems of living" stem from interacting with other people? In such instances, Szasz says it is inconsistent to refer to that person's social problems as "mental illness" and treat them through a medical model that prescribes drugs. If the person who believes that his body is already dead does nothing more than offend or frighten other people with his bizarre belief, then what right do mental health professionals have to label him "mentally ill" and administer drugs to him? What right do they have to force him into treatment? Szasz has even gone so far as to compare psychiatry to slavery (Szasz, 2002).

Ken Kesey's novel *One Flew over the Cuckoo's Nest*, published in 1962, explores just such a tragedy. The antihero, McMurphy, is a social outsider who opts to go to a mental institution instead of prison. Unfortunately for him, the hospital staff do not take kindly to his unruliness. He is treated with drugs and electroshock therapy until he loses his identity. Kesey wrote his bestseller based on his experiences in working at a mental hospital.

A poignant example of dealing with "problems of living" can be found in the origins of dissociative identity disorder (having two or more distinct personalities or selves; Braun, 1985). Children whose parents have dissociative identity disorder may develop signs of the disorder as a learned behaviour. One possibility is that these children learn by imitating their parents' behaviour. Another is that they develop symptoms as a way of coping with their abnormal circumstances. This tragedy may be compounded by diagnosing such children as "having" the psychological disorder and treating them with drugs. For Szasz, the treatment of such children should be sociocultural in nature (such as removing them from unhealthy environments and placing them in healthy ones) and may involve behavioural techniques.

Szasz's critique extends to suggesting that the so-called insanity defence be abolished. He says that finding people not criminally responsible because of a mental disorder means that they have a psychological disorder, which he disputes; otherwise, by committing a crime, they are misbehaving, in which case they should be held responsible. Stripping them of responsibility and yet depriving them of liberty for a longer period than they would have served for a criminal conviction is doing them no favour.

Szasz's critics reply that there is sound evidence that biological factors are implicated in psychological disorders, including mood disorders and schizophrenia (Torrey, 2005). They also argue that many psychological disorders are now successfully treated using drug therapies that were unavailable when Szasz first published his arguments. When it comes to the insanity defence, critics argue that imprisoning someone suffering from a psychological disorder for a crime is much less humane than providing him or her with treatment aimed at curing the disorder.

Szasz's supporters counter that defining an individual's problems as illness only labels them and encourages them to lose hope. Masson (1998, page 2) comments, "There is a heightened awareness of the dangers inherent in labeling somebody with a disease category like schizophrenia, and many people are beginning to realize that there is no such entity."

If any resolution to this controversy is in sight, it is that everyone agrees that further research is needed to clarify what disorders like "depression" and "schizophrenia" really are. Nobody wants to inappropriately label, misdiagnose, or mistreat people who are already suffering.

What do you think?

- When do you think it is appropriate to label someone as having a psychological disorder?
- When do you think medical interventions for mental disorders are appropriate?
- Under what circumstances, if any, is the insanity defence an acceptable legal alternative? Why?

Labels can be damaging when they draw attention to one aspect of a person and ignore others (Sarason & Sarason, 2005). For example, the label of "mental patient" or of any disorder, such as anxiety disorder, often has negative connotations, such as incompetent, dangerous, and socially unacceptable. Negative labels can reduce a person's self-esteem and cause the person to be discriminated against. Also, when people feel they might be stigmatized, they may be reluctant to seek help because they don't want to be labelled "mentally ill" or "crazy." Further, even when a person who has had a psychological disorder improves, the label may nevertheless stay with the person. As detailed in the Critical Reflections box, some individuals have gone so far as to argue that psychological disorders are a myth.

Although psychologists usually go along with the *DSM-IV*, psychiatrists are more satisfied with it because of its medical approach. Even though the *DSM-IV* has its critics, it is still the most comprehensive classification system available.

> **reflect and review**

1 **Discuss the characteristics and classification of abnormal behaviours.**

- Define abnormal behaviour.
- Summarize the biological, psychological, and sociocultural approaches to psychological disorders.
- Describe the classification of psychological disorders and evaluate its advantages and disadvantages.

Ed Gein, a serial killer from Wisconsin, admitted to murdering two women in the 1950s and to robbing bodies from graves. He made corpse parts into ornaments and clothes that he wore to replicate the image of his dead mother. Gein was acquitted by reason of insanity and committed to a mental institution. He was the inspiration for Psycho and The Silence of the Lambs. Do you think Gein should have been acquitted? What do you think about the "insanity" defence?

2 ANXIETY DISORDERS

Generalized — Panic — Phobic — Obsessive- — Post-Traumatic
Anxiety   Disorder   Disorders   Compulsive   Stress
Disorder   Disorder   Disorder

What are the characteristics of the various anxiety disorders?

Anxiety is a diffuse, vague, highly unpleasant feeling of fear and apprehension. People with high levels of anxiety worry a lot, but their anxiety does not necessarily impair their ability to function in the world. **Anxiety disorders** are psychological disorders that feature motor tension (jumpiness, trembling, inability to relax); hyperactivity (dizziness, a racing heart, or possibly perspiration); and apprehensive expectations and thoughts (Rachman, 2004). According to Health Canada (2002a), combined anxiety disorders afflict 12 percent of Canadians. A 1990 Ontario survey found that 16 percent of women and 9 percent of men experienced an anxiety disorder in the year preceding the survey (Ontario Ministry of Health, 1990; Antony & Swinson, 1996). Approximately 19.1 million American adults from 18 to 54 years of age, or about 13.3 percent of people in this age group, are diagnosed with an anxiety disorder in any given year (U. S. National Institute of Mental Health, 2001a). The five types of anxiety disorders are generalized anxiety disorder, panic disorder, phobic disorders, obsessive-compulsive disorder, and post-traumatic stress disorder.

Generalized Anxiety Disorder

Anna, who is 27 years old, has just arrived for her visit with the psychologist. She was very nervous, wringing her hands, crossing and uncrossing her legs, and playing nervously with strands of her hair. She said her stomach felt like it was in knots, that her hands were cold, and that her neck muscles were so tight they hurt. She said that lately arguments with her husband had escalated. In recent weeks, Anna indicated that she had felt more and more nervous throughout the day as if something bad were about to happen. If the doorbell sounded or the phone rang, her heart beat rapidly and her breathing quickened. When she was around people, she had a difficult time speaking. She began to isolate herself. Her husband became impatient with Anna, so she decided to see a psychologist. (Goodstein & Calhoun, 1982)

Anna has a **generalized anxiety disorder**, an anxiety disorder that consists of persistent anxiety for a period of at least one month; the individual with generalized anxiety disorder is unable to specify the reasons for the anxiety (Heimberg, Turk, &

anxiety disorders Psychological disorders that include these features: motor tension, hyperactivity, and apprehensive expectations and thoughts.

generalized anxiety disorder An anxiety disorder that consists of persistent anxiety over at least one month; the individual with this disorder cannot specify the reasons for the anxiety.

Mennin, 2004; Ladouceur & Dugas, 2002). People with generalized anxiety disorder are nervous most of the time. They may worry about their work, their relationships, or their health. They may also worry about minor things in life, such as being late for an appointment or whether their clothes fit just right. Their anxiety often shifts from one aspect of life to another. Health Canada (2002a) reports that 1.1 percent of Canadians have generalized anxiety disorder in any given year. Approximately four million Americans from 18 to 54 years of age, or about 2.8 percent of people in this age group, have generalized anxiety disorder in any given year (U. S. National Institute of Mental Health, 2001a).

What is the etiology of generalized anxiety disorder? (The term *etiology* here means investigating the causes or significant antecedents of a mental disorder). Among the biological factors involved in generalized anxiety disorder are a genetic predisposition (Eley & Gregory, 2004; Stein, Jang, & Livesley, 1999) and a deficiency in the neurotransmitter GABA (Lydiard, 2003; Nutt, 2001). Among the psychological and sociocultural factors are having harsh self-standards that are virtually impossible to achieve or maintain, intolerance of uncertainty, having parents who were overly strict and critical (which can produce low self-esteem and excessive self-criticism), automatic negative thoughts in the face of stress, and a history of uncontrollable stressors or traumas, such as an abusive parent (Dugas & Ladouceur, 2000; Dugas, Marchand, & Ladouceur, 2005).

Edvard Munch's *The Scream*. Many experts interpret Munch's painting as an expression of the terror brought on by a panic attack.

Panic Disorder

Panic disorder is an anxiety disorder marked by the recurrent sudden onset of intense apprehension or terror (De Silva & Rachman, 1996; Rachman, 2004). The individual often has a feeling of impending doom but may not feel anxious all the time. Panic attacks, the defining feature of panic disorder, often strike without warning and produce severe palpitations, extreme shortness of breath, chest pains, trembling, sweating, dizziness, and a feeling of helplessness (Cox & others, 1994). Victims are seized by fear that they will die, go crazy, or do something they cannot control. Health Canada (2002a) reports that 0.7 percent of Canadians have panic disorder in any given year. Approximately 2.4 million Americans from 18 to 54 years of age, or about 1.7 percent of the people in this age group, have panic disorder in any given year (U. S. National Institute of Mental Health, 2001a).

In *DSM-IV*, panic disorder can be classified as with or without **agoraphobia**, a cluster of fears centred on public places and an inability to escape or find help should one become incapacitated (Marcaurelle & others, 2005). Crowded public places; travelling away from home, especially by public transportation; feeling confined or trapped; and being separated from a place or person can all produce agoraphobia, which causes some people to remain housebound (Antony & Swinson, 2000). It usually appears first in early adulthood, with 2.5 percent of individuals in the United States classified as having the disorder. Females are likelier than males to have panic disorder. The following individual was classified as having panic disorder with agoraphobia:

> Mrs. Reiss is a 48-year-old woman who is afraid to go out alone, a fear that she has had for six years but which has intensified in the last two years. The first signs of her fear appeared after an argument with her husband. After the argument, she went to the mailbox to get the mail and began to feel very anxious and dizzy. It was a struggle for her to get back to the house. Her fear lessened for several years, but reappeared even more intensely after she learned that her sister had cancer. Her fear continued to escalate after arguments with her husband. She became increasingly apprehensive about going outside alone. When she did try

panic disorder An anxiety disorder marked by the recurrent sudden onset of intense apprehension or terror.

agoraphobia A cluster of fears centred around public places and being unable to escape or to find help should one become incapacitated.

Acrophobia	Fear of high places
Aerophobia	Fear of flying
Ailurophobia	Fear of cats
Algophobia	Fear of pain
Amaxophobia	Fear of vehicles, driving
Arachnophobia	Fear of spiders
Astrapophobia	Fear of lightning
Cynophobia	Fear of dogs
Gamophobia	Fear of marriage
Hydrophobia	Fear of water
Melissophobia	Fear of bees
Mysophobia	Fear of dirt
Nyctophobia	Fear of darkness
Ophidiophobia	Fear of nonpoisonous snakes
Thanatophobia	Fear of death
Xenophobia	Fear of strangers

FIGURE 13.3
Phobias
This is only a partial listing.

phobic disorder Commonly called phobia, an anxiety disorder in which the individual has an irrational, overwhelming, persistent fear of a particular object or situation.

to leave, her heart would pound, she would perspire, and she would begin to tremble. After being outside only briefly, she would quickly go back into her house. (Greenberg, Szmulker, & Tantum, 1986).

What is the etiology of panic disorder? In terms of biological factors, individuals may have a predisposition for the disorder, which runs in families and occurs more often in identical than in fraternal twins (Goldstein & others, 1997). One line of research builds on the finding that selective serotonin reuptake inhibitors, drugs that affect the functioning of the neurotransmitter serotonin, are effective in treating panic disorder (Kasper & Resinger, 2001). This finding led researchers to demonstrate reduced serotonin binding (Maron & others, 2004) and genetic variants related to reduced serotonin function (Maron & others, 2005) in the brains of patients with panic disorder. The result may be that individuals who experience panic disorder have an autonomic nervous system that is predisposed to be overly active (Rachman, 2004). Other researchers have proposed that either or both of two other neurotransmitters, norepinephrine and GABA, may also be involved (Sand & others, 2001; Versiani & others, 2002). In yet another biological link, panic attacks involve hyperventilation or overbreathing (Abelson & others, 2001; Nardi & others, 2001).

In terms of psychological factors, in many instances, a stressful life event occurred in the six months prior to the onset of panic disorder, most often a threatened or actual separation from a loved one or a change in job. Once panic attacks begin, agoraphobia may follow. According to the *fear-of-fear hypothesis*, in these cases the agoraphobia may not represent a fear of public places per se but rather a fear of having a panic attack in public places.

In terms of sociocultural factors, North American women are twice as likely as men to have panic attacks with or without agoraphobia (Fodor & Epstein, 2002). However, in India, men are far likelier to have panic disorders, probably because in India and other Eastern and Middle Eastern countries, women rarely leave home alone (McNally, 1994). Reasons for North American women having a higher incidence of panic disorder with or without agoraphobia than men include gender socialization (boys are encouraged to be more independent, girls are protected more) and traumatic experiences (women are more often victims of rape and child sexual abuse; Fodor & Epstein, 2002).

Phobic Disorders

A **phobic disorder**, commonly called a *phobia*, is an anxiety disorder in which the individual has an irrational, overwhelming, persistent fear of a particular object or situation. Individuals with generalized anxiety disorder cannot pinpoint the cause of their nervous feelings; individuals with phobias can (Barlow, 2001). A fear becomes a phobia when an individual dreads a situation so much that he or she goes to almost any lengths to avoid it. Some phobias are more debilitating than others. An individual with a fear of automobiles has a more difficult time functioning in our society than a person with a fear of snakes, for example. Health Canada (2002a) reports that 6.2–8 percent of Canadians have a specific phobia disorder in any given year and 6.7 percent have a social phobia. Keep in mind that these statistics include individuals suffering from both types of disorder simultaneously. Approximately 6.3 million Americans from 18 to 54 years of age, or about 4.4 percent of the people in this age group, have a phobic disorder in any given year (U. S. National Institute of Mental Health, 2001a).

Phobias come in many forms. Some of the most common phobias involve social situations, dogs, height, dirt, flying, and snakes. Figure 13.3 labels and describes a number of phobias. Let's look at one person with a phobic disorder.

Agnes is an unmarried 30-year-old who has been unable to go higher than the second floor of any building for more than a year. When she tried to overcome her fear of heights by going up to the third, fourth, and fifth floor, she became overwhelmed by anxiety. She remembers how it all began. One evening she was working alone and was seized by an urge to jump out of an eighth-storey window. She was so frightened by her impulse that she hid behind a file cabinet for more than two hours until she calmed down enough to gather her belongings and

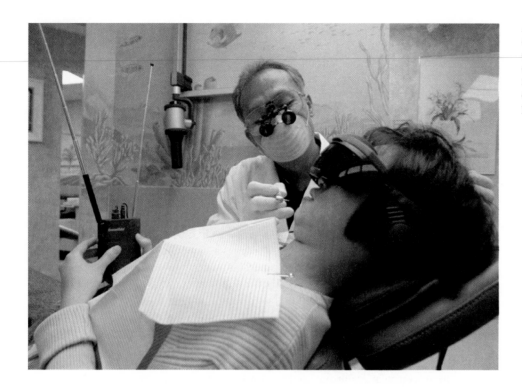

As Dr. Howard Lim works in his Toronto office, his patients can wear goggles containing a tiny TV monitor so they can watch TV. Dental phobia is usually rooted in childhood experiences and dentists are going to great lengths to put patients at ease.

go home. As she reached the first floor of the building, her heart was pounding and she was perspiring heavily. After several months, she gave up her position and became a lower-paid salesperson so she could work on the bottom floor of the building (Cameron, 1963).

Let's examine another phobia. *Social phobia* is an intense fear of being humiliated or embarrassed in social situations. Figure 13.4 shows the percentage of people in the United States who say they have experienced a social phobia in their lifetimes (Kessler, Stein & Berglund, 1998). Individuals with this phobia are afraid that they will say or do the wrong thing. As a consequence, they might avoid speaking up in a conversation, giving a speech, going out to eat, or attending a party. Their intense fear of such contexts can severely restrict their social life and increase their loneliness (Erwin & others, 2002; McLean & Wood, 2001).

What is the etiology of phobic disorders? In terms of biological factors, about 16 percent of first-degree relatives of individuals with social phobia have an increased risk of developing the phobia, compared with only 5 percent of the relatives of people without social phobia (Kessler, Olfson, & Bergland, 1998). A number of neurotransmitters may be involved in social phobia, especially serotonin (Van Ameringen & others, 2000; Van Ameringen & Mancini, 2001). Also, a neural circuit has been proposed for social phobia that includes the thalamus, amygdala, and cerebral cortex (Li, Chokka, & Tibbo, 2001). For example, Cottraux (2005) has suggested that a core feature of social phobia may be enhanced amygdala activation to novel faces. In turn, enhanced processing of unfamiliar faces may make social phobics more sensitive to the expression of negative emotions, especially by strangers (Eastwood & others, 2005) and more likely to avoid social situations.

Different theoretical perspectives provide different psychological explanations (Coupland, 2001; Kendler, Myers, & Prescott, 2002; Wilson & Rapee, 2005). Psychodynamic theorists, for example, say phobias develop as defence mechanisms to ward off threatening or unacceptable impulses—Agnes hid behind a file cabinet because she feared she would jump out of an eighth-storey window. Learning theorists, however, explain phobias differently. They say phobias are learned fears (Stein, Chavira, & Jang, 2001). In Agnes's case, she may have fallen from a high place when she was a little girl. As a result, she associates falling with pain and now fears high places (a classical conditioning explanation). Or she may have heard about or seen other people who were afraid of high places (an observational-learning explanation). Cognitive-behavioural

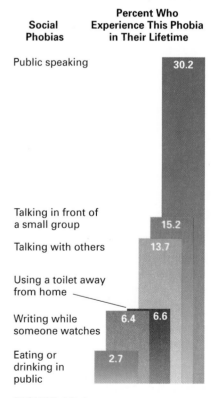

FIGURE 13.4

Social Phobias in the United States
In a national survey, the most common social phobia was public speaking.

"He always times '60 Minutes.'" © The New Yorker Collection
1983 Mischa Richter from cartoonbank.com. All Rights Reserved.

Jack Nicholson portrayed an individual with obsessive-compulsive disorder in the movie *As Good As It Gets*.

obsessive-compulsive disorder (OCD) An anxiety disorder; the individual has anxiety-provoking thoughts that will not go away (obsession) and/or urges to perform repetitive, ritualistic behaviours to prevent or produce some future situation (compulsion).

post-traumatic stress disorder (PTSD) An anxiety disorder that develops through exposure to a traumatic event, severely oppressive situations, severe abuse, and natural and unnatural disasters.

theorists propose that catastrophic thinking plays a strong mediating role in phobias. For example, Wilson & Rapee (2005) have proposed that catastrophic interpretations of negative social situations may be modified by cognitive-behaviour therapy.

Obsessive-Compulsive Disorder

Earlier, you read about 30-year-old Ralph, who has an obsessive-compulsive disorder. Twenty-seven-year-old Bob also has this disorder. As a young adult, he found himself ensnared in an exacting ritual in which he would remove his clothes in a prearranged sequence, then scrub every inch of his body from head to toe. He dresses himself in an order precisely the opposite to the order in which he takes off his clothes. If he deviates from this order, he feels compelled to start the sequence all over again. Sometimes Bob performs the cleansing ritual four or five times a day. Even though he is aware that the ritual is absurd, he simply cannot stop performing it (Meyer & Osborne, 1982).

Obsessive-compulsive disorder (OCD) is an anxiety disorder in which the individual has anxiety-provoking thoughts that will not go away (obsession) and/or urges to perform repetitive, ritualistic behaviours to prevent or produce some future situation (compulsion). Individuals with OCD repeat and rehearse normal doubts and daily routines, sometimes hundreds of times a day (Citkowska-Kisielewska & Aleksandrowicz, 2005). According to Health Canada (2002a) reports that 1.8 percent of Canadians have OCD in any given year. Approximately 3.3 million Americans from 18 to 54 years of age, or about 2.3 percent of the people in this age group, have OCD in any given year (U. S. National Institute of Mental Health, 2001a).

The most common compulsions are excessive checking, cleansing, and counting. For example, a young man feels he has to check his apartment for gas leaks and make sure the windows are locked. His behaviour is not compulsive if he does this once, but if he checks five or six times and then constantly worries that he might not have checked carefully enough, his behaviour is compulsive. According to Robert Ladouceur, of Université Laval, who focuses on understanding and treating anxiety disorders, most individuals do not enjoy their ritualistic behaviour. Instead, they feel anxious when they do not carry it out (Bouchard, Rhéaume, & Ladouceur, 1999). Such individuals can benefit from therapy (Freeston & Ladouceur, 2000).

What is the etiology of obsessive-compulsive disorder? There seems to be a genetic component, because OCD runs in families (Bellodi & others, 2001). Also, researchers using positron emission tomography (PET) and other brain-imaging techniques have found neurological links for OCD (Cavedini & others, 2002). One interpretation of these data is that the frontal cortex or basal ganglia are so active in OCD that numerous impulses reach the thalamus, generating obsessive thoughts or compulsive actions (see Figure 13.5; Rappaport, 1989). Depletion of the neurotransmitter serotonin is likely involved in the neural circuitry linked with OCD (Jenike, 2001). In fact, selective serotonin reuptake inhibitors, drugs that affect the functioning of the neurotransmitter serotonin, are also somewhat effective in treating panic disorder (Fineberg & Gale, 2005).

Late onset OCD, usually in late adolescence or early adulthood, often occurs during a period of life stress, such as childbirth, a change in occupational status, or a change in marital status. Early onset OCD, which emerges in young children, is associated with other clinical features such as hoarding and a history of tics (Millet & others, 2004). According to the cognitive perspective, what differentiates individuals with OCD from those who do not have it is the ability to turn off negative, intrusive thoughts by ignoring or dismissing them (Salkovskis & others, 1997).

Post-Traumatic Stress Disorder

Post-traumatic stress disorder (PTSD) is a psychological disorder that develops through exposure to a traumatic event, such as terrorist attacks or war; severely oppressive situations, such as the Holocaust; severe abuse, as in rape; natural disasters, such as

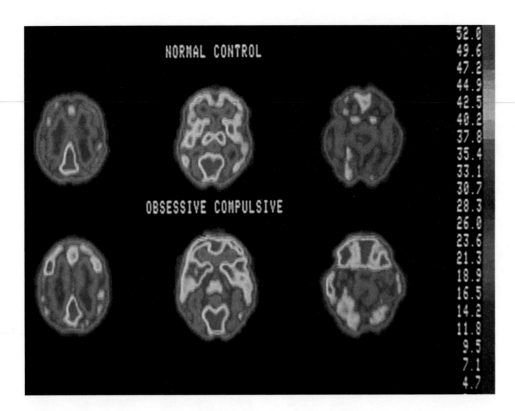

FIGURE 13.5
PET Scans of Individuals with Obsessive-Compulsive Disorder
(*Top*) Brain images of normal individuals. (*Bottom*) Brain images of individuals with obsessive-compulsive disorder (OCD). The brain images of the individuals with OCD show more activity in the frontal cortex, basal ganglia, and thalamus than the brain images of normal individuals.

floods and tornados; and unnatural disasters, such as plane crashes (Wilson & Keane, 2004; Shalev & Freedman, 2005). Approximately 5.2 million Americans between the ages of 18 and 54, or about 3.6 percent of people in this age group, have PTSD in any given year (U. S. National Institute of Mental Health, 2001a).

PTSD Symptoms The symptoms of PTSD vary but can include the following:

- Flashbacks, in which the individual relives the event
- Constricted ability to feel emotions, often reported as feeling numb, resulting in an inability to experience happiness, sexual desire, or enjoyable interpersonal relationships
- Excessive arousal, resulting in an exaggerated startle response, or inability to sleep
- Difficulties with memory and concentration
- Feelings of apprehension, including nervous tremors
- Impulsive outbursts of behaviour, such as aggressiveness, or sudden changes in lifestyle

Not every individual exposed to the same disaster develops PTSD. PTSD overloads the individual's usual coping abilities (Norris & others, 2001). For example, about 15 to 20 percent of Vietnam veterans, including tens of thousands of Canadians (Stretch, 1990, 1991), experienced post-traumatic stress disorder (PTSD). Even "peacekeeping" is stressful (Gray, Bolton, & Litz, 2004). Up to 10 percent of Canadian peacekeepers develop PTSD (Carbonneau, 1994). Soldiers with decision-making authority are less likely to develop PTSD than soldiers who have no option but to follow orders. Also, preparation for a trauma reduces the likelihood that an individual will develop PTSD.

PTSD can also strike closer to home. Shootings like the 1989 murder of 14 women at the École Polytechnique in Montreal turn bystanders into victims. Further, some experts consider sexual abuse and assault victims to be the single largest group of PTSD sufferers (Koss & Boeschen, 1998; Feuer, Nishith, & Resick, (2005). According to a report of the Prairie Women's Health Centre of Excellence (2001), PTSD is a significant problem among immigrant women and Aboriginal women living in Saskatchewan. PTSD has even been transmitted from Holocaust survivors to their offspring (Baranowsky & others, 1998).

Post-traumatic stress disorder (PTSD) can be caused by a variety of traumatic events, including war (PTSD has been a common disorder in Canadians serving in peace-keeping activities and, more recently, in Afghanistan), abuse (such as spousal abuse or rape), unnatural disasters (such as terrorist attacks), and natural disasters (such as hurricanes).

Developmental Course of PTSD PTSD is characterized by anxiety symptoms that may either immediately follow the trauma or be delayed by months or even years (Baranowsky, Gentry, & Schultz, 2005). Most people who are exposed to a traumatic, stressful event experience some of the symptoms in the days and weeks following exposure (U.S. National Center for PTSD, 2005). Overall, approximately 8 percent of men and 20 percent of women go on to develop PTSD, and about 30 percent of these individuals develop a chronic form that persists through their lifetimes.

The course of PTSD typically involves periods of symptom increase followed by remission or decrease, although for some individuals the symptoms may be unremitting and severe. Ordinary events can serve as reminders of the trauma and trigger flashbacks or intrusive images.

A flashback can make the person lose touch with reality and reenact the event for a period of seconds, hours or, very rarely, days. A person having a flashback, which can come in the form of images, sounds, smells, and/or feelings, usually believes that the traumatic event is happening all over again.

Combat and War-Related Traumas Much of what is known about PTSD comes from individuals who have developed the disorder because of combat and war-related traumas (Jones & Wessely, 2005). One study examined 276 surviving Canadians who had participated in the disastrous raid on Dieppe in World War II, in which two thirds of the original Canadian force was killed and many others were held as prisoners of war for almost three years. Fifty years later, 43 percent of the survivors who had been held as prisoners of war still suffered from PTSD. Thirty percent of the survivors who had not been captured also suffered from PTSD (Beal, 1995).

Similarly, the Holocaust produced many individuals who developed PTSD. In a study of 124 survivors of the Holocaust, almost half were still suffering from PTSD 40 years after experiencing this traumatic event (Kuch & Cox, 1992). Further, Holocaust survivors with PTSD show signs of accelerated aging relative to Holocaust survivors without PTSD (Yehuda & others, 2005). In another study, 10 percent of Vietnamese, Hmong, Laotian, and Cambodian refugees who left their war-torn countries to live in California had PTSD (Gong-Guy, 1986). A study of Bosnian refugees just after they had come to the United States indicated that as many as 65 percent had PTSD (Weine & others, 1995; Spahic-Mihajlovic, Crayton, & Neafsey, 2005). This figure may be this high because many of these Bosnian refugees had experienced numerous atrocities including organized mass rapes, and murders of relatives and neighbours.

Rather than waiting years for the effects of the stress of combat to take its toll on those who have served in the military, branches of the Canadian and U.S. armed forces now use military psychologists—those who specialize in research and application to military problems—and other mental health professionals in preventive efforts in combat zones around the world (Rabasca, 2000). The mental health units typically have a psychologist, social worker, and several mental health technicians. Units also might have a psychiatrist, psychiatric nurses, and occupational therapists. The front-line teams take a rapid, short-term, on-site approach. Treatment is prompt—beginning as soon as possible after a service member shows symptoms such as tremors, nightmares, or headaches. How effective is this new approach? The military believes that it is much more effective than the old practice of sending troubled individuals to the rear. Their data indicate that 70 to 90 percent of service members return to active duty within several days when they are treated at the front (Rabasca, 2000).

Abuse Abuse can come in many forms, including abuse of a spouse, the sexual abuse of rape or incest, and emotional abuse (as when parents harshly criticize and belittle their children; Hanson & others, 2001; Trowell & others, 2002). Researchers have found that approximately 95 percent of rape survivors experience PTSD symptoms in the first two weeks following the traumatic event. About 50 percent still have symptoms three months later, and as many as 25 percent have symptoms four to five years after the rape (Foa & Riggs, 1995). Consider the following case (U. S. National Institute of Mental Health, 2001a):

> I started having flashbacks. They kind of came over me like a splash of water. I would be terrified. Suddenly I was reliving the rape. Every instant was startling. I felt like my entire head was moving a bit, shaking, but that wasn't so at all. I would get flushed or a very dry mouth and my breathing changed.... And it was scary. Having a flashback can wring you out. You're really shaken.

Natural and Unnatural Disasters Natural disasters such as tornados, hurricanes, earthquakes, and fires can cause the individuals involved in these traumatic events to develop PTSD (Auger & others, 2000; Goenjian & others, 2001). In one study of children who lived through Hurricane Andrew, which wreaked havoc in the Bahamas, Florida, and Louisiana, in 1992, 20 percent still had PTSD one year later (La Greca & others, 1996). In the massive 2003 earthquake in Turkey, even a quarter of the search and rescue workers showed significant levels of PTSD two months afterward (Ozen & Sir, 2004).

Unnatural disasters such as plane crashes and terrorist attacks can cause individuals to develop post-traumatic stress disorder. Terrorist attacks around the world, from Israel and Iraq to those in western countries like the United States, Spain, and England regularly trigger post-traumatic stress disorder in many of the survivors of the attacks (Shalev & Freedman, 2005; Norris & others, 2001).

> **> reflect and review**
>
> **(2) Distinguish among the various anxiety disorders.**
>
> - Define anxiety disorders and characterize generalized anxiety disorder.
> - State the key features of panic disorder.
> - Identify the sources of anxiety in phobic disorders.
> - Explain obsessive-compulsive disorder.
> - Describe post-traumatic stress disorder.
>
> *Family members and friends of individuals with obsessive-compulsive disorder frequently tell them to stop their obsessions and compulsions. However, just telling someone to stop these obsessions and compulsions does not usually work. If you had a friend with this disorder, what would you try to do about it?*

---

(3) DISSOCIATIVE DISORDERS

— Dissociative — Dissociative
   Amnesia   Identity
   and Fugue   Disorder

What are the dissociative disorders?

Dissociative disorders are psychological disorders that involve a sudden loss of memory or change in identity. Dissociative disorders are relatively rare. Under extreme stress or shock, the individual's conscious awareness becomes dissociated (separated or split) from previous memories and thoughts (Gast & others, 2001; Simeon & others, 2002).

Recall that, in chapter 6, we discussed Ernest Hilgard's (1986) *hidden observer* concept, which he used to explain hypnosis. In Hilgard's view, people can develop a special divided state of consciousness, a sort of splitting of consciousness into separate components. One component is active and includes conscious awareness; the other is passive, registering and storing information in memory without being aware that the information has been processed, as if a hidden observer is watching and recording events in people's lives without their awareness.

For most of us, the active and passive dimensions of consciousness connect our experiences so effectively that we don't detect any division between them (Nolen-Hoeksema, 2004). However, individuals who develop dissociative disorders may have problems integrating the active and passive dimensions of consciousness (Dell, 2002; Hilgard, 1992; Kihlstrom, 1992). That is, in some individuals, dimensions of the conscious mind remain split, and function independently of each other.

Three kinds of dissociative disorders are dissociative amnesia, dissociative fugue, and dissociative identity disorder (Oltmanns, Emery, & Taylor, 2006).

Dissociative Amnesia and Fugue

dissociative disorders Psychological disorders that involve a sudden loss of memory or change in identity.

dissociative amnesia A dissociative disorder involving extreme memory loss caused by extensive psychological stress.

Amnesia is the inability to recall important events (LaBar & others, 2002). Amnesia can be caused by a blow to the head, causing trauma to the brain. But **dissociative amnesia** is a dissociative disorder characterized by extreme memory loss that is caused by extensive psychological stress. For example, an individual showed up at a hospital and said he did not know who he was. After several days in the hospital, he awoke one morning and

FIGURE 13.6
The Three Faces of Eve
Chris Sizemore, the subject of *The Three Faces of Eve*, is shown here with a work she painted, titled *Three Faces in One*.

demanded to be released. Eventually he remembered that he had been involved in an automobile accident in which a pedestrian had been killed. The extreme stress of the accident and the fear that he might be held responsible triggered the amnesia.

Dissociative fugue (*fugue* means "flight") is a dissociative disorder in which the individual not only develops amnesia but also travels away from home unexpectedly and assumes a new identity. Consider the following example of this disorder:

> One day a woman named Barbara vanished without a trace. Two weeks later, looking more like a teenager—with her hair in a ponytail and wearing bobby socks—than a 31-year-old woman, Barbara was picked up by police in a nearby city. When her husband came to see her, Barbara asked, "Who are you?" She could not remember anything about the last 2 weeks of her life. During psychotherapy, she gradually began to recall her past. She had left home with enough money to buy a bus ticket to the town where she grew up as a child. She spent days walking the streets and standing near a building where her father had worked. Later she went to the motel with a man. According to the motel manager, she entertained a series of men there over a three-day period. (Goldstein & Palmer, 1975).

Dissociative Identity Disorder

Dissociative identity disorder (DID), formerly called *multiple personality disorder*, is the most dramatic but least common dissociative disorder. Individuals suffering from this disorder have two or more distinct personalities or selves, like the fictional Dr. Jekyll and Mr. Hyde of Robert Louis Stevenson's short story. Each personality has its own memories, behaviours, and relationships; one personality dominates the individual at one time, and another personality takes over at another time (Korol, Craig, & Firestone, 2003). The shift from one personality to the other usually occurs under distress (Dell, 2002; Gleaves, May, & Cardena, 2001).

Jenny, who you read about at the beginning of this chapter, had DID (Ross, 1994). One of the most famous cases of dissociative identity disorder involves the "three faces of Eve" (see figure 13.6; Thigpen & Cleckley, 1957):

> Eve White was the original dominant personality. She had no knowledge of her second personality, Eve Black, although Eve Black had been alternating with Eve White for a number of years. Eve White was bland, quiet, and serious—a rather dull personality. By contrast, Eve Black was carefree, mischievous, and uninhibited. She would "come out" at the most inappropriate times, leaving Eve White with hangovers, bills, and a reputation in local bars that she could not explain. During treatment, a third personality, Jane, emerged. More mature than the other two, Jane seemed to have developed as a result of therapy.

dissociative fugue A dissociative disorder in which the individual not only develops amnesia but also unexpectedly travels away from home and establishes a new identity.

dissociative identity disorder (DID) Formerly called multiple personality disorder, this is the most dramatic but least common dissociative disorder; individuals suffering from this disorder have two or more distinct personalities.

In some cases, therapists have been ascribed responsibility for creating a second or third personality. At one point, Eve said that her therapist had created one of her personalities.

A summary of research on dissociative identity disorder suggests that the disorder is characterized by an inordinately high rate of sexual or physical abuse during early childhood (McAllister, 2000; Stafford & Lynn, 2002). Sexual abuse occurred in 56 percent of reported cases of the disorder. Note, though, that the majority of individuals who have been sexually abused do not develop dissociative identity disorder. Mothers of individuals who develop this disorder tend to be rejecting and depressed; fathers distant, alcoholic, and abusive. The vast majority of individuals with dissociative identity disorder are adult females. When males develop the disorder, they show more aggression than females with the disorder (Ross & Norton, 1989). A genetic predisposition might exist, as the disorder tends to run in families (Dell & Eisenhower, 1990). Some research suggests that a person's different personalities have different EEG patterns (Allen & Movius, 2000).

Fascinating as it is, the reality of dissociative identity disorder has long been controversial (Piper & Merskey, 2004a, b). Until the 1980s, only about 300 cases had ever been reported. Yet in the past few decades, hundreds more have been labelled "dissociative identity disorder." According to Merskey (1992), this increase, at best, represents a diagnostic fad and at worst, an example of an *iatrogenic* illness, one brought on by the doctor. It is also quite easy to fake multiple personalities (Spanos, 1994). It is possible that if clinicians suggest the possibility, clients entranced with stories of dissociative identity disorder might act out the clinicians' suggestions. Others believe that dissociative identity disorder is not rare but has been frequently misdiagnosed as schizophrenia (Welburn & colleagues, 2003). Improved techniques for assessing physiological changes that occur when individuals change personalities increase the likelihood that more accurate rates of occurrence can be determined.

> **reflect and review**

③ Describe the dissociative disorders.

- Define dissociative disorders.
- Explain dissociative amnesia and fugue.
- Discuss dissociative identity disorder.

Imagine that you are on the jury in a trial in which an individual who has been accused of killing someone claims that he suffers from dissociative identity disorder and doesn't remember committing the murder. How difficult would it be for you and the other jury members to determine if he really has this disorder? What questions would you want answered before making your decision about the individual?

---

④ MOOD DISORDERS

 Depressive Disorders — Bipolar Disorder — Causes of Mood Disorders — Suicide

What are the symptoms and causes of mood disorders, and who is at risk for depression and suicide?

mood disorders Psychological disorders in which there is a primary disturbance in mood (prolonged emotion that colours the individuals entire emotional state). Two main types are the depressive disorders and bipolar disorder.

The **mood disorders** are psychological disorders in which there is a primary disturbance of mood (prolonged emotion that colours the individual's entire emotional state). The mood disturbance can include cognitive, behavioural, and somatic (physical) symptoms, as well as interpersonal difficulties (Nevid & Greene, 2005). Two main types of mood disorders are the depressive disorders and bipolar disorder. Depression can occur alone, as in the depressive disorders, or it can alternate with mania (an overexcited, unrealistically optimistic state), as in bipolar disorder. Recall Norman Endler's descriptions of his battles with bipolar disorder, at the beginning of the chapter, in which he oscillated between manic highs and terrifying depressions. Health Canada (2002a) reports that about 8.3 percent percent of Canadians have a mood disorder in any given year. Similarly, approximately 18.8 million Americans between the ages 18 and 54, or about 9.5 percent of the people in this age group, have a mood disorder in any given year (U. S. National Institute of Mental Health, 2001a).

Depressive Disorders

The **depressive disorders** are mood disorders in which the individual suffers depression without ever experiencing mania. The severity of the depressive disorders varies. Some individuals experience what is classified as *major depressive disorder*, whereas others are given the diagnosis of *dysthymic disorder* (more chronic depression with fewer symptoms than major depression; Klein & Santiago, 2003; Dozois & Dobson, 2002).

Consider a person with a depressive disorder:

> Peter had been depressed for several months. Nothing cheered him up. As he reflected, "My brain is like on time out. I just can't get anything done. I feel virtually exhausted all of the time. I try to study but I read the same pages over and over again and can't remember a thing I've read. I feel like the bottom is falling out of my life. It's so empty." Nothing cheered Peter up. His depression began when the girl he wanted to marry decided that marriage was not for her, at least not marriage to Peter. Peter's emotional state deteriorated to the point at which he didn't leave his room for days at a time, he kept his shades down and the room dark, and he could hardly get out of bed in the morning. When he managed to leave the room, he had trouble maintaining a conversation. By the time Peter contacted his college counselling centre, he had gone from being mildly depressed to being in the grip of major depression.

Peter was diagnosed with **major depressive disorder**, a disorder in which the individual experiences a major depressive episode and depressed characteristics, such as lethargy and hopelessness, for at least two weeks. The individual's daily functioning becomes impaired. In any given year 4.6 percent of Canadians have major depressive disorder (Canadian Psychiatric Association, 2001; Health Canada, 2002a). Similarly, 9.9 million Americans from 18 to 54 years of age, or about 5 percent of the people in this age group, have major depressive disorder in any given year (U. S. National Institute of Mental Health, 2001a).

Nine symptoms define a major depressive episode (of which at least five must be present during a two-week period):

1. Depressed mood most of the day
2. Reduced interest or pleasure in all or most activities
3. Significant weight loss or gain, or significant decrease or interest in appetite
4. Trouble sleeping or sleeping too much
5. Psychomotor agitation or retardation
6. Fatigue or loss of energy
7. Feeling worthless or guilty in an excessive or inappropriate manner
8. Problems in thinking, concentrating, or making decisions
9. Recurrent thoughts of death and suicide

Dysthymic disorder is generally more chronic and has fewer symptoms than major depressive disorder (Klein & Santiago, 2003; Ryder, Bagby, & Dion. 2001). The individual is in a depressed mood for most days for at least two years as an adult or at least one year as a child or adolescent. To be classified as having dysthymic disorder, a major depressive episode must not have occurred, and the two-year period of depression must not have been broken by a normal mood lasting more than two months. Two or more of these six symptoms must be present: poor appetite or overeating, sleep problems, low energy or fatigue, low self-esteem, poor concentration or difficulty making decisions, and feelings of hopelessness (Munoz, 1998). Health Canada (2002a) reports

This painting by Vincent Van Gogh, *Portrait of Dr. Gachet,* reflects the extreme melancholy that characterizes the depressive disorders.

depressive disorders Mood disorders in which the individual suffers depression without ever experiencing mania.

major depressive disorder Indicated by a major depressive episode and depressed characteristics, such as lethargy and hopelessness, lasting at least two weeks.

dysthymic disorder A depressive disorder that is generally more chronic and has fewer symptoms than major depressive disorder.

Are You Depressed?

Below is a list of the ways that you might have felt or behaved in the past week. Indicate what you felt by putting an X in the appropriate box for each item.

During the past week

	Rarely or None of the Time (Less Than 1 Day)	Some or a Little of the Time (1–2 Days)	Occasionally or a Moderate Amount of the Time (3–4 Days)	Most or All of the Time (5–7 Days)
1. I was bothered by things that usually don't bother me.	☐	☐	☐	☐
2. I did not feel like eating; my appetite was poor.	☐	☐	☐	☐
3. I felt that I could not shake off the blues even with help from my family and friends.	☐	☐	☐	☐
4. I felt that I was just as good as other people.	☐	☐	☐	☐
5. I had trouble keeping my mind on what I was doing.	☐	☐	☐	☐
6. I felt depressed.	☐	☐	☐	☐
7. I felt that everything I did was an effort.	☐	☐	☐	☐
8. I felt hopeful about the future.	☐	☐	☐	☐
9. I thought my life had been a failure.	☐	☐	☐	☐
10. I felt fearful.	☐	☐	☐	☐
11. My sleep was restless.	☐	☐	☐	☐
12. I was happy.	☐	☐	☐	☐
13. I talked less than usual.	☐	☐	☐	☐
14. I felt lonely.	☐	☐	☐	☐
15. People were unfriendly.	☐	☐	☐	☐
16. I enjoyed life.	☐	☐	☐	☐
17. I had crying spells.	☐	☐	☐	☐
18. I felt sad.	☐	☐	☐	☐
19. I felt that people disliked me.	☐	☐	☐	☐
20. I could not get going.	☐	☐	☐	☐

For items 4, 8, 12, and 16, give yourself a 3 each time you checked Rarely or None, 2 each time you checked Some or a Little, 1 each time you checked Occasionally or Moderate, and a 0 each time you checked Most or All of the Time. For the remaining items, give yourself a 0 each time you checked Rarely or None, 1 each time you checked Some or a Little, 2 each time you checked Occasionally or Moderate, and 3 each time you checked Most or All of the Time. Total up your score for all 20 items.

If your score is around 7, then you are like the average male in terms of how much depression you have experienced in the past week. If your score is around 8 or 9 your score is similar to the average female's. Scores less than the average for either males or females indicate that depression has probably not been a problem for you during the past week. If your score is 16 or more and you are bothered by your feelings, you might benefit from professional help.

Keep in mind, though, that self-diagnosis is not always accurate and to adequately diagnose anyone, the professional judgment of a qualified clinician is required.

that between 0.8 and 3.1 percent of Canadians will have dysthymic disorder in any given year. Approximately 10.9 million people in the United States, or about 5.4 percent of the population, will have dysthymic disorder in their lifetimes (U. S. National Institute of Mental Health, 2001a).

Although most people do not spiral into major depression as Peter did, everyone feels "blue" sometimes (Flett, Vredenburg, & Krames, 1997). In our stress-filled world, people often use the term *depression* to describe brief bouts of normal sadness or discontent over life's problems. Perhaps you haven't done well in a class or things aren't working out in your love life. You feel down in the dumps and say you are depressed. In most instances, though, your depression won't last as long or be as intense as Peter's; after a few hours, days, or weeks, you snap out of your gloomy state and begin to cope more effectively with your problems. Nonetheless, depression is so widespread that it has been called the "common cold" of mental disorders; more than 250,000 individuals are hospitalized every year for the disorder. Students, professors, corporate executives, labourers—no one is immune to depression, not even F. Scott Fitzgerald, Ernest Hemingway, Virginia Woolf, Leonard Cohen, Kurt Cobain, or Winston Churchill—each of whom experienced depression. After years of depression, Hemingway eventually took his own life, as did Cobain. Suicide is discussed later in this section.

The inadequate care that results from a lack of understanding or a misunderstanding of depression is tragic. Given the range of psychological and pharmacological treatments available today, individuals who go untreated suffer needlessly. To evaluate whether you might be depressed, see the Personal Reflections box.

Bipolar Disorder

Although she had experienced extreme mood swings since she was a child, Mrs. M. was first admitted to a mental hospital at the age of 38. At 33, shortly before the birth of her first child, she became very depressed. One month after the baby was born, she became agitated and euphoric. Mrs. M. signed a year's lease on an apartment, bought furniture, piled up debts. Several years later other manic and depressive mood swings occurred. In one of her excitatory moods, Mrs. M. swore loudly and created a disturbance at a club where she was not a member. Several days later she began divorce proceedings. On the day prior to her admission to the mental hospital, she went on a spending spree and bought 57 hats. Several weeks later, she became despondent, saying, "I have no energy. My brain doesn't work right. I have let my family down. I don't have anything to live for." In a subsequent manic bout, Mrs. M. pursued a romantic relationship with a doctor. (Kolb, 1973).

Bipolar disorder is a mood disorder that is characterized by extreme mood swings that include one or more episodes of mania (an overexcited, unrealistically optimistic state; Brickman, LoPiccolo, & Johnson, 2002; Olley & others, 2005). *Bipolar* means that the person may experience both depression and mania. Most bipolar individuals experience multiple cycles of depression interspersed with mania. Less than 10 percent of bipolar individuals tend to experience manic-type episodes without depression. Between 0.2 and 0.6 percent of Canadians experience bipolar disorder in any given year (Health Canada, 2002a). Approximately 2.3 million Americans, or about 1.2 percent of the U.S. population 18 years and older, have bipolar disorder in any given year (U. S. National Institute of Mental Health, 2001a).

A manic episode is like the flip side of a depressive episode (Miklowitz, 2002). Instead of feeling depressed, the person feels euphoric and on top of the world. However, as the manic episode unfolds, the person can experience panic and eventually depression. Instead of feeling fatigued, as many depressed individuals do, when individuals experience mania they have tremendous energy and might sleep very little. Individuals in a manic state often manifest an impulsivity that can get them in trouble in business and legal transactions. For example, they might spend their life savings on a foolish business venture. By definition in the *DSM-IV* classification, manic episodes must last one week. They average 8 to 16 weeks. Individuals with bipolar disorder can have manic and depressive episodes that occur four or more times a year, but they are usually separated by six months to a year.

Bipolar disorder is much less common than depressive disorders (MacKinnon & others, 2002), but unlike depressive disorders (which are likelier to occur in females), bipolar disorder is equally common in females and males. About 1 or 2 in 100 people are estimated to experience bipolar disorder at some point in their lifetimes (Kessler & others, 1994).

Causes of Mood Disorders

Mood disorders, such as Peter's depression and Mrs. M.'s bipolar disorder, can involve biological, psychological, and sociocultural factors. We distinguish between depressive disorders and bipolar disorder in discussing the causes of mood disorders.

Biological Factors The links between biology and mood disorders are well established. Biological explanations of mood disorders include heredity, neurophysiological abnormalities, neurotransmitter deregulation, and hormonal factors (Nolen-Hoeksema, 2004). Stress is seen as triggering biological abnormalities which, in turn, lead to depression (and are compounded by depression) especially in individuals more prone to depression (van Praag, de Kloet, & van Os, 2004).

Heredity Depressive and bipolar disorders tend to run in families, although the family link is stronger for bipolar disorder than for depressive disorders (Bradbury, 2001). One of the greatest risks for developing a mood disorder is having a biological parent who suffers from a mood disorder. In bipolar disorder, the rate of the disorder in first-degree

bipolar disorder A mood disorder characterized by extreme mood swings that include one or more episodes of mania.

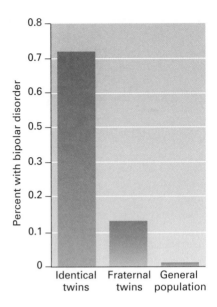

FIGURE 13.7

Risk of Bipolar Disorder in Identical Twins, Fraternal Twins, and the General Population
Notice how much stronger the incidence of bipolar disorder is in identical twins compared with fraternal twins and the general population; these statistics suggest a strong genetic role in the disorder.

relatives (parents, siblings) is 10 to 20 times higher than in the general population (MacKinnon, Jamison, & DePaulo, Jr., 1997). An individual with an identical twin who has bipolar disorder has a more than 60 percent probability of also having the disorder, and a fraternal twin more than 10 percent, whereas the rate of bipolar disorder in the general population is 1 to 2 percent (see figure 13.7). Recent work suggests that more than one gene is responsible for bipolar disorder (Payne, Potash, & DePaulo, Jr., 2005).

Neurobiological Abnormalities One of the most consistent findings of neurobiological abnormalities in individuals with mood disorders is altered brain-wave activity during sleep (Wilson & Nutt, 2005). Depressed individuals experience less slow-wave sleep (which contributes to a feeling of being rested and restored) and go into rapid-eye-movement (REM) sleep earlier in the night than nondepressed individuals (Benca, 2001). These neurobiological abnormalities correspond to the reports of depressed individuals that they have difficulty going to sleep at night or remaining asleep, that they often wake up early in the morning and can't get back to sleep, and that they do not feel rested after they sleep.

Neuroimaging studies also reveal decreased metabolic activity in the cerebral cortex of individuals with severe major depressive disorder (Buchsbaum & others, 1997). Figure 13.8 shows the metabolic activity of an individual cycling through depressive and manic phases of bipolar disorder. Notice the decrease in metabolic activity in the brain during depression and the increase in metabolic activity during mania (Baxter, Jr. & others, 1995).

Most areas of the brains of depressed individuals are underactive. For example, one section of the prefrontal cortex, which is involved in generating actions, is underactive in depressed individuals. However, certain brain areas are overactive. For example, recent studies using brain imaging techniques revealed that the amygdala, a part of the limbic system, is overactive in depression (Van Elst, Ebert, & Trimble, 2001; Anand & others, 2005a).

Some of depression's symptoms may be explained by this change in brain activity in the amygdala, which helps to store and recall emotionally charged memories and sends information to the prefrontal cortex at the sight of something fearful. In turn, the prefrontal cortex should signal the amygdala to slow down when the source of the fear is gone. But in depression, the prefrontal cortex may fail to send the all-clear signal. Thus, the amygdala may continue sending signals that keep triggering extended rumination about sad events (Bagby & Parker, 2001). Interestingly, antidepressant drugs may enhance communication between cortex and the limbic system (Anand & others, 2005b).

FIGURE 13.8 **Brain Metabolism in Mania and Depression**
PET scans of an individual with bipolar disorder, who is described as a rapid-cycler because of how quickly severe mood changes occurred in the individual. (*Top, bottom*) The person's brain in a depressed state. (*Middle*) A manic state. The PET scans reveal how the brain's energy consumption falls in depression and rises in mania. The red areas in the middle row reflect rapid consumption of glucose.

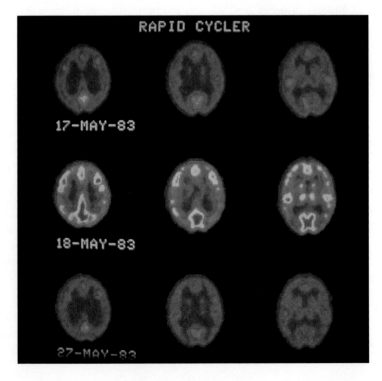

Another neurobiological abnormality in depression is neuron death or disability. Recent research studies revealed that depressive disorders are linked to neuron death or disability (Manji, 2001; Manji, Drevets, & Charney, 2001). Individuals with depression seem to have fewer neurons in some parts of their brain, including the prefrontal cortex, which should be sending the slowdown signals to the amygdala (Drevets, 2001).

Neurotransmitter Deregulation Deregulation of a number of neurotransmitters is likely involved in depression (Stahl, 2002). Researchers have also found abnormalities in a number of monoamine neurotransmitters in individuals with mood disorders (Elhwuegi, 2004). Abnormalities in the monoamine neurotransmitters, such as norepinephrine, serotonin, and dopamine, have been implicated in mood disorders. An imbalance in the monoamine neurotransmitters in one direction is thought to be involved in depression, an imbalance in the other direction in mania. For example, individuals with major depressive disorder appear to have too few receptors for serotonin and norepinephrine. Recent studies have also revealed that changes in the neurotransmitter glutamate occur in bipolar disorder (Shaldubina, Agam, & Belmaker, 2001). Still other research suggests that regulation of a neurotransmitter called substance P is involved in depression (Pacher & others, 2001).

Hormones Depressed individuals show chronic hyperactivity in the neuroendocrine glandular system and an inability to return to normal functioning following a stressful experience (Young & Korzun, 1998). In turn, the excess hormones produced by the neuroendocrine glands (such as the pituitary gland and adrenal cortex) may be linked to the deregulation of the monoamine neurotransmitters just discussed.

Also in regard to the role of hormones in depression, it has been argued that women's increased vulnerability to depression is linked to their ovarian hormones, estrogen and progesterone. However, the evidence that women's moods are tied to their hormones is mixed at best (Nolen-Hoeksema, 2004). Some women do experience more depression during the postpartum period, menopause, and other times when their hormone levels are changing. Nonetheless, the extent to which hormonal changes in women account for their higher rate of depression compared with men is less clear.

Psychological Factors Psychodynamic, behavioural, and cognitive theories have all proposed explanations for depression. These ideas are significant for their influence on the treatment of these disorders, as discussed in chapter 14.

Psychodynamic Explanations Psychodynamic theories emphasize that depression stems from individuals' childhood experiences that prevented them from developing a strong, positive sense of self (Nolen-Hoeksema, 2004). According to John Abela, of McGill University, and his colleagues, children who are insecurely attached to their parents, especially if the parents themselves suffer from depression, experience more depressive symptoms (Abela & others, 2005). Further, adults who are insecurely attached also experience more depressive symptoms (Hankin, Kassel, & Abela, 2005).

Many modern psychodynamic theorists still rely on Freud's (1917) theory that depression is a turning inward of aggressive instincts. Freud theorized that a child's early attachment to a love object (usually the mother) contains a mixture of love and hate. When the child loses the love object or when his or her dependency needs are frustrated, feelings of loss coexist with anger. Because the child cannot openly accept such angry feelings toward the individual he or she loves, the hostility is turned inward and experienced as depression. The unresolved mixture of anger and love is carried forward to adolescence and adulthood, when loss can bring back these early feelings of abandonment.

Behavioural Explanations Peter Lewinsohn and his colleagues (Lewinsohn & Gottlib, 1995; Lewinsohn, Joiner, Jr., & Rohde, 2001) proposed that life's stresses can lead to depression by reducing the positive reinforcers in a person's life. The sequence goes like this: When people experience considerable stress in their lives, they may withdraw from the stress. The withdrawal produces a further reduction in positive reinforcers, which can lead to more withdrawal, which leads to even fewer positive reinforcers.

All-or-nothing thinking	You see things in black-and-white categories. If your performance falls short of perfect, you see yourself as a total failure.
Overgeneralization	You see a single negative event as a never-ending pattern of defeat.
Mental filter	You pick out a single negative detail and dwell on it exclusively so that your vision of all reality becomes darkened, like the drop of ink that discolors the entire beaker of water.
Disqualifying the positive	You reject positive experiences by insisting they "don't count" for some reason or other. In this way you can maintain a negative belief that is contradicted by your everyday experiences.
Jumping to conclusions	You make a negative interpretation even though there are no definite facts that convincingly support your conclusion. (a) *Mind reading*. You arbitrarily conclude that someone is reacting negatively to you, and you don't bother to check this out. (b) *The Fortune Teller Error*. You anticipate that things will turn out badly, and you feel convinced that your prediction is an already-established fact.
Magnification (catastrophizing) or minimization	You exaggerate the importance of things (such as your goof-up or someone else's achievement), or you inappropriately shrink things until they appear tiny (your own desirable qualities or other fellow's imperfections). This is also called the "binocular trick."
Emotional reasoning	You assume that your negative emotions necessarily reflect the way things really are: "I feel it, therefore it must be true."
Should statements	You try to motivate yourself with shoulds and shouldn'ts, as if you had to be whipped and punished before you could be expected to do anything. "Musts" and "oughts" are also offenders. The emotional consequence is guilt. When you direct should statements toward others, you feel anger, frustration, and resentment.
Labelling and mislabelling	This is an extreme form of overgeneralization. Instead of describing your error, you attach a negative label to yourself: "I'm a *loser*." When someone else's behaviour rubs you the wrong way, you attach a negative label to him: "He's a . . . louse." Mislabelling involves describing an event with language that is highly coloured and emotionally loaded.
Personalization	You see yourself as the cause of some negative external event which in fact you were not primarily responsible for.

FIGURE 13.9

Cognitive Distortions that Can Contribute to Depression

Another behavioural view of depression focuses on **learned helplessness**, which occurs when individuals are exposed to aversive stimulation, such as prolonged stress, over which they have no control LoLordo, 2001). The inability to avoid such aversive stimulation produces an apathetic state of helplessness. Martin Seligman (1975) proposed that learned helplessness is one reason that some individuals become depressed. When individuals cannot control the stress they encounter, they eventually feel helpless and depressed.

Research on learned helplessness led Susan Nolen-Hoeksema (2000; Treynor, Gonzalez, & Nolen-Hoeksema, 2003) to examine the ways people cope when they are depressed. She found that some depressed individuals use a *ruminative coping style*, in which they focus intently on how they feel (their sadness and hopelessness) but do not try to do anything about the feelings: They just ruminate about their depression. Nolen-Hoeksema, Larson, & Grayson (1999) have found that individuals with depression remain depressed longer when they use a ruminative coping style rather than an action-oriented coping style. Women are more likely to ruminate when they are depressed than men are. Verhaeghen, Joorman, & Khan, (2005) have proposed that creative people are also more likely to ruminate and that this may be why they are more prone to depression.

Cognitive Explanations The cognitive approach provides another perspective on mood disorders (Gibb & others, 2004). Individuals who are depressed rarely think positive thoughts. They interpret their lives in self-defeating ways and have negative expectations about the future (Gilbert, 2001). Beck (1967) believed such negative thoughts reflect schemas that shape the depressed individual's experiences. These habitual negative thoughts magnify and expand a depressed person's negative experiences (Lau & Segal, 2003). A person given a slightly negative work evaluation might, through catastrophic thinking, expect to be fired and to be unable to find another job. Canadian researchers such as Zindel Segal of the University of Toronto, have conducted much useful research on distortions due to negative self-schemas in depression (Scher, Segal,

learned helplessness Occurs when individuals are exposed to aversive stimulation, such as prolonged stress, over which they have no control. The inability to avoid such aversive stimulation can produce an apathetic state of helplessness.

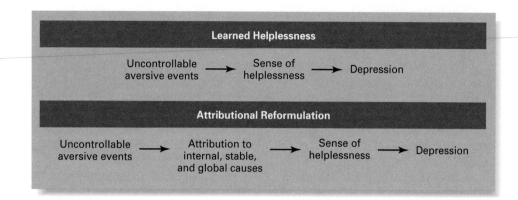

FIGURE 13.10

Learned Helplessness and Attributional Reformulation of Learned Helplessness

& Ingram, 2004; Rector, Segal, & Gemar, 1998). For example, Tripp, Catano, & Sullivan (1997) have explored the relationship of attributional style, expectancies, and self-esteem in depression. Figure 13.9 describes a number of cognitive distortions that can contribute to depression (Nolen-Hoeksema, 2000).

Another cognitive view of depression involves a cognitive reformulation of the hopelessness involved in learned helplessness (Joiner, Jr. & others, 2001). It focuses on people's attributions, as discussed in chapter 12. When people make attributions, they attempt to explain what caused something to happen. In this attributional view of depression, individuals who regularly explain negative events as being caused by internal ("It is my fault I failed the exam"), stable ("I'm going to fail again and again"), and global ("Failing this exam shows how I won't do well in any of my courses") causes, blame themselves for these negative events, expect the negative events to recur in their lives in the future, and tend to experience negative events in many areas of their lives (see figure 13.10; Abramson, Seligman, & Teasdale, 1978).

Closely related to the attributional view of learned helplessness is a distinction between optimistic and pessimistic cognitive styles. Recall from chapter 12 that being either optimistic or pessimistic can have profound effects on a person's well-being, with optimistic individuals showing better physical and mental health. In one study, researchers interviewed first-year students at two universities and distinguished those with an optimistic style from those with a pessimistic style (Alloy, Abramson, & Francis, 1999). They interviewed the students on a regular basis over the next 2 1/2 years. In this time frame, among students with no prior history of depression, 17 percent of the students with a pessimistic style developed major depression, whereas only 1 percent of those with an optimistic style did. Also, among students with a prior history of depression, 27 percent of those who had a pessimistic style relapsed into depression over the 2 1/2 years, but only 6 percent of those with the optimistic style did.

Another cognitive explanation of depression focuses on what is called depressive realism (McKendree-Smith & Scogin, 2000). Some people who are depressed may be seeing their world accurately and realistically (Keller, Lipkus, & Rimer, 2002). That is, there really are negative things going on in their lives that make them depressed. In one classic study, when depressed individuals are asked to make judgments about how much control they have over situations that actually cannot be controlled, they are accurate in saying that they do not have control (Alloy & Abramson, 1979). In contrast, nondepressed individuals overestimate the amount of control they have in such situations. Thus, nondepressed individuals often have an illusion of control over their world that depressed individuals do not. In this view, it may not be accurate, realistic thinking that prevents individuals from becoming depressed but optimism and a perceived sense of illusory control over one's world.

Sociocultural Factors   Among the sociocultural factors involved in depression are relationships with other people, socioeconomic and ethnic variations, cultural variations, and gender (Blazer, 2005).

Interpersonal Relationships One view of depression is that it may stem from problems that develop in relationships with other people (Segrin, 2001). Both proximal (recent) and distal (distant, earlier) interpersonal experiences might be involved in depression. In terms of a proximal factor, recent marital conflict might trigger depression. In terms of distal factors, possibly inadequate early relationships with parents are carried forward to influence whether depression occurs later in a person's life. In support of the view that interpersonal relationships contribute to depression, one study of university students found that those with an anxious, insecure attachment style were likelier to have depressive symptoms than their counterparts with secure attachment styles (Roberts, Gotlib, & Kassel, 1996).

The British psychiatrist John Bowlby (1989) suggested that both interpersonal relationships and cognitive factors can explain the development of depression. He believes a combination of an insecure attachment to the mother, a lack of love and affection as a child, and the actual loss of a parent during childhood gives rise to a negative cognitive set, or schema. The schema built up during childhood causes the individual to interpret later losses as yet other failures in the effort to establish enduring and close positive relationships.

Socioeconomic and Ethnic Factors Individuals with a low socioeconomic status (SES), especially those living in poverty, are more likely to develop depression than their higher SES counterparts. In addition, in one study, Latinos in the United States had a higher incidence of depression than whites (Blazer & others, 1994; Blazer, 2005). The higher rate of depression among Latinos may be due to their higher incidence of poverty. Very high rates of depression have also been found in Aboriginal groups, among many of whom poverty, hopelessness, and alcoholism are widespread (Manson & others, 1990). However, SES may not always be associated with depression. One Canadian study found that Jewish Canadians have higher rates of depression than English Canadians do and that Asian Canadians have the lowest rates of depression, even when socioeconomic factors are taken into account (Wu & others, 2003).

Cultural Variations According to Seligman (1989), the reason so many young North Americans face depression is our society's emphasis on self, independence, and individualism, along with an erosion of connectedness to others, family, and religion, which has spawned a widespread sense of hopelessness Kirsh & Kuiper, 2002). To make matters worse, people who do feel depressed also face being stigmatized (Endler, 1990b), increasing the sense of disconnection even further.

Depressive disorders are found in virtually all cultures in the world, but their incidence, intensity, and components vary across cultures. The incidence of depressive disorders is lower in less industrialized, less modernized countries than in more industrialized, modernized countries (Cross-National Collaborative Group, 1992). This difference is likely due to the fast-paced, stressful lifestyles of individuals in industrialized, modernized countries and the stronger family and community orientation of people in less industrialized, less modernized countries.

Gender Bipolar disorder occurs about equally among women and men, but women are about twice as likely as men to develop depression (Nolen-Hoeksema & Keita, 2003; Kuehner, 2003). This gender difference occurs in many countries (see figure 13.11; Weissman & Olfson, 1995).

Janet Stoppard (1999, 2000; Stoppard & McMullen, 2003), of the University of New Brunswick, has stressed the need to understand women's depression in a socio-cultural context. This perspective focuses on the extent to which external factors may create more severe life stresses for many women, which, in turn, may be more likely to contribute to depression in women than in men. In other words, women may not be more prone to depression than men are; it is just that many women are often under higher life stress than many men. Men exposed to similar levels of external stress may also be at greater risk for developing depression. For example, Leadbeater, Bishop, & Raver (1996) found that young women are more vulnerable to depression through interpersonal relations—being, for example, more reactive to stressful events involving

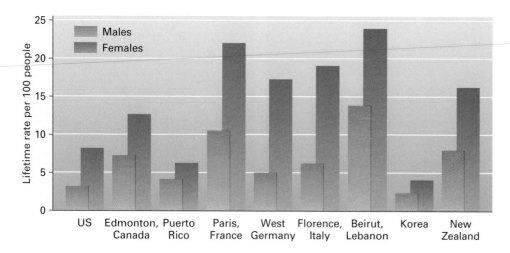

FIGURE 13.11

Gender Differences in Depression Across Cultures
One study showed that women were more likely than men to have major depression in nine cultures.

others. Studies have shown that depression is especially high among single women who are the head of the household, unhappily married women, mothers of young children, and young married women who work at unsatisfying, dead-end jobs (Bernstein, 2001).

In the same vein, and as we saw earlier, poverty may be a pathway to depression. Twenty percent of all Canadian children and 54 percent of all Canadian lone-parent mothers lived in poverty in 1997 (Ross, Scott, & Smith, 2000). Three of every four people living in poverty in the United States are women and children. Minority women are also a high-risk group for depression.

Careful diagnosis of depression in women is critical (Kornstein & Clayton, 2002). According to the American Psychological Association's Task Force on Women and Depression, depression is misdiagnosed at least 30 to 50 percent of the time in women (McGrath & others, 1990). Approximately 70 percent of prescriptions for antidepressants are given to women, too often with improper diagnosis and monitoring.

Suicide

Severe depression and other psychological disorders can cause individuals to want to end their lives. This was the effect of his bipolar disorder on Norman Endler (Sareen & others, 2005). Although attempting suicide is abnormal behaviour, it is not uncommon for individuals to contemplate suicide at some point in their lives. For example, as many as two of every three university students have thought about suicide on at least one occasion.

Approximately 4000 Canadians (Sakinofsky, 1998; Canadian Alliance on Mental Illness and Mental Health, 2003) and 29,000 Americans commit suicide every year. The number of *parasuicides*, or attempted suicides, is estimated at 8 to 25 for every successful suicide (U.S. National Center for Health Statistics, 2000a).

After about the age of 15, the suicide rate begins to rise rapidly (Weissman & others, 1999). Suicide is the third leading cause (after automobile accidents and homicides) of death today among adolescents 13 to 19 years of age (U.S. National Center for Health Statistics, 2000a).

Females are likelier than males to attempt suicide, but males are more likely to actually commit suicide. This difference may be due to the fact that males tend to use lethal means, such as guns, whereas females tend to cut their wrists or take overdoses of sleeping pills, both less likely to result in death (Maris, 1998).

Biological Factors Genetic factors appear to play a role in suicide, which tends to run in families (Fu & others, 2002). One famous family that has been plagued by suicide is the Hemingway family. Five members of this family, spread across generations, have committed suicide. The best-known of the five Hemingways are the writer Ernest Hemingway and his granddaughter, actress Margaux (who committed suicide on the 35th anniversary of her father's suicide).

Suicide tends to run in families. Five suicides occurred in different generations of the Hemingway family, including famous author Ernest (*left*) and his granddaughter Margaux (*right*).

A number of studies have linked suicide with low levels of the neurotransmitter serotonin (Mann & Arango, 1999; van Praag, 2000). Postmortem analyses of the brains of individuals who have committed suicide show abnormally low levels of this transmitter. Also, individuals who attempt suicide and who have low levels of serotonin are 10 times likelier to attempt suicide again than attempters who have high levels of serotonin (Roy, 1992).

Poor physical health, especially when it is long-standing and chronic, is another risk factor for suicide. For example, Ernest Hemingway had been in failing health for a number of years when he committed suicide.

Psychological Factors Psychological factors that can contribute to suicide include mental disorders and traumas, such as sexual abuse. Approximately 90 percent of individuals who commit suicide are estimated to have a diagnosable mental disorder (U. S. National Institute of Mental Health, 2001a). The most common mental disorder among individuals who commit suicide is depression (Fergusson & Woodward, 2002).

Immediate and highly stressful circumstances, such as the loss of a job, flunking out of school, or an unwanted pregnancy can lead people to threaten and/or commit suicide (Rudd, Joiner, Jr., & Rajab, 2001). Also, substance abuse is linked with suicide more today than it was in the past.

Sociocultural Factors Suicide rates vary from country to country. In 1990, the highest suicide rates in the world were found in Hungary (with 39.9/100,000) followed by Sri Lanka and Finland, while the lowest rates are found in Azerbaijan (with 1.6/100,000) followed by Mexico and Malta. By way of comparison, the Canadian rate was 12.7/100,000 and the U. S. rate was 12.4/100,000 (Lester & Yang, 2005). One trend in these data is that suicide rates tend to be higher in the more developed countries. Another is that suicide is relatively uncommon in Islamic countries, likely because of stronger cultural and religious norms against suicide.

Within a country, there is also a link between suicide and life circumstances, such as a long-standing history of family instability and unhappiness. Chronic economic hardship can be a factor in suicide. In one study, 8.5 percent of people living below the poverty line, compared with 5.4 percent living above the line, said that they had contemplated suicide (Crosby, Cheltenham, & Sacks, 1999). In Canada (Health Canada, 1999, 2002b) and the United States (Hendin, 1995), Aboriginal peoples have the highest suicide rate of all demographic groups, followed by whites. Also, recent life events, such as the loss of a loved one through death, divorce, or separation can lead to a suicide attempt (Heikkinen, Aro, & Loennqvist, 1992). Poor health can also be a trigger, such as receiving an HIV/AIDS diagnosis (Meel & Leenaars, 2005). Similarly, hospitalization can lead to suicide attempts in the elderly (Tsoh & others, 2005)

Psychologists cannot prevent suicidal impulses with certainty. But there is a need to improve suicide prevention programs, especially in schools (Leenaars, Lester, & Wenckstern, 2005). Psychologists believe that the most effective intervention comes from those who have had special training. Figure 13.12 provides some good advice on what to do and what not do when someone is threatening suicide.

What to Do	**What Not to Do**
1. Ask direct, straightforward questions in a calm manner. For example, "Are you thinking about hurting yourself?"	1. Don't ignore the warning signs.
2. Be a good listener and be supportive. Emphasize that unbearable pain can be survived.	2. Don't refuse to talk about suicide if the person wants to talk about it.
3. Take the suicide threat very seriously. Ask questions about the person's feelings, relationships, and thoughts about the type of method to be used. If a gun, pills, rope, or other means is mentioned and a specific plan has been developed, the situation is dangerous. Stay with the person until help arrives.	3. Don't react with horror, disapproval, or repulsion.
	4. Don't offer false reassurances ("Everything will be all right") or make judgments ("You should be thankful for . . .").
4. Encourage the person to get professional help and assist him or her in getting help. If the person is willing, take the person to a mental health facility or hospital.	5. Don't abandon the person after the crisis seems to have passed or after professional counselling has begun.

FIGURE 13.12 **What to Do and What Not to Do When Someone Is Threatening Suicide**

> **reflect and review**

4 **Compare the mood disorders and specify risk factors for depression and suicide.**

- Define the mood disorders.
- Distinguish between depressive disorders and normal feelings of sadness.
- Describe the mood disturbances that characterize bipolar disorder.
- Discuss the causes of mood disorders.
- Explain the factors that can lead to suicide.

Do any of the theories about the causes of depression seem better at accounting for depression in university students? Explain.

5 SCHIZOPHRENIA

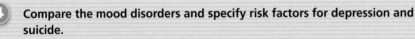

Types of Schizophrenia — Causes of Schizophrenia

What is the nature of schizophrenia and its different forms?

One day, while I was in the principal's office, suddenly the room became enormous, illuminated by a dreadful electric light that cast false shadows. Everything was exact, smooth, artificial, extremely tense; the chairs and tables seemed models placed here and there. Pupils and teachers were puppets revolving without cause, without objective. I recognized nothing, nobody. It was as though reality, attenuated, had slipped away from all these things and these people. Profound dread overwhelmed me, and as though lost, I looked around desperately for help. I heard people talking, but I did not grasp the meaning of their words. The voices were metallic, without warmth or color. From time to time, a word detached itself from the rest. It repeated itself over and over in my head, absurd, as though cut off by a knife. (Sechehaye,1951).

This passage was written by a man with **schizophrenia**, a severe psychological disorder that is characterized by highly disordered thought processes. Individuals with schizophrenia may show odd communication, inappropriate emotion, abnormal motor behaviour, and social withdrawal (Heinrichs, 2001). The term *schizophrenia* comes from the Latin words *schizo*, meaning "split," and *phrenia*, meaning "mind." It signifies that the individual's mind is split from reality and that personality disintegrates.

schizophrenia A severe psychological disorder that is characterized by highly disordered thought processes.

Schizophrenia is not the same as dissociative identity disorder, which sometimes is called "split personality." Schizophrenia involves the split of an individual's personality from reality, not the coexistence of several personalities within one individual. In Canada, 1 percent of the population suffers from schizophrenia in any given year (Health Canada, 2002a). Similarly, 2.2 million adults in the United States, or about 1.1 percent of the population 18 years and older, have schizophrenia in any given year (U. S. National Institute of Mental Health, 2001a).

Schizophrenia is a serious, debilitating mental disorder (Neufeld & others, 2003). About half of the patients in mental hospitals are individuals with schizophrenia. More often now than in the past, individuals with schizophrenia live in society and return to mental hospitals periodically for treatment. Drug therapy is primarily responsible for fewer individuals with schizophrenia being hospitalized. The "rule of fourths" characterizes outcomes for individuals with schizophrenia: One-fourth get well and stay well; one-fourth go on medication, do relatively well, and are able to live independently; another one-fourth are well enough to live in a group home; and one-fourth do poorly and are usually institutionalized.

Schizophrenia produces a bizarre set of symptoms and wreaks havoc on the individual's personality (VandenBos, 2000). According to Walter Heinrichs, of York University, profound neurocognitive deficits are at the core of these symptoms (Heinrichs, 2005). Heinrichs & Zakzanis (1998) surveyed 204 studies and found that schizophrenics showed poorer performance in 22 different tasks ranging from selective verbal memory and general intelligence to visual and auditory attention and language. Neurocognitive deficits include *delusions*, or false beliefs. One individual might think he is Jesus Christ, another Napoleon, for example. Individuals with schizophrenia might also hear, see, feel, smell, and taste things that are not there. These *hallucinations* often take the form of voices. An individual with schizophrenia might think that he hears two people talking about him. Or, on another occasion, he might say, "Hear that rumbling noise in the pipe? That is one of my men watching out for me." John Nash, the mathematician whose life story became the focus of the film *A Beautiful Mind*, finally overcame his hallucinations by rejecting them.

Often individuals with schizophrenia do not make sense when they talk or write. For example, one individual with schizophrenia might say, "Well, Rocky, babe, help is out, happening, but where, when, up, top, side, over, you know, out of the way, that's it. Sign off." Such speech has no meaning. These incoherent, loose word associations are called *word salad*.

The motor behaviour of the individual with schizophrenia can be bizarre, sometimes taking the form of an odd appearance, pacing, statuelike postures, or strange mannerisms. Some individuals with schizophrenia withdraw from their social world, totally absorbed in their own thoughts.

Types of Schizophrenia

There are four main types of schizophrenia: disorganized, catatonic, paranoid, and undifferentiated. Their outward behaviour patterns vary, but they have in common the characteristics of disordered thought processes.

Disorganized Schizophrenia In **disorganized schizophrenia**, an individual has delusions and hallucinations that have little or no recognizable meaning—hence, the label "disorganized." An individual with disorganized schizophrenia may withdraw from human contact and may regress to silly, childlike gestures and behaviour. Many of these individuals were isolated or maladjusted during adolescence.

Catatonic Schizophrenia **Catatonic schizophrenia** is characterized by bizarre motor behaviour, which sometimes takes the form of a completely immobile stupor (see figure 13.13; Fink & Taylor, 2003). Even in this stupor, individuals with catatonic schizophrenia are completely conscious of what is happening around them. In a catatonic state, the individual sometimes shows waxy flexibility; for example, if the person's

disorganized schizophrenia A type of schizophrenia in which an individual has delusions and hallucinations that have little or no recognizable meaning.

catatonic schizophrenia A type of schizophrenia that is characterized by bizarre motor behaviour, which sometimes takes the form of a completely immobile stupor.

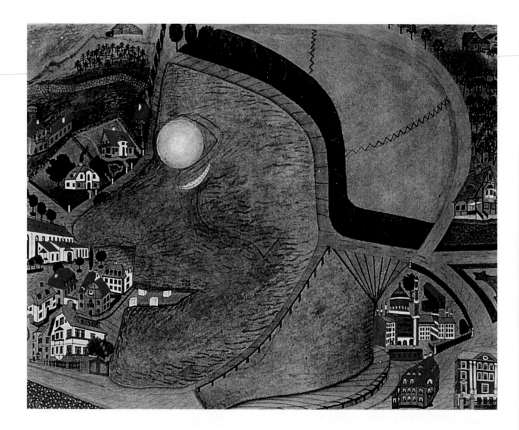

Landscape, by August Neter, who was a successful electrical engineer until he developed schizophrenia in 1907. He lost interest in his work as his mind became disorganized.

FIGURE 13.13

A Person with Catatonic Schizophrenia Unusual motor behaviours are prominent symptoms in catatonic schizophrenia. Individuals may cease to move altogether, sometimes holding bizarre postures.

arm is raised and then allowed to fall, the arm stays in the new position. The following excerpt describes an individual with catatonic schizophrenia:

> Todd, a 16-year-old high school student, began to change for the worse. A few months ago, he began to take Tai Chi lessons and often stood for long periods of time in karate-like positions, oblivious to what was going on around him. When his parents tried to get him out of bed in the morning, he lay motionless. When he was taken to see a mental health professional, Todd stood motionless in the centre of the room with his head flexed forward and his hands at his sides. He seemed unresponsive to much of what was going on around him. When the mental health professional placed Todd's hands in an awkward position, he remained frozen in that position for several minutes. (Carson, Butcher, & Mineka, 2000).

Paranoid Schizophrenia **Paranoid schizophrenia** is characterized by delusions of reference, grandeur, and persecution (Freeman & Garety, 2004). The delusions usually form a complex, elaborate system based on a complete misinterpretation of actual events. It is not unusual for individuals with paranoid schizophrenia to develop all three delusions in the following order: First, they sense that they are special and have been singled out for attention (delusions of reference). Individuals with delusions of reference misinterpret chance events as being directly relevant to their own lives—a thunderstorm, for example, might be perceived as a personal message from God. Second, they believe that this special attention is the result of their admirable and special characteristics (delusions of grandeur). Individuals with delusions of grandeur think of themselves as exalted beings—the pope or the prime minister, for example. Third, they think that others are so jealous and threatened by these characteristics that they spy and plot against them (delusions of persecution). Individuals with delusions of persecution often feel that they are the target of a conspiracy, as in Bob's case:

> Bob began to miss work. He spent his time watching his house from a rental car parked inconspicuously down the street and following his fellow employees as they left work to see where they went and what they were doing. He kept a little black book in which he scribbled cryptic notes. When he went to the water cooler at work, he pretended to drink but instead looked around the room to observe if anyone looked guilty or frightened. Bob's world

paranoid schizophrenia A type of schizophrenia that is characterized by delusions of reference, grandeur, and persecution.

FIGURE 13.14

Lifetime Risk of Developing Schizophrenia, According to Genetic Relatedness
As genetic relatedness to an individual with schizophrenia increases, so does the risk of developing schizophrenia.

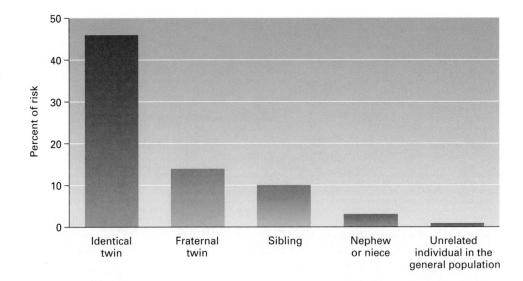

seemed to be closing in on him. After an explosive scene at the office one day, he became very agitated. He left and never returned. By the time Bob arrived home, he was in a rage. He could not sleep that night and the next day he kept his children home from school. All day he kept the shades pulled on every window. The next night he maintained his vigil. At 4 a.m., he armed himself and burst out of the house, firing shots in the air while daring his enemies to come out. (McNeil, 1967).

Undifferentiated Schizophrenia **Undifferentiated schizophrenia** is characterized by disorganized behaviour, hallucinations, delusions, and incoherence. This diagnosis is used when an individual's symptoms either do not meet the criteria for one of the other types or meet the criteria for more than one of the other types.

Causes of Schizophrenia

Like the mood disorders, schizophrenia may have biological, psychological, and sociocultural causes. Schizophrenia is a heavily researched mental disorder, with recent research focusing on biological factors.

Biological Factors There is strong research support for biological explanations of schizophrenia. Particularly compelling is the evidence for a genetic predisposition, but structural abnormalities and neurotransmitters also seem to be linked to this devastating disorder.

Heredity If you have a relative with schizophrenia, what are the chances you will develop schizophrenia? It depends on how closely related you are. As genetic similarity increases, so does a person's risk of becoming schizophrenic. As shown in figure 13.14, an identical twin of an individual with schizophrenia has a 48 percent chance of developing the disorder, a fraternal twin 17 percent, a sibling 13 percent, a nephew or niece 4 percent, and an unrelated individual in the general population 1 percent (Cowan, Kopnisky, & Hyman, 2002). Such data strongly suggest that genetic factors are involved in schizophrenia. Researchers are seeking to pinpoint the chromosomal location of genes involved in schizophrenia. They have recently found possible genetic markers for schizophrenia on a number of chromosomes including 13 and 22 (Bassett & others, 2001; Cowan, Kopnisky, & Hyman, 2002).

The role of heredity in schizophrenia may be illustrated through the story of the Genain quadruplets, who have been extensively studied at the U.S. National Institute of Mental Health (NIMH). Henry Genain had forgotten to buy his wife a birthday present, so she suggested that he give her a child for their third wedding anniversary instead. The wish came true, but there were four presents instead of one. Their birth in a midsize midwestern U.S. town was a celebrated occasion; one paper ran a contest to name

undifferentiated schizophrenia A type of schizophrenia that is characterized by disorganized behaviour, hallucinations, delusions, and incoherence.

the girls and received 12,000 entries. The family was given a rent-free house and a baby carriage for four, and a dairy company donated milk. Newspaper stories appeared from time to time about the quadruplets, portraying their similarities, especially their drama talent and a song-and-dance routine they had developed.

The quadruplets' problems emerged by the time they reached high school. It became clear then that the girls had serious mental problems. By the time they were in their twenties, each had been diagnosed with schizophrenia. A perceptive doctor recognized their symptoms and contacted NIMH. A research team led by David Rosenthal (1963) began extensive evaluation of the schizophrenic quadruplets.

About 20 years later, psychologist Alan Mirsky invited the quadruplets back to NIMH to determine how they might have changed. The scientists also wanted to know if recently developed techniques could discover something special about their biological makeup (Buchsbaum & others, 1984). PET scans revealed an unusually high rate of energy use in the rear portion of the quadruplets' brains (see figure 13.15). Their brains also showed much less alpha-wave activity than the brains of normal individuals. Remember that alpha-wave activity appears in individuals in a relaxed state. Scientists speculate that the onset of hallucinations might possibly block alpha-wave activity.

Environmental experiences may have contributed to the Genain quadruplets' schizophrenia as well. Their father placed strict demands on his daughters, delighted in watching them undress, and would not let them play with friends or participate in school or church activities. He refused to let the quadruplets participate in social activities even as adults, and he followed them to their jobs and opened their mail.

What makes the Genain quadruplets so fascinating is their uniqueness—identical quadruplets occur once in every 16 million births, only half survive to adulthood, and only 1 in 100 develops schizophrenia. The chances of all of them surviving and developing schizophrenia are one in tens of billions of births, a figure much greater than the current world population.

In a follow-up of the Genain quadruplets when they were 66 years of age, significant variations in the courses of their lives were apparent (Mirsky & others, 2000). Myra worked, married, and raised a family despite having schizophrenia. Hester never completed high school and has never been able to function independently outside a group home or institution. Nora and Iris fared somewhat better than Hester but have never married or had substantial careers. The Genain quadruplets' thought processes remained stable or even improved somewhat as they got older, supporting the idea that schizophrenia is not a degenerative disorder, as many mental health professionals previously believed.

Structural Brain Abnormalities   Structural abnormalities in the brain have been found in individuals with schizophrenia. Imaging techniques, such as the PET scan, clearly show enlarged ventricles in the brains of these people (Puri & others, 2001). Ventricles

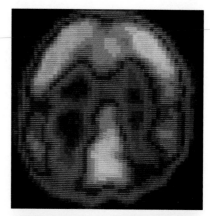
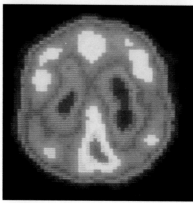

FIGURE 13.15

PET Scans of the Genain Quadruplets
In a normal brain (*top*), the areas of high energy use are at the top, in the frontal lobes. The quadruplets all showed abnormal energy use in the visual areas (*red area, bottom*). *Are these hallucinations?*

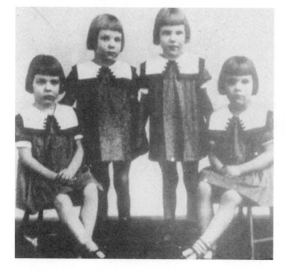

The Genain quadruplets as children and as middle-aged adults. All four had been diagnosed with schizophrenia by the time they were in their 20s.

are fluid-filled spaces in the brain, and enlargement of the ventricles indicates atrophy or deterioration in other brain tissue. Individuals with schizophrenia also have a small frontal cortex (the area in which thinking, planning, and decision making take place) and show less activity than is seen in individuals who do not have schizophrenia (Cotter & others, 2002). Among the questions raised by such findings are: Do these deficits cause the disorder? Or are they simply symptoms of a disorder whose true origin lies deeper in the brain, in the genes, or in the environment?

Neurotransmitter Deregulation An early biological explanation for schizophrenia stated that individuals with schizophrenia produce higher than normal levels of the neurotransmitter dopamine and that the excess dopamine causes schizophrenia. That theory is probably too simple, although there is good evidence that dopamine does play a role in schizophrenia (Kapur & Lecrubier, 2003).

Psychological Factors Although contemporary theorists do not propose psychological factors as stand-alone causes of schizophrenia, stress may be a contributing factor. The **diathesis-stress model** argues that a combination of biogenetic disposition and stress causes schizophrenia (Davison & Neale, 2006). The term *diathesis* means physical vulnerability or predisposition to a particular disorder. A defective gene makeup might produce schizophrenia only when the individual lives in a stressful environment. For example, Louis Schmidt, of McMaster University, and his colleagues have proposed a diathesis-stress model of extreme shyness in children (Schmidt, Polak, & Spooner, 2001) and have identified childhood shyness and early sociability problems as risk factors in the emergence of schizophrenia later in life (Goldberg & Schmidt, 2001). Advocates of the diathesis-stress view emphasize the importance of stress reduction and family support in treating schizophrenia.

Sociocultural Factors Disorders of thought and emotion are common to schizophrenia in all cultures, but the type and incidence of schizophrenic disorders may vary from culture to culture (Jenkins & Barrett, 2004). Individuals living in poverty are likelier to have schizophrenia than people at higher socioeconomic levels. The link between schizophrenia and poverty is correlational, and contemporary theorists do not believe that poverty causes schizophrenia (Schiffman & Walker, 1998).

> **> reflect and review**
>
> **5** **Characterize schizophrenia.**
> - Describe the different types of schizophrenia.
> - Explain the causes of schizophrenia.
>
> *Imagine that you are a clinical psychologist who has been given the opportunity to interview the Genain quadruplets. What questions would you want to ask them in an effort to sort through why the paths of their schizophrenia varied through their adult years?*

diathesis-stress model A model of schizophrenia that proposes a combination of biogenetic disposition and stress as the cause of the disorder.

6 PERSONALITY DISORDERS

— **Odd/Eccentric Cluster** — **Dramatic/ Emotionally Problematic Cluster** — **Chronic-Fearfulness/ Avoidant Cluster**

personality disorders Chronic, maladaptive cognitive-behavioural patterns that are thoroughly integrated into the individual's personality.

What behaviour patterns are typical of personality disorders?
Personality disorders are chronic, maladaptive cognitive-behavioural patterns that are thoroughly integrated into the individual's personality, and that are troublesome to

others or whose pleasure sources are either harmful or illegal (Davison & Neale, 2006; Serin & Marshall, 2003). The patterns are often recognizable by adolescence or earlier. Personality disorders usually are not as bizarre as schizophrenia, and they do not have the intense, diffuse feelings of fear and apprehension that characterize the anxiety disorders (Evans & others, 2002). From 6 to 9 percent of the population of the United States and, by extrapolation, Canada, have a personality disorder (Health Canada, 2002a).

In the *DSM-IV*, the personality disorders are grouped into three clusters: odd/eccentric, dramatic/emotionally problematic, and chronic-fearfulness/avoidant.

Odd/Eccentric Cluster

The odd/eccentric cluster includes the paranoid, schizoid, and schizotypal disorders:

Individuals with paranoid personality disorder show chronic and pervasive mistrust and suspicion of other people that is not warranted.

- *Paranoid*. These individuals have a lack of trust in others and are suspicious. They see themselves as morally correct yet vulnerable and envied.
- *Schizoid*. They do not form adequate social relationships. They show shy, withdrawn behaviour and have difficulty expressing anger. Most are considered to be "cold" people.
- *Schizotypal*. They show odd thinking patterns that reflect eccentric beliefs, overt suspicion, and overt hostility. The following case describes an individual with schizotypal personality disorder.

Mr. S. was 35-year-old chronically unemployed man who was thought to have a vitamin deficiency. This was believed to have occurred because Mr. S. avoided any foods that could have been contaminated by a machine. He had started to develop alternative ideas about food and diet in his 20s. He left his family to study an eastern religion. As he said, "It opened my third eye, corruption is all about." Later, Mr. S. moved to live by himself on a small farm, attempting to grow his own food. He spent his days and evenings researching the mechanisms of food contamination. (Quality Assurance Project, 1990).

As you can see, some personality disorders have names that are similar to other disorders described in other categories earlier in the chapter, such as schizotypal personality disorder and schizophrenic disorders. However, individuals with schizotypal disorder are not as clearly bizarre in their thinking and behaviour as individuals with schizophrenia.

Dramatic/Emotionally Problematic Cluster

The dramatic and emotionally problematic cluster consists of the histrionic, narcissistic, borderline, and antisocial personality disorders.

- *Histrionic*. These individuals need a lot of attention and tend to overreact. They respond more dramatically and intensely than is required by the situation, thus the term histrionic. The disorder is more common in women than men.
- *Narcissistic*. These individuals have an unrealistic sense of self-importance, can't take criticism, manipulate people, and lack empathy. These characteristics lead to substantial problems in relationships.
- *Borderline*. These individuals are often emotionally unstable, impulsive, unpredictable, irritable, and anxious. They are also prone to abuse their intimates (Dutton, 1998). Their behaviour is similar to that of individuals with schizotypal personality disorder, but they are not as consistently withdrawn and bizarre.
- *Antisocial*. They are guiltless, law-breaking, exploitive, self-indulgent, irresponsible, and intrusive. They are impulsive (Parker & Bagby, 1997). They often resort to a life of crime and violence. This disorder is far more common in men than in women.

Based on U. S. data, Health Canada (2002a) estimates that 6 to 9 percent of individuals have a personality disorder and that up to 50 percent of prisoners may have the disorder. The following individual has an antisocial personality disorder:

Paul Bernardo is a classic case of a personality disorder. By the time he attended the University of Toronto, he was beating up the women he dated and preferred forceful anal sex. As the Scarborough rapist, he sexually assaulted at least 14 young women in southern Ontario between 1987 and 1991. On December 24, 1990, Bernardo and his former wife Karla Homolka, who served 12 years for manslaughter, drugged and raped her 15-year-old sister Tammy, who choked to death on her own vomit. In June 1991, they repeatedly raped Leslie Mahaffy in their Port Dalhousie home for nearly 24 hours, then strangled her, dismembered the body and disposed of the parts in Lake Gibson. In April, 1992, they held Kristen French hostage for almost 72 hours, brutally raping her before strangling her to death. Bernardo, who was officially declared a dangerous offender, will likely spend the rest of his life in prison, ineligible for parole.

Mark, 22 years old, is awaiting trial for car theft and armed robbery. He has a long history of arrests beginning at nine years of age, when he was arrested for vandalism. He was expelled from high school for truancy and disruptive behaviour. He ran away from home on numerous occasions. He has not held a job for more than two days at a time, even though his charming manner enables him to obtain work rather easily. Mark is a loner with few friends and, although initially charming, he soon antagonizes the people he meets with his aggressive, self-oriented behaviour. While Mark was awaiting trial, he skipped bail and left town (Carson, Butcher, & Mineka, 2000).

A pervasive pattern of antisocial behaviour occurring in children younger than 15 is labelled *conduct disorder*. When the antisocial behaviour persists beyond the age of 15 into adulthood, it is labelled *antisocial personality disorder*. It is much more common in males than in females. These individuals represent a small percentage of the population but commit a disproportionately large percentage of violent and property crimes (Hare, 2001; Health Canada, 2002a). The disorder is very difficult to treat (Hare, 2002; Hemphill, Hare, & Wong, 1998).

Explanations for the causes of antisocial personality disorder include biological, psychological, and sociocultural factors. In terms of biological factors, a genetic predisposition for the disorder may be present (Goldstein, Prescott, & Kendler, 2001) since the disorder is more likely to appear in identical twins than in fraternal twins (Eley, Lichtenstein, & Moffitt, 2003).

Robert Hare, of the University of British Columbia, has distinguished between the closely related concepts of antisocial personality disorder, which focuses on antisocial behaviour, and *psychopathy*, which focuses on the lack of a capacity to experience feelings like empathy, remorse, guilt, anxiety, or loyalty. Many psychopaths engage in antisocial behaviour. In an experiment, Hare and his colleagues (Williamson, Harpur, & Hare, 1991) compared the brain waves of normal participants with those of psychopaths. Normal participants took longer recognizing emotionally-laden words like "cancer," while psychopaths recognized words like "cancer" as quickly as words like "table," suggesting that psychopaths do not process emotional connotations for words. Hare and his colleagues (Intrator and others, 1997) showed that normal participants process emotionally-laden words in the areas around the ventromedial frontal cortex and amygdala, whereas psychopaths show brain activity only in the cortex and not the amygdala, "the seat of emotion."

These results suggest that psychopaths do not experience the integration of cognition and emotion that normal people do (Hervé, Hayes, & Hare, 2003). In terms of psychological factors, the impulsive and aggressive behaviour that characterizes individuals with antisocial personality disorders suggests that they have not adequately learned how to delay gratification. In terms of sociocultural factors, inadequate socialization regularly appears in the history of individuals who develop antisocial personality disorder (Sutker & Allain, 1993). Parents of these children may be neglectful or inconsistent and punitive in their discipline.

Chronic-Fearfulness/Avoidant Cluster

The chronic-fearfulness/avoidant cluster includes the avoidant, dependent, passive-aggressive, and obsessive-compulsive personality disorders:

- *Avoidant*. These individuals are shy and inhibited yet desire interpersonal relationships, which distinguishes them from the schizoid and schizotypal disorders. They often have low self-esteem and are extremely sensitive to rejection. This disorder is close to being an anxiety disorder but is not characterized by as much personal distress.
- *Dependent*. These individuals lack self-confidence and do not express their own personalities. They have a pervasive need to cling to stronger personalities, whom they allow to make decisions for them. The disorder is far more common in women than in men.

- *Passive-Aggressive*. These individuals often pout and procrastinate; they are stubborn or are intentionally inefficient in an effort to frustrate others. Passive-aggressive personality disorder was removed from the Axis II Personality Disorders of the *DSM-IIIR* because of controversy regarding the category. It is currently located in Appendix B, "Criteria Sets and Axes Provided for Further Study" of the *DSM-IV* and is being considered for inclusion in future revisions.

- *Obsessive-Compulsive*. This personality disorder is often confused with obsessive-compulsive anxiety disorder. Generally, obsessive-compulsive anxiety disorder impairs function much more than obsessive-compulsive personality disorder, which usually centres on a preoccupation with perfection and order. A person with obsessive-compulsive personality disorder may chronically create sets of lists, rules, and goals. People with obsessive-compulsive personality disorder may nevertheless be successful achievers, although often at the expense of professional and personal relationships. And, in the personality disorder, the person does not become upset or distressed about his or her lifestyle. These individuals are obsessed with rules, are emotionally insensitive, and are oriented toward a lifestyle of productivity and efficiency.

> **reflect and review**

 6 **Identify the behaviour patterns typical of personality disorders.**

- Define personality disorders.
- Discuss the odd/eccentric cluster.
- Explain the dramatic/emotionally problematic cluster.
- Describe the chronic-fearfulness/avoidant cluster.

We described a possible psychological cause for antisocial personality disorder. Go down the list of other personality disorders and try to come up with psychological causes for them.

Psychological Disorders

1 UNDERSTANDING PSYCHOLOGICAL DISORDERS

- Defining Abnormal Behaviour
- Theoretical Approaches to Psychological Disorders
- Classifying Abnormal Behaviour

2 ANXIETY DISORDERS

- Generalized Anxiety Disorder
- Panic Disorder
- Phobic Disorders
- Obsessive-Compulsive Disorder
- Post-Traumatic Stress Disorder

3 DISSOCIATIVE DISORDERS

- Dissociative Amnesia and Fugue
- Dissociative Identity Disorder

4 MOOD DISORDERS

- Depressive Disorders
- Bipolar Disorder
- Causes of Mood Disorders
- Suicide

5 SCHIZOPHRENIA

- Types of Schizophrenia
- Causes of Schizophrenia

6 PERSONALITY DISORDERS

- Odd/Eccentric Cluster
- Dramatic/ Emotionally Problematic Cluster
- Chronic-Fearfulness/ Avoidant Cluster

At the beginning of the chapter, we posed six chapter questions and encouraged you to review material related to these questions at the end of each major section (see pages 518, 526, 528, 539, 544, and 547). Use the following reflection and review features for further your understanding of the chapter material.

CHAPTER REFLECTIONS

1. Spend 15 to 20 minutes observing in an area with a large number of people (a mall, the cafeteria, etc.) and identify behaviours that you would classify as abnormal. How does your list of behaviours compare with the definition of abnormal in the text? What would change on the list if you were in a different setting (a church, a bar, a library)? What does this tell you about defining abnormal behaviour?

2. Imagine the following events. For each event, describe the kind of anxiety or dissociative disorder that might be most likely to develop. Is it likelier that the person would or would not develop a disorder?

   a. Marcy was bitten by a dog as a young child.
   b. Alex came under fire as a peacekeeper with the Canadian Armed Forces in Afghanistan.
   c. Andy was involved in a serious automobile accident.
   d. Sam's parents were always critical about her behaviour and sometimes locked her in a room for several days at a time when she was growing up.

3. After reading information on psychological disorders, students often feel like they may be suffering from one or two of those disorders themselves. This is often referred to as "medical student's disease" or the "common cold of psychological disorder." Did you experience this difficulty? Did anyone else you know who is taking this course? What does this tell you about defining "abnormality?

4. The Internet provides a wealth of mental health information. Find a site (such as www.mental-health.com) that gives more information about personality disorders or schizophrenia. What information can you find that's not discussed in the text? Does it change your view of either disorder?

5. Visit www.dsm5.org, the Web site of the DSM-V revision process. How would you characterize the process of creating a new revision of the DSM?

CHAPTER REVIEW

Discuss the characteristics and classifications of psychological disorders.

- Psychologists define abnormal behaviour as behaviour that is deviant, maladaptive, or personally distressful. Only one of these criteria is necessary for the classification of abnormal behaviour, but two or three can be present. There are a number of myths about abnormal behaviour, and a thin line often exists between normal and abnormal behaviour.

- Theoretical perspectives on the causes of psychological disorders include biological, psychological, and sociocultural approaches. In terms of biological factors, the medical model describes psychological disorders as diseases with a biological origin. Structural, biochemical, and genetic views have also been proposed. Psychological approaches include the psychodynamic perspective, the behavioural/social cognitive perspective, and the humanistic perspective. The sociocultural approach places more emphasis on the larger social context in which a person lives than on psychological factors. Sociocultural contexts include the individual's marriage or family, neighbourhood, socioeconomic status, ethnicity, gender, and culture. The biopsychosocial approach is an interactionist approach to understanding psychological disorders.

- The classification of mental disorders gives mental health professionals a shorthand to use in their communications and allows clinicians to make predictions about disorders and determine what kind of treatment is appropriate. The Diagnostic and Statistical Manual of Mental Disorders (DSM), published by the American Psychiatric Association, is the classification system used by clinicians to diagnose and treat psychological disorders. The DSM-IV features a multiaxial diagnostic system that enables clinicians to characterize an individual on the basis of five dimensions. Some psychologists contend that DSM-IV perpetuates the medical model of psychological disorders and labels as psychological disorders some everyday problems that are not considered deviant or maladaptive.

Distinguish among the various anxiety disorders.

- Anxiety is a diffuse, vague, highly unpleasant feeling of fear and apprehension. The main features of anxiety disorders are motor tension, hyperactivity, and apprehensive expectations and thoughts. Generalized anxiety disorder is defined as anxiety that persists for at least one month with no specific reason for the anxiety. Biological, psychological, and sociocultural factors may be involved.

- Recurrent panic attacks marked by the sudden onset of intense apprehension or terror characterize panic disorder. Panic disorder can occur with or without agoraphobia. Biological and psychological factors may contribute to the development of panic disorder.

- Phobic disorders involve an irrational, overwhelming fear of a particular object, such as snakes, or situation, such as flying. Biological and psychological factors have been proposed as causes of phobias.

- Obsessive-compulsive disorder (OCD) is an anxiety disorder in which the individual has anxiety-provoking thoughts that will not go away (obsession) and/or urges to perform repetitive, ritualistic behaviours to prevent or produce some future situation (compulsion). Biological and psychological factors are likely involved in OCD.

- Post-traumatic stress disorder (PTSD) is an anxiety disorder that develops through exposure to traumatic events, such as war; severely oppressive situations, such as the Holocaust; severe abuse, as in rape; natural disasters, such as floods and tornados; and unnatural disasters, such as plane crashes and terrorist attacks. Symptoms include flashbacks, which may appear immediately after the trauma or may be delayed.

Describe the dissociative disorders.

- Dissociative disorders are characterized by a sudden loss of memory or change in identity. Under extreme stress, conscious awareness becomes dissociated (separated or split) from previous memories and thoughts. Hilgard's hidden observer concept has been applied to understanding the dissociative disorders.

- Dissociative amnesia involves memory loss caused by extensive psychological stress. Dissociative fugue also involves a loss of memory, but individuals with this disorder also unexpectedly travel away from home or work, assume a new identity, and do not remember the old one.

- Dissociative identity disorder, formerly called multiple personality disorder, involves the presence of two or more distinct personalities in the same individual. This disorder is rare.

Compare the mood disorders and specify the risk factors for depression and suicide.

- Mood disorders are psychological disorders in which there is a primary disturbance of mood. The mood disturbance can include cognitive, behavioural, and somatic (physical) symptoms, as well as interpersonal difficulties. Two main types of mood disorders are depressive disorders and bipolar disorder. The depressive disorders are mood disorders in which the individual suffers depression without experiencing mania. In major depressive disorder, the individual experiences a major depressive episode and depressed characteristics, such as lethargy and hopelessness, for two weeks or longer. Dysthymic disorder is generally more chronic and has fewer symptoms than major depressive disorder.

- Bipolar disorder is characterized by extreme mood swings that include one or more episodes of mania (an overexcited, unrealistic, optimistic state). *Bipolar* means that the person may experience both depression and mania. Less than 10 percent of bipolar individuals experience mania without depression.

- Biological explanations of mood disorders focus on heredity, neurophysiological abnormalities, neurotransmitter deregulation, and hormonal factors. Psychological explanations include psychoanalytic, behavioural, and cognitive perspectives. Sociocultural explanations emphasize interpersonal relationships, socioeconomic and ethnic factors, cultural variations, and gender.

- Severe depression and other psychological disorders can cause individuals to want to end their lives. Biological, psychological, and sociocultural explanations of suicide have been proposed.

Characterize schizophrenia.

- Schizophrenia is a severe psychological disorder that is characterized by highly disordered thought processes. Individuals with schizophrenia may show odd communication, inappropriate emotion, abnormal motor behaviour, and social withdrawal. There are four main types of schizophrenia: disorganized, catatonic, paranoid, and undifferentiated. In disorganized schizophrenia, an individual has delusions and hallucinations that have little or no recognizable meaning. Catatonic schizophrenia is characterized by bizarre motor behaviour, which may take the form of a completely immobile stupor. Paranoid schizophrenia is characterized by delusions of reference, grandeur, and persecution. Undifferentiated schizophrenia is characterized by disorganized behaviour, hallucinations, delusions, and incoherence.

- Biological factors (heredity, structural brain abnormalities, and neurotransmitter deregulation), psychological factors (diathesis-stress view), and sociocultural factors may be involved in schizophrenia. Psychological and sociocultural factors are not viewed as stand-alone causes of schizophrenia.

Identify the behaviour patterns typical of personality disorders.

- Personality disorders are chronic, maladaptive cognitive-behavioural patterns that are throughly integrated into the individual's personality. The three main clusters of personality disorders are odd/eccentric, dramatic/emotionally problematic, and chronic fearfulness/avoidant.

- The odd/eccentric cluster includes the paranoid, schizoid, and schizotypal personality disorders.

- The dramatic/emotionally problematic cluster consists of the histrionic, narcissistic, borderline, and antisocial personality disorders. Biological, psychological, and sociocultural explanations of antisocial personality disorder have been proposed.

- The chronic-fearfulness/avoidant cluster includes the avoidant, dependent, passive-aggressive, and obsessive-compulsive personality disorders.

CONNECTIONS

For extra help in mastering the material in the chapter, see the review questions and practice quizzes in the Student Study Guide and the Online Learning Centre.

CORE TERMS

abnormal behaviour, p. 511
medical model, p. 512
DSM-IV, p. 514
anxiety disorders, p. 518
generalized anxiety disorder, p. 518
panic disorder, p. 519
agoraphobia, p. 519
phobic disorder, p. 520
obsessive-compulsive disorder (OCD), p. 522

post-traumatic stress disorder, p. 522
dissociative disorders, p. 526
dissociative amnesia, p. 526
dissociative fugue, p. 527
dissociative identity disorder (DID), p. 527
mood disorders, p. 528
depressive disorders, p. 529
major depressive disorder, p. 529
dysthymic disorder, p. 529

bipolar disorder, p. 531
learned helplessness, p. 534
schizophrenia, p. 539
disorganized schizophrenia, p. 540
catatonic schizophrenia, p. 540
paranoid schizophrenia, p. 541
undifferentiated schizophrenia, p. 542
diathesis-stress model, p. 544
personality disorders, p. 544

14 Therapies

CHAPTER QUESTIONS

1 What are the biological therapies?

2 What is a definition of psychotherapy and what are four types of psychotherapies?

3 What are the sociocultural approaches and the issues in treatment that arise?

4 What is the effectiveness of psychotherapy?

In 1995, Susan Aglukark released a CD entitled *This Child*, which catapulted her onto the world stage. Born on Hudson Bay and often singing in her native language, Inuktitut, Aglukark sings songs that deal with the many ills that tear at the social fabric of Aboriginal peoples, such as the tidal wave of suicide that washes over many communities. In *Kathy I*, a heart-breaking song on her album *This Child*, Aglukark laments the loss of Kathy, her cousin and good friend, who killed herself.

C. Murray Sinclair, a First Nations member from Winnipeg, shared his experiences at a conference on suicide prevention (Sinclair, 1998). For him, growing up Aboriginal in Canada was a "difficult and sometimes traumatic experience." According to Sinclair, the treatment of Aboriginal peoples by Canadian governments for much of the twentieth century, although well intentioned, was a form of cultural genocide (see also Waldram, 1997). It rested on the belief that Aboriginal societies were inferior and must be destroyed to save Aboriginal peoples, a belief also held by Australian governments towards Australian aboriginals (Leenaars & others, 1999).

Under the *Indian Act*, traditional chiefs in Canada could be removed from office and Aboriginal people could be prevented from competing economically with whites, leaving their reservations without permission, or benefiting from natural resources on their lands. Subsequent amendments made it an offence for Aboriginals to participate in tribal ceremonies or wear traditional costumes, and legally required Aboriginal children to attend residential schools, where they were often abused. This policy destroyed traditional leadership and tribal institutions without replacing them with appropriate alternatives, which resulted in social chaos and an inevitable toll of depression, alcoholism, abuse, and suicide.

What can be done? It is not always helpful to treat individuals suffering from these complaints without considering the broader social context. The usual image of an individual therapist healing an individual patient must, in this case, be augmented by tribal and national healing. Sinclair

Susan Aglukark sings about, and speaks out on behalf of, the disenfranchised in remote northern Canadian communities.

advocates that Aboriginal peoples must take control and look to their own cultural heritage, as well as to the future, to heal. Chandler & Lalonde (1998) have presented evidence that Sinclair is right. They showed that suicide rates vary widely across British Columbia's nearly 200 Aboriginal groups: some communities show rates 800 times the national average, while in others suicide is rare. They also showed that lower suicide rates were associated with Aboriginal bands that are actively working to preserve and rehabilitate their own cultures (see also Chandler & others, 2003). In fact, Leenaars and others (1999) note that, historically, suicide was relatively rare among Aboriginal peoples living within their own cultural contexts.

In Chapters 12 and 13 we explained the biological, psychological, and sociocultural factors relevant to personality and pyschological disorders. With this foundation, we turn to a discussion of the biological, psychological, and sociocultural factors underlying the use of therapy to improve the lives of people with psychological disorders (Sharf, 2004). The chapter begins with the biological therapies, which often involve the use of medication to treat psychological disorders. Later, the chapter examines the wide range of mental health professionals who provide therapy.

① BIOLOGICAL THERAPIES

━━ **Drug**   ━━ **Electroconvulsive** ━━ **Psychosurgery**
      Therapy   **Therapy**

What are the biological therapies?

Biological therapies are treatments to reduce or eliminate the symptoms of psychological disorders by altering the way an individual's body functions. Drug therapy is the most common form of biomedical therapy. Electroconvulsive therapy and psychosurgery are much less widely used biomedical therapies. Recall from chapter 1 that psychiatrists, who are medical doctors, can administer drugs as part of therapy. However, psychologists, who are not trained as medical doctors, cannot administer drugs as part of therapy. Psychologists and other mental health professionals may provide **psychotherapy** to help individuals recognize and overcome their problems in conjunction with the biological therapy administered by psychiatrists and other medical doctors. Indeed, in many instances, a combination of psychotherapy and medication is a desirable course of treatment (Winston, Been, & Serby, 2005).

Drug Therapy

Although medicine and herbs have long been used to alleviate symptoms of emotional distress, it was not until the twentieth century that drug treatments began to revolutionize mental health care. Psychotherapeutic drugs are used mainly in three diagnostic categories: anxiety disorders, mood disorders, and schizophrenia. This section discusses the effectiveness of drugs in these areas, beginning with drugs used to treat anxiety.

Antianxiety Drugs   **Antianxiety drug**s are commonly known as *tranquilizers* (Julien, 2005). These drugs reduce anxiety by making individuals calmer and less excitable. *Benzodiazepines* are the antianxiety drugs that most often offer the greatest relief for anxiety symptoms. They are relatively fast-acting medications, taking effect within hours. Benzodiazepines work by binding to the receptor sites of neurotransmitters that become overactive during anxiety (Spiegel, 2003). The most frequently prescribed benzodiazepines include alprazolam (Xanax), Diazepam (Valium) and lorazepam (Ativan). A nonbenzodiazepine—buspirone (BuSpar)—is also commonly used to treat generalized anxiety disorder. However, Buspirone must be taken daily for 2 to 3 weeks before it takes effect (Roy-Byrne & Cowley, 2002).

Benzodiazepines, like all drugs, have some side effects (Roy-Byrne & Cowley, 2002). They can be addicting. Also, drowsiness, loss of coordination, fatigue, and mental slowing can accompany their use. These effects can be hazardous when driving or operating some types of machinery, especially when the person first starts taking benzodiazepines. Stewart (2005) has suggested that the long-term use of benzodiazepines may lead to impaired cognitive processing, including speed of processing, verbal learning, and visuospatial ability. Benzodiazepines have also been linked to abnormalities in babies born to mothers who took them during pregnancy (Perault & others, 2000).

When benzodiazepines are combined with other medications, problems can result. When combined with alcohol, anaesthetics, antihistamines, sedatives, muscle relaxants, and some prescription pain medications, benzodiazepines can lead to depression (Dalfen & Stewart, 2001; Gutierrez-Lobos & others, 2001).

Antianxiety medications are controlled drugs that should be used only temporarily for symptomatic relief. They can be overused and, as mentioned earlier, can become addictive. Further, while antianxiety drugs may bring relief from high levels of anxiety and stress, they may not always be helpful. For example, antianxiety drugs may be helpful for panic and anxiety (Cox & others, 1992; Allgulander & others, 2003) but not for phobia, which is better dealt with via systematic desensitization. Similarly, because of their side effects, benzodiazepines are less preferable for the long-term treatment of anxiety disorders. Instead, antidepressants, especially SSRIs (see the next section) are recommended

---

biological therapies Treatments to reduce or eliminate the symptoms of psychological disorders by altering the way an individual's body functions.

psychotherapy The process used by mental health professionals to help individuals recognize, define, and overcome their psychological and interpersonal difficulties.

antianxiety drugs Commonly known as tranquilizers, they reduce anxiety by making people calmer and less excitable.

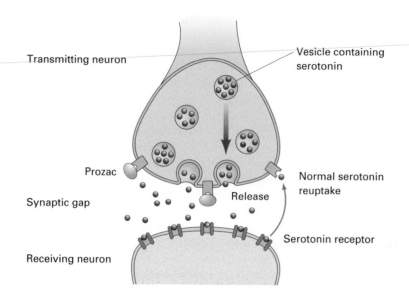

FIGURE 14.1

How the Antidepressant Prozac Works
Serotonin is secreted by a transmitting neuron, moves across the synaptic gap, and then binds to receptors in a receiving neuron. Excess serotonin in the synaptic gap is normally reabsorbed by the transmitting neuron. However, Prozac blocks the reuptake of serotonin to the transmitting neuron, which leaves excess serotonin in the synaptic gap. The excess serotonin will be transmitted to the receiving neuron and circulated through the brain, thus reducing the serotonin deficit found in depressed individuals.

for the long-term treatment of most of the anxiety disorders (Greist & others, 2003; Pollack & others, 2003; Stein & others, 2003; Van Ameringen & others, 2003).

In general, the anxiety disorders may be better dealt with by combining biological and psychological interventions (Gauthier, 1999). The preferred psychological intervention for most anxiety disorders is cognitive-behaviour therapy (Greist & others, 2003; Pollack & others, 2003; Van Ameringen & others, 2003).

Antidepressant Drugs

Linda has a good marriage and her second child, a healthy boy, was just born, so you would think that everything is great in her life. However, she describes her life as if it were an unbearable weight on her shoulders. Usually energetic and focused, Linda considers it a major accomplishment to get through the day. These feelings continue for several months and finally she decides to see a psychiatrist, who prescribes an antidepressant drug for treating her depression, along with psychotherapy. After several weeks of being on the medication and participating in psychotherapy, Linda begins to feel better. The dreary Midwest winter and the responsibility involved in caring for her young children no longer overwhelm her. (Nathan, Gorman, & Salkind, 1999).

Antidepressant drugs regulate mood. The three main classes of antidepressant drugs are tricyclics, such as amitriptyline (Elavil); MAO inhibitors, such as phenelzine (Nardil); and SSRI drugs, such as fluoxetine (Prozac) (Julien, 2005).

The *tricyclics*, so called because of their three-ringed molecular structure, are believed to work by increasing the level of certain neurotransmitters, especially norepinephrine and serotonin (Julien, 2005). The tricyclics reduce the symptoms of depression in approximately 60 to 70 percent of cases. The tricyclics usually take two to four weeks to improve mood. Sometimes they have adverse side effects, such as restlessness, faintness, trembling, sleepiness, and difficulty remembering.

The *MAO (monoamine oxidase) inhibitors* reduces the ability of the enzyme monoamine oxidase to break down dopamine, norepinephrine, and serotonin, thus increasing the effect of these mood-elevating neurotransmitters. MAO inhibitors are not as widely used as the tricyclics because they are more toxic. However, some individuals who do not respond to the tricyclics do respond to the MAO inhibitors. The MAO inhibitors may be especially risky because of their potential interactions with certain foods and drugs. Cheese and other fermented foods, as well as some alcoholic beverages such as red wine, can interact with the MAO inhibitors to increase blood pressure and eventually cause a stroke.

Psychiatrists are increasingly prescribing a newer type of antidepressant drug called *selective serotonin reuptake inhibitors (SSRIs)*. SSRI drugs work mainly by interfering with the reabsorption of serotonin (5-HT) in the brain (Spiegel, 2003). Figure 14.1 shows how this process works.

antidepressant drugs Drugs that regulate mood.

Three widely prescribed SSRI antidepressants are fluoxetine (Prozac), paroxetine (Paxil), and sertraline (Zoloft). Their popularity is based on their effectiveness in reducing the symptoms of depression with fewer side effects than the other antidepressant drugs (Nemeroff & Schatzberg, 2002; Polsky & others, 2002). Nonetheless, they can have negative effects, including insomnia, anxiety, headache, and diarrhea. They can also impair sexual functioning and produce severe withdrawal symptoms if their use is ended too abruptly (Clayton & others, 2001). Most importantly, recent reports link antidepressant use with an increased risk of suicide (Culpepper & others, 2004).

Antidepressant drugs are not only used to treat mood disorders but are also often effective for a number of anxiety disorders, including generalized anxiety disorder, panic disorder, obsessive-compulsive disorder, social phobia, and post-traumatic stress disorder (Greist & others, 2003; Pollack & others, 2003; Stein & others, 2003; Van Ameringen & others, 2003). In addition, eating disorders, especially bulimia nervosa, may be amenable to treatment with antidepressant drugs (Devlin & others, 2000).

Although antidepressant drugs, especially the SSRI drugs, have been effective in treating many cases of depression, at least 25 percent of individuals with major depressive disorders do not respond to any antidepressant drug (Shelton & Hollon, 2000). Several factors related to nonresponse include the presence of a personality disorder or psychotic symptoms.

Lithium is widely used to treat bipolar disorder (Carney & Goodwin, 2005). The amount of lithium that circulates in the bloodstream must be carefully monitored because the effective dosage is precariously close to toxic levels. Kidney and thyroid gland complications can arise as a consequence of lithium therapy (Keck, McElroy, & Arnold, 2001).

The use of antidepressant drugs to treat depression is not without controversy. According to Breggin and Breggin (1995), some of the original studies of Prozac found that people taking a placebo actually became less depressed than those in the treatment group who were taking Prozac. The general question of the effectiveness of Prozac and other antidepressants, as compared with placebos, has since been a focus of ongoing investigations. One meta-analysis included 19 clinical double-blind trials involving 2318 patients randomly assigned to antidepressant or placebo conditions. The results revealed that placebos produced 75 percent of the effectiveness of actual drugs and that drug and placebo effects were very highly correlated (+.90). Further, active drugs that were not antidepressants also produced strong effects. The conclusion of the researchers was that the effects of antidepressant drugs may be due to an active placebo effect (Kirsch & Sapperstein, 1998).

Although this conclusion is open to argument (Gartlehner & others, 2004), it does raise the question of how a placebo might alleviate depression and just what depression is. Feeling down now and then is part of living and may be psychologically healthy in some cases. Immediately using drugs to treat common despondent moods, such as a "disorder," may interrupt normal processes of grieving or self-evaluation, possibly blocking healthy development. Also, a diet rich in refined carbohydrates and alcohol may produce some depression. The choice, then, may not be between Prozac and other antidepressant medications but between drug and "natural" interventions such as dietary improvements and exercise. Another benefit: such natural interventions do not have the side effects that antidepressants do, such as a tendency toward increased violence in some people and an increase in the risk of suicide.

lithium A drug that is widely used to treat bipolar disorder.

antipsychotic drugs Powerful drugs that diminish agitated behaviour, reduce tension, decrease hallucinations, improve social behaviour, and produce better sleep patterns in people who have a severe psychological disorder, such as schizophrenia.

Antipsychotic Drugs **Antipsychotic drugs** are powerful drugs that diminish agitated behaviour, reduce tension, decrease hallucinations, improve social behaviour, and produce better sleep patterns in individuals who have a severe psychological disorder, especially schizophrenia. Before antipsychotic drugs were developed in the 1950s, few, if any, interventions brought relief from the torment of psychotic symptoms. Once the effectiveness of these medications was apparent, the medical community significantly reduced more intrusive interventions, such as brain surgery, for schizophrenia (Spiegel, 2003).

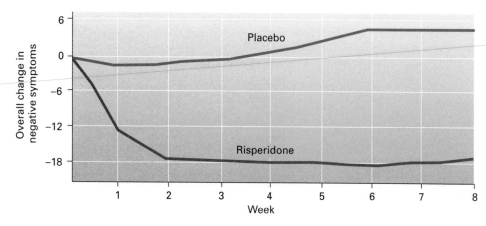

FIGURE 14.2 Effects of Risperidone (Risperdal) on Schizophrenics' Negative Symptoms
In one study, researchers found that by just one week after starting treatment with risperidone, negative symptoms (such as disorganized thought and uncontrolled hostility/excitement) were substantially reduced in schizophrenics. Negative symptoms in the placebo group actually increased slightly over the eight weeks of the study.

The *neuroleptics* are the most widely used class of antipsychotic drugs (Bradford, Stroup, & Lieberman, 2002). The most widely accepted explanation for the effectiveness of the neuroleptics is their ability to block the dopamine system's action in the brain. Schizophrenics have too much of the neurochemical messenger dopamine. Numerous well-controlled investigations reveal that when used in sufficient doses, the neuroleptics reduce a variety of schizophrenic symptoms, at least in the short term (Friedman, Temporini, & Davis, 1999; Tsirigotis & Gruszczynski, 2004).

The neuroleptics do not cure schizophrenia; they only treat the symptoms of schizophrenia, not its causes. If an individual with schizophrenia stops taking the drug, the symptoms return. Neuroleptic drugs have substantially reduced the length of hospital stays for individuals with schizophrenia. However, although these individuals are able to return to the community because drug therapy keeps their symptoms from reappearing, most have difficulty coping with the demands of society, and most are chronically unemployed. Also, the neuroleptics can have severe side effects.

Tardive dyskinesia is a major side effect of neuroleptics; it is a neurological disorder characterized by grotesque, involuntary movements of the facial muscles and mouth, as well as extensive twitching of the neck, arms, and legs. As many as 20 percent of individuals with schizophrenia who take neuroleptics develop this disorder. Older women are especially vulnerable. Long-term neuroleptic therapy is also associated with increased depression and anxiety. Nonetheless, for the majority of schizophrenics, the benefits of neuroleptic treatment outweigh its risk and discomforts.

A group of medications called *atypical antipsychotic medications* was introduced in the 1990s. Like the SSRI drugs, atypical antipsychotic medications block the reuptake of the neurotransmitter serotonin. The two most widely used drugs in this group are clozapine (Clozaril) and risperidone (Risperdal), which show promise for reducing schizophrenia's symptoms without the side effects of neuroleptics (Lublin, Eberhard, & Levander, 2005; Buckley & others, 2001). Figure 14.2 shows the substantial reduction in negative symptoms when schizophrenics take risperidone (Marder, Davis, & Chouinard, 1997).

Strategies to increase the effectiveness of the antipsychotic drugs involve administering small dosages over time, rather than a large initial dose, and combining drug therapy with psychotherapy. The fact that only a small percentage of schizophrenics are able to hold jobs suggests that drugs alone will not help them be contributing members of society. They also need training in vocational, family, and social skills.

A summary of the drugs used to treat various psychological disorders, the disorders for which they are used, their effectiveness, and their side effects are shown in figure 14.3. Notice that for some types of anxiety disorders, antidepressant drugs might be used rather than antianxiety drugs.

Psychological Disorder	Drug	Effectiveness	Side Effects
Everyday Anxiety and Anxiety Disorders			
Everyday anxiety	Antianxiety drugs; antidepressant drugs	Substantial improvement short-term	Antianxiety drugs: less powerful the longer people take them; may be addictive Antidepressant drugs: see below under depressive disorders
Generalized anxiety disorder	Antianxiety drugs SSRI drugs	Not very effective	Antianxiety drugs: less powerful the longer people take them; may be addictive SSRI drugs: fewer side-effects with longer-term use
Panic disorder	Antianxiety drugs SSRI drugs	About half show improvement	Antianxiety drugs: less powerful the longer people take them; may be addictive SSRI drugs: fewer side-effects with longer-term use
Agoraphobia	Tricyclic drugs and MAO inhibitors	Majority show improvement	Tricyclics: restlessness, fainting, and trembling MAO inhibitors: toxicity
Specific phobias	Antianxiety drugs	Not very effective	Less powerful the longer people take them; may be addictive
Mood Disorders			
Depressive disorders	Tricyclic drugs, MAO inhibitors, and SSRI drugs	Majority show moderate improvement	Tricylics: cardiac problems, mania, confusion, memory loss, fatigue MAO inhibitors: toxicity SSRI drugs: nausea, nervousness, insomnia, and in a few cases possible suicidal thoughts
Bipolar disorder	Lithium	Large majority show substantial improvement	Toxicity
Schizophrenic Disorders			
Schizophrenia	Neuroleptics; atypical antipsychotic medications	Majority show partial improvement	Neuroleptics: irregular heartbeat, low blood pressure, uncontrolled fidgeting, tardive dyskinesia, and immobility of face Atypical antipsychotic medications: Less extensive side effects than with neuroleptics, but can have a toxic effect on white blood cells.

FIGURE 14.3
Drug Therapy for Psychological Disorders

**electroconvulsive therapy
(ECT)** Commonly called shock therapy, this treatment is used for severely depressed individuals; it causes a seizure to occur in the brain.

Electroconvulsive Therapy

Electroconvulsive therapy (ECT), commonly called *shock therapy*, is used mainly to treat severely depressed individuals. The goal of ECT is to cause a seizure in the brain much like what happens spontaneously in some forms of epilepsy. A small electric current lasting for one second or less passes through two electrodes placed on the individual's head. The current excites neural tissue, stimulating a seizure that lasts for approximately one minute.

ECT has been used for more than 40 years. In earlier years it was often used indiscriminately, sometimes even to punish patients. ECT is still used with as many as 60,000 North Americans per year, mainly to treat major depressive disorder. Today ECT is given mainly to individuals who have not responded to drug therapy or psychotherapy. You may think that ECT would entail intolerable pain, but the manner in which it is administered today involves little discomfort. The patient is given anaesthesia and muscle relaxants before the current is applied; this allows the individual to sleep through the procedure, minimizes convulsions, and reduces the risk of physical injury. The individual awakens shortly afterward with no conscious memory of the treatment.

How effective is electroconvulsive therapy? Two meta-analyses of the use of electroconvulsive therapy have found that ECT is more effective in treating depression than antidepressant drugs (Pagnin & others, 2004; Carney & others, 2003).

Critics reply by noting that despite such positive findings, little is known about how ECT actually works. Further, usually ECT must be repeatedly administered. Also, most of the adverse side effects, such as memory loss and other cognitive impairments, are more severe than drug side effects, and in extreme cases can lead to brain damage. One possible exception is that ECT appears to reduce suicidal thinking (McCall, 2005) while antidepressants may actually increase it. A positive aspect of ECT is that its beneficial effects appear in a matter of days, whereas the beneficial effects of antidepressant drugs can take weeks, and those of cognitive therapy, months, to appear (Dannon & others, 2002).

Psychosurgery

Psychosurgery is a biological therapy that involves removing or destroying brain tissue to improve the individual's adjustment. The effects of psychosurgery are irreversible. In the 1930s, Portuguese physician Egas Moniz developed a procedure known as a *prefrontal*

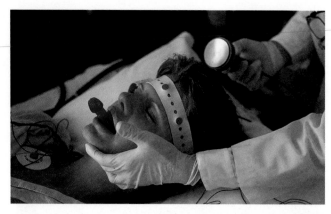

Electroconvulsive therapy (ECT), commonly called *shock therapy*, causes a seizure in the brain. ECT is still given to as many as 60,000 North Americans per year, mainly to treat major depressive disorder.

lobotomy. In this procedure, a surgical instrument is inserted into the brain and rotated, severing fibres that connect the frontal lobe, which is important in higher thought processes, and the thalamus, important in emotion. Moniz theorized that by severing the connections between these brain structures, the symptoms of severe mental disorders could be alleviated. Prefrontal lobotomies were conducted on thousands of patients from the 1930s through the 1950s. Moniz was awarded the Nobel Prize for his work (Tierney, 2000). However, whereas some patients may have benefited from the lobotomies, many were left in a vegetable-like state because of the massive assaults on their brains.

These crude lobotomies are no longer performed. Since the 1960s, psychosurgery has become more precise. When psychosurgery isperformed now , a small lesion is made in the amygdala or another part of the limbic system. Today, only a few hundred North Americans patients who have severely debilitating conditions undergo psychosurgery each year. It is used only as a last resort and with extreme caution.

> ## > reflect and review
>
> **1** **Describe the biological therapies.**
>
> - Identify the types of drugs used to treat psychological disorders and evaluate their effects.
> - Explain what electroconvulsive therapy is and when it is used.
> - Discuss psychosurgery.
>
> *Before prescribing drug therapy for an individual, what might be some important factors for a psychiatrist or other medical doctor (such as a general practitioner) to consider?*

② PSYCHOTHERAPIES

— Psychodynamic — Humanistic — Behaviour — Cognitive
Therapies   Therapies   Therapies   Therapies

What is psychotherapy and what are the four main types of psychotherapy?

Psychotherapy is the process used by mental health professionals to help individuals recognize, define, and overcome their psychological and interpersonal difficulties and improve their adjustment. Psychotherapists use a number of strategies to accomplish these goals: talking, interpreting, listening, rewarding, and modelling, for example. Both psychologists and psychiatrists use psychotherapy in treating people who have psychological problems (Prochaska, 2003).

psychosurgery A biological therapy that involves removal or destruction of brain tissue to improve an individual's adjustment.

"Looking good!"

© The New Yorker Collection 1994. Gahan Wilson from cartoonbank.com. All Rights Reserved.

This section focuses on four main approaches to psychotherapy: psychodynamic, humanistic, behavioural, and cognitive. The term **insight therapy** characterizes both psychodynamic and humanistic therapies, because they encourage insight and self-awareness. The psychodynamic therapies are the oldest of these approaches.

Psychodynamic Therapies

The **psychodynamic therapies** stress the importance of the unconscious mind, extensive interpretation by the therapist, and the role of early-childhood experiences in the development of an individual's problems. The goal of the psychodynamic therapies is to help individuals recognize the maladaptive ways in which they have been coping with problems and the sources of their unconscious conflicts (Nolen-Hoeksema, 2004). Many psychodynamic approaches grew out of Freud's psychoanalytic theory of personality. Today some therapists with a psychodynamic perspective practise Freudian techniques, but others do not (Moursund, 2004).

Freud's Psychoanalysis Freud once said that if you give psychoanalysis your little finger, it will soon have your whole hand. As you read about the basic philosophy of psychoanalysis and its therapy techniques, you will see that Freud believed that the therapist acts like a psychological detective, sometimes taking the smallest clue and using it as a springboard for understanding the individual's major problems. The following shows how one analyst approached an individual's problems (Davison & Neale, 1994):

> A 50-year-old business executive came to therapy because he felt depressed and anxious and these feelings would not go away. Although he was perceived as being very successful by his family and business associates, he perceived himself to be weak and incompetent. Through many sessions, the psychoanalyst had begun to suspect that the man's feelings of failure stemmed from his childhood experiences with a critical and punitive father. The father never seemed satisfied with the son's efforts. Following is an exchange between the analyst and the businessman that occurred one year into therapy:
>
> Client: "I don't really feel like talking today."
>
> Analyst: Remains silent for several minutes, then says, "Perhaps you would like to talk about why you don't feel like talking."
>
> Client: "There you go again, making demands on me, insisting I do what I just don't feel up to doing. (Pause) Do I always have to talk here, when I don't feel like it? (Voice becomes angry and petulant) Can't you just get off my back? You don't really care how I feel."
>
> Analyst: "I wonder why you feel I don't care?"
>
> Client: "Because you're always pressuring me to do what I feel I can't do."

This exchange was interpreted by the analyst as an expression of resentment by the client of his father's pressures that were put on him and had little to do with the analyst himself. The transfer of the client's feelings from the father to the analyst was regarded as significant by the analyst and was used in subsequent sessions to help the client overcome his fear of expressing anger toward his father.

Psychoanalysis is Freud's therapeutic technique for analyzing an individual's unconscious thoughts. Freud believed that clients' current problems could be traced to childhood experiences, many of which involved conflicts about sexuality. He also recognized that the early experiences were not readily available to the individual's conscious mind. Only through extensive questioning, probing, and analyzing was Freud able to put the pieces of the person's personality together and help the individual become aware of how these early experiences were affecting present adult behaviour.

insight therapy Encourages insight and self-awareness; includes the psychodynamic and humanistic therapies.

psychodynamic therapies Stress the importance of the unconscious mind, extensive interpretation by the therapist, and the role of experiences in the early-childhood years. The goal of the psychodynamic therapies is to help individuals recognize their maladaptive ways of coping and the sources of their unconscious conflicts.

psychoanalysis Freud's psychotherapeutic technique for analyzing an individual's unconscious thoughts. Freud believed that clients' current problems could be traced to childhood experiences, involving conflicts about sexuality.

To encourage his patients to relax, Freud had them recline on this couch while he sat in the chair on the left, out of their view.

To reach the shadowy world of the unconscious, psychoanalytic therapists often use the following therapeutic techniques: free association, catharsis, interpretation, dream analysis, analysis of transference, and analysis of resistance, each of which we discuss in turn.

Free association consists of encouraging individuals to say aloud whatever comes to mind no matter how trivial or embarrassing (Hoffer & Youngren, 2004). When Freud detected a person resisting the spontaneous flow of thoughts, he probed further. He believed that the crux of the person's emotional problem probably lurked below this point of resistance. Encouraging people to talk freely, Freud thought, would help emotional feelings to emerge. **Catharsis** is the psychoanalytic term for the release of emotional tension a person experiences when reliving an emotionally charged and conflicting experience.

Interpretation plays an important role in psychoanalysis. As the therapist interprets free association and dreams, the person's statements and behaviour are not taken at face value. To understand what is truly causing the person's conflicts, the therapist constantly searches for symbolic, hidden meanings in what the individual says and does. From time to time the therapist suggests possible meanings of the person's statements and behaviour.

The following case study reveals how a psychoanalyst used interpretation to improve a woman's understanding of her problems (Langs, 1978):

> Mrs. A. H. began her session with a psychoanalyst by describing how her husband, a businessman, had been caught in a financial squeeze and had anxiously gone to the bank to raise additional funds. She was in a state of panic, even though there was a good chance that her husband would be able to obtain a loan from the bank. The previous night she had diarrhea and had dreamed that her two sisters were discussing her mother, saying that she seldom did all that she promised to others. Mrs. A. H. then commented that her mother had been wealthy and could have provided all the money her husband needed. Her father could have too, she said, but he was hard to deal with. She went on to recall her mother's involvement with another man and the illness her mother had when Mrs. A. H. was an infant. Her sisters, who were considerably older, had taken care of their mother, but Mrs. A. H. wondered why they criticized her mother who had been briefly hospitalized. They tended to blame poor health habits for her illness. Mrs. A. H. also reviewed her adolescent years, during which her mother denied the impact of her absence. She thought her mother's attitude was rather strange.
>
> The psychoanalytic session seemed to be prompted by her husband's financial crisis and the repercussions it had for Mrs. A. H.'s longings for her mother, who would rescue her and

free association The psychoanalytic technique of having individuals say aloud whatever comes into their minds.

catharsis The psychoanalytic term for people's release of emotional tension when they relive an emotionally charged and conflicting experience.

Sexual Theme	Objects or Activities in Dreams That Symbolize Sexual Themes
Male genitals, especially penis	Umbrellas, knives, poles, swords, airplanes, guns, serpents, neckties, tree trunks, hoses
Female genitals, especially vagina	Boxes, caves, pockets, pouches, the mouth, jewel cases, ovens, closets
Sexual intercourse	Climbing, swimming, flying, riding (a horse, an elevator, a roller coaster)
Parents	Kings, queens, emperors, empresses
Siblings	Little animals

FIGURE 14.4

Freudian Interpretation of Sexual Symbolism in Dreams
The painting is the right panel (Hell) from the *Garden of Earthly Delight*, painted around 1500 by Hieronymus Bosch.

her husband; her rage at her mother for her absence and possible unfaithfulness; and some implied concerns regarding her husband's ability to handle the business situation. There was little in the session to suggest what unconscious thoughts were evoking the gastrointestinal symptoms.

However, this session is intriguing in the light of the next session that took place. In that session, Mrs. A. H. revealed that she inadvertently had forgotten to mention an incident that had occurred prior to the previous session. One of her girlfriends had seen her husband having a drink at a local restaurant with an attractive woman. In this context, the psychoanalyst was able to gain more insight into what Mrs. A. H. had said in the previous session. In fact, she had used the past to conceal the present. She had used her mother as a screen to hide her most active and meaningful conflicts and unconscious fantasies about her husband. In the second session, her free associations related to fears of finding out that her husband was having an affair, to her dread of confronting him, and to her anxiety that others would be talking about his having an affair. The associations revealed her rage, her wishes to humiliate him in public, and her death wishes toward him. The sister in the dream had also been suspected of having an affair. The bowel symptoms actually related to fantasies of defecating on and soiling her husband in an uncontrolled release of aggression, according to the analyst.

Dream analysis is the psychotherapeutic technique used by psychoanalysts to interpret a person's dream. Psychoanalysts believe dreams contain information about the individual's unconscious thoughts and conflicts. Freud distinguished between the dream's manifest and latent content. *Manifest content* is the psychoanalytic term for the conscious, remembered aspects of a dream. *Latent content* is the psychoanalytic term for the unconscious, unremembered, symbolic aspects of a dream. The psychoanalyst interprets the dream by analyzing the manifest content for disguised unconscious wishes and needs, especially those that are sexual and aggressive in nature. For some examples of the sexual symbols psychoanalysts use to interpret dreams, see figure 14.4. But even Freud cautioned against overinterpreting. As he once quipped, "Sometimes a cigar is just a cigar."

© The New Yorker Collection 1973. Dana Fradon from cartoonbank.com. All Rights Reserved.

Freud believed transference was an inevitable and essential aspect of the analyst-patient relationship. **Transference** is the psychoanalytic term for the person's relating to the analyst in ways that reproduce or relive important relationships in the individual's life. A person might interact with an analyst as if the analyst were a parent or lover, for example. When transference dominates therapy, the person's comments may become directed toward the analyst's personal life. Transference is often difficult to overcome in psychotherapy. However, transference can be used therapeutically as a model of how individuals relate to important people in their lives (Marcus, 2002). *Counter-transference* occurs when the analyst relates to the patient in ways that echo important relationships in the therapist's life. When appropriately contained by the analyst, counter-transference can be an important element in analysis (Vaslamatzis, 2005). Otherwise, counter-transference can interfere with analysis.

Resistance is the psychoanalytic term for the person's unconscious defence strategies that prevent the analyst from understanding the person's problems. Resistance occurs because it is painful to bring conflicts into conscious awareness. By resisting therapy, individuals do not have to face their problems. Showing up late or missing sessions, arguing with the psychoanalyst, or faking free associations are examples of resistance. Some people go on endlessly about a trivial matter to avoid facing their conflicts. A major goal of the analyst is to break through this resistance (Davy & Cross, 2004).

Contemporary Psychodynamic Therapies Although the face of psychodynamic therapy has changed extensively since its inception almost a century ago, many contemporary psychodynamic therapists still probe a person's unconscious thoughts about early childhood experiences to obtain clues to the person's current problems (Teyber, 2006; Sugarman & DePottel, 2002). Many contemporary psychodynamic therapists also try to help individuals gain insight into their emotionally laden, repressed conflicts (Ogden, 2005; Sonnenberg & Ursano, 2002). Today, only a small percentage of psychodynamic therapists rigorously follow Freud's guidelines. Although many psychodynamic therapists still emphasize the importance of unconscious thought and early family experiences, they also accord more power to the conscious mind, current relationships, and emotions (Greenberg & Paivio, 1997; Orfanos, 2002) in understanding a person's problems.

When psychoanalysis is practised today, it can still involve more than one session per week over a period of many years. Just like psychoanalysis, some contemporary psychodynamic therapies can be intensive and extensive, also lasting for years. However, in many cases, contemporary psychodynamic therapy is shorter, involving a few months rather than many years, even in dramatic cases (e.g. Ryle, 2005).

Contemporary psychodynamic approaches emphasize the development of the self in social contexts (Erikson, 1968; Kohut, 1977; Ogden, 2005). In Heinz Kohut's view, early relationships with attachment figures, such as one's parents, are critical (Banai, Mikulincer, & Shaver, 2005). As we develop we do not relinquish these attachments; we continue to need them. Kohut's prescription for therapy involves getting the person to identify and seek out appropriate relationships with others. He also wants individuals to develop more realistic appraisals of relationships. Kohut (1977) believes therapists need to interact with individuals in ways that are empathic and understanding. Empathy and understanding are absolute cornerstones for humanistic therapists, who encourage individuals to further their sense of self.

Humanistic Therapies

The underlying philosophy of humanistic therapies is captured by the metaphor of how an acorn, if provided with appropriate conditions, will grow in positive ways, pushing naturally toward its actualization as an oak (Corey, 2005; Schneider, 2002). In the **humanistic therapies**, people are encouraged to understand themselves and to grow personally. The humanistic therapies are unique in their emphasis on the person's self-healing capacities. In contrast to the psychodynamic therapies, the humanistic therapies emphasize conscious rather than unconscious thoughts, the present rather than the past, and growth and self-fulfillment rather than illness.

dream analysis The psychotherapeutic technique used by psychoanalysts to interpret a person's dream. Psychoanalysts believe dreams contain information about the individual's unconscious thoughts and conflicts.

transference The psychoanalytic term for the person's relating to the analyst in ways that reproduce or relive important relationships in the individual's life.

resistance The psychoanalytic term for the person's unconscious defence strategies that prevent the analyst from understanding the person's problems.

humanistic therapies Encourage people to understand themselves and to grow personally. The humanistic therapies are unique in their emphasis on self-healing capacities.

FREDERICK (FRITZ) PERLS (1893–1970)

The founder of gestalt therapy.

active listening: feed back what client FELT not said.

Client-Centred Therapy

Therapist: Everything's lousy, huh? You feel lousy. [Silence of 39 seconds]

Want to come in Friday at 12 at the usual time?

Client: [Yawns and mutters something unintelligible. Silence of 48 seconds]

Therapist: Just kind of feel sunk way down deep in those lousy, lousy feelings, hm? Is that something like it?

Client: No.

Therapist: No? [Silence of 20 seconds]

Client: No. I'm just no good to anybody, never was, and never will be.

Therapist: Feeling that now, hm? That you're no good to yourself, no good to anybody. Just that you're completely worthless, huh? Those are really lousy feelings. Just feel that you're no good at all, hm?

This is an excerpt from a therapy session conducted by a client-centred therapist with a young man who was depressed. The therapist was Carl Rogers (Meador & Rogers, 1979). Notice how Rogers unconditionally accepted the client's feelings. **Client-centred therapy** is a form of humanistic therapy developed by Carl Rogers (1961, 1980), in which the therapist provides a warm, supportive atmosphere to improve the client's self-concept and encourage the client to gain insight about problems. Compared with psychodynamic therapies, which emphasize analysis and interpretation by the therapist, the client-centred approach places far more emphasis on the client's self-reflection (Kirschenbaum & Jourdan, 2005).

The relationship between the therapist and the person is an important aspect of Rogers's therapy. The therapist must enter into an intensely personal relationship with the client, not as a physician diagnosing a disease but as one human being to another. Consistent with his vision, Rogers referred to the "client" and, later in his career, the "person," but never the "patient."

You might recall from chapter 12 that Rogers believed each of us grows up with a sense of worth we receive from others that has strings attached; in other words, with *conditional positive regard*. We usually do not receive love and praise unless we conform to the standards and demands of others. This causes us to be unhappy and have low self-esteem. Rarely do we feel that we measure up to such standards or that we are as good as others expect us to be.

To free a person from worry about society's demands, the therapist engages in *unconditional positive regard*, in which the therapist creates a warm and caring environment, never disapproving of the client. Rogers believed this unconditional positive regard improves the person's self-esteem. The therapist's role is *nondirective*, that is, he or she does not lead the client to any particular revelation. The therapist is there to listen sympathetically to the client's problems and to encourage positive self-regard, independent self-appraisal, and decision making. Though client-centred therapists give approval of the person, they do not always approve of the person's behaviour.

In addition to unconditional positive regard, Rogers advocated the use of these three techniques in client-centred therapy:

- *Genuineness* (also called *congruence*), which involves letting a client know the therapist's feelings and not hiding behind a facade.
- *Active listening*, which consists of giving total attention to what the person says and means. One way therapists improve active listening is to restate and support what the client has said and done.
- *Empathic understanding*, which focuses on the therapist's identification with the client. Rogers believed that therapists must sense what it is like to be the client at any moment in the client–therapist relationship.

Gestalt Therapy **Gestalt therapy** is a humanistic therapy developed by Fritz Perls (1893–1970), in which the therapist challenges clients to help them become more aware of their feelings and face their problems. Perls was trained in Europe as a Freudian psychoanalyst, but he developed his own ideas and eventually parted from some of Freud's teachings.

client-centred therapy Rogers's humanistic therapy in which the therapist provides a warm, supportive atmosphere to improve the client's self-concept and encourage the client to gain insight about problems.

gestalt therapy Perls's humanistic therapy in which the therapist challenges clients to help them become more aware of their feelings and face their problems.

Perls (1969) agreed with Freud that psychological problems originate in unresolved past conflicts and that these conflicts need to be acknowledged and worked through. Also like Freud, Perls stressed that interpretation of dreams is an important aspect of therapy. But, in other ways, Perls and Freud were far apart. Perls believed that unresolved conflicts should be brought to bear on the here and now of the individual's life. The therapist *pushes* clients into deciding whether they will continue to allow the past to control their future or whether they will choose right now what they want to be in the future. To this end, Perls both confronted individuals and encouraged them to actively control their lives and to be open about their feelings (Rosenberg & Lynch, 2002).

Gestalt therapists use a number of techniques to encourage individuals to be open about their feelings, to develop self-awareness, and to actively control their lives. The therapist sets examples, encourages congruence between verbal and nonverbal behaviour, and uses role playing. To stimulate change, the therapist often openly confronts the client. To demonstrate an important point to a client, the Gestalt therapist might exaggerate a client's characteristics.

In the following excerpt from a gestalt therapy session, the therapist (in this case, gestalt therapy founder Fritz Perls) exaggerates a phrase the client uses:

Perls: Now talk to your Top Dog! Stop nagging.

Jane: [Loud, pained] Leave me alone.

Perls: Yah, again.

Jane: Leave me alone.

Perls: Again.

Jane: [Screaming it and crying] Leave me alone!

Perls: Again.

Jane: [She screams it, a real blast.] Leave me alone! I don't have to do what you say! [Still crying] I don't have to be in this chair! I don't have to. You make me. You make me come here! [Screams] Aarhh. You make me pick my face [crying], that's what you do. [Screams and cries] Aarhh! I'd like to kill you.

Perls: Say this again.

Jane: I'd like to kill you.

Perls: Again.

Jane: I'd like to kill you.

Another technique used in gestalt therapy is role playing, either by the client, the therapist, or both. For example, if an individual is bothered by conflict with her mother, the therapist might play the role of the mother and reopen the quarrel. The therapist might encourage the individual to act out her hostile feelings toward her mother by yelling, swearing, or kicking the couch, for example. In this way, gestalt therapists hope to help individuals better manage their feelings instead of letting their feelings control them.

As you probably noticed, the gestalt therapist is much more directive than the client-centred therapist. By being more directive, the gestalt therapist provides more interpretation and feedback (Zahm & Gold, 2002). Nonetheless, both of these humanistic therapies encourage individuals to take responsibility for their feelings and actions, to truly be themselves, to understand themselves, to develop a sense of freedom, and to look at what they are doing with their lives.

Behaviour Therapies

Having explored the insight therapies—the psychodynamic and humanistic approaches— we turn to therapies that take a different approach to reducing people's problems and improving their adjustment: the behaviour therapies. Behaviour therapies offer action-oriented strategies to help people change what they are doing (L. K. Miller, 2006; Spiegler & Guevremont, 2003).

Behaviour therapies use principles of learning to reduce or eliminate maladaptive behaviour. Behaviour therapies are based on the behavioural and social cognitive theories of learning and personality. Behaviour therapists do not search for unconscious

behaviour therapy Uses principles of learning to reduce or eliminate maladaptive behaviour. It places an emphasis on self-healing capacities.

1. A month before an examination
2. Two weeks before an examination
3. A week before an examination
4. Five days before an examination
5. Four days before an examination
6. Three days before an examination
7. Two days before an examination
8. One day before an examination
9. The night before an examination
10. On the way to the university on the day of an examination
11. Before the unopened doors of the examination room
12. Awaiting distribution of examination papers
13. The examination paper lies face-down before her
14. In the process of answering the exam questions

FIGURE 14.5

A Desensitization Hierarchy Involving Test Anxiety
In the above hierarchy, the individual begins with her least feared circumstance (a month before the exam) and moves through each of the circumstances until reaching her most feared circumstance (being in the process of answering the exam questions). At each step of the way, the person replaces fear with deep relaxation and successful visualizations.

systematic desensitization A method of behaviour therapy based on classical conditioning that treats anxiety by getting the person to associate deep relaxation with increasingly intense anxiety-producing situations.

conflicts, as psychodynamic therapists do, or encourage individuals to develop accurate perceptions of their feelings and selves as humanistic therapists do. Insight and self-awareness are not the keys to helping individuals develop more adaptive behaviour patterns, say the behaviour therapists.

Behaviour therapists assume that the overt maladaptive symptoms are the problem (Miltenberger, 2004). Individuals can become aware of why they are depressed and still be depressed, say the behaviour therapists. The behaviour therapist tries to eliminate the depressed symptoms or behaviours themselves rather than trying to get individuals to gain insight or awareness of why they are depressed (Forsyth & Savsevitz, 2002; Lazarus, 1996).

The behaviour therapies were initially based almost exclusively on the learning principles of classical and operant conditioning. As social cognitive theory grew in popularity, however, behaviour therapists increasingly included observational learning, cognitive factors, and self-instruction in their efforts to help people with their problems (Meichenbaum, 1977, 1991, 2003; Andersson & others, 2005). In self-instruction, therapists try to get people to change what they say to themselves. We will have more to say about these self-instructional strategies later in this section and in the next chapter when we discuss coping with stress. For now, though, we'll focus on classical and operant conditioning.

Techniques Based on Classical Conditioning Some behaviours, especially fears, can be acquired or learned through classical conditioning. If such fears can be learned, possibly they can be unlearned as well (S. E. Taylor, 2002a). If an individual has learned to fear snakes or heights through classical conditioning, perhaps the individual can unlearn the fear through counterconditioning. Two types of counterconditioning involve systematic desensitization and aversive conditioning.

Systematic Desensitization **Systematic desensitization** is a behaviour therapy method based on classical conditioning that treats anxiety by getting the person to associate deep relaxation with increasingly intense anxiety-producing situations (Wolpe, 1963). Consider the common fear of taking an exam. Using systematic desensitization, the behaviour therapist first asks the person which aspects of the feared situation—in this case, taking an exam—are the most and least frightening. Then the behaviour therapist arranges these circumstances in order from most to least frightening. An example of this type of desensitization hierarchy is shown in figure 14.5.

The next step is to teach individuals to relax. Clients are taught to recognize the presence of muscular contractions or tensions in various parts of their bodies and then how to contract and relax different muscles. Once individuals are relaxed, the therapist asks them to imagine the least feared stimulus in the hierarchy. Subsequently, the therapist moves up the list of items, from least to most feared, while clients remain relaxed. Eventually, individuals are able to imagine the most fearsome circumstance without being afraid—in our example, being in the process of answering exam questions. In this manner, individuals learn to relax while thinking about the exam instead of feeling anxious.

FIGURE 14.6
Systematic Desensitization
Systematic desensitization is often used to help eliminate phobias. In this systematic desensitization treatment, the individual progresses from handling rubber snakes (*top left*), to peering at snakes in an aquarium (*top right*), to handling snakes with rubber gloves (*bottom left*), to handling live but harmless snakes (*bottom right*).

Researchers have found that systematic desensitization is often an effective treatment for a number of phobias, such as fear of giving a speech, fear of heights, fear of flying, fear of dogs, and fear of snakes (Barlow, 2001). If you were afraid of snakes, for instance, the therapist might initially have you watch someone handle a snake. Then the therapist would ask you to engage in increasingly more feared behaviours—you might first just go into the same room with the snake, next you would approach the snake, subsequently you'd touch the snake, and eventually you would play with the snake. Figure 14.6 shows a desensitization treatment with individuals who were afraid of snakes.

Desensitization involves exposing someone to a feared situation in a real or imagined way. A more intense form of exposure involves *flooding*, which consists of exposing individuals to feared stimuli or situations to an excessive degree while not allowing them to avoid the object or situation (Miller, 2002). The following case reveals how flooding works (Meyer & Osborne, 1982):

> A 45-year-old divorced woman suffered from an obsessive-compulsive disorder that involved washing and cleansing rituals whenever she came into contact with objects she thought might be even remotely linked with death. For example, holding a newspaper article about someone she did not know who had been killed made her intensely anxious. The disorder first occurred when she was 15 years old, at the time of her mother's death.
>
> When the woman sought treatment, she was to be remarried in two weeks. She did not believe that she could handle the marriage in her current condition of almost daily experiencing panic attacks related to her fear of contamination. The therapist used flooding to alleviate her problem. Most of the treatment took place in her home, although the first treatment was in a hospital mortuary. There the woman and the therapist became "contaminated" by handling a corpse, which produced intense anxiety. Later, the therapist gave her "contaminated" objects related to death, such as newspaper articles about death, photographs of funerals, dead animal meat, and so on, in her home during hour-long therapy sessions. After 12 days of flooding, the woman reported considerable progress and was married.

With the advent of more sophisticated computer technologies, virtual reality systems have come to play an increasing role in therapies based on systematic desensitization and flooding. To learn more about the role of virtual reality in therapy see the Critical Reflections box.

Virtual Reality Therapy

Imagine what life was like for Miss Muffet:

Our first spider-phobia patient, nick-named Miss Muffet, had suffered from this anxiety disorder for nearly 20 years and had acquired a number of obsessive-compulsive behaviours. She routinely fumigated her car with smoke and pesticides to get rid of spiders. Every night she sealed all her bedroom windows with duct tape after scanning the room for spiders. She searched for the arachnids wherever she went and avoided walkways where she might find one. After washing her clothes, she immediately sealed them inside a plastic bag to make sure they remained free of spiders. Over the years her condition grew worse. When her fear made her hesitant to leave home, she finally sought therapy (Hoffman, 2004).

Systematic desensitization has a new format. Virtual reality technology is being used by some therapists to expose individuals to more vivid situations than their imagination might generate. Here, an individual with a fear of spiders is wearing a virtual reality headset and has become immersed in a vivid, three-dimensional world in which spiders appear very real.

Any yet, after just ten one-hour sessions, Miss Muffet, Hunter Hoffman's first spider-phobia patient, was able to allow a live tarantula to crawl up her arm. Hoffman, of the University of Washington, in Seattle, achieved this dramatic success using virtual reality therapy. The patient wears a headset that projects slightly different images to each eye, creating a vivid, three-dimensional image. She also uses a glove or a joystick to move around in this world. While the resulting experience not quite as immersive as the world imagined in the Wachowski brother's Matrix movies, it can be quite compelling.

Virtual reality therapy is the use of digital technology to create virtual experiences that are therapeutically helpful. Miss Muffet used a joystick to manoeuvre herself closer and closer to a virtual tarantula in a virtual kitchen. Then she wore a glove that she could experience in the virtual spider world to "touch" the spider. In the end she also touched a toy spider while also touching the spider in the virtual world, to add in the feeling of the furry little object.

Researchers like Hoffman have been especially enthusiastic about the use of virtual reality therapy in the treatment of phobias, including arachnophobia (fear of spiders; Hoffman & others, 2003), aviophobia (fear of flying; Arbona & others, 2004), as well as acrophobia (fear of heights), claustrophobia (fear of enclosed spaces), fear of medical procedures, fear of driving, and social phobia (Wiederhold & Wiederhold, 2005). Virtual reality treatments have also been created for other psychological disorders (Giuseppe, 2005) such as eating disorders (Myers & others, 2004) and other anxiety disorders such as, including panic disorder, obsessive-compulsive disorder, and post-traumatic stress disorder (Wiederhold & Wiederhold, 2005).

Because virtual reality therapy is based on proven behavioural techniques, it is, in principle, applicable in a wide variety of situations. To date it has been exceptionally useful in implementing systematic desensitization and flooding. In these contexts, virtual reality therapy offers some unique advantages as well. One traditional method of implementing systematic desensitization and flooding is though active visualization. A patient with a phobia of, say, cockroaches, might be asked to visualize the insects coming progressively closer. Compared with active imagining, virtual reality therapy can offer most patients more vivid images than those they can create for themselves.

The other traditional method is *in vivo* exposure. Patients encounter the source of their fears in the real world. For someone with ophidiophobia (fear of snakes), an actual snake would be used as a part of the therapy. But this is not always practical. With virtual reality therapy a patient with fear of flying can experience the fearful situation without actually paying to go up in an airplane. Someone with a fear of height can experience being 50 stories up in a glass elevator without traveling to a tall building and someone with a war-related post-traumatic stress disorder can re-experience battlefield trauma without going back into combat.

Aside from practicality, virtual reality therapy also allows the therapist to exercise precise control over what the patient experiences and patient can feel safer in the privacy of the therapist's office (Botella & others, 2004). These advantages, coupled with evidence that virtual reality therapy is just as at least as effective as traditional methods (e.g. Klinger & others, 2005), guarantees a bright future for this innovative technology.

What do you think?

- Do you think virtual reality offers an effective alternative to in vivo exposure?
- Would you avail yourself of virtual reality therapy if it was appropriate? Why? Why not?

Aversive Conditioning The other behaviour therapy technique involving classical conditioning is **aversive conditioning**, which consists of repeated pairings of the undesirable behaviour with aversive stimuli to decrease the behaviour's rewards. Aversive conditioning is used to teach people to avoid such behaviours as smoking, eating, and drinking. Electric shocks, nausea-inducing substances, and verbal insults are some of the noxious stimuli used in aversive conditioning. How could aversive conditioning be

aversive conditioning A classical conditioning treatment which consists of repeated pairings of the undesirable behaviour with aversive stimuli to decrease the behaviour's rewards.

used to reduce a person's alcohol consumption? Every time a person drank an alcoholic beverage, he or she also would consume a mixture that induced nausea. In classical conditioning terminology, the alcoholic beverage is the conditioned stimulus and the nausea-inducing agent is the unconditioned stimulus. By repeatedly pairing alcohol with the nausea-inducing agent, alcohol becomes the conditioned stimulus that elicits nausea, the conditioned response. As a consequence, alcohol is no longer associated with something pleasant but rather something highly unpleasant. Figure 14.7 illustrates how classical conditioning is the backbone of aversive conditioning.

Operant Conditioning Approaches The basic philosophy of using operant conditioning as a therapy approach is that, because maladaptive behaviour patterns are learned, they can be unlearned. Therapy involves conducting a careful analysis of the person's environment to determine what factors need to be modified (L. K. Miller, 2006). Especially important is changing the consequences of the person's behaviour to ensure that behavioural responses are followed by positive reinforcement.

Operant therapy's techniques focus on **behaviour modification**, the application of operant conditioning principles to change human behaviour; its main goal is to replace unacceptable, maladaptive behaviours with acceptable, adaptive ones. Consequences for behaviour are established to ensure that acceptable actions are reinforced and unacceptable ones are not (Kearney & Vecchio, 2002; Poling & Carr, 2002). Advocates of behaviour modification believe that many emotional and behavioural problems are caused by inadequate (or inappropriate) response consequences (Miltenberger, 2004).

A behaviour modification system in which behaviours are reinforced with tokens (such as poker chips) that later can be exchanged for desired rewards (such as candy, money, or going to a movie) is called a *token economy*. Token economies have been established in classrooms, institutions for the mentally retarded, homes for young offenders, and mental hospitals (Field & others, 2004).

Behaviour modification does not always work. One person may become so wedded to the tokens that when they are no longer given, the positive behaviour associated with them may disappear. Yet, another person might continue the positive behaviour without the tokens as rewards. Some critics object to behaviour modification because they believe such extensive control of another person's behaviour unethically infringes on the individual's rights. But, as in the case of the university student with an intense fear of exams, maladaptive responses can be turned into adaptive ones through behaviour modification.

To end this discussion of behaviour therapies, consider a case in which behaviour modification helped an individual replace maladaptive responses with more adaptive ones to reduce his depression (Rosenfeld, 1985):

> Henry Greene is a 36-year-old lawyer who wrestled with depression for months before finally seeking psychotherapy. His initial complaints were physical—fitful sleep, often ending at 3 a.m., lack of appetite, weight loss of 15 pounds, and a disinterest in sex. Henry began to move more slowly and his voice became monotonous. He reached the point where he could hardly bear to cope with life. Henry finally let his guard down and confessed that, although he looked successful on the outside, he felt like a failure on the inside. He said that he actually was a third-rate lawyer, husband, lover, and father. He felt that he was bound to remain that way.

How would a behaviourist treat Henry Greene? Peter Lewinsohn and his colleagues (1984) developed the "Coping with Depression Course" for such individuals. A basic principle of this approach is that feelings are caused by behaviours. Behaviour therapists encourage people to increase the ratio of positive life events to negative life events

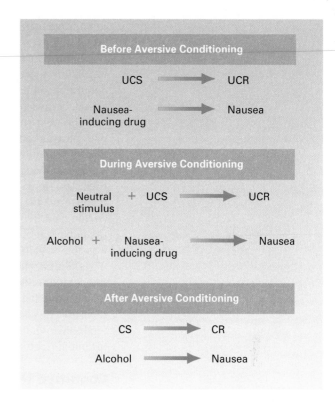

FIGURE 14.7

Classical Conditioning: The Backbone of Aversive Conditioning The above illustrates how classical conditioning can provide a conditional aversion to alcohol. After the association of the drug with alcohol, the alcohol becomes a conditioned stimulus for nausea. Recall these abbreviations: UCS (unconditioned stimulus), UCR (unconditioned response), CS (conditioned stimulus), and CR (conditioned response).

behaviour modification The application of operant conditioning principles to change human behaviours, especially to replace unacceptable, maladaptive behaviours with acceptable, adaptive behaviours.

to improve their mood. To accomplish the desired ratio, most individuals require a variety of skill exercises.

Henry Greene was first given the assignment of monitoring his moods. This task forced him to pay attention to his daily mood changes, and the information was used to determine which events are associated with which moods. Relaxation training followed, because relaxation skills improve an individual's sense of well-being.

The next step for Henry Greene was to determine how his moods are associated with pleasant and unpleasant events in his life. Henry was asked to fill out a "Pleasant Events Schedule" and an "Unpleasant Events Schedule." Each week, Henry completed a graph showing the number of pleasant and unpleasant events, as well as his mood, for each day. Henry was able to see a close relation between pleasant events and pleasant moods and between unpleasant events and unpleasant moods. The therapist then encouraged Henry to increase the amount of time he spends in pleasant activities with the hope that more positive moods would follow. The positive outcome was that Henry was able to gain control over his moods.

The final stage for Henry was maintenance planning. Henry was asked to identify the components of behaviour therapy that were the most successful in changing his maladaptive behaviour. Once Henry identified these, he was encouraged to continue their use. He also was required to develop emergency plans for those times when stress might overwhelm him. Henry continued to go to follow-up sessions for six months after his initial treatment.

Cognitive Therapies

Rahul, an undergraduate, thinks he is a failure in school and to his parents. He is preoccupied with negative thoughts, dwells on his problems, and exaggerates his faults. According to University of Calgary psychologist Keith Dobson, cognitive therapies were developed to help alter such thinking, which is common among depressed individuals (Dobson, 2001; Dobson & Dozois, 2001; Dozois & Dobson, 2004). The **cognitive therapies** emphasize that individuals' cognitions or thoughts are the main source of abnormal behaviour and psychological problems. Cognitive therapies use cognitive restructuring to change a pattern of thought that is presumed to be causing maladaptive behaviour or emotion. Cognitive therapies differ from psychoanalytic therapies by focusing on overt symptoms instead of unconscious thoughts, by structuring the individual's thoughts, and by being less concerned about the origin of the problem (Dobson, Backs-Dermott, & Dozois, 2000). Cognitive therapies differ from humanistic therapies by providing more structure, more analysis, and more specific cognitive techniques. Cognitive therapies have been applied to depression (Dozois & Dobson, 2004), panic disorder (Chambless & Peterman, 2004), pathological gambling (Boutin & others, 2003) and obsessive-compulsive disorder (Clark, 2004).

Cognitive therapists guide individuals in identifying their irrational and self-defeating thoughts. Then they use various techniques to get clients to challenge these thoughts and consider different, more positive ways of thinking. One exciting new development in cognitive therapy is a growing realization that we construct meaning through language, metaphor, and narrative. According to Lynne Angus, of York University, and her colleagues, healthy people tell healthy, open-ended stories about themselves and the process of psychotherapy involves helping people tell healthier stories about themselves (Angus & Bouffard, 2004; Goncalves, Korman, & Angus, 2000). Linda McMullen, of the University of Saskatchewan, focuses on the metaphors we use in the construction of our narratives (McMullen, 1996), especially our unhealthy ones (McMullen, 1999, 2003). For example, Levitt, Korman, & Angus (2000) explored one metaphor common among depressed patients, that of feeling burdened, and suggested that a successful therapeutic outcome can result when the patient begins to describe "unburdening" himself or herself.

The two main forms of cognitive therapy are Albert Ellis's rational-emotive behaviour therapy and Aaron Beck's cognitive therapy. Cognitive-behaviour therapy uses a combination of cognitive and behavourial techniques.

cognitive therapies Emphasize that individuals' cognitions or thoughts are the main source of abnormal behaviour and psychological problems.

Rational-Emotive Behaviour Therapy Rational-emotive behaviour therapy **(REBT)** is based on Albert Ellis's assertion that individuals develop a psychological disorder because of their beliefs, especially irrational and self-defeating beliefs. Ellis (1962, 2002, 2004) says that we usually talk to ourselves when we experience stress; too often the statements are irrational, making them more harmful than helpful.

Ellis (2002, 2004) believes that many individuals construct three basic demands: (1) I *absolutely must* perform well and win the approval of other people; (2) Other people *have to* treat me kindly and fairly; and (3) My life conditions *should not* be frustrating but rather *should be* enjoyable. Once people convert their important desires into demands, they often create dysfunctional, exaggerated beliefs, such as "Because I'm not performing well, as I *absolutely must*, I'm an inadequate person."

The goal of REBT is to get the person to eliminate self-defeating beliefs by rationally examining them. Clients are shown how to dispute their dysfunctional beliefs—especially their absolute musts—and change them to realistic and logical thoughts. Homework assignments provide them opportunities to engage in the new self-talk and experience the positive results of not viewing life in such a catastrophic way.

Beck's Cognitive Therapy Aaron Beck (1976, 1993) developed a somewhat different form of cognitive therapy to treat psychological problems, especially depression. A basic assumption Beck makes is that psychological problems such as depression result when people think illogically about themselves, the world they live in, and the future. Beck's approach shares with Ellis's the idea that the goal of therapy should be to help people to recognize and discard self-defeating cognitions.

In the initial phases of therapy, individuals are taught to make connections between their patterns of thinking and their emotional responses. The therapist helps them to identify their own automatic thoughts and to keep records of their thought content and emotional reactions. With the therapist's assistance, they learn about logical errors in their thinking and learn to challenge the accuracy of these automatic thoughts. Logical errors in thinking can lead an individual to erroneous beliefs such as (Butcher, Mineka, & Hooley, 2004):

- Perceiving the world as harmful while ignoring evidence to the contrary, for example, still feeling worthless even though a friend has just told her how much other people like her
- Overgeneralizing on the basis of limited examples, such as seeing himself as worthless because one individual stopped dating him
- Magnifying the importance of undesirable events, such as seeing the loss of a dating partner as the end of the world
- Engaging in absolutist thinking, such as exaggerating the importance of someone's mildly critical comment and perceiving it as proof of total inadequacy.

Figure 14.8 describes some of the most widely used cognitive therapy techniques.

The following case study involves a cognitive therapist guiding a depressed 26-year-old graduate student to understand the connection between how she interprets her experiences and the way she feels and to begin seeing the inaccuracy of her interpretations (Beck & others, 1979):

> Student: I agree with the description of me but I guess I don't agree that the way I think makes me depressed.
> Therapist: How do you understand it?
> Student: I get depressed when things go wrong. Like when I fail a test.
> Therapist: How can failing a test make you depressed?
> Student: Well, if I fail I'll never get into law school.
> Therapist: So failing the test means a lot to you. But if failing a test could drive people into clinical depression, wouldn't you expect everyone who failed the test to have depression? Did everyone who failed the test get depressed enough to require treatment?
> Student: No, but it depends on how important the test was to the person.
> Therapist: Right, and who decides the importance?

rational-emotive behaviour therapy (REBT) Based on Ellis's assertion that individuals develop a psychological disorder because of their beliefs, especially those that are irrational and self-defeating; the goal of REBT is to get the person to eliminate self-defeating beliefs by rationally examining them.

Cognitive Therapy Technique	Description	Example
Challenge idiosyncratic meanings	Explore personal meaning attached to the client's words and ask the client to consider alternatives.	When a client says he will be "devastated" by his spouse leaving, ask just how he would be devastated and ways he could avoid being devastated.
Question the evidence	Systematically examine the evidence for the client's beliefs or assertions.	When a client says she can't live without her spouse, explore how she lived without the spouse before she was married.
Reattribution	Help the client distribute responsibility for events appropriately.	When a client says that his son's failure in school must be his fault, explore other possibilities, such as the quality of the school.
Examine options and alternatives	Help the client generate alternative actions to maladaptive ones.	If a client considers leaving school, explore whether tutoring or going part-time to school are good alternatives.
Decatastrophize	Help the client evaluate whether he is overestimating the nature of a situation.	If a client states that failure in a course means she must give up the dream of medical school, question whether this is a necessary conclusion.
Fantasize consequences	Explore fantasies of a feared situation: If unrealistic, the client may recognize this; if realistic, work on effective coping strategies.	Help a client who fantasizes "falling apart" when asking the boss for a raise to role-play the situation and develop effective skills for making the request.
Examine advantages and disadvantages	Examine advantages and disadvantages of an issue, to instill a broader perspective.	If a client says he "was just born depressed and will always be that way," explore the advantages and disadvantages of holding that perspective versus other perspectives.
Turn adversity to advantage	Explore ways that difficult situations can be transformed to opportunities.	If a client has just been laid off, explore whether this is an opportunity for her to return to school.
Guided association	Help the client see connections between different thoughts or ideas.	Draw the connections between a client's anger at his wife for going on a business trip and his fear of being alone.
Scaling	Ask the client to rate her emotions or thoughts on scales to help gain perspective.	If a client says she was overwhelmed by an emotion, ask her to rate it on a scale from 0 (not at all present) to 100 (I fell down in a faint).
Thought stopping	Provide the client with ways of stopping a cascade of negative thoughts.	Teach an anxious client to picture a stop sign or hear a bell when anxious thoughts begin to snowball.
Distraction	Help the client find benign or positive distractions to take attention away from negative thoughts or emotions temporarily.	Have a client count to 200 by 13s when he feels himself becoming anxious.
Labelling of distortions	Provide labels for specific types of distorted thinking to help the client gain more distance and perspective.	Have a client keep a record of the number of times a day she engages in all-or-nothing thinking—seeing things as all bad or all good.

FIGURE 14.8

Cognitive Therapy Techniques

Student: I do.

Therapist: And so, what we have to examine is your way of viewing the test or the way that you think about the test and how it affects your chances of getting into law school. Do you agree?

Student: Right . . .

Therapist: Now what did failing mean?

Student: (Tearful) That I couldn't get into law school.

Therapist: And what does that mean to you?

Student: That I'm just not smart enough.

Therapist: Anything else?

Student: That I can never be happy.

Therapist: And how do these thoughts make you feel?

Student: Very unhappy.

Therapist: So it is the meaning of failing a test that makes you very unhappy. In fact, believing that you can never be happy is a powerful factor in producing unhappiness. So, you get yourself into a trap—by definition, failure to get into law school equals, "I can never be happy."

As we mentioned earlier, Beck's and Ellis's cognitive therapies have some similarities. However, there are also some differences: Rational-emotive behaviour therapy is very directive, persuasive, and confrontational. In contrast, Beck's cognitive therapy involves more of an open-ended dialogue between the therapist and the individual. In Beck's approach, the aim of this dialogue is to get individuals to reflect on personal issues and discover their own misconceptions. Beck also encourages individuals to gather information about themselves and to try out unbiased experiments that reveal the inaccuracies of their beliefs.

Cognitive-Behaviour Therapy **Cognitive-behaviour therapy** consists of a combination of cognitive therapy, with its emphasis on reducing self-defeating thoughts, and behaviour therapy, with its emphasis on changing behaviour. Donald Meichenbaum, of the University of Waterloo, one of the founders of cognitive-behaviour therapy (Meichenbaum, 1977, 1991, 2003), holds that how individuals control their minds shapes their behaviour.

Self-instructional methods are cognitive-behaviour techniques aimed at teaching individuals to modify their own behaviour (Dowd, 2002; Meichenbaum, 1977, 2003). The therapist gives the client examples of constructive statements, known as "reinforcing self-statements," that the client can repeat in order to take positive steps to cope with stress or meet a goal. The therapist will also encourage the client to practise the statements through role playing and will strengthen the client's newly acquired skills through reinforcements. Following is a series of examples of self-instructional methods that individuals can use to cope with stressful situations (Meichenbaum, Turk, & Burstein, 1975):

Preparing for anxiety or stress:
What do I have to do?
I'm going to map out a plan to deal with it.
I'll just think about what I have to do.
I won't worry. Worry doesn't help anything.
I have a lot of different strategies I can call on.
Confronting and handling the anxiety or stress:
I can meet the challenge.
I'll keep on taking one step at a time.
I can handle it. I'll just relax, breathe deeply, and use one of the strategies.
I won't think about the pain. I will think about what I have to do.
Coping with feelings at critical moments:
What is it I have to do?
I was supposed to expect the pain to increase. I just have to keep myself in control.
When the pain comes, I will just pause and keep focusing on what I have to do.
Reinforcing self-statements:
Good, I did it.
I handled it well.
I knew I could do it.
Wait until I tell other people how I did it!

An important aspect of cognitive-behaviour therapy is *self-efficacy*, Albert Bandura's (1997, 2000b) concept that one can master a situation and produce positive outcomes. Bandura believes that self-efficacy is the key to successful therapy. At each step of the therapy process, people need to bolster their confidence by telling themselves, "I'm going to master my problem," "I can do it, " "I'm improving," "I'm getting better," and so on. As people gain confidence and engage in adaptive behaviour, the successes become intrinsically motivating. Before long, individuals persist with considerable effort in their attempts to solve personal problems because of the positive outcomes that were set in motion by self-efficacy.

Now that we have examined three of the most widely used cognitive therapy approaches—Ellis's rational-emotive behaviour therapy, Beck's cognitive therapy, and Meichenbaum's cognitive-behaviour therapy—we'll examine how effective cognitive therapy is in treating psychological disorders.

cognitive-behaviour therapy Consists of a combination of cognitive therapy and behaviour therapy; self-efficacy is an important goal of cognitive-behaviour therapy.

FIGURE 14.9

Effects of Cognitive-Behaviour Therapy on Children's Anxiety About School

Children and their parents participated in a 10-week cognitive-behaviour therapy program. Compared with a control group of children, the children in the cognitive therapy program were less likely to have an anxiety disorder through 24 months after the therapy.

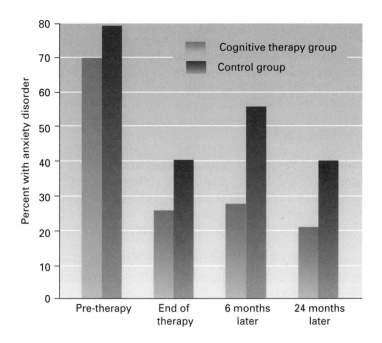

Using Cognitive Therapy to Treat Psychological Disorders Cognitive therapy has been used effectively in the treatment of some anxiety disorders, mood disorders, schizophrenia, and personality disorders (Barlow, 2001; Beck, 2002). In many instances, cognitive therapy used conjointly with drug therapy is an effective treatment for psychological disorders (Barlow & others, 2000; Ressler & others, 2004).

Among the anxiety disorders to which cognitive therapy has been applied is panic disorder (Hoffart & Sexton, 2002). In one study, a combination of an SSRI drug and cognitive therapy was effective in treating panic disorder (Azhar, 2001). Cognitive therapy has shown considerable promise in the treatment of post-traumatic stress disorder, especially when individuals are encouraged to relive traumatic experiencesso they can come to grips with the threatening cognitions precipitated by those events (Ehlers & others, 2005).

Cognitive therapy has also been successful in treating generalized anxiety disorder, certain phobias, and obsessive-compulsive disorder (Tafet, 2005; Wells & Papageorgiou, 2001). Figure 14.9 shows the results of an experiment that studied the effects of cognitive-behaviour therapy on children's anxiety. Robert Ladouceur, of Université Laval, has successfully applied cognitive therapy to pathological gambling, a growing problem in Canada (Ladouceur & Shaffer, 2005; Ladouceur, 2000). Many gamblers have a real problem staying away from casinos, to the point that casinos themselves have begun to provide self-exclusion programs (Ladouceur and others, 2000). The basic treatment focuses on improving the gamblers' understanding of the concept of randomness and correcting the erroneous beliefs held by gamblers (Ladouceur, 2005; Ladouceur & others, 2001).

One of the earliest applications of cognitive therapy was in the treatment of depression. A number of studies have shown that cognitive therapy can be just as successful as drug therapy in the treatment of depressive disorders (DeRubeis & others, 2005; Dunner, 2001). Some studies have also shown that individuals treated with cognitive therapy are less likely to relapse into depression than individuals treated with drug therapy (Jarrett & others, 2001).

Considerable strides have been made in recent years in applying cognitive therapy to the treatment of schizophrenia. Although not a substitute for drug therapy, cognitive therapy has been effective in reducing the schizophrenic's belief in delusions and lowering the probability that the schizophrenic will act out in an impulsive fashion (Rector, 2004; Rector & Beck, 2001).

Cognitive therapy has also been used effectively in treating personality disorders. The focus is on using cognitive therapy to change individuals' core beliefs and to reduce their automatic negative thoughts.

	Topic		
	Cause of Problem	**Therapy Emphasis**	**Nature of Therapy and Techniques**
Psychodynamic Therapies	Client's problems are symptoms of deep-seated, unresolved unconscious conflicts.	Discover underlying unconscious conflicts and work with client to develop insight.	Psychoanalysis, including free association, dream analysis, resistance, and transference: therapist interprets heavily.
Humanistic Therapies	Client is not functioning at an optimal level of development.	Develop awareness of inherent potential for growth.	Client-centred therapy, including unconditional positive regard, genuineness, accurate empathy, and active listening; Gestalt therapy, including confrontation to encourage honest expression of feelings; self-appreciation emphasized.
Behaviour Therapies	Client has learned maladaptive behaviour patterns.	Learn adaptive behaviour patterns through changes in the environment or cognitive processes.	Observation of behaviour and its controlling conditions; specific advice given about what should be done; therapies based on classical conditioning, operant conditioning.
Cognitive Therapies	Client has developed inappropriate thoughts.	Change feelings and behaviours by changing cognitions.	Conversation with client designed to get him or her to change irrational and self-deflating beliefs.

FIGURE 14.10 Therapy Comparisons

So far in this chapter we have studied the biological therapies and psychotherapies. A comparison of the four psychotherapies—psychodynamic, humanistic, behavioural, and cognitive—is presented in figure 14.10.

> ## > reflect and review

 Define psychotherapy and characterize four types of psychotherapies.

- Explain what psychotherapy is.
- Describe the psychodynamic therapies.
- Discuss the humanistic therapies.
- Summarize the classical conditioning and operant conditioning approaches to behavioural therapies.
- Distinguish among three cognitive therapies.

Imagine that you are a psychotherapist and that you diagnose an individual as having a depressive disorder. Which of the psychotherapies would you use to treat the individual? Explain your choice.

3 SOCIOCULTURAL APPROACHES AND ISSUES IN TREATMENT

—	Group Therapy	—	Family and Couples Therapy	—	Self-Help Support Groups	—	Community Mental Health	—	Cultural Perspectives

What treatment needs do the sociocultural approaches address?

In the treatment of psychological disorders, biological therapies change the person's body, behavioural therapies modify the person's behaviour, and cognitive therapies alter the person's thinking. This section focuses on sociocultural approaches to the treatment of psychological disorders. These approaches view the individual as part of a social system of

Because many psychological problems develop in the context of interpersonal relationships and group experiences—within family, marriage, work or social group—group therapy can be an important context for learning how to cope more effectively with these problems.

relationships, influenced by various social and cultural factors, and believe that these sociocultural aspects must be dealt with in the treatment of psychological disorders (Nolen-Hoeksema, 2004). The sociocultural approaches and issues include group therapy, family and couples therapy, self-help support groups, community mental health, and cultural perspectives on therapy.

Group Therapy

A major issue in therapy is how to structure it to reach more people at less cost. One way to address this problem is for the therapist to see clients in a group (MacKenzie, 2002).

Nine people make their way into a room, each looking tentatively at the others. Although each person has met the therapist during a diagnostic interview, no one knows any of the other clients. Some of the people seem reluctant, others enthusiastic. All are willing to follow the therapist's recommendation that group therapy might help each of them learn to cope better with their problems. As they sit down and wait for the session to begin, one thinks, "Will they really understand me?" Another thinks, "Do the others have problems like mine?" Yet another thinks, "How can I stick my neck out with these people?"

Individual therapy is often expensive and time-consuming. Freud believed that therapy is a long process and saw clients as often as three to five times a week for a number of years. Advocates of group therapy stress that individual therapy is limited because the client is seen outside the normal context of relationships, relationships that may hold the key to successful therapy (Gladding, 2002; Kline, 2003). Many psychological problems develop in the context of interpersonal relationships—within one's family, marriage, or peer group, for example. By taking into account the context of these important groups, therapy may be more successful (Capuzzi, 2003; Gazda, Horne, & Ginter, 2001).

Group therapy is diversified. Psychodynamic, humanistic, behaviour, and cognitive therapies are all used in group therapy, in addition to approaches that are not based on the major psychotherapeutic perspectives. Six features make group therapy an attractive treatment format (Yalom, 1995):

1. *Information*. The individual receives information about his problem from either the group leader or other group members.
2. *Universality*. Many individuals develop the sense that no one else has frightening and unacceptable impulses. In the group, individuals observe that others feel anguish and suffering as well.
3. *Altruism*. Group members support one another with advice and sympathy and learn that they have something to offer others.
4. *Corrective recapitulation of the family group*. A therapy group often resembles a family (in family therapy the group is a family), with the leaders representing parents and the other members' siblings. In this "new" family, old wounds may be healed and new, more positive "family" ties made.
5. *Development of social skills*. Corrective feedback from peers may correct flaws in the individual's interpersonal skills. A self-centred individual may see that he is self-centred if five other group members inform him about his self-centredness; in individual therapy he might not believe the therapist.
6. *Interpersonal learning*. The group can serve as a training ground for practising new behaviours and relationships. A hostile woman may learn that she can get along better with others by behaving less aggressively, for example.

Family and Couples Therapy

"A friend loves you for your intelligence, a mistress for your charm, but your family's love is unreasoning; you were born into it and are of its flesh and blood. Nevertheless, it can irritate you more than any group of people in the world," commented the French biographer André Maurois. As his statement suggests, the family may be the source of an individual's problems.

Family therapy is group therapy with family members (Lebow, 2005). **Couples therapy** is group therapy with married or unmarried couples whose major problem is their relationship (Harway, 2004). These approaches stress that, although one person may have some abnormal symptoms, the symptoms are a function of the family or couple relationships (Capuzzi & Gross, 2003; Griffin, 2002). Psychodynamic, humanistic, and behaviour therapies may be used in family and couples therapy.

Consider the following case study to gain an understanding of how family therapy works (Sheras & Worchel, 1979):

Family therapy has become increasingly popular in recent years. In family therapy, the assumption is that psychological adjustment is related to patterns of interaction within the family unit.

> Father: I just don't understand. We have had a happy family all along until Tommy started acting up. . . .
> Therapist: Have you ever had to hit Tommy?
> Father: Sure, a couple of times, but it didn't seem to do any good.
> Tommy (Son): Yeah, he hit me a lot, for no reason at all!
> Mother: Now, that's not true, Tommy. If you behaved yourself a little better, you wouldn't get hit. . . .
> Therapist: I get the feeling that people in this family would like for things to be different. Bob, I can see how frustrating it must be for you to work so hard and not be able to relax when you get home. And Ginny, your job is not easy either. You have a lot to do at home and Bob can't be there to help a lot of the time. It must be hard for you, Tommy, to be catching so much flack these days.

Therapist now looks at each person briefly and then says, "There seems to be a lot going on. What I would like to do is talk with you together a little longer, then see the parents alone and then Tommy alone, to hear the different sides of what is going on. I would like for each of you to think about how you would change the other family members so that you would be happier as a family."

Four of the most widely used family therapy techniques are:

1. *Validation*. The therapist expresses an understanding and acceptance of each family member's feelings and beliefs and thus validates the person. When the therapist talks with each family member, she finds something positive to say.
2. *Reframing*. The therapist helps families reframe problems as family problems, not as an individual's problems. A delinquent adolescent boy's problems are reframed in terms of how each family member contributed to the situation. The father's lack of attention to his son and marital conflict may be involved, for example.
3. *Structural change*. The family systems therapist tries to restructure the coalitions in a family. In a mother-son coalition, the therapist might suggest that the father take a stronger disciplinarian role to relieve some of the burden from the mother. Restructuring might be as simple as suggesting that parents explore satisfying ways to be together; the therapist may recommend that once a week the parents go out for a quiet dinner together, for example.
4. *Detriangulation*. In some families, one member is the scapegoat for two other members who are in conflict but pretend not to be. For example, in the triangle of two parents and one child, the parents may insist that their marriage is fine but find themselves in subtle conflict over how to handle the child. The therapist tries to disentangle, or detriangulate, this situation by shifting attention away from the child to the conflict between the parents (Goldenthal, 2005).

Couples therapy proceeds in much the same way as family therapy. Conflict in marriages and in relationships between unmarried individuals frequently involves poor communication. In some instances, communication has broken down entirely. The therapist tries to improve the communication between the partners. In some cases, she will focus on the roles partners play: one may be "strong," the other "weak;" one may be "responsible," the other "spoiled," for example. Couples therapy addresses diverse problems such as jealousy, sexual messages, delayed childbearing, infidelity, gender roles, two-career families, divorce, and remarriage (Harway, 2004).

family therapy Group therapy with family members.

couples therapy Therapy with married or unmarried couples whose major problem is within their relationship.

Self-Help Support Groups

Self-help support groups are voluntary organizations of individuals who get together on a regular basis to discuss topics of common interest. The groups are not conducted by a professional therapist but rather by a paraprofessional or a member of the common interest group. A paraprofessional is someone who has been taught by a professional to provide some mental health services but who does not have formal mental health training. The group leader and members provide support to help individuals with their problems. Self-help support groups play an important role in our mental health, with as many as 10 million North Americans participating in such groups each year, often over the Internet (Meier, 2005). In addition to reaching so many people in need of help, these groups are important because they use community resources and are relatively inexpensive. They also serve people who are less likely to receive help otherwise, such as less educated adults, individuals living in low-income circumstances, and homemakers.

Self-help support groups provide members with a sympathetic audience for confession, sharing, and emotional release (Burlingame & Davies, 2002). The social support, role modelling, and sharing of concrete strategies for solving problems that unfolds in self-help groups adds to their effectiveness. A woman who has been raped might not believe a male therapist who tells her that, with time, she will be able to put back together the pieces of her shattered life and work through much of the psychological pain. But the same message from another rape survivor—someone who has had to work through the same feelings of rage, fear, and violation—might be more believable.

Alcoholics Anonymous (AA), founded in 1935 by a reformed alcoholic and a physician, is one of the best-known self-help groups. Mental health professionals often recommend AA for their alcoholic clients (Vaillant, 2005). There are myriad self-help groups, such as those for victims of terrorism, Parents Without Partners, lesbian and gay support groups, cocaine abuse support groups, Weight Watchers and TOPS (Take Off Pounds Sensibly), child abuse support groups, and many medical (heart disease, cancer) support groups. Figure 14.11 lists a sampling of the variety of self-help groups available in one province. Also, the Internet is now an invaluable tool for connecting people with self-help groups. For example, the Self-Help Resource Centre (www.selfhelp.on.ca) provides many online resources, including access to self-help groups across Canada.

Self-help support groups have broad, though not universal, appeal. For people who tend to cope by seeking information and affiliation with similar peers, such groups can reduce stress and promote adjustment. However, as with any group therapy, there is the possibility that negative emotions will spread through the group, especially if the members face circumstances that deteriorate over time, such as terminal cancer patients. Group leaders who are sensitive to the spread of negative emotions can minimize such effects.

Community Mental Health

The community mental health movement was born in the 1960s when it became apparent that the North American mental health care system was not reaching the poor and when the care of large numbers of individuals with psychological disorders was transferred from mental institutions to community-based facilities. In Canada, 78 percent of the in-patient beds were closed, despite a rapidly increasing population (Freeman, 1994). This transfer (called *deinstitutionalization*) came about largely because of the development of new drugs for treating individuals with psychological disorders, especially schizophrenia.

In 1963, The Canadian Mental Health Association published *More for the Mind*, the charter document for deinstitutionalization in Canada (Tyhurst, 1963). As envisaged there, teams working at community mental health centres were intended to meet two basic goals: (1) to provide community-based mental health services, and (2) to commit resources to help prevent, as well as treat, mental disorders (Burns, 2004). Out-patient care is an important community health centre service. Individuals can attend therapy sessions at the centre and still keep their job and live with their family. Prevention takes one of three courses: primary, secondary, or tertiary.

Social Concerns	

Gamblers Anonymous
Hope for Youth Foundation
Kids Help Phone
Victim Services
St. John's Rape Crisis and Information
   Centre
	Canadian Association of Retired Persons
	(North East Avalon Chapter)
	St. John's Native Friendship Centre
	   Association
	CHANNAL—Adult Survivors of Child
	   Sexual Abuse (C.A.S.C.S.A.)

Bereavement	
Adolescent Grief Group Bereavement Group	Janeway Bereaved Parents Support Group Survivors of Suicide Group (S.O.S.)

Alcohol/Substance Abuse	
Addictions Services Alcoholics Anonymous (A.A.)	Coping Without Smoking (C.W.S.) Narcotics Anonymous

Parenting	

St. John's Parents Rights Group
   Newfoundland and Labrador
Association for Gifted Children
Single Parent Association of
   Newfoundland (S.P.A.N.)
Breastfeeding Support Group
   Program (BFSGP)
	Autism Society—Parent Support Group
	Parents of Children With a Disability
	Newfoundland and Labrador Association
	   for Spina Bifida and Hydrocephalus
	Support for Parents of Adolescents (SPA)
	Foster Families Association—
	   Newfoundland and Labrador

Health	
Lupus Society of Newfoundland Epilepsy Newfoundland and Labrador Chronic Pain Support Group Thyroid Foundation of Canada	St. John's Stroke Survivors Support Group Schizophrenia Society of Newfoundland and Labrador Support Group Canadian Hard of Hearing Association

FIGURE 14.11

Examples of Self-Help Groups
A partial listing of self-help groups in Newfoundland and Labrador, from the Web site of the Canadian Mental Health Association, Newfoundland and Labrador Division.

In *primary prevention*, efforts are made to reduce the number of new cases of psychological disorders. In some instances, high-risk populations are targeted for prevention, such as children of alcoholics, children with chronic illnesses, and children in poverty.

In *secondary prevention*, screening for early detection of problems and early intervention may take place. Secondary prevention programs seek to reach large numbers of people. One way they do this is by educating paraprofessionals, individuals without formal mental health training, about preventing psychological problems and by having them work with psychologists. One type of early intervention involves screening schoolchildren to find those who show early signs of problems and provide them with psychological services.

In *tertiary prevention*, an effort is made to treat psychological disorders that were not prevented or arrested early in the course of the disorders. Tertiary programs are often geared toward people who once required long-term care or hospitalization but who are now living in the community. An example of a tertiary intervention is halfway houses (community residences for individuals who no longer require institutionalization but who still need support in readjusting to the community) for formerly hospitalized schizophrenics.

An explicit goal of community mental health is to help people who are disenfranchised from society, such as those living in poverty, to lead happier, more productive lives. A key concept involved in this effort is empowerment, which consists of assisting individuals to develop the skills they need to control their own lives. A more recent goal of community mental health is to marshal resources in response to large-scale emergencies, such as natural disasters or terrorist attacks (Ursano, Fullerton, Norwood, 2003; Laor & others, 2005).

As an infant, Cornelia Wieman was removed from her home on the Little Grand Rapids Reserve in northern Manitoba, made a ward of the Crown, and was eventually adopted by a Dutch couple in Thunder Bay. Later, she reconnected with her Aboriginal roots and went on to become Canada's first practicing female Aboriginal psychiatrist.

Laurence Kirmayer is a professor of psychiatry and director of the Division of Social and Transcultural Psychiatry at McGill University. He is also director of the Culture and Mental Health Research Unit at the Institute of Community and Family Psychiatry of the Sir Mortimer B. Davis Jewish General Hospital. He has a special interest in Canadian Aboriginal peoples and has done clinical work and field research among the Inuit of northern Quebec.

Cultural Perspectives

The psychotherapies that were discussed earlier in the chapter—psychodynamic, humanistic, behavioural, and cognitive—focus mainly on the individual. This approach is compatible with the needs of many people in Western cultures, such as Canada, where the focus is on the individual rather than the group—family, community, or ethnic group. However, these psychotherapies may not be as effective with people who live in cultures that place more importance on the group—called *collectivist* cultures. Some psychologists argue that family therapy is likely to be more effective with people in cultures that place a high value on the family, such as Asian cultures (Tharp, 1991).

Ethnicity Many ethnic minority individuals are reluctant to discuss problems with mental health professionals (Atkinson & Hackett, 2004; Gibson & Mitchell, 2003). Cornelia Wieman, Canada's first female Aboriginal psychiatrist, believes that therapy progresses best when the therapist and the client are from the same ethnic background. Dr. Wieman has practised psychiatry on the Six Nations Reserve, southeast of Hamilton, Ontario (Wieman, 2000) and is currently in the Indigenous Health Research Development Program at the University of Toronto. When there is an ethnic match between the therapist and the client and when ethnic-specific services are provided, clients are less likely to drop out of therapy early and may have better treatment outcomes (Jackson & Greene, 2000; Nystul, 2006).

Nonetheless, therapy can be effective when the therapist and client are from different ethnic backgrounds if the therapist has excellent clinical skills and is culturally sensitive (Gibson & Mitchell, 2003; Pederson & Carey, 2003). Culturally skilled psychotherapists have good knowledge of the cultural groups they work with, understand the sociopolitical influences involved, and have skills in working with culturally diverse groups (Toukmanian & Brouwers, 1998).

For example, Laurence Kirmayer, a psychiatrist at McGill University, stresses the need to conceptualize the mental health problems of Canada's Aboriginal peoples as continuing responses to Canada's history of colonization. The disruption of Aboriginal cultures can be related to high rates of alcoholism, violence, depression, and suicide in many communities (Kirmayer, Brass, & Tait,, 2000; Leenaars & others,1999; Tester & McNicoll, 2004). While Susan Aglukark makes us more aware of the plight of the Inuit, researchers are working on building healthy Inuit communities (Allen, 2000) and dealing with the difficult problem of Inuit suicides (Kirmayer, Boothroyd, & Hodgins, 1998).

Gender One by-product of changing gender roles for women and men is evaluation of the goals of psychotherapy (Nolen-Hoeksema, 2004; Vatcher & Bogo, 2001). Women have argued that autonomy, the traditional goal of psychotherapy, is often more central in the lives of men than of women, for whom relatedness and connection with others may be more central (Nutt, 2005; Worell & Remer, 2003). For example, Janet Stoppard, of the University of New Brunswick, proposes a sociocultural view of depression rather than the view that it is an individual pathology to be treated medically (Stoppard, 1999; Stoppard & McMullen, 2003).

Because traditional therapy has often not adequately addressed the specific concerns of women in a sexist society, several nontraditional approaches have arisen (Henderson & others, 2005). These nontraditional therapies emphasize the importance of helping people break free from traditional gender roles and stereotypes. Feminist therapists believe that traditional psychotherapy continues to carry considerable gender bias and that female clients cannot realize their full potential without becoming aware of society's sexism (Stoppard, 2000).

The goals of feminist therapists are no different from other therapists' goals, and feminist therapists make no effort to turn clients into feminists. However, they do want the female client to be fully aware of how the nature of the female role in North American society can contribute to the development of a psychological disorder. Feminist therapists believe that women must become aware of the bias and discrimination in their own lives to achieve their mental health goals (Stoppard & Gammell, 2003).

> **reflect and review**

3 **Explain the sociocultural approaches and issues in treatment.**

- Define group therapy.
- Describe family and couples therapy.
- Discuss the features of self-help support groups.
- Explain the community mental health approach.
- Identify cultural perspectives that can affect the success of treatment.

Which therapy setting do you think you would benefit from the most—individual or group? Why?

4 THE EFFECTIVENESS OF PSYCHOTHERAPY

Research on the Effectiveness of Psychotherapy	Common Themes in Psychotherapy	Integrative Therapies	Funding and Finding Therapy	Mental Health Professionals	Guidelines for Seeking Professional Help

How effective is psychotherapy?

Do individuals who go through therapy get better? Are some approaches more effective than others? Or is the situation similar to that of the Dodo in *Alice's Adventures in Wonderland*? Dodo was asked to judge the winner of a race. He decided, "Everybody has won and all must have prizes." How would we evaluate the effectiveness of psychotherapy? Would we take the client's word? The therapist's word? What would be our criteria for effectiveness? Would it be "feeling good," "adaptive behaviour," "improved interpersonal relationships," "autonomous decision making," or "more positive self-concept," for example? During the past several decades an extensive amount of thought and research has addressed these questions (Brems, 2001; Moras, 2002).

Research on the Effectiveness of Psychotherapy

Over five decades ago, Hans Eysenck (1952) came to the shocking conclusion that psychotherapy is ineffective. Eysenck analyzed 24 studies of psychotherapy and found that approximately two-thirds of the individuals with neurotic symptoms improved. Sounds impressive so far. But Eysenck also found that a similar percentage of neurotic individuals on waiting lists to see a psychotherapist also showed marked improvement, even though they were not given any psychotherapy at all.

Eysenck's pronouncement prompted a flurry of research on psychotherapy's effectiveness (Lambert, 2001; Orlinsky & Howard, 2000; Pilkonis, 1999; Pilkonis & Krause, 1999). Hundreds of studies on the outcome of psychotherapy have now been conducted.

One strategy for analyzing these diverse studies is called **meta-analysis**, in which the researcher statistically combines the results of many different studies (Rosenthal & DiMatteo, 2001). In one classic meta-analysis of psychotherapy research, 475 studies were statistically combined (Smith, Glass, & Miller, 1980). Only studies in which a therapy group had been compared with an untreated control group were used. The results showed greater psychotherapy effectiveness than Eysenck's earlier results: On 88 percent of the measures, individuals who received therapy improved more than those who did not. This meta-analysis and others (Lipsey & Wilson, 1993) document that psychotherapy is effective in general, but they do not inform us about the specific ways in which different therapies might be effective.

Figure 14.12 provides a summary of numerous studies and reviews of research in which clients were randomly assigned to a no-treatment control group, a placebo control

meta-analysis Statistical analysis that combines the results of many different studies.

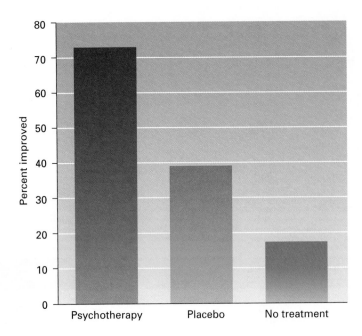

FIGURE 14.12

The Effects of Psychotherapy
In a recent review of studies, more than 70 percent of individuals who saw a therapist improved, whereas fewer than 40 percent who received a placebo and fewer than 20 percent who received no treatment improved.

group, or a psychotherapy treatment (Lambert, 2001; Lambert & Ogles, 2002). As you can see, individuals who did not get treatment improved, probably because they sought help from friends, family, the clergy, or others. Individuals who were in a placebo control group fared better than nontreated individuals, probably because they had had contact with a therapist, they expected to be helped, or they were given reassurance and support during the study. However, by far the best outcomes were for individuals who were given psychotherapy.

People who are thinking about seeing a psychotherapist want to know not only whether psychotherapy in general is effective but also especially which form of psychotherapy is most effective for their particular problem. Similarly, more recent meta-analyses have tended to focus on more narrow comparisons between forms of therapy and particular disorders. For example, Eddy and colleagues (2004) found that behavioural, cognitive-behavioural, and drug therapies are all beneficial in the treatment of obsessive-compulsive disorder. However, their results specifically singled out individual psychotherapies and SSRI drugs as yielding the best results, although they also caution that OCD symptoms are only moderated, not abolished. Similarly, Bradley and colleagues (2005) found that a variety of brief psychotherapies are effective in treating post-traumatic stress disorder. They qualify these results by noting that combat-related PTSD is the least responsive to treatment, perhaps because it is more severe than most other forms of PTSD. They also suggest that success rates are much lower for patients suffering from other psychological disorders, along with PTSD.

Research that evaluates the effectiveness of a psychotherapy usually includes a comparison group—either a control group of individuals who do not experience the therapy or a group that receives a different type of psychotherapy (Alloy, Riskind, & Manos, 2005). When a control group is included, it often consists of individuals waiting to see a psychotherapist but who, as yet, have not been given therapy (this is called a *wait-list control group*). Why is it so important for psychotherapy research to include a control or comparison group? Because it gives us some idea of how many people in the study who experienced the targeted psychotherapy (such as cognitive therapy for depression) would have gotten better without the psychotherapy.

We present here one study that illustrates how control and comparison groups are used in psychotherapy research. Addis and colleagues (2004) compared patients with panic disorder treated with cognitive behavioural therapy (CBT) with another type of control group, *treatment as usual (TAU)*. Individuals in this type of control group continue to receive whatever treatment they were receiving before entering the study. Eighty individuals were randomly assigned to receive CBT or TAU. After 12 to 15 weeks in treatment, 43 percent of the individuals in the CBT group, compared to 19 percent of individuals in the TAU control group, showed clinically meaningful improvement, a significant difference. Addis and colleagues (2004) concluded that CBT was of value in treating panic disorder. If CBT had shown no greater improvement than TAU, their conclusion would have been quite different.

Using these sorts of research methods, researchers have found that therapies are more effective than others in treating some disorders (Seligman, 2006; Nathan & Gorman, 2002; Nathan, Stuart, & Dolan, 2000):

● Cognitive therapies and behaviour therapies have been successful in treating anxiety disorders (Provencher, Dugas, & Ladouceur, 2004; Landon, & Barlow, 2004; Barlow, 2001).
● Cognitive therapies and behaviour therapies have been successful in treating depressive disorders (Beevers & Miller, 2005; Craighead & Craighead, 2001).
● Relaxation therapy (discussed in chapter 15) has also been successful in treating anxiety disorders (Arntz, 2003; Hidalgo & Davidson, 2001).

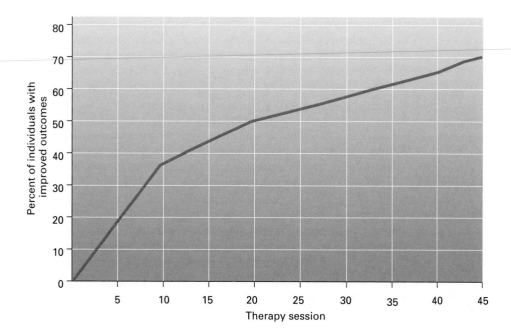

FIGURE 14.13
Number of Therapy Sessions and Improvement
In one recent study, a large number of people undergoing therapy rated their well-being (based on symptoms, interpersonal relations, and quality of life) before each treatment session (Anderson & Lambert, 2001). The percentage of people who showed improved outcomes after each additional session of treatment indicated that about one-third of the individuals recovered by the 10th session, 50 percent by the 20th session, and 70 percent by the 45th session.

Individuals who see a therapist also want to know how long it will take them to get better. In one study, individuals showed substantial improvement in therapy over the course of the first six months, with diminishing returns after that (Howard & others, 1996). In another study, individuals rated their symptoms, interpersonal relations, and quality of life on a weekly basis before each treatment session (Anderson & Lambert, 2001). Figure 14.13 shows that one-third of individuals had improved outcomes by the 10th session, 50 percent by the 20th session, and 70 percent by the 45th session. In sum, therapy benefits most individuals with psychological problems at least through the first six months of therapy and possibly longer.

Common Themes in Psychotherapy

Another approach to understanding psychotherapy seeks to uncover the effective components, or elements, which all psychotherapies have in common (Frank & Frank, 2004). After carefully studying the nature of psychotherapy for more than 25 years, Jerome Frank (1982; Frank & Frank, 2004) concluded that effective psychotherapies have the common components of expectations, mastery, and emotional arousal. By inspiring expectations of help, the effective therapist motivates the client to continue coming to therapy (Jennings & Skovholt, 1999). These expectations are powerful morale builders and symptom relievers in themselves (Arnkoff, Glass, &Shapiro, 2002). The therapist also increases the client's sense of mastery and competence (Brammer & MacDonald, 2003). For example, clients begin to feel that they can cope effectively with their world. Therapy also arouses the individual's emotions, an essential motivator for behaviour change, according to Frank.

The therapeutic relationship is another important component in successful psychotherapy (Norcross, 2002). Confidence and trust in the therapist is essential to effective psychotherapy. In one study, the most common ingredient in the success of different psychotherapies was the therapist's supportiveness (Wallerstein, 1989). The client and therapist engage in a "healing ritual," which requires the active participation of both the client and the therapist. In a supportive therapeutic relationship, the client can constructively retell his or her life narrative (Angus & Hardtke, 1994).

Integrative Therapies

In the single-therapy approach, the therapist believes that one particular kind of therapy works best. However, an ever-growing percentage of practising therapists do not identify themselves as adhering to one particular approach but rather refer to themselves as "integrative" or "eclectic" (Norcross, Hedges, & Prochaska, 2002; Gold, 2002;). **Integrative**

integrative therapies Combinations of techniques from different therapies based on the therapist's judgment of which particular techniques will provide the greatest benefit for the client.

therapies are combinations of techniques from different therapies based on the therapist's judgment of which particular techniques will provide the greatest benefit for the client.

Integrative therapies are characterized by an openness to various ways of integrating diverse therapies. For example, a therapist might use a behavioural approach to treat an individual with panic disorder and a cognitive therapy approach to treat an individual with major depressive disorder. There is no single well-defined integrative therapy that ties all of the therapy approaches together.

In the past two decades, integrative therapies have grown dramatically (Norcross & Goldfried, 2005). What has fostered the movement toward integrative therapies? The motivating factors include the proliferation of therapies, the inadequacy of a single therapy that is relevant to all clients and all problems, a lack of evidence that one therapy is better than others, and recognition that therapy commonalities play an important role in therapy outcomes (Norcross, 2005).

At their best, integrative therapies are effective, systematic uses of a variety of therapy approaches (Corey, 2005). However, one worry about integrative therapies is that their increased use will result in an unsystematic, haphazard eclecticism, which some therapists say would be no better than a narrow, dogmatic approach to therapy (Norcross, 2005).

With the increased diversity of client problems and populations, future integrative therapies are likely to include more attention to ethnic and cultural factors in treating clients (Sue, 2000). This increased ethnic and cultural diversity will also require therapists to integrate spiritual concerns into their therapy approach (Sollod, 2005).

Integrative therapies are also at work when individuals are treated with both psychotherapy and drug therapy. For example, combined drug therapy and cognitive therapy has been effective in treating anxiety and depressive disorders (Dunner, 2001). And combined drug therapy and cognitive therapy holds promise in treating schizophrenia (Rector & Beck, 2001; Rector, 2004). This integrative approach might be conducted by a mental health team that includes a psychiatrist and a clinical psychologist.

Integrative therapies are conceptually compatible with the biopsychosocial model of abnormal behaviour described in chapter 13. That is, many therapists believe that abnormal behaviour involves biological, psychological, and social factors. Many single-therapy approaches focus on one aspect of the person more than others; for instance, drug therapies focus on biological factors, and cognitive therapies focus on psychological factors. Integrative therapies often taken a broader look at individuals' problems.

Funding and Finding Therapy

The need to control rising health-care costs in Canada has led governments to restructure the delivery of health care, including mental health care. In response, the Canadian Mental Health Association has developed an influential framework for mental health policy (Pomeroy, Trainor, & Pape, 2002; Trainor, Pomeroy, & Pape, 1999). The framework is structured around the Community Resource Base, which assumes the perspective of the person living at the centre—the person with a mental health problem. Surrounding that person are four key components:

- The traditional mental health services, which continue to have a role to play in psychosocial rehabilitation
- Family and friends, which are the largest and most influential group of caregivers
- Consumer groups and organizations, which constitute a new and growing body of stakeholders with the capacity to develop self-help services
- Generic community services and groups, such as welfare and family services as well as religious organizations and service clubs, which must be integrated into an overall support plan

In the United States, rising costs led to the development of private managed care. **Managed care** consists of strategies for controlling health care costs, including mental health treatment, and demands for accountability of treatment success. Emerging in the 1980s (Corcoran, Gorin, & Moniz, 2005), managed care providers attempt to offer services at lower costs by limiting traditional services, using stringent review procedures, and using

managed care Consists of strategies for controlling health care costs, including mental health treatment, and demands for accountability of treatment success.

Professional Type	Degree	Education Beyond Bachelor's Degree	Nature of Training
Clinical psychologist	Ph.D. or Psy.D	5–7 years	Some American universities offer Psy.D. programs, which lead to a professional degree with a stronger emphasis on clinical work than research. Under some circumstances it is possible to complete a Psy.D. degree in the United States and go on into clinical practice in Canada.
Psychiatrist	M.D.	7–9 years	Four years of medical school, plus an internship and residency in psychiatry are required. A psychiatry residency involves supervision in therapies, including psychotherapy and biomedical therapy.
Counselling psychologist	M.A., Ph.D., Psy.D., or Ed.D.	3–7 years	Similar to clinical psychologist but with emphasis on counselling and therapy. Some counselling psychologists specialize in vocational counselling. Some counsellors complete master's degree training, others Ph.D. or Ed.D training, in graduate schools of psychology or education.
School psychologist	M.A., Ph.D., Psy.D., or Ed.D.	3–7 years	Training in graduate programs of education or psychology. Emphasis on psychological assessment and counselling practices involving students' school-related problems. Training is at the master's or doctoral level.
Social worker	M.S.W./D.S.W. or Ph.D.	2–5 years	Graduate work in a school of social work that includes specialized clinical training in mental health facilities.
Psychiatric nurse	R.N., M.A., or Ph.D.	0–5 years	Graduate work in a school of nursing with special emphasis on care of mentally disturbed individuals in hospital settings and mental health facilities.
Occupational therapist	B.S., M.A., or Ph.D.	0–5 years	Emphasis on occupational training with focus on physically or psychologically handicapped individuals. Stresses getting individuals back into the mainstream of work.
Pastoral counsellor	None to Ph.D. or D.D. (Doctor of Divinity)	0–5 years	Requires ministerial background and training in psychology. An internship in a mental health facility as a chaplain is recommended.
Counsellor	M.A. or M.Ed.	2 years	Graduate work in a department of psychology or department of education with specialized training in counselling techniques.

FIGURE 14.14 **Main Types of Mental Health Professionals**

lower-cost brief treatment options. Managed care has been criticized for stressing cost control at the expense of effective treatment. Grembowski (2003) has argued that managed care has made primary physicians less likely to refer clients for mental health care in the first place (Grembowski, 2003). Even when mental health care is prescribed, expensive treatments, such as long-term community-based care, are difficult to obtain (Schied, 2003).

Mental Health Professionals

Psychotherapy is practised by a variety of mental health professionals, including clinical psychologists, psychiatrists, and counsellors. Recall that psychiatrists have a medical degree. Clinical psychologists, in contrast, are trained in graduate programs in psychology. Figure 14.14 lists the main types of mental health professionals, their degrees, the years of education required, and the nature of their training.

Licensing and certification are two ways that society retains control over individuals who practise psychotherapy (Remley & Herlihy, 2005). Laws at the provincial level are used to license or certify someone as a psychologist (although the use of the professional designation "psychotherapist" is much less regulated; Evans, 1997). The requirements vary but generally they consist of advanced academic qualifications, supervised clinical experience, and some form of competency examination. Once psychologists become licensed to practise they must maintain high standards of competence as specified by the Canadian Psychological Association's Canadian Code of Ethics for Psychologists (Evans, 1997).

Licensing and certification also require mental health practitioners to engage in ethical practices. Laws typically address the importance of doing no harm to clients, protecting the privacy of clients, and avoiding inappropriate relationships with clients. Violations of ethical codes can result in a loss of the licence to practise psychotherapy (Evans, 1997; Hecker & Thorpe, 2005).

Guidelines for Seeking Professional Help

Ling felt anxious most of the time. But what caused her the greatest difficulty was that she became so anxious during exams in her classes that she would nearly freeze. Her mind would go blank, and she would begin to sweat and shake all over. It was such a problem that she was failing her classes. She told one of her professors that this was the problem with her grades. He told her that it sounded as if she had a serious case of test anxiety and that she should get some help. Ling decided that she should take his advice and wanted to find a psychotherapist. How would she go about finding a therapist? Are certain professionals more qualified than others? How could she know that she was going to see someone who could help her rather than someone who would not be helpful, or would perhaps even make things worse? These are only a few of the questions people commonly have when they want to find a therapist.

When trying to find a therapist, Ling could consider a psychologist, psychiatrist, social worker, counsellor, or any number of other helping professionals. Each of these mental health professionals is qualified to provide psychotherapeutic services. They all practise any one of a combination of the therapeutic orientations discussed in this chapter. They may also see people on an individual, one-to-one basis or in small groups, as in group therapy. The critical question is, of course, how does someone go about selecting a therapist to help him or her? This is not as easy a question as it may appear at first glance. We may face many of the same problems when we try to find a "good" medical doctor, accountant, or dentist; however, the way that most people go about finding these other professional services may not be the best way of selecting a therapist. Asking a friend to recommend a good therapist ignores the fact that some approaches to therapy work better with some problems than others. Also, every therapeutic relationship is different, so one person's experience in therapy is not translatable to another person's. Following are some general suggestions when looking for a therapist.

Identify the Professional's Credentials   Although all different types of mental health professionals may be competent, psychologists, psychiatrists, and social workers all differ in their approach to therapy based on differences in training: Psychologists tend to be focused on the person's emotions and behaviours; psychiatrists are trained as medical doctors, so their perspective is likely to involve physical aspects of psychological problems; and social workers are inclined to take a person's entire family and social situation into account. Regardless of the specific profession, some minimal credentials should be considered important. All provinces have licensing regulations for professionals who provide public services. Thus every province licenses or certifies individuals to practise as psychologists (but, in general, the provinces exercise less control over the term "psychotherapist"). In addition, in some cases it may be important for a professional to have some advanced, specialized training in a certain area. For example, if a person is seeking help with a specific problem, such as drug abuse, alcohol abuse, or a sexual problem, the therapist should have some training in that area. You should ask about the professional's credentials either before or during a first visit.

Give Therapy Some Time   Making changes is very difficult. Expecting too much too soon can result in premature dissatisfaction and disappointment. Because a large part of therapy involves the development of a relationship with the therapist, it may take several meetings to really know if things are going well. One suggestion is to give therapy between four and six weekly meetings. If it does not seem as if things are going the way you would like, it is a good idea to discuss your progress with the therapist and ask what you should expect with regard to making progress. Setting specific goals with specific time expectations can be helpful. If your goals are not being met, consider a new therapist.

Evaluating Whether You Need a Therapist

There are no hard-and-fast rules about when people should go to a psychotherapist for help with their personal problems. However, to get a sense of whether you should see a psychotherapist, evaluate whether you have recently experienced the following:

- I feel sad or blue a lot.
- My self-esteem is really low.
- I feel like other people are always out to get me.
- I feel so anxious that it is hard for me to function.
- I have trouble concentrating on my academic work.
- I don't do anything social and spend much of my spare time alone.

- I have a tendency to alienate people when I don't really want to.
- I'm frightened by things that I know should not be fear-provoking.
- I hear voices that tell me what I should do.
- I know I have problems, but I just don't feel I can talk with anyone about them.

If any of these statements describe your life, consider talking over your concerns with a qualified therapist. Most colleges and universities have counselling or mental health services that are covered by your student fees. This is a good place to start in seeking mental health consultation.

Be a Thoughtful and Careful Consumer of Mental Health Services With mental health services, as is true when you seek any services, the more informed you are about the services provided, the better decision you can make about whether or not they are the right services for you. The Canadian Psychological Association Web site offers information about deciding whether or not to see a psychologist, how to choose one, and what to expect if you go (www.cpa.ca/Psychologist). There you will also find links to provincial licensing boards and psychology associations (www.cpa.ca/provs.html) while the Canadian Register of Health Service Providers in Psychology (www.crhspp.ca) maintains a voluntary listing of appropriately qualified health service providers in psychology. Calling around and asking specific questions about approaches and specializations is one way to become informed about the services offered by therapists. You may also want to learn more about their theoretical orientation to therapy as described in this chapter. Another way to find out more about a therapist is to ask these kinds of questions during your first visit. Most professionals are quite comfortable talking about their background and training. Your confidence and trust in the professional is an important part of how well therapy will work for you.

Use these general guidelines when first looking for a therapist. Remember that people should continually evaluate their own progress throughout therapy and, when they are dissatisfied with how it is going, they should discuss this feeling with their therapists. Remember that therapy is like other services: When dissatisfied, you can always look for another therapist. Don't think that just because one therapist has not been helpful, none will be. All therapists and therapeutic relationships are different. Finding the right therapist is one of the most important factors in therapy success. See the Personal Reflections box to help evaluate whether you should see a therapist.

> reflect and review

4 **Evaluate the effectiveness of psychotherapy.**

- Discuss research on psychotherapy effectiveness.
- Describe common themes in psychotherapy.
- Explain integrative therapies.
- List the kinds of health professionals who are qualified to provide mental health treatment and state the effects of managed care on mental health treatment.
- Summarize the guidelines for seeking professional help.

Explain why a control group is important in research on psychotherapy effectiveness.

> review your learning goals

Therapies

1 BIOLOGICAL THERAPIES

- Drug Therapy
- Electroconvulsive Therapy
- Psychosurgery

2 PSYCHOTHERAPIES

- Psychodynamic Therapies
- Humanistic Therapies
- Behaviour Therapies
- Cognitive Therapies

3 SOCIOCULTURAL APPROACHES AND ISSUES IN TREATMENT

- Group Therapy
- Family and Couples Therapy
- Self-Help Support Groups
- Community Mental Health
- Cultural Perspectives

4 THE EFFECTIVENESS OF PSYCHOTHERAPY

- Research on the Effectiveness of Psychotherapy
- Common Themes in Psychotherapy
- Integrative Therapies
- Funding and Finding Therapy
- Mental Health Professionals
- Guidelines for Seeking Professional Help

At the beginning of the chapter, we posed six chapter questions and encouraged you to review material related to these questions at the end of each major section (see pages 559, 575, 581, and 587). Use the following reflection and review features for further your understanding of the chapter material.

CHAPTER REFLECTIONS

1. The chapter describes some types of psychosurgery previously performed on patients. Use the Internet to research the kinds of problems that are currently treated with psychosurgery. Do you think psychosurgery should still be used?

2. Think critically about the use of antidepressant and antipsychotic drugs. Using your library, do some research for evidence that drug therapy works. If you were diagnosed with a psychological disorder, would you take a drug? Why or why not?

3. Behavioural and cognitive approaches may be helpful to change behaviours that wouldn't be considered abnormal but that you might want to change (for example, procrastinating, eating unhealthy food, or watching too much TV). Think about a behaviour that you would like to do more, or less, frequently; then, think like a behavioural or cognitive therapist and describe the kinds of recommendations you might hear during a therapy session.

4. Think about the sociocultural approaches to therapy. For which kinds of problems would you be most likely to choose one of these approaches? Which approach would you choose? Do some research and see whether you can find a local group or therapist that would be helpful to someone with this kind of problem. What would you do if none were available in your area?

5. Imagine that a good friend confesses that he or she has been having some difficulties coping with some aspects of his or her life and asks you for advice in finding a psychotherapist. Based on the therapies and their effectiveness discussed in the text, what kind of advice would you give your friend?

6. Visit the Web site of the Canadian Psychological Association for information on deciding whether or not to see a psychologist, how to choose one, and what to expect if you go (www.cpa.ca/Psychologist/). Is the information you found there helpful?

CHAPTER REVIEW

Describe the biological therapies.

- Psychotherapeutic drugs that are used to treat psychological disorders fall into three main categories: antianxiety drugs, antidepressant drugs, and antipsychotic drugs. Antianxiety drugs are commonly known as tranquilizers. Benzodiazepines are the most commonly used antianxiety drugs. Antidepressant drugs regulate mood; the three main classes are tricyclics, MAO inhibitors, and SSRI drugs. Lithium is often successful in treating bipolar disorder. The antidepressant drugs are increasingly being used to treat some anxiety disorders as well. Antipsychotic drugs are powerful drugs that are used to treat people with severe psychological disorders, especially schizophrenia. Psychotherapeutic drugs have varying effectiveness and side effects.

- Electroconvulsive therapy, commonly called shock therapy, is used to treat severe depression when other strategies have not worked.

- Psychosurgery is an irreversible procedure in which brain tissue is destroyed in an attempt to improve adjustment. Today, psychosurgery is rarely used and is more precise than the early prefrontal lobotomies.

Define psychotherapy and characterize four types of psychotherapy.

- Psychotherapy is the process used by mental health professionals to help individuals recognize, define, and overcome their psychological and interpersonal difficulties and improve their adjustment. Psychotherapists use a number of strategies to accomplish these goals: talking, interpreting, listening, rewarding, and modelling, for example. The insight therapies consist of the psychodynamic therapies and the humanistic therapies.

- Psychodynamic therapies stress the importance of the unconscious mind, early family experiences, and extensive interpretation by therapists. In Freudian psychoanalysis, psychological disorders are caused by unresolved unconscious conflicts, believed to originate in early family experiences. A therapist's interpretation of free association, dreams, transference, and resistance provide tools for understanding the client's unconscious conflicts. Although psychodynamic therapy has changed, many contemporary psychodynamic therapists still probe the unconscious mind for early family experiences that might provide clues to clients' current problems. The development of the self in social contexts is an important theme in Kohut's contemporary approach.

- In humanistic therapy, clients are encouraged to understand themselves and to grow personally. The humanistic therapies emphasize conscious thoughts, the present, and growth and fulfillment. Client-centred therapy was developed by Carl Rogers. In this therapy, the therapist provides a warm, supportive atmosphere to improve the client's self-concept and to encourage the client to gain insight into problems. Client-centred techniques include unconditional positive regard, genuineness, empathy, and active listening to raise the client's self-esteem. Fritz Perls developed gestalt therapy, in which therapists question and challenge clients to help them become more aware of their feelings and face their problems. Gestalt psychologists use such therapy techniques as setting examples and role playing. Gestalt therapy's techniques are more directive than Rogers' client-centred techniques.

- Behaviour therapies use principles of learning to reduce or eliminate maladaptive behaviour. They are based on the behavioural and social cognitive theories of personality. Behaviour therapies seek to eliminate the symptoms of behaviours rather than to help individuals to gain insight into their problems. Behaviour therapists increasingly use observational learning, cognitive factors, and self-instruction in their efforts to help people with their problems. Classical conditioning and operant conditioning techniques are used in behaviour therapies. The two main therapy techniques based on classical conditioning are systematic desensitization and aversive conditioning. In systematic desensitization, anxiety is treated by getting the individual to associate deep relaxation with increasingly intense anxiety-producing situations. A concentrated form of desensitization is flooding. In aversive conditioning, pairings of the undesirable behaviour with aversive stimuli are repeated to decrease the behaviour's rewards. In operant conditioning approaches to therapy, a careful analysis of the person's environment is conducted to determine which factors need to be modified. Behaviour modification is the application of operant conditioning to change human behaviour. Its main goal is to replace unacceptable, maladaptive behaviours with acceptable, adaptive ones. A token economy is a behaviour modification system in which behaviours are reinforced with tokens that later can be exchanged for desired rewards.

- Cognitive therapies emphasize that the individual's cognitions or thoughts are the main source of abnormal behaviour. Cognitive therapies attempt to change the person's feelings and behaviours by changing cognitions. Three main forms of cognitive therapy are Ellis's rational-emotive behaviour therapy, Beck's cognitive therapy, and Meichenbaum's cognitive-behaviour therapy. Ellis's approach is based on the assertion that individuals develop psychological disorders because of their beliefs, especially those that are irrational and self-defeating. Beck's cognitive therapy has been especially effective in treating depression. In Beck's therapy, the therapist assists the client in learning about logical errors in thinking and then guides the client in challenging these thinking errors. Ellis's approach is more directive, persuasive, and confrontational than Beck's. Meichenbaum's cognitive-behaviour therapy combines cognitive therapy and behaviour therapy techniques. Self-efficacy and self-instructional methods are used in this approach. Cognitive therapy has been demonstrated to be effective in treating a number of psychological problems.

Explain the sociocultural approaches and issues in treatment.

- Group therapies emphasize that relationships can hold the key to successful therapy. Psychodynamic, humanistic, behaviour, and cognitive therapies, as well as unique group approaches, are used in group therapy.

- Family therapy is group therapy with family members. Four widely used family therapy techniques are validation, reframing, structural change, and detriangulation. Couples therapy is group therapy with married or unmarried couples whose major problem is within their relationship.

- Self-help support groups are voluntary organizations of individuals who get together on a regular basis to discuss topics of common interest. They are conducted without a professional therapist.

- The community mental health movement was born out of the belief that the mental health–care system was not adequately reaching people in poverty and people who had been deinstitutionalized. Community mental health emphasizes primary, secondary, and tertiary prevention. Empowerment is often a goal of community mental health.

- Psychotherapies have mainly focused on the individual, which may work well in individualized cultures such as those in North America. However, these psychotherapies may not work as well in collectivist cultures. Many ethnic minority individuals prefer to discuss problems with parents, friends, and relatives rather than with mental health professionals. Therapy is often more effective when there is an ethnic match between the therapist and the client, although effective therapy can be provided by a culturally sensitive therapist who is from a different ethnic background. The emphasis on autonomy in psychotherapies may produce a problem for many women, who place a strong emphasis on connectedness in relationships. Some feminist-based therapies have emerged.

Evaluate the effectiveness of psychotherapy.

- Psychotherapy is generally effective. Researchers have found, using meta-analysis, that the cognitive and behaviour therapies are successful in treating anxiety and depressive disorders. Relaxation therapy also has been effective in treating anxiety disorders.

- Successful psychotherapy commonly includes positive expectations of help, increasing the client's sense of mastery, arousing the client's emotions, and developing the client's confidence and trust in the therapist.

- More and more practising therapists refer to themselves as "integrative" or "eclectic." Integrative therapies use a combination of techniques from different therapies based on the therapist's judgment of which particular techniques will provide the greatest benefit for the client. In some instances, a combination of a particular type of psychotherapy and drug therapy is most effective in treating a psychological disorder.

- Psychotherapy can be expensive, which has led to substantial changes in the delivery of mental health care. Canada has adopted the idea of the Community Resource Base, while the U.S. has developed managed care, which has received its share of criticism.

- Mental health professionals include clinical and counselling psychologists, psychiatrists, school psychologists, social workers, psychiatric nurses, occupational therapists, pastoral counsellors, and counsellors. These mental health professionals have different degrees, education, and training. Society retains some control over individuals who practise psychotherapy through licensing and certification.

- Guidelines for seeking professional mental health care include identifying the professional's credentials, giving therapy some time before judging its usefulness, and being a thoughtful and careful consumer of mental health services.

CONNECTIONS

For extra help in mastering the material in the chapter, see the review questions and practice quizzes in the Student Study Guide and the Online Learning Centre.

CORE TERMS

biological therapies, p. 554
psychotherapy, p. 554
antianxiety drugs, p. 554
antidepressant drugs, p. 555
lithium, p. 556
antipsychotic drugs, p. 556
electroconvulsive therapy (ECT), p. 558
psychosurgery, p. 559
insight therapy, p. 560
psychodynamic therapies, p. 560
psychoanalysis, p. 560

free association, p. 561
catharsis, p. 561
dream analysis, p. 563
transference, p. 563
resistance, p. 563
humanistic therapies, p. 563
client-centred therapy, p. 564
gestalt therapy, p. 564
behaviour therapy, p. 565
systematic desensitization, p. 566
aversive conditioning, p. 568

behaviour modification, p. 569
cognitive therapies, p. 570
rational-emotive behaviour therapy, p. 571
cognitive-behaviour therapy, p. 573
family therapy, p. 577
couples therapy, p. 577
meta-analysis, p. 581
integrative therapies, p. 583
managed care, p. 584

15 Stress, Coping, and Health

CHAPTER QUESTIONS

1. What is the scope of health psychology and behavioural medicine?

2. What is stress and what are its sources?

3. How do people respond to stress?

4. What are the links between stress and illness?

5. What are some strategies for coping with stress?

6. How can health be promoted?

Americaner Norman Cousins (1915–1990) was a life-long optimist, publicly advocating for human freedom and justice as well as world peace. As the longtime editor of the magazine *Saturday Review*, Cousins wrote extensively on these subjects and actively worked to shape American policies throughout his lifetime. His achievements were recognized with hundreds of awards including the 1963 Eleanor Roosevelt Peace Award, the 1968 Family of Man Award, and the 1971 United Nations Peace Medal.

Norman Cousins also displayed his extraordinary humanism and optimism in facing his own personal health challenges (Irwin, 2005). In the 1960's Cousins was stricken with ankylosing spondylitis, a degenerative disease characterized by the breakdown of collagen, the fibrous tissue that gives structure to the body's cells. Facing paralysis and given only months to live, Cousins moved from the hospital to a hotel where he consumed megadoses of vitamin C and humour. He recovered from his illness and went on to write about his experience in his 1979 book, *Anatomy of an Illness as Perceived by the Patient: Reflections on Healing and Regeneration*, which became a best-seller. About the role of humour, he said, "Hearty laughter is a good way to jog internally without having to go outdoors."

Fifteen years later, Cousins had a heart attack and is reputed to have remarked to the doctors in the emergency room, "Gentlemen, I want you to know that you're looking at the darnedest healing machine that's ever been wheeled into this hospital." Once again he recovered and wrote about his experiences, this time in his 1983 book *The Healing Heart: Antidotes to Panic and Helplessness*.

Following his retirement from the *Saturday Review*, Cousins became an adjunct professor of medical humanities at the UCLA School of Medicine. Today, the Cousins Center of Psychoneuroimmunology at UCLA continues to investigate the role of positive psychology in mental and physical health (Irwin, 2005).

Researchers continue to be inspired by the example of positive psychology pioneers like Norman Cousins (e.g., Fleshner & Laudenslager, 2004). Several avenues of research will be explored in this chapter, from the role of stress in our mental and physical health to the importance of how we respond to stress and the challenges of healthy living. For example, several tests have been developed to measure stress. How do you fare on the stress test in Figure 15.1?

NORMAN COUSINS (1915–1990)

Rate yourself on each item, using a scale of 1–5:

1 = almost always	2 = often	3 = sometimes	4 = seldom	5 = never

1 1. I eat at least one hot, balanced meal a day.

3 2. I get 7 to 8 hours of sleep at least four nights a week.

1 3. I give and receive affection regularly.

1 4. I have at least one relative within 80 kilometres whom I can rely on.

1 5. I exercise to the point of perspiration at least twice a week.

1 6. I smoke less than half a pack of cigarettes a day.

5 7. I have fewer than five alcoholic drinks a week.

3 8. I am the appropriate weight for my height.

4 9. I have an income adequate to meet my basic expenses.

5 10. I get strength from my religious beliefs.

5 11. I regularly attend church.

1 12. I have a network of friends and acquaintances.

1 13. I have one or more friends to confide in about personal matters.

2 14. I am in good health (including eyesight, hearing, teeth).

2 15. I am able to speak openly about my feelings when angry or worried.

2 16. I have regular conversations with the people I live with about domestic problems (e.g., chores, money, and daily living issues).

1 17. I do something for fun at least once a week.

4 18. I am able to organize my time effectively.

2 19. I drink fewer than three cups of coffee (or tea or cola drinks) a day.

4 20. I take quiet time for myself during the day.

Total: _____

To get your total score, add your answers and subtract 20. Any number over 30 indicates a vulnerability to stress. You are seriously vulnerable if your score is between 50 and 75, extremely vulnerable if it is over 75.

FIGURE 15.1 **How Stressed Are You?**

❶ HEALTH PSYCHOLOGY AND BEHAVIOURAL MEDICINE

(Top) Members of this Masai tribe in Kenya, Africa, can stay on a treadmill for a long time because of their active lives. Heart disease is extremely low in the Masai tribe, which also can be attributed to their energetic lifestyle. *(Bottom)* North Americans are increasingly recognizing the health benefits of exercise and an active lifestyle. The role of exercise in health is one of health psychology's many interests.

health psychology Emphasizes psychology's role in promoting and maintaining health and in preventing and treating illness.

behavioural medicine An interdisciplinary field that focuses on developing and integrating behavioural and biomedical knowledge to promote health and reduce illness.

What is the scope of health psychology and behavioural medicine?

For hundreds of years the *medical model* prevailed in Western society. Health was defined as the absence of disease and illness was conceptualized as due to biological factors such as bacterial infections or the deterioration of organs like the heart or lungs. That is, health was thought to involve only bodily factors, not mental factors. Often people's complaints were dismissed with the phrase "It's all in your mind."

Today, in part due to the example set by Norman Cousins, we live with a growing awareness that health is not merely an absence of illness, but is a positive state of well-being toward which we strive and which we seek to maintain (Health Canada, 2001). The ultimate responsibility for influencing health rests not with doctors but with individuals themselves. In addition, both the body *and* mind can exert important influences on health. Indeed, a combination of biological, psychological, and social factors may be explored as possible causes of health or illness. The *biopsychosocial model* that we discussed in chapter 13 applies to health psychology as well (Oakley, 2004). Figure 15.2 contrasts health care as conceptualized within the medical model of the past with that of the biopsychosocial model of the future.

Two relatively new fields of study—health psychology and behavioural medicine—reflect the belief that lifestyles and psychological states can play important roles in health. **Health psychology** emphasizes psychology's role in promoting and maintaining health and in preventing and treating illness. **Behavioural medicine** is an interdisciplinary field that focuses on developing and integrating behavioural and biomedical knowledge to promote health and reduce illness. Behavioural medicine and health psychology are overlapping, and sometimes indistinguishable, fields. But when distinctions are made, behavioural medicine is viewed as a broader field that focuses on both behavioural and biomedical factors, whereas health psychology tends to focus on cognitive and behavioural factors. A joint survey of the health of Canadians and Americans revealed that 88 percent of Canadians and 85 percent of Americans reported being in excellent, very good, or good health (Statistics Canada, 2003).

The interests of health psychologists and behavioural medicine researchers are broad (Lyons & Chamberlain, 2006; Boll & others, 2002). They include examining how stress affects an individual's immune functioning, why we do or do not comply with medical advice, how effective media campaigns are in reducing smoking, what psychological factors play a part in losing weight, and how exercise helps in reducing stress (Wood, 2001).

Changing patterns of illness in developed countries have fuelled the increased interest in health psychology and behavioural medicine. Just a century ago, the leading causes of death were infectious diseases such as influenza, tuberculosis, polio, typhoid fever, rubella, and smallpox. Today, none of these diseases are among the major causes of death in developed countries. Rather, 7 of the 10 leading causes of death in the United States today are related to personal habits and lifestyles. Similarly, the various forms of cardiovascular disease (stroke, heart attack) and cancer alone accounted for 63 percent of all deaths in Canada in 1996 (Health Canada, 1999). Other chronic diseases such as diabetes are also major contributors to disability and death. Health behaviours often play key roles in these diseases, as they did in Norman Cousins' recoveries from his own health challenges (Taylor, 2006).

In 1999, health-care spending cost the Canadian federal and provincial governments $86 billion (Statistics Canada, 2001) and costs continue to rise rapidly. Health experts hope to make a dent in these costs by encouraging people to live healthier lives. Many corporations now recognize that health promotion for their employees is cost effective.

Health experts are also acknowledging that psychological and social factors are involved in many chronic diseases (Forshaw, 2002). In fact, the fields of health psychology and behavioural medicine evolved partly to examine these factors and to find ways to help people cope more effectively (Conner & Norman, 2005; Zwaal & others, 2003; Prkachin & others, 2002). One of the main areas of research in health psychology and

Components of Health

Care Models	Medical Model (Past)	Biopsychosocial Model (Future)
Focus	Fighting sickness	Building Health
Emphasis	Environmental factors	Behavioural factors
Causes of disease	Pathogen	Host-pathogen interaction
Patient role	Passive recipient of treatment	Active in treatment and health
Belief system of patient	Irrelevant Determiner of treatment and healing	Critically important Collaborator in treatment and healing
Physician role	process	process

behavioural medicine is the link between stress and illness (Dougall & Baum, 2001). Researchers are finding that our psychological and physical well-being are related to how much stress we face and how we cope with it. These topics are the focus of this chapter.

FIGURE 15.2

Past and Future Approaches to Health Care

Source: Based on Oakley, 2004.

> **reflect and review**

1 **Describe the scope of health psychology and behavioural medicine.**

- Define health psychology and behavioural medicine and describe how they seek to promote health and reduce illness.

How high would you estimate your stress level to be? Do you think stress affects your health? What are the signs that it does?

2 STRESS AND ITS SOURCES

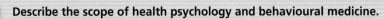

Personality Factors   Environmental Factors   Sociocultural Factors

What is stress and what are its sources?

Stress is inevitable in human lives, given the conflict between our needs and desires and the realities of our environment and relationships. Sometimes stress is useful, but extreme stress often leads to serious health problems. Thus, human beings have long sought to understand what factors are involved in causing stress, in managing it effectively, and in maintaining a healthy lifestyle.

In 1994–95, over 25 percent of Canadians reported high chronic stress levels while almost half (47 percent) of lone female parents experienced high chronic stress (Health Canada, 1999). Stress is a major contributor to coronary heart disease, cancer, lung disease, accidental injuries, cirrhosis of the liver, and suicide—six of the leading causes of death in North America. Antianxiety drugs and ulcer medications are among the best-selling prescription drugs in North America today.

Stress is a sign of the times. Everywhere you look, people are trying to reduce the effects of excessive tension by jogging, going to health clubs, and following special diets. Even corporations have developed elaborate stress management programs. No one really knows whether we experience more stress than our parents or grandparents did, but it seems as if we do.

"I think we can rule out stress."

© Sidney Harris.

Type **Z** behaviour

© The New Yorker Collection 1987. Donald Reilly from cartoonbank.com. All Rights Reserved.

Initially, the word *stress* was loosely borrowed from physics. Humans, it was thought, are in some ways similar to physical objects such as metals, which resist moderate outside forces but lose their resilience under greater pressure. But, unlike metals, human beings can think and reason, and they experience a myriad social and environmental circumstances that make defining stress more complex in psychology than in physics (Hobfoll, 2002). Thus, in psychological terms, we can define **stress** as the response of individuals to stressors, the circumstances and events that threaten them and tax their coping abilities.

To understand stress, we need to examine its sources. They include personality factors, environmental factors, and sociocultural factors.

Personality Factors

Do certain personality characteristics help people cope more effectively with stress and make them less vulnerable to illness? The answer to this question is yes and focuses on three aspects of personality that have been studied extensively in relation to stress: Type A/Type B behaviour patterns, hardiness, and personal control.

Type A/Type B Behaviour Patterns In the late 1950s, a secretary for two California cardiologists, Meyer Friedman and Ray Rosenman, observed that the chairs in their waiting rooms were tattered and worn, but only on the front edges. The cardiologists had also noticed the impatience of their cardiac patients, who often arrived exactly on time for an appointment and were in a great hurry to leave. Intrigued by this consistency, they conducted a classic study of 3000 healthy men between the ages of 35 and 59 over a period of eight years to find out whether people with certain behavioural characteristics might be prone to heart problems (Friedman & Rosenman, 1974). During the eight years, one group of men had twice as many heart attacks or other forms of heart disease as the other men. And autopsies of the men who died revealed that this same group had coronary arteries that were more obstructed than those of the other men.

Friedman and Rosenman described the common personality characteristics of the men who developed coronary disease as the **Type A behaviour pattern**. They theorized that a cluster of characteristics—being excessively competitive, hard-driven, impatient, and hostile—is related to the incidence of heart disease. Rosenman and Friedman labelled the behaviour of the healthier group, who were commonly relaxed and easygoing, the **Type B behaviour pattern**.

Research on the link between Type A behaviour and coronary disease reveals greater complexity than Friedman and Rosenman believed (Frieman, 2002; Jamal, 2005). Researchers have examined components of Type A behaviour, such as hostility, competitiveness, time pressure, goal orientation, and impatience, to determine a more precise link with coronary risk and have found that hostility is most consistently associated with coronary problems (T. W. Smith & others, 2004; Boyle & others, 2004; Markovitz, Jonas, & Davidson, 2001).

Further research has shown that hostility is itself a complex construct (Zwaal & others, 2003). On the one hand, outwardly hostile people may also be especially vulnerable to coronary heart disease (McDermott, Ramsay, & Bray, 2001; Miller & others; 1996). On the other hand, anger-defensive individuals also show elevated cardiovascular responses to some stressors (Miller, 1993). Similarly, Greenglass (1996) has shown that Canadian managers who suppress their anger and show cynical distrust are more vulnerable to coronary problems. Regardless, Redford Williams, of the Duke University Medical Center, believes that hostile people have the ability to control their anger and develop more trust in others, which he thinks can reduce their risk for heart disease (R. B. Williams, 2001, 2002).

stress The response of individuals to stressors, the circumstances and events that threaten and tax their coping abilities.

Type A behaviour pattern A cluster of characteristics—being excessively competitive, hard-driven, and hostile—thought to be related to the incidence of heart disease.

Type B behaviour pattern A relaxed and easygoing personality.

Hardiness **Hardiness** is a personality style characterized by a sense of commitment (rather than alienation), control (rather than powerlessness), and a perception of problems as challenges (rather than threats).

In the classic Chicago Stress Project, male business managers were studied over a five-year period during which most of them experienced stressful events, such as divorce, job transfers, the death of a close friend, and working with an unpleasant boss (Kobasa, Maddi, & Kahn, 1982; Kobasa & others, 1986). Managers who developed an illness (ranging from the flu to a heart attack) were compared with those who did not (Kobasa, Maddi, & Kahn, 1982). The latter group was more likely to have a hardy personality. In another study, when hardiness was combined with exercise and social support, the level of illness dropped even further (Kobasa, Maddi, & Kahn, 1982). That is, when all three factors were present in an executive's life the level of illness dropped dramatically (see Figure 15.3).

Immigrants have also been a focus of hardiness research, due to the stress they face when adapting to their new country. In one study, Australian researchers showed that hardier Latin American immigrants experienced less stress in adapting to life in Melbourne (Lopez, Haigh, & Burney, 2004). Similarly, Dion, Dion, & Pak (1992) studied the hardiness of members of Toronto's Chinese community and found that the relationship between experienced discrimination and psychological symptoms was stronger among respondents low in hardiness than in those high in hardiness.

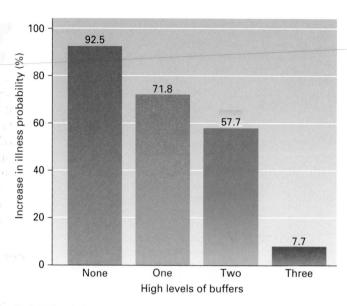

FIGURE 15.3 **Illness in High-Stress Business Executives**
In one study of high-stress business executives (all of whom were selected for this analysis because they were above the stress mean for the entire year of the study), a low level of all three buffers (hardiness, exercise, and social support) involved a high probability of at least one serious illness in that year. High levels of one, two, and all three buffers decreased the likelihood of at least one serious illness occurring in the year of the study.

Other researchers have also found support for the role of hardiness in illness, health, and posttraumatic growth (Almedom, 2005; Pengilly & Dowd, 2000). The results of hardiness research suggest the power of multiple factors, rather than any single factor, in buffering stress and maintaining health (Ouellette & DiPlacido, 2001).

Personal Control An important aspect of stress is the extent to which people can do something to control or reduce the stress, as well as their *perception* of a sense of control (Taylor, 2006; Thompson, 2001). As discussed in chapter 13, perceived lack of control in the face of stress can produce learned helplessness (Seligman, 1975), which can lead to depression.

In contrast, having a general sense of control reduces stress and can lead to the development of problem-solving strategies to cope with the stress. A person with a good sense of personal control might say, "If I stop smoking now, I will not develop lung cancer," or "If I exercise regularly, I won't develop cardiovascular disease."

A sense of control is important for people experiencing stressful events (Taylor & others, 2003). It may be especially important for people who are vulnerable to health problems, such as medical patients (including people with cancer), children, and older adults. You might recall, from chapter 4, the study by Judith Rodin and Ellen Langer (1977), in which a group of elderly nursing home residents were given greater control over their environment. Not only was their overall health better than the health of their counterparts who remained dependent on nursing home staff, but the more independent residents were also less likely to die within the 18-month time frame of the study.

A sense of personal control may also help people avoid a risky lifestyle that involves health-compromising behaviours. Consider a study of East German migrants to West Germany who found themselves unemployed (Mittag & Schwarzer, 1993). They often turned to heavy drinking for solace unless they had a sense of personal control (as measured by such survey items as, "When I'm in trouble, I can rely on my ability to deal with the problem effectively"). Across a wide range of studies, a sense of personal control over the stressful events that go on around people has been related to emotional well-being, successful coping with a stressful event, behaviour change that can promote good health, and good health (Decruyenaere & others, 2000; Pickering, 2001; Taylor & others, 2003).

hardiness A personality style characterized by a sense of commitment (rather than alienation), control (rather than powerlessness), and a perception of problems as challenges (rather than threats).

The events listed below commonly occur in the lives of university students. Check the space provided for the events that have occurred in your life during the past 12 months. When you have checked off all the events that have happened in the past 12 months, total the point values in parentheses for each checked item.

(100)	✓ Death of a close family member	4 ~~100~~	(25)	____ Problems with your boss or professor
(80)	✓ Jail term	63	(25)	____ Outstanding personal achievement
(63)	✓ Final year or first year in university	53	(25)	✓ Failure in some course
(60)	____ Pregnancy (yours or caused by you)	45	(20)	✓ Final exams
(53)	✓ Severe personal illness or injury	40	(20)	✓ Increased or decreased dating
(50)	____ Marriage	40	(20)	____ Change in working conditions
(45)	✓ Any interpersonal problems	40	(20)	____ Change in your major
(40)	✓ Financial difficulties	30	(18)	✓ Change in your sleeping habits
(40)	____ Death of a close friend	30	(15)	✓ Several-day vacation
(40)	✓ Arguments with your roommate (more than every other day)	30	(15)	✓ Change in eating habits
(40)	✓ Major disagreements with your family	25	(15)	✓ Family reunion
(30)	✓ Major change in personal habits	20	(15)	✓ Change in recreational activities
(30)	✓ Change of living environment	20	(15)	✓ Minor illness or injury
(30)	✓ Beginning or ending a job		(11)	____ Minor violations of the law

~~596~~

Total Life Events Score 599

2
5~~3~~6
18
15
15
15
599

Your total may predict the frequency of serious illness you will experience in the coming year. If your life events score totals 300 points or more, you have an 80 percent chance of having a significant illness in the coming year. If your total score is 299 to 150, you have a 50 percent chance of having a significant illness. If your total score is 149 points or less, your risk of significant illness decreases to 30 percent.

Keep in mind, in interpreting your life events total score, that such events checklists don't take into account how you cope with such events. Some people who experience stressful life events cope and adjust well to them, and others do not.

FIGURE 15.4

Impact of Life Events: Social Readjustment Scale

Environmental Factors

Many circumstances, large and small, can produce stress in our lives. In some instances, cataclysmic events, such as war, an automobile accident, a fire, or the death of a loved one, produce stress. But often the everyday pounding of being overloaded with work, dealing with a difficult situation, or being frustrated in an unhappy relationship produces stress.

Life Events and Daily Hassles Think about your own life. What events have created the most stress for you? Were they big problems like a change in financial status, getting fired, a divorce, the death of someone you loved, a personal injury? Or were they the everyday circumstances of your life, such as not having enough time to study, arguing with your girlfriend or boyfriend, not getting enough credit for the work you do at your job?

Some health psychologists have proposed that significant life events are the main environmental source of stress. Some psychologists have studied the effects of individual life events, such as a tornado or volcanic eruption; others have evaluated the effects of *clusters* of events. Thomas Holmes and Richard Rahe (1967) devised a scale to measure the possible cumulative effect of clusters of life events and their possible influence on illness. Their widely used Social Readjustment Rating Scale includes events ranging from the death of a spouse (100 stress points) to minor violations of the law (11 stress points). Figure 15.4 provides an opportunity for you to evaluate the stressfulness of life events you have experienced in the past year.

People who experience clusters of stressful life events are likelier to become ill than they normally would be (Pagano & others, 2004). However, the ability to predict illness from life events alone is modest. Total scores of life-events scales such as the Social Readjustment Rating Scale are frequently ineffective at predicting future health problems. A life-events checklist tells us nothing about a person's physiological makeup, constitutional strengths and weaknesses, ability to cope with stressful circumstances, support systems, or the nature of the social relationships involved—all of which are important in understanding how stress is related to illness. A divorce, for example, might be less stressful than a marriage filled with day-to-day tension. And the changes related to positive events in the Social Readjustment Scale, such as reconciling with a spouse and gaining a new family member, are not as difficult to cope with as the changes that result from negative events.

Because of these limitations, some health psychologists believe information about daily hassles and daily uplifts provide better clues than life events about the effects of stress (Gaudet, Clément, & Deuzeman, 2005; Crowther & others, 2001; DaCosta & others, 2000). Enduring a boring and tense job and living in poverty do not show up on scales of major life events. Yet the everyday tension involved in these living conditions creates a highly stressful life and, in some cases, psychological disorder or illness (Bottos & Dewey, 2004). In one study, students who experienced the most daily hassles were more likely to suffer from depression and anxiety (D'Angelo & Wierzbicki, 2003).

What are the biggest hassles for university students? One study showed that they included changes in sleeping or eating habits, changes in social activities, and increased workload. The fear of failing in our success-oriented world also often plays a role in university students' depression (Martin & Marsh, 2003). The small things in life—having fun, laughing, going to movies, getting along well with friends, and completing a task—can also provide university students with daily uplifts.

The daily-hassles approach can also be criticized as facing some of the same problems as the life-events scales approach. For example, knowing about a person's daily irritations and problems tell us nothing about her or his physiological resilience to stress, coping ability or strategies, or perceptions of stress. Further, the daily-hassles and -uplifts scale has not been consistently related to objective measures of health and illness. Another criticism is that daily hassles can be conceived of as dependent measures rather than as causes. People who complain about things, who report being anxious and unhappy, and who see the bad side of everything are likely to see more problems in their daily lives than people with an optimistic outlook are. From this perspective, problems do not predict bad moods; bad moods predict problems. But supporters of the daily-hassles and -uplifts concept reply that information about daily events can be used in concert with information about a person's physiological reactions, coping, and perceptions of stress to provide a more complete picture of the causes and consequences of stress.

Conflict Stress researchers who are interested in the effects of daily environmental experiences have studied a number of specific types of environmental stimuli. One such stimulus is conflict, which occurs when we must decide between two or more incompatible options. There are three major types of conflict, which were initially investigated by Neal Miller (1959):

- **Approach/approach conflict:** Conflict in which the individual must choose between two attractive stimuli or circumstances. Should you go out with the cute music lover or with the cute sports lover? Which car should you buy, a Kia Spectra or a Saturn Ion? The approach/approach conflict is the least stressful of the three types of conflict because either choice leads to a positive result.
- **Avoidance/avoidance conflict:** Conflict in which the individual must choose between two unattractive stimuli or circumstances. Do you go through the stress of giving an oral presentation in class or not show up and get a zero? You want to avoid both, but you must choose one or the other. Obviously, this conflict is more stressful than having the luxury of two enticing choices. In many instances, we delay our decision about the avoidance/avoidance conflict until the last possible moment.
- **Approach/avoidance conflict:** Conflict involving a single stimulus or circumstance that has both positive and negative characteristics. Let's say you really like the person you are going out with and are thinking about getting married. On the one hand, you are attracted by the steady affection and love that marriage might bring, but, on the other hand, marriage is a commitment you

approach/approach conflict A conflict in which the individual must choose between two attractive stimuli or circumstances.

avoidance/avoidance conflict A conflict in which the individual must choose between two unattractive stimuli or circumstances.

approach/avoidance conflict A conflict involving a single stimulus or circumstance that has both positive and negative characteristics.

What creates stress for workers?

might not feel ready to make. On a more mundane level, you might look at a menu and face a dilemma—the double chocolate delight would be sumptuous, but is it worth the extra half kilo of weight? Our world is full of approach/avoidance conflicts, and they can be highly stressful. In these circumstances, we often vacillate before deciding.

Overload Daily hassles can also result in a stress reaction called *overload*. Sometimes stimuli become so intense that we can no longer cope with them. For example, persistent high levels of noise overload our adaptability to other stimuli. Overload can occur with work as well. How often have you said to yourself, "There are not enough hours in the day to do all I have to do." In today's computer age especially, we are faced with information overload. It is easy to develop the uncomfortable feeling that we don't know as much about a topic as we should, even if we are experts.

According to Michael Leiter, of Acadia University, and his colleagues, overload can lead to a state of physical and emotional exhaustion that includes a hopeless feeling, chronic fatigue, and low energy (Leiter, 2005; Leiter & Maslach, 2001; Maslach, Schaufeli, & Leiter, 2001). **Burnout** does not usually occur because of one or two traumatic events but because of a gradual accumulation of everyday stresses (Demerouti & others, 2001; Leiter & Maslach, 1998). Burnout is most likely to occur among individuals who deal with others in highly emotional situations (such as nurses and social workers), but who have only limited control over the behaviour of their clients or patients or the results of the cases they handle (Alexander & Klein, 2001; DiGiacomo & Adamson, 2001; Schwarzer & Greenglass, 1999).

In poor economic times, corporate downsizing and restructuring can add to employee stress (Greenglass & Burke, 2000a). Ronald Burke and Esther Greenglass, of York University, have shown that nurses in Canada have been very vulnerable to burnout (Greenglass, Burke, & Moore, 2003). Not only do they work in emotional situations over which they have limited control, but they have also had to deal with shrinking health-care budgets. The resulting restructuring of health care has added more stress to an already stressful work environment (Greenglass & Burke, 2000b; Burke & Greenglass, 2000).

Burnout also affects one-quarter of the students at some universities. On a number of university campuses, burnout is the most frequent reason students leave school before earning their degrees. Most university counselling services have professionals who can effectively work with students to alleviate the sense of being overloaded and overwhelmed by life.

Work-Related Stress More North American workers are working harder and longer than they have in past decades just to maintain their standard of living. In one generation, the number of hours Americans work each week has increased by 8 percent to a current average of 47. Twenty percent of Americans are working 49 hours or more per week (U.S. National Institute for Occupational Safety and Health, 2001). Thirty-nine percent of Canadian workers in primary industries work more than 40 hours a week, while 12 percent work 60 hours a week or more (Statistics Canada, 2001).

The predictable result is greater work-related stress and increased risk for psychological and physical health problems (Nelson, Quick, & Simmons, 2001; Sulsky & Smith, 2005). Researchers have found that one-quarter to one-third of American workers have high job stress and are emotionally drained at the end of a workday (U.S. National Institute for Occupational Safety and Health, 2001). North American workers' stress levels have also increased because economic dips and downsizing trends among corporations have made their jobs less secure. In a study spanning the years 1996–2002, Statistics Canada (2005a) has also identified work-related stress as a factor in early retirement.

The stress level of workers also increases when their jobs do not meet their expectations (Rabasca, 1999). Employees who find their work personally rewarding are better able to handle workplace stress. North Americans want jobs that are secure, offer advancement, provide them with some control over the work they do rather than it being completely dictated by others, offer a sense of community among co-workers, and allow them

burnout A feeling of overload, including mental and physical exhaustion, that usually results from a gradual accumulation of everyday stresses.

to use their creative and problem-solving skills. For example, co-worker support is an important buffer against burnout among teachers (Greenglass, Burke, & Konarski, 1998) and in self-managed work teams (Elloy, Terpening, & Kohls, 2001).

Earlier in the chapter, we indicated that perceptions of personal control influence stress. Work-related stress usually increases when job demands are high and the individual has little choice in deciding how to meet the demands (low autonomy, high external control). In one classic study of Swedish workers, men who held jobs that were demanding and low in autonomy reported high levels of exhaustion; depression; insomnia, tranquilizer and sleeping pill use; and sick leave (Karacek, 1979). In another study, a combination of personal and job factors placed individuals at risk for getting sick (Schaubroeck, Jones, & Xie, 2001). Employees who perceived they had control over their job responsibilities but did not have confidence in their problem-solving abilities or who blamed themselves for bad outcomes were the likeliest to experience stress.

This North American Chinese family association has helped its members cope with acculturative stress. *What are some strategies for coping with acculturative stress?*

These types of job situations placed these employees at risk for getting infections.

Psychologists and policy makers also worry that work-related stress can carry over and influence well-being in other areas of a person's life, especially the family (European Agency for Safety and Health at Work, 2002). The degree to which work-related problems home and home-related problems to work depends upon the worker's family support and the availability of leisure time (Michailidis & Georgiou, 2005). It also depends on gender. While work sources are the main precursors of burnout in men, in women both work and family variables, such as marital satisfaction, can precede burnout (Greenglass, 1991). For example, female veterinarians experience significantly more marital and family stress on their careers than male veterinarians do (Phillips-Miller, Morrison, & Campbell, 2001).

Sociocultural Factors

The personality and environmental factors described so far are not the only sources of stress. Sociocultural factors also help to determine which stressors individuals are likely to encounter, whether they are likely to perceive events as stressful or not, how they believe stressors should be confronted and how the stressors affect their health (Kawachi & Kennedy, 2001; Brydon & others, 2004). Sociocultural factors involved in stress include conflict between cultures and poverty (Beiser, 1999; Rummens, Beiser & Noh, 2003; Gurung, 2006).

Acculturative Stress Moving to a new place is a stressful experience in the best of circumstances. It is even more stressful when a person from one culture moves into a different culture. **Acculturative stress** refers to the negative consequences that result from contact between two distinctive cultural groups. Many immigrants to North America have experienced acculturative stress (Uppaluri, Schumm, & Lauderdale, 2001; Lee, Koeske, & Sales, 2004; Gurung, 2006).

Florida teacher Daniel Arnoux (1998) called out a student's name in class and asked if she was Haitian. The student became so embarrassed that she slid under her seat and disappeared from view. Arnoux realized how stressful school was for many immigrant students, some of whom were beaten and harassed for being Haitian, and began developing lessons to help students gain empathy and tolerance for people from different ethnic and cultural backgrounds.

acculturative stress The negative consequences that result from contact between two distinctive cultural groups.

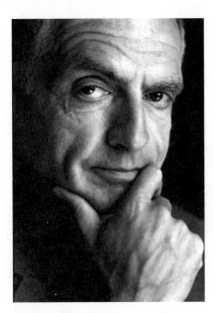

Morton Beiser, of the University of Toronto, studied Vietnamese "boat people" in Canada for 10 years (Beiser, 1999). His work has focused on the health problems faced by immigrants, refugees, and First Nations people in Canada.

In an influential formulation, Queen's University cross-cultural psychologist John Berry (1980) believes that when people like the young Florida schoolgirl experience cultural change, they can adapt in one of four main ways:

- *Assimilation* occurs when individuals relinquish their native cultural identity and adopt an identity that helps them blend into the larger society. If enough individuals follow this path, the nondominant group is absorbed into the established mainstream. Sometimes assimilation occurs when many groups merge to form a new society (what is often called a "melting pot").
- *Integration* implies that people move into the larger culture but, in contrast to assimilation, maintain many aspects of their distinctive cultural identity. In this circumstance, a number of ethnic groups all cooperate within a large social system (a "mosaic").
- *Separation* refers to self-imposed withdrawal from the larger culture. If imposed by the larger society, however, separation becomes segregation. People might maintain their traditional way of life because they desire an independent existence (as in the case of "separatist" movements) or the dominant culture may exercise its power to exclude the other culture (as in the circumstance of slavery and apartheid).
- *Marginalization* refers to the process in which nondominant groups lose cultural and social contact with both their traditional society and the larger, dominant society. This involves confusion and anxiety because the essential features of one's culture are lost but are not replaced by the larger society. Thus, marginalization involves feelings of alienation and a loss of identity. Marginalization does not mean that a group has no culture. . It indicates that this culture may be disorganized and doesn't support the acculturating individual.

Separation and marginalization are the least adaptive responses to acculturation. Separation can sometimes have benefits, but it may be especially stressful for individuals who seek separation while most members of their group seek assimilation. Integration and assimilation are healthier adaptations to acculturative pressures. But assimilation means some cultural loss, so it may be more stressful than integration.

While Canadians generally hold positive attitudes about the idea of a multicultural society, their attitudes toward ethnocultural groups vary (Berry, 1993). Schwean and others (1999) found that cultural minority people are vulnerable to negative psychosocial outcomes not because of cultural differences but because of acculturative stress, especially in the case of the Aboriginal peoples of Canada (Herring & Young, 2002; Waldram, 2004). For example, Canadians still hold negative social stereotypes of the Innu, based mainly upon information derived from television and newspapers (Claxton-Oldfield & Keefe, 1999).

Poverty Poverty can cause considerable stress for individuals and families (Beiser & others, 2002; Landrine & Klonoff, 2001; Wadsworth & others, 2005). Chronic conditions such as inadequate housing, dangerous neighbourhoods, crowding, burdensome responsibilities, and economic uncertainties are potent stressors in the lives of the poor (Adler, 2001; Evans & English, 2002).

The poor are disproportionately made up of ethnic minority families and female-headed families (Statistics Canada, 2001). Many people who become poor during their lives remain so for only one or two years. However, ethnic minority groups and female heads of household are especially at risk for persistent poverty.

Poverty is also related to threatening and uncontrollable life events (Russo, 1990). Poor women are more likely to experience crime and violence than middle-class women are. And poverty undermines sources of social support that play a role in buffering the effects of stress. Poverty is related to marital unhappiness and with having spouses who are unlikely to serve as confidants. Children growing up in poverty are more likely to experience family instability, have a depressed parent, and have their own emotional difficulties (Evans & English, 2002). Further, poverty means having to depend on many overburdened and unresponsive bureaucratic systems for financial, housing, and health assistance, which may contribute to a person living in poverty feeling powerless—itself a factor in stress.

> **reflect and review**

2 **Define stress and identify its sources.**

- Define stress.
- Explain the role of personality factors in stress.
- Identify environmental factors in stress.
- Evaluate the effects of sociocultural factors on stress.

What are the main sources of stress in your life? Would you classify them as personality factors, environmental factors, or sociocultural factors?

3 **STRESS RESPONSES**

 General Adaptation Syndrome — Fight or Flight, Tend and Befriend — Cognitive Appraisal

How do people respond to stress?

When we experience stress, we may respond physiologically and cognitively. Physiological responses to stress are discussed first.

General Adaptation Syndrome

When we experience stress, our body readies itself to handle the assault of stress and a number of physiological changes take place. Those changes were the main interest of Hans Selye (1974, 1983), who spent his research career at the Université de Montréal and founded the area of stress research. He defined stress as the wear and tear on the body due to the demands placed on it. After observing patients with different problems—the death of someone close, loss of income, arrest for embezzlement—Selye concluded that any number of environmental events or stimuli will produce the same stress response. Regardless of which problem the patient had, similar symptoms appeared: loss of appetite, muscular weakness, and decreased interest in the world.

General adaptation syndrome (GAS) is Selye's term for the common effects on the body when demands are placed on it. The GAS consists of three stages: alarm, resistance, and exhaustion (see figure 15.5). Selye's model is especially useful in helping us understand the link between stress and health.

Alarm The body's first reaction to a stressor is the *alarm stage*. This is a temporary state of shock, a time at which resistance to illness and stress falls below normal limits. In trying to cope with the initial effects of stress, the body quickly releases hormones that, in a short time, adversely affect the immune system's functioning. It is during this time that the individual is prone to infections from illness and injury. Fortunately, the alarm stage passes rather quickly.

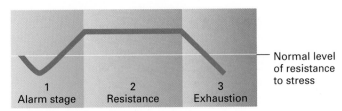

FIGURE 15.5 Selye's General Adaptation Syndrome

The general adaptation syndrome (GAS) describes an individual's general response to stress in terms of three stages: (1) alarm, in which the body mobilizes its resources; (2) resistance, in which resistance levels off; and (3) exhaustion, in which resistance becomes depleted.

general adaptation syndrome (GAS) Selye's term for the common effects on the body when demands are placed on it. The GAS consists of three stages: alarm, resistance, and exhaustion.

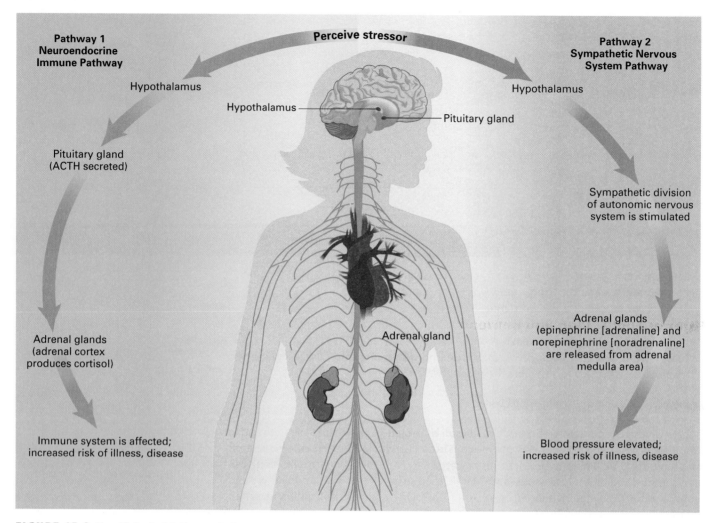

Pathway 1
Neuroendocrine
Immune Pathway

Hypothalamus

Pituitary gland
(ACTH secreted)

Adrenal glands
(adrenal cortex
produces cortisol)

Immune system is affected;
increased risk of illness, disease

Perceive stressor

Hypothalamus

Pituitary gland

Adrenal gland

Pathway 2
Sympathetic Nervous
System Pathway

Hypothalamus

Sympathetic division
of autonomic nervous
system is stimulated

Adrenal glands
(epinephrine [adrenaline] and
norepinephrine [noradrenaline]
are released from adrenal
medulla area)

Blood pressure elevated;
increased risk of illness, disease

FIGURE 15.6 Two Biological Pathways in Stress

Scientists today are zeroing in on some more precise descriptions of the biological changes in the stress–body linkage that takes place during the alarm stage. Many scientists now agree that two main biological pathways between the brain and the endocrine system respond to stress (Anderson, 2000; Taylor, 2006): the neuroendocrine-immune pathway and the sympathetic nervous system pathway.

As shown in figure 15.6, the neuroendocrine-immune pathway (pathway 1) goes through the hypothalamus and pituitary gland to the adrenal glands, from which cortisol is released. Cortisol is a steroid that is good for the body over the short term because it causes cellular fuel—glucose—to move to muscles. But over the long term, high levels of cortisol can be bad for the body, suppressing the immune system and straining the brain's cellular functioning. Too much cortisol also increases appetite and can cause weight gain.

In the sympathetic nervous pathway (pathway 2), the route is through the hypothalamus and then the sympathetic nervous system (rather than the pituitary gland). When the signal reaches the adrenal glands, epinephrine and norepinephrine (but not cortisol) are released. Recall from chapter 11 that the sympathetic nervous system is the subsystem of the autonomic nervous system that is responsible for the body's arousal. It produces a quick response to a stressor (often referred to as the "fight-or-flight" response). The release of the hormones epinephrine and norepinephrine causes a number of physiological changes, including elevated blood pressure. Over time, high blood pressure can lead to increased risk of illness and disease, such as cardiovascular disease.

Resistance In the second stage, or *resistance stage* of Selye's general adaptation syndrome, a number of glands throughout the body begin to manufacture different hormones that protect the individual in many ways. Endocrine and sympathetic nervous system activity are not as high as in the alarm stage, although they still are elevated.

During the resistance stage, the body's immune system can fight off infection with remarkable efficiency. Similarly, hormones that reduce the inflammation normally associated with injury circulate at high levels.

Exhaustion If the body's all-out effort to combat stress fails and the stress persists, the individual moves into the final stage, the *exhaustion stage*. At this point, the wear and tear on the body takes its toll—the person might collapse in a state of exhaustion, and be more vulnerable to disease. Some type of serious, possibly irreversible damage to the body, or even death, may occur in the exhaustion stage.

One of the main criticisms of Selye's general adaptation syndrome is that human beings do not always react to stress in the uniform way he proposed. There is more to understanding stress in humans than knowing their physical reactions to it. We also need to know about their personalities, their physical makeup, their perceptions, and the contexts in which the stressors occurred.

Fight or Flight, Tend and Befriend

Selye's concept of alarm reaction—the first stage of the general adaptation syndrome—is essentially the same as the fight-or-flight response. The central notion of both concepts is that the body's physiological resources are mobilized quickly to prepare the organism to deal with threats to survival.

The fight-or-flight response was first observed by Walter Cannon (1929) when he studied the reaction of cats suddenly confronted by a dog. Cannon noted that the cats experienced such changes as more rapid blood circulation, muscular tension, and heavy breathing. He concluded that these changes were adaptive ones: they prepared the cats for survival. He called the entire reaction "fight or flight" because it prepared the animals for engaging in one of these two behaviours when confronted with a threatening situation.

Today, it is understood that threats to survival are not the only situations that generate the fight-or-flight response. Virtually any threat that taxes an individual's coping abilities might trigger this response.

Shelley Taylor, of the University of California, Los Angeles, has proposed that females are less likely to respond to stressful and threatening situations with a fight-or-flight response than males are. She argues that females are likelier to "tend and befriend." That is, females often respond to stressful situations by protecting themselves and their young through nurturing behaviours (the *tend* part of the model) and forming alliances with a larger social group, especially one populated by other women (the *befriend* part of the model; S. E. Taylor, 2002b).

Although females do show the same immediate hormonal and sympathetic nervous system response to acute stress that males do, other factors can intervene and make the fight-or-flight response less likely in females. In terms of the fight response, male aggression is regulated by androgen hormones, such as testosterone, and is linked to sympathetic nervous system reactivity and hostility. In contrast, female aggression appears to be more cerebral in nature, moderated more by social circumstances, learning, culture, and the particular situation. In terms of the flight response, fleeing too quickly at the first sign of danger can place offspring at risk and reduce reproductive success. Evolutionarily, this would have been a poor choice, especially for females.

Cognitive Appraisal

Most of us think of stressors as environmental events that place demands on our lives, such as losing one's notes from a class, being yelled at by a friend, failing a test, or being in a car wreck. But, although our bodies may have a similar response to

Shelley Taylor, a leading expert in health psychology (Taylor, 2003), believes that recent trends in medicine, psychology, and health care have combined to make health psychology an important area of psychology. These trends include the rise of chronic or lifestyle-related illnesses, the expanding role of health care in the economy, the realization that psychological and social factors are often important factors in health and illness, and the demonstrated importance of psychological interventions in improving people's health care. Taylor and her colleagues developed the tend-and-befriend model, a reinterpretation of fight or flight that takes into account the motivation of females in threatening contexts.

Health psychologists such as Shelley Taylor usually have a doctoral degree in psychology. At the graduate level, many doctoral programs in clinical, counselling, social, or experimental psychology have a specialized track in some area of health psychology.

Step 1:
Primary Appraisal

Do I perceive the event as
(a) harmful?
(b) threatening?
(c) challenging?

Step 2:
Secondary Appraisal

What coping resources do
I have available?

FIGURE 15.7

Lazarus's Cognitive Appraisal View of Stress
Perceiving a stressor as harmful and/or threatening in step 1 and having few or no coping resources available in step 2 yields high stress. Perceiving a stressor as challenging in step 1 and having good coping resources available in step 2 reduces stress.

stressors, not everyone perceives the same events as stressful. For example, one person may perceive an upcoming job interview as threatening, whereas another person may perceive it as merely challenging. One person may perceive a D on a paper as threatening; another person may perceive the same grade as an incentive to work harder. To some degree, then, what is stressful depends on how people cognitively appraise and interpret events. This view has been most clearly presented by Richard Lazarus (1993, 2000). **Cognitive appraisal** is Lazarus's term for individuals' interpretation of the events in their lives as harmful, threatening, or challenging and how they determine whether they have the resources to effectively cope with the events.

In Lazarus's view, events are appraised in two steps: primary appraisal and secondary appraisal (see figure 15.7). In primary appraisal, individuals interpret whether an event involves harm or loss that has already occurred, a threat of some future danger, or a challenge to be overcome. Lazarus believes that perceiving a stressor as a challenge to be overcome, rather than as a threat, is a good strategy for reducing stress. This strategy fits with the concept of hardiness, a personality factor involved in stress, which was discussed earlier.

To understand Lazarus' concept of primary appraisal, consider two students, each of whom has a failing grade in their psychology class at midterm. Student A is almost frozen by the stress of the low grade and looks at the rest of the term as a threatening circumstance. In contrast, student B does not become overwhelmed by the harm already done and the threat of future failures. She looks at the low grade as a challenge that she can address and overcome.

In secondary appraisal, individuals evaluate their resources and determine how effectively they can be used to cope with the event. This appraisal is secondary because it comes after primary appraisal and depends on the degree to which the student appraised the event as harmful, threatening, or challenging. For example, student A might have some helpful resources for coping with her low midterm grade, but she views the stressful circumstance as so harmful and threatening that she doesn't use her resources. Student B would instead evaluate the resources she can call on to improve her grade during the second half of the term. These include asking the instructor for suggestions about how to study better for the tests in the course, setting up a time management program to include more study hours, and asking several students who are doing well in the class about their strategies.

In many instances, viewing stress as a challenge during primary appraisal paves the way for finding effective coping resources during secondary appraisal. However, sometimes people do not have adequate resources for coping with an event they have defined as a challenge. For example, if student B is extremely shy, she might lack the courage and skills to talk to the instructor or to ask several students in the class about their strategies for doing well in the course.

cognitive appraisal Lazarus's term for individuals' interpretation of events in their lives as threatening, harmful, or challenging and their determination of whether they have the resources to effectively cope with the events.

> **reflect and review**

 Explain how people respond to stress.

- Describe the general adaptation syndrome.
- Discuss the differences between the fight-or-flight response and the tend-and-befriend response.
- Explain the nature of cognitive appraisal.

How do your body and mind react when you face a stressful experience?

④ STRESS AND ILLNESS

Stress and the Immune System	Stress and Cardiovascular Disease	Stress and Cancer	Positive Emotions, Illness, and Health

How are stress and illness linked?

It has already been mentioned several times that stress makes the body more vulnerable to illness. This section examines what research has revealed about links between stress and specific types of illness. In particular, stress has been identified as a factor in weakened immune systems, cardiovascular disease, and cancer. The good news, which is also discussed, is that positive emotions have been shown to help stave off illness and maintain health.

Stress and the Immune System

Inspired by the example of pioneers like Norman Cousins, researchers have become very interested in links between the immune system and stress (Herberman, 2002; Kiecolt-Glaser & others, 2002a, 2002b; Fleshner & Laudenslager, 2004). Their theory and research constitute a new field of scientific inquiry, **psychoneuroimmunology**, which explores connections among psychological factors (such as attitudes and emotions), the nervous system, and the immune system (Ader, 2003a; Irwin, 2005).

The immune system keeps us healthy by recognizing foreign materials such as bacteria, viruses, and tumours, and then destroying them. Its machinery consists of billions of white blood cells located in the lymphatic system. The number of white blood cells and how effective they are in killing foreign viruses or bacteria are related to stress levels. When a person is in the alarm or exhaustion stage, for example, the immune system functions poorly. During these stages, viruses and bacteria are likelier to multiply and cause disease (Vedhara, 2005).

The immune system and the central nervous system at first glance appear to be organized in different ways. The brain is usually regarded as a command centre for the nervous system, sending and receiving electronic signals along fixed pathways, much like a telephone network. In contrast, the immune system is decentralized: its organs (spleen, lymph nodes, thymus, and bone marrow) are located throughout the body. The immune system communicates by releasing immune cells into the bloodstream. From there, they float to new locations to deliver their messages.

However, scientists are increasingly recognizing that the central nervous system and immune system are in fact more similar than different in how they receive, recognize, and integrate signals from the external environment (Taylor, 2006). The central nervous system and the immune system both possess "sensory" elements, which receive information from the environment and other parts of the body, and "motor" elements, which carry out an appropriate response. Both systems also rely on chemical mediators for communication. A key hormone shared by the central nervous system and the immune system is corticotropin-releasing hormone (CRH), which is produced in the hypothalamus and unites the stress and immune responses.

Three lines of research provide support for the conclusion that the immune system and stress are linked (Anderson, 2000; Anderson, Golden-Kreutz, & DiLillo, 2001; Kiecolt-Glaser & others, 2002a, 2002b; Taylor, 2006). This is what researchers have found:

- Acute stressors (sudden, one-time life events or stimuli) can produce immunological changes (Cao & others, 2004). For example, in relatively healthy HIV-infected individuals, as well as in individuals with cancer, acute stressors are associated with poorer immune system functioning (Roberts, Anderson, & Lubaroff, 1994). According to Theoharides & Cochrane, (2004) acute stress can activate mast cells, which results in a worsening of a variety of inflammatory conditions including migraines, arthritis, multiple sclerosis, and irritable bowel syndrome.

psychoneuroimmunology The field that explores connections among psychological factors (such as attitudes and emotions), the nervous system, and the immune system.

FIGURE 15.8

NK Cells and Cancer
Two natural killer (NK) cells (*yellow*) are shown attacking a leukemia cell (*red*). Notice the blisters that the leukemia cell developed to defend itself. Nonetheless, the NK cells are surrounding the leukemia cell and are about to destroy it.

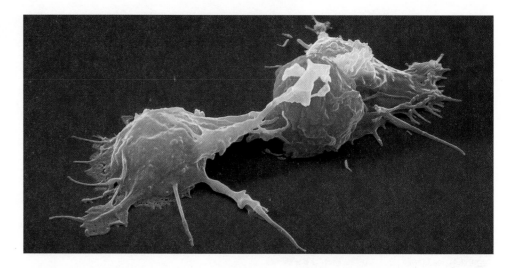

- Chronic stressors (those that are long-lasting) decrease immune system responsiveness, rather than adaptation (Irwin, 2002; Kiecolt-Glaser & others, 2002a, 2002b). This effect has been documented in a number of circumstances that include living next to a damaged nuclear reactor, burdensome caregiving for a family member with progressive illness, and failures in close relationships (divorce, separation, and marital distress; Robles & Kiecolt-Glaser, 2003).
- Positive social circumstances and low stress are associated with increased ability to fight illness (Ryff. 2001). For example, having good social relationships and support is often linked with higher NK-cell levels (NK stands for "natural killer"), whereas a high degree of stress is often related to lower NK-cell levels (Levy & others, 1990). NK cells can attack tumour cells (see figure 15.8).

Psychoneuroimmunology is relatively young. Much of what we know needs to be clarified, explained, and verified further. Researchers hope to clarify the precise links among psychological factors, the brain, and the immune system (Daruna, 2004). Some preliminary hypotheses about the interaction that causes vulnerability to disease include the following: (1) Stressful experiences lower the efficiency of immune systems, making individuals more susceptible to disease; (2) stress directly promotes disease-producing processes; and (3) stressful experiences may cause the activation of dormant viruses that diminish the individual's ability to cope with disease. These hypotheses may lead to clues for more successful treatments for some of the most baffling diseases—among them, cancer and AIDS (Vedhara, 2005).

In a classic example of research on psychoneuroimmunology, conducted by Sheldon Cohen and his colleagues (1998), adults who faced interpersonal or work-related stress for at least one month were likelier than people who were less stressed to catch a cold after being exposed to viruses. Cohen concluded that stress-triggered changes in the immune system and hormones might create greater vulnerability to infection. The findings suggest that when we know we are under stress, we need to take better care of ourselves than usual, although often we do just the opposite (S. Cohen, 2002; Cohen, Miller, & Rabin, 2001). Cohen (2004) has also proposed that positive social ties with friends and family provide a protective buffer that helps to prevent people from catching a cold when they are exposed to cold viruses. For example, Pressman and her colleagues (2004) showed that influenza shots are less helpful to first-year university and college students who are more lonely and have smaller social support networks.

Stress and Cardiovascular Disease

You may have heard someone say something like "It's no wonder she died of a heart attack with all of the stress he put her through." But is it true that emotional stress can cause a person to have a heart attack? A clear link has not been found, but there is evidence that chronic emotional stress is associated with high blood pressure, heart disease, and early death (Rozanski, Blumenthal, & Kaplan, 1999). One possibility is that stress triggers an influx of immune system T-cells into the blood stream, which, in turn, speeds up the rate at which arteries clog (Bosch & others, 2003).

In one study of 103 couples, each with one mildly hypertensive (high blood pressure) spouse, the researchers found that a happy marriage was linked with lower blood pressure and an unhappy marriage was related to higher blood pressure (B. Baker, 2001). Over the three-year time frame of the study, the blood pressure of the mildly hypertensive spouse in a happy marriage fell by six points on average, whereas the blood pressure of the mildly hypertensive spouse in an unhappy marriage rose by six points on average.

Emotional stress can contribute to cardiovascular disease in several other ways. For instance, people who have had major life changes (loss of a spouse or other close relative, loss of a job) have a higher incidence of cardiovascular disease and early death (Taylor, 2006). And, as discussed earlier in the chapter, people who are quick to anger or who display frequent hostility have an increased risk of cardiovascular disease (R. B. Williams, 2001; Smith & others, 2004).

The body's internal reactions to stress are not the only risk. People who live in a chronically stressed condition are likelier to take up smoking, start overeating, and avoid exercising. All of these stress-related behaviours are linked with the development of cardiovascular disease (Schneiderman & others, 2001).

Stress and Cancer

In addition to finding that stress is linked to immune system weaknesses and cardiovascular disease, researchers have found links between stress and cancer. Barbara Anderson (2000; Anderson, Golden-Kreutz, & DiLillo, 2001) believes that the link between stress and cancer can be best understood by examining three factors:

- *Quality of life*. Although negative life events, such as finding out that one has cancer, do not always produce stress and lowered quality of life, a number of studies have documented acute stress at the time cancer is diagnosed (Turner & others, 2005; Strange & others, 2000). Lengthy cancer treatments and the disruptions the disease creates in family, social, economic, and/or occupational functioning can cause chronic stress. As has been shown, these stressors can suppress the body's ability to fight off many types of disease, including cancer.
- *Behavioural factors*. An increase in negative health behaviours and/or a decrease in positive health behaviours can accompany cancer. For instance, in terms of negative health behaviours, individuals with cancer may become depressed or anxious and more likely to medicate with alcohol and other drugs (Turner & others, 2005). Also, individuals who are stressed by cancer may abandon their previous positive health behaviours, such as participating in regular exercise. These health factors may in turn affect immunity. For example, substance abuse directly suppresses immunity and is associated with poor nutrition, which indirectly affects health (Anderson, 2000). Also, there is growing evidence that positive health behaviours such as exercise can have positive effects on both the immune and endocrine systems, even among individuals with chronic diseases (Phaneuf & Leeuwenburgh, 2001; Kendall & others, 2005).
- *Biological pathways*. As you already have seen, stress sets in motion biological changes involving the autonomic, endocrine, and immune systems. If the immune system is not compromised, it appears to help provide resistance to cancer and slow its progression (Anderson, 2000). But researchers have found that the physiological effects of stress inhibit a number of cellular immune responses (Anderson & others, 2001). Cancer patients have diminished NK-cell activity in the blood. Low NK-cell activity is linked with the development of further malignancies, and the length of survival for the cancer patient is related to NK-cell activity (Levy & others, 1990).

FIGURE 15.9

Some Links Between Positive Emotions and Health

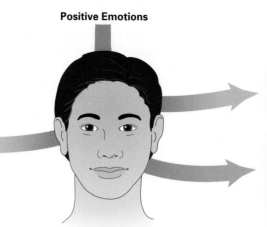

Positive Emotions

Physiological Effects
• Improved cardiovascular health
• Improved immune activity
• Higher levels of S-IgA (antibody that fights colds)
• Fewer illnesses and uses of medical services when faced with stress

Social Effects
• More social support

Behavioural Effects
• More health-promoting behaviours
• More confidence in ability to take steps to relieve illness
• Greater ability to cope with problems

Positive Emotions, Illness, and Health

Researchers have mainly focused on the role of negative factors, such as emotional stress and anger, in illness. However, the recent interest in positive psychology has sparked research on the role that positive emotions might play in reducing illness and promoting health (Tugade, Fredrickson, & Barrett, 2004; Taylor & Sherman, 2004).

Although the data concerning the effects of negative states are more extensive, positive emotional states are thought to be associated with healthy patterns of physiological functioning in both the cardiovascular system and the immune system (Nyklícek, Temoshok, & Vingerhoets, 2004).

Positive emotions have been linked with the release of secretory immunoglobulin A (S-IgA), the antibody that is believed to be the first line of defence against the common cold (Salovey & others, 2000; Ogden, 2004). The positive experiences associated with singing in a choir (Kreutz & others, 2004), writing poetry (Lowe, Beckett, & Lowe, 2003), and petting dogs (Charnetski, Riggers, & Brennan, 2004) are all associated with increased S-IgA levels.

Moods can also influence people's beliefs about their health, including their willingness to carry out health-promoting behaviours. For example, happy individuals are likelier to engage in health-promoting behaviours and have more confidence that these behaviours will relieve their illness than sad individuals (Salovey & others, 2000). Rod Martin (2001, 2004) has suggested that positive moods lead people to believe they are healthier even though they are not.

Recall from chapter 11 Barbara Frederickson's (2001) belief that the main function of positive emotions is to facilitate the ability to cope with problems. In one study, individuals who experienced more positive emotions (such as happiness) used broader coping strategies than those who experienced more negative emotions (such as sadness). For example, individuals who experienced positive emotions were likelier to think about ways to deal with the problem and to step back from the situation and be more objective than individuals who experienced negative emotions (Frederickson & Joiner, Jr., 2002; Fredrickson & Branigan, 2005).

Social support, such as caring family and friends, is another important factor in stress and coping that is likely linked with positive emotions (Hogan, Linden, & Najarian, 2002; Salovey & others, 2000). Emotional experience and social support are reciprocally linked: Not only does social support improve a person's emotional state, but a person's emotional state also influences the likelihood that the support will be provided. Researchers have found that positive emotions are correlated with people having more family members and friends they could count on in times of need (Cohen, 2004).

In sum, positive emotions do appear to be involved in helping to reduce illness and promote health (see figure 15.9). However, much more research needs to be carried out to determine the precise linkages (R. A. Martin, 2001, 2004). See the Critical Reflections box for more information.

Positive Emotions and Health: Placebo Effect or Meaning Response?

If your best friend offered you a piece of candy when you had the flu and told you that it would make you better, would you believe her? What if the candy came from a famous medical doctor who told you the candy contained powerful medicine? What would it mean if you ate the candy and your achiness and fever disappeared?

According to the medical model, the cause of your flu was a *specific* pathogen, probably a bacteria or virus. In the absence of a treatment specifically targeted at the pathogen, you might have improved simply because the illness had run its course, and you would have felt better even if you hadn't eaten the candy. Or you might have experienced the placebo effect, a change believed to have been brought about by a medically inactive substance.

The word placebo stems from the Latin for "I shall please" and commonly refers to a medication prescribed more for the mental or emotional relief of the patient than because of any actual curative properties. The placebo effect has been known for centuries. In the second century, the Greek physician Galen noted, "He cures most successfully in whom the people have the most confidence." In the intervening centuries, doctors have been divided over whether to deliberately use the placebo effect to help their patients. Recently, the placebo effect has again become the focus of considerable controversy.

Seen from the perspective of the biopsychosocial model that underlies health psychology, disease arises from an interaction of biological, psychological and social factors (Ader, 2003a). While a *specific* pathogen probably did trigger your flu, *nonspecific* factors, such as your pre-illness stress levels, your beliefs about your health, and your social support also have a role to play, both in the onset of illness and in recovery. Within the medical model, these nonspecific factors are lumped together and referred to, sometimes dismissively, as the *placebo effect*. Benefits of placebos are often seen as being "in the patient's head" and the doctor who deliberately tries to trigger placebo effects is often seen as acting unethically (Moerman, 2002).

In sharp contrast, within the biopsychosocial model, the term *meaning response* is sometimes used instead (Benedetti, Maggi, & Lopiano, 2003). Far from being inappropriate, maximum healing comes from deliberately helping to create a positive meaning context around the illness (Moerman, 2002; Ader, 2003a). As you read earlier in this chapter, various psychological factors, like hardiness and positive emotions, and social factors, like social support, can influence illness and health. The effect of these nonspecific factors is to allow the patient to create a meaningful context within which he or she can become more optimistic, more prepared to engage in health-promoting behaviours, and more cooperative with health caregivers.

Benedetti, Maggi, & Lopiano (2003) have demonstrated the role of nonspecific factors in the treatment of illness through a comparison of open vs. hidden medical treatments across several medical circumstances. In one case, they administered morphine as a painkiller to patients recovering from thoracic surgery. In one treatment, the patients were aware of their treatment since they were accurately informed that a painkiller was being administered as a doctor carried out the injection in full view. In the other treatment, patients received their injections unawares via an infusion machine. Both sets of patients received the identical injections of morphine at the same times so the only difference between the two groups was their awareness that the injections were taking place. The results showed that the morphine was not as effective as a painkiller when patients did not know it was being administered. From the biopsychosocial perspective, patients receiving hidden treatments could not construct a meaningful context around those injections and, thus, did not benefit from the nonspecific factors that modulate the specific effects of the treatment.

In another demonstration of the efficacy of nonspecific factors, researchers from the University of British Columbia (de la Fuente-Fernandez & others, 2001) injected patients suffering from Parkinson's disease with either a drug (apomorphine) or a placebo (an inactive salt solution). Using PET scans, they showed that the drug produced improvement by initiating the release of the neurotransmitter dopamine in the brain. Surprisingly, PET scans revealed a similar release of dopamine in patients who were given the placebo injection. From the biopsychosocial perspective, the nonspecific factors activated by placebo injection allowed for a positive meaning response from the patients.

The status of the placebo effect (or meaning response, if you prefer) is still open to question. In one meta-analysis, patients who received placebo treatment fared no better than those left untreated (Hróbjartsson & Gotzsche, 2001). Similarly, although Rod Martin (2001, 2004) found evidence that positive moods lead people to believe they are healthier, he found little evidence that positive moods actually lead to better health. Robert Ader (2003b), who initially coined the term *psychoneuroimmunology*, suggests that progress will be made only when researchers begin to sort out which nonspecific factors or combinations of factors are relevant to different medical circumstances.

What do you think?

- Have you ever been aware of a connection between a positive attitude in yourself and good health?
- How could you design an experiment to test whether positive thinking fosters better health?
- Here are some positive attitudes associated with an optimistic mindset: being very optimistic; having a strong belief in a higher power; thinking of the future, not the past; thinking people are good; being very trusting; thinking you control your life; and thinking you control your health. Is this list complete? What other attitudes might you add to the list? Why?

> **reflect and review**

 Discuss the links between stress and health.

- Outline the findings of psychoneuroimmunology.
- Evaluate the link between stress and cardiovascular disease.
- Explain the connection between stress and cancer.
- Describe how positive emotions, illness, and health are related.

Think about the last few times you were sick. Did you experience any stressful circumstances prior to getting sick? Might they have contributed to your illness?

5 COPING STRATEGIES

| Problem-Focused and Emotion-Focused Coping | — | Optimism and Positive Thinking | — | Social Support | — | Assertive Behaviour | — | Religion | — | Stress Management Programs |

What are some good strategies for coping with stress?

A stressful circumstance is rendered considerably less stressful when a person successfully copes with it (Endler, 1997; Preece & DeLongis, 2005). Successful coping is associated with a number of factors, including a sense of personal control, a healthy immune system, personal resources, and positive emotions. What precisely is coping? **Coping** involves managing taxing circumstances, expending effort to solve life's problems, and seeking to master or reduce stress.

Keep in mind that multiple strategies often work better than a single strategy alone, especially for people who have experienced a stressful life event or a cluster of life events (such as the death of a parent, a divorce, and a significant reduction in income). A multiple-strategy plan for coping might include engaging in problem-focused coping, using positive self-talk, seeking social support, and practising relaxation. Norman Endler, of York University, along with James Parker and Laura Summerfeldt, of Trent University, have developed the widely-used CHIP (Coping with Health, Injuries and Problems) Scale for measuring how well people are coping with physical health problems (Endler, Parker, & Summerfeldt, 1993, 1998; Endler & Parker, 2000).

Problem-Focused and Emotion-Focused Coping

In the discussion of stress earlier in this chapter, we described Richard Lazarus's (1993, 2000) view that cognitive appraisal is critical to coping. Lazarus believes that people can make two general types of coping efforts: problem-focused coping and emotion-focused coping.

Problem-focused coping is Lazarus's term for the cognitive strategy of squarely facing one's troubles and trying to solve them. For example, if you are having trouble with a class, you might go to the study skills centre at your college or university and enter a training program to learn how to study more effectively. You have thus faced your problem and attempted to do something about it.

Emotion-focused coping is Lazarus's term for responding to stress in an emotional manner, especially by using defensive mechanisms. Norman Endler and James Parker developed the Coping Inventory for Stressful Situations, which measures both problem- and emotion-focused coping as well as a third coping style, *avoidance coping* (Endler & Parker, 1993). Emotion-focused and avoidance coping involve defence mechanisms. In emotion-focused coping we might rationalize what has happened to us, joke about it, or say it doesn't matter. In avoidance coping we might deny what happened, distract ourselves with other people, or avoid going to class. In one study, avoidance

coping Managing taxing circumstances, expending effort to solve life's problems, and seeking to master or reduce stress.

problem-focused coping Lazarus's term for the cognitive strategy of squarely facing one's troubles and trying to solve them.

emotion-focused coping Lazarus's term for responding to stress in an emotional manner, especially using defensive appraisal.

was linked with symptoms of depression, anxiety, and somatization (the conversion of psychological symptoms into physical symptoms) (Tull & others, 2004).

Sometimes emotion-focused or avoidance coping is adaptive. Forgiveness is one effective emotion-focused coping style (Worthington, Jr. & Scherer, 2004). Also, denial is one of the main protective mechanisms enabling people to cope with the flood of feelings that occur when the reality of death or dying becomes too great. Denial can also be used to avoid the destructive impact of shock by postponing the time when you have to deal with stress. At other times, emotion-focused or avoidance coping is maladaptive (Zeidner & Saklofske, 1996). Denying that the person you were dating doesn't love you any more when that person has actually become engaged to someone else is not adaptive and keeps you from getting on with your life.

Many individuals successfully use both problem-focused and emotion-focused coping when adjusting to a stressful circumstance. For example, in one classic study, individuals said they used both problem-focused and emotion-focused coping strategies in 98 percent of the stressful encounters they face (Folkman & Lazarus, 1980). Over the long term, though, problem-focused coping rather than emotion-focused coping is what usually works best (Heppner & Lee, 2001).

© 1999 Tom Cheney from cartoonbank.com. All Rights reserved.

Optimism and Positive Thinking

Thinking positively and avoiding negative thoughts is generally a good coping strategy when trying to handle stress more effectively. A positive mood improves our ability to process information more efficiently, makes us more altruistic, and gives us higher self-esteem. In addition, in most cases, an optimistic attitude is better than a pessimistic one because it gives us a sense that we are controlling our environment. In chapter 12, we discussed the positive benefits of being optimistic rather than pessimistic. Although some individuals at times use a strategy of defensive pessimism to improve their ability to cope with stress, overall a positive feeling of optimism is the best strategy.

There is evidence that optimism is important in promoting health. In one study, older men and women who expressed a positive outlook toward life were less likely to suffer heart attacks than those who expressed a negative outlook (Ostir & others, 2001). The effect of positive thinking can even be lifelong. Analysis of brief autobiographies written more than 60 years ago by Catholic nuns when they were in their 20s suggests that those with a positive outlook lived longer than nuns who wrote about their lives in more neutral terms (Danner, Snowdon, & Friesen, 2001).

Cognitive Restructuring and Positive Self-Talk   Linda Seligman (2006) believes the best tools for overcoming chronic pessimism lie in cognitive therapy, one of the major psychotherapies discussed in chapter 14. In cognitive therapy, the client is encouraged to think positively and talk back to negative thoughts in an optimistic style that limits self-blame and negative generalizations.

Many cognitive therapists believe the process of *cognitive restructuring*—modifying the thoughts, ideas, and beliefs that maintain an individual's problems—can also be used to get people to think more positively and optimistically. The process is often aided by changes in *self-talk* (also called *self-statements*), the soundless, mental speech that we use when we think about something, plan, or solve problems. Positive self-talk can foster the confidence that frees us to use our talents to the fullest. Because self-talk has a way of being self-fulfilling, unopposed negative thinking can spell trouble. That's why it's so important to monitor your self-talk.

Several strategies can help you to monitor your self-talk. First, at random times during the day, ask yourself, "What am I saying to myself right now?" Then, if you can, write down your thoughts along with a few notes about the situation you are in and how you're feeling. At the beginning, it is important to record your self-talk without

Situation	Negative Self-Statements	Positive Self-Statements
Having a long, difficult assignment due the next day	"I'll never get this work done by tomorrow."	"If I work real hard I may be able to get it all done by tomorrow." "This is going to be tough but it is still possible to do it." "Finishing this assignment by tomorrow will be a real challenge." "If I don't get it finished, I'll just have to ask the teacher for an extension."
Losing one's job	"I'll never get another job."	"I'll just have to look harder for another job." "There will be rough times ahead, but I've dealt with rough times before." "Hey, maybe my next job will be a better deal altogether." "There are agencies that can probably help me get some kind of job."
Moving away from friends and family	"My whole life is left behind."	"I'll miss everyone, but it doesn't mean we can't stay in touch." "Just think of all the new people I'm going to meet." "I guess it will be kind of exciting moving to a new home." "Now I'll have two places to call home."
Breaking up with a person you love	"I have nothing to live for. He/she was all I had."	"I really thought our relationship would work, but it's not the end of the world." "Maybe we can try again in the future." "I'll just have to try to keep myself busy and not let it bother me." "If I met him (her), there is no reason why I won't meet someone else someday."
Not getting into graduate school	"I guess I'm really dumb. I don't know what I'll do."	"I'll just have to reapply next year." "There are things I can do with my life other than going to grad school." "I guess a lot of good students get turned down. It's just so unbelievably competitive." "Perhaps there are a few other programs that I could apply to."
Having to participate in a class discussion	"Everyone else knows more than I do, so what's the use of saying anything."	"I have as much to say as anyone else in the class." "My ideas may be different, but they're still valid." "It's OK to be a bit nervous; I'll relax when I start talking." "I may as well say something; how bad could it sound?"

FIGURE 15.10

Replacing Negative Self-Statements with Positive Ones

any censorship. But your goal is to fine-tune your self-talk to make it as accurate and positive as possible.

You can also use uncomfortable emotions or moods—such as stress, depression, and anxiety—as cues for listening to your self-talk. When this happens, identify the feeling as accurately as possible. Then ask yourself, "What was I saying to myself right before I started feeling this way?" or "What have I been saying to myself since I've been feeling this way?"

Situations that you anticipate might be difficult for you are also excellent opportunities to assess your self-talk. Write down a description of the coming event. Then ask yourself, "What am I saying to myself about this event?" If your thoughts are negative, think how you can use your strengths to turn these disruptive feelings into more positive ones and help turn a potentially difficult experience into a success.

You might also compare your self-talk predictions (what you thought would or should happen in a given situation) with what actually took place. If the reality conflicts with your predictions—as it often does when your self-talk is in error—pinpoint how you can adjust your self-talk to fit reality.

You are likely to have a subjective view of your own thoughts. So you might try to enlist the assistance of a sympathetic but objective friend, partner, or therapist who is willing to listen, discuss your self-assessment with you, and help you to identify ways in which your self-talk is distorted and might be improved. Some examples of positive self-statements that might replace negative self-statements in coping with various stressful situations are presented in figure 15.10.

Positive Self-Illusion For a number of years, mental health professionals believed that seeing reality as accurately as possible was the best path to health. Recently, though, researchers have found increasing evidence that maintaining some positive illusions about oneself and the world is healthy. Happy people often have falsely high opinions of themselves, give self-serving explanations for events, and have exaggerated beliefs about their ability to control the world around them (Taylor & others, 2000). Similarly, as mentioned previously, while happiness may lead people to believe they are healthier, it may not actually lead to better health (R. A. Martin, 2002, 2004).

Illusions, whether positive or negative, are related to one's sense of self-esteem. Having too grandiose an idea of yourself or thinking too negatively about yourself both have negative consequences (Johnson, 2004). Rather, the ideal overall orientation may be to have mildly-inflated illusions or a reality orientation (Baumeister, 1989; see figure 15.11).

A negative outlook can increase our chances of getting angry, feeling guilty, and magnifying our mistakes. And for some people, seeing things too accurately can lead to depression. Seeing one's suffering as meaningless and random does not help a person cope and move forward, even if the suffering is random and meaningless. An absence of illusions may also thwart individuals from undertaking the risky and ambitious projects that may yield the greatest rewards (Simonton & Baumeister, 2005). In some cases, though, a strategy of defensive pessimism may actually work best in handling stress. By imagining negative outcomes, people can prepare for stressful circumstances. The honours student who is worried that she will flunk the next test may not be paralyzed but instead may be motivated to do everything necessary to ensure that things go smoothly.

Among other qualities, people with more positive outlooks often have a good sense of humour (Lefcourt, 2003). Rod Martin, of the University of Western Ontario, has investigated the impact of humour on self-concept and well-being (R. A. Martin, 2004). He has proposed that a greater level of humour in a person is associated with a more positive self-concept, more positivity in the face of stress (Martin, 1996), and greater positive affect in response to both positive and negative life events (Kuiper & Martin, 1998).

Self-Efficacy Earlier, we indicated that perceived control is an important factor in stress. Closely linked with the concept of perceived control is self-efficacy, the belief that one can master a situation and produce positive outcomes. **Self-efficacy** can be an effective strategy in coping with stress and challenging circumstances.

As you read in chapter 11, Albert Bandura (1997, 2000b, 2001) and others have shown that people's self-efficacy affects their behaviour in a variety of circumstances, ranging from solving personal problems to going on diets. Self-efficacy influences whether people even try to develop healthy habits, how much stress they experience, how much effort they expend in coping with stress, and how long they persist in the face of obstacles (Luszczynska & Schwarzer, 2005; Maddux, 2001).

Researchers have found that self-efficacy can improve individuals' ability to cope and be mentally healthy (Bandura, 2001). In one study, University of Athens students who felt challenged by their examinations experienced greater self-efficacy and reported fewer psychological symptoms such as feelings of isolation, anxiety, depression and negative well-being. In contrast, students who felt threatened by their exams reported lower self-efficacy and more psychological symptoms (Karademas & Kalantzi-Azizi, 2004). In a study of parents with young children, researchers established that parents high in self-efficacy experience less anxiety and depression than parents low in self-efficacy (Kwok & Wong, 2000).

Social Support

Our crowded, polluted, noisy, and achievement-oriented world can make us feel overwhelmed and isolated. Now more than ever, we may need support systems such as family members, friends, and co-workers to buffer stress (Cohen, 2004). **Social support** means information and feedback from others that one is loved and cared for, esteemed and valued, and included in a network of communication and mutual obligation.

Social support has three types of benefits: tangible assistance, information, and emotional support (Taylor, 2006).

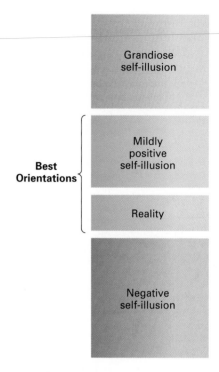

FIGURE 15.11

Reality and Self-Illusion
Individuals often have self-illusions that are slightly above average. However, having too grandiose an opinion or thinking negatively can have negative consequences. For some individuals, seeing things too accurately can be depressing. Overall, in most contexts, a reality orientation or a mildly inflated self-illusion might be most effective.

self-efficacy The belief that one can master a situation and produce positive outcomes.

social support Information and feedback from others that one is loved and cared for, esteemed and valued, and included in a network of communication and mutual obligation.

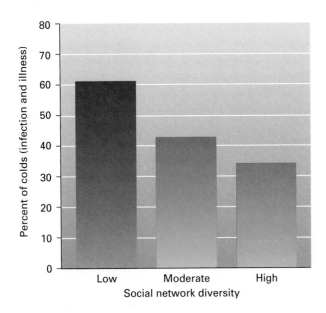

FIGURE 15.12

Diversity of Social Roles and the Common Cold
In one study, the more social roles (diversity) involved in individuals' social networks, the less likely they were to develop a cold after being infected by a cold virus (Cohen & others, 1997). Note that low = 1 to 3 social roles; moderate = 4 to 5 social roles; and high = 6 or more social roles.

- *Tangible assistance.* Family and friends can provide actual goods and services in stressful circumstances. For example, gifts of food are often given after a death in the family occurs, so that bereaved family members won't have to cook for themselves and visiting relatives at a time when their energy and motivation is low.
- *Information.* Individuals who provide support can also recommend specific actions and plans to help the person under stress cope more effectively. Friends may notice that a co-worker is overloaded with work and suggest ways for him or her to manage time more efficiently or delegate tasks more effectively.
- *Emotional support.* In stressful situations, individuals often suffer emotionally and may develop depression, anxiety, and loss of self-esteem. Friends and family can reassure the person under stress that he or she is a valuable individual who is loved by others. Knowing that others care allows a person to approach stress and cope with stress with greater assurance.

Researchers have consistently found that social support helps individuals cope with stress (Cutrona, Russell, & Gardner, 2005). For example, in one study, single mothers were compared with married mothers. The reduced social support experienced by single mothers was related to a greater incidence of depression (Cairney & others, 2003). In other studies, social support predicted the mortality of patients with heart disease, especially by reducing sedentary behaviour (Brummett & others, 2005).

Having diverse social ties may be especially important in coping with stress. People who participate in more diverse social networks—for example, having a close relationship with a partner; interacting with family members, friends, neighbours, and fellow workers; and belonging to social and religious groups—report better health than people with fewer types of social relationships (Zunzunegui & others, 2004). One study investigated the effects of diverse social ties on susceptibility to getting a common cold (Cohen & others, 1998). Individuals reported the extent of their participation in 12 types of social ties. Then they were given nasal drops containing a cold virus and monitored for the appearance of a cold. Individuals with more diverse social ties were less likely to get a cold than their counterparts with less diverse social networks (see figure 15.12).

Keep in mind that the studies of social support are correlational. What does that mean about interpreting their results?

Assertive Behaviour

We have just seen that social ties, especially diverse ties, play important roles in helping people cope more effectively with stress in their lives. Another aspect of social relationships that can affect coping is how we deal with conflict in these relationships. Assertive expression has become a communication ideal.

However, not everyone acts assertively. We can deal with conflict in our lives in four main ways: aggressively, manipulatively, passively, and assertively.

- *Acting aggressively.* People who respond aggressively to conflict run roughshod over others. They are demanding, abrasive, and hostile. Aggressive people are often insensitive to the rights of others.
- *Acting manipulatively.* Manipulative people try to get what they want by making other people feel sorry for them or feel guilty. They don't take responsibility for meeting their own needs. Instead, manipulative people play the role of the victim or martyr to get others to do things for them. They work indirectly to get their needs met.
- *Acting passively.* Passive people act in nonassertive, submissive ways. They let others run roughshod over them. Passive people don't express their feelings. They don't let others know what they want or need.

Dealing with Conflict

Think about the following situations one at a time. Check which response is most typical of the way you would behave in that situation.

	Assertive	Aggressive	Manipulative	Passive
You are being kept on the phone by a salesperson trying to sell you something you don't want.		✓		
You want to break off a relationship that is no longer working for you.			✓	
You are sitting in a movie and the people behind you are talking.	✓			
Your doctor keeps you waiting more than 20 minutes.				✓
You are standing in line and someone moves in front of you.	✓			
Your friend has owed you money for a long time and it is money you could use.		✓		
You receive food at a restaurant that is over- or undercooked.	✓			
You want to ask a major favour of your friend, romantic partner, or roommate.			✓	
Your friends ask you to do something that you don't feel like doing.				✓
You are in a large lecture hall. The instructor is speaking too softly and you know other students are having trouble hearing what is being said.	✓			
You want to start a conversation at a gathering, but you don't know anyone there.	✓			
You are sitting next to someone who is smoking, and the smoke bothers you.	✓			
You are talking to someone about something that is important to you, but they don't seem to be listening.		✓		
You are speaking and someone interrupts you.		✓		
You receive an unjust criticism from someone.		✓		

In most circumstances, being assertive is the best strategy. However, there may be some situations in which a different style of interaction is needed. Look at each situation again and determine if the assertive style is always the best strategy and whether there is any circumstance in which one of the other styles might work best.

- *Acting assertively.* Assertive individuals express their feelings, ask for what they want, and say "no" to something they don't want. When individuals act assertively, they act in their own best interests and stand up for their legitimate rights. In the view of assertiveness experts Robert Alberti and Michael Emmons (2001), assertiveness builds equal relationships.

The Personal Reflections box, "Dealing with Conflict," gives you a chance to evaluate the styles that you use.

Following are some strategies for becoming more assertive (Bourne, 2000):

- *Set up a time for discussing what you want to discuss.* Talk with the other person to establish a mutually convenient time to talk. Omit this step when you need to be assertive on the spot.
- *State the problem in terms of its consequences for you.* Outline your point of view clearly to give the other person a better sense of your position. Describe the problem as objectively as you can without blaming or judging the other person. For example, you might tell a roommate or family member, "I'm having a problem with the loud music you are playing. I'm studying for a test tomorrow and the music is so loud I can't concentrate."
- *Express your feelings.* Go ahead and express your feelings openly—but noncombatively. You need to let the other person know how important the issue is to you. Suppressing your feelings prolongs the problem.
- *Make your request.* A key part of being assertive is asking for what you want in a straightforward, direct way.

Religious interest is widespread around the world. Of the world's 5.5 billion people, approximately two-thirds either are involved in a religion or have been affected by religion in important ways. (*Centre*) Worshippers at the Makka (Mecca) mosque in Saudi Arabia. (*Top left*) A Jewish rabbi reading a prayer. (*Top right*) Temple of the Thousand Buddhas in Bangkok, Thailand. (*Lower left*) A congregation singing at a North American Protestant church. (*Lower right*) Worshippers at the World Youth Day mass in Toronto, Summer 2002. *How might religion be linked to physical and mental health?*

Religion

Might religion have an effect on a person's physical and mental health? Individuals in the religious mainstream generally experience a positive relationship between religion and both physical and psychological health (Koenig, 2002; Wink, Dillon, & Larsen, 2005). Researchers have found that religious commitment helps to moderate blood pressure and hypertension (Walsh, 1998). Also, a number of studies have confirmed that religious participation is related to a longer life (Marks & other, 2005; McCullough & others, 2000).

How might religion promote physical health? Part of the answer may be simply that some religious organizations provide some health-related services. Another possible explanation is that religious individuals have healthier life styles (for example, they use fewer drugs).

In general, various dimensions of religion can also help some people cope more effectively with the stress in their lives (Fabricatore & others, 2004; Koenig & Cohen, 2002). Religious thoughts can play a role in maintaining hope and stimulating motivation for recovery. Although the evidence is not clear, it has also been argued that prayer might be associated with positive health-related changes in the face of stress, such as decreased perception of pain and reduced muscle tension.

Yet another explanation for the link between religion and good health is that religious organizations sponsor social connections. It is well documented that socially connected individuals have fewer health problems (Brannon & Feist, 2004). The social connections promoted by religious activity can forestall anxiety and depression and can help to prevent isolation and loneliness (Salsman & others, 2005).

Stress Management Programs

Because many people have difficulty managing stress themselves, psychologists have developed a variety of techniques that can be taught to individuals (Linden, 2005). **Stress management programs** teach individuals how to appraise stressful events, how to develop skills for coping with stress, and how to put these skills into use in their everyday lives. Some stress management programs are broad in scope, teaching a variety of techniques to handle stress; others may teach a specific technique, such as relaxation or assertiveness training.

Stress management programs are often taught through workshops, which are being offered more often in the workplace (Taylor, 2006). Aware of the high cost in lost productivity due to stress-related disorders, many organizations have become increasingly motivated to help their workers identify and cope with stressful circumstances in their lives. Universities are also developing stress management programs for students. If you are finding the experience of university extremely stressful and are having difficulty coping with taxing circumstances in your life, you might want to consider enrolling in a stress management program at your university or in your community. Some stress management programs are also taught to individuals who are experiencing similar kinds of problems—such as migraine headache sufferers or individuals with chronically high blood pressure.

Do stress management programs work? In one recent study, men and women with hypertension (blood pressure greater than 140/90) were randomly assigned to one of three groups. One group received 10 hours of individual stress management training; a second group was placed in a wait-list control group and eventually received stress management training; and a third group (a control group) received no stress management training (Linden, Lenz, & Con, 2001). In the two groups that received the stress management training, blood pressure was significantly reduced. The control group experienced no reduction in blood pressure. Also, the reduced blood pressure in the first two groups was linked to a reported reduction in psychological stress and improved ability to cope with anger.

The following two techniques are often used in stress management programs.

Meditation and Relaxation At one time, meditation was believed to have more in common with mysticism than with science. But it has been an important part of life in Asia for centuries and has become popular in North America.

Meditation is the practice and system of thought that incorporates exercises that help the individual to attain bodily or mental control and well-being, as well as enlightenment (Shapiro & Walsh, 2003; Gillani & Smith, 2001). The strategies of meditation vary but usually take one of two forms: concentrative meditation or mindfulness meditation.

Concentrative meditation is the practice of focusing the attention, usually on the breath or a sound (mantra), in order to calm the mind and heighten awareness. *Transcendental meditation (TM)* is a form of concentrative meditation derived from an ancient Indian technique. Popular in North America, TM involves using a *mantra*, which is a resonant sound or phrase that is repeated mentally or aloud to focus attention. One widely used TM mantra is the phrase *Om mani padme hum*. By concentrating on this phrase, the individual replaces other thoughts with the syllables Om mani padme hum. In transcendental meditation the individual learns to associate a mantra with a special meaning, such as beauty, peace, or tranquility.

In contrast, **mindfulness meditation** is the practice of opening attention to an awareness of the ongoing stream of sensations, thoughts, and feelings in order to develop

Meditation has been an important dimension of Asian life for centuries.

stress management programs Teach individuals to appraise stressful events, to develop skills for coping with stress, and to put these skills into use in their everyday lives.

meditation The practice and system of thought that incorporates exercises to attain bodily or mental control and well-being, as well as enlightenment.

concentrative meditation The practice of focusing of attention, usually on the breath or a sound (mantra), in order to calm the mind and heighten awareness.

mindfulness meditation The practice of opening attention to an awareness of the ongoing stream of sensations, thoughts, and feelings in order to develop a non-reactive, clear state of mind.

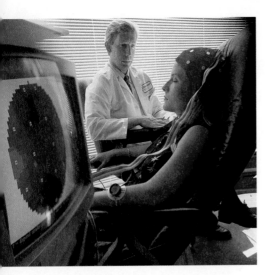

In biofeedback, instruments monitor physiological activities and give individuals information about them so they can learn to voluntarily control the activities.

a non-reactive, clear state of mind. If concentrative meditation is like the zoom lens of a camera, serving to focus attention on a narrow part of the field of experience, mindfulness meditation is like a wide-angle lens, opening up attention to the fuller field of experience.

As a physiological state, meditation is often described as an altered state of consciousness that shows qualities of both sleep and wakefulness, yet it is distinct from either of them. It resembles a hypnagogic state, which is the transition from wakefulness to sleep, but at the very least it is prolongation of that state (Vaitl & others, 2005).

Early research on meditation's effects on the body found that it lowers oxygen consumption, slows heart rate, increases blood flow in the arms and forehead, and produces EEG patterns that are predominantly of the alpha variety—regular and rhythmic (Wallace & Benson, 1972). Some researchers have found support for the notion that meditation causes positive physiological changes and believe that meditation is superior to relaxation in reducing body arousal and anxiety (Eppley, Abrams, & Shear, 1989; Bishop, 2002); other researchers acknowledge meditation's positive physiological effects but believe that relaxation is just as effective (Holmes, 1988).

Researchers have found that the practice of either form of meditation activates neural structures involved in attention and control of the autonomic nervous system (Valentine & Sweet, 1999; Lazar & others, 2000). In one study, mindfulness meditation was effective in decreasing mood disturbance and stress symptoms in cancer patients (Speca & others, 2000). In another study, meditation lowered blood pressure in young people (Barnes & others, 2004).

Would you like to feel what a state of meditation is like? If so, you can probably reach that feeling state by following some simple instructions. First, you need to find a quiet place to sit. Sit quietly and upright in a comfortable chair. Let your chin rest comfortably on your chest, your hands in your lap. Close your eyes. Then pay attention to your breathing. Notice every time you inhale and every time you exhale. Pay attention to the sensations of air flowing through your body, the feeling of your lungs filling and emptying. After you have focused on several breaths, begin to repeat silently to yourself a single word every time you breathe out. The word you choose does not have to mean anything: You can make up a word, you can use the word *one*, or you can try a word that is associated with the emotion you want to produce, such as *trust*, *love*, *patience*, or *happy*. Try several different words to see which one works for you. At first, you will find that thoughts are intruding and that you are no longer attending to your breathing. Just return to your breathing and say the word each time you exhale.

After you have practiced this exercise for 10 to 15 minutes, twice a day, every day for two weeks, you will be ready for a shortened version. If you notice that you are experiencing stressful thoughts or circumstances, simply meditate on the spot for several minutes. If you are in public, you don't have to close your eyes; just fix your gaze on some nearby object, attend to your breathing, and say your word silently every time you exhale.

Audiotapes that induce the relaxation response are available in most bookstores. They usually include soothing background music along with instructions on how to meditate. These audiotapes can help you become more relaxed especially before you go to bed at night.

Biofeedback For many years, operant conditioning was believed to be an effective technique only when dealing with voluntary behaviours such as aggression, shyness, and achievement. Behaviour modification helped people to reduce their aggression, to be more assertive and outgoing, and to get better grades, for example. Involuntary physiological behaviours, such as blood pressure, muscle tension, pulse rate, and brain waves were thought to be outside the boundaries of operant conditioning and more appropriate for classical conditioning. Beginning in the 1960s though, psychologist Neal Miller (1969) and others began to demonstrate that people can control internal behaviours.

Biofeedback is the process in which individuals' internal physiological activities are monitored by instruments; then, the information from the instruments is given (fed back) to the individuals so that they can learn to voluntarily control their physiological activities. How does biofeedback work? Consider the problem of reducing an individual's muscle tension. The individual's muscle tension is monitored, and the level of tension is fed back to him or her. Often the feedback is in the form of an audible tone. As muscle tension rises, the tone becomes louder; as it drops, the tone becomes softer. The reinforcement in biofeedback is the raising and lowering of the tone (or in some cases, seeing a dot move up or down on a screen) as the individual learns to control muscle tension (Schwartz & Andrasik, 2003).

Researchers have found that biofeedback can help people reduce the intensity of migraine headaches and chronic pain (Scharff, Marcus, & Masek, 2002). But is biofeedback more effective than less expensive, simpler methods of relaxation? This issue has not been completely resolved, but several large-scale studies have found no distinct advantage of biofeedback over meditation and relaxation techniques (Schwartz & Andrasik, 2003). Indeed, relaxation is believed to be a key aspect of how biofeedback works.

> ## > reflect and review

5 **Outline strategies for coping with stress.**

- Evaluate problem-focused and emotion-focused coping.
- Understand the importance of optimism and positive thinking.
- Describe the role of social support in coping.
- Explain assertive behaviour and its benefits.
- Discuss the link between religion and health.
- Summarize what stress management programs are like.

Think about a stressful circumstance that has occurred during the past year in your life. How effectively did you cope with it? Now that you have read about various coping strategies, would you have been better off if you had used one or more of them? Explain.

6 HEALTHFUL LIVING

— Exercising Regularly   — Eating Healthily   — Quitting Smoking   — Making Sound Sexual Decisions

What are some ways to promote your own health?

Effectively coping with stress is essential for physical and mental health. But we can do a great deal more to promote better health. Healthful living—establishing healthy habits and evaluating and changing our behaviours that interfere with good health—helps avoid the damaging effects of stress (Lyons & Chamberlain, 2006). Among the essential ingredients of a healthier lifestyle are regular exercise and good nutrition. Not smoking and sound sexual decision making are also important in improving the quality of our health.

Exercising Regularly

Canadians have recently begun to recognize that they need to get more exercise. In the 1996–97 National Population Health Survey, almost half of all Canadians had changed some health-related behaviour, such as exercise, in the previous year (Health Canada, 1999). By the time of the 2001 Canadian Community Health Survey, 41 percent of Canadians were classified as active or moderately active during their leisure time

biofeedback The process in which individuals' internal biological activities are monitored by instruments. The information from the instruments is fed back to the individuals so that they can learn to voluntarily control their physiological activities.

FIGURE 15.13
Moderate and Vigorous Physical Activities

Moderate	Vigorous
Walking, briskly (5–7 km/h)	Walking, briskly uphill or with a load
Cycling for pleasure or transportation (≤16 km/h)	Cycling, fast or racing (>16 km/h)
Swimming, moderate effort	Swimming, fast treading crawl
Conditioning exercise, general calisthenics	Conditioning exercise, stair ergometer, ski machine
Racquet sports, table tennis	Racquet sports, singles tennis, racquetball
Golf, pulling cart or carrying clubs	Golf, practice at driving range
Canoeing, leisurely (3–6 km/h)	Canoeing, rapidly (≥7 km/h)
Home care, general cleaning	Moving furniture
Mowing lawn, power mower	Mowing lawn, hand mower
Home repair, painting	Fix-up projects

(Statistics Canada, 2002c). Without question, people are jogging, cycling, and taking exercise classes more today than in the past, but we are getting far less exercise in our daily lives. Too many of us drive instead of walk, take the elevator instead of climbing the stairs, and hire somebody else to do the little physical work that remains in our lives. Far too many of us spend most of our leisure time sitting in front of the TV or the computer screen.

One of the main reasons that health experts want us to exercise is that it helps to prevent heart disease (Billman, 2002; Blumenthal & others, 2005). Although exercise designed to strengthen muscles and bones or to improve flexibility is important to fitness, many health experts stress aerobic exercise. **Aerobic exercise** is sustained activity—jogging, swimming, or cycling, for example—that stimulates heart and lung functioning. A pioneering long-term study of 17,000 male alumni of Harvard University found that those who exercised strenuously on a regular basis had a lower risk of heart disease and were likelier to still be alive in their middle adulthood years than their more sedentary counterparts (Paffenbarger & others, 1986; Lee, Hsieh, & Paffenbarger, 1995).

People in some occupations get more vigorous exercise than those in others. (Howley, 2001). For example, longshoremen who are on their feet all day and who lift, push, and carry heavy cargo have about half the risk of fatal heart attacks as such co-workers as crane drivers and clerks, who have physically less demanding jobs.

Some health experts conclude that, regardless of other risk factors (smoking, high blood pressure, being overweight, heredity), if you exercise enough to burn more than 2000 calories a week, you can cut your risk of heart attack by an impressive two-thirds (Sherwood, Light, & Blumenthal, 1989). But burning up 2000 calories a week through exercise requires a lot of effort, far more than most of us are willing to expend. To burn 300 calories a day through exercise, you would have to do one of the following: swim or run for about 25 minutes, walk for 45 minutes at about 4 miles an hour, or participate in aerobic dancing for 30 minutes.

As a more realistic goal, many health experts recommend that adults engage in 30 minutes or more of moderate physical activity on most, preferably all, days of the week. Most recommend that you should try to raise your heart rate to at least 60 percent of your maximum heart rate. However, only about one-fifth of adults are active at these recommended levels of physical activity. Examples of the physical activities that qualify as moderate (and, for comparison, vigorous activities) are listed in figure 15.13.

Researchers have found that exercise benefits not only physical health but also mental health (Penedo & Dahn, 2005; Pennix & others, 2002). In particular, exercise

aerobic exercise Sustained exercise that stimulates heart and lung activity.

improves self-concept and reduces anxiety and depression. In one study, 109 nonexercising volunteers were randomly assigned to one of four conditions: high-intensity aerobic training, moderate-intensity aerobic training, low-intensity nonaerobic training, and waiting list (Moses & others, 1989). In the high-intensity aerobic group, participants engaged in a continuous walk-jog program that elevated their heart rate to between 70 and 75 percent of maximum. In the moderate-intensity aerobic group, participants engaged in walking or jogging that elevated their heart rate to 60 percent of maximum. In the low-intensity nonaerobic group, participants engaged in strength, mobility, and flexibility exercises in a slow, discontinuous manner for about 30 minutes. Those who were assigned to exercise programs worked out three to five times a week. Those who were on the waiting list did not exercise. The programs lasted for 10 weeks. As expected, the group assigned to the high-intensity aerobic program showed the greatest aerobic fitness on a 12-minute walk-run. Fitness also improved for those assigned to moderate- and low-exercise programs. However, only the people assigned to the moderate-intensity aerobic training programs showed psychological benefits. These benefits appeared immediately in the form of reduced tension and anxiety and, after three months, in the form of improved ability to cope with stress.

Moderate or intense exercise benefits physical and mental health.

Why were the psychological benefits superior in the moderate-intensity aerobic condition? Perhaps the participants in the high-intensity program found the training too demanding, not so surprising as these individuals were nonexercisers prior to the study. The superiority of the moderate-intensity aerobic training program over the nonaerobic low-intensity exercise program suggests that a minimum level of aerobic conditioning may be required to obtain important psychological benefits.

Research on the benefits of exercise suggests that both moderate and intense activities may produce important physical and psychological gains (Brannon & Feist, 2004). Some people enjoy rigorous, intense exercise. Others enjoy moderate exercise. The enjoyment and pleasure we derive from exercise added to its aerobic benefits makes exercise one of life's most important activities.

Following are some helpful strategies for building exercise into your life:

- *Reduce TV time.* In one study, adults who had watched more television when they were younger were now carrying more fat, and had poorer respiratory fitness and higher cholesterol (Hancox, Milne, & Poulton, 2004). Replace some of your TV time with exercise time.
- *Chart your progress.* Systematically recording your exercise workouts will help you to chart your progress. This strategy is especially helpful in maintaining an exercise program over an extended period.
- *Get rid of excuses.* People make up all kinds of excuses for not exercising. A typical excuse is "I just don't have enough time." You probably do have the time to make exercise a priority.
- *Imagine the alternative.* Ask yourself whether you are too busy to take care of your own health. What will your life be like if your lose your health?
- *Learn more about exercise.* The more you know about exercise, the more you are likely to start an exercise program and continue it.

Eating Healthily

In chapter 11, we discussed many aspects of eating and weight. Obesity is a serious and pervasive health problem, with about one-third of the North American population overweight enough to be at increased health risk. According to a joint Canadian/U.S. health survey, 15 percent of Canadians and 21 percent of Americans are obese (Statistics Canada, 2003). On the other hand, the pressure to be thin can lead to harmful effects for people who are not overweight. Researchers have found that the most effective component of weight loss programs is regular exercise.

Despite the growing variety of choices North Americans can make in the grocery store, many of us are unhealthy eaters. We take in too much sugar and not enough

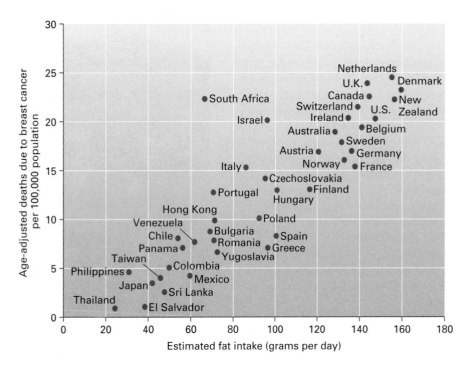

FIGURE 15.14 **Cross-Cultural Comparisons of Diet and Breast Cancer Rates**
In countries in which individuals have a low daily intake of fat, the rate of breast cancer is low (in Thailand, for example). In countries in which individuals have a high daily intake of fat, the rate of breast cancer is high (the Netherlands, for example).

foods high in vitamins, minerals, and fibre, such as fruits, vegetables, and grains. We eat too much fast food and too few well-balanced meals, choices that increase our fat and cholesterol intake, both of which are implicated in long-term health problems.

Evidence for the negative effects of poor nutritional choices comes from both animal and cross-cultural research. For example, mice fed a high-fat diet are likelier to develop breast cancer than mice fed on a low-fat diet. And a cross-cultural study of women found a strong positive correlation between fat consumption and death rates from breast cancer (see figure 15.14; Cohen, 1987).

One telling comparison linking fat intake and cancer is between Canada, the United States, and Japan. These three countries have similar levels of industrialization and education, as well as high medical standards. Although the overall cancer rates of the three countries are similar, cancers of the breast, colon, and prostate are common in Canada and the United States but rare in Japan. Within two generations, descendants of Japanese immigrants to Hawaii, California, and British Columbia have developed breast cancer rates that are significantly higher than those in Japan and that approach the rates of other North Americans. Many researchers believe that the high fat intake of North Americans and the low fat intake of the Japanese are implicated in the countries' different cancer rates.

North American nutritional standards have changed over time, adding to our confusion about which foods we should eat. Only a few decades ago, eggs and dairy foods were promoted as virtually ideal food sources. Most recently, however, the moderate intake of these foods has been endorsed.

Today, nutritionists believe that proper nutrition involves more than merely taking in an appropriate number of calories. It involves carefully selecting foods that provide appropriate nutrients along with their calories. A sound nutritional plan provides the right amounts of all the nutrients we need—fat, carbohydrates, proteins, vitamins, minerals, and water.

Several health goals can be accomplished through a sound nutritional plan. Not only does a well-balanced diet provide more energy but it can also lower blood pressure and lessen our risk of cancer and even tooth decay.

Quitting Smoking

Shifts toward promoting health are most obvious in the area of smoking prevention. Governments in Canada and the United States have developed public antismoking campaigns. Some have even undertaken massive litigation against tobacco companies. Tobacco companies are finally accepting some responsibility and are negotiating to limit their liability for health-related damages. Nevertheless, 19 percent of Canadians and 17 percent of Americans still smoke daily (Statistics Canada, 2003).

Converging evidence from a number of studies underscores the dangers of smoking or being around those who do (Friedman, 2002; Millis, 1998). For example, smoking is linked to 30 percent of cancer deaths, 21 percent of heart disease deaths, and 82 percent of chronic pulmonary disease deaths. Put another way, in Canada it has been estimated that smoking leads to nearly one in five deaths—more than deaths from suicide, vehicle crashes, AIDS, and murder combined (Statistics Canada, 2001). Second-hand smoke is implicated in as many as 9000 lung cancer deaths a year in the United States. Children of smokers are at special risk for respiratory and middle-ear diseases.

Fewer people smoke today than in the past, and almost half of the living adults who ever smoked have quit. The prevalence of smoking in men has dropped from over 50 percent in 1965 to about 28 percent today (U.S. National Center for Health Statistics, 2000c). However, more than 7 million Canadians still smoke cigarettes today, about 22 percent. And cigar smoking and tobacco chewing, which have risk levels similar to those of cigarette smoking, have increased.

Most smokers would like to quit, but their addiction to nicotine often makes quitting a challenge. Nicotine, the active drug in cigarettes, is a stimulant that increases the smoker's energy and alertness, a pleasurable and reinforcing experience (Rukstalis & others, 2005; Seidman, Rosecan, & Role, 1999). Nicotine also stimulates neurotransmitters that have a calming or pain-reducing effect. Smoking also works as a negative reinforcer by ending a smoker's painful craving for nicotine. The immediate gratification of smoking is hard to overcome even for those who recognize that smoking is "suicide in slow motion." Figure 15.15 shows that when individuals quit smoking, over time their risk of fatal lung cancer declines.

How can smokers quit? Five main methods are used to help smokers abandon their habit (Abrams & others, 2003):

- *Using a substitute source of nicotine.* Nicotine gum, the nicotine patch, the nicotine inhaler, and nicotine spray work on the principle of supplying small amounts of nicotine to diminish the intensity of withdrawal (Cepeda-Benito, Reynoso, & Erath, 2004). Nicotine gum, now available without a prescription, is a drug that smokers can take orally when they get the urge to smoke. The nicotine patch is a nonprescription adhesive pad that delivers a steady dose of nicotine to the individual. The dose is gradually reduced over an 8- to 12-week period. Success rates for nicotine substitutes have been encouraging. The percentage of study participants who are still not smoking after five months ranges from 18 percent for the nicotine patch to 30 percent for the nicotine spray (Centers for Disease Control and Prevention, 2001b).
- *Taking an antidepressant.* Bupropion SR, an antidepressant sold as Zyban, helps smokers control their cravings while they ease off nicotine. Zyban works at the neurotransmitter level in the brain by inhibiting the uptake of dopamine, serotonin, and norepinephrine. In recent research, smokers using Zyban to quit have had a 30 percent average success rate after five months of taking the antidepressant (Centers for Disease Control and Prevention, 2001b; Gonzales & others, 2001; Steele, 2001). Some deaths have been reported as a consequence of Zyban, however, which has led to screening for the seizures that may occur in some individuals (Bhattacharjee & others, 2001).

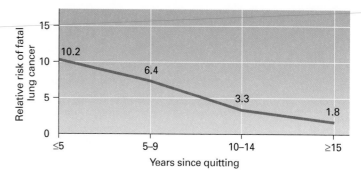

FIGURE 15.15

Fatal Lung Cancer and Years Since Quitting Smoking
One study compared more than 43,000 former male smokers with almost 60,000 males who had never smoked (Enstrom, 1999). For comparison purposes, a zero level was assigned as the risk of fatal lung cancer for men who had never smoked. Over time, the relative risk for smokers who had quit declined, but even after 15 years it was still above that of nonsmokers.

- *Controlling stimuli associated with smoking.* This behaviour modification technique sensitizes the smoker to social cues associated with smoking. For example, the individual might associate a morning cup of coffee or a social drink with smoking. Stimulus control strategies help the smoker to avoid these cues or learn to substitute other behaviours for smoking. This approach has met with mixed results.
- *Undergoing aversive conditioning.* Chapter 14 discussed the behavioural therapy technique of aversive conditioning, which involves repeated pairings of an undesirable behaviour with aversive stimuli to decrease the behaviour's rewards. Imagine smoking as many cigarettes as possible until the ashtray overflows, the smell of stale cigarettes seems permanently embedded in your fingertips, your throat is dry and scratchy, and you feel nauseated. The concept behind aversive conditioning is to make smoking so unpleasant that you won't want to smoke anymore. Sometimes this technique works, sometimes it doesn't.
- *Going cold turkey.* Some people succeed by simply stopping smoking without making any major changes in their lifestyle. They decide they are going to quit and they do. Lighter smokers usually have more success with this approach than heavier smokers.

As you can see, no one method is foolproof for quitting smoking. Often a combination of these methods is the best approach. And, often, truly quitting requires more than one try.

Making Sound Sexual Decisions

Chapter 11 discussed sexual motivations and sexual orientations. This section focuses on the importance of making healthy decisions in your sex life.

Sexual Knowledge According to Health Canada (2003), sexual health and the ability to make sound sexual decisions begins with sexual knowledge, including knowledge relevant to creating and maintaining personal sexual health as well as knowledge relevant to understanding cultural and individual differences in beliefs about sexual health. Unfortunately, many people are still quite uninformed about basic sexual health. Even more problematic are the unfounded sexual myths we believe. According to Barrett and colleagues (1997), young Canadians get most of their information about sex from television and their friends. In one study, a majority of adolescents believed that pregnancy risk is greatest during menstruation. There is a serious need to improve our sexual awareness and knowledge, which can help to reduce unwanted pregnancies and promote sexual self-awareness. For an assessment of your own sexual knowledge, see figure 15.16.

Read each of the following statements and check whether you think it is true or false.

	True	False		True	False
1. There is a right way and a wrong way to have sexual intercourse.	☑	☐	7. You can tell immediately if you have a sexually transmitted disease.	☐	☑
2. It is important for couples to have simultaneous orgasms.	☑	☐	8. Gonorrhea, syphilis, and AIDS can be contracted from toilet seats.	☐	☑
3. Individuals should not have sexual intercourse at any time during pregnancy.	☐	☑	9. Masturbation can cause mental disorders.	☐	☑
4. Once individuals are sterilized, their interest in sex diminishes.	☐	☑	10. Females rarely masturbate.	☐	☑
5. You can tell the size of a man's penis by the size of his hands and feet.	☐	☑	11. Only homosexual males and intravenous drug abusers are at risk for contracting AIDS.	☐	☑
6. If you contract a sexually transmitted disease and treat it effectively, you can't get it again.	☐	☑	12. Most sexual dysfunctions are due to physical problems.	☑	☐

Most people mark one or more of the above items true. However, according to experts on human sexuality, all of the above statements are myths (Crooks & Bauer, 1999; Greenberg, Bruess, & Mullen, 1992). Thus, although sexuality is an integral part of life, many people have misconceptions about it.

FIGURE 15.16 Sexual Myths and Realities

Contraception Most couples in North America want to control whether and when they will conceive a child. For them it is important to have accurate knowledge about contraception. But inadequate knowledge about, and inconsistent use of, effective contraceptive methods has resulted in an adolescent pregnancy rate in Canada of about 22–24 per 1000 births. While these rates are high compared to many other industrialized countries, the United States reports rates of 60 adolescent pregnancies per 1000 live births, by far the highest rates in the industrialized world (Public Health Agency of Canada, 1999).

Although the rate of contraceptive use among teenagers is improving, many still do not use contraception (Child Trends, 2000) or may overestimate the effectiveness of some of the unreliable methods (Weisman & others, 2002). According to Irwin (2004), about 85 percent of adolescent pregnancies in the United States are unintended, resulting in hundreds of thousands of abortions each year. Adolescent pregnancy is linked with a host of problems for the mother, such as less future education and lower socioeconomic status, and for the offspring (Leadbeater & Way, 2001; Whitman & others, 2001).

In this regard, the distribution of information about contraception, and contraceptives themselves, to adolescents is a major public health challenge. One common stereotype is that of the sexually active adolescent as a risk taker who is encouraged to take even more risks as contraceptives are made more available (Irwin, 2004). Attempts to restrict the availability of contraceptives or knowledge of contraception or to mandate that adolescents can only access contraceptives with parental consent tend to drive adolescent sexual activity underground, a factor which might be contributing to the adolescent pregnancy rate (Jones & others, 2005).

No method of contraception is best for everyone (Hyde & DeLamater, 2006). When choosing a method of contraception, couples need to consider such factors as their physical and emotional concerns, the method's effectiveness, the nature of their relationship, their values and beliefs, and the method's convenience. Calculations of the effectiveness of a contraceptive method are often based on the failure rates during the first year of use. It is estimated that if no contraceptive method were used, about 90 percent of women would become pregnant in their first year of being heterosexually active (Hatcher & others, 2004).

Sexually Transmitted Infections **Sexually transmitted infections (STIs)** are infections that are contracted primarily through sex—oral–genital and anal–genital sex as well as intercourse. STIs were previously labeled *venereal diseases or sexually transmitted diseases (STDs)*. The newer label, STI, is more inclusive, encompassing both symptomatic and asymptomatic infections. For example, HIV infection is classified as an STI even though the symptoms of the disease, AIDS, may not be present. STIs affect about one of every six adults (U.S. National Center for Health Statistics, 2001). The main STIs are caused by bacterial infections, as in the case of gonorrhea and syphilis, or viruses, as in the case of genital herpes and AIDS.

No single STI has had a greater impact on sexual behaviour, or created more fear, in the past decades than has AIDS. **Acquired immunodeficiency syndrome (AIDS)** is caused by the *human immunodeficiency virus (HIV)*, a sexually transmitted disease that destroys the body's immune system. A person who has contracted HIV is thus vulnerable to germs that a normal immune system could destroy. Once an individual is infected with HIV, the prognosis is likely progression to AIDS and eventual death. In a hopeful development, new drug "cocktails," referred to as *HAART (Highly Active Anti-Retroviral Therapy)*, are allowing 90 percent of treated individuals to live ten years after they have been diagnosed with HIV infection (K. Porter & others, 2003).

According to the World Health Organization (2004), at the end of 2003, about 56,000 Canadian men, women, and children were infected with HIV/AIDS, about 0.3 percent of the population. Just under a quarter of the cases were women. While the overall infection rate in Canada has levelled off, infection rates are down for injection drug use and up for both homosexual and heterosexual contact.

sexually transmitted infections (STIs) Infections that are contracted primarily through sex—oral–genital and anal–genital sex as well as intercourse.

acquired immunodeficiency syndrome (AIDS) Caused by the human immunodeficiency virus (HIV), a sexually transmitted disease that destroys the body's immune system.

Pat Hawkins is deputy director of the Whitman-Walker Clinic in Washington, D.C., helping HIV and AIDS patients. She came to the clinic as a volunteer in 1983, just after HIV/AIDS exploded into an epidemic.

Hawkins says that she would not do anything else but community work. "Nothing gets you engaged so fast as getting involved," she comments. "We often keep the academic world separate from the real world, and we desperately need psychologists' skills in the real world."

Why does she like working in a nonprofit organization? "I knew I wanted to treat people clinically, but I wanted a broader impact," she says. "In private clinical work, you might see 1000 people in a whole lifetime. I wanted to do more than that."

Hawkins was a double major in psychology and sociology as an undergraduate and then went on to obtain her Ph.D. in community psychology.

Although the incidence of HIV/AIDS is relatively low in Canada, according to UNAIDS, the United Nations Programme on HIV/AIDS, the infection has reached epidemic proportions in sub-Saharan Africa, where the virus first affected human populations (UNAIDS, 2004). At the end of 2004, over 25 million people, or 7.5 percent of all adults in sub-Saharan Africa, were infected with HIV. There were 3.1 million new infections and 2.3 million deaths due to AIDS in 2004 alone. AIDS has become the leading cause of death in adolescents and young adults in sub-Saharan Africa (Centers for Disease Control and Prevention, 2001a).

Remember that it is not who you are but what you do that puts you at risk for HIV. Experts (Hyde & DeLamater, 2006) say that HIV can be transmitted only by:

● sexual contact
● other direct contact of cuts or mucous membranes with blood and sexual fluids
● sharing hypodermic needles
● blood transfusions (which in the past few years have been tightly monitored)

Anyone who is sexually active or uses intravenous drugs is at risk. No one is immune (Hynie, 1998). The only safe behaviour is abstinence from sex, which is not perceived as an option by most individuals. Beyond abstinence, there is only safer behaviour, such as sexual behaviour without exchange of semen, vaginal fluids, or blood, and sexual intercourse with a condom (King, 2005; Perloff, 2001).

Just asking a date about his or her previous sexual behaviour does not guarantee protection from HIV and other sexually transmitted diseases (Delega & others, 2004). In one disquieting investigation, 655 university students were asked to answer questions about lying and sexual behaviour (Cochran & Mays, 1990). Of the 422 respondents who said they were sexually active, 34 percent of the men and 10 percent of the women said they had lied so their partner would have sex with them. Much higher percentages—47 percent of the men and 60 percent of the women—said they had been lied to by a potential sexual partner. When asked what aspects of their pasts they would be likeliest to lie about, more than 40 percent of the men and women said they would understate the number of their sexual partners. Twenty percent of the men, but only 4 percent of the women, said they would lie about their results from an HIV blood test.

There are some good strategies for protecting against HIV and other sexually transmitted diseases (King, 2005; Fisher & others, 2002). They include:

● *Abstinence*. With the rise of the AIDs pandemic, sex education has returned to promoting the merits of abstinence before marriage, and especially abstinence from casual, risky sex (Moran, 2002).
● *Knowing your and your partner's risk status*. Anyone who has had previous sexual activity with another person might have contracted an STI without being aware of it. Spend time getting to know a prospective partner before you have sex. Use this time to inform the other person of your STI status and inquire about your partner's. Remember that many people lie about their STI status.
● *Obtaining medical examinations*. Many experts recommend that couples who want to begin a sexual relationship have a medical checkup to rule out STIs before they engage in sex. If cost is an issue, contact your campus health service or a public health clinic.
● *Having protected, not unprotected, sex*. When correctly used, latex condoms help to prevent many STIs from being transmitted. Condoms are most effective in

preventing gonorrhea, syphilis, chlamydia, and HIV. They are less effective against the spread of herpes.

 Not having sex with multiple partners. One of the best predictors of getting STIs is having sex with multiple partners. Having more than one sex partner elevates the likelihood that you will encounter an infected partner.

> **> reflect and review**

6 **Summarize how to promote health.**

- Explain why exercise is important to good health.
- Evaluate the role of nutrition in health.
- Describe why quitting smoking is important and how it might be accomplished.
- Discuss sound sexual decision making.

How good are you at maintaining a regular exercise program, eating nutritiously and healthily, not smoking, and engaging in sound sexual decision making? Has your lifestyle and behaviour in these areas affected your health? Might they affect your health in the future? Explain.

Stress, Coping, and Health

1 HEALTH PSYCHOLOGY AND BEHAVIOURAL MEDICINE

2 STRESS AND ITS SOURCES

— Personality Factors — Environmental Factors — Sociocultural Factors

3 STRESS RESPONSES

— General Adaptation Syndrome — Fight or Flight, Tend and Befriend — Cognitive Appraisal

4 STRESS AND ILLNESS

— Stress and the Immune System — Stress and Cardiovascular Disease — Stress and Cancer — Positive Emotions, Illness, and Health

5 COPING STRATEGIES

— Problem-Focused and Emotion-Focused Coping — Optimism and Positive Thinking — Social Support — Assertive Behaviour — Religion — Stress Management Programs

6 HEALTHFUL LIVING

— Exercising Regularly — Eating Healthily — Quitting Smoking — Making Sound Sexual Decisions

At the beginning of the chapter, we posed six chapter questions and encouraged you to review material related to these questions at the end of each major section (see pages 595, 603, 606, 612, 621, and 629). Use the following reflection and review features for further your understanding of the chapter material.

CHAPTER REFLECTIONS

1. The text distinguishes between the medical model and the biopsychosocial model and describes personality, environment, and sociocultural influences as three factors contributing to stress. What are the advantages and disadvantages of categorizing factors in this manner and considering them separately? Can you think of examples of stressors in which these factors clearly interact? Or in which these factors don't seem to play a role?

2. The text describes physiological stress responses in terms of the damage they cause to our health. If stress responses are so damaging, why do we have them? What purpose might physiological stress responses serve? Why might people differ in their physiological stress responses (for example, men and women)?

3. The links between stress and illness are currently based primarily on correlational studies. Take one of the specific examples described in the text and explain how you would test whether there is a causal link between stress and illness.

4. Do an Internet search on the topic of "stress management" or "coping with stress." Visit three or four sites and critically evaluate the suggestions made on the sites. How are they similar to the suggestions given in the text? How much information is available to evaluate the claims on the sites? Based on your critical evaluation, is the advice something you would follow or not?

5. One method that has helped to decrease unhealthy behaviours such as smoking is to make them more expensive. Currently, some people are calling for a tax on unhealthy foods. Why would such a tax be useful? Would you be in favour of such a tax, or opposed? Why?

CHAPTER REVIEW

Describe the scope of health psychology and behavioural medicine.

-   Health psychology is grounded in the biopsychosocial model, a multidimensional approach to health that emphasizes psychological factors, lifestyle, and the nature of the health care delivery system. Closely aligned with health psychology is behavioural medicine, which combines medical and behavioural knowledge to reduce illness and promote health.

-   Psychological and social factors are often involved in chronic diseases. A special interest is the link between stress and illness.

Define stress and identify its sources.

-   Stress is the response of individuals to the circumstances and events, called stressors, that threaten them and tax their coping abilities.

-   Personality factors involved in stress include the Type A/Type B behaviour pattern, hardiness, and personal control. The Type A behaviour pattern is a cluster of personality characteristics—such as being hostile, excessively competitive, impatient, and hard driven—that seem to be related to cardiovascular disease. The dimension of the Type A cluster most consistently related to heart disease is hostility. The Type B behaviour pattern includes being relaxed and easygoing. Hardiness—which involves a sense of commitment, a sense of control, and a perception of problems as challenges rather than threats—is a stress buffer and is related to reduced illness. Another important aspect of stress is the extent to which people can control or reduce stress, as well as a related personality characteristic: their perception of control. Across a wide range of studies, a sense of personal control over stressful events has been related to emotional well-being, successful coping with a stressful event, and behaviour change that can promote good health.

-   Environmental factors involved in stress include life events, daily hassles, conflict, overload, and work-related stress. People who experience clusters of life events tend to become ill; daily hassles, ongoing daily annoyances, can also produce health-sapping stress. Everyday conflicts can be stressful. The three types of conflict are approach/approach (least stressful), avoidance/avoidance, and approach/avoidance. Daily hassles can result in overload, which can lead to burnout. The stress level of workers increases when their jobs do not meet their expectations, when job demands are high, and when workers have little choice in deciding how to meet the demands.

- Sociocultural sources of stress include acculturation and poverty. Acculturative stress refers to the negative consequences that result from contact between two distinctive cultural groups. People can adapt to cultural change in one of four ways: assimilation, integration, separation, and marginalization. Poverty can cause considerable stress for individuals and families and is related to threatening and uncontrollable life events.

Explain how people respond to stress.

- Selye proposed the general adaptation syndrome as a model of how the body responds to stress. It consists of three stages: alarm, resistance, and exhaustion. Many scientists now agree that two main biological pathways can be involved in the stress response: the neuroendocrine-immune pathway and the sympathetic nervous system pathway.
- A quick response to stress may take the form of a fight-or-flight response. The central notion of this concept is that the body's physiological resources are mobilized to prepare the organism to deal with threats to survival. However, females are less likely to respond to a threatening situation with a fight-or-flight response than males are. Rather, females responding to threatening circumstances are likelier to tend (protect themselves and their young through nurturing behaviours) and befriend (form alliances with a larger social group, especially one populated by women).
- Lazarus believes that how people respond to stress depends on the way in which they cognitively appraise events. Cognitive appraisal consists of primary appraisal (Is the stressful event harmful, threatening, or challenging?) and secondary appraisal (What resources do I have available to cope with the stressful event?).

Discuss links between stress and illness.

- Psychoneuroimmunology is the field that explores connections among psychological factors (such as attitudes and emotions), the nervous system, and the immune system. Researchers have found that acute stressors can produce immunological changes in healthy individuals. Chronic stressors are associated with a downturn in immune system functioning. Research with cancer patients shows that a good quality of life is associated with a healthier immune system.

- Emotional stress is likely an important factor contributing to cardiovascular disease. People who live in a chronically stressed condition are likelier to smoke, overeat, and not exercise. All of these stress-related behaviours are linked with cardiovascular disease.
- The link between stress and cancer can best be understood by considering connections between stress and quality of life, behavioural factors, and biological pathways.
- The recent interest in positive psychology has sparked research on the role that positive emotions might play in reducing illness and promoting health. In general, positive emotional states are thought to be associated with healthy patterns of physiological functioning in both the cardiovascular and the immune systems.

Outline strategies for coping with stress.

- Lazarus distinguished between problem-focused coping, which involves squarely facing stressors and trying to solve them, and emotion-focused coping, which consists of responding to stress in an emotional manner and usually takes the form of defensive appraisal. Problem-focused coping is usually the better coping strategy.
- Many cognitive therapists believe cognitive restructuring, including positive self-talk, can be used to get people to think more positively and optimistically. Positive self-talk is often helpful in cognitive restructuring. Individuals' ability to cope often benefits from mildly positive self-illusion, although some people cope best by facing reality. Grandiose self-illusion and negative self-illusion are generally not good coping strategies, although some people use defensive pessimism to prepare for stressful situations. Bandura has shown that self-efficacy, the belief that one can master a situation and produce positive outcomes, is an effective strategy in many domains of coping.
- Social support consists of information and feedback from others that one is loved and cared for, esteemed and valued, and included in a network of communication and mutual obligation. Three important benefits are tangible assistance, information, and emotional support. Researchers consistently find that social support, especially diverse social ties, helps people to cope with stress and to live healthier lives.
- People can deal with conflict aggressively, manipulatively, passively, or assertively. Assertive behaviour has become the communication ideal.

- A positive link or neutral link has been found between religion and physical health. Various dimensions of religion can help people cope with stress in their lives.
- Stress management programs teach people how to appraise stressful events, to develop skills for coping with stress, and to put these skills into use in their everyday lives. These programs are often taught through workshops. Meditation, relaxation, and biofeedback are used in stress management. Both concentrative and mindfulness medition are systems of thought that incorporates exercise to attain bodily or mental control and well-being, as well as enlightenment. Researchers have found that meditation reduces body arousal and anxiety, but whether it is more effective than relaxation is debated. Biofeedback is the process in which individuals' internal biological activities are monitored by instruments and the information from the instruments is fed back to the individuals so that they can learn to voluntarily control the activities. Biofeedback has been successful in reducing muscle tension and blood pressure.
- Multiple coping strategies often work better than a single coping strategy.

Summarize how to promote health.

- Both moderate and intense exercise produce important physical or psychological gains, such as lowered risk of heart disease and reduced anxiety.

- Too many people are unhealthy eaters, taking in too much sugar and eating unbalanced meals. Healthy food selections can lower blood pressure, risk for cancer, and even tooth decay.
- Smoking is linked to 30 percent of cancer deaths, 21 percent of heart disease deaths, and 82 percent of chronic pulmonary disease deaths. Second-hand smoke is implicated in thousands of lung cancer deaths a year. Strategies for quitting smoking include nicotine substitutes, Zyban (an antidepressant), stimulus control, aversive conditioning, and going cold turkey. Combining strategies may have the best results.
- Inadequate knowledge about sex, especially contraception, and inconsistent use of effective methods, results in many unwanted adolescent pregnancies. The United States has the highest adolescent pregnancy rates in the industrialized world. Thus becoming knowledgeable about sex and planning contraception before having sex are both aspects of sound sexual decision making. Sexually transmitted infections (STIs) are contracted primarily through sex—oral–genital and anal–genital sex as well as intercourse. The most devastating STI is HIV/AIDS. A special concern is the extremely high rate of HIV/AIDS in sub-Saharan African countries. Some good strategies for protecting against STIs are (1) abstinence, (2) knowing your and your partner's risk status, (3) obtaining medical examinations, (4) having protected, not unprotected, sex, and (5) avoiding sex with multiple partners.

CONNECTIONS

For extra help in mastering the material in the chapter, see the review questions and practice quizzes in the Student Study Guide and the Online Learning Centre.

CORE TERMS

16 Social Psychology

CHAPTER QUESTIONS

1 How do people think about the social world?

2 How are people are influenced in social settings?

3 What are intergroup relations?

4 How do aggression and altruism characterize social interaction?

5 What is the nature of relationships?

Now retired, Canadian General Roméo Dallaire was the commander of 3000 UN Peacekeepers when the 1994 genocide broke out in Rwanda. Early on, when he still had an excellent chance of preventing a slaughter, he repeatedly confronted his superiors, requesting more forces and the authorization to confront Hutu militias. Instead, after the deaths of 10 Belgian peacekeepers, the United Nations withdrew all but 500 peacekeepers. Given responsibility without authority, Dallaire was left a virtually helpless witness to a killing spree in which machete-wielding Hutu extremists slaughtered over 800,000 Tutsis within the span of a hundred days.

The United States refused to help and even called for a complete withdrawal of the peacekeepers. Three days after the genocide began, Dallaire was reduced to watching a well-equipped 1000-strong European force arrive in the capital of Kigali for the sole purpose of evacuating European nationals. A few days into the massacre, he was ordered to withdraw his remaining forces by then-United Nations General Secretary Boutros Ghali. He refused since, by then, he was protecting about 20,000 people in areas under his control, people who would certainly also have been slaughtered.

Left suffering from post-traumatic stress disorder, Dallaire was haunted by memories of piles of hacked-off limbs and the eyes of those who begged him for help that he could not give. He became depressed and even tried to commit suicide. In Dallaire's 2004 award-winning book about his experiences *Shake Hands With the Devil*, he describes his personal torment and systematically indicts the international community for their callous inaction. Today there is general consensus that Dallaire was right: the massacre could have been avoided.

Think about the times in your life when you have faced the pressure to conform to what peers or authority figures wanted you to do. Did you go along to avoid conflict? Or did you have the courage of Roméo Dallaire and resist their pressure? Was it easy? Probably not. What makes it so hard for human beings to follow their consciences? Later in the chapter, the factors that are related to the pressure to conform are examined.

But, more generally, this chapter is about **social psychology**—the study of how people think about, influence, and relate to other people (Alcock, Carment, & Sadava, 2005). Social psychology differs from sociology in that social psychology focuses more on the individual as a social being, whereas sociology places more emphasis on society at large. In keeping with the social psychological focus on the individual, we begin this chapter by examining how individuals think about the social world around them. We then reverse perspective to examine how the social world influences individuals. With this foundation, we turn our attention to intergroup relations and the roles that aggression and altruism play in social interaction. We close the chapter with an examination of how individuals form relationships.

Roméo Dallaire, a true Canadian hero. Dallaire's courage in the face of an impossible situation has been honoured with many awards, including the Order of Canada and the United States Legion of Merit. His book, *Shake hands with the devil: The failure of humanity in Rwanda* won the Governor General's Award in 2004. In 2005, he was called to Canada's Senate and continues to speak out as a humanitarian.

social psychology The study of how people think about, influence, and relate to other people.

❶ SOCIAL THINKING

Attribution ▬▬ Social
Perception ▬▬ Attitudes

How do people think about the social world?
Many aspects of social life engage people. One of the most intriguing is how people think about the social world. This area of social psychology, which is often referred to as *social cognition*, involves how people select, interpret, remember, and use social information. Each person may have a unique combination of expectations, memories, and attitudes based on his or her social history. Nevertheless, certain common principles apply to the way people process information in a social situation (D. T. Miller, 2006; Bordens & Horowitz, 2002; Moskowitz, 2001). The most important of these principles focuses on the way people attribute causes to behaviour, the processes of social perception, and the link between attitudes and behaviour.

Attribution

Human beings are curious, seeking answers to all sorts of questions about their social world. We often try to figure out why something has happened or is happening. We might be curious about why someone is yelling at another person, why someone is in love with a particular person, or why someone joined a certain organization.

Finding causal, meaningful explanations for these and many other social circumstances is a complex task. We can observe people's behaviour and listen to what they say, but to determine the underlying cause of their behaviour, we often have to make inferences from these observations. For example, when we observe someone make a nasty remark to another person, do we infer that the person deserved to be talked to that way, or do we infer that the negative comment occurred because of the perpetrator's hostile personality?

Given the fact that determining the causes of behaviour is a challenge, our desire to find causal explanations is a bit of a puzzle. Why is it so important to us? Attribution theorists argue that we want to know why people do the things they do because the knowledge will enable us to cope more effectively with the situations that confront us (Alderman, 2004). Recall from chapter 11 that **attribution theory** views people as motivated to discover the underlying causes of behaviour as part of their effort to make sense of the behaviour. Thus attributions are thoughts about why people behave the way they do. Attribution theorists say people are, in a way, a lot like detectives or scientists, seeking the reasons for human actions.

The Dimensions of Causality The attributions people make vary along three dimensions (Michener, DeLamater, & Myers, 2004):

- *Internal/external causes.* Chapter 11 explained that an important attribution people make is whether achievement is attributed to external causes or internal causes. *Internal attributions* include all causes internal to the person, such as personality traits, intelligence, attitudes, and health. *External attributions* include all causes external to the person, such as social pressure, aspects of the social situation, money, the weather, and luck. Fritz Heider (1958) argued that this internal/external dimension is the central issue in attribution.

  Consider the attributions we are likely to make in this situation: Josh and Lisa have been dating for several months when Lisa breaks off the relationship. When we speculate about the reasons (as human beings are apt to do), we might observe that Lisa says she is ending the relationship because of pressure from her parents, who want her to tone down her social life and study more (external cause). But, we might wonder, is that the true reason she is breaking off the relationship? Possibly the vivacious Lisa is dumping Josh because she has grown tired of his introverted personality (internal cause).

attribution theory Views people as motivated to discover the underlying causes of behaviour as part of their effort to make sense of the behaviour.

- *Stable/unstable causes*. Our perception of whether the cause is stable or unstable is also involved in making attributions. Is the cause relatively enduring and permanent or is it temporary? If Lisa has inferred that Josh's introverted personality is not going to change, she perceives a stable cause of his behaviour. Alternatively, if Lisa believes that Josh just isn't putting forth enough effort but is capable of being more outgoing, she perceives an unstable cause. These are both internal causes. If Lisa's parents never like anybody she dates, that is an external stable cause. If they don't like Josh but will approve of someone else Lisa dates, that is an external unstable cause.
- *Controllable/uncontrollable causes*. Whether a cause is perceived as controllable or uncontrollable is another dimension of causality (Weiner, 1986). We perceive that we can control some causes but not others. This dimension can coexist with any combination of internal/external and stable/unstable dimensions. Consider these examples of causes that we can control and causes that we can't control: An internal unstable cause such as effort or mood is usually thought of as controllable; an external unstable cause such as luck is generally seen as uncontrollable.

According to Bernard Weiner (1986), successful outcomes that we attribute to ourselves increase our self-esteem more than outcomes attributed to external causes like luck. Attributions regarding controllability are of particular importance because personal responsibility is involved. Attributions of controllability for personal failure are linked with such emotions as guilt, shame, and humiliation. We also hold others responsible for failures attributed to controllable causes and may feel angry toward them. On the other hand, we might feel sympathy toward people whose failures stem from circumstances beyond their control. For example, consider the situation in which a vase is accidentally knocked off a table and broken, in one instance by a child with a disability, in another by a drunken adult. The child with the disability is likely to elicit sympathy, the drunken adult, anger. One interesting aspect of attribution theory is the degree to which we believe in a just world (Hafer & Bègue, 2005; Hafer & Olson, 2003). Someone who strongly believes the world is a just place is more likely to accept his or her own personal deprivation as just but is also more likely to respond negatively to innocent victims.

Attributional Errors and Biases   So far, what we have said about attribution suggests that it is a rational process. However, some common errors and biases infiltrate our attributions. The *fundamental attribution error* is important in understanding how people assign causes to their own behaviour and the behaviour they observe. The *self-serving bias* is people's tendency to be overly positive about their own behaviour, characteristics, and beliefs.

The Fundamental Attribution Error   In attribution theory, the person who acts or produces the behaviour to be explained is called the *actor*. The onlooker, or the person who offers a causal explanation of the actor's behaviour or experience, is called the *observer*. Attribution theorists have observed that actors often explain their own behaviour in terms of external causes. In contrast, observers frequently explain the actor's behaviour in terms of internal causes. The **fundamental attribution error** means that observers overestimate the importance of internal traits and underestimate the importance of external situations when they seek explanations of an actor's behaviour (see figure 16.1).

The fundamental attribution error suggests that when most people encounter examples of social behaviour, they have a tendency to explain the behaviour in terms of the personalities of the people involved rather than of the situation the people are in (Aronson, Wilson, & Akert, 2005). For example, when we try to explain why people do repugnant or bizarre things, our tendency is to describe them as flawed human beings. For example, with founder Luc Jouret leading the way, 74 members of the Order of the Solar Temple "departed" for the star Sirius in the early 1990s. Their suicides, including those in St. Casmir and Morin Heights, Quebec, were intended as a triumphant escape from a "planet of fools." Delusion on such a scale is hard to fathom, and it was easy to conclude that all involved were "kooks." But Jouret was highly charismatic and exerted enormous pressure on his acolytes to go along with him. The public's emphasis on the traits of the actors, without considering how they may have been overpowered by the social forces of the situation, reflects the fundamental attribution error.

fundamental attribution error The tendency for observers to overestimate the importance of traits and underestimate the importance of situations when they seek explanations of a person's behaviour.

FIGURE 16.1

The Fundamental Attribution Error
In this situation, the female supervisor
is the observer and the male employee
is the actor. *If the employee has made
an error in his work, how are the
employee and his supervisor likely to
differ in their explanations of his
behaviour, based on your knowledge of
actor/observer differences and the fundamental attribution error?*

Actor

Tends to give external,
situational explanations of
own behaviour

"I'm late with my report
because other people keep
asking me to help them with
their projects."

Observer

Tends to give internal, trait
explanations of actor's
behaviour

"He's late with his report
because he can't concentrate
on his own responsibilities."

Self-Serving Bias Behaviour is determined by a number of factors, so it is not surprising that our lives are full of squabbling and arguing about the causes of behaviour
(Harvey & Weber, 2002). In addition, as you have just learned, actors and observers
have different ideas about what causes behaviour. What accounts for these differences
in attributions is often bias (Krull, 2001). Our personal attitudes and experiences shape
our perceptions of causes.

When explaining our own actions, our bias is usually self-serving. That is, we tend
to be self-enhancing in the way that we attribute the causes of our behaviour, and we
often exaggerate positive beliefs about ourselves (Sedikides & others, 1998). We often
believe that we are more trustworthy, moral, and physically attractive than other people are. We also tend to believe that we are above-average teachers, managers, and
leaders. We maintain these exaggerated positive beliefs about ourselves through self-
serving bias (Duval & Silvia, 2002).

Self-serving bias especially emerges when our self-esteem is threatened. We may
attribute our successes to internal factors and our failures to external factors: That is, we
tend to take credit for our successes and blame our failures on others or on the situation. In the case of Lisa breaking up with Josh, Josh might find it a lot easier to accept
Lisa's external attribution—that she is doing it because of her parents—than the internal attribution—that he is too introverted. Josh's attribution helps to protect him from
harsh self-criticism.

Social Perception

When we think about our social world and try to make sense of it, we not only make
attributions but also engage in these social perceptions: We develop impressions of
other people, gain self-knowledge by comparing ourselves with others, and present
ourselves to others in such a way as to influence the way they perceive us.

Developing Impressions of Others As we move through the world, we develop
shortcuts for evaluating which people to seek out and which to avoid. Often we use
broad, polar dimensions to categorize them—good or bad, happy or sad, introvert or
extravert, for example. If someone asked for your impression of your psychology professor, you might respond, "She's great. She's dynamic and well organized." From this
description we can infer that you have a positive impression of her.

Our first encounter with someone contributes to the impression we form. First
impressions are often enduring. *Primacy effect* is the term used to describe the enduring
quality of initial impressions. One reason for the primacy effect is that we pay more
attention to what we first learn about a person and less attention to subsequent information (Anderson, 1965). The next time you want to impress someone, a wise strategy
is to make sure that you put your best foot forward in your first encounter.

As we form impressions of others, we cognitively organize the information in two
important ways:

- *We unify our impressions.* Traits, actions, appearance, and all the other information we have obtained about a person are closely connected in memory even though the information may have been obtained in an interrupted or random fashion. We might obtain some information today, more next week, some more in two months. During those two months, we interacted with many other people and developed impressions of them as well. Nonetheless, we usually perceive the information about a particular person as unified, as a continuous block of information (Breckler, 2006).
- *We integrate our impressions.* We reach beyond the spotty information we may have about a person—adding to, manipulating, and modifying it—to form a whole impression. Solomon Asch's original work (1946) uncovered this principle. Participants in his study were asked to think of a short list of traits for an individual. Asch then asked the participants to write character sketches based on a brief list of traits. The sketches included many different combinations of the traits and went far beyond the original list, indicating the tendency to integrate impressions of the person.

When we integrate information about people, we follow certain rules. **Implicit personality theory** is the term given to the public's or a layperson's conception of which personality traits go together (Bruner & Tagiuri, 1954). One person might have an implicit personality theory that all extraverted people are optimistic. The integration of these traits might be based on a thought process similar to this: "Because most of my friends who are extravertedare also optimistic, I assume all extraverted people are optimistic." Such theories serve as organizers of our social perceptions.

Another rule shaping the integration of information about people is that we use some evaluative dimensions more than others. According to the classic formulation by Norman Anderson (1974, 1989), we use three dimensions more than any others to categorize people. The most common dimension is *good/bad*. Think for a moment about the people you know. Chances are you categorize each of them as either good or bad. Our tendency to categorize people as good or bad is so strong that Anderson calls this *the* evaluation dimension. Potency (*strong/weak*) and activity (*active/passive*) are two other dimensions we often use to categorize people (see figure 16.2).

Recall from the discussion in chapter 8 that a *schema* is a conceptual framework that we use to organize information. When we read a book, we do not remember every paragraph word for word; rather, we get the gist of what the author says and fit the information into the schemas in our mind. We "read" people in a similar way. We don't remember everything about what they are like and what they do, but we get the gist of their personality and behaviour, and we fit the information about them into existing categories of memory.

By classifying people as members of groups or categories with which we are familiar we simplify the task of understanding them. Normally we supplement our categorical knowledge of people with some knowledge of their individual characteristics. *Stereotyping* refers to the categorization of an individual without any consideration of that person's individual characteristics. Imagine meeting a sales representative. You develop an impression of him based on the "sales representative" schema in your mind. Without seeking any additional information, you might perceive that person as pushy, self-serving, and materialistic.

We do not always respond to others on the basis of categories, however. As you interact with the sales representative, you might discover that he is actually interesting, modest, bright, and altruistic. You would then have to revise your impression and perceive him differently. When we discover information that is inconsistent with a category, or when we simply become more personally involved with someone, we tend to take an individual approach rather than an oversimplifying category-based approach to impression formation.

Comparing Ourselves with Others How many times have you asked yourself questions such as "Am I as smart as Jill?" "Is Sergei better looking than I am?" or "Is my taste as good as Carmen's?" We gain self-knowledge from our own behaviour, of course; but

Good-bad

Strong-weak

Active-passive

FIGURE 16.2

Developing Impressions of Others: Three Dimensions We Use to Categorize People Look at the individual running. What is your impression of her? You will almost certainly categorize her as good and possibly as strong and active.

implicit personality theory The term given to the public or layperson's conception of which personality traits go together in an individual.

"Randall, my old college nemesis, I was hoping I'd find you here."

Copyright © 1996, *USA Today*. Reprinted with permission.

we also gain it from others through *social comparison*, the process by which individuals evaluate their thoughts, feelings, behaviours, and abilities in relation to other people. Social comparison helps individuals to evaluate themselves, tells them what their distinctive characteristics are, and aids them in building an identity.

Some years ago, social psychologist Leon Festinger (1954) proposed a theory of social comparison. He stressed that when no objective means is available to evaluate our opinions and abilities, we compare ourselves with others. Festinger believed that we are more likeley to compare ourselves with others who are similar to us than dissimilar to us. He reasoned that if we compare ourselves with someone who is very different from us, we will not be able to obtain an accurate appraisal of our own behaviour and thoughts. We will develop more accurate self-perceptions if we compare ourselves, for example, with people in communities similar to where we live, with people who have similar family backgrounds, and with people of the same sex or sexual orientation. Social comparison theory has been extended and modified over the years and continues to provide an important rationale for why we affiliate with others and how we come to know ourselves (White & Lehman, 2005).

Festinger studied social comparison with those who are similar to us; other researchers have focused on social comparison with those whom we consider to be inferior to us. Individuals under threat (from negative feedback, low self-esteem, depression, and illness, for example) try to improve their mental and physical well-being by comparing themselves with others who are less fortunate (Bailis, Chipperfield, & Perry, 2005). It can be comforting to tell ourselves, "Well, at least I'm not as badly off as that guy." According to Buunk, Oldersma, & de Dreu, (2001), we also use downward social comparison with other relationships to make us feel better about our own relationship.

Presenting Ourselves to Others At the same time we form impressions of others, others are forming impressions of us. In most cases, of course, we want others to think the best of us. But how can we influence others to perceive us more positively? Is it better to try to act naturally and be ourselves, or should we deliberately change our behaviour to get other people to have a more favourable impression? Two aspects of presenting ourselves to others are *impression management* and *self-monitoring*.

Impression Management **Impression management** (or **self-presentation**) involves acting in a way that will present an image of you to others as a certain sort of person, which might or might not be who you really are. In most instances, we try to present ourselves to look better than we really are. We spend years and small fortunes rearranging our faces, bodies, minds, and social skills. We especially use impression management in our business relationships (Tsai, Chen, & Chiu, 2005) and with potential romantic partners (Leary & others, 1994).

Nonverbal cues are a key element of successful impression management. Certain facial expressions, patterns of eye contact, and body postures or movements are part of the reason we are liked or disliked. Although impression management is common among people in all cultures, the specific techniques that work in one cultural setting may not work in another. For example, Americans tend to believe that an open, friendly style makes a positive impression on others. But in some parts of Canada people are more impressed by reserve. In particular, appreciation and flattery are often culture bound. For example, in some Eastern European countries, if one person expresses great admiration for another's watch, courtesy dictates that the watch should be given to the admirer. In the culture of the Sioux, it's considered courteous to open a conversation with a compliment.

One setting in which most of us especially want to make a good impression is a job interview, and a great deal has been written about how to do it. For example, to improve the likelihood that an interviewer will have a favourable impression of you, you are advised to use the right nonverbal cues: smile often, lean forward, maintain a high degree of eye contact, and frequently nod your head in agreement with what the interviewer says. In general, researchers have found that individuals who use these impression management techniques receive more favourable ratings than individuals who do

impression management (self-presentation) Involves acting in a way to present an image of oneself as a certain type of person, which might or might not be who one really is.

These statements concern personal reactions to a number of situations. No two statements are exactly alike, so consider each statement carefully before answering. If a statement is true or mostly true as applied to you, check True. If a statement is false or not usually true as applied to you, check False.

	True	False			True	False
1. I find it hard to imitate the behaviour of other people.	☐	☑	6. In different situations and with different people, I often act like very different persons.	☑	☐	
2. I guess I put on a show to impress or entertain people.	☑	☐	7. I can only argue for ideas I already believe.	☐	☑	
3. I would probably make a good actor.	☑	☐	8. In order to get along and be liked, I tend to be what people expect me to be.	☐	☑	
4. I sometimes appear to others to be experiencing deeper emotions than I actually am.	☐	☑	9. I may deceive people by being friendly when I really dislike them.	☑	☐	
5. In a group of people, I am rarely the centre of attention.	☐	☑	10. I'm not always the person I appear to be.	☑	☐	

Scoring: Give yourself one point for 1, 5, and 7 if you answered False. Give yourself one point for each of the remaining questions that you answered True. Add up your points. If you are a good judge of yourself and scored 7 or above, you are probably a high-self-monitoring individual; 3 or below, you are probably a low-self-monitoring individual.

not (Riggio, 2005). In one early study, researchers observed that individuals who were selected for engineering apprenticeships were indeed the ones who had smiled more, maintained greater eye contact with the interviewer, and more often nodded their heads affirmatively during their interviews than rejected applicants did (Forbes & Jackson, 1980). Some people use nonverbal cues such as these more naturally than others. But even if you do not normally behave this way when you are interacting with someone, you can make a conscious effort to control your nonverbal behaviour.

Three other techniques of impression management are conforming to situational norms (for example, adopting the same form of dress and the same type of language and etiquette as other people in that setting), showing appreciation of others, and behavioural matching (engaging in behaviour that the other person displays, such as clasping one's hands together).

As with most forms of manipulation, impression management can become counterproductive. You overdo it if you use so many positive nonverbal cues that the other individual perceives you to be insincere. And remember that impression management goes only so far: One study found that the frequent use of nonverbal cues had favourable outcomes in a job interview only when the applicants also had the qualifications to do the job (Rasmussen, 1984).

Self-Monitoring Some people are more concerned about and aware of the impressions they make than others are (Snyder & Stukas, Jr., 1999). **Self-monitoring** is paying attention to the impressions you make on others and the degree to which you fine-tune your performance to optimize the impressions you make. Lawyers and actors are among the best self-monitors; salespeople, con artists, and politicians are not far behind. As Raymond Perry, of the University of Manitoba, and his colleagues have shown, effective self-monitoring can also lead directly to greater personal control, for example, academically (Perry & others, 2001) and health-wise (Chipperfield & others, 1999).

Individuals who are very skilled at self-monitoring seek information about appropriate ways to present and improve themselves and invest considerable time in trying to "read" and understand others (Levine & Feldman, 2002). In and of itself, such behaviour is neither good nor bad. Nobody can be a successful member of a family or a community without attention to the expectations and opinions of others. The danger is that the energy spent in self-monitoring in order to present ourselves favourably might reduce the amount of energy we can devote to trying to understand and improve ourselves. To get an idea of your skill at self-monitoring, see figure 16.3.

FIGURE 16.3
Self-Monitoring

self-monitoring Individuals' attention to the impressions they make on others and the degree to which they fine-tune their performances accordingly.

Attitudes

Social thinking involves not only attributions and social perceptions but also attitudes. **Attitudes** are beliefs or opinions about people, objects, and ideas (Oskamp & Schultz, 2005). We have attitudes about all sorts of things, such as "Most people are out for themselves," "Money is evil," and "Television has caused family members to talk less with one another." We also live in a world in which people try to influence others' attitudes, such as when politicians try to get your vote and advertisers try to convince you that their product is the best. Social psychologists are interested not only in how attitudes are changed but also in whether changing an individual's attitude will actually have an effect on his or her behaviour—or whether changing an individual's behaviour will lead to an attitude change (Petty, Wegener, & Fabrigar, 1997).

Can Attitudes Predict Behaviour? People sometimes say one thing but do another. For example, they might respond in a poll that they prefer one candidate and then actually vote for another. But, often, what people say is what they do. Studies over the course of the past half century indicate some of the conditions under which attitudes guide actions (Eagly & Chaikin, 1998; Smith & Fabrigar, 2000):

- *When the person's attitudes are strong* (Ajzen, 2001; Petty & Krosnick, 1995). For example, people whose attitudes toward gambling are "highly favourable" are more likely to buy lottery tickets or visit a casino than their counterparts who have only "moderately favourable" attitudes toward gambling.
- *When the person shows a strong awareness of his or her attitudes and when the person rehearses and practices them* (Fazio & others, 1982). For example, we would expect a person who vigorously argues for a ban on snowmobiles in Canada's national parks to avoid driving one; a person with the same desire to protect our national parks from snowmobiles but who hasn't had to put it into words or define it in public might be likelier to try riding a snowmobile.
- *When the attitudes are relevant to the behaviour.* For example, one study found that general attitudes toward birth control were virtually unrelated to the use of birth control pills in the following two years; however, a specific attitude toward taking birth control pills showed a much higher correlation with actual use in the following two years (Davidson & Jacard, 1979). The more relevant the attitude is to the behaviour, the better it will predict the behaviour.

Can Behaviour Predict Attitudes? "The actions of men are the best interpreters of their thoughts," asserted seventeenth-century English philosopher John Locke. Does doing change believing? If you quit drinking, will you then have a negative attitude toward drinking? If you take up an exercise program, are you then likely to extol the benefits of cardiovascular fitness when someone asks about your attitude toward exercise?

Ample evidence exists that changes in behaviour can precede changes in attitudes (Bandura, 1989). Merely repeatedly expressing attitudes increases their importance to us (Roese & Olson, 1994). Two main explanations of why behaviour influences attitudes have been offered. The first view is that we have a strong need for cognitive consistency; we change our attitudes to make them more consistent with our behaviour (Carkenord & Bullington, 1995). The second view is that our attitudes are not completely clear even to us, so we observe our own behaviour and make inferences about it to determine what our attitudes should be.

Cognitive Dissonance Theory **Cognitive dissonance**, a concept developed by social psychologist Leon Festinger (1957), refers to an individual's motivation to reduce the discomfort (dissonance) caused by two inconsistent thoughts. According to the theory, we are likely to feel uneasy if we can't justify to ourselves the difference between what we believe and what we do.

We can reduce cognitive dissonance in one of two general ways: change our attitudes or change our behaviours. For example, most smokers believe that it is unhealthy to smoke; yet they can't seem to resist lighting up. This discrepancy between attitude and

attitudes Beliefs or opinions about people, objects, and ideas.

cognitive dissonance A concept developed by Festinger that refers to an individual's motivation to reduce the discomfort (dissonance) caused by two inconsistent thoughts.

behaviour creates discomfort. To reduce the dissonance, the smoker must either stop smoking or decide that smoking really isn't so bad. "No one has proven smoking kills people" and "I'll have to die from something" are both dissonance-reducing attitudes.

Social psychologists have refined Festinger's original theory. For instance, dissonance theory predicts that individuals will avoid information inconsistent with their views. Early attempts to document this selective exposure failed. However, more recently, researchers have found that people will avoid unpleasant information—but only if they think they cannot refute the uncomfortable argument, and they are highly committed to their way of thinking or behaving. Perhaps you have a friend or relative who has strong political or religious opinions that are not only at odds with yours but that seem contrary to common sense. You may have tried and tried, to no avail, to introduce facts that would convince the other person to change his or her mind. Interestingly, if we become aware that we are caught in a cognitive inconsistency, our degree of discomfort is also reduced (McGregor, Newby-Clark, & Zanna, 1999).

Researchers have also focused on the specific situations that are linked with dissonance. Sometimes cognitive dissonance causes us to justify things in our lives that are unpleasant (Aronson, 2003). As playwright George Bernard Shaw said of his father's alcoholism; "If you cannot get rid of the family skeleton, you may as well make it dance." "Making the family skeleton dance" helped Shaw to reduce the tension between his attitude about his father's drinking problem and its actual occurrence. Sometimes cognitive dissonance causes us to justify world events. For example, Carolyn Hafer, of Brock University, and James Olson, of the University of Western Ontario, have shown that the need to justify our belief in, and desire for, a just world can lead us to negatively perceive the innocent victims of tragic events, presumably to reduce the dissonance which arises because it is inconsistent to believe that innocent people can suffer in a just world (Hafer & Olson, 1998; Hafer, 2000).

Christopher Burris, of the University of Waterloo, and his colleagues have shown that dissonance can also be reduced through transcendence, essentially an appeal to a higher principle (Burris & others, 1997). For example, a religious person might reconcile the suffering of innocents with a belief in a just world by concluding that there is no contradiction from God's point of view.

We especially have a strong need to justify the effort we put forth in life—a process called *effort justification*. In general, goals that require considerable effort are the ones that we value most highly. If we put forth considerable effort, yet still do not reach the goal, we develop dissonance. We could reduce the dissonance by convincing ourselves that we did not work as hard as we actually did, or we could say that the goal was not all that important in the first place. Think of the person who goes to a lot of trouble to get a particular job but gets passed over. The person might justify the effort by saying that she should have followed up more diligently, or she might say that the job really wasn't a good match with her skills and career goals.

Our most intense justifications of our actions take place when our self-esteem is involved (Aronson, 2000; Aronson, Cohen, & Nails, 1999). If you do something cruel, then it follows that you have to perform some mental gymnastics to keep yourself from thinking you are a cruel person. The clearest results in the hundreds of research studies on cognitive dissonance occur when self-esteem is involved, and the most dissonance results when individuals with the highest self-esteem act in cruel ways. What about individuals with low self-esteem? They probably experience less dissonance because acting in a cruel way is consistent with their attitudes toward themselves—indicated by such self-labels as *loser, jerk, zero,* or *bad guy*. Put another way, individuals who think of themselves as bad might do bad things because it keeps dissonance at a minimum. The emphasis on self-esteem in understanding cognitive dissonance suggests that dissonance is not produced by a discrepancy between two cognitions (as Festinger believed) but rather by a discrepancy between a cognition about a particular behaviour and the person's self-image (Aronson, 2000). Not all our thoughts and behaviours are aimed at reducing dissonance, however. Some of us learn from our mistakes. We catch ourselves doing something we don't approve of, look in the mirror, and say, "You blew it. Now what can you do to prevent that from happening again?" Eliot Aronson (2003) offers

	Cognitive Dissonance Theory	**Self-Perception Theory**
Theorist	Festinger	Bem
Nature of theory	We are motivated toward consistency between attitude and behaviour and away from inconsistency.	We make inferences about our attitudes by perceiving and examining our behaviour and the context in which it occurs, which might involve inducements to behave in certain ways.
Example	"I hate my job. I need to develop a better attitude toward it or else quit."	"I am spending all of my time thinking about how much I hate my job. I really must not like it."

these three suggestions for avoiding the treadmill of dissonance reduction—that is, simply trying to justify the bad things in our lives and the bad things we do:

- Know your defensive and dissonance-reducing tendencies. Be able to sense them before you get in over your head.
- Realize that behaving in stupid and cruel ways does not necessarily mean that you are a stupid and cruel person.
- Develop enough strengths and competencies to be able to tolerate your mistakes without having to rationalize them away.

Self-Perception Theory Not all social psychologists believe that the theory of cognitive dissonance explains the influence of behaviour on attitudes. Daryl Bem (1967), for example, believes that the cognitive dissonance view relies too heavily on internal factors, which are difficult to measure. Bem argues that we should move away from such fuzzy and nebulous concepts as "cognitions" and "psychological discomfort" and replace them with more behavioural terminology. **Self-perception theory** is Bem's idea about the connection between attitudes and behaviour; it stresses that individuals make inferences about their attitudes by perceiving their behaviour. For example, consider the remark, "I am spending all of my time thinking about the test I have next week. I must be anxious." Or, "This is the third time I have gone to the student union in two days. I must be lonely." Bem believes we look to our own behaviour when our attitudes are not completely clear. Figure 16.4 provides a comparison of cognitive dissonance theory and self-perception theory.

Which theory is right: cognitive dissonance or self-perception? The pattern of research on cognitive dissonance suggests that people do change their attitudes to avoid feeling cheap or stupid or guilty about their behaviour. But, at the same time, Bem's self-perception theory is compelling. People who are not strongly committed to attitudes before acting on them do seem to analyze their behaviour for hints about their true opinions (Aronson, Wilson, & Akert, 2005). Self-perception theory has also been more useful in explaining what happens to people's attitudes when they are offered an inducement to do something they would want to do anyway. In sum, cognitive dissonance theory and self-perception theory both have merit in explaining the connection between attitudes and behaviour (Oskamp & Schultz, 2005).

How Are People's Attitudes Changed? We spend many hours of our lives trying to persuade people to do certain things. You've probably tried to persuade your friends to go to a movie or to play the game that you are interested in. If you're a parent, you've probably tried to persuade your children to eat their peas or to go to bed early. At some point in your life, you have also likely tried to persuade someone to buy something from you.

Professional persuaders have similar goals, but they use more polished techniques based on extensive research on attitude change (Brock & Green, 2005). What makes people decide to give up their original attitudes and to adopt new ones instead? What makes people decide to act on an attitude that they haven't acted on before? Teachers, lawyers, and sales representatives study techniques that will help them sway their audiences (children, juries, and buyers, respectively). Politicians have armies of speech writers and image

self-perception theory Bem's theory about the connection between attitudes and behaviour; stresses that individuals make inferences about their attitudes by perceiving their behaviour.

consultants to ensure that their words are as persuasive as possible. Perhaps most skilled of all are advertisers, who combine the full array of techniques in an effort to sell cars, insurance policies, and cornflakes.

A full review of the factors involved in persuasion and attitude change could fill volumes. But here are a few findings of social psychologists, organized around the main elements of the communication process: who conveys the message (the source), what the message is (the communication), how the message is conveyed (the medium), and who receives the message (the target, or audience; Oskamp & Schultz, 2005).

The Communicator (Source) Suppose you are running for president of the student body. You tell your fellow students that you are going to make life at your university better. Would they believe you? That would likely depend on some of your characteristics as a communicator. Whether or not we believe someone depends in large part on his or her expertise or credibility. If you have held other elective offices, students would be likelier to believe you have the expertise to be their president. Trustworthiness, power, attractiveness, likeability, and similarity are all credibility characteristics that help a communicator change people's attitudes or convince them to act (O'Keefe, 2002).

The Message What kind of a message is persuasive? One line of research has focused on whether a rational or an emotional strategy is more effective. Is it better to use basic motivators such as love, sex, or fear to persuade someone? Or is it better to use facts or logic?

Emotional appeals are very powerful. Negative appeals often play to the audience's emotions, whereas positive appeals are often directed at the audience's logical, rational thinking. The less informed we are, the likelier it is that we will respond to an emotional appeal.

All other things being equal, the more frightened we are, the more we will change our attitudes. Advertisers sometimes take advantage of our fears to stimulate attitude change. You may have seen the Michelin tire ad that shows a baby playing near tires or the life insurance company ad that shows a widow and her young children moving out of their home because they did not have enough insurance.

Not all emotional appeals are negative, though. Music is widely used to make us feel good about a message. Think about how few television commercials you have seen without some form of music either in the background or as a prominent part of the message. When we watch such commercials, we may associate the pleasant feelings of the music with the product, even though the music itself provides us with no information about the product.

The less informed we are about the topic of the message, the likelier we are to respond to an emotional appeal. However, most people are persuaded only when rational and emotional appeals are used together. The emotional appeal arouses our interest, and the facts give us a logical reason for going along with the message. These days, for example, Greenpeace and other environmental organizations do not rely solely upon emotional appeals in crafting their environmental messages. Instead, they also back up their emotional appeals with sound empirical arguments based on scientific research. Or consider an ad for a new cell phone. Our emotions might be aroused by images of people using the cell phone to call for help or to keep in touch with someone attractive. But then we are given the facts that make the cell phone an appealing purchase. Perhaps the cost is reasonable, it is engineered to reduce static and broken connections, or it combines in one device the capabilities of a phone, a digital camera, and an Internet connection.

One model that has been proposed to explain the relation between emotional and rational appeals is the **elaboration likelihood model**. It proposes two ways to persuade: a central route and a peripheral route (Petty & others, 2005; Petty, Wheeler, & Bizer, 2000). The central route to persuasion works by engaging someone thoughtfully. The peripheral route involves nonmessage factors, such as the source's credibility and attractiveness or emotional appeals. The peripheral route is effective when people are not paying close attention to what the communicator is saying. As you might guess, television commercials often involve the peripheral route to persuasion on the assumption that during the commercials you are probably not paying full attention to the screen. However, the central route is more persuasive when people have the ability, and are motivated, to pay attention to the facts (Lammers, 2000).

elaboration likelihood model States that there are two ways to persuade—by a central route and by a peripheral route.

Another aspect of the message that has been of interest to social psychologists is the order in which arguments are presented. Should you wait until the end of your presentation to make your strongest points or put your best foot forward at the beginning? The *foot-in-the-door strategy* involves presenting a weaker point at the beginning or making a small request with which the listeners will probably comply, saving the strongest point until the end. In the words of social psychologist Robert Cialdini (2001), "Start small and build." For example, a sales pitch for a health spa might offer you four weeks' use of the facility for $10 and hope that, after the four weeks, you will pay $200 for a one-year membership.

In contrast, the *door-in-the-face strategy* involves a communicator making the strongest point or demand in the beginning, which the listeners probably will reject. Then a weaker point or moderate "concessionary" demand is made toward the end. For example, the salesperson for the health spa might offer you the one-year membership for $200, which you turn down, and then offer you a "bargain" four-weeks-for-$10 package.

The Medium Another persuasion factor is which medium or technology to use to get the message across. Consider the difference between watching a political debate on television and reading about it in the newspaper. Television lets us see how the candidates deliver their messages, what their appearance and mannerisms are like, and so on. Because it presents live images, television is often considered to be a more powerful medium for changing attitudes. In one classic study, the winners of various political contests were predicted by the amount of media exposure they had (Grush, 1980). On the other hand, the written format is most effective for communicating more complex information, like information about health (Byrne & Curtis, 2000).

The Target (Audience) Age and attitude strength are two characteristics of the audience that determine whether a message will be effective. Younger people are likelier to change their attitudes than older ones. If the attitudes of the audience are weak, attitude change is likelier; if audience attitudes are strong, the communicator will have more difficulty changing them (Cialdini, 2001).

> ## > reflect and review
>
> **Describe how people think about the social world.**
>
> - Explain attribution.
> - Discuss the three main elements of social perception.
> - Identify the relationship between attitudes and behaviour.
>
> *Which television ads do you like the best? Have they persuaded you to buy the products that are being advertised? What is it about the ads that is persuasive?*

② SOCIAL INFLUENCE

— Conformity   — Group   — Leadership
and Obedience   Influence

How are people influenced in social settings?

Another topic that social psychologists are interested in is how our behaviour is influenced by other people and groups (Brehm, & Kassin, & Fein, 2005). The section on social thinking discussed how we present ourselves to others to influence their perceptions of us and how we can change other people's attitudes and behaviour. This section explores some other aspects of social influence: conformity and obedience, group influence, and cultural and ethnic influences.

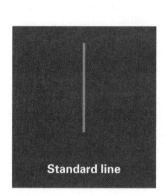

Conformity and Obedience

Research on conformity and obedience started in earnest after World War II. Psychologists began to seek answers to the disturbing question of how ordinary people could be influenced to commit the sorts of atrocities inflicted on Jews, Roma, and other minority groups during the Holocaust. How extensively will people change their behaviour to coincide more with what others are doing? How readily do people obey someone in authority? What factors influence whether people will resist such social influences? These questions are still relevant when we try to understand contemporary events such as vicious group attacks on ethnic minorities or gays. They are also relevant in trying to understand everyday human behaviour.

Conformity **Conformity** is a change in a person's behaviour to coincide more closely with a group standard. Conformity comes in many forms and affects many aspects of people's lives. Conformity is at work when a person takes up snowboarding because everyone else is doing it. Conformity is also at work when an individual cuts her hair short one year because short hair is fashionable and then lets it grow long the next year because long hair has become the vogue.

Although conformity has some unpleasant or unattractive aspects, it is not entirely a negative thing. People's conformity to rules and regulations allows society to run more smoothly. Consider how chaotic it would be if most people did not conform to social norms such as stopping at red lights, driving on the correct side of the road, going to school regularly, and not punching others in the face. However, some of the most dramatic and insightful work on conformity has examined how we sometimes act against our better judgment in order to conform.

Asch's Conformity Experiment Put yourself in this situation: You are taken into a room in which you see five other people seated around a table. A person in a white lab coat enters the room and announces that you are about to participate in an experiment on perceptual accuracy. The group is shown two cards, the first having only a single vertical line on it, the second card three vertical lines of varying length. You are told that the task is to determine which of the three lines on the second card is the same length as the line on the first card. You look at the cards and think, "What a snap. It's so obvious which is the same" (see figure 16.5).

What you do not know is that the other people in the room are actually in league with the experimenter. They've been hired to perform in ways the experimenter dictates. On the first several trials, everyone agrees about which line matches the standard. Then, on the fourth trial, each of the others picks an incorrect line. As the last person to make a choice, you have the dilemma of responding as your eyes tell you or conforming to what the others before you said. How do you think you would answer?

FIGURE 16.5

Asch's Conformity Experiment
The figures on the left show the stimulus materials for the Asch conformity experiment on group influence. The photograph shows the puzzlement of one subject after five confederates of the experimenter chose the incorrect line.

conformity Involves a change in a person's behaviour to coincide more with a group standard.

Solomon Asch conducted this classic experiment on conformity in 1951. He believed few of his volunteer participants would yield to group pressure. To test his hypothesis, Asch instructed the hired accomplices to give incorrect responses on 12 of the 18 trials. To his surprise, Asch (1951) found that the volunteer participants conformed to the incorrect answers 35 percent of the time. Subsequent research has shown that the pressure to conform is strong (Pines & Maslach, 2002). Even when faced with clear-cut information such as the lines in the Asch experiment, we often conform to what others say and do. We do not want to be laughed at or make others angry with us.

In the Asch experiments, the pressure to conform was explicit and participants were consciously aware of that pressure. But conformity also occurs when there is no explicit pressure and can occur unconsciously. One interesting example is *behavioural mimicry* (or the *chameleon effect*), the unconscious tendency to mimic other people's facial expressions, postures, and mannerisms. In one study, female participants thought they were participating in an ice cream taste test along with other participants. However, one participant was a confederate of the experimenter. On some occasions she ate more ice cream during the taste test. Sometimes she ate less. Without any explicit pressure, the actual participants followed the lead of the confederate, mimicking her ice cream consumption (Johnston, 2002).

Factors that Contribute to Conformity Many factors influence whether an individual will conform or not (Cialdini & Goldstein, 2004). But, in general, people conform because of either normative social influence or informational social influence.

Normative social influence is the influence that other people have on us to conform because we seek their approval or seek to avoid their disapproval. So, if a group is important to us, we might wear a particular kind of clothing that people in the group wear, adopt a particular hairstyle, use the same slang words, and adopt a certain set of attitudes that characterize the group's members. This is true whether the group is an inner-city gang or members of a profession, such as medicine or law.

Whereas normative social influence causes people to conform because they want to be liked, **informational social influence** causes people to conform because they want to be right (Taylor, Peplau, & Sears, 2006). The tendency to conform based on informational social influence depends especially on two factors: how confident we are in our own independent judgment and how well informed we perceive the group to be. Thus, if you don't know much about computers and three of your acquaintances who work in the computer industry tell you not to buy a particular brand of computer, you are likely to conform to their recommendation.

Researchers have found some other factors that are involved in conforming or not conforming:

- *Unanimity of the group*. In Asch's study with lines on cards, the group's opinion was unanimous. When the group's opinion is divided, individuals feel less pressure to conform.
- *Prior commitment*. If you do not have a prior commitment to an idea or action, you are likelier to be influenced by others. However, if you have publicly committed to an idea or action, conformity to another idea or action is less likely.
- *Personal characteristics*. People with lower self-esteem and doubts about their abilities, who look for external validation, are likelier to conform (Arndt & others, 2002).
- *Group members' characteristics*. You are likelier to conform if the group members are experts, attractive to you, or similar to you in any way.
- *Cultural values*. In experiments conducted in 14 countries, conformity rates were lower in individualistic cultures (such as those of Canada and the United States), in which people tend to pursue their own interests, and higher in collectivistic cultures (such as that of China), in which people typically seek to contribute to the group's success (Bond & Smith, 1996).

normative social influence The influence that other people have on us because we seek their approval or to avoid their disapproval.

informational social influence The influence other people have on us because we want to be right.

obedience Behaviour that complies with the explicit demands of the individual in authority.

Obedience **Obedience** is behaviour that complies with the explicit demands of the individual in authority. That is, we are obedient when an authority figure demands that we do something and we do it. How is obedience different from conformity? In conformity, people change their thinking or behaviour so that it will be more like that of others. In contrast to obedience, there is no explicit demand to conform.

Obedient behaviour can sometimes be distressingly cruel. The massacre of Tutsis, described at the beginning of the chapter, and the Nazi crimes against Jews and others in World War II are examples of cruel obedience. A more recent example is the obedience of radical Muslims who are instructed to participate in suicide attacks and other acts of aggression against Israelis and Westerners. Acts like these seem wrong, yet millions of people throughout history have obeyed commands to commit them.

A classic experiment by Stanley Milgram (1965, 1974) provides insight into such obedience. Imagine that, as part of an experiment in psychology, you are asked to deliver a series of painful electric shocks to another person. You are told that the purpose of the study is to determine the effects of punishment on memory. Your role is to be the "teacher" and punish the mistakes made by the "learner." Each time the learner makes a mistake, you are to increase the intensity of the shock by a certain amount.

You are introduced to the learner, a nice 50-year-old man who mumbles something about having a heart condition. He is strapped to a chair in the next room; he communicates with you through an intercom. The apparatus in front of you has 30 switches, ranging from 15 volts (light) to 450 volts (marked as dangerous, "severe shock XXX"). Before this part of the experiment began, you had been given a 75-volt shock to see how it felt.

As the trials proceed, the learner quickly runs into trouble and is unable to give the correct answers. Should you shock him? As you increase the intensity of the shock, the learner says he's in pain. At 150 volts, he demands to have the experiment stopped. At 180 volts, he cries out that he can't stand it anymore. At 300 volts, he yells about his heart condition and pleads to be released. But if you hesitate in shocking the learner, the experimenter tells you that you have no choice; the experiment must continue.

By the way, the 50-year-old man is in league with the experimenter. He is not being shocked at all. Of course the so-called teachers are completely unaware that the learner is only pretending to be shocked.

As you might imagine, the teachers in this experiment were uneasy about shocking the learner. At 240 volts, one teacher responded, "240 volts delivered; aw, no. You mean I've got to keep going with that scale? No sir, I'm not going to kill that man—I'm not going to give him 450 volts!" (Milgram,1965). At the very strong voltage, the learner quit responding. When the teacher asked the experimenter what to do, the experimenter simply instructed the teacher to continue the experiment and told him that it was his obligation to complete the job.

Forty psychiatrists were asked how they thought individuals would respond to this situation. The psychiatrists predicted that most teachers would go no further than 150 volts, that fewer than 1 in 25 would go as far as 300 volts, and that only 1 in 1000 would deliver the full 450 volts. The psychiatrists, it turns out, were way off the mark. The majority of the teachers obeyed the experimenter. In fact, almost two-thirds delivered the full 450 volts. Figure 16.6 shows the results of the Milgram study.

In subsequent studies, Milgram set up a storefront in Bridgeport, Connecticut, and recruited volunteers through newspaper ads. Milgram wanted to create a more natural environment for the experiment and to use a wider cross section of volunteers. In these additional studies, close to two-thirds of the individuals still selected the highest level of shock for the learner.

In variations of the experiment, Milgram discovered that more people would disobey in certain circumstances. Disobedience was more common when participants could see others disobey, when the authority figure was not perceived to be legitimate and was not close by, and when the victim was made to seem more human.

An important point has been raised about the Milgram experiments: How ethical were they? The volunteer teachers in Milgram's experiment clearly felt anguish, and some were very disturbed about "harming" another individual. After the experiment was completed, they were told that the learner was not actually shocked. But even though they were debriefed and told that they really had not shocked or harmed anyone, was the anguish imposed on them ethical?

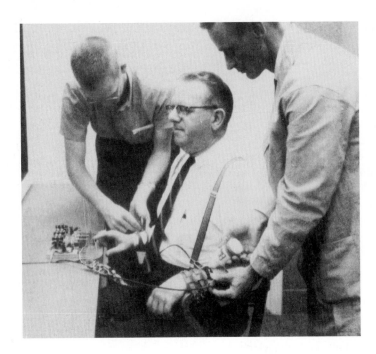

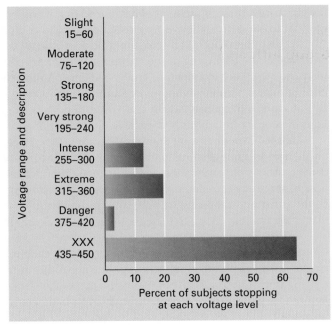

FIGURE 16.6

Milgram Obedience Study
A 50-year-old man, the "learner," is strapped into a chair. The experimenter makes it look as if a shock generator is being connected to his body through several electrodes. The chart at the right shows the percentage of "teachers" who stopped shocking the learner at each voltage level.

In 1989, Chinese students led a massive demonstration against the government in Beijing. The students resisted the government's social influence by putting together resources to challenge the Chinese authorities; however, the government eventually eliminated the protests, massacring hundreds.

Milgram argued that we have learned a great deal about human nature from the experiments. He claimed that they tell us how far individuals will go in their obedience, even if it means being cruel to someone. The volunteers were interviewed later, and more than four-fifths said that they were glad they had participated in the study; none said that they were sorry they had participated.

When Milgram conducted his studies on obedience, the ethical guidelines for research were not as stringent as they are today. The current ethical guidelines of the Canadian and American psychological associations and the Tri-Council Policy Statement (2003) stress that researchers should obtain informed consent from their volunteers. Deception should be used only for very important purposes. Individuals are supposed to feel as good about themselves when the experiment is over as they did when it began. Under today's guidelines, it is unlikely that the Milgram experiment would be conducted.

Resistance to Social Influence "If a man does not keep pace with his companions, perhaps it is because he hears a different drummer. Let him step to the music which he hears, however measured or far away." Thoreau's words suggest that some of us resist social influence, just as General Roméo Dallaire did during the 1994 genocide in Rwanda. Most of us would prefer to think of ourselves as stepping to our own music, maybe even setting the rhythms for others, rather than trying to keep pace with our companions. However, a certain degree of conformity is required if society is to function at all. As we go through our lives, we are both conformists and nonconformists. Sometimes we are overwhelmed by the persuasion and influence of others. In other circumstances we resist and gain personal control over our lives. It is important to remember that our relation to the social world is reciprocal. Individuals may be trying to control us, but we can exert personal control over our actions and influence others in turn (Bandura, 1986).

If you believe that someone in a position of authority is making an unjust request or ordering you to do something wrong, what choice of action do you have?

- You can comply.
- You can give the appearance of complying but secretly do otherwise.
- You can publicly dissent by showing doubts and disenchantment but still follow the request/order.
- You can openly disregard the order and refuse to comply.
- You can challenge or confront the authority.
- You can get higher authorities to intervene or organize a group of people who agree with you to show the strength of your view.

Resistance to authority can be difficult, but living with the knowledge that you compromised your own moral integrity may be more difficult in the long run.

Group Influence

A student joining a campus organization, a jury making a decision about a criminal case, a president of a company delegating authority, a prejudiced remark against a minority group, conflict among nations, and attempts to reach peace—all of these circumstances reflect our lives as members of groups. They range in size from dyads, which consist of two people, to immense groups of all the people who are linked by national identity, religion, ethnicity, or gender. Some groups we choose, others we do not. We choose to belong to a club, but we are all born into a particular family, for example.

Regardless of their size, groups serve a useful human purpose. They satisfy our personal needs, reward us, provide information, raise our self-esteem, and give us an identity. We might join a group because we think it will be enjoyable and exciting and satisfy our need for affiliation and companionship. We might join a group because we will receive rewards, either material or psychological. For example, by taking a job with a company, we not only get paid to work as part of a group but we also reap a portion of the company's prestige and recognition. Groups are also an important source of information. For example, as we listen to other members talk in a Weight Watchers group, we learn about their strategies for losing weight.

Many of the groups of which we are members—family, university, company, ethnic—also provide identities; when asked who we are, we often answer in terms of which groups we belong to.

Some of the important questions about group relations that interest social psychologists are these: What is the structure of groups? How does group performance compare with individual performance? How do people in groups interact and make decisions?

The Structure of Groups Any group to which you belong has certain things in common with all other groups. One is the existence of *norms*, or rules that are specific to that group and apply to all of its members (Kenrick, Neuberg, & Cialdini, 2005). Norms can be formal or informal. An example of a formal norm is an employer's requirement that all of its workers wear socks or Mensa's requirement that all of its members demonstrate a high IQ. Informal norms are such things as the subtle pressure you face to sit in the same seat or the same area of a lecture hall every time you attend a certain class.

Another characteristic that all groups have in common is a set of *roles*, or expectations that govern certain positions in the group. Roles define how different people in the group behave. In a family, parent is one role, sibling is another role, and grandparent is yet another role. A parent isn't expected to behave the same way toward the children in a family as siblings or grandparents are expected to behave. On a football team, many different roles must be fulfilled: on offence alone, centre, guard, tackle, end, quarterback, running back, and wide receiver; each member of the team has a different job to do to accomplish the group's goals.

Group Performance The very first experiment in social psychology examined the question of whether individuals perform better in a group or when alone. Norman Triplett (1898) found that bicyclists performed better when they raced against each other than when they raced alone against the clock. Triplett also built a "competition machine" made out of fishing reels. The machine allowed two individuals to turn the reels side by side. Observing 40 children, he discovered that those who reeled next to another child worked faster than those who reeled alone.

Since Triplett's work over a century ago, many investigations of group versus individual performance have been conducted. Some studies reveal that we do better in groups, others that we are more productive when we work alone (Franzoi, 2003). We can make sense out of these contradictory findings by looking more closely at the circumstances in which performance is being analyzed.

Social Facilitation **Social facilitation** occurs when an individual's performance improves because of the presence of others. Robert Zajonc (1965) argued that the

Do you perform better as a member of a group or as an individual?

social facilitation Occurs when an individual's performance improves because of the presence of others.

We can become deindividuated in groups. People can lose their individual identities in situations such as Mardi Gras (*top*) and in national patriotism crowds (*bottom*).

presence of other individuals arouses us. The arousal produces energy and facilitates our performance in groups. According to Coleman & Cater (2005), when adolescents congregate in unsupervised settings, social facilitation can lead to binge drinking. If our arousal is too high, however, we won't be able to learn new or difficult tasks efficiently. Social facilitation, then, improves our performance on well-learned tasks. For new or difficult tasks, we might be best advised to work things out on our own before trying them in a group.

In one early investigation, expert and poor pool players were observed in a student union (Michaels & others, 1982). When they were observed unobtrusively, the experts hit 71 percent of their shots, the poor players 36 percent. When four individuals walked up to observe their play, the experts improved, making 80 percent of their shots. The poor players got worse, however, making only 25 percent of their shots.

Social Loafing   Another factor in group performance is how closely our behaviour is monitored. **Social loafing** refers to each person's tendency to exert less effort in a group because of reduced accountability for individual effort. The effect of social loafing is lowered group performance. Social loafing is common when a group of students is assigned a school project (North, Linley, & Hargreaves, 2000). Also, the larger the group, the likelier it is that a person can loaf without being detected. Unsurprisingly, people low in achievement motivation are more likely to engage in social loafing (Hart & others, 2004).

The tendency to socially loaf is linked to gender and culture. Men are likelier to loaf than women (Karau & Williams, 1993). Why might this be the case? Because women are more likely to care about the welfare of others in the group and the group's collective performance. In contrast, men tend to be more individualistic, focusing on their own needs and performances (Wood, 1987). The tendency to socially loaf is stronger in individualistic Western cultures such as Canada and the United States than in collectivistic Eastern cultures such as China and Japan (Karau & Williams, 1993).

Some ways to decrease social loafing are increasing the identifiability and uniqueness of individual contributions, making it easier to evaluate these contributions, and making the task more attractive (Karau & Williams, 1993).

Under certain conditions, working with others can increase, rather than decrease, individual effort (Baron & Byrne, 2003). For example, a person who views the group's task as important and who does not expect other group members to contribute adequately to the group's performance is likely to work harder than usual.

Deindividuation   Individuals in groups also can become deindividuated and thus behave much differently than they would on their own (Silke, 2003). **Deindividuation** occurs when being part of a group reduces personal identity and erodes the sense of personal responsibility. As early as 1895, Gustav LeBon observed that being in a group can foster uninhibited behaviour, ranging from wild celebrations to mob activity. Mardi Gras wild times, riots after sporting events or rock concerts, and nationalistic fervour might be due to deindividuated behaviour.

One explanation of deindividuation is that groups give us anonymity (Silke, 2003). We may act in a disinhibited way because we believe that authority figures and victims are unlikely to identify us as the culprits.

Group Interaction and Decision Making   Many of the decisions we make take place in groups—juries, teams, families, clubs, school boards, Parliament, or a class vote, for example (Spector, 2005; Levine & Moreland, 1998). What happens when people put their minds to the task of making a group decision? How do they decide whether a criminal is guilty, whether a country should attack another country, whether a family should stay home or go on vacation, or whether sex education should be part of a school curriculum? Three aspects of group decision making bear special mention: the *risky shift* and *group polarization*, *groupthink*, and *majority-minority influence*.

The Risky Shift and Group Polarization   When we make decisions in a group, do we take risks and stick our necks out, or do we compromise our opinions and move toward the centre? The evidence is mixed.

Some research indicates that many times group decisions are riskier than individual decisions. The **risky shift** is the tendency for a group decision to be riskier than the

social loafing Each person's tendency to exert less effort in a group because of reduced monitoring.

deindividuation Occurs when being part of a group reduces personal identity and the sense of responsibility.

risky shift The tendency for a group decision to be riskier than the average decision made by individual group members.

average decision made by the individual group members (Franzoi, 2003). In one classic investigation, fictitious dilemmas were presented, and participants were asked how much risk the characters in the dilemmas were willing to take (Stoner, 1961). When the individuals discussed the dilemmas as a group, they were more willing to respond that the characters would make risky decisions than when they were queried alone. Many studies have been conducted on this topic with similar results (Goethals & Demorest, 1995).

We do not always make riskier decisions in a group than when alone; hundreds of research studies show that being in a group moves us more strongly in the direction of the position we initially held (Fiske, 2004). The **group polarization effect** is the solidification and further strengthening of a position as a consequence of a group discussion. For instance, imagine an environmentalist and a representative of the logging industry who listen to hours of discussion about sustainable logging of an old-growth forest in B.C. Research indicates that neither is likely to be converted to a different point of view. After hours of deliberation, each will be even more strongly committed to his or her position than before the deliberation began. Initially held views often become more polarized because of group discussion.

Group polarization may occur because people hear new, more persuasive arguments that strengthen their original position and they dismiss the arguments that do not support their position. Group polarization also might occur because of social comparison. We may find that our opinion is not as extreme as others' opinions and be influenced to take a stand at least as strong as the most extreme advocate's position.

Groupthink In 1961, when John F. Kennedy was president, the United States sent a group of Cuban exiles into Cuba on a mission to overthrow Communist dictator Fidel Castro. The plan failed miserably: The exiles were either captured or killed, Castro remained in power, and the United States looked rather foolish. How could the very intelligent men in the Kennedy administration have agreed to go through with such a fiasco as the Bay of Pigs?

According to social psychologist Irving Janis (1972), the answer is **groupthink**, which refers to group members' impaired decision making and avoidance of realistic appraisal in order to maintain group harmony. Groupthink evolves because members are motivated to boost each other's egos and increase each other's self-esteem in search of conformity, especially in the face of stress. Groupthink involves many heads, but only one group mind. This ubiquitous motivation for harmony and unanimity can result in disastrous decisions (Baron, 2005).

Following are some of the symptoms of groupthink and how they worked in the Kennedy administration's Bay of Pigs decision:

- *Overestimation of the power and morality of the group.* The Kennedy decision makers believed that they could keep news of their involvement secret and that the world would think the Cuban dissidents were acting on their own. Although at least two group members had misgivings about the plan's morality, these were either not voiced or not evaluated in meetings, which reflects a symptom of groupthink: ignoring moral consequences.
- *Closed-mindedness.* After a group has selected a course of action, it is difficult for the group to change that course, even when the course of action is going badly. As they recommit to past decisions, group members collectively rationalize what they have decided to do, discounting warnings and other negative indications that might call previous policy decisions into question. The Kennedy group believed that Castro's forces would be easy to overcome, an example of such discounting. However, the Cuban Air Force shot down half of the U.S. planes sent to protect the invading exiles and bombed the invaders when they arrived on Cuban shores.
- *Pressures toward uniformity.* Members pressure those who momentarily express misgivings to conform to the plan supported by the majority. President Kennedy did not provide adequate time to discuss dissidents' concerns and played down the criticisms of the one group member who had serious doubts about the Bay of Pigs invasion. Some members may act as "mindguards" to suppress dissenting views or information that conflicts with the group's decision. For instance, the

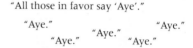

"All those in favor say 'Aye'."

"Aye."   "Aye."
      "Aye."   "Aye."
              "Aye."

© The New Yorker Collection 1979.
Henry Martin from cartoonbank.com.
All Rights Reserved.

group polarization effect The solidification and further strengthening of a position as a consequence of a group discussion.

groupthink Involves impaired decision making and avoidance of realistic appraisal to maintain group harmony.

Certain individuals in the minority have played important roles in history. (*Top*) Martin Luther King, Jr., helped African Americans gain important rights. (*Bottom*) Corazon Aquino, who became president of the Philippines after defeating Ferdinand Marcos, toppled a corrupt political regime and reduced the suffering of many Philippine citizens.

Secretary of State kept the group from learning about the concerns raised by the director of the United States Information Agency. Group members also tend to suppress their own doubts.

Canadian governments are not immune to groupthink. On October 30, 1995, Canada almost came apart. The "No" side in the Quebec referendum on separation had won by the slim margin of 50.56 percent to 49.44 percent. The inactivity of "No" side leaders may have been due to groupthink. Early polls showing the "No" side far ahead convinced "No" leaders that victory was inevitable. As decision day approached, the "No" side advantage collapsed, especially when Lucien Bouchard became leader of the "Yes" side. Yet the "No" side leaders did nothing until just before the referendum. At that time, thousands of non-Quebeckers travelled to Quebec to make personal appeals to Quebeckers to stay in Canada. While it will never be known for certain, it is possible that without this populist action, groupthink might have torn Canada apart.

Here are some helpful strategies for avoiding groupthink:

- *Reduce isolation.* Invite people who are not part of the decision-making group to attend meetings. Encourage them to give their opinions and criticize plans without any retribution.
- *Make leadership impartial.* To encourage a wide range of options, leaders should not state their own preferences and expectations up front.
- *Use outside experts.* They may put a different perspective on the issues at hand and can challenge core beliefs of the group.
- *Discuss with trusted subordinates.* Before final consensus, each member should report to the group what their own associates outside of the group have to say about the topic under consideration.
- *Hold second-chance meetings and review sessions.* After the "final" decision has been made, meet again to provide a second chance to object to the group decision before it is implemented.

Majority and Minority Influence In most groups—even when groupthink is not involved—the majority of the members tend to hold sway over the minority. Think about the groups in which you have been a member. The majority exerts both normative and informational pressure on the group: It sets the group's norm; those who do not go along may be ignored or even given the boot. The majority also has a greater opportunity to provide information that will influence decision making.

Although in most cases the majority wins, sometimes the minority has its day (Kerr, 2002). The minority cannot win through normative pressure because it is outnumbered; so, it must do its work through informational pressure. If the minority presents its view consistently and confidently, then the majority is likelier to listen to the minority's views.

Certain individuals within the minority may play a crucial role. For instance, those who can command the attention of others have a better opportunity to shape and direct the group's decision making. To achieve such influence, individuals have to distinguish themselves in various ways from the rest of the group. They have to make themselves noticed by the opinions they express, the jokes they tell, or their nonverbal style. They might be the first ones to raise a new idea, to disagree with a prevailing point of view, or to propose a creative alternative solution to a problem. People who have a strong social conscience are often willing to be different.

Individuals with a history of taking minority stands also have influence. They may trigger others to dissent by showing them that disagreement is possible and may indeed be the best course. Such is the basis of some of history's greatest moments. When Martin Luther King galvanized the civil rights movement in the United States when he spoke out against racism; when Corazon Aquino became a candidate for president of the Philippines, few people thought Ferdinand Marcos could be beaten.

The influence of the minority has been studied in jury room deliberations (Hastie, 2001). Researchers have found that the people on a jury with a minority view often convince the majority to change their minds. Is that a good thing or a bad thing? Although trials would proceed faster if the jury's initial majority vote determined the defendant's innocence or guilt, a number of social psychologists believe that the minority opinion is useful in the deliberation process (Aronson, Wilson, & Akert, 2005). First, forcing juries to reach a unanimous verdict with both majority and minority coming to an agreement makes everyone consider the evidence more carefully. Second, even if the minority seldom succeeds in convincing the majority to change their opinion about guilt or innocence, the minority often does change opinions about the degree of guilt. In criminal trials, juries often have some discretion about the type of guilty verdict, such as first-degree murder, second-degree murder, or manslaughter.

Leadership

What makes people leaders? What makes them so influential within a group that others willingly follow them into difficult or even dangerous endeavours? Is it a set of personality traits, the situations in which leaders emerge, or some combination of the two (Nahavandi, 2003)?

The *great-person theory* states that some individuals have certain traits that are best suited for leadership positions. Leaders are commonly thought to be assertive, cooperative, decisive, dominant, energetic, self-confident, tolerant of stress, willing to assume responsibility, diplomatic and tactful, and persuasive. "I am certainly not one of those who needs to be prodded," the British Prime Minister Winston Churchill once said of himself. "In fact, if anything, I am the prod." This is a classic statement of the great-person theory. However, although we can list traits and skills possessed by leaders, a large number of research studies conclude that we cannot predict who will become a leader solely from the individual's personality characteristics (G. L. Wilson, 2002).

Is it the situation, then, that produces leaders? The *situational view* of leadership argues that the needs of a group change from time to time. The individual who emerges as the leader in one particular circumstance will not necessarily be the individual who becomes the leader in another circumstance. But what determines which member of a group emerges as leader in a particular situation?

The *contingency model* of leadership states that both personality characteristics and situational influences determine who will become a leader. It views leadership as a complex undertaking in which leaders influence their followers and followers influence their leaders (Graen & Hui, 2001). The contingency model notes that leaders have two basic styles: They direct their efforts either toward getting a task completed or toward helping group members get along. If a group is working under very favourable or very unfavourable conditions, a task-oriented leader is better, but if working conditions are moderate, a relationship-oriented leader is better. These ideas have not been fully tested by researchers, but the concept that leadership is a function of both personality characteristics and situational influences is an important one.

The idea of different leadership styles has been useful to social psychologists studying the increasing number of women in leadership roles that were once reserved for men. Reviews of research on gender and leadership conclude that men appear to be more directive and task-oriented leaders, whereas women are more democratic and interpersonally oriented (O'Leary & Flanagan, 2001). A man might just tell people what to do, whereas a woman might say, "Let's discuss how we should go about doing this and let's also get some more opinions."

By adopting a participative and collaborative style, women may be able to overcome others' resistance to their leadership, win their acceptance, gain self-confidence, and be effective (Lips, 2003). And, indeed, women have proved to be very effective leaders. In one study, ratings of 9000 female and male managers by subordinates and peers indicated that women were perceived as more effective leaders than men were (Center for Leadership Studies, 2000). This outcome may reflect more than just preference for relationship-oriented leadership or the influence of gender roles. It may also reflect the tendency for women to have to meet a higher standard than men to attain leadership positions and then to have to maintain a higher standard of performance. Another factor that may play a role in this outcome could be some relaxation of the persistent sexism which has contributed to the higher standard which women have long had to meet.

> **reflect and review**

2 **Identify how people are influenced in social settings.**

- Describe the factors that affect conformity and obedience.
- Discuss group performance.
- Summarize the factors that influence leadership.

How do you think you would have responded in the Asch conformity and Milgram obedience experiments? What makes you say so? Have you ever been in a situation in which social circumstances seemed to pressure you to do something against your values?

3 INTERGROUP RELATIONS

— **Group Identity: Us Versus Them** — **Prejudice** — **Ways to Improve Interethnic Relations**

What affects relations between groups?

Conflicts among groups, especially ethnic and cultural groups, are rampant around the world (Forsyth, 2006; Chirot & Seligman, 2001). Groups like Al Qaeda attack Western countries that they perceive to be too secular and materialistic. The West retaliates, invading Afghanistan and Iraq. Israelis and Palestinians fight over territory in the Middle East, each claiming religious rights to disputed land. Across Africa, tribal chiefs try to craft a new social order favourable to their own rule. In Northern Ireland and Spain, clashes still break out. Such conflicts occur in Canada, between Aboriginals and police, and between English- and French-speakers, but with much less violence. Prejudice, stereotyping, ethnocentrism, and other concepts introduced by social psychologists can help us understand the intensity of such cultural and ethnic conflicts and how to reduce these conflicts (Ellemers, Spears, & Doosje, 2002; Hewstone, Rubin, & Willis, 2002).

Group Identity: Us Versus Them

Think about the groups of which you are a member—possibly social organizations, your ethnicity, your nationality. When someone asks you to identify yourself, how often do you respond by mentioning these group memberships? And how much does it matter to you whether the people you associate with are members of the same groups?

Social Identity **Social identity** refers to the way we define ourselves in terms of our group membership (Ashmore, Deaux, McLaughlin-Volpe, 2004; Deaux, 2001). In contrast to personal identity, which can be highly individualized, social identity assumes some commonalities with others. A person's social identity might include identifying with a religious group, a country, a social organization, a university or college, and many others. To identify with a group does not necessarily mean that we know or interact with every other member of the group. However, it does mean that we believe that we share numerous features with other members of the group.

Many forms of social identity exist, reflecting the many ways in which people connect to other groups and social categories. Social psychologist Kay Deaux (2001) identified five distinct types of social identity: ethnic and religious, political, vocations and avocations, personal relationships, and stigmatized groups (see figure 16.7).

For many people, ethnic identity and religious identity are central aspects of their social identity (Eriksen, 2001; Phinney, 2005). Social psychologist Henry Tajfel (1978), a Jewish survivor of the Holocaust, wanted to explain the extreme violence and prejudice that his religious group experienced. Tajfel's **social identity theory** states that when individuals are assigned to a group, they invariably think of their group as an in-group (Tajfel & Turner, 2004). This occurs because they want to have a positive self-image.

social identity Refers to the way we define ourselves in terms of group memberships.

social identity theory Tajfel's theory that when individuals are assigned to a group, they invariably think of it as an in-group.

(*Top*) A Palestinian-Israeli clash in the Gaza Strip. (*Bottom*) An outbreak of violence in Northern Ireland. *How might a group's social identity be involved in such violence?*

Ethnicity and Religion

Asian
Jewish
Quebecois
West Indian

Political Affiliation

Feminist
Conservative
Environmentalist

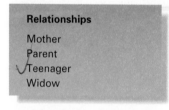

Vocations and Avocations

Psychologist
Artist
Athlete
Military veteran

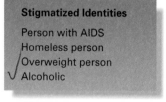

Relationships

Mother
Parent
Teenager
Widow

Stigmatized Identities

Person with AIDS
Homeless person
Overweight person
Alcoholic

FIGURE 16.7

Types of Identity

Self-image consists of both a personal identity and many different social identities. Tajfel argues that individuals can improve their self-images by enhancing either their personal or their social identities, but he believes that social identity is especially important. Think about how you introduce yourself to a stranger. Are you more likely to say, "Hi, I'm an ambitious hard-working idealist"? Or are you more likely to say, "Hi, I'm a student at Trent and I'm a member of the psychology society"? Chances are you are more likely to tell people about the groups with which you identify.

We are continually comparing our groups (*in-groups*) with other groups (*out-groups*). In the process, we often focus more on the groups' differences than on their similarities. Imagine two fans of pro football teams, one a Calgary Stampeders fan, the other a Hamilton Tiger Cats fan. These fans are less likely to discuss how much they both like football than to argue about the virtues of their teams. As they strive to promote their social identities, they soon lapse into self-congratulatory remarks about their own team and nasty comments about the opposing team. The theme of the conversation has become "My team is good and I am good. Your team is bad and you are bad." And so it goes with the sexes, ethnic groups, nations, socioeconomic groups, religions, sororities, fraternities, and countless other groups. Curiously, people perceive discrimination

Group members often show considerable pride in their group identity, as reflected in Caribbean Canadians' celebration of Caribana, gays' and lesbians' celebration of Gay Pride Day, Aboriginals' celebration of their heritage, and Polish Canadians' celebration of their cultural background.

against their group as more severe than discrimination against themselves personally (Hodson & Esses, 2002; Taylor, Ruggiero, & Louis, 1996). Dion & Kawakami (1996) studied six minorities in Toronto (blacks, Chinese, South Asians, Italians, Jews, and Portuguese) and found that all of them experienced a *personal/group discrimination discrepancy*. Regardless, these comparisons often lead to competition and even discrimination against other groups.

Tajfel (1978) showed how easy it is to lead people to think in terms of "we" and "they." In one experiment, he assigned those who overestimated the number of dots on a screen to one group and those who underestimated the number to another group. Once assigned to the two groups, the participants were asked to award money to the other participants. Invariably, individuals awarded money only to members of their own group. If we favour our own group on such trivial criteria, it is no wonder that we show intense in-group favouritism when differences are not so trivial (Jussim, Ashmore, & Wilder, 2001).

Ethnocentrism At the beginning of the twenty-first century, group pride—especially group pride based on ethnicity and culture—has mushroomed. There's Gay Pride and Black Pride. The Scots grow more Scottish, the Brazilians more Brazilian, Canadians even more Canadian. The tendency to favour one's own group over other groups is called **ethnocentrism**. Ethnocentrism's positive side is that it fosters a sense of pride in the group that fulfills the human urge to attain and maintain a positive self-image. Of course, the negative side of ethnocentrism is that it encourages in-group/out-group, we/they thinking.

ethnocentrism The tendency to favour one's own ethnic group over other groups.

There is something paradoxical, though, about ethnic pride. Most members of an ethnic group celebrate their own heritage and culture and set themselves apart from, and even above, others. But, still, they often attest that they do not discriminate against others. As African-American activist Stokely Carmichael said, "I'm for the Negro. I'm not against anything." In reality, however, members of ethnic groups often stress differences with others rather than emphasizing pride in their own group. One explanation for this paradox may be that individuals do not experience any *explicit* (conscious) ethnocentrism even though they are *implicitly* (unconsciously) ethnocentric (Cunningham, Nezlek, & Banaji, 2004).

In-group pride does not always reflect ethnocentrism. Members of some marginalized groups (such as women, Aboriginal Canadians, and gays and lesbians) often assert in-group pride to counter the negative messages about their group transmitted by society (Crocker, Major, & Steele, 1998).

Prejudice

Understanding the antagonism that develops between groups requires knowledge about prejudice and the stereotyping and discrimination that often accompany it (Dovidio, Glick, & Rudman, 2005; Dion, 2003; Fishbein, 2002). Like most people, you probably do not consider yourself prejudiced. But, in fact, each of us has prejudices. **Prejudice** is an unjustified negative attitude toward an individual based on the individual's membership in a group. The group can be made up of people of a particular race, sex, age, religion, or nationality or can share some other detectable difference from the prejudiced individual (Jones, 2002; Nelson, 2002).

Prejudice, as a worldwide phenomenon (Plous, 2003), has often erupted into hatred and violence in human history. The Taliban were so prejudiced against women that they tried to make them invisible. Serbs were so prejudiced against Bosnians that they pursued a policy of "ethnic cleansing." Roméo Dallaire was forced to witness the Hutus in Rwanda go on a murderous rampage against the Tutsis because of the Hutu prejudice against Tutsis. Europeans were so prejudiced against Native Americans and Canadians that they systematically robbed them of their property and self-respect, killed them, and herded the survivors like animals onto reservations.

Why do people develop prejudice? The simplest approach holds that prejudice stems from stereotypes: a person who stereotypes all out-group members as lazy will experience prejudice toward that out-group. However, Mark Zanna, of the University of Waterloo, and his colleagues, have shown that prejudice is based on more than stereotypes (Haddock & Zanna, 1998; Haddock, Zanna, & Esses, 1994; Zanna, 1994). For example, Gardner (1994) showed that English-Canadian prejudice toward French Canadians has little relationship to stereotypes of French Canadians. In Zanna's theory, prejudice arises from four interrelated factors: stereotypes, symbolic beliefs, emotions, and past experience. Symbolic beliefs are beliefs about whether a group helps or hinders the reaching of important values. For example, a negative symbolic belief that an outgroup prevents a person from getting a job can also lead to prejudice. In addition, emotions experienced about outgroups and past experiences of outgroups can also lead to prejudice.

Zanna (1994) asked Canadian university students their opinions of four Canadian outgroups: French Canadians, Aboriginal Canadians, Pakistanis, and homosexuals. Degree of prejudice was better predicted by combining stereotype, emotional factors, and symbolic beliefs. For example, these students stereotyped Aboriginal Canadians as alcoholic and lazy; in addition, Aboriginals gave rise to feelings of anger and uneasiness in the students, who also held symbolic beliefs of Aboriginal Canadians violating peace. The students stereotyped homosexuals as effeminate, normal, and friendly; homosexuals also gave rise to feelings of disgust, confusion, and discomfort in the students, who held symbolic beliefs of homosexuals promoting freedom, blocking the traditional family, and promoting peace. In subsequent work, the fourth factor, quality of past experience, was also shown to improve the prediction of degree of prejudice toward Aboriginal Canadians (Haddock, Zanna, & Esses, 1994).

prejudice An unjustified negative attitude toward an individual based on the individual's membership in a group.

Mark Zanna, of the University of Waterloo, is interested in how we form attitudes, and the relationship of those attitudes to our behaviour. He is especially interested in the topics of open-mindedness versus closed-mindedness, discrimination, and prejudice.

Social psychologists also give the following reasons for prejudice (Myers, 2005; Monteith, 2000):

- *Individual personality*. Some years ago social psychologist Theodor Adorno and his colleagues (1950) described the *authoritarian personality*: strict adherence to conventional ways of behaving, aggression against people who violate conventional norms, rigid thinking, and exaggerated submission to authority. According to Robert Altemeyer, of the University of Manitoba, individuals with an authoritarian personality are likely to be prejudiced (Altemeyer, 1996), lack self-awareness (Altemeyer, 1999), and be dominating (Altemeyer, 2004b). However, not all individuals who harbour prejudice have an authoritarian personality.
- *Competition between groups over scarce resources*. Feelings of hostility and prejudice can develop when a society does not have enough jobs or land or power or status—or any of a number of other material and social resources—to go around (Stephan & others, 2005; Jackson & Esses, 2000; Dion, 2001). Given the historical distributions of resources in a particular society, certain groups may regularly be involved in competing with each other and thus be likelier to develop prejudice toward each other. For instance, immigrants often compete with established low-income members of a society for jobs, leading to persistent conflict between the two groups.
- *Motivation to enhance self-esteem*. As Tajfel (1978; Tajfel & Turner, 2004) stated, individuals derive a sense of self-esteem through their identification as members of a particular group and, to the extent that their group is viewed more favourably than other groups, their self-esteem will be further enhanced. In this view, prejudice against other groups leads to a positive social identity and higher self-esteem.
- *Cognitive processes that contribute to a tendency to categorize and stereotype others*. Human beings are limited in their capacity for careful and thorough thought (Allport, 1954; Jones, 2002). The social environment is extremely complex and makes many demands on our limited information processing capacity, which can produce an unfortunate consequence: simplification of the social environment through categorization and stereotyping. Once stereotypes are in place, prejudice is often not far behind.
- *Cultural learning*. Families, friends, traditional norms, and institutionalized patterns of discrimination provide plenty of opportunities for individuals to be exposed to the prejudice of others. In this manner, others' prejudiced belief systems can be incorporated into one's own system. Children often show prejudice before they even have the cognitive abilities or social opportunities to develop their own attitudes (Berry & others, 2002).

Stereotyping One important aspect of prejudice is a **stereotype**, a generalization about a group's characteristics that does not consider any variations from one individual to the next (Giliovich, Keltner, & Nisbett, 2005; Kite, 2001). Think about your image of a step-parent. Most of us would probably describe such a person as caring less about his or her stepchildren than the children's biological parent. In fact, the step-parent has been treated as "wicked" in fairy tales for centuries. But characterizing all step-parents in such negative terms is a clear example of a stereotype (Claxton-Oldfield, 2000; Claxton-Oldfield & others, 2002).

We are less likely to detect variations among individuals who belong to "other" groups than among individuals who belong to "our" group (Wells & Olson, 2001). Emotions like anger can also be involved (Bodenhausen & others, 2001). The result is a tendency to view members of other groups as having homogeneous and undesirable qualities.

Further, according to Jacquie Vorauer, of the University of Manitoba, and her colleagues, our perception of individuals who belong to "other groups" is filtered through our own *meta-stereotypes*, our stereotyped images of how others see us (Vorauer & others, 2000). Take Albert, a white professional male working in Ottawa. His meta-stereotype of Aboriginal Canadians is that they have a negative stereotype of white

stereotype A generalization about a group's characteristics that does not consider any variations from one individual to another.

Canadians. No matter how accurate his meta-stereotype actually is (perhaps Aboriginal Canadians hold positive views of white Canadians), Albert unfortunately develops negative emotions about intergroup interaction with Aboriginal Canadians, which increases his own tendency to stereotype them (Vorauer & others, 2000; Vorauer, Main, & O'Connell, 1998).

Stereotypes are directly harmful because they can lead to stigma (Major & O'Brien, 2005) and discrimination toward group members, a topic we will consider shortly. But they are also indirectly harmful because the victims of stereotypes face *stereotype threat*. In the face of a negative stereotype of a group, anything an individual does which might fit the stereotype seems to confirm the stereotype, even to that individual. This can cause extra pressure, leading to poorer performance in possible stereotype confirming situations. In the original demonstration of stereotype threat, Steele & Aronson (1995), African-American and white students were administered questions from the Scholastic Achievement Test. African-American participants showed impaired performance relative to white participants when they were asked to record their race, but not otherwise. Being asked about their race activated negative stereotypes about intellectual abilities and generated stereotype threat for the African-American participants. The resulting stress impaired their performance. Stereotype threat has also been demonstrated in the memory performance of older people who face the negative stereotype of poor memories in the aged (Chasteen & others, 2005) and in the mathematics performance of women, who face the negative stereotype of poor mathematics abilities in women (Cadinu & others, 2005).

Although stereotyping can be harmful, we should remember that all people stereotype. As we explained in chapter 9, people use categories, or schemas, when thinking about groups and individuals from these groups (Brown, 2006; Fiske, 1998), often unawares (Chugh, 2004). The problem is not that we use these categories but that we limit our perceptions of others to the rough outlines of the schema; we don't add information about the individual's characteristics.

Discrimination Holding a stereotype does not mean that you have to act on it. But if you do act on your prejudices, you may be guilty of **discrimination**, an unjustified negative or harmful action toward a member of a group simply because the person belongs to that group (Dion, 2002). Discrimination results when negative emotional reactions combine with prejudiced beliefs and are translated into behaviour.

Early research on discrimination focused on overt forms of discrimination in which the target (person or group), the action, and the intention of the actor were clear and identifiable. Overt discrimination is the outcome, for example, of old-fashioned racism or sexism. The actor tries to maintain self-esteem by using the power of being a member of a particular group to treat, for example, women or individuals from ethnic minority groups unfairly.

Overt discrimination is no longer acceptable in mainstream North American society, however. In Canada, the *Canadian Charter of Rights and Freedoms*, along with changing attitudes expressed widely in popular media, have made it "politically incorrect" to publicly discriminate. But more subtle forms of discrimination have arisen. Subtle forms of racism, for example, have appeared, described by such terms as symbolic racism, aversive racism, ambivalent racism, and modern racism (Blair, 2001). They involve negative feelings, but not traditional stereotypes, about minority groups. Symbolic racism assumes that, because discrimination is no longer acceptable, it must not exist; any difficulties that individuals in minority groups might face is their own fault. It encompasses the ideas that Canadian Aboriginals, for example, are alcoholic, uneducated, and poor (Claxton-Oldfield & Keefe, 1999) and that African Americans, for example, are pushing too hard, too fast, for equality, are making unfair demands and are getting undeserved special attention, such as favouritism in job hiring and college admissions (Taylor, Peplau, & Sears, 2006).

This more subtle form of racism is based on discrimination that is covert rather than overt, unconscious rather than conscious, and denied rather than acknowledged (Monteith & Voils, 2001).

discrimination An unjustified negative or harmful action toward a member of a group simply because he or she is a member of that group.

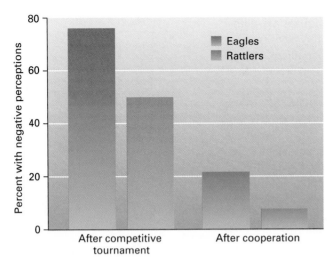

FIGURE 16.8

Attitudes Toward the Out-group Following Competitive and Cooperative Activities
In Sherif's research, hostility peaked after an athletic tournament, as reflected in the high percentage of Eagles and Rattlers who perceived the other group unfavourably following this event. However, after the groups worked together to reach a goal, their unfavourable attitudes toward each other dropped considerably.

Ways to Improve Interethnic Relations

Martin Luther King, Jr., once said, "I have a dream that my four little children will one day live in a nation where they will not be judged by the colour of their skin but by the content of their character." How might we possibly reach the world King envisioned, a world without prejudice and discrimination? Frances Aboud, of McGill University, and her colleagues, have shown that not talking about issues of race (being "colour blind") is unhelpful. It only teaches children to feel uneasy around people of different ethnic groups (Aboud, Mendelson, & Purdy, 2003; Aboud & Doyle, 1996). Indeed, researchers have consistently found that contact alone—attending the same school or living next door to each other or working in the same company—does not necessarily improve relations with people from other ethnic backgrounds (Brewer & Brown, 1998). They have found that more focused efforts, such as task-oriented cooperation and intimate contact, are needed to break down barriers based on prejudice (Aboud & Levy, 2000).

Task-Oriented Cooperation Decades ago, social psychologist Muzafer Sherif and his colleagues (1961) fuelled "we/they" competition between two groups of 11-year-old boys at a summer camp called Robbers Cave in Oklahoma. In the first week, one group hardly knew the other group existed. One group became known as the Rattlers (a tough, cursing group whose shirts were emblazoned with a snake insignia), and the other was known as the Eagles.

Near the end of the first week each group learned of the other's existence. It took little time for "we/they" talk to surface ("They had better not be on our ball field." "Did you see the way one of them was sneaking around?"). Sherif, who disguised himself as a janitor so he could unobtrusively observe the Rattlers and Eagles, arranged for the two groups to compete in baseball, touch football, and tug-of-war. Counsellors manipulated and judged events so the teams were close. Each team perceived the other to be competing unfairly. Raiding the other group's area, burning the other group's flag, and fighting resulted. The Rattlers and Eagles further derided one another, holding their noses in the air as they passed each other. Rattlers described all Rattlers as brave, tough, and friendly and called all Eagles sneaky and smart alecks. The Eagles reciprocated by calling the Rattlers crybabies.

After "we/they" conflict transformed the Rattlers and Eagles into opposing "armies," Sherif devised ways to reduce hatred between the groups. He tried noncompetitive contact, but that didn't work. Only when both groups were required to work cooperatively to solve a problem did the Rattlers and Eagles develop a positive relationship. Sherif created tasks that required the efforts of both groups: working together to repair the only water supply to the camp, pooling their money to rent a movie, and cooperating to pull the camp truck out of a ditch. Figure 16.8 shows how competitive and cooperative activities changed perceptions of the out-group.

Might Sherif's idea—creating cooperation between groups rather than competition—be applied to ethnic groups? When the schools in Austin, Texas, were desegregated through extensive busing, increased racial tension among African Americans, Mexican Americans, and whites resulted in violence in the schools. The superintendent consulted Eliot Aronson, a prominent social psychologist, who was at the University of Texas at Austin at the time. Aronson (2004) thought it was more important to prevent ethnic hostility than to control it. He observed a number of elementary school classrooms in Austin and saw how fierce the competition was between children of unequal status.

Aronson stressed that the reward structure of the classrooms needed to be changed from a setting of unequal competition to one of cooperation among equals, without making any curriculum changes. To accomplish this, he put together the jigsaw classroom. The jigsaw classroom works by creating a situation in which all of the students

Eliot Aronson developed the concept of the jigsaw classroom to reduce ethnic conflict. *How does the jigsaw classroom work?*

have to pull together to get the "big picture." Let's say we have a class of 30 students, some white, some Caribbean, and some Aboriginal. The academic goal is to learn about the Canadian prairies. The class might be broken up into five study groups of six students each, with the ethnic composition and academic achievement level of the groups being as equal as possible. Learning about the Canadian prairies becomes a class project divided into six parts, with one part given to each member of the six-person group. The components might be early immigration to the prairies, animals and plants of the prairies, prairie crops, cities on the prairies, and so on. The parts are like the pieces of a jigsaw puzzle. Each group has to put the parts together to form the complete puzzle.

Each student has an allotted time to study her or his part. Then the group meets, and each member tries to teach her or his part to the group. Each student must learn the entire lesson, so learning depends on the cooperation and effort of other members. After an hour or so each student is tested on the Canadian prairies. Aronson believes that cooperatively working to reach a common goal increases students' interdependence.

The strategy of emphasizing cooperation rather than competition and the jigsaw approach have been widely used in classrooms in North America. A number of studies reveal that this type of cooperative learning is associated with increased self-esteem, better academic performance, friendships among classmates, and improved interethnic perceptions (Johnson & Johnson, 2003; Aronson, 2004).

It is not easy to get groups who do not like each other to cooperate. The air of distrust and hostility is hard to overcome. Creating goals that require both groups to cooperate is one viable strategy, as shown in Sherif's and Aronson's work. Other strategies involve spreading positive information about the "other" and reducing the potential threat of each group.

Intimate Contact We stated earlier that contact by itself does not improve inter-ethnic relations. However, one form of contact—intimate contact—can (Eller & Abrams, 2004; Brislin, 1993). Intimate contact in this context does not mean sexual relations; rather, it involves sharing one's personal worries, troubles, successes, failures, personal ambitions, and coping strategies. When people reveal personal information about themselves, they are likelier to be perceived as individuals than as members of a category. And the sharing of personal information often produces the discovery that others have many of the same feelings, hopes, and concerns that we have, which can help to break down in-group/out-group, "we/they" barriers. Sharing intimate information and becoming friendly with someone from another ethnic group helps to make people more tolerant and less prejudiced toward the other ethnic group (Brewer & Gaertner, 2001; Pettigrew & Tropp, 2000).

Intimate personal contact that involves sharing doubts, hopes, problems, ambitions, and much more is one way to improve interethnic relations.

In one of the initial investigations of extensive interethnic contact, African-American and white residents in a U.S. integrated housing project were studied (Deutsch & Collins, 1951). Initially, any conversations focused on such nonintimate matters as washing machines. Over time the whites and African Americans discovered that they shared a number of similar concerns, such as jobs and work, the quality of schools for their children, taxes, and so on. This revelation helped to diminish in-group/out-group thoughts and feelings.

Richard Clément, of the University of Ottawa, and his colleagues have explored shared language, one important variable mediating intimate contact. Intimate contact is virtually impossible between people who cannot speak to each other (Clément, Baker, & MacIntyre, 2003; Clément & Bourhis, 1996; Clément, Noels, & Deneault, 2001). In a study of Chinese undergraduates in Canada, Noels, Pon, & Clément (1996) found that self-confidence in using Chinese and English was an important part of the student's adjustment. Similarly, linguistic self-confidence mediates interethnic contact between French and English Canadians (McIntyre & others, 2003; Noels & Clément, 1996). These sorts of findings underscore the value of bilingual education in Canada (McIntyre & others, 2003; Noels & Clément, 1998).

> **> reflect and review**

> **3 Discuss intergroup relations.**
> - Identify how group identity leads to "we/they" thinking.
> - Describe the relationships among prejudice, stereotyping, and discrimination.
> - Explain two effective strategies for improving interethnic relations.
>
> *What personal experiences have you had with prejudice, stereotyping, and discrimination? Explain why you think these occurred.*

4 SOCIAL INTERACTION

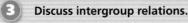

Aggression   Altruism

How do aggression and altruism characterize social interaction?

Our social interactions can bring us experiences we would rather forget, moments that are charged with conflict and harm. They can also bring us warm and cherished acts of kindness (A. G. Miller, 2004). Let's explore these two faces of social interaction: the negative side—aggression—and the positive side—altruism.

Aggression

The danger of aggression was captured vividly by the wise Yoda in the classic film *The Empire Strikes Back*: "Beware of the dark side. Anger, fear, aggression. Easily they flow. Once you start down the dark path, it will forever dominate your destiny and consume your will." Is this dark side biologically based or is it learned?

Biological Influences   There is nothing new about human aggression. The primate ancestors of human beings and the earliest humans are thought to have committed aggressive acts against others of their own kind. Ancient writings describe the violent ways of the Assyrian king Ashurbanipal, who delighted in beheading his enemies and blinding and mutilating his prisoners. The Russian czar Ivan the Terrible bludgeoned his own son to death and destroyed the second largest city in his empire, Novgorod, in the sixteenth century. In the 1970s, four million Cambodians were killed by their fellow Cambodians. Murders in North America take place at the rate of 20,000 per year, assaults at the rate of 700,000 per year; there are at least 200,000 reports of rape per year in North America. In the twentieth century, 80 to 100 million people were violently killed. Asked Shakespeare, "Is there any cause in nature that makes these hard hearts?" Is aggression an inborn characteristic of the human species?

Evolutionary Views Ethologists say that aggression is biologically based; certain stimuli release *innate* aggressive responses (Lorenz, 1965; Tinbergen, 1969). For example, a male robin will attack another male when it sees the red patch on the other bird's breast. When the patch is removed, however, no attack takes place.

While fighting does occur in the animal kingdom, most encounters do not escalate to killing or even severe harm. Much fighting is ritualistic and involves threat displays. For example, elephant seals show approximately 65 threat displays for every fight that actually takes place (LeBoeuf & Peterson, 1969). The type of threat display varies from one species to the next: a cat arches its back, bares its teeth, and hisses; a chimpanzee stares, stomps the ground, and screams.

Evolutionary theorists believe that, when it comes to aggression, human beings are not very different from other animals (Blanchard & Blanchard, 2003). A basic theme of their theory is the survival of the fittest. Thus they conclude that early in human evolution, the survivors were probably aggressive individuals. Hunters and food gatherers not only had to kill animals to eat but also had to compete for the best food territories if they were to survive. There may even be an evolutionary underpinning for homicide (Daly & Wilson, 1988, 2001).

Freud's Theory of Aggression Freud (1917) also argued that aggression is biologically based. He said we have a self-destructive urge he called *thanatos*, the *death instinct*. Because the death instinct comes in conflict with our self-preserving life instinct, the death instinct is redirected toward others in the form of aggression.

Most psychologists feel uneasy about the concept of instinct when discussing human behaviour. But instinct theorists often support their belief that humans have an instinct for aggression by pointing out examples of how common aggression is. However, simply calling aggression an instinct does not prove that it is one.

Genetic Basis Even though a human instinct for aggression has not been proved, genes are important in understanding the biological basis of aggression. The selective breeding of animals provides evidence. After a number of breedings among only aggressive animals and among only docile animals, vicious and timid strains of animals emerge. The vicious strains attack nearly anything in sight; the timid strains rarely fight, even when attacked.

The genetic basis for aggression is more difficult to demonstrate with humans (Brennan, Mednick, & Kandel, 1991). Nonetheless, in one investigation of 573 sets of adult twins, identical twins had more similar aggressive tendencies than did fraternal twins (Rushton & others, 1986).

Neurobiological Factors Rather than an instinct for aggression, what may have evolved is an aggressive capacity wired into the human neuromuscular system. Researchers point to the behaviour of children born deaf and blind, who still show aggressive patterns—foot stomping, teeth clenching, and fist making—even though they have had no opportunity to observe these behaviours (Eibl-Eibesfeldt, 1977).

Studies by neuroscientists indicate how the brain is involved in the biological processes of aggression (Niehoff, 1999). In an extreme example, in 1966 Charles Whitman climbed to the top of the campus tower at the University of Texas at Austin. As he looked down, he pulled the trigger of a high-powered rifle and killed 15 people. Then he took his own life. An autopsy revealed a tumour in the limbic system of Whitman's brain, an area associated with emotion. Kiehl and others (2001) demonstrated that criminal psychopaths show abnormally low levels of limbic activation in emotional situations. In another instance, an electrode was implanted in the amygdala (an area of the brain that is part of the limbic system) of a meek female mental patient. Immediately after an electric current stimulated the amygdala, the mild-mannered woman became vicious (King, 1961). We do not appear to have a specific aggression centre in the brain, but, when the lower, more primitive, areas of the brain (such as the limbic system) are stimulated by fine electric currents, aggressive behaviour often results (Gontkovsky, 2005).

Neurotransmitters have also been linked to highly aggressive behaviour (Filley & others, 2001). Individuals with depressive disorders who commit suicide by violent means (such as using a gun) have been found to have lower levels of the neurotransmitter

Aggression has been pervasive throughout the past. (*Top*) Russian czar Ivan the Terrible killed his own son. (*Bottom*) In the 1970s, four million Cambodians were killed by fellow Cambodians.

serotonin than most people do (Van Winkle, 2000). In one study, young men whose serotonin levels were low relative to those of other men their age were far likelier to have committed a violent crime (Goveas, Csernansky, & Coccaro, 2004). Also, children who show high rates of aggression have lower levels of serotonin than children who display low rates of aggression (Holmes, Slaughter, & Kashani, 2000).

Alcohol, which acts on the brain to stifle our inhibitions, has been strongly linked to violence and aggression. Individuals under the influence of alcohol are more easily provoked than they would be when they are sober to unleash harsh words, throw a punch, or pull the trigger of a gun (Fillmore & Weafer, 2004). People under the influence of alcohol commit almost one-half of rapes and other violent crimes (Abbey, Ross, & McDuffie, 1993). Unfortunately, the people who are already prone to aggression are also the ones who are likely to drink and then become violent when they become intoxicated (Seto & Barbaree, 1995).

Hormones are another biological factor that may play a role in aggression (Susman & others, 1996). For example, Sam, a bull, was a terror. With hooves scratching, eyes glazed, and nostrils snorting, he roared across a field at an intruder. Barely escaping with his life, the intruder (who turned out to be a tractor salesman) filed a complaint against the bull's owner. The local sheriff convinced the owner it was time to do something about Sam. What was Sam's fate? He was castrated, which changed him from a simmering volcano into a docile ox. The castration reduced Sam's motivation to terrorize by acting on his male hormone system. However, a clear link between testosterone and aggressive behaviour has not been found in humans (Moore, 2001; Brain & Susman, 1997).

Psychological Factors Numerous psychological factors appear to be involved in aggression (Morgan, 2005). They include individuals' responses to certain circumstances, cognitive and learning factors, and sociocultural factors.

Frustrating and Aversive Circumstances Some years ago, John Dollard and his colleagues (1939) proposed that frustration, the blocking of an individual's attempts to reach a goal, triggers aggression. Their *frustration-aggression hypothesis* states that frustration always leads to aggression. Not much later, however, psychologists found that aggression is not the only possible response to frustration. Some individuals who experience frustration become passive, for example (Miller, 1941).

Psychologists later recognized that a broad range of aversive experiences besides frustration can also cause aggression. They include physical pain, personal insults, and unpleasant events such as divorce. Aversive circumstances can also include the physical environment. Environmental psychologists have demonstrated how such factors as noise, weather, and crowding can stimulate aggression. Murder, rape, and assault increase when temperatures are the hottest (during the third quarter of the year), as well as in the hottest years and in the hottest cities (Bushman, Wang, & Anderson, 2005; Anderson & Bushman, 2002). Our everyday encounters with other people also produce aversive experiences that can trigger aggressive responses (Schwartz, 1999). For example, when someone cuts into a line in front of us (such as at a ticket booth), we may respond aggressively toward that person (Milgram & others, 1986).

Cognitive Factors Whether we respond aggressively to aversive situations is determined by our interpretation of the event (Baumeister, 1999; Berkowitz, 1990):

- *Expectations.* You expect to be jostled on a crowded bus, but you don't expect someone to run into you when there are only five or six people on the bus. Thus you might respond more aggressively when you are bumped on a relatively empty bus than on a crowded one.
- *Equity.* If you perceive that an aversive experience is not fair, or justified, you might respond aggressively. For example, if you deserve a D in a class, you are less likely to say nasty things about the professor than if you perceive the grade to be unfair.
- *Intentions.* If you think someone has intentionally tripped you, you are more likely to respond aggressively than if you think the individual's feet accidentally became tangled with yours.

• *Responsibility*. When you perceive that other people are responsible for frustrating or aversive actions, you are more likely to behave aggressively toward them. For example, when are you more likely to respond aggressively: when an 8-year-old child runs into you with a shopping cart in a store, or when her assertive, healthy, 30-year-old mother does the same thing? You are likely to perceive that the mother is more responsible for her own behaviour than the young girl is, so you would probably respond more aggressively toward the mother.

Reinforcement and Observational Learning   Behavioural and social cognitive theorists believe that aggression is learned through the processes of reinforcement and observational learning. Aggression is reinforced when it helps people attain money, attention, sex, power, or status. For example, a young adolescent who succeeds in getting the seat he wants by glowering at the schoolmate who is occupying it may try the same sort of aggressive tactic again. If he gets no such response, he begins to learn that aggression is not the key to success.

Aggression can also be learned by watching others engage in aggressive actions (Bandura, 1989). One of the most frequent opportunities people have to observe aggression in our culture is to watch violence on television, which is discussed further in the next section.

Sociocultural Factors   Aggression not only involves biological and cognitive factors but is also linked with factors in the wider social world. Among the sociocultural factors involved in aggression are variations across cultures and the extent to which people watch violence on TV.

Cross-cultural Variations   The incidence of aggression and violence has varied throughout human history. We think of our own era as relatively violent, but, in the past, hunters and food gatherers had to be even more aggressive just to survive. However, as anthropologist Loren Eiseley commented, "The need is now for a gentler, a more tolerant people than those who won for us against the ice, the tiger, and the bear."

Even today, aggression and violence are more common in some cultures than others (Matsumoto & Juang, 2004; Bellesiles, 1999). The homicide rate in Canada ranks 32 among 65 countries surveyed (United Nations, 1999; U.S. Bureau of Justice Statistics, 2001). The rate for the United States is much higher than in many other countries—about four times as high as in Canada and six times as high as in Europe. Crime rates tend to be higher in countries with a considerable gap between the rich and the poor (Triandis, 1994).

Cultural differences in aggression and violence are related to the circumstances that people in a culture face. Imagine yourself on a barren mountainside away from civilization in the country of Uganda. For about 2000 years, your ancestors lived as nomadic hunters, but, early in this century, the government of Uganda turned your hunting grounds into a national park. Hunting is forbidden in the park, so you are now forced to farm its steep, barren mountain areas. Famine, crowding, and drought have led to tremendous upheaval in families and moral values. You were sent out to live on your own at the age of six with no life supports; you fight and maim others to obtain food and water (Turnbull, 1972). This may seem like an exaggeration, but it is a description of normal life for the Ik people for most of the twentieth century. The world of the Ik involved many frustrating and aversive circumstances that produced pain and hunger. If you were placed in the same circumstances, wouldn't you become more callous and aggressive?

Media Violence   Violence is pictured as a way of life throughout the popular media: on the news and on television shows, in movies, in video games, and in song lyrics (Carter & Weaver, 2003). Evil doers kill and get killed; police and detectives violently uphold or even break society's laws; sports announcers glorify players, whether or not their behaviour is sportsmanlike or contributes to their team's success. It is easy to get the message that aggression and violence are the norm—in fact, are the preferred mode of behaviour—in North American society.

Part of the reason that violence seems so glamorous is that it is usually portrayed unrealistically. Viewers rarely see its lasting effects, whether the violence is real or fictitious.

Calvin and Hobbes
by Bill Watterson

Calvin & Hobbes © 1995 Watterson. Reprinted with permission of Universal Press Syndicate. All rights reserved.

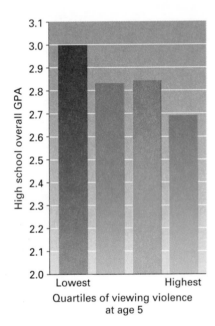

FIGURE 16.9

Girls' High School Grade Point Average by Quartiles of Violence Viewing at Age 5
Girls who watched the least TV violence at age 5 had a higher grade point average in high school than girls who watched more TV violence at age 5. The bar on the left represents the 25 percent of girls who watched the least violence at age 5, the second bar the next 25 percent of girls, and so on.

In real life, an injured person may not recover for weeks, for months, or perhaps not at all, but on television recovery is either assumed or takes only 30 to 60 minutes.

The amount of aggression in the media, and especially on television is a special problem for children (DeGaetano, 2005). In recent years, violent video games have also begun to elicit concern, although not so much yet in the case of girls (de Castell & Bryson, 1998). Between 1998 and 2003, Canadians watched an average of 22 hours of television a week. Canadian children are watching somewhat less television than they did in previous decades, mainly because of Internet use. It grew among children under eighteen from 41 percent in 1999 to 73 percent in 2003 (Statistics Canada, 2005b).

Almost every day of their lives, children watch someone being stabbed, maimed, or slaughtered. Does such pervasive exposure to violence merely stimulate children to go out and buy wrestling dolls or toy guns, or can it even trigger aggressive attacks on playmates and increase the likelihood that children will violently attack or murder someone when they grow up (McCreary, 1997)?

In one early study of the effects of TV violence, children were randomly assigned to one of two groups: One watched violent Saturday morning cartoon shows on 11 different days; the second group watched the same cartoon shows with the violence removed (Steur, Applefield, & Smith, 1971). The children were then observed during play at their preschool. The children who saw the TV cartoon shows with violence were likelier to kick, choke, and push their playmates than the children who saw the cartoon shows with the violence removed.

What children watch on TV is related not only to their aggression but also to their cognitive skills and achievement. In one recent longitudinal study, viewing educational programs as preschoolers was associated with a host of desirable characteristics in adolescence: getting higher grades, reading more books, placing a higher value on achievement, being more creative, and acting less aggressively (Anderson & others, 2001). These associations were more consistent for boys than girls. However, girls who were more frequent viewers of violent TV programs in the preschool years had lower grades in adolescence than girls who infrequently watched violent TV programs in the preschool years (see figure 16.9).

Some critics have argued that research results do not warrant the conclusion that TV violence causes aggression (Savage, 2004). But many experts insist that TV violence can cause aggressive or antisocial behaviour in children (Anderson & others, 2003; Bushman & Huesmann, 2001). Of course, television violence is not the *only* cause of aggression. There is no one cause of any social behaviour. Aggression, like all other social behaviours, has multiple determinants (Donnerstein, 2001). Television violence does not affect adults in isolation from such other factors as aggressive tendencies, marital problems, and job stress. Likewise, the link between TV violence and aggression in children is influenced by children's aggressive tendencies, by their attitudes toward violence, and by the monitoring of children's exposure to it.

Another aspect of media violence involves whether watching pornography leads to violence against women. To read further about this topic, see the Critical Reflections box.

Does Pornography Lead to Violence Against Women?

In 1993, 80 percent of Canadian female university students reported experiencing violence in a dating relationship (DeKeseredy & Kelly, 1993). In 1999, there were 383,000 rapes, attempted rapes, and sexual assaults in the United States, according to the U.S. Justice Department's annual National Crime Victimization Survey. Statistics like these fuel concerns that pornography contributes to a climate in which some men feel that sexual violence toward women is acceptable. Critics of pornography have repeatedly called for laws restricting access to pornography, especially now that it is freely available on the Internet (Mehta, 2001). Defenders, often claiming the right to freedom of expression, argue against such laws on the grounds that no clear link has been demonstrated between pornography and sexual violence against women. (Hawkins & Zimring, 1988; Seto, Maric, & Barbaree, 2001). Psychologists have entered the fray to scientifically evaluate whether or not the consumption of pornography, in fact, can lead to violence against women.

The most widely accepted explanation of how pornography may affect men's behaviour toward women comes from social cognitive theory (Bandura, 2000a, 2001). Studies suggest that children who regularly watch violence on television may learn to become more violent. So perhaps men who watch pornography learn to become sexually violent toward women or at least become desensitized to sexual violence.

Based on several meta-analyses and on research of their own, Neil Malamuth and his colleagues (Malamuth, Addison, & Koss, 2000) concluded that pornography consumption does have a small effect on male sexual aggression, but they caution that it is only one of a number of factors that may lead to sexual violence against women. They stress that the nature of pornographic material, the characteristics of the men viewing pornography, and the surrounding culture all combine to produce an effect. In other words, no one factor (such as pornography) is likely to control a complex behaviour (such as men's violence against women).

Adding to the complexity of the controversy over pornography is the absence of agreement on a definition of pornography. To some people, pornography means all sexually explicit materials. In contrast, the report of the U.S. Attorney General's Commission on Pornography (1986) distinguished between erotica and pornography: *Erotica* depicts nudity and explicit consensual sex, whereas *pornography* depicts the domination and humiliation of women, as well as explicit sexual violence toward women. When a further distinction is drawn between nonviolent and violent pornography, the consumption of erotica and even nonviolent pornography are not associated with increases in sexual violence toward women (Malamuth & others, 2000). Apparently, the most problematic materials are those that depict women enjoying being the victims of male sexual violence.

Such violent pornography reinforces the rape myth, the false belief that women actually desire coercive sex.

Further, most men are not prone to sexual violence against women (Malamuth & others, 2000). Rather, men who score higher on self-report measures of attraction to sexual aggression, hostile masculinity, and/or low intelligence appear to be prone to sexual violence against women (Bogaert, Woodard, & Hafer, 1999). In addition, they come from backgrounds in which gender equality is deemphasized and education about sexuality limited. In other words, some men are vulnerable to believing in the rape myth that women desire rape and deserve sexual abuse. When such at-risk men are exposed to violent pornography, they are even more likely to become perpetrators of sexual violence against women (Donnerstein, 2001).

Cultural variables may also be important (Lips, 2003). For example, research conducted after the legalization of pornography in Denmark failed to find evidence of increased criminal sexual acts as a function of the wider availability of pornography (Kutchinsky, 1991). It seems that public attitudes toward pornography vary with the cultural environment. The Danes generally enjoy a more natural approach to sex. Public nudity, for example, is more common and more accepted in Denmark than in the United States. Perhaps their more relaxed attitudes make the Danes less vulnerable to the effects of pornography.

One of the most difficult aspects of interpreting research on the effects of pornography on sexual violence against women is distinguishing between correlation and causality. Consider the Danish experience. The relationship between the wider availability of pornography and a lower rate of reported sexual violence is probably not a causal relationship. More likely, broader changes in Danish society underlie both variables. Similarly, it may be that high-risk men need greater stimulation, which is not satisfied even by heavy exposure to pornography. If so, pornography use may be a symptom of an underlying compulsion. Alternatively, it may be that the use of pornography raises an already high level of sexual aggressiveness above a threshold necessary to elicit actual behaviour. In this case, pornography would be a contributing cause. Further research is needed to determine whether one or both of these explanations is correct.

What do you think?

- Do you think the distinction between erotica, nonviolent pornography, and violent pornography is a helpful one?
- Do you think that the availability of sexually explicit materials should be restricted?
- How could you use experimental methods to investigate whether sexually explicit materials contribute to sexual violence against women?

Aggression and Gender Our stereotypes clearly tag boys and men as more aggressive than girls and women. In general, research has supported this view (Eagly, Beall, & Sternberg, 2004; Gussler-Burkhardt & Giancola, 2005). As children, boys are more likely to engage in rough-and-tumble play and get in more fights in which they are physically aggressive toward each other. As adolescents, males are more likely to be members of gangs and to commit violent acts. Children and adolescents who are diagnosed with conduct disorder (a pattern of offensive behaviour that violates the basic rights of others) are three times more likely to be boys than girls (Cohen & others, 1993). As adults, men are much more likely to be chronically hostile and to murder or rape than women are (Archer, 2004; Lalumière & others, 2005).

In a classic analysis of research studies, the following conclusions were reached about aggression and gender (Maccoby & Jacklin, 1974):

- Males are more aggressive than females in all cultures.
- Males are more aggressive than females from early in life, with differences consistently appearing as early as two years of age.
- Aggression is more common among males than among females, in animals as well as humans.

These findings often have been interpreted as supporting the view that gender differences in aggression are biologically based.

However, environment and culture also contribute to gender differences in aggression (White, 2001). In one study, individuals in 12 countries were asked to write stories in response to conflicts presented to them (Archer & McDaniel, 1995). In all 12 countries, males wrote stories with more violent themes than females did, suggesting a biological interpretation of gender differences in aggression. However, the degree of violence used in the descriptions varied considerably across the cultures, suggesting an environmental or cultural interpretation.

Despite the strong evidence that gender is a factor in aggression, we need to remind ourselves of an important point about the conclusions drawn from psychological research. When we say that males are more aggressive than females, we cannot jump to the conclusion that all males are more aggressive than all females (Hyde & Mezulis, 2002). In any given culture and time, some females will be more aggressive than some males. According to Artz (1998, 2004, 2005), young North American females are under more and more social pressure to use violence to achieve the social goals of becoming popular and sexy.

In addition, we need to consider the type of aggression. Researchers have found stronger gender differences in physical aggression than in verbal aggression (Eagly & Steffen, 1986). One longitudinal study found no gender differences in verbal aggression among eight-year-old children (Björkqvist, Österman, & Lagerspetz, 1994). However, at age 18, females displayed more verbal aggression than males.

"All I'm saying is, giving a little something to the arts might help our image."

© The New Yorker Collection 1989. Peter Steiner from cartoonbank.com. All Rights Reserved.

Ways to Reduce Aggression You might recall that chapter 11 explored the powerful, negative emotion of anger, which can generate aggression. Several strategies for reducing anger were examined that apply to our evaluation of aggression here. Among them is *catharsis*, the release of anger by directly engaging in anger or aggression. According to psychodynamic and ethological theories, behaving angrily or watching others behave angrily reduces subsequent anger or aggression. But social cognitive theorists disagree strongly. They believe that by acting aggressively people are often rewarded for their aggression and that by watching others behave aggressively, people learn to be aggressive themselves. Researchers have found more support for the social cognitive view than for the psychoanalytic and ethological views on reducing aggression (Bandura, 2000a, 2001). Thus, good possible strategies that will reduce aggression are decreasing rewards for aggression and allowing people to observe fewer incidences of aggression.

Parents have been specially targeted to help children to reduce aggression. English criminologist David Farrington (2005) lists parental attitude and conflict along with poor parental supervision and parental discipline as risk factors for antisocial behaviours in children. Recommended parenting strategies include encouraging young children to develop empathy toward others and better monitoring of adolescents' activities.

Schools are also seeking ways to reduce aggression (McCurdy, Mannella, & Eldridge, 2003). Strategies for reducing aggression that are being tried in many schools are teaching conflict management skills to students and having students serve as peer counsellors. The students discuss real and hypothetical problem situations and work together to develop positive, nonaggressive solutions. Children in these programs are taught to analyze their thoughts and to consider alternatives to aggression.

Altruism

We know from experience that social interaction is not all a matter of aggression. We often hear or read about acts of generosity and courage, such as the rock concerts and fundraisers to help the victims of the Asian tsunamis of December 26, 2004 or the terrorist attacks on September 11, 2001, the police and firefighters who risked their lives to save the people in the World Trade Center towers, and the volunteers who rushed to the various scenes of the disaster to offer their services to victims and rescuers (Oliner, 2001). On a more mundane level, you may have placed some of your hard-earned cash in the palm of a homeless person or perhaps cared for a wounded cat. What all of these acts have in common is **altruism**, an unselfish interest in helping someone else (Penner & others, 2005).

Psychological and Sociocultural Foundations of Altruism How do psychologists account for such acts of human altruism? One key aspect is the concept of *reciprocity*, which encourages us to do unto others as we would have them do unto us (Fehr & Rockenbach, (2004). It is present in every widely practised religion in the world—Judaism, Christianity, Buddhism, and Islam, for example. Complex human sentiments are involved in reciprocity: Trust in the people with whom we are interacting is probably the most important principle over the long run. But reciprocity can involve more negative sentiments, such as guilt, if we do not reciprocate a favour, and anger, if someone else does not reciprocate. One study found that university students were more likely to pledge to the charity of someone who had previously bought them candy (Webster & others, 1999). Reciprocity was more likely when the donor's name was made public to the recipient, but even when the recipient did not know who the donor was, reciprocity occurred, although at a lower level.

Not all altruism is motivated by reciprocity, but this view alerts us to the importance of considering interactions between oneself and others to understand altruism. And not all seemingly altruistic behaviour is unselfish. Some psychologists argue that a distinction between altruism and egoism is possible, while others argue that true altruism has never been demonstrated (Cialdini & others, 1987). **Egoism** involves giving to another person to ensure reciprocity, to gain self-esteem, to present oneself as powerful, competent, or caring, or to avoid social and self-censure for failing to live up to society's expectations. In contrast, altruism is giving to another person with the ultimate goal of benefiting that other person. Any benefits that come to the giver are unintended.

Altruism is determined by the nature of both the person and the situation (Post & others, 2002; Sober, 2001). Describing individuals as having altruistic or egoistic motives implies that psychological variables—a person's ability to empathize with the needy or to feel a sense of responsibility for another person's welfare—are important in understanding altruistic behaviour. The stronger these personality dispositions are, the less we would expect situational variables to influence whether giving, kindness, or helping occurs. But, as with any human behaviour, characteristics of the situation influence the strength of altruistic motivation. Some of these characteristics include the degree of need shown by the other individual, the needy person's responsibility for his plight, the cost of assisting the needy person, and the extent to which reciprocity is expected (Batson, 2002; Batson & Powell, 2003).

altruism An unselfish interest in helping someone else.

egoism Giving to another person to ensure reciprocity, to gain self-esteem, to present oneself as powerful, competent, or caring, or to avoid social and self-censure for failing to live up to normative expectations.

(*Top*) An example of animal altruism—a baboon plucking bugs from another baboon. Most acts of animal altruism involve kin. (*Bottom*) A young woman assists a child with a disability.

The Biological Foundations of Altruism   Evolutionary psychologists look for biological explanations of altruism rather than psychological or situational ones. They emphasize that some types of altruism help to perpetuate our genes (Ruse, 2002; Simpson & Gangestad, 2001). An act in the biological realm is considered altruistic if it simply increases another organism's prospects for survival and opportunity to reproduce (Fehr & Rockenbach, 2004).

Evolutionary psychologists believe that tremendous benefits can accrue to individuals who form cooperative, reciprocal relationships (Trivers, 1971). By being good to someone now, individuals increase the likelihood that they will receive a benefit from the other person in the future. Through this reciprocal process, both gain something beyond what they could have by acting alone (Krebs, 1998; Krebs & Denton, 2005).

Evolutionary psychologists also stress that those who carry our genes—our children—have a special place in the domain of altruism. Natural selection favours parents who care for their children and improve their probability of surviving. A parent feeding its young is performing a biologically altruistic act because the offspring's chance of survival is increased. So is a mother bird who tries to lure predators away from the fledglings in her nest. She is willing to sacrifice herself so that three or four of her young offspring will have the chance to survive, thus preserving her genes.

Human beings also often show more empathy toward relatives, who share their genes or have the potential to perpetuate their genes. In the case of a natural disaster, people's uppermost concern is their family. In one study involving a hypothetical decision to help in life-or-death situations, university students chose to aid close kin over distant kin, the young over the old, the healthy over the sick, the wealthy over the poor, and premenopausal women over postmenopausal woman (Burnstein, Crandall, & Kitayama, 1994). In this same study, when an everyday favour rather than a life-or-death situation was involved, the university students gave less weight to kinship and chose to help either the very young or the very old over those of intermediate age, the sick over the healthy, and the poor over the wealthy.

The Bystander Effect   One of the most widely studied aspects of altruism is why one person will help a stranger in distress whereas another won't lift a finger. Social psychologists have found that it often depends on the circumstances.

More than 30 years ago a young woman named Kitty Genovese was brutally murdered. She was attacked at about 3 a.m. in a respectable area of New York City. The murderer left and returned three times; he finally put an end to Kitty's life as she crawled to her apartment and screamed for help. It took the slayer about 30 minutes to kill Kitty. Thirty-eight neighbours watched the gory scene and heard Kitty Genovese's screams. No one helped or even called the police. This incident prompted social psychologists to study

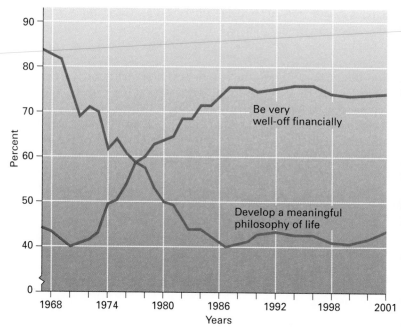

FIGURE 16.10

Changing First-year Student Life Goals, 1968–2001
In the past three decades, a significant change has occurred in first-year students' life goals. A far greater percentage of today's first-year university students state that a "very important" life goal is to be well-off financially; far fewer state that developing a meaningful philosophy of life is a "very important" life goal.

the **bystander effect**, the tendency for individuals who observe an emergency to help less when other people are present than when the observers are alone. The bystander effect helps to explain the apparent cold-blooded indifference to Kitty Genovese's murder.

Social psychologists John Darley and Bibb Latané (1968) first documented the bystander effect in a number of simulated criminal and medical emergencies. Most of the bystander intervention studies show that, when alone, a person will help 75 percent of the time, but when another bystander is present, the figure drops to 50 percent. Apparently the difference is due to the diffusion of responsibility among witnesses and the tendency to look to the behaviour of others for clues about what to do. We may think that someone else will call the police or that, because no one else is helping, possibly the person does not need help.

Many other aspects of the situation influence whether the individual will intervene and come to the aid of the person in distress. Bystander intervention is less likely to occur in the following situations (Shotland, 1985; Penner & others, 2005):

- The situation is not clear.
- The individuals struggling or fighting appear to be married or related.
- The victim is perceived to be intoxicated.
- The victim is thought to be from a different ethnic group.
- Intervention might lead to personal harm or retaliation by the criminal.
- Helping requires considerable time, such as days in court testifying.
- Bystanders have no prior history of victimization themselves, have seen few crimes and intervention efforts, or have not had training in first aid, rescue, or police tactics.

Trends in Altruistic Behaviour How altruistic are people today? Are they less altruistic than they were several decades ago? Over the past two decades, university students have shown an increased concern for personal well-being and a decreased concern for the well-being of others, especially the disadvantaged (Sax & others, 2003). And, as shown in figure 16.10, today's first-year university students are more strongly motivated to be well-off financially and less motivated to develop a meaningful philosophy of life than their counterparts were some 30 years ago (Sax & others, 2001).

However, today's university students also show some signs of shifting toward a stronger interest in the welfare of our society. For example, between 1986 and 1998, there was an increase in the percentage of first-year university students who said they were strongly interested in participating in community action programs (16.9 percent

bystander effect The concept that individuals who observe an emergency help less when someone else is present than when they are alone.

in 1990 compared to 25.3 percent in 2003; Sax & others, 2003). These trends are a good sign. For successful adjustment in adult life, it is important to seek self-fulfillment *and* to have a strong commitment to others.

Altruism and Gender Who are more helping and caring, males or females? The stereotype is that females are. However, as in most domains, it is a good idea to think about gender in context (Eagly, Beall, & Sternberg, 2004).

Researchers have found that females are more likely than males to help when the context involves nurturing, as when volunteering time to help a child with a personal problem. For example, in North America women are more likely than men to volunteer (Penner & others, 2005). However, males are more likely to help in situations in which a perceived danger is present and they feel competent to help (Eagly & Crowley, 1986). For example, males are more likely than females to help a person who is stranded by the roadside with a flat tire. An automobile problem is an area in which many males feel a sense of competence. Males are also more likely than females to give a ride to a hitchhiker, because of the perceived danger in this situation.

> ### reflect and review

 Explain how aggression and altruism characterize social interaction.

- Discuss the influence of aggressive behaviour.
- Describe what social psychologists know about altruism.

Analyze the acts of altruism surrounding the September 11, 2001, terrorist attacks. Can you determine which acts likely were altruistic and which acts likely were egoistic?

---

⑤ RELATIONSHIPS

— Attraction — Love — Relationships — Loneliness
and Gender

What is the nature of relationships?

Our close relationships are among the most important aspects of our lives. In some cases, these relationships are extremely positive, in others they can be highly conflicted (Harvey & Weber, 2002). Perhaps worst of all is the lack of relationships, which creates the deeply unsettling feeling of loneliness.

Social psychologists have explored several aspects of social relationships. Attraction, love, and intimacy are key dimensions (Berscheid & Regan, 2005). This section begins with a discussion on the formation of relationships.

Attraction

What attracts us to others and motivates us to spend more time with them? Does just being around someone increase the likelihood a relationship will develop? Or are we likely to seek out and associate with those who are similar to us? How important is physical attraction in the initial stages of a relationship?

Familiarity and Similarity Familiarity breeds contempt, as the old saying goes, but social psychologists have found that familiarity is a necessary condition for a close relationship to develop. For the most part, friends and lovers are people who have been around each other for a long time; they may have grown up together, gone to high school or university together, worked together, or gone to the same social events (Brehm, 2002).

Once we have been exposed to someone for a while, what is it that creates friendship and even love? Another old saying, "Birds of a feather flock together," also helps to explain attraction. One of the most powerful lessons generated by the study of close relationships is that we like to associate with people who are similar to us (Berscheid, 2000; Berscheid & Regan, 2005). Our friends and lovers are much more like us than unlike us. We have similar attitudes, behaviour patterns, and personal characteristics, as well as similar taste in clothes, intelligence, personality, other friends, values, lifestyle, physical attractiveness, and so on. In some limited cases and on some isolated characteristics, opposites may attract. An introvert may wish to be with an extravert, or someone with little money may wish to associate with someone who has a lot of money, for example. But overall we are attracted to individuals with similar rather than opposite characteristics. One study, for example, found that depressed university students preferred to meet unhappy others, whereas nondepressed university students preferred to meet happy others (Wenzlaff & Prohaska, 1989). The fact that individuals are attracted to each other on the basis of similar characteristics and attitudes is reflected in the questions that computer dating services ask their clients.

The concept of *consensual validation* explains why people are attracted to others who are similar to them. Our own attitudes and behaviour are supported when someone else's attitudes and behaviour are similar to ours—their attitudes and behaviour validate ours. Another reason that similarity matters is that people tend to shy away from the unknown. We often prefer to be around people whose attitudes and behaviour we can predict. And similarity implies that we will enjoy doing things with another person who likes the same things and has similar attitudes. In several studies, this sort of similarity was shown to be important in successful marriages (Swann, De La Ronde, & Hixon, 1994; Priest & Thein, 2003).

Physical Attraction   You may be thinking at this point that something is missing from our discussion of attraction. As important as familiarity and similarity may be, they do not explain the spark that often ignites a romantic relationship: physical attraction (Mehrabian & Blum, 2003).

How important is physical attraction in a romantic relationship? According to advertising agencies it is the most important factor in establishing and maintaining a relationship. Perhaps in guilty agreement, people intentionally under-report the impact of physical attractiveness on their dating preferences (Hadjistavropoulos & Genest, 1994). However, people do differ on the importance they place on good looks when they seek an intimate partner (Dion & Dion, 1995). According to Shackelford, Schmitt, & Buss (2005), cross-cultural data reveal that men are more likely than women to value physical attractiveness when choosing a mate. They also found that physical attractiveness was only one consideration when choosing a mate. Others include: love, status, dependability, education, and desire for a home and family.

Complicating research on the role of physical attraction in romantic relationships is changing standards of what is deemed attractive. The criteria for beauty can differ, not just *across* cultures, but over time *within* cultures as well (Lamb & others, 1993). In the 1950s, the ideal of female beauty in North America was typified by the well-rounded figure of Marilyn Monroe. As a result of the current preoccupation with health, Monroe's 60-kilo, 160-centimetre physique is regarded as overweight by today's standards. Today, the ideal physique for both men and women is neither pleasingly plump nor extremely slender. Instead, a low body-fat physically fit shape has become desirable among both men and women.

Social psychologists have found that the force of similarity also operates at a physical level. We usually seek out someone at our own level of attractiveness in both physical characteristics and social attributes. Research validates the *matching hypothesis*—which states that, although we may prefer a more attractive person in the abstract, in the real world we end up choosing someone who is close to our own level (Kalick & Hamilton, 1986; Wong & others, 1991).

We should take some of these findings with a grain of salt. Much of the research on physical attraction has focused on initial or short-term encounters; researchers have not

Eric Stoltz's portrayal of Rocky Dennis in the movie *Mask*. Rocky was unloved and unwanted as a young child because of his grotesque features. But, as his mother and peers got to know him, they became attracted to him.

DILBERT reprinted by permission of United Feature Syndicate, Inc.

often evaluated attraction over the course of months and years. As relationships endure, physical attraction assumes less importance. Rocky Dennis, as portrayed in the movie *Mask*, is a case in point. His peers and even his mother initially wanted to avoid Rocky, whose face was severely distorted, but over the course of his childhood and adolescent years, the avoidance turned into attraction and love as people got to know him. As Rocky's story demonstrates, familiarity can overcome even severely negative initial reactions to a person.

Love

Some relationships never progress much beyond the attraction stage. But some relationships deepen to friendship and perhaps to love in one of its guises (Vohs & Baumeister, 2004; Harvey & Weber, 2002). Three types of love that have been described by social psychologists are romantic love, affectionate love, and consummate love.

Romantic Love **Romantic love** is also called *passionate love*. Poets, playwrights, and musicians through the ages have lauded the fiery passion of romantic love—and lamented the searing pain when it fails. Think for a moment about songs and books that hit the top of the charts. Chances are they are about love. When we say we are "in love," we mean romantic love, and for most of us, this means physical, sexual attraction. Although sexual desire and romantic love often co-occur, they are not identical. Sexual desire is related to the short-term concern of sexual mating while romantic love is related to the long-term concern of pair-bonding (Diamond, 2004).

Romantic love is especially important among university students (Berscheid & Regan, 2005). One study of unattached university men and women found that over half identified a romantic partner, rather than a parent, sibling, or friend, as their closest relationship (Bersheid, Snyder, & Omoto, 1989). Another study found that romantic loves were more likely than friends to be the cause of depression (Berscheid & Fei, 1977).

University of Toronto psychologists Kenneth and Karen Dion found that people with an individual (as opposed to collective) value orientation were less likely to have experienced romantic love. When individualistic people did experience romantic love, they experienced less affective involvement with their partners (Dion & Dion, 1991).

Paradoxically, in societies with an individual value orientation (such as Canada and the U.S.), greater stress is placed on romantic love and personal fulfillment in marriage than in societies with a collective value orientation (such as China and India). This may be because psychological individualism makes achieving romantic love more difficult (and hence desirable) whereas in societies with a collective value orientation intimacy is likely to be diffused across a network of family relationships (Dion & Dion, 1993).

Affectionate Love Love is more than just passion. **Affectionate love**, also called *companionate love*, is the type of love that occurs when someone desires to have the other person near and has a deep, caring affection for the person.

romantic love Also called passionate love; the type of love that has strong components of sexuality and infatuation and often predominates in the early part of a love relationship.

affectionate love Also called companionate love; the type of love that occurs when individuals desire to have the other person near and have a deep, caring affection for the person.

There is a growing belief that the early stages of love have more romantic ingredients but that as love matures passion tends to give way to affection (Berscheid & Reis, 1998; Harvey & Weber, 2002). The initial phase of romantic love is a time that is fuelled by a mixture of sexual attraction and gratification, a reduced sense of loneliness, uncertainty about the security of developing an attachment, and excitement from exploring the novelty of another human being. With time sexual attraction wanes, attachment anxieties either lessen or produce conflict and withdrawal, and novelty is replaced with familiarity.

Couples who experience the secure attachment of a deeply caring affectionate love report higher levels of life satisfaction compared to couples still experiencing romantic love (Kim & Hatfield, 2004). Other couples become distressed—feeling bored, disappointed, lonely, or hostile, for example. In the latter case, one or both partners may eventually seek a different close relationship.

Consummate Love   So far we have discussed two forms of love: romantic (or passionate) and affectionate (or companionate). Robert J. Sternberg (1988) described a third form of love, *consummate love*, which he said is the strongest, fullest type of love. Sternberg proposed that love can be thought of as a triangle with three main dimensions—passion, intimacy, and commitment. Passion, as described earlier, is physical and sexual attraction to another. Intimacy is emotional feelings of warmth, closeness, and sharing in a relationship. Commitment is our cognitive appraisal of the relationship and our intent to maintain the relationship even in the face of problems (Rusbult & others, 2001).

Sternberg's theory states that the ideal form of love involves all three dimensions (see figure 16.11). If passion is the only ingredient in a relationship (with intimacy and commitment low or absent), we are merely *infatuated*. An affair or a fling in which there is little intimacy and even less commitment would be an example. A relationship marked by intimacy and commitment but low or lacking in passion is *affectionate love*, a pattern often found among couples who have been married for many years. If passion and commitment are present but intimacy is not, Sternberg calls the relationship *fatuous love*, as when one person worships another from a distance. But if couples share all three dimensions—passion, intimacy, and commitment—they will experience consummate love.

The Personal Reflections box, "What Is Your Love Like?" will help you determine what kind of relationship you have with a particular person in your life.

Passion

FIGURE 16.11

Sternberg's Triangle of Love.
Sternberg identified three dimensions that shape the experience we call love: passion, intimacy, and commitment. Various combinations of the three dimensions produce particular types of love.

Types of Love	Passion	Intimacy	Commitment
Infatuation	Present	Absent or low	Absent or low
Companionate (affectionate) love	Absent or low	Present	Present
Fatuous love	Present	Absent or low	Present
Consummate love	Present	Present	Present

Present   Absent or low

What Is Your Love Like?

Imagine the blank spaces filled in with the name of one person you love or care about deeply. Then rate each of the items from 1 to 9 with 1 = not at all, 5 = moderately, and 9 = extremely.

_____ 1. I actively support _____'s well-being.

_____ 2. I have a warm relationship with _____.

_____ 3. I can count on _____ in times of need.

_____ 4. _____ is able to count on me in times of need.

_____ 5. I am willing to share myself and my possessions with _____.

_____ 6. I receive considerable emotional support from _____.

_____ 7. I give considerable emotional support to _____.

_____ 8. I communicate well with _____.

_____ 9. I value _____ greatly in my life.

_____ 10. I feel close to _____.

_____ 11. I have a comfortable relationship with _____.

_____ 12. I feel that I really understand _____.

_____ 13. I feel that _____ really understands me.

_____ 14. I feel that I can really trust _____.

_____ 15. I share deeply personal information about myself with _____.

_____ 16. Just seeing _____ excites me.

_____ 17. I find myself thinking about _____ frequently during the day.

_____ 18. My relationship with _____ is very romantic.

_____ 19. I find _____ to be very personally attractive.

_____ 20. I idealize _____.

_____ 21. I cannot imagine another person making me as happy as _____.

_____ 22. I would rather be with _____ than anyone.

_____ 23. There is nothing more important to me than my relationship with _____.

_____ 24. I especially like physical contact with _____.

_____ 25. There is something special about my relationship with _____.

_____ 26. I adore _____.

_____ 27. I cannot imagine my life without _____.

_____ 28. My relationship with _____ is passionate.

_____ 29. When I see romantic movies and read romantic books I think of _____.

_____ 30. I fantasize about _____.

_____ 31. I know that I care about _____.

_____ 32. I am committed to maintaining my relationship with _____.

_____ 33. Because of my commitment to _____, I would not let other people come between us.

_____ 34. I have confidence in the stability of my relationship with _____.

_____ 35. I could not let anything get in the way of my commitment to _____.

_____ 36. I expect my love for _____ to last for the rest of my life.

_____ 37. I will always feel a strong responsibility for _____.

_____ 38. I view my commitment to _____ as a solid one.

_____ 39. I cannot imagine ending my relationship with _____.

_____ 40. I am certain of my love for _____.

_____ 41. I view my relationship with _____ as permanent.

_____ 42. I view my relationship with _____ as a good decision.

_____ 43. I feel a sense of responsibility toward _____.

_____ 44. I plan to continue my relationship with _____.

_____ 45. Even when _____ is hard to deal with, I remain committed to our relationship.

Add up your score for each of the three areas of love: 1–15 (intimacy), 16–30 (passion), and 31–45 (commitment). Below are the average scores of a group of women and men (average age 5 31) who either were married or in a close relationship:

Intimacy	Passion	Commitment	Percentile
93	73	85	15
102	85	96	30
111	98	108	50
120	110	120	70
129	123	131	85

The fourth column (percentile) shows the percentage of adults who scored at that level or above. Thus, if your intimacy score is 122, your intimacy is greater than 70 percent of the adults whose scores are averaged here.

Relationships and Gender

Do women and men hold different views of love? One recent study found that men conceptualize love in terms of passion, whereas women think of love more in terms of friendship (Fehr & Broughton, 2001). However, both women and men view love in affectionate terms.

One aspect of relationships that seems to be linked to gender is caring (Brannon, 2005). Recall the discussion of Carol Gilligan's care perspective in chapter 4. Gilligan (1982, 2003) believes that social relationships are more important to females than they are to males and that females are more sensitive in social relationships. In contrast, she argues that males are more individualistic and self-oriented. Even as children, boys often define themselves apart from their caregivers and peers, whereas girls emphasize social ties. Researchers have indeed found that adult females are often caring, supporting, and empathic, whereas adult males are independent, self-reliant, and unexpressive (Brannon, 2005; Paludi, 2002). And, once the novelty, unpredictability, and urgency of sexual attraction in a love relationship have abated, women are more likely than men to detect deficiencies in caring that indicate the relationship has problems. Perhaps that sensitivity is why wives are almost twice as likely as husbands to initiate a divorce (U.S. National Center for Health Statistics, 2000a).

Another aspect of relationships that seems to be linked to gender is communication styles (Lips, 2003). Deborah Tannen (1990. 2001) highlighted the differences between women and men in her analyses of their talk. She reported that a common complaint women have about their husbands is, "He doesn't listen to me any more." Another is "He doesn't talk to me any more." Lack of communication, although high on women's lists of reasons for divorce, is much less often mentioned by men.

Tannen distinguishes between rapport talk and report talk. *Rapport talk* is the language of conversation. It is a way of establishing connections and negotiating relationships. Women prefer to engage in rapport talk. Women enjoy private conversations more than men do, and it is men's lack of interest in rapport talk that bothers many women. *Report talk* is talk that is designed to give information, which includes public speaking. Men prefer to engage in report talk. Men hold centre stage through such verbal performances as telling stories and jokes. They learn to use talk as a way of getting and keeping attention.

Tannen (1990, 2001) argues that these gender differences are the result of girls and boys being socialized differently as they grow up. Mothers have participated far more in rearing children than fathers have and have modelled a stronger interest in relationships when interacting with their daughters than when interacting with their sons. Tannen (1990, 2001) and others (Levant, 2001; Levant & Brooks, 1997) recommend that men develop a stronger interest in relationships and make women feel more comfortable in public speaking contexts. Tannen (1990, 2001) also recommends that women seek more report-talk opportunities, including speaking up in groups.

Many females show a stronger interest in relationships than many males do. *What has been your experience with the gender differences in relationship orientation that have been discussed? If you are a female, do you have a strong interest in relationships? If you are a male, do you have less interest in relationships than most females you know?*

Loneliness

In chapter 11, we described the importance of the motive for affiliation and relatedness. People have a basic human desire to seek the company of others (DiTommaso, Brannen, & Burgess, 2005). Because of this strong human tendency, people who do not interact with others in close relationships on a regular basis may feel lonely. Lonely people may feel that no one knows them very well. They might feel isolated and sense that they do not have anyone to turn to in times of need and stress.

Each of us has times in our lives when we feel lonely, but for some people loneliness is a chronic condition. More than just an unwelcome social situation, chronic loneliness is linked with impaired physical and mental health (Brehm, 2002; Cattan & others, 2005). Chronic loneliness can even lead to an early death (Cuijpers, 2001). In one study, lonely university students had higher levels of stress-related hormones and poorer sleep patterns than students who had relationships with others (Cacioppo & others, 2000).

Our society's emphasis on self-fulfillment and achievement, the importance we attach to commitment in relationships, and a decline in stable close relationships are among the reasons loneliness is common today. Researchers have found that married individuals are less lonely than their nonmarried counterparts (never married, divorced, or widowed) in studies conducted in more than 20 countries (Perlman & Peplau, 1998).

Males and females attribute their loneliness to different sources, with men tending to blame themselves an d women tending to blame external factors. Men are socialized to initiate relationships, whereas women are traditionally socialized to wait and then respond. Perhaps men blame themselves because they feel they should do something about their loneliness, whereas women wonder why no one calls.

How do you determine if you are lonely? Scales of loneliness, such as the UCLA Loneliness Scale ask you to respond to items such as "I don't feel in tune with the people around me" and "I can find companionship when I want it." If you consistently respond that you never or rarely feel in tune with people around you and rarely or can never find companionship when you want it, you are likely to fall into the category of people who are described as moderately or intensely lonely (Russell, 1996).

Loneliness and Life's Transitions Loneliness is interwoven with how people pass through life transitions, such as a move to a different part of the country, a divorce, or the death of a close friend or family member. Another situation that often creates loneliness is studying at university or college (Bauer & Rokach, 2004). When students leave the familiar world of their hometown and family to enter university, they can feel especially lonely. Many first-year university students feel anxious about meeting new people, and developing a new social life can create considerable anxiety. As one student commented,

> My first year here at the university has been pretty lonely. I wasn't lonely at all in high school. I lived in a fairly small town—I knew everybody and everyone knew me. I was a member of several clubs and played on the basketball team. It's not that way at the university. It is a big place and I've felt like a stranger on so many occasions. I'm starting to get used to my life here and the last few months I've been making myself meet people and get to know them, but it has not been easy.

As this comment illustrates, first-year students rarely bring their popularity and social standing from high school into the university environment. There may be a dozen high school basketball stars, Canadian Millennium scholars, and former student council presidents in a single dormitory wing. Especially if students attend university away from home, they face the task of forming completely new social relationships. Loneliness is not reserved for first-year students, though. Senior students are often lonely as well (Bauer & Rokach, 2004). In one study of more than 2600 undergraduates, lonely individuals were less likely to actively cope with stress than individuals who were able to make friends (Cacioppo & others, 2000).

Loneliness and Technology One of the factors that may be contributing to loneliness in contemporary society is technology (Morahan-Martin & Schumacher, 2003). Although the invention of the telephone more than a century ago seems to have decreased social isolation for many individuals and families, psychologists have found a link between TV viewing and loneliness (Perse & Rubin, 1990). Similarly, one study focused on 169 individuals during their first several years online (Kraut & others, 1998). In this study, greater use of the Internet was associated with declines in participants' communication with family members in the household and increases in depression and loneliness.

However, correlation does not equal causation. While it may seem plausible that television or the Internet can contribute to social disengagement, it is also possible that people who are lonelier turn to these media. Amichai-Hamburger & Ben-Artzi (2003) have provided evidence that lonely women use the Internet in an attempt to reduce their loneliness.

Further, as Amichai-Hamburger (2002) suggests, not everyone uses the Internet for the same purposes. Some people use the Internet to provide a safe way to begin contacts that eventually lead to face-to-face meetings and possibly even intimate relationships (Clay, 2000).

Strategies for Reducing Loneliness If you are lonely, how can you become better connected with others? Following are some strategies:

"What I'm trying to say, Mary, is that I want *your* site to be linked to *my* site."

© The New Yorker Collection 2000. Mick Stevens from cartoonbank.com. All Rights Reserved.

- *Participate in activities that you can do with others.* Join organizations or volunteer your time for a cause you believe in. You will likely get to know others whose views are similar to yours. Going to just one social gathering can help you develop social contacts. When you go, introduce yourself to others and start a conversation. Another strategy is to sit next to new people in your classes or find someone to study with.
- *Be aware of the early warning signs of loneliness.* People often feel bored or alienated before loneliness becomes pervasive. Head off loneliness by becoming involved in new social activities.
- *Draw a diagram of your social network.* Determine whether the people in the diagram meet your social needs. If not, pencil in the people you would like to get to know.
- *Engage in positive behaviours when you meet new people.* You will improve your chances of developing enduring relationships if, when you meet new people, you are nice, considerate, honest, trustworthy, and cooperative. Have a positive attitude, be supportive of the other person, and make positive comments about him or her.
- *See a counsellor or read a book on loneliness.* If you can't get rid of your loneliness on your own, you might want to contact the counselling services at your university or college. The counsellor can talk with you about strategies for reducing your loneliness. You also might want to read a good book on loneliness, such as *The Loneliness Workbook* by Mary Ellen Copeland (2000).

> **reflect and review**

 Understand the nature of relationships.

- Describe the factors involved in attraction.
- Identify three types of love.
- Explain how gender affects relationships.
- Discuss some causes of loneliness and strategies for reducing it.

Think about the people to whom you are attracted. What is it about them that attracts you?

You have arrived at the end of this book. You should be able to look back and say you have learned a lot about both yourself and other human beings. You should also see that, although many unanswered questions remain, psychology's quest to understand human behaviour produces information we can use to make our lives more enjoyable and humane. What could be more intriguing and important to all of us than psychology's mission of describing, explaining, and predicting the behaviour of the human species?

Social Psychology

1 SOCIAL THINKING

— Attribution — Social Perception — Attitudes

2 SOCIAL INFLUENCE

— Conformity and Obedience — Group Influence — Leadership

3 INTERGROUP RELATIONS

— Group Identity: Us Versus Them — Prejudice — Ways to Improve Interethnic Relations

4 SOCIAL INTERACTION

— Aggression — Altruism

5 RELATIONSHIPS

— Attraction — Love — Relationships and Gender — Loneliness

At the beginning of the chapter, we posed six chapter questions and encouraged you to review material related to these questions at the end of each major section (see pages 646, 656, 664, 674, and 681). Use the following reflection and review features for further your understanding of the chapter material.

CHAPTER REFLECTIONS

1. We're often unaware of how many attributions we make about the behaviour of others. To demonstrate this to yourself, spend some time in a crowded area observing the interactions of others (or you could watch some scenes in television shows or movies). Take careful notes about the social behaviours that occur and then indicate your impression of why the people behaved the way they did. What cues did you use to make your decision about their behaviour? Did your knowledge of the fundamental attribution error influence your attributions?

2. The text discusses stereotyping and prejudice as two factors affecting intergroup relations. Many of our stereotypes and prejudices are quite subtle, and we can be unaware of them. To help you better appreciate the effects of these subtle influences, search the Web for the phrase "implicit association test" and take one of the tests (or go to https://implicit.harvard.edu/implicit/). Knowing the results, how can you use the suggestions in the text to change your attitudes or behaviour?

3. Find a movie that shows an example of aggression (or altruism). Look at the scene and assess the influences that caused the characters to behave aggressively (or altruistically). In what ways are these influences consistent with those discussed in the text, and in what ways do they differ?

4. Many of the conclusions about the nature of relationships are based on correlational studies. Discuss the factors that contribute to the difficulty of conducting experiments on relationships, and describe an experiment that you might conduct to test one of the factors described as contributing to attraction or loneliness.

CHAPTER REVIEW

Describe how people think about the social world.

- Attributions are our thoughts about why people behave the way they do and about who or what is responsible for the outcome of events. Attribution theory views people as motivated to discover the causes of behaviour as part of their effort to make sense of it. The dimensions that we use to make sense of the causes of human behaviour include internal/external, stable/unstable, and controllable/uncontrollable. The fundamental attribution error states that observers overestimate the importance of traits and underestimate the importance of situations when they seek explanations of an actor's behaviour. When our self-esteem is threatened, we might depart from the fundamental attribution error and engage in a self-serving bias, attributing our successes to internal causes and our failures to external causes.

- Social perception involves the impressions we develop of others, comparisons of ourselves with others, and presentation of ourselves to others to influence others' perceptions. Our impressions of others are unified and integrated. An individual's notions of which traits go together is called implicit personality theory. We use social schemas, or prototypes, to evaluate others. We simplify our impressions by categorizing others. In some instances, though, we develop a more individualized approach to impressions. First impressions are important and influence later impressions. As for social comparison, we evaluate ourselves by comparison with others. Festinger stresses that social comparison is an important source of self-knowledge, especially when no other objective means is available. We tend to compare ourselves with similar others. Self-presentation to influence others' social perceptions includes two dimensions: impression management to present a favourable self-image and self-monitoring to fine-tune the impressions we are making.

- Attitudes are beliefs or opinions about people, objects, and ideas. We are better able to predict behaviour from attitudes when the person's attitudes are strong, when the person is very aware of his or her attitudes and expresses them often, and when the attitudes are specifically relevant to the behaviour. Sometimes changes in behaviour precede changes in attitude. Cognitive dissonance theory, developed by Festinger, argues that we have a strong need for cognitive consistency. We change our attitudes to make them more consistent with our behaviour in order to reduce dissonance. In many cases, we reduce dissonance by justifying our actions. Justification is most intense when self-esteem is involved. Bem's more behavioural approach, called self-perception theory, stresses the importance of making inferences about attitudes by observing our own behaviour, especially when our attitudes are not clear. Success in changing someone's attitudes may involve the communicator (source), the message, the medium, and the target (audience).

Identify how people are influenced in social settings.

- Conformity involves a change in a person's behaviour to coincide with a group standard. Asch's classic study on judgments of line length illustrated the power of conformity. Many factors influence whether we will conform, including normative social influence and informational social influence. Obedience is behaviour that complies with the explicit demands of an individual in authority. Milgram's classic experiment demonstrated the power of obedience. Participants obeyed the experimenter's directions even though they thought they were hurting someone. As we go through our lives, we are both conformist and non-conformist, obedient and not obedient. Sometimes we are overwhelmed by persuasion. At other times, we exert personal control and resist such influence.

- Groups satisfy our personal needs, reward us, provide us with information, raise our self-esteem, and enhance our identity. Every group has norms and rules. Our performance in groups can be improved through social facilitation and lowered because of social loafing. In a group, we also can experience deindividuation—a loss of personal identity and a decrease in responsibility. The risky shift is the tendency for a group decision to be riskier than the average decision made by the individual group members. The group polarization effect is the solidification and further strengthening of a position as a consequence of group discussion. Groupthink involves impaired decision making and avoidance of realistic appraisal to maintain harmony in the group. The majority usually gets its way in group influence, but occasionally the minority has its day.

- Theories of group leadership include the great-person theory (leaders are born), the situational approach (leaders are made), and the person-situation view, known as the contingency model of leadership (leaders are people who have the ability to take charge when the situation requires it). As leaders, men tend to be more directive and task-

oriented, whereas women are more likely to be more democratic and interpersonally oriented.

Discuss intergroup relations.

- Social identity is how we define ourselves in terms of our group memberships. Tajfel proposed social identity theory, which states that when individuals are assigned to a group they invariably think of it as the in-group, or "we." Identifying with the group allows them to have a positive self-image. Ethnocentrism is the tendency to favour one's own group over other groups. Ethnocentrism can have positive or negative outcomes.

- Prejudice is an unjustified negative attitude toward an individual based on the individual's membership in a group. Among the reasons given for why people develop prejudice are an individual's personality (authoritarian), competition between groups over scarce resources, motivation to enhance one's self-esteem, cognitive processes that contribute to a tendency to categorize and stereotype others, and cultural learning. Prejudice is based on stereotyping, a generalization about a group's characteristics that does not consider any variations from one individual to the next. The cognitive process of stereotyping can lead to discrimination, an unjustified negative or harmful action toward a member of a group simply because he or she is a member of that group. It can also lead to stereotype threat, the extra pressure members of stereotyped groups feel when they are in stereotype confirming situations. Discrimination results when negative emotional reactions combine with prejudiced beliefs and are translated into behaviour.

- Contact between ethnic groups, by itself, does not decrease conflict and improve relations. Two effective strategies are to set up task-oriented cooperation and for members of different ethnic groups to share intimate information.

Explain how aggression and altruism characterize social interaction.

- One view of the biological basis of aggression is that, early in human evolution, the most aggressive individuals were likely to be the survivors. Freud proposed an instinct theory of aggression, but that view has not been supported. There is some evidence for the genetic basis of aggression, however. Neurobiological factors involved in aggressive behaviour include the amygdala, the neurotransmitter serotonin, alcohol's disinhibiting effects, and hormones. Psychological factors in aggression include frustrating and aversive circumstances, expectations, equity, intentions, responsibility, and reinforcement and observational learning. Sociocultural factors include cross-cultural variations and the extensive violence North American children watch on TV. Gender is also a factor. Males are consistently more physically aggressive than females, but gender differences in verbal aggression are not consistent.

- Altruism is an unselfish interest in helping someone else. Reciprocity is often involved in altruism. The motivation for helping others can be altruistic or egoistic. Psychologists have studied both person and situation variables in altruism. Evolutionary psychologists stress that altruism increases prospects of survival, as well as reproduction. Evolutionary examples involve favouritism toward kin, as well as a parental care for offspring. The bystander effect is the concept that individuals who observe an emergency help less when someone else is present than when they are alone. The altruistic behaviour of university students has fluctuated over the years. When examining the link between altruism and gender, context is important. Females are likelier to help in situations that are not dangerous and involve care giving. Males are likelier to help in situations that involve danger or in which they feel competent.

Understand the nature of relationships.

- Familiarity precedes a close relationship. We also like to associate with people who are similar to us.

The principles of consensual validation and matching can explain the appeal of similarity. Physical attraction is usually more important in the early part of a relationship. Criteria for physical attractiveness vary across cultures and over time.

- Romantic love (or passionate love) is involved when we say we are "in love." It includes passion, sexuality, and a mixture of emotions, not all of which are positive. Affectionate love (or companionate love) is the type of love that usually becomes more important as relationships mature. Sternberg proposed a triarchic model of love involving passion, intimacy, and commitment. Consummate love occurs in relationships in which all three elements are present.

- Females have a stronger interest in relationships than males do. Tannen suggests that another gender difference in relationships relates to communication styles. Females prefer rapport talk, and males prefer report talk.

- Men tend to blame themselves for their loneliness, whereas women tend to blame external sources. Loneliness often emerges when people make life transitions, so it is not surprising that loneliness is common among first-year university students. Technology, such as the telephone, television, and the Internet, can affect loneliness. A number of strategies can help to reduce loneliness, including participating in activities that one can do with others and taking positive steps to meet new people.

For extra help in mastering the material in the chapter, see the review questions and practice quizzes in the Student Study Guide and the Online Learning Centre.

CORE TERMS

social psychology, p. 635
attribution theory, p. 636
fundamental attribution error, p. 637
implicit personality theory, p. 639
impression management (self-presentation), p. 640
self-monitoring, p. 641
attitudes, p. 642
cognitive dissonance, p. 642
self-perception theory, p. 644
elaboration likelihood model, p. 645

conformity, p. 647
normative social influence, p. 648
informational social influence, p. 648
obedience, p. 648
social facilitation, p. 651
social loafing, p. 652
deindividuation, p. 652
risky shift, p. 652
group polarization effect, p. 653
groupthink, p. 653
social identity, p. 656

social identity theory, p. 656
ethnocentrism, p. 658
prejudice, p. 659
stereotype, p. 660
discrimination, p. 661
altruism, p. 671
egoism, p. 671
bystander effect, p. 673
romantic love, p. 676
affectionate love, p. 676

Glossary

A

abnormal behaviour Behaviour that is deviant, maladaptive, or personally distressful. p. 511

absolute threshold The minimum amount of stimulus energy that people can detect. p. 179

accommodation Occurs when individuals adjust their schemas to new information. p. 128

acculturative stress The negative consequences that result from contact between two distinctive cultural groups. p. 601

achievement tests Tests that measure what a person has learned or the skills that a person has mastered. p. 390

acquired immunodeficiency syndrome (AIDS) Caused by the human immunodeficiency virus (HIV), a sexually transmitted disease that destroys the body's immune system. p. 627

acquisition (in classical conditioning) The initial learning of the stimulus-response link, which involves a neutral stimulus being associated with a UCS and becoming a conditioned stimulus (CS) that elicits the CR. p. 270

action potential The brief wave of electrical charge that sweeps down the axon during the transmission of a nerve impulse. p. 85

activation-synthesis theory States that dreaming occurs when the cerebral cortex synthesizes neural signals emanating from activity in the lower part of the brain. p. 246

addiction A pattern of behaviour characterized by an overwhelming need to use the drug and to secure its supply. p. 259

adrenal glands Important endocrine glands that are instrumental in regulating moods, energy level, and the ability to cope with stress. p. 104

advance organizer A reference frame for encountering new information that results in better comprehension and memory for textual material. p. 32

aerobic exercise Sustained exercise that stimulates heart and lung activity. p. 622

affectionate love Also called companionate love; the type of love that occurs when individuals desire to have the other person near and have a deep, caring affection for the person. p. 676

afferent nerves Sensory nerves that transport information to the brain. p. 81

agonist A drug that mimics or increases a neurotransmitter's effects. p. 88

agoraphobia A cluster of fears centred around public places and being unable to escape or to find help should one become incapacitated. p. 519

alcoholism A disorder that involves long-term, repeated, uncontrolled, compulsive, and excessive use of alcoholic beverages and that impairs the drinker's health and work and social relationships. p. 255

algorithms Strategies that guarantee a solution to a problem. p. 355

all-or-none principle Once an electrical impulse reaches a certain level of intensity, it fires and moves all the way down the axon without losing any of its intensity. p. 85

altruism An unselfish interest in helping someone else. p. 671

amnesia The loss of memory. p. 337

androgens The main class of male sex hormones. pp. 145, 435

anorexia nervosa An eating disorder that involves the relentless pursuit of thinness through starvation. p. 433

antagonist A drug that blocks a neurotransmitter's effects. p. 88

anterograde amnesia A memory disorder that affects the retention of new information or events p. 337

antianxiety drugs Commonly known as tranquilizers, they reduce anxiety by making people calmer and less excitable. p. 554

antidepressant drugs Drugs that regulate mood. p. 555

antipsychotic drugs Powerful drugs that diminish agitated behaviour, reduce tension, decrease hallucinations, improve social behaviour, and produce better sleep patterns in people who have a severe psychological disorder, such as schizophrenia. p. 556

anxiety disorders Psychological disorders that include these features: motor tension, hyperactivity, and apprehensive expectations and thoughts. p. 518

apparent movement The perception that a stationary object is moving. p. 200

applied behaviour analysis (behaviour modification) The application of operant conditioning principles to change human behaviour. p. 287

approach/approach conflict A conflict in which the individual must choose between two attractive stimuli or circumstances. p. 599

approach/avoidance conflict A conflict involving a single stimulus or circumstance that has both positive and negative characteristics. p. 599

aptitude tests Tests that predict an individual's ability to learn. p. 390

archetypes The name Jung gave to the emotionally laden ideas and images in the collective unconscious that have rich and symbolic meaning. p. 478

artificial intelligence (AI) The science of creating machines capable of performing activities that require intelligence when they are done by people. p. 349

assimilation Occurs when individuals incorporate new information into existing knowledge. p. 128

association cortex Region of the cerebral cortex in which the highest intellectual functions, including thinking and problem solving, occur (also called association areas). p. 96

associative learning Learning in which a connection is made between two events. p. 268

Atkinson-Shiffrin theory The view that memory involves a sequence of three stages: sensory memory, short-term memory, and long-term memory. p. 309

attachment The close emotional bond between an infant and its caregiver. p. 136

attitudes Beliefs or opinions about people, objects, and ideas. p. 642

attribution theory Views people as motivated to discover the underlying causes of behaviour as part of their effort to make sense of the behaviour. pp. 443, 636

auditory nerve Carries neural impulses to the brain's auditory area. p. 206

authoritarian parenting A restrictive, punitive style in which the parent exhorts the child to follow the parent's directions and value hard work and effort. p. 139

authoritative parenting A parenting style that encourages children's independence (but still places limits and controls on their behaviour), includes extensive verbal give-and-take, and warm and nurturant interactions with the child. p. 139

automatic processes States of consciousness that require little attention and do not interfere with other ongoing activities. p. 230

autonomic nervous system Division of the PNS that communicates with the body's internal organs. It consists of the sympathetic and parasympathetic nervous systems. p. 80

availability heuristic A prediction about the probability of an event based on the frequency of the event's past occurrences. p. 365

aversive conditioning A classical conditioning treatment which consists of repeated pairings of the undesirable behaviour with aversive stimuli to decrease the behaviour's rewards. p. 568

avoidance/avoidance conflict A conflict in which the individual must choose between two unattractive stimuli or circumstances. p. 599

axon The part of the neuron that carries information away from the cell body to other cells; each neuron has only one axon. p. 83

B

barbiturates Depressant drugs that decrease the activity of the central nervous system. p. 255

basal ganglia Located above the thalamus and under the cerebral cortex, these large clusters of neurons work with the cerebellum and the cerebral cortex to control and coordinate voluntary movements p. 93

basal metabolism rate (BMR) The minimal amount of energy an individual uses in a resting state. p. 430

basic-skills-and-phonetics approach Stresses that reading instruction should emphasize the basic rules for translating written patterns into sounds. p. 378

behaviour Everything we do that can be directly observed. p. 5

behaviour modification The application of operant conditioning principles to change human behaviour; especially to replace unacceptable, maladaptive behaviours with acceptable, adaptive behaviours. p. 569

behaviour therapy Uses principles of learning to reduce or eliminate maladaptive behaviour. Emphasis on self-healing capacities. p. 565

behavioural approach Emphasizes the scientific study of behaviour and asserts that behaviour is shaped by the environment. p. 9

behavioural medicine An interdisciplinary field that focuses on developing and integrating behavioural and biomedical knowledge to promote health and reduce illness. p. 594

behavioural neuroscience approach Views understanding the brain and nervous system as central to understanding behaviour, thought, and emotion. p. 12

belief perseverance The tendency to hold on to a belief in the face of contradictory evidence. p. 364

big five factors of personality Openness to experience, conscientiousness, extroversion, agreeableness, and neuroticism (emotional stability). p. 492

binding The bringing together and integration of what is processed through different pathways or cells. p. 192

binocular cues Depth cues that are based on the combination of the images on the left and right eyes and on the way the two eyes work together. p. 197

biofeedback The process in which individuals' muscular or visceral activities are monitored by instruments. The information from the instruments is fed back to the individuals so that they can learn to voluntarily control their physiological activities. p. 621

biological rhythms Periodic physiological fluctuations in the body. p. 233

biological therapies Treatments to reduce or eliminate the symptoms of psychological disorders by altering the way an individual's body functions. p. 554

bipolar disorder A mood disorder characterized by extreme mood swings that include one or more episodes of mania. p. 531

bottom-up processing Processing that begins with sensory receptors registering environmental information and sending it to the brain for integration and cognitive processing. p. 176

brain stem The region of the brain that includes most of the hindbrain (excluding the cerebellum) and the midbrain. p. 91

bulimia nervosa An eating disorder in which the individual consistently follows a binge-and-purge eating pattern. p. 433

burnout A feeling of overload, including mental and physical exhaustion, that usually results from a gradual accumulation of everyday stresses. p. 600

bystander effect The concept that individuals who observe an emergency help less when someone else is present than when they are alone. p. 673

C

Cannon-Bard theory States that emotion and physiological states occur simultaneously. p. 453

case study An in-depth look at a single individual. p. 52

catatonic schizophrenia A type of schizophrenia that is characterized by bizarre motor behaviour, which sometimes takes the form of a completely immobile stupor. p. 540

catharsis The release of anger or aggressive energy by directly or vicariously engaging in anger or aggression; the catharsis hypothesis states that behaving angrily or watching others behave angrily reduces subsequent anger. pp. 462, 561

cell body Part of the neuron that contains the nucleus, which directs the manufacture of substances that the neuron needs for growth and maintenance. p. 82

central nervous system (CNS) The brain and spinal cord. p. 80

cerebral cortex Highest level of the forebrain, where the highest mental functions, such as thinking and planning, take place. p. 95

chromosomes Threadlike structures that contain genes and DNA. Humans have 23 chromosome pairs in the nucleus of every cell. Each parent contributes one chromosome to each pair. p. 105

circadian rhythms Daily behavioural or physiological cycles, such as the sleep/wake cycle. p. 234

classical conditioning Learning by which a neutral stimulus becomes associated with a meaningful stimulus and acquires the capacity to elicit a similar response. p. 269

classical model States that all instances of a concept share defining properties. p. 352

client-centred therapy Rogers's humanistic therapy in which the therapist provides a warm, supportive atmosphere to improve the client's self-concept and encourage the client to gain insight about problems. p. 564

cognition The way in which information is processed and manipulated in remembering, thinking, and knowing. p. 348

cognitive appraisal Lazarus's term for individuals' interpretation of events in their lives as threatening, harmful, or challenging and their determination of whether they have the resources to effectively cope with the events. p. 606

cognitive approach Focuses on the mental processes involved in knowing: how we direct our attention, perceive, remember, think, and solve problems. p. 11

cognitive dissonance A concept developed by Festinger that refers to an individual's motivation to reduce the discomfort (dissonance) caused by two inconsistent thoughts. p. 642

cognitive theory of dreaming Proposes that dreaming can be understood by relying on the same cognitive processes that are used in studying the waking mind. p. 245

cognitive therapies Emphasize that individuals' cognitions or thoughts are the main source of abnormal behaviour and psychological problems. p. 570

cognitive-behaviour therapy Consists of a combination of cognitive therapy and behaviour therapy; self-efficacy is an important goal of cognitive-behaviour therapy. p. 573

collective unconscious Jung's term for the impersonal, deepest layer of the unconscious mind, shared by all human beings because of their common ancestral past. p. 478

concentrative meditation The practice of focusing attention, usually on the breath or a sound (mantra), in order to calm the mind and heighten awareness. p. 619

concepts Mental categories that are used to group objects, events, and characteristics. p. 350

concrete operational stage The third Piagetian stage of cognitive development (approximately 7 to 11 years of age) in which thought becomes operational, replacing intuitive thought with logical reasoning in concrete situations. p. 131

conditioned response (CR) The learned response to the conditioned stimulus that occurs after the CS-UCS pairing. p. 270

conditioned stimulus (CS) A previously neutral stimulus that eventually elicits the conditioned response after being associated with the unconditioned stimulus. p. 270

cones The receptors in the retina that process information about colour. p. 189

confirmation bias The tendency to search for and use information that supports, rather than refutes, our ideas. p. 364

conformity Involves a change in a person's behaviour to coincide more with a group standard. p. 647

connectionism (parallel distributed processing) The theory that memory is stored throughout the brain in connections between neurons, several of which may work together to process a single memory. p. 320

consciousness Awareness of external events and internal sensations, including awareness of the self and thoughts about one's experiences. p. 228

control group A comparison group that is treated in every way like the experimental group except for the manipulated factor. p. 55

controlled processes The most alert states of consciousness. p. 231

convergent thinking Thinking that produces one correct answer; characteristic of the type of thinking required on traditional intelligence tests. p. 405

coping Managing taxing circumstances, expending effort to solve life's problems, and seeking to master or reduce stress. p. 612

corpus callosum A large bundle of axons that connect the brain's two hemispheres. p. 98

correlational research Research with the goal of describing the strength of the relationship between two or more events or characteristics. p. 52

counterconditioning A classical conditioning procedure for weakening a CR by associating the fear-provoking stimulus with a new response that is incompatible with the fear. p. 274

couples therapy Therapy with married or unmarried couples whose major problem is within their relationship. p. 577

creativity The ability to think about something in novel and unusual ways and come up with unconventional solutions to problems. p. 405

critical thinking The process of thinking reflectively and productively, as well as evaluating evidence. p. 25

crystallized intelligence An individual's accumulated information and verbal skills. p. 161

culture-fair tests Intelligence tests that are intended to be culturally unbiased. p. 392

D

decay theory States that when something new is learned, a neurochemical memory trace is formed, but over time this trace tends to disintegrate. p. 335

decision making Involves evaluating alternatives and making choices among them. p. 363

deductive reasoning Reasoning from the general to the specific. p. 363

defence mechanisms The ego's protective methods for reducing anxiety by unconsciously distorting reality. p. 475

deindividuation Occurs when being part of a group reduces personal identity and the sense of responsibility. p. 652

dendrites Branches of a neuron that receive and orient information toward the cell body; most neurons have numerous dendrites. p. 82

deoxyribonucleic acid (DNA) A complex molecule that contains genetic information; makes up chromosomes. p. 106

dependent variable The factor that can change in an experiment in response to changes in the independent variable. p. 55

depressants Psychoactive drugs that slow down mental and physical activity. p. 253

depressive disorders Mood disorders in which the individual suffers depression without ever experiencing mania. p. 529

depth perception The ability to perceive objects three-dimensionally. p. 197

descriptive statistics Mathematical procedures that are used to describe and summarize samples of data in a meaningful way. p. 58

development The pattern of change in human capabilities that begins at conception and continues throughout the life span. p. 118

diathesis-stress model A model of schizophrenia that proposes a combination of biogenetic disposition and stress as the cause of the disorder. p. 544

difference threshold Also called just noticeable difference, this concept refers to the smallest difference in stimulation required to discriminate one stimulus from another 50 percent of the time. p. 181

discrimination An unjustified negative or harmful action toward a member of a group simply because he or she is a member of that group. pp. 279, 661

discrimination (in classical conditioning) The process of learning to respond to certain stimuli and not to others. p. 271

discrimination (in operant conditioning) The tendency to only respond to stimuli that signal whether a behaviour will or will not be reinforced. p. 271

disease model of addiction Describes addictions as biologically based, lifelong diseases that involve a loss of control over behaviour and require medical and/or spiritual treatment for recovery. p. 259

disorganized schizophrenia A type of schizophrenia in which an individual has delusions and hallucinations that have little or no recognizable meaning. p. 540

display rules Sociocultural standards that determine when, where, and how emotions should be expressed. p. 459

dissociative amnesia A dissociative disorder involving extreme memory loss caused by extensive psychological stress. p. 526

dissociative disorders Psychological disorders that involve a sudden loss of memory or change in identity. p. 526

dissociative fugue A dissociative disorder in which the individual not only develops amnesia but also unexpectedly travels away from home and establishes a new identity. p. 527

dissociative identity disorder (DID) Formerly called multiple personality disorder, this is the most dramatic but least common dissociative disorder; individuals suffering from this disorder have two or more distinct personalities. p. 527

divergent thinking Thinking that produces many answers to the same question; characteristic of creativity. p. 405

dominant-recessive genes principle If one gene of a pair governing a given characteristic (such as eye colour) is dominant and one is recessive, the dominant gene overrides the recessive gene. A recessive gene exerts its influence only if both genes in a pair are recessive. p. 106

double-blind experiment An experiment that is conducted so that neither the experimenter nor the participants are aware of which participants are in the experimental group and which are in the placebo control group until after the results are calculated. p. 57

dream analysis The psychotherapeutic technique used by psychoanalysts to interpret a person's dream. Psychoanalysts believe dreams contain information about the individual's unconscious thoughts and conflicts. p. 563

drive An aroused state that occurs because of a physiological need. p. 422

DSM-IV Diagnostic and Statistical Manual of Mental Disorders, fourth edition; the APA's major classification of psychological disorders. p. 514

dysthymic disorder A depressive disorder that is generally more chronic and has fewer symptoms than major depressive disorder. p. 529

E

efferent nerves Motor nerves that carry the brain's output. p. 81

ego The Freudian structure of personality that deals with the demands of reality. p. 474

egoism Giving to another person to ensure reciprocity, to gain self-esteem, to present oneself as powerful, competent, or caring, or to avoid social and self-censure for failing to live up to normative expectations. p. 671

elaboration The extensiveness of processing at any given level of memory. p. 307

elaboration likelihood model States that there are two ways to persuade-by a central route and by a peripheral route. p. 645

electroconvulsive therapy (ECT) Commonly called shock therapy, this treatment is used for severely depressed individuals; it causes a seizure to occur in the brain. p. 558

emotion Feeling, or affect, that can involve physiological arousal, conscious experience, and behavioural expression. p. 450

emotion-focused coping Lazarus's term for responding to stress in an emotional manner, especially using defensive appraisal. p. 612

emotional intelligence The ability to monitor one's own and others' emotions and feelings, to discriminate among them, and to use this information to guide one's thinking and actions. p. 400

empirically keyed test Relies on items to predict some criterion that discriminates between groups individually. p. 499

encoding The way in which information gets into memory storage. p. 305

endocrine system A set of glands that regulate the activities of certain organs by releasing hormones into the bloodstream. p. 104

episodic memory The retention of information about the where and when of life's happenings. p. 314

estrogens The main class of female sex hormones. pp. 145, 435

ethnic gloss Involves using an ethnic label, such as "Aboriginal" or "Asian," in a superficial way that portrays the ethnic group as more homogeneous than it really is. p. 67

ethnocentrism The tendency to favour one's own ethnic group over other groups. p. 658

evolutionary psychology approach Emphasizes the importance of functional purpose and adaptation in explaining why behaviours are formed, are modified, and survive. p. 13

experiment A carefully regulated procedure in which one or more factors believed to influence the behaviour being studied are manipulated and all other factors are held constant. p. 55

experimental group A group in a research study whose experience is manipulated. p. 55

experimenter bias The influence of the experimenter's own expectations on the outcome of the research. p. 56

explicit memory (declarative memory) The conscious recollection of information, such as specific facts or events and, at least in humans, information that can be verbally communicated. p. 314

extinction (in classical conditioning) The weakening of the conditioned response in the absence of the unconditioned stimulus. p. 272

extinction (in operant conditioning) A previously reinforced behaviour is no longer reinforced, and there is a decreased tendency to perform the behaviour. p. 281

extrinsic motivation Involves external incentives, such as rewards and punishments. p. 424

F

facial feedback hypothesis States that facial expressions can influence emotions, as well as reflect them. p. 458

factor analysis A statistical procedure that examines various items or measures and identifies factors that are correlated with each other. p. 396

family therapy Group therapy with family members. p. 577

feature detectors Neurons in the brain's visual system that respond to particular lines or other features of a stimulus. p. 191

figure-ground relationship People organize the perceptual field into stimuli that stand out (figure) and those that are left over (background). p. 196

fixation Involves using a prior problem-solving strategy and failing to look at a problem from a new perspective. p. 356

fluid intelligence One's ability to reason abstractly. p. 161

folk psychology The common-sense conceptual framework we use to make sense of our behaviour and that of other people and animals. p. 4

forebrain The highest and most recently evolved level of the brain. Key structures in the forebrain are the limbic system, thalamus, basal ganglia, hypothalamus, and cerebral cortex. p. 92

formal operational stage The fourth and final Piagetian stage of cognitive development (emerging from about 11 to 15 years of age) in which thinking becomes more abstract, idealistic, and logical. p. 131

free association The psychoanalytic technique of having individuals say aloud whatever comes into their minds. p. 561

frequency theory Perception of a sound's frequency is due to how often the auditory nerve fires. p. 206

frontal lobe The part of the cerebral cortex just behind the forehead that is involved in the control of voluntary muscles, intelligence, and personality. p. 95

functional fixedness A type of fixation in which individuals fail to solve a problem because they are fixated on a thing's usual functions. p. 356

functionalism An early school of psychology that emphasized the interaction between the mind and the outside environment. p. 7

fundamental attribution error The tendency for observers to overestimate the importance of traits and underestimate the importance of situations when they seek explanations of a person's behaviour. p. 637

G

gate-control theory of pain The spinal column contains a neural gate that can be open (allowing the perception of pain) or closed (blocking the perception of pain). p. 213

gender role Expectations for how females and males should think, act, and feel. p. 146

general adaptation syndrome (GAS) Selye's term for the common effects on the body when demands are placed on it. The GAS consists of three stages: alarm, resistance, and exhaustion. p. 603

generalization (in classical conditioning) The tendency of a new stimulus that is similar to the original stimulus to elicit a response that is similar to the conditioned response. p. 271

generalization (in operant conditioning) Giving the same response to similar stimuli. p. 279

generalized anxiety disorder An anxiety disorder that consists of persistent anxiety over at least one month; the individual with this disorder cannot specify the reasons for the anxiety. p. 518

genes The units of hereditary information. They are short segments of chromosomes, composed of DNA. p. 106

genotype An individual's genetic heritage, the actual genetic material. p. 119

gestalt psychology An early school of psychology that emphasized that, in perception, the whole is greater than the sum of the parts. pp. 8, 196

gestalt therapy Perls's humanistic therapy in which the therapist challenges clients to help them become more aware of their feelings and face their problems. p. 564

gifted Individuals who have an IQ of 120 or higher and/or superior talent in a particular domain. pp. 403

glial cells Provide support and nutritional functions in the nervous system. p. 82

group polarization effect The solidification and further strengthening of a position as a consequence of a group discussion. p. 653

groupthink Involves impaired decision making and avoidance of realistic appraisal to maintain group harmony. p. 653

H

hallucinogens Psychoactive drugs that modify a person's perceptual experiences and produce visual images that are not real. p. 258

hardiness A personality style characterized by a sense of commitment (rather than alienation), control (rather than powerlessness), and a perception of problems as challenges (rather than threats). p. 597

health psychology Emphasizes psychology's role in promoting and maintaining health and in preventing and treating illness. p. 594

heritability The fraction of the variance in IQ in a population that is attributed to genetics. p. 409

heuristics Strategies or guidelines that suggest, but do not guarantee, a solution to a problem. p. 355

hierarchy of needs Maslow's view that individuals' main needs are satisfied in the following sequence: physiological, safety, love and belongingness, esteem, and self-actualization. p. 436

hindbrain The lowest level of the brain, consisting of the medulla, cerebellum, and pons. p. 90

hindsight bias The tendency to falsely report, after the fact, that we accurately predicted an event. p. 365

homeostasis The body's tendency to maintain an equilibrium, or steady state. p. 423

hormones Chemical messengers manufactured by the endocrine glands. p. 104

human sexual response pattern Identified by Masters and Johnson; consists of four phases—excitement, plateau, orgasm, and resolution. p. 435

humanistic movement An emphasis on a person's capacity for personal growth, freedom to choose a destiny, and positive qualities. p. 17

humanistic perspectives Stress the person's capacity for personal growth, freedom to choose a destiny, and positive qualities. p. 485

humanistic therapies In these therapies people are encouraged to understand themselves and to grow personally. The humanistic therapies are unique in their emphasis on self-healing capacities. p. 563

hypnosis A psychological state or possibly altered attention and awareness in which the individual is unusually responsive to suggestions. p. 247

hypothalamus Forebrain structure involved in regulating eating, drinking, and sex; directing the endocrine system through the pituitary gland; and monitoring emotion, stress, and reward. p. 93

hypothesis An idea that is a testable prediction, often arrived at logically from a theory. p. 42

I

id The Freudian structure of personality that consists of instincts, which are the individual's reservoir of psychic energy. p. 474

identity versus identity confusion Erikson's fifth psychological stage in which adolescents face the challenge of finding out who they are, what they are all about, and where they are going in life. p. 151

implicit memory (nondeclarative memory) Memory in which behaviour is affected by prior experience without that experience being consciously recollected. p. 316

implicit personality theory The term given to the public or layperson's conception of which personality traits go together in an individual. p. 639

impression management (self-presentation) Involves acting in a way to present an image of oneself as a certain type of person, which might or might not be who one really is. p. 640

imprinting The tendency of an infant animal to form an attachment to the first moving object it sees and/or hears. p. 137

independent variable The manipulated, influential, experimental factor in an experiment. p. 55

individual psychology The term for Adler's approach, which views people as motivated by purposes and goals, being creators of their own lives. p. 479

inductive reasoning Reasoning from the specific to the general. p. 362

indulgent parenting A parenting style in which parents are involved with their children but place few limits on them. p. 139

inferential statistics Mathematical methods that are used to draw conclusions about data. p. 61

infinite generativity The ability to produce an infinite number of sentences using a finite set of words and rules. p. 367

informational social influence The influence other people have on us because we want to be right. p. 648

inner ear Consists of oval window, cochlea, and basilar membrane. p. 205

insight learning A form of problem solving in which the organism develops a sudden insight or understanding of the problem's solution. p. 295

insight therapy Encourages insight and self-awareness; includes the psychodynamic and humanistic therapies. p. 560

instinct An innate (unlearned), biological pattern of behaviour that is assumed to be universal throughout a species. p. 422

instinctive drift The tendency of animals to revert to instinctive behaviour that interferes with learning. p. 295

integrative therapy Combinations of techniques from different therapies based on the therapist's judgment of which particular techniques will provide the greatest benefit for the client. p. 583

intelligence Problem-solving skills and the ability to adapt to and learn from life's everyday experiences. p. 386

intelligence quotient (IQ) Consists of an individual's mental age divided by chronological age multiplied by 100. p. 387

interference theory States that people forget, not because memories are actually lost from storage but because other information gets in the way of what we want to remember. p. 336

intrinsic motivation Based on internal factors, such as self-determination, curiosity, challenge, and effort. p. 424

J

James-Lange theory States that emotion results from physiological states triggered by stimuli in the environment. p. 452

K

kinesthetic senses Provide information about movement, posture, and orientation. p. 217

L

language A form of communication, whether spoken, written, or signed, that is based on a system of symbols. p. 366

latent content In Freud's view, the dream's hidden content; its unconscious meaning. p. 245

latent learning Unreinforced learning that is not immediately reflected in behaviour. p. 294

law of effect Thorndike's concept that behaviours followed by positive outcomes are strengthened, whereas behaviours followed by negative outcomes are weakened. p. 276

learned helplessness Occurs when individuals are exposed to aversive stimulation, such as prolonged stress, over which they have no control. The inability to avoid such aversive stimulation can produce an apathetic state of helplessness. p. 534

learning A relatively permanent change in behaviour that occurs through experience. p. 268

levels of processing theory States that memory is on a continuum from shallow to deep, with deeper processing producing better memory. p. 306

limbic system Loosely connected network of structures—including the amygdala and hippocampus—that play important roles in memory and emotion. p. 92

lithium A drug that is widely used to treat bipolar disorder. p. 556

locus of control Individuals' beliefs about whether the outcomes of their actions depend on what they do (internal control) or on events outside of their personal control (external control). p. 483

long-term memory A relatively permanent type of memory that holds huge amounts of information for a long period of time. p. 313

M

major depressive disorder Indicated by a major depressive episode and depressed characteristics, such as lethargy and hopelessness, lasting at least two weeks. p. 529

managed care Consists of strategies for controlling health-care costs, including mental health treatment, and demands for accountability for treatment success. p. 584

manifest content In Freud's view, the dream's surface content, which contains symbols that distort and disguise the dream's true meaning. p. 245

mean A statistical measure of central tendency that is calculated by adding all the scores and then dividing by the number of scores. p. 58

median A statistical measure of central tendency that falls exactly in the middle of a distribution of scores after they have been arranged (or ranked) from highest to lowest. p. 59

medical model A biological approach that describes psychological disorders as medical diseases with a biological origin. p. 512

meditation The practice and system of thought that incorporates exercises to attain bodily or mental control and well-being, as well as enlightenment. p. 619

memory The retention of information over time through encoding, storage, and retrieval. p. 304

mental age (MA) An individual's level of mental development relative to that of others. p. 387

mental processes The thoughts, feelings, and motives that each of us experiences privately but that cannot be observed directly. p. 5

mental retardation A condition of limited mental ability in which the individual has a low IQ, usually below 70, has difficulty adapting to everyday life, and has an onset of these characteristics in the so-called developmental period. p. 402

mental set A type of fixation in which an individual tries to solve a problem in a particular way that has worked in the past. p. 357

meta-analysis Statistical analysis that combines the results of many different studies. p. 581

midbrain Located between the hindbrain and forebrain, a region in which many nerve-fibre systems ascend and descend to connect the higher and lower portions of the brain. p. 9

middle ear Consists of eardrum, hammer, anvil, and stirrup. p. 204

mindfulness meditation The practice of opening attention to an awareness of the ongoing stream of sensations, thoughts, and feelings in order to develop a non-reactive, clear state of mind. p. 619

Minnesota Multiphasic Personality Inventory (MMPI) The most widely used and researched self-report personality test. p. 499

mode A statistical measure of central tendency, the score that occurs most often. p. 59

monocular cues Depth cues that can be extracted from the images in either eye. p. 197

mood disorders Psychological disorders in which there is a primary disturbance in mood (prolonged emotion that colours the individuals entire emotional state). Two main types are the depressive disorders and bipolar disorder. p. 528

morphology A language's rules for word formation. p. 367

motivation Why people behave, think, and feel the way they do. Motivated behaviour is energized, directed, and sustained. p. 422

motor cortex Area of the frontal lobe that processes information about voluntary movement. p. 95

multiple-factor theory Thurstone's theory that intelligence consists of seven primary mental abilities: verbal comprehension, number ability, word fluency, spatial visualization, associative memory, reasoning, and perceptual speed. p. 397

myelin sheath A layer of fat cells that encases and insulates most axons. The myelin sheath speeds up the transmission of nerve impulses. p. 83

N

natural selection The principle that the organisms that are best adapted to their environment are the most likely to survive, reproduce, and pass on their genes to their offspring. p. 6

naturalistic observation Observations of behaviour in real-world settings with no effort made to manipulate or control the situation. p. 49

nature An organism's biological inheritance. p. 119

need A deprivation that energizes the drive to eliminate or reduce the deprivation. p. 422

need for achievement The desire to accomplish something, to reach a standard of excellence, and to expend effort to excel. p. 443

need for affiliation The motive to be with other people. p. 448

negative punishment A behaviour decreases when a positive stimulus is removed from it. p. 284

negative reinforcement The frequency of a behaviour increases because it is followed by the removal of an aversive (unpleasant) stimulus. p. 281

neglectful parenting A parenting style in which parents are uninvolved in their child's life. p. 139

nerve A collection of axons carrying information from one cluster of neurons to another outside the brain. p. 81

nervous system The body's electrochemical communication circuitry, made up of billions of neurons. p. 76

neural networks Clusters of neurons that are interconnected to process information. p. 81

neuron Nerve cell that is specialized for processing information. Neurons are the basic units of the nervous system. p. 82

neurotransmitters Chemicals that carry information across the synaptic gap from one neuron to the next. p. 86

noise Irrelevant and competing stimuli. p. 180

normal distribution A symmetrical, bell-shaped curve with a majority of the scores falling in the middle of the possible range and few scores appearing toward the extremes of the range. p. 388

normative social influence The influence that other people have on us because we seek their approval or to avoid their disapproval. p. 648

nucleus (pl. nuclei) A group of specialized nerve cells in the brain or spinal cord. p. 81

nurture An organism's environmental experience. p. 119

O

obedience Behaviour that complies with the explicit demands of the individual in authority. p. 648

observational learning Also called imitation or modelling; learning that occurs when a person observes and imitates another's behaviour. p. 290

obsessive-compulsive disorder (OCD) An anxiety disorder; the individual has anxiety-provoking thoughts that will not go away (obsession) and/or urges to perform repetitive, ritualistic behaviours to prevent or produce some future situation (compulsion). p. 522

occipital lobe The part of the cerebral cortex at the back of the head that is involved in vision. p. 95

Oedipus complex In Freud's theory, the young child's development of an intense desire to replace the same-sex parent and enjoy the affections of the opposite-sex parent. p. 476

olfactory epithelium Located in the roof of the nasal cavity, a sheet of receptor cells for smell. p. 217

operant conditioning Also called instrumental conditioning; a form of learning in which the consequences of behaviour change the probability of the behaviour's occurrence. p. 277

operational definition A circumstance or behaviour defined in such a way that it can be objectively observed and measured. p. 44

opiates Opium and its derivatives; they depress the central nervous system's activity. p. 256

opponent-process theory Cells in the visual system respond to red-green and blue-yellow colors; a given cell might be excited by red and inhibited by green, whereas another might be excited by yellow and inhibited by blue. p. 194

outer ear Consists of the pinna and the external auditory canal. p. 204

overconfidence bias The tendency to have more confidence in judgments and decisions than we should based on probability or past occurrence. p. 364

P

pain The sensation that warns us that damage to our bodies is occurring. p. 213

panic disorder An anxiety disorder marked by the recurrent sudden onset of intense apprehension or terror. p. 519

papillae Bumps on the tongue that contain taste buds, the receptors for taste. p. 215

parallel processing The simultaneous distribution of information across different neural pathways. p. 192

paranoid schizophrenia A type of schizophrenia that is characterized by delusions of reference, grandeur, and persecution. p. 541

parasympathetic nervous system The division of the autonomic nervous system that calms the body. p. 80

parietal lobe Area of the cerebral cortex at the top of the head that is involved in registering spatial location, attention, and motor control. p. 95

perception The brain's process of organizing and interpreting sensory information to give it meaning. p. 176

pedagogical tools Activities that aid in the active construction of knowledge or skill. p. 30

perceptual constancy Recognition that objects are constant and unchanging even through sensory input about them is changing. p. 200

perceptual set A predisposition or readiness to perceive something in a particular way. p. 185

peripheral nervous system (PNS) The network of nerves that connects the brain and spinal cord to other parts of the body. It is divided into the somatic nervous system and the autonomic nervous system. p. 80

personality A pattern of enduring, distinctive thoughts, emotions, and behaviours that characterize the way an individual adapts to the world. p. 472

personality disorders Chronic, maladaptive cognitive-behavioural patterns that are thoroughly integrated into the individual's personality. p. 545

phenotype The expression of an individual's genotype in observable, measurable characteristics. p. 119

pheromones Odorous substances released by animals which are powerful attractants. p. 437

phobic disorder Commonly called phobia, an anxiety disorder in which the individual has an irrational, overwhelming, persistent fear of a particular object or situation. p. 520

phonology A language's sound system. p. 367

physical dependence The physical need for a drug, accompanied by unpleasant withdrawal symptoms when the drug is discontinued. p. 252

pituitary gland An important endocrine gland at the base of the skull that controls growth and regulates other glands. p. 104

place theory A theory of hearing that states that each frequency produces vibrations at a particular spot on the basilar membrane. p. 206

placebo An innocuous, inert substance or condition that may be given to participants instead of a presumed active agent, such as a drug, to determine if it produces effects similar to those of the active agent. p. 57

placebo effect The influence of participants' expectations, rather than the experimental treatment, on experimental outcome. p. 57

plasticity The brain's special capacity for modification and change. p. 77

polygraph A machine that monitors changes in physiological thought to be influenced by emotional states; it is used by examiners to try to determine if someone is lying. p. 452

population The entire group that the investigator wants to learn about. p. 45

positive psychology movement A strong emphasis on the experiences that people value subjectively (such as happiness),

positive individual traits (such as the capacity for love), and positive group and civic values (such as responsibility). p. 17

positive punishment A behaviour decreases when it is followed by an unpleasant stimulus. p. 284

positive reinforcement The frequency of a behaviour increases because it is followed by a rewarding stimulus. p. 281

post-traumatic stress disorder (PTSD) An anxiety disorder that develops through exposure to a traumatic event, severely oppressive situations, severe abuse, and natural and unnatural disasters. p. 522

prejudice An unjustified negative attitude toward an individual based on the individual's membership in a group. p. 659

preoperational stage The second Piagetian stage of cognitive development (approximately two to seven years of age) in which thought becomes more symbolic, egocentric, and intuitive rather than logical; but the child cannot yet perform operations. p. 129

preparedness The species-specific biological predisposition to learn in certain ways. p. 296

primary reinforcement The use of reinforcers that are innately satisfying. p. 281

priming A type of implicit memory; information that people already have in storage is activated to help them remember new information better and faster. p. 317

proactive interference Occurs when material that was learned earlier disrupts the recall of material learned later. p. 336

problem solving An attempt to find an appropriate way of attaining a goal when the goal is not readily available. p. 354

problem-focused coping Lazarus's term for the cognitive strategy of squarely facing one's troubles and trying to solve them. p. 612

procedural memory Memory for skills. p. 317

projective test Personality assessment tool that presents individuals with an ambiguous stimulus and then asks them to describe it or tell a story about it; based on the assumption that the ambiguity of the stimulus allows individuals to project their personalities onto it. p. 496

prospective memory Remembering information about doing something in the future. p. 316

prototype model People decide whether an item reflects a concept by comparing it with the most typical item(s) of that concept that they know about. p. 352

psychoactive drugs Drugs that act on the nervous system to alter consciousness, modify perceptions, and change moods. p. 251

psychoanalysis Freud's psychotherapeutic technique for analyzing an individual's unconscious thoughts. Freud believed that clients' current problems could be traced to childhood experiences, involving conflicts about sexuality. p. 560

psychodynamic approach Emphasizes the unconscious aspects of the mind, conflict between biological instincts and society's demands, and early family experiences. p. 11

psychodynamic perspectives View personality as primarily unconscious (that is, beyond awareness) and as occurring in stages. Most psychoanalytic perspectives emphasize that early experiences with parents play a role in sculpting personality. p. 473

psychodynamic therapies Stress the importance of the unconscious mind, extensive interpretation by the therapist, and the role of experiences in the early-childhood years. The goal of the psychodynamic therapies is to help individuals recognize their maladaptive ways of coping and the sources of their unconscious conflicts. p. 560

psychological dependence The strong desire and craving to repeat the use of the drug for emotional reasons. p. 252

psychology The scientific study of behaviour and mental processes. p. 5

psychoneuroimmunology The field that explores connections among psychological factors (such as attitudes and emotions), the nervous system, and the immune system. p. 607

psychophysics The field that studies links between the physical properties of stimuli and a person's experience of them. p. 179

psychosurgery A biological therapy that involves removal or destruction of brain tissue to improve an individual's adjustment. p. 559

psychotherapy The process used by mental health professionals to help individuals recognize, define, and overcome their psychological and interpersonal difficulties. p. 554

puberty A period of rapid skeletal and sexual maturation that occurs mainly in early adolescence. p. 149

punishment A consequence that decreases the likelihood that a behaviour will occur. p. 283

R

random assignment Assignment of participants to experimental and control groups by chance. p. 56

random sample A sample in which every member of the population has an equal chance of being selected. p. 45

range A statistical measure of variability that is the distance between the highest and lowest scores. p. 59

rational-emotive behaviour therapy Based on Ellis's assertion that individuals develop a psychological disorder because of their beliefs, especially those that are irrational and self-defeating; the goal of REBT is to get the person to eliminate self-defeating beliefs by rationally examining them. p. 571

reasoning The mental activity of transforming information to reach conclusions. p. 362

reinforcement The process by which a stimulus or event strengthens or increases the probability of an event that it follows. p. 281

reliability The extent to which a test yields a consistent, reproducible measure of performance. p. 391

REM sleep (Rapid-eye-movement sleep) Stage 5 of sleep, in which most dreaming occurs. p. 237

representativeness heuristic Making faulty decisions based on how well something matches a prototype—the common or representative example—rather than on its relevance to the particular situation. p. 365

research participant bias The influence of research participants' expectations on their behaviour within an experiment. p. 56

resistance The psychoanalytic term for the person's unconscious defence strategies that prevent the analyst from understanding the person's problems. p. 563

resting potential The stable, negative charge of an inactive neuron. p. 84

reticular formation A midbrain system that consists of a diffuse collection of neurons involved in stereotypical behaviours such as walking, sleeping, or turning to attend to a sudden noise. p. 91

retina The light-sensitive surface in the back of the eye that houses light receptors called rods and cones. p. 189

retrieval The memory process of taking information out of storage. p. 324

retroactive interference Occurs when material learned later disrupts the retrieval of information learned earlier. p. 336

retrograde amnesia A memory disorder that involves memory loss for a segment of the past but not for new events. p. 337

retrospective memory Remembering the past. p. 316

risky shift The tendency for a group decision to be riskier than the average decision made by individual group members. p. 652

rods The receptors in the retina that are sensitive to light but are not very useful in colour vision. p. 189

romantic love Also called passionate love; the type of love that has strong components of sexuality and infatuation and often predominates in the early part of a love relationship. p. 676

Rorschach inkblot test A widely used projective test; it uses an individual's perception of inkblots to determine his or her personality. p. 496

S

sample The subset of the population that the investigator has chosen for study. p. 45

schedules of reinforcement "Timetables" that determine when a behaviour will be reinforced. p. 282

schema A concept or framework that already exists at a given moment in a person's mind and that organizes and interprets information. pp. 128, 319

schizophrenia A severe psychological disorder that is characterized by highly disordered thought processes. p. 539

science In psychology, the use of systematic methods to observe, describe, predict, and explain behaviour. p. 5

script A schema for an event. p. 320

secondary reinforcement Acquires its positive value through experience. p. 281

secure attachment An important aspect of socioemotional development in which infants use the caregiver, usually the mother, as a secure base from which to explore the environment. p. 137

selective attention Focusing on a specific aspect of experience while ignoring others. p. 183

self-actualization The highest and most elusive of Maslow's needs; the motivation to develop one's full potential as a human being. p. 426

self-concept A central theme in Rogers's and other humanists' views; self-concept refers to individuals' overall perceptions of their abilities, behaviour, and personalities. p. 486

self-efficacy The belief that one can master a situation and produce positive outcomes. pp. 482, 615

self-esteem The person's overall evaluation of self-worth or self-image. p. 488

self-monitoring Individuals' attention to the impressions they make on others and the degree to which they fine-tune their performances accordingly. p. 641

self-perception theory Bem's theory about the connection between attitudes and behaviour; stresses that individuals make inferences about their attitudes by perceiving their behaviour. p. 644

self-report tests Also called objective tests or inventories, they directly ask people whether items (usually true/false or agree/disagree) describe their personality traits or not. p. 498

semantic memory A person's knowledge about the world. p. 315

semantics The meaning of words and sentences in a particular language. p. 367

semicircular canals Located in the inner ear; contain the sensory receptors that detect head motion. p. 218

sensation The process of receiving stimulus energies from the environment. p. 176

sensorimotor stage The first Piagetian stage of cognitive development (birth to about two years of age), in which infants construct an understanding of the world by coordinating sensory experiences (such as seeing and hearing) with motor (physical) actions. p. 128

sensory adaptation A change in the responsiveness of the sensory system based on the average level of surrounding stimulation. p. 185

sensory cortex Area of the parietal lobe that processes information about body sensations. p. 95

sensory memory Holds information from the world in its original form only for an instant, not much longer than the brief time it is exposed to the visual, auditory, and other senses. p. 310

sensory receptors Specialized cells that detect and transmit stimulus information to sensory neurons and the brain. p. 177

serial position effect The tendency for items at the beginning and at the end of a list to be recalled more readily. p. 325

set point The weight maintained when no effort is made to gain or lose weight. p. 430

sexually transmitted infections (STIs) Infections that are contracted primarily through sex—oral-genital and anal-genital sex as well as intercourse. p. 627

shaping The process of rewarding approximations of desired behaviour. p. 278

short-term memory A limited-capacity memory system in which information is retained for only as long as 30 seconds unless strategies are used to retain it longer. p. 311

signal detection theory Focuses on decision making about stimuli in the presence of uncertainty; detection depends on a variety of factors besides the physical intensity of the stimulus and the sensory abilities of the observer. p. 182

social cognitive behaviour view of hypnosis Views hypnosis as a result of social factors associated with the hypnotic context, coupled with cognitive events involved in the efforts of the hypnotized person to immerse himself or herself in the role of the hypnotized person. p. 249

social cognitive theory Stesses that behaviour is determined not only by environmental conditions but also by how thoughts modify the impact of environment on behaviour. pp. 10, 481

social facilitation Occurs when an individual's performance improves because of the presence of others. p. 651

social identity Refers to the way we define ourselves in terms of group memberships. p. 656

social identity theory Tajfel's theory that when individuals are assigned to a group, they invariably think of it as an in-group. p. 656

social loafing Each person's tendency to exert less effort in a group because of reduced monitoring. p. 652

social psychology The study of how people think about, influence, and relate to other people. p. 635

social support Information and feedback from others that one is loved and cared for, esteemed and valued, and included in a network of communication and mutual obligation. p. 615

sociocultural approach Emphasizes social and cultural influences on behaviour. p. 14

somatic nervous system Division of the PNS consisting of sensory nerves, whose function is to convey information to the CNS, and motor nerves, whose function is to transmit information to the muscles. p. 80

spacing effect The finding that for a given amount of study time, it is better to distribute studying across time than to mass it together. p. 32

spontaneous recovery The process in classical conditioning by which a conditioned response can recur after a time delay without further conditioning. p. 272

standard deviation A statistical measure of variability that involves how much the scores vary on the average around the mean of the sample. p. 60

standardization Involves developing uniform procedures for administering and scoring a test, as well as creating norms for the test. p. 391

standardized test An oral or written assessment for which an individual receives a score indicating how the individual responded relative to others. p. 51

stereotype A generalization about a group's characteristics that does not consider any variations from one individual to another. p. 660

stimulants Psychoactive drugs that increase the central nervous system's activity. p. 256

storage Ways in which information is retained over time and how it is represented in memory. p. 309

stream of consciousness James's concept that the mind is a continuous flow of sensations, images, thoughts, and feelings. p. 228

stress The response of individuals to stressors, the circumstances and events that threaten and tax their coping abilities. p. 596

stress management programs Teach individuals to appraise stressful events, to develop skills for coping with stress, and to put these skills into use in their everyday lives. p. 619

structuralism An early school of psychology that attempted to discover basic elements (structures) of the human mind. p. 7

subgoaling Involves setting intermediate goals or defining intermediate problems that put you in a better position to reach the final goal or solution. p. 355

subliminal perception The ability to detect information below the level of conscious awareness. p. 180

superego The Freudian structure of personality that deals with morality. p. 474

suprachiasmatic nucleus (SCN) A small structure in the hypothalamus that registers changes in light. p. 234

sympathetic nervous system The division of the autonomic nervous system that arouses the body. p. 80

synapses Tiny junctions between two neurons, generally where the axon of one neuron meets the dendrites or cell body of another neuron. p. 86

syntax A language's rules for the way words are combined to form acceptable phrases and sentences. p. 367

systematic desensitization A method of behaviour therapy based on classical conditioning that treats anxiety by getting the person to associate deep relaxation with increasingly intense anxiety-producing situations. p. 566

T

temperament An individual's behavioural style and characteristic way of responding. p. 138

temporal lobe The portion of the cerebral cortex just above the ears that is involved in hearing, language processing, and memory. p. 95

thalamus Forebrain structure that functions as a relay station to sort input and direct it to different areas of the cerebral cortex. It also has ties to the reticular formation. p. 92

Thematic Apperception Test (TAT) An ambiguous projective test designed to elicit stories that reveal something about an individual's personality. p. 497

theory A broad idea or set of closely related ideas that attempt to explain and predict observations. p. 42

thermoreceptors Located under the skin, they respond to increases and decreases in temperature. p. 212

thinking Manipulating information, as when we form concepts, solve problems, think critically, reason, and make decisions. p. 350

tolerance The need to take increasing amounts of the drug to produce the same effect. p. 252

top-down processing Processing of perceptual information that starts out with cognitive processing at the higher levels of the brain. p. 176

tract A collection of axons carrying information from one cluster of neurons to another inside the brain. p. 81

trait An enduring personality characteristic that tends to lead to certain behaviours. p. 490

tranquilizers Depressant drugs that reduce anxiety and induce relaxation. p. 255

transcendental meditation (TM) The most popular form of meditation in the United States, derived from an ancient Indian technique; involves using a mantra. p. 619

transduction The process of transforming physical energy into electrochemical energy. p. 176

transference The psychoanalytic term for the person's relating to the analyst in ways that reproduce or relive important relationships in the individual's life. p. 563

triarchic theory Sternberg's theory that there are three main types of intelligence: analytical, creative, and practical. p. 399

trichromatic theory Colour perception is based on the existence of three types of receptors that are maximally sensitive to different, but overlapping, ranges of wavelengths. p. 193

two-factor theory Spearman's theory that individuals have both general intelligence (g) and a number of specific abilities (s). p. 396

two-factor theory of emotion Schachter and Singer's theory that emotion is determined by two main factors: physiological arousal and cognitive labelling. p. 455

Type A behaviour pattern A cluster of characteristics—being excessively competitive, hard-driven, and hostile—thought to be related to the incidence of heart disease. p. 596

Type B behaviour pattern A relaxed and easygoing personality. p. 596

U

unconditional positive regard Rogers's term for accepting, valuing, and being positive toward another person regardless of the person's behaviour. p. 486

unconditioned response (UCR) An unlearned response that is automatically elicited by the UCS. p. 270

unconditioned stimulus (UCS) A stimulus that produces a response without prior learning. p. 269

unconscious thought Freud's concept of a reservoir of unacceptable wishes, feelings, and thoughts that are beyond conscious awareness. p. 228

undifferentiated schizophrenia A type of schizophrenia that is characterized by disorganized behaviour, hallucinations, delusions, and incoherence. p. 542

V

validity The extent to which a test measures what it is intended to measure. p. 390

vestibular sense Provides information about balance and movement. p. 217

visual illusion A discrepancy or incongruency between reality and the perceptual representation of it. p. 201

volley principle A cluster of nerve cells can fire neural impulses in rapid succession, producing a volley of impulses. p. 206

W

Weber's law The principle that two stimuli must differ by a constant minimum percentage (rather than a constant amount) to be perceived as different. p. 182

whole language approach Stresses that reading instruction should parallel a child's natural language learning; so reading materials should be whole and meaningful. p. 378

wisdom Expert knowledge about the practical aspects of life. p. 163

wish fulfillment Freud's concept of dreaming as an unconscious attempt to fulfill needs (especially for sex and aggression) that cannot be expressed, or that go ungratified while awake. p. 245

working memory A three-part system that temporarily holds information. Working memory is a kind of mental workbench on which information is manipulated and assembled to perform other cognitive tasks. p. 312

Y

Yerkes-Dodson law States that performance is best under conditions of moderate arousal than under those of low or high arousal. p. 423

Z

zone of proximal development According to Vygotsky, the gap between what is already known and what, with assistance, can be learned. p. 133

References

* denotes Canadian research

A

Abbey, A., Ross, L. T., & McDuffie, D. (1993). Alcohol's role in sexual assault. In R. R. Watson (Ed.), *Drug and alcohol abuse reviews. Vol. 5: Addictive behaviors in women*. Totowa, NJ: Humana Press.

Abdel-Hamid, T. K. (2003). Exercise and diet in obesity treatment: An integrative system dynamics perspective. *Medicine & Science in Sports & Exercise, 35(3),* 400–413.

Abela, J. R. Z., Hankin, B. L., Haigh, E. A. P., Adams, P., Vinokuroff, T., & Trayhern, L. (2005). Interpersonal vulnerability to depression in high-risk children: The role of insecure attachment and reassurance seeking. *Journal of Clinical Child & Adolescent Psychology, 34(1),* 182–192.*

Abelson, J. L., Weg, J. G., Nesse, R. M., & Curtis, G. C. (2001). Persistent respiratory irregularity in patients with panic disorder. *Biological Psychiatry, 49,* 588–595.

Abernethy, G., Gill, D. P., Parks, S. L., & Packer, S. T. (2001). Expertise and the perception of kinematic and situational probability information. *Perception, 30,* 233–252.

Aboud, F. E., & Dennis, S. C. (1998). Adolescent use and abuse of alcohol. In D. Pushkar, & W. M. Bukowski (Eds.), *Improving competence across the lifespan: Building interventions based on theory and research*. New York: Plenum Press.*

Aboud, F. E., & Doyle, A. B. (1996). Does talk of race foster prejudice or tolerance in children? *Canadian Journal of Behavioural Science, 28,* 161–170.*

Aboud, F. E., & Levy, S. R. (2000). Interventions to reduce prejudice and discrimination in children and adolescents. In S. Oskamp (Ed.), *Reducing prejudice and discrimination: The Claremont Symposium on Applied Social Psychology*. Mahwah, NJ: Erlbaum.*

Aboud, F. E., Mendelson, M. J., & Purdy, K. T. (2003). Cross-race peer relations and friendship quality. *International Journal of Behavioral Development, 27(2),* 165–173.*

Abrams, D. B., Brown, R., Niaura, R. S., Emmons, K., Goldstein, M., & Monti, P. M. (2003). *The tobacco dependence treatment handbook: A guide to best practices*. New York, Guilford.

Abramson, L. Y., Seligman, M. E. P., & Teasdale, J. (1978). Learned helplessness in humans: Critique and reformulation. *Journal of Abnormal Psychology, 87,* 49–74.

Abu-Rabia, S., & Kehat, S. (2004). The critical period for second language pronunciation: Is there such a thing? Ten case studies of late starters who attained a native-like Hebrew accent. *Educational Psychology, 24(1),* 77–98.

Achat, H., Kawachi, I., Spiro, A., DeMolles, D. A., & Sparrow, D. (2000). Optimism and depression as predictors of physical and mental health functioning: The Normative Aging Study. *Annals of Behavioral Medicine, 22,* 127–130.

Addis, D. R., Moscovitch, M., Crawley, A. P. & McAndrews, M. P. (2004). Recollective qualities modulate hippocampal activation during autobiographical memory retrieval. *Hippocampus, 14,* 752–762.*

Addis, K. M., & Kahana, M. J. (2004). Decomposing serial learning: What is missing from the learning curve? *Psychonomic Bulletin & Review, 11(1),* 118–174.

Addis, M. E., Hatgis, C., Krasnow, A. D., Jacob, K., Bourne, L., & Mansfield, A. (2004). Effectiveness of cognitive-behavioral treatment for panic disorder versus treatment as usual in a managed care setting. *Journal of Consulting & Clinical Psychology, 72(4),* 625–635.

Ader, R. (1974). Letter to the editor: Behaviorally conditioned immunosuppression. *Psychosomatic Medicine, 36,* 183–184.

Ader, R. (2003a). Psychosocial factors and the therapeutic response to drugs. *Prevention & Treatment, 6,* Article 2. Retrieved August 19, 2005, from http://journals.apa.org/prevention/volume6/pre0060001a.html.

Ader, R. (2003b). Conditioned immunomodulation: Research needs and directions. *Brain, Behavior & Immunity. Special Biological mechanisms of psychosocial effects on disease: Implications for cancer control, 17(Suppl1),* S51–S57.

Ader, R., & Cohen, N. (1975). Behaviorally conditioned immunosuppression. *Psychosomatic Medicine, 37,* 333–340.

Ader, R., & Cohen, N. (2000). Conditioning and immunity. In R. Ader, D. L. Felton, & N. Cohen (Eds.), *Psychoneuroimmunology (3rd ed.)*. San Diego: Academic Press.

Adlaf, E. M., & Paglia, A. (2003). Drug use among Ontario students, 1977–2003: Detailed OSDUS findings. *CAMH Research Document Series, No. 13. Toronto: Centre for Addiction and Mental Health*. Retrieved March 19, 2005 from http://www.camh.net/pdf/OSDUS03-drugdetail-final.pdf.

Adler, A. (1927). *The theory and practice of individual psychology*. Fort Worth: Harcourt Brace.

Adler, N. E. (2001). A consideration of multiple pathways from socioeconomic status to health. In J. A. Auerbach, & B. K. Krimgold (Eds.), *Income, socioeconomic status, and health*. Washington: National Policy Association.

Adler, T. (1991, January). Seeing double? Controversial twins study is widely reported, debated. *APA Monitor, 22,* 1, 8.

Adorno, T. W., Frenkel-Brunswick, E., Levinson, D. J., & Sanford, R. N. (1950). *The authoritarian personality*. New York: Harper & Row.

Agnew, N. McK., & Pyke, S. W. (1993). *The science game: An introduction to research in the social sciences*. Englewood Cliffs, NJ: Prentice Hall.*

Ahasan, M. R., Lewko, J., Campbell, D., & Slamoni, A. (2001). Adaptation to night shifts and synchronization processes of night workers. *Journal of Physiological Anthropology, 20,* 215–226.

Aiken, L. R. (2006). *Psychological testing and assessment (12th ed.)*. Boston: Allyn & Bacon.

Ainsworth, M. D. S. (1979). Infant-mother attachment. *American Psychologist, 34,* 932–937.

Aizenstein, H. J., MacDonald, A. W., Stenger, V. A., Nebes, R. D., & Larson, J. K., Jeris, K., Ursu, S., & Carter, C. S. (2000). Complementary category learning systems identified using event-related functional MRI. *Journal of Cognitive Neuroscience, 12,* 977–987.

Ajzen, I. (2001). Nature and operation of attitudes. *Annual Review of Psychology, 52,* 27–58.

Alberti, R., & Emmons, M. (2001). *Your perfect right (8th ed.)*. San Luis Obispo, CA: Impact.

Alberto, P., & Troutman, A. C. (2003). *Applied behavior analysis for teachers (6th ed.)*. Englewood Cliffs, NJ: Prentice Hall.

Albrecht, U. (2002). Invited review: Regulation of mammalian circadian clock genes. *Journal of Applied Physiology, 92,* 1348–1355.

Alcock, J. E. (2003). Give the null hypothesis a chance: Reasons to remain doubtful about the existence of psi. *Journal of Consciousness Studies, 10(6-7),* 29–50.*

Alcock, J. E., Burns, J., & Freeman, A. (2003). *Psi wars: Getting to grips with the paranormal*. Exeter, UK: Imprint Academic Press.*

Alcock, J. E., Carment, D. W., & Sadava, S. M. (2005). *A textbook of social psychology (6th ed.)*. Toronto: Prentice Hall.*

Aldenkamp, A., & Arends, J. (2004). The relative influence of epileptic EEG discharges, short nonconvulsive seizures, and type of epilepsy on cognitive function. *Epilepsia, 45(1),* 54–63.

Alderman, M. K. (2004). *Motivation for achievement (2nd ed.)*. Mahwah, NJ: Erlbaum.

Alexander, A. L., Wickens, C. D., & Merwin, D. H. (2005). Perspective and coplanar cockpit displays of traffic information: Implications for manoeuvre choice, flight safety, and mental workload. *International Journal of Aviation Psychology, 15(1),* 1–21.

Alexander, D. A., & Klein, S. (2001). Caring for others can seriously damage your health. *Hospital Medicine, 62,* 264–267.

Al-Issa, I. (1982). Does culture make a difference in psychopathology? In I. Al-Issa (Ed.), *Culture and psychopathology*. Baltimore: University Park Press.

Alkire, M. T., Haier, R. J., & James, H. F. (1998). Toward the neurobiology of consciousness: Using brain imaging and anesthesia to investigate the anatomy of consciousness. In S. Hameroff, A. Kaszniak, & A. Scott (Eds.), *Toward a science of consciousness II*. Cambridge MIT Press.

Allan, K., Wolf, H. A., Rosenthal, C. R., & Rugg, M. D. (2001). The effects of retrieval cues on post-retrieval monitoring in episodic memory: An electrophysiological study. *Brain Research, 12,* 289–299.

Allen, J. J. B. (1998). DSM-IV. In H. S. Friedman (Ed.), *Encyclopedia of mental health (Vol. 2)*. San Diego: Academic Press.

Allen, J. J. B., & Movius, H. L. (2000). The objective assessment of amnesia in dissociative identity disorder using event-related potentials. *International Journal of Psychophysiology, 38,* 21–41.

Allen, J., Kraus, N., & Bradlow, A. (2000). Neural representation of consciously imperceptible speech sound differences. *Perception and Psychophysics, 62,* 1383–1393.

Allen, K. (2000). Negotiating health: Meanings of building a healthy community in Igloolik. In L. J. Kirmayer, M. E. Macdonald, & G. M. Brass (Eds.), *Proceedings of the Montreal Advanced Study Institute: The mental health of indigenous peoples*. Montreal: McGill University Division of Transcultural Psychiatry.*

Alexander, M. P., Stuss, D. T., & Benson, D. F. (1979). Capgras syndrome: A reduplicative phenomenon. *Neurology, 29,* 334–339.*

Allgulander, C., Bandelow, B., Hollander, E., Montgomery, S. A., Nutt, D. J., Okasha, A., Pollack, M. H., Stein, D. J., & Swinson, R. P. (2003). WCA recommendations for the long-term treatment of generalized anxiety disorder. *CNS Spectrums, 8 (8, Suppl1),* 53–61.*

Allison R., Harris, L. R, Jenkin, M., Pintilie, G., Redlick, F. P., & Zikovitz, D. C. (2000). First steps with a rideable computer. *IEEE International Conference on Virtual Reality, 2,* 169--175.*

Alloy, L. B., & Abramson, L. Y. (1979). Judgment of contingency in depressed and nondepressed students: Sadder but wiser? *Journal of Experimental Psychology: General, 108,* 441–485.

Alloy, L. B., Abramson, L. Y., & Francis, E. L. (1999). Do negative cognitive styles confer vulnerability to depression? *Current Directions in Psychological Science, 8,* 128–132.

Alloy, L. B., Riskind, J. H., & Manos, M. (2005). *Abnormal psychology: Current perspectives (9th ed.).* New York: McGraw-Hill.

Allport, G. W. (1937). *Personality: A psychological interpretation.* New York: Holt.

Allport, G. W. (1954). *The nature of prejudice.* Reading, MA: Addison-Wesley.

Al-Mashaan, O. S. (2001). Job stress and job satisfaction in relation to neuroticism, type A behavior, and locus of control among Kuwaiti personnel. *Psychological Reports, 88,* 1145–1152.

Almedom, A. M. (2005). Resilience, hardiness, sense of coherence, and posttraumatic growth: All paths leading to "light at the end of the tunnel"? *Journal of Loss & Trauma, 10(3),* 253–265.

Altemeyer, B. (1996). *The authoritarian specter.* Cambridge Harvard University Press.*

Altemeyer, B. (1999). To thine own self be untrue: Self-awareness in authoritarians. *North American Journal of Psychology, 1(2),* 157–164.*

Altemeyer, B. (2004a). The decline of organized religion in western civilization. *International Journal for the Psychology of Religion, 14(2),* 77–89.*

Altemeyer, B. (2004b). Highly dominating, highly authoritarian personalities. *Journal of Social Psychology, 144(4),* 421–447.*

Altemeyer, B., & Hunsberger, B. (2004). A revised religious fundamentalism scale: the short and sweet of it. *International Journal for the Psychology of Religion, 14(1),* 47–54.*

Alterman, A. I., Gariti, P., & Mulvaney, F. (2001). Short- and long-term smoking cessation for three levels of intensity of behavioral treatment. *Psychology and Addictive Behavior, 15,* 261–264.

Amato, P. R., & Cheadle, J. (2005). The long reach of divorce: Divorce and child well-being across three generations. *Journal of Marriage & Family, 67(1),* 191–206.

Ambady, N., & Rosenthal, R. (1992). Thin slices of expressive behavior as predictors of interpersonal consequences: A meta-analysis. *Psychological Bulletin, 777,* 256–274.

Ambady, N., & R. Rosenthal, R. (1993). Half a minute: Predicting teacher evaluations from thin slices of nonverbal behavior and physical attractiveness. *Journal of Personality & Social Psychology, 64,* 431–41.

Ambady, N., LaPlante, D., & Johnson, E. (2001). Thin slice judgments as a measure of interpersonal sensitivity. In J. Hall, & F. Bernieri (Eds.), *Interpersonal sensitivity: Measurement and applications.* Mahwah, NJ: Erlbaum.

American Academy of Pediatrics. (2001). Health care supervision for children with Williams syndrome. *Pediatrics, 107,* 1192–1204.

American Association on Mental Retardation. (2002). *Mental retardation: Definition, classification, and systems of supports (10th ed.).* Washington: American Association on Mental Retardation.

American Psychiatric Association. (1994). *Diagnostic and statistical manual of mental disorders (4th ed.).* Washington: American Psychiatric Press.

American Psychiatric Association. (2000). *Diagnostic and statistical manual of mental disorders (4th ed.) Text revision.* Washington: American Psychiatric Press.

American Psychiatric Association. (2001). *Mental illness.* Washington: American Psychiatric Press.

American Psychological Association. (1994). Interim report of the working group on investigation of memories of childhood abuse. Washington: APA Press

American Sleep Apnea Association. (2001). *Sleep apnea: General information packet.* Washington: American Sleep Apnea Association.

Amichai-Hamburger, Y. (2002). Internet and personality. *Computers in Human Behavior, 18,* 1–10.

Amichai-Hamburger, Y., & Ben-Artzi, E. (2003). Loneliness and Internet use. *Computers in Human Behavior, 19(1),* 71–80.

Amsel, E., & Byrnes, J. (2001). Symbolic communication and cognitive development. In J. Byrnes, & E. Amsel (Eds.), *Language, literacy, and cognitive development.* Mahwah, NJ: Erlbaum.

Anand, A., Li, Y., Wang, Y., Wu, J., Gao, S., Bukhari, L., Mathews, V. P., Kalnin, A., & Lowe, M. J. (2005a). Activity and connectivity of brain mood regulating circuit in depression: A functional magnetic resonance study. *Biological Psychiatry, 57(10),* 1079–1088.

Anand, A., Li, Y., Wang, Y., Wu, J., Gao, S., Bukhari, L., Mathews, V. P., Kalnin, A., & Lowe, M. J. (2005b). Antidepressant effect on connectivity of the mood-regulating circuit: An fMRI study. *Neuropsychopharmacology, 30(7),* 1334–1344.

Anastasi, A., & Urbina, S. (1996). *Psychological testing (7th ed.).* Englewood Cliffs, NJ: Prentice Hall.

Anderson, B. L. (1998). Cancer. In H. S. Friedman (Ed.), *Encyclopedia of mental health (Vol. 1).* San Diego: Academic Press.

Anderson, B. L. (2000). Cancer. In A. Kazdin (Ed.), *Encyclopedia of psychology.* Washington, & New York: APA Press and Oxford.

Andersen, R. A., & Bruneo, C. A. (2002). Intentional maps in posterior parietal cortex. *Annual Review of Neuroscience, 25,* 189–220.

Anderson, B. L., Golden-Kreutz, D. M., & DiLillo, V. (2001). Cancer. In A. Baum, T. A. Revenson, & J. E. Singer (Eds.), *Handbook of health psychology.* Mahwah, NJ: Erlbaum.

Anderson, B. L., Kiecolt-Glaser, J. K., & Glaser, R. (1994). A biobehavioral model of cancer stress and disease course. *American Psychologist, 49,* 389–404.

Anderson, C. A., Berkowitz, L., Donnerstein, E., Huesmann, L. R., Johnson, J. D., Linz, D., Malamuth, N. M., & Wartella, E. (2003). The influence of media violence on youth. *Psychological Science in the Public Interest, 4(3),* 81–110.

Anderson, C. A., & Bushman, B. J. (2002). Human aggression. *Annual Review of Psychology, 53,* 27–51.

Anderson, D. R., Huston, A. C., Schmitt, K., Linebarger, D., & Wright, J. C. (2001). Early television viewing and adolescent behavior: The recontact study. *Monographs of the Society for Research in Child Development, 66 (1, Serial No. 264.)*

Anderson, E. M., & Lambert, M. J. (2001). A survival analysis of clinically significant change in outpatient psychotherapy. *Journal of Clinical Psychology, 57,* 875–888.

Anderson, J. R. (2005). *Cognitive psychology and its implications (6th ed.).* New York: Worth.

Anderson, J. R., Douglass, S., & Qin, Y. (2005). How should a theory of learning and cognition inform instruction? In A. F. Healy (Ed.), *Experimental cognitive psychology and its applications.* Washington: APA Press.

Anderson, M. (2005). Cortex forum on the concept of general intelligence in neuropsychology. *Cortex, 41(2),* 99–100.

Anderson, M. C. (2003). Rethinking interference theory: Executive control and the mechanisms of forgetting. *Journal of Memory & Language, 49(4),* 415–445.

Anderson, M. C., & Green, C. (2001, March 15). Suppressing unwanted memories by executive control. *Nature, 410,* 366–369.

Anderson, M. C., Ochsner, K. N., Kuhl, B., Cooper, J., Robertson, E., Gabrieli, S. W., Glover, G. H., & Gabrieli, J. D. E. (2004). Neural systems underlying the suppression of unwanted memories. *Science, 303,* 232–235.

Anderson, N. H. (1965). Primacy effects in personality impression formation using a generalized order effect paradigm. *Journal of Personality & Social Psychology, 2,* 1–9.

Anderson, N. H. (1974). Cognitive algebra: Integration theory applied to social attribution. In L. Berkowitz (Ed.), *Advances in experimental social psychology (Vol. 7).* New York: Academic Press.

Anderson, N. H. (1989). Functional memory and on-line attribution. In J. N. Bassili (Ed.), *On-line cognition in person perception.* Mahwah, NJ: Erlbaum.

Andersson, G, Asmundson, G. J. G., Carlbring, P., Ghaderi, A., Hofmann, S. G., & Stewart, S. H. (2005). Is CBT already the dominant paradigm in psychotherapy research and practice? *Cognitive Behaviour Therapy, 34(1),* 1–2.

Andrews, D., Nonnecke, B., & Preece, J. (2003). Electronic survey methodology: A case study in reaching hard-to-involve Internet users. *International Journal of Human-Computer Interaction, 16,* 185–210.*

Andrews, J. J. W., Saklofske, D. H., & Janzen, H. L. (Eds.). (2001). *Handbook of psychoeducational assessment: Ability, achievement, and behavior in children.* San Diego, CA: Academic Press.*

Angold, A., Costello, E. J., & Worthman, C. M. (1998). Puberty and depression: The roles of age, pubertal status, and pubertal timing. *Psychological Medicine, 28,* 51–61.

Angus, L., & Bouffard, B. (2004). The search for emotional meaning and self-coherence in the face of traumatic loss in childhood: A narrative process perspective. In J. D. Raskin, & S. K. Bridges (Eds.), *Studies in meaning 2: Bridging the personal and social in constructivist psychology.* New York: Pace University Press.*

Angus, L., & Hardtke, K. (1994). Narrative processes in psychotherapy. *Canadian Psychology, 35(2),* 190–203.*

Antle, M. C., & Mistlberger, R. E. (2005). Circadian rhythms. In I. Q. Whishaw & B. Kolb (Eds.) *The behavior of the laboratory rat: A handbook with tests.* London: Oxford.*

Antonucci, T. C. (2001). Social relations. In J. E. Birren, & K. W. Schaie (Eds.), *Handbook of the psychology of aging (5th ed.).* San Diego: Academic Press.

Antonucci, T. C., Vandewater, E. A., & Lansford, J. E. (2000). Adult development and aging: Social processes and development. In A. Kazdin (Ed.), *Encyclopedia of psychology.* Washington, & New York: APA Press and Oxford.

Antony, M. M., & Swinson, R. P. (1996). *Anxiety disorders and their treatment: A critical review of the evidence-based literature.* Ottawa: Health Canada (Downloaded July 26, 2005 from http://www.hc-sc.gc.ca/hppb/mentalhealth/pdfs/anxiety_review.pdf).*

Antony, M. M., & Swinson, R. P. (2000). Panic disorder and agoraphobia. In M. M. Antony, & R. P. Swinson (Eds.), *Phobic disorders and panic in adults: A guide to assessment and treatment.* Washington: APA Press.*

Arana-Ward, M. (1997). As technology advances, a bitter debate divides the deaf. *Washington Post, A1.*

Arbona, C. B., Osma, J., Garcia-Palacios, A., Quero, S., & Baños, R. M. (2004). Treatment of flying phobia using virtual reality: Data from a 1-year follow-up using a multiple baseline design. *Clinical Psychology & Psychotherapy, 11(5),* 311–323.

Archer, D., & Gartner, R. (1976). Violent acts and violent times: A comparative approach in postwar homicide. *American Sociological Review, 41,* 937–963.

Archer, D., & McDaniel, P. (1995). Violence and gender: Differences and similarities across societies. In R. B. Ruback, & N. A. Weiner (Eds.), *Interpersonal violent behaviors: Social and cultural aspects.* New York: Springer.

Archer, J. (2004). Sex differences in aggression in real-world settings: A meta-analytic review. *Review of General Psychology, 8(4),* 291–322.

Archer, R. P., Handel, R. W., Greene, R. L., Baer, R. A., & Elkins, D. E. (2001). An evaluation of the usefulness of the MMPI-2 F (p) scale. *Journal of Personality Assessment, 76,* 282–285.

Archibald, A. B., Graber, J. A., & Brooks-Gunn, J. (2003). Pubertal processes and physical growth in adolescence. In G. R. Adams, & M. Berzonsky (Eds.),

Blackwell handbook of adolescence. Malden, MA: Blackwell.

Archibald, C. J., & Fisk, J. D. (2000). Information processing efficiency in patients with multiple sclerosis. *Journal of Clinical and Experimental Neuropsychology, 22,* 686–701.*

Armitage, R., Emslie, G. J., Hoffman, R. F., Rintelmann, J., & Rush, A. J. (2001). Delta sleep EEG in depressed adolescent females and healthy controls. *Journal of Affective Disorders, 63,* 139–148.

Arndt, J., Schimel, J., Greenberg, J., & Pyszczynski, T. (2002). The intrinsic self and defensiveness: Evidence that activating the intrinsic self reduces self-handicapping and conformity. *Personality and Social Psychology Bulletin, 28,* 671–683.

Arnell, K. M., & Jenkins, R. (2004). Revisiting within-modality and cross-modality attentional blinks: Effects of target-distractor similarity. *Perception & Psychophysics, 66(7),* 1147–1161.*

Arnell, K. M., & Jolicoeur, P. (1999). The attentional blink across stimulus modalities: Evidence for a central processing limitation. *Journal of Experimental Psychology: Human Perception and Performance, 25,* 630–648.*

Arnett, J. J. (2000). Emerging adulthood: A theory of development from the late teens through the twenties. *American Psychologist, 55,* 469–480.

Arnett, J. J. (2002). Adolescents in Western countries in the 21st century: Vast opportunities—for all? In B. B. Brown, R. W. Larson, & T. S. Saraswathi (Eds.), *The world's youth: Adolescence in eight regions of the globe.* Boston: Cambridge.

Arnett, J. J. (2004). *Emerging adulthood: The winding road from late teens through the twenties.* New York: Oxford.

Arnett, J. J., & Galambos, N. L. (Eds.). (2003). *New directions for child and adolescent development: Exploring cultural conceptions of the transition to adulthood.* San Francisco: Jossey-Bass.*

Arnkoff, D. B., Glass, C. R., & Shapiro, S. J. (2002). Expectations and preferences. In J. C. Norcross (Ed.), *Psychotherapy relationships that work.* New York: Oxford.

Arntz, A. (2003). Cognitive therapy versus applied relaxation as treatment of generalized anxiety disorder. *Behaviour Research & Therapy, 41(6),* 633–646.

Arnoux, D. (1998, September). *Description of teaching experiences prepared for John Santrock's text, Educational Psychology.* New York: McGraw-Hill.

Aron, A., Aron, E., & Coups, E. (2006). *Statistics for the behavioral and social sciences: A brief course (4th ed.).* Englewood Cliffs, NJ: Prentice Hall.

Aronson, E. (2000). *Nobody left to hate.* New York: Freeman.

Aronson, E. (2003). *The social animal (9th ed.).* New York: Worth/Freeman.

Aronson, E. (2004). Reducing hostility and building compassion: Lessons from the jigsaw classroom. In A. G. Miller (Ed.), *The social psychology of good and evil.* New York: Guilford.

Aronson, E., Wilson, T. D., & Akert, R. M. (2005). *Social psychology (5th ed.).* Englewood Cliffs, NJ: Prentice Hall.

Aronson, J., Cohen, G., & Nails, P. R. (1999). Unwanted consequences and the self: In search of the motivation for dissonance reduction. In E. Harmon-Jones, & J. Mills (Eds.), *Cognitive dissonance.* Washington: APA Press.

Artz, S. (1998). *Sex, power, & the violent school girl.* Toronto: Trifolium Books.*

Artz, S. (2004). Violence in the schoolyard: School girls' use of violence. In C. Alder, & A. Worall (Eds.), *Girls' violence: Myths and realities.* New York: SUNY Press.*

Artz, S. (2005). To die for: Violent adolescent girls' search for male attention. In D. J. Pepler, K. C. Madsen, C. D. Webster, & K. S. Levene (Eds.), *The development and treatment of girlhood aggression.* Mahwah, NJ: Erlbaum.*

Arvanitogiannis, A., & Amir, S. (1999). Circadian clock resetting by ultra-short light flashes. *Neuroscience Letters, 261,* 159–162.*

Arvanitogiannis, A., & Amir, S. (2001). A novel, associative process modulating photic resetting of the circadian clock. *Neuroscience, 104,* 615–618.*

Arvanitogiannis, A., Beaulé, C., Robinson, B., & Amir, S. (2000). Calbindin-D28k immunoreactivity in the suprachiasmatic nucleus and the circadian response to constant light in the rat. *Neuroscience, 99,* 397–401.*

Arvind, S., & Rogers, E. M. (2003). *Combating AIDS: Communication strategies in action.* Thousand Oaks, CA: Sage.

Asch, S. E. (1946). Forming impressions of personality. *Journal of Personality & Social Psychology, 41,* 248–290.

Asch, S. E. (1951). Effects of group pressure on the modification and distortion of judgments. In H. S. Guetzkow (Ed.), *Groups, leadership, and men.* Pittsburgh: Carnegie University Press.

Ashby, F. G., & Maddox, W. T. (2005). Human category learning. *Annual Review of Psychology, 56,* 149–78.

Ashcraft, M. H., & Kirk, E. P. (2001). The relationships among working memory, math anxiety, and performance. *Journal of Experimental Psychology: General, 130,* 224–237.

Ashcroft, D. (2003). *Personality theories workbook (2nd ed.).* Belmont, CA: Wadsworth.

Asher, J., & Garcia, R. (1969). The optimal age to learn a foreign language. *Modern Language Journal, 53,* 334–341.

Ashida, H., Seiffert, A. E., & Osaka, N. (2001). Inefficient visual search for second-order motion. *Journal of the Optical Society of America, 18,* 2255–2266.

Ashmore, R. D., Deaux, K., & McLaughlin-Volpe, T. (2004). An organizing framework for collective identity: Articulation and significance of multidimensionality. *Psychological Bulletin, 130,* 80–114.

Ashton, M. C., Jackson, D. N., Helmes, E., & Paunonen, S. V. (1998a). Joint factor analysis of the Personality Research Form and the Jackson Personality Inventory: Comparisons with the Big Five. *Journal of Research in Personality, 32,* 243–250.*

Ashton, M. C., & Lee, K. (2005). A defence of the lexical approach to the study of personality structure. *European Journal of Personality, 19(1),* 5–24.*

Ashton, M. C., Lee, K., & Goldberg, L. R. (2004). A hierarchical analysis of 1,710 english personality-descriptive adjectives. *Journal of Personality & Social Psychology, 87(5),* 707–721.*

Ashton, M. C., Paunonen, S. V., Helmes, E., & Jackson, D. N. (1998b). Kin altruism, reciprocal altruism, and the Big Five personality factors. *Evolution and Human Behavior, 19,* 243–255.*

Asplund, R. (2003). Nightmares relation to health, sleep and somatic symptoms in the elderly. *Sleep in & Hypnosis, 5(4),* 175–181.

Atkinson, D. R. & Hackett, G. (2004). *Counseling diverse populations (3rd ed.).* New York: McGraw-Hill.

Atkinson, J. W., & Raynor, I. O. (1974). *Motivation and achievement.* Washington: Winston.

Atkinson, R. C., & Shiffrin, R. M. (1968). Human memory: A proposed system and its control processes. In K. W. Spence, & J. T. Spence (Eds.), *The psychology of learning and motivation (Vol. 2).* San Diego, CA: Academic Press.

Attaca, B., & Berry, J. W. (2002). Psychological, sociocultural and martial adaptation of Turkish immigrant couples in Canada. *International Journal of Psychology, 37,* 13–26.*

Atwood, J. D. (Ed.). (2001). *Family systems/family therapy.* Binghamton, NY: Haworth Press.

Auger, C., Latour, S., Trudel, M., & Fortin, M. (2000). Post-traumatic stress disorder: After the flood in Saguenay. *Canadian Family Physician, 46,* 2420–2427.*

Auld, F., Hyman, M., & Rudzinski, D. (2005). *Resolution of inner conflict: An introduction to psychoanalytic therapy (2nd ed.).* Washington: APA Press.*

Austin, J. L., Lee, M., & Carr, J. P. (2004). The effects of guided notes on undergraduate students' recording of lecture content. *Journal of Instructional Psychology, 31(4),* 314–320.

Ausubel, D. P. (1963). *The psychology of meaningful verbal learning.* New York: Grune & Stratton.

Ausubel, D. P. (1968). *Educational psychology: A cognitive view.* New York: Rinehart & Winston.

Ausubel, D. P. (1978). In defense of advance organizers: A reply to the critics. *Review of Educational Research, 48,* 251–257.

Averill, J. R. (1983). Studies on anger and aggression: Implications for theories of emotion. *American Psychologist, 38,* 1145–1160.

Avis, N. E. (1999). Women's health at midlife. In S. L. Willis, & J. D. Reid (Eds.), *Life in the middle: Psychological and social development in middle age.* San Diego: Academic.Press

Azar, S. T. (2002). Parenting and child maltreatment. In M. Bornstein (Ed.), *Handbook of parenting (2nd ed.).* Mahwah, NJ: Erlbaum.

Azhar, M. Z. (2001). Comparison of Fluvoxamine alone, Fluvoxamine and cognitive psychotherapy and psychotherapy alone in the treatment of panic disorder in Kelantan: Implications for management by family doctors. *Medical Journal of Malaysia, 55,* 402–408.

B

Baars, B. (1999). Psychology in a world of sentimental, self-knowing beings: A modest utopian fantasy. In R. L. Solso (Ed.), *Mind and brain sciences in the 21st century.* Cambridge MIT Press.

Bachman, J. (1997). *Smoking, drinking, and drug use in young adulthood: The impact of new freedoms and responsibilities.* Mahwah, NJ: Erlbaum.

Backman, L., Small, B. J., & Wahlin, A. (2001). Aging and memory. In J. E. Birren, & K. W. Schaie (Eds.), *Handbook of the psychology of aging (5th ed.).* San Diego: Academic Press.

Baddeley, A. D., & Hitch, G. (1974). Working memory. In G. H. Bower (Ed.), *The psychology of learning and motivation (Vol. 8).* San Diego: Academic Press.

Baddeley, A. D. (1992). Working memory. *Science, 255,* 556–560.

Baddeley, A. D. (2000). Short-term and working memory. In E. Tulving, & F. I. M. Craik (Eds.), *The Oxford handbook of memory.* New York: Oxford.

Baddeley, A. D. (2001). *Is working memory still working?* Paper presented at the meeting of the American Psychological Association, San Francisco.

Baddeley, A. D. (2003). Working memory: Looking back and looking forward. *Nature Reviews Neuroscience, 4(10),* 829-839.

Badgaiyan, R. D. (2005). Conscious awareness of retrieval: An exploration of the cortical connectivity. *International Journal of Psychophysiology, 55(2),* 257–262.

Badgaiyan, R. D., Schacter, D. L., & Alpert, N. M. (2001). Priming within and across modalities: Exploring the nature of rCBF increases and decreases. *NeuroImage, 13,* 272–282.

Baehr, E. K., Revelle, W., & Eastman, C. I. (2000). Individual differences in the phase and amplitude of the human circadian temperature rhythm with an emphasis on morningness-eveningness. *Journal of Sleep Research, 9,* 117–127.

Bagby, R., M., & Parker, J. D. A. (2001). Relation of rumination and distraction with neuroticism and extraversion in a sample of patients with Major Depression. *Cognitive Therapy and Research, 25,* 91–102.*

Bagozzi, R. P., & Dholakia, U. M. (2005). Three roles of past experience in goal setting and goal striving. In T. Betsch, & S. Haberstroh (Eds.), *The routines of decision making.* Mahwah, NJ: Erlbaum.

Bailis, D. S., Chipperfield, J. G., & Perry, R. P. (2005). Optimistic social comparisons of older adults low in primary control: A prospective analysis of hospitalization and mortality. *Health Psychology, 24(4),* 393–401.*

Baillargeon, R. (1997). The object concept revisited. In C. E. Granrud (Ed.), *Visual perception and cognition in infancy.* Mahwah, NJ: Erlbaum.

Baillargeon, R. (2004). Infants' reasoning about hidden objects: Evidence for event-general and event-specific expectations. *Developmental Science. 7(4)*, 391-424.

Bain, S. K., & Allin, J. D. (2005). Stanford-Binet Intelligence Scales, (5th Edition). *Journal of Psychoeducational Assessment, 23(1)*, 87–95.

Baity, M. R., & Hilsenroth, M. J. (1999). Rorschach aggression variables: A study of reliability and validity. *Journal of Personality & Assessment, 72*, 93–110.

Baker, B. (2001, March). *Marital interaction in mild hypertension*. Paper presented at the meeting of the American Psychosomatic Association, Monterey, CA.

Baker, L. R. (2001). Folk psychology. In R. A. Wilson & F. C. Keil (Eds.), *MIT Encyclopedia of the Cognitive Sciences*. Cambridge MIT Press.

Baker, M. C. (2004). Socially learned antipredator behavior in black-capped chickadees (Poecile atricapillus). *Bird Behavior, 16(1–2)*, 13–19.

Bakkum, D. J., Shkolnik, A. C., Ben-Ary, G., Gamblen, P., DeMaarse, T. B. and Potter, S. M. (2004). Removing some 'A' from AI: Embodied cultured networks. In Iida, F., Pfeifer, R., Steels, L. & Kuniyoshi, Y. (Eds.), *Embodied artificial intelligence*. New York: Springer.

Baldo, M. V., Kihra, A. H., Namba, J., & Klein, S. A. (2002). Evidence for an attentional component of the perceptual misalignment between moving and flashing stimuli. *Perception, 31*, 17–30.

Baldo, O., & Eardley, I. (2005). Diagnosis and investigation of men with erectile dysfunction. *Journal of Men's Health & Gender, 2(1)*, 79–86.

Baldwin, J. D., & Baldwin, J. I. (1998). Sexual behavior. In H. S. Friedman (Ed.), *Encyclopedia of mental health (Vol. 3)*. San Diego: Academic Press.

Baldwin, J. D., & Baldwin, J. I. (2001). *Behavior principles in everyday life*. Englewood Cliffs, NJ: Prentice Hall.

Bales, J. (1988, December). Vincennes: Findings could have averted tragedy, scientists tell Hill panel. *APA Monitor*, pp. 10–11.

Baltes, P. B. (1993). The aging mind: Potentials and limits. *Gerontologist, 33*, 580–594.

Baltes, P. B. (2000). Life-span developmental theory. In A. Kazdin (Ed.), *Encyclopedia of psychology*. Washington, & New York: APA Press and Oxford.

Baltes, P. B., & Kunzmann, U. (2003). Wisdom. *Psychologist, 16(3)*, 131–133.

Baltes, P. B., Lindenberger, U., & Staudinger, U. M. (1998). Life-span theory in developmental psychology. In W. Damon (Ed.), *Handbook of child psychology (5th ed., Vol. 1)*. New York: Wiley.

Banai, E., Mikulincer, M., & Shaver, P. R. (2005). "Selfobject" needs in Kohut's self psychology: Links with attachment, self-cohesion, affect regulation, and adjustment. *Psychoanalytic Psychology, 22(2)*, 224–260.

Bandura, A. (1965). Influences of models' reinforcement contingencies on the acquisition of imitative responses. *Journal of Personality & Social Psychology, 1*, 589–596.

Bandura, A. (1977). *Social learning theory*. Englewood Cliffs, NJ: Prentice Hall.

Bandura, A. (1986). *Social foundations of thought and action*. Englewood Cliffs, NJ: Prentice Hall.

Bandura, A. (1989). Social cognitive theory. In R. Vasta (Ed.), *Six theories of child development*. Greenwich, CT: JAI Press.

Bandura, A. (1997). *Self-efficacy: The exercise of self-control*. New York: Freeman.

Bandura, A. (2000a). Social cognitive theory. In A. Kazdin (Ed.), *Encyclopedia of psychology*. Washington, and New York: APA Press and Oxford.

Bandura, A. (2000b). Self-efficacy. In A. Kazdin (Ed.), *Encyclopedia of psychology*. Washington, & New York: APA Press and Oxford.

Bandura, A. (2001). Social cognitive theory: An agentic perspective. *Annual Review of Psychology, 52*, 1–26.

Bandura, A. (2004). Model of causality in social learning theory. In A. Freeman, M. J. Mahoney, P. DeVito, & D. Martin (Eds.), *Cognition and psychotherapy (2nd ed.)*. New York: Springer.

Banich, M. T., & Mack, M. (Eds). (2002). *Mind, brain , and language: Multidisciplinary perspectives*. Mahwah, NJ: Erlbaum.

Banks, J. (2006). *Cultural diversity and education: foundations, curriculum, and teaching (5th ed.)*. Boston: Allyn & Bacon.

Banks, J. (2003). *Teaching strategies for ethnic studies (7th ed.)*. Boston: Allyn & Bacon.

Bannerman, K., Lemaire, M., Yee, K., Iversen, D., Oswald, P., Good, A., & Rawlins, G. A. (2002). Selective cytotoxic lesions of the retrohippocampal region produce a mild deficit in social recognition memory. *Experimental Brain Research, 142*, 395–401.

Baranowsky, A. B., Young, M., Johnson-Douglas, S., Williams-Keeler, L., & McCarrey, M. (1998). PTSD transmission: A review of secondary traumatization in Holocaust survivor families. *Canadian Psychology, 39(4)*, 247–256.*

Baard, P. P., Deci, E. L., & Ryan, R. M. (2004). Intrinsic need satisfaction: A motivational basis of performance and well-being in two work settings. *Journal of Applied Social Psychology, 34(10)*, 2045–2068.

Baranowsky, A. B., Gentry, J. E., & Schultz, D. F. (2005). *Trauma practice: Tools for stabilization and recovery*. Ashland, OH: Hogrefe & Huber.*

Bard, P. (1934). Emotion. In C. Murchison (Ed.), *Handbook of general psychology*. Worcester, MA: Clark University Press.

Barker, L. M. (2001). *Learning and behavior (3rd ed.)*. Englewood Cliffs, NJ: Prentice Hall.

Barkow, J. H. (2005). *Missing the revolution: Darwinism for social scientists*. New York: Oxford.*

Barlow, D. H. (2001). *Anxiety and its disorders (2nd ed.)*. New York: Guilford.

Barlow, D. H. & Durand, V. M. (2005). *Abnormal psychology: An integrative approach (4th ed.)*. Belmont, CA: Wadsworth.

Barlow, D. H., Durand, V. M. & Stewart, S. H. (2006). *Abnormal psychology: An integrative approach (1st Canadian ed.)*. Toronto: Thomson.

Barlow, D. H., Gorman, J. M., Shear, M. K., & Woods, S. W. (2000). Cognitive-behavioral therapy, imipramine, or their combination for panic disorder: A randomized controlled trial. *Journal of the American Medical Association, 283*, 2229–2236.

Barman, J. (1996). Aboriginal education at the crossroads: The legacy of residential schools and the way ahead. In D. A. Long, & O. P. Dickason (Eds.), *Visions of the heart: Canadian aboriginal issues*. Toronto: Harcourt Brace Canada.*

Barnes, V. A., Davis, H. C., Murzynowski, J. B., & Treiber, F. A. (2004). Impact of meditation on resting and ambulatory blood pressure and heart rate in youth. *Psychosomatic Medicine, 66(6)*, 909–914.

Barnett, R. C. (2002). Work-family balance. In J. Worell (Ed.), *Encyclopedia of women and gender*. San Diego: Academic Press.

Barnett, R. C. (2004). Women and multiple roles: Myths and reality. *Harvard Review of Psychiatry, 12(3)*, 158–164.

Barnett, R. C. (2005). Dual-earner couples: Good/Bad for her and/or him? In D. F. Halpern, & S. E. Murphy (Eds.), *From work-family balance to work-family interaction: Changing the metaphor*. Mahwah, NJ: Erlbaum.

Barnett, R. C., Gareis, K. C., James, J. B., & Steele, J. (2001, August). *Planning ahead: College seniors' concerns about work-family conflict*. Paper presented at the meeting of the American Psychological Association, San Francisco.

Baron, N. (1992). *Growing up with language*. Reading, MA: Addison-Wesley.

Bar-On, R., & Parker, J. D. A. (2000). *Handbook of emotional intelligence*. San Francisco, CA: Jossey-Bass.*

Baron, R. S. (2005). So right it's wrong: Groupthink and the ubiquitous nature of polarized group decision making In M. P. Zanna (Ed.), *Advances in experimental social psychology (Vol. 37)*. San Diego, CA: Elsevier.

Baron, R. A., & Byrne, D. (2003). *Social psychology (10th ed.)*. Boston: Allyn & Bacon.

Barrett, M. C., King, A., Lévy, J., Maticka-Tyndale, E., & McKay, A. (1997). Canada. In R. T. Francoeur (Ed.), *The International encyclopedia of sexuality (Vol 1): Argentina to Greece*. New York: Continuum.*

Barron, K. E., & Harackiewicz, J. M. (2001). Achievement goals and optimal motivation: Testing multiple goal models. *Journal of Personality & Social Psychology, 80*, 706–722.

Barron, R. W. (1994). The sound-to-spelling connection: Orthographic activation in auditory word recognition and its implications for the acquisition of phonological awareness and literacy skills. In V. W. Berninger (Ed.), *The varieties of othographic knowledge I: Theoretical and developmental issues*. Dordrecht, the Netherlands: Kluwer Academic Press.

Barry, H., Child, I. L., & Bacon, M. K. (1959). Relation of child training to subsistence cconomy. *American Anthropologist, 61*, 51–63.

Bartlett, F. C. (1932). *Remembering*. Cambridge: Cambridge University Press.

Bartoshuk, L. M. (2004). Psychophysics: A journey from the laboratory to the clinic. *Appetite, 43(1)*, 15–18.

Bartoshuk, L. M., & Beauchamp, G. K. (1994). Chemical senses. *Annual Review of Psychology, 45*, 419–449.

Baruss, I. (2003). *Alterations of consciousness: An empirical analysis for social scientists*. Washington: APA Press.

Bartzokis, G, Sultzer, D, Lu, P. H, Neuchterlein, K. H, Mintz, J, & Cummings, J. L. (2004). Heterogeneous age-related breakdown of white matter structural integrity: Implications for cortical "disconnection" in aging and Alzheimer's disease. *Neurobiology of Aging, 25*, 843–851.

Bassett, A. S., Cohw, E. W., Waterworth, D. M., & Brzustowicz, L. (2001). Genetic insights into schizophrenia. *Canadian Journal of Psychiatry, 46*, 121–122.*

Basso, M. R., Schefft, B. K., Ris, M. D., & Dember, W. N. (1996). Mood and global-local visual processing. *Journal of the International Neuropsychological Society, 2*, 249–255.

Bates, T. C. (2005). Auditory inspection time and intelligence. *Personality & Individual Differences, 38(1)*, 115–127.

Batson, C. D. (2002). Addressing the altruism question experimentally. In S. G. Post, L. G. Underwood, J. P. Schloss, & W. B. Hurlbut (Eds.), *Altruism and altruistic love*. New York: Oxford.

Batson, C. D., & Powell, A. A. (2003). Altruism and prosocial behavior. In T. Millon, & M. J. Lerner (Eds.), *Handbook of psychology: Personality and social psychology (Vol. 5)*. New York: Wiley.

Bauer, N. & Rokach, A. (2004). The experience of loneliness in university: A cross-cultural study. *International Journal of Adolescence & Youth, 11(4)*, 283–302.*

Baumeister, R. F. (1989). The optimal margin of illusion. *Journal of Social and Clinical Psychology, 8*, 176–189.

Baumeister, R. F. (1991). *Meanings of life*. New York: Guilford.

Baumeister, R. F. (1997). Identity, self-concept, and self-esteem. In R. Hogan, J. Johnson, & S. Briggs (Eds.), *Handbook of personality psychology*. San Diego: Academic Press.

Baumeister, R. F. (1999). *Evil: Inside human violence and cruelty*. New York: Freeman.

Baumeister, R. F., & Butz, D. (2005). Roots of evil, violence, and hate. In R. Sternberg (Ed.), *The psychology of hate*. Washington: APA Press.

Baumeister, R. F., Campbell, J. D., Krueger, J. I., & Vohs, K. D. (2003). Does high self-esteem cause better performance, interpersonal success, happiness, or healthier lifestyles? *Psychological Science in the Public Interest. 4(1)*, 1–44.*

Baumrind, D. (1971). Current patterns of parental authority. *Developmental Psychology Monographs, 4 (1, Pt. 2)*.

Baumrind, D. (in press). Patterns of parental authority and adolescent autonomy. In J. Smetana (Ed.), *New directions for child development: Changes in parental authority during adolescence*. San Francisco: Jossey-Bass.

Baxter, Jr., L. R., Phelps, M. E., Mazziotta, J. C., Schwartz, J. M., Gerner, R. H., Selin, C. E., et al. (1995). Cerebral metabolic rates for glucose in mood disorders: Studies with positron emission tomography and fluorodeoxyglucose F 18. *Archives of General Psychiatry, 42*, 441–447.

Baylor, D. (2001). *Seeing, hearing, and smelling the world*. Retrieved August 29, 2005 from http://www.hhmi.org/senses.

Beal, A. L. (1995). Post-traumatic stress disorder in prisoners of war and combat veterans of the Dieppe Raid: A 50-year follow-up. *Canadian Journal of Psychiatry, 40(4),* 177–184.*

Beal, A. L., Dumont, R. P., Cruse, C. L., & Branche, A. H. (1996). Practical implications of differences between the American and Canadian norms for WISC-III and a short form for children with learning disabilities. *Canadian Journal of School Psychology, 12,* 7–14.*

Beauchamp, M. S., Less, K. E., Haxby, J. V., & Martin, A. (2002). Parallel visual motion processing streams for manipulable objects and human movements. *Neuron, 34,* 149–159.

Beaupré, M. G., & Hess, U. (2005). Cross-cultural emotion recognition among Canadian ethnic groups. *Journal of Cross-Cultural Psychology, 36(3),* 355–370.*

Bechara, A., Damasio, H., Tranel, D., & Damasio, A. R. (1997). Deciding advantageously before knowing the advantageous strategy. *Science, 275,* 1293–1295.

Bechara, A., Damasio, H., Tranel, D., & Damasio, A. R. (2005). The Iowa Gambling Task and the somatic marker hypothesis: Some questions and answers. *Cognitive Sciences, 9(4),* 159–162.

Beck, A. T. (1967). *Depression*. New York: Harper & Row.

Beck, A. T. (1976). *Cognitive therapies and the emotional disorders*. New York: International Universities Press.

Beck, A. T. (1993). Cognitive therapy: Past, present, and future. *Journal of Consulting and Clinical Psychology, 61,* 194–198.

Beck, A. T. (2004). Cognitive patterns in dreams and daydreams. In R. I. Rosner, & W. J. Lyddon (Eds.), Cognitive therapy and dreams. New York: Springer Publishing.

Beck, A. T., Rush, A. J., Shaw, B. F., & Emery, G. (1979). *Cognitive therapy of depression*. New York: Guilford.

Beck, J. (2002). Beck therapy approach. In M. Hersen, & W. H. Sledge (Eds.), *Encyclopedia of psychotherapy*. San Diego: Academic Press.

Beck, R. C. (2004). *Motivation: Theories and principles (5th ed.)*. Englewood Cliffs, NJ: Prentice Hall.

Becker, A. J., Uckert, S., Stief, C. G., Scheller, F., Knapp, W. H., et al. (2002). Cavernous and systematic plasma levels of norepinephrine and epinephrine during different penile conditions in healthy men and patients with erectile dysfunction. *Urology, 59,* 281–286.

Bednar, R. L., Wells, M. G., & Peterson, S. R. (1995). *Self-esteem (2nd ed.)*. Washington: APA Press.

Beevers, C. G., & Miller, I. W. (2005). Unlinking negative cognition and symptoms of depression: Evidence of a specific treatment effect for cognitive therapy. *Journal of Consulting & Clinical Psychology, 73(1),* 68–77.

Begg, I. M. (1983). Imagery instruction and the organization of memory. In J. C. Yuille (Ed.), *Imagery, memory and cognition*. Mahwah, NJ: Erlbaum.*

Begg, I. M., Needham, D. R., & Bookbinder, M. (1993). Do backward messages unconsciously affect listeners? No. *Canadian Journal of Experimental Psychology, 47(1),* 1–14.*

Behrend, D. A., Beike, D. R., & Lampinen, J. M. (2004). *The self and memory*. Hove, UK: Psychology Press.

Behrens, H. & Gut, U. (2005). The relationship between prosodic and syntactic organization in early multiword speech. *Journal of Child Language, 32(1),* 1–34.

Behrmann, M., Avidan, G., Marotta, J. J. & Kimchi, R. (in press). Detailed exploration of face-related processing in congenital prosopagnosia: 1. Behavioral findings. *Journal of Cognitive Neuroscience.**

Beilock, S. L., Kulp, C. A., Holt, L. E., Carr, T. H. (2004). More on the fragility of performance: Choking under pressure in mathematical problem solving. *Journal of Experimental Psychology: General, 133(4),* 584–600.

Beiser, M. (1999). *Strangers at the gate: The 'boat people's' first ten years in Canada*. Toronto: University of Toronto Press, 1999.*

Beiser, M., Hou, F., Hyman, I., & Tousignant, M. (2002). Poverty, family process, and the mental health of immigrant children in Canada. *American Journal of Public Health, 92,* 220–227.*

Békésy, G. von (1960). Vibratory patterns of the basilar membrane. In E. G. Wever (Ed.), *Experiments in hearing*. New York: McGraw-Hill.

Belicki, K., & Cuddy, M. (1996). Identifying a history of sexual trauma from patterns of dream and sleep experience. In D. Barrett (Ed.), *Trauma & dreams*. Boston: Harvard University Press.*

Belicki, K., Chambers, E., & Ogilvie, R. (1997). Nightmares and sleep quality. *Sleep Research, 26,* 637.*

Belicki, K., Correy, B., Cuddy, M., Dunlop, A., & Boucock, A. (1993). Examining the authenticity of reports of sexual abuse. *Canadian Psychology, 34,* 284.*

Belk, A., & Ruse, M. (2000). Why should evolutionary psychology be a science? *Psychological Inquiry, 11,* 22–23.

Bell, A. P., Weinberg, M. S., & Mammersmith, S. K. (1981). *Sexual preference*. New York: Simon & Schuster.

Bellesiles, M. A. (1999). *Lethal imagination*. New York: New York University Press.

Bellodi, L., Cavallini, M. C., Bertelli, S., Chiapparino, D., Riboldi, C., & Smeraldi, E. (2001). Morbidity risk for obsessive-compulsive spectrum disorders in first-degree relatives of patients with eating disorders. *American Journal of Psychiatry, 158,* 563–569.

Belsky, J. K. (1999). *The psychology of aging (3rd ed.)*. Belmont, CA: Wadsworth.

Bem, D. (1967). Self-perception: An alternative explanation of cognitive dissonance phenomena. *Psychological Review, 74,* 183–200.

Benca, R. M. (2001). Consequences of insomnia and its therapies. *Journal of Clinical Psychiatry, 62(Suppl. 10),* 33–38.

Benedetti, F., Maggi, G., & Lopiano, L. (2003). Open versus hidden medical treatments: The patient's knowledge about a therapy affects the therapy outcome. *Prevention & Treatment, 6,* Article 1. Retrieved from http://journals.apa.org/prevention/volume6/pre0060001a.html August 19, 2005.

Benini, A. L., Camilloni, M. A., Scordato, C., Lezzi, G., Savia, G., Oriani, G., et al. (2001). Contribution of weight cycling to serum leptin in human obesity. *International Journal of Obesity and Related Metabolic Disorders, 25,* 721–726.

Benjafield, J. G. (1997). *Cognition (2nd ed.)*. Englewood Cliffs, NJ: Prentice Hall.*

Benjafield, J. G. (2004). *A history of psychology (2nd ed.)*. Boston: Allyn & Bacon.*

Ben-Shakhar, G., Bar-Hillel, M., & Kremnitzer, M. (2002). Trial by polygraph: Reconsidering the use of the guilty knowledge technique in court. *Law & Human Behavior, 26(5),* 527–541.

Bennardo, G. (2003). Language, mind, and culture: From linguistic relativity to representational modularity. In M. T. Banich, & M. Mack (Eds.), *Mind, brain, and language: Multidisciplinary perspectives*. Mahwah, NJ: Erlbaum.

Benson, J., Greaves, W., O'Donnell, M., & Taglialatela, J. (2002). Evidence for symbolic language processing in a Bonobo (Pan paniscus). *Journal of Consciousness Studies, 9(12),* 33–56.*

Ben-Shakhar, G., Bar-Hillel, M., Yoram, B., Ben-Abba, E., & Flug, A. (1986). Can graphology predict occupational success? Two empirical studies and some methodological ruminations. *Journal of Applied Psychology, 71,* 645–653.

Ben-Zur, H., Rappaport, B., & Uretzky, G. (2004). Pessimism, lifestyle, and survival: A follow-up study of open-heart surgery patients in Israel. *Illness, Crisis & Loss, 12(4),* 299–306.

Bereiter, C. (2002). *Education and mind in the Knowledge Age*. Mahwah, NJ: Erlbaum.*

Bereiter, C., & Scardamalia, M. (1996). Rethinking learning. In D. R. Olson, & N. Torrance (Eds.), *Handbook of education and human development: New models of learning, teaching and schooling*. Cambridge Basil Blackwell.*

Bereiter, C., & Scardamalia, M. (2000). Commentary on part I: Process and product in problem-based learning (PBL) research. In D. H. Evensen, & C. E. Hmelo (Eds.), *Problem-based learning: A research perspective on learning interactions*. Mahwah, NJ: Erlbaum.*

Berenbaum, S. A., & Hines, M. (1992). Early androgens are related to childhood sex-typed toy preferences. *Psychological Science, 3,* 203–206.

Berg, C. (2000). Intellectual development in adulthood. In R. J. Sternberg (Ed.), *Handbook of intelligence*. New York: Cambridge.

Berg, F. M. (1998). Is yo-yo dieting dangerous? In S. Nolen-Hoeksema (Ed.), *Clashing views on abnormal psychology: A Taking Sides custom reader*. Guilford, CT: Dushkin/McGraw-Hill.

Bering, J. M., & Shackelford, T. K. (2004). The causal role of consciousness: A conceptual addendum to human evolutionary psychology. *Review of General Psychology, 8(4),* 227–248.

Berko, J. (1958). The child's learning of English morphology. *World, 14,* 150–157.

Berkowitz, L. (1990). On the formation and regulation of anger and aggression: A cognitive neoassociationistic analysis. *American Psychologist, 45,* 494–503.

Bernstein, A. B. (2001). Motherhood, health status, and health care. *Women's Health Issues, 11,* 173–184.

Berridge, C. W., & O'Neil, J. (2001). Differential sensitivity to the wake-promoting actions of norepinephrine within the medial preoptic area and the substantia innominata. *Behavioral Neuroscience, 115,* 165–174.

Berridge, K. C. (2004). Motivation concepts in behavioral neuroscience. *Physiology & Behavior. Special Reviews on Ingestive Science, 81(2),* 179–209.

Berry, J. W. (1976). *Human ecology and cognitive style*. New York: Sage.*

Berry, J. W. (1980). Acculturation as varieties of adaptation. In A. Padilla (Ed.), *Acculturation: Theory, model, and new new findings*. Washington: American Association for the Advancement of Science.*

Berry, J. W. (1993). Psychology in and of Canada: One small step toward a universal psychology. In U. Kim, & J. W. Berry (Eds.), *Indigenous psychologies: Research and experience in cultural context*. Newbury Park, CA: Sage.*

Berry, J. W. (1996). A cultural ecology of cognition. In I. Dennis, & P. Tapsfield (Eds.), *Human abilities: Their nature and measurement*. Mahwah, NJ: Erlbaum.*

Berry, J. W. (1999). Intercultural relations in plural societies. *Canadian Psychology, 40(1),* 12–21.*

Berry, J. W. (2001). Contextual studies of cognitive adaptation. In J. M. Collis, & S. Messick (Eds.), *Intelligence and personality: Bridging the gap in theory and measurement*. Mahwah, NJ: Erlbaum.*

Berry, J. W., & Bennett, J. A. (1992). Cree conceptions of cognitive competence. *International Journal of Psychology, 27,* 73–88.*

Berry, J. W., Phinney, J. S, Sam, D. L. & Vedder, P. (2005). *Immigrant youth in cultural transition*. Mahwah, NJ: Erlbaum.*

Berry, J. W., Poortinga, Y. H., Segall, M. H., & Dasen, P. R. (2002). *Cross-cultural psychology: Research and applications (2nd ed.)*. New York: Cambridge.*

Berry, J. W., & Triandis, H. C. (2004). Cross-cultural psychology. In C. Speilberger (Ed.), *Encyclopaedia of applied psychology (Vol. 1)*. San Diego: Elsevier/Academic Press.*

Berscheid, E. (2000). Attraction. In A. Kazdin (Ed.), *Encyclopedia of psychology*. Washington, & New York: APA Press and Oxford.

Berscheid, E., & Fei, J. (1977). Sexual jealousy and romantic love. In G. Clinton, & G. Smith (Eds.), *Sexual jealousy*. Englewood Cliffs, NJ: Prentice Hall.

Berscheid, E. & Regan, P. (2005). *The psychology of interpersonal relationships*. Englewood Cliffs, NJ: Prentice Hall.

Berscheid, E., & Reis, H. T. (1998). Attraction and close relationships. In D. T. Gilbert, S. T. Fiske, & G. Lindzey (Eds.), *Handbook of social psychology (4th ed., Vol. 2)*. New York: McGraw-Hill.

Berscheid, E., Snyder, M., & Omoto, A. M. (1989). Issues in studying close relationships: Conceptualizing and measuring closeness. In C. Hendrick (Ed.), *Close relationships*. Newbury Park, CA: Sage.

Berthier, N. E., Rosenstein, M. T., & Barto, A. G. (2005). Approximate optimal control as a model for motor learning. *Psychological Review, 112(2),* 329–346.

Besner, D., Risko, E. F., Sklair, N. (2005). Spatial attention as a necessary preliminary to early processes in reading. *Canadian Journal of Experimental Psychology, 59(2),* 99–108.*

Besner, D., & Stolz, J. A. (1999). What kind of attention modulates the Stroop effect? *Psychonomic Bulletin & Review, 6,* 99–105.*

Best, D. (2002). Cross-cultural gender roles. In J. Worell (Ed.), *Encyclopedia of women and gender*. New York: Oxford.

Betsch, T. & Haberstroh, S. (Eds.). (2005). *The routines of decision making*. Mahwah, NJ: Erlbaum.

Betsch, T., Haberstroh, S., Glockner, A., Haar, T., & Fiedler, K. (2001). The effects of routine strength on adaptation and information search in recurrent decision making. *Organizational Behavior and Human Decision Processes, 84,* 23–53.

Bettman, J. (2001). *Learning*. Unpublished manuscript, Fuqua School of Business, Duke University, Durham, NC.

Bhattacharjee, C., Smith, M., Todd, F., & Gillepsie, M. (2001). Bupropion overdose: A potential problem with the new "miracle" anti-smoking drug. *International Journal of Clinical Practice, 55,* 221–222.

Bi, G., & Poo, M. (2001). Synaptic modification by correlated activity: Hebb's postulate revisited. *Annual Review of Neuroscience, 24,* 139–166.

Bialystok, E. (Ed.) (1991). *Language processing in bilingual children*. London: Cambridge.*

Bialystok, E. (1995). Towards a definition of metalinguistic awareness. In H. Dechert (Ed.), *Metacognition and second language acquisition*. Clevedon, England: Multilingual Matters.*

Bialystok, E. (1997). Effects of bilingualism and biliteracy on children's emerging concepts of print. *Developmental Psychology, 33,* 429–440.*

Bialystok, E. (2001). *Bilingualism in development: Language, literacy, and cognition*. New York: Cambridge.*

Bialystok, E., & Herman, J. (1999). Does bilingualism matter for early literacy? *Bilingualism: Language and Cognition, 2,* 35–44.*

Bialystok, E., Luk, G., & Kwan, E. (2005). Bilingualism, biliteracy, and learning to read: Interactions among languages and writing systems. *Scientific Studies of Reading, 9(1),* 43–61.*

Bialystok, E., & Mitterer, J. (1987). Metalinguistic differences among three kinds of readers. *Journal of Educational Psychology, 79(2),* 147–153.*

Billman, G. E. (2002). Aerobic exercise conditioning: A nonpharmacological antiarrhythmic intervention. *Journal of Applied Physiology, 92,* 446–454.

Billman, J. (2003). *Observation and participation in early childhood setting: A practicum guide (2nd ed.)*. Boston: Allyn & Bacon.

Billmann, S. J., & Ware, J. C. (2002). Marital satisfaction of wives of untreated sleep apneic men. *Sleep Medicine, 3,* 55–59.

Bird, L. R., Roberts, W. A., Abroms, B., Kit, K. A., & Crupi, C. (2003). Spatial memory for food hidden by rats (Rattus norvegicus) on the radial maze: Studies of memory for where, what, and when. *Journal of Comparative Psychology, 117(2),* 176–187.*

Birdsong, D., & Molis, M. (2001). On the evidence for maturational constraints in second-language acquisition. *Journal of Memory & Language, 44(2),* 235–249.

Birnbaum, M. H. (2004). Human research and data collection via the Internet. *Annual Review of Psychology, 55,* 803–832.

Birren, J. E., & Schaie, K. W. (Eds.). (2001). *Handbook of the psychology of aging (5th ed.)*. San Diego: Academic Press.

Bisanz, J., Bisanz, G. L., & Korpan, C. A. (1994). Inductive reasoning. In R. J. Sternberg (Ed.), *Handbook of perception and cognition: Vol. 12. Thinking and problem solving*. Orlando, FL: Academic Press.*

Bishop, S. R. (2002). What do we really know about mindfulness-based stress reduction? *Psychosomatic Medicine, 64,* 71–83.

Bjorklund, D. F. (2004). *Children's thinking (4th ed.)*. Belmont, CA: Wadsworth.

Bjorklund, D. F., Yunger, J. L., & Pellegrini, A. D. (2002). The evolution of parenting and evolutionary approaches to childrearing. In M. Bornstein (Ed.), *Handbook of parenting (2nd ed.)*. Mahwah, NJ: Erlbaum.

Björkqvist, K., Österman, K., & Lagerspetz, K. M. J. (1994). Sex differences in covert aggression among adults. *Aggressive Behavior, 20,* 27–33.

Black, I. B. (1998). Plasticity. In M. S. Gazzaniga (Ed.), *The new cognitive neurosciences (2nd ed.)*. Cambridge MIT Press.

Blackwell, J. C., Thurston, W. E., & Graham, K. M. (1996). Canadian women and substance use: overview and policy implications. In M. Adrian, C. Lundy, & M. Eliany (Eds.), *Women's use of alcohol and other drugs in Canada*. Toronto: Addiction Research Foundation.*

Blair, C. (2002). School readiness: Integrating cognition and emotion in a neurobiological conceptualization of children's functioning at school entry. *American Psychologist, 57,* 111–127.

Blair, C., & Ramey, C. (1996). Early intervention with low birth weight infants: The path to second generation research. In M. J. Guralnick (Ed.), *The effectiveness of early intervention*. Baltimore: Paul H. Brookes.

Blair, I. V. (2001). Implicit stereotypes and prejudice. In G. B. Moscowitz (Ed.), *Cognitive social psychology*. Mahwah, NJ: Erlbaum.

Blais, F. C., Morin, C. M., Boisclair, A., Greiner, V., & Guay, B. (2001). Insomnia. *Canadian Family Physician, 47,* 759–767.*

Blake, R. (2000). Vision and sight: Structure and function. In A. Kazdin (Ed.), *Encyclopedia of psychology*. Washington, & New York: APA Press and Oxford.

Blake, R., Palmeri, T., Marois, R. & Kim, C.-Y. (2005). On the perceptual reality of synesthesia. In L. C. Robertson, & N. Sagiv (Eds.), *Synesthesia: Perspectives from cognitive neuroscience*. New York: Oxford.

Blanchard, D. C., & Blanchard, R. J. (2003). What can animal aggression research tell us about human aggression? *Hormones & Behavior, 44(3),* 171–177.

Blatt, S. J. (2000). Projective techniques. In A. Kazdin (Ed.), *Encyclopedia of psychology*. Washington; DC, & New York: APA Press and Oxford.

Blazer, D. G. (2005). *The age of melancholy: "Major depression" and its social origins*. New York: Routledge.

Blazer, D. G., Kessler, R. C., McGonagle, K. A., & Swartz, M. S. (1994). The prevalence and distribution of major depression in a national community sample: The National Comorbidity Study. *American Journal of Psychiatry, 151,* 979–986.

Blenkiron, P. (2005). Stories and analogies in cognitive behaviour therapy: A clinical review. *Behavioural & Cognitive Psychotherapy, 33(1),* 45–59.

Bless, H., & Igou, E. R. (2005). Mood and the use of general knowledge structures in judgment and decision making. In T. Betsch, & S. Haberstroh (Eds.), *The routines of decision making*. Mahwah, NJ: Erlbaum.

Blittner, M., Goldberg, J., & Merbaum, M. (1978). Cognitive self-control factors in the reduction of smoking behavior. *Behavior Therapy, 9,* 553–561.

Block, J. (2002). *Personality as an affect processing system*. Mahwah, NJ: Erlbaum.

Bloom, B. (1985). *Developing talent in young people*. New York: Ballantine.

Bloom, F., Nelson, C.A., & Lazerson, A. (2001). *Brain, mind and behavior (3rd ed.)*. New York: Worth.

Bloom, P. (2000). *How children learn the meaning of words*. Cambridge MIT Press.

Blum, H. P. (2001). Freud's private mini-monograph on his own dreams. *International Journal of Psychoanalysis, 82,* 953–964.

Blumenthal, J. A., Sherwood, A., Babyak, M. A., Watkins, L. L., Waugh, R., Georgiades, A., et al. (2005). Effects of exercise and stress management training on markers of cardiovascular risk in patients with ischemic heart disease: A randomized controlled trial. *Journal of the American Medical Association, 293(13),* 1626–1634.

Blunt, A. & Pychyl, T. A. (2005). Project systems of procrastinators: A personal project-analytic and action control perspective. *Personality & Individual Differences, 38(8),* 1771–1780.*

Blyth, D. (2000). Community approaches to improving outcomes for urban children, youth, and families. In A. Booth, & A. C. Crouter (Eds.), *Does it take a village?* Mahwah, NJ: Erlbaum.

Blythe, S. B. (2004). *The well balanced child: Movement and early learning*. Gloucestershire, England: Hawthorn Press.

Bobocel, D. R., & Debeyer, M. (1998). Explaining controversial organizational decisions: To legitimize the means or the ends? *Social Justice Research, 11,* 21–40.*

Bobocel, D. R., Agar, S. E., Meyer, J. P., & Irving, P. G. (1998). Managerial accounts and fairness perceptions in conflict resolution: Differentiating the effects of minimizing responsibility and providing justification. *Basic & Applied Social Psychology, 20,* 133–143.*

Bobocel, D. R., Son Hing, L. S., Holmvall, C. M., & Zanna, M. P. (2002). Policies to redress social injustice: Is the concern for justice a cause both of support and of opposition? In M. Ross, & D. Miller (Eds.), *The justice motive in everyday life*. New York: Cambridge.*

Bobocel, D. R., & Zdaniuk, A. (2005). How can explanations be used to foster organizational justice? In J. Greenberg, & J. A. Colquitt (Eds.), *Handbook of organizational justice*. Mahwah, NJ: Erlbaum.*

Bochner, S., & Jones, J. (2003). *Child language development: Learning to talk*. London: Whurr.

Bodenhausen, G. V., Mussweiler, T., Gabriel, S., & Moreno, K. N. (2001). Affective influences on stereotyping and intergroup relations. In J. P. Forgas (Ed.), *Handbook of affect and cognition*. Mahwah, NJ: Erlbaum.

Boekaerts, M, Pintrich, P. R., & Zeidner, M. (Eds.). (2000). *Handbook of self-regulation*. San Diego: Academic Press.

Bogaert, A. F. (2005a). Sibling sex ratio and sexual orientation in men and women: New tests in two national probability samples. *Archives of Sexual Behavior, 34(1),* 111–116.*

Bogaert, A. F. (2005b). Gender role/identity and sibling sex ratio in homosexual men. *Journal of Sex & Marital Therapy, 31(3),* 217–227.*

Bogaert, A. F., Woodard, U., & Hafer, C. L. (1999). Intellectual ability and reactions to pornography. *Journal of Sex Research, 36,* 283–291.*

Bogdan, R. J. (1999). *Minding minds*. Cambridge MIT Press.

Bohart, A. C., & Greening, T. (2001). Humanistic psychology and positive psychology. *American Psychologist, 56,* 81–82.

Boll, T. J., Johnon, B., Perry, N., & Rozensky, R. H. (Eds.). (2002). *Handbook of clinical health psychology (Vol. 1)*. Washington: APA Press.

Bond, R., & Smith, P. B. (1996). Culture and conformity: A meta-analysis of studies using Asch's (1952, 1956) line judgment task. *Psychological Bulletin, 119,* 111–137.

Bonds-Raacke, J. M., Fryer, L. S., Nicks, S. D., & Durr, R. T. (2001). Hindsight bias demonstrated in the prediction of a sporting event. *Journal of Social Psychology, 141(3),* 349–352.

Bonebakker, A. E., Bonke, B., Klein, M. D., Wolters, G., Stijnen, T., Passchier, J., & Merikle, P. M. (1996). Information processing during general anesthesia: Evidence for unconscious memory. *Memory & Cognition, 24,* 766–776.*

Booth, A., & Crouter, A. C. (Eds.). (2000). *Does it take a village?* Mahwah, NJ: Erlbaum.

Bonham, V., Warshauer-Baker, E., & Collins, F. S. (2005). Race and ethnicity in the genome era: The complexity of the constructs. *American Psychologist, 60(1),* 9–15.

Boraud, T., Bezard, E., Bioulac, B., & Gross, C. E. (2002). From single extracellular unit recording in experimental and human Parkinsonism to the development of a functional concept of the role played by the basal ganglia in motor control. *Progress in Neurobiology, 66,* 265–283.

Borckardt, J. J. (2002). Case study examining the efficacy of a multi-modal psychotherapeutic intervention for hypertension. *International Journal of Clinical and Experimental Hypnosis, 50,* 189–201.

Bordens, K. S., & Barrington, B. (2005). *Research design and methods with PowerWeb (6th ed.).* New York: McGraw Hill.

Bordens, K. S., & Horowitz, I. A. (2002). *Social psychology (2nd ed.).* Mahwah, NJ: Erlbaum.

Borman, W. C., Ilgen, D. R., Klimoski, R. J., Irving, B., Weiner, I. B. (Eds.). (2003). *Handbook of psychology: Industrial and organizational psychology.* New York: Wiley.

Bornstein, M. H., & Bradley, R. H. (Eds.). (2003). *Socioeconomic status, parenting, and child development.* Mahwah, NJ: Erlbaum.

Bornstein, M. H., & Tamis-LeMonda, C. S. (2001). Mother-infant interaction. In A. Fogel & G. Bremmer (Eds.), *Blackwell handbook of infant development.* London: Blackwell.

Bornstein, R. F., & Masling, J. M. (Eds.). (2005). *Scoring the Rorschach: Seven validated systems.* Mahwah, NJ: Erlbaum.

Borrelli, B., Hogan, J. W., Bock, B., Pinto, B., Roberts, M., & Marcus, B. (2002). Predictors of quitting and dropout among women in a clinic-based smoking cessation program. *Psychology of Addictive Behaviors, 16,* 22–27.

Borrelli, B., Spring, B., Niaura, R., Hitsman, B., & Papandonatos, G. (2001). Influences of gender and weight gain on short-term relapse to smoking in a cessation trial. *Journal of Consulting and Clinical Psychology, 69(3),* 511–15.

Bosch, J. A., Berntson, G. G., Cacioppo, J. T., Dhabhar, F. S., & Marucha, P. T. (2003). Acute stress evokes selective mobilization of T cells that differ in chemokine receptor expression: A potential pathway linking immunologic reactivity to cardiovascular disease. *Brain, Behavior & Immunity, 17(4),* 251–259.

Botella, C., Villa, H., García-Palacios, A., Baños, R. M., Perpiña, C., & Alcañiz, M (2004). Clinically significant virtual environments for the treatment of panic disorder and agoraphobia. *CyberPsychology & Behavior, 7(5),* 527–535.

Bottos, S., & Dewey, D. (2004). Perfectionists' appraisal of daily hassles and chronic headache. *Headache, 44(8),* 772–779.

Bouchard, C., Rhéaume, J., & Ladouceur, R. (1999). Responsibility and perfectionism in OCD: An experimental study. *Behavior Research and Therapy, 37,* 239–248.*

Bouchard, P., & St-Amant, J. C. (1996). Garçons et filles, stéréotypes et réussite scolaire, *Montréal,* Éditions du Remue-ménage.*

Bouchard, P., Boily, I. & Proulx, M.-C. (2003). *School success by gender: A catalyst for the masculinist discourse.* Ottawa: Status of Women Canada. Retrieved April 18, 2005 from http://www.swc-cfc.gc.ca/pubs/ 0662882857/200303_0662882857_1_e.html.*

Bouchard, Jr., T. J., Lykken, D. T., Tellegen, A., & McGue, M. (1996). Genes, drives, environment, and experience. In D. Lubinski & C. Benbow (Eds.), *Psychometrics and social issues concerning intellectual talent.* Baltimore: Johns Hopkins University Press.

Bouchard, Jr., T. J. (2004). Genetic influence on human psychological traits: A survey. *Current Directions in Psychological Science, 13(4),* 148–151.

Bouchard Jr., T. J., Lykken, D. T., Tellegen, A., & McGue, M. (1996). Genes, drives, environment, and experience. In D. Lubinski & C. Benbow (Eds.), *Psychometrics and social issues concerning intellectual talent.* Baltimore: Johns Hopkins University Press.

Bou-Flores, C., & Berger, A. J. (2001). Gap junctions and inhibitory synapses modulate inspiratory motoneuron synchronization. *Journal of Neurophysiology, 85,* 1543–1551.

Bouman, M., Maas, L., & Kok, G. (1998). Health education in television entertainment: Medisch Centrum West: A Dutch drama serial. *Health Education Research, 13(4),* 503–518.

Bourne, E. J. (2000). *The anxiety and phobia workbook (3rd ed.).* Oakland, CA: New Harbinger.

Boutin, C., Dumont, M., Ladouceur, R., & Montecalvo, P. (2003). Excessive gambling and cognitive therapy: How to address ambivalence. *Clinical Case Studies, 2(4),* 259–269.*

Bouton, M. E. (2004). Context and behavioral processes in extinction. *Learning & Memory, 11(5),* 485–494.

Bower, G. H., Clark, M., Winzenz, D., & Lesgold, A. (1969). Hierarchical retrieval schemes in recall of categorized word lists. *Journal of Verbal Learning and Verbal Behavior, 3,* 323–343.

Bowers, K. S. (1973). Situationism in psychology: An analysis and critique. *Psychological Review, 80,* 307–336.*

Bowlby, J. (1969). *Attachment and loss (Vol. 1).* London: Hogarth Press.

Bowlby, J. (1989). *Secure and insecure attachment.* New York: Basic Books.

Bowman, M. L. (2000). The diversity of diversity: Canadian-American differences and their implications for clinical training and APA accreditation. *Canadian Psychology, 41(4),* 230–243.*

Boyle, S. H., Williams, R. B., Mark, D. B., Brummett, B. H., Siegler, I. C., Helms, M. J., & Barefoot, J. C. (2004). Hostility as a predictor of survival in patients with coronary artery disease. *Psychosomatic Medicine, 66(5),* 629–632.

Bozarth, J. D., Zimring, F. M., & Tausch, R. (2001). Client-centered therapy: The evolution of a revolution. In D. J. Cain & J. Seeman (Eds.), *Humanistic psychotherapies.* Washington: APA Press.

Bradbury, J. (2001). Teasing out the genetics of bipolar disorder. *Lancet, 357,* 156.

Bradford, D., Stroup, S., & Lieberman, J. (2002). Pharmacological treatments for schizophrenia. In P. Nathan & J. M. Gorman (Eds.), *A guide to treatments that work (2nd ed.).* New York: Oxford.

Bradley, M. T., & Rettinger, J. (1992). Awareness of crime relevant information and the guilty knowledge test. *Journal of Applied Psychology, 77(1),* 55–59.*

Bradley, R., Greene, J., Russ, E., Dutra, L., & Westen, D. (2005). A multidimensional meta-analysis of psychotherapy for PTSD. *American Journal of Psychiatry, 162(2),* 214–227.

Brain, P. F., & Susman, E. J. (1997). Hormonal aspects of aggression and violence. In D. M. Stoff, J. Breiling, & J. D. Maser (Eds.), *Handbook of antisocial personality disorder.* New York: Wiley.

Brammer, L. M., & MacDonald, G. (2003). *The helping relationship (8th ed.).* Boston: Allyn & Bacon.

Brannon, L. (2005). *Gender: Psychological perspectives (4th ed.).* Boston: Allyn & Bacon.

Brannon, L., & Feist, J. (2004). *Health psychology: An introduction to behavior and health (5th ed.).* Belmont, CA: Wadsworth.

Bransford, J. D., & Stein, B. S. (1993). *The IDEAL problem solver.* New York: Freeman.

Braun, B. G. (1985). Transgenerational incidence of dissociation and multiple personality disorder: A preliminary report. In R. P. Kluft (Ed.), *Childhood antecedents of multiple personality.* Washington: American Psychiatric Press.

Bray, G. A. (2005). Drug treatment of obesity. *Psychiatric Clinics of North America, 28(1),* 193–217.

Brébion, G., David, A. S., Bressan, R. A., & Pilowsky, L. (2005). Word frequency effects on free recall and recognition in patients with schizophrenia. *Journal of Psychiatric Research, 39(2),* 215–222.

Breckler, S. J. (2006). *Social psychology alive.* Belmont, CA: Wadsworth.

Breggin, P. R., & Breggin, G. R. (1995). *Talking back to Prozac: What doctors aren't telling you about today's most controversial drug.* New York: St. Martin's Press.

Brehm, S. S. (2002). *Intimate relationships (3rd ed.).* New York: McGraw-Hill.

Brehm, S. S., & Kassin, S. M., & Fein, S. (2005). *Social psychology (6th ed.).* Boston: Houghton Mifflin.

Breland, K., & Breland, M. (1961). The misbehavior of organisms. *American Psychologist, 16,* 681–684.

Bremner, J. G. (2005). Perception and knowledge of objects in infancy. In J. B. Hopkins, R. G. Barr, G. F. Michel, & P. Rochat (Eds.), *Cambridge encyclopaedia of developmental psychology.* Cambridge: Cambridge University Press.

Brems, C. (2001). *Basic skills in psychotherapy and counseling.* Belmont, CA: Wadsworth.

Brennan, F. X., & Charnetski, C. J. (2000). Explanatory style and immunglobin A (IgA). *Integration of Physiology and Behavioral Science, 35,* 251–255.

Brennan, P., Mednick, S., & Kandel, E. (1991). Congenital determinants of violent and property offencing. In D. Pepler, & K. Rubin (Eds.), *The development and treatment of childhood aggression.* Mahwah, NJ: Erlbaum.

Brennan, P. A., & Keverne, E. B. (2004). Something in the air? New insights into mammalian pheromones. *Biology, 14(2),* R81–R89.

Brewer, J. B., Zuo, Z., Desmond, J. E., Glover, G. H., & Gabrieli, J. D. E. (1998). Making memories: Brain activity that predicts how well visual experience will be remembered. *Science, 281,* 1185–1187.

Brewer, M. B., & Gaertner, S. L., (2001). Toward reduction of prejudice: Intergroup contact and social categorization. In R. Brown & S. L. Gaertner (Eds.), *Handbook of social psychology: Intergroup processes.* Malden, MA: Blackwell.

Brewer, M. B., & Brown, R. J. (1998). Intergroup relations. In D. T. Gilbert, S. T. Fiske, & G. Lindzey (Eds.), *Handbook of social psychology (4th ed., Vol. 2).* New York: McGraw-Hill.

Brickman, A. L., LoPiccolo, C. J., & Johnson, S. L. (2002). Screening for bipolar disorder. *Psychiatric Services, 53,* 349.

Brickman, P., Coates, D., & Janoff-Bulman, R. J. (1978). Lottery winners and accident victims: Is happiness relative? *Journal of Personality & Social Psychology, 36,* 917–927.

Bridges, L. J. (2003). Trust, attachment, and relatedness. In M. H. Bornstein, L. Davidson, C. L. M. Keyes, & K. A. Moore (Eds.), *Well-being: Positive development across the life course.* Mahwah, NJ: Erlbaum.

Brim, O. (1999). *The McArthur Foundation study of midlife development.* Vero Beach, FL: The McArthur Foundation.

Brisch, K. H., & Kronenberg, K. (2002). *Treating attachment disorders: From theory to therapy.* New York: Guilford.

Brislin, R. (1993). *Understanding culture's influence on behavior.* Fort Worth, TX: Harcourt Brace.

Brody, N. (2000). Intelligence. In A. Kazdin (Ed.), *Encyclopedia of psychology.* Washington, & New York: APA Press and Oxford.

Brody, N. (2004). What cognitive intelligence is and what emotional intelligence is not. *Psychological Inquiry, 15(3),* 234–238.

Brock, T. C., & Green, M. C. (Eds.). (2005). *Persuasion: Psychological insights and perspectives (2nd ed.).* Thousand Oaks, CA: Sage.

Bronfenbrenner, U. (2000). Ecological systems theory. In A. Kazdin (Ed.), *Encyclopedia of psychology.* Washington, and New York: APA Press and Oxford.

Bronfenbrenner, U., & Morris, P. (1998). The ecology of developmental processes. In W. Damon (Ed.), *Handbook of child psychology (5th ed., Vol. 1)*. New York: Wiley.

Bronzaft, A. L. (2002). Noise pollution: A hazard to physical and mental well-being. In R. B. Bechtel, & A. Churchman (Eds.), *Handbook of environmental psychology*. NY:Wiley.

Brooks, D. C. (2000). Recent and remote extinction cues reduce spontaneous recovery. *Quarterly Journal of Experimental Psychology, 3*, 25–58.

Brooks, J. G., & Brooks, M. G. (2001). *In search of understanding: The case for the constructivist classroom*. Englewood Cliffs, NJ: Prentice Hall.

Brooks, L. R. (1978). Nonanalytic concept formation and memory for instances. In E. Rosch, & B. B. Lloyd (Eds.), *Cognition and categorization*. Mahwah, NJ: Erlbaum.*

Brooks, L. R. (2005). The blossoms and the weeds. *Canadian Journal of Experimental Psychology. Special Issue on 2003 Festschrift for Lee R. Brooks, 59(1)*, 62–74.*

Brooks-Gunn, J., & Warren, M. P. (1989). The psychological significance of secondary sexual characteristics in 9- to 11-year-old girls. *Child Development, 59*, 161–169.

Brosvic, G. M., Dihoff, R. E., & Fama, J. (2002). Age-related susceptibility to the Muller-Lyer and the horizontal-vertical illusion. *Perceptual and Motor Skills, 94*, 229–234.

Broughton, R. J., & Ogilvie, R. D. (Eds.). (1992). *Sleep, arousal and performance: Problems and promises*. Boston: Birkhauser.*

Broughton, R., & Shimisu, T. (1995). Sleep-related violence: a medical and forensic challenge. *Sleep, 18*, 727–730.*

Broughton, R., Billings, R., Cartwright, R., Doucette, D., Edmeads, J., Edwardh, M., et al. (1994). Homicidal somnambulism: a case report. *Sleep, 17(3)*, 253–64.*

Broughton, W. A., & Broughton, R. J. (1994). Psychosocial impact of narcolepsy. *Sleep, 17(8 Suppl)*, 45–9.*

Brouwer, W. H., Withaar, F. K., Tant, M. L., & van Zomeren, A. H. (2002). Attention and driving in traumatic brain injury: A question of coping with time pressure. *Journal of Head and Trauma Rehabilitation, 17*, 1–15.

Brown, E., Deffenbacher, K., & Sturgill, W. (1977). Memory for faces and the circumstances of encounter. *Journal of Applied Psychology, 62*, 311–318.

Brown, J. D. (2006). *Social psychology*. New York: McGraw-Hill.

Brown, J. D., Steele, J. R., & Walsh-Childers, K. (Eds.). (2002). *Sexual teens, sexual media*. Mahwah, NJ: Erlbaum.

Brown, J. F., Spencer, K., & Swift, S. (2002). A parent training programme for chronic food refusal: A case study. *British Journal of Learning Disabilities, 30(3)*, 118–121.

Brown, L. S. (1989). New voices, new visions: Toward a lesbian/gay paradigm for psychology. *Psychology of Women Quarterly, 13*, 445–458.

Brown, R. (1973). *A first language: The early stages*. Cambridge Harvard University Press.

Brown, R., & McNeill, D. (1966). The "tip of the tongue" phenomenon. *Journal of Verbal Learning & Verbal Behavior, 5(4)*, 325–337.

Brumberg, J. J. (1997). *The body project: An intimate history of American girls*. New York: Random House.

Brummett, B. H., Mark, D. B., Siegler, I. C., Williams, R. B., Babyak, M. A., Clapp-Channing, N. E., & Barefoot, J. C. (2005). Perceived social support as a predictor of mortality in coronary patients: Effects of smoking, sedentary behavior, and depressive symptoms. *Psychosomatic Medicine, 67(1)*, 40–45.

Bruner, J. S., & Tagiuri, R. (1954). The perception of people. In G. Lindzey (Ed.), *Handbook of social psychology (Vol. 2)*. Boston: Addison-Wesley.

Bruning, R. H., Schraw, G. J., Norby, M., & Ronning, R. R. (2004). *Cognitive psychology and instruction (4th ed.)*. Mahwah, NJ: Prentice Hall.

Bryden, M. P. (1986). The nature of complementary specialization. In F. Lepore, M. Ptito, & H. H. Jasper (Eds.), *Two hemispheres–One brain: Functions of the corpus callosum*. New York: Alan R. Liss.*

Brydon, L., Edwards, S., Mohamed-Ali, V., & Steptoe, A. (2004). Socioeconomic status and stress-induced increases in interleukin-6. *Brain, Behavior & Immunity, 18(3)*, 281–290.

Bryson, M., & Scardamalia, M. (1996). Fostering reflectivity in the argumentative thinking of students with different learning histories. *Reading & Writing Quarterly: Overcoming Learning Difficulties, 12*, 351–384.*

Budak, F., Filiz, T. M., Topsever, P., & Tan, Ü. (2005). Correlations between nonverbal intelligence and nerve conduction velocities in right-handed male and female subjects. *International Journal of Neuroscience, 115(5)*, 613–623.

Buchanan, L., & Besner, D. (1993). Reading aloud: Evidence for the use of a whole word nonsemantic pathway. *Canadian Journal of Experimental Psychology, 47(2)*, 133–152.*

Buchsbaum, M. S., Mirsky, A. F., DeLisi, L. E., Morihisa, J., Karson, C. N., Mendelson, W. B., et al. (1984). The Genain quadruplets: Electrophysiological, positron emission, and X-ray tomographic studies. *Psychiatry Research, 13(1)*, 95–108.

Buchsbaum, M. S., Someya, T., Wu, J. C., Tang, C. Y., & Bunney, W. E. (1997). Neuroimaging bipolar illness with positron emission tomography and magnetic resonance imaging. *Psychiatric Annals, 27*, 489–495.

Buckley, P. F., Miller, D. D., Singer, B., & Donenwirth, K. (2001). The evolving clinical profile of a atypical antipsychotic medications. *Canadian Journal of Psychiatry, 46*, 285.*

Buckner, R. L., & Schacter, D. L. (2004). Neural correlates of memory's successes and sins. In M. S. Gazzaniga (Ed.), *The cognitive neurosciences III*. Cambridge MIT Press.

Bukatko, D., & Daehler, M. W. (2001). *Child development (4th ed.)*. Boston: Houghton Mifflin.

Bulmer, M. (2003). *Francis Galton: Pioneer of heredity and biometry*. Baltimore: Johns Hopkins University Press.

Burack, J. A., Enns, J. T., Iarocci, G., & Randolph, B. (2000). Age differences in visual search for compound patterns: Long versus short range grouping. *Developmental Psychology, 36*, 731–740.*

Burbach, M. E., Matkin, G. S., & Fritz, S. M. (2004). Teaching critical thinking in an introductory leadership course utilizing active learning strategies: A confirmatory study. *College Student Journal, 38(3)*, 482–493.

Buree, B. U., Papageorgis, D., & Hare, R. D. (1990). Eating in anorexia nervosa and bulimia nervosa: An application of the tripartite model of anxiety. *Canadian Journal of Behavioral Science, 22(2)*, 207–218.*

Burgess, P. W., Quayle, A., & Frith, C. D. (2001). Brain regions involved in prospective memory as determined by positron emission tomography. *Neuropsychologica, 39*, 545–555.

Burke, G. L., Arnold, A. M., Bild, D., Cushman, M., Fried, O., Newman, A., et al. (2001). Factors associated with healthy aging. *Journal of the American Geriatric Society, 49*, 254–262.

Burke, R. J., & Greenglass, E. R. (2000). Effects of hospital restructuring on full time and part time nursing staff in Ontario. *International Journal of Nursing Studies, 37*, 163–171.*

Burlingame, G., & Davies, R. (2002). Self-help groups. In M. Hersen & W. H. Sledge (Eds.), *Encyclopedia of psychotherapy*. San Diego: Academic Press.

Burnett, R. C., Medin, D. L., Ross, N. O. & Blok, S. V. (2005). Ideal is typical. *Canadian Journal of Experimental Psychology. Special Issue on 2003 Festschrift for Lee R. Brooks, 59(1)*, 3–10.

Burns, D. D. (1980). *Feeling good: The new mood therapy*. New York: Morrow.

Burns, T. (2004). *Community mental health teams: A guide to current practices*. New York: Oxford.

Burnstein, E., Crandall, C., & Kitayama, S. (1994). Some neo-Darwinian decision rules for altruism: Weighing cues for inclusive fitness as a function of the biological importance of the decision. *Journal of Personality & Social Psychology, 67*, 773–789.

Burris, C. T., Harmon-Jones, E., & Tarpley, W. R. (1997). "By Faith Alone": Religious agitation and cognitive dissonance. *Basic & Applied Social Psychology, 19*, 17–31.*

Bushman, B. J. (2002). Does venting anger feed or extinguish the flame? Catharsis, rumination, distraction, anger and aggressive responding. *Personality & Social Psychology Bulletin, 28(6)*, 724–731.

Bushman, B. J., & Huesmann, L. R. (2001). Effects of televised violence on aggression. In D. Singer & J. Singer (Eds.), *Handbook of children and the media*. Thousand Oaks, CA: Sage.

Bushman, B. J., Wang, M. C., & Anderson, C. A. (2005). Is the curve relating temperature to aggression linear or curvilinear? Assaults and temperature in Minneapolis reexamined. *Journal of Personality & Social Psychology, 89(1)*, 62–66.

Buss, A. H., & Plomin, R. (1987). Commentary. In H. H. Goldsmith, A. H. Buss, R. Plomin, M. K. Rothbart, A. Thomas, A. Chess, R. R. Hinde, & R. B. McCall (Eds.), Roundtable: What is temperament? Four approaches. *Child Development, 58*, 505–529.

Buss, D. M. (2000). The evolution of happiness. *American Psychologist, 55*, 15–23.

Buss, D. M. (2004). *Evolutionary psychology: The new science of the mind, (2nd ed.)*. Boston: Allyn & Bacon.

Buss, D. M., Abbott, M., Angleitner, A., Biaggio, A., Blanco-Villasenor, A., Bruchon-Schweitzer, M., et al. (1990). International preferences in selecting mates: A study of 37 cultures. *Journal of Cross-Cultural Psychology, 21*, 5–47.

Butcher, J. N. (2005). *A beginner's guide to the MMPI-2 (2nd ed.)*. Washington: APA Press.

Butcher, J. N., Mineka, S., & Hooley, J. (2004). *Abnormal psychology and modern life (12th ed.)*. Boston: Allyn & Bacon.

Buunk, B. P., Oldersma, F. L., & de Dreu, C. K. W. (2001). Enhancing satisfaction through downward comparison: The role of relational discontent and individual differences in social comparison orientation. *Journal of Experimental Social Psychology, 37(6)*, 452–467.

Buxton, W. (2001). Less is more (More or less). In P. Denning (Ed.), *The invisible future: The seamless integration of technology in everyday life*. New York: McGraw-Hill.*

Buxton, W., Fitzmaurice, G. Balakrishnan, R., & Kurtenbach, G. (2000). Large displays in automotive design. *IEEE Computer Graphics and Applications, 20(4)*, 68–75.*

Byers, E. S. (2001). Evidence for the importance of relationship satisfaction for women's sexual functioning. *Women & Therapy, 24*, 23–26.*

Byers, E. S., Purdon, C., & Clark, D. A. (1998). Sexual intrusive thoughts of college students. *Journal of Sex Research, 35(4)*, 359–369.*

Byrne, M., & Curtis, R. (2000). Designing health communication: Testing the explanations for the impact of communication medium on effectiveness. *British Journal of Health Psychology, 5(Part2)*, 189–199.

Byrne, S. M., & McLean, N. J. (2002). The cognitive-behavioral model of bulimia nervosa: A direct evaluation. *International Journal of Eating Disorders, 31*, 17–31.

C

Cabeza, R. C., Nyberg, L., & Park, D. (2005) (Eds.), *Cognitive neuroscience of aging: Linking cognitive and cerebral aging*. London: Oxford.

Caciopppo, J. T., & Gardner, W. L. (1999). Emotions. *Annual Review of Psychology, 50*, 191–214.

Cacioppo, J. T., Ernst, J. M., Burleson, M. H., McClintock, M. K., Malarkey, W. B., Hawkley, L. C., et al. (2000). Lonely traits and concomitant physiological processes: The MacArthur Social Neuroscience Studies. *International Journal of Psychophysiology, 35*, 143–154.

Cadinu, M., Maass, A., Rosabianca, A., & Kiesner, J. (2005). Why do women underperform under stereotype threat? Evidence for the role of negative thinking. *Psychological Science, 16(7)*, 572–578.

Calhoun, S. L. & Dickerson-Mayes, S. (2005). Processing speed in children with clinical disorders. *Psychology in the Schools, 42(4)*, 333–343.

Cain, D. J. (2001). Defining characteristics, history, and evolution of humanistic psychotherapies. In D. J. Cain, & J. Seeman (Eds.), *Humanistic psychotherapies*. Washington: APA Press.

Cairney, J., Boyle, M., Offord, D. R., & Racine, Y. (2003). Stress, social support and depression in single and married mothers. *Social Psychiatry & Psychiatric Epidemiology, 38(8)*, 442–449.*

Callan, J. E. (2002). Gender development: Psychoanalytic perspectives. In J. Worell (Ed.), *Encyclopedia of women and gender*. San Diego: Academic Press.

Callister, L. C. (2003). Cultural influences on pain perceptions and behaviors. *Home Health Care Management & Practice, 15(3)*, 207–211.

Cameron, J., Banko, K. M., & Pierce, W. D. (2001). Pervasive negative effects of rewards on intrinsic motivation: The myth continues. *Behavior Analyst, 24(1)*, 1–44.*

Cameron, J., & Pierce, W. D. (2002). *Rewards and intrinsic motivation: Resolving the controversy*. Westport, CO: Bergin & Garvey.*

Cameron, N. (1963). *Personality development and psychopathology*. Boston: Houghton Mifflin.

Campbell, C (2004) The role of collective action in the prevention of HIV/AIDS in South Africa. In D. Hook, N. Mkhize, P. Kiguwa and A. Collins (Eds.), *Critical Psychology in South Africa*. Cape Town: Juta/University of Cape Town Press.

Campbell, C. & Foulis, C. (2004) Creating contexts for effective home-based care of people dying of AIDS in South Africa. *Curationis, 27 (3)*, pp. 5–14.

Campbell, C. & Murray, M. (2004). Community health psychology: Promoting analysis and action for social change. *Journal of Health Psychology, 9(2)*, 187–196.*

Campbell, F. A., Pungello, E. P., Miller-Johnson, S., Burchinal, M., & Ramey, C. T. (2001). The development of cognitive and academic abilities: Growth curves from an early childhood educational experiment. *Developmental Psychology, 37*, 231–243.

Campbell, L., Campbell, B., & Dickinson, D. (2003). *Teaching and learning through multiple intelligences (3rd ed.)*. Boston: Allyn & Bacon.

Campbell, N. A., Reece, J. B., & Mitchell, L. G. (2002). *Biology (6th ed.)*. Reading, MA, & Menlo Park, CA: Benjamin/Cummings.

Campfield, L. A., Smith, F. J., Gulsez, Y., Devos, R., & Burn, P. (1995). Mouse OB protein: Evidence for a peripheral signal linking adiposity and central neural networks. *Science, 269*, 546–549.

Canadian Alliance on Mental Illness and Mental Health (2003). *A call for action: Building consensus for a national action plan on mental illness and mental health*. Guelph. ON: Canadian Alliance on Mental Illness and Mental Health. Retrieved July 25, 2005 from http://www.camimh.ca/callforaction.htm.*

Canadian Council on Social Development (2000). *The Canadian fact book on poverty 2000*. Retrieved August 29, 2005 from http://www.ccsd.ca/pubs/2000/fbpov00/index.htm.*

Canadian Press & Leger Marketing (2002). *Child abuse report*. Montréal, PQ: Canadian Press & Leger Marketing.*

Canadian Psychiatric Association (2001). *Clinical practice guidelines for the treatment of depressive disorders*. Ottawa: Canadian Psychiatric Association. Retrieved August 29, 2005 from http://www.cpa-apc.org/Publications/Clinical_Guidelines/depression/clinicalGuidelinesDepression.asp.*

Canadian Psychological Association (1996). *Guidelines for the use of animals in research and instruction in psychology: Commentary and elaboration*. Ottawa: Canadian Psychological Association. Retrieved August 29, 2005 from http://www.cpa.ca/guide7.html.*

Canadian Psychological Association (2000). *Canadian code of ethics for psychologists (3rd ed.)*. Ottawa:

Canadian Psychological Association. Retrieved March 24, 2005 from http://www.cpa.ca/ethics2000.html.*

Canadian Psychological Association (2001). *Guidelines for psychologists addressing recovered memories*. Ottawa: Canadian Psychological Association. Retrieved March 24, 2005 from http://www.cpa.ca/memory.html.*

Cannon, W. B. (1927). The James-Lange theory of emotions: A critical examination and an alternative theory. *American Journal of Psychology, 39*, 106–124.

Cannon, W. B. (1929). *Bodily changes in pain, hunger, fear, and rage (2nd ed.)*. New York: Appleton-Century-Crofts.

Cannon, W. B., & Washburn, A. L. (1912). An explanation of hunger. *American Journal of Physiology, 29*, 444–454.

Cao, L., Martin, A., Polakos, N., & Moynihan, J. A. (2004). Stress causes a further decrease in immunity to herpes simplex virus-1 in immunocompromised hosts. *Journal of Neuroimmunology, 156(1–2)*, 21–30.

Caporael, L. (2001). Evolutionary psychology: Toward a unifying theory and a hybrid science. *Annual Review of Psychology, 52*, 607–628.

Capuzzi, D. (2003). *Approaches to group counseling*. Englewood Cliffs, NJ: Prentice Hall.

Capuzzi, D., & Gross, D. R. (2003). *Counseling and psychotherapy (3rd ed.)*. Englewood Cliffs, NJ: Prentice Hall.

Carbonneau, L. (1994). When bullets have ceased: Critical incident stress is the biggest source of morbidity in Canada's peacekeepers. *Medical Post, 30*, 9.*

Carkenord, D. M., & Bullington, J. (1995). Bringing cognitive dissonance to the classroom. In M. E. Ware, & D. E. Johnson (Eds.), *Demonstrations and activities in teaching of psychology (Vol. 3)*. Mahwah, NJ: Erlbaum.

Carlin, M. T., Soraci, S. A., & Strawbridge, C. P. (2005). Generative learning during visual search for scene changes: Enhancing free recall of individuals with and without mental retardation. *American Journal on Mental Retardation, 110(1)*, 13–22.*

Carlson, N. R. (2000). Neuron. In A. Kazdin (Ed.), *Encyclopedia of psychology*. Washington, & New York: APA Press and Oxford.

Carlson, N. R. (2005). *Physiology of behavior (8th ed.)*. Boston: Allyn & Bacon.

Carney, S. M., Cowen, P., Geddes, J., Goodwin, G., Rogers, R., Dearness, K., Tomlin, A., Eastaugh, J., Freemantle, N., Lester, H., Harvey, A., & Scott, A. (2003). Efficacy and safety of electroconvulsive therapy in depressive disorders: A systematic review and meta-analysis. *Lancet, 361(9360)*, 799–808.

Carney, S. M., & Goodwin, G. M. (2005). Lithium: A continuing story in the treatment of bipolar disorder. *Acta Psychiatrica Scandinavica, 111(Suppl426)*, 7–12.

Carroll, C. R. (2003). *Drugs in modern society (6th ed.)*. New York: McGraw-Hill.

Carroll, J. B. (1993). *Human cognitive abilities: A survey of factor-analytic studies*. New York: Cambridge.

Carskadon, M. A., Acebo, C., & Seifer, R. (2001). Extended nights, sleep loss, and recovery sleep in adolescents. *Archives of Italian Biology, 139*, 301–312.

Carskadon, M. A., Labyak, S. E., Acebo, C., & Seifer, R. (1999). Intrinsic circadian period of adolescent humans measured in conditions of forced desynchrony. *Neuroscience Letters, 260*, 129–132.

Carskadon, M. A., Wolfson, A. R., Acebo, C., Tzischinsky, O., & Seifer, R. (1998). Adolescent sleep patterns, circadian timing, and sleepiness at a transition to early school days. *Sleep, 21*, 873–884.

Carson, R. C., Butcher, J. N., & Mineka, S. (2000). *Abnormal psychology and modern life (11th ed.)*. Boston: Allyn & Bacon.

Carstensen, L. L., & Turk-Charles, S. (1994). The salience of emotion across the adult life span. *Psychology and Aging, 9*, 262.

Carstensen, L. L., Pasupathi, M., & Mayr, U. (1998). *Emotion experience in the daily lives of older and younger adults*. Unpublished manuscript, Stanford University.

Carstensen, L. L., Pasupathi, M., & Nesselroade, J. R. (2000). Emotional experience in everyday life across the life span. *Journal of Personality & Social Psychology, 79*, 644–655.

Carswell, R. S. (1992). Graphology: Canadian legal implications. In B. Bayerstein, & G. Bayerstein (Eds.), *The write stuff*. Buffalo, NY: Prometheus.*

Carter, C., & Weaver, C. K. (2003). *Violence and the media*. Philadelphia: Open University Press.

Cartwright, R. D. (2004). The role of sleep in changing our minds: A psychologist's discussion of papers on memory reactivation and consolidation in sleep. *Learning & Memory, 11(6)*, 660–663.

Carver, C. S., & Scheier, M. F. (2001). Optimism. In C. R. Synder, & S. J. Lopez (Eds.), *Handbook of positive psychology*. New York: Oxford.

Case, R. (1991). *The mind's staircase: Exploring the conceptual underpinnings of children's thought and knowledge*. Mahwah, NJ: Erlbaum.*

Case, R., Demetriou, A., Platsidou, M., & Kazi, S. (2001). Integrating concepts and tests of intelligence from the differential and developmental traditions. *Intelligence, 29(4)*, 307–336.*

Caspi, O., & Burleson, K. O. (2005). Methodological challenges in meditation research. *Advances in Mind-Body Medicine, 21(1)*, 4–11.

Castro-Alamancos, M. A., & Calcagnotto, M. E. (2001). High-pass filtering of corticothalamic activity by neuromodulators released during arousal. *Journal of Neurophysiology, 85*, 1489–1497.

Catano, V., Cronshaw, S. F., Hackett, R., Wiesner, W., & Methot, L. (1997). *Recruitment and selection in Canada*. Toronto: ITP Nelson.*

Cattan, M., White, M., Bond, J., & Learmouth, A. (2005). Preventing social isolation and loneliness among older people: A systematic review of health promotion interventions. *Ageing & Society, 25(1)*, 41–67.

Cavaco, S., Anderson, S. W., Allen, J. S., Castro-Caldas, A., & Damasio, H. (2004). The scope of preserved procedural memory in amnesia. *Brain, 127(8)*, 1853–1867.

Cavedini, P., Riboldi, G., Keller, R., D'Annucci, A., & Bellodi, K. L. (2002). Frontal lobe dysfunction in pathological gambling patients. *Biological Psychiatry, 15*, 334–341.

Ceballo, R., McLoyd, V. C., & Toyokawa, T. (2004). The influence of neighborhood quality on adolescents' educational values and school effort. *Journal of Adolescent Research, 19(6)*, 716–739.

Ceci, S. J. (2003). Cast in six ponds and you'll reel in something: Looking back on 25 years of research. *American Psychologist, 58(11)*, 855–864.

Ceci, S. J., & Gilstrap, L. L. (2000). Determinants of intelligence: Schooling and intelligence. In A. Kazdin (Ed.), *Encyclopedia of Psychology*. Washington, & New York: APA Press and Oxford.

Center for Leadership Studies. (2000). *Multifactor Leadership Questionnaire: Norms*. Retrieved August 29, 2005 from http://cls.binghamton.edu/mlq.htm.

Centers for Disease Control and Prevention. (2001a). *AIDS*. Atanta: Centers for Disease Control and Prevention.

Centers for Disease Control and Prevention. (2001b). *How to quit*. Atlanta, GA: Centers for Disease Control and Prevention.

Centre for Addiction and Mental Health (2004). Drug use among Ontario students: Does it differ from American students? *CAMH Population Studies eBulletin, Jan/Feb 2004, Vol. 5, No. 1*. Toronto, Ontario: Centre for Addiction and Mental Health. Retrieved March 19, 2005 from http://www.camh.net/pdf/ebv5n1_OSDUSvsMTF2003.pdf.*

Cepeda-Benito, A., Reynoso, J. T., & Erath, S. (2004). Meta-analysis of the efficacy of nicotine replacement therapy for smoking cessation: Differences between men and women. *Journal of Consulting & Clinical Psychology, 72(4)*, 712–722.

Chabas, D., Taheri, S., Renier, C., & Mignot, E. (2003). The genetics of narcolepsy. *Annual Review of Genomics and Human Genetics, 4*, 459–483.

Chaikelson, J. S., Arbuckle, T., Lapidus, S., & Gold, D. (1994). Measurement of lifetime alcohol consumption. *Journal of Studies on Alcohol, 55*, 133–140.*

Chambers, E., & Belicki, K. (1998). Using sleep dysfunction to explore the nature of resilience in adult survivors of childhood abuse or trauma. *Child Abuse & Neglect, 22*, 753–758.*

Chambless, D. L., & Peterman, M. (2004). Evidence on cognitive-behavioral therapy for generalized anxiety disorder and panic disorder: The second decade. In R. L. Leahy (Ed.), *Contemporary cognitive therapy: Theory, research, and practice.* New York: Guilford.

Chance, P. (2006). *Learning and behavior (5th ed.).* Belmont, CA: Wadsworth.

Chandler, M. J., & Lalonde, C. E. (1998). Cultural continuity as a hedge against suicide in Canada's First Nations. *Transcultural Psychiatry, 35(2),* 193–211.*

Chandler, M. J., Lalonde, C. E., Sokol, B. W., & Hallett, D. (2003). Personal persistence, identity development, and suicide: A study of Native and non-Native North American adolescents. *Monographs of the Society for Research in Child Development, 68(2),* vii–130.

Changeux, J., & Chavillion, J. (1995). *Origins of the human brain.* New York: Oxford.

Chao, J., & Nestler, E. J. (2004). Molecular neurobiology of drug addiction. *Annual Review of Medicine, 55,* 113–132.

Chaplin, T. M., Cole, P. M. & Zahn-Waxler, C. (2005). Parental socialization of emotion expression: Gender differences and relations to child adjustment. *Emotion, 5(1),* 80–88.

Charles, C.M., & Senter, G.W. (2004). *Building classroom discipline (8th ed.).* Boston: Allyn & Bacon.

Charnetski, C. J., Riggers, S., & Brennan, F. X. (2004). Effect of petting a dog on immune system function. *Psychological Reports, 95(3,Pt2),* 1087–1091.

Chase, W. G., & Simon, H. A. (1973). Perception in chess. *Cognitive Psychology, 4,* 55–81.

Chastain, G., & Landrum, R. E. (1999). *Protecting human subjects.* Washington: APA Press.

Chasteen, A. L., Bhattacharyya, S., Horhota, M., Tam, R., & Hasher, L. (2005). How feelings of stereotype threat influence older adults' memory performance. *Experimental Aging Research, 31(3),* 235–260.*

Chaves, J. F. (2000). Hypnosis. In A. Kazdin (Ed.), *Encyclopedia of psychology.* Washington DC, and New York: APA Press and Oxford.

Cheasty, M., Condren, R., & Cooney, C. (2002). Altered sexual preference and behavior in a man with vascular ischemic lesions in the temporal lobe. *International Journal of Geriatric Psychiatry, 17,* 87–88.

Chen, C., & Stevenson, H. W. (1989). Homework: A cross-cultural comparison. *Child Development, 60,* 551–561.

Chen, Z. (2002). Analogical problem solving: A hierarchical analysis of procedural similarity. *Journal of Experimental Psychology, 28,* 81–98.

Chess, S., & Thomas, A. (1977). Temperamental individuality from childhood to adolescence. *Journal of Child Psychiatry, 16,* 218–226.

Cheyne, D., Roberts, L. E., Gaetz, W., Bosnyak, D., Nahmias, C., Christoforou, N., & Weinberg, H. (1998). Somatotopic organization of human somatosensory cortex: A comparison of EEG, MEG and fMRI methods. In Y. Koga, K. Nagata, & K. Hirata (Eds.), *Brain topography today.* Amsterdam: Excerpta Medica International Congress Series, Elsevier.*

Child Trends. (2000). *Trends in sexual activity and contraceptives among teens.* Child Trends Research Brief. Washington: Author.

Chipperfield, J. G., Perry, R. P., & Menec, V. H. (1999). Primary and secondary control-enhancing strategies: Implications for health in later life. *Journal of Aging & Health, 11,* 517–539.*

Chirot, D., & Seligman, M. E. P. (Eds.). (2001). *Ethnopolitical warfare.* Washington: APA Press.

Chizuko, I. (Ed.). (1999). *On human memory: Evolution, progress, and reflections on the 30th anniversary of the Atkinson-Shiffrin model.* Mahwah, NJ: Erlbaum.

Chodorow, N. (1978). *The reproduction of mothering.* Berkeley: University of California Press. Chodorow, N. (1989). *Femininism and psychoanalytic theory.* New Haven, CT: Yale University Press.

Chodorow, N. J. (2004). Psychoanalysis and women: A personal thirty-five-year retrospect. *Annual of Psychoanalysis, 32,* 101–129.

Chomsky, N. (1975). *Reflections on language.* New York: Pantheon.

Chorney, M. J., Chorney, K., Seese, N., Owen, M. J., Daniels, J., McGuffin, P., et al. (1998). A quantitative trait locus associated with cognitive ability in children. *Psychological Science, 9,* 159–166.

Christian, K., Bachnan, H. J., & Morrison, F. J. (2001). Schooling and cognitive development. In R. J. Sternberg, & E. L. Grigorenko (Eds.), *Environmental effects on cognitive development.* Mahwah, NJ: Erlbaum.

Christiansen, L. B. (2001). *Experimental methodology (8th ed.).* Boston: Allyn & Bacon.

Christie, I. C., & Friedman, B. H. (2004). Autonomic specificity of discrete emotion and dimensions of affective space: A multivariate approach. *International Journal of Psychophysiology, 51(2),* 143–153.

Christie, J., & Klein, R. (1998). *The relative merits of using simple path and gateway metaphors in Graphic User Interface design.* Nortel Technologies Technical Report.*

Chu, S., Handley, V., & Cooper, S. R. (2003). Eliminating context-dependent forgetting: changing contexts can be as effective as reinstating them. *Psychological Record, 53(4),* 549–559.

Chugh, D. (2004). Societal and managerial implications of implicit social cognition: Why milliseconds matter. *Social Justice Research, 17(2),* 203–222.

Chung, K., & Chung, J. M. (2001). Sympathetic sprouting in the dorsal root ganglion after spinal nerve ligation: Evidence of regenerative collateral sprouting. *Brain Research, 895,* 204–212.

Church, R. M., & Kirkpatrick, K. (2001). Theories of conditioning and timing. In R. R. Mowrer, & S. B. Klein (Eds.), *Handbook of contemporary learning theories.* Mahwah, NJ: Erlbaum.

Cialdini, R. B. (2001). *Influence: Science and practice (4th ed.).* Boston: Allyn & Bacon.

Cialdini, R. B., & Goldstein, N. J. (2004). Social influence: Compliance and conformity. *Annual Review of Psychology, 55,* 591–621.

Cialdini, R. B., Schaller, M., Houlihan, D., Arps, K., Fultz, J., & Beaman, A. L. (1987). Empathy-based helping: Is it selflessly or selfishly motivated? *Journal of Personality & Social Psychology, 52,* 749–758.

Cicourel, A. V. (2005). Word meaning and ecological validity. *Journal of the Learning Sciences, 14(2),* 285–291.

Citkowska-Kisielewska, A., & Aleksandrowicz, J. W. (2005). Obsessive-compulsive disorder: Psychopathology and therapy. *Archives of Psychiatry & Psychotherapy, 7(1),* 29–42.

Clark, D., Boutros, N. & Mendez, M. (2005). *The Brain and behavior, (2nd ed.).* Cambridge: Cambridge University Press.

Clark, D. A. (2004). Cognitive-behavioral theory and treatment of obsessive-compulsive disorder: Past contributions and current developments. In R. L. Leahy (Ed.), *Contemporary cognitive therapy: Theory, research, and practice.* New York: Guilford.

Clark, D. A. (2005). *Intrusive thoughts in clinical disorders: Theory, research, and treatment.* New York: Guilford.*

Clark, E. V. (1983). Meanings and concepts. In P. H. Mussen (Ed.), *Handbook of child psychology (4th ed., Vol. 2).* New York: Wiley.

Clark, N. M., & Dodge, J. A. (1999). Exploring self-efficacy as a predictor of disease management. *Health Education & Behavior, 26,* 72–89.

Clark, T. (2001). Post-traumatic stress disorder: Baby should not be thrown out with the bath water. *British Journal of Medicine, 322,* 1303–1304.

Clarke, V. A., Lovegrove, H., Williams, H., & Macpherson, M. (2000). Unrealistic optimism and the health belief model. *Journal of Behavioral Medicine, 25,* 367–376.

Claxton-Oldfield, S. (2000). Deconstructing the myth of the wicked stepparent. *Marriage & Family Review. Special Issue: Macro/micro dynamics and the family, 30(1–2),* 51–58.*

Claxton-Oldfield, S., Goodyear, C., Parsons, T., & Claxton-Oldfield, J. (2002). Some possible implications of negative stepfather stereotypes. *Journal of Divorce & Remarriage, 36(3–4),* 77–88.*

Claxton-Oldfield, S, & Keefe, S. M. (1999). Assessing stereotypes about the Innu of Davis Inlet, Labrador. *Canadian Journal of Behavioural Science, 31(2),* 86–9.*

Clay, R. A. (2000, April). Linking up online: Is the Internet enhancing interpersonal connections or leading to greater isolation? *Monitor on Psychology,* 20–23.

Clayton, A. H., McGarvey, E. L., Abouesh, A. L., & Pinkerton, R. C. (2001). Substitution of an SSRI with bupropion sustained release following SSRI-induced sexual dysfunction. *Journal of Clinical Psychiatry, 62,* 185–190.

Cleary, T. J., & Zimmerman, B. J. (2004). Self-regulation empowerment program: A school-based program to enhance self-regulated and self-motivated cycles of student learning. *Psychology in the Schools, 41(5),* 537–555.

Clément, R., Baker, S. C., & MacIntyre, P. D. (2003). Willingness to communicate in a second language: The effects of context norms, and vitality. *Journal of Language & Social Psychology, 22(2),* 190–209.*

Clément, R., & Bourhis, R. Y. (1996). Bilingualism and intergroup communication. *International Journal of Psycholinguistics, 12(2),* 171–191.*

Clément, R., Noels, K. A., & Deneault, B. (2001). Interethnic contact, identity, and psychological adjustment: The mediating and moderating roles of communication. *Journal of Social Issues, 57,* 559–577.*

Clifford, R. M., Harms, T., Pepper, S., & Stuart, B. (1992). Assessing quality in family day care. In D. R. Peters, & A. R. Pence (Eds.), *Family day care: Current research for informed public policy.* New York: Teachers College Press.*

Cloninger, C. R. (2004). *Feeling good: The science of well being.* New York: Oxford.

Close, C. E., Roberts, P. L., & Berger, R. E. (1990). Cigarettes, alcohol, and marijuana are related to pyospermia in infertile men. *Journal of Urology, 144,* 900–903.

Cobb, N. J. (2004). *Adolescence (5th ed.).* New York: McGraw-Hill.

Cochran, S. D., & Mays, V. M. (1990). Sex, lies, and HIV. *New England Journal of Medicine, 322,* 774–775.

Cohen, A. J. (2000). Film music: Perspectives from cognitive psychology. In J. Buhler, C. Flinn, & D. Neumeyer (Eds.), *Music and cinema.* Hanover: Wesleyan University Press.*

Cohen, A. J. (2001). Music as a source of emotion in film. In P. Juslin, & J. Sloboda (Eds.), *Music and emotion.* Oxford: Oxford University Press.*

Cohen, L. A. (1987). Diet and cancer. *Scientific American, 257(5),* 128–137.

Cohen, L., De Moor, C., & Amato, R. J. (2001). The association between treatment-specific optimism and depressive symptomatology in patients enrolled in a Phase I cancer clinical trial. *Cancer, 91,* 1949–1953.

Cohen, P., Cohen, J., Kasen, S., Velez, C. N., Hartmark, C., Johnson, J., et al. (1993). An epidemiological study of disorders in late adolescence: I. Age- and gender-specific prevalence. *Journal of Child Psychology & Psychiatry, 6,* 851–867.

Cohen, R. J., & Swerdlik, M. E. (2005). *Psychological testing and assessment (6th ed.).* New York: McGraw-Hill.

Cohen, R. L., & Borsoi, D. (1996). The role of gestures in description-communication: A cross-sectional study of aging. *Journal of Nonverbal Behavior, 20,* 45–64.*

Cohen, S. (2002). Psychosocial stress, social networks, and susceptibility to infection. In H. G. Koenig, & H. J. Cohen (Eds.), *The link between religion and health.* New York: Oxford.

Cohen, S. (2004). Social relationships and health. *American Psychologist, 59(8),* 676–684.

Cohen, S., Evans, G. W., Krantz, D. S., Stokols, D., & Kelly, S. (1981). Aircraft noise and children: Longitudinal and cross-sectional evidence on adaptation to noise and the effectiveness of noise abatement. *Journal of Personality & Social Psychology, 40,* 331–345.

Cohen, S., Frank, E., Doyle, W., Skoner, D. P., Rabin, B. S., & Gwaltney, J. M. (1998). Types of stressors that increase susceptibility to the common cold in healthy adults. *Health Psychology, 17,* 214–223.

Cohen, S., Glass, D. C., & Singer, J. E. (1973). Apartment noise, auditory discrimination, and reading ability in children. *Journal of Experimental Psychology, 9,* 407–422.

Cohen, S., Miller, G. E., & Rabin, B. S. (2001). Psychological stress and antibody response to immunization. *Psychosomatic Medicine, 63,* 7–18.

Cohen, S. I. (2002). Treatment of insomnia. *Lancet, 359,* 1433–1434.

Colby, A., Kohlberg, L., Gibbs, J., & Lieberman, M. (1983). A longitudinal study of moral judgment. *Monographs of the Society for Research in Child Development, 48 (21, Serial No. 201).*

Cole, C. F., Richman, B. A., & Brown, S. K. (2001). The world of Sesame Street research. In S. M. Fisch, & R. T. Truglio (Eds.), *"G" is for growing: Thirty years of research on children and Sesame Street.* Mahwah, NJ: Erlbaum.

Cole, M. (1999). Culture in development. In M. H. Bornstein, & M. E. Lamb (Eds.), *Developmental psychology: An advanced textbook (4th ed.).* Mahwah, NJ: Erlbaum.

Cole, M., Cole, S. R., & Lightfoot, C. (2005). *The development of children (5th ed.).* New York:Worth.

Coleman, B. L., Stevens, M. J., & Reeder, G. G. (2001). What makes recovered-memory testimony compelling to jurors? *Law and Human Behavior, 25,* 317–338.

Coleman, L., & Cater, S. (2005). Underage 'binge' drinking: A qualitative study into motivations and outcomes. *Drugs: Education, Prevention & Policy, 12(2),* 125–136.

Coleman, P. D. (1986, August). *Regulation of dendritic extent: Human aging brain and Alzheimer's disease.* Paper presented at the meeting of the American Psychological Association, Washington.

Coley, J., Shafto, P., Stepanova, O., & Baraff, E. (2005). Knowledge and category-based induction. In A. Woo-kyoung, R. L. Goldstone, B. C. Love, A. B. Markman, & P. Wolff (Eds.), (2005). *Categorization inside and outside the laboratory: Essays in honor of Douglas L. Medin.* Washington: APA Press.

Collins, M. (1996, Winter). The job outlook for '96 grads. *Journal of Career Planning,* 51–54.

Collins, W. A., Maccoby, E. E., Steinberg, L., Hetherington, E. M. & Bornstein, M. H. (2003). Contemporary research on parenting: The case for nature and nurture. In M. E. Hertzig, & E. A. Farber (Eds.), *Annual progress in child psychiatry and child development: 2000-2001.* New York: Brunner-Routledge.

Colom, R., Lluis-Font, J. M., & Andrés-Pueyo, A. (2005). The generational intelligence gains are caused by decreasing variance in the lower half of the distribution: Supporting evidence for the nutrition hypothesis. *Intelligence, 33(1),* 83–91.

Combs, M. (2002). *Readers and writers in the primary grades (2nd ed.).* Upper Saddle River, NJ: Prentice Hall.

Comer, R. J. (2005). *Fundamentals of abnormal psychology (4th ed.).* New York: Worth.

Committee on the Rights of the Child (2003) *UN Doc CRC/C/15/Add215.* New York: United Nations.

Commons, M. L., & Richards, F. A. (2003). Four postformal stages. In J. Demick, & C. Andreoletti (Eds.), *Handbook of adult development.* New York: Plenum.

Compas, B. E., Connor-Smith, J. K., Saltzman, H., Thomsen, A. H., & Wadsworth, M. E. (2001). Coping with stress during childhood and adolescence: Problems, progress, and potential in theory and research. *Psychological Bulletin, 127,* 87–127.

Comunian, A. L. (2004). Construction of a scale for measuring development of moral judgement. *Psychological Reports, 94(2),* 613–618.

Conklin, C. A., & Tiffany, S. T. (2002). Applying extinction research and theory to cue-exposure addiction treatments. *Addiction, 97,* 155–167.

Conner, M., & Norman, P. (2005). *Predicting health behaviour (2nd ed.).* New York: McGraw-Hill.

Conway, M. (Ed.). (2002). *Levels of processing 30 years on.* Hove, UK: Psychology Press.

Conway, M., & Rubin, D. (1993). The structure of autobiographical memory. In A. F. Collins, S. E. Gathercole, M. A. Conway, & P. E. Morris (Eds.), *Theories of memory.* Mahwah, NJ: Erlbaum.

Cooper, M. J. (2005). Cognitive theory in anorexia nervosa and bulimia nervosa: Progress, development and future directions. *Clinical Psychology Review, 25(4),* 511–531.

Cooper, R. M., & Zubek, J. P. (1958). Effects of enriched and restricted early environments on the learning ability of bright and dull rats. *Canadian Journal of Psychology, 12,* 159–164.*

Cooper, R. P., Yule, P., Fox, J., & Glasspool, D. W. (2002). *Modeling high-level cognitive processes.* Mahwah, NJ: Erlbaum.

Copeland, M. E. (2000). *The loneliness workbook: A guide to developing and maintaining lasting connections.* Oakland, CA: New Harbinger Publications.

Corballis, P. M., Funnell, M. G., & Gazzaniga, M. S. (2002). Hemispheric asymmetries for simple visual judgments in the split brain. *Neuropsychologia, 40,* 401–410.

Corcoran, K., Gorin, S., & Moniz, C. (2005). Managed care and mental health. In S. A. Kirk (Ed.), *Mental disorders in the social environment: Critical perspectives. Foundations of social work knowledge.* New York: Columbia University Press.

Coren, S. (1996). *Sleep thieves: An eye-opening exploration into the science and mysteries of sleep.* New York: Free Press.*

Coren, S. (1999). Psychology applied to animal learning. In D. A. Bernstein, & A. Stec (Eds.), *Psychology: Fields of application.* Houghton Mifflin: Boston.*

Coren, S., & Hewitt, P. L. (1998). Is anorexia nervosa associated with elevated rates of suicide? *American Journal of Public Health, 88,* 1206–1207.*

Coren, S., Ward, L. M., & Enns, J. T. (2004). *Sensation and perception (6th ed.).* New York: Wiley.*

Corey, G. (2005). *Theory and practice of counseling and psychotherapy (7th ed.).* Belmont, CA: Wadsworth.

Corey, G., & Corey, M. S. (2002). *I never knew I had a choice (7th ed.).* Belmont, CA: Wadsworth.

Corkin, S. (2002). What's new with the amnesic patient H.M.? *Nature Reviews Neuroscience, 3,* 153–160.

Cornoldi, C., & Vecchi, T. (2003). *Visuo-spatial working memory and individual differences.* New York: Psychology Press.

Corr, C. A. (1993). Coping with dying: Lessons that we should and should not learn from the work of Elisabeth Kübler-Ross. *Death Studies, 17(1),* 69–83.

Correa-Chávez, M., Rogoff, B., & Arauz, R. M. (2005). Cultural patterns in attending to two events at once. *Child Development, 76(3),* 664–678.

Cosmides, L., Tooby, J. Cronin, H., & Curry, O. (2003). *What is evolutionary psychology? Explaining the new science of the mind.* New Haven, CT: Yale University Press.

Costa, P. T., & McCrae, R. R. (1992). *Revised NEO personality inventory.* Odessa, FL: Psychological Assessment Resources.

Côté, J. E. (2000). *Arrested adulthood: the changing nature of identity and maturity in the late-modern world.* New York: New York University Press.

Cotter, D., Mackay, D., Chana, G., Beasley, C., Landau, S., & Everall, I. P. (2002). Reduced neuronal size and glial density in area 9 of the dorsolateral prefrontal cortex in subjects with major depressive disorder. *Cerebral Cortex, 12,* 386–394.

Cottraux, J. (2005). Recent developments in research and treatment for social phobia (social anxiety disorder). *Current Opinion in Psychiatry, 18(1),* 51–54.

Coupland, D. (2005). *Terry.* London: Douglas & McIntyre.

Coupland, N. J. (2001). Social phobia: Etiology, neurobiology, and treatment. *Journal of Clinical Psychiatry, 62 (Suppl. 1),* 25–35.*

Coupland, N. J. (2002). Worry WARTS have generalized anxiety attacks. *Canadian Journal of Psychiatry, 47,* 197.*

Cousins, N. (1979). *Anatomy of an Illness as perceived by a patient: Reflections on healing and regeneration.* New York: Norton.

Cousins, N. (1983). *The healing heart: Antidotes to panic and helplessness.* New York: Norton.

Cowan, N. (2005). *Working memory capacity.* Hove, UK: Psychology Press.

Cowan, P. A., & Cowan, C. P. (2001). What an intervention design reveals about how parents affect their children's academic achievement and social competence. In J. Borkowski, S. Landesman-Ramey, & M. Bristol (Eds.), *Parenting and the child's world: Multiple influences on intellectual and social-emotional development.* Mahwah, NJ: Erlbaum.

Cowan, W. M., Kopnisky, K. L., & Hyman, S. E. (2002). The human genome project and its impact on psychiatry. *Annual Review of Neuroscience, 25,* 1–50.

Cowley, G. (1988, May 23). The wisdom of animals. *Newsweek,* pp. 52–58.

Cowley, M. A., Smart, J. L., Rubinstein, M., Cerdan, M. G., Diano, S., Horvath, T. L., et al. (2001). Leptin activates anorexigenic POMC neurons through a neural network in the arcuate nucleus. *Nature, 411,* 480–484.

Cox, B. J., Endler, N. S., Lee, P. S., & Swinson, R. P. (1992). A meta-analysis of treatments for panic disorder with agoraphobia: imipramine, alprazolam, and in vivo exposure. *Journal of Behavior Therapy and Experimental Psychiatry, 23,* 175–182.*

Cox, B. J., Swinson, R. P., Endler, N. S., & Norton, G. R. (1994). The symptom structure of panic attacks. *Comprehensive Psychiatry, 35,* 349–353.*

Cox, R., Baker, S. E., Macdonald, D. W., & Berdoy, M. (2004). Protecting egg prey from Carrion Crows: The potential of aversive conditioning. *Applied Animal Behaviour Science, 87(3–4),* 325–342.

Cozby, P. C. (2004). *Methods and behavioral research (8th ed.).* New York: McGraw-Hill.

Crabbe, J. C. (2002). Genetic contributions to alcoholism. *Annual Review of Psychology, 53,* 435–462.

Craighead, W. E., & Craighead, L. W. (2001). The role of psychotherapy in treating psychiatric disorders. *Medical Clinics of North America, 85,* 617–629.

Craik, F. I. M., & Bialystok, E. (2005). Intelligence and executive control: Evidence from aging and bilingualism. *Cortex, 41(2),* 222-224.*

Craik, F. I. M., & Lockhart, R. S. (1972). Levels of processing; A framework for memory research. *Journal of Verbal Learning and Verbal Behavior, 11,* 671–684.*

Craik, F. I. M., & Salthouse, T. A. (Eds.) (2000). *The handbook of aging and cognition.* Mahwah, NJ: Erlbaum.*

Craik, F. I. M., & Tulving, E. (1975). Depth of processing and retention of words in episodic memory. *Journal of Experimental Psychology: General, 104,* 268–294.*

Craik, F. I. M., Moroz, T. M., Moscovitch, M., Stuss, D. T., Winocur, G., Tulving, E., & Kapur, S. (1999). In search of self: A PET investigation of self-referential information. *Psychological Science, 10,* 26–34.*

Cramer, P. (1999). Future directions for the Thematic Apperception Test. *Journal of Personality Assessment, 72,* 74–92.

Cramer, P., & Brilliant, M. A. (2001). Defense use and defense understanding in children. *Journal of Personality, 69,* 297–322.

Cramer, P., & Tracy, A. (2005). The pathway from child personality to adult adjustment: The road is not straight. *Journal of Research in Personality, 39(3),* 369–394.

Crandall, C. S., & Schaller, M. (2004). Scientists and science: How individual goals shape collective norms. In M. Schaller, & C. S. Crandall (Eds.), *The psychological foundations of culture.* Mahwah, NJ: Erlbaum.*

Crandall, R., & Jones, A. (1991). Issues in self-actualization measurement. In A. Jones & R. Crandall (Eds.), Handbook of self-actualization (Special Issue). *Journal of Social Behavior and Personality, 6,* 339–344.

Crawford, T. N., Cohen, P., Johnson, J. G., Sneed, J. R., & Brook, J. S. (2004). The course and psychosocial correlates of personality disorder symptoms in adolescence: Erikson's developmental theory revisited. *Journal of Youth & Adolescence, 33(5)*, 373–387.

Crick, F., & Koch, C. (1998). Consciousness and neuroscience. *Cerebral Cortex, 8*, 97–107.

Crocker, J. (2001, August). *The costs of seeking self-esteem.* Paper presented at the meeting of the APA Press, San Francisco.

Crocker, J., Major, B., & Steele, C. (1998). Social stigma. In D. T. Gilbert, S. T. Fiske, & G. Lindzey (Eds.), *Handbook of social psychology (4th ed., Vol. 2)*. New York: McGraw-Hill.

Crocker, J., & Park, L. E. (2004). The costly pursuit of self-esteem. *Psychological Bulletin, 130(3)*, 392–414.

Crooks, R., & Bauer, K. (2005). *Our sexuality (9th ed.).* Belmont, CA: Wadsworth.

Crosby, A. E., Cheltenham, M. P., & Sacks, J. J. (1999). Incidence of suicidal ideation and behavior in the United States, 1994. *Suicide and Life-Threatening Behavior, 29*, 131–140.

Cross-National Collaborative Group (1992). The changing rate of major depression. *Journal of the American Medical Association, 268*, 3098–3105.

Crowther, J. H., Sanftner, J., Bonifazi, D. Z., & Shepherd, K. L. (2001). The role of daily hassles in binge eating. *International Journal of Eating Disorders, 29*, 449–454.

Csikszentmihalyi, M. (1990). *Flow: The psychology of optimal experience.* New York: HarperPerennial.

Csikszentmihalyi, M. (1996). *Creativity.* New York: HarperCollins.

Csikszentmihalyi, M., & Beattie, O. (1979). Life themes: A theoretical and empirical exploration of their origins and effects. *Journal of Humanistic Psychology, 19*, 677–693.

Cuddy, L. L. (1997). Tonal relations. In I. Deliege, & J. Sloboda (Eds.), *Perception and cognition of music.* Hove, England: Psychology Press.*

Cuffe, S. P., McKeown, R. E., Addy, C. L., & Garrison, C. Z. (2005). Family and psychosocial risk factors in a longitudinal epidemiological study of adolescents. *Journal of the American Academy of Child & Adolescent Psychiatry, 44(2)*, 121–129.

Cuijpers, P. (2001). Mortality and depressive symptoms in inhabitants of residential homes. *International Journal of Geriatric Psychiatry, 16*, 131–138.

Cullen, M., & Bradley, M. T. (2004). Positions of truthfully answered controls on control question tests with the polygraph. *Canadian Journal of Behavioural Science, 36(3)*, 167–176.*

Culpepper, L., Davidson, J. R., Dietrich, A. J., Goodman, W. K., Kroenke, K., & Schwenk, T. L. (2004). Suicidality as a possible side effect of antidepressant treatment. *Journal of Clinical Psychiatry, 65*, 742–749.

Culross, R. R. (2004). Individual and contextual variables among creative scientists: The new work paradigm. *Roeper Review, 26(3)*, 126–127.

Cumming, B. G., & DeAngelis, G. C. (2001). The physiology of stereopsis. *Annual Review of Neuroscience, 24*, 203–238.

Cummings, M. (2003). *Human heredity (6th ed.).* Belmont, CA: Wadsworth.

Cunningham, W. A., Nezlek, J. B., & Banaji, M. R. (2004). Implicit and explicit ethnocentrism: Revisiting the ideologies of prejudice. *Personality & Social Psychology Bulletin, 30(10)*, 1332–1346.

Curran, K., DuCette, J., Eisenstein, J., & Hyman, I. A. (2001, August). *Statistical analysis of the cross-cultural data: The third year.* Paper presented at the meeting of the American Psychological Association, San Francisco.

Currie, E. (2005). *The road to whatever: Middle-class culture and the crisis of adolescence.* New York: Holt.

Curtiss, S. (1977). *Genie.* New York: Academic Press.

Cushner, K. (2003). *Human diversity in action: Developing multicultural competencies for the classroom. (2nd ed.).* Boston: McGraw-Hill.

Cutrona, C. E., Russell, D. W., & Gardner, K. A. (2005). The relationship enhancement model of social support. In T. A. Revenson, K. Kayser, & G.

Bodenmann (Eds.), *Couples coping with stress: Emerging perspectives on dyadic coping.* Washington: APA Press.

Czienskowski, U., & Giljohann, S. (2002). Intimacy, concreteness, and the "self-reference" effect. *Experimental Psychology, 49*, 73–79.

D

DaCosta, D., Larouche, J., Dritsa, M., & Brender, W. (2000). Psychosocial correlates of prepartum and postpartum depressed mood. *Journal of Affective Disorders, 59*, 31–40.

Dadds, M. R., Holland, D. E., Barrett, P. M., & Spence, S. H. (1999). Early intervention and prevention of anxiety disorders in children: Results at 2-year follow-up. *Journal of Consulting & Clinical Psychology, 67*, 145–150.

Dagenais, D., & Berron, C. (2001). Promoting multilingualism through French immersion and language maintenance in three immigrant families. *Language, Culture & Curriculum, 14*, 142–155.*

Dahua, W., Yan, T., Liqing, Z., & Jiliang, S. (2004). Inner-mechanisms between intergenerational social support and subjective well-being of the elderly. *Acta Psychologica Sinica, 36(1)*, 78–82.

Dalfen, A. K., & Stewart, D. E. (2001). Who develops severe or fatal adverse drug reactions to selective serotonin reuptake inhibitors? *Canadian Journal of Psychology, 46*, 258–263.*

Dallaire, R. (2004). *Shake hands with the devil: The failure of humanity in Rwanda.* Toronto: Random House Canada.*

Daly, M., & Wilson, M. (1983). *Sex, evolution, and behavior.* Boston: Willard Grant Press.*

Daly, M., & Wilson, M. (1998). *The truth about Cinderella: A Darwinian view of parental love.* London: Weidenfeld & Nicolson.*

Daly, M., & Wilson, M. (2001). Risk-taking, intrasexual competition, and homicide. In J. A. French, A. C. Kamil, & D. Leger (Eds.), *Evolutionary psychology and motivation. Volume 47 of the Nebraska symposium on motivation.* Lincoln, NE: University of Nebraska Press.*

Damasio, A. (Ed.). (2001). *The Scientific American book of the brain.* New York: Scientific American.

Damasio, A., & Anderson, S. W. (2003). The frontal lobes. In K. M. Heilman, & E. Valenstein, (Eds). *Clinical neuropsychology (4th ed.).* London: Oxford.

Daneman, M. (1991). Working memory as a predictor of verbal fluency. *Journal of Psycholinguistic Research, 20*, 445–464.*

Daneman, M., & Merikle, P. M. (1996). Working memory and comprehension: A meta-analysis. *Psychonomic Bulletin & Review, 3*, 422–433.*

D'Angelo, B. & Wierzbicki, M. (2003). Relations of daily hassles with both anxious and depressed mood in students. *Psychological Reports, 92(2)*, 416–418.

Danner, D. D., Snowdon, D. A., & Friesen, W. V. (2001). Positive emotions in early life and longevity: Findings from the nun study. *Journal of Personality & Social Psychology, 80(5)*, 804–813.

Dannon, P. N., Dolberg, O. T., Schrieber, S., & Grunhaus, L. (2002). Three and six-month outcome following courses of either ECT or rTMS in a population of severly depressed individuals: Preliminary report. *Biological Psychiatry, 51*, 687–690.

Danziger, K. (1980). The history of introspection reconsidered. *Journal of the History of the Behavioral Sciences, 16*, 240–262.*

Danziger, K. (1997). *Naming the mind: How psychology found its language.* London: Sage.*

Darley, J. M., & Latané, B. (1968). Bystander intervention in emergencies: Diffusion of responsibility. *Journal of Personality & Social Psychology, 8*, 377–383.

Darou, W. S. (1992). Native Canadians and intelligence testing. *Canadian Journal of Counselling, 26(2)*, 96–99.*

Daruna, J. H. (2004). *Introduction to psychoneuroimmunology.* San Diego: Elsevier.

Darwin, C. (1872/1965). *The expression of the emotions in man and animals.* Chicago: University of Chicago Press.

Darwin, C. (1859/1979). *The origin of species.* New York: Avenal Books.

Das, J. P. (1998). A popular primer on mental retardation. *Developmental Disabilities Bulletin, 26*, 43–58.*

Das, J. P. (2000). Mental retardation. In A. Kazdin (Ed.), *Encyclopedia of psychology.* Washington, & New York: APA Press and Oxford.*

Das, J. P. (2002). A better look at intelligence. *Current Directions in Psychological Science, 11*, 28–33.*

Dattilio, F. M. (Ed.) (2001). *Case studies in couple and family therapy.* New York: Guilford.

Davidhizar, R., & Giger, J. N. (2004). A review of the literature on care of clients in pain who are culturally diverse. *International Nursing Review, 51(1)*, 47–55.

Davidson, A. R., & Jacard, J. J. (1979). Variables that moderate the attitude-behavior relation: Results of a longitudinal survey. *Journal of Personality & Social Psychology, 37*, 1364–1376.

Davidson, G. C., & Neale, J. M. (2001). *Abnormal psychology (8th ed.).* New York: Wiley.

Davidson, J. E., & Callery, C. (2001). Care of the obesity surgery patient requiring immediate-level or intensive care. *Obesity Surgery, 11*, 93–97.

Davidson, P. S., & Glisky, E. L. (2002). Is flashbulb memory a special instance of source memory? Evidence from older adults. *Memory, 10*, 99–111.

Davidson, R. J., Scherer, K. R., & Goldsmith, H. H. (Eds.), (2002). *Handbook of affective sciences.* New York: Oxford.

Davidson, R. J., Shackman, A., & Pizzagalli, D. (2002). The functional neuroanatomy of emotion and affective style. In R. J. Davidson, K. R. Scherer, & H. H. Goldsmith (Eds.), *Handbook of affective sciences.* New York: Oxford.

Davies, K. (2001). *Cracking the genome.* New York: Free Press.

Davis, S. F., & Smith, R. A. (2005). *Introduction to statistics and research methods: Becoming a psychological detective.* Englewood Cliffs, NJ: Prentice Hall.

Davison, G. C., & Neale, J. M. (1994). *Abnormal psychology (6th ed.).* New York: Wiley.

Davison, G. C., & Neale, J. M. (2006). *Abnormal psychology (10th ed.).* San Francisco: Jossey-Bass.

Davy, J., & Cross, M. (2004). *Barriers, defences and resistance.* New York: McGraw-Hill.

Dawson, K. A. (2004). Temporal organization of the brain: Neurocognitive mechanisms and clinical implications. *Brain & Cognition, 54(1)*, 75–94.

Day, D. E., & Roberts, M. W. (1983). An analysis of the physical punishment component of a parent training program. *Journal of Abnormal Child Psychology, 11*, 141–152.

Day, R. J. F. (2000). *Multiculturalism and the history of Canadian diversity.* Toronto: University of Toronto Press.*

de Castell, S., & Bryson, M. (1998). Retooling play: Dystopia, dysphoria, and difference. In J. Cassell, & H. Jenkins (Eds.), *From Barbie to Mortal Kombat: Gender and computer games.* Cambridge MIT Press.*

De Silva, W. P., & Rachman, S. J. (1996). *Panic disorder: The facts.* New York: Oxford.

Dean, G. A., Kelly, I. W., Saklofske, D. H., & Furnham, A. (1992). Graphology and human judgment. In B. Bayerstein & G. Bayerstein (Eds.), *The write stuff.* Buffalo, NY: Prometheus.

Deaux, K. (2001). Social identity. In J. Worell (Ed.), *Encyclopedia of gender and women.* San Diego: Academic Press.

DeBattista, C., Solvason, H. B., & Schatzberg, A. F. (1998). Mood disorders. In H. S. Friedman (Ed.), *Encyclopedia of mental health (Vol. 2).* San Diego: Academic Press.

deCatanzaro, D. (1999). *Motivation and emotion: Evolutionary, physiological, developmental, and social perspectives.* Englewood Cliffs, NJ: Prentice Hall.*

de St Aubin, E., McAdams, D. P, & Kim, T.-C. (2004). *The generative society: Caring for future generations.* Washington: APA Press.

Deary, I. J., & Der, G. (2005). Reaction time, age, and cognitive ability: Longitudinal findings from age 16 to

63 years in representative population samples. *Aging, Neuropsychology, & Cognition, 12(2)*, 187–215.

Debiec, J., & Ledoux, J. E. (2004). Disruption of reconsolidation but not consolidation of auditory fear conditioning by noradrenergic blockade in the amygdala. *Neuroscience, 129(2)*, 267–272.

Deci, E. L., Koestner, R., & Ryan, R. M. (2001). Extrinsic rewards and intrinsic motivation in education: Reconsidered once again. *Review of Educational Research, 71(1)*, 1–27.*

Deci, E. L., & Ryan, R. M. (Eds.). (2002). *Handbook of self-determination research.* Rochester, NY: University of Rochester Press.

Deckers, L. (2005). *Motivation: Biological, psychological, and environmental (2nd ed.).* Boston: Allyn & Bacon.

DeCourville, N., & Sadava, S. W. (1997). The structure of problem drinking in adulthood: A confirmatory approach. *Journal of Studies on Alcohol, 58*, 146–154.*

Deco, G., Rolls, E. T., & Horwitz, B. (2004). "What" and "Where" in visual working memory: A computational neurodynamical perspective for integrating fMRI and single-neuron data. *Journal of Cognitive Neuroscience, 16(4)*, 683–701.

Decruyenaere, M., Evers-Kiebooms, G., Welkenhuysen, M., Denayer, L., & Claes, E. (2000). Cognitive representations of breast cancer, emotional distress, and preventive health behavior: A theoretical perspective. *Psychooncology, 9*, 528–536.

DeGaetano, G. (2005). The impact of media violence on developing minds and hearts. In S. Olfman (Ed.), *Childhood lost: How American culture is failing our kids.* Westport, CT: Praeger Publishers.

De Guise, E., Leblanc, J., Feyz, M., Thomas, H., & Gosselin, N. (2005). Effect of an integrated reality orientation programme in acute care on post-traumatic amnesia in patients with traumatic brain injury. *Brain Injury, 19(4)*, 263–269.*

Dehaene, S., & Naccache, L. (2001). Towards a neuroscience of consciousness: Basic evidence and a workspace format. *Cognition, 79*, 1–37.

de Jong, F., Kollöffel, B., van der Meijden, H., Staarman, J. K., & Janssen, J. (2005). Regulative processes in individual, 3D and computer supported cooperative learning contexts. *Computers in Human Behavior, 21(4)*, 645–670.

DeJong, M. (2004). Metaphor and the mentoring process. *Child & Youth Care Forum, 33(1)*, 3–17.*

DeKeseredy, W., & Kelly, K. (1993). The incidence and prevalence of woman abuse in Canadian university and college dating relationships: Results from a national survey. Ottawa: Health Canada.*

de la Fuente-Fernández, R., Ruth, T. J., Sossi, V., Schulzer, M., Calne, D. B., & Stoessl, A. J. (2001). Expectation and dopamine release: Mechanism of the placebo effect in Parkinson's disease. *Science, 293(5532)*, 1164–1166.

Delega, V. J., Winstead, B. A., Greene, K., Serovich, J., & Elwood, W. N. (2004). Reasons for HIV disclosure/nondisclosure in close relationships: Testing a model of HIV-disclosure decision making. *Journal of Social & Clinical Psychology, 23(6)*, 747–767.

Dell, P. F. (2002). Dissociative phenomena of dissociative identity disorder. *Journal of Nervous and Mental Disorders, 190*, 10–15.

Dell, P. F., & Eisenhower, J. W. (1990). Adolescent multiple personality disorder: A preliminary study of eleven cases. *Journal of the American Academy of Child & Adolescent Psychiatry, 29*, 359–366.

Demakis, G. (1997). Hindsight bias and the Simpson trial: Use in introductory psychology. *Teaching of Psychology, 24*, 190–191.

Demaree, H. A., Everhart, D. K., Youngstrom, E. A., & Harrison, D. W. (2005). Brain lateralization of emotional processing: Historical roots and a future incorporating "dominance". *Behavioral & Cognitive Neuroscience Reviews, 4(1)*, 3–20.

Dement, W. C. (1978). *Some must watch while some must sleep.* New York: Norton.

Dement, W. C. (1999). *The promise of sleep.* New York: Delacorte Press.

Demerouti, E., Bakker, A. B., Nachreiner, F., & Schaufeli, W. B. (2001). The job demands-resources model of burnout. *Journal of Applied Psychology, 86*, 499–512.

Denmark, F. L., Russo, N. F., Frieze, I. H., & Eschuzur, J. (1988). Guidelines for avoiding sexism in psychological research: A report of the ad hoc committee on nonsexist research. *American Psychologist, 43*, 582–585.

Denmark, F. L., Rabinowitz, V. C., & Sechzer, J. A. (2005). *Engendering psychology: Women and gender revisited (2nd ed.).* Boston: Allyn & Bacon.

Derlega, V. J., Winstead, B. A., & Jones, W. H. (2005). *Personality: Contemporary theory and research (3rd ed.).* Belmont, CA: Wadsworth.

Derryberry, D., & Reed, M. (2002). Information processing approaches to individual differences in emotional reactivity. In R. J. Davidson, K. R. Scherer, & H. H. Goldsmith (Eds.), *Handbook of affective sciences.* New York: Oxford.

DeRubeis, R. J., Hollon, S. D., Amsterdam, J. D., Shelton, R. C., Young, P. R., Salomon, R. M., O'Reardon, J. P., et al. (2005). Cognitive therapy vs medications in the treatment of moderate to severe depression. *Archives of General Psychiatry, 62*, 409–416.

Deutsch, M., & Collins, M. (1951). *Interracial housing: A psychological evaluation of a social experiment.* Minneapolis: University of Minnesota Press.

DeVellis, B. M., & DeVellis, R. F. (2001). Self-efficacy and health. In A. Baum, T. A. Revenson, & J. E. Singer (Eds.), *Handbook of health psychology.* Mahwah, NJ: Erlbaum.

Devi, G., & Silver, J. (2000). Approaches to memory loss in neuropsychiatric disorders. *Seminars in Clinical Neuropsychiatry, 5*, 259–265.

Devlin, M. J., Golfein, J. A., Crino, J. S., & Wolk, S. L. (2000). Open treatment of overweight binge eaters with phentermine and fluoxetine as an adjunct to cognitive-behavioral therapy. *International Journal of Eating Disorders, 28*, 325–332.

Devries, L. K. (1998). *Insomnia.* New York: Harold Shaw.

Dewey, J. (1933). *How we think.* Lexington, MA: Heath.

Diamond, A. (2002). Normal development of prefrontal cortex from birth to young adulthood: Cognitive functions, anatomy, and biochemistry. In D. T. Stuss, & R. T. Knight (Eds), *Principles of frontal lobe function.* New York: Oxford.

Diamond, L. M. (2004). Emerging perspectives on distinctions between romantic love and sexual desire. *Current Directions in Psychological Science, 13(3)*, 116–119.

Dickens, W. T., & Flynn, J. R. (2001). Heritability estimates versus large environmental effects: The IQ paradox resolved. *Psychological Review, 108*, 346–369.

Dickson, G. L. (1990). A feminist post-structuralist analysis of the knowledge of menopause. *Advances in Nursing Science, 12*, 15–31.

Diener, E. (1984). Subjective well-being. *Psychological Bulletin, 109*, 542–575.

Diener, E. (1999). Introduction to the special section on the structure of emotion. *Journal of Personality & Social Psychology, 76*, 803–804.

Diener, E. (2000). Subjective well-being: The science of happiness and a proposal for a national index. *American Psychologist, 55*, 34–43.

Diener, E., Oishi, S., & Lucas, R. E. (2003). Personality, culture, and subjective well-being: Emotional and cognitive evaluations of life. *Annual Review of Psychology, 54*, 403–425.

Diener, E., & Seligman, M. E. P. (2002). Very happy people. *Psychological Science, 13*, 81–84.

Diener, E., Oishi, S., & Lucas, R. E. (2003). Personality, culture, and subjective well-being: Emotional and cognitive evaluations of life. *Annual Review of Psychology, 54*, 403–425.

Diener, E., Suh, E. M., Lucas, R. E., & Smith, H. L. (1999). Subjective well-being: Three decades of progress. *Psychological Bulletin, 125*, 276–301.

Dihoff, R. E., Brosvic, G. M., Epstein, M. L. & Cook, M. J. (2004). Provision of feedback during preparation for academic testing: Learning is enhanced by immedi-

ate but not delayed feedback. *Psychological Record, 54(2)*, 207–231.

DiGiacomo, M., & Adamson, B. (2001). Coping with stress in the workplace: Implications for new health professionals. *Journal of Allied Health, 30*, 106–111.

DiLalla, L. F. (Ed.) (2004). *Behavior genetic principles: Perspectives in development, personality, and psychopathology.* Washington: APA Press.

Dinsmoor, J. A. (1998). Punishment. In W. O'Donohue (Ed.), *Learning and behavior therapy.* Boston: Allyn & Bacon.

Dion, K. L. (2001). Immigrants' perceptions of housing discrimination in Toronto: The Housing New Canadians study. *The Journal of Social Issues, 57(3)*, 523–539.*

Dion, K. L. (2002). The social psychology of perceived prejudice and discrimination. *Canadian Psychology, 43(1)*, 1–10.*

Dion, K. L. (2003). Prejudice, racism, and discrimination. In T. Millon, & M. J. Lerner (Eds.), *Personality and social psychology. The comprehensive handbook of psychology (Vol. 5).* New York: Wiley.*

Dion, K. L., Dion, K. K., & Pak, A. W. (1992). Personality-based hardiness as a buffer for discrimination-related stress in members of Toronto's Chinese community. *Canadian Journal of Behavioural Science, 24(4)*, 517–536.*

Dion, K. L., & Kawakami, K. (1996). Ethnicity and perceived discrimination in Toronto: Another look at the personal/group discrimination discrepancy. *Canadian Journal of Behavioural Science, 28(3)*, 203–213.*

Dion, K. K., & Dion, K. L. (1991). Psychological individualism and romantic love. *Journal of Social Behavior and Personality, 6(1)*, 17–33.*

Dion, K. K., & Dion, K. L. (1993). Individualistic and collectivistic perspectives on gender and the cultural context of love and intimacy. *Journal of Social Issues, 49(3)*, 53–69.*

Dion, K. K., & Dion, K. L. (1995). On the love of beauty and the beauty of love: Two psychologists study attraction. In G. G. Brannigan, & M. R. Merrens (Eds.), *The social psychologists: Research adventures.* New York: McGraw-Hill.*

DiTommaso, E., Brannen, C., & Burgess, M. (2005). The universality of relationship characteristics: A cross-cultural comparison of different types of attachment and loneliness in Canadian and visiting Chinese students. *Social Behavior & Personality, 33(1)*, 57–68.*

Dixon, M. J., Smilek, D., Cudahy, C., & Merikle, P. M. (2000). Five plus two equals yellow. *Nature, 406*, 365.*

Dixon, M. J., Smilek, D., & Merikle, P. M. (2004). Not all synaesthetes are created equal: Projector versus associator synaesthetes. *Cognitive, Affective, & Behavioral Neuroscience, 4(3)*, 335–343.*

Dixon, R. A., Bäckman, L., & Nilsson, L.-G. (Eds.). (2004). *New frontiers in cognitive aging.* Oxford: Oxford University Press.*

Dixon, R. A., & de Frias, C. M. (2004). The Victoria Longitudinal Study: From characterizing cognitive aging to illustrating changes in memory compensation. *Aging Neuropsychology, and Cognition, 11*, 346–376.*

Dixon, R. A., Wahlin, Å., Maitland, S. B., Hultsch, D. F., Hertzog, C. & Bäckman, L. (2004). Episodic memory change in late adulthood: Generalizability across samples and performance indices. *Memory & Cognition, 32(5)*, 768–778.*

Dobson, K. S. (1995). Psychology in Canada: The future is not the past. *Canadian Psychology, 36(1)*, 1–11.*

Dobson, K. S. (Ed.). (2001). *Handbook of cognitive-behavioral therapy (2nd ed.).* New York: Guilford.*

Dobson, K. S., & Breault, L. (1998). The Canadian code of ethics and the regulation of psychology. *Canadian Psychology, 39(3)*, 212–218.*

Dobson, K. S., Backs-Dermott, G. J., & Dozois, D. J. A. (2000). Cognitive and cognitive-behavioral therapies. In C. R. Snyder, & R. E. Ingram (Eds.), *Handbook of psychological change: Psychotherapy processes and practices for the 21st century.* New York: Wiley.*

Dobson, K. S., & Dozois, D. J. A. (2001). Historical and philosophical bases of the cognitive-behavioral therapies. In K. S. Dobson (Ed.), *Handbook of cognitive-behavioral therapies (2nd ed.)*. New York: Guilford.*

Dobzhansky, T. G. (1977). *Evolution*. New York: Freeman.

Dodson, C. S., & Schacter, D. L. (2002). When false recognition meets metacognition: The distinctiveness heuristic. *Journal of Memory & Language, 46(4)*, 782–803.

Dollard, J., Doob, L. W., Miller, N. E., Mowrer, O. H., & Sears, R. R. (1939). *Frustration and aggression*. New Haven, CT: Yale University Press.

Dolphin, W. D. (2002). *Biological investigations (6th ed.)*. New York: McGraw-Hill.

Domhoff, G. W. (1999). New directions in the study of dream content using the Hall/Van de Castle coding system. *Dreaming, 9*, 115–137.

Domhoff, G. W. (2001). A new neurocognitive theory of dreams. *Dreaming, 11*, 13–33.

Domhoff, G. W., & Schneider, A. (1998). New rationales and methods for quantitative dream research outside the laboratory. *Sleep, 21*, 398–404.

Domjan, M. (2005). *The essentials of conditioning and learning (3rd ed.)*. Belmont, CA: Wadsworth.

Domjan, M. (2006). *The principles of learning and behavior: Active learning edition (5th ed.)*. Belmont, CA: Wadsworth.

Donnerstein, E. (2001). Media violence. In J. Worell (Ed.), *Encyclopedia of gender and women*. San Diego: Academic Press.

Dooley, D. (2001). *Social science research methods (4th ed.)*. Englewood Cliffs, NJ: Prentice Hall.

Doran, S. M., Van Dongen, H. P., & Dinges, D. F. (2001). Sustained attention performance during sleep deprivation. *Archives of Italian Biology, 139*, 253–267.

Doty, R. L., & Muller-Schwarze, D. (Eds.). (1992). *Chemical signals in vertebrates 6*. New York: Plenum Press.

Dougall, A. L., & Baum, A. (2001). Stress, health, and illness. In A. Baum, T. A. Revenson, & J. E. Singer (Eds.), *Handbook of health psychology*. Mahwah, NJ: Erlbaum.

Dovidio, J. F., Glick, P., & Rudman, L. A. (Eds.). (2005). *On the nature of prejudice: Fifty years after Allport*. Malden, MA: Blackwell.

Dovidio, J. E., & Penner, L. A. (2001). Helping and altruism. In M. Hewstone, & M. Brewer (Eds.), *Handbook of social psychology*. London: Blackwell.

Dowd, E. T. (2002). Self-statement modification. In M. Hersen & W. H. Sledge (Eds.), *Encyclopedia of psychotherapy*. San Diego: Academic Press.

Dozois, D. J. A., & Dobson, K. S. (2002). Depression. In M. M. Antony, & D. H. Barlow (Eds.), *Handbook of assessment and treatment planning for psychological disorders*. New York: Guilford.*

Dozois, D. J. A., & Dobson, K. S. (Eds.), (2004). *The prevention of anxiety and depression: Theory, research, and practice*. Washington: APA Press.*

Drapeau, M. (2004). An exploratory study of the wishes and fears of pedophiles: An Eriksonian perspective. *Archives of Psychiatry & Psychotherapy, 6(1)*, 37–43.*

Drevets, W. C. (2001). Neuroimaging and neuropathological studies of depression: Implications for the cognitive-emotional features of mood disorders. *Current Opinion in Neurobiology, 11*, 240–249.

Driver, J. L., & Gottman, J. M. (2004). Daily marital interactions and positive affect during marital conflict among newlywed couples. *Family Process, 43(3)*, 301–314.

Driver, J. L., Tabares, A., Shapiro, A., Nahm, E. Y., & Gottman, J. M. (2003). Interactional patterns in marital success and failure: Gottman laboratory studies. In F. Walsh (Ed), *Normal family processes: Growing diversity and complexity (3rd ed.)*. New York: Guilford.

Drobes, D. J., Miller, E. J., Hillman, C. H., Bradley, M. M., Cuthbart, B. N., & Lang, P. J. (2001). Food deprivation and emotional reaction to food cues: Implications for eating disorders. *Biological Psychology, 57*, 153–177.

Druckman, D., & Bjork, R. A. (Eds.) (1994). *Learning, remembering, and believing*. Washington: National Academy Press.

Dryfoos, J. G. (1990). *Adolescents at risk: Prevalence and prevention*. New York: Oxford.

Duchowny, M. (2004). Neurobehavioral teratogenicity in antiepileptic drugs: The new Pandora's box. *Neurology, 62(1)*, 8–9.

Dugas, M. J., & Ladouceur, R. (2000). A new cognitive-behavioral treatment for generalized anxiety disorder: Evaluation in a single-case design. *Behavior Modification, 24*, 635–657.*

Dugas, M. J., Marchand, A., & Ladouceur, R. (2005). Further validation of a cognitive-behavioral model of generalized anxiety disorder: Diagnostic and symptom specificity. *Journal of Anxiety Disorders, 19(3)*, 329–343.*

Duka, T., Weissenborn, R., & Dienes, Z. (2001). Two state-dependent effects of alcohol on recollective experiences, familiarity, and awareness on memories. *Psychopharmacology, 153*, 295–306.

Duncan, J. (2005). Task models in prefrontal cortex. In U. Mayr, E. Awh, & S. W. Keele (Eds.), *Developing individuality in the human brain: A tribute to Michael I. Posner*. Washington: APA Press.

Dunner, D. L. (2001). Acute and maintenance treatment of chronic depression. *Journal of Clinical Psychiatry, 62* (Suppl. 6), 10–16.

Dunner, D. L., Hendricksen, H. E., Bea, C., Budech, C. B., & Friedman, S. D. (2002). Dysthmic disorder: Treatment with citalopram. *Depression and Anxiety, 15*, 18–22.

Dunnett, S. B. (1989). Neural transplantation: Normal brain function and repair after damage. *Psychologist, 1*, 4–8.

Durand-Bush, N., & Salmela, J. H. (2001). The development of talent in sport. In R. N. Singer, H. A. Hausenblas, & C. Janelle (Eds.), *Handbook of sport psychology (2nd ed.)*. New York: Wiley.*

Durgin, F. H. (2000). Sensory adaptation. In A. Kazdin (Ed.), *Encyclopedia of psychology*. Washington, & New York: APA Press and Oxford.

Durrant, J. E. (1996). Public attitudes toward corporal punishment in Canada. In D. Frehsee, W. Horn, & K.-D. Bussman (Eds.), *Family violence against children: A challenge for society*. Berlin: de Gruyter.*

Durrant, J. E. (2000). Trends in youth crime and well-being since the abolition of corporal punishment in Sweden. *Youth and Society, 31(4)*, 437–455.*

Durrant, J. E., Broberg, A. G., & Rose-Krasnor, L. (1999). Predicting use of physical punishment during mother-child conflicts in Sweden and Canada. In P. Hastings, & C. Piotrowski (Eds.), *Maternal beliefs about child rearing: New directions for child development*. San Francisco, CA: Jossey-Bass.*

Durrant, J. E., Ensom, R., and Coalition on Physical Punishment of Children and Youth (2004). *Joint statement on physical punishment of children and youth*. Ottawa: Coalition on Physical Punishment of Children and Youth. Retrieved March 21, 2005 from http://www.cheo.on.ca/english/1120.html.*

Durrant, J. E., & Janson, S. (in press). Law reform, corporal punishment and child abuse: The case of Sweden. *International Review of Victimology.*

Durrant, J. E., Rose-Krasnor, L., & Broberg, A. G. (2003). Maternal beliefs about physical punishment in Sweden and Canada. *Journal of Comparative Family Studies, 34*, 586–604.*

Dutton, D. G. (1998). *The abusive personality: Violence and control in intimate relationships*. New York: Guilford.*

Dutton, D., & Aron, A. (1974). Some evidence for heightened sexual attraction under conditions of high anxiety. *Journal of Personality & Social Psychology, 30*, 510–517.*

Dutton, R. C., Maurer, A. J., Sonner, J. M., Fanselow, M. S., Laster, M. J., & Eger, E. I. (2002). Isoflurane causes anterograde but not retrograde amnesia for Pavlovian fear conditioning. *Anesthesiology, 96*, 1223–1229.

Duval, T. S., & Silvia, P. J. (2002). Self-awareness, probability of improvement, and the self-serving bias. *Journal of Personality & Social Psychology, 82(1)*, 49–61.

d'Ydewalle, G., Bouckaert, D., & Brunfaut, E. (2001). Age-related differences and complexity of ongoing activities in time- and event-based prospective memory. *American Journal of Psychology, 114*, 411–423.

Dywan, J. (1995). The illusion of familiarity: An alternative to the report-criterion account of hypnotic recall. *International Journal of Clinical & Experimental Hypnosis, 43(2)*, 194–211.

E

Eagly, A. H. (2000). Gender roles. In A. Kazdin (Ed.), *Encyclopedia of psychology*. Washington, and New York: APA Press and Oxford.

Eagly, A. H. (2001). Social role theory of sex differences and similarities. In J. Worell (Ed.), *Encyclopedia of women and gender*. San Diego: Academic Press.

Eagly, A. H., Beall, A. E., & Sternberg, R. J. (Eds.). (2004). *The psychology of gender (2nd Ed.)*. New York: Guilford.

Eagly, A. H., & Chaiken, S. (1998). Attitude structure and function. In D. T. Gilbert, S. T. Fiske, & G. Lindzey (Eds.), *Handbook of social psychology (4th ed., Vol. 2)*. New York: McGraw-Hill.

Eagly, A. H., & Crowley, M. (1986). Gender and helping behavior: A meta-analytic review of the social psychological literature. *Psychological Bulletin, 100*, 283–308.

Eagly, A. H., & Steffen, V. J. (1986). Gender and aggressive behavior: A meta-analytic review of the social psychological literature. *Psychological Bulletin, 111*, 3–22.

Eastwood, J. D., Smilek, D., Oakman, J. M., Farvolden, P., van Ameringen, M., Mancini, C., & Merikle, P. M. (2005). Individuals with social phobia are biased to become aware of negative faces. *Visual Cognition, 12(1)*, 159–179.*

Eccles, J. S., & Wigfield, A. (2002). Motivational beliefs, values, and goals. *Annual Review of Psychology, 53*, 109–132.

Eccles, J. S., Wigfield, A., & Schiefele, U. (1998). Motivation to succeed. In W. Damon (Ed.), *Handbook of child psychology (Vol. 3)*. New York: Wiley.

Eckardt, M. H. (2005). Karen Horney: A portrait: The 120th anniversary, Karen Horney, September 16, 1885. *American Journal of Psychoanalysis, 65(2)*, 95–101.

Eddy, K. T., Dutra, L., Bradley, R., & Westen, D. (2004). A multidimensional meta-analysis of psychotherapy and pharmacotherapy for obsessive-compulsive disorder. *Clinical Psychology Review, 24(8)*, 1011–1030.

Edinger, J. D., Wohlgemuth, W. K., Radtke, R. A., Marsh, G. R., & Quillian, R. E. (2001). Cognitive behavioral therapy for treatment of chronic primary insomnia. *Journal of the American Medical Association, 285*, 1856–1864.

Edwards, C. D. (1999). *How to handle a hard-to-handle kid*. Los Angeles: Free Spirit Pub.

Edwards, C. P., & Liu, W. (2002). Parenting toddlers. In M. H. Bornstein (Ed.), *Handbook of parenting (2nd ed.)*. Mahwah, NJ: Erlbaum.

Edwards, J. R., & Rothbard, N. P. (1999). Work and family stress and well-being: An examination of person-environment fit in the work and family domains. *Organizational Behavior and Human Decision Processes, 77*, 85–129.

Edwards, R. R., Ness, T. J., Weigent, D. A., & Fillingim, R. B (2003). Individual differences in diffuse noxious inhibitory controls (DNIC): Association with clinical variables. *Pain, 106(3)*, 427–437.

Edwards, S. (2005). Constructivism does not only happen in the individual: Sociocultural theory and early childhood education. *Early Child Development & Care, 175(1)*, 37–47.

Ehlers, A., Clark, D. M., Hackmann, A., McManus, F., & Fennell, M. (2005). Cognitive therapy for post-traumatic stress disorder: Development and evaluation. *Behaviour Research & Therapy, 43(4),* 413–431.

Ehrhardt, A. A. (1987). A transactional perspective on the development of gender differences. In J. M. Reinisch, L. A. Rosenblum, & S. A. Sanders (Eds.), *Masculinity/femininity: Basic perspectives.* New York: Oxford.

Eibl-Eibesfeldt, I. (1977). Evolution of destructive aggression. *Aggressive Behavior, 3,* 127–144.

Eimer, B. N. (2000). Clinical applications of hypnosis for brief and efficient pain management psychotherapy. *American Journal of Clinical Hypnosis, 43,* 17–40.

Einstein, G. O., & McDaniel, M. A. (1996). Remembering to do things: Remembering a forgotten topic. In D. J. Hermann, C. McEvoy, C. Hertzog, P. Hertel, & M. K. Johnson (Eds.), *Basic and applied memory research: Practical applications (Vol. 2).* Mahwah, NJ: Erlbaum.

Einstein, G. O., McDaniel, M. A., Mazi, M., Cochran, B., & Baker, M. (2000). Prospective memory and aging: Forgetting intentions over short delays. *Psychology and Aging, 15,* 671–683.

Eisenberg, N., & Valiente, C. (2002). Parenting and children's prosocial and moral development. In M. H. Bornstein (Ed.), *Handbook of parenting (2nd ed.).* Mahwah, NJ: Erlbaum.

Ekman, P. (1980). *The face of man.* New York: Garland.

Ekman, P. (1996). Lying and deception. In N. L. Stein, C. Brainerd, P. A. Ornstein, & B. Tversky (Eds.), *Memory for everyday emotional events.* Mahwah, NJ: Erlbaum.

Ekman, P. (2003). *Emotions revealed: Recognizing faces and feelings to improve communication and emotional life.* New York: Times BooksEkman, P., & Friesen, W. V. (1968). The repertoire of nonverbal behavior: Categories, origins, usage, and coding. *Semiotica, 1,* 49–98.

Ekman, P., & Friesen, W. V. (1971). Constants across cultures in the face and emotion. *Journal of Personality & Social Psychology, 17,* 124–129.

Ekman, P., & O'Sullivan, M. (1991). Facial expressions: Methods, means, and moues. In R. S. Feldman, & B. Rime (Eds.), *Fundamentals of nonverbal behavior.* Cambridge: Cambridge University Press.

Ekman, P., Levenson, R. W., & Friesen, W. V. (1983). Autonomic nervous system activity distinguishes among emotions. *Science, 223,* 1208–1210.

Eley, T. C., & Gregory, A. M. (2004). Behavioral genetics. In T. L. Morris, & J. S. March (Eds.), *Anxiety disorders in children and adolescents (2nd ed.).* New York: Guilford.

Eley, T. C., Lichtenstein, P., & Moffitt, T. E. (2003). A longitudinal behavioral genetic analysis of the etiology of aggressive and nonaggressive antisocial behavior. *Development & Psychopathology, 15(2),* 383–402.

Elhwuegi, A. S. (2004). Central monoamines and their role in major depression. *Progress in Neuro-Psychopharmacology & Biological Psychiatry, 28(3),* 435–451.

Eliasson, A., Eliasson, A., King, J., Gould, B., & Eliasson, A. (2002). Association of sleep and academic performance. *Sleep and Breathing, 6,* 45–48.

Eliot, L. (2001). *What's going on in there? How the brain and mind develop in the first five years of life.* New York: Bantam Doubleday.

Elkind, D. (1978). Understanding the young adolescent. *Adolescence, 13,* 127–134.

Ellemers, N., Spears, R., & Doosje, B. (2002). Self and social identity. *Annual Review of Psychology, 53,* 161–186.

Eller, A. & Abrams, D. (2004). Come together: Longitudinal comparisons of Pettigrew's reformulated intergroup contact model and the Common Ingroup Identity Model in Anglo-French and Mexican-American contexts. *European Journal of Social Psychology, 34(3),* 229–256.

Ellis, A. (1962). *Reason and emotion in psychotherapy.* New York: Lyle Stuart.

Ellis, A. (2002). Rational emotive behavior therapy. In M. Hersen, & W. H. Sledge (Eds.), *Encyclopedia of psychotherapy.* San Diego: Academic Press.

Ellis, A. (2004). Why rational emotive behavior therapy is the most comprehensive and effective form of behavior therapy. *Journal of Rational-Emotive & Cognitive Behavior Therapy, 22(2),* 85–92.

Elloy, D. F., Terpening, W., & Kohls, J. (2001). Causal model of burnout among self-managed work team members. *Journal of Psychology: Interdisciplinary & Applied, 135(3),* 321–334.

Ellsworth, P. C. (2002). Appraisal processes in emotion. In R. J. Davidson, K. R. Scherer, & H. H. Goldsmith (Eds.), *Handbook of affective sciences.* New York: Oxford.

Elzinga, B. M., & Bremner, J. D. (2002). Are the neural substrates of memory the final common pathway in posttraumatic stress disorder (PTSD)? *Journal of Affective Disorders, 70(1),* 1–17.

Emurian, H. H. (2004). A programmed instruction tutoring system for Java-super(TM): Consideration of learning performance and software self-efficacy. *Computers in Human Behavior, 20(3),* 423–459.

Endler, N. S. (1990a). *Holiday of darkness (revised ed.).* Toronto: Wall & Thompson Publishers.*

Endler, N. S. (1990b). Sociopolitical factors and stigma in depression. In C. D. McCann, & N. S. Endler (Eds.), *Depression: New directions in theory, research and practice.* Toronto: Wall & Emerson, Inc.*

Endler, N. S. (1993). Personality: An interactional perspective. In P. J. Hettema, & I. J. Deary (Eds.), *Foundations of personality.* Dordrecht, Netherlands: Kluwer Academic Publishers.*

Endler, N. S. (1997). Stress, anxiety and coping: The multidimensional interaction model. *Canadian Psychology, 38,* 136–153.*

Endler, N. S., & Parker, J. D. A. (1991). Personality research: Theories, issues and methods. In M. Hersen, A. E. Kazdin, & A. S. Bellack (Eds.), *The clinical psychology handbook (2nd ed.).* New York: Pergamon Press.*

Endler, N. S., & Parker, J. D. A. (1993). The multidimensional assessment of coping: Concepts, issues, and measurement. In G. L. Van Heck, & P. Bonaiuto, (Eds.), *Personality psychology in Europe (Vol. 4).* Tilburg, Netherlands: Tilburg University Press.*

Endler, N. S., & Parker, J. D. A. (2000). *Coping with Health, Injuries and Problems (CHIP): Manual.* Toronto: Multi-Health Systems.* Endler, N. S., Parker, J. D. A., & Butcher, J. N. (2003). A factor analytic study of coping styles and the MMPI-2 content scales. *Journal of Clinical Psychology, 59(10),* 1049–1054.*

Endler, N. S., Parker, J. D. A., & Summerfeldt, L. J. (1993). Coping with health problems: Conceptual and methodological issues. *Canadian Journal of Behavioural Science, 25,* 384–399.*

Endler, N. S., Parker, J. D. A., & Summerfeldt, L. J. (1998). Coping with health problems: Developing a reliable and valid multidimensional measure. *Psychological Assessment, 10,* 195–205.*

Engel, A. K., & Singer, W. (2001). Temporal binding and the neural correlates of sensory awareness. *Trends in Cognitive Science, 5,* 16–25.

Enger, E., & Ross, F. (2005). *Concepts in biology (11th ed.).* New York: McGraw-Hill.

Enns, J. T. (2004). *The thinking eye, the seeing brain.* New York: Norton.

Enns, J. T. & Trick, L. (in press). A framework for studying individual differences in visual attention: Developmental factors. In E. Bialystok & G. Craik (Ed.), *Lifespan cognition: Mechanisms of change.* New York: Oxford.

Enoch, M. A., & Goldman, D. (2002). Problem drinking and alcoholism: diagnosis and treatment. *American Family Physician, 65,* 449–450.

Enstrom, J. E. (1999). Smoking cessation and mortality trends among two United States populations. *Journal of Clinical Epidemiology, 52,* 813–825.

Enzle, M. E., & Anderson, S. C. (1993). Surveillant intentions and intrinsic motivation. *Journal of Personality & Social Psychology, 64(2),* 257–266.*

Enzle, M. E., Roggeveen, J., & Look, S. C. (1991). Self- versus other-reward administration and intrinsic motivation. *Journal of Experimental Social Psychology, 27,* 468–479.*

Ephraim, D. (2000). Culturally relevant research and practice with the Rorschach comprehensive system in Iberoamerica. In R. H. Dana (Ed.), *Handbook of cross-cultural and multicultural personality assessment.* Mahwah, NJ: Erlbaum.

Eppley, K. R., Abrams, A. I., & Shear, J. (1989). Differential effects of relaxation effects on trait anxiety. *Journal of Clinical Psychology, 45,* 957–974.

Epstein, N. B., & Baucom, D. H. (2002). *Enhanced cognitive-behavioral therapy for couples.* Washington: APA Press.

Erdelyi, M. H. (2004). Subliminal perception and its cognates: Theory, indeterminacy, and time. *Consciousness & Cognition: An International Journal, 13(1),* 73–91.

Ericsson, K. A., Krampe, R. T., & Tesch-Römer, C. (1993). The role of deliberate practice in the acquisition of expert performance. *Psychological Review, 100,* 363–406.

Ericsson, K. A. (2005). Superior decision making as an integral quality of expert performance: Insights into the mediating mechanisms and their acquisition through deliberate practice. In H. Montgomery, R. Lipshitz & B. Brehmer (Eds.), *How professionals make decisions. Expertise: Research and applications.* Mahwah, NJ: Erlbaum.

Eriksen, T. H. (2001). Ethnic identity, national identity, and intergroup conflict: The significance of personal experiences. In R. D. Ashmore, L. Jussim, & D. Wilder (Eds.), *Social identity, intergroup conflict, and conflict resolution.* New York: Oxford.

Erikson, E. H. (1968). *Identity: Youth and crisis.* New York: Norton.

Erikson, E. H. (1969). *Gandhi's truth.* New York: Norton.

Erwin, B. A., Heimberg, R. G., Juster, H., & Mindlin, M. (2002). Comorbid anxiety and mood disorders among persons with social anxiety disorder. *Behavior Research and Therapy, 40,* 19–35.

Esses, V. M., Jackson, L. M., & Armstrong, T. L. (1998). Intergroup competition and attitudes toward immigrants and immigration: An instrumental model of group conflict. *Journal of Social Issues, 54,* 698–724.*

Esses, V. M., Dovidio, J. F., Jackson, L. M., & Armstrong, T. L. (2001). The immigration dilemma: The role of perceived group competition, ethnic prejudice, and national identity. *Journal of Social Issues, 57,* 389–412.*

Esses, V. M. & Dovidio, J. F., Jackson, L. M., & Semenya, A. H. (in press). Attitudes toward immigrants and immigration: The role of national and international identities. In D. Abrams, J. M. Marques, & M. A. Hogg (Eds.), *The social psychology of inclusion and exclusion.* Philadelphia: Psychology Press.*

Etaugh, C., & Bridges, J. S. (2004). *Psychology of women: A life-span perspective (2nd ed.).* Boston: Allyn & Bacon.

European Agency for Safety and Health at Work. (2002). *Research on work-related stress.* Retrieved August 29, 2005, from http://osha.eu.int/ew2002/pubs/facts8_en.pdf.

Evans, D. L., Herbert, J. D., Nelson-Gray, R. O., & Gaudiano, B. A. (2002). Determinants of diagnostic prototypicality judgments of the personality disorders. *Journal of Personality Disorders, 16,* 95–106.

Evans, D. R. (1997). *The law, standards of practice, and ethics in the practice of psychology.* Toronto: Emond Montgomery Publications.*

Evans, G. W., & English, K. (2002). The environment of poverty: Multiple stressor exposure, psychophysiological stress, and socioemotional adjustment. *Child Development, 73(4),* 1238–1248.

Evertson, C. M., Emmer, E. T., & Worsham, M. E. (2003). *Classroom management for elementary teachers, (5th ed.).* Boston: Allyn & Bacon.

Eysenck, H. J. (1952). The effects of psychotherapy: An evaluation. *Journal of Consulting Psychology, 16,* 319–324.

Eysenck, H. J. (1967). *The biological basis of personality.* Springfield, IL: Thomas.

F

Fabrega, Jr., H. (2004). Culture and the origins of psychopathology. In U. P. Gielen, J. M. Fish, & Draguns, J. G. (Eds.), *Handbook of culture, therapy, and healing.* Mahwah, NJ: Erlbaum.

Fabricatore, A. N., Randal, P. J., Rubio, D. M., & Gilner, F. H. (2004). Stress, religion, and mental health: Religious coping in mediating and moderating roles. *International Journal for the Psychology of Religion, 14(2),* 97–108.

Fancher, R. E. (1998). Alfred Binet: General psychologist. In G. Kimble, & M. Wertheimer (Eds.), *Portraits of pioneers in psychology (Vol. 3).* Washington DC: APA.

Fanselow, M. S., & Poulos, A. M. (2005). The neuroscience of mammalian associative learning. *Annual Review of Psychology, 56,* 207–234.

Farthing, G. W. (1992). *The psychology of consciousness.* Englewood Cliffs, NJ: Prentice Hall.

Farrington, D. P. (2005). Childhood origins of antisocial behavior. *Clinical Psychology & Psychotherapy. Special Forensic Psychology, 12(3),* 177–190.

Farris, P. J. (2004). *Teaching reading: A balanced approach for today's classrooms.* New York: McGraw-Hill.

Farvolden, P., & Woody, E. Z. (2004). Hypnosis, memory, and frontal executive functioning. *International Journal of Clinical & Experimental Hypnosis, 52(1),* 3–26.*

Fauconnier, G., & Turner, M. (2002). *The way we think: Conceptual blending and the mind's hidden complexities.* New York: Basic Books.

Fazio, R. H., Chen, J., McDonel, E. C., & Sherman, S. J. (1982). Attitude accessibility, attitude-behavior consistency, and the strength of the object-evaluation association. *Journal of Experimental Social Psychology, 18,* 339–357.

Feehan, G. G., & Enzle, M. E. (1991). Subjective control over rewards: Effects of perceived choice of reward schedule on intrinsic motivation and behavior maintenance. *Perceptual and Motor Skills, 72(3),* 995–1006.*

Fehr, B., & Broughton, R. (2001). Gender and personality differences in conceptions of love: An interpersonal theory analysis. *Personal Relationships, 8,* 115–136.*

Fehr, E., & Rockenbach, B. (2004). Human altruism: Economic, neural, and evolutionary perspectives. *Current Opinion in Neurobiology, 14(6),* 784–790.

Feist, J., & Feist, G. J. (2006). *Theories of personality (6th ed.).* New York: McGraw-Hill.

Feldhusen, J. F. (1999). Giftedness and creativity. In M. A. Runco, & S. Pritzker (Eds.), *Encyclopedia of creativity.* San Diego: Academic Press.

Feldhusen, J. F., & Westby, E. L. (2003). Creative and affective behavior: Cognition, personality, and motivation. In J. Houtz (Ed.), *The educational psychology of creativity. Perspectives on creativity.* Cresskill, NJ: Hampton Press.

Feldman, J., & Singh, M. (2005). Information along contours and object boundaries. *Psychological Review, 112(1),* 243–252.

Feldman, M. A., & Case, L. (1997). Effectiveness of self-instructional audiovisual materials in teaching child-care skills to parents with intellectual disabilities. *Journal of Behavioral Education, 7,* 235–257.*

Feldman, R. (1999, January). Commentary on Murray, B.: This architect builds a career in psychology. *APA Monitor, 13.*

Fellous, J.-M., & Ledoux, J. E. (2005). Toward basic principles for emotional processing: What the fearful brain tells the robot. In J.-M. Fellous, & Arbib, M. A. (Eds.), *Who needs emotions?: The brain meets the robot..* New York: Oxford.

Feng, A. S., & Ratnam, R. (2000). Neural basis of hearing in real world situations. *Annual Review of Psychology, 51,* 699–725.

Fentress, J. C. (1999). *The Organization of Behavior* revisited. *Canadian Journal of Experimental Psychology, 53(1),* 8–19.*

Ferber, S. G. (2004). The nature of touch in mothers experiencing maternity blues: The contribution of parity. *Early Human Development, 79(1),* 65–75.

Fergusson, D. M., & Woodward, L. J. (2002). Mental health, educational, and social role outcomes of adolescents with depression. *Archives of General Psychiatry, 59,* 225–231.

Festinger, L. (1954). A theory of social comparison processes. *Human Relations, 7,* 117–140.

Festinger, L. (1957). *A theory of cognitive dissonance.* Evanston, IL: Row Peterson.

Feuer, C. A., Nishith, P., & Resick, P. (2005). Prediction of numbing and effortful avoidance in female rape survivors with chronic PTSD. *Journal of Traumatic Stress, 18(2),* 165--170.

Field, A. J. (2002). *Altruistically inclined? The behavioral sciences, evolutionary theory, and the origins of reciprocity.* Ann Arbor, MI: University of Michigan Press.

Field, C. E., Nash, H. M., Handwerk, M. L., & Friman, P. C. (2004). A modification of the token economy for nonresponsive youth in family-style residential care. *Behavior Modification. Special Introduction to Special Issue on Adolescent Conduct Problems, 28(3),* 438–457.

Field, G. D., Alapakkam P. S., & , Rieke, F. (2005). Retinal processing near absolute threshold: From behavior to mechanism. *Annual Review of Physiology, 67,* 491–514.

Field, J. (2004). *Psycholinguistics: The key concepts.* Hove, UK: Psychology Press.

Field, T. M. (2001). Massage therapy facilitates weight gain in preterm infants. *Current Directions in Psychological Science, 10,* 51–53.

Field, T. M. (2003). *Touch.* Cambridge: MIT Press.

Field, T. M., Grizzle, N., Scafidi, F., & Schanberg, S. (1996). Massage and relaxation therapies' effects on depressed adolescent mothers. *Adolescence, 31,* 903–911.

Field, T. M., Scafidi, F., & Schanberg, S. (1987). Massage of preterm newborns to improve growth and development. *Pediatric Nursing, 13,* 386–388.

Field, T. M., Schanberg, S. M., Scafidi, F., Bauer, C. R., Vega-Lahr, N., Garcia, R., et al. (1986). Tactile/kinesthetic stimulation effects on preterm neonates. *Pediatrics, 77,* 654–658.

Fifer, B., & Grose-Fifer, J. (2002). Prenatal development and risk. In A. Fogel, & G. Bremmer (Eds.), *Blackwell handbook of infant development.* London: Blackwell.

Filley, C. M., Price, B. H., Nell, V., Morgan, A. S., Bresnahan, J. F., Pincus, J. H., et al. (2001). Toward an understanding of violence: Neurobehavioral aspects of unwarranted physical aggression. *Neuropsychiatry, 14,* 1–14.

Fillmore, M. T., & Weafer, J. (2004). Alcohol impairment of behavior in men and women. *Addiction, 99(10),* 1237–1246.

Fils-Aime, M.-L., Eckardt, M. J., George, D. T., Brown, G. L., Mefford, I., & Linnoila, M. (1996). Early-onset alcoholics have lower cerebrospinal fluid 5-hydroxyindoleacetic acid levels than late-onset alcoholics. *Archives of General Psychiatry, 53,* 211–216.

Findley, L. C., & Ste-Marie, D. M. (2004). A reputation bias in figure skating judging. *Journal of Sport & Exercise Psychology, 26(1),* 154–166.*

Fine, S. A., & Cronshaw, S. F. (1999). *Functional job analysis: A foundation for human resources management.* Mahwah, NJ: Erlbaum.*

Fineberg, N. A., & Gale, T. M. (2005). Evidence-based pharmacotherapy of obsessive-compulsive disorder. *International Journal of Neuropsychopharmacology, 8(1),* 107–129.

Fink, M., & Taylor, M. A. (2003). *Catatonia: A clinician's guide to diagnosis and treatment.* London: Cambridge.

Finke, K., Bublak, P., Neugebauer, U., & Zihl, J. (2005). Combined processing of what and where information within the visuospatial scratchpad. *European Journal of Cognitive Psychology, 17(1),* 1–22.

Firestone, P., & Marshall, W. L. (Eds.). (2003). *Abnormal psychology: perspectives (2nd ed.).* Toronto: Prentice Hall.*

First, M. B., & Pincus, H. A. (2002). The DSM-IV text revision: Rationale and potential impact on clinical practice. *Psychiatric Services, 53,* 288–292.

Fisch, S. M., & Truglio, R. T. (Eds.). (2001). *"G" is for growing: Thirty years of research on children and Sesame Street.* Mahwah, NJ: Erlbaum.

Fischer, A. R., Jome, L. R., & Atkinson, D. R. (1998). Reconceptualizing multicultural counseling: Universal healing conditions in a culturally specific context. *Counseling Psychologist, 26,* 525–588.

Fischer, J., & Gochros, H. L. (1975). *Planned behavior change.* New York: Free Press.

Fish, J. M. (2002). The myth of race. In J. M. Fish (Ed.), *Race and intelligence: Separating science from myth.* Mahwah, NJ: Erlbaum.

Fishbein, H. D. (2002). *Peer prejudice and discrimination (2nd ed.).* Mahwah, NJ: Erlbaum.

Fisher, J. D., Fisher, W. A., Bryan, A. D., & Misovich, S. J. (2002). Information-motivation-behavioral skills model-based HIV risk behavior change intervention for inner-city high school youth. *Health Psychology, 21(2),* 177–186.

Fiske, S. T. (1998). Stereotyping, prejudice, and discrimination. In D. T. Gilbert, S. T. Fiske, & G. Lindzey (Eds.), *The handbook of social psychology (4th ed., Vol. 2).* New York: McGraw-Hill.

Fiske, S. T. (2004). *Social beings: A core motives approach to social psychology.* New York: Wiley.

Flavell, J. H., Miller, P. H., & Miller, S. A. (2002). *Cognitive development (4th ed.).* Upper Saddle River, NJ: Prentice Hall.

Fleischman, D. A., Wilson, R. S., Gabrieli, J. D. E., Bienias, J. L., & Bennett, D. A. (2004). A longitudinal study of implicit and explicit memory in old persons. *Psychology & Aging, 19(4),* 61–625.

Fleming, J. S., & Courtney, B. E. (1984). The dimensionality of self-esteem. *Journal of Personality & Social Psychology, 46,* 404–421.

Fleshner, M., & Laudenslager, M. L. (2004). Psychoneuroimmunology: Then and now. *Behavioral & Cognitive Neuroscience Reviews, 3(2),* 114–130.

Fletcher, J. S., & Banasik, J. L. (2001). Exercise self-efficacy. *Clinical Excellence in Nursing Practice, 5,* 134–143.

Flett, G. L., Vredenburg, K., & Krames, L. (1997). The continuity of depression in clinical and nonclinical samples. *Psychological Bulletin, 121,* 395–416.*

Flynn, J. R. (1999). Searching for justice: The discovery of IQ gains over time. *American Psychologist, 54,* 5–20.

Frischholz, E. (1995). *Clinical hypnosis and memory: Guidelines for clinicians and for forensic hypnosis.* Des Plaines, IL: American Society of Clinical Hypnosis Press.

Foa, E. B., & Riggs, D. S. (1995). Posttraumatic stress disorder following assault: Theoretical considerations and empirical findings. *Current Directions in Psychological Science, 4,* 61–65.

Fodor, I., & Epstein, J. (2002). Agoraphobia, panic disorder, and gender. In J. Worell (Ed.), *Encyclopedia of women and gender.* San Diego: Academic Press.

Folayan M. O., Idehen E. E., & Ojo O. O. (2004). The modulating effect of culture on the expression of dental anxiety in children: a literature review. *International Journal of Paediatric Dentistry. 14,* 241–245.

Folkman, S., & Lazarus, R. S. (1980). An analysis of coping in a middle-aged community sample. *Journal of Health and Social Behavior, 21,* 219–239.

Fontaine, K. R., Barofsky, I., Bartlett, S. J., Franckowiak, S. C., & Andersen, R. E. (2004). Weight loss and health-related quality of life: Results at 1-year follow-up. *Eating Behaviors, 5(1),* 85–88.

Forbes, R. J., & Jackson, P. R. (1980). Non-verbal behavior and the outcome of selection interviews. *Journal of Occupational Psychology, 53,* 65–72.

Forshaw, M. (2002). *Essential health psychology.* New York: Oxford.

Forsyth, D. R. (2006). *Group dynamics (4th ed.).* Belmont, CA: Wadsworth.

Forsyth, J. P., & Savsevitz, J. (2002). Behavior therapy: Historical perspective and overview. In M. Hersen, & W. H. Sledge (Eds.), *Encyclopedia of psychotherapy*. San Diego: Academic Press.

Foulkes, D. (1993). Cognitive dream theory. In M. A. Carskadon (Ed.), *Encyclopedia of sleep and dreams*. New York: Macmillan.

Foulkes, D. (1999). *Children's dreaming and the development of consciousness*. Cambridge Harvard University Press.

Foulks, E. (2002). Cultural issues. In M. Hersen, & W. H. Sledge (Eds.), *Encyclopedia of psychotherapy*. San Diego: Academic Press.

Fournier, J. F., Calmels, C., Durand-Bush, N., & Salmela, J. H. (2005). Effects of a season-long PST program on gymnastic performance and on psychological skill development. *International Journal of Sport & Exercise Psychology, 3(1)*, 59–77.*

Fouts, R. S. & Waters, G. (2001). Chimpanzee sign language and Darwinian continuity: Evidence for a neurology continuity of language. *Neurological Research, 23*, 787–794.

Fowler, C. A., Wolford, G., Slade, R., & Tassinary, L. (1981). Lexical access without awareness. *Journal of Experimental Psychology: General, 110*, 341–362.

Fox, B., & Hull, M. (2002). *Phonics for the teacher of reading (8th ed.)*. Upper Saddle River, NJ: Prentice Hall.

Fox, S. I. (2004). *Human physiology (8th ed.)*. New York: McGraw-Hill.

FPT Heads of Prosecutions Committee Working Group (2005). *Report on the prevention of miscarriages of justice*. Ottawa, ON: Justice Canada. Retrieved March 27, 2005, from http://canada.justice.gc.ca/en/dept/pub/hop/.*

Frager, R., & Fadiman, J. (2005). *Personality and personal growth (6th ed.)*. Upper Saddle River, NJ: Prentice Hall.

Frase, L. T. (1975). Prose processing. In G. H. Bower (Ed.), *The psychology of learning and motivation (Vol. 9)*. New York: Academic Press.

Friedman, H. S. (2002). *Health psychology (2nd ed.)*. Upper Saddle River, NJ: Prentice Hall.

Frank, J. D. (1982). Therapeutic components shared by all psychotherapies. In J. H. Harvey, & M. M. Parks (Eds.), *Psychotherapy research and behavior change*. Washington: APA Press.

Frank, J. D., & Frank, J. (2004). Therapeutic components shared by all psychotherapies. In A. Freeman, M. J. Mahoney, P. DeVito, & D. Martin (Eds.), *Cognition and psychotherapy (2nd ed.)*. New York: Springer.

Frankenberger, K. D. (2004). Adolescent egocentrism, risk perceptions, and sensation seeking among smoking and nonsmoking youth. *Journal of Adolescent Research, 19(5)*, 576–590.

Frankl, V. (1946/1984). *Man's search for meaning*. New York: Pocket Books.

Franzoi, S. L. (2003). *Social psychology (3rd ed.)*. New York: McGraw-Hill.

Fraser, J., Maticka-Tyndale, E., & Smylie, L. (2004). Sexuality Of Canadian women at midlife. *Canadian Journal of Human Sexuality, 13(3–4)*, 171–188.*

Fraser, S. (Ed.). (1995). *The Bell Curve wars: Race, intelligence, and the future of America*. New York: Basic Books.

Frederich, R. C., Hamann, A., Anderson, S., & others (1995). Leptin levels reflect body lipid content in mice: Evidence for diet-induced resistance to leptin action. *Nature Medicine, 1*, 1311–1314.

Frederickson, B. L. (2001). The role of positive emotions in positive psychology. *American Psychologist, 56*, 218–226.

Fredrickson, B. L., & Branigan, C. (2005). Positive emotions broaden the scope of attention and thought-action repertoires. *Cognition & Emotion, 19(3)*, 313–332.

Frederickson, B. L., & Joiner, Jr., T. E. (2002). Positive emotions trigger upward spirals of well being. *Psychological Science, 13*, 172–176.

Frederickson, B. L., & Levenson, R. W. (1998). Positive emotions speed recovery from the cardiovascular sequelae of negative emotions. *Cognition and Emotion, 12*, 191–220.

Frederikse, M., Lu, A., Aylward, E., Barta, P., Sharma, T., & Pearlson, G. (2000). Sex differences in inferior lobule volume in schizophrenia. *American Journal of Psychiatry, 157*, 422–427.

Freed, C. R., Greene, P. E., Breeze, R. E., Tsai, W. Y., DuMouchel, W., Kao, R., et al. (2001). Transplantation of embryonic dopamine neurons for severe Parkinson's disease. *New England Journal of Medicine, 344*, 710–719.

Freeman, A., & Reinecke, M. A. (1995). Cognitive therapy. In A. S. Gurman (Ed.), *Essential psychotherapies*. New York: Guilford.

Freeman, D., & Garety, P. A. (2004). *Paranoia: the psychology of persecutory delusions*. New York: Routledge.

Freeman, L. M. Y., & Gil, K. M. (2004). Daily stress, coping, and dietary restraint in binge eating. *International Journal of Eating Disorders, 36(2)*, 204–212.

Freeman, S. J. J. (1994). An overview of Canada's mental health system. In L. L. Bachrach, P. Goering, & D. Wasylenki (Eds.), *Mental health care in Canada: New directions for mental health services*. San Francisco, CA: Jossey-Bass.*

Freeston, M. H., & Ladouceur, R. (2000). Exposure and response prevention for obsessional thoughts. *Cognitive and Behavioral Practice. 6*, 362–383.*

Freud, S. (1917). *A general introduction to psychoanalysis*. New York: Washington Square Press.

Freud, S. (1900/1953). The interpretation of dreams. In J. Strachey (Ed.), *The standard edition of the complete psychological works of Sigmund Freud*. New York: Washington Square Press.

Friedman, H. S., & Schustack, M. W. (1999). *Personality: Classic theories and modern research*. Boston: Allyn & Bacon.

Friedman, J. I., Temporini, H., & Davis, K. L. (1999). Pharmacologic strategies for augmenting cognitive performance in schizophrenia. *Biological Psychiatry, 45*, 1–16.

Friedman, M., & Rosenman, R. (1974). *Type A behavior and your heart*. New York: Knopf.

Frieman, J. L. (2002). *Learning and adaptive behavior*. Belmont, CA: Wadsworth.

Friston, K. J. (2005). Models of brain function in neuroimaging. *Annual Review of Psychology, 56*, 57–87.

Fromm, E. (1947). *Man for himself*. New York: Holt, Rinehart & Winston.

Fry, A. F., & Hale, S. (2000). Relationships among processing speed, working memory, and fluid intelligence in children. *Biological Psychology, 54*, 1–34.

Fu, Q., Heath, A. C., Bucholz, K. K., Nelson, E. C., Glowinski, A. L., Goldberg, J., et al. (2002). A twin study of genetic and environmental influences on suicidality in men. *Psychological Medicine, 32*, 11–24.

Fujita, T., & Horiuchi, T. (2004). Self-reference effect in an independence/remember-know procedure. *Japanese Journal of Psychology, 74(6)*, 547–551.

Funder, D. C. (2001). Personality. *Annual Review of Psychology, 52*, 197–221.

Funder, D. C. (2004). *The personality puzzle (3rd ed.)*. New York: Norton.

Fung, H. H. & Carstensen, L. L. (2004). Motivational changes in response to blocked goals and foreshortened time: Testing alternatives to socioemotional selectivity theory. *Psychology & Aging, 19(1)*, 68–78.

Furth, H. G. (1971). Linguistic deficiency and thinking: Research with deaf subjects. *Psychological Bulletin, 75*, 52–58.

Furth, H. G., & Wachs, H. (1975). *Thinking goes to school*. New York: Oxford.

Furumoto, L. (1991). "Paired associates" to a psychology of self: The intellectual odyssey of Mary Whiton Calkins. In G. A. Kimble, M. Wertheimer, & C. L. White (Eds.), *Portraits of pioneers in psychology*. Washington: APA Press.

Fugelsang, J. A., Stein, C. B., Green, A. E., & Dunbar, K. N. (2004). Theory and data interactions of the scientific mind: Evidence from the molecular and the cognitive laboratory. *Canadian Journal of Experimental Psychology, 58(2)*, 86–95.

Furnham, A., Chamorro-Premuzic, T., & Callahan, I. (2003). Does graphology predict personality and intelligence? *Individual Differences Research, 1(2)*, 78–94.

G

Gable, S. L., Reis, H. T., Impett, E., & Asher, E. R. (2004). What do you do when things go right? The intrapersonal and interpersonal benefits of sharing positive events. *Journal of Personality & Social Psychology, 87*, 228–245.

Gadzella, B. M. (1995). Differences in processing information among psychology course grade groups. *Psychological Reports, 77*, 1312–1314.

Gage, F. H. (2000). Mammalian neural stem cells. *Science, 287*, 1433–1438.

Gage, F. H. (2004). Structural plasticity of the adult brain. *Dialogues in Clinical Neuroscience, 6*, 135–141.

Gage, F. H., & Bjorklund, A. (1986). Cholinergic septal grafts into the hippocampal formation improve spatial learning and memory in aged rats by an atropine-sensitive mechanism. *Journal of Neuroscience, 6*, 2837–2847.

Gagné, M., & Deci, E. L. (2005). Self-determination theory and work motivation. *Journal of Organizational Behavior, 26(4)*, 331–362.*

Gais, S. & Born, J. (2004). Declarative memory consolidation: Mechanisms acting during human sleep. *Learning & Memory, 11(6)*, 679–685.

Galambos, N. L., Barker, E. T., & Tilton-Weaver, L. C. (2003). Who gets caught at maturity gap? A study of pseudomature, immature and mature adolescents. *International Journal of Behavioral Development, 27(3)*, 253–263.*

Galambos, N. L., & Tilton-Weaver, L. C. (1998). Multiple-risk behavior in adolescents and young adults. *Health Reports, 10*, 9–20.*

Galef, Jr., B. G. (2005). Social learning. In I. Q. Whishaw, & B. Kolb, (Eds.), *The behavior of the laboratory rat: A handbook with tests*. London: Oxford.*

Galef, Jr., B. G., & Whiskin, E. E. (2004). Effects of environmental stability and demonstrator age on social learning of food preferences by young Norway rats. *Animal Behaviour, 68(4)*, 897–902.

Galotti, K. M. (2002). *Making decisions that matter: How people face important life choices*. Mahwah, NJ: Erlbaum.

Gallup Organization (1999). *The 31st annual Phi Delta Kappa/Gallup Poll*. Princeton, NJ: Author.

Gamache, G. (2004). *Essentials in human factors*. San Mateo, CA: Usernomics. Garb, H. N., Wood, J. M., Lilienfeld, S. O., & Nezworski, M. T. (2005). Roots of the Rorschach controversy. *Clinical Psychology Review, 25(1)*, 97–118.

Garb, H. N., Wood, J. M., Nezworski, M. T., Grove, W. M., & Stejskal, W. J. (2001). Toward a resolution of the Rorschach controversy. *Psychological Assessment, 13*, 432–448.

Garbarino, S., Beelke, M., Costa, G., Violani, C., Lucidi, F., Ferrillo, F. & Sannita, G. (2002). Brain function and effects of shift work: implications for clinical neuropharmacology. *Neuropsychobiology, 45*, 50–56.

Garcia, E. E., Bravo, M. A., Dickey, L. M., Cun, K., & Sun-Irminger, X. (2002). Rethinking school reform in the context of cultural and linguistic diversity. In L. Minaya-Rowe (Ed.), *Teaching training and effective pedagogy in the context of cultural diversity*. Greenwich, CT: IAP.

Garcia, J. (1989). Food for Tolman: Cognition and cathexis in concert. In T. Archer, & L. Nilsson (Eds.), *Aversion, avoidance, and anxiety*. Mahwah, NJ: Erlbaum.

Garcia, J., Ervin, F. E., & Koelling, R. A. (1966). Learning with prolonged delay of reinforcement. *Psychonomic Science, 5*, 121–122.

García-Junco-Clemente, P., Linares-Clemente, P., & Fernández-Chacón, R. (2005). Active zones for presynaptic plasticity in the brain. *Molecular Psychiatry, 10(2)*, 185–200.

Gardner, B. T., & Gardner, R. A. (1971). Two-way communication with an infant chimpanzee. In A.

Schreir, & F. Stollnitz (Eds.), *Behavior of nonhuman primates (Vol. 4)*. New York: Academic Press.

Gardner, H. (1983). *Frames of mind*. New York: Basic Books.

Gardner, H. (1985). *The mind's new science*. New York: Basic Books.

Gardner, H. (1993). *Multiple intelligences*. New York: Basic Books.

Gardner, H. (1999). *The disciplined mind*. New York: Simon & Schuster.

Gardner, H. (2002). The pursuit of excellence through education. In M. Ferrari (Ed.), *Learning from extraordinary minds*. Mahwah, NJ: Erlbaum.

Gardner, H. (2003). *Multiple intelligences after twenty years*. Invited Address, American Educational Research Association, April, 2003. Retrieved July 7, 2005 from http://www.pz.harvard.edu/PIs/HG_MI_after_20_years.pdf.

Gardner, R. C. (1994). Stereotypes as consensual beliefs. In M. P. Zanna, & J. M. Olson (Eds.), *The psychology of prejudice: The Ontario symposium (Vol. 7)*. Mahwah, NJ: Erlbaum.*

Gardner, R. C., & Tremblay, P. F. (1995). On motivation: Measurement and conceptual considerations. *Modern Language Journal, 78*, 524–527.*

Garnets, L. D. (2002) Sexual orientation in perspective. *Cultural Diversity and Ethnic Minority Psychology, 8*, 115–129.

Gartlehner, G., Hansen, R. A., Kahwati, L., Lohr, K. N., Gaynes, B., & Carey, T. (2004). *Drug class review on second generation antidepressants*. Portland, OR: Oregon Evidence-based Practice Center. Retrieved August 2, 2005 from http://www.ohsu.edu/drugeffectiveness/reports/documents/Second%20Generation%20Antidepressants%20Final%20Report.pdf.

Gast, U., Roodewald, F., Nickel, V., & Emrich, H. M. (2001). Prevalence of dissociative disorders among psychiatric patients in a German university clinic. *Journal of Nervous and Mental Disorders, 189*, 249–257.

Gatchel, R. J. (2005). *Clinical essentials of pain management*. Washington: APA Press.

Gau, S-F., & Soong, W-T. (2003). The transition of sleep-wake patterns in early adolescence. *Sleep: Journal of Sleep & Sleep Disorders Research, 26(4)*, 449–454.

Gaudet, S., Clément, R., & Deuzeman, K. (2005). Daily hassles, ethnic identity and psychological adjustment among Lebanese-Canadians. *International Journal of Psychology, 40(3)*, 157–168.*

Gauthier, J. G. (1999). Bridging the gap between biological and psychological perspectives in the treatment of anxiety disorders. *Canadian Psychology, 40(1)*, 1–11.*

Gazda, G. M., Horne, A., & Ginter, E. (2001). *Group counseling and psychotherapy*. Boston: Allyn & Bacon.

Gazzaniga, M. S., Ivry, R. B., & Mangun, G. R. (2002). *Cognitive neuroscience: The biology of the mind (2nd ed.)*. New York: Norton.

Gear, A., Wizniak, R., & Cameron, J. (2004). Rewards for reading: A review of seven programs. *Alberta Journal of Educational Research, 50(2)*, 200–203.*

Geary, N. (2004). Endocrine controls of eating: CCK, leptin, and ghrelin. *Physiology & Behavior, 81(5)*, 719–733.

Gedo, J. E. (2002). The enduring scientific contributions of Sigmund Freud. *Perspectives in Biology and Medicine, 45*, 200–211.

Gegenfurtner, K. R., & Kiper, D. C. (2003). Color vision. *Annual Review of Neuroscience, 26*, 181–206.

Gehring, W. J., & Knight, R. T. (2002). Lateral prefrontal damage affects processing selection but not attention switching. *Cognitive Brain Research, 13*, 267–279.

Gentner, D., & Lowenstein, J. (2001). Relational thinking and relational language. In J. Byrnes, & E. Amsel (Eds.), *Language, literacy, and cognitive development*. Mahwah, NJ: Erlbaum.

George, L. K. (2001). The social psychology of health. In R. H. Binstock, & L. K. George (Eds.), *Handbook of the psychology of aging (5th ed.)*. San Diego: Academic Press.

German, T. P., & Barrett, H. C. (2005). Functional fixedness in a technologically sparse culture. *Psychological Science, 16(1)*, 1–5.

Gernsbacher, M. A., & Robertson, D. A. (2005). Watching the Brain Comprehend Discourse. In A. F. Healy (Ed.), *Experimental cognitive psychology and its applications*. Washington: APA Press.

Gershkoff-Stowe, L., & Thelen, E. (2004). U-shaped changes in behavior: A dynamic systems perspective. *Journal of Cognition & Development, 5(1)*, 1–36.

Gershoff, E. T. (2002). Corporal punishment by parents and associated child behaviors and experiences: A meta-analytic and theoretical review. *Psychological Bulletin, 128(4)*, 539–579.

Geschwind, N., & Galaburda, A. M. (1987). *Cerebral lateralization*. Cambridge: MIT Press.

Gesell, A. (1934). *Infancy and human growth*. New York: Macmillan. Gevins, A. S. (1999). What to do with your own personal brain scanner. In R. L. Solso (Ed.), *Mind and brain sciences in the 21st century*. Cambridge: MIT Press.

Gibb, B. E., Alloy, L. B., Abramson, L. Y., Beevers, C. G. & Miller, I. W. (2004). Cognitive vulnerability to depression: A taxometric analysis. *Journal of Abnormal Psychology, 113(1)*, 81–89.

Gibb, J. L., & Taylor, P. J. (2003). Past experience versus situational employment: Interview questions in a New Zealand social service agency. *Asia Pacific Journal of Human Resources, 41(3)*, 371–382.

Gibbs, J. T., & Huang, L. N. (1989). A conceptual framework for assessing and treating minority youth. In J. T. Gibbs, & L. N. Huang (Eds.), *Children of color*. San Francisco: Jossey-Bass.

Gibson, E. J. (2001). *Perceiving the affordances*. Mahwah, NJ: Erlbaum.

Gibson, R. L., & Mitchell, M. H. (2003). *Introduction to counseling and guidance (6th ed.)*. Upper Saddle River, NJ: Prentice Hall.

Gifford, R. (2002). *Environmental psychology: Principles and practice (3rd ed.)*. Colville, WA: Optimal Books.*

Gigerenzer, G., & Selton, R. (Eds.). (2001). *Bounded rationality*. Cambridge MIT Press.

Gila, A., Castro, J., Cesena, J., & Toro, J. (2005). Anorexia nervosa in male adolescents: Body image, eating attitudes and psychological traits. *Journal of Adolescent Health, 36(3)*, 221–226.

Gilbert, P. (2001). *Overcoming depression*. New York: Oxford.

Gilbert, S. J., & Shallice, T. (2002). Task switching: A PDP model. *Cognitive Psychology, 44*, 297–337.

Gilovich, T., Keltner, D., & Nisbett, R. (2005). *Social psychology*. New York: Norton.

Gillani, N. B., & Smith, J. C. (2001). Zen meditation and ABC relaxation theory. *Journal of Clinical Psychology, 57*, 839–846.

Gilligan, C. (1982). *In a different voice*. Cambridge Harvard University Press.

Gilligan, C. (1996). The centrality of relationships in psychological development. In G. Noam, & K. W. Fischer (Eds.), *Development and vulnerability in close relationships*. Mahwah, NJ: Erlbaum.

Gilligan, C. (1998). *Minding women: Reshaping the educational realm*. Cambridge Harvard University Press.

Gilligan, C. (2003). Hearing the difference: Theorizing connection. *Anuario de Psicologia, 34(2)*, 155–161.

Gilman, S. L. (2001). Karen Horney, M. D., 1885–1952. *American Journal of Psychoanalysis, 158*, 1205.

Giorgi, A. (2005). Remaining challenges for humanistic psychology. *Journal of Humanistic Psychology, 45(2)*, 204–216.

Giuseppe, R. (2005). Virtual reality in psychotherapy: Review. *CyberPsychology & Behavior. Special Use of Virtual Environments in Training and Rehabilitation: International Perspectives, 8(3)*, 220–230.

Gjerde, P. F., Block, J., & Block, J. H. (1991). The preschool family context of 18-year-olds with depressive symptoms: A prospective study. *Journal of Research on Adolescence, 1*, 63–92.

Gladding, S. T. (2002). *Family therapy (3rd ed.)*. Englewood Cliffs, NJ: Prentice Hall.

Gladwell, M. (2005). *Blink: The power of thinking without thinking*. New York: Little, Brown.

Glancy, G., & Saini, M. A. (2005). An evidenced-based review of psychological treatments of anger and aggression. *Brief Treatment & Crisis Intervention, 5(2)*, 229–248.

Gleason, J. B. (2005). *The development of language (6th ed.)*. Boston: Allyn & Bacon.

Gleaves, D. H., May, M. C., & Cardena, E. (2001). An examination of the diagnostic validity of dissociative identity disorder. *Clinical Psychology Review, 21*, 577–608.

Gnatkovsky, V., Uva, L., & de Curtis, M. (2004). Topographic distribution of direct and hippocampus-mediated entorhinal cortex activity evoked by olfactory tract stimulation. *European Journal of Neuroscience, 20(7)*, 189–1905.

Godbout, L., Cloutier, P., Bouchard, C., Braun, C. M. J., & Gagnon, S. (2004). Script generation following frontal and parietal lesions. *Journal of Clinical & Experimental Neuropsychology, 26(7)*, 857–873.*

Goddard, M. J. (1997). Spontaneous recovery in US extinction. *Learning and Motivation, 28*, 118–128.*

Godden, D. R., & Baddeley, A. D. (1975). Context-dependent memory in two natural environments: On land and under water. *British Journal of Psychology, 66*, 325–331.

Goel, V. (1995). *Sketches of thought*. Cambridge MIT Press.*

Goel, V. (2005a). Can there be a cognitive neuroscience of central cognitive systems? In C. E. Erneling, & D. M. Johnson (Eds.), *The mind as a scientific object: Between brain and culture*. London: Oxford.*

Goel, V. (2005b). Cognitive neuroscience of deductive reasoning. In K. Holyoak, & R. Morrison (Eds.), *Cambridge handbook of thinking & reasoning*. Cambridge: Cambridge University Press.*

Goel, V., & Dolan, R. J. (2004). Differential involvement of left prefrontal cortex in inductive and deductive reasoning. *Cognition, 93(3)*, 109–121.

Goelman, H. (2000). Training, quality and the lived experience of child care. In G. Cleveland, & M. Krashinsky (Eds.), *Our children's future: Child care policy in Canada*. Toronto: University of Toronto Press.*

Goelman, H., Andersen, C. J., Anderson, J. Gouzouasis, P., Kendrick, M., Kindler, A. M., Porath, M., & Koh, J. (2003). Early childhood education. In W. M. Reynolds & G. E. Miller (Eds.) *Handbook of psychology: Educational psychology (Vol. 7)*. New York: Wiley.

Goenjian, A. K., Molina, L., Steinberg, A. M., Fairbanks, L. A., Alvarez, M. L., Goenjian, H. A., et al. (2001). Post-traumatic stress and depression reactions among Nicaraguan adolescents after Hurricane Mitch. *American Journal of Psychiatry, 158*, 788–794.

Goethals, G. R., & Demorest, A. P. (1995). The risky shift is a sure bet. In M. E. Ware, & D. E. Johnson (Eds.), *Demonstrations and activities in teaching of psychology (Vol. 3)*. Mahwah, NJ: Erlbaum.

Gold, B. (2002). Integrative approaches to psychotherapy. In M. Hersen, & W. H. Sledge (Eds.), *Encyclopedia of psychotherapy*. San Diego: Academic Press.

Goldberg, D., & Goodyer, I. M. (2005). *The origins and course of common mental disorders*. New York: Routledge.

Goldberg, J. O., & Schmidt, L. A. (2001). Shyness, sociability, and social dysfunction in schizophrenia. *Schizophrenia Research, 48*, 343–349.*

Goldberg, R. (2003). *Clashing views on controversial issues in drugs and society (5th ed.)*. New York: McGraw-Hill.

Golden, J. (2005). *Message in a bottle: The making of fetal alcohol syndrome*. Cambridge: Harvard University Press.

Goldenthal, P. (2005). *Helping children and families: A new treatment model integrating psychodynamic, behavioral, and contextual approaches*. San Francisco: Jossey-Bass.

Goldsmith, H. H. (2002). Genetics of emotional development. In R. J. Davidson, K. R. Scherer, & H. H. Goldsmith (Eds.), *Handbook of affective sciences*. New York: Oxford.

Goldsmith, T. H., & Zimmerman, W. F. (2001). *Biology, evolution, and human nature*. New York: Wiley.

Goldstein, E. B. (2002). *Sensation and perception (6th ed.)*. Belmont, CA: Wadsworth. Goldstein, I. (2004). Androgen physiology in sexual medicine. Sexuality & Disability. *Special Proceedings of the Boston University School of Medicine Conference on Erectile Dysfunction, 22(2)*, 165–169.

Goldstein, I. L., & Ford, K. (2002). *Training in organizations*. Belmont, CA: Wadsworth.

Goldstein, J. M., Seidman, L. J., Horton, N. J., Makris, N., Kennedy, D. N., Caviness, V. S., et al. (2001). Normal sexual dimorphism of the adult human brain assessed by in vivo magnetic resonance imaging. *Cerebral Cortex, 11*, 490–497.

Goldstein, M. J. & Palmer, J. O. (1975). *The experience of anxiety: A casebook*. Oxford: Oxford University Press.

Goldstein, R. B., Prescott, C. A., & Kendler, K. S. (2001). Genetic and environmental factors in conduct problems and adult antisocial behavior among adult female twins. *Journal of Nervous and Mental Disorders, 189*, 201–209.

Goldstein, R. B., Wickramaratne, P. J., Horwath, E., & Weissman, M. M. (1997). Familal aggregation and phenomenology of "early"-onset (at or before age 20 years) panic disorder. *Archives of General Psychiatry, 54*, 271–278.

Goleman, D. (1995). *Emotional intelligence*. New York: Bantam.

Goleman, D., Kaufman, P., & Ray, M. (1993). *The creative mind*. New York: Plume.

Gomez Beldarrain, M., Gafman, J., Ruiz De Velasco, J., & Pascual-Leone, A. (2002). Prefrontal lesions impair the implicit and explicit learning of sequences in visuomotor tasks. *Experimental Brain Research, 142*, 529–538.

Goncalves, O. F., Korman, Y., & Angus, L. (2000). Constructing psychopathology from a cognitive narrative perspective. In R. A. Neimeyer, & J. D. Raskin (Eds.), *Constructions of disorder: Meaning-making frameworks for psychotherapy*. Washington: APA Press.*

Gong-Guy, E. (1986). *Depression in students of Chinese and Japanese ancestry: An acculturation, vulnerability and stress model*. Unpublished dissertation, University of California, Los Angeles.

Gontkovsky, S. T. (2005). Neurobiological bases and neuropsychological correlates of aggression and violence. In J. P. Morgan (Ed.), *Psychology of aggression*. Hauppauge, NY: Nova Science Publishers.

Gonzales, D. H., Nides, M. A., Ferry, L. H., Kustra, R. P., Jamerson, B. D., Segall, N., et al. (2001). Bupropion SR as an aid to smoking cessation in smokers previously treated with bupropion: A randomized placebo-controlled study. *Clinical and Pharmacology Therapy, 69*, 438–444.

Gonzales, P., Guzmán, J. C., Partelow, L., Pahlke, E., Kastberg, L. & Williams, T. (2004). *Highlights From the Trends in International Mathematics and Science Study (TIMSS) 2003 (NCES 2005–005)*. U.S. Department of Education, National Center for Education Statistics. Downloaded August 26, 2005 from http://nces.ed.gov/pubs2005/timss03/.

González-Ibáñez, Á., Rosel, P., & Moreno, I. (2005). Evaluation and treatment of pathological gambling. *Journal of Gambling Studies, 21(1)*, 35–42.

Goodale, M. A., & Humphrey, G. K. (2001). Separate visual systems for action and perception. In E. B. Goldstein (Ed) *Blackwell handbook of perception*. Malden, MA: Blackwell.*

Goodale, M. A., Milner, A. D., Jakobson, L. S., & Carey, D. P. (1991). A neurological dissociation between perceiving objects and grasping them. *Nature, 349*, 154–156.*

Goodstein, I. K., & Calhoun, J. F. (1982). *Understanding abnormal behavior*. Reading, MA: Addison-Wesley.

Gorenstein, E. E. (1997). *Case studies in abnormal psychology*. New York: Longman.

Gorman, P. (2003). *Motivation and emotion*. Philadelphia: Psychology Press.

Gottlieb, G. (2002a). Origin of the species: The potential significance of early experience for evolution. In W. W. Hartup, & R. A. Weinberg (Eds.), *Child psychology in retrospect and prospect*. Mahwah, NJ: Erlbaum.

Gottlieb, G. (2002b). Nature and nurture theories. In A. Kazdin (Ed.), *Encyclopedia of psychology*. Washington, & New York: APA Press and Oxford.

Gottlieb, G., Wahlsten, D., & Lickliter, R. (1998). The significance of biology for human development: A developmental psychobiological systems view. In W. Damon (Ed.), *Handbook of child psychology (5th ed.)*. New York: Wiley.*

Gottman, J. M. (1994). *What predicts divorce?* Mahwah, NJ: Erlbaum.

Gottman, J. M., & Silver, N. (1999). *The seven principles for making marriages work*. New York: Crown.

Gottman, J. M., Coan, J., Carrere, S., & Swanson, C. (1998). Predicting marital happiness and stability from newlywed interactions. *Journal of Marriage and the Family, 60*, 5–22.

Gottman, J. M., Katz, L. F., & Hooven, C. (1997). *Meta-emotion: How families communicate*. Mahwah, NJ: Erlbaum.

Gottman, J. M., Ryan, K. D., Carrere, S., & Erley, A. M. (2002). Toward a scientifically based marital therapy. In H. A. Liddle, D. A. Santisteban, et al. (Eds.), *Family psychology: Science-based interventions*. Washington: APA Press.

Gottselig, J. M., Bassetti, C. L., & Achermann, P. (2002). Power and coherence of sleep spindle frequency activity following hemispheric stroke. *Brain, 125*, 373–383.

Gotz, M. E., Janetzky, B., Pohli, S., Gottschalk, S., Gsell, A., Tatshchner, T., et al. (2001). Chronic alcohol consumption and cerebral indices of oxidative stress: Is there a link? *Alcoholism: Clinical and Experimental Research, 25*, 717–725.

Gould, E., Reeves, A. J., Graziano, M. S., & Gross, C. G. (1999). Neurogenesis in the neocortex of adult primates. *Science, 286 (1)*, 548–552.

Gould, S. J. (1981). *The mismeasure of man*. New York: Norton.

Goveas, J. S., Csernansky, J. G., & Coccaro, E. F. (2004). Platelet serotonin content correlates inversely with life history of aggression in personality-disordered subjects. *Psychiatry Research, 126(1)*, 23–32.

Grabowski, J. (1999, January). *Addicted to addictions?* APA Monitor, p. 8.

Graen, G. B., & Hui, C. (2001). Approaches to leadership: Toward a complete contingency model of face-to-face leadership. In M. Erez, U. Kleinbeck & H. Thierry (Eds.), *Work motivation in the context of a globalizing economy*. Mahwah, NJ: Erlbaum.

Graf, P., & Schacter, D. L. (1985). Implicit and explicit memory for new associations in normal and amnesiac subjects. *Journal of Experimental Psychology: Learning, Memory and Cognition, 11*, 501–518.*

Graf, P., & Uttl, B. (2001). Prospective memory: A new focus for research. *Consciousness & Cognition: An International Journal, 10(4)*, 437–450.*

Graham, S. (1992). Most of the subjects were white and middle class. *American Psychologist, 47*, 629–637.

Graham-Bermann, S., Eastin, J. A., & Bermann, E. A. (2002). Stress and coping. In J. Worell (Ed.), *Encyclopedia of women and gender*. New York: Oxford.

Grant, A. M., Langer, E. J., Falk, E., & Capodilupo, C. (2004). Mindful creativity: Drawing to draw distinctions. *Creativity Research Journal, 16(2-3)*, 261–265.

Grau, C., Polo, M. D., Yago, E., Gual, A., & Escera, C. (2002). Auditory sensory memory as indicated by a mismatch negativity in chronic alcoholism. *Clinical Neurophysiology, 112*, 728–731.

Gravetter, F. J., & Wallnau, L. B. (2004). *Statistics for the behavioral sciences (6th ed.)*. Belmont, CA: Wadsworth.

Gray, C. (2002). Pediatricians taking a new look at corporal-punishment issue. *Canadian Medical Association Journal, 167*, 793.

Gray, J. (1992). *Men are from Mars, women are from Venus*. New York: Harper Collins.

Gray, J. E., Shone, M. A., & Liddle, P. F. (2000). *Canadian mental health law and policy*. Markham, ON: Butterworths Canada.*

Gray, J. R. (2001). Emotional modulation of cognitive control: Approach-withdrawal states double-dissociate spatial from verbal two-back task performance. *Journal of Experimental Psychology: General, 130*, 436–452.

Gray, M. J., Bolton, E. E., & Litz, B. T. (2004). A longitudinal analysis of PTSD symptom course: Delayed-onset PTSD in Somalia peacekeepers. *Journal of Consulting & Clinical Psychology, 72(5)*, 909–913.

Graziano, W. J. (1995). Evolutionary psychology: Old music, but now on CDs? *Psychological Inquiry, 6*, 41–44.

Green, C. D. (2004). The hiring of James Mark Baldwin and James Gibson Hume at Toronto in 1889. *History of Psychology, 7*, 130–153.*

Green, C. D. (2005). Was Babbage's Analytical Engine intended to be a mechanical model of the mind? *History of Psychology. Special: The Roles Of Instruments In Psychological Research, 8(1)*, 35–45.*

Green, C. D., & Groff, P. R. (2003). *Early psychological thought: Ancient accounts of mind and soul*. Westport, CT: Praeger.*

Green, C. D., Shore, M., & Teo, T. (Eds.). (2001). *The transformation of psychology: Influences of 19th-century philosophy, technology, and natural science*. Washington: APA Press.*

Greenberg, D. L. (2004). President Bush's false 'flashbulb' memory of 9/11/01. *Applied Cognitive Psychology, 18(3)*, 363–370.

Greenberg, L., & Bolger, L. (2001). An emotion focussed approach to the over-regulation of emotion and emotional pain. *Journal of Clinical Psychology: In-Session, 57(2)*, 197–211.*

Greenberg, L., & Paivio, S. (1997). *Working with emotion in psychotherapy*. New York: Guilford.*

Greenberg, L., Korman, L., & Paivio, S. (2001). Emotion in humanistic therapy. In D. Cain, & J. Seeman, (Eds.), *Humanistic psychotherapies: Handbook of research and practice*. Washington: APA Press.*

Greenberg, M., Szmukler, G., & Tantam, D. (1986). *Making sense of psychiatric cases*. Oxford: Oxford University Press.

Greenfield, S. (1996, April). *Neural assemblies*. Paper presented at the conference on "Toward a science of consciousness," Tucson, AZ.

Greenglass, E. R. (1991). Burnout and gender: Theoretical and organizational implications. *Canadian Psychology, 32(4)*, 562–574.*

Greenglass, E. R. (1996). Anger suppression, cynical distrust, and hostility: Implications for coronary heart disease. In C. D. Spielberger, & I. G. Sarason (Eds.), *Stress and emotion: Anxiety, anger, and curiosity (Vol 16)*. Washington: Taylor & Francis.*

Greenglass, E. R. (1998). Gender differences in mental health. In H. S. Friedman (Ed.), *Encyclopedia of mental health (Vol. 2)*. San Diego: Academic Press.*

Greenglass, E. R., & Burke, R. J. (2000a). Organizational restructuring, downsizing and employee well-being. In S. B. Dahiya (Ed.), *The current state of business disciplines*. New Delhi: Spellbound Publications.*

Greenglass, E. R., & Burke, R. J. (2000b). The relationship between hospital restructuring, anger, hostility and psychosomatics in nurses. *Journal of Community and Applied Social Psychology. 10*, 155–161.*

Greenglass, E. R., Burke, R. J., & Konarski, R. (1998). Components of burnout, resources, and gender-related differences. *Journal of Applied Social Psychology, 28(12)*, 1088–1106.*

Greenglass, E. R., Burke, R. J., & Moore, K. A. (2003). Reactions to increased workload: Effects on professional efficacy of nurses. *Applied Psychology: An International Review, 52(4)*, 580–597.*

Greenough, W. T. (2000). Brain development. In A. Kazdin (Ed.), *Encyclopedia of psychology*. Washington, & New York: APA Press and Oxford.

Greenough, W. T. (2001). Commentary. *In J. W. Santrock, Child Development (9th ed.)*. Boston: McGraw-Hill.

Gregory, R. L. (2000). Visual illusions. In A. Kazdin (Ed.), *Encyclopedia of psychology*. Washington, & New York: APA Press and Oxford.

Greist, J. H., Bandelow, B., Hollander, E., Marazziti, D., Montgomery, S. A., Nutt, D. J., Okasha, A., et al. (2003). WCA recommendations for the long-term treatment of obsessive-compulsive disorder in adults. *CNS Spectrums, 8(8, Suppl1)*, 7–16.*

Grembowski, D. (2003). Managed care organizations and access to mental health specialists: It's a jungle out there. *General Hospital Psychiatry, 25(3)*, 147–148.

Griffin, B., & Hesketh, B. (2004). Why openness to experience is not a good predictor of job performance. *International Journal of Selection & Assessment, 12(3)*, 243–251.

Griffin, W. A. (2002). Family therapy. In M. Hersen, & W. H. Sledge (Eds.), *Encyclopedia of psychotherapy*. San Diego: Academic Press.

Griggs, R. A. (1999). Introductory psychology textbooks: Assessing levels of difficulty. *Teaching of Psychology, 26*, 248–253.

Grigorenko, E. L. (2000). Heritability and intelligence. In R. J. Sternberg (Ed.), *Handbook of intelligence*. New York: Cambridge.

Grigorenko, E. L. (2005). The inherent complexities of gene-environment interactions. *Journals of Gerontology: Series B: Psychological Sciences & Social Sciences. Special Research on Environmental Effects in Genetic Studies of Aging, 60B(1,SpecIssue)*, 53–64.

Grimshaw, G. M., Adelstein, A., Bryden, M P., & MacKinnon, G. E. (1998). First-language acquisition in adolescence: Evidence for a critical period for verbal language development. *Brain & Language, 63(2)*, 237–255.*

Grodzinsky, Y. (2001). The neurology of syntax: Language use without Broca's area. *Behavior and Brain Sciences, 23*, 1–21.

Grossenbacher, P. G. (2001). *Finding consciousness in the brain: A neurocognitive approach*. Amsterdam: John Benjamins.

Grubin, D., & Madsen, L. (2005). Lie detection and the polygraph: A historical review. *Journal of Forensic Psychiatry & Psychology, 16(2)*, 357–369.

Grusec, J. E., Goodnow, J. J., & Kuczynski, L. (2000). New directions in analyses of parenting contributions to children's acquisition of values. *Child Development, 71(1)*, 205–211.*

Grush, J. E. (1980). Impact of candidate expenditures, regionality, and prior outcomes on the 1976 Democratic presidential primaries. *Journal of Personality & Social Psychology, 38*, 337–347.

Guilbault, R. L., Bryant, F. B., Brockway, J. H., & Posavac, E. J. (2004). A meta-analysis of research on hindsight bias. *Basic & Applied Social Psychology, 26(3)*, 103–117.

Guilford, J. P. (1967). *The structure of intellect*. New York: McGraw-Hill.

Guillery-Girard, B., Desgranges, B., Urban, C., Piolino, P., de la Sayette, V., & Eustache, F. (2004). The dynamic time course of memory recovery in transient global amnesia. *Journal of Neurology, Neurosurgery & Psychiatry, 75(11)*, 1532–1540.

Gunn, R., & Linden, R. (1994). The processing of child sexual abuse cases. In J. V. Roberts, & R. M. Mohr (Eds.), *Confronting sexual assault: A decade of legal and social change*. Toronto: University of Toronto Press.*

Gupta, P., & Dell, G. S. (1999). The emergence of language from serial order and procedural memory. In B. MacWhinney (Ed.), *The emergence of language*. Mahwah, NJ: Erlbaum.

Gurung, R. A. R. (2006). *Health psychology: A cultural approach*. Belmont, CA: Wadsworth.

Gurung, R. A. R. (2003). Pedagogical aids and student performance. *Teaching of Psychology, 30*, 92–95.

Gurung, R. A. R. (2004). Pedagogical aids: Learning enhancers or dangerous detours? *Teaching of Psychology, 31*, 164–166.

Gussler-Burkhardt, N. L., & Giancola, P. R. (2005). A further examination of gender differences in alcohol-related aggression. *Journal of Studies on Alcohol, 66(3)*, 413–422.

Guthrie, R. V. (2004). *Even the rat was white: A historical view of psychology (2nd ed.)*. Boston: Allyn & Bacon.

Gutierrez-Lobos, K., Frohlich, S., Quiner, S., Haring, C., & Barnas, C. (2001). Prescription patterns and quality of information provided for consumers of benzodiazepines. *Acta Medica Austrica, 28*, 56–59.

Guttman, N., & Kalish, H. I. (1956). Discriminability and stimulus generalization. *Journal of Experimental Psychology, 51*, 79–88.

Gwynn, M. I., & Spanos, N. P. (1996). Hypnotic responsiveness, nonhypnotic suggestibility, and responsiveness to social influence. In R. G. Kunzendorf, N. P. Spanos, & B. Wallace (Eds.), *Hypnosis and imagination*. Amityville, NY: Baywood Publishing.*

H

Hacking, I. (1998). *Mad travelers: Reflections on the reality of transient mental illness*. Charlottesville, VA: University Press of Virginia.*

Haddock, G., & Zanna, M. P. (1998). Assessing the structure of anti-gay attitudes: The impact of right-wing authoritarianism and values on anti-gay prejudice and discrimination. In G. M. Herek (Ed.), *Stigma and sexual orientation: Understanding prejudice against lesbians, gay men, and bisexuals*. Thousand Oaks, CA: Sage.*

Haddock, G., Zanna, M. P., & Esses, V. M. (1994). The (limited) role of trait-laden stereotypes in predicting attitudes toward Native Peoples. *British Journal of Social Psychology, 33*, 83–106.*

Hadjistavropoulos, T., & Genest, M. (1994). The underestimation of the role of physical attractiveness in dating preferences: Ignorance or taboo? *Canadian Journal of Behavioural Science, 26(2)*, 298–318.*

Hadjistavropoulos, T., Malloy, D., Sharpe, D., Green, S. & Fuchs-Lacelle, S. (2002). The Canadian model of ranking ethical principles and the code of ethics of the American Psychological Association. *Canadian Psychology, 43*, 254–259.*

Hafer, C. L. (2000). Do innocent victims threaten the belief in a just world? Evidence from a modified Stroop task. *Journal of Personality & Social Psychology, 79*, 165–173.*

Hafer, C. L., & Bègue, L. (2005). Experimental research on just-world theory: problems, developments, and future challenges. *Psychological Bulletin, 131(1)*, 128–167.*

Hafer, C. L., & Olson, J. M. (1998). Individual differences in the belief in a just world and responses to personal misfortune. In L. Montada, & M. J. Lerner, (Eds.), *Responses to victimizations and belief in a just world. Critical issues in social justice*. New York: Plenum Press.*

Hafer, C. L., & Olson, J. M. (2003). An analysis of empirical research on the scope of justice. *Personality & Social Psychology Review, 7(4)*, 311–323.*

Haier, R. J. (2003). Brain imaging studies of intelligence: Individual differences and neurobiology. In R. J. Sternberg, & J. Lautrey (Eds.), *Models of intelligence: International perspectives*. Washington: APA Press.

Haier, R. J., White, N. S., & Alkire, M. T. (2003). Individual differences in general intelligence correlate with brain function during nonreasoning tasks. *Intelligence, 31(5)*, 429–441.

Haier, R. J., Jung, R. E,, Yeo, R. A,, Head, K, & Alkire, M. T. (2004). Structural brain variation and general intelligence. *NeuroImage, 23*, 425–433.

Haier, R. J., Jung, R. E., Yeo, R. A., Head, K. & Alkire, M. T. (2005). The neuroanatomy of general intelligence: sex matters. *NeuroImage, 25*, 320–327.

Hakuta, K. (1999). The debate on bilingual education. *Developmental and Behavioral Pediatrics, 20*, 36–37.

Hakuta, K., Bialystok, E., & Wiley, E. (2003). Critical evidence: A test of the critical-period hypothesis for second-language acquisition. *Psychological Science, 14(1)*, 31–38.*

Hakuta, K., Butler, Y. G., & Witt, D. (2000). *How long does it take English learners to attain proficiency? (Linguistic Minority Institute Policy Report 2000–2001)*. Berkeley: University of California.

Hakuta, K., & Garcia, E. E. (1989). Bilingualism and education. *American Psychologist, 44*, 374–379.

Haladyna, T. M. (2002). *Essentials of standardized testing*. Boston: Allyn & Bacon.

Hall, G. B, Witelson, S.F., Szechtman, H. & Nahmias C. (2004). Sex differences in functional activation patterns revealed by increased emotion processing demands. *Neuroreport, 15(2)*, 219–23.*

Hall, K. H. (2002). Reviewing intuitive decision-making and uncertainty: The implications for medical education. *Medical Education, 36(3)*, 216–224.

Hall, R. V., & Hall, M. L. (1998). *How to select reinforcers (2nd ed.)*. Austin: Pro-Ed.

Hallahan, D. P., & Kauffman, J. M. (2006). *Exceptional learners (10th ed.)*. Boston: Allyn & Bacon.

Halpern, D. F. (1998). Teaching critical thinking for transfer across domains: Dispositions, skills, structure training, and metacognitive monitoring. *American Psychologist, 53*, 449–455.

Halpern, D. F. (2000). Critical thinking. In N. J. Smelser, & P. B. Baltes (Eds.), *International encyclopedia of the social and behavioral sciences*. Amsterdam: Pergamon.

Halpern, D. F. (2001). Sex difference research: Cognitive abilities. In J. Worell (Ed.), *Encyclopedia of women and gender*. New York: Oxford.

Halpern, D. F. (2002). Teaching for critical thinking: A four-part model to enhance thinking skills. In S. Davis, & W. Buskist (Eds.), *The teaching of psychology: Essays in honor of Wilbert J. McKeachie and Charles L. Brewer*. Mahwah, NJ: Erlbaum.

Halpern, D. F. (2003). *Thought and knowledge: An introduction to critical thinking (4th ed.)*. Mahwah, NJ: Erlbaum.

Halpern, D. F. (2004). A cognitive-process taxonomy for sex differences in cognitive abilities. *Current Directions in Psychological Science, 13(4)*, 135–139.

Hamann, S. B., Ely, T. D., Hoffman, J. M., & Kilts, C. D. (2002). Ecstasy and agony: Activation of human amygdala in positive and negative emotion. *Psychological Science, 13(2)*, 135–141.

Hambrick, D. Z., & Oswald, F. L. (2005). Does domain knowledge moderate involvement of working memory capacity in higher-level cognition? A test of three models. *Journal of Memory & Language, 52(3)*, 377–397.

Hamermesh, D. S., & Parker, A. M. (2005). Beauty in the classroom: Professorial pulchritude and putative pedagogical productivity. *Economics of Education Review, 24(4)*, 369–376. Retrieved July 1, 2005 from http://www.eco.utexas.edu/faculty/Hamermesh/Beautystuff.html.

Hampton, R. R., & Shettleworth, S. J. (1996). Hippocampal lesions impair memory for location but not color in passerine birds. *Behavioral Neuroscience, 110*, 831–835.*

Hancock, P. A., & Desmond, P. A. (2000). *Stress, workload, and fatigue*. Mahwah, NJ: Erlbaum.

Hancock, P. A., & Ganey, H. C. N. (2003). From the inverted-U to the extended-U: The evolution of a law of psychology. *Journal of Human Performance in Extreme Environments, 7(1)*, 5–14.

Hancox, R. J., Milne, B. J., & Poulton, R. (2004). Association between child and adolescent television viewing and health: A longitudinal birth cohort study. *Lancet, 364 (9430)*, 257–262.

Hankin, B. L., Kassel, J. D., & Abela, J. R. Z. (2005). Adult attachment dimensions and specificity of emotional distress symptoms: Prospective investigations of cognitive risk and interpersonal stress generation as mediating mechanisms. *Personality & Social Psychology Bulletin, 31(1)*, 136–151.*

Hannigan, J. H., Spear, L. P., Spear, N. E., & Goodlet, C. R. (Eds.). (1999). *Alcohol and alcoholism*. Mahwah, NJ: Erlbaum.

Hannon, B., & Craik, F. I. M. (2001). Encoding specificity revisited: The role of semantics. *Canadian Journal of Experimental Psychology, 55*, 231–243.*

Hansell, J. H., & Damour, L. (2004). *Abnormal psychology*. San Francisco: Jossey-Bass.

Hanson, R. F., Saunders, B., Kilpatrick, D., Resnick, H., Crouch, J. A., & Duncan, R. (2001). Impact of childhood rape and aggravated assault on adult mental health. *American Journal of Orthopsychiatry, 71*, 108–119.

Hardy, C. L., & van Leeuwen, S. A. (2004). Interviewing young children: Effects of probe structures and focus of rapport-building talk on the qualities of young children's eyewitness statements. *Canadian Journal of Behavioural Science, 36(2)*, 155–165.*

Hare, R. D. (2001). Psychopaths and their nature: Some implications for understanding human predatory violence. In J. Sanmartin, & A. Raine (Eds.), *Violence and psychopathy.* Dordrecht, The Netherlands: Kluwer.*

Hare, R. D. (2002). Psychopathy and risk for recidivism and violence. In N. Gray, J. Laing, & L. Noaks (Eds.), *Criminal justice, mental health, and the politics of risk.* London: Cavendish Publishing.*

Harkness, S., & Super, C. M. (2002). Culture and parenting. In M. Bornstein (Ed.), *Handbook of parenting (2nd ed.).* Mahwah, NJ: Erlbaum.

Harlow, H. F., & Zimmerman, R. R. (1959). Affectional responses in the infant monkey. *Science, 130*, 421–432.

Harrington, M. (2006). *The design and analysis of experiments in neuroscience.* Belmont, CA: Wadsworth.

Harris, J. R. (1998). *The nurture assumption.* New York: Free Press.

Harris, L. R., & Jenkin, M. (Eds.) (1998). *Vision and action.* New York: Cambridge.*

Harris, L. R., Jenkin, M., & Zikovitz, D. C. (1999). *Vestibular cues and virtual environments: choosing the magnitude of the vestibular cue.* IEEE International Conference on Virtual Reality, 229–236.*

Harris, R. B. S., Bowen, H. M., & Mitchell, T. D. (2003). Leptin resistance in mice is determined by gender and duration of exposure to high-fat diet. *Physiology & Behavior, 78(4-5)*, 543–555.

Harrison, Y., & Horne, J. A. (2000). The impact of sleep deprivation on decision making: A review. *Journal of Experimental Psychology: Applied, 6*, 236–249.

Hart, B., & Risley, T. R. (1995). *Meaningful differences in the everyday experience of young Americans.* Baltimore: Paul H. Brookes.

Hart, J. W., Karau, S. J., Stasson, M. F., & Kerr, N. A. (2004). Achievement motivation, expected coworker performance, and collective task motivation: Working hard or hardly working? *Journal of Applied Social Psychology, 34(5)*, 984–1000.

Harter, S. (1998). The development of self-representations. In W. Damon (Ed.), *Handbook of child psychology (5th ed., Vol. 3).* New York: Wiley.

Hartmann, E. (1993). Nightmares. In M. A. Carskadon (Ed.), *Encyclopedia of sleep and dreams.* New York: Macmillan.

Harvey, A. G. (2001). Insomnia: Symptom or diagnosis? Clinical Psychology Review, 21, 1037–1059.

Harvey, J. H., & Weber, A. L. (2002). Odyssey of the heart (2nd ed.). Mahwah, NJ: Erlbaum.

Harway, M. (Ed.). (2004). *Handbook of couples therapy.* San Francisco, CA: Jossey-Bass.

Hasher, L., Goldstein, D., & May, C. P. (2005). It's about time: Circadian rhythms, memory, and aging. In C. Izawa, & N. Ohta, (Eds.) *Human learning and memory: Advances in theory and application: The 4th Tsukuba International Conference on Memory.* Mahwah, NJ: Erlbaum.*

Hassall, R., Rose, J., & McDonald, J. (2005). Parenting stress in mothers of children with an intellectual disability: The effects of parental cognitions in relation to child characteristics and family support. *Journal of Intellectual Disability Research, 49(6)*, 405–418.

Hastie, R. (2001). Problems for judgment and decision making. *Annual Review of Psychology, 52*, 653–683.

Hastie, R., & Dawes, R. (2001). *Rational choice in an uncertain world.* Thousand Oaks, CA: Sage.

Hatcher, R. A., Trussell, J., Stewart, F., Nelson A., Cates, W., Guest F., & Kowal, D. (2004). *Contraceptive technology: Eighteenth revised edition.* New York: Ardent Media.

Hatton, C., & Emerson, E. (2004). The relationship between life events and psychopathology amongst children with intellectual disabilities. *Journal of Applied Research in Intellectual Disabilities, 17(2)*, 109–117.

Hatzakis, G, & Tsoukas, C. (2002). Use of artificial intelligence in monitoring HIV disease. *American Clinical Laboratory, 21(1)*, 25–28.*

Hauptmann, B., & Karni, A. (2002). From primed to learn: the saturation of repetition priming and the induction of long-term memory. *Brain Research: Cognitive Brain Research, 13*, 313–322.

Hausknecht, K. A., Acheson, A., Farrar, A. M., Kieres, A. K., Shen, R-Y., Richards, J. B., & Sabol, K. E. (2005). Prenatal alcohol exposure causes attention deficits in male rats. *Behavioral Neuroscience, 119(1)*, 302–310.

Hawkins, F. H. (1987). *Human factors in flight.* Aldershot, England: Gower Technical Press.

Hawkins, G., & Zimring, F. E. (1988). *Pornography in a free society.* New York: Cambridge.

Hayes, N. (1997, July). The distinctive skills of a psychology graduate. *APA Monitor, 33*.

Hayflick, L. (1997). The cellular basis for biological aging. In C. E. Finch, & L. Hayflick (Eds.), *Handbook of the biology of aging.* New York: Van Nostrand.

Health Canada (1999). *Statistical report on the health of Canadians.* Ottawa: Health Canada. Retrieved September 5, 2005 from http://www.phac-aspc.gc.ca/ph-sp/phdd/report/stat/index.html.*

Health Canada (2001). *Achieving health for all: A framework for health promotion.* Ottawa: Health Canada. Retrieved August 10, 2005 from http://www.hc-sc.gc.ca/hcs-sss/pubs/care-soins/2001-frame-plan-promotion/index_e.html.*

Health Canada (2002a). *A report on mental illnesses in Canada.* Ottawa: Health Canada. Retrieved July 25, 2005 from http://www.phac-aspc.gc.ca/publicat/miic-mmac/index.html.*

Health Canada (2002b). *National Native Alcohol and Drug Abuse Program.* Ottawa: Health Canada. Retrieved March 18, 2005 from http://www.hc-sc.gc.ca/fnihb/cp/nnadap/index.htm.*

Health Canada (2003). *Canadian guidelines for sexual health education, 2003.* Ottawa: Health Canada. Retrieved August 22, 2005 from http://www.phac-aspc.gc.ca/publicat/cgshe-ldnemss/index.html.*

Health Canada (2004). *HIV/AIDS EPI Updates, May 2004.* Ottawa: Health Canada. Retrieved March 19, 2005 from http://www.phac-aspc.gc.ca/publicat/epiu-aepi/epi_update_may_04/pdf/epi_may_2004_e.pdf.*

Health Canada (2005). *Canada's drug strategy.* Ottawa: Health Canada. Available from Health Canada (online at http://www.hc-sc.gc.ca/). Retrieved March 18, 2005 from http://www.hc-sc.gc.ca/hecs-sesc/cds/index.htm.*

Healy, A. F. (Ed.). (2005). *Experimental cognitive psychology and its applications.* Washington: APA Press.

Heath, A. C., Todorov, A. A., Nelson, E. C., Madden, P. A., Bucholz, K. K., & Martin, N. G. (2002). Gene-environment interaction effects on behavioral variation and risk of complex disorders: the example of alcoholism and other psychiatric disorders. *Twin Research, 5*, 30–37.

Heath, Y., & Gifford, R. (2002). Extending the theory of planned behavior: Predicting the use of public transportation. *Journal of Applied Social Psychology. 32(10)*, 2154–2185.*

Heatherton, T. F., & Polivy, J. (1992). Chronic dieting and eating disorders; a spiral model. In J. H. Crowther, S. E. Hobfoll, M. A. P. Stephens, & D. L. Tennenbaum (Eds.), *The etiology of bulimia: The individual and familial context.* Washington: Hemisphere Publishers.*

Hebb, D. O. (1949/1961). *The organization of behavior: A neuropsychological theory.* New York: Wiley.*

Hebb, D. O. (1980). *Essay on mind.* Mahwah, NJ: Erlbaum.*

Hébert, S., & Cuddy, L. L. (2002). Detection of metric structure in auditory figural patterns. *Perception & Psychophysics, 64(6)*, 909–918.*

Hecker, J. E., & Thorpe, G. L. (2005). *Introduction to clinical psychology.* Boston: Allyn & Bacon.

Heeger, D. (2003). *Signal detection theory.* Department of Psychology, New York University. Retrieved on March 7, 2005 from http://www.cns.nyu.edu/~david/sdt/sdt.html.

Heekeren, H. R., Marrett, S., Bandettini, P. A, & Ungerleider, L. G. (2004). A general mechanism for perceptual decision-making in the human brain. *Nature, 431*, 859–861.

Hefferman, D. D., Harper, S. M., & McWilliam, D. (2002). Women's perceptions of the outcome of weight loss diets: A signal detection approach. *International Journal of Eating Disorders, 31*, 339–343.

Hege, A. C. G., & Dodson, C. S. (2004). Why distinctive information reduces false memories: Evidence for both impoverished relational-encoding and distinctiveness heuristic accounts. *Journal of Experimental Psychology: Learning, Memory, & Cognition, 30(4)*, 787–795.

Heider, F. (1958). Attitudes and cognitive organization. *Journal of Psychology, 21*, 107–122.

Heikkinen, M., Aro, H., & Loennqvist, J. (1992). Recent life events and their role in suicide as seen by the spouses. *Acta Psychiatrica Scandinavica, 86*, 489–494.

Heim, C., & Nemeroff, C. B. (2002). Neurobiology of early life stress: Clinical studies. *Seminars in Clinical Psychiatry, 7*, 147–159.

Heiman, J. R. (2002). Sexual dysfunction: Overview of prevalence, etiological factors, and treatments. *Journal of Sex Research. Special Promoting Sexual Health And Responsible Sexual Behavior, 39(1)*, 73–78.

Heimberg, R. G., Turk, C. L., & Mennin, D. S. (Eds.). (2004). *Generalized anxiety disorder: Advances in research and practice.* New York: Guilford.

Heimpel, S. A., Wood, J. V., Marshall, M. A., & Brown, J. D. (2002). Do people with low self-esteem really want to feel better? Self-esteem differences in motivation to repair negative moods. *Journal of Personality & Social Psychology, 82*, 128–147.*

Heinrichs, R. W. (2001). *In search of madness.* New York: Oxford.*

Heinrichs, R. W. (2005). The primacy of cognition in schizophrenia. *American Psychologist, 60(3)*, 229–242.*

Heinrichs, R. W., & Zakzanis, K. K. (1998). Neurocognitive deficit in schizophrenia: A quantitative review of the evidence. *Neuropsychology, 12*, 426–445.*

Helgeson, V. S. (2005). *The psychology of gender (2nd ed.).* Englewood Cliffs, NJ: Prentice Hall.

Heller, W., Nitschke, J. B., Etienne, M. A., & Miller, G. A. (1997). Patterns of regional activity differentiates types of anxiety. *Journal of Abnormal Psychology, 106*, 376–385.

Helmholtz, H. von. (1852). On the theory of compound colors. *Philosophical Magazine, 4*, 519–534.

Hemphill, J. F., Hare, R. D., & Wong, S. (1998). Psychopathy and recidivism: A review. *Legal and Criminological Psychology, 3*, 139–170.*

Henderson, C., Smith, C., Smith, S. & Stevens, A. (Eds.), (2005). *Women & psychiatric treatment.* London: Routledge.

Henderson, V. L., & Dweck, C. S. (1990). Motivation and achievement. In S. S. Feldman, & G. R. Elliott (Eds.). *At the threshold: The developing adolescent.* Cambridge Harvard University Press.

Hendin, H. (1995). *Suicide in America.* New York: Norton.

Heppner, P., & Lee, D. (2001). Problem-solving appraisal and psychological adjustment. In C. R. Snyder, & S. J. Lopez (Eds.), *Handbook of positive psychology.* New York: Oxford.

Herberman, R. B. (2002). Stress, natural killer cells, and cancer. In H. G. Koenig, & H. J. Cohen (Eds.), *The link between religion and health.* New York: Oxford.

Hergenhahn, B. R. (2001). *An introduction to the history of psychology (4th ed.).* Belmont, CA: Wadsworth.

Hergenhahn, B. R., & Olson, M. H. (2001). *An introduction to theories of learning (6th ed.).* Upper Saddle River, NJ: Prentice Hall.

Herman, C. P., & Polivy, J. (2004). The self-regulation of eating: Theoretical and practical problems. In T. F. Baumeister, & K. D. Vohs (Eds.), *Handbook of self-regulation: Research, theory, and applications.* New York: Guilford.*

Herman, C. P., Roth, D. A., & Polivy, J. (2003). Effects of the presence of others on food intake: A normative interpretation. *Psychological Bulletin, 129(6),* 873–886.*

Herold, E. S., Maticka-Tyndale, E., & Mewhinney, D. (1998). Predicting intentions to engage in casual sex. *Journal of Social & Personal Relationships, 15,* 502–516.*

Herring, D. A., & Young, T. K. (2002). *Aboriginal health in Canada.* Toronto: University of Toronto Press.*

Herrnstein, R. J., & Murray, C. (1994). *The Bell Curve: Intelligence and class structure in American life.* New York: Macmillan.

Hertzman, C., Goelman, H. & Kershaw, P. (2005). *What does the research say about the QUAD child care principles?* Vancouver, BC: Human Early Learning Partnership, University of British Columbia. Retrieved April 7, 2005 from http://www.earlylearning.ubc.ca/documents/HELPs_QUAD_Research_Summary.pdf.*

Hertzsprung, M. E. A., & Dobson, K. S. (2000). Diversity training: Conceptual issues and practices for Canadian clinical psychology programs. *Canadian Psychology, 41(3),* 184–191.*

Hervé, H. F., Hayes, P. J., & Hare, R. D. (2003). Psychopathy and sensitivity to the emotional polarity of metaphorical statements. *Personality & Individual Differences, 35(7),* 1497–1507.*

Herxheimer, A., & Waterhouse, J. (2003). The prevention and treatment of jet lag. *British Medical Journal, 326(7384),* 296–297.

Herzberg, E. (2000). Use of TAT in multicultural societies: Brazil and the United States. In R. H. Dana (Ed.), *Handbook of cross-cultural and multicultural personality assessment.* Mahwah, NJ: Erlbaum.

Herzog, H. A. (1995). Discussing animal rights and animal research in the classroom. In M. E. Ware, & D. E. Johnson (Eds.), *Demonstrations and activities in teaching of psychology (Vol. 1).* Mahwah, NJ: Erlbaum.

Hetherington, E. M., & Kelly, S. (2002). *For better or for worse: Divorce reconsidered.* New York: Norton.

Hetherington, E. M., Parke, R. D., & Schmuckler, M. A. (2005). *Child psychology: A contemporary viewpoint (2nd Canadian ed.).* Toronto: McGraw-Hill.*

Hetherington, E. M., & Stanley-Hagan, M. (2002). Parenting in divorced and remarried families. In M. Bornstein (Ed.), *Handbook of parenting (2nd ed.).* Mahwah, NJ: Erlbaum.

Hevern, V. W. (2004). Threaded identity in cyberspace: Weblogs and positioning in the dialogical self. *Identity: An International Journal of Theory and Research, 4(4),* 321–335.

Hewstone, M., Rubin, M., & Willis, H. (2002). Intergroup bias. *Annual Review of Psychology, 53,* 575–604.

Heyes, C. M., & Galef, Jr., B. G. (Eds.) (1996). *Social learning in animals: The roots of culture.* San Diego: Academic Press.*

Hidalgo, R. B., & Davidson, J. R. (2001). Generalized anxiety disorder: An important clinical concern. *Medical Clinics of North America, 85,* 691–710.

Higgins, N. C., & Hay, J. (2003). Attributional style predicts causes of negative life events on the Attributional Style Questionnaire. *Journal of Social Psychology, 143(2),* 253–271.*

Higgins, N. C., & Shaw, J. K. (1999). Attributional style moderates the impact of causal controllability information on helping behaviour. *Social Behavior and Personality, 27(3),* 221–236.*

Hilgard, E. R. (1965). *Hypnotic suggestibility.* Ft. Worth, TX: Harcourt Brace.

Hilgard, E. R. (1986). *Divided consciousness: Multiple controls in human thought and action.* New York: Wiley.

Hilgard, E. R. (1992). Dissociation and theories of hypnosis. In E. Fromm, & M. R. Nash (Eds.), *Contemporary hypnosis research.* New York: Guilford.

Hiller, J. (2004). Speculations on the links between feelings, emotions and sexual behaviour: Are vasopressin and oxytocin involved? *Sexual & Relationship Therapy, 19(4),* 393–429.

Hilsenroth, M. J. (2000). Rorschach test. In A. Kazdin (Ed.), *Encyclopedia of psychology.* Washington, & New York: APA Press and Oxford.

Hines, M. (1982). Prenatal gonadal differences in human behavior. *Psychological Bulletin, 92,* 56–80.

Hines, M. (2004). Androgen, estrogen, and gender: Contributions of the early hormone environment to gender-related behavior. In A. H. Eagly, A. E. Beall, & R. J. Sternberg (Eds.), *The psychology of gender (2nd ed.).* New York: Guilford.

Hinkel, E. (Ed.). (2005). *Handbook of research in second language teaching and learning.* Mahwah, NJ: Erlbaum.

Hirstein, W., Kolak, D., Mandik, P., & Waskan, J. (2006). *Cognitive science.* Philadelphia: Taylor & Francis.

Hobfoll, S. E. (2002). Social and psychological resources and adaptation. *Review of General Psychology, 6(4),* 307–324.

Hobson, J. A. (2000). Dreams: Physiology. In A. Kazdin (Ed.), *Encyclopedia of psychology.* Washington, & New York: APA Press and Oxford.

Hobson, J. A. (2001). *Consciousness.* New York: Freeman.

Hobson, J. A., & McCarley, R. W. (1977). The brain as a dream state generator: An activation-synthesis hypothesis of the dream process. *American Journal of Psychiatry, 134(12),* 1335–1348.

Hobson, J. A., Pace-Schott, E. F., & Stickgold, R. (2000). Dreaming and the brain. *Behavior and Brain Sciences, 23,* 793–842.

Hodges, J. R. (2000). Memory in the dementias. In E. Tulving, & F. I. M. Craik (Eds.), *Oxford handbook of memory.* New York: Oxford.

Hodson, G., & Esses, V. M. (2002). Distancing oneself from negative attributes and the personal/group discrimination discrepancy. *Journal of Experimental Social Psychology, 38(5),* 500–507.*

Hoff, E., & Tian, C. (2005). Socioeconomic status and cultural influences on language. *Journal of Communication Disorders, 38(4),* 271–278.

Hoffart, A., & Sexton, H. (2002). The role of optimism in the process of schema-focused cognitive therapy of personality problems. *Behaviour Research & Therapy, 40(6),* 611–623.

Hoffer, A., & Youngren, V. R. (2004). Is free association still at the core of psychoanalysis? *International Journal of Psychoanalysis, 85(6),* 1489–1492.

Hoffman, H. G. (2004). Virtual-reality therapy. *Scientific American, 291(2),* 58–65. Hoffman, H. G., Garcia-Palacios, A., Carlin, C., Furness, T. A., III, & Botella-Arbona, C. (2003). Interfaces that heal: Coupling real and virtual objects to cure spider phobia. *International Journal of Human-Computer Interaction, 16,* 283–300.

Hogan, B. E., Linden, W., & Najarian, B. (2002). Social support interventions: Do they work? *Clinical Psychology Review, 22,* 381–440.*

Hogan, E. H., Hornick, B. A., & Bouchoux, A. (2002). Focus on communications: Communicating the message: Clarifying the controversies about caffeine. *Nutrition Today, 37,* 28–35.

Hogan, J. (1986). *Hogan Personality Inventory manual.* Minneapolis: National Computer Systems.

Hogarth, L. A., Roberts, W. A., & Roberts, S., & Abroms, B. (2000). Spatial localization of a goal: Beacon and landmark piloting by rats on a radial maze. *Animal Learning & Behavior, 28,* 43–58.*

Holaday, M., Smith, D. A., & Sherry, A. (2000). Sentence completion tests: A review of the literature and results of a survey of members of the Society for Personality Assessment. *Journal of Personality Assessment, 74,* 371–383.

Holden, R. R. (1995). Response latency detection of fakers on personnel tests. *Canadian Journal of Behavioural Science, 27,* 343–355.*

Holden, R. R., & Hibbs, N. (1995). Incremental validity of response latencies for detecting fakers on a personality test. *Journal of Research in Personality, 29,* 362–372.*

Holden, R. R., & Kroner, D. G. (1992). Relative efficacy of differential response latencies for detecting faking on a self-report measure of psychopathology.

Psychological Assessment: A Journal of Consulting and Clinical Psychology, 4, 170–173.*

Holmes, D. S. (1988). The influence of meditation versus rest on physiological considerations. In M. West (Ed.), *The psychology of meditation.* New York: Oxford.

Holmes, S. E., Slaughter, J. R., & Kashani, J. (2001). Risk factors in childhood that lead to the development of conduct disorder and antisocial personality disorder. *Child Psychiatry and Human Development, 31,* 183–193.

Holmes, T. H., & Rahe, R. H. (1967). The social readjustment rating scale. *Journal of Psychosomatic Research, 11,* 213–218.

Holtzmann, W. (1982). Cross-cultural comparisons of personality development in Mexico and the United States. In D. Wagner, & H. W. Stevenson (Eds.), *Cultural perspectives on child development.* San Francisco: Jossey-Bass.

Hong, W., Thong, J. Y. L., & Tam, K. Y. (2004). Designing product listing pages on e-commerce websites: An examination of presentation mode and information format. *International Journal of Human-Computer Studies, 61(4),* 481–503.

Honts, C. (1998, June). *Commentary.* APA Monitor, p. 30.

Hood, A. S., & Morrison, J. D. (2002). The dependence of binocular contrast sensitivities on binocular single vision in normal and amblyopic human subjects. *Journal of Physiology, 540,* 607–622.

Hood, D. C., Frishman, L. J., Saszik, S., & Viswanathan, S. (2002). Retinal origins of the primate multifocal ERG: Implications for the human response. *Investigative Ophthalmology and Visual Science, 43,* 1673–1685.

Hooper, J., & Teresi, D. (1993). *The 3-pound universe.* New York: Tarcher/Putnam.

Horn, J. L., & Donaldson, G. (1980). Cognitive development II: Adulthood development of human abilities. In O. G. Brim, & J. Kagan (Eds.), *Constancy and change in human development.* Cambridge: Harvard University Press.

Horney, K. (1945). *Our inner conflicts.* New York: Norton.

Horst, J. S., Oakes, L. M., & Madole, K. L. (2005). What does it look like and what can it do? Category structure influences how infants categorize. *Child Development, 76(3),* 614–631.

Horton, D. M. (2001). The disappearing bell curve. *Journal of Secondary Gifted Education, 12,* 185–188.

Hough, L. M., & Furnham, A. (2003). Use of personality variables in work settings. In W. C. Borman, D. R. Ilgen & R. J. Klimoski (Eds), *Handbook of psychology: Industrial and organizational psychology (Vol. 12).* New York: Wiley.

Houghton, G. (Ed.) (2005). *Connectionist models in cognitive psychology.* Philadelphia: Taylor & Francis.

Howard, I. P., & Rogers, B. J. (1995). *Binocular vision and stereopsis.* New York: Oxford.*

Howard, I. P., & Rogers, B. J. (2001a) *Seeing in depth (Vol. I). Basic mechanisms.* Toronto: Porteous Publishing.*

Howard, I. P., & Rogers, B. J. (2001b) *Seeing in depth (Vol. II). Basic mechanisms.* Toronto: Porteous Publishing.*

Howard, K. I., Moras, K., Brill, P. L., Martinovich, Z., & Lutz, W. (1996). Evaluation of psychotherapy: Efficacy, effectiveness, and patient progress. *American Psychologist, 51,* 1059–1064.

Howard, R. W. (2001). Searching the real world for signs of rising population intelligence. *Personality and Individual Differences, 30,* 1039–1058.

Howe, E. R. (2004). Canadian and Japanese teachers' conceptions of critical thinking: A comparative study. *Teachers & Teaching: Theory & Practice, 10(5),* 505–525.*

Howell, A. J., Jahrig, J. C., & Powell, R. A. (2004). Sleep quality, sleep propensity and academic performance. *Perceptual & Motor Skills, 99(2),* 525–535.*

Howell, D. (2004). *Fundamental statistics for the behavioral sciences, (5th ed.).* Boston: Thomson.

Howley, E. T. (2001). Type of activity: Resistance, aerobic and leisure versus occupational physical activity. *Medical Science and Sports Exercise, 33 (Suppl.),* S364–369.

Hoyer, W. J., Rybash, J. M., & Roodin, P. A. (2004). *Adult development and aging (5th ed.).* New York: McGraw-Hill.

Hróbjartsson, A., & Gotzsche, P. (2001). Is the placebo powerless? An analysis of clinical trials comparing placebo with no treatment. *New England Journal of Medicine, 344,* 1594–1602.

Hsu, P., Yu, F., Feron, F., Pickles, J. O., Sneesby, K., & Mackay-Sim, A. (2001). Basic fibroblast growth factor and fibroblast growth factor receptors in adult olfactory epithelium. *Brain Research, 896,* 188–197.

Hu, M. T., Taylor-Robinson, S. D., Chaudhuri, K. R., Bell, J. D., Labbe, C., Cunningham, V. J., et al. (2000). Cortical dysfunction in non-demented Parkinson's disease patients: A combined (31)P-MRS and (18)FDG-PET study. *Brain, 123,* 340–352.

Huang, L., & Pashler, H. (2005). Attention capacity and task difficulty in visual search. *Cognition, 94(3),* B101–B111.

Hubel, D. H., & Wiesel, T. N. (1965). Receptive fields and functional architecture in two nonstriate areas (18 and 19) of the cat. *Journal of Neurophysiology, 28,* 229–289.*

Hublin, C., Kaprio, J., Partinen, M., & Koskenvu, M. (2001). Parasomnias: Co-occurrence and genetics. *Psychiatric Genetics, 11,* 65–70.

Huffcutt, A. I., Conway, J. M., Roth, P. L., & Stone, N. J. (2001). Identification and meta-analytic assessment of psychological constructs measured in employment interviews. *Journal of Applied Psychology, 86,* 897–913.

Hunsley, J., & Bailey, J. M. (1999). The clinical utility of the Rorschach: Unfulfilled promises and an uncertain future. *Psychological Assessment, 11(3),* 266–277.*

Hunsley, J., Lee, C. M., & Wood, J. M. (2003). Controversial and questionable assessment techniques. In S. O. Lilienfeld, S. J. Lynn, & J. M. Lohr (Eds.), *Science and pseudoscience in clinical psychology.* New York: Guilford.*

Hunt, E. (2002). *Précis of thoughts on thought.* Mahwah, NJ: Erlbaum.

Hunt, E. B. (1995). *Will we be smart enough? A cognitive analysis of the coming workforce.* New York: Russell Sage Foundation.

Hunt, H. T. (1995). *On the nature of consciousness: Cognitive, phenomenological, and transpersonal perspectives.* New Haven, CT: Yale University Press.*

Hunt, M. (1974). *Sexual behavior in the 1970s.* Chicago: Playboy.

Hunt, M. (1993). *The story of psychology.* New York: Anchor Books.

Hunter, J. P., Katz, J., & Davis, K. D. (2003). The effect of tactile and visual sensory inputs on phantom limb awareness. *Brain, 126(3),* 579–589.

Hurley, S. R., & Tinajero, J. V. (2001). *Literacy assessment of second-language learners.* Boston: Allyn & Bacon.

Huttenlocher, J., Haight, W., Bruk, A., Selzer, M., & Lyons, T. (1991). Early vocabulary growth: Relation to language input and gender. *Developmental Psychology, 27,* 236–248.

Huttenlocher, J., Vasilyeva, M., Cymerman, E., & Levine, S. (2002). Language input and child syntax. *Cognitive Psychology, 45(3),* 337–374.

Huttenlocher, P. R., & Dabholkar, A. S. (1997). Regional differences in synaptogenesis in human cerebral cortex. *Journal of Comparative Neurology, 37(2),* 167–178.

Hyde, J. S. (2004). *Half the human experience: The psychology of women (6th ed.).* Boston: Houghton Mifflin.

Hyde, J. S., & DeLamater, J. D. (2006). *Understanding human sexuality (9th ed.).* New York: McGraw-Hill.

Hyde, J. S. (2005). The gender similarities hypothesis. *American Psychologist, 60(6),* 581–592.

Hyde, J. S., & Mezulis, A. H. (2002). Gender difference research: Issues and critique. In J. Worell (Ed.), *Encyclopedia of women and gender.* San Diego: Academic Press.

Hynie, M. (1998). The AIDS/ HIV pandemic. In F. Aboud (Ed.), *Health psychology in global perspective.* Beverly Hills, CA: Sage.*

I

Idson, L. C., & Mischel, W. (2001). The personality of familiar and significant people: The lay perceiver and the social-cognitive theorist. *Journal of Personality & Social Psychology, 80,* 585–596.

Ilgen, D. R. (2000). Industrial and organizational psychology. In A. Kazdin (Ed.), *Encyclopedia of psychology.* Washington, & New York: APA Press and Oxford.

Ilgen, D. R. (2001). Industrial psychology. In W. E. Craighead & C. B. Nemeroff (Eds.), *The Corsini encyclopedia of psychology and behavioral science (3rd ed.).* New York: Wiley.

Impara, J. C., & Plake, B. S. (Eds.) (2001). *The fourteenth mental measurements yearbook.* Lincoln, NE: University of Nebraska Press.

Insel, T. R., & Fernald, F. D. (2004). How the brain processes social information: Searching for the social brain. *Annual Review of Neuroscience, 27,* 697–722.

Intrator, J., Hare, R., Strizke, P., Brichtswein, K., Dorfman, D., Harpur, T., et al. (1997). Brain imaging (SPECT) study of semantic and affective processing in psychopaths. *Biological Psychiatry, 42,* 96–103.*

Irwin, C. E. (2004). Emergency contraception for adolescents: The time to act is now. *Journal of Adolescent Health, 35(4),* 257–258.

Irwin, M. (2002). Psychoneuroimmunology of depression: Clinical implications. *Brain, Behavior, and Immunity, 16,* 1–16.

Irwin, M. (2005). Images in psychoneuroimmunology: Norman Cousins. *Brain, Behavior & Immunity, 19,* 268–269.

Isotani, T., Tanaka, H., Lehmann, D., Pascual-Marqui, R. D., Kochi, K., Saito, N., et al. (2001). Source localization of EEG activity during hypnotically induced anxiety and relaxation. *International Journal of Psychophysiology, 41,* 143–153.

Israelashvili, M. & Wegman-Rozi, O. (2003). Advancement of preschoolers' resilience: The A.R.Y.A. project. *Early Childhood Education Journal, 31(2),* 101–105.

Ivanco, T. L., & Racine, R. J. (2000). Long-term potentiation in the pathways between the hippocampus and neocortex in the chronically implanted, freely moving, rat. *Hippocampus, 10,* 143–152.*

Iverson, G. L., & Barton, E. (1999). Interscorer reliability of the MMPI-2: Should TRIN and VRIN be computer scored? *Journal of Clinical Psychology, 55,* 65–70.*

J

Jackowski, A. P., & Schultz, R. T. (2005). Foreshortened dorsal extension of the central sulcus in Williams syndrome. *Cortex. Special: The Neurobiology of Developmental Disorders, 41(3),* 282–290.

Jackson, D. N. (1991). Computer-assisted personality test interpretation: The dawn of discovery. In T. B. Gutkin & S. L. Wise (Eds.), *The computer and the decision-making process. Buros-Nebraska Symposium on Measurement & Testing, (Vol 4).* Mahwah, NJ: Erlbaum.*

Jackson, L. C., & Greene, B. (2000). *Psychotherapy with African-American women.* New York: Guilford.

Jackson, L. M., & Esses, V. M. (2000). Effects of perceived economic competition on people's willingness to help empower immigrants. *Group Processes & Intergroup Relations, 3,* 419–435.*

Jacobs, M. (2003). *Sigmund Freud.* Thousand Oaks, CA: Sage.

Jacoby, L. L. (1998). Invariance in automatic influences of memory: Toward a user's guide for the process-dissociation procedure. *Journal of Experimental Psychology: Learning, Memory, and Cognition, 24,* 3–26.*

Jafari, M.-R., Zarrindast, M.-R., & Djahanguiri, B. (2004). Effects of different doses of glucose and insulin on morphine state-dependent memory of passive avoidance in mice. *Psychopharmacology, 175(4),* 457–462.

Jäger, B., Liedtke, R., Lamprecht, F., & Freyberger, H. (2004). Social and health adjustment of bulimic women 7–9 years following therapy. *Acta Psychiatrica Scandinavica, 110(2),* 138–145.

Jakel, R. J., & Marangos, W. F. (2000). Neuronal cell death in Huntington's disease: A potential role for dopamine. *Trends in Neuroscience, 23,* 239–245.

Jamal, M. (2005). Short communication: Personal and organizational outcomes related to job stress and Type-A behavior: A study of Canadian and Chinese employees. *Stress & Health: Journal of the International Society for the Investigation of Stress, 21(2),* 129–137.

James, R. K., & Gilliland, B. E. (2003). *Theories and strategies in counseling and psychotherapy (5th ed.).* Boston: Allyn & Bacon.

James, T. W., Culham, J., Humphrey, G. K., Milner, A. D., & Goodale, M. A. (2003). Ventral occipital lesions impair object recognition but not object-directed grasping: An fMRI study. *Brain, 126(11),* 2463–2475.*

James, W. (1890/1950). *Principles of psychology.* New York: Dover.

Jameson, D., & Hurvich, L. M. (1989). Essay concerning color constancy. *Annual Review of Psychology, 40,* 1–22.

Jamieson, G. A., & Sheehan, P. W. (2004). An empirical test of Woody and Bowers's dissociated-control theory of hypnosis. *International Journal of Clinical & Experimental Hypnosis, 52(3),* 232–249.

Jamurtas, A. Z., Goldfarb, A. H., Chung, S. C., Hegde, S., & Marino, C. (2000). Beta-endorphin infusion during exercise in rats. *Medical Science and Sports Exercise, 32,* 1570–1575.

Janicki, M., & Krebs, D. L. (1998). Evolutionary approaches to culture. In C. Crawford & D. L. Krebs (Eds.), *Handbook of evolutionary psychology: Ideas, issues, and applications.* Mahwah, NJ: Erlbaum.*

Janis, I. (1972). *Victims of groupthink: A psychological study of foreign-policy decisions and fiascos.* Boston: Houghton Mifflin.

Jansen, A., Theunissen, N., Slechten, K., Nederkoorn, C., Boon, B., Mulkens, S., & Roefs, A. (2003). Overweight children overeat after exposure to food cues. *Eating Behaviors, 4(2),* 197–209.

Jarrett, R. B., Kraft, D., Doyle, J., Foster, B. M., Eaves, G. G., & Silver, P. C. (2001). Preventing recurrent depression using cognitive therapy with and without a continuation phase: A randomized clinical trial. *Archives of General Psychiatry, 58,* 381–388.

Jarvin, L., & Sternberg, R. J. (2003). Alfred Binet's contributions to educational psychology. In B. J. Zimmerman, & D. H. Schunk (Eds.), *Educational psychology: A century of contributions.* Mahwah, NJ: Erlbaum.

Jausovec, N., & Jausovec, K. (2000). Correlations between ERP parameters and intelligence: A reconsideration. *Biological Psychology, 55,* 137–154.

Jausovec, N., & Jausovec, K. (2001). Differences in EEG current density related to intelligence. *Brain Research: Cognitive Brain Research, 12,* 55–60.

Jay, T. B. (2003). *Psychology of language.* Upper Saddle River, NJ: Prentice Hall.

Jenike, M. A. (2001). An update on obsessive-compulsive disorder. *Bulletin of the Menninger Clinic, 65,* 4–25.

Jenkins, J. H., & Barrett, R. J. (Eds.). (2003). *Schizophrenia, culture and subjectivity. The edge of experience.* Cambridge: Cambridge University Press.

Jenkins, S. (2002). Race and human diversity. In M. Hersen, & W. H. Sledge (Eds.), *Encyclopedia of psychotherapy.* San Diego: Academic Press.

Jennings, L., & Skovholt, T. M. (1999). The cognitive, emotional, and relational characteristics of master therapists. *Journal of Counseling Psychology, 46,* 3–11.

Jensen, A. R. (1969). How much can we boost IQ and scholastic achievement? *Harvard Educational Review, 39,* 1–123.

Jensen, S. M., Barabasz, A., Barabasz, M., & Warner, D. (2001). EEG P300 event-related markers of hypnosis. *American Journal of Clinical Hypnosis, 44,* 127–139.

Jeong, J., Kim, D. J., Kim, S. Y., Chae, J. H., Go, H. J., & Kim, K. S. (2001). Effect of total sleep deprivation on the dimensional complexity of the waking EEG. *Sleep, 15,* 197–202.

Jernigan, T. L., Ostergaard, A. L., & Fennema-Notestine, C. (2001). Mesial temporal, diencephalic, and striatal contributions to single word reading, word priming, and recognition memory. *Journal of the International Neuropsychological Society, 7,* 67–78.

Johnson, D. D. P. (2004). *Overconfidence and war: The havoc and glory of positive illusions.* Cambridge Harvard University Press.

Johnson, D. W., & Johnson, F. P. (2003). *Joining together: Group theory and group skills. (8th ed.).* Boston: Allyn & Bacon.

Johnson, G. B. (2003). *The living world (3rd ed.).* New York: McGraw-Hill.

Johnson, M. H. (2000). Infancy: Biological processes. In A. Kazdin (Ed.), *Encyclopedia of psychology.* Washington, & New York: APA Press and Oxford.

Johnson, M. H. (2002). Functional brain development during infancy. In G. Bremmer & A. Fogel (Eds.), *Blackwell handbook of infant development.* Malden, MA: Blackwell.

Johnson, S. (2005). *Everything bad is good for you: How today's popular culture is actually making us smarter.* New York: Riverhead.

Johnson-Laird, P. N. (2000). Thinking: Reasoning. In A. Kazdin (Ed.), *Encyclopedia of psychology.* Washington, & New York: APA Press and Oxford.

Johnston, L. (2002). Behavioral mimicry and stigmatization. *Social Cognition, 20(1),* Feb 2002, 18–35.

Johnston, L. D., Bachman, J. G., & O'Malley, P. M. (1989, February 24). *Teenage drug use continues decline* [News release]. Ann Arbor: University of Michigan, Institute for Social Research.

Joiner, Jr., T. E., Steer, R. A., Abramson, L. Y., Mealsky, G. I., & Schmidt, N. B. (2001). Hopelessness depression as a distinct dimension of depressive symptoms among clinical and non-clinical samples. *Behavior Research and Therapy, 39,* 523–536.

Jones, A., & Crandall, R. (1986). Validation of a short index of self-actualization. *Personality and Social Psychology Bulletin, 12,* 63–73.

Jones, B. T. (2003). Alcohol consumption on the campus. *Psychologist, 16(10),* 523–525.

Jones, E. & Wessely, S. (2005). *Shell shock to PTSD : Military psychiatry from 1900 to the Gulf War.* New York: Routledge.

Jones, J. M., Bennett, S., Olmsted, M. P., Lawson, M. L., & Rodin, G. (2001). Disordered eating attitudes and behaviours in teenaged girls: a school-based study. *Canadian Medical Association Journal, 165,* 547–52.*

Jones, M. (2002). *Social psychology of prejudice.* Upper Saddle River, NJ: Prentice Hall.

Jones, M. C. (1924). A laboratory study of fear: The case of Peter. *Journal of Genetic Psychology, 31,* 308–315.

Jones, R., Kemenes, G., & Benjamin, P. R. (2001). Selective expression of electrical correlates of differential appetitive classical conditioning in a feedback network. *Journal of Neurophysiology, 85,* 89–97.

Jones, R. K., Purcell, A., Singh, S., & Finer, L. B. (2005). Adolescents' reports of parental knowledge of adolescents' use of sexual health services and their reactions to mandated parental notification for prescription contraception. *Journal of the American Medical Association, 293(3),* 340–348.

Jones, R. N. (2003). Racial bias in the assessment of cognitive functioning of older adults. *Aging & Mental Health, 7(2),* 83–102.

Jonides, J., Lacey, S. C. & Nee, D. E. (2005). Processes of working memory in mind and brain. *Current Directions in Psychological Science, 14(1),* 2–5.

Jordan, C. H., Spencer, S. J., & Zanna, M. P. (2005). Types of high self-esteem and prejudice: How implicit self-esteem relates to racial discrimination among high explicit self-esteem individuals. *Personality & Social Psychology Bulletin, 31(5),* 693–702.*

Judge, T. A., & Bono, J. E. (2001). Relationship of core self-evaluation traits—self-esteem, generalized self-efficacy, locus of control, and emotional stability—with job satisfaction and job performance: A meta-analysis. *Journal of Applied Psychology, 86,* 80–92.

Julien, R. M. (2005). *A primer of drug action: A comprehensive guide to the actions, uses, and side effects (10th ed.).* New York: Worth.

Jung, C. (1917). *Analytic psychology.* New York: Moffat, Yard.

Jusczyk, P. W., & Hohne, E. A. (1997). Infants' memory for spoken words. *Science, 277,* 1984–1986.

Jussim, L., Ashmore, R., & Wilder, D. (2001). Introduction: Social identity and intergroup conflict. In R. D. Ashmore, L. Jussim, & D. Wilder (Eds.), *Social identity, intergroup conflict, and conflict resolution.* New York: OxfordKagan, J. (1992). Yesterday's premises, tomorrow's promises. *Developmental Psychology, 28,* 990–997.

K

Kagan, J. (1998). Biology and the child. In W. Damon (Ed.), *Handbook of child psychology (5th ed., Vol. 3).* New York: Wiley.

Kagan, J. (2000). Temperament. In A. Kazdin (Ed.), *Encyclopedia of psychology.* Washington, & New York: APA Press and Oxford.

Kagan, J. (2003). Biology, context, and developmental inquiry. *Annual Review of Psychology, 54,* 1–23.

Kagan, S., & Madsen, M. C. (1972). Experimental analysis of cooperation and competition of Anglo-American and Mexican children. *Developmental Psychology, 6,* 49–59.

Kahn, D., & Hobson, J. A. (2003). Dreaming and hypnosis as altered states of the brain-mind. *Sleep & Hypnosis, 5(2),* 2003, 58–71.

Kahneman, D., & Tversky, A. (1995). Conflict resolution: A cognitive perspective. In K. Arrow, R. H. Mnookin, L. Ross, A. Tversky, & R. Wilson (Eds.), *Barriers to conflict resolution.* New York: Norton.

Kaiser, P. K., & Boynton, R. M. (1996). *Human color vision (2nd ed.).* Washington: Optical Society of America.*

Kalat, J. W. (2004). *Biological psychology (8th ed.).* Belmont, CA: Wadsworth.

Kales, A., Tan, T. L., Kolar, E. J., Naitoh, P., Preston, T. A., & Malmstrom, E. J. (1970). Sleep patterns following 205 hours of sleep deprivation. *Psychosomatic Medicine, 32,* 189–200.

Kalick, S. M., & Hamilton, T. E. (1986). The matching hypothesis reexamined. *Journal of Personality & Social Psychology, 51,* 673–682.

Kallio, S. & Revonsuo, A. (2003). Hypnotic phenomena and altered states of consciousness: A multilevel framework of description and explanation. *Contemporary Hypnosis, 20(3),* 111–164.

Kamin, C. S., O'Sullivan, P. S., Younger, M., & Deterding, R. (2001). Measuring critical thinking in problem-based learning discourse. *Teaching and Learning in Medicine, 13,* 27–35.

Kamin, L. J. (1968). Attention-like processes in classical conditioning. In M. R. Jones (Ed.), *Miami symposium on the prediction of behavior: Aversive stimuli.* Coral Gables, FL: University of Miami Press.*

Kammrath, L. K., Mendoza-Denton, R., & Mischel, W. (2005). Incorporating if...then...personality signatures in person perception: beyond the person-situation dichotomy. *Journal of Personality & Social Psychology, 88(4),* 605–618.

Kampf, M., Babkoff, H., & Nachson, I. (2005). Laterality in familiar face recognition: A meta-analysis. *International Journal of Neuroscience, 115(1),* 23–33.

Kandel, E. R., & Schwartz, J. H. (1982). Molecular biology of learning: Modulation of transmitter release. *Science, 218,* 433–443.

Kandel, E. R., Schwartz, J. H., & Jessell, T. M. (2003). *Principles of neuroscience (5th ed.).* New York: McGraw-Hill.

Kane, M. J., Hambrick, D. Z., & Conway, A. R. (2005). Working memory capacity and fluid intelligence are strongly related constructs: Comment on Ackerman, Beier, and Boyle. *Psychological Bulletin, 131(1),* 66–71.

Kanner, A. M., & Balabanov, A. (2002). Depression and epilepsy: How closely related are they? *Neurology, 58,* S27–S39.

Kantowitz, B. H., Roediger, H. L., & Elmes, D. G. (2005). *Experimental psychology: Understanding psychological research (8th ed.).* Belmont, CA: Wadsworth/Thomson.

Kanwisher, N., & Moscovitch, M. (2000). The cognitive neuropsychology of face processing: An introduction. *Cognitive Neuropsychology, 17,* 1–12.*

Kaplan, R. M., & Kerner, D. N. (1998). Behavioral medicine. In H. S. Friedman (Ed.), *Encyclopedia of mental health (Vol. 1).* San Diego: Academic Press.

Kaplan, R. M., & Saccuzzo, D. P. (2005). *Psychological testing: Principles, applications, and issues (6th ed.).* Belmont, CA: Wadsworth.

Kapur, S., & Lecrubier, Y. (Eds.). (2003). *Dopamine in the pathophysiology and treatment of schizophrenia: New findings.* Washington: Taylor & Francis.

Karacek, R. (1979). Job demands, job decision latitude, and mental strain: Implications for job redesign. *Administrative Science Quarterly, 24,* 285–307.

Karademas, E. C., & Kalantzi-Azizi, A. (2004). The stress process, self-efficacy expectations, and psychological health. *Personality & Individual Differences, 37(5),* 1033–1043.

Karau, S. J., & Williams, K. D. (1993). Social loafing: A meta-analytic review and theoretical integration. *Journal of Personality & Social Psychology, 65,* 681–706.

Kasper, S. & Resinger, E. (2001). Panic disorder: The place of benzodiazepines and selective serotonin reuptake inhibitors. *European Neuropsychopharmacology, 11(4),* 307–321.

Kassin, S. M., Tubb, V. A., Hosch, H. M., & Memon, A. (2001). On the "general acceptance" of eyewitness testimony research. *American Psychologist, 56,* 405–416.

Kataria, S. (2004). A clinical guide to pediatric sleep: Diagnosis and management of sleep problems. *Journal of Developmental & Behavioral Pediatrics, 25(2),* 132–133.

Katz, L.F., & Windecker-Nelson, B. (2004). Parental meta-emotion philosophy in families with conduct-problem children: Links with peer relations. *Journal of Abnormal Child Psychology, 32(4),* 385–398.

Kaufman, A. S., & Lichtenberger, E. O. (2006). *Assessing adolescent and adult intelligence (3rd ed.).* New York: Wiley.

Kaufmann, G. (2003). What to measure? A new look at the concept of creativity. *Scandinavian Journal of Educational Research, 47(3),* 235–251.

Kaufman, J. C., & Baer, J. (2005). *Creativity across domains: Faces of the muse.* Mahwah, NJ: Erlbaum.

Kawachi, I., & Kennedy, B. P. (2001). How income inequality affects health: Evidence from research in the United States. In J. A. Auerbach, & B. K. Krimgold (Eds.), *Income, socioeconomic status, and health.* Washington: National Policy Association.

Kaye, W., Frank, G. K., Bailer, U. F., Henry, S. E., Meltzer, C. C., Price, J. C., et al. (2004). Serotonin alterations in anorexia and bulimia nervosa: New insights from imaging studies. *Physiology & Behavior. Special Proceedings from the 2004 Meeting of the Society for the Study of Ingestive Behavior (SSIB), 85(1),* 73–81.

Kaye, W., Strober, M., & Rhodes, L. (2002). Body image disturbance and other core symptoms in anorexia and bulimia nervosa. In D. J. Castle, & K. A. Phillips (Eds.), *Disorders of body image.* Petersfield, England: Wrightson Biomedical Publishing.

Kazdin, A. E. (2000). *Essentials of conditioning and learning (2nd ed.).* Belmont, CA: Wadsworth.

Kearney, C. A., & Vecchio, J. (2002). Contingency management. In M. Hersen, & W. H. Sledge (Eds.), *Encyclopedia of psychotherapy.* San Diego: Academic Press.

Keck, P. E., McElroy, S. L., & Arnold, I. M. (2001). Bipolar disorder. *Medical Clinics of North America, 85,* 645–661.

Keefe, F. J., Abernethy, A. P., & Campbell, L. C. (2005). Psychological approaches to understanding and treating disease-related pain. *Annual Review of Psychology, 56,* 601–630.

Keenan, T., Olson, D., & Marini, Z. A. (1998). Working memory and children's developing understanding of mind. *Australian Journal of Psychology, 50,* 76–82.*

Keillor, J. M., Barrett, A. M., Crucian, G. P., Kortenkamp, S., & Heilman, K. M. (2002). Emotional experience and perception in the absence of facial feedback. *Journal of the International Neuropsychological Society, 8,* 130–135.

Keller, P. A., Lipkus, I. M., & Rimer, B. K. (2002). Depressive realism and health risk accuracy: The negative consequences of positive mood. *Journal of Consumer Research, 29(1),* 57–69.

Kelley, C. M., & Jacoby, L. L. (1996). Memory attributions: Remembering, knowing and feeling of knowing. In L. M. Reder (Ed.), *Implicit memory and metacognition.* Mahwah, NJ: Erlbaum.*

Kellogg, R. T., Friedman, A., Johnson, P., & Rickard, T. C. (2005). Domain-specific knowledge in intellectual skills: A symposium in honor of Lyle E. Bourne, Jr. In A. F. Healy (Ed.), *Experimental cognitive psychology and its applications.* Washington: APA Press.*

Kelly, W. E. (2004). Sleep-length and life satisfaction in a college student sample. *College Student Journal, 38(3),* 42–430.

Keltner, D., & Ekman, P. (2000). Emotion: An overview. In A. Kazdin (Ed.), *Encyclopedia of psychology.* Washington, & New York: APA Press and Oxford.

Kendall, A. R., Mahue-Giangreco, M., Carpenter, C. L., Ganz, P. A., & Bernstein, L. (2005). Influence of exercise activity on quality of life in long-term breast cancer survivors. *Quality of Life Research: An International Journal of Quality of Life Aspects of Treatment, Care & Rehabilitation, 14(2),* 361–371.

Kendler, K. S., Myers, J., & Prescott, C. A. (2002). The etiology of phobias: An evaluation of the diathesis-stress model. *Archives of General Psychiatry, 59,* 242–248.

Kennaway, D. J., & Wright, H. (2002). Melatonin and circadian rhythms. *Current Topics in Medicinal Chemistry, 2,* 199–209.

Kennedy, P. G. E., & Folk-Seang, J. F. (1986). Studies on the development, antigenic phenotype and function of human glial cells in tissue culture. *Brain, 109,* 1261–1277.

Kenrick, D. T., Neuberg, S. L., & Cialdini, R. B. (2005). *Social psychology: Unraveling the mystery (3rd ed.).* Boston: Allyn and Bacon.

Kensinger E. A., & Corkin, S. (2003). Effects of negative emotional content on working memory and long-term memory. *Emotion, 3,* 378–393.

Kerr, N. L. (2002). When is a minority a minority?: Active versus passive minority advocacy and social influence. *European Journal of Social Psychology, 32(4),* 471–483.

Kershaw, T. S., Ickovics, J. R., Lewis, J. B., Niccolai L. M., Milan, S., and Ethier, K. A. (2004). Sexual risk following a sexually transmitted disease diagnosis: The more things change the more they stay the same. *Journal of Behavioral Medicine, 27(5),* 445–461.

Kesey, K. (1962). *One flew over the cuckoo's nest.* New York: Viking Press.

Kessler, R. C., McGonagle, K. A., Zhao, S., Nelson, C. B, Hughes, M., Eshleman, S., et al. (1994). Lifetime and 12-month prevalence of DSM-III-R psychiatric disorders in the United States: Results from the National Comorbidity Study. *Archives of General Psychiatry, 51,* 8–19.

Kessler, R. C., Olfson, M., & Berglund, P. A. (1998). Patterns and predictors of treatment contact after first onset of psychiatric disorders. *American Journal of Psychiatry, 155,* 62–69.

Kessler, R. C., Stein, M. B., & Berglund, P. (1998). Social phobia subtypes in the National Comorbidity Survey. *American Journal of Psychiatry, 155,* 613–619.

Key, W. B. (1973). *Subliminal seduction: Ad media's manipulation of a not so innocent America.* Englewood Cliffs, NJ: Prentice Hall.*

Key, W. B. (2003). Subliminal sexuality: The fountainhead for America's obsession. In T. Reichert, & J. Lambiase, (Eds.) *Sex in advertising: Perspectives on the erotic appeal.* Mahwah, NJ: Erlbaum.*

Kiecolt-Glaser, J. K., McGuire, L., Robles, T. F., & Glaser, R. (2002a). Psychoneuroimmunology and psychosomatic medicine: Back to the future. *Psychosomatic Medicine, 64,* 15–28.

Kiecolt-Glaser, J. K., McGuire, L., Robles, T. F., & Glaser, R. (2002b). Emotions, morbidity, and mortality: New perspectives from psychoneuroimmunology. *Annual Review of Psychology, 53,* 83–107.

Kiehl, K. A., Smith, A. M., Hare, R. D., Mendrek, A., Forster, B. B., et al. (2001). Limbic abnormalities in affective processing by criminal psychopaths as revealed by functional magnetic resonance imaging. *Biological Psychiatry, 50,* 677–684.*

Kiernan, M., Kraemer, H. C., Winckleby, M. A., King, A. C., & Taylor, C. B. (2001). Do logistic regression and signal detection identify different subgroups at risk? *Psychological Methods, 6,* 35–48.

Kihlstrom, J. F. (1992). Dissociation and dissociations: A comment on consciousness and cognition. *Consciousness & Cognition: An International Journal, 1,* 47–53.

Kikyo, H., Ohki, K., & Sekihara, K. (2001). Temporal characterization of memory retrieval process: An fMRI study of the "tip-of-the-tongue" phenomenon. *European Journal of Neuroscience, 14,* 887–892.

Kilgore, K., Snyder, J. & Lentz, C. (2000). The contribution of parental discipline, parental monitoring, and school risk to early-onset conduct problems in African American boys and girls. *Developmental Psychology, 36(6),* 835–845.

Killen, M., & Smetana, J. G. (Eds.). (2005). *Handbook of moral development.* Mahwah, NJ: Erlbaum.

Kim, J. & Hatfield, E. (2004). Love types and subjective well-being: A cross cultural study. *Social Behavior & Personality, 32(2),* 173–182.

Kimmel, A. (1996). *Ethical issues in behavioral research.* Cambridge Blackwell.

Kimura, D. (1999). *Sex and cognition.* Cambridge Bradford.*

Kinder, A., & Shanks, D. R. (2003). Neuropsychological dissociations between priming and recognition: A single-system connectionist account. *Psychological Review, 110(4),* 728–744.

King, B. E. (2005). *Human sexuality today (5th ed.).* Englewood Cliffs, NJ: Prentice Hall.

King, H. E. (1961). Psychological effects of excitement of the limbic system. In D. E. Sheer (Ed.), *Electrical stimulation of the brain.* Austin: University of Texas Press.

King, R. N., & Koehler, D. J. (2000). Illusory correlations in graphological inference. *Journal of Experimental Psychology: Applied, 6,* 336–348.

Kingdom, F. A. A. (2003). Colour brings relief to human vision. *Nature Neuroscience, 6,* 641–644.*

Kinsey, A. C., Pomeroy, W. B., & Martin, E. E. (1948). *Sexual behavior in the human male.* Philadelphia: W. B. Saunders.

Kircher, J. C., & Raskin, D. C. (2002). Computer methods for the psychophysiological detection of deception. In M. Kleiner, (Ed.), *Handbook of polygraph testing.* San Diego, CA: Academic Press.

Kirmayer, L. J., Boothroyd, L. J., & Hodgins, S. (1998). Attempted suicide among Inuit youth: Psychosocial correlates and implications for prevention. *Canadian Journal of Psychiatry, 43,* 816–822.*

Kirmayer, L. J., Brass, G. M., & Tait, C. L. (2000). The mental health of Aboriginal peoples: Transformations of identity and community. *Canadian Journal of Psychiatry, 45,* 607–616.*

Kirsch, I., Lynn, S. J., Vigorito, M., & Miller, R. R. (2004). The role of cognition in classical and operant conditioning. *Journal of Clinical Psychology, 60(4),* 369–392.

Kirsch, I., & Sapirstein, G. (1998). Listening to Prozac but hearing placebo: A meta-analysis of antidepressant medication. *Prevention and Treatment, 1,* Article 0002a. Retrieved August 1, 2005 from http://www.journals.apa.org/prevention/volume1/pre0010002a.html.

Kirschenbaum, H., & Jourdan, A. (2005). The current status of Carl Rogers and the person-centered approach. *Psychotherapy: Theory, Research, Practice, Training, 42(1),* 37–51.

Kirsh, G. A., & Kuiper, N. A. (2002). Individualism and relatedness themes in the context of depression, gender, and a self-schema model of emotion. *Canadian Psychology, 43(2),* 76–90.*

Kisilevsky, B. S., Hains, S. M. J., Jacquet, A.-Y., Granier-Deferre, C & Lecanuet, J. P., (2004). Maturation of fetal responses to music. *Developmental Science, 7(5),* 550–559.*

Kitayama, S. (2002). Culture and basic psychological processes—Toward a system view of culture: Comment on Oyserman et al. (2002). *Psychological Bulletin, 128,* 89–96.

Kite, M. (2001). Gender stereotypes. In J. Worell (Ed.), *Encyclopedia of women and gender.* San Diego: Academic Press.

Kitzmann, K., & Gaylord, N. K. (2002). Divorce and child custody. In J. Worell (Ed.), *Encyclopedia of women and gender.* New York: Oxford.

Klein, K., & Boals, A. (2001). Expressive writing can increase working memory capacity. *Journal of Experimental Psychology: General, 130,* 520–533.

Kleespies, P. K. (2004). *Life and death decisions: Psychological and ethical considerations in end-of-life care.* Washington: APA Press.

Klein, D. N., & Santiago, N. J. (2003). Dysthymia and chronic depression: Introduction, classification, risk factors, and course. *Journal of Clinical Psychology, 59(8),* 807–816.

Klein, D. W., & Kihlstrom, J. F. (1986). Elaboration, organization, and the self-reference effect in memory. *Journal of Experimental Psychology: General, 115,* 26–38.

Klein, R. M. (2004). On the control of visual orienting. In M. I. Posner (Ed.), *Cognitive neuroscience of attention.* New York: Guilford.

Klein, R. M. (2005). On the role of endogenous orienting in the inhibitory aftermath of exogenous orienting. In U. Mayr, E. Awh & S. W. Keele (Eds.), *Developing individuality in the human brain: A tribute to Michael I. Posner.* Washington: APA Press.* Kline, W. B. (2003). *Interactive group work.* Upper Saddle River, NJ: Prentice Hall.

Klinger, E. (2000). Daydreams. In A. Kazdin (Ed.), *Encyclopedia of psychology.* Washington, & New York: APA Press and Oxford.

Klinger, E., Bouchard, S., Légeron, P., Roy, S., Lauer, F., Chemin, I., & Nugues, P. (2005). Virtual reality therapy versus cognitive behavior therapy for social phobia: A preliminary controlled study. *CyberPsychology & Behavior, 8(1),* 76–88.*

Klug, W. S., & Cummings, M. R. (2003). *Genetics: A molecular perspective.* Upper Saddle River, NJ: Prentice Hall.

Kluznik, J. C., Walbek, N. H., Farnsworth, M. G., & Melstrom, K. (2001). Clinical effects of a randomized switch of patients from clozaril to generic clozapine. *Journal of Clinical Psychiatry, 62,* (Suppl. 5), 14–17.

Koolstra, C. M., Van Zanten, J., Lucassen, N., & Ishaak, N. (2004). The formal pace of Sesame Street over 26 years. *Perceptual & Motor Skills, 99(1),* 354–360.

Knauff, M., Mulack, T., Kassubek, J., Salih, H. R., & Greenlee, M. W. (2002). Spatial imagery in deductive reasoning: A functional MRI study. *Cognitive Brain Research, 13(2),* 203–212.

Knight, J. A. (2000). The biochemistry of aging. *Advances in Clinical Chemistry, 35,* 1–62.

Knox, G. W. (1999). A comparison of cults and gangs: Dimensions of coercive power and malevolent authority. *Journal of Gang Research, 6(4),* 1–39.

Knox, J. M. (2003). *Archetype, attachment, analysis: Jungian psychology and the emergent mind.* Hove, Netherlands: Brunner-Routledge.

Kobasa, S. C., Maddi, S. R., & Kahn, S. (1982). Hardiness and health: A prospective study. *Journal of Personality & Social Psychology, 42,* 168–177.

Kobasa, S. C., Maddi, S. R., Puccetti, M. C., & Zola, M. (1986). Relative effectiveness of hardiness, exercise, and social support as resources against illness. *Journal of Psychosomatic Research, 29,* 525–533.

Koch, C. (2004). *The quest for consciousness: A neurobiological approach.* Englewood, CO: Roberts and Co.

Koenig, C. S., Daly, K. D., Griggs, R. A., Marek, P., & Andrew, N. C., (2004). A compendium of introductory pychology texts. *The Society for the Teaching of Psychology's Office of Teaching Resources in Psychology.* Retrieved September 3, 2005 from http://www.lemoyne.edu/OTRP/introtexts.html.

Koenig, H. G. (2001). Religion and medicine: II. Religion, mental health, and related behaviors. *International Journal of Psychiatry, 31,* 97–109.

Koenig, H. G. (2002). *The link between religion and health: Psychoneuroimmunology and the faith factor.* New York: Oxford.

Koenig, H. G., & Cohen, H. J. (Eds.). (2002). *The link between religion and health.* New York: Oxford.

Kohlberg, L. (1958). *The development of modes of moral thinking and choice in the years 10 to 16.* Unpublished doctoral dissertation, University of Chicago.

Kohlberg, L. (1969). Stage and sequence: The cognitive-developmental approach to socialization. In D. A. Goslin (Ed.), *Handbook of socialization theory and research.* Chicago:Rand McNally.

Kohlberg, L. (1976). Moral stages and moralization: The cognitive-developmental approach. In T. Lickona (Ed.), *Moral development and behavior.* New York: Holt, Rinehart, & Winston.

Kohlberg, L. (1986). A current statement on some theoretical issues. In S. Modgil, & C. Modgil (Eds.), *Lawrence Kohlberg.* Philadelphia: Falmer.

Köhler, W. (1925). *The mentality of apes.* New York: Harcourt Brace Jovanovich.

Kohut, H. (1977). *Restoration of the self.* New York: International Universities Press.

Kolb, B. (1989). Brain development, plasticity, and behavior. *American Psychologist, 44,* 1203–1212.*

Kolb, B. (1990). Recovery from occipital stroke: A self-report and an inquiry into visual processes. *Canadian Journal of Psychology, 44(2),* 130–147.*

Kolb, B., Forgie, M., Gibb, R., Gorny, G., & Rowntree, S. (1998). Age, experience, and the changing brain. *Neuroscience and Biobehavioral Reviews, 22,* 143–159.*

Kolb, B., Gibb, R., & Gorny, G. (2003). Experience-dependent changes in dendritic arbor and spine density in neocortex vary with age and sex. *Neurobiology of Learning and Memory, 79(1),* 1–10.

Kolb, B., Gibb, R., & Robinson, T. E. (2003). Brain plasticity and behavior. *Current Directions in Psychological Science, 14,* 1–5.

Kolb, B., & Whishaw, I. Q. (2003). *Fundamentals of human neuropsychology (5th ed.).* New York: Worth.*

Kolb, B., & Whishaw, I.Q. (2005) *Introduction to brain and behavior (2nd ed.).* New York: Freeman-Worth,

Kolb, B., Forgie, M., Gibb, R., Gorny, G., & Rowntree, S. (1998). Age, experience, and the changing brain. *Neuroscience and Biobehavioral Reviews, 22,* 143–159.*

Kolb, L. (1973). *Modern clinical psychiatry (8th ed.).* Philadelphia: Saunders.

Kolchakian, M. R., & Hill, C. E. (2002). Dream interpretation with heterosexual dating couples. *Dreaming, 12,* 1–16.

Kondziolka, D., Wechsler, L., Goldstein, S., Meltzer, C., Thulborn, K. R., Gebel, J., et al. (2000). Transplantation of cultured human neuronal cells for patients with stroke. *Journal of Neurology, 55,* 565–569.

Kornstein, S. G., & Clayton, A. H. (Eds.). (2002). *Women's mental health.* New York: Guilford.

Korol, C., Craig, K. D., & Firestone, P. (2003). Dissociative and somatoform disorders. In P. Firestone, & W. L. Marshall (Eds.), *Abnormal psychology: Perspectives (2nd ed.).* Toronto: Prentice Hall.*

Kosambi, D. D. (1965). *The culture and civilisation of ancient India in historical outline.* London: Routledge & Kegan Paul.

Koss, M., & Boeschen, L. (1998). Rape. In H. S. Friedman (Ed.), *Encyclopedia of mental health (Vol. 3).* San Diego: Academic Press.

Kosslyn, S. M. (1994). *Image and brain: The resolution of the imagery debate.* Cambridge MIT Press.

Kotani, S., Kawahara, S., & Kirino, Y. (2002). Classical eyeblink conditioning in decerebrate guinea pigs. European *Journal of Neuroscience, 15,* 1267–1270.

Kovas, Y., Hayiou-Thomas, M. E., Oliver, B., Dale, P. S., Bishop, D. V. M., & Plomin, R. (2005). Genetic influences in different aspects of language development: The etiology of language skills in 4.5-year-old twins. *Child Development, 76(3),* 632–651.

Kowalski, T. J. (2004). The future of genetic research on appetitive behavior. *Appetite, 42(1),* 11–14.

Kozma, A., & Stones, M. J. (1980). The measurement of happiness: Development of the Memorial University of Newfoundland Scale of Happiness (MUNSH). *Journal of Gerontology, 35,* 906–912.*

Kozma, A., Stones, M. J., & McNeil, K. V. (1991). *Psychological well-being in later life.* Toronto: Butterworths.*

Kramer, D. A. (2003). The ontogeny of wisdom in its variations. In J. Demick, & C. Andreoletti (Eds.), *Handbook of adult development.* New York: Kluwer.

Kramer, M. S., Cutler, N., Feighner, J., Shrivastava, R., Carman, J., Sramek, J. J., et al. (1998). Distinct mechanism for antidepressant activity by blockade of central substance P receptors. *Science, 281,* 1640–1645.

Krause, J. B., Taylor, J. G., Schmidt, D., Hautzel, H., Mottaghy, F. M., & Muller-Gartner, H. W. (2000). Imaging and neural modelling in episodic and working memory processes. *Neural Networks, 13,* 847–859.

Krauss, J. K., & Jankovic, J. (2002). Head injury and posttraumatic movement disorders. *Neurosurgery, 50,* 927–940.

Kraut, R., Patterson, M., Lundmark, V., Kiesler, S., Mukopadhyay, T., & Scherlis, W. (1998). Internet paradox. *American Psychologist, 53,* 1017–1031.

Krebs, D. L. (1998). The evolution of moral behaviours. In C. Crawford, & D. L. Krebs (Eds.), *Handbook of evolutionary psychology: Ideas, issues and applications.* Mahwah, NJ: Erlbaum.*

Krebs, D. L. & Denton, K. (2005). Toward a more pragmatic approach to morality: A critical evaluation of Kohlberg's model. *Psychological Review, 112(3),* 629–649.*

Kreitler, S. (2005). Alexithymia as an affecto-cognitive personality construct. In S. P. Shohov (Ed.), *Advances in psychology research (Vol. 34).* Hauppauge, NY: Nova Science Publishers.

Kreitler, S. & Kreitler, H. (2004). The motivational and cognitive determinants of defense mechanisms. In U. Hentschel, G. Smith, J. G. Draguns, & W. Ehlers (Eds.), *Defense mechanisms: Theoretical, research and clinical perspectives.* Oxford: Elsevier.

Kreutz, G., Bongard, S., Rohrmann, S., Hodapp, V., & Grebe, D. (2004). Effects of choir singing or listening on secretory immunoglobulin A, cortisol, and emotional state. *Journal of Behavioral Medicine, 27(6),* 623–635.

Krogh, D. (2003). *Biology (2nd ed.).* Upper Saddle River, NJ: Prentice Hall.

Krull, D. S. (2001). On partitioning the fundamental attribution error. In G. B. Moskowitz (Ed.), *Cognitive social psychology.* Mahwah, NJ: Erlbaum.

Kubke, M. F., Massoglia, D. P., & Carr, C. E. (2002). Developmental changes underlying the formation of the specialized time coding circuits in barn owls (Tyto alba). *Journal of Neuroscience, 22(17),* 7671–7679.

Kübler-Ross, E. (1969). *On death and dying.* New York: Macmillan.

Kubzansky, L. D., Wright, R. J., Cohen, S., Rosner, B., Weiss, S., & Sparrow, D. (2002). Breathing easy: A prospective study of optimism and pulmonary function in the Normative Aging Study. *Annals of Behavioral Medicine, 24(4),* 345–353.

Kuch, K., & Cox, B. J. (1992). Symptoms of PTSD in 124 survivors of the Holocaust. *American Journal of Psychiatry, 149,* 337–340.

Kuehner, C. (2003). Gender differences in unipolar depression: an update of epidemiological findings and possible explanations. *Acta Psychiatrica Scandinavica, 108(3),* 163–174.

Kuhl, P. K. (2004). Early language acquisition: Cracking the speech code. *Nature Reviews Neuroscience, 5(11),* 831–841Kuhn, M., Weinstock, M., & Flaton, R. (1994). How well do jurors reason? Competence dimensions of individual variation in a juror reasoning task. *Psychological Science, 5,* 289–296.

Kuiper, N. A., & Martin, R. A. (1998). Laughter and stress in daily life: Relation to positive and negative affect. *Motivation and Emotion, 22(2),* 133–153.*

Kutchinsky, B. (1991). Pornography and rape: Theory and practice? Evidence from crime data in four countries where pornography is easily available. *International Journal of Law and Psychiatry, 14,* 47–64.

Kuterovac-Jagodic, G. (2003). Posttraumatic stress symptoms in Croatian children exposed to war: A prospective study. *Journal of Clinical Psychology, 59(1),* 9–25.

Kwok, S., & Wong, D. (2000). Mental health of parents with young children in Hong Kong: The roles of parenting stress and parenting self-efficacy. *Child & Family Social Work, 5(1),* 57–65.

Kymlicka, W. (1998). *Finding our way: Rethinking ethno-cultural relations in Canada.* New York: Oxford.*

L

La Greca, A., Silverman, W. K., Vernberg, E. M., & Prinstein, M. J. (1996). Symptoms of post-traumatic stress in children after Hurricane Andrew: A prospective study. *Journal of Consulting and Clinical Psychology, 64,* 712–723.

LaBar, K. S., & LeDoux, J. E. (2002). Emotional learning circuits in animals and man. In R. J. Davidson, K. R. Scherer, & H. H. Goldsmith (Eds.), *Handbook of affective sciences.* New York: Oxford.

LaBar, K. S., Gitelman, D. R., Parrish, T. B., & Mesulam, M. M. (2002). Functional changes in temporal lobe activity during transient global amnesia. *Neurology, 58,* 638–641.

Labouvie-Vief, G. (1986, August). *Modes of knowing and life-span cognition.* Paper presented at the meeting of the American Psychological Association, Washington.

Lac, G., & Chamoux, A. (2004). Biological and psychological responses to two rapid shiftwork schedules. *Ergonomics, 47(12),* 1339–1349.

Lacerda, F., von Hofsten, C., & Heimann, M. (Eds.). (2000). *Emerging cognitive abilities in early infancy.* Mahwah, NJ: Erlbaum.

Lachman, M. E. (2004). Development in midlife. *Annual Review of Psychology, 55,* 305–331.

Lachman, M. E., & Firth, K. M. P. (2004). The adaptive value of feeling in control during midlife. In O. G. Brim, C. D. Ryff, & R. Kessler (Eds) *How healthy are we: A national study of wellbeing in midlife.* Chicago: University of Chicago Press.

Lackner, J. R., & DiZio, P. (2005). Vestibular, proprioceptive, and haptic contributions to spatial orientation. *Annual Review of Psychology, 56,* 115–147.

Ladouceur, R. (1996). Prevalence of pathological gamblers in Canada and related issues. *Journal of Gambling Studies, 12,* 129–142.*

Ladouceur, R. (2000). Review of pathological gambling: The making of a medical problem. *New England Journal of Medicine, 343,* 1050–1051.*

Ladouceur, R. (2005). Controlled gambling for pathological gamblers. *Journal of Gambling Studies, 21(1),* 51–59.*

Ladouceur, R., & Dugas, M. J. (2002). Generalized anxiety disorder. In M. Hersen, & L. K. Porzelius (Eds.), *Diagnosis, conceptualization, and treatment planning for adults: A step-by-step guide.* Mahwah, NJ: Erlbaum.*

Ladouceur, R., Boisvert, J.-M., Pépin, M., Loranger, M., & Sylvain, C. (1994). Social costs of pathological gambling. *Journal of Gambling Studies, 10,* 399–409.*

Ladouceur, R., Jacques, C., Giroux, I., Ferland, F., & Leblond, J. (2000). Analysis of a casino's self-exclusion program. *Journal of Gambling Studies, 16,* 453–460.*

Ladouceur, R., & Shaffer, H. J. (2005). Treating problem gamblers: Working towards empirically supported treatment. *Journal of Gambling Studies, 21(1),* 1–4.*

Ladouceur, R., Sylvain, C., Boutin, C., Doucet, C., Leblond J., et al. (2002). *Understanding and treating the pathological gambler.* San Francisco, CA: Jossey-Bass.*

Ladouceur, R., Sylvain, C., Boutin, C., Lachance, S., Doucet, C., et al. (2001). Cognitive treatment of pathological gambling. *Journal of Nervous & Mental Disease, 189,* 774–780.*

Laing, E., Grant, J., Thomas, M., Parmigiani, C., Ewing, S., & Karmiloff-Smith, A. (2005). Love is...an abstract word: The influence of lexical semantics on verbal short-term memory in Williams syndrome. *Cortex, 41(2)*, 169–179.

Laird, R. D., Pettit, G. S., Dodge, K. A., & Bates, J. E. (2003). Change in parents' monitoring knowledge: Links with parenting, relationship quality, adolescent beliefs, and antisocial behavior. *Social Development, 12(3)*, 401–419.

Lalumière, M. L., Blanchard, R., & Zucker, K. J. (2000). Sexual orientation and handedness in men and women: A meta-analysis. *Psychological Bulletin, 126(4)*, 575–592.*

Lalumière, M. L., Harris, G. T., Quinsey, V. L., & Rice, M. E. (2005). *The causes of rape: Understanding individual differences in male propensity for sexual aggression.* Washington: APA Press.*

Lamb, C. S., Jackson, L. A., Cassiday, P. B., & Priest, D. J. (1993). Body figure preferences of men and women: A comparison of two generations. *Sex Roles, 28*, 345–358.

Lambert, K., & Kinsley, C. (2005). *Clinical neuroscience.* New York: Worth.

Lambert, M. J. (2001). The effectiveness of psychotherapy: What a century of research tells us about the effects of treatment. *Psychotherapeutically speaking: Updates from the Division of Psychotherapy (29).* Washington: APA Press.

Lambert, M. J., & Ogles, B. M. (2002). The efficacy and effectiveness of psychotherapy. In M. J. Lambert (Ed.), *Handbook of psychotherapy and behavior change (5th ed.).* New York: Wiley.

Lambert, W. E., & Anisfeld, E. (1969). A note on the relationship of bilingualism and intelligence. *Canadian Journal of Behavioural Science, 1*, 123–128.*

Lambert, W. E., & Tucker, R. (1972). *Bilingual education of children: The St. Lambert study.* Rowley, MA: Newburg House.*

Lambert, W. E., Genesee, F., Holobow, N., & Chartrand, L. (1993). Bilingual education for majority English-speaking children. *European Journal of Psychology of Education, 8*, 3–22.*

Lammers, H. B. (2000). Effects of deceptive packaging and product involvement on purchase intention: An elaboration likelihood model perspective. *Psychological Reports, 86*, 546–550.

Landon, T. M., & Barlow, D. H. (2004). Cognitive-behavioral treatment for panic disorder: Current status. *Journal of Psychiatric Practice, 10(4)*, 211–226.

Landrine, H., & Klonoff, E. A. (2001). Cultural diversity and health psychology. In A. Baum, T. A. Revenson, & J. E. Singer (Eds.), *Handbook of health psychology.* Mahwah, NJ: Erlbaum.

Landy, F. J., & Conte, J. M. (2004). *Work in the 21st century: An introduction to industrial and organizational psychology.* Boston: McGraw-Hill.

Lang, P. J., Davis, M., & Ohman, A. (2000). Fear and anxiety: Animal models and human cognitive psychophysiology. *Journal of Affective Disorders, 61*, 137–159.

Lange, C. G. (1922). *The emotions.* Baltimore: Williams & Wilkins.

Langenfeld, M. C., Cipani, E., & Borckardt, J. J. (2002). Hypnosis for the control of HIV/ AIDS-related pain. *International Journal of Clinical and Experimental Hypnosis, 50*, 170–188.

Langens, T. A., & Schmalt, H.-D. (2002). Emotional consequences of positive daydreaming: The moderating role of fear of failure. *Personality & Social Psychology Bulletin, 28(12)*, 1725–1735.

Langer, E. J. (1989). *Mindfulness.* Reading, MA: Addison-Wesley.

Langer, E. J. (1997). *The power of mindful learning.* Reading, MA: Addison-Wesley.

Langer, E. J. (2000). Mindful learning. *Current Directions in Psychological Science, 9*, 220–223.

Langer, L. L. (1991). *Holocaust testimonies: The ruins of memory.* New Haven: Yale University Press.

Langs, R. (1978). *Technique in transition.* New York: Jason Aronson.

Langston, W. (2005). *Research methods manual for psychology (2nd ed.).* Belmont, CA: Wadsworth.

Lanham, S. L. (2003). *Relational remembering: Rethinking the memory wars.* Boulder, CO: Rowman and Littlefield.

Laor, N., Wiener, Z., Spirman, S., & Wolmer, L. (2005). Community mental health in emergencies and mass disasters: The Tel-Aviv model. *Journal of Aggression, Maltreatment & Trauma, 10(3-4)*, 681–694.

Larson, R. (2000). Toward a psychology of positive youth development. *American Psychologist, 55*, 170–183.

Larsen, R. J., & Buss, D. M. (2005). *Personality psychology (2nd ed.).* New York: McGraw-Hill.

Lashley, K. (1950). In search of the engram. *Society for Experimental Biology, 4*, 454–482.

Latham, G. P., & Pinder, C. C. (2005). Work motivation theory and research at the dawn of the twenty-first century. *Annual Review of Psychology, 56*, 485–516.

Lau, M. A., & Segal, Z. V. (2003). Mood disorders and suicide. In P. Firestone, & W. L. Marshall (Eds.), *Abnormal psychology: Perspectives (2nd ed.).* Toronto: Prentice Hall.*

Lau, S., Nicholls, J., Thorkildsen, T. A., & Patashnick, M. (2000). Chinese and American adolescents' perceptions of the purposes of education and beliefs about the world of work. *Social Behavior & Personality, 28(1)*, 73–89.

Laurent, G., Stopfer, M., Friedrich, R. W., Rabinovich, M. I., Volkovskii, A., & Abarbanel, H. D. (2001). Odor encoding as an active, dynamical process. *Annual Review of Neuroscience, 24*, 263–297.

Lauterbach, E. C. (2004). The neuropsychiatry of Parkinson's disease and related disorders. *Psychiatric Clinics of North America. Special Addictive Disorders, 27(4)*, 801–825.

Lavie, P. (2001). Sleep-wake as a biological rhythm. *Annual Review of Psychology, 52*, 277–303.

Lazar, S. W, Bush, G., Gollub, R. L., Fricchione, G. L., Khalsa, G., & Benson, H. (2000). Functional brain mapping of the relaxation response and meditation. *Neuroreport, 15*, 1581–1585.

Lazarus, R. S. (1991). On the primacy of cognition. *American Psychologist, 39*, 124–129.

Lazarus, R. S. (1993). Coping theory and research: Past, present, and future. *Psychosomatic Medicine, 55*, 234–247.

Lazarus, R. S. (1999). The cognition-emotion debate: A bit of history. In T. Dalgleish, & M. J. Power (Ed.), *Handbook of cognition and emotion.* New York: Wiley.

Lazarus, R. S. (2000). Toward better research on stress and coping. *American Psychologist 55*, 665–673.

Leadbeater, B. J., & Way, N. (2001). *Growing up fast.* Mahwah, NJ: Erlbaum.*

Leadbeater, B. J., Bishop, S., & Raver, C. (1996). Quality of mother-toddler interactions, maternal depressive symptoms and behavior problems in preschoolers of adolescent mothers. *Developmental Psychology, 32*, 280–288.*

Leary, M. R. (2004). *Introduction to behavioral research methods (4th ed.).* Boston: Allyn and Bacon.

Leary, M. R., Nezlek, J. B., Downs, D., Radford-Davenport, J., Martin, J., & McMullen, A. (1994). Self-presentation in everyday interactions. *Journal of Personality & Social Psychology, 67*, 664–673.

LeBlanc, G., & Bearison, D. J. (2004). Teaching and learning as a bi-directional activity: Investigating dyadic interactions between child teachers and child learners. *Cognitive Development, 19(4)*, 499–515.

LeBoeuf, B. J., & Peterson, R. S. (1969). Social status and mating activity in elephant seals. *Science, 163*, 91–93.

Le Bourdais, C., & Lapierre-Adamcyk, E. (2004). Changes in conjugal life in Canada: Is cohabitation progressively replacing marriage? *Journal of Marriage & Family, 66(4)*, 929–942.*

Lebow, J. (Ed.). (2005). *Handbook of clinical family therapy.* San Francisco, CA: Jossey-Bass.

Lederman, S. J., Howe, R. D., Klatzky, R. L., & Hamilton, C. (2004). Force variability during surface contact with bare finger or rigid probe. 12th International Symposium on Haptic Interfaces for Virtual Environment and Teleoperator Systems,154–160.*

Lederman, S. J., & Klatsky, R. (1998, June). Commentary in B. Azar's "From surgery to robotics, touch is the key," *APA Monitor*, 21.*

Lederman, S. J., & Klatzky, R. L. (2004). Haptic identification of common objects: Effects of constraining the manual exploration process. *Perception & Psychophysics, 66(4)*, 618-628.*

LeDoux, J. E. (2000). Emotion circuits in the brain. *Annual Review of Neuroscience, 23*, 155–184.

LeDoux, J. E. (2002). *The synaptic self.* New York: Viking.

Lee, G., & Farhat, N. H. (2001). The bifurcating neuron network. *Neural Networks, 14*, 115–131.

Lee, G. P., Meador, K. J., Loring, D. W., Allision, J. D., Brown, W. S., Paul, L. K., Pillai, J. J., & Lavin, T. B. (2004). Neural substrates of emotion as revealed by functional magnetic resonance imaging. *Cognitive & Behavioral Neurology, 17(1)*, 9–17.

Lee, I., Hsieh, C., & Paffenbarger, O. (1995). Exercise intensity and longevity in men. *Journal of the American Medical Association, 273*, 1179–1184.

Lee, J.-S., Koeske, G. F., & Sales, E. (2004). Social support buffering of acculturative stress: A study of mental health symptoms among Korean international students. *International Journal of Intercultural Relations, 28(5)*, 399–414.

Lee, K., & Ashton, M. C. (2004). Psychometric properties of the HEXACO Personality Inventory. *Multivariate Behavioral Research, 39(2)*, 329–358.*

Lee, K., & Ashton, M. C. (2005). Psychopathy, Machiavellianism, and narcissism in the five-factor model and the HEXACO model of personality structure. *Personality & Individual Differences, 38(7)*, 1571–1582.*

Lee, Y. S., Cheung, Y. M., & Wurm, L. H. (2000). Levels-of-processing effects on Chinese character completion: The importance of lexical processing and test cue. *Memory and Cognition, 28*, 1398–1405.

Leenaars, A. A., Brown, C., Taparti, L., Anowak, J. & Hill-Keddie, T. (1999). Genocide and suicide among Indigenous people: The North meets the South. *The Canadian Journal of Native Studies, 19(2)*, 337–363.*

Leenaars, A. A., Lester, D., & Wenckstern, S. (2005). Coping with: The art and the research. In R. I. Yufit, & D. Lester (Eds.), *Assessment, treatment, and prevention of suicidal behavior.* New York: Wiley.*

Lefcourt, H. M. (2003). Humor as a moderator of life stress in adults. In C. E. Schaefer (Ed.), *Play therapy with adults.* New York: Wiley.*

Lefebvre, L., & Giraldeau, L.-A. (1996). Is social learning an adaptive specialization? In C. M. Heyes, & B. G. Galef Jr. (Eds.), *Social learning in animals: The roots of culture.* San Diego: Academic Press.*

Legault, G., Smith, C. T., & Beninger, R. J. (2004). Scopolamine during the paradoxical sleep window impairs radial arm maze learning in rats. *Pharmacology, Biochemistry & Behavior, 79(4)*, 715–721.*

Lehar, S. M. (2002). *The world in your head.* Mahwah, NJ: Erlbaum.

Lehman, D. R., Chiu, C.-Y., & Schaller, M. (2004). Psychology and culture. *Annual Review of Psychology, 55*, 689–714.*

Lehtonen, S., Stringer, A. Y., Millis, S., Boake, C., Englander, J., Hart, T., et al. (2005). Neuropsychological outcome and community re-integration following traumatic brain injury: The impact of frontal and non-frontal lesions. *Brain Injury, 19(4)*, 239–256.

Leiter, M. P. (2005). Perception of risk: An organizational model of occupational risk, burnout, and physical symptoms. *Anxiety, Stress & Coping: An International Journal, 18(2)*, 131–144.*

Leiter, M. P., & Maslach, C. (1998). Burnout. In H. S. Friedman (Ed.), *Encyclopedia of mental health (Vol. 1).* San Diego: Academic Press.*

Leiter, M. P., & Maslach, C. (2001). Burnout and health. In A. Baum, T. A. Revenson, & J. E. Singer (Eds.), *Handbook of health psychology.* Mahwah, NJ: Erlbaum.*

Lemke, G. E. (2001). Glial control of neuronal development. *Annual Review of Neuroscience, 24*, 87–105.

Lenneberg, E. H. (1967). *The biological foundations of language*. New York: Wiley.

Lenneberg, E. H., Rebelsky, F. G., & Nichols, I. A. (1965). The vocalization of infants born to deaf and hearing parents. *Human Development, 8,* 23–37.

Leon, G. R. (1990). *Case histories of psychopathology (4th ed.)*. Boston: Allyn & Bacon.

Lepper, M., Greene, D., & Nisbett, R. E. (1973). Undermining children's intrinsic interest with extrinsic rewards. *Journal of Personality & Social Psychology, 28,* 129–137.

Lessow-Hurley, J. (2005). *Foundations of dual language instruction (4th ed.)*. Boston: Allyn & Bacon.

Lester, D. (1992). Cooperative/competitive strategies and locus of control. *Psychological Reports, 71(2),* 594.

Lester, D., & Yang, B. (2005). Regional and time-series studies of suicide in nations of the world. *Archives of Suicide Research, 9(2),* 123–133.

LeUnes, A., & Nation, J. (2002). *Sport psychology (3rd ed.)*. Belmont, CA: Wadsworth.

Levant, R. F. (2001). Men and masculinity. In J. Worell (Ed.), *Encyclopedia of women and gender*. San Diego: Academic Press.

Levant, R. F. (2003). Treating male alexithymia. In L. B. Silverstein, & T. J. Goodrich (Eds.), *Feminist family therapy: Empowerment in social context*. Washington: APA Press.

Levant, R. F., & Brooks, G. R. (1997). *Men and sex: New psychological perspectives*. New York: Wiley.

LeVay, S. (1991). A difference in the hypothalamic structure between heterosexual and homosexual men. *Science, 253,* 1034–1037.

Leventhal, H., & Tomarken, A. J. (1986). Emotion: Today's problems. *Annual Review of Psychology, 37,* 565–610.

Levine, B., Cabeza, R., Black, S. E., Sinden, M., Toth, J. B., Tulving, E., et al. (1997). Functional and structural neuroimaging correlates of selective retrograde amnesia: A case study with MRI and PET. *Brain and Cognition, 35,* 372–376.*

Levine, B., Turner, G. T., Tisserand, D. J., Graham, S. I., Hevenor, S. J., & McIntosh, A. R. (2004). The functional neuroanatomy of episodic and semantic autobiographical remembering: a prospective study. *Journal of Cognitive Neuroscience, 16(9),* 1633–1646.*

Levine, J. D., Gordon, N. C., & Fields, H. L. (1979). Naloxone dose dependently produces analgesia and hyperalgesia in postoperative pain. *Nature, 278,* 740–741.

Levine, J. H., & Moreland, R. H. (1998). Small groups. In D. T. Gilbert, S. T. Fiske, & G. Lindzey (Eds.), *Handbook of social psychology (4th ed., Vol. 2)*. New York: McGraw-Hill.

Levine, L. J., & Bluck, S. (2004). Painting with broad strokes: Happiness and the malleability of event memory. *Cognition & Emotion, 18(4),* 559–574.

Levine, R. L. (2002). Endocrine aspects of eating disorders in adolescents. *Adolescent Medicine, 13,* 129–144.

Levine, S. P., & Feldman, R. S. (2002). Women and men's nonverbal behavior and self-monitoring in a job interview setting. *Applied H.R.M. Research, 7(1-2),* 1–14.

Levinson, D. J. (1978). *The seasons of a man's life*. New York: Knopf.

Levinson, D. J. (1996). *Seasons of a woman's life*. New York: Knopf.

Levitt, H., Korman, Y., & Angus, L. (2000). A metaphor analysis in treatments of depression: Metaphor as a marker of change. *Counselling Psychology Quarterly, 13,* 23–35.*

Levy, S. M., Herberman, R. B., Lee, J., Whiteside, T., Kirckwood, J., & McFreeley, S. (1990). Estrogen receptor concentration and social factors as predictors of natural killer cell activity in early-stage breast cancer patients. *Natural Immunity and Cell Growth Regulation, 9,* 313–324.

Levy, T. M. (Ed.). (1999). *Handbook of attachment interventions*. San Diego: Academic Press.

Lewinsohn, P. M. (1987). The coping with depression course. In R. F. Munoz (Ed.), *Depression prevention*. New York: Hemisphere.

Lewinsohn, P. M., & Gotlib, I. H. (1995). Behavioral therapy and treatment of depression. In E. E. Beckham, & W. R. Leber (Eds.), *Handbook of depression (2nd ed.)*. New York: Guilford.

Lewinsohn, P. M., Antonuccio, D. O., Steinmetz, J., & Teri, L. (1984). *The Coping with Depression course: A psychoeducational intervention for unipolar depression*. Eugene, OR: Castalia.

Lewinsohn, P. M., Joiner, Jr., T. E., & Rohde, P. (2001). Evaluation of cognitive diathesis-stress models in predicting major depressive disorder in adolescence. *Journal of Abnormal Psychology, 110,* 203–215.

Lewinsohn, P. M., Striegel-Moore, R. H., & Seeley, J. R. (2000). Epidemiology and natural course of eating disorders in young women from adolescence to young adulthood. *Journal of American Academy of Child and Adolescent Psychiatry, 39,* 1284–1292.

Lewis, J. (2000). Controlling lap dancing: Law, morality and sex work. In R. Weitzer (Ed.), *Sex as work: Prostitution, pornography, and the sex industry*. New York: Routledge.*

Lewis, J., & Maticka-Tyndale, E. (2000). Licensing sex work: Public policy and women's lives. *Canadian Public Policy, 16,* 1–13.*

Lewis, M. (1997). *Altering fate: Why the past does not predict the future*. New York: Guilford.

Lewis, R. (2004). *Life (5th ed.)*. New York: McGraw-Hill.

Lewis, R. (2005). *Human genetics (6th ed.)*. New York: McGraw-Hill.

Lewis, T. L., & Maurer, D. (2005). Multiple sensitive periods in human visual development: Evidence from visually deprived children. *Developmental Psychobiology. Special Critical Periods Re-examined: Evidence from Human Sensory Development, 46(3),* 163–183.*

Li, D., Chokka, P., & Tibbo, P. (2001). Toward an integrative understanding of social phobia. *Journal of Psychiatry and Neuroscience, 26,* 190–202.*

Liddell, A., & Locker, D. (2000). Changes in levels of dental anxiety as a function of dental experience. *Behavior Modification, 24,* 57–68.*

Lieber, C. S. (1997). Gender differences in alcohol metabolism and susceptibility. In S. C. Wilsnack, & R. W. Wilsnack (Eds.), *Gender and alcohol*. New Brunswick, NJ: Rutgers Center of Alcohol Studies.

Lieberman, D. A. (2004). *Learning and memory: An integrative approach*. Belmont, CA: Wadsworth.

Lieberman, P. (2002). A biological view of the evolution of language. In M. H. Christiansen, & S. Kirby (Eds.), *Language evolution: The states of the art*. Oxford: Oxford University Press.

Lilienfeld, S. O., Wood, J. M., & Garb, H. N. (2000). The scientific status of projective techniques. *Psychological Science in the Public Interest, 1(2),* 27–66.

Lin, C.-C., & Tsay, H.-F. (2005). Relationships among perceived diagnostic disclosure, health locus of control, and levels of hope in Taiwanese cancer patients. *Psycho-Oncology, 14(5),* 376–385.

Lindemann, B. (2001). Receptors and transduction in taste. *Nature, 413,* 219–225.

Linden, W. (2005). *Stress management: From basic science to better practice*. Thousand Oaks, CA: Sage.

Linden, W., Lenz, J. W., & Con, A. H. (2001). Individualized stress management for primary hypertension: A randomized trial. *Archives of Internal Medicine, 161,* 1071–1080.

Lindqvist, R., & Aberg, H. (2002). Locus of control in relation to smoking cessation during pregnancy. *Scandinavian Journal of Public Health, 30,* 30–35.

Lindsay, J., & Anderson, B. A. (2003). Dementia and Alzheimer's disease. Ottawa: Public Health Agency of Canada. Retrieved March 5, 2005 from http://www.phac-aspc.gc.ca/publicat/whsr-rssf/chap_19_e.html.*

Lindvall, O. (2001). Parkinson disease: Stem cell transplanation. *Lancet, 358 [Supplement],* S48.

Lingjaerde, O., Foreland, A. R., & Engvik, H. (2001). Personality structure in patients with winter depression, assessed in a depression-free state according to the five-factor model of personality. *Journal of Affective Disorders, 62,* 165–174.

Lips, H. M. (2003). *A new psychology of women: Gender, culture, and ethnicity (2nd ed.)*. New York: McGraw-Hill.

Lipsey, M. W., & Wilson, D. B. (1993). The efficacy of psychological, educational, and behavioral treatment: Confirmation from meta-analysis. *American Psychologist, 48,* 1181–1209.

Lister, P. (1992, July). A skeptic's guide to psychics. *Redbook,* pp. 103–105, 112–113.

Liu, R., & Gong, Y. (1999). Preliminary application of the Memorial University of New Foundland Scale of Happiness. Chinese *Journal of Clinical Psychology, 7,* 107–108, 110.

Livanou, M., Basoglu, M., Marks, I. M., De, S. P., Noshirvani, H., & Lovell, K. (2002). Beliefs, sense of control, and treatment outcome in post-traumatic stress disorder. *Psychological Medicine, 32,* 157–165.

Livingston, J. D., Wilson, D., Tien, G., & Bond, L. (2003). A follow-up study of persons found not criminally responsible on account of mental disorder in British Columbia. *Canadian Journal of Psychiatry, 48(6),* 408–415.

Lodge, M., & Taber, C. S. (2005). The automaticity of affect for political leaders, groups, and issues: An experimental test of the hot cognition hypothesis. *Political Psychology, 26(3),* 455–482.

Lochman, J. J. (2000). A perception-action perspective on tool use development. *Child Development, 71,* 137–144.

Locke, E. A. (2001). Setting goals for life and happiness. In C. R. Snyder, & S. J. Lopez (Eds.). *Handbook of positive psychology*. New York: Oxford.

Locke, J. L. (1993). *The child's path to spoken language*. Cambridge Harvard University Press.

Löckenhoff, C. E., & Carstensen, L. L. (2004). Socioemotional selectivity theory, aging, and health: The increasingly delicate balance between regulating emotions and making tough choices. *Journal of Personality: Special Emotions, Personality, and Health, 72(6),* 1395–1424.

Loftus, E. F. (1975). Spreading activation within semantic categories. *Journal of Experimental Psychology, 104,* 234–240.

Loftus, E. F. (1979). *Eyewitness testimony*. Cambridge: Harvard University Press.

Loftus, E. F. (1993). Psychologists in the eyewitness world. *American Psychologist, 48,* 550–552.

Loftus, E. F. (2003). Memory in Canadian courts of law. *Canadian Psychology, 44(3),* 207–212.

Loftus, E. F. (2003). Make-believe memories. *American Psychologist, 58(11),* 867–873.

Loftus, E. F., & Bernstein, D. M. (2005). Rich false memories: The royal road to success. In A.F. Healy, (Ed.), *Experimental cognitive psychology and its applications*. Washington: APA Press.

Loftus, E. F., & Ketcham, K. (1994). *The myth of repressed memory: False memories and allegations of abuse*. New York: St. Martin's Press.

Logie, R. H., Cocchini, G., Delia Sala, S., & Baddeley, A. D. (2004). Is there a specific executive capacity for dual task coordination? Evidence from Alzheimer's disease. *Neuropsychology, 18(3),* 504–513.

Lohman, D. F. (2005). Reasoning abilities. In R. J. Sternberg, & E. Pretz (Eds.), *Cognition and intelligence: Identifying the mechanisms of the mind*. New York: Cambridge.

LoLordo, V. M. (2001). Learned helplessness and depression. In M. E. Carroll, & J. B. Overmier, (Eds.), *Animal research and human health: Advancing human welfare through behavioral science*. Washington: APA Press.*

Longo, D. A., Lent, R. W., & Brown, S. D. (1992). Social cognitive variables in the prediction of client motivation and attribution. *Journal of Counseling Psychology, 39,* 447–452.

Lopez, O., Haigh, C., & Burney, S. (2004). Relationship between hardiness and perceived stress in two generations of Latin American migrants. *Australian Psychologist, 39(3),* 238–243.

López, S. R., & Guarnaccia, P. J. (2000). Cultural psychopathology: Uncovering the social world of mental illness. *Annual Review of Psychology, 51,* 571–598.

López, S. R., & Guarnaccia, P. J. (2005). Cultural dimensions of psychopathology: The social world's impact on mental illness. In J. E. Maddux, & B. A.

Winstead (Eds.), *Psychopathology: Foundations for a contemporary understanding.* Mahwah, NJ: Erlbaum.

Lorenz, K. Z. (1965). *Evolution and the modification of behavior.* Chicago: University of Chicago Press.

Lott, B., & Maluso, D. (2002). Gender development: Social learning. In J. Worell (Ed.), *Encyclopedia of women and gender.* New York: Oxford.

Lovett, M. C. (2002). Problem solving. In H. Pashler, & D. Medin (Eds.), *Steven's handbook of experimental psychology (3rd ed.). Vol. 2: Memory and cognitive processes.* New York: Wiley.

Lowe, G., Beckett, J., & Lowe, G. (2003). Poetry writing and secretory immunoglobulin A. *Psychological Reports, 92(3),* 847–848.

Lowe, R. (2004). Interrogation of a dynamic visualization during learning. *Learning & Instruction, 14(3),* 257–274.

Lu, Z-L., & Sperling, G. (2003). Measuring sensory memory: Magnetoencephalography habituation and psychophysics. In Z.-L. Lu, & L. Kaufman (Eds.), *Magnetic source imaging of the human brain.* Mahwah, NJ: Erlbaum.

Lubinski, D. (2000). Scientific and social significance of assessing individual differences: "Sinking shafts at a few critical points." *Annual Review of Psychology, 51,* 405–444.

Lublin, H., Eberhard, J., & Levander, S. (2005). Current therapy issues and unmet clinical needs in the treatment of schizophrenia: A review of the new generation antipsychotics. *International Clinical Psychopharmacology, 20(4),* 183–198.

Lumley, M. A. (2004). Alexithymia, emotional disclosure, and health: A program of research. *Journal of Personality. Special Emotions, Personality, and Health, 72(6),* 1271–1300.

Luria, A. R. (1968). *The mind of a mnemonist.* New York: Basic Books.

Luria, A. R. (1973). *The working brain.* New York: Penguin.

Luszczynska, A., & Schwarzer, R. (2005). The role of self-efficacy in health self-regulation. In W. Greve, K. Werner, D. Rothermund, & D. Wentura (Eds.), (2005). *The adaptive self: Personal continuity and intentional self-development.* Ashland, OH: Hogrefe & Huber.

Lutz, D. J., & Sternberg, R. J. (1999). Cognitive development. In M. H. Bornstein, & M. E. Lamb (Eds.), *Developmental psychology: An advanced textbook (4th ed.).* Mahwah, NJ: Erlbaum.

Lyall, V., Alam, R. I., Phan, D. Q., Heck, G. L., & DeSimone, J. A. (2002). Excitation and adaptation in the detection of hydrogen ions by taste receptor cells: A role for cAMP and CA (2+). *Journal of Neurophysiology, 87,* 399–408.

Lydiard, R. B. (2003). The role of GABA in anxiety disorders. *Journal of Clinical Psychiatry. Special The role of GABA in neuropsychiatric disorders: A review of GABA agents, 64(Suppl3),* 21–27.

Lykken, D. T. (2001). Lie detection. In W. E. Craighead, & C. B. Nemeroff (Eds.), *The Corsini Encyclopedia of psychology and behavioral science (3rd ed.).* New York: Wiley.

Lynn, R. (1996). Racial and ethnic differences in intelligence in the U.S. on the Differential Ability Scale. *Personality and Individual Differences, 26,* 271–273.

Lynn, S. J., Neuschatz, J., & Fite, R. (2002). Hypnosis and memory: Implications for the courtroom and psychotherapy. In M. L. Eisen, (Ed.), *Memory and suggestibility in the forensic interview.* Mahwah, NJ: Erlbaum.

Lynn, S. J., Rhue, J. W., & Spanos, N. P. (1994). Hypnosis. In *Encyclopedia of human behavior.* New York: Academic Press.*

Lyons, A., & Chamberlain, K. (2006). *Health psychology.* New York: Cambridge.

Lyubomirsky, S., Sheldon, K. M., & Schkade, D. (2005). Pursuing happiness: The architecture of sustainable change. *Review of General Psychology. Special Positive Psychology, 9(2),* 111–131.

M

Maas, J. (1998). *Power sleep.* New York: Villard.

Macaluso, E., Frith, C. D., & Driver, J. (2002). Directing attention to locations and to sensory modalities: Multiple levels of selective processing revealed with PET. *Cerebral Cortex, 12,* 357–368.

Maccoby, E. E., & Jacklin, C. N. (1974). *The psychology of sex differences.* Palo Alto, CA: Stanford University Press.

MacIntyre, P. D., Baker, S. C., Clément, R., & Conrod, S. (2001). Willingness to communicate, social support, and language-learning orientations of immersion students. *Studies in Second Language Acquisition, 23,* 369–388.*

MacIntyre, P. D., Baker, S. C., Clément, R., & Donovan, L. (2003). Sex and age effects on willingness to communicate, anxiety, perceived competence, and L2 motivation among junior high school French immersion students. *Language Learning, 53(Suppl1),* 137–166.*

MacIntyre, P. D., Clément, R., Dörnyei, Z., & Noels, K. A. (1998). Conceptualizing willingness to communicate in L2: A situational model of L2 confidence and affiliation. *The Modern Language Journal, 82,* 545–562.*

Mack, A., & Rock, I. (1998). *Inattentional blindness.* Cambridge: MIT Press.

MacKenzie, R. (2002). Group psychotherapy. In M. Hersen, & W. H. Sledge (Eds.), *Encyclopedia of psychotherapy.* San Diego: Academic Press.

MacKinnon, D. F., Jamison, K. R., & DePaulo, Jr., J. R. (1997). Genetics of manic depressive illness. *Annual Review of Neuroscience, 20,* 355–373.

MacKinnon, D. F., Zandi, P. P., Cooper, J., Potash, J. B., Simpson, S. G., & Gershon, E. (2002). Comorbid bipolar disorder and panic disorder in families with a high prevalence of bipolar disorder. *American Journal of Psychiatry, 159,* 30–35.

MacLaren, V. V. (2001). A qualitative review of the Guilty Knowledge Test. *Journal of Applied Psychology, 86,* 674–683.*

MacLeod, C. M. (1992). The Stroop task: The "gold standard" of attentional measures. *Journal of Experimental Psychology: General, 121,* 12–14.*

MacLeod, C. M., Rutherford, E., Campbell, L., Ebsworthy, G., & Holker, L. (2002). Selective attention and emotional vulnerability: Assessing the casual basis of their association through the experimental manipulation of attentional bias. *Journal of Abnormal Psychology, 111,* 107–123.*

MacLeod, C. M., & Sheehan, P. W. (2003). Hypnotic control of attention in the Stroop task: A historical footnote. *Consciousness & Cognition: An International Journal, 12(3),* 347–353.*

MacWhinney, B. (Ed.). (1999). *The emergence of language.* Mahwah, NJ: Erlbaum.

MacWhinney, B. (2005). Language evolution and human development. In B. J. Ellis, & D. F. Bjorklund (Eds.), *Origins of the social mind: Evolutionary psychology and child development.* New York: Guilford.

Mace, B. L., Bell, P. A., & Loomis, R. J. (2004). Visibility and natural quiet in national parks and wilderness areas: Psychological considerations. *Environment and Behavior, 36,* 5–31.

Maddux, J. (2001). Self-efficacy. In C. R. Snyder & S. J. Lopez (Eds.), *Handbook of positive psychology.* New York: Oxford.

Mader, S. S. (2004). *Human biology (8th ed.).* New York: McGraw-Hill.

Mader, S. S. (2006). *Inquiry into life (11th ed.).* New York: McGraw-Hill.

Mager. R.F. (1997). *Goal analysis: How to clarify your goals so you can actually achieve them. (3rd ed.).* Atlanta, GA: Center for Effective Performance.

Magnavita, J. J. (2005). Components of a unified treatment approach: psychopathology, personality theory, and psychotherapy. In J. J. Magnavita (Ed.), *Personality-guided relational psychotherapy.* Washington: APA Press.

Magnusson, R. S. (2004). Euthanasia: above ground, below ground. *Journal of Medical Ethics, 30(5),* 441–446.

Mah, K., & Binik, Y. M. (2001). The nature of human orgasm: A critical review of major trends. *Clinical Psychology Review, 21(6),* 823–856.*

Mahendran, R. (2001). Characteristics of patients referred to an insomnia clinic. Singapore Medical Journal, 42, 64–70.

Mahoney, J. L., Larson, R. W. & Eccles, J. S. (2005). *Organized activities as contexts of development: Extracurricular activities, after-school and community programs.* Mahwah, NJ: Erlbaum.

Mai, X.-Q., Luo, J., Wu, J.-H., & Luo, Y.-J. (2004). "Aha!" effects in a guessing riddle task: An event-related potential study. *Human Brain Mapping, 22(4),* 261–271.

Maibom, H. (2004). Minding minds. *Philosophical Psychology, 17(2),* 314–317.*

Maier, N. R. F. (1931). Reasoning in humans. *Journal of Comparative Psychology, 12,* 181–194.

Majeres, R. L. (1999). Sex differences in phonological processes: Speeded matching and word reading. *Memory and Cognition, 27,* 246–253.

Major, B., & O'Brien, L. T. (2005). The social psychology of stigma. *Annual Review of Psychology, 56,* 393–421.

Malamuth, N. M., Addison, T., & Koss, M. (2000). Pornography and sexual aggression: Are there reliable effects and can we understand them? *Annual Review of Sex Research, 11,* 26–91.

Malapani, C., Deweer, B., & Gibbon, J. (2002). Separating storage from retrieval dysfunction of temporal memory in Parkinson's disease. *Journal of Cognitive Neuroscience, 14,* 311–322.

Malott, R. W., & Trojan Suarez, E. A. (2004). *Principles of behavior (5th ed.).* Upper Saddle River, NJ: Prentice Hall.

Mamen, M. (2004). *Pampered child syndrome: How to recognize it, how to manage it and how to avoid it.* Carp, ON: Creative Bound.*

Mandler, G. (1980). Recognizing: The judgment of previous occurrence. *Psychological Review, 87,* 252–271.

Mandler, J. M. (1998). Representation. In W. Damon (Ed.), *Handbook of child psychology (5th ed., Vol. 2).* New York: Wiley.

Mandzia, J. L., Black, S. E., McAndrews, M. P., Grady, C., & Graham, S. (2004). fMRI Differences in encoding and retrieval of pictures due to encoding strategy in the elderly. *Human Brain Mapping, 21(1),* 1–14.*

Manes, F., Sahakain, B., Clark, L., Rogers, R., Antoun, N., Aitken, M., & Robbins, T. (2002). Decision-making processes following damage to the frontal lobe. *Brain, 125* (Pt. 3), 624–639.

Mangels, J. A., Picton, T. W., & Craik, F. I. M. (2001). Attention and successful episodic encoding: An event-related potential study. *Brain Research, 11,* 77–95.*

Manitoba Justice (2001). *The inquiry regarding Thomas Sophonow: The investigation, prosecution and consideration of entitlement to compensation.* Winnipeg, MB: Department of Justice. Retrieved August 29, 2005, from http://www.gov.mb.ca/justice/publications/sophonow/toc.html.*

Manji, H. K. (2001). Strategies for gene and protein expression studies in neuropsychopharmacology and biological psychiatry. *International Journal of Neuropsycho-pharmacology, 4,* 45.

Manji, H. K., Dreverts, W. C., & Charney, D. S. (2001). The cellular neurobiology of depression. *Nature Medicine, 7,* 541–547.

Mann, J. J., & Arango, V. (1999). The neurobiology of suicidal behavior. In D. G. Jacobs (Ed.), *The Harvard Medical School guide to suicide assessment and intervention.* San Francisco: Jossey-Bass.

Manson, S. M., Ackerson, L. M., Dick, R. W., & Baron, A. E. (1990). Depressive symptoms among American Indian adolescents: Psychometric characteristics of the Center for Epidemiologic Studies Depression Scale (CES-D). *Psychological Assessment, 2,* 231–237.

Mantere, T., Tupala, E., Hall, H., Sarkoja, T., Rasanen, P., Bergstrom, K., et al. (2002). Serotonin transporter distribution and density in the cerebral cortex of alcoholic and nonalcoholic comparison subjects: A whole-hemisphere autoradiograph study. *American Journal of Psychiatry, 159*, 599–606.

Mäntylä, T. (2003). Assessing absentmindedness: Prospective memory complaint and impairment in middle-aged adults. *Psychological Assessment, 31(1)*, 15–25.

Maratsos, M. (1999). Some aspects of innateness and complexity in grammar acquisition. In M. Barrett (Ed.), *The development of language*. Philadelphia: Psychology Press.

Marcaurelle, R., Bélanger, C., Marchand, A. Katerelos, T. E., & Mainguy, N. (2005). Marital predictors of symptom severity in panic disorder with agoraphobia. *Journal of Anxiety Disorders, 19(2)*, 211–232.*

Marcia, J. E. (1980). Ego identity development. In J. Adelson (Ed.), *Handbook of adolescent psychology*. New York: Wiley.*

Marcia, J. E. (2002). Identity and psychosocial development in adulthood. *Identity, 2(1)*, 7–28.*

Marcus, E. (2002). Psychoanalytic psychotherapy and psychoanalysis: An overview. In M. Hersen, & W. H. Sledge (Eds.), *Encyclopedia of psychotherapy*. San Diego: Academic Press.

Marcus, G. (2004). *The birth of the mind: How a tiny number of genes creates the complexities of human thought*. New York: Basic Books.

Marder, S. R., Davis, J. M., & Chouinard, G. (1997). The effects of risperidone on the five dimensions of schizophrenia derived by factor analysis: Combined results of the North American trials. *Journal of Clinical Psychiatry, 58*, 538–546.*

Maril, A., Wagner, A. D., & Schacter, D. L. (2001). On the tip of the tongue: An event-related fMRI study of semantic retrieval failure and cognitive conflict. *Neuron, 31*, 653–660.

Maris, R. W. (1998). Suicide. In H. S. Friedman (Ed.), *Encyclopedia of mental health (Vol. 3)*. San Diego: Academic Press.

Markman, A., & Gentner, D. (2001). Thinking. *Annual Review of Psychology, 52*, 223–247.

Markman, H. J. (2000). Marriage. In A. Kazdin (Ed.), *Encyclopedia of psychology*. Washington, & New York: APA Press and Oxford.

Markovitz, J. H., Jonas, B. S., & Davidson, K. (2001). Psychological factors as precursors to hypertension. *Current Hypertension Reports, 3*, 25–32.

Marks, I. M. (1987). *Fears, phobias, and rituals*. New York: Oxford.

Marks, L., Nesteruk, O., Swanson, M., Garrison, B., & Davis, T. (2005). Religion and health among African Americans: A qualitative examination. *Research on Aging, 27(4)*, 447–474.

Maron, E., Kuikka, J. T., Shlik, J., Vasar, V., Vanninen, E., & Tiihonen, J. (2004). Reduced brain serotonin transporter binding in patients with panic disorder. *Psychiatry Research: Neuroimaging, 132(2)*, 173–181.

Maron, E., Lang, A., Tasa, G., Liivlaid, L., Tõru, I., Must, A., et al. (2005). Associations between serotonin-related gene polymorphisms and panic disorder. *International Journal of Neuropsychopharmacology, 8(2)*, 261–266.

Marotta, J. J., Keith, G. P., & Crawford, J. D. (2005). Task-specific sensorimotor adaptation to reversing prisms. *Journal of Neurophysiology, 93*, 1104–1110.*

Marotta, J. J., McKeeff, T. J. & Behrmann, M. (2002). The effects of rotation and inversion on face processing in prosopagnosia. *Cognitive Neuropsychology, 19(1)*, 31–47.*

Marr, D. (1982). *Vision*. New York: Freeman.

Marra, M., Polito, A., De Filippo, E., Cuzzolar, M., Ciarapica, D., Contaldo, F., et al. (2002). Are the general equations to predict BMR applicable to patients with anorexia nervosa? *Eating and Weight Disorders, 7*, 53–59.

Marriott, L. K., & Wenk, G. L. (2004). Neurobiological consequences of long-term estrogen therapy. *Current Directions in Psychological Science, 13(5)*, 173–176.

Marschark, M. (2003a). Interactions of language and cognition in deaf learners: From research to practice. *International Journal of Audiology, 42(Suppl1)*, S41–S48.

Marschark, M. (2003b). Cognitive functioning in deaf adults and children. In M. Marschark, & P. E. Spencer (Eds.), *Oxford handbook of deaf studies, language, and education*. London: Oxford.

Marsella, A. J. (2000). Culture and mental health. In A. Kazdin (Ed.), *Encyclopedia of psychology*. Washington, & New York: APA Press and Oxford.

Marshall, V. J., McGregor, A., Good, M., & Honey, R. C. (2004). Hippocampal lesions modulate both associative and nonassociative priming. *Behavioral Neuroscience, 118(2)*, 377–382.

Martens, B. K., & Witt, J. C. (2004). Competence, persistence, and success: The positive psychology of behavioral skill instruction. *Psychology in the Schools. Special Positive Psychology and Wellness in Children, 41(1)*, 19–30.

Martin, A. J., & Marsh, H. W. (2003). Fear of failure: Friend or foe? *Australian Psychologist, 38(1)*, 31–38.

Martin, C. L., & Dinella, L. (2001). Gender development: Gender schema theory. In J. Worell (Ed.), *Encyclopedia of women and gender*. New York: Oxford.

Martin, C. L., & Ruble, D. (2004). Children's search for gender cues: Cognitive perspectives on gender development. *Current Directions in Psychological Science, 13(2)*, 67–70.

Martin, D. W. (2004). *Doing psychology experiments (6th ed.)*. Belmont, CA: Wadsworth.

Martin, G., & Pear, J. (2003). *Behavior modification (7th ed.)*. Upper Saddle River, NJ: Prentice Hall.*

Martin, L. (1986). "Eskimo words for snow": A case study in the genesis and decay of an anthropological example. *American Anthropologist, 88(2)*, 418–423.

Martin, R. A. (1996). Humour as therapeutic play: Stress-moderating effects of humor. *Journal of Leisurability, 23(4)*, 8–15.*

Martin, R. A. (2001). Humor, laughter, and physical health: Methodological issues and research findings. *Psychological Bulletin, 127(4)*, 504–519.*

Martin, R. A. (2004). Sense of humor and physical health: Theoretical issues, recent findings, and future directions. *Humor: International Journal of Humor Research, 17(1–2)*, 1–19.*

Martin, W. E., & Swartz-Kulstad, J. L. (Eds.). (2000). *Person-environment psychology and mental health*. Mahwah, NJ: Erlbaum.

Martini, F. (2004). *Fundamentals of anatomy and physiology (6th ed.)*. Upper Saddle River, NJ: Prentice Hall.

Martins, Y., & Pliner, P. (1999). Restrained eating among vegetarians: Does a vegetarian eating style mask concerns about weight? *Appetite, 32(1)*, 145–154.*

Maslach, C., Schaufeli, W. B., & Leiter, M. P. (2001). Job burnout. *Annual Review of Psychology, 52*, 397–422.*

Masland, R. H., & Raviola, E. (2000). Confronting complexity: Strategies for understanding the microcircuitry of the retina. *Annual Review of Neuroscience, 23*, 249–284.

Maslow, A. (1954). *Motivation and personality*. New York: Harper & Row.

Maslow, A. (1971). *The farther reaches of human nature*. New York: Viking.

Masoro, E. J., & Austad, S. N. (Eds.) (2001). *Handbook of the biology of aging (5th ed.)*. San Diego: Academic Press.

Massimini, F., & Delle Fave, A. (2000). Individual development in bio-cultural perspective. *American Psychologist, 55*, 24–33.

Masson, J. M. (1988). *Against therapy*. New York: Atheneum.

Masson, M. E. J., & MacLeod, C. M. (1997). Episodic enhancement of processing fluency. In D. L. Medin (Ed.), *The psychology of learning and motivation (Vol. 37)*. San Diego, CA: Academic Press.*

Masten, A. S. (2001). Ordinary magic: Resilience processes in development. *American Psychologist, 56*, 227–238.

Masten, A. S., & Reed, M-G. J. (2002). Resilience in development. In C. R. Snyder, & S. J. Lopez (Eds.).

Handbook of positive psychology. Oxford: Oxford University Press.

Masters, W. H., & Johnson, V. E. (1966). *Human sexual response*. Boston: Little, Brown.

Matthews, G., Deary, I. J., & Whiteman, M. C. (2003). *Personality traits (2nd ed.)*. Malden, MA: Blackwell.

Matthews, G., Schwean, V. L., Campbell, S. E., Saklofske, D. H., & Mohamed, A. (2000). Personality, self-regulation and adaptation: A cognitive-social framework. In M. Boekaerts, P. Pintrich, & M. Zeidner (Eds.), *Handbook of self-regulation*. San Diego, CA: Academic Press.*

Mathias, J. L., & Mansfield, K. M. (2005). Prospective and declarative memory problems following moderate and severe traumatic brain injury. *Brain Injury, 19(4)*, 271–282.

Maticka-Tyndale, E. (2001). Sexual health and Canadian youth: How do we measure up? *Canadian Journal of Human Sexuality, 10(1-2)*, 1–17.*

Maticka-Tyndale, E., Herold, E. S., & Mewhinney, D. (1998). Casual sex on spring break: Intentions and behaviors of Canadian students. *Journal of Sex Research, 35*, 254–264.*

Maticka-Tyndale, E., & Herold, E. S. (1999). Condom use on spring-break vacation: The influence of intentions, prior use, and context. *Journal of Applied Social Psychology, 29*, 1010–1027.*

Maticka-Tyndale, E., Lewis, J., & Street, M. (2005). Making a place for escort works: A case study. *Journal of Sex Research. Special Sexuality and Place, 42(1)*, 46–53.*

Maticka-Tyndale, E., Lewis, J., Clark, J., Zubick, J., & Young, S. (2000). Exotic dancing and health. *Women and Health, 31*, 87–108.*

Matlin, M. M. (2004). *Cognition (6th Ed.)*. San Francisco, CA: Jossey-Bass.

Matochik, J. A., Eldreth, D. A., Cadet, J-L., & Bolla, K. I. (2005). Altered brain tissue composition in heavy marijuana users. *Drug & Alcohol Dependence, 77(1)*, 23–30.

Matsumoto, A. (Ed.). (2000). *Sexual differentiation of the brain*. Boca Raton, FL: CRC Press.

Matsumoto, D. (2000). *Culture and social behavior*. Belmont, CA: Wadsworth.

Matsumoto, D., & Juang, L. (2004). *Culture and psychology: People around the world (3rd ed.)*. Belmont, CA: Wadsworth.

Matsumoto, D., Yoo, S. H., Hirayama, S., & Petrova, G. (2005). Development and validation of a measure of display rule knowledge: The display rule assessment inventory. *Emotion, 5(1)*, 23–40.

Matthews, G., & Dreary, I. J. (1998). *Personality traits*. Cambridge: Cambridge University Press.

Matthews, G., Schwean, V. L., Campbell, S. E., Saklofske, D. H., & Mohamed, A. (2000). Personality, self-regulation and adaptation: A cognitive-social framework. In M. Boekaerts, P. Pintrich, & M. Zeidner (Eds.), *Handbook of self-regulation*. San Diego, CA: Academic Press.*

Mattson, M. P. (2002). Neurogenetics: White matter matters. *Trends in Neuroscience, 25*, 135–136.

Mattys, S. L., & Jusczyk, P. W. (2001). Phonotactic cues for segmentation of fluent speech by infants. *Cognition, 78*, 91–121.

Maurer, D., Lewis, T. L., & Mondloch, C. J. (2005). Missing sights: Consequences for visual cognitive development. *Trends in Cognitive Sciences. 9(3)*, 144–151.*

Mawhinney, T. A. (1983). A picture vocabulary test for the Eastern James Bay Cree. In S. H. Irvine, & J. W. Berry (Eds.), *Human assessment and cultural factors*. New York: Plenum.*

Mayer, E. L. (2002). Freud and Jung: the boundaried mind and the radically connected mind. *Journal of Analytical Psychology, 47*, 91–99.

Mayer, R. (2000). Problem solving. In M. A. Runco, & S. Pritzker (Eds.), *Encyclopedia of psychology*. San Diego: Academic Press.

Maylor, E. A., Chater, N., & Brown, G. D. (2001). Scale invariance in the retrieval of retrospective and prospective memories. *Psychonomic Bulletin Review, 8,* 162–167.

Mazur, J. E. (2006). *Learning and behavior (6th ed.).* Upper Saddle River, NJ: Prentice Hall.

McAdams, D. P. (1993). *The stories we live by.* New York: Morrow.

McAllister, M. M. (2000). Dissociative identity disorder: A literature review. *Journal of Psychiatric and Mental Health Nursing, 7,* 25–33.

McAnulty, R., & Burnette, M. M. (2004). *Exploring human sexuality: Making healthy decisions (2nd ed.).* Boston: Allyn & Bacon.

McCabe, R., McFarlane, T., Polivy, J., & Olmsted, M. P. (2001). Eating disorders, dieting, and the accuracy of self-reported weight. *International Journal of Eating Disorders, 29,* 59–64.*

McCall, W. V. (2005). Concerns over antidepressant medications and suicide: What does it mean for ECT? *Journal of ECT, 21(1),* 1–2.

McCann, C. D., & Endler, N. S. (Eds.). (1990). *Depression: New directions in theory, research and practice.* Toronto: Wall & Emerson, Inc.*

McCann, C. D., & Flett, G. (2004). Norman S. Endler (1931-2003). *American Psychologist, 59(2),* 120.

McCann, R. S. (2001, March/April). Human factors psychology at NASA. *Psychological Science Agenda, 14,* 11.

McClelland, D. C. (1955). Some social consequences of achievement motivation. In M. R. Jones (Ed.), *Nebraska Symposium of Motivation.* Lincoln: University of Nebraska Press.

McClelland, D. C. (1978). Managing motivation to expand human freedom. *American Psychologist, 33,* 201–210.

McClelland, D. C., Atkinson, J. W., Clark, R., & Lowell, E. L. (1953). *The achievement motive.* New York: Appleton-Century-Crofts.

McConaghy, N. (1993). *Sexual behavior: Problems and management.* New York: Plenum Press.

McCormick, C. M., & Witelson, S. F. (1994). Functional cerebral asymmetry in homosexual men and women. *Behavioral Neuroscience, 108,* 525–531.*

McCormick, C. M., Witelson, S. F., & Kingstone, E. (1990). Left-handedness in homosexual men and women: neuroendocrine implications. *Psychoneuroendocrinology, 15(1),* 69–76.*

McCormick, R. M. (2000). Aboriginal traditions in the treatment of substance abuse. *Canadian Journal of Counselling. Special Issue: Counselling First Nations people in Canada, 34,* 25–32.*

McCrae, R. R., & Costa, P. T. (2001). A five-factor theory of personality. In L. A. Pervin, & O. P. John (Eds.), *Handbook of personality.* New York: Guilford.

McCrae, R. R., Costa, P. T. Jr., & Martin, T. A. (2005). The NEO-PI-3: A more readable revised NEO Personality Inventory. *Journal of Personality Assessment, 84(3),* 261–270.

McCrae, R. R., & Terracciano, A. (2005). Universal features of personality traits from the observer's perspective: Data from 50 cultures. *Journal of Personality & Social Psychology, 88(3),* 547–561.

McCreary, D. R. (1997). Media influences. In S. W. Sadava & D. R. McCreary (Eds.), *Applied social psychology.* Englewood Cliffs, NJ: Prentice Hall.*

McCullough, M. E., Hoyt, W. T., Larson, D. B., Koenig, H. G., & Thoresen, C. (2000). Religious involvement and mortality: A meta-analytic review. *Health Psychology, 19,* 211–222.

McCurdy, B. L., Mannella, M. C., & Eldridge, N. (2003). Positive behavior support in urban schools: Can we prevent the escalation of antisocial behavior? *Journal of Positive Behavior Interventions, 5(3),* 158–170.

McDermott, M. R., Ramsay, J. M. C., & Bray, C. (2001). Components of the anger-hostility complex as risk factors for coronary artery disease severity: A multi-measure study. *Journal of Health Psychology, 6(3),* 309–319.

McDonnell, P. M., Corkum, V. L., & Wilson, D. L. (1989). Patterns of movement in the first 6 months of life: New directions. *Canadian Journal of Psychology, 43(2),* 320–339.*

McDougall, W. (1908). *Social psychology.* New York: Putnam.

McDowell, M. J. (2001). Principle of organization: A dynamic-systems view of the archetype-as-such. *Journal of Analytical Psychology, 46,* 637–654.

McFarlane, T., Polivy, J., & Herman, C. P. (1998). Dieting. In H. S. Friedman (Ed.), *Encyclopedia of mental health (Vol. 1).* San Diego: Academic Press.*

McFarlane, T., Polivy, J., & McCabe, R. (1999). Help, not harm: Psychological foundation for a nondieting approach toward health. *Journal of Social Issues, 55,* 261–276.*

McGaugh, J. L., & Cahill, L. (2002). Emotion and memory. In R. J. Davidson, K. R. Scherer, & H. H. Goldsmith (Eds.), *Handbook of affective sciences.* New York: Oxford.

McGrath, E., Strickland, B. R., Keita, G. P., & Russo, N. F. (Eds.). (1990). *Women and depression: Risk factors and treatment issues.* Washington: APA Press.

McGrath, R. E., Pogge, D. L., Stokes, J. M., Cragnolino, A., Zaccario, M., Hayman, J., et al. (2005). Field reliability of comprehensive system scoring in an adolescent inpatient sample. *Assessment, 12(2),* 199–209.

McGregor, I., Newby-Clark, I. R., & Zanna, M. P. (1999). Remembering dissonance: Simultaneous accessibility of inconsistent cognitive elements moderates epistemic discomfort. In E. Harmon-Jones, & J. Mills (Eds.), *Cognitive dissonance: Progress on a pivotal theory in social psychology.* Washington: APA Press.*

McGue, M., Bouchard, T. J., Iacono, W. G., & Lykken, D. T. (1993). Behavioral genetics of cognitive ability: A life-span perspective. In R. Plomin, & G. E. McClearn (Eds.), *Nature, nurture, and psychology.* Washington: APA Press.

McGuigan, F. J. (2004). *Biological psychology: A cybernetic science.* Upper Saddle River, NJ: Prentice Hall.

McIntosh, A. R. (2000). Towards a network theory of cognition. *Neural Networks, 13,* 861–870.*

McIntyre, C. K., Pal, S. N., Marriott, L. K., & Gold, P. E. (2002). Competition between memory systems: acetylcholine release in the hippocampus correlates negatively with good performance on an amygdala-dependent task. *Journal of Neuroscience, 22,* 1171–1176.

McIver, T. (1988). Backward masking and other backward thoughts about music. *Skeptical Inquirer, 13,* 50–63.

McKay, D., & Tryon, W. W. (2002). Behavior therapy: Theoretical bases. In M. Hersen & W. H. Sledge (Eds.), *Encyclopedia of psychotherapy.* San Diego: Academic Press.

McKelvie, S. J., & Drumheller, A. (2001). The availability heuristic with famous names: A replication. *Perceptual and Motor Skills, 92,* 507–516.*

McKendree-Smith, N., & Scogin, F. (2000). Depressive realism: Effects of depression severity and interpretation time. *Journal of Clinical Psychology, 56,* 1601–1608.

McKim, M. K., Cramer, K. M., Stuart, B., & O'Connor, D. H. (1999). Infant care decisions and attachment security: The Canadian Transition to Child Care Study. *Canadian Journal of Behavioral Science, 31(2),* 92–106.*

McLean, P. D., & Wood, S. R. (2001). *Anxiety disorders in adults.* New York: Oxford.

McLoyd, V. C. (2000). Poverty. In A. Kazdin (Ed.), *Encyclopedia of psychology.* Washington, & New York: American Psychological Association and Oxford.

McMahon, S., & Koltzenburg, M. (2005). *Wall & Melzacks textbook of pain (5th ed.).* London: Churchill Livingstone.

McMillan, J. H. (2004a). *Educational research: Fundamentals for the consumer (4th ed.).* Boston: Allyn & Bacon.

McMillan, J. H. (2004b). *Classroom assessment (3rd ed.).* Boston: Allyn & Bacon.

McMillan, J. H., & Wergin, J. F. (2002). *Understanding and evaluating educational research (2nd ed.).* Englewood Cliffs, NJ: Prentice Hall.

McMullen, L. M. (1996). Studying the use of figurative language in psychotherapy: The search for research-able questions. *Metaphor and Symbolic Activity, 11,* 241–255.*

McMullen, L. M. (1999). Metaphors in the talk of "depressed" women in psychotherapy. *Canadian Psychology, 40,* 102–111.*

McMullen, L. M. (2003). "Depressed" women's constructions of the deficient self. In J. M. Stoppard, & L. M. McMullen (Eds.), *Situating sadness: Women and depression in social context.* New York: New York University Press.*

McMullen, L. M., & Conway, J. B. (1997). Dominance and nurturance in the narratives told by clients in psychotherapy. *Psychotherapy Research, 7,* 83–99.*

McNally, R. J. (1994). *Panic disorder: A critical analysis.* New York: Guilford.

McNally, R. J. (1998). Panic attacks. In H. S. Friedman (Ed.), *Encyclopedia of mental health (Vol. 3).* San Diego: Academic Press.

McNeil, E. B. (1967). *The quiet furies.* Englewood Cliffs, NJ: Prentice Hall.

McShane, D. A., & Plas, J. M. (1984). The cognitive functioning of American Indian school children: Moving from the WISC to the WISC-R. *School Psychology Review, 13,* 61–73.

McVey, G., Tweed, S., & Blackmore, E. (2004). Dieting among preadolescent and young female adolescents. *Canadian Medical Association Journal, 170(10),* 1559–1561.*

Meade, C. S., & Ickovics, J. R. (2005). Systematic review of sexual risk among pregnant and mothering teens in the USA: Pregnancy as an opportunity for integrated prevention of STD and repeat pregnancy. *Social Science & Medicine, 60(4),* 661–678.

Meador, B. D., & Rogers, C. R. (1979). Person-centered therapy. In R. J. Corsini (Ed.), *Current psychotherapies (2nd ed.).* Itasca, IL: Peacock.

Mealey, L. (2000). *Sex differences: Developmental and evolutionary perspectives.* San Diego: Academic Press.

Mechler, F., & Ringach, D. L. (2002). On the classification of simple and complex cells. *Vision Research, 42,* 1017–1033.

Medin, D. L., Lynch, E. B., & Solomon, K. O. (2000). Are there kinds of concepts? *Annual Review of Psychology, 51,* 121–147.

Medin, D. L., Proffitt, J. B., & Schwartz, H. C. (2000). Concepts: Structure. In A. Kazdin (Ed.), *Encyclopedia of psychology.* Washington, & New York: APA Press and Oxford.

Meel, B. L., & Leenaars, A. A. (2005). Human immunodeficiency virus (HIV) and suicide in a region of Eastern Province ("Transkei"), South Africa. *Archives of Suicide Research, 9(1),* 69–75.*

Mehrabian, A., & Blum, J. S. (2003). Physical appearance, attractiveness, and the mediating role of emotions. In N. J. Pallone (Ed.), *Love, romance, sexual interaction: Research perspectives from Current Psychology.* New Brunswick, NJ: Transaction Publishers.

Mehta, M. D. (2001). Pornography in Usenet: A study of 9,800 randomly selected images. *CyberPsychology & Behavior, 4(6),* 695–703.*

Meichenbaum, D. (1977). *Cognitive-behavior modification: An integrative approach.* Plenum Press: New York.*

Meichenbaum, D. (1991). Evolution of cognitive behavior therapy: Origins, tenets and clinical examples. In J. Zeig (Ed.), *The evolution of psychotherapy, II.* New York: Brunner/ Mazel.*

Meichenbaum, D. (2003). Cognitive-behavior therapy: Folktales and the unexpurgated history. *Cognitive Therapy & Research, 27(1),* 125–129.*

Meichenbaum, D., Turk, D., & Burstein, S. (1975). The nature of coping with stress. In I. Sarason, & C. Spielberger (Eds.), *Stress and anxiety.* Washington: Hemisphere.*

Meier, A. (2005). In-person counseling and internet self-help groups: Synthesizing new forms of social work practice. In G. L. Greif, & P. H. Ephross (Eds.), *Group work with populations at risk (2nd ed.).* New York: Oxford.

Melinder, K. A., & Andersson, R. (2001). The impact of structural factors on the injury rate in different

European countries. *European Journal of Public Health, 11*, 301–308.

Melis, M., Camarin, R., Ungless, M. A., & Bonci, A. (2002). Long-lasting potentiation of GABAergic synapses in dopamine neurons after a single in vivo ethanol exposure. *Journal of Neuroscience, 22*, 2074–2982.

Meller, R., Harrison, P. J., Elliott, J. M., & Sharp, T. (2002). In vitro evidence that 5-hydroxytryptamine increases efflux of glial glutamate via 5-HT2a receptor activation. *Journal of Neuroscience Research, 67*, 399–405.

Melzack, R. (1973). *The puzzle of pain.* New York: Basic Books.*

Melzack, R. (1989). Phantom limbs, the self, and the brain. *Canadian Psychology, 30(1)*, 1–16.*

Melzack, R. (1993). Pain: Past, present and future. *Canadian Journal of Experimental Psychology, 47(4)*, 615–629.*

Melzack, R., & Wall, P. D. (1965). Pain mechanisms: A new theory. *Science, 150*, 971–979.*

Melzack, R. (1999). From the gate to the neuromatrix. *Pain. Special A tribute to Patrick D. Wall, Suppl 6*, pS121–S126.*

Memmler, R. L., Cohen, B. J., Wood, D. L., & Schwegler, J. (1995). *The human body in health and disease (8th ed.).* Philadelphia: Lippincott Williams & Wilkins.

Memon, A., & Yarmey, D. (1999). The cognitive interview and earwitness testimony. *Perceptual and Motor Skills, 88*, 797–807.*

Mendez, M. F., Chow, T., Ringman, J., Twitchell, G., & Hinkin, C. H. (2000). Pedophilia and temporal lobe disturbances. *Journal of Neuropsychiatry and Clinical Neurosciences, 12*, 71–76.

Merikle, P. M., & Daneman, M. (1996). Memory for unconsciously perceived events: Evidence from anesthetized patients. *Consciousness and Cognition, 5*, 525–541.*

Merikle, P. M., & Daneman, M. (1998). Psychological investigations of unconscious perception. *Journal of Consciousness Studies, 5*, 5–18.*

Merikle, P.M., Smilek, D., & Eastwood, J.D. (2001). Perception without awareness: Perspectives from cognitive psychology. *Cognition, 79(1-2)*, 115–134.*

Merskey, H. (1992), The manufacture of personalities: The production of multiple personality disorder. *British Journal of Psychiatry, 160*, 327–340.*

Mesquita, B. (2002). Emotions as dynamic cultural phenomena. In R. J. Davidson, K. R. Scherer, & H. H. Goldsmith (Eds.), *Handbook of affective sciences.* New York: Oxford.

Messer, W. S., & Griggs, R. A. (1989). Student belief and involvement in the paranormal and performance in introductory psychology. *Teaching of Psychology, 16*, 187–191.

Messinger, J. C. (1971). Sex and repression in an Irish folk community. In D. S. Marshall, & R. C. Suggs (Eds.), *Human sexual behavior.* New York: Basic Books.

Metcalfe, J., & Mischel, W. (1999). A hot/cool system analysis of delay of gratification: Dynamics of will power. *Psychological Review, 106*, 3–19.

Meyer, G. J. (2001). Introduction to the special section in the special series on the utility of the Rorschach for clinical assessment. *Psychological Assessment, 13*, 419–422.

Meyer, G. J., & Archer, R. P. (2001). The hard science of Rorschach research: What do we know and where do we go from here? *Psychological Assessment, 13*, 486–491.

Meyer, R. G., & Osborne, Y. V. H. (1982). *Case studies in abnormal behavior.* Boston: Allyn & Bacon.

Meyer, G. J., Mihura, J. L., & Smith, B. L. (2005). The interclinician reliability of Rorschach interpretation in four data sets. *Journal of Personality Assessment, 84(3)*, 29–314.

Meyer, R. (2002). *Phonics exposed: Understanding and resisting systematic direct intense phonics instruction.* Mahwah, NJ: Erlbaum.

Micarelli, A., & Sciarrone, F. (2004). Anatomy and empirical evaluation of an adaptive web-based information filtering system. *User Modeling & User-Adapted Interaction. Special User Modeling for Web Information Retrieval, 14(2-3)*, 159–200.

Michael, R. T., Gagnon, J. H., Laumann, E. O., & Kolata, G. (1994). *Sex in America.* Boston: Little, Brown.

Michaels, J. W., Bloomel, J. M., Brocato, R. M., Linkous, R. A., & Rowe, J. S. (1982). Social facilitation and inhibition in a natural setting. *Replications in Social Psychology, 2*, 21–24.

Michailidis, M., & Georgiou, Y. (2005). Employee occupational stress in banking. *Work: Journal of Prevention, Assessment & Rehabilitation, 24(2)*, 123–137.

Michener, H. A., DeLamater, J. D., & Myers, D. J. (2004). *Social psychology (5th ed.).* Belmont, CA: Wadsworth.

Michinov, E., & Michinov, N. (2001). The similarity hypothesis: A test of the moderating role of social comparison orientation. *European Journal of Social Psychology, 31*, 549–555.

Middleton, F. A., & Strick, P. L. (2001). Cerebellar projections to the prefrontal cortex of the primate. *Journal of Neuroscience, 21*, 700–712.

Mignot, E. (2001). A hundred years of narcolepsy research. *Archives of Italian Biology, 139*, 207–220.

Mignot, E., & Thorsby, E. (2001). Narcolepsy and the HLA system. *New England Journal of Medicine, 344(9)*, 692.

Miklowitz, D. J. (2002). *The bipolar disorder survival guide: What you and your family need to know.* New York: Guilford.

Milgram, P., Vigehesa, H., & Weinstein, P. (1992). Adolescent dental fear and control. *Behavior Research and Therapy, 30*, 367–373.

Milgram, S. (1965). Some conditions of obedience and disobedience to authority. *Human Relations, 18*, 56–76.

Milgram, S. (1974). *Obedience to authority.* New York: Harper & Row.

Milgram, S., Liberty, H. J., Toledo, R., & Wackenhut, J. (1986). Response to intrusion in waiting lines. *Journal of Personality & Social Psychology, 51*, 683–689.

Miller, A. G. (Ed.). (2004). *The social psychology of good and evil.* New York: Guilford.

Miller, C. (2002). Flooding. In M. Hersen, & W. H. Sledge (Eds.), *Encyclopedia of psychotherapy.* San Diego: Academic Press.

Miller, D. T. (2006). *An invitation to social psychology.* Belmont, CA: Wadsworth.

Miller, E. K., & Cohen, J. D. (2001). An integrative theory of prefrontal cortex function. *Annual Review of Neuroscience, 24*, 167–202.

Miller, G. (2004). Brain cells may pay the price for a bad night's sleep. *Science, 306*, 1126.

Miller, G. A. (1956). The magical number seven, plus or minus two: Some limits on our capacity for information processing. *Psychological Review, 48*, 337–442.

Miller, L. K. (2006). *Principles of everyday behavior analysis (4th ed.).* Belmont, CA: Wadsworth.

Miller, L. T., & Vernon, P. A. (1996). Intelligence, reaction time, and working memory in 4- to 6- year-old children. *Intelligence, 22*, 155–190.*

Miller, N. E. (1941). The frustration-aggression hypothesis. *Psychological Review, 48*, 337–442.

Miller, N. E. (1959). Liberalization of basic S-R concepts: Extension to conflict behavior, motivation, and social learning. In S. Koch (Ed.), *Psychology: A study of science.* New York: McGraw-Hill.

Miller, N. E. (1969). Learning of visceral glandular responses. *Science, 163*, 434–445.

Miller, N. E. (1985). The value of behavioral research on animals. *American Psychologist, 40*, 432–440.

Miller, S. B. (1993). Cardiovascular reactivity in anger-defensive individuals: The influence of task demands. *Psychosomatic Medicine, 55(1)*, 79–85.*

Miller, S. B., Dolgoy, L., Friese, M., & Sita, A. (1996). Dimensions of hostility and cardiovascular response to interpersonal stress. *Journal of Psychosomatic Research, 41(1)*, 81–95.*

Millet, B., Kochman, F., Gallarda, T., Krebs, M. O., Demonfaucon, F., Barrot, I., et al. (2004). Phenomenological and comorbid features associated in obsessive-compulsive disorder: Influence of age of onset. *Journal of Affective Disorders, 79(1-3)*, 241–246.

Millis, R. M. (1998). Smoking. In H. S. Friedman (Ed.), *Encyclopedia of mental health (Vol. 3).* San Diego: Academic Press.

Mills, J. A. (1998). *Control: A history of behavioral psychology.* New York: New York University Press.*

Mills, J. (2004). Clarifications on Trieb: Freud's theory of motivation reinstated. *Psychoanalytic Psychology, 21(4)*, 673–677.*

Milner, A. D., & Goodale, M. A. (1995). *The visual brain in action.* New York: Oxford.*

Milner, A. D., & Goodale, M. A. (2002). The visual brain in action. In A. Noë, & E. Thompson, (Eds.) *Vision and mind: Selected readings in the philosophy of perception.* Cambridge MIT Press.*

Milner, B., Corkin, S., & Teuber, H. L. (1968). Further analysis of the hippocampal amnesic syndrome: 14-year follow-up study of H. M. *Neuropsychologia, 6*, 215–234.*

Milner, P. M. (1991). Brain-stimulation reward: A review. *Canadian Journal of Psychology, 45(1)*, 1–36.*

Miltenberger, R. G. (2004). *Behavior modification (3rd ed.).* Belmont, CA: Wadsworth.

Minda, J. P., & Smith, J. D. (2001). Prototypes in category learning: The effects of category size, category structure, and stimulus complexity. *Journal of Experimental Psychology: Learning, Memory, and Cognition, 27*, 775–799.

Mindell, J. A., & Owens, J. A. (2003). *A clinical guide to pediatric sleep: Diagnosis and management of sleep problems in children and adolescents.* Philadelphia: Lippincott, Williams & Wilkins.

Mineka, S., & Nugent, K. (1995). Mood-congruent memory biases in anxiety and depression. In D. L. Schacter, J. T. Coyle, G. D. Fischbach, M. M. Mesulam, & L. E. Sullivan (Eds.), *Memory distortion: How minds, brains, and societies reconstruct the past.* Cambridge Harvard University Press.

Minnes, P. (1998). Mental retardation: The impact upon the family. In J. A. Burack, R. M. Hodapp, &. E. Zigler (Eds.), *Handbook of mental retardation and development.* New York: Cambridge.*

Mirsky, A. F., Bieliauskas, L. M., Van Kammen, D. P., Jonsson, E., & Sedvall, G. (2000). A 39-year followup of the Genain quadruplets. *Schizophrenia Bulletin, 3*, 5–18.

Mischel, W. (1968). *Personality and assessment.* New York: Wiley.

Mischel, W. (1973). Toward a cognitive social learning theory reformulation of personality. *Psychological Review, 80*, 252–283.

Mischel, W. (2004). Toward an integrative science of the person. *Annual Review of Psychology, 55*, 1–22.

Mischel, W., & Ayduk, O. (2004). Willpower in a cognitive-affective processing system: The dynamics of delay of gratification In R. F. Baumeister, & K. D. Vohs (Eds.), *Handbook of self-regulation.* New York: Guilford.

Mischel, W., & Moore, B. S. (1980). The role of ideation in voluntary delay for symbolically presented rewards. *Cognitive Therapy and Research, 4*, 211–221.

Mischel, W., & Shoda, Y. (2001). Integrating dispositions and processing dynamics within a unified theory of personality: The cognitive-affective personality system. In L. A. Pervin, & O. P. John (Eds.), *Handbook of personality.* New York: Guilford.

Mischel, W., Shoda, Y., & Mendoza-Denton, R. (2002). Situation-behavior profiles as a locus of consistency in personality. *Current Directions in Psychological Science, 11*, 50–53.

Misra, A., Arora, N., Mondal, S., Pandey, R. M., Jailkhani, B., Peshin, S., et al. (2001). Relation between plasma leptin and anthropometric and metabolic covariates in lean and obese diabetic and hyperlipidaemic Asian Northern Indian subjects. *Diabetes, Nutrition, and Metabolism, 14*, 18–26.

Mitchell, D. E. (1989). Normal and abnormal visual development in kittens: Insights into the mechanisms that underlie visual development in humans. *Canadian Journal of Psychology, 43(2)*, 141–164.*

Mitchell, J. P., Macrae, C. N., & Banaji, M. R. (2004). Encoding-specific effects of social cognition on the neural correlates of subsequent memory. *Journal of Neuroscience, 24(21)*, 4912–4917.

Mittag, W., & Schwarzer, R. (1993). Interaction of employment status and self-efficacy on alcohol consumption: A two-wave study on stressful life transitions. *Psychology and Health, 8*, 77–87.

Mitterer, J. (1982). There are at least two kinds of poor reader: Whole-word poor readers and recoding poor readers. *Canadian Journal of Psychology, 36*, 445–461.*

Mitterer, J., & Begg, I. (1979). Can meaning be extracted from meaningless stimuli? *Canadian Journal of Psychology, 33*, 193–198.*

Miyashita, Y., & Hayashi, T. (2000). Neural representation of visual objects: Encoding and top-down activation. *Current Opinions in Neuroscience, 10*, 187–194.

Mizes, J. S., & Miller, K. J. (2000). Eating disorders. In M. Herson, & R. T. Ammerman (Eds.), *Advanced abnormal child psychology (2nd ed.)*. Mahwah, NJ: Erlbaum.

Mizutani, A., Chahl, J. S., & Srinivasan, M. V. (2003). Motion camouflage in dragonflies. *Nature, 423(6940)*, 604.

Moerman, D. E. (2002). The meaning response and the ethics of avoiding placebos. *Evaluation & the Health Professions. Special Recent Advances in Placebo Research, 25(4)*, 399–409.

Molina V., Sanz J., Sarramea F., Benito C., & Palomo T. (2005). Prefrontal atrophy in first episodes of schizophrenia associated with limbic metabolic hyperactivity. *Journal of Psychiatry Research, 39(2)*, 117–27.

Monahan, J. L., Murphy, S. T., & Zajonc, R. B. (2000). Subliminal mere exposure: Specific, general, and diffuse effects. *Psychological Science, 11*, 462–466.

Monahan, J. S. (2001). Coloring single Stroop elements: Reducing automaticity or slowing color processing? *Journal of General Psychology, 138*, 98–112.

Mondloch, C. J., Geldart, S., Maurer, D., & Le Grand, R. (2003). Developmental changes in face processing skills. *Journal of Experimental Child Psychology, 86*, 67–84.*

Mondor, T. A., & Lacey, T. E. (2001). Facilitative and inhibitory effects of cuing sound duration, intensity, and timbre. *Perception & Psychophysics, 63*, 726–736.*

Monk, T. H. (1993). Shiftwork. In M. A. Carskadon (Ed.), *Encyclopedia of sleep and dreaming*. New York: Macmillan.

Monsell, S., Taylor, T. J., & Murphy, K. (2001). Naming the color of a word: Is it responses or task sets that compete? *Memory and Cognition, 29*, 137–151.

Montagne, B., Kessels, R. P. C., Frigerio, E., de Haan, E. H. F., & Perrett, D. I. (2005). Sex differences in the perception of affective facial expressions: Do men really lack emotional sensitivity? *Cognitive Processing, 6(2)*, 136–141.

Monte, C. F., & Sollod, R. N. (2003). *Beneath the mask: An introduction to theories of personality (7th ed.)*. New York: Wiley.

Monteith, M. J. (2000). Prejudice. In A. Kazdin (Ed.), *Encyclopedia of psychology*. Washington, & New York: APA Press and Oxford.

Monteith, M. J., & Voils, C. I. (2001). Exerting control over prejudiced responses. In G. B. Moscowitz (Ed.), *Cognitive social psychology*. Mahwah, NJ: Erlbaum.

Montgomery, H., Lipshitz, R., & Brehmer, B. (Eds.). (2005). *How professionals make decisions. Expertise: Research and applications*. Mahwah, NJ: Erlbaum.

Moodley, R., & Palmer, S. (Eds.). (2006). *Race, culture and psychotherapy*. London: Routledge.

Mook, D. (2004). *Classic experiments in psychology*. Westport, CT: Greenwood Press.

Moore, T. E. (1995). Subliminal self-help auditory tapes: An empirical test of perceptual consequences. *Canadian Journal of Behavioural Science, 27*, 9–20.*

Moore, T. O. (2001). Testosterone and male behavior: Empirical research with hamsters does not support the use of castration to deter human sexual aggression. *North American Journal of Psychology, 3(3)*, 503–520.

Moore-Ede, M. C., Sulzman, F. M., & Fuller, C. A. (1982). *The clocks that time us*. Cambridge: Harvard University Press.

Morahan-Martin, J., & Schumacher, P. (2003). Loneliness and social uses of the Internet. *Computers in Human Behavior, 19(6)*, 659–671.

Moran, J. P. (2002). *Teaching sex: The shaping of adolescence in the 20th century*. Cambridge Harvard University Press.

Moras, K. (2002). Research on psychotherapy. In M. Hersen, & W. H. Sledge (Eds.), *Encyclopedia of psychotherapy*. San Diego: Academic Press.

Morgan, D. L. (2002). *Essentials of learning and cognition*. New York: McGraw-Hill.

Morgan, J. P. (Ed.). (2005). *Psychology of aggression*. Hauppauge, NY: Nova Science Publishers.

Morgan, T., & Cummings, A. L. (1999). Change experienced during group therapy of female survivors of childhood sexual abuse. *Journal of Consulting and Clinical Psychology, 67*, 28–36.*

Morgan, W. G. (2002). Origin and history of the earliest thematic apperception test pictures. *Journal of Personality Assessment, 79(3)*, 422–445.

Morley K. I., & Montgomery G. W. (2001). The genetics of cognitive processes: Candidate genes in humans and animals. *Behavior Genetics, 31(6)*, 511–531.

Morris, C. A. (2005). The dysmorphology, genetics, and natural history of Williams syndrome. In C. A. Morris, P. P. Wang, & H. Lenhoff (Eds.), *Williams-Beuren syndrome: Research and clinical perspectives*. Baltimore, MD: Johns Hopkins University Press.

Moses, J., Steptoe, A., Mathews, A., & Edwards, S. (1989). The effects of exercise training on mental well-being in a normal population: A controlled trial. *Journal of Psychosomatic Research, 33*, 47–61.

Moskowitz, G. B. (Ed.). (2001). *Cognitive social psychology*. Mahwah, NJ: Erlbaum.

Moursund, J. P. (2004). *Integrative psychotherapy: The art and science of relationship*. Belmont, CA: Wadsworth.

Muchinsky, P. M. (2003). *Psychology applied to work (7th ed.)*. Belmont, CA: Wadsworth.

Muir, D., & Hains, S. (2004). The U-shaped developmental function for auditory localization. *Journal of Cognition & Development, 5(1)*, 123–130.

Muir, D., & Slater, A. (2003). The scope and methods of developmental psychology. In A. Slater, & G. Bremmer (Eds) *An introduction to developmental psychology*. Malden, MA: Blackwell.*

Mulvihill, C. B., Davies, G. J., & Rogers, P. J. (2002). Dietary restraint in relation to nutrient intake, physical activity, and iron status in adolescent females. *Journal of Human Nutrition-Dietetics, 15*, 19–31.

Mumford, M., & Porter, P. P. (1999). Analogies. In M. A. Runco, & S. Pritzker (Eds.), *Encyclopedia of creativity*. San Diego: Academic Press.

Munoz, R. F. (1998). Depression: Applied aspects. In H. S. Friedman (Ed.), *Encyclopedia of mental health (Vol. 1)*. San Diego: Academic Press.

Murdock, B. B. (1999). The buffer 30 years later: Working memory in a theory of distributed associative model (TODAM). In C. Izawa (Ed.), *On human memory*. Mahwah, NJ: Erlbaum.*

Murphy, R. A., Baker, A. G., & Fouquet, N. (2001). Relative validity effects with either one or two more valid cues in Pavlovian and instrumental conditioning. *Journal of Experimental Psychology: Animal Processes, 27*, 59–67.

Murray, H. A. (1938). *Explorations in personality*. Cambridge Harvard University Press.

Murray, M., Nelson, G., Poland, B., Maticka-Tyndale, E., & Ferris, L. (2004). Assumptions and values of community health psychology. *Journal of Health Psychology, 9*, 315–325.*

Murray, S. L., Rose, P., Bellavia, G. M., Holmes, J. G., & Kusche, A. G. (2002). When rejection stings: How self-esteem constrains relationship-enhancement processes. *Journal of Personality & Social Psychology, 83(3)*, 556–573.

Murtha, S., Fitch, T., DelCarpio, R., Bergman, H., Chertkow, H. (1998). Does atrophy of the temporal lobes predict decline to dementia. *Journal of Canadian Congress of Neurological Sciences, Supple. 1*, S28.*

Myers, A. (2003). *Experimental psychology (5th ed.)*. Belmont, CA: Wadsworth.

Myers, D. G. (2000). *The American paradox*. New Haven, CT: Yale University Press.

Myers, D. G. (2005). *Social psychology (8th ed.)*. New York: McGraw-Hill.

Myers, T. C., Swan-Kremeier, L., Wonderlich, S., Lancaster, K., & Mitchell, J. E. (2004). The use of alternative delivery systems and new technologies in the treatment of patients with eating disorders. *International Journal of Eating Disorders, 36(2)*, 123–143.

Myerson, J., Rank, M. R., Raines, F. Q., & Schnitzler, M. A. (1998). Race and general cognitive ability: The myth of diminishing returns in education. *Psychological Science, 9*, 139–142.

N

Nachshen, J. S., Woodford, L., & Minnes, P. (2003). The Family Stress and Coping Interview for families of individuals with developmental disabilities: A lifespan perspective on family adjustment. *Journal of Intellectual Disability Research. Special Issue on Family Research, 47(4–5)*, 285–290.*

Nadon, R., Laurence, J.-R., & Perry, C. W. (1991). The two disciplines of scientific hypnosis: A synergistic model. In S. J. Lynn, & J. W. Rhue (Eds.), *Theories of hypnosis: Current models and perspectives*. New York: Guilford.*

Nagel, T. (1974). What is it like to be a bat? *The Philosophical Review, 83*, 435–450.

Nahavandi, A. (2003). *The art and science of leadership (3rd ed.)*. Englewood Cliffs, NJ: Prentice Hall.

Nairn, S. L., Ellard, J. E., Scialfa, C. T., & Miller, C. D. (2003). At the core of introductory psychology: A content analysis. *Canadian Psychology, 44.*

Nakamura, J., & Csikszentmihalyi, M. (2002). The concept of flow. In C. R. Snyder, & S. J. Lopez (Eds.), *Handbook of positive psychology*. New York: Oxford.

Nakamura, J., & Csikszentmihalyi, M. (2003). The motivational sources of creativity as viewed from the paradigm of positive psychology. In L. G. Aspinwall, & U. M. Staudinger (Eds.), *A psychology of human strengths: Fundamental questions and future directions for a positive psychology*. Washington: APA Press.

Nakashima, M., & Canda, E. R. (2005). Positive dying and resiliency in later life: A qualitative study. *Journal of Aging Studies, 19(1)*, 109–125.

Nardi, A. E., Valenca, A. M., Nascimento, I., Mezzalama, M. A., & Zin, W. A. (2001). Hyperventilation in panic disorder and social phobia. *Psychopathology, 34*, 123–127.

Nash, J. M. (1997, February 3). Fertile minds. *Time*, pp. 50–54.

Nash, M. R. (2001). The truth and the hype about hypnosis. *Scientific American, 285(1)*, 46–49, 52–55.

Nash, M. R., & Nadon, R. (1997). The scientific status of research on hypnosis. In D. L. Faigman, D. H. Kaye, M. K. Saks, & J. Sanders (Eds.), *The West companion of scientific evidence*. St. Paul, MN: West Publishing.*

Naslund, E., Hellstrom, P. M., & Krail, G. (2001). The gut and food intake: An update for surgeons. *Journal of Gastrointestinal Surgeons, 5*, 556–567.

Nathan, P. E., & Gorman, J. M. (Eds.) (2002). *A guide to treatments that work (2nd ed.)*. New York: Oxford.

Nathan, P. E., & Langenbucher, J. W. (1999). Psychopathology: Description and classification. *Annual Review of Psychology, 50*, 79–107.

Nathan, P. E., Gorman, J. M., & Salkind, N. J. (1999). *Treating mental disorders*. New York: Oxford.

Nathan, P. E., Stuart, S. P., & Dolan, S. L. (2000). Research on psychotherapy efficacy and effectiveness: Between Scylla and Charybdis? *Psychological Bulletin, 126*, 964–981.

Neath, I., Gordon D. A., Brown, M. P., & Claudette F. C. (Eds.). (2005). *Short term/working memory: Special issue for the second Quebec conference on short-term/working memory*. Hove, UK: Psychology Press.

Nehlig, A. (Ed.). (2004). *Coffee, tea, chocolate, and the brain*. Boca Raton, FL: CRC Press.

Nehra, A., Blute, M. L., Barrent, D. M., & Moreland, R. B. (2002). Rationale for combination therapy of intraurethal prostaglandin E (1) and sildenafil in the salvage of erectile dysfunction patients during noninvasive therapy. *International Journal of Impotency Research, 14 (Suppl. 1),* S38–S42.

Neisser, U., Boodoo, G., Bouchard, T. J., Boykin, A. W., Brody, N., Ceci, S. J., et al. (1996). Intelligence: Knowns & unknowns. *American Psychologist, 51,* 77–101.

Nelson, D. L., Quick, J. C., & Simmons, B. L. (2001). Preventive management of work stress: Current themes and future challenges. In A. Baum, T. A. Revenson, & J. E. Singer (Eds.), *Handbook of health psychology*. Mahwah, NJ: Erlbaum.

Nelson, M. E., Fiatarone, M. A., Moranti, C. M., Trice, I., Greenberg, R. A., & Evans, W. J. (1994). Effects of high-intensity strength training on multiple risk factors for osteoporotic fractures: A randomized controlled trial. *Journal of the American Medical Association, 272,* 1909–1914.

Nelson, T. D. (2002). *Psychology of prejudice*. Boston: Allyn & Bacon.

Nemeroff, C. B., & Schatzberg, A. F. (2002). Pharmacological treatments for unipolar depression. In P. Nathan, & J. M. Gorman (Eds.), *A guide to treatments that work (2nd ed.)*. New York: Oxford.

Neufeld, R. W. J., Carter, J. R., Nicholson, I. R., & Vollick, D. N. (2003). Schizophrenia. In P. Firestone & W. L. Marshall (Eds.), *Abnormal psychology: Perspectives (2nd ed.)*. Toronto: Prentice Hall.*

Neufeldt, A. H. (1989). Applying psychology: Some real-world possibilties for scientists and practitioners. *Canadian Psychology, 30(4),* 681–691.*

Neumeister, A. (2004). Neurotransmitter depletion and seasonal affective disorder: Relevance for the biologic effects of light therapy. *Primary Psychiatry. Special Neurotransmitter Depletion, 11(6),* 44–48.

Neverlien, P. O., & Johnsen, T. B. (1991). Optimism-pessimism dimension and dental anxiety in children aged 10–12. *Community Dentistry and Oral Epidemiology, 19,* 342–346.

Nevid, J. S., & Greene, B. (2005). *Abnormal psychology in a changing world, media and research update (5th ed.)*. Upper Saddle River, NJ: Prentice Hall.

Neville, H. J. (2005). Development and plasticity of human cognition. In U. Mayr, E. Awh, & S. W. Keele (Eds.), *Developing individuality in the human brain: A tribute to Michael I. Posner*. Washington: APA Press.

Newstead, S. E., Handley, S. J., Harley, C., Wright, H., & Farelly, D. (2004). Individual differences in deductive reasoning. *Quarterly Journal of Experimental Psychology: Human Experimental Psychology, 57A(1),* 33–60.

Nicholls, J. G., Cobb, P., Wood, T., Yackel, E., & Patashnick, M. (1990). Assessing students' theories of success in mathematics: Individual and classroom differences. *Journal for Research in Mathematics Education, 21,* 109–122.

Nichols, C. D., & Sanders-Bush, E. (2002). A single dose of lysergic acid diethyamide influences gene expression patterns with the mammalian brain. *Neuropsychopharmacology, 26,* 634–642.

Nichols, T., & Dutton, D.G. (2001) Violence committed by women against intimates. *Journal of Couples Therapy, 10(1),* 41–57.*

Nicholson, I. A. M. (2003). *Inventing personality: Gordon Allport and the science of selfhood*. Washington: APA Press.*

Nickels, W. G., McHugh, J. M., & McHugh, S. M. (2005). *Understanding business (7th ed.)*. New York: McGraw-Hill.

Nickerson, R. S. (2004). *Cognition and chance: The psychology of probabilistic reasoning*. Mahwah, NJ: Erlbaum.

Nickerson, R. S., & Adams, M. J. (1979). Long-term memory for a common object. *Cognitive Psychology, 11,* 287–307.

Niedzwienska, A. (2004). Metamemory knowledge and the accuracy of flashbulb memories. *Memory, 12(5),* 603–613.

Niehoff, D. (1999). *The biology of violence*. New York: The Free Press.

Nielsen, M., Dissanayake, C., & Kashima, Y. (2003). A longitudinal investigation of self-other discrimination and the emergence of minor self-recognition. *Infant Behavior & Development, 26(2),* 213–226.

Niki, K., & Luo, J. (2002). An fMRI study on the time-limited role of the medial temporal lobe in long-term topographical autobiographical memory. *Journal of Cognitive Neuroscience, 14,* 500–507.

Niraula, S., Mishra, R. C., & Dasen, P. R. (2004). Linguistic relativity and spatial concept development in Nepal. *Psychology & Developing Societies, 16(2),* 99–124.

Nisbett, R. E. (2005). Heredity, environment, and race differences in IQ: A commentary on Rushton and Jensen (2005). *Psychology, Public Policy, and Law, 11(2),* 302–310.

Nobel, P. A., & Shiffrin, R. M. (2001). Retrieval processes in recognition and cued recall. *Journal of Experimental Psychology: Learning, Memory, and Cognition, 27,* 384–413.

Nock, S. (1995). A comparison of marriages and cohabiting relationships. *Journal of Family Issues, 16,* 53–76.

Noddings, N. (2005). Care and moral education. H. S. Shapiro, & D. E. Purpel (Eds) *Critical social issues in American education: Democracy and meaning in a globalizing world (3rd ed.)*. Mahwah, NJ: Erlbaum.

Noël, P. H., & Pugh, J. A. (2002). Management of overweight and obsese adults. *British Medical Journal, 325(7367),* 757–761.

Noels, K. A., & Clément, R. (1996). Communicating across cultures: Social determinants and acculturative consequences. *Canadian Journal of Behavioural Science, 28(3),* 214–228.*

Noels, K. A., & Clément, R. (1998). Language in education: Bridging educational policy and social psychological research. In J. Edwards (Ed.), *Language in Canada*. Cambridge: Cambridge University Press.*

Noels, K. A., Clément, R., & Pelletier, L. G. (1999). Perceptions of teachers' communicative style and students' intrinsic and extrinsic motivation. *Modern Language Journal, 83,* 23–34.*

Noels, K. A., Pelletier, L. G., Clément, R., & Vallerand, R. J. (2000). Why are you learning a second language? Motivational orientations and self-determination theory. *Language Learning, 50,* 57–85.*

Noels, K. A., Pon, G., & Clément, R. (1996). Language, identity, and adjustment: The role of linguistic self-confidence in the acculturation process. *Journal of Language and Social Psychology, 15(3),* 246–264.*

Nolen-Hoeksema, S. (2000). The role of rumination in depressive disorders and mixed anxiety/depressive symptoms. *Journal of Abnormal Psychology, 109,* 504–511.

Nolen-Hoeksema, S. (2004). *Abnormal psychology (3rd ed.)*. New York: McGraw-Hill.

Nolen-Hoeksema, S., & Keita, G. P. (2003). Women and depression: Introduction. *Psychology of Women Quarterly, 27(2),* 89–90.

Nolen-Hoeksema, S., Larson, J., & Grayson, C. (1999). Explaining the gender difference in depressive symptoms. *Journal of Personality & Social Psychology, 77,* 1061–1072.

Norcross, J. C. (Ed.) (2002). *Psychotherapy relationships that work*. New York: Oxford.

Norcross, J. C. (2005). A primer on psychotherapy integration. In J. C. Norcross, & M. R. Goldfried (Eds.), *Handbook of psychotherapy integration (2nd ed.)*. London: Oxford.

Norcross, J. C., & Goldfried, M. R. (Eds.). (2005). *Handbook of psychotherapy integration (2nd ed.)*. London: Oxford.

Norcross, J. C., Hedges, M., & Prochaska, J. O. (2002). The face of 2010: A Delphi poll on the future of psychotherapy. *Professional Psychology: Research & Practice, 33(3),* 316–322.

Norman, G. (2005). Research in clinical reasoning: Past history and current trends. *Medical Education, 39(4),* 418–427.*

Norris, F. N., Bryne, C. M., Diaz, E., & Kaniasty, K. (2001). *The range, magnitude, and duration of effects of natural and human-caused disasters: A review of the empirical literature*. Washington: National Center for PTSD.

North, A. C., Linley, A., & Hargreaves, D. J. (2000). Social loafing in a co-operative classroom task. *Educational Psychology, 20(4),* 389–392.

Northcutt, R. G. (2004). Taste buds: Development and evolution. *Brain, Behavior & Evolution, 64(3),* 198–206.

Notman, M. T., & Nadelson, C. C. (2002). Women's issues. In M. Hersen, & W. H. Sledge (Eds.), *Encyclopedia of psychotherapy*. San Diego: Academic Press.

Nottelmann, E. D., Susman, E. J., Blue, J. H., Inoff-Germain, G., Dorn, L. D., Loriaux, D. L., et al. (1987). Gonadal and adrenal hormone correlates of adjustment in early adolescence. In R. M. Lerner, & T. T. Foch (Eds.), *Biological-psychological interactions in early adolescence*. Mahwah, NJ: Erlbaum.

Nucci, L. P. (2001). *Education in the moral domain*. New York: Cambridge.

Nutt, D. J. (2001). Neurobiological mechanisms in generalized anxiety disorder. *Journal of Clinical Psychology, 62 (Suppl. 11),* 22–27.

Nutt, R. L. (2005). Feminist and contextual work. In M. Harway (Ed.), *Handbook of couples therapy*. New York: Wiley.

Nyberg, L., Forkstam, C., Petersson, K. M., Cabeza, R., & Ingvr, M. (2002). Brain imaging of human memory systems: between-systems similarities and within-system differences. *Brain Research: Cognitive Brain Research, 13,* 281–292.

Nyklícek, I, Temoshok, L., & Vingerhoets, A. (Eds.). (2004). *Emotional expression and health*. Hove, UK: Psychology Press.

Nystul, M. S. (2006). *Introduction to counseling (3rd ed.)*. Boston: Allyn & Bacon.

O

Oakley, R. (2004). How the mind hurts and heals the body. *American Psychologist, 59(1),* 29–40.

Oaksford, M., Roverts, L., & Chater, N. (2002). Relative informativeness of quantifiers used in syllogistic reasoning. *Memory & Cognition, 30,* 138–149.

Oberbauer, A. M., Rundstadler, J. A., Murray, A. D., & Havel, P. J. (2001). Obesity and elevated plasma leptin concentration in oMTIA-o growth hormone transgenic mice. *Obesity Research, 9,* 51–58.

O'Brien, G., & Opie, J. (1999). A connectionist theory of phenomenal experience. *Behavior and Brain Sciences, 1,* 127–148.

O'Connell, A. N., & Russo, N. F. (Eds.) (1983). *Models of achievement: Reflections of eminent women in psychology*. New York: Columbia University Press.*

O'Connor, E. (2001, February). Marketing medications. *Monitor on Psychology, 32(2),* 33.

O'Donnell, L., Stueve, A., San Doval, A., et al. (1999). Violence prevention and young adolescents' participation in community service. *Journal of Adolescent Health, 24,* 28–37.

Offer, D., Ostrov, E., Howard, K. I., & Atkinson, R. (1988). *The teenage world: Adolescents' self-image in ten countries*. New York: Plenum.

Ogbu, J. U. (2004). Collective identity and the burden of "acting white" in black history, community, and education. *Urban Review, 36(1),* 1–35.

Ogbu, J. U., & Stern, P. (2001). Caste status and intellectual development. In R. J. Sternberg, & E. L. Grigorenko (Eds.), *Environmental effects on cognitive abilities*. Mahwah, NJ: Erlbaum.

Ogden, J. (2004). *Health psychology: A textbook (3rd ed.)*. New York: McGraw-Hill.

Ogden, T. H. (2005). *This art of psychoanalysis*. London: Routledge.

Ogilvie, R. D. (1993). Sleep onset. In M. Carskadon, A. Rechtschaffen, G. Richardson, T. Roth, & J. Siegel (Eds.), *Encyclopedia of sleep and dreaming*. New York: Macmillan.*

Ogilvie, R. D., & Harsh, J. R. (Eds.). (1994). *Sleep onset: Normal and abnormal processes*. Washington: APA Press.*

Ogilvie, R. D., & Wilkinson, R. T. (1988). Behavioral versus EEG-based monitoring of all-night sleep/wake patterns. *Sleep, 11(2)*, 139–155.*

O'Hara, M., & Taylor, E. (2000). Humanistic psychology. In A. Kazdin (Ed.), *Encyclopedia of psychology*. Washington, & New York: APA Press and Oxford.

Ogloff, J. (2004). Invited introductory remarks to the special issue: Forensic psychology. *Canadian Journal of Behavioural Science, 36(2)*, 84–85.*

Ohayon, M. M. (2004). Interactions between sleep normative data and sociocultural characteristics in the elderly. *Journal of Psychosomatic Research, 56(5)*, 479–486.

Okagaki, L. (2000). Determinants of intelligence: Socialization of intelligence. In A. Kazdin (Ed.), *Encyclopedia of psychology*. Washington, & New York: APA Press and Oxford.

Okazawa, M., Takao, K., Hori, A., Shiraki, T., Matsumura, K., & Kobayashi, S. (2002). Ionic basis of cold receptors acting as thermostats. *Journal of Neuroscience, 22(10)*, 3994–4001.

O'Keefe, D. J. (2002). *Persuasion: Theory and research (2nd ed.)*. London: Sage.

Olds, J. M. (1958). Self-stimulation experiments and differential reward systems. In H. H. Jasper, L. D. Proctor, R. S. Knighton, W. C. Noshay, & R. T. Costello (Eds.), *Reticular formation of the brain*. Boston: Little, Brown.*

Olds, J. M., & Milner, P. M. (1954). Positive reinforcement produced by electrical stimulation of the septal area and other areas of the rat brain. *Journal of Comparative and Physiological Psychology, 47*, 419–427.*

O'Leary, V. E., & Flanagan, E. H. (2001). Leadership. In J. W. Worell (Ed.), *Encyclopedia of gender and women*. San Diego: Academic Press.

Olff, M. (1999). Stress, depression, and immunity. *Psychiatry Research, 85*, 7–16.

Oliet, S. H., Piet, R,, Poulain, D. A., & Theodosis, D. T. (2004). Glial modulation of synaptic transmission: Insights from the supraoptic nucleus of the hypothalamus. *Glia, 47(3)*, 258–67.

Oliner, S. P. (2001). Ordinary people: Faces of heroism and altruism. In S. G. Post, L. G. Underwood, J. P. Schloss, & W. B. Hurlbut (Eds.), *Altruism and altruistic love*. New York: Oxford.

Olio, K. A. (2004). The truth about "false memory syndrome". In P. J. Caplan, & L. Cosgrove (Eds.), *Bias in psychiatric diagnosis. A project of the association for women in psychology*. Northvale, NJ: Jason Aronson.

Olley, A., Malhi, G. S., Mitchell, P. B., Batchelor, J., Lagopoulos, J., & Austin, M.-P. V. (2005). When euthymia is just not good enough: The neuropsychology of bipolar disorder. *Journal of Nervous & Mental Disease, 193(5)*, 323–330.

Olshausen, B. A., & Field, D. J. (2005). How close are we to understanding V1? *Neural Computation, 17(8)*, 1665–1699.

Olszewski, P. K., Li, D., Grace, M. K., Billington, C. J., Kotz, C. M., & Levine, A. S. (2003). Neural basis of orexigenic effects of ghrelin acting within lateral hypothalamus. *Peptides, 24(4)*, 597–602.

Olthof, A., & Roberts, W. A. (2000). Summation of symbols by pigeons (Columba livia): The importance of number and mass of reward items. *Journal of Comparative Psychology, 114*, 158–166.*

Olthof, A., Sutton, J. E., Slumskie, S. V., D'Addetta, J-A., & Roberts, W. A. (1999). In search of the cognitive map: Can rats learn an abstract pattern of rewarded arms on the radial maze? *Journal of Experimental Psychology: Animal Behavior Processes, 25*, 352–362.*

Oltmanns, T. F., Emery, R. E., & Taylor, S. (2006). *Abnormal psychology (2nd Canadian ed.)*. Toronto: Pearson.

Oltmanns, T. F., Neale, J. M., & Davison, G. C. (1986). *Case studies in abnormal psychology (2nd ed.)*. New York: Wiley.

O'Neill, P. (1999). Ethical issues in working with communities in crisis. In R. Gist, & B. Lubin (Eds.), *Response to disaster: Psychosocial, community, and ecological approaches*. Philadelphia: Taylor & Francis.*

O'Neill, P. (2000). Cognition in social context: Contributions to community psychology. In J.

Rappaport, & E. Seidman (Eds.), *Handbook of community psychology*. Dordrecht, Netherlands: Kluwer Academic Publishers.*

O'Neill, P. (2005) The ethics of problem definition. *Canadian Psychology, 46*, 13–20.*

Ontario Ministry of Health (1990). *Ontario health survey, 1990*. Toronto: Ontario Ministry of Health.*

Onwuegbuzi, A. J., & Daley, C. E. (2001). Racial differences in IQ revisited: A synthesis of nearly a century of research. *Journal of Black Psychology, 27*, 209–220.

Oren, D. A., & Terman, M. (1998). Tweaking the human circadian clock with light. *Science, 279*, 333–334.

Orfanos, S. D. (2002). Relational psychoanalysis. In M. Hersen, & W. H. Sledge (Eds.), *Encyclopedia of psychotherapy*. San Diego: Academic Press.

Orlinsky, D. E., & Howard, K. L. (2000). Psychotherapy: Research. In A. Kazdin (Ed.), *Encyclopedia of psychology*. Washington, & New York: APA Press and Oxford.

Orne, M. T. (1959). The nature of hypnosis: Artifact and essence. *Journal of Abnormal & Social Psychology, 58*, 277–299.

Osborne, L., & Pober, B. (2001). Genetics of childhood disorders: XXVII. Genes and cognition in Williams syndrome. *Journal of the Academy of Child and Adolescent Psychiatry, 40*, 732–735.

Oshima, J., Scardamalia, M., & Bereiter, C. (1999). Collaborative learning processes associated with high and low conceptual progress. *Instructional Science, 24*, 125–155.*

Osipow, S. (2000). Work. In A. Kazdin (Ed.), *Encyclopedia of psychology*. Washington, and New York: APA Press and Oxford.*

Oskamp, S. & Schultz, P. W. (2005). *Attitudes and opinions (3rd ed.)*. Mahwah, NJ: Erlbaum.

Ost, L. (1991). Acquisition of blood and injection phobia and anxiety response patterns in clinical patients. *Behavior and Research Therapy, 23*, 263–282.

Ostir, G. V., Markides, K. S., Peek, M. K., & Goodwin, J. S. (2001). The association between emotional well-being and the incidence of stroke in older adults. *Psychosomatic Medicine, 63(2)*, 210–215.

Otten, L. J., Henson, R. N., & Rugg, M. D. (2001). Depth of processing effects on neural correlates of memory encoding. *Brain, 124*, 399–412.

Ouellette, S. C., & DiPlacido, J. (2001). Personality's role in the protection and enhancement of health: Where the research has been, where it is stuck, how it might move. In A. Baum, T. A. Revenson, & J. E. Singer (Eds.), *Handbook of health psychology*. Mahwah, NJ: Erlbaum.

Oving, A. B., Veltman, J. A., & Bronkhorst, A. W. (2004). Effectiveness of 3-D audio for warnings in the cockpit. *International Journal of Aviation Psychology, 14(3)*, 257–277.

Owen, A. M. (1997). Cognitive planning in humans: Neuropsychological, neuroanatomical, and neuropharmacological perspectives. *Progress in Neurobiology, 53(4)*, 431–450.

Oxenkrug, G. F., & Requintina, P. J. (2003). Melatonin and jet lag syndrome: Experimental model and clinical implications. *CNS Spectrums, 8(2)*, 139–148.

Oyserman, D., Coon, H. M., & Kemmelmeir, M. (2002). Rethinking individualism and collectivism: Evaluation of theoretical assumptions and meta-analyses. *Psychological Bulletin, 128*, 3–72.

Ozen, S., & Sir, A. (2004). Frequency of PTSD in a group of search and rescue workers two months after 2003 Bingol (Turkey) earthquake. *Journal of Nervous & Mental Disease, 192(8)*, 573–575.

Ozer, D. J. (2001). Four principles for personality assessment. In L. A. Pervin, & O. P. John (Eds.), *Handbook of personality*. New York: Guilford.

P

Pacheco-Lopez, G., Niemi, M. B., Kou, W., Harting, M., Fandrey, J., & Schedlowski, M. (2005). Neural substrates for behaviorally conditioned immunosup-

pression in the rat. *Journal of Neuroscience, 25(9)*, 2330–2337.

Pacher, P., Kohegyi, E., Kecskemeti, V., & Furst, S. (2001). Current trends in the development of new antidepressants. *Current Medicine and Chemistry, 8*, 89–100.

Paffenbarger, O., Hyde, R. T., Wing, A. L., & Hsieh, C. (1986). Physical activity, all-cause mortality, and longevity of college alumni. *New England Journal of Medicine, 324*, 605–612.

Pagano, M. E., Skodol, A. E., Stout, R. L., Shea, M. T., Yen, S., Grilo, C. M., et al. (2004). Stressful life events as predictors of functioning: Findings from the Collaborative Longitudinal Personality Disorders Study. *Acta Psychiatrica Scandinavica, 110(6)*, 421–429.

Pagnin, D., de Queiroz, V., Pini, S., & Cassano, G. B. (2004). Efficacy of ECT in Depression: A meta-analytic review. *Journal of ECT, 20(1)*, 13–20.

Paivio, A. (1971). *Imagery and verbal processes*. New York: Holt, Rinehart & Winston.*

Paivio, A. (1986). *Mental representations: A dual coding approach*. New York: Oxford.*

Palmer, S. E. (2003). Perceptual organization and grouping. In R. Kimchi, M. Behrmann, & C. R. Olson (Eds.), *Perceptual organization in vision: Behavioral and neural perspectives*. Mahwah, NJ: Erlbaum.

Palmer, E. D., Brown, T. T., Petersen, S. E. & Schlaggar, B. L. (2004). Investigation of the functional neuroanatomy of single word reading and its development. *Scientific Studies of Reading, 8(3)*, 203–223.

Paludi, M. A. (2002). *Psychology of women (2nd ed.)*. Upper Saddle River, NJ: Prentice Hall.

Panda, S., & Hogenesch, J. B. (2004). It's all in the timing: Many clocks, many outputs. *Journal of Biological Rhythms, 19(5)*, 374–387.

Panksepp, J. (2003). At the interface of the affective, behavioral, and cognitive neurosciences: Decoding the emotional feelings of the brain. *Brain & Cognition, 52(1)*, 4–14.

Panksepp, J. (2004). *Affective neuroscience: The foundations of human and animal emotions*. Oxford England: Oxford.

Panksepp, J. (2005). Affective consciousness: Core emotional feelings in animals and humans. *Consciousness & Cognition: An International Journal. Special Issue on the Neurobiology of Animal Consciousness, 14(1)*, 30–80.

Paradis, C. M., Solomon, L. Z., Florer, F., & Thompson, T. (2004). Flashbulb memories of personal events of 9/11 and the day after for a sample of New York City residents. *Psychological Reports, 95(1)*, 304–310.

Park, D. C., Nisbett, R., & Hedden, T. (1999). Aging, culture, and cognition. *Journal of Gerontology, 54B*, P75–P84.

Park, N. W., Conrod, B., Rewilak, D., Kwon, C., Gao, F., & Black, S. E. (2001). Automatic activation of positive but not negative attitudes after brain injury. *Neuropsychologia, 39*, 7–24.*

Parker, J. D. A. (2000). Emotional intelligence: Clinical and therapeutic implications. In R. Bar-On, & J. D. A. Parker (Eds.), *Handbook of emotional intelligence*. San Francisco, CA: Jossey-Bass.*

Parker, J. D. A., & Bagby, R. M. (1997). The measurement of impulsivity. In C. D. Webster, & M. A. Jackson (Eds.), *Impulsivity: A foundation for the understanding of psychopathy and violence*. New York: Guilford.*

Parker, J. D. A., Creque, R., Barnhart, D., Harris, J., Majeski, S. A., Wood, L.M., & Hogan, M. J. (2004) Academic achievement in high school: Does emotional intelligence matter? *Personality & Individual Differences, 37(7)*, 1321–1330.*

Parker, J. D. A., Saklofske, D. H., Wood, L. M., Eastabrook, J. M., & Taylor, R. N. (2005). Stability and change in emotional intelligence: Exploring the transition to young adulthood. *Journal of Individual Differences, 26(2)*, 100–106.*

Parker, J. D. A., Summerfeldt, L. J., Hogan, M. J., & Majeski, S. A. (2004) Emotional intelligence and academic success: examining the transition from high school to university. *Personality & Individual Differences, 36(1)*, 163–172.*

Parker, L. A., & Joshi, A. (1998). Naloxone-precipitated morphine withdrawal induced place aversion: Effects of naloxone at 24 hr post-morphine. *Pharmacology, Biochemistry and Behavior, 61*, 331–333.*

Parker, P. D., Prkachin, K. M., & Prkachin, G. C. (2005). Processing of facial expressions of negative emotion in alexithymia: The influence of temporal constraint. *Journal of Personality, 73(4)*, 1087–1107.*

Pascual-Leone, J., & Johnson, J. (1999). A dialectical constructivist view of representation. In I. E. Sigel (Ed.), *Development of mental representation*. Mahwah, NJ: Erlbaum.*

Pascual-Leone, J. & Johnson, J. (2004). A dialectical constructivist view of developmental intelligence. In O. Wilhelm & . R. W. Engle (Eds.) *Handbook of understanding and measuring intelligence*. Newbury Park, CA: Sage.*

Pashler, H., Johnston, J. C., & Ruthruff, E. (2001). Attention and performance. *Annual Review of Psychology, 52*, 629–651.

Passingham, R. E., Stephan, K. E., & Kötter, R. (2002). The anatomical basis of functional localization in the cortex. *Nature Reviews Neuroscience, 3*, 606–616.

Patterson, C. J. (2000). Family relationships of lesbians and gay men. *Journal of Marriage and the Family, 62*, 1052–1069.

Patterson, C. J. (2003). Children of lesbian and gay parents. In L. D. Garnets & D. C. Kimmel (Eds.), *Psychological perspectives on lesbian, gay, and bisexual experiences (2nd ed.)*. New York: Columbia University Press.

Patterson, D. R. (2004). Treating pain with hypnosis. *Current Directions in Psychological Science, 13(6)*, 252–255.

Paul, B. M., Elvevåg, B., Bokat, C. E., Weinberger, D. R., & Goldberg, T. E. (2005). Levels of processing effects on recognition memory in patients with schizophrenia. *Schizophrenia Research, 74(1)*, 101–110.

Paulson, D. S. (2004). The nearing death process and pastoral counseling. *Pastoral Psychology, 52(4)*, 339–352.

Paunonen, S. V., & Ashton, M. C. (1998). The structured assessment of personality across cultures. *Journal of Cross-Cultural Psychology, 29*, 150–170.*

Paunonen, S. V. & Ashton, M. C. (2002). The nonverbal assessment of personality; the NPQ and the FF-NPQ. In B. de Raad (Ed.), *Big five assessment*. Ashland, OH: Hogrefe & Huber.

Paunonen, S. V., Ashton, M. C., & Jackson, D. N. (2001). Nonverbal assessment of the Big Five personality factors. *European Journal of Personality, 15*, 3–18.*

Paunonen, S. V., Haddock, G., Forsterling, F., & Keinonen, M. (2003). Broad versus narrow personality measures and the prediction of behaviour across cultures. *European Journal of Personality, 17(6)*, 413–433.*

Paunonen, S. V., Jackson, D. H., Trzebinski, J., & Forsterling, F. (1992). Personality structures across cultures: A multimethod evaluation. *Journal of Personality & Social Psychology, 62*, 447–456.*

Paunovic, N. (2002). Prolonged exposure counterconditioning (PEC) as a treatment for chronic post-traumatic stress disorder and major depression in an adult survivor of repeated child sexual and physical abuse. *Clinical Case Studies, 1(2)*, 148–169.

Paus, T., Collins, D. L., Evans, A. C., Leonardf, G., Pike, B., & Zijdenbros, A. (2001). Maturation of white matter in the human brain: A review of magnetic resonance imaging. *Brain Research Bulletin, 54*, 255–266.

Pavlov, I. P. (1927). *Conditioned reflexes*. New York: Dover.

Payne, D. G., Lang, V. A., & Blackwell, J. M. (1995). Mixed versus pure display format in integration and nonintegration visual display. *Human Factors, 37*, 507–527.

Payne, J. L., Potash, J. B., & DePaulo, Jr., J. R. (2005). Recent findings on the genetic basis of bipolar disorder. *Psychiatric Clinics of North America, 28(2)*, 481-498.

Pearce, J., & Bouton, M. E. (2001). Theories of associative learning in animals. *Annual Review of Psychology, 52*, 111–139.

Pease, B., & Pease, A. (1998), *Why men don't listen and women can't read maps*. New York: Broadway Books.

Peckford, T., Templer, D. I., & Ruff, C. F. (1975). American bias of WAIS administered to Canadian patients. *Canadian Journal of Behavioural Science, 7*, 446–448.*

Pedersen, P. B., & Carey, J. C. (2003). *Multicultural counseling in schools (2nd ed.)*. Boston: Allyn & Bacon.

Pederson, D. R., Gleason, K. E., Moran, G., & Bento, S. (1998). Maternal attachment representations, maternal sensitivity, and infant-mother attachment. *Developmental Psychology, 34*, 925–933.*

Pegram, G. V., McBurney, J., Harding, S. M., & Makris, C. M. (2004). Normal sleep and sleep disorders in adults and children. In J. M. Raczynski, & L. C. Leviton (Eds.), *Handbook of clinical health psychology: (Vol 2). Disorders of behavior and health*. Washington: APA Press.

Pelletier, J. G., & Paré, D. (2004). Role of amygdala oscillations in the consolidation of emotional memories. *Biological Psychiatry, 55(6)*, 559–562.

Pence, A. R. (Ed.) (1988). *Ecological research with children and families: From concepts to methodology*. New York: Teachers College Press.*

Pence, A. R. (1989). In the shadow of mother-care: Contexts for an understanding of child day care in North America. *Canadian Psychology, 30(2)*, 140–147.*

Penedo, F. J., & Dahn, J. R. (2005). Exercise and well-being: A review of mental and physical health benefits associated with physical activity. *Current Opinion in Psychiatry, 18(2)*, 189–193.

Penfield, W. (1947). Some observations in the cerebral cortex of man. *Proceedings of the Royal Society, 134*, 349.*

Penfield, W., & Rasmussen, T. (1950). *The cortex of man*. New York: Macmillan.*

Peng, J., Qiao. H., & Xu, Z. B. (2002). A new approach to stability of neural networks with time-varying delays. *Neural Networks, 15*, 95–103.

Pengilly, J. W., & Dowd, E. T. (2000). Hardiness and social support as moderators of stress. *Journal of Clinical Psychology, 56*, 813–820.

Pennebaker, J. W., & Beall, S. K. (1986). Confronting a traumatic event: Toward an understanding of inhibition and disease. *Journal of Abnormal Psychology, 95(3)*, 274–281.

Pennebaker, J. W. (1997a). *Opening up: The healing power of expressing emotions (Rev. ed.)*. New York: Guilford.

Pennebaker, J. W. (1997b). Writing about emotional experiences as a therapeutic experience. *Psychological Science, 8*, 162–166.

Pennebaker, J. W. (2001). Dealing with a traumatic emotional experience immediately after it occurs. *Advances in Mind-Body Medicine, 17*, 160–162.

Pennebaker, J. W. (2004). *Writing to heal: A guided journal for recovering from trauma and emotional upheaval*. Oakland, CA: New Harbinger Press.

Pennebaker, J. W., & Graybeal, A. (2001). Patterns of natural language use: Disclosure, personality, and social integration. *Current Directions in Psychological Science, 32*, 90–93.

Pennebaker, J. W., Kiecolt-Glaser, J. D., & Glaser, G. (1988). Disclosure of traumas and immune function: Health implications for psychotherapy. *Journal of Consulting and Clinical Psychology, 56*, 239–245.

Penner, L. A., Dovidio, J. F., Piliavin, J. A., & Schroeder, D. A. (2005). Prosocial behavior: Multilevel perspectives. *Annual Review of Psychology, 56*, 365–392.

Pennix, B. W., Rejeski, W. J., Pandya, J., Miller, M. E., Di Bari, M., Applegate, W. B., et al. (2002). Exercise and depressive symptoms: A comparison of aerobic and resistance exercise effects on emotional and physical function in older persons with high and low depressive symptomatology. *Journal of Gerontology: Psychological Sciences, 57*, P124–P132.

Perault, M. C., Favreliere, S., Minet, P., & Remblier, C. (2000). Benzodiazepines and pregnancy. *Therapy, 55*, 587–595.

Perea, M., & Rosa, E. (2002). Does "whole-word shape" play a role in visual word recognition? *Perception & Psychophysics, 64(5)*, 785–794.

Peregoy, S., & Boyle, O. (2005). *Reading, writing, and learning in ESL (4th ed.)*. Boston: Allyn & Bacon.

Perkins, D. (1994, September). Creativity by design. *Educational Leadership*, pp. 18–25.

Perkins, K. A., Marcus, M. D., Levine, M. D., D'Amico, D., Miller, A., Broge, M. & others (2001). Cognitive-behavioral therapy to reduce weight concerns improves smoking cessation outcome in weight-concerned women. *Journal of Consulting and Clinical Psychology, 69*, 604–613.

Perlman, D., & Peplau, L. A. (1998). Loneliness. In H. S. Friedman (Ed.), *Encyclopedia of mental health (Vol. 2)*. San Diego: Academic Press.*

Perlman, M., & Ross, H. S. (1997). The benefits of parent intervention in children's disputes: An examination of concurrent changes in children's fighting styles. *Child Development, 68(4)*, 690–700.*

Perloff, R. M. (2001). *Persuading people to have safer sex*. Mahwah, NJ: Erlbaum. Perls, F. (1969). *Gestalt therapy verbatim*. Lafayette, CA: Real People Press.

Perry, C. (2004). Can anecdotes add to an understanding of hypnosis? *International Journal of Clinical & Experimental Hypnosis, 52(3)*, 218–231.*

Perry, R. P., Hladkyj, S., Pekrun, R. H., & Pelletier, S. T. (2001). Academic control and action control in the achievement of college students: A longitudinal field study. *Journal of Educational Psychology, 93*, 776–789.*

Perse, E. M. & Rubin, A. M. (1990). Chronic loneliness and television use. *Journal of Broadcasting & Electronic Media, 34(1)*, 37–53.

Person, L., & Taylor, E. J. (2002). Managing pain in outpatients: There are particular challenges to pain control in outpatient settings. *American Journal of Nursing, 102*, Supplement, 24–27.

Pert, A. B., & Snyder, S. H. (1973). Opiate receptor: Demonstration in a nervous tissue. *Science, 179*, 1011.

Pervin, L. A. (2003). *The science of personality (2nd ed.)*. London: Oxford.

Pervin, L. A., Cervone, D., & John, O. P. (2005). *Personality: Theory and research (9th ed.)*. Hoboken, NJ: Wiley. Pervin, L. A., & John, O. P. (Eds.). (2001). *Handbook of personality*. New York: Guilford.

Peters, S. L., van den Bos, K. & Bobocel, D. R. (2004). The moral superiority effect: Self versus other differences in satisfaction with being overpaid. *Social Justice Research, 17(3)*, 257–273.*

Peterson, C. (2000). The future of optimism. *American Psychologist, 55*, 44–55.

Peterson, C., & Seligman, M. E. P. (2004). Open-mindedness [Judgment, Critical Thinking]. In C. Peterson & M. E. P. Seligman. *Character strengths and virtues: A handbook and classification*. Washington: APA Press.

Peterson, C., Seligman, M. E. P., & Vaillant, G. E. (1988). Pessimistic explanatory style is a risk factor for physical illness: A thirty-five year longitudinal study. *Journal of Personality & Social Psychology, 55*, 23–27.

Peterson, G. B. (2004). A day of great illumination: B. F. Skinner's discovery of shaping. *Journal of the Experimental Analysis of Behavior, 82(3)*, 317–328.

Peterson, J. B. (1999). *Maps of meaning: The architecture of belief*. Routledge.*

Petry, N. M., Petrakis, I., Trevisan, L., Wiredu, G., Boutros, N. N., Martin, B., et al. (2001). Contingency management interventions: From research to practice. *American Journal of Psychiatry, 158*, 694–702.

Pettifor, J. L. (1998). The Canadian code of ethics for psychologists: A moral context for ethical decision-making in emerging areas of practice. *Canadian Psychology, 39(3)*, 231–238.*

Pettigrew, T. F., & Tropp, L. R. (2000). Does intergroup contact reduce prejudice? Recent meta-analytic findings. In S. Oskamp (Ed.), *Reducing prejudice and discrimination*. Mahwah, NJ: Erlbaum.

Petty, R. E., Cacioppo, J. T., Strathman, A. J., & Priester, J. R. (2005). To think or not to think: Exploring two routes to persuasion. In T. C. Brock, & M. C. Green (Eds.), *Persuasion: Psychological insights and perspectives (2nd Ed.)*. Thousand Oaks, CA: Sage.

Petty, R. E., & Krosnick, J. A. (Eds.), (1995). *Attitude strength: Antecedents and consequents*. Mahwah, NJ: Erlbaum.*

Petty, R. E., Wegener, D. T., & Fabrigar, L. R. (1997). Attitudes and attitude change. *Annual Review of Psychology, 48*, 609–647.*

Petty, R. E., Wheeler, S. C., & Bizer, G. Y. (2000). Attitude functions and persuasion: An elaboration likelihood approach to matched versus mismatched messages. In G. R. Maio, & J. M. Olson (Eds.), *Why we evaluate*. Mahwah, NJ: Erlbaum.*

Pezdek, K., & Banks, K. W. (Eds.). (1996). *The recovered memory/false memory debate*. San Diego, CA: Academic Press.

Phan, K. L., Wager, T. D., Taylor, S. F., & Liberzon, I. (2004). Functional neuroimaging studies of human emotions. *CNS Spectrums, 9(4)*, 258–266.

Phaneuf, S., & Leeuwenburgh, C. (2001). Apoptosis and exercise. *Medical Science and Sports Exercise, 33*, 393–396.

Philip P. (2005). Sleepiness of occupational drivers. *Industrial Health, 43(1)*, 30–33.

Philips, H. C., & Rachman, S. (1996). *The psychological management of chronic pain (2nd ed.)*. New York: Springer.*

Phillips-Miller, D., Morrison, C., & Campbell, N. J. (2001). Same profession, different career: A study of men and women in veterinary medicine. In F. Columbus (Ed.), *Advances in psychology research (Vol. 5)*. Hauppauge, NY: Nova Science Publishers.

Phinney, J. S. (2005). Ethnic identity in late modern times: A response to Rattansi and Phoenix. *Identity. 5(2)*, 187–194.

Piaget, J. (1952). *The origins of intelligence in children*. New York: Oxford.

Piaget, J., & Inhelder, B. (1969). *The child's conception of space*. New York: Norton.

Pickering, T. G. (2001). Mental stress as a causal factor in the development of hypertension and cardiovascular disease. *Current Hypertension Reports, 3*, 249–254.

Pierce, W. D., & Cheney, C. D (2004). *Behavior analysis and learning (3rd ed.)*. Mahwah, NJ: Erlbaum.*

Pikona-Sapir, A., Melamed, Y., & Elizur, A. (2001). The insanity defense: Examination of the extent of congruence between psychiatric recommendation and adjudication. *Medicine and Law, 20*, 93–100.

Pilkonis, P. A. (1999). Introduction: Paradigms for psychotherapy outcome research. *Journal of Clinical Psychology, 55*, 145–146.

Pilkonis, P. A., & Krause, M. S. (1999). Summary: Paradigms for psychotherapy outcome research. *Journal of Clinical Psychology, 55*, 201–206.

Pinel, J. P. J. (2006). *Biopsychology (6th ed.)*. Boston: Allyn & Bacon.*

Pinel, J. P.J., Assanand, S., & Lehman, D. R. (2000). Hunger, eating, and ill health. *American Psychologist, 55(10)*, 1105–1116.*

Pines, A. M., & Maslach, C. (2002). *Experiencing social psychology (4th ed.)*. New York: McGraw-Hill.

Pinker, S. (1999). *How the mind works*. New York: Norton.

Pinker, S. (2002) *The blank slate: The modern denial of human nature*. New York: Viking.

Pinker, S., & Jackendoff, R. (2005). The faculty of language: What's special about it? *Cognition, 95(2)*, 201–236.

Pintrich, P. R., & Schunk, D. H. (Eds.). (2002). *Motivation in education (2nd ed.)*. Upper Saddle River, NJ: Prentice Hall.

Piper, A., & Merskey, H. (2004a). The persistence of folly: A critical examination of dissociative identity disorder. Part I. The excesses of an improbable concept. *Canadian Journal of Psychiatry, 49(9)*, 592–600.*

Piper, A., & Merskey, H. (2004b). The persistence of folly: A critical examination of dissociative identity disorder. Part II. The defence and decline of multiple personality or dissociative identity disorder, *Canadian Journal of Psychiatry, 49(10)*, 678–683.*

Pipher, M. (1995). *Hunger pains: The modern woman's tragic quest for thinness*. New York: Ballantine.

Piran, N. (2002). Eating disorders and disordered eating. In J. Worell (Ed.), *Encyclopedia of women and gender*. New York: Oxford.

Pirolli, P. (2003). A theory of information scent. In J. Jacko, & C. Stephanidis (Eds.) *Human-computer interaction (Vol. 1)*. Mahwah, NJ: Erlbaum.

Pirolli, P. (in press). Rational analyses of information foraging on the Web. *Cognitive Science*.

Pittenger, D. (2003). *Behavioral research design and analysis*. New York: McGraw-Hill.

Pliner, P., & Mann, N. (2004). Influence of social norms and palatability on amount consumed and food choice. *Appetite, 42(2)*, 227–237.*

Plomin, R. (1999). Genetics and general cognitive ability. *Nature, 402 (Suppl.)*, C25–C29.

Plomin, R., & Craig, I. (2001). Genetics, environment, and cognitive abilities: Review and work in progress toward a genome scan for quantitative trait locus associations using DNA pooling. *British Journal of Psychiatry, 40*, 41–48.

Plous, S. (Ed.). (2003). *Understanding prejudice and discrimination*. New York: McGraw-Hill.

Plutchik, R. (1980). *Emotion: A psychoevolutionary synthesis*. New York: Harper & Row.

Plutchik, R. (2003). *Emotions and life: Perspectives from psychology, biology, and evolution*. Washington: APA Press.

Poling, A., & Carr, J. E. (2002). Operant conditioning. In M. Hersen, & W. H. Sledge (Eds.), *Encyclopedia of psychotherapy*. San Diego: Academic Press.

Polivy, J., & Herman, C. P. (1985). Dieting and bingeing: A causal analysis. *American Psychologist, 40*, 193–201.*

Polivy, J., & Herman, C. P. (1999). The effects of resolving to diet on restrained and unrestrained eaters: The "False Hope Syndrome." *International Journal of Eating Disorders, 26*, 434–447.*

Polivy, J., & Herman, C. P. (2000). The False Hope Syndrome: Unfulfilled expectations of self-change. *Current Directions in Psychological Science, 9*, 128–131.*

Polivy, J., & Herman, C. P. (2002). Causes of eating disorders. *Annual Review of Psychology, 53*, 187–213.*

Pollack, M. H., Allgulander, C., Bandelow, B., Cassano, G. B., Greist, J. H., Hollander, E., et al. (2003). WCA recommendations for the long-term treatment of panic disorder. *CNS Spectrums, 8(8,Suppl1)*, 17–30.*

Pollmacher, T., Schuld, A., Kraus, T., Haack, M., Hinze-Selch, D., & Mullington, J. (2000). Experimental modulation, sleep, and sleepiness in humans. *Annals of the New York Academy of Science, 917*, 488–499.

Polsky, D., Onesirosan, P., Bauer, M. S., & Glick, H. A. (2002). Duration of therapy and health care costs of fluoxetine, paroxetine, and sertraline in 6 health plans. *Journal of Clinical Psychiatry, 63*, 156–164.

Pomeroy, E., Trainor, J., & Pape, B. (2002). Citizens shaping policy: The Canadian Mental Health Association's framework for support project. *Canadian Psychology, 43*, 11–20.*

Pomplum, M., Reingold, E. M., & Shen, J. (2001). Investigating the visual span in comparative search: The effects of task difficulty and divided attention. *Cognition, 81*, B57–67.

Ponterotto, J. G., Casas, J. M., Suzuki, L. A., & Alexander, C. M. (Eds.). (2001). *Handbook of multicultural counseling*. Thousand Oaks, CA: Sage.

Poole, G. D., Matheson, D. H., & Cox, D. (2000). *The psychology of health and health care: A Canadian perspective*. Toronto: Prentice Hall.*

Pope-Davis, D. B., Coleman, H. L. K., Liu, W. M. & Toporek, R. L. (Eds.) (2003). *Handbook of multicultural competencies in counseling and psychology*. Thousand Oaks, CA: Sage.

Popham, W. J. (2005). *Classroom assessment: What teachers need to know (4th ed.)*. Boston: Allyn & Bacon.

Porter, K. (2003). *The mental athlete: Inner training for peak performance in all sports*. Stanningley, Leeds: Human Kinetics Europe.

Porter, K., Babiker, A. G., Darbyshire, J. H., & Pezzotti, P. (2003). Determinants of survival following HIV-1 seroconversion after the introduction of HAART. *The Lancet, Oct. 18, 362*, 1267–1274.

Porter, S., Campbell, M. A., Birt, A. R., & Woodworth, M. T. (2003). "He said, she said": A psychological perspective on historical memory evidence in the courtroom. *Canadian Psychology, 44(3)*, 190–206.

Post, S. G., Underwood, L. G., Scholls, J. P., & Hurlbut, W. B. (Eds.) (2002). *Altruism and altruistic love*. New York: Oxford.

Post, S. G. (2005). Altruism, happiness, and health: It's good to be good. International *Journal of Behavioral Medicine, 12(2)*, 66–77.

Postle, B. R., & Brush, L. N. (2004). The neural bases of the effects of item-nonspecific proactive interference in working memory. *Cognitive, Affective & Behavioral Neuroscience, 4(3)*, 379–392.

Potter, S. M., Wagenaar, D. A., & DeMaarse. T. B. (in press). Closing the loop: Stimulation feedback systems for embodied MEA cultures. In M. Taketani, & M. Baudry (Eds.), *Advances in network electrophysiology using multi-electrode arrays*. New York: Kluwer.

Potts, A., Gavey, N., Grace, V. M. & Vares, T. (2003). The downside of Viagra: Women's experiences and concerns. *Sociology of Health & Illness, 25(7)*, 697–719.

Poulin-Dubois, D., Serbin, L. A., Eichstedt, J. A., Sen, M. G., & Beissel, C. F. (2002). Men don't put on make-up: Toddlers' knowledge of the gender stereotyping of household activities. *Social Development, 11(2)*, 166–181.*

Powell, D. R. (2001). Early intervention and risk. In A. Fogel, & G. Bremmer (Eds.), *Blackwell handbook of infant development*. London: Blackwell.

Powell, R. A., Symbaluk, D. G., & Macdonald, S. E. (2005). *Introduction to learning and behavior (3rd ed.)*. Belmont, CA: Wadsworth.

Prairie Women's Health Centre of Excellence (2001). *Post traumatic stress disorder: The lived experience of immigrant, refugee and visible minority women*. Retrieved July 27, 2005 from http://www.pwhce.ca/ptsd-immigrant.htm.*

Pratt, M. W., Danso, H. A., Arnold, M. L., Norris, J. E., & Filyer, R. (2001). Adult generativity and the socialization of adolescents. *Journal of Personality, 69*, 89–120.

Preece, M., & DeLongis, A. (2005). A contextual examination of stress and coping processes in stepfamilies. In T. A. Revenson, K. Kayser, & G. Bodenmann (Eds.), *Couples coping with stress: Emerging perspectives on dyadic coping*. Washington: APA Press.

Predebon, J. (2004). Selective attention and asymmetry in the Müller-Lyer illusion. *Psychonomic Bulletin & Review, 11(5)*, 916–920.

Premack, D. (1986). *Gavagai! The future history of the ape language controversy*. Cambridge MIT Press.

Pressley, M. (2000). What should comprehension instruction be the instruction of? In M. Kamil (Ed.), *Handbook of reading research*. Mahwah, NJ: Erlbaum.

Pressley, M., & Hilden, K. R. (2005). Commentary on three important directions in comprehension assessment research. In S. G. Paris, & S. A. Stahl, (Eds.), *Children's reading comprehension and assessment. Center for improvement of early reading achievement (CIERA)*. Mahwah, NJ: Erlbaum.

Pressman, S. D., Cohen, S., Miller, G. E., Barkin, A., Rabin, B. S., & Treanor, J. J. (2005). Loneliness, social network size, and immune response to influenza vaccination in college freshmen. *Health Psychology, 24(3)*, 297–306.*

Preston, J. M. (1998). From mediated environments to the development of consciousness. In J. Gackenbach (Ed.), *Psychology and the Internet: Intrapersonal, interpersonal, and transpersonal implications*. San Diego, CA: Academic Press.*

Preuger, V. J., & Rogers, T. B. (1993). Development of a scale to measure cross-cultural sensitivity in the Canadian context. *Canadian Journal of Behavioral Science, 25(4),* 615–621.*

Priest, R. F., & Thein, M. T. (2003). Humor appreciation in marriage: Spousal similarity, associative mating, and disaffection. *Humor: International Journal of Humor Research, 16(1),* 63–78.

Prieto, M., & Giralt, M. T. (2001). Effects of N-(2-chlorethyl)-N-ethyl-2-bromobenzylamine on alpha2-adrenoceptors which regulate the synthesis and release of noradrenaline in the rat brain. *Pharmacological Toxology, 88,* 152–158.

Prifitera, A., Saklofske, D.H., & Weiss, L.G. (2005). *WISC-IV clinical use and interpretation.* San Diego: Elsevier/Academic Press.*

Priluck, R. & Till, B. D. (2004). The role of contingency awareness, involvement, and need for cognition in attitude formation. *Journal of the Academy of Marketing Science, 32(3),* 329–344.

Prkachin, K. M. (2005). Effects of deliberate control on verbal and facial expressions of pain. *Pain, 114(3),* 328–338.*

Prkachin, K. M., Schultz, I., Berkowitz, J., Hughes, E., & Hunt, D. (2002). *Behaviour Research & Therapy, 40(5),* 595–607.*

Prochaska, J. O. (2003). *Systems of psychotherapy: A transtheoretical analysis (5th ed.).* Belmont, CA: Wadsworth.

Proctor, R. W., & Wang, H. (2002). Influences of different combinations of conceptual, perceptual, and structural similarity on stimulus-response compatibility. *Quarterly Journal of Experimental Psychology, 55,* 59–74.

Provencher, M. D., Dugas, M. J., & Ladouceur, R. (2004). Efficacy of problem-solving training and cognitive exposure in the treatment of generalized anxiety disorder: A case replication series. *Cognitive & Behavioral Practice, 11(4),* 404–414.*

Provenzo, E. F. (2002). *Teaching, learning, and schooling in American culture: A critical perspective.* Boston: Allyn & Bacon.

Public Health Agency of Canada (1999). *Measuring up: A health surveillance update on Canadian children and youth.* Retrieved August 22, 2005 from http://www.phac-aspc.gc.ca/publicat/meas-haut/index.html.*

Pugh, G. M., & Boer, D. G. (1989). An examination of culturally appropriate items for the WAIS-R Information subtest with Canadian subjects. *Journal of Psychoeducational Assessment, 7,* 131–140.*

Pugh, G. M., & Boer, D. G. (1991). Normative data on the validity of Canadian subtest items for the WAIS-R Information subtest. *Canadian Journal of Behavioral Science, 23(2),* 149–158.*

Punamaki, R., & Joustie, M. (1998). The role of culture, violence, and personal factors affecting dream content. *Journal of Cross-Cultural Psychology, 29,* 320–343.

Puri, B. K., Huttson, S. B., Saeed, N., Oatridge, A., Hajnal, J. V., Duncan, L., et al. (2001). A serial longitudinal quantitative MRI study of cerebral changes in first-episode schizophrenia using image segmentation and subvoxel registration. *Psychiatry Research, 106,* 141–150.

Putnam, S. P., Sanson, A. V., & Rothbart, M. K. (2002). Child temperament and parenting. In M. Bornstein (Ed.), *Handbook of parenting (2nd ed.).* Mahwah, NJ: Erlbaum.

Pyke, S. W. (1997). Education and the "woman question." *Canadian Psychology, 38(3),* 154–163.*

Pylyshyn, Z. W. (1981). The imagery debate: Analogue media versus tacit knowledge. *Psychological Review, 88,* 16–45.*

Pylyshyn, Z. (2003). Return of the mental image: Are there really pictures in the brain? *Trends in Cognitive Sciences, 7(3),* 113–118.

Q

Quality Assurance Project (1990). Treatment outlines for paranoid, schizotypal, and schizoid personality disorders. *Australian & New Zealand Journal of Psychiatry, 24,* 339–350.

Quinlin, M., Mayhew, C., & Bohle, P. (2001). The global expansion of precarious employment. *International Journal of Health Services, 31,* 507–536.

R

Rabasca, L. (1999, May). Stress caused when jobs don't meet expectations. *APA Monitor, 30,* 24–25.

Rabasca, L. (2000, June) More psychologists in the trenches. *Monitor on psychology, 31,* 50–51.

Rachman, S. (2004). *Anxiety (2nd. ed.),* New York: Routledge.*

Rahman, Q., & Wilson, G. D. (2003). Born gay? The psychobiology of human sexual orientation. *Personality & Individual Differences, 34(8),* 1337–1382.

Rains, G. D. (2002). *Principles of human neuropsychology.* New York: McGraw-Hill.

Rakic, P. (2002). Neurogenesis in adult primate neocortex: An evaluation of the evidence. *Nature Reviews: Neuroscience, 3,* 65–71.

Ramachandran, V. S., & Hubbard, E. M. (2003). Hearing colors, tasting shapes: People with synesthesia —whose senses blend together—are providing valuable clues to understanding the organization and functions of the human brain. *Scientific American, 288(5),* 52–60.

Ramesch, M., & Roberts, G. (2002). Use of night-time benzodiazepines in an elderly inpatient population. *Journal of Clinical and Pharmacological Therapy, 27,* 93–97.

Ramey, C. T., & Campbell, F. A. (1984). Preventive education for high-risk children: Cognitive consequences of the Carolina Abecedarian Project. *American Journal of Mental Deficiency, 88,* 515–523.

Ramey, C. T., & Ramey, S. L. (2004). Early learning and school readiness: can early intervention make a difference? *Merrill-Palmer Quarterly. Special 50th Anniversary Issue: Part II The maturing of the human developmental sciences: appraising past, present, and prospective agendas, 50(4),* 471–491.

Ramey, C. T., Ramey, S. L., & Lanzi, R. G. (2001). Intelligence and experience. In R. J. Sternberg & E. L. Grigorenko (Eds.), *Environmental effects on cognitive abilities.* Mahwah, NJ: Erlbaum.

Ramey, S. L., & Ramey, S. T. (2000). Early childhood experiences and developmental competence. In S. Danzinger, & J. Waldfogel (Eds.), *Securing the future: Investing in children from birth to college.* New York: Russell Sage Foundation.

Ramirez, J. M., Alvarado, J. M., & Santisteban, C. (2004). Individual differences in anger reaction to noise. *Individual Differences Research, 2(2),* 125–136.

Ramphal, C. (1962). *A study of three current problems in education.* Unpublished doctoral dissertation, University of Natal, India.

Randi, J. (1997). *An encyclopedia of claims, frauds, and hoaxes of the occult and supernatural.* New York: St. Martin's Press.

Rapaport, D. (1967). On the psychoanalytic theory of thinking. In M. M. Gill (Ed.), *The collected papers of David Rapaport.* New York: Basic Books.

Rapaport, S. (1994, November 28). Interview. *U.S. News and World Report,* p. 94.

Rappaport, J. L. (1989). The biology of obsessions and compulsions. *Scientific American, 260(3),* 83–89.

Rasinski, T., & Padak, N. (2004). Beyond consensus— beyond balance: Toward a comprehensive literacy curriculum. *Reading & Writing Quarterly: Overcoming Learning Difficulties, 20(1),* 91–102.

Raskin, D. C., & Yuille, J. C. (1989). Problems in evaluating interviews of children in sexual abuse cases. In S. J. Ceci, D. F. Ross, & M. P. Toglia (Eds.), *Perspectives on children's testimony.* New York: Springer-Verlag.*

Rasmussen, K. G. (1984). Nonverbal behavior, verbal behavior, resume credentials, and selection interview outcomes. *Journal of Applied Psychology, 69,* 551–556.

Rathus, R., Nevid, J., & Fichner-Rathus, L. (2005). *Human sexuality in a world of diversity (6th ed.).* Boston: Allyn & Bacon.

Raven, P. H., & Johnson, G. B. (2002). *Biology (6th ed.).* New York: McGraw-Hill.

Raymond, J. E., Shapiro, K. L., & Arnell, K. M. (1992). Temporary suppression of visual processing in an RSVP task: An attentional blink? *Journal of Experimental Psychology: Human Perception & Performance, 18,* 849–860.*

Raz, N., Gunning-Dixon, F., Head, D., Williamson, A., & Acker, J. D. (2001). Age and sex differences in the cerebellum and the ventral pons. *American Journal of Neuroradiology, 22,* 1161–1167.

Rector, N. A. (2004). Cognitive theory and therapy of schizophrenia. In R. L. Leahy (Ed.), *Contemporary cognitive therapy: Theory, research, and practice.* New York: Guilford.*

Rector, N. A., & Beck, A. T. (2001). Cognitive behavioral therapy for schizophrenia: An empirical review. *Journal of Nervous and Mental Disorders, 189,* 278–287.*

Rector, N. A., Segal, Z. V., & Gemar, M. (1998). Schema research in depression: A Canadian perspective. *Canadian Journal of Behavioural Science. 30(4),* 213–224.*

Reed, S. K. (2004). *Cognition (6th ed.).* Belmont, CA: Wadsworth.

Reed, T. E., Vernon, P. A., & Johnson, A. M. (2004). Confirmation of correlation between brain nerve conduction velocity and intelligence level in normal adults. *Intelligence, 32(6),* 563–572.*

Reid, P. T., & Zalk, S. R. (2001). Academic environments: Gender and ethnicity in U.S. higher education. In J. Worrell (Ed.), *Encyclopedia of women and gender.* New York: Oxford.

Reid, R. C. (2000). Sensory systems. In A. Kazdin (Ed.), *Encyclopedia of psychology.* Washington, & New York: APA Press and Oxford University Press.

Reisberg, D. & Hertel, P. (Eds.). (2004). *Memory and emotion. Series in affective science.* London, Oxford.

Reiss, S., & Havercamp, S. M. (2005). Motivation in developmental context: A new method for studying self-actualization. *Journal of Humanistic Psychology, 45(1),* 41–53.

Remley, T. P., & Herlihy, B. (2005). *Ethical, legal, and professional issues in counseling (2nd ed.).* Upper Saddle River, NJ: Prentice Hall.

Rennie, J. (2005). *Roberton's textbook of neonatology (4th ed.).* San Diego: Elsevier/Academic Press.

Rescorla, R. A. (1966). Predictability and number of pairings in Pavlovian fear conditioning. *Psychonomic Science, 4,* 383–384.

Rescorla, R. A. (1988). Pavlovian conditioning: It's not what you think it is. *American Psychologist, 43,* 151–160.

Rescorla, R. A. (1996). Spontaneous recovery after training with multiple outcomes. *Animal Learning & Behavior, 24,* 11–18.

Rescorla, R. A. (2001). Experimental extinction. In R. R. Mowrer & S. B. Klein (Eds.), *Handbook of contemporary learning theories.* Mahwah, NJ: Erlbaum.

Rescorla, R. A. (2003). Contemporary study of Pavlovian conditioning. *Spanish Journal of Psychology, 6(2),* 185–195.

Rescorla, R. A. (2004). Spontaneous recovery. *Learning & Memory, 11(5),* 501–509.

Ressler, K. J., Rothbaum, B. O., Tannenbaum, L., Anderson, P., Graap, K., Zimand, E., et al. (2004). Cognitive enhancers as adjuncts to psychotherapy: Use of d-cycloserine in phobic individuals to facilitate extinction of fear. *Archives of General Psychiatry, 61(11),* 1136–1144.

Revitch, E., & Schlesinger, L. B. (1978). Murder: Evaluation, classification, and prediction. In I. L. Kutash, S. B. Kutash, & O. B. Schlesinger (Eds.), *Violence.* San Francisco: Jossey-Bass.

Reynolds, C. R., Livingston, R. & Willson, V. (2006). *Measurement and assessment in education.* Boston: Allyn & Bacon.

Reynolds, J. H., & Glaser, R. (1964). Effects of repetition and spaced review upon retention of a complex learning task. *Journal of Educational Psychology, 55,* 297–308.

Rex, T. S., Lewis, G. P., Geller, S. F., & Fisher, S. K. (2002). Differential expression of cone opsin mRNA levels following experimental retinal detachment and reattachment. *Molecular Vision, 8,* 114–118.

Reynolds, C. R. (2001). Employment tests. In W. E. Craighead, & C. B. Nemeroff (Eds.), *The Corsini encyclopedia of psychology and behavioral science (3rd ed.).* New York: Wiley.

Rezvani, A. H., & Levin, E. D. (2001). Cognitive effects of nicotine. *Biological Psychiatry, 49,* 258–267.

Riggio, R. E. (2005). Business applications of nonverbal communication. In R. E. Riggio, & R. S. Feldman (Eds.), *Applications of nonverbal communication.* Mahwah, NJ: Erlbaum.

Rijsdijk, F. V., & Boomsma, D. I. (1997). Genetic mediation of the correlation between peripheral nerve conduction velocity and IQ. *Behavior Genetics, 27,* 87–98.

Rijsdijk, F. V., Boomsma, D. I., & Vernon, P. A. (1995). Genetic analyses of peripheral nerve conduction velocity in men and its relation with IQ. *Behavior Genetics, 25,* 341–348.*

Rijsdijk, F. V., Vernon, P. A., & Boomsma, D. I. (1998). The genetic basis of the relation between speed-of-information-processing and IQ. *Behavior and Brain Research, 95,* 77–84.*

Rilling, J. K., & Seligman, R. A. (2002). A quantitative morphometric comparative analysis of the primate temporal lobe. *Journal of Human Evolution, 42,* 505–533.

Rips, L. J. (2002). Reasoning. In H. Paschler, & D. Medin (Eds.), *Steven's handbook of experimental psychology (3rd ed), Vol. 2: Memory and cogniitive processes.* New York: Wiley.

Risen, M. L., Jodi A. Quas. J. A., & Goodman, G. S. (2002). *Memory and suggestibility in the forensic interview.* Mahwah, NJ: Erlbaum.

Risko, E. F., Stolz, J. A., & Besner, D. (2005). Basic processes in reading: Is visual word recognition obligatory? *Psychonomic Bulletin & Review, 12(1),* 119–124.*

Rivera-Gaxiola, M., Silva-Pereyra, J., & Kuhl, P. K. (2005). Brain potentials to native and non-native speech contrasts in 7- and 11-month-old American infants. *Developmental Science, 8(2),* 162–172.

Robbins, T. W. (2000). From arousal to cognition: The integrative position of the prefrontal cortex. *Progress in Brain Research, 126,* 469–483.

Roberti, J. W. (2004). A review of behavioral and biological correlates of sensation seeking. *Journal of Research in Personality, 38(3),* 256–279.

Roberts, B. W., & Hogan, R. (Eds.). (2001). *Personality psychology in the workplace.* Washington: APA Press.

Roberts, D., Anderson, B. L., & Lubaroff, A. (1994). *Stress and immunity at cancer diagnosis.* Unpublished manuscript, Dept. of Psychology, Ohio State University, Columbus.

Roberts, J. (2000). Paediatric HIV/AIDS: School implications. *Canadian Journal of School Psychology, 15(2),* 35–40.*

Roberts, J., & Marshall, A. (2001). Preparing counsellors for HIV positive youth: A model for curriculum development. *Canadian Journal of Counselling, 35(3),* 229–236.*

Roberts, J., Pettifor, J., Cairns, K., & DeMatteo, D. (2000). Serving children with HIV/AIDS in Canadian public schools: An interpretation of the CPA guidelines for non-discriminatory practice. *Canadian Journal of School Psychology, 15(2),* 41–50.*

Roberts, J. E., Gotlib, I. H., & Kassel, J. D. (1996). Adult attachment security and symptoms of depression: The mediating roles of dysfunctional attitudes and low self-esteem. *Journal of Personality & Social Psychology, 60,* 310–320.

Roberts, M. A., & Besner, D. (2005). Stroop dilution revisited: Evidence for domain-specific, limited-capacity processing. *Journal of Experimental Psychology: Human Perception & Performance, 31(1),* 3–13.*

Roberts, W. A. (1998). *Principles of animal cognition.* Boston: McGraw-Hill.*

Roberts, W. A., & Roberts, S. (2002). Two tests of the stuck-in-time hypothesis. *Journal of General Psychology, 129,* 415–429.*

Roberts, W. A., Roberts, S., & Kit, K. A. (2002). Pigeons presented with sequences of light flashes use behavior to count but not to time. *Journal of Experimental Psychology: Animal Behavior Processes, 28,* 137–150.

Robertson, L. C. (2003). Binding, spatial attention and perceptual awareness. *Nature Reviews Neuroscience, 4(2),* 93–102.

Robertson, L. C., & Sagiv, N. (2005). *Synesthesia: Perspectives from cognitive neuroscience.* New York: Oxford.

Robins, L., & Regier, D. (Eds.). (1991). *Psychiatric disorders in America.* New York: Free Press.

Robins, R. W., Trzesniewski, K. H., Tracey, J. L., Potter, J., & Gosling, S. D. (2002). Global self-esteem across the lifespan. *Psychology and Aging, 17,* 423–434.

Robinson, M., Laurence, J., Hogue, A., Zacher, J. E., German, A., & Jenkin, M. (2002). IVY: Basic design and construction details. Proc ICAT 2002, Tokyo, Japan.*

Robles, T. F., & Kiecolt-Glaser, J. K. (2003). The physiology of marriage: Pathways to health. *Physiology & Behavior, 79(3),* 409–416.

Robson, A. L. (1997). Low birthweight and parenting stress during early childhood. *Journal of Pediatric Psychology, 22,* 297–311.*

Roedema, T. M., & Simons, R. F. (1999). Emotion-processing deficit in alexithymia. *Psychophysiology, 36(3),* 379–387.

Rodin, J. (1993). *Body traps.* New York: Morrow.

Rodin, J., & Langer, E. J. (1977). Long-term effects of a control-relevant intervention with the institutionalized aged. *Journal of Personality & Social Psychology, 35,* 397–402.

Rodrigues, M. S., & Cohen, S. (1998). Social support. In H. S. Friedman (Ed.), *Encyclopedia of mental health (Vol. 3).* San Diego: Academic Press.

Roeckelein, J. E. (2004). *Imagery in psychology: A reference guide.* Westport, CT: Praeger.

Roehrs, T., & Roth, T. (1998). Reported in Maas, J. (1998). *Power sleep.* New York: Villard, 44.

Roesch, R., Hart, S. D., & Ogloff, J. R. P. (Eds.). (1999). *Psychology and law: The state of the discipline.* New York: Kluwer Academic/Plenum.*

Roese, N. J., & Olson, J. M. (1994). Attitude importance as a function of repeated attitude expression. *Journal of Experimental Social Psychology, 30(1),* 39–51.*

Rogers, C. R. (1961). *On becoming a person.* Boston: Houghton Mifflin.

Rogers, C. R. (1974). In retrospect: Forty-six years. *American Psychologist, 29,* 115–123.

Rogers, C. R. (1980). *A way of being.* Boston: Houghton Mifflin.

Rogers, R. D., Andrews, T. C., Grasby, P.M., Brooks, D. J., & Robbins, T. W. (2000). Contrasting cortical and subcortical activations produced by attentional-set shifting and reversal learning in humans. *Journal of Cognitive Neuroscience, 12,* 142–162.

Rogers, T. B., Kuiper, N. N., & Kirker, W. S. (1977). Self-reference and the encoding of personal information. *Journal of Personality & Social Psychology, 35,* 677–688.

Rogers, T. T., & McClelland, J. L. (2004). *Semantic cognition: A parallel distributed processing approach.* Cambridge: MIT Press.

Rogers, R. (2001). *Handbook of diagnostic and structured interviewing.* New York: Guilford.

Rogers, T. B., Kuiper, N. A., & Kirker, W. S. (1977). Self-reference and the encoding of personal information. *Journal of Personality & Social Psychology, 35,* 677–688.

Rogoff, B. (1998). Cognition as a collaborative process. In W. Damon (Ed.), *Handbook of child psychology (5th ed., Vol. 2).* New York: Wiley.

Rogoff, B. (2003). *The cultural nature of human development.* London: Oxford.

Rohde, P., Lewinsohn, P. M., Clarke, G. N., Hops, H., & Seeley, J. R. (2005). The Adolescent Coping With Depression Course: A cognitive-behavioral approach to the treatment of adolescent depression.

In E. D. Hibbs, & P. S. Jensen, (Eds.), *Psychosocial treatments for child and adolescent disorders: Empirically based strategies for clinical practice (2nd ed.).* Washington: APA Press.

Roid, G. H. (2003). *Stanford-Binet Intelligence Scales, (5th ed.), Examiner's manual.* Itasca, IL: Riverside.

Rooy, D. L., Pipe, M-E., & Murray, J. E. (2005). Reminiscence and hypermnesia in children's eyewitness memory. *Journal of Experimental Child Psychology, 90(3),* 235–254.

Rosch, E. (1973). On the internal structure of perceptual and semantic categories. In T. E. Moore (Ed.), *Cognition and the acquisition of language.* San Diego: Academic Press.

Rosch, E. (2002). Principles of categorization. In D. J. Levitin (Ed.), *Foundations of cognitive psychology: Core readings.* Cambridge MIT Press.

Rose, R. J., Koskenvuo, M., Kaprio, J., Sarna, S., & Langinvainio, H. (1988). Shared genes, shared experiences, and similarity of personality: Data from 14,228 adult Finnish co-twins. *Journal of Personality & Social Psychology, 54,* 161–171.

Rose-Krasnor, L., Rubin, K. H., Booth, C. L., Coplan, R. (1996). The relation of maternal directiveness and child attachment security to social competence in preschoolers. *International Journal of Behavioral Development, 19,* 309–325.*

Rosenbaum, M., Leibel, R. L., & Hirsch, J. (1997). Medical progress: Obesity. *New England Journal of Medicine, 337,* 396–407.

Rosenberg, S. S., & Lynch, J. E. (2002). Fritz Perls revisited: A micro-assessment of a live clinical session. *Gestalt Review, 6(3),* 184–202.

Rosenbloom, M. (2002). Chlorpromazine and the psychopharmacological revolution. *Journal of the American Medical Association, 287,* 1860–1861.

Rosenfeld, A. H. (1985, June). Depression: Dispelling despair. *Psychology Today,* pp. 28–34.

Rosenhan, D. L. (1973). On being sane in insane places. *Science, 179,* 250–258.

Rosenthal, D. (1963). *The Genain quadruplets.* New York: Basic Books.

Rosenthal, R. (1994). Interpersonal expectancy effects: A 30-year-perspective. *Current Dimensions in Psychological Science, 3,* 176–179.

Rosenthal, R., & DiMatteo, M. R. (2001). Meta-analysis: Recent developments in quantitative methods for literature reviews. *Annual Review of Psychology, 52,* 59–62.

Rosenthal, R., & Jacobsen, L. (1968). *Pygmalion in the classroom.* Fort Worth: Harcourt Brace.

Rosenthal, R., & Lawson, R. (1964). A longitudinal study of the effects of experimenter bias on the operant learning of laboratory rats. *Journal of Psychiatric Research, 2(2),* 61–72.

Rosenzweig, M. R., Bennett, E. L., & Diamond, M. C. (1972). Brain changes in response to experience. *Scientific American, 226(2),* 22–29.

Rosnow, R. L., & Rosenthal, R. (2002). *Beginning behavioral research (4th ed.).* Englewood Cliffs, NJ: Prentice Hall.

Ross, B. H. (2000). Concepts: Learning. In A. Kazdin (Ed.), *Encyclopedia of psychology.* Washington, and New York: APA Press and Oxford.

Ross, C. A. (1994). *The Osiris complex: Case-studies in multiple personality disorder.* Toronto: University of Toronto Press.*

Ross, C. A., & Norton, G. R. (1989). Differences between men and women with multiple personality disorder. *Hospital & Community Psychiatry, 40,* 186–188.*

Ross, D. P., Scott, K., & Smith, P. (2000). *The Canadian fact book on poverty 2000.* Ottawa: Canadian Council on Social Development. Highlights retrieved August 29, 2005, from www.ccsd.ca/pubs/2000/fbpov00/hl.htm.*

Ross, H. E., & Plug. C. (2002). *The mystery of the moon illusion: Exploring size perception.* Oxford: Oxford University Press.

Ross, S. E., Neibling, B. C., & Heckert, T. M. (1999). Sources of stress among college students. *College Student Journal, 33(2),* 312–317.

Rossi, A. S. (2004). The menopausal transition and aging processes. In O. G. Brim, C. D. Ryff, & R. Kessler (Eds) *How healthy are we: A national study of wellbeing in midlife.* Chicago, IL: Univ. Chicago Press.

Rossi, F., Saggiorato, C., & Strata, P. (2002). Target-specific innervation of embryonic cerebellar transplants by regenerating olivocerebellar axons in the adult rat. *Experimental Neurology, 172,* 205–212.

Rotenberg, K. J., Carte, L., & Speirs, A. (2005). The effects of modeling dietary restraint on food consumption: Do restrained models promote restrained eating? *Eating Behaviors, 6(1),* 75–84.

Roth, D., Eng, W., & Heimberg, R. G. (2002). Cognitive behavior therapy. In M. Hersen, & W. H. Sledge (Eds.), *Encyclopedia of psychotherapy.* San Diego: Academic Press.

Rothbart, M. K., & Bates, J. E. (1998). Temperament. In W. Damon (Ed.), *Handbook of child psychology (5th ed., Vol. 3).* New York: Wiley.

Rotter, J. B. (1966). Generalized expectancies for internal versus external control of reinforcement. *Psychological Monographs, 80, (1, Whole No. 609).*

Rouby, C., Schaal, B., & Holley, A. (2002). *Olfaction taste and cognition.* Cambridge: Cambridge University Press.

Rouleau, M., Levichek, Z., & Koren, G. (2003). Are mothers who drink heavily in pregnancy victims of FAS? *Journal of FAS International, 1,* e4. Retrieved April 14, 2005 from http://www.motherisk.org/JFAS/pdf/Heavily_drinking_mothers_victims.pdf.*

Rowe, D. C. (1994). *The limits of family influence: Genes, experience, and behavior.* New York: Guilford.

Rowe, J. W., & Kahn, R. L. (1997). *Successful aging.* New York: Pantheon.

Roy, A. (1992). Genetics, biology, and suicide in the family. In R. W. Maris, A. L. Berman, J. T. Maltsberger, & R. I. Yufit (Eds.), *Assessment and prediction of suicide.* New York: Guilford.

Roy-Byrne, P. P., & Cowley, D. S. (2002). Pharmacological treatments for panic disorders, phobias, and generalized anxiety disorder. In P. Nathan, & J. M. Gorman (Eds.), *A guide to treatments that work (2nd ed.).* New York: Oxford.

Royden, C. S. (2000). Motion perception. In A. Kazdin (Ed.), *Encyclopedia of psychology.* Washington, & New York: APA Press and Oxford.

Rozanski, A., Blumenthal, J. A., Kaplan, J. (1999). Impact of psychological factors on the pathogenesis of cardiovascular disease and implications for therapy. *Circulation, 99,* 2192–2217.

Rubel, E. W., & Fritzsch, B. (2002). Auditory system development: Primary auditory neurons and their targets. *Annual Review of Neuroscience, 25,* 51–101.

Rubenzer, S., Ones, D. Z., & Faschingbauer, T. (2000, August). *Personality traits of U.S. presidents.* Paper presented at the meeting of the American Psychological Association, Washington.

Rubin, D. C., & Kozin, M. (1984). Vivid memories. *Cognition, 16,* 81–95.

Rubin, Z., & Mitchell, C. (1976). Couples research as couples counseling. *American Psychologist, 31,* 17–25.

Ruby, N. F., Dark, J., Burns, D. E., Heller, H. C., & Zucker, I. (2002). The suprachiasmatic nucleus is essential for circadian body temperature rhythms in hibernating ground squirrels. *Journal of Neuroscience, 22,* 357–364.

Rudd, M. D., Joiner, Jr., T. E., & Rajab, M. H. (2001). *Treating suicidal behavior.* New York: Guilford.

Rudolf, K. I., Chang, S., Lee, H., Gottlieb, G. J., Greider, C., & DePinto, R. A. (1999). Longevity, stress, response, and cancer in aging telomerase-deficient mice. *Cell, 96,* 701–712.

Rueckl, J. G., & Galantucci, B. (2005). The locus and time course of long-term morphological priming. *Language & Cognitive Processes, 20(1),* 115–138.

Rukstalis, M., Jepson, C., Strasser, A., Lynch, K. G., Perkins, K., Patterson, F., & Lerman, C. (2005). Naltrexone reduces the relative reinforcing value of nicotine in a cigarette smoking choice paradigm. *Psychopharmacology, 180(1),* 41–48.

Rummens, J., Beiser, M., & Noh, S. (Eds.) (2003). *Immigration, ethnicity and health.* University of Toronto Press.*

Runco, M. A. (2003). Idea evaluation, divergent thinking, and creativity. In M. A. Runco (Ed.). *Critical creative processes. Perspectives on creativity research.* Cresskill, NJ: Hampton Press.

Runco, M. A. (2004). Creativity. *Annual Review of Psychology, 55,* 657–687.

Rusbult, C. E., Olsen, N., Davis, J. L., & Hannon, P. A. (2001). Commitment and relationship maintenance mechanisms. In J. H. Harvey, & A. Wenzel (Eds.), *Close romantic relationships.* Mahwah, NJ: Erlbaum.

Ruse, M. (2002). A Darwinian naturalists's perspective on altruism. In S. G. Post, L. G. Underwood, J. P. Schloss, & W. B. Hurlbut (Eds.), *Altruism and altruistic love.* New York: Oxford.

Rushton, J. P., Fulker, D. W., Neal, M. C., Nias, D. K. B., & Eysenck, H. J. (1986). Altruism and aggression: The heritability of individual differences. *Journal of Personality & Social Psychology, 50,* 1192–1198.*

Rushton, J. P., & Jensen, A. R. (2005). Thirty years of research on race differences in cognitive ability. *Psychology, Public Policy, and Law, 11(2),* 235–294.

Russell, D. W. (1996). UCLA Loneliness Scale (Version 3): Reliability, validity, and factor structure. *Journal of Personality, Assessment, 66,* 20–43.

Russell, J. A., & Fernandez-Dols, J.-M. (Eds.) (1997). *The psychology of facial expression.* New York: Cambridge.*

Russell, S. & Norvig, P. (2003). *Artificial intelligence: A modern approach (2nd ed.).* Englewood Cliffs, NJ: Prentice Hall.

Russo, N. F. (1990). Overview: Forging research priorities for women's health. *American Psychologist, 45,* 373–386.

Ryan, J. M. (2001). Pharmacologic approach to aggression in neuropsychiatric disorders. *Seminars in Clinical Neuropsychiatry, 5,* 238–249.

Ryan, R. M., & Deci, E. L. (2000). Self-determination theory and the facilitation of intrinsic motivation, social development, and well-being. *American Psychologist, 55,* 68–78.

Ryan, R. M., & LaGuardia, J. G. (2000). What is being optimized? Self-determination theory and basic psychological needs. In S. H. Qualls, & N. Abeles (Eds.), *Psychology and the aging revolution.* Washington: APA Press.

Ryckman, R. M. (2004). *Theories of personality (8th ed.).* Belmont, CA: Wadsworth.

Ryder, A. G., Bagby, R. M., & Dion, K. L. (2001). Chronic, low-grade depression in a nonclinical sample: Depressive personality or dysthymia? *Journal of Personality Disorders, 15,* 84–93.*

Ryff, C. D. (2001). *Emotion, social relationships, and health.* New York: Oxford.

Ryff, C. D., & Singer, B. H. (1998). Middle age and well-being. In H. S. Friedman (Ed.), *Encyclopedia of mental health (Vol. 2).* San Diego: Academic Press.

Ryff, C. D., & Singer, B. H. (2005). Social environments and the genetics of aging: Advancing knowledge of protective health mechanisms. *Journals of Gerontology: Series B: Psychological Sciences & Social Sciences. Special Research on Environmental Effects in Genetic Studies of Aging, 60B(1, SpecIssue),* 12–23.

Ryle, A. (2005). Cognitive analytic therapy. In J. C. Norcross, & M. R. Goldfried (Eds.), *Handbook of psychotherapy integration (2nd ed.).* London: Oxford.

Rymer, R. (1993). *Genie.* New York: HarperCollins.

S

Sacks, O. (1985). *The man who mistook his wife for a hat.* New York: Summit Books.

Sadava, S. W. (1987). Interactional theory. In H. T. Blane, & K. E. Leonard (Eds.), *Psychological theories of drinking and alcoholism.* New York: Guilford.*

Sadoski, M., & Paivio, A. (2001). *Imagery and text: A dual coding theory of reading and writing.* Mahwah, NJ: Erlbaum.*

Sakinofsky, I. (1998). The epidemiology of suicide in Canada. In A. A. Leenaars, S. Wenckstern, I. Sakinofsky, R. J. Dyck, M. J. Kral, & R. C. Bland (Eds.), *Suicide in Canada.* Toronto: University of Toronto Press.*

Saklofske, D. H. (1996). Using the WISC-III Canadian Study results in academic research. In D. Wechsler *WISC-III manual Canadian supplement.* Toronto: The Psychological Corporation.*

Saklofske, D. H., Austin, E. J., & Minski, P. S. (2003). Factor structure and validity of a trait emotional intelligence measure. *Personality and Individual Differences, 34(4),* 707–721.*

Saklofske, D. H., Bartell, R., Derevensky, J., Hahn, G., Holmes, B., & Janzen, H. L. (2000). School psychology in Canada: Past, present, and future perspectives. In T. Fagan. & P. Wise (Eds.), *School psychology (2nd ed.).* Bethesda, MD: NASP.*

Saklofske, D. H., Caravan, G., & Schwartz, C. (2000). Concurrent validity of the Wechsler Abbreviated Scale of Intelligence (WASI) with a sample of Canadian children. *Canadian Journal of School Psychology, 16(1),* 87–94.*

Saklofske, D. H., & Eysenck, H. J. (1994). Extraversion-introversion. In V. S. Ramachandran (Ed.). *Encyclopedia of human behavior (Vol. 2).* San Diego, CA: Academic Press.*

Saklofske, D. H., Hildebrand, D. K., Reynolds, C. R., & Wilson, V. L. (1998). Substituting symbol search for coding on the WISC-III; Canadian normative tables for Performance and Full Scale IQ scores. *Canadian Journal of Behavioural Science, 20,* 57–68.*

Saklofske, D. H., Tulsky, D. S., Wilkins, C., & Weiss, L. G. (2003). Canadian WISC-III directional base rates of score discrepancies by ability level. *Canadian Journal of Behavioural Science, 35(3),* 210–218.*

Saklofske, D. H., Weiss, L. G., Beal, A. L., & Coalson, D. (2003). The Wechsler Scales for assessing children's intelligence: Past to present. In J. Georgas (Ed.), *Culture and children's intelligence: Cross-cultural analysis of the WISC-III.* San Diego, CA: Academic Press.*

Sakmar, T. P., Menon, S. T., Marin, E. P. & Awad, E. S. (2002). Rhodopsin: Insights from recent structural studies. *Annual Review of Biophysics and Biomolecular Structure, 31,* 443–484.

Salkind, N. J. (2003). *Exploring research (5th ed.).* Englewood Cliffs, NJ: Prentice Hall.

Salkovskis, P. M., Westbrook, D., Davis, J., Jeavons, A., & Gledhill, A. (1997). Effects of neutralizing on intrusive thoughts: An experiment investigating the etiology of obsessive-compulsive disorder. *Behaviour Research & Therapy, 35,* 211–219.

Salmon, D. P. (2000). Alzheimer's disease. In A. Kazdin (Ed.), *Encyclopedia of psychology.* Washington, & New York: APA Press and Oxford.

Salovey, P., & Mayer, J. D. (1990). Emotional intelligence. *Imagination, Cognition, and Personality, 9,* 185–211.

Salovey, P., Rothman, A., Detweiler, J. B., & Steward, W. T. (2000). Emotional states and physical health. *American Psychologist, 55,* 110–121.

Salsman, J. M., Brown, T. L., Brechting, E. H., & Carlson, C. R. (2005). The link between religion and spirituality and psychological adjustment: The mediating role of optimism and social support. *Personality & Social Psychology Bulletin, 31(4),* 522–535.

Salthouse, T. A. (1994). The aging of working memory. *Neuropsychology, 8,* 535–543.

Salthouse, T. A. (1994). The nature of the influence of speed on adult age differences in cognition. *Developmental Psychology, 30,* 240–259.

Salthouse, T. A. (2000). Adult development and aging: Cognitive processes and development. In A. Kazdin (Ed.), *Encyclopedia of psychology.* Washington, & New York: APA Press and Oxford.

Salthouse, T. A. (2004). What and when of cognitive aging. *Current Directions in Psychological Science, 13(4),* 140–144.

Sam, D. L., & Berry, J. W. (Eds) (2004). *Cambridge handbook of acculturation psychology.* Cambridge: Cambridge University Press.*

Sameroff, A. J., Peck, S. C., & Eccles, J. S. (2004). Changing ecological determinants of conduct problems from early adolescence to early adulthood. *Development & Psychopathology. Special Transition from Adolescence to Adulthood, 16(4),* 873–896.

Samson, J.-M., Levy, J. J., Dupras, A., & Tessier, D. (1993). Active oral-genital sex among married or cohabiting heterosexual adults. *Sexological Review, 1(1),* 143–156.*

Sand, P. G., Godau, C., Riederer, P., Peters, C., Franke, P., Nothen, M. M., et al. (2001). Exonic variants of the GABA (B) receptor gene and panic disorder. *Psychiatry and Genetics, 10,* 191–194.

Sandahl, C., Gerge, A., & Herlitz, K. (2004). Does treatment focus on self-efficacy result in better coping? Paradoxical findings from psychodynamic and cognitive-behavioral group treatment of moderately alcohol-dependent patients. *Psychotherapy Research, 14(3),* 388–397.

Sandell, J. (2000). Vision and sight: Behavioral and functional aspects. In A. Kazdin (Ed.), *Encyclopedia of psychology.* Washington, & New York: APA Press and Oxford.

Sangha, S., McComb, C., Scheibenstock, A., Johannes, C., & Lukowiak, K. (2002). The effects of continuous versus partial reinforcement schedules on associative learning, memory, and extinction in Lymnaea Stagnalis. *Journal of Experimental Biology, 205,* 1171–1178.

Sanson, A., Hemphill, S. A., & Smart, D. (2002). Temperament and social development. In P. Smith & C. Hart (Eds.), *Blackwell handbook of childhood social development.* Malden, MA: Blackwell.

Sanson, A., Hemphill, S. A., & Smart, D. (2004). Connections between temperament and social development: A review. *Social Development, 13(1),* 142–170.

Santrock, J. W. (2002). *Life-span development (8th ed.).* New York: McGraw-Hill.

Santrock, J. W. (2004). *Child development (10th ed.).* New York: McGraw-Hill.

Santrock, J.W. (2005a). *Children (8th ed.).* New York: McGraw-Hill.

Santrock, J. W. (2005b). *Adolescence (10th ed.).* New York: McGraw-Hill.

Santrock, J. W., & Halonen, J. A. (2006). *Your guide to college success (4th ed.).* Belmont, CA: Wadsworth.

Santrock, J. W., MacKenzie-Rivers, A., Leung, K. H. & Malcomson, T. (2005). *Life-span development (2nd Canadian ed.).* Whitby, ON: McGraw-Hill Ryerson.*

Santrock, J., Woloshyn, V. E., Gallagher, T. L., Di Petta, T., & Marini, Z. (2004). *Educational psychology (1st Canadian ed.).* Whitby, ON: McGraw-Hill Ryerson.*

Sarason, I. G., & Sarason, B. R. (2005). *Abnormal psychology (11th ed.).* Mahwah, NJ: Prentice Hall.

Sareen, J., Houlahan, T., Cox, B. J. & Asmundson, G. J. G. (2005). Anxiety disorders associated with suicidal ideation and suicide attempts in the national comorbidity survey. *Journal of Nervous & Mental Disease, 193(7),* 450–454.

Saretzki, G., & von Zglinicki, T. (2002). Replicative aging, telomeres, and oxidative stress. *Annals of the New York Academy of Sciences, 959,* 24–29.

Sarigiani, P. A., & Petersen, A. C. (2000). Adolescence: Puberty and biological maturation. In A. Kazdin (Ed.), *Encyclopedia of psychology.* Washington, & New York: APA Press and Oxford.

Sarouphim, K. M. (2004). Discover in middle school: Identifying gifted minority students. *Journal of Secondary Gifted Education, 15(2),* 61–69.

Sateia, M. J., & Nowell, P. D. (2004). Insomnia. *Lancet, 364(9449),* 1959–1973.

Saunders, D., & Thagard, P. (2005). Creativity in computer science. In J. C. Kaufman, & J. Baer (Ed.), *Creativity across domains: Faces of the muse.* Mahwah, NJ: Erlbaum.*

Savage, J. (2004). Does viewing violent media really cause criminal violence? A methodological review. *Aggression & Violent Behavior, 10(1),* 99–128.

Savage-Rumbaugh, E. S., Murphy, J., Sevcik, R. A., Brakke, K. E., Williams, S. L., & Rumbaugh, D. M. (1993). Language comprehension in ape and child. *Monographs of the Society for Research in Child Development, Serial No. 233 (Vol. 58, Nos. 3–4).*

Savage-Rumbaugh, S., Shanker, S., & Taylor, T. (1998). *Apes, language, and mind.* New York: Oxford.*

Savic, I. (2002). Sex differences in hypothalamic activation by putative pheromones. *Molecular Psychiatry, 7,* 335–336.

Sax, L. J., Astin, A. W., Korn, W. S., & Mahoney, K. M. (1995). *The American college freshman: National norms for fall, 1995.* Los Angeles: University of California at Los Angeles Higher Education Research Institute.

Sax, L. J., Astin, A. W., Lindholm, J. A., Saenz, V. B., Korn, W. S., & Mahoney, K. M. (2003). *The American freshman: National norms for fall 2003.* Los Angeles: Higher Education Research Institute, UCLA.

Sax, L. J., Lindholm, J. A., Astin, A. W., Korn, W. S., & Mahoney, K. M. (2001). *The American freshman: National norms for fall 2001.* Los Angeles: Higher Education Research Institute, UCLA.

Scafidi, F., & Field, T. M. (1996). Massage therapy improves behavior in neonates born to HIV-positive mothers. *Journal of Pediatric Psychology, 21,* 889–897.

Scarborough, E., & Furumoto, L. (1987). *Untold lives: The first generation of American women psychologists.* New York: Columbia University Press.

Scardamalia, M., & Bereiter, C. (1999). Schools as knowledge building organizations. In D. Keating, & C. Hertzman (Eds.), *Today's children, tomorrow's society: The developmental health and wealth of nations.* New York: Guilford.*

Scardamalia, M., & Bereiter, C. (2003). Knowledge building. In *Encyclopedia of education (2nd ed.).* New York: Macmillan.*

Scarpa, A., & Luscher, K. (2002). Self-esteem, cortisol reactivity, and depressed mood mediated by perceptions of control. *Biological Psychology, 59(2),* 93–103.

Scarr, S., & Weinberg, R. A. (1983). The Minnesota adoption studies: Genetic differences and malleability. *Child Development, 54,* 182–259.

Schachter, S., & Singer, J. E. (1962). Cognitive, social, and physiological determinants of emotional state. *Psychological Review, 69,* 379–399.

Schacter, D. L. (2000). Memory: Memory systems. In A. Kazdin (Ed.), *Encyclopedia of psychology.* Washington, & New York: APA Press and Oxford.

Schacter, D. L. (2001). *The seven sins of memory.* Boston: Houghton Mifflin.

Schaffer, H. R., & Emerson, P. E. (1964). The development of social attachments in infancy. *Monographs of the Society for Research in Child Development, 29 (3, Serial No. 94).*

Schaie, K. W. (1983). Consistency and changes in cognitive functioning of the young-old and old-old. In M. Bergner, U. Lehr, E. Lang, & R. Schmidt-Scherzer (Eds.), *Aging in the eighties and beyond.* New York: Springer.

Schaie, K. W. (1994). The life course of adult intellectual development. *American Psychologist, 49,* 304–313.

Schaie, K. W. (1996). *Intellectual development in adulthood: The Seattle Longitudinal Study.* New York: Cambridge.

Schaie, K. W., & Willis, S. L. (2001). *Adult development and aging (5th ed.).* Upper Saddle River, NJ: Prentice Hall.

Schaie, K. W. (2005). *Developmental influences on adult intelligence: The Seattle longitudinal study.* London, Oxford.

Schall, J. D. (2003). On building bridges between brain and behavior. *Annual Review of Psychology, 55,* 23–50.

Schaller, M., & Crandall, C. S. (2004). *The psychological foundations of culture.* Mahwah, NJ: Erlbaum.*

Schank, R., & Abelson, R. (1977). *Scripts, plans, goals, and understanding.* Mahwah, NJ: Erlbaum.

Scharff, L., Marcus, D. A., & Masek, B. J. (2002). A controlled study of minimal-contact thermal biofeedback treatment in children with migraine. *Journal of Pediatric Psychology, 27,* 109–119.

Scharfman, H. E. (2002). Epilepsy as an example of neural plasticity. *Neuroscientist, 8,* 154–173.

Schaubroeck, J., Jones, J. R., & Xie, J. L. (2001). Individual differences in utilizing control to cope with job demands: Effects on susceptibility to infectuous disease. *Journal of Applied Psychology, 86,* 265–298.

Scher, C. D., Segal, Z. V., & Ingram, R. E. (2004). Beck's theory of depression: Origins, empirical status, and future directions for cognitive vulnerability. In R. L. Leahy (Ed.), *Contemporary cognitive therapy: Theory, research, and practice.* New York: Guilford.*

Scheid, T. L. (2003). Managed care and the rationalization of mental health services. *Journal of Health & Social Behavior, 44(2),* 142–161.

Schiffman, J., & Walker, E. (1998). Schizophrenia. In H. S. Friedman (Ed.), *Encyclopedia of mental health (Vol. 2).* San Diego: Academic Press.

Schilling, M. A. (2005). A "Small-World" network model of cognitive insight. *Creativity Research Journal, 17(2–3),* 131–154.

Schleicher, S. S., & Gilbert, L. A. (2005). Heterosexual dating discourses among college students: Is there still a double standard? *Journal of College Student Psychotherapy, 19(3),* 7–23.

Schliecker, E., White, D. R., & Jacobs, E. (1991). The role of daycare quality in the prediction of children's vocabulary. *Canadian Journal of Behavioral Science, 23(1),* 12–24.*

Schmid, D. A., Held, K., Ising, M., Uhr, M., Weikel, J. C., & Steiger, A. (2005). Ghrelin stimulates appetite, imagination of food, GH, ACTH, and cortisol, but does not affect leptin in normal controls. *NeuroPsychopharmacology, 30(6),* 1187–1192.

Schmidt, L. A., Polak, C. P., & Spooner, A. L. (2001). Biological and environmental contributions to childhood shyness: A diathesis-stress model. In W. R. Crozier, & L. E. Alden (Eds.), *International handbook of social anxiety: Concepts, research and interventions relating to the self and shyness.* New York: Wiley.*

Schmolck, H., Buffalo, E. A., & Squire, L. R. (2000). Memory distortions develop over time: Recollections of the O. J. Simpson trial verdict after 15 and 32 months. *Psychological Science, 11(1),* 39–45.

Schneider, K. J. (2002). Humanistic psychotherapy. In M. Hersen, & W. H. Sledge (Eds.), *Encyclopedia of psychotherapy.* San Diego: Academic Press.

Schneider, S. L. (2001). In search of realistic optimism: Meaning, knowledge, and warm fuzziness. *American Psychologist, 56,* 250–263.

Schneiderman, N., Antoni, M. H., Saab, P. G., & Ironson, G. (2001). Health psychology: Psychological and biobehavioral aspects of chronic disease management. *Annual Review of Psychology, 52,* 555–580.

Scholnick, E. K. (1999). Piaget's legacy: Heirs to the house that Jean built. In E. K. Scholnick, K. Nelson, S. A. Gelman, & P. H. Miller (Eds.), *Conceptual development: Piaget's legacy.* Mahwah, NJ: Erlbaum.

Schooler, C. (1998) Environmental complexity and the Flynn effect. In U. Neisser (Ed.), *The rising curve: Long-term gains in IQ and related measures.* Washington: APA Press.

Scholnick, E. K., Nelson, K., Gelman, S. A., & Miller, P. H. (Eds.). (1999). *Conceptual development: Piaget's legacy.* Mahwah, NJ: Erlbaum.

Schore, A. N. (2003). *Affect dysregulation and disorders of the self.* New York: Norton.

Schouwenburg, H. C., Lay, C., Pychyl, T., & Ferrari, J. R. (Eds.) (2004). *Counseling the procrastinator in academic settings.* Washington: APA Press.*

Schredl, M., Ciric, P., Götz, S., & Wittmann, L. (2004). Typical dreams: Stability and gender differences. *Journal of Psychology: Interdisciplinary & Applied, 138(6),* 485–494.

Schretlen, D., Pearlson, G. D., Anthony, J. C., Aylward, E. H., Augustine, A. M., Davis, A., et al. (2000). Elucidating the contributions of processing speed, executive ability, and frontal lobe volume to normal age-related differences in fluid intelligence. *Journal of the International Neuropsychology Society, 6,* 52–61.

Schulenberg, J., & Maggs, J. L. (2002). A developmental perspective on alcohol use and heavy drinking during adolescence and the transition to young adulthood. *Journal Of Studies On Alcohol, Supplement No. 14.*

Schulenberg, J., O'Malley, P. M., Bachman, J. G., & Johnston, L. D. (2000). "Spread your wings and fly": The course of health and well-being during the transition to young adulthood. In L. Crockett, & R. Silbereisen (Eds.), *Negotiating adolescence in times of social change.* New York: Cambridge.

Schultheiss, O. C., & Brunstein, J. C. (1999). Goal imagery: Bridging the gap between implicit motives and explicit goals. *Journal of Personality, 67,* 1–38.

Schultz, D. P., & Schultz, S. E. (2005). *Theories of personality (8th ed.).* Pacific Grove, CA: Brooks/Cole.

Schultz, R., & Curnow, C. (1988). Peak performance and age among superathletes: Track and field, swimming, baseball, tennis, and golf. *Journal of Gerontology, 43,* 113–120.

Schunk, D. H. (2004a). *Learning theories (4th ed.).* Englewood Cliffs, NJ: Prentice Hall.

Schunk, D. H. (2004b). *Theories of learning applied to education (4th ed.).* Upper Saddle River, NJ: Merrill.

Schwartz, B. (2000). Self-determination: The tyranny of freedom. *American Psychologist, 55,* 79–88.

Schwartz, B., & Ward, A. (2004). Doing better but feeling worse: The paradox of choice. In P. A. Linley, & S. Joseph (Ed.), *Positive psychology in practice.* New York: Wiley.

Schwartz, B. L. (2002). *Tip-of-the-tongue states.* Mahwah, NJ: Erlbaum.

Schwartz, M. S., & Andrasik, F. (Eds.). (2003). *Biofeedback: A practitioner's guide (3rd ed.).* New York: Guilford.

Schwartz, T. (1999). *Kids and guns.* New York: Franklin Watts.

Schwarzer, R., & Greenglass, E. (1999). Teacher burnout from a social-cognitive perspective: A theoretical position paper. In R. Vandenberghe, & A. M. Huberman (Eds.), *Understanding and preventing teacher burnout: A sourcebook of international research and practice.* New York: Cambridge.*

Schwean, V. L., Mykota, D, Robert, L, & Saklofske, D. H. (1999). Determinants of psychosocial disorders in cultural minority children. In V. L. Schwean, & D. H. Saklofske (Eds.), *Handbook of psychosocial characteristics of exceptional children.* New York: Kluwer Academic/Plenum Publishers.*

Sechehaye, M. (1951). *Autobiography of a schizophrenic girl.* New York: Grune & Stratton.

Sedikides, C., Campbell, W. K., Reeder, G. D., & Elliot, A. J. (1998). The self-serving bias in relational context. *Journal of Personality & Social Psychology, 74,* 378–386.

Segal, D. L., & Coolidge, F. L. (2000). Assessment. In A. Kazdin (Ed.), *Encyclopedia of psychology.* Washington, & New York: APA Press and Oxford.

Segall, M. H., Dasen, P. R., Berry, J. W., & Poortinga, Y. H. (1990). *Human behavior in global perspective.* New York: Pergamon.*

Segalowitz, N. (1997). Individual differences in second language acquisition. In A. de Groot, & J. Kroll (Eds.), *Tutorials in bilingualism.* Mahwah, NJ: Erlbaum.*

Segalowitz, S. J. (1983). *Two sides of the brain: Brain lateralization explored.* Englewood Cliffs, NJ: Prentice Hall.*

Segraves, T., & Althof, S. (2002). Psychotherapy and pharmacotherapy for sexual dysfunctions. In P. E. Nathan & J. M. Gorman (Eds.), *A guide to treatments that work (2nd ed.).* London: Oxford.

Segrin, C. (2001). *Interpersonal processes in psychological disorders.* New York: Guilford.

Seidman, D. F., Rosecan, J., & Role, L. (1999). Biological and clinical perspectives on nicotine addiction. In D. F. Seidman, & L. S. Covey (Eds.), *Helping the hard-core smoker.* Mahwah, NJ: Erlbaum.

Sekuler, A. B., Gaspar, C. M., Gold, J. M., & Bennett, P. J. (2004). Inversion leads to quantitative, not qualitative, changes in face processing. *Current Biology, 14,* 391–396.*

Sekuler, R., & Blake, R. (2006). *Perception (5th ed.).* New York: McGraw-Hill.

Seligman, C., Olson, J. M., & Zanna, M. P. (Eds.). (1996). *The psychology of values.* Mahwah, NJ: Erlbaum.*

Seligman, L. (2006). *Theories of counseling and psychotherapy: Systems, strategies, and skills (2ⁿᵈ ed.).* Upper Saddle River, NJ: Prentice Hall.

Seligman, M. E. P. (1970). On the generality of the laws of learning. *Psychological Review, 77,* 406–418.

Seligman, M. E. P. (1975). *Helplessness: On depression, development and death.* New York: Freeman.

Seligman, M. E. P. (1989). *Why is there so much depression today? The waxing of the individual and the waning of the common.* In The G. Stanley Hall Lecture Series. Washington: APA Press.

Seligman, M. E. P. (1990). *Learned optimism.* New York: Knopf.

Seligman, M. E. P. (2002). *Authentic happiness: Using the new positive psychology to realize your potential for lasting fulfillment.* New York: Free Press/Simon and Schuster.

Seligman, M. E. P., & Csikszentmihalyi, M. (2000). Positive psychology: An introduction. *American Psychologist, 55,* 5–14.

Selye, H. (1974). *Stress without distress.* Philadelphia: W. B. Saunders.*

Selye, H. (1983). The stress concept: Past, present, and future. In C. I. Cooper (Ed.), *Stress research.* New York: Wiley.*

Semel, E., & Rosner. S. (2003). *Understanding Williams syndrome: Behavioural patterns and interventions.* Mahwah, NJ: Erlbaum.

Serbin, L. A., Poulin-Dubois, D., & Eichstedt, J. A. (2002). Infants' response to gender-inconsistent events. *Infancy, 3(4),* 531–542.*

Serin, R. C., & Marshall, W. L. (2003). The personality disorders. In P. Firestone, & W. L. Marshall (Eds.), *Abnormal psychology: Perspectives (2nd ed.).* Toronto: Prentice Hall.*

Serpell, R. (2000). Determinants of intelligence: Culture and intelligence. In A. Kazdin (Ed.), *Encyclopedia of psychology.* Washington, & New York: APA Press and Oxford.

Service, R. F. (1994). Will a new type of drug make memory-making easier? *Science, 266,* 218–219.

Seto, M. C., & Barbaree, H. E. (1995). The role of alcohol in sexual aggression. *Clinical Psychology Review, 15,* 545–566.*

Seto, M. C., Maric, A., & Barbaree, H. E. (2001). The role of pornography in the etiology of sexual aggression. *Aggression & Violent Behavior, 6(1),* 35–53.*

Seutter, R. A., & Rovers, M. (2004). Emotionally absent fathers: Furthering the understanding of homosexuality. *Journal of Psychology & Theology, 32(1),* 43–49.*

Sévigny, S., Cloutier, M., Pelletier, M-F., & Ladouceur, R. (2005). Internet gambling: Misleading payout rates during the "demo" period. *Computers in Human Behavior, 21(1),* 153–158.*

Shackelford, T. K., Schmitt, D. P., & Buss, D. M. (2005). Universal dimensions of human mate preferences. *Personality & Individual Differences, 39(2),* 447–458.

Shaffer D., Wood, E. & Willoughby, T. (2005). *Developmental psychology: Childhood and adolescence (2nd Canadian ed.).* Toronto; Nelson/Thomson.*

Shakesby, A. C., Anwyl, R., & Rowan, M. J. (2002). Overcoming the effects of stress on synaptic plasticity in the intact hippocampus: rapid actions of serotonergic and antidepressant agents. *Journal of Neuroscience, 22,* 3638–3644.

Shaldubina, A., Agam, G., & Belmaker, R. H. (2001). The mechanism of lithium: State of the art, ten years later. *Progress in Neuropsychology and Biological Psychiatry, 25,* 855–866.

Shanker, S. G, Savage-Rumbaugh, E. S., & Taylor, T. J. (1999). Kanzi: A new beginning. *Animal Learning & Behavior, 27(1),* 24–25.*

Shanker, S. G., & Taylor, T. J. (2005). The significance of ape language research. In C. E.

Erneling, & D. M. Johnson (Eds.), *The mind as a scientific object: Between brain and culture.* London: Oxford.*

Shanks, D. R. (1991). Categorization by a connectionist network. *Journal of Experimental Psychology: Learning, Memory, and Cognition, 17,* 433–443.

Shapiro, S. L., & Walsh, R. (2003). An analysis of recent meditation research and suggestions for future directions. *Humanistic Psychologist. Special Transpersonal psychology, 31(2-3),* 86–114.

Sharf, R. S. (2004). *Theories of psychotherapy and counseling: Concepts and cases (3ʳᵈ ed.).* Belmont, CA: Wadsworth.

Sharkey, K. M., & Eastman, C. I. (2002). Melatonin phase shifts human circadian rhythms in a placebo-controlled simulated night-work study. *American Journal of Physiology: Regulatory, Integrative, and Comparative Physiology, 282,* R454–R463.

Sharpe, L. (2002). A reformulated cognitive-behavioral model of problem gambling: A biopsychosocial perspective. *Clinical Psychology Review, 22,* 1–25.*

Shaughnessy, J. J., Zechmeister, E. B., Zechmeister, J. S. (2006). *Research methods in psychology (7th ed.).* New York: McGraw-Hill.

Shaver, P. R., & Mikulincer, M. (2005). Attachment theory and research: Resurrection of the psychodynamic approach to personality. *Journal of Research in Personality, 39(1),* 22–45.

Shalev, A. Y., & Freedman, S. (2005). PTSD following terrorist attacks: A prospective evaluation. *American Journal of Psychiatry, 162(6),* 1188–1191.

Shaw, M. L. (2003). Creativity and whole language. In J. Houtz, (Ed.), *The educational psychology of creativity.* Cresskill, NJ: Hampton Press.

Shay, J. W., & Wright, W. E. (2000). The use of telomerized cells for tissue engineering. *Nature Biotechnology, 18,* 22–23.

Shaywitz, B. A, Shaywitz, S. E., Pugh, K. R., Constable, R. T., et al. (1995). Sex differences in the functional organization of the brain for language. *Nature, 373,* 607–609.

Shea, A., Walsh, C., MacMillan, H. & Steiner, M. (2005). Child maltreatment and HPA axis dysregulation: Relationship to major depressive disorder and post traumatic stress disorder in females. *Psychoneuroendocrinology, 30(2),* 162–178.*

Sheldon, K. M. (2004). *Optimal human being: An integrated multi-level perspective.* Mahwah, NJ: Erlbaum.

Sheldon, K. M. (in press). Getting older, getting better? Recent psychological evidence. In M. Csikszentmihalyi (Ed.), *A life worth living: Perspectives from positive psychology.* Washington: Gallup.

Sheldon, K. M., & Kasser, T. (2001). Getting older, getting better? Personal strivings and psychological maturity across the life span. *Developmental Psychology, 37(4),* 491–501.

Shelton, R. C., & Hollon, S. D. (2000). Antidepressants. In A. Kazdin (Ed.), *Encyclopedia of psychology.* Washington, & New York: APA Press and Oxford.

Shepard, R. N. (1967). Recognition memory for words, sentences, and pictures. *Journal of Verbal Learning and Verbal Behavior, 6,* 156–163.

Sher, K. J. (1993). Children of alcoholics and the intergenerational transmission of alcoholism: A biopsychological perspective. In J. S. Baer, G. A. Marlatt, & R. J. McMahon (Eds.), *Addictive behaviors across the life span.* Newbury Park, CA: Sage.

Sheras, P., & Worchel, S. (1979). *Clinical psychology: A social psychological approach.* New York: Van Nostrand.

Sherif, M., Harvey, O. J., White, B. J., Hood, W. R., & Sherif, C. W. (1961). *Intergroup cooperation and competition: The Robbers Cave experiment.* Norman, OK: University of Oklahoma Press.

Sherwood, A., Light, K. C., & Blumenthal, J. A. (1989). Effects of aerobic exercise training on hemodynamic responses during psychosocial stress in normotensive and borderline hypertensive Type A men: A preliminary report. *Psychosomatic Medicine, 51,* 123–136.

Shettleworth, S. J. (1998). *Cognition, evolution, and behavior.* New York: Oxford.*

Shettleworth, S. J. (2003). Memory and hippocampal specialization in food-storing birds: Challenges for research on comparative cognition. *Brain, Behavior & Evolution, 62(2),* 108–116.*

Shettleworth, S. J., & Hampton, R. R. (1998). Adaptive specializations of spatial cognition in food-storing birds? Approaches to testing a comparative hypothesis. In R. P. Balda, I. M. Pepperberg, & A. C. Kamil (Eds.), *Animal cognition in nature: The convergence of psychology and biology in laboratory and field.* San Diego: Academic Press.*

Shevrin, H. (2000). "Experimental psychology and psychoanalysis: What we can learn from a century of misunderstanding": Comment. *Neuro-psychoanalysis, 2,* 255–258.

Shevrin, H. (2001). Event-related markers of unconscious processes. International Journal of Psychophysiology. *Special Issue: A "snapshot" of Psychophysiology at the end of the twentieth century, 42,* 209–218.

Shields, S. A. (1991). Gender in the psychology of emotion. In K. T. Strongman (Ed.), *International review of studies of emotion (Vol. 1).* New York: Wiley.

Shields, S. A., & Eyssell, K. M. (2002). History of the study of gender psychology. In J. Worell (Ed.), *Encyclopedia of women and gender.* New York: Oxford.

Shier, D., Butler, J., & Lewis, R. (2003). *Human anatomy and physiology (9th ed.).* New York: McGraw-Hill.

Shiffrin, R. M., & Schneider, W. (1977). Controlled and automatic human information processing: II. Perceptual learning, automatic attending, and a general theory. *Psychological Review, 84,* 127–190.

Shnek, Z. M., Irvine, J., Stewart, D., & Abbey, S. (2001). Psychological factors and depressive symptoms in ischemic heart disease. *Health Psychology, 20,* 141–145.

Shore, D. I., McLaughlin, E. N., & Klein, R. M. (2001). Modulation of the attentional blink by differential resource allocation. *Canadian Journal of Experimental Psychology, 55,* 318–324.*

Shotland, R. L. (1985, June). When bystanders just stand by. *Psychology Today,* pp. 50–55.

Shrum, L. J. (2004). *The psychology of entertainment media: Blurring the lines between entertainment and persuasion.* Mahwah, NJ: Erlbaum.

Shulman, B. H. (2004). Cognitive therapy and the individual psychology of Alfred Adler. In A. Freeman, M. J. Mahoney, P. DeVito, & D. Martin (Eds.), *Cognition and psychotherapy (2nd ed.).* New York: Springer.

Shulman, R. G., & Reiser, M. F. (2004). Freud's theory of mind and functional imaging experiments. *Neuro-psychoanalysis, 6(2),* 133–142.

Shultz, R. T., Grelotti, D. J., & Pober, B. (2001). Genetics of childhood disorders: XXVI. Williams syndrome and brain-behavior relationships. *Journal of the American Academy of Child and Adolescent Psychiatry, 40,* 606–609.

Shuper, P. A., Sorrentino, R. M., Otsubo, Y., Hodson, G., & Walker, A. M. (2004). A theory of uncertainty orientation: Implications for the study of individual differences within and across cultures. *Journal of Cross-Cultural Psychology, 35(4),* 460–480.*

Siebner, H. R., Limmer, C., Peinemann, A., Drzezga, A., Bloem, B. R., Schwaiger, M., et al. (2002). Long-term consequences of switching handedness: A positron emission tomography study on handwriting in "converted" left handers. *Journal of Neuroscience, 22,* 2816–2825.

Siegel, S. (1979). The role of conditioning in drug tolerance and addiction. In J. D. Keehn (Ed.), *Psychopathology in animals.* New York: Academic Press.*

Siegel, S. (1983). Classical conditioning, drug tolerance, and drug dependency. In Y. Israel, F. B. Slower, H. Kalant, R. E. Popham, W. Schmidt, & R. G. Smart (Eds.), *Research advances in alcohol and drug abuse (Vol. 7).* New York: Plenum.*

Siegel, S. (1988). State dependent learning and morphine tolerance. *Behavioral Neuroscience, 102,* 228–232.*

Siegel, S. (1999). Drug anticipation and drug addiction. The 1998 H. David Archibald Lecture. *Addiction, 94(8),* 1113–1124.*

Siegel, S. (2001). Pavlovian conditioning and drug overdose: When tolerance fails. *Addiction Research & Theory, 9(5),* 503–513.*

Siegel, S., Hinson, R. E., Krank, M. D., & McCully, J. (1982). Heroin "overdose" death: Contribution of drug-associated environmental cues. *Science, 216,* 436–7.*

Siegel, S., Parker, L. A., & Moroz, I. (1995). Morphine-induced taste avoidance is attenuated with multiple conditioning trials. *Pharmacology, Biochemistry and Behavior, 50,* 299–303.*

Siegel, S., & Ramos, B. M. C. (2002). Applying laboratory research: Drug anticipation and the treatment of drug addiction. *Experimental & Clinical Psychopharmacology. Special Issue: Clinical research in Psychopharmacology and substance abuse, 10(3),* 162–183.*

Siegle, G. J., Steinhauer, S. R., Thase, M. E., Stenger, V. A., & Carter, C. S. (2002). Can't shake that feeling: event-related fMRI assessment of sustained amygdala activity in response to emotional information in depressed individuals. *Biological Psychiatry, 51,* 693–707.

Siegler, R. S. (2004). *Children's thinking (4th ed.).* Mahwah, NJ: Erlbaum.

Siegler, R. S. (2004). Learning about learning. *Merrill-Palmer Quarterly. Special: The Maturing of the Human Developmental Sciences: Appraising Past, Present, and Prospective Agendas, 50(3),* 353–368.

Siffre, M. (1975). Six months alone in a cave. *National Geographic, 147,* 426–435.

Sifneos, P. E. (1972). The prevalence of "alexithymic" characteristics in psychosomatic patients. *Psychotherapy & Psychosomatics, 22(2–6),* 255–262.

Silke, A. (2003). Deindividuation, anonymity, and violence: Findings from Northern Ireland. *Journal of Social Psychology, 143(4),* 493–499.

Silverstein, S. M., Menditto, A. A., & Stuve, P. (2001). Shaping attention span: An operant conditioning procedure to improve neurocognition and functioning in schizophrenia. *Schizophrenia Bulletin, 27,* 247–257.

Silverthorne, C. (2004). *Common sense statistics (4th ed.).* Englewood Cliffs, NJ: Prentice Hall.

Simeon, D., Guralnik, O., Knutelska, M., & Schmeidler, J. (2002). Personality factors associated with dissociation: Temperament, defenses, and cognitive schemata. *American Journal of Psychiatry, 159,* 489–491.

Simner, M. L., & Goffin, R. D. (2003). A position statement by the International Graphonomics Society on the use of graphology in personnel selection testing. *International Journal of Testing, 3(4),* 353–364.

Simon, H. A. (1969). *The sciences of the artificial.* Cambridge MIT Press.

Simon, H. A. (2000). Artificial intelligence. In A. Kazdin (Ed.), *Encyclopedia of psychology.* Washington, & New York: APA Press and Oxford.

Simons-Morton, B., Chen, R., Abroms, L., & Haynie, D. L. (2004). Latent growth curve analyses of peer and parent influences on smoking progression among early adolescents. *Health Psychology, 23(6),* 612–621.

Simonton, D. K., & Baumeister, R. F. (2005). Positive psychology at the summit. *Review of General Psychology. Special Positive Psychology, 9(2),* 99–102.

Simpson, J. A., & Gangestad, S. W. (2001). *Evolution and relationships: A call for integration.* Personal Relationships, 8, 341–356.

Simpson, K. J. (2002). Anorexia nervosa and culture. *Journal of Psychiatric and Mental Health Nursing, 9,* 65–71.

Sinclair, C. (1998). Nine unique features of the Canadian code of ethics for psychologists. *Canadian Psychology, 39(3),* 167–176.*

Sinclair, C. M. (1998). Suicide in First Nations people. In A. A. Leenaars, S. Wenckstern, I. Sakinofsky, R. J. Dyck, M. J. Kral, & R. C. Bland (Eds.), *Suicide in Canada.* Toronto: University of Toronto Press.*

Singer, M., Gagnon, N., & Richards, E. (2002). Strategies of text retrieval: A criterion shift account. *Canadian Journal of Experimental Psychology, 56,* 41–57.

Singer, W., & Gray, C. M. (1995). Visual feature integration and the temporal correlation hypothesis. *Annual Review of Neuroscience, 18,* 555–586.

Singh, P. G., & Bregman, A. S. (1997). The influence of different timbre attributes on the perceptual segregation of complex-tone sequences. *Journal of the Acoustical Society of America, 102(4),* 1943–1952.*

Skinner, A. M., & Turker, M. S. (2005). Oxidative mutagenesis, mismatch repair, and aging. *Science of Aging Knowledge Environment, 9,* re3.

Skinner, B. F. (1938). *The behavior of organisms: An experimental analysis.* New York: Appleton-Century-Crofts.

Skinner, B. F. (1948). *Walden Two.* New York: Macmillan.

Skinner, B. F. (1957). *Verbal behavior.* New York: Appleton-Century-Crofts.

Skog, O.-J. (2003). Alcohol consumption and fatal accidents in Canada, 1950-98. *Addiction, 98(7),* 883–893.

Slavin, R. E. (2006). *Educational psychology (8th ed.).* Boston: Allyn & Bacon.

Slife, B., & Yanchar, S. C. (2000). Unresolved issues in psychology. In B. Slife (Ed.), *Taking sides (11th ed.).* New York: Duskin McGraw-Hill.

Sloan, P., Arsenault, L., Hilsenroth, M., & Harvill, L. (1996). Rorschach measures of post-traumatic stress in Persian Gulf War veterans: A three-year follow-up study. *Journal of Personality Assessment, 66,* 54–64.

Slobin, D. (1972, July). Children and language: They learn the same way around the world. *Psychology Today,* 71–76.

Slobin, D. (2003). Language and thought online: Cognitive consequences of linguistic relativity. In D. Gentner, & S. Goldin-Meadow (Eds.), *Language in mind: Advances in the study of language and thought.* Cambridge MIT Press.

Smetana, J. G., & Campione, N. (2003). Parenting styles. In J. J. Ponzetti, Jr. (Ed.), *The international encyclopedia of marriage and family relationships (Vol. 3, 2nd ed.).* New York: Macmillan.

Smallwood, J. M., Baracaia, S. F., Lowe, M., & Obonsawin, M. (2003). Task unrelated thought whilst encoding information. *Consciousness & Cognition: An International Journal, 12(3),* 452–484.

Smilek, D., & Dixon, M. J. (2002). Towards a synergistic understanding of synaesthesia: Combining current experimental findings with synaesthetes' subjective descriptions. *Psyche, 8(01).*

Smith, C. T., Aubrey, J. B., & Peters, K. R. (2004). Different roles for REM and Stage 2 sleep in motor learning: A proposed model. *Psychologica Belgica. Special Cognition in Slumberland: Mechanisms of Information Processing in the Sleep-Wake Cycle, 44(1–2),* 81–104.*

Smith, D. V., & Margolskee, R. F. (2001). Making sense of taste. *Scientific American, 284(3),* 32–39.

Smith, K. H., & Rogers, M. (1994). Effectiveness of subliminal messages in television commercials. *Journal of Applied Psychology, 79,* 866–874.

Smith, L. (2001). Piaget's model. In U. Goswami (Ed.), *Blackwell handbook of childhood cognitive development.* Malden, MA: Blackwell.

Smith, M. B. (2001). Humanistic psychology. In W. E. Craighead, & C. B. Nemeroff (Eds.), *The Corsini encyclopedia of psychology and behavioral science (3rd ed.).* New York: Wiley.

Smith, M. L., Glass, G. V., & Miller, R. L. (1980). *The benefit of psychotherapy.* Baltimore: Johns Hopkins University Press.

Smith, N. (2003). Dissociation and modularity: Reflections on language and mind. In M. T. Banich, & M. Mack, (Eds.), *Mind, brain, and language: Multidisciplinary perspectives.* Mahwah, NJ: Erlbaum.

Smith, R. E., & Bayen, U. J. (2004). Multinomial model of event-based prospective memory. *Journal of Experimental Psychology: Learning, Memory, & Cognition, 30(4),* 756–777.

Smith, S. L., Fry, M. D., Ethington, C. A., & Li, Y. (2005). The effect of female athletes' perceptions of their coaches' behaviors on their perceptions of the motivational climate. *Journal of Applied Sport Psychology, 17(2),* 170–177.

Smith, S. M., & Fabrigar, L. R. (2000). Attitudes: An overview. In A. Kazdin (Ed.), *Encyclopedia of psychology.* Washington, & New York: APA Press and Oxford.*

Smith, S. M., Stinson, V., & Prosser, M. A. (2004). Do they all look alike? An exploration of decision-making strategies in cross-race facial identifications. *Canadian Journal of Behavioural Science. Special Forensic Psychology, 36(2),* 146–154.*

Smith, S. M., & Vela, E. (2001). Environmental context-dependent memory: A review and meta-analysis. *Psychonomic Bulletin Review, 8,* 203–220.*

Smith, T. W., Glazer, K., Ruiz, J. M., & Gallo, L. C. (2004). Hostility, anger, aggressiveness, and coronary heart disease: An interpersonal perspective on personality, emotion, and health. *Journal of Personality. Special Emotions, Personality, and Health, 72(6),* 1217–1270.

Smither, J. W., London, M., & Richmond, K. R. (2005). The relationship between leaders' personality and their reactions to and use of multisource feedback: A longitudinal study. *Group & Organization Management, 30(2),* 181–210.

Smitson, A. W. (2001). Action in infancy—Perspectives, concepts, and challenges: The development of reaching and grasping. In G. Bremner, & A. Fogel (Eds), *Blackwell handbook of infant development.* Malden, MA: Blackwell.

Snook, B., Canter, D., & Bennell, C. (2002). Predicting the home location of serial offenders: A preliminary comparison of the accuracy of human judges with a geographic profiling system. *Behavioral Sciences & the Law, 20,* 109–118.*

Snook, B., Taylor, P. J. and Bennell, C. (2004). Geographic profiling: The fast, frugal and accurate way. Applied *Cognitive Psychology, 18,* 105–121.*

Snook, B., Zito, M., Bennell, C. & Taylor, P. J. (2005). On the complexity and accuracy of geographic profiling strategies. *Journal of Quantitative Criminology, 21(1),* 1–26.*

Snow, C. E. (1998). *Preventing reading difficulties in young children.* Washington: U.S. Department of Education.

Snowden, D. A. (1997). Aging and Alzheimer's disease: Lessons from the nun study. *Gerontologist, 37,* 150–156.

Snowden, D. A. (2001). *Aging with grace: What the nun study teaches us about longer, healthier, and more meaningful lives.* New York: Bantam.

Snyder, M., & Stukas, Jr., A. A. (1999). Interpersonal processes: The interplay of cognitive, motivational, and behavioral activities in social interaction. *Annual Review of Psychology, 50,* 273–303.

Sober, E. (2001). The ABC's of altruism. In S. G. Post, L. G. Underwood, J. P. Schloss, & W. B. Hurlbut (Eds.), *Altruism and altruistic love.* New York: Oxford.

Sobolewski, J. M., & Amato, P. R. (2005). Economic hardship in the family of origin and children's psychological well-being in adulthood. *Journal of Marriage & Family, 67(1),* 141–156.

Soderstrom, M., Dolbier, C., Leiferman, J., & Stenhardt, M. (2000). The relationship of hardiness, coping strategies, and perceived stress to symptoms of illness. *Journal of Behavioral Medicine, 23,* 311–328.

Sofroniew, M. V., Howe, C. L., & Mobley, W. C. (2001). Nerve growth factor signaling, neuroprotection, and neural repair. *Annual Review of Neuroscience, 24,* 1217–1281.

Soja, P. J., Pang, W., Taepavarapruk, N., & McErlane, S. A. (2001). Spontaneous spike activity of spinoreticular tract neurons during sleep and waking. *Sleep, 24,* 18–25.

Sollod, R. N. (2005). Integrating spirituality with psychotherapy. In J. C. Norcross, & M. R. Goldfried (Eds.), *Handbook of psychotherapy integration (2nd ed.).* London: Oxford.

Solms, M. (1997). *The neuropsychology of dreams.* Mahwah, NJ: Erlbaum.

Solso, R. L., MacLin, M. K., & MacLin, O. H. (2005). *Cognitive psychology (7th ed)*. Allyn and Bacon.

Sommer, B. (2002). Menopause. In J. Worell (Ed.), *Encyclopedia of women and gender.* New York: Oxford.

Sonnenberg, S. M., & Ursano, R. (2002). Psychoanalysis and psychoanalytic psychotherapy: Technique. In M. Hersen, & W. H. Sledge (Eds.), *Encyclopedia of psychotherapy.* San Diego: Academic Press.

Sorensen, A., Adam, C. L., Findlay, P. A., Marie, M., Thomas, L., Travers, M. T., et al. (2002). Leptin secretion and hypothalamic neuropeptide receptor gene expression in sheep. *American Journal of Physiology: Regulatory, Integrative, and Comparative Physiology, 282,* R1227–R1235.

Sorensen, B. K., Hojrup, P., Ostergard, E., Jorgensen, C. S., Enghild, J., Ryder, L. R., et al. (2002). Silver staining of proteins of electroblotting membranes and intensification of silver staining of proteins separated by polyacrylamide gel. *Annals of Biochemistry, 304,* 33-41.

Sorrentino, R. M., Otsubo, Y., Yasunaga, S., Nezlek, J., Kouhara, S., & Shuper, P. (2005). Uncertainty orientation and social behavior: individual differences within and across cultures. In R. M. Sorrentino, & D. Cohen (Eds.), *Cultural and social behavior: The Ontario Symposium (Vol 10).* Mahwah, NJ: Erlbaum.*

Sorrentino, R. M., & Roney, C. R. J. (2000). *The uncertain mind: Individual differences in facing the unknown.* Philadelphia: Psychology Press.*

Sothern, M. S., Schumacher, H., von Almen, T. K., Carlisle, L. K., & Udall, J. N. (2002). Committed to kids: an integrated, 4-level team approach to weight management in adolescents. *Journal of the American Dietetic Association, 102,* S81–S85.

Soussignan, R. (2002). Duchenne smile, emotional experience, and autonomic reactivity: A test of the facial feedback hypothesis. *Emotion, 2(1),* 52–74.

Spahic-Mihajlovic, A., Crayton, J. W., & Neafsey, E. J. (2005). Selective numbing and hyperarousal in male and female Bosnian refugees with PTSD. *Journal of Anxiety Disorders, 19(4),* 383–402.

Spanos, N. P. (1991). A sociocognitive approach to hypnosis. In S. J. Lynn, & J. W. Rhue (Eds.), *Theories of hypnosis: Current models and perspectives.* New York: Guilford.

Spanos, N. P. (1994). Multiple identity enactments and multiple personality disorder: A sociocognitive perspective. *Psychological Bulletin, 116,* 143–165.*

Spanos, N. P., & Chaves, J. F. (Eds.). (1989). *Hypnosis: The cognitive-behavior perspective.* Buffalo, NY: Prometheus.*

Spanos, N. P., & Chaves, J. F. (1991). History and historiography of hypnosis. In S. J. Lynn, & J. W. Rhue (Eds.), *Theories of hypnosis: Current models and perspectives.* New York: Guilford.*

Spanos, N. P., Burgess, C. A., Burgess, M. F., Samuels, C., & Blois, W. O. (1999). Creating false memories of infancy with hypnotic and non-hypnotic procedures. *Applied Cognitive Psychology, 13,* 201–218.*

Spearman, C. (1904). "General intelligence," objectively determined and measured. *American Journal of Psychology, 15,* 201–293.

Speca, M., Carlson, L. E., Goodey, E., & Angen, M. (2000). A randomized, wait-list controlled clinical trial: The effect of a mindfulness meditation-based stress reduction program on mood and symptoms of stress in cancer outpatients. *Psychosomatic Medicine, 62,* 613–622.

Spector, A. C., & Kopka, S. L. (2002). Rats fail to discriminate quinine from denatonium: implications for the neural coding of bitter-tasting compounds. *Journal of Neuroscience, 22,* 1937–1941.

Spector, P. E. (2005). *Industrial and organizational psychology: Research and practice (4th ed.).* New York: Wiley.

Spelke, E. (2002). Developmental neuroimaging: A developmental psychologist looks ahead. *Developmental Science, 5(3),* 392–396.

Spellman, B., & Willingham, D. T. (Eds.). (2004). *Current directions in cognition.* Englewood Cliffs, NJ: Prentice Hall.

Spence, C., Kingstone, A., Shore, D. I., & Gazzaniga, M. S. (2001). Representation of visuotac-

tile space in the split brain. *Psychological Science, 12,* 90–93.

Spencer, M. B. (2000). Ethnocentrism. In A. Kazdin (Ed.), *Encyclopedia of psychology.* Washington, and New York: APA Press and Oxford.

Spera, S. P., Buhrfeind, E. D., & Pennebaker, J. W. (1994). Expressive writing and coping with job loss. *Academy of Management Journal, 37,* 722–733.

Sperling, G. (1960). The information available in brief presentations. *Psychological Monographs, 74 (Whole No. 11).*

Sperry, L. (2003). *Handbook of diagnosis and treatment of DSM-IV personality disorders (2nd ed.).* New York: Routledge.

Sperry, R. W. (1968). Hemisphere deconnection and unity in conscious awareness. *American Psychologist, 23,* 723–733.

Sperry, R. W. (1974). Lateral specialization in surgically separated hemispheres. In F. O. Schmitt, & F. G. Worden (Eds.), *The neurosciences: Third study program.* Cambridge MIT Press.

Spetea, M., Rydelius, G., Nylander, I., Ahmed, M., Blieviciute-Ljungar, I., Lundeberg, T., et al. (2002). Alteration in endogenous opioid systems due to chronic inflammatory pain conditions. *European Journal of Pharmacology, 435,* 245–252.

Spiegel, R. (2003). *Psychopharmacology: An introduction.* New York: Wiley.

Spiegler, M. D., & Guevremont, D. C. (2003). *Contemporary behavior therapy (4th ed.).* Belmont, CA: Wadsworth.

Spinella, M. (2005). Compulsive behavior in tobacco users. *Addictive Behaviors, 30(1),* 183–186.

Springer, S. P., & Deutsch, G. (1998). *Left brain, right brain.* New York: Freeman.

Squire, L. R. (1990, June). *Memory and brain systems.* Paper presented at the meeting of the American Psychological Society, Dallas.

Squire, L. R. (2004). Memory systems of the brain: A brief history and current perspective. *Neurobiology of Learning & Memory, 82,* 171–177.

Squire, L. R., & Kandel, E. R. (2000). *Memory: From mind to molecule.* New York: Worth.

Squire, L. R., & Schacter, D. L. (Eds.) (2002). *Neuropsychology of memory (3rd ed.).* New York: Guilford.

Stack, D. M., & Tsonis, M. (1999). Infants' haptic perception of texture in the presence and absence of visual cues. *British Journal of Development Psychology, 17,* 97–110.*

Staddon, J. E., Chelaru, I. M., & Higa, J. J. (2002). A tune-trace theory of interval-timing dynamics. *Journal of the Experimental Analysis of Behavior, 77,* 105–124.

Stafford, J., & Lynn, S. J. (2002). Cultural scripts, memories of childhood abuse, and multiple identities: A study of role-played enactments. *International Journal of Experimental Hypnosis, 50,* 67–85.

Stahl, S. M. (2002). The psychopharmacology of energy and fatigue. *Journal of Clinical Psychiatry, 63,* 7–8.

Stanley, M. A., & Turner, S. M. (1995). Current status of pharmacological and behavioral treatment of obsessive-compulsive disorder. *Behavior Therapy, 26,* 163–177.

Stanovich, K. E. (1999). *Who is rational? Individual differences in reasoning.* Mahwah, NJ: Erlbaum.*

Stanovich, K. E. (2004). *How to think straight about psychology (7th ed.).* Boston: Allyn & Bacon.*

Stanovich, K. E., & West, R. E. (2000). Individual differences in reasoning: Implications for the rationality debate? *Behavior and Brain Sciences, 23,* 645–665.*

Stark, C. (2000). Women and Canadian psychology: Writing our own pasts and our futures. *History and Philosophy of Psychology Bulletin, 12(1),* 3–10.*

Stark-Adamec, C. (1992). Sexism in research: The limits of academic freedom. *Women and Therapy, 12(4),* 103–111.*

Stark-Adamec, C., & Kimball, M. (1984). Science free of sexism: A psychologist's guide to the conduct of nonsexist research. *Canadian Psychology, 25(1),* 23–34.*

Statistics Canada (2001). *Canada year book 2001.* Ottawa: Statistics Canada.*

Statistics Canada (2002a). *Life expectancy: Abridged life table, at birth and confidence interval, by sex, Canada, provinces and territories.* Retrieved March 4, 2005 from http://www.statcan.ca/english/freepub/84F0211XIE/2002/tables/html/t027_en.htm.*

Statistics Canada (2002b). *Proportion of common-law couples, selected countries, Canada and regions.* Retrieved March 5, 2005 from http://www12.statcan.ca/english/census01/Products/Analytic/companion/fam/clcintnl.cfm.*

Statistics Canada (2002c). *Canadian Community Health Survey: A first look.* Ottawa: Statistics Canada. Retrieved August 10, 2005 from http://www.statcan.ca/Daily/English/020508/d020508a.htm.*

Statistics Canada (2003). *Joint Canada/United States survey of health, 2002-2003.* Ottawa: Statistics Canada. Retrieved August 22, 2005 from http://www.statcan.ca:8096/bsolc/english/bsolc?catno=82-005-X20040027421.*

Statistics Canada (2004a). *Divorces.* The Daily, May 24, 2004. Retrieved March 5, 2005 http://www.statcan.ca/Daily/English/040504/d040504a.htm.*

Statistics Canada (2004b). *Canada e-Book.* Retrieved June 22, 2005 from http://142.206.72.67/r000_e.htm.

Statistics Canada (2004c). *Canadian Community Health Survey.* Retrieved July 13, 2005 from http://www.statcan.ca/Daily/English/040615/d040615b.htm.*

Statistics Canada (2004b). *Joint Canada/United States Survey of Health.* Retrieved July 13, 2005 from http://www.statcan.ca/Daily/English/040615/d040615b.htm.*

Statistics Canada (2005a). *Study: Job strain and retirement.* The Daily, March 31, 2005. Ottawa: Statistics Canada. Retrieved August 29, 2005 from http://www.statcan.ca/Daily/English/050331/d050331b.htm.*

Statistics Canada (2005b). *Television viewing.* The Daily, March 31, 2005. Ottawa: Statistics Canada. Retrieved August 24, 2005 from http://www.statcan.ca/Daily/English/050331/d050331b.htm.*

Ste-Marie, D. M. (1996). International bias in gymnastic judging: Conscious or unconscious influences? *Perceptual and Motor Skills, 83,* 963–975.*

Steele, C. (2001). Zyban: An effective treatment for nicotine addiction. *Hospital Medicine, 61,* 785–788.

Steers, W., Guay, A. T., Leriche, A., Gingell, C., Hargeave, T. B., Wright, P. J., et al. (2001). Assessment of the efficacy and safety of Viagra (sildenafil citrate) in men with erectile dysfunction during long-term treatment. *International Journal of Impotence Research, 13,* 261–267.

Stefanick, M. L. (1999). Estrogen, progesterons, and cardiovascular risk. *Journal of Reproductive Medicine, 44,* 221–226.

Stein, D. J., Bandelow, B., Hollander, E., Nutt, D. J., Okasha, A., Pollack, M. H., Swinson, R. P., & Zohar, J. (2003). WCA recommendations for the long-term treatment of posttraumatic stress disorder. *CNS Spectrums, 8(8, Suppl1),* 31–39.*

Stein, M. B., Chavira, D. A., & Jang, K. L. (2001). Bringing up bashful baby: Developmental pathways to social phobia. *Psychiatric Clinics of North America. Special Issue: Social anxiety disorder, 24,* 661–675.*

Stein, M. B., Jang, K. L., & Livesley, W. J. (1999). Heritability of anxiety sensitivity: A twin study. *American Journal of Psychiatry, 156,* 246–251.*

Stein, M. T., & Ferber, R. (2001). Recent onset of sleepwalking in early adolescence. *Journal of Development, Behavior, and Pediatrics, 22,* S33–S35.

Steele, C. M., & Aronson, J. (1995). Stereotype threat and the intellectual test performance of African Americans. *Journal of Personality & Social Psychology, 69(5),* 797–781.

Stephan, W. G., Renfro, C. L., Esses, V. M., Stephan, C. W., & Martin, T. (2005). The effects of feeling threatened on attitudes toward immigrants. *International Journal of Intercultural Relations, 29(1),* 1–19.

Sternberg, R. J. (1986). *Intelligence applied.* Fort Worth: Harcourt Brace.

Sternberg, R. J. (1988). *The triangle of love.* New York: Basic Books.

Sternberg, R. J. (1994, December). *Commentary.* APA Monitor, 22.

Sternberg, R. J. (1997a). Inspection time for inspection time. *American Psychologist, 52,* 1144–1147.

Sternberg, R. J. (1997b). *Successful intelligence.* New York: Simon & Schuster.

Sternberg, R. J. (Ed.). (1997c). *Career paths in psychology.* Washington: APA Press.

Sternberg, R. J. (1997d). Educating intelligence: Infusing the triarchic theory into instruction. In R. J. Sternberg, & E. Grigorenko (Eds.), *Intelligence, heredity, and environment.* New York: Cambridge.

Sternberg, R. J. (1999). Intelligence. In M. A. Runco, & S. Pritzker (Eds.). *Encyclopedia of creativity.* San Diego: Academic Press.

Sternberg, R. J. (2000). The holy grail of general intelligence. *Science, 289,* 399–401.

Sternberg, R. J. (2001). Is there a heredity-environment paradox? In R. J. Sternberg, & E. L. Grigorenko (Eds.), *Environmental effects on cognitive abilities.* Mahwah, NJ: Erlbaum.

Sternberg, R. J. (2002). Intelligence: The triarchic theory of intelligence. In J. W. Gutherie (Ed.). *Encyclopedia of education (2nd ed.).* New York: Macmillan.

Sternberg, R. J. (2003a). *Cognitive psychology (3rd ed.).* Belmont, CA: Wadsworth.

Sternberg, R. J. (2003b). Creative thinking in the classroom. *Scandinavian Journal of Educational Research, 47(3),* 325–338.

Sternberg, R. J. (2005). The importance of converging operations in the study of human intelligence. *Cortex, 41(2),* 243–244.

Sternberg, R. J., & Grigorenko, E. L. (Eds.). (2001). *Environmental effects on cognitive abilities.* Mahwah, NJ: Erlbaum.

Sternberg, R. J., Grigorenko, E. L., & Kidd, K. K. (2005). Intelligence, race, and genetics. *American Psychologist, 60(1),* 46–59.

Sternberg, R. J., & O'Hara, L. A. (2000). Intelligence and creativity. In R. J. Sternberg (Ed.), *Handbook of intelligence.* New York: Cambridge.

Sternberg, R. J., & Spear-Swerling, P. (1996). *Teaching for thinking.* Washington: APA Press.

Steur, F. B., Applefield, J. M., & Smith, R. (1971). Televised aggression and the interpersonal aggression of preschool children. *Journal of Experimental Child Psychology, 11,* 442–447.

Stevenson, H. W. (1992). Learning from Asian schools. *Scientific American, 267(6),* 70–76.

Stevenson, H. W. (2000). Middle childhood: Education and schooling. In A. Kazdin (Ed.), *Encyclopedia of psychology.* Washington, & New York: APA Press and Oxford.

Stevenson, H. W., Lee, S., & Stigler, J. W. (1986). Mathematics achievement of Chinese, Japanese, and American children. *Science, 231,* 693–699.

Stewart, D. D., Stewart, C. B., Tyson, C., Vinci, G., & Fioti, T. (2004). Serial position effects and the picture-superiority effect in the group recall of unshared information. *Group Dynamics, 8(3),* 166–181.

Stewart, S., McWilliams, L. A., Blackburn, J. R. & Klein, R. M. (2002). A laboratory-based investigation of relations among video lottery terminal (VLT) play, negative mood, and alcohol consumption in regular VLT players. *Addictive Behaviors, 27(5),* 819–835.*

Stewart, S. A. (2005). The effects of benzodiazepines on cognition. *Journal of Clinical Psychiatry, 66(Suppl2),* 9–13.

Stickgold, R. (2001). Watching the sleeping brain watch us: Sensory processing during sleep. *Trends in Neuroscience, 24,* 307–309.

Stickgold, R., & Hobson, J. A. (2000). Visual discrimination learning requires sleep after training. *Nature Neuroscience, 3,* 1237–1238.

Stigler, J. W., & Hiebert, J. (1997, September). Understanding and improving classroom mathematics instruction. *Phi Delta Kappan, 79,* 14–21.

Stipek, D. (2001). *Motivation to learn (4th ed.).* Boston: Allyn & Bacon.

Stockhorst, U., & Pietrowsky, R. (2004). Olfactory perception, communication, and the nose-to-brain pathway. *Physiology & Behavior, 83(1),* 3–11.

Stolarz-Fantino, S., & Fantino, E. (2005). The rules we choose by. *Behavioural Processes. Special Proceedings of the meeting of the Society for the Quantitative Analyses of Behavior (SQAB 2004), 69(2),* 151–153.

Stoner, J. (1961). *A comparison of individual and group decisions, including risk.* Unpublished master's thesis, School of Industrial Management, MIT.

Stones, M. J., & Kozma, A. K. (1989). Happiness and activities in later life: A propensity formulation. *Canadian Psychology, 30(3),* 526–537.*

Stoppard, J. M. (1999). Why new perspectives are needed for understanding depression in women. *Canadian Psychology, 40(2),* 79–90.*

Stoppard, J. M. (2000). *Understanding depression: Feminist social constructionist approaches.* London: Routledge.*

Stoppard, J. M., & Gammell, D. J. (2003). Depressed women's treatment experiences: Exploring themes of medicalization and empowerment. In In J. M. Stoppard, & L. M. McMullen (Eds.), *Situating sadness: Women and depression in social context.* New York: New York University Press.*

Stoppard, J. M., & McMullen, L. M. (Eds.). (2003). *Situating sadness: Women and depression in social context.* New York: New York University Press.*

Strange, K. S., Kerr, L. R., Andrews, H., Emerman, J. T., & Weinberg, J. (2000). Psychosocial stressors and mouse mammary tumor growth: An animal model. *Neurotoxicology and Teratology, 22,* 89–102.*

Stratton G. M. (1897). Vision without inversion of the retinal image. *Psychological Review, 4,* 463–481.

Straus, M. A., Sugarman, D. B., & Giles-Sims, J. (1997). Spanking by parents and subsequent antisocial behavior of children. *Archives of Pediatrics & Adolescent Medicine, 151,* 761–767.

Stretch, R. H. (1990). Post traumatic stress disorder and the Canadian Vietnam veteran. *Journal of Traumatic Stress, 3,* 239–254.*

Stretch, R. H. (1991). Psychosocial readjustment of Canadian Vietnam veterans. *Journal of Consulting and Clinical Psychology, 59,* 188–189.*

Striedter, G. F. (2005). *Principles of brain evolution.* Sunderland, MA: Sinauer Associates.

Striefel, S. (1998). *How to teach through modeling and imitation.* Austin, TX: Pro-Ed.

Striegel-Moore, R. H., Silberstein, L. R., & Rodin, J. (1993). The social self in bulimia nervosa: Public self-consciousness, social anxiety, and perceived fraudulence. *Journal of Abnormal Psychology, 102,* 297–303.

Strober, M. (2005). The future of treatment research in anorexia nervosa. *International Journal of Eating Disorders. Special Anorexia Nervosa, 37(Suppl),* S90–S94.

Stuart, M. (2005). Phonemic analysis and reading development: Some current issues. *Journal of Research in Reading. Special Literacy Research in Retrospect and Prospect: A special issue in recognition of the contributions of Tony Pugh and Greg Brooks to the Journal of Research in Reading, 28(1),* 39–49.

Stuss, D. T., & Alexander, M. P. (2000). The anatomical basis of affective behavior, emotion and self-awareness: A specific role of the right frontal lobe. In G. Hatano, N. Okada, & H. Tanabe (Eds.), *Affective minds. The 13th Toyota conference.* Amsterdam: Elsevier.

Stuss, D. T., & Anderson, V. (2004). The frontal lobes and theory of mind: Developmental concepts from adult focal lesion research. *Brain & Cognition, 55(1),* 69–83.*

Stuss, D. T., & Knight, R. T. (Eds.). (2002). *Principles of frontal lobe function.* London: Oxford.

Stuss, D. T., Picton, T. W., & Alexander, M. P. (2001). Consciousness, self-awareness, and the frontal lobes. In S. P. Salloway, & P. F. Malloy (Eds.), *The* *frontal lobes and neuropsychiatric illness.* Washington: American Psychiatric Publishing.*

Stuss, D. T., Winocur, G., & Robertson, I. H. (1999). *Cognitive neurorehabilitation.* New York: Oxford.*

Sue, S. (2000). Ethnocultural psychotherapy. In A. Kazdin (Ed.), *Encyclopedia of psychology.* Washington, & New York: APA Press and Oxford.

Sue, D. (2002). Culture specific psychotherapy. In M. Hersen, & W. H. Sledge (Eds.), *Encyclopedia of psychotherapy.* San Diego: Academic Press.

Suedfeld, P. (2004). Canadian space psychology: The future may be almost here. *Canadian Psychology, 44(2),* 85–92.*

Sugarman, A., & DePottel, C. (2002). The unconscious. In M. Hersen, & W. H. Sledge (Eds.), *Encyclopedia of psychotherapy.* San Diego: Academic Press.

Suhner, A., Schlagenhauf, P., Hofer, I., Johnson, R., Tschopp, A., & Steffen, R. (2001). Effectiveness and tolerability of melatonin and zopidem for the alleviation of jet lag. *Aviation, Space, and Environmental Medicine, 72,* 638–646.

Suinn, R. M. (1976, July). Body thinking: Psychology for Olympic champions. *Psychology Today, 10,* 38–41.

Suinn, R. M. (1984). *Fundamentals of abnormal psychology.* Chicago: Nelson-Hall.

Sullivan, H. S. (1953). *The interpersonal theory of psychiatry.* New York: Norton.

Sulsky, L., & Smith, C. (2005). *Work stress.* Belmont, CA: Wadsworth.

Sun, R. (2002). *Duality of the mind: A bottom-up approach toward cognition.* Mahwah, NJ: Erlbaum.

Susman, E. J., & Rogol, A. (2003). Puberty and psychological development. In R. M. Lerner, & L. Steinberg (Eds.), *The handbook of adolescent psychology.* New York: Wiley.

Susman, E. J., Worrall, B. K., Murowchick, E., Frobose, C. A., & Schwab, J. E. (1996). Experience and neuroendocrine parameters of development: Aggressive behaviors and competencies. In D. M. Stoff, & R. B. Cairns (Eds.), *Aggression and violence.* Mahwah, NJ: Erlbaum.

Sussman, E., Ceponiene, R., Shestakova, A., Naatanen, R., & Winkler, I. (2001). Auditory stream segregation processes operate similarly in school-aged children and adults. *Hearing Research, 153,* 108–114.

Sussman, S. (2001). School-based tobacco use prevention and cessation: Where are we going? *American Journal of Health Behavior, 25,* 191–199.

Sutker, P. B., & Allain, A. N. (1993). Behavior and personality assessment in men labeled adaptive sociopaths. *Journal of Behavioral Assessment, 5,* 65–79.

Suzuki, L., & Aronson, J. (2005). The cultural malleability of intelligence and its impact on the racial/ethnic hierarchy. *Psychology, Public Policy, and Law, 11(2),* 320–327.

Sutton, J. E., Olthof, A., & Roberts, W. A. (2000). Landmark use by squirrel monkeys (Saimiri sciureus). *Animal Learning & Behavior, 28,* 28–42.*

Swaab, D. F., Chung, W. C., Kruijver, F. P., Hofman, M. A., & Ishunina, T. A. (2001). Structural and functional sex differences in the human hypothalamus. *Hormones and Behavior, 40,* 93–98.

Swann, W. B., De La Ronde, C., & Hixon, J. G. (1994). Authenticity and positive strivings in marriage and courtship. *Journal of Personality & Social Psychology, 66,* 857–869.

Swanson, J. (Ed.). (1999). *Sleep disorders sourcebook.* New York: Omnigraphics.

Swartz-Kulstad, J. L., & Martin, W. E. (2000). Culture as an essential aspect of person-environment fit. In W. E. Martin, & J. L. Swartz-Kulstad (Eds.), *Person-environment psychology and mental health.* Mahwah, NJ: Erlbaum.

Sylvain, C., Ladouceur, R., & Boisvert, J.-M. (1997). Cognitive and behavioral treatment of pathological gambling: A controlled study. *Journal of Consulting and Clinical Psychology, 65,* 727–732.*

Symons, L. A., Hains, S. M. J., & Muir, D. (1998). Look at me: Five-month-old infants' sensitivity to very small deviations in eye-gaze during social interactions. *Infant Behavior & Development, 21(3),* 531–536.*

Szasz, T. S. (1961). *The myth of mental illness: Foundations of a theory of personal conduct.* New York: Hoeber-Harper.

Szasz, T. (2002). *Liberation by oppression: A comparative study of slavery and psychiatry.* New Brunswick, NJ: Transaction Publishers.

Szasz, T. (2004). Psychiatric fraud and force: A critique of E. Fuller Torrey. *Journal of Humanistic Psychology, 44(4),* 416–430.

T

Tafet, G. E., Feder, D. J., Abulafia, D. P. & Roffman, S. S. (2005). Regulation of hypothalamic-pituitary-adrenal activity in response to cognitive therapy in patients with generalized anxiety disorder. *Cognitive, Affective & Behavioral Neuroscience, 5(1),* 37–40.

Tager-Flusberg, H. (1999). Language development in atypical children. In M. Barrett (Ed.), *The development of language.* Philadelphia: Psychology Press.

Tajfel, H. (1978). The achievement of group differentiation. In H. Tajfel (Ed.), *Differentiation between social groups.* London: Academic Press.

Tajfel, H., & Turner, J. C. (2004). The social identity theory of intergroup behavior. In J. T. Jost, & J. Sidanius (Eds.), *Political Psychology: Key readings.* New York: Psychology Press.

Takeuchi, T., Miyasia, A., Inugami, M., & Yamamoto, Y. (2001). Intrinsic dreams are not produced without REM sleep mechanisms. *Journal of Sleep Research, 10,* 43–52.

Takeuchi, T., Ogilvie, R. D., Murphy, T. I., & Ferrelli, A. V. (2003). EEG activities during elicited sleep onset REM and NREM periods reflect different mechanisms of dream generation. *Clinical Neurophysiology, 114(2),* 210–220.*

Takeyama, H., Itani, T., Tachi, N., Sakamura, O., Murata, K., Inoue, T., et al. (2005). Effects of shift schedules on fatigue and physiological functions among firefighters during night duty. *Ergonomics, 48(1),* 1–11.

Tam, E. M, Lam, R. W, & Levitt, A. J. (1995). Treatment of seasonal affective disorder: A review. *Canadian Journal of Psychiatry, 40(8),* 457–66.*

Tanaka-Matsumi, J. (2001). Abnormal psychology and culture. In D. Matsumoto (Ed.), *The handbook of culture and psychology.* New York: Oxford.

Tang, Y. P., Shimizu, E., Dube, G. R., Rampon, C., Kerchner, G. A., Zhuo, M., et al. (1999). Genetic enhancement of learning and memory in mice. *Nature, 401,* 63–69.

Tannen, D. (1990). *You just don't understand!* New York: Ballantine.

Tannen, D. (2001). But what do you mean? Women and men in conversation. In J. M. Henslin (Ed.), *Down to earth sociology: Introductory readings (11th ed.).* New York: Free Press.

Tardif, T., Gelman, S. A., & Xu, F. (1999). Putting the "noun bias" in context: A comparison of English and Mandarin. *Child Development, 70(3),* 620–635.

Tavris, C. B. (1988). *Women and health psychology (Vols 1 & 2).* Mahwah, NJ: Erlbaum.

Tavris, C. B., & Wade, C. (1984). *The longest war: Sex differences in perspective (2nd ed.).* Fort Worth: Harcourt Brace.

Tavris, C. (1989). *Anger: The misunderstood emotion.* New York: Touchstone Books.

Tavris, C. B. (1992). *The mismeasure of woman.* New York: Simon & Schuster.

Taylor, D. M. (1997). The quest for collective identity: The plight of disadvantaged ethnic minorities. *Canadian Psychology, 38 (3),* 174–189.*

Taylor, D. M. (2002). *The quest for identity: From ethnic minorities to Generation X.* New York: Praeger Publications.*

Taylor, D. M., Lydon, J. E., Bougie, E., & Johannesen, K., (2004). "Street Kids": Towards an understanding of their motivational context. *Canadian Journal of Behavioural Science, 36(1),* 1–16.*

Taylor, D. M., Ruggiero, K. M., & Louis, W. R. (1996). Personal/group discrimination discrepancy: Towards a two-factor explanation. *Canadian Journal of Behavioural Science, 28(3),* 193–202.*

Taylor, G. J., Ryan, D., Bagby, R. M. (1985). Toward the development of a new self-report alexithymia scale. *Psychotherapy and Psychosomatics. 44,* 191–199.*

Taylor, J. L., O'Hara, R., Mumenthaler, M. S., Rosen, A. C., & Yesavage, J. A. (2005). Cognitive ability, expertise, and age differences in following air-traffic control instructions. *Psychology and Aging, 20(1),* 117–133.

Taylor, S. E. (2002a). Classical conditioning. In M. Hersen, & W. H. Sledge (Eds.), *Encyclopedia of psychotherapy.* San Diego: Academic Press.

Taylor, S. E. (2002b). *The tending instinct: how nurturing is essential to who we are and how we live.* New York: Henry Holt.

Taylor, S. E. (2006). *Health psychology (6th ed.).* New York: McGraw-Hill.

Taylor, S. E., Kemeny, M. E., Reed, G. M., Bower, J. E., & Gruenewald, T. L. (2000). Psychological resources, positive illusions, and health. *American Psychologist, 55(1),* 99–109.

Taylor, S. E., Klein, L. S., Lewis, B. P., Gurenewald, T. L., Gurun, R. A., & Updegraff, J. A. (2000). Biobehavioral responses in females: Tend-and-befriend, not fight-or-flight. *Psychological Review, 107,* 411–429.

Taylor, S. E., Lerner, J. S., Sherman, D. K., Sage, R. M. & McDowell, N. K. (2003). Are self-enhancing cognitions associated with healthy or unhealthy biological profiles? *Journal of Personality & Social Psychology, 85(4),* 605–615.

Taylor, S. E., Peplau, L. A., & Sears, D. O. (2006). *Social psychology (12th ed.).* Englewood Cliffs, NJ: Prentice Hall.

Taylor, S. E., & Sherman, D. K. (2004). positive psychology and health psychology: A fruitful liaison. In P. A. Linley, & Joseph, S. (Eds.), *Positive psychology in practice.* New York: Wiley.

Temple, E. C., Hutchinson, I., Lang, D. G., & Jinks, A. L. (2002). Taste development: Differential growth rates of tongue regions in humans. *Brain Research: Developmental Brain Research, 135,* 65–70.

Templer, D. I., Tomeo, M. E., Arikawa, H., & Williams, R. (2003). Asian-Black differences in aptitude and difficulty of chosen academic discipline. *Personality & Individual Differences. 35(1),* 237–241.

Terman, L. (1925). *Genetic studies of genius (Vol. 1): Mental and physical traits of a thousand gifted children.* Stanford, CA: Stanford University Press.

Tesser, A., Stapel, D. A., & Wood. J. V. (Eds.) (2002). *Self and motivation: Emerging psychological perspectives.* Washington: APA Press.*

Tester, F. J., & McNicoll, P. (2004). Isumagijaksaq: Mindful of the state: Social constructions of Inuit suicide. *Social Science & Medicine, 58(12),* 2625–2636.

Teti, D. M., & Candelaria, M. (2002). Parenting competence. In M. H. Bornstein (Ed.), *Handbook of parenting (2nd ed.).* Mahwah, NJ: Erlbaum.

Tetreault, M. K. T. (1997). Classrooms for diversity: Rethinking curriculum and pedagogy. In J. A. Banks, & C. A. Banks (Eds.), *Multicultural education (3rd ed.).* Boston: Allyn & Bacon.

Teyber, E. (2006). *Interpersonal process in therapy: An integrative model (5th ed.).* Belmont, CA: Wadsworth.

Tharp, R. G. (1991). Cultural diversity and treatment of children. *Journal of Consulting & Clinical Psychology, 59,* 799–812.

Thelen, E. (2000). Infancy: Perception and motor development. In A. Kazdin (Ed.), *Encyclopedia of psychology.* Washington, & New York: Oxford.

Theoharides, T. C., & Cochrane, D. E. (2004). Critical role of mast cells in inflammatory diseases and the effect of acute stress. *Journal of Neuroimmunology, 146(1-2),* 1–12.

Thiedke, C. C. (2001). Sleep disorders and sleep problems in childhood. *American Family Physician, 63*, 277–284.

Thigpen, C. H., & Cleckley, H. M. (1957). *Three faces of Eve*. New York. McGraw-Hill.

Thijssen, J. H. (2002). Relations of androgens and selected aspects of human behavior. *Maturitas, 41*, Supplement, 47–54.

Thomas, E. L., & Robinson, H. A. (1972). *Improving reading in every class: A sourcebook for teachers*. Boston: Allyn & Bacon.

Thomas, E. M. (2004). *Aggressive behaviour outcomes for young children: Change in parenting environment predicts change in behaviour*. Ottawa, ON: Statistics Canada. Retrieved March 22, 2005 from http://www.statcan.ca/cgi-bin/downpub/listpub.cgi?catno=89-599-MIE2004001.*

Thomas, J. C., & Segal, D. L. (Eds.). (2005). *Comprehensive handbook of personality and psychopathology (Vol 1): Personality and everyday functioning*. San Francisco: Jossey-Bass.

Thomas, M., Sing, H., Belenky, G., Holcomb, H., Mayberg, H., Dannals, R., et al. (2001). Neural basis of alertness and cognitive performance impairments during sleepiness: I. Effects of 24 hours of sleep deprivation on waking human regional brain activity. *Journal of Sleep Research, 9*, 335–352.

Thomas, R. M. (2001). *Recent human development theories*. Thousand Oaks, CA: Sage.

Thompson, M. J., Raynor, A., Cornah, D., Stevenson, J., & Sonuga-Barke, E. J. (2002). Parenting behavior described by mothers in a general population sample. *Child: Care, Health and Development, 28*, 149–155.

Thompson, P. M., Giedd, J. N., MacDonald, D., Evans, A. C., & Toga, A. W. (2000). Growth patterns in the developing brain by using continuum sensor maps. *Nature, 404*, 190–193.

Thompson, R. (2000). Early experience and socialization. In A. Kazdin (Ed.), *Encyclopedia of psychology*. Washington, & New York: APA Press and Oxford.

Thompson, R. F. (2005). In search of memory traces. *Annual Review of Psychology, 56*, 1–23.

Thompson, S. C. (2001). The role of personal control in adaptive functioning. In C. R. Snyder, & S. J. Lopez (Eds.), *Handbook of positive psychology*. New York: Oxford.

Thompson, V. A. (1996). Reasoning from false premises: The role of soundness in making logical deductions. *Canadian Journal of Experimental Psychology, 50(3)*, 315–319.*

Thorne, B. M. (2001). Introversion-extraversion. In W. E. Craighead & C. B. Nemeroff (Eds.), *The Corsini encyclopedia of psychology and behavioral science (3rd ed.)*. New York: Wiley.

Thrybom, T., Rooth, P., & Lindstrom, P. (2001). Effect of serotonin reuptake inhibitor on syndrome development in obese hyperglycemic mice. *Metabolism, 50*, 144–150.

Thurstone, L. L. (1938). *Primary mental abilities*. Chicago: University of Chicago Press.

Tierney, A. J. (2000). Egas Moniz and the origins of psychosurgery: A review commemorating the 50th anniversary of Moniz's Nobel Prize. *Journal of the History of the Neurosciences, 9(1)*, 22–36.

Tierney, J. P., Grossman, J. B., & Resch N. L. (1995). Making a difference: *An impact study of Big Brothers/Big Sisters*. Philadelphia: Public/Private Ventures. Retrieved March 24, 2005 from http://www.ppv.org/ppv/publications/assets/111_publication.pdf.

Timmerman, T. A. (2004). Relationships between NEO PI-R personality measures and job performance ratings of inbound call center employees. *Applied H.R.M. Research, 9(1–2)*, 35–38.

Tinbergen, N. (1969). *The study of instinct*. New York: Oxford.

Tisserand, D. J., Bosma, H., Van Boxtel, M. P., & Jolles, J. (2001). Head size and cognitive ability in nondemented older adults are related. *Neurology, 56*, 969–971.

Tjepkema, M. (2004). *Alcohol and illicit drug dependence*. Statistics Canada, Supplement to Health Reports, Volume 15, Catalogue 82-003. Retrieved March 19, 2005 from http://www.statcan.ca/english/freepub/82-003-SIE/2004000/pdf/82-003-SIE20040007447.pdf.*

Tobach, E. (2002). Development of sex and gender: Biochemistry, physiology, and experience. In J. Worell (Ed.), *Encyclopedia of women and gender*. New York: Oxford.

Todd, G. S., & Gigerenzer, G. (2001). Precis of simple heuristics that make us smart. *Behavior and Brain Sciences, 23*, 727–741.

Tolman, E. C. (1932). *Purposive behavior in animals and man*. New York: Appleton-Century-Crofts.

Tolman, E. C. (1948). Cognitive maps in rats and men. *Psychological Review, 55*, 189–208.

Tolman, E. C., & Honzik, C. H. (1930). Degrees of hunger, reward and non-reward, and maze performance in rats. *University of California Publications in Psychology, 4*, 21–256.

Tomasello, M. (2003). *Constructing a language: A usage-based theory of language acquisition*. Cambridge Harvard University Press.

Tomkins, S. S. (1962). *Affect, imagery, and consciousness (Vol. 1)*. New York: Springer.

Tomkins, S. S. (1981). The quest for primary motives: Biography and autobiography of an idea. *Journal of Personality & Social Psychology, 41*, 306–329.

Toukmanian, S. G., & Brouwers, M. C. (1998). Cultural aspects of psychotherapy and self-disclosure. In S. Kazarian, & D. R. Evans (Eds.), *Cultural clinical psychology: Theory, research, and practice*. Toronto: Oxford.*

Toppelberg, C. O. & Collins, B. (2004). Constructing a language: A usage-based theory of language acquisition. *Journal of the American Academy of Child & Adolescent Psychiatry, 43(10)*, 1305–1306.*

Torrey, E. F. (2005). Psychiatric fraud and force: A Reply to Szasz. *Journal of Humanistic Psychology, 45(3)*, 397–402.

Trainor, J., Pomeroy, E., & Pape, B. (1999). A new framework for support. In J. Trainor, E. Pomeroy, & B. Pape (Eds.), *Building a framework for support: A community development approach to mental health policy*. Toronto: Canadian Mental Health Association.*

Trainor, L. J., McDonald, K. L., & Alain, C. (2002). Automatic and controlled processing of melodic contour and interval information measured by electrical brain activity. *Journal of Cognitive Neuroscience, 14*, 430–432.

Trantham-Davidson, H., & Lavin, A. (2004). Acute cocaine administration depresses cortical activity. *NeuroPsychopharmacology, 29(11)*, 2046–2051.

Treasure, D. C., & Roberts, G. C. (2001). Students' perceptions of the motivational climate, achievement beliefs, and satisfaction in physical education. *Research Quarterly on Exercise and Sport, 72*, 165–175.

Trehub, S. E., & Thorpe, L. A. (1989). Infant's perception of rhythm: Categorization of auditory sequences by temporal structure. *Canadian Journal of Psychology, 43(2)*, 217–229.*

Trepel, C., & Racine, R. J. (1998). Long-term potentiation in the neocortex of the adult, freely moving rat. *Cerebral Cortex, 8*, 719–729.*

Trepel, C., & Racine, R. J. (1999). Blockade and disruption of neocortical long-term potentiation following electroconvulsive shock in the adult, freely moving rat. *Cerebral Cortex, 9*, 300–305.*

Treynor, W., Gonzalez, R., & Nolen-Hoeksema, S. (2003). Rumination reconsidered: A psychometric analysis. *Cognitive Therapy & Research, 27(3)*, 247–259.

Triandis, H. C. (1994). *Culture and social behavior*. New York: McGraw-Hill.

Triandis, H. C. (2001). Individualism and collectivism. In D. Matsumoto (Ed.), *The handbook of culture and psychology*. New York: Oxford.

Triandis, H. C. (2005). Issues in individualism and collectivism research. In R. M. Sorrentino, D. Cohen, J. M. Olson, & M. P. Zanna (Eds.), *Culture and social behavior: The Ontario symposium (Vol. 10)*. Mahwah, NJ: Erlbaum.

Triandis, H. C., & Suh, E. M. (2002). Cultural influences on personality. *Annual Review of Psychology, 53*, 133–160.

Trick, L., & Enns, J. T. (2004). Driving and selective attention: a conceptual framework for understanding the role of selective attention in driving. In A. G. Gale, I. D., Brown, C. M. Haslegrave, & S. P. Taylor (Eds.), *Vision in Vehicles X*. Amsterdam: Elsevier.*

Tri-Council Policy Statement (2003). *Ethical conduct for research involving humans*. Ottawa: Medical Research Council of Canada. Retrieved April 6, 2005 from http://www.pre.ethics.gc.ca/english/policystatement/policystatement.cfm.*

Triplett, N. (1898). The dynamogenic factors in peace-making and competition. *American Journal of Psychology, 9*, 507–533.

Tripp, D. A., Catano, V., & Sullivan, M. J. L. (1997). The contributions of attributional style, expectancies, depression, and self-esteem in a cognition-based depression model. *Canadian Journal of Behavioural Science, 29(2)*, 101–111.*

Trivers, R. (1971). The evolution of reciprocal altruism. *Quarterly Review of Biology, 46*, 35–57.

Trocmé, N., MacLaurin, B., Fallon, B., Daciuk J., et al. (2001). *Canadian Incidence Study of Reported Child Abuse and Neglect*. Ottawa: National Clearinghouse on Family Violence. Retrieved March 24, 2005 from http://www.phac-aspc.gc.ca/publicat/cissr-ecirc/.*

Tropp, L. R., & Pettigrew, T. F. (2005). Differential relationships between intergroup contact and affective and cognitive dimensions of prejudice. *Personality & Social Psychology Bulletin, 31(8)*, 1145–1158.

Trottier, K., Polivy, J., & Herman, C. P. (2005). Effects of exposure to unrealistic promises about dieting: Are unrealistic expectations about dieting inspirational? *International Journal of Eating Disorders, 37(2)*, 142–149.*

Trowell, J., Kolvin, I., Weeramanthri, T., Sadowski, H., Berelowitz, M., Glasser, D., et al. (2002). Psychotherapy for abused girls. *British Journal of Psychiatry, 180*, 234–247.

Tryon, R. C. (1940). *Genetic differences in maze-learning ability in rats*. In 39th Yearbook, National Society for the Study of Education. Chicago: University of Chicago Press.

Tsai, W.-C., Chen, C.-C., & Chiu, S.-F. (2005). Exploring boundaries of the effects of applicant impression management tactics in job interviews. *Journal of Management, 31(1)*, 108–125.

Tsao, F-M., Liu, H.-M., & Kuhl, P. K. (2004). Speech perception in infancy predicts language development in the second year of life: A longitudinal study. *Child Development, 75(4)*, 1067–1084.

Tsien, J. Z. (2000). Linking Hebb's coincidence-detection to memory formation. *Current Opinions in Neurobiology, 10*, 266–273.

Tsirigotis, K., & Gruszczynski, W. (2004). Personality functioning of outpatients with schizophrenia treated with classic neuroleptics and risperidone. *Archives of Psychiatry & Psychotherapy, 6(3)*, 23–36.

Tsoh, J., Chiu, H. F. K., Duberstein, P. R., Chan, S. S. M., Chi, I., Yip, P. S. F., & Conwell, Y. (2005). Attempted suicide in elderly Chinese persons: A multi-group, controlled study. *American Journal of Geriatric Psychiatry, 13(7)*, 562–571.

Tugade, M. M., Fredrickson, B. L., & Barrett, L. F. (2004). Psychological resilience and positive emotional granularity: Examining the benefits of positive emotions on coping and health. *Journal of Personality. Special Emotions, Personality, and Health, 72(6)*, 1161–1190.

Tull, M. T., Gratz, K. L., Salters, K., & Roemer, L (2004). The role of experiential avoidance in posttraumatic stress symptoms and symptoms of depression, anxiety, and somatization. *Journal of Nervous & Mental Disease, 192(11)*, 754–761.

Tulving, E. (1972). Episodic and semantic memory. In E. Tulving, & W. Donaldson (Eds.), *Origins of memory*. San Diego: Academic Press.*

Tulving, E. (1983). *Elements of episodic memory*. New York: Oxford.*

Tulving, E. (1985). Memory and consciousness. *Canadian Psychology, 26*, 1–12.*

Tulving, E. (1989). Remembering and knowing the past. *American Scientist, 77*, 361–367.*

Tulving, E. (1999a). On the uniqueness of episodic memory. In L.-G. Nilsson, & H. J. Markowitsch (Eds.), *Cognitive neuroscience of memory.* Göttingen, Netherlands: Hogrefe & Huber.*

Tulving, E. (Ed.). (1999b). *Memory, consciousness, and the brain: The Tallinn Conference.* Philadelphia: Psychology Press.*

Tulving, E. (2000). Concepts of memory. In E. Tulving, & F. I. M. Craik (Eds.), *The Oxford handbook of* memory. New York: Oxford.*

Tulving, E. (2002). Episodic memory: From mind to brain. *Annual Review of Psychology, 53*, 1–25.*

Tulving, E., & Lepage, M. (2000). Where in the brain is awareness of one's past? In D. L. Schacter, & E. Scarry. (Eds.), *Memory, brain, and belief.* Cambridge Harvard University Press.*

Tulving, E., & Markowitsch, H. J. (1998). Episodic and declarative memory: Role of the hippocampus. *Hippocampus, 8*, 198–204.*

Tulving, E., & Thomson, D. M. (1973). Encoding specificity and retrieval processes in episodic memory. *Psychological Review, 80*, 352–373.*

Turk, D. C., & Melzack. R. (2001). *Handbook of pain assessment.* New York: Guilford.*

Turkheimer, E., Haley, A., Waldron, M., D'Onofrio, B., & Gottesman, I. I. (2003). Socioeconomic status modifies heritability of IQ in young children. *Psychological Science, 14(6)*, 623–628.*

Turnbull, C. (1972). *The mountain people.* New York: Simon & Schuster.

Turner, J., Kelly, B., Swanson, C., Allison, R., & Wetzig, N. (2005). Psychosocial impact of newly diagnosed advanced breast cancer. *Psycho-Oncology, 14(5)*, 396–407.

Tversky, A., & Fox, C. R. (1995). Weighing risk and uncertainty. *Psychological Review, 102*, 269–283.

Tyhurst, J. (Ed.) (1963). *More for the mind.* Toronto: Canadian Mental Health Association.*

Tyler, C. (1983). Sensory processing of binocular disparity. In C. M. Schor & K. J. Ciuffreda (Eds.), *Vergence eye movements.* Boston: Butterworth.

U

U. S. Attorney General's Commission on Pornography. (1986). *Final report.* Washington: U.S. Department of Justice.

U. S. Bureau of Justice Statistics. (2001). *Homicide rates.* Washington: Author.

U. S. Department of Energy Human Genome Project. (2003). *Genomics and its impact on science and society.* Washington: U. S. Department of Energy. Retrieved September 3, 2005 from http://www.ornl.gov/sci/techresources/Human_Genome/publicat/primer2001/primer11.pdf.

U. S. National Association for the Education of Young Children. (1996). NAEYC position statement: Responding to linguistic and cultural diversity. *Young Children, 51*, 4–12.

U. S. National Center for Health Statistics. (2000a). *Births, deaths, marriages, and divorces.* Atlanta: Centers for Disease Control and Prevention.

U. S. National Center for Health Statistics. (2000b). *Prevalence of overweight among children and adolescents.* Hyattsville, MD: U.S. Department of Health and Human Services.

U. S. National Center for Health Statistics. (2000c). *Smoking.* Atlanta, GA: Centers for Disease Control and Prevention.

U. S. National Center for Health Statistics. (2001). *AIDS.* Atlanta: Centers for Disease Control and Prevention.

U. S. National Center for PTSD. (2005). *What is post-traumatic stress disorder?* Washington: National Center for PTSD. Retrieved July 27, 2005 from http://www.ncptsd.va.gov/facts/general/fs_what_is_ptsd.html.

U. S. National Commission on Sleep Disorders Research. (1993, January). *Report of the National Commission on Sleep Disorders Research.* Report submitted to the United States Congress and to the Secretary of the U.S. Department of Health and Human Services.

U. S. National Institute for Occupational Safety and Health. (2001). *Job stress in American workers.* Washington: Centers for Disease Control and Prevention.

U. S. National Institute of Mental Health. (2000). In harms way: *Suicide in America.* Washington: National Institute of Mental Health. Retrieved July 25, 2005 from http://www.nimh.nih.gov/publicat/harmsway.cfm.

U. S. National Institute of Mental Health. (2001a). *Mental disorders in America.* Bethesda, MD: Author.

U. S. National Institute of Mental Health. (2001b). *Post-traumatic stress disorder.* Washington: Author.

U. S. National Institute of Neurological Disorders and Stroke. (2004). *Brain basics: Understanding sleep.* Washington: National Institutes of Health.

U. S. National Institute on Drug Abuse. (2001). *Common drugs of abuse.* Washington: National Institutes of Health.

U. S. National Reading Panel. (2000). *Report of the National Reading Panel: Teaching children to read.* Washington: National Institute of Child Health and Human Development. Retrieved July 2, 2005 from http://www.nationalreadingpanel.org/Publications/subgroups.htm.

Ubell, C. (1992, December 6). We can age successfully. *Parade*, pp. 14–15.

Uekermann, J., Daum, I., Schlebusch, P., & Trenckmann, U. (2005). Processing of affective stimuli in alcoholism. *Cortex, 41(2)*, 189–194.

Ullian, E. M., Sapperstein, S. K., Christopherson, K. S., & Barres, B. A. (2001). Control of synapse number by glia, *Science, 291*, 657.

UNAIDS (2004). *Sub-Saharan Africa.* New York: United Nations. Retrieved August 19, 2005 from http://www.unaids.org/EN/geographical+area/by+region/sub-saharan+africa.asp.

UNDCP (2003). *Global illicit drug trends.* Geneva, Switzerland: United Nations. Retrieved March 18, 2005 from http://www.unodc.org/unodc/en/global_illicit_drug_trends.html.

Ungerleider, L. G., & Mishkin, M. (1982). Two cortical visual systems. In D. J. Engle, M. A. Goodale, & R. J. Mansfield (Eds.), *Analysis of visual behavior.* Cambridge MIT Press.

UNICEF Innocenti Research Centre (2005). *Child poverty in rich countries 2005.* Florence, Italy: UNICEF Innocenti Research Centre.

United Nations. (1999). *Demographic yearbook.* Geneva, Switzerland: United Nations.

Uppaluri, C. R., Schumm, I. P., & Lauderdale, D. S. (2001). Self-reports of stress in Asian immigrants: Effects of ethnicity and acculturation. *Ethnic Distribution, 11*, 107–144.

Ursano, R. J., Fullerton, C. S., & Norwood, A. E. (Eds.), (2003). *Terrorism and disaster: Individual and community responses to extraordinary events.* London: Cambridge.

V

Vaillant, G. E. (1983). *The natural history of alcoholism.* Cambridge Harvard University Press.

Vaillant, G. E. (1992). Is there a natural history of addiction? In C. P. O'Brien, & J. H. Jaffe (Eds.), *Addictive states.* Cambridge Harvard University Press.

Vaillant, G. E. (2002). *Aging well.* Boston: Little Brown.

Vaillant, G. E. (2005). Alcoholics Anonymous: Cult or cure? *Australian and New Zealand Journal of Psychiatry, 39(6)*, 431–436.

Vaitl, D., Birbaumer, N., Gruzelier, J., Jamieson, G. A., Kotchoubey, B., Kubler, A., et al. (2005). Psychobiology of altered states of consciousness. *Psychological Bulletin, 131(1)*, 98–127.

Valencia, R. R., & Suzuki, L. A. (2001). *Intelligence testing and minority students.* Thousand Oaks, CA: Sage.

Valentine, E. R., & Sweet, P. L. G. (1999). Meditation and attention: A comparison of the effects of concentrative and mindfulness meditation on sustained attention. *Mental Health, Religion & Culture, 2(1)*, 59–70.

Vallone, R. P., Griffin, D. W., Lin, S., & Ross, L. (1990). Overconfident prediction of future actions and outcomes by self and others. *Journal of Personality & Social Psychology, 58*, 582–592.

Van Ameringen, M., Allgulander, C., Bandelow, B., Greist, J. H., Hollander, E., Montgomery, S. A., et al. (2003). WCA recommendations for the long-term treatment of social phobia. *CNS Spectrums, 8(8, Suppl1)*, 40–52.*

Van Ameringen, M., Lane, R. M., Walker, J. R., Rudaredo, C., Chooka, P. R., et al. (2001). Sertaline treatment of generalized social phobia: 20-week, double-blind, placebo-controlled study. *American Journal of Psychiatry, 158*, 275–281.*

Van Ameringen, M., & Mancini, C. (2001). Pharmacotherapy of social anxiety disorder at the turn of the millennium. *Psychiatric Clinics of North America. Special Issue: Social anxiety disorder, 24(4)*, 783–803.*

Van Ameringen, M., Mancini, C., Farvolden, P., & Oakman, A. J. (2000). The neurobiology of social phobia: From pharmacology to brain imaging. *Current Psychiatry Reports, 2*, 358–366.*

van Dielen, F. M., van 't Veer, C., Buurman, W. A., & Greve, J. W. (2002). Leptin and soluble leptin receptor levels in obese and weight-losing individuals. *Journal of Clinical Endocrinology and Metabolism, 87*, 1708–1716.

Van Elst, L. T., Ebert, D., & Trimble, M. R. (2001). Hippocampus and amygdala pathology in depression. *American Journal of Psychiatry, 158*, 652–653.

Van Goozen, S. H. M., Matthys, W., Cohen-Kettenis, P. T., Thijssen, J. H., & van Engeland, H. (1998). Adrenal androgens and aggression in conduct disorder prepubertal boys and normal control. *Biological Psychiatry, 43*, 156–158.

van Praag, H. M., de Kloet, E R; van Os, J. (2004). *Stress, the brain and depression.* New York: Cambridge.

van Vreeswijk, C. (in press) What is the neural code? In J. L. van Hemmen, & T. J. Sejnowski (Eds.) *23 problems in system neuroscience.* Oxford, England: Oxford.

Van Winkle, E. (2000). The toxic mind: The biology of mental illness and violence. *Medical Hypotheses, 55*, 356–368.

Vandell, D. L. (2004). Early child care: The known and the unknown. *Merrill-Palmer Quarterly. Special The maturing of the human developmental sciences: Appraising past, present, and prospective agendas, 50(3)*, 387–414.

Vandell, D. L., Pierce, K. M., & Dadisman, K. (2005). Out-of-school settings as a developmental context for children and youth. In R. Kail (Ed.), *Advances in child development (Vol 33).* Oxford: Elsevier.

VandenBos, G. R. (2000). Schizophrenia. In A. Kazdin (Ed.), *Encyclopedia of psychology.* Washington, & New York: APA Press and Oxford.

Varela, J. G., Boccaccini, M. T., Scogin, F., Stump, J., & Caputo, A. (2004). Personality testing in law enforcement employment settings: A meta-analytic review. *Criminal Justice & Behavior, 31(6)*, 649–675.

Vaslamatzis, G. (2005). Projective identification, containment and sojourn in the psyche: Clinical notes on a specific type of transference-countertransference interaction. *International Forum of Psychoanalysis, 14(2)*, 116–119.

Vatcher, C. A., & Bogo, M. (2001). The feminist/emotionally focused therapy practice model: An integrated approach for couple therapy. *Journal of Marital and Family Therapy, 27*, 69–83.

Vaughn, S., Bos, C. S., & Schumm, J. S. (2006). *Teaching exceptional, diverse, and at-risk students in the general education classroom, IDEA 2004 Update Edition, (3rd ed.).* Boston: Allyn & Bacon.

Vedhara, K. (2005). *Human psychoneuroimmunology.* New York: Oxford.

Veitch, J. A., & Gifford, R. (1996). Assessing beliefs about lighting effects on health, performance, mood, and social behavior. *Environment and Behavior, 28*, 446–470.*

Verhaeghen, P., Joorman, J., & Khan, R. (2005). Why we sing the blues: The relation between self-reflective rumination, mood, and creativity. *Emotion, 5(2),* 226–232.

Verhoeff, N. P., Christensen, B. K., Hussey, D., Lee, M., Paptheodorou, et al. (2003). Effects of catecholamine depletion on D-sub-2 receptor binding, mood and attentiveness in humans: A replication study. *Pharmacology, Biochemistry & Behavior, 74(2),* 425–432.

Vernon, P. A. (2000). Determinants of intelligence: Biological theories. In A. Kazdin (Ed.), *Encyclopedia of psychology.* Washington, & New York: APA Press and Oxford.*

Vernoy, M. W., & Kyle, D. (2003). *Behavioral statistics in action (3rd ed.).* New York: McGraw-Hill.

Versiani, M., Cassano, G., Perugi, G., Benedetti, A., Mastalli, L. et al. (2002). Reboxetine, a selective norepinephrine reuptake inhibitor, is an effective and well-tolerated treatment for panic disorder. *Journal of Clinical Psychiatry, 63,* 31–37.

Verschuere, B., Crombez, G., & Koster, E. H. W. (2004). Orienting to guilty knowledge. *Cognition & Emotion, 18(2),* 265-279.

Viana, del Pena, E., & Belmonte, C. (2002). Specificity of cold thermotransduction is determined by differential ionic channel expression. *Nature Neuroscience, 5,* 254–260.

Videon, T. M. (2005). Parent-child relations and children's psychological well-being: Do dads matter? *Journal of Family Issues, 26(1),* 55–78.

Viglione, D. J., & Hilsenroth, M. J. (2001). The Rorschach: Facts, fictions, and future. *Psychological Assessment, 13,* 452–471.

Viney, W., & King, D. B. (2003). *History of psychology (3rd ed.).* Boston: Allyn & Bacon.

Vishton, P. M. (2005). Using kitchen appliance analogies to improve students' reasoning about neurological results. *Teaching of Psychology, 32(2),* 107–110.

Vokey, J. R., & Read, J. D. (1985). Subliminal messages: Between the devil and the media. *American Psychologist, 40,* 1231–1239.

Vohs, K. D., & Baumeister, R. F. (2004). Sexual passion, intimacy, and gender. In D. J. Mashek, & A. P. Aron (Eds.), *Handbook of closeness and intimacy.* Mahwah, NJ: Erlbaum.

Von Lengerke, T. (2005). Distinctiveness of disease prototypes in lay illness diagnosis: An exploratory observational study. *Psychology, Health & Medicine, 10(1),* 108–121.

Vorauer, J. D., Hunter, A. J., Main, K. J., & Roy, S. A. (2000). Meta-stereotype activation: Evidence from indirect measure for specific evaluative concerns experienced by members of dominant groups in intergroup interaction. *Journal of Personality & Social Psychology, 78,* 690–707.*

Vorauer, J. D., Main, K. J., & O'Connell, G. B. (1998). How do individuals expect to be viewed by members of lower status groups? Content and implications of meta-stereotypes. *Journal of Personality & Social Psychology, 75,* 917–937.*

Vrij, A. (2000). *Detecting lies and deceit.* Chichester, UK: Wiley.

Vygotsky, L.S. (1978). *Mind and society: The development of higher mental processes.* Cambridge Harvard University Press.

W

Wachs, T. D., & Kohnstamm, G. A. (Eds.). (2001). *Temperament in context.* Mahwah, NJ: Earlbaum.

Wachs, T. D., Bishry, Z., Sobhy, A., McCabe, G., Galal, O., & Shaeen, F. (1993). Relation of rearing environment to adaptive behavior of Egyptian toddlers. *Child Development, 54,* 396–407.

Wadden, T. A., Foser, G. D., Stunkard, A. J., & Conill, A. M. (1996). Effects of weight cycling on the resting energy expenditure and body composition of obese women. *Eating Disorders, 19,* 5–12.

Wadsworth, M. E., Raviv, T., Compas, B. E., & Connor-Smith, J. K. (2005). Parent and adolescent responses to poverty-related stress: Tests of mediated and moderated coping models. *Journal of Child and Family Studies, 14(2),* 283–298.

Wagenaar, D. A., Madhavan, R., Pine, J., & Potter, S. M. (2005). Controlling bursting in cortical cultures with closed-loop multi-electrode stimulation. *Journal of Neuroscience, 25(3),* 680–688.

Wagner, K. D., & Ambrosini, P. J. (2001). Childhood depression: Pharmacological therapy. *Journal of Clinical Child Psychology, 30,* 88–97.

Wagner, R. K. (1997). Intelligence, training, and employment. *American Psychologist. Special Intelligence & Lifelong Learning, 52(10),* 1059–1069.

Wagner, R. K., & Sternberg, R. J. (1986). Tacit knowledge and intelligence in the everyday world. In R. J. Sternberg, & R. K. Wagner (Eds.), *Practical intelligence: Nature and origins of competence in the everyday world.* Cambridge: Cambridge University Press.

Wagner, U., Gais, S., & Born, J. (2001). Emotional memory formation is enhanced across sleep intervals with high amounts of rapid eye movement sleep. *Learning and Memory, 8,* 112–119.

Wagstaff, G., Brunas-Wagstaff, J., Cole, J., & Wheatcroft, J. (2004). New directions in forensic hypnosis: Facilitating memory with a focused meditation technique. *Contemporary Hypnosis, 21(1),* 14–27.

Wahlsten, D. (1994). The intelligence of heritability. *Canadian Psychology, 35,* 244–258.*

Wahlsten, D. (1996). Advances in genetic analysis of IQ await a better understanding of environment. In D. K. Detterman (Ed.), *Current topics in human intelligence, (Vol. 5).* Norwood, NJ: Ablex Publishing.

Wahlsten, D. (1997). The malleability of intelligence is not constrained by heritability. In B. Devlin, S. E. Fienburg, D. P. Resnick, & K. Roeder (Eds.), *Intelligence, genes, and success: Scientists respond to the Bell Curve.* New York: Copernicus (Springer Verlag).*

Wahlsten, D. (2000). Behavioral genetics. In A. Kazdin (Ed.), *Encyclopedia of psychology.* Washington, & New York: APA Press and Oxford.*

Wahlsten, D., & Gottlieb, G. (1997). The invalid separation of effects of nature and nurture: Lessons from animal experimentation. In R. J. Sternberg, & E. L. Grigorenko (Eds.), *Intelligence, heredity and environment.* Cambridge: Cambridge University Press.*

Walhovd, K. B., Fjell, A. M., Reinvang, I., Lundervold, A., & others (2005). Cortical volume and speed-of-processing are complementary in prediction of performance intelligence. *Neuropsychologia, 43(5),* 704–713.

Waldmann, M. R., & Hagmayer, Y. (2005). Seeing versus doing: Two modes of accessing causal knowledge. *Journal of Experimental Psychology: Learning, Memory, and Cognition, 31(2),* 216–227.

Waldram, J. B. (1997). The aboriginal peoples of Canada: Colonialism and mental health. In I. Al-Issa, & M. Tousignant (Eds.), *Ethnicity, immigration, and psychopathology.* New York: Plenum.*

Waldram, J. B. (2004). *Revenge of the Windigo: The construction of the mind and mental health of North American Aboriginal peoples.* Toronto: University of Toronto Press.*

Walker, L. E. (1999). Psychology and domestic violence around the world. *American Psychologist, 54,* 6–20.

Walker, L. J., & Pitts, R. C. (1998). Naturalistic conceptions of moral maturity. *Developmental Psychology, 34,* 403–419.*

Wall, P. D., & Melzack, R. (1999). *Textbook of pain (4th ed.).* Philadelphia: Saunders.*

Wall, P. L., Botly, L. C. P., Black, C. M. , & Shettleworth, S. J. (2004). The geometric module in the rat: Independence of shape and feature learning in a food-finding task. *Learning & Behavior, 32,* 289–298.*

Wall, T. L., Shea, S. H., Chan, K. K., & Carr, L. G. (2001). A genetic association with the development of alcohol and other substance use in Asian Americans. *Journal of Abnormal Psychology, 110,* 173–178.

Wallace, B. E., Wagner, A. K., Wagner, E. P., & McDeavit, J. T. (2001). A history and review of quantitative electroencephalography in traumatic brain disorders. *Journal of Head and Trauma Rehabilitation, 16,* 165–190.

Wallace, R. K., & Benson, H. (1972). The physiology of meditation. *Scientific American, 226(2),* 84–90.

Wallerstein, J. S., & Lewis, J. M. (2004). The unexpected legacy of divorce: Report of a 25-year study. *Psychoanalytic Psychology, 21(3),* 353–370.

Wallerstein, R. S. (1989). The psychotherapy research project of the Menninger Foundation: An overview. *Journal of Consulting and Clinical Psychology, 57,* 195–205.

Wallston, K. A. (2001). Conceptualization and operationalization of perceived control. In A. Baum, T. A. Revenson, & J. E. Singer (Eds.), *Handbook of health psychology.* Mahwah, NJ: Erlbaum.

Walsh, A. (1998). Religion and hypertension: Testing alternative explanations among immigrants. *Behavioral Medicine, 24(3),* 122–130.

Walsh, W. B., & Betz, N. E. (2001). *Tests and measurement (4th ed.).* Upper Saddle River, NJ: Prentice Hall.

Wang, Q., & Conway, M. A. (2004). The stories we keep: Autobiographical memory in American and Chinese middle-aged adults. *Journal of Personality, 72(5),* 911–938.

Wang, S. S., & Brownell, K. D. (2005). Public policy and obesity: The need to marry science with advocacy. *Psychiatric Clinics of North America, 28(1),* 235–252.

Ward, R. A., & Grashial, A. F. (1995). Using astrology to teach research methods to introductory psychology students. In M. E. Ware, & D. E. Johnson (Eds.), *Demonstrations and activities in teaching of psychology (Vol. 1).* Mahwah, NJ: Erlbaum.

Warnecke, R. B., Morera, O., Turner, L., Mermelstein, R., Johnson, T. P., Parsons, J., et al. (2001). Changes in self-efficacy and readiness for smoking cessation among women with high school or less education. *Journal of Health and Social Behavior, 42,* 97–109.

Wathen, C. N., Feig, D. S., Feightner, J. W., Abramson, B. W., & Cheung, A. M. (2004). Hormone replacement therapy for the primary prevention of chronic diseases: Recommendation statement from the Canadian Task Force on Preventive Health Care. *Canadian Medical Association Journal, 170(10),* 1535-1537. Retrieved September 20, 2005 from http://www.cmaj.ca/cgi/content/full/170/10/1535.*

Watkins, C. E., Campbell, V. L., Nieberding, R., & Hallmark, R. (1995). Contemporary practice of psychological assessment by clinical psychologists. *Professional Psychology: Research and Practice, 26,* 54–60.

Watkins, E., & Subich, L. M. (1995). Career development, reciprocal work/nonwork interaction, and women's workforce participation. *Journal of Vocational Behavior, 47,* 109–163.

Watling, R., & Schwartz, I. S. (2004). Understanding and implementing positive reinforcement as an intervention strategy for children with disabilities. *American Journal of Occupational Therapy, 58(1),* 113–116.

Watras, J. (2002). *The foundations of educational curriculum and diversity: 1565 to the present.* Boston: McGraw-Hill.

Watson, D. L., & Tharp, R. G. (2003). *Self-directed behavior (8th ed.).* Belmont, CA: Wadsworth.

Watson, D. (2001). Positive affectivity: The disposition to experience pleasurable emotional states. In C. R. Snyder, & S. J. Lopez (Eds.), *Handbook of positive psychology.* New York: Oxford.

Watson, D., Wiese, D., Vaidya, J., & Tellegen, A. (1999). The two general activation systems of affect: Structural findings, evolutionary considerations, and psychobiological evidence. *Journal of Personality & Social Psychology, 76,* 820–838.

Watson, J. B. (1913). Psychology as the behaviorist views it. *Psychological Review, 20,* 158–177.

Watson, J. B. (1928). *Psychological care of the infant and child.* Philadelphia: Lippincott.

Watson, J. B., & Rayner, R. (1920). Conditioned emotional reactions. *Journal of Experimental Psychology, 3,* 1–14.

Wauters, M., Mertens, I. K., Chagnon, M., Rankinen, T., Considine, R. V., Chagnon, Y. C., et al. (2001). Polymorphisms in the leptin receptor gene, body composition, and fat distribution in overweight and obese women. *International Journal of Obesity and Related Metabolic Disorders, 25,* 714–720.

Webb, W. B. (2000). Sleep. In A. Kazdin (Ed.), *Encyclopedia of psychology.* Washington, & New York: APA Press and Oxford.

Webster, J. M., Smith, R. H., Rhodes, A., & Whatley, M. A. (1999). The effect of a favor on public and private compliance: How internalized is the norm of reciprocity? *Basic and Applied Social Psychology, 21,* 251–260.

Wechsler, D. (1939). *The measurement of adult intelligence.* Baltimore: Williams & Wilkins.

Wechsler, H., Davenport, A., Sowdall, G., Moetykens, B., & Castillo, S. (1994). Health and behavioral consequences of binge drinking in college. *Journal of the American Medical Association, 272,* 1672–1677.

Wechsler, H., Lee, J. E., Kuo, M., & Lee, H. (2000). College binge drinking in the 1990s—A continuing health problem: Results of the Harvard University School of Public Health 1999 College Alcohol Study. *Journal of American College Health, 48,* 199–210.

Weich, S., Lewis, G., & Jenkins, S. P. (2001). Income inequality and the prevalence of common mental disorders in Britain. *British Journal of Psychiatry, 178,* 222–227.

Weidemann, G., Georgilas, A., & Kehoe, E. J. (1999). Temporal specificity in patterning of the rabbit nictitating membrane response. *Animal Learning & Behavior, 27,* 99–109.

Weigel, V. B. (2001). *Deep learning for a digital age.* San Francisco, CA: Jossey-Bass.

Weine, S. M., Becker, D. F., McGlashan, T. H., Laub, D., Lazrove, S., Vojvoda, D., et al. (1995). Psychiatric consequences of "ethnic cleansing": Clinical assessments and trauma testimonies of newly resettled Bosnian refugees. *American Journal of Psychiatry, 152,* 536–542.

Weiner, B. (1986). *An attributional theory of motivation and emotion.* New York: Springer-Verlag.

Weiner, I. B. (2003). *Principles of Rorschach interpretation (2nd ed.).* Mahwah, NJ: Erlbaum.

Weiner, I. B., Exner, J. E., & Sciara, A. (1996). Is the Rorschach welcome in the courtroom? *Journal of Personality Assessment, 67,* 422–424.

Weinraub, M., Hill, C., & Hirsh-Pasek, K. (2002). Child care: Options and outcomes. In J. Worell (Ed.), *Encyclopedia of women and gender.* New York: Oxford.

Weisman, C. S., Maccannon, D. S., Henderson, J. T., Shortridge, E., & Orso, C. L. (2002). Contraceptive counseling in managed care. *Women's Health Issues, 12,* 79–95.

Weiss, L. H., & Schwarz, J. C. (1996). The relationship between parenting types and older adolescents' personality, academic achievement, adjustment, and substance use. *Child Development, 67(5),* 2101–2114.

Weissberg, R. P., & Greenberg, M. T. (1998). School and community competence-enhancement and prevention programs. In W. Damon (Ed.), *Handbook of child psychology (5th ed., Vol. 4).* New York: Wiley.

Weissman, M. M., Bland, R. C., Canino, G. J., Greenwald, S., et al. (1999). Prevalence of suicide ideation and suicide attempts in nine countries. *Psychological Medicine, 29,* 9–18.

Weissman, M., & Olfson, M. (1995). Depression in women: Implications for health care research. *Science, 269,* 799–801.

Welburn, K. R., Fraser, G. A., Jordan, S. A. Cameron, C., Webb, L. M., & Raine, D. (2003). Discriminating dissociative identity disorder from schizophrenia and feigned dissociation on psychological tests and structured interview. *Journal of Trauma & Dissociation, 4(2),* 109–130.*

Wells, A., & Papageorgiou, C. (2001). Brief cognitive therapy for social phobia: A case series. *Behavior Research and Therapy, 39,* 713–720.

Wells, G. L., & Olson, E. A. (2001). The other-race effect in eyewitness identification: What do we do about it? *Psychology, Public Policy, & Law, 7(1),* 230–246.

Wenke, D., Frensch, P. A., & Funke, J. (2005). Complex problem solving and intelligence: Empirical relation and causal direction. In R. J. Sternberg, & E.

Pretz (Eds.), *Cognition and intelligence: Identifying the mechanisms of the mind.* New York: Cambridge.

Wenzlaff, R. M., & Prohaska, M. L. (1989). When misery loves company: Depression, attributions, and responses to others' moods. *Journal of Experimental Social Psychology, 25,* 220–223.

Wessel, I., & Wright, D. B. (Eds.). (2004). *Emotional memory failures.* Hove, UK: Psychology Press.

West, R., & Craik, F. I. M. (2001). Influences on the efficiency of prospective memory in younger and older adults. *Psychology and Aging, 16,* 682–696.*

Westermeyer, J. F. (2004). Predictors and characteristics of Erikson's life cycle model among men: A 32-year longitudinal study. *International Journal of Aging & Human Development, 58(1),* 29–48.

Whipple, B., Ogden, G., & Komisaruk, B. (1992). Analgesia produced in women by genital self-stimulation. *Archives of Sexual Behavior, 9,* 87–99.

Whitbourne, S. K. (2005). *Adult development and aging: Biopsychosocial perspectives (2nd ed.).* New York: Wiley.

White, G. L., & Taytroe, L. (2003). Personal problem-solving using dream incubation: Dreaming, relaxation, or waking cognition? *Dreaming, 13(4),* 193–209.

White, J. W. (2001). Aggression and gender. In J. Worell (Ed.), *Encyclopedia of gender and women.* San Diego: Academic Press.

White, K., & Lehman, D. R. (2005). Culture and social comparison seeking: The role of self-motives. *Personality & Social Psychology Bulletin, 31(2),* 232–242.*

Whitehead, C. (2004). Everything I believe might be a delusion. Whoa!: Tucson 2004: Ten years on, and are we any nearer to a science of consciousness? *Journal of Consciousness Studies, 11(12),* 68–88.

Whiting, W. L., Madden, D. J., Pierce, T. W., & Allen, P. A. (2005). Searching from the top down: Ageing and attentional guidance during singleton detection. Quarterly *Journal of Experimental Psychology: Human Experimental Psychology. Special Cognitive Gerontology: Cognitive Change in Old Age, 58A(1),* 72–97.

Whitman, T. L., Borkowski, J. G., Keogh, D. A., & Weed, K. (2001). *Interwoven lives.* Mahwah, NJ: Erlbaum.

Whorf, B. L. (1956). *Language, thought, and creativity.* New York: Wiley.

Wickett, J. C., Vernon, P. A., & Lee, D. H. (2000). Relationships between factors of intelligence and brain volume. *Personality & Individual Differences, 29,* 1095–1122.*

Wicks, S. R., & Rankin, C. H. (1997). The effects of tap withdrawal response habituation on other withdrawal behaviors: The localization of habituation in the nematode Caenorhabditis elegans. *Behavioral Neuroscience, 111,* 342–353.*

Wicks, S. R., Roehrig, C. J., & Rankin, C. H. (1996). A dynamic network simulation of the nematode tap withdrawal circuit: Predictions concerning synaptic function using behavioral criteria. *Journal of Neuroscience, 16,* 4017–4031.*

Widiger, T. A. (2005). Classification and diagnosis: Historical development and contemporary issues. In J. E. Maddux, & B. A. Winstead (Eds.), *Psychopathology: Foundations for a contemporary understanding.* Mahwah, NJ: Erlbaum.

Widiger T. A., Costa, P. T., Jr., & McCrae, R. R. (2002). Proposal for Axis II: Diagnosing personality disorders using the Five-Factor Model. In P. T. Costa, Jr., & T. A. Widiger (Eds.), *Personality disorders and the five-factor model of personality.* Washington: APA Press.

Widiger, T. A., & Simonsen, E. (2005). Introduction to the special section: The American Psychiatric Association's research agenda for the DSM-V. *Journal of Personality Disorders, 19(2),* 103–109.

Wiederhold, B. K., & Wiederhold, M. D. (2005). Posttraumatic stress disorder. In B. K. Wiederhold, & M. D. Wiederhold (Eds), *Virtual reality therapy for anxiety disorders: Advances in evaluation and treatment.* Washington: APA Press.

Wiederhold, B. K., & Wiederhold, M. D. (Eds.). (2005). *Virtual reality therapy for anxiety disorders: Advances in evaluation and treatment.* Washington: APA Press.

Wiederman, M. W., & Whitley, B. E. (Eds.). (2002). *Handbook for conducting research on human sexuality.* Mahwah, NJ: Erlbaum.

Wielandt, H., Bolden, J., & Knudsen, L. B. (2002). The prevalent use of contraception among teenagers in Denmark and the corresponding low pregnancy rate. *Journal of Biosocial Science, 34,* 1–11.

Wieman, C. (2000). An overview of Six Nations mental health services. In L. J. Kirmayer, M. E. Macdonald, & G. M. Brass (Eds.), *Proceedings of the Montreal Advanced Study Institute: The mental health of indigenous peoples.* Montreal: McGill University Division of Transcultural Psychiatry.*

Wigfield, A., & Eccles, J. (Eds.). (2002). *Development of achievement motivation.* San Diego: Academic Press.

Wiggins, J. S. (Ed.). (1996). *The five-factor model of personality: Theoretical perspectives.* New York: Guilford.*

Wiggins, J. S. (1997). In defense of traits. In R. Hogan, J. A. Johnson, & S. R. Briggs (Eds.), *Handbook of personality psychology.* San Diego: Academic Press.*

Wiggins, J. S., & Pincus, A. L. (1992). Personality: Structure and assessment. *Annual Review of Psychology, 43,* 473–504.

Wiggins, J. S., & Trapnell, P. D. (1997). Personality structure: The return of the big five. In R. Hogan, J. Johnson, & S. Briggs (Eds.), *Handbook of personality research.* San Diego: Academic Press.*

Wilens, T. E., Spencer, T. J., Biederman, J., Girard, K., Doyle, R., Polisner, J., et al. (2001). A controlled clinical trial of bupropion for attention deficit hyperactivity disorder in adults. *American Journal of Psychiatry, 158,* 282–188.

Wiley, E., Bialystok, E., & Hakuta, K. (2005). New approaches to using census data to test the critical-period hypothesis for second-language acquisition. *Psychological Science, 16(4),* 341–343.*

Williams, C. (2001). *You snooze, you lose? – Sleep patterns in Canada.* Statistics Canada Catalogue No. 11-008. Ottawa, ON: Statistics Canada. Retrieved March 13, 2005, from http://www.statcan.ca/english/kits/pdf/social/sleep2.pdf.*

Williams, C. C., & Zacks, R. T. (2001). Is retrieval-induced forgetting an inhibitory process? *American Journal of Psychology, 114,* 329–354.

Williams, G., Cai, X. J., Elliott, J. C., & Harrold, J. A. (2004). Anabolic neuropeptides. *Physiology & Behavior. Special Reviews on Ingestive Science, 81(2),* 211–222.

Williams, J. D., & Gruzelier, J. H. (2001). Differentiation of hypnosis and relaxation by analysis of narrow band theta and alpha frequencies. *International Journal of Clinical and Experimental Hypnosis, 49,* 185–206.

Williams, P. T. (2001). Health effects resulting from exercise versus those from body fat. *Medical Science and Sports Exercise, 33 (Suppl.),* S611–621.

Williams, R. B. (2001). Hostility (and other psychosocial risk factors): Effects on health and the potential for successful behavioral approaches to prevention and treatment. In A. Baum, T. A. Revenson, & J. E. Singer (Eds.), *Handbook of health psychology.* Mahwah, NJ: Erlbaum.

Williams, R. B. (2002). Hostility, neuroendocrine changes, and health outcomes. In H. G. Koenig, & H. J. Cohen (Eds.), *The link between religion and health.* New York: Oxford.

Williamson, S. E., Harpur, T. J., & Hare, R. D. (1991). Abnormal processing of affective words by psychopaths. *Psychophysiology, 28(3),* 260–273.*

Willis, S. L., & Schaie, K. W. (1994). Assessing everyday competence in the elderly. In C. Fisher, & R. Lerner (Eds.), *Applied developmental psychology.* Mahwah, NJ: Erlbaum.

Willis, S. L., & Schaie, K. W. (1999). Intellectual functioning in midlife. In S. L. Willis, & J. D. Reid (Eds.), *Life in the middle: Psychological and social development in middle age.* San Diego: Academic Press.

Wills, A. J. (Ed.). (2005). *New directions in human associative learning.* Mahwah, NJ: Erlbaum.

Wilson, G. L. (2002). *Groups in context: Leadership and participation in small groups (6th ed.).* New York: McGraw-Hill.

Wilson, J. F. (2003). *Biological foundations of human behavior.* Belmont, CA: Wadsworth.

Wilson, J. H. (2005). *Essential statistics.* Englewood Cliffs, NJ: Prentice Hall.

Wilson, J. K., & Rapee, R. M. (2005). The interpretation of negative social events in social phobia: Changes during treatment and relationship to outcome. *Behaviour Research & Therapy, 43(3),* 373–389.

Wilson, J. P., & Keane, T. M. (Eds.). (2004). *Assessing psychological trauma and PTSD (2nd ed.).* New York: Guilford.

Wilson, M., & Daly, M. (2002) Infanticide. In M. Pagel, (Ed.), *Encyclopedia of evolution.* Oxford: Oxford University Press.*

Wilson, S. J., & Nutt, D. J. (2005). Sleep research and affective disorders. In E. J. L. Griez, C. Faravelli, Nutt, D. J. & Zohar, J. (Eds.), *Mood disorders: Clinical management and research issues.* New York: Wiley.

Wilson, T. D. (2002). *Strangers to ourselves: Discovering the adaptive unconscious.* Cambridge Harvard University Press.

Wink, P., Dillon, M., & Larsen, B. (2005). Religion as moderator of the depression-health connection: findings from a longitudinal study. *Research on Aging, 27(2),* 197–220.

Winman, A. (2004). Do perfume additives termed human pheromones warrant being termed pheromones? *Physiology & Behavior, 82(4),* 697–701.

Winner, E. (1996). *Gifted children: Myths and realities.* New York: Basic Books.

Winner, E. (2000). The origins and ends of giftedness. *American Psychologist, 55,* 159–169.

Winner, E. (2003). Creativity and talent. In M. H. Bornstein, and L. Davidson et al. (Eds.), *Well-being: Positive development across the life course.* Mahwah, NJ: Erlbaum.

Winstead, B. A. & Sanchez, J. (2005). Gender and psychopathology. In J. E. Maddux & B. A. Winstead (Eds.), *Psychopathology: Foundations for a contemporary understanding.* Mahwah, NJ: Erlbaum.

Winston, A., Been, H., & Serby, M. (2005). Psychotherapy and psychopharmacology: Different universes or an integrated future? *Journal of Psychotherapy Integration, 15(2),* 213–223.

Winter, D. G. (2005). Things I've learned about personality from studying political leaders at a distance. *Journal of Personality, 73(3),* 557–584.

Winter, E., & McGhie-Richmond, D. (2005). Using computer conferencing and case studies to enable collaboration between expert and novice teachers. *Journal of Computer Assisted Learning, 21(2),* 118–129.*

Winters, J., Clift, R. J. W., & Dutton, D. G. (2004). An exploratory study of emotional intelligence and domestic abuse. *Journal of Family Violence, 19(5),* 255–267.

Wise, J. A., & Hopkins, V. D. (Eds.). (2000). *Human factors in certification.* Mahwah, NJ: Erlbaum.

Wisniewski, E. (2000). Concepts: Combinations. In A. Kazdin (Ed.), *Encyclopedia of psychology.* Washington, & New York: APA Press and Oxford.

Witelson, S. F. (1985). The brain connection: The corpus callosum is larger in left handers. *Science, 229,* 665–668.*

Witelson, S. F., & Kigar, D. L. (1992). Sylvian fissure morphology and asymmetry in men and women: Bilateral differences in relation to handedness in men. *Journal of Comparative Neurology, 323,* 326–340.*

Witelson, S. F., Kigar, D. L., & Harvey, T. (1999). The exceptional brain of Albert Einstein. *Lancet, 353,* 2149–2153.*

Wixted, J. T. (2005). A theory about why we forget what we once knew. *Current Directions in Psychological Science, 14(1),* 6–9.

Wogalter, M. S., Malpass, R. S., & Mcquiston, D. E. (2004). A national survey of US police on preparation and conduct of identification lineups. *Psychology, Crime & Law, 10(1),* 69-82.

Wolpe, J. (1963). Behavior therapy in complex neurotic states. *British Journal of Psychiatry, 110,* 28–34.

Wong, F. Y., McCreary, D. R., Bowden, C. C., & Jenner, B. (1991). The matching hypothesis: Factors influencing dating preferences. *Psychology: A Journal of Human Behavior, 28(3-4),* 27–31.*

Wong, G., & Picot, G. (2001). Working time in comparative perspective. In G. Wong, & G. Picot (Eds.), *Patterns, trends, and policy implications of earnings inequality and unemployment.* Kalamazoo, MI: Upjohn Institute for Employment Research.*

Wong, P. T. P. (1989). Personal meaning and successful aging. *Canadian Psychology, 30(3),* 516–525.*

Wong, S. K. (1999). Acculturation, peer relations, and delinquent behavior of Chinese-Canadian youth. *Adolescence, 34,* 108–119.*

Wong, S. K. (2001). Acculturation, language use, and Chinese delinquency: An examination of four theoretical models. In F. Columbus (Ed.), *Advances in psychology research (Vol. 5).* Huntington, NY: Nova Science Publishers.*

Woo-kyoung, A., Goldstone, R. L., Love, B. C., Markman, A. B. & Wolff, P. (Eds.). (2005). *Categorization inside and outside the laboratory: Essays in honor of Douglas L. Medin.* Washington: APA Press.

Wood, A. G., Harvey, A. S., Wellard, R. M., Abbott, D. F., Anderson, V. Kean, M., et al. (2004). Language cortex activation in normal children. *Neurology, 63(6),* 1035–1044.

Wood, D. (2001). Established and emerging cardiovascular risk factors. *American Heart Journal, 141 (Suppl. 2),* S49–57.

Wood, G. (1986). *Myth of neurosis: Overcoming the illness excuse.* New York: Perennial.

Wood, J. M., Nezworski, M. T., & Garb, H. N. (2003). What's right with the Rorschach? *Scientific Review of Mental Health Practice, 2(2),* 142–146.

Wood, J. M., Nezworski, M. T., Lilienfeld, S. O., & Garb, H. N. (2003). *What's wrong with the Rorschach? Science confronts the controversial inkblot test.* San Francisco, CA: Jossey-Bass.

Wood, J. T. (2001). *Gendered lives (4th ed.).* Belmont, CA: Wadsworth.

Wood, J. V., Heimpel, S. A., & Michela, J. L. (2003). Savoring versus dampening: Self-esteem differences in regulating positive affect. *Journal of Personality & Social Psychology. 85(3),* 566–580.

Wood, W. (1987). Meta-analytic review of sex differences in group performance. *Psychological Bulletin, 102,* 53–71.

Woody, E. Z., & Bowers, K. S. (1994). A frontal assault on dissociated control. In S. J. Lynn, & J. W. Rhue (Eds.), *Dissociation: Clinical and theoretical perspectives.* New York: Guilford.*

Worell, J. (Ed.). (2002). *Encyclopedia of women and gender.* New York: Oxford.

Worell, J., & Remer, P. (2003). *Feminist perspectives in therapy: Empowering diverse women (2nd ed.).* New York: Wiley.

World Health Organization (2000). *The World Health Report.* Geneva, Switzerland: World Health Organization.

World Health Organization (2004). *Epidemiological fact sheets on HIV/AIDs and sexually transmitted diseases , 2004 update: Canada.* Geneva: World Health Organization. Generated August 21, 2005 from http://www.who.int/hiv/pub/epidemiology/pubfacts/en/.

Worthington, Jr., E. L. & Scherer, M. (2004). Forgiveness is an emotion-focused coping strategy that can reduce health risks and promote health resilience: Theory, review, and hypotheses. *Psychology & Health, 19(3),* 385–405.

Wright, J. C., Huston, A. C., Scantlin, R., & Kotler, J. (2001). The early window project: Sesame Street prepares children for school. In S. M. Fisch, & R. T. Truglio (Eds.), *"G" is for growing.* Mahwah, NJ: Erlbaum.

Wright, M. J., & Myers, C. R. (Eds.). (1982). *History of academic psychology in Canada.* Toronto: C. J. Hogrefe.*

Wrightsman, L., Greene, E., Nietzel, M. T., & Fortune, W. H. (2002). *Psychology and the legal system.* Belmont, CA: Wadsworth.

Wu, J. C., Iacono, R., Ayman, M., Salmon, E., Lin, S. D., Carlson, J., et al. (2000). Correlation of intellectual impairment in Parkinson's disease with FDG PET scan. *Neuroreport, 11,* 2139–2144.

Wu, Z., Noh, S., Kaspar, V., & Schimmele, C. M. (2003). Race, ethnicity, and depression in Canadian society. *Journal of Health & Social Behavior. Special Race, Ethnicity and Mental Health, 44(3),* 426–441.*

Wu, Z. & Schimmele, C. M. (2005). Repartnering after first union disruption. *Journal of Marriage & Family, 67(1),* 27–36.*

Wyatt, R. C. (2004). Thomas Szasz: Liberty and the practice of psychotherapy. *Journal of Humanistic Psychology, 44(1),* 71–85.

Y

Yalom, I. D. (1995). *The theory and practice of group psychotherapy (4th ed.).* New York: Basic Books.

Yamamoto, J., Frequet, N., & Sandner, G. (2002). Conditioned taste aversion using four different means to deliver sucrose to rats. *Physiology and Behavior, 75,* 387–396.

Yanovski, S. Z., & Yanovski, J. A. (2002). Obesity. *New England Journal of Medicine, 346,* 591–602.

Yapko, M. (2001). Hypnosis in treating symptoms and risk factors of major depression. *American Journal of Clinical Hypnosis, 44,* 97–108.

Yarmey, A. D. (1973). I recognize your face but I can't remember your name: Further evidence for the tip-of-the-tongue phenomenon. *Memory and Cognition, 1,* 287–290.*

Yarmey, A. D. (2001). Earwitness descriptions and speaker identification. *Forensic Linguistics, 8,* 113–122.*

Yarmey, A. D. (2003). Eyewitness identification: Guidelines and recommendations for identification procedures in the United States and in Canada. *Canadian Psychology, 44(3),* 181–189.

Yatvin, J. (2005). Making whole language disappear: How the National Reading Panel worked its magic. In L. Poynor, & P. M. Wolfe (Eds.), *Marketing fear in America's public schools: The real war on literacy.* Mahwah, NJ: Erlbaum.

Yehuda, R., Golier, J. A., Harvey, P. D., Stavitsky, K., Kaufman, S., Grossman, R. A., et al. (2005). Relationship between cortisol and age-related memory impairments in Holocaust survivors with PTSD. *Psychoneuroendocrinology, 30(7),* 678–687.

Yonkers, K. A., Wisner, K. L., Stowe, Z., Leibenluft, E., Cohen, L., Miller, L., et al. (2004). Management of bipolar disorder during pregnancy and the postpartum period. *American Journal of Psychiatry, 161(4),* 608–620.

Yost, W. (2000). *Fundamentals of hearing: An introduction.* San Diego: Academic Press.

Young, E., & Korzun, A. (1998). Psychoneuroendocrinology of depression: Hypothalamic-pituitary-gonadal axis. *Psychiatric Clinics of North America, 21,* 309–323.

Young, T. (1802). On the theory of light and colors. *Philosophical Transactions of the Royal Society of London, 92,* 12–48.

Yovel, I., Revelle, W., Mineka, S. (2005). Who sees trees before forest? The obsessive-compulsive style of visual attention. *Psychological Science, 16(2),* 123–129.

Ypsilanti, A., Grouios, G., Alevriadou, A., & Tsapkini, K. (2005). Expressive and receptive vocabulary in children with Williams and Down syndromes. *Journal of Intellectual Disability Research, 49(5),* 353–364.

Yuille, J. C. (1997). Interviewing children is a complex task. *Contemporary Psychology, 42(9),* 803–804.*

Yuille, J. C., & Daylen, J. (1998). The impact of traumatic events on eyewitness memory. In C. Thompson, D. Herrmann, D. Read, D. Payne, & M. Toglia (Eds.), *Eyewitness memory: Theoretical and applied perspectives.* Mahwah, NJ: Erlbaum.*

Yuille, J. C., Hunter, R., Joffe, R., & Zaparniuk, J. (1993). Interviewing children in sexual abuse cases. In G. Goodman, & B. Bottoms (Eds.), *Understanding and improving children's testimony: Clinical, developmental and legal implications.* New York: Guilford.*

Yuille, J. C., & Wells, G. L. (1991). Concerns about the applications of research findings: The issue of ecological validity. In J. Doris (Ed.), *The suggestibility of children's recollections: Implications for eyewitness testimony.* Washington: APA Press.*

Z

Zacks, J. M., & Tversky, B. (2001). Event structure in perception and conception. *Psychological Bulletin, 127,* 3–21.

Zahm, S., & Gold, E. (2002). Gestalt therapy. In M. Hersen, & W. H. Sledge (Eds.), *Encyclopedia of psychotherapy.* San Diego: Academic Press.

Zaimovic, G. G., Zambelli, U., Timpano, M., Reali, N., Bernasconi, S., & Brambilla, F. (2000). Neuroendocrine responses to psychological stress in adolescents with anxiety disorder. *Neuropsychobiology, 42,* 82–92.

Zajonc, R. B. (1965). Social facilitation. *Science, 149,* 269–274.

Zajonc, R. B. (1984). On the primacy of affect. *American Psychologist, 39,* 117–123.

Zalla, T., Koechlin, E., Pietrini, P., Basso, G., Aquino, P., et al. (2000). Differential amygdala responses to winning and losing. *European Journal of Neuroscience, 15,* 1764–1770.

Zanna, M. P. (1994). On the nature of prejudice. *Canadian Psychology, 35,* 11–23.*

Zarit, S. H., Pearlin, L. I., & Schaie, K. W. (Eds.). (2002). *Personal control in social and life contexts.* New York: Springer.

Zeidner, M., & Saklofske, D. H. (1996). Adaptive and maladaptive coping. In M. Zeidner, & N. S. Endler (Eds.), *Handbook of coping: Theory, research, applications.* New York: Wiley.

Zeki, S. (1991). Cerebral akinetopsia (Visual motion blindness): A review. *Brain, 114,* 811–824.

Zeki, S. (2001). Localization and globalization in conscious vision. *Annual Review of Neuroscience, 24,* 57–86.

Zelazo, P. D., Craik, F. I. M., & Booth, L. (2004). Executive function across the life span. *Acta Psychologica, 115(2–3),* 167–183.*

Zetik, D. C., & Stuhlmacher, A. F. (2002). Goal setting and negotiation performance: A meta-analysis. *Group Processes & Intergroup Relations, 5(1),* 35–52.

Ziegert, K. A. (1983). The Swedish prohibition of corporal punishment: A preliminary report. *Journal of Marriage and the Family, 45,* 917–926.

Zikovitz, D. C., & Harris, L. R. (1999). Head tilt during driving. *Ergonomics, 42,* 740–746.*

Zilbergeld, B. (1992). *The new male sexuality.* New York: Bantam Books.

Zilbergeld, B., & Zilbergeld, G. (2004). *Better than ever: Love and sex at midlife.* Williston, VT: Crown House Publishing.

Zillman, D. (1998). Anger. In H. S. Friedman (Ed.) *Encyclopedia of mental health (Vol. 1).* San Diego: Academic Press.

Zimmerman, B. J. (2001). Theories of self-regulated learning and academic achievement. In B. J. Zimmerman, & D. H. Schunk (Eds.), *Self-regulated learning and academic achievement.* Mahwah, NJ: Erlbaum.

Zimmerman, B. J., & Campillo, M. (2003). Motivating self-regulation problem solvers. In J. E. Davidson, & R. J. Sternberg (Eds.), *The psychology of problem solving.* New York: Cambridge.

Zimmerman, C., Bisanz, G. L., &, Bisanz, J. (1998). Everyday scientific literacy: Do students use knowledge about the social context and methods of research to evaluate news briefs about science? *Alberta Journal of Educational Research, Theme Issue, Literacy in the 21st Century, 44,* 188–207.*

Zisapel, N. (2001). Circadian rhythm sleep disorders: Pathophysiology and potential approaches to management. *CNS Drugs, 15(4),* 311–328.

Zola, S. M., & Squire, L. R. (2001). Relationship between magnitude of damage to the hippocampus and impaired recognition in monkeys. *Hippocampus, 11,* 92–98.

Zuckerman, M. (2000). Sensation seeking. In A. Kazdin (Ed.), *Encyclopedia of psychology.* Washington, & New York: APA Press and Oxford.

Zuckerman, M. (2002). Genetics of sensation seeking. In J. Benjamin, R. P. Ebstein, & R. H. Belmake (Eds.), *Molecular genetics and the human personality.* Washington: American Psychiatric Publishing.

Zunzunegui, M. V., Koné, A., Johri,M., Béland, F., Wolfson, C., & Bergman, H. (2004). Social networks and self-rated health in two French-speaking Canadian community dwelling populations over 65. *Social Science & Medicine, 58(10),* 2069–2081.*

Zupanc, G. (2003). *Behavioral neurobiology: An integrative approach.* Oxford: Oxford University Press.

Zwaal, C., Prkachin, K. M., Husted, J. & Stones, M. (2003). Components of hostility and verbal communication of emotion. *Psychology & Health, 18(2),* 261–273.*

Zwaan, R. A., Stanfield, R. A., & Yaxley, R. H. (2002). Language comprehenders mentally represent the shape of objects. *Psychological Science, 13(2),* 168–171.

Zwislocki, J. J. (2002). *Auditory sound transmission.* Mahwah, NJ: Erlbaum.

Credits

Text and Line Art Credits

Chapter 1

p. 24 Personal Reflections Box From Jane Halonen and John Santrock, *Psychology: Contexts and Applications,* Third Edition, McGraw-Hill, 1999 © 1999 The McGraw-Hill Companies. Reprinted with the permission of the McGraw-Hill Companies.

Chapter 3

Figures 3.6, 3.7 From R. Lewis, Life, 3rd edition. © 1998 by the McGraw-Hill Companies. Reproduced with the permission of the McGraw-Hill Companies. Figures 3.9, 3.20 From *Mapping the Mind* by Rita Carter, 1998. Reprinted by permission of Weidenfeld & Nicolson. Figures 3.13, 3.18 From *Brain, Mind, and Behavior* by Floyd Bloom, Charles A. Nelson, Arlyne Lazerson. © 1985, 1988, 2001 by Educational Broadcasting Corporation. Used with permission of W. H. Freeman and Company. Figure 3.23 From John Santrock, *Psychology,* 6th edition, Module on Evolution and Heredity, Figure 12. Reprinted with permission from the McGraw-Hill Companies.

Chapter 4

Figure 4.3 From T. Field, S. M. Schanberg, F. Scafidi, C. R. Bauer, N. Vega-Lahr, R. Garcia, J. Nystrom, C. M. Kuhn, "Tactile/Kinesthetic Stimulation Effects on Preterm Neonates, *Pediatrics,* 77, 1986, p. 657, Figure 1. Reproduced with permission of publisher. Figures 4.16, 4.20, 4.21, 4.27, 4.28, 4.29 From John W. Santrock, *Life-Span Development,* 8th edition. Figure 4.19 From "The Development of Competence in Favorable and Unfavorable Environments" by A. Masten & J. D. Coatsworth, *American Psychologist,* 553, pp. 205–220. © 1998 by the American Psychological Association. Adapted with permission. Figure 4.24 From Grant Jarding, *USA Today,* January 5, 1999, p. 4. Figures 4.30, 4.31 From "The Nature of the Influence of Speed on Adult Age Differences in Cognition," in *Developmental Psychology,* 1994, 30, pp. 240–259. © 1994 by the American Psychological Association. Adapted with permission. Figure 4.32 From L. L. Carstensen and S. Turk-Charles, *Psychology and Aging,* 9, p. 262. © 1994 by the American Psychological Association. Adapted with permission. Figure 4.33 From *Aging Well* by George Vaillant. © 2002 by George E. Vaillant, M.D. by permission of Little, Brown and Company, Inc.

Chapter 5

Figure 5.17 Reproduced with permission from Ishihara's Tests for Colour Deficiency, published by Kanehara Trading Inc., located in Tokyo, Japan. Test for colour deficiency cannot be conducted with this material. For accurate testing, the original plates should be used. Figure 5.18 From *Introduction to Psychology,* 7th ed., by Hilgard, Atkinson, and Atkinson. © 2003 Thomson Learning. Reprinted with permission of Wadsworth, an imprint of the Wadsworth Group, a division of Thomson Learning. Fax 800-730-2215. Figure 5.29 From James J. Gibson, *The Perception of the Visual World.* © 1950 by Houghton Mifflin Company. Reprinted with permission. Figure 5.36 From *Brain, Mind, and Behavior,* by Floyd Bloom, Charles A. Nelson, Arlyne Lazerson. © 1985, 1988, 2001, by Educational Broadcasting Corporation. Used with the permission of W. H. Freeman and Company.

Chapter 6

Figure 6.6 Reprinted with permission from H. P. Roffwarg, J. N. Muzio, and W. C. Dement, "Ontogenetic Development of Human Dream-Sleep-Cycle," *Science,* 152, pp. 604–609. © 1966 American Association for the Advancement of Science. Figure 6.7 From *Brain, Mind, and Behavior,* by Floyd Bloom, Charles A. Nelson, Arlyne Lazerson. © 1985, 1988, 2001, by Educational Broadcasting Corporation. Used with the permission of W. H. Freeman and Company. p. 243 Personal Reflections Box Quiz and Strategies: From *Power Sleep* by James B. Maas. © 1998 by James B. Maas, Ph.D. Used by permission of Villard Books, a division of Random House, Inc. Figure 6.10 National Institute of Drug Abuse, 2001, Teaching Packet for Psychoactive Drugs, slide 9. Figure 6.12 From *Journal of the American Medical Association,* 1994, 272, pp. 1672–1677. With permission from the American Medical Association. Figure 6.13 National Institute of Drug Abuse, 2001, Teaching Packet for Psychoactive Drugs, slides 12 and 13.

Chapter 8

Figure 8.11 Figure from "Retrieval Time for Semantic Memory," by A. M. Collins and M. R. Quillan, in *Journal of Verbal Learning and Verbal Behavior,* vol. 3, pp. 240–248. © 1969 Elsevier Science (USA). Reproduced by permission of publisher. Figure 8.12 From R. Lachman et al., *Cognitive Psychology and Information Processing.* © 1979 Lawrence Erlbaum Associates, Inc. Reprinted with permission of publisher. Figure 8.13 From J. C. Bartlett, *Remembering,* Cambridge, England: Cambridge University Press, 1932. Reprinted with permission. Figure 8.16 From B. Murdock, Jr., *Human Memory: Theory and Data.* © 1974 Lawrence Erlbaum Associates, Inc. Reprinted with permission. Figure 8.19 D. C. Rubin and M. Kozin, "Vivid Memories," in *Cognition,* 16, pp. 81–95. © 1984 Associated Scientific Publishers, Amsterdam, Netherlands. Reprinted with permission. Figure 8.20 From Kassin, Tubb, Hosch, and Memon, *American Psychologist,* 56, pp. 405–416. © 2001 by the American Psychological Association. Adapted with permission. Figure 8.21 www.exploratorium.edu/exhibits/common_cents/index.html. © Exploratorium. With permission from the Exploratorium, San Francisco. Figure 8.22 From Hermann Ebbinghaus, *Memory: A Contribution to Experimental Psychology,* 1885. Translated by Henry A. Ruger and Clara E. Bussenius, 1913. Figure 8.24 Illustration by Greg Devitt.

Chapter 9

Figure 9.1 With permission from Dr. Ursula Bellugi; Figures 9.4, 9.5 © 2002 The McGraw-Hill Companies, Inc. Reproduced with the permission of the McGraw-Hill Companies. Figure 9.7 From *The Universe Within: A New Science Explores the Human*

Mind, by Morton Hunt, 1982. © 1982 Morton Hunt. Reprinted with permission from Simon & Schuster. **Figures 9.11, 9.13** From John W. Santrock, *Educational Psychology.* © 2001 The McGraw-Hill Companies, Inc. Reprinted by permission of The McGraw-Hill Companies.

Chapter 10

Figure 10.1 From John W. Santrock, *Children,* 5th ed. © 1997 The McGraw-Hill Companies, Inc. Reprinted by permission of The McGraw-Hill Companies. **Figure 10.3** © Monkmeyer Press/Merrim. **Figure 10.4** *Raven Standard Progressive Matrices,* F-A5. Reprinted by permission of J. C. Raven Ltd. **Figure 10.6** From John W. Santrock, *Educational Psychology.* © 2001 The McGraw-Hill Companies, Inc. Reprinted by permission of the McGraw-Hill Companies. **Figure 10.7** From John W. Santrock, *Mental Retardation: Definition, Classification, and Systems of Supports.* © 1992 by the American Association on Mental Retardation/AAMR. Reproduced with permission of American Association on Mental Retardation/AAMR in the format Textbook via Copyright Clearance Center.

Chapter 11

Figure 11.5 Reprinted with permission of Simon & Schuster Adult Publishing Group, from *Overweight: Causes, Cost and Control* by Jean Mayer. © 1968 by Prentice-Hall Inc. **Figure 11.7** W. H. Masters and V. E. Johnson, *Human Sexual Response,* 1966, Little, Brown and Company. Reprinted by permission. **Figure 11.8** From John W. Santrock, *Life-Span Development,* 8th ed. © 2002 The McGraw-Hill Companies, Inc. Reproduced with the permission of the McGraw-Hill Companies.

Chapter 12

Figure 12.1 From *Psychology: A Scientific Study of Human Behaviour,* by L. S. Wrightsman, C. K. Sigelman, and F. H. Sanford. © 1979, 1975, 1970, 1965, 1961 Brooks/Cole Publishing Company, a division of International Thomson Publishing Inc. By permission of the publisher. **Figure 12.10** © Courtesy Dr. Hans J. Eysenck. **Figure 12.15** © From *MMPI-2 (Minnesota Multiphasic Personality Inventory-2) Manual for Administration, Scoring, and Interpretation,* Revised Edition. © 2001 by the Regents of the University of Minnesota. All rights reserved. Used by permission of University of Minnesota Press. "MMPI-2" and "Minnesota Multiphasic Personality-2" are trademarks owned by the

Regents of the University of Minnesota. **Figure 12.16** N. S. Jacobson et al., "Toward a Behavioural Profile of Marital Distress," in *Journal of Consulting and Clinical Psychology,* 48:696–703. © 1980 by the American Psychological Association. All rights reserved.

Chapter 13

Figure 13.7 With permission from the *Annual Review of Neuroscience,* Volume 20. © 1997 by Annual Reviews, www.AnnualReviews.org. **Figure 13.9** From *Feeling Good: The New Mood Therapy,* by David D. Burns, 1980. New York: William Morrow & Company. © 1980 David D. Burns, M.D. Reprinted with permission from HarperCollins Publishers (William Morrow). **Figure 13.11** Reprinted with permission of *Science,* 269, p. 779, Figure 1. © 1995, American Association for the Advancement of Science. **Figure 13.12** From *Living with 10-to-15-Year-Olds: A Parent Education Curriculum.* © 1982, 1987 by the Center for Early Adolescence, Carrboro, NC. Used with permission. **Figure 13.14** From I. I. Gottesman and J. Shields, *Schizophrenia: The Epigenetic Puzzle.* © 1992, Cambridge University Press. Reprinted with permission of Cambridge University Press.

Chapter 14

Figure 14.2 From Stephen R. Marder, M.D., et al., *The Journal of Clinical Psychiatry,* Volume 58, pp. 538–546, 1997. © 1997 Physicians Postgraduate Press. Reprinted by permission. **Figure 14.8** From A. Freeman and M. A. Reinecke, "Cognitive Therapy," in A. S. Gurman, ed., *Essential Psychotherapies,* Guilford, 1995. Reprinted with permission. **Figure 14.9** From *Journal of Consulting and Clinical Psychology,* 1999, 67, pp. 145–150. © 1990 by the American Psychological Association. Adapted with permission. **Figure 14.12** Reprinted with permission of Michael J. Lambert, Brigham Young University. **Figure 14.13** From "A Survival Analysis of Clinically Significant Change in Outpatient Psychotherapy," by Anderson & Lambert, from *Journal of Clinical Psychology,* 57, pp. 875–888. © 2001 John Wiley & Sons, Inc. Reprinted by permission of the publisher.

Chapter 15

Figure 15.1 "Vulnerability to Stress Scale," from the *Stress Audit,* developed by Lyle H. Miller & Alma Dell Smith. © 1987 Biobehavioral Institute, Brookline, MA. Reprinted with permission. **Figure 15.2** Oakley, R. 2004, "How the mind hurts and

heals the body," *American Psychologist,* 59(1), 29–40. **Figure 15.3** Reprinted from *Journal of Psychosomatic Research,* Volume 29, S. C. Kobasa, S. R. Maddi, M. C. Puccette, and M. Zola, pp. 525–533. © 1986 Elsevier Science. With permission from Elsevier Science. **Figure 15.5** From J. Selye, *The Stress of Life.* © 1976 by the McGraw-Hill Companies. Reproduced with the permission of the McGraw-Hill Companies. **Figure 15.10** From *Contemporary Behavior Therapy,* 2nd edition, by M. D. Spiegler and D. C. Guevremont. © 1993 Wadsworth Group. Reprinted with permission of Brooks/Cole, an imprint of the Wadsworth Group, a division of Thomson Learning. Fax 800-730-2215. **Figure 15.12** From *Journal of the American Medical Association,* 277, pp. 1940–1944. Reprinted with permission. **Figure 15.14** From *Scientific American,* November 1997 issue, p. 44. Reprinted by permission of Slim Films.

Chapter 16

Figure 16.3 From "Self-Monitoring," by Mark Snyder, *Journal of Personality and Social Psychology,* Volume 30, pp. 562–537. © 1974 by the American Psychological Association. Reprinted by permission. **Figure 16.6** From Stanley Milgram, "Behavioral Study of Obedience," in *Journal of Abnormal and Social Psychology,* Volume 67, pp. 371–378, 1963. Reprinted with permission. **Figure 16.7** Figure "Types of Identity," by K. Deaux, in *Encyclopedia of Women and Gender: Sex Similarities and Differences and the Impact of Society on Gender,* 2-volume set, edited by Judith Worell. © 2001 Elsevier Science (USA). Reproduced by permission of the publisher. **Figure 16.8** From M. Sherif, O. J. Harvey, B. J. White, W. E. Hood, and C. W. Sherif, "Intergroup Conflict and Cooperation: The Robber's Cave Experiment," University of Oklahoma Press/Book Exchange, 1953. Reprinted with permission. **Figure 16.9** From D. Anderson et al., "Early Television Viewing and Adolescent Behavior: The Recontact Study," *Monographs of the Society for Research in Child Development,* Serial No. 264. Reprinted with permission from the Society for Research in Child Development. **Figure 16.10** Dey et al., *The American Freshmen: National Norms for Fall 1992,* 1992; A. W. Astin et al., *The American Freshman: National Norms for Fall 1993,* 1993; A. W. Astin et al., *The American Freshman: National Norms for Fall 1994,* 1994. All works © Higher Education Research Institute, UCLA. Used with permission. **Figure 16.11** From *The Triangle of Love,* by Robert J. Sternberg. © 1988 by Basic Books, Inc. Reprinted by permission of Basic Books, a division of HarperCollins Publishers, Inc.

Photographs and Cartoons

Chapter 1

p. 3 © CP/Larry MacDougal; p. 5 *PEANUTS* reprinted by permission of United Feature Syndicate, Inc.; p. 7 (top and bottom) Archives of the History of American Psychology—The University of Akron; p. 8 Archives of the History of American Psychology—The University of Akron; p. 10 © Corbis; p. 11 Hulton-Deutsch Collection/Corbis; p. 13 Courtesy Mark R. Rosenzweig; p. 13 (bottom) © Tom McHugh/Photo Researchers, Inc.; p. 14 (left) © Jay Dickman; p. 14 (right) © CP/Phill Snel/Maclean's; p. 15 © CP/Larry MacDougal; p. 16 © AP/Guatam Singh; p. 17 © Digital Vision; p. 18 Courtesy Mihaly Csikszentmihalyi; p. 19 © Mel Evans; p. 20 © The New Yorker Collection, 1994, Sam Gross from Cartoonbank.com. All rights reserved.; p. 21 (top) Courtesy Sandra Witelson, from *New Scientist*, March 18, 2000; p. 21 (bottom) Courtesy Sibylle Artz; p. 22 (top) Courtesy James Parker; p. 22 (bottom) Chris Hughes, UW Graphics; p. 23 (top) Courtesy Cannie Stark, uregina.ca/~starkc; p. 23 (bottom) © CP/Paul Chiasson; p. 26 © Bios/M. Gunter/Peter Arnold, Inc.; p. 27 © Corbis

Chapter 2

p. 39 © CBS/Courtesy Everett Collection STREVT; p. 40 (top left) © NOAA; p. 40 (bottom left) © Brand X Pictures/PunchStock; p. 40 (top right) © NASA; p. 40 (bottom right) © Chase Jarvis/Getty Images; p. 42 © John Mitterer; p. 44 © Bob Daemmrich; p. 46 © Russell Kaye/Getty Images/Stone; p. 48 THE FAR SIDE © 1985 FARWORKS, INC. Used by permission. All rights reserved.; p. 49 © Jeff Greenberg/Photo Researchers, Inc.; p. 50 (top) © Ken Regan Pictures; p. 50 (bottom) Drawing by Chas Adams, © 1982 The New Yorker Magazine, Inc.; p. 51 (top) Courtesy David Clark, people.unb.ca/~clark; p. 51 (bottom) © Laura Dwight/PhotoEdit; p. 52 © Bettmann/Corbis; p. 54 © CP/Andrew Vaughan; p. 57 © Doug Martin/Photo Researchers, Inc.; p. 67 (top) © AFP/Corbis; p. 67 (bottom) © Bob Daemmrich/Stock Boston; p. 68 Courtesy Victoria Esses

Chapter 3

p. 75 Courtesy Brian Kolb; p. 78 © Jonathan Nourok/PhotoEdit; p. 79 (top) © Steven Peterson; p. 79 (bottom) Courtesy Vinod Goel; p. 89 (left and right) Courtesy Steve M. Potter, Georgia Institute of Technology; p. 90 © Lennart Nilsson/Albert Bonniers Forlag AB; p. 93 © John Wiley,

California Institute of Technology, estate of James Olds; p. 94 © A. Glauberman/Photo Researchers; p. 95 From H. Damasio, T. Grabowski, R. Frank, A. M. Galaburda, and A. R. Damasio, "The Return of Phineas Gage: Clues about the brain from a famous patient," in *Science*, 264: 1102–1105, 1994. Department of Neurology and Image Analysis Facility, University of Iowa. © 1994 American Association for the Advancement of Science; p. 103 © Steven Binder; p. 108 © Rick Rickman/Matrix; p. 109 © Enrico Ferorelli; p. 111 CALVIN AND HOBBES © Watterson. Reprinted with permission of UNIVERSAL PRESS SYNDICATE. All rights reserved.

Chapter 4

p. 117 © Digital Vision/Getty Images; p. 121 © Tom Rosenthal/SuperStock; p. 123 (all) © Lennart Nilsson, A Child Is Born/Dell Publishing Company/Albert Bonniers Forlag AB; p. 124 Courtesy Dr. Tiffany Field/Touch Research Institutes; p. 126 (top) Photo by Monica Hurt; p. 126 (bottom) From John W. Santrock, *Life-Span Development*, 8th edition; p. 129 (left and right) © D. Goodman/Photo Researchers, Inc.; p. 130 © Paul Fusco/Magnum Photos, Inc.; p. 133 © Yves DeBraine/Black Star; p. 134 © Corbis; p. 136 © Martin Rogers/Stock Boston; p. 137 (top) Reprinted with permission of Operation Migration; p. 137 (bottom) © Penny Tweedie/Getty Images/Stone; p. 140 Courtesy Maggie Mamen; p. 142 © Richard Hutchings/PhotoEdit; p. 143 Harvard University Press; p. 144 Courtesy Carol Gilligan; p. 145 (top and bottom) © Custom Medical Stock Photo; p. 146 (top) Cathy © Cathy Guisewite. Reprinted with permission of UNIVERSAL PRESS SYNDICATE. All rights reserved; p. 146 (bottom) © Digital Stock; p. 149 © Getty Images/Verve Commissioned Series; p. 150 From Penguin Dreams and Stranger Things by Berke Breathed. © 1985 by the Washington Post Company. By permission of Little, Brown and Company; p. 151 © The New Yorker Collection 1988. Edward Koren from cartoonbank.com. All rights reserved; p. 152 © USA Today Photo Library, photo by Robert Deutsch; p. 153 Courtesy Jillian Roberts, www.educ.uvic.ca/epls/faculty/roberts/roberts.htm; p. 156 © William Hubbell/Woodfin Camp and Associates; p. 158 (top) From Grant Jarding, *USA Today*, January 5, 1999, p. 4; p. 158 (bottom) © Pascal Parrot/Sygma; p. 159 (top) © John Goodman; p. 159 (bottom) © CP/TRSTR; p. 160 (top left and top right) From Charles Carroll and Dean Miller, *Health: The Science of Human Adaptation*, 5/e.

© 1991 Wm. C. Brown Communications, Inc. Dubuque, IA. All rights reserved. Reprinted by permission; p. 160 (margin top) Courtesy Office of Development, School Sisters of Notre Dame, Mankato, MN; p. 160 (margin bottom) © Steve Liss/Timepix; p. 163 Elizabeth Crews; p. 164 © 1985; Reprinted courtesy of Bunny Hoest; p. 165 Photo by Sharon M. Fentiman; p. 166 Leo Cullum © 1984 from the New Yorker Collection. All rights reserved; p. 167 © Rim Light/PhotoLink/Getty Images

Chapter 5

p. 175 © Tretyakov Gallery, Moscow/SuperStock; p. 177 © Zig Leszczynski/Animals Animals; p. 182 © Doug Plummer/Photo Researchers, Inc.; p. 188 Courtesy Gretag-Macbeth; p. 189 © Frank S. Werblin; p. 190 Used with permission from "ABCs of the Human Body," 1987 by The Reader's Digest Association, Inc., Pleasantville, New York, www.rd.com. Photograph by Morris Karol; p. 191 © Burrton McNeely/Getty Images/The Image Bank; p. 195 THE FAR SIDE © FARWORKS, Inc. Used by permission. All rights reserved; p. 196 *Relativity*, by M. C. Escher. © 2002 Cordon Art-Baarn-Holland. All rights reserved; p. 198 © 1994, Jun Oi; p. 199 Reprinted by permission of the Art Gallery of Ontario and the family of Lawren S. Harris; p. 200 (top) From Wathern-Dunn, *Models for the Perception of the Visual Form*. © MIT Press. Reprinted by permission; p. 200 (bottom) © Lawrence Migdale; p. 201 © Sidney Harris; p. 202 (top left) © Herman Eisen beiss/Photo Researchers, Inc.; p. 202 (top right) © Emilio Mercado/Jeroboamp; p. 202 (bottom) Courtesy Allison B. Sekuler, McMaster University, www.psychology.mcmaster.ca/sekuler; p. 207 © AP/Wide World Photos; p. 208 (left) © Chuck Kuhn/Getty Images/The Image Bank; p. 208 (middle) © CP/MTLP/Martin Chamberland; p. 208 (right) © PhotoDisc; p. 209 © Merlin D. Tuttle/Photo Researchers, Inc.; p. 210 © Dana Fineman/Sygma; p. 212 (left and right) Provided courtesy SRI International, Menlo Park, California; p. 214 (left) © J. P. Laffont/Sygma; p. 214 (right) Courtesy Peabody Museum of Salem, Salem, Massachusetts. Photograph by Mark Sexton; p. 216 © Chip Simons; p. 218 © AP/Kevork Kjansezian; p. 218 (inset) © Lennart Nilsson/Albert Bonniers Forlag AB; p. 219 © King Features. Reprinted with special permission of King Features Syndicate; p. 220 Courtesy Dr. Robert McCann

Chapter 6

p. 227 © Image Source/PunchStock; p. 229 (top) © Barry Christensen/Stock Boston; p. 229 (top middle) © Randy Duchane/The Stock Market; p. 229 (middle) © David Young-Wolff/Picture Quest; p. 229 (bottom middle) © Steve Dunwell/Getty Images/The Image Bank; p. 229 (bottom) © Pictor International/Picture Quest; p. 229 (bottom) © The New Yorker Collection, 1983, Edward Frascino from cartoonbank.com. All rights reserved; p. 232 (top) © Dean Press Images/The Image Works; p. 232 (bottom) © image100/SuperStock; p. 235 (top) © Karen Hunt H. Mason/Corbis; p. 235 (bottom) © Philip Lee Harvey/Getty Images/Stone; p. 237 (top left) © Stephen Dalton/Photo Researchers, Inc.; p. 237 (bottom left) © J. Stephens/SuperStock; p. 237 (bottom right) Courtesy San Diego Historical Society Union Tribune Collection; p. 238 (top) Courtesy Roger Broughton; p. 238 (bottom) © Richard Hutchings/PhotoEdit; p. 239 (top) © Will and Deni McIntyre/Photo Researchers, Inc.; p. 239 (bottom) © 1990 by Sidney Harris; p. 241 © J. Allan Hobson & Hoffman-LaRouche, Inc.; p. 246 (left) © Erich Lessing/Art Resource, NY; p. 246 (right) © Chagall, Marc. I and the Village. 1911. Oil on canvas. 6′ 3-5/8″ × 59-5/8″ (192.1cm × 151.4cm). The Museum of Modern Art, New York. Mrs. Simon Guggenheim Fund. Photograph © 2002, The Museum of Modern Art, New York; p. 248 © James Wilson/Woodfin Camp & Associates; p. 249 Stanford News Service; p. 257 (left and right) Reprinted with permission from Elsevier Science (*The Lancet*, 1998, vol. 352, pp. 1433–1437); p. 258 © PhotoDisc; p. 259 © Kelly & Massa Photography

Chapter 7

p. 267 © CP/TRSUN; p. 270 © The Granger Collection, New York; p. 273 Courtesy Professor Benjamin Harris; p. 278 © Nina Leen, Life Magazine/Timepix; p. 279 © Richard Cummins/Corbis; p. 280 © 1999, Jack Ziegler from cartoonbank.com. All rights reserved; p. 282 © Bob Krist/Leo de Wys; p. 285 © Bob Daemmrich/The Image Works; p. 286 (left) © Kevin Mackintosh/Getty Images/Stone; p. 286 (middle) © Image 100/Royalty-Free/Corbis; p. 286 (right) © Spencer Grant/PhotoEdit; p. 293 © Leo Cullum; p. 294 (all) © SuperStock; p. 296 Courtesy Animal Behaviour Enterprises, Inc.; p. 297 © Paul Chesley/National Geographic Society Image Collection

Chapter 8

p. 303 Reprinted with permission from *The Globe and Mail*; p. 305 (left, middle, and right) © 2002, Exploratorium, www.exploratorium.edu; p. 308 © Michael Fredericks/The Image Works; p. 310 © PhotoDisc; p. 314 Courtesy Endel Tulving; p. 315 Courtesy Endel Tulving; p. 317 FRANK & ERNEST reprinted by permission of Newspaper Enterprise Association, Inc.; p. 320 © The New Yorker Collection, 1986, Edward Koren from cartoonbankc.com. All rights reserved; p. 321 (left) © James L. Shaffer; p. 321 (middle) © G. Aschendorf/Photo Researchers, Inc.; p. 321 (right) © Bob Krist/Getty Images/Stone; p. 326 (left) © AP/Wide World Photos; p. 326 (right) © Reuters/Rick Wilking/Archive Photos; p. 329 (left) © AFP/Corbis; p. 329 (right) © AP/Vincent Thian; p. 333 © CP/Heather Spears; p. 334 Courtesy the Wellcome Institute Library, London; p. 339 © Sidney Harris

Chapter 9

p. 347 Courtesy J. R. Verougstraete; p. 348 Photograph and digital finishing by Marilyn Klein; p. 349 © PhotoDisc; p. 350 (top) © Peter Menzel/Stock Boston; p. 350 (bottom) © The New Yorker Collection, 1986, Edward Koren from cartoonbank.com. All rights reserved; p. 351 (top) Palazzo de Mula, Venice, Chester Dale Collection. © 2002 National Gallery of Art, Washington, 1908. Oil on canvas, .620 × .811 (24-1/2 × 31-7/8), framed .863 × 1.054 × .107 (34 × 41-1/2 × 4-1/4); p. 351 (bottom left) © Scala/Art Resource, NY; p. 351 (bottom right) Paul Klee, *Dance You Monster to my Soft Song*. 1972. Gift, Solomon R. Guggenheim, 1938. Photograph by Lee B. Ewing © The Solomon R. Guggenheim Foundation, New York. (FN 38.508); p. 354 © Stock Montage; p. 358 © Reuters NewMedia, Inc./Corbis; p. 359 © 1998 Sam Gross from cartoonbank.com. All rights reserved; p. 360 The pictures in this photo collage are from the Institute of Child Study, Ontario Institute for Studies in Education, University of Toronto. Knowledge Forum® is published by Learning in Motion, Inc.; p. 364 © The New Yorker Collection, 1990, Eric Teitelbaum from cartoonbank.com. All rights reserved; p. 365 (top) © Focus Films/Everett Collection STREVT; p. 365 (bottom) © Everett Collection STREVT/François Duhamel; p. 367 FRANK & ERNEST reprinted by permission of Newspaper Enterprise Association, Inc.; p. 368 (top) © Holton/SuperStock; p. 368 (bottom) © SuperStock; p. 369 (top)

Reprinted courtesy Omni Magazine © 1982; p. 369 (bottom) © James Balog; p. 370 © Enrico Ferorelli; p. 371 (top) From Curtiss, *Genie: A Psycholinguistic Study of a Modern Day "Wild Child."* © 1977 Academic Press, Orlando, FL; p. 371 (bottom) © AFP/Corbis; p. 373 © Digital Vision/Getty Images; p. 376 © Anthony Bannister/Animals Animals/Earth Scenes; p. 377 Courtesy Ellen Bialystok

Chapter 10

p. 385 (left) © AP/Wide World Photos; p. 385 (right) © 1985 FAR WORKS, Universal Press Syndicate; p. 387 Courtesy National Library of Medicine; p. 390 Courtesy Don Saklofske; p. 393 © The New Yorker Collection, 1987, Edward Koren, from cartoonbank.com. All rights reserved; p. 394 © 1980 Universal Press Syndicate. Reprinted with permission. All rights reserved; p. 397 © Erich Lessing/Art Resource, NY; p. 398 (top) © Shooting Start; p. 398 (bottom) © Project Spectrum; p. 399 © Donald Reilly, 1988, from The New Yorker Collection. All rights reserved; p. 403 © Jill Cannefax/EKM Nepenthe; p. 404 (top) © J. L. Bulcao/Getty Images; p. 404 (bottom) © Sidney Harris; p. 405 © John Alxom/Zuma; p. 406 (left) © CP/Frank Gunn; p. 406 (middle) © CP/Phill Snel; p. 406 (right) Courtesy Jim Cox/Salk Institute; p. 412 Courtesy Douglas Wahlsten; p. 413 (top left) © David Austen/Stock Boston; p. 413 (top right) © Gen Simmons/The Stock Market; p. 413 (bottom) © Sidney Harris

Chapter 11

p. 421 (top) © CP/Associated Press/Christophe Ena; p. 421 (bottom) © CP/Jon Murray; p. 429 © Dr. J. Sholtis, The Rockefeller University, New York, NY; p. 432 Courtesy Janet Polivy; p. 433 © Robert Hepler/Everett Collection Strevt; p. 438 (top left) © Bob Coyle; p. 438 (top right) © Anthony Mercieca/Photo Researchers, Inc.; p. 438 (bottom left) © Seven-Olof Lindblad/Photo Researchers, Inc.; p. 438 (bottom right) © Jan Cannefax/EKM Nepenthe; p. 439 © Barry O'Rourke/The Stock Market; p. 441 © Corbis; p. 443 Calvin and Hobbes © 1991 Watterson. Reprinted with permission of Universal Press Syndicate. All rights reserved; p. 446 © Robert A. Isaacs/Photo Researchers, Inc.; p. 448 Courtesy Natalie Durand-Bush; p. 452 © Bernard Gotfry/Woodfin Camp and Associates; p. 456 (top and bottom) © Donald Dutton; p. 458 (top left) © Dale Durfee/Getty Images/Stone; p. 458 (top middle) © SuperStock; p. 458 (top right) © Richard Lord/The Image Works; p. 458

(bottom left) © SuperStock; p. 458 (bottom middle) © SuperStock; p. 458 (bottom right) © Index Stock Imagery; p. 459 (left) © PhotoDisc; p. 459 (middle left) © PhotoDisc; p. 459 (middle right) © Paul Eckman; p. 459 (right) © Paul Eckman; p. 460 © Robert Harding Library; p. 464 (top) Richard Cline © 1988 from The New Yorker Collection. All rights reserved; p. 464 (bottom) © CP/KEL/Gary Moore; p. 465 (left) Courtesy Albert Kozma; p. 465 (right) Courtesy Michael Stones

Chapter 12

p. 471 (top) © National Portrait Gallery, Smithsonian Institution/Art Resource, NY; p. 471 (bottom) © CP/Fred Chartrand; p. 473 © Bettmann/Corbis; p. 474 © The New Yorker Collection, 1979, Dana Fradon from cartoonbank.com. All rights reserved; p. 477 © Bettmann/Corbis; p. 478 (top) © Bettmann/Corbis; p. 478 (bottom) © The Granger Collection, New York; p. 479 © Lucas Film; p. 482 © Bettmann/Corbis; p. 484 © Courtesy Martin Seligman; p. 486 © Center for the Study of the Person; p. 488 © CP/Fred Chartrand; p. 496 © Sidney Harris; p. 498 © Reprinted by permission of the publishers from Henry A. Murray, "Thematic Apperception Test," Cambridge, MA: Harvard University Press. © 1943 by the President and Fellows of Harvard College; p. 501 © Michael Newman/PhotoEdit; p. 502 Courtesy Douglas Jackson

Chapter 13

p. 509 Courtesy Norman Endler; p. 511 © CP/SKTN/Richard Marjan; p. 519 © Scala/Art Resource, NY; p. 521 © CP/TRSTR/Michael Stuparyk; p. 522 (top) © The New Yorker Collection, 1983, Mischa Richter from cartoonbank.com. All rights reserved; p. 522 (bottom) © Rex USA; p. 523 © Lewis Baxter/Peter Arnold Inc.; p. 524 (top left) © CP/Jonathan Hayward; p. 524 (top middle) © Monica Anderson/Stock Boston; p. 524 (top right) © AFP/Corbis; p. 524 (bottom) © Christopher Brown/Stock Boston; p. 527 © 1974 The Washington Post. Photo by Gerald Martineau; p. 529 © Erich Lessing/Art Resource, NY; p. 532 Courtesy Lewis Baxter and Michael Phelps/UCLA School of Medicine; p. 538 (left)

© Bettmann/Corbis; p. 538 (right) © Alain Benainous/Getty Images; p. 541 (left) © *Landscape*, 1907 by August Neter. Reprinted by permission of Prinzhorn-Sammlung der Psychiatrischen Universitätsklinik Heidelberg; p. 541 (right) © Grunnitus/Monkmeyer Press; p. 543 (top) © Monte S. Buchsbaum, M.D., Mt. Sinai School of Medicine, New York, NY; p. 543 (bottom left) © Monte S. Buchsbaum, M.D., Mt. Sinai School of Medicine, New York, NY; p. 543 (bottom right) © Courtesy the Genain quadruplets; p. 545 © Bob Daemmrich/The Image Works; p. 546 © CP/Phill Snel

Chapter 14

p. 553 © AP/Tina Fineberg/Stringer; p. 559 © W&O McIntyre/Photo Researchers, Inc.; p. 560 © The New Yorker Collection, 1994, Gahan Wilson from cartoonbank.com. All rights reserved; p. 561 © Historical Pictures/Stock Montage; p. 562 (left) © Scala/Art Resrouce, NY; p. 562 (right) © The New Yorker Collection, 1973, Dana Fradon from cartoonbank.com. All rights reserved; p. 564 © Courtesy Deke Simon; p. 566 © David Frazier Photo Library, Inc.; p. 567 (all) Courtesy Albert Bandura; p. 568 © Mary Levin/University of Washington; p. 576 © Michael Newman/PhotoEdit; p. 577 © Bob Daemmrich/Stock Boston; p. 580 (top) Courtesy Cornelia Wieman; p. 580 (bottom) Courtesy Laurence Kirmayer

Chapter 15

p. 593 Courtesy www.normancousins.org and Dr. Michael Irwin; p. 594 (top) © George V. Mann, Sc.D., M.D.; p. 594 (bottom) © David Stoecklein/The Stock Market; p. 595 © Sidney Harris; p. 596 © The New Yorker Collection, 1987, Donald Reilly from cartoonbank.com. All rights reserved; p. 600 © SuperStock; p. 601 © Catherine Gehm; p. 602 www.mortonbeiser.com. Photo by David Morgan, New York; p. 605 Photo by Todd Cheney. Courtesy Dr. Shelley Taylor; p. 608 © Mckes/Ottawa/Photo Researchers; p. 613 © 1999, Tom Cheney, from cartoonbank.com. All rights reserved; p. 618 (main photo) © Nabeel Turner/Getty Images/Stone; p. 618 (top left) © Don Smetzer/Getty Images/Stone; p. 618 (top

right) © David Austen/Getty Images/Stone; p. 618 (bottom left) © David Austen/Getty Images/Stone; p. 618 (bottom right) © CP/Kevin Frayer; p. 619 © Cary Wolkinsky/Stock Boston; p. 620 © Peter Gregoire Photography; p. 623 © John P. Kelly/Getty Images/The Image Bank; p. 624 © John Elk; p. 628 © Lloyd Wolf

Chapter 16

p. 635 © CP/Ryan Remiorz; p. 638 © Romilly Lockyear/Getty Images/The Image Bank; p. 639 © John P. Kelly/Getty Images/The Image Bank; p. 640 © 1996, USA Today. Reprinted with permission; p. 647 © William Vandivert; p. 650 (top) © 1965 by Stanley Milgram, from the film Obedience, distributed by Penn State Media Sales; p. 650 (bottom) © AP/Wide World Photos; p. 651 (top) © Scott T. Smith/Corbis; p. 651 (bottom) © Hughes Martin/Corbis; p. 652 (top) © Andrea Pistolesi/Getty Images/The Image Bank; p. 652 (bottom) © CP/Paul Chaisson; p. 653 © The New Yorker Collection, 1979, Henry Martin from cartoonbank.com. All rights reserved; p. 654 (top) © AP/Wide World Photos; p. 654 (bottom) © Alberto Garcia/Getty Images; p. 657 (top and bottom) © Reuters New Media Inc./Corbis; p. 658 (top left) © Bill Gillette/Stock Boston; p. 658 (top middle) © CP/TRSTR/Melanie Sochan; p. 658 (top right) © Larry Kolvoord/The Image Works; p. 658 (bottom) © Alison Derry; p. 660 Courtesy Mark Zanna; p. 663 (top) © Cleo Photography; p. 663 (bottom) © Mary Kate Denny/PhotoEdit; p. 665 (top) © Bettmann/Corbis; p. 665 (bottom) © AP/Wide World Photos; p. 668 Calvin & Hobbes © 1995 Watterson. Reprinted with permission of Universal Press Syndicate. All rights reserved; p. 670 © The New Yorker Collection, 1989, Peter Steiner from cartoonbank.com. All rights reserved; p. 672 (left) © Kent Reno/Jeroboam; p. 672 (right) © David Young-Wolff/PhotoEdit; p. 673 © David W. Hamilton/Getty Images/The Image Bank; p. 676 (left) © Courtesy the Academy of Motion Picture Arts and Sciences; p. 676 (right) DILBERT reprinted by permission of United Features Syndicate, Inc.; p. 679 © David Young-Wolff/PhotoEdit; p. 680 © The New Yorker Collection, 2000, Mick Stevens from cartoonbank.com. All rights reserved.

Name Index

Subject Index

AIR COMMAND

FIGHTERS AND BOMBERS OF WORLD WAR II

Jeffrey L. Ethell

Lowe & B. Hould
Publishers

This edition published in 1997 by Lowe and B. Hould, an imprint of Borders, Inc., 515 East Liberty, Ann Arbor, MI 48104 Lowe & B. Hould Publishers is a trademark of Borders Properties, Inc.

BOMBER COMMAND first published in 1994 by Motorbooks International Publishers & Wholesalers, 729 Prospect Ave, PO Box 1, Osceola, WI 54020-0001 USA

© Jeffrey L. Ethell, 1994

All rights reserved. With the exception of quoting brief passages for the purposes of review no part of this publication may be reproduced without prior written permission from the Publisher

Motorbooks International is a certified trademark, registered with the United States Patent Office

The information in this book is true and complete to the best of our knowledge. All recommendations are made without any guarantee on the part of the author or Publisher, who also disclaim any liability incurred in connection with the use of this data or specific details

We recognize that some words, model names and designations, for example, mentioned herein are the property of the trademark holder. We use them for identification purposes only. This is not an official publication

Library of Congress Cataloging-in-Publication Data Available
ISBN 0-681-22745-1

On the front cover: The Republic P-47D Thunderbolt was powered by an air cooled, radial eighteen cylinder Pratt & Whitney R-2800 Double Wasp engine that enabled the big fighter to reach maximum speeds of 428 miles per hour. *Warren Bodie*

On the frontispiece: Copilot Lieutenant William C. Rowland from New Castle, Pennsylvania, off to war from England in a B-24. Relationships on the flight deck could be good, could be bad. A great deal depended upon the attitude of the aircraft commander in the left seat. Some gave their copilots half of the flying time, while others were of the "gear up, flaps up, shut up" variety. *USAF*

Printed in Hong Kong

Contents

Introduction

At its height in World War II, the US Army Air Forces had 2,411,294 men and women in uniform. By the time the war was over, the Army Air Forces would take delivery of almost 230,000 aircraft to be flown by 193,440 pilots. By far the majority of the Army Air Forces' effort went into manning the service's bombers, the very heart of American air power doctrine. The numbers built of each type were staggering: 12,677 B-17s at $204,370 each in 1944; 18,188 B-24s (more than any single American aircraft in history) for $215,515 each; 9,815 B-25s at $142,194 each; 5,157 B-26s at $192,427 each; 3,760 B-29s for $605,360 each; 7,230 A-20s at $100,800 each; and 2,446 A-26s at $192,457 each.

Between Pearl Harbor and VJ-Day, the army aircrew training machine used 475 facilities, 30,000 aircraft, and a million people to train 497,533 aircraft and engine mechanics, 347,236 gunners, 195,422 radio mechanics and operators, 50,976 navigators, 47,354 bombardiers, and 193,440 pilots. Between December 1942 and August 1945, most of these personnel ended up in or worked on a bomber. Over 29,350 heavy bombardment crews were formed, and 7,600 medium and light bomber crews were created.

The army gave these men a base pay, to which could be added flying pay and foreign-service pay. In 1945 a technical sergeant made $114 a month; with flying pay added, that went up to $171. Total pay for service overseas came to $193.80 a month. A captain earned $200 per month; if he flew, his pay climbed to $300. On foreign service, the total could be $320.

Of all the combat jobs in the American services during World War II, from infantryman to submariner, no job was more dangerous, statistically, than that of a man in a bomber over Germany. The Eighth and Fifteenth Air Forces took a higher percentage of losses than any other American fighting force, from foxhole to destroyer deck. Though the glamour of the Army Air Corps (as it continued to be known regard-

Two red flares arc up from a 381st Bomb Group B-17 on short final at Ridgewell—wounded aboard! The Dodge "meat wagon" was a standard fixture at all Eighth Air Force fields. A bomb group usually had more than one on hand at the end of a mission. USAF

less of the name change in 1941) seemed to shine throughout the war, the air war was not clean or safe. It was murderous.

Flying 264,618 bomber and 257,321 fighter sorties from England, the Eighth Air Force lost 4,148 B-17s and B-24s; 2,042 fighters were also lost, with 43,742 airmen killed or missing and another 1,923 seriously wounded. The Fifteenth Air Force flew 148,955 bomber and 87,732 fighter sorties out of Italy, losing a proportionate number of men. Once transferred from the Mediterranean, the Ninth Air Force, though mostly a fighter air force, flew 368,500 sorties to lose 2,139 fighters and 805 bombers (and a few other types). The Twelfth Air Force, based in North Africa, Sicily, and Italy, flew 430,681 sorties, losing 2,667 aircraft. Royal Air Force Bomber Command, though supposedly protected by flying at night, lost 55,573 men, a 20 percent casualty rate, greater than any single fighting force except the German U-boats. To be in a bomber of any kind during World War II was not a safe proposition.

Nevertheless, in spite of severe testing of even the highest morale, particularly during the summer and fall of 1943, American bomber crews did their jobs day after day, going up against the roughest flak and fighter defenses ever conceived. Because prewar planners believed bombers could get through without fighter protection had a great deal to do with the number of American losses. Army Air Forces commander General Henry H. "Hap" Arnold had the integrity to say it was the service's own fault that the P-51 did not arrive on the scene until late 1943.

When some bomber commanders remained stubbornly insistent that their bombers could still get through without fighters, Arnold quickly removed them from command, placed them elsewhere, and put aggressive believers in the fighter in their place. American bomber losses dropped from 9.1 percent per mission in October 1943 to 3.5 percent in March 1944 as long-range fighters engaged Luftwaffe fighters intent on getting to the bombers. By that time, planners had finally concentrated on what turned out to be the most vital enemy target, oil production, and the German war machine quickly ground to a halt in spite of increased industrial production.

Regardless of the continual banter between the bomber crews and the fighter pilots who flew escort for them, each held nothing but the highest respect for the other when it came down to doing their jobs. There was nothing more gut wrenching than watching a bomber go down out of control with men trapped inside . . . or a fighter outnumbered and trying to fight off a swarm of German fighters to protect the bombers, then getting clobbered in the process. There were no foxholes in the air.

As a companion volume to my book *Fighter Command* (Motorbooks International, 1991), *Bomber Command* has the same aim of turning a black-and-white war into one of color, brought to life with first person narrative. A few years ago I would have thought it nearly impossible to get enough vintage color to write more than one all-color book on World War II, but I have been proven wonderfully wrong by the generosity of the veterans and fellow historians who supplied the photos you see here. Fortunately for history, some Army Air Forces personnel carried their cameras, often against regulations, and asked for Kodachrome instead of cookies in their letters home.

To the following I owe a great debt of gratitude for trusting me to bring their wartime color to a new generation: Robert Astrella; Fred Bamberger; Duane J. Reed at the US Air Force Academy; Joe Kingsbury; Ole Griffith; Roger Freeman (for access to his files and for permission to quote interviews with Sam Wilson, John Ramsey, Lalli Coppinger, and Pecos Reeves); Arnold Delmonico; Byron Trent; Al Keeler (who also provided wartime memories); National Air & Space Museum staff members Dan Hagedorn, Melissa Keiser, Tim Cronen, and Mark Avino; Jack Havener (who provided not only his slides but also permission to quote from his excellent writing); Norman Jackson; Morris and Richard Davidson; Bill Skinner; James Wilson; Claude Porter; Lyle McCarty of the 459th Bomb Group Association (who also gave permission to quote from his wartime memoir *Coffee Tower*); John Devney, also of the 459th Bomb Group Association; David Menard; Mrs. M. M. Leigh; Jim Dietz; John Meyers; Albert Krassman; Roland Scott; Glenn Tessmer; Stan Piet; Leslie Peterson; Clark B. Rollins, Jr.; F. M. "Pappy" Grove (who also wrote an extensive series of recollections to go along with his slides); D. C. R. "Chris" Elliott and Andrew Renwick at the Royal Air Force Museum; Claude Murray and Ed Hoffman of the 7th Photo Group Association; Richard H. Denison; Jim Stitt; Herb Rutland; Cal Sloan; and Larry Hendel.

Photos alone could never bring the air war to life. The planes were maintained and flown by people who, happily, knew how to tell their experiences in such a way as to bring the reader back in time with them. That bomber war has come alive in a unique way thanks to all of you who took the time and effort to let me know how it really was: Bob DeGroat, both father and son (who provided an extensive series of memoirs called *Adventures in Military Flying* and *POW File*); Mark Hutchins (for interviews with Richard Fitzhugh, Bob Nourie, and Bud Abbot); Fred Alexander (for tapes of Corrine Wall and Bob Morgan); Ben Smith (for permission to quote from his book *Chick's Crew*, self-published, 1983); Tom Gabay (for sharing his father John's memoirs); Roy Kennett; Bob and Willetta Shoens; Bob Gillman (for permission to quote from his *Memoirs of War and Peace*); Mary Lou Neale; Charles Watry (for permission to quote from his book *Washout!*, California Aero Press, 1983); B. C. Reed; Philip Ardery (for permission to quote from his book *Bomber Pilot*, University Press of Kentucky, 1978); Ken Kailey; Ken Hamilton; Jim Bakewell; A. H. Albrecht; Ralph J. Watson, Jr. (for permission to quote from his father's memoirs); Fritz Nowosad; Hubert Cripe; Robert Keir; Ed Leighty; Johnny Miller; Frank Morrison; C. E. "Bud" Anderson (for permission to quote from his book *To Fly and Fight*, St. Martin's Press, 1990); Bud Guillot; Louis Kandl; George Meshko; Bob Kennedy; Alfred Price (my long time co-historian, who supplied a constant stream of material); Hans Iffland; Friedrich Stehle; Lowell Watts; John Flottorp; and Fred Weiner.

CHAPTER 1

Bomber Crew

Richard Fitzhugh
B-17 pilot, 457th Bomb Group

When I was a youngster, about five years old, my father was a traveling salesman. One week out of the month Ralph took him to one of the local country stores in the county. Sometimes he would take me with him. We stopped for lunch with sardines and the cheese box and crackers, and he would put me up on the counter when some of the lunch bunch at the country store would come by, and he'd say, "Dickie, what do you want to be when you grow up?" I'd say, "I want to fight the Germans!" I don't know where I got this from. This would be in about 1927. I was born in 1922. I guess somewhere in my early youth I'd been hearing about World War I, but this was in my mind. I started early in making model airplanes of balsa wood. I'd take them up on the roof of the house, line them up, set them on fire, and watch them go sailing off.

Of course, I knew about Lindbergh. I remember a barnstormer came to our hometown of Charlottesville, Virginia. I must have been probably seven years old at this point, and I wanted to go touch the airplane. The sign said, "Don't touch." I wanted to go touch it anyway, and the pilot came over, and very gruffly said, "Get away! You might stick your finger through it." I was taken aback a little bit.

Somehow or other I had just developed an interest in airplanes. I used to go up to Washington, D.C., and spend summers out on Columbia Pike in Arlington. At that time, the national airport was Hoover Field, where the Pentagon is now. They had a swimming pool there—the airport swimming pool. We would walk down Columbia Pike to the swimming pool; you could walk across the runway in those days. They had a gate like you do at a railroad track. We'd go down there and watch what was known then as the "Great Silver Fleet" take off: beautiful Eastern Airlines and American Airlines airplanes. I think it was Eastern that was called the "Great Silver Fleet." These were all C-47s and DC-3s. Just spectacular as a kid to stand there by the run-

Bomber transition B-17Fs at sunset after a long day surviving the rigors of teaching new crews how to handle a heavy bomber. Zone of Interior (ZI or stateside) training aircraft were worn out at a furious pace, from both use and accidents. Never before had such a large-scale experiment been attempted in teaching neophytes to handle state-of-the-art technology. *USAF*

The Air Corps that was, and was never to be again, in the calm before the storm. These US Army Air Corps officers and their beautiful friends stand in front of the massive Boeing XB-15 at Bolling Field, Washington, D.C., in the winter snow of 1940. Though the underpowered B-15 was never destined to be much more than a prototype, it paved the way for heavy bomber development, the core of airpower doctrine that would shape the strategies of World War II. *NASM Arnold Collection*

way and watch these things go. I think some of that had to do with me wanting to get into the Army Air Corps. I wasn't much into the movies; I'd much rather be making model airplanes and setting them on fire or watching the real thing!

One day I was out to lunch, and I passed the recruiting station. Big signs out there showed the B-17—all these beautiful recruiting posters. Somebody was with me, and we both decided to go in and sign up, so we did. Just like that. That was in May of '42, and they didn't call me until October.

B. C. Reed
B-18 copilot, 17th Bomb Group

This little boy's dream came true when I graduated from the Air Corps Advanced Fly-

ing School, Class of 40-E, at Kelly Field, Texas, on August 30, 1940, as a second lieutenant, US Army Air Corps, with rating as pilot. "I wanted Wings." Now I officially wore silver wings! And a Sam Browne belt with a saber. Wow!

Several of us became copilots in the three squadrons of the 17th Group. We didn't realize it at the time, but we were enjoying the last days of the old peacetime Air Corps, with Wednesday and Friday afternoons off, and completely free weekends (one Saturday morning a month we had a dress parade). We were considered "student officers" for three more months, with more ground school.

We expected to remain copilots and second lieutenants for years. In 1940, second

lieutenants were told to expect serving seven years before making first lieutenant, and then *at least* five more years before even being considered for captain, *if* we were good enough to still be on active duty.

Bob DeGroat
PT-23 pilot, primary flight training

At one point we got alternating aerobatic maneuvers. I could hardly wait to get in my snap-and-a-half specialty. I announced my intentions and concentrated hard. The maneuver came out solidly and precisely. As I proudly looked into the rearview mirror for approval and respect from my instructor in the rear cockpit, I was horrified to see nobody there. I immediately righted the trainer and began sweeping turns, looking for a parachute or a falling body. At last I saw a slight bobbing motion in the rear cockpit and recognized the top of a helmet just barely showing as it rocked with mirth.

My instructor had lowered his seat to the bottom while I was preparing my show-off maneuver and curled himself out of sight. He finished me off with his own top maneuver, which was to go inverted, do two clearing turns while inverted, and then enter into an inverted spin.

I knew when I'd been topped.

A brand spanking new Boeing B-17D Flying Fortress assigned to Wright Field's Air Development Center for service tests in 1941. Advanced versions of this single type would dominate wartime planning, carrying a new generation of crews into combat around the world. In spite of prewar isolationism, the "Fort" was ready for mass production on a hitherto unheard of scale. *NASM Groenhoff Collection*

13

Engine change on an early Douglas A-20 Havoc during the 1941 Louisiana Maneuvers, which attempted for the first time to combine air and ground forces in some form of cohesive whole. Lighter attack aircraft (most twin-engine types) were the other side of the newly renamed US Army Air Forces' bomber doctrine. There was some serious attention to tactical, or close air support, aviation, though this aspect of the service was somewhat of a stepchild. That would change drastically by 1944, when tactical air forces were looked upon as vital to moving troops forward in the field. *NASM Arnold Collection*

Charles Watry
PT-22 pilot, primary flight training

Dubbed the "Maytag Messerschmitt," the PT-22 had a fighter-plane look about it and handled as well as a fighter, too. The engine had a distinctive *pockata-pockata* sound to it, giving the impression of a slow-turning engine, which it was. Even on takeoff, the engine sounded as if it were not turning up enough revs to get the trainer off the ground.

Ben Smith
B-17 radio operator, 303rd Bomb Group

We came east on a troop train that seemed to make no progress at all. It toiled on for days, chugging and wheezing and clanking along, stopping for hours at a time, then backing up for miles, then stopping and starting again. Our route took us through the Royal Gorge of Colorado, the only bright spot of the trip. Sometimes we would sit on a siding, sweating and dirty, as a streamliner flashed by us at lightning speed, compounding our discomfort. We could see the fat cats in the dining car giving us the fish eye over their horn-rimmed spectacles as they had their morning coffee, ham and eggs, and newspapers. We ate our powdered eggs and cursed them roundly. The troop trains were pulled by the old iron-horse locomotives. Because of the heat we rode with

Shortly after the attack on Pearl Harbor, many Army and Navy units were assigned to coastal patrol because of fear of an enemy invasion. One of the more promising new medium bombers in line squadrons at the time was the North American B-25 Mitchell. This B-25A of the 2nd Bomb Group was based on the East Coast in early 1942 for antisubmarine patrol. *NASM Arnold Collection*

With the B-17E, which first rolled out in September 1941, came the definitive shape of the Flying Fortress that would become so famous in World War II. With numerous improvements, particularly in defensive fire power, and with the addition of a tail gunner's position, this version carried the brunt of the Army Air Forces' initial strategic bombing effort over Europe and the Pacific. *USAF*

16

the windows up. There was no air conditioning. The cinders were flying about like sooty snowflakes. Rivulets of dirty sweat streamed down our faces, our clothes became filthy, and we stank abominably. Of all the humbling experiences I ever had, there was nothing to compare with a troop train.

Right off the bat O'Hearn and I got caught for being out of uniform and were put on K.P. for the duration of the trip eastward. It was not so great a transgression—they needed some full time K.P.s, and we were elected. One of the cars was set aside for the preparation and cooking of food. We had been on duty for eighteen hours and

were about to go off. I had a bright idea. We would make some bologna sandwiches, wrap them up in wax paper, and peddle them to the officers. This was no problem as we had the kitchen to ourselves. We did a land-office business for the rest of the trip and made a lot of money. The mess officer could not understand what was happening to all his bologna. We did not enlighten him.

Ken Hamilton
AT-6 mechanic, factory airfield

At times us Yanks got a good dose of British upper-class ways, and it wasn't often we could get some satisfaction. Few of us

A never-to-be-forgotten sight for a new Army Air Forces cadet: the entrance to the West Point of the air, Randolph Field, Texas, where the Army centered the training of its pilots. When President Franklin Roosevelt issued his prewar call for building 50,000 planes a year, the military services pushed up their student pilot quotas to meet the demand. This influx of men and machines proved to be a crucial factor in helping the United States to withstand the early dark days of World War II. *Fred E. Bamberger*

will forget one of the arrivals made by the British squadron leader assigned to American factories in southern California. Approaching from the east in a Douglas Boston, he started to let down with the gear up. The North American and Douglas flight ramp mechanics ran out, wildly waving, trying to get him to go around. He looked out the open left side of the cockpit window, acknowledged the waving with a snappy salute, flared beautifully at gear-down height, plopped onto the runway, and slid to a halt. He climbed out, strode rapidly to a car, and left without a word.

Bob DeGroat
BT-13 pilot, basic flight training

Stages could be considered as landing performance exams. They taxied a BT over to the west side of the field and used it as a radio control and reviewing stand for the instructors who were to do the evaluating. The cadets were to make four three-point landings. Evaluation was based on approach, landing control, form, and proximity to a hypothetical spot directly in front of the parked control plane.

As luck would have it, I was really "on" this day. I strung together probably the best four BT landings that I ever made, and stuck them in with my wing tip dead in front of the "judges." After my fourth landing (which I thought at the time was only ordinary), I got a faint, garbled instruction that disappointingly did not release me to return to the main field, but to make still another landing. So I took off again and came around for landing—only this time I overshot a little.

To set it down right in front of the con-

17

America in 1942 was a burgeoning flurry of technology, from military aircraft to entertainment, and new pilots took to both with more than enough eagerness. The award-winning film, *Mrs. Miniver* and the stage show, *At Ease* are playing here at Radio City Music Hall in the summer of that year (not that anyone actually wanted to see the long-legged Rockettes kick up their heels). New York City was a magnet for men with wings.
Albert J. Keeler

trol plane, I had to fly it onto the ground with the tail high. I had no sooner done this when the radio exploded again in unintelligible chaos, ending with sending me back to the main field.

The mystery was cleared up when I next saw my instructor. He greeted me with, "Boy, did you put on a show yesterday! You not only put in four perfect landings, but when they asked you to try an extra one and make it a wheel landing, you stuck that one in, too." I never let on.

Ben Smith
B-17 radio operator, 303rd Bomb Group

The B-17 was never used as a night bomber, yet strangely enough, almost all of our cross-country flying training was done at night. Once on a night mission we were almost involved in a midair collision, the first of many. There were no radar stations handling air traffic, as nowadays. Our mission took us by Pensacola, Florida, where there was a big naval flying school. We blundered right into the traffic pattern of a bunch of student pilots shooting night landings. Chick pulled sharply to miss one airplane that was heading straight toward us. We had it hot and heavy there for a few moments. All of us went to the windows to watch out for the tiny airplanes that were buzzing all around us. I'll bet we scared them a lot worse than they scared us.

Bob DeGroat
AT-10 pilot, advanced twin engine flight training

The last day before graduation (which

The "Washing Machine" . . . there was no better description of the Boeing Stearman PT-17 Kaydet. For most cadets, this was the first aircraft they would fly in primary— a rude awakening for most. Large and prone to ground-looping because of its narrow landing gear and a high center of gravity, this aircraft was very difficult for inexperienced pilots to master, getting its nickname from "washing out" so many cadets from flight training. *NASM Groenhoff Collection*

meant receiving your wings and lieutenant's bars at last) was supposed to be a relaxed, fun flying day. The assignment was a low-level cross-country designed to sharpen identification of physical checkpoints and map reading, but was understood by student and instructor alike to be a legalized "buzz job." In my own case, during the early moments of the trip, every time I glanced at my instructor in the copilot seat, his hand seemed to subtly indicate that I was too high. It was great fun. We went down val-leys, climbed over tree lines and high tension wires, scared some livestock, and even startled a few people driving on the highway.

Bob Gillman
B-24 pilot, advanced four engine bomber transition

Following graduation, my orders were to go to the Student Training Detachment at Smyrna, Tennessee, which was twelve miles south of Nashville, for transition into the B-

Eric W. Holtz with a Stearman during primary at Union City, Tennessee, in the summer of 1943. Clearly the airplane has been worked hard—with fading, old Army Air Corps blue and yellow paint, nonstandard by this time, and a replacement aileron painted with silver dope. No one was really worried about matching paint because of the hectic pace of training so many pilots. *Albert J. Keeler*

The view from Army cadet Ole Griffith's primary training PT-17 at Dorr Field, Alabama, in 1943. The flight line was always crowded and always busy, with instructors, students, and linemen sending a continual stream of junior birdmen into the air. Though the Stearman was a throwback to an earlier age of baling wire and fabric biplanes, it was an excellent introduction to handling large aircraft prone to ground loops. *Ole C. Griffith*

24 Liberator bomber. SAAF [Smyrna Army Air Field] was an excellent base with mostly brick buildings, an officers club, and bachelor officer quarters. Other facilities included an officers bowling alley, swimming pools, and several Hamburger Havens, even on the flight line. Now, this was a "real" military air base, where flying took place around the clock. Nevertheless, we were still basking in the glory of being saluted and addressed as "Sir!" We also realized that this was where the really serious business began.

On February 25, 1944, we were taken down to the flight line and shown the B-24. Four student officers were assigned to an instructor, who spent two hours going over the entire aircraft, inside and out. I will never forget climbing up on the flight deck and seeing the cockpit for the first time. The instrument panel stretched from the extreme left to the extreme right of the cockpit and was covered entirely with instruments. There were controls and levers on the left side of the pilot's area from the front panel to behind the seat back, and from the window sill to the floor. Same on the right side. The center pedestal held not only the four throttles, but also four mixture controls, four turbocharger controls, four propeller controls, four cowl flap switches, and four of many other things. Landing gear and flap levers were by the pilot's and copilot's knees, respectively. Even the ceiling was covered with radio controls from front to rear and left to right. Immediately below the landing

The intermediate training step in an Army pilot's career was basic, where the Vultee BT-13 Valiant provided a bit more complexity. Better known as the "Virbrator," this fixed gear, 450 horsepower craft had most of the systems common to more advanced types, including a controllable-pitch propeller and flaps. For the most part, pilots couldn't wait to get out of basic flight training and into their advanced phase. *Fred E. Bamberger*

gear lever, by the pilot's right leg, was a red "T" handle, which was the bomb salvo lever. Pulled up to the first notch, it opened the bomb bay doors. Pulling further to the limit dropped the entire bomb load. This was obviously a true emergency control, which I did not realize at that moment would be used before the year 1944 was past. Needless to say, we were all overwhelmed by what we had just witnessed and hardly believed we would ever master this cockpit!

Bob DeGroat
B-24 pilot, advanced four engine bomber transition

My first close-up examination of a Con-solidated B-24 Liberator was to stand up and view the inside through the lower waist hatch of a parked aircraft. I looked in wonder at the barn-like space, having only just graduated from Globe AT-10s. I had been quoted in my early transition training as comparing the flight deck visibility in the B-24 to "flying a hotel from the basement window."

Visualize a flight line full of fledgling pilots all trying to taxi their first tricycle-geared aircraft. It not only has twice the engines and throttles, but also is twice the size of anything they have handled before. Note that this is under the impatient guidance of disgruntled instructors who are trying to get off the ground and on with their boring day of instructing extremely green pilots.

One of the first instructions that my co-student received when he first got in the left seat was to adjust the seat fore-and-aft and up-and-down to get comfortable, then check his position so he could be assured of making the same seat adjustments the next time. Therefore, when it became time for me to take the left seat in the air midway through the flying period, I looked for a surefire check for seat height. Looking out the window on my side, I found that I could just see the marker light on the wing tip over the outboard engine nacelle.

The next day, when it was my turn to be first in the left seat, I tried to use this check

Intrepid Army basic student Ole Griffith climbs into his BT-13 at Gunter Field, Alabama, September 1943 on his way to becoming a photo-mapping pilot in F-10s, the photo version of the B-25 Mitchell. *Ole C. Griffith*

Lieutenant Johnny King flying a North American BT-14 out of Randolph Field, Texas, May 1942. Though the BT-14 looked a great deal like its bigger brother, the AT-6, it was actually an older fixed gear aircraft with less power and a fabric-covered fuselage. When the BT-13 became available in large numbers, the older '14 left the scene, having served since well before the beginning of the war. *Fred E. Bamberger*

At last—advanced twin-engine pilot training. A Beechcraft AT-10 Wichita from Freeman Field, Indiana, late 1943. The AT-10 was a wood-and-fabric airplane with a single purpose for existence: getting multi-engine pilots trained as fast as possible and pushing them into operational units. As a result, the AT-10 was born, lived, and died all within the war years. *Ole C. Griffith*

to adjust the seat height, but my head hit the canopy and my feet wouldn't reach the rudder pedals. That long Davis wing of the B-24 was very limber and flexed as much as three feet in flight—I had proof. Later, on a cross-country trip in turbulent air, I was able to see motion not unlike a jump rope when I viewed the wing from the nose compartment. Impressive, but quite frightening.

I was familiar with engine-out procedures, with their accompanying drag and corrective trim techniques, from flying the Globe AT-10 in Advanced Training. However, I was not ready for the drag problems of an outboard engine failure in the B-24. For-

tunately, the rudder pedals on the B-24 were large enough to accommodate both feet, and I was encouraged to do this by my instructor, at least until I became familiar enough with the engine-out procedure to get corrective trim in quickly. Some instructors, mine included, might occasionally "pull" an outboard engine on you and then refuse to let you use trim for correction. The alternative was to put both feet on the one pedal to hold opposite rudder, lock your knees, then hope that your seat belt was snug enough to keep you from sliding up the back of the seat. It didn't take long for the strain to set your legs to quaking from the unrelieved pres-

The Cessna AT-17, or UC-78, Bobcat served across the United States as a multi-engine advanced trainer. Originally developed as a civil light transport, Cessna's first twin came along at just the right time to be ordered in great numbers for the war effort. Nicknamed the "Bamboo Bomber" for its wood-and-fabric construction, the bulbous aircraft got stuck with a number of other less flattering names, including the "Useless 78" and the "Double-Breasted Cub." *USAF*

Another in a string of advanced multi-trainers was the Curtiss AT-9 Jeep, certainly the oddest and the most difficult twin to handle of the lot. With only two seats, the jeep was small, a beast of a ground-looper, and difficult to fly on one engine. If a pilot got through its quirks and graduated, he could fly just about anything given to him. *USAF*

sure. Many a sadistic instructor took out his frustrations in viewing the vibrating, sweating student that he had created.

Bob Nourie
B-26 pilot, advanced twin engine bomber transition

We flew a few copilot missions in AT-23s or the B-26, towing targets in planes that were being flown by the WASP pilots—some of the most experienced WASP pilots that they had. Boy, those girls could fly. They were people with a lot of flying time, cer-

tainly more experienced than most new military pilots. These were relatively young women. Those very experienced ones were in their thirties, maybe thirty-five, thirty-eight. Very experienced pilots. I flew copilot for some of those. Some of them flew B-24s, and they had to practice for the gunners.

Mary Lou Neale
A-20 pilot, Women Airforce Service Pilot

In ferrying, love of flying *had* to win over fondness for comfort, if one wanted to stay in that command. Primary trainers and fight-

When bombardiers went to school, they flew in the Beechcraft AT-11 fitted with a Norden bombsight, a full set of bomb release gadgets, and an internal bomb bay—just like the real thing. These AT-11s are heading back from the range to the SAAAF Bomb School at Concho, Texas, January 1943 with their cadet bombardiers aboard. *Fred E. Bamberger*

A bombardier cadet (left) sits with his instructor in the nose of a SAAAF Bomb School AT-11, January 1943. Quite often these men were washed-out, would-be pilots assigned to bombardier or navigator school, much to their disappointment. The stigma was one not easily gotten over, though bombardiers were crucial to the success of the bombers' missions. At least pilots had a skill they could transfer to peacetime. What would a bombardier do? *Fred E. Bamberger*

An AT-11 is fueled up
on the line at Ontario
Army Air Base,
California, in late
1944. The snow-capped
mountains to the
north formed a
stunning backdrop to
this field, which
primarily served as a
major P-38 transition
base. The AT-11s had
to fly over this range
to get to the dry lake
bed bombing range at
Muroc, an ideal site
for dropping all kinds
of exploding ordnance.
Norman W. Jackson

ers had one thing in common—both had miserable cockpits for the long haul. One was either hot or cold, rattling around in a windswept cavern or cramped into a miniature oven. But now and then appeared a miracle—like the cushiony A-20. Orders to take this sturdy beauty with its luxurious armchair in a glassed-in room to Canada seemed like a gift too good to be true. It was. There was another name on it: "Staff Sergeant Louis Stamp, Radio Operator." These A-20s, named "Bostons" by the British, were not equipped with cockpit radio for ferrying, so a crew member sitting in the nose was necessary.

Staff Sergeant Stamp turned out to be a short, muscular, stone-faced veteran of few

words, mostly grunts. On rotation after overseas duty, he and four other sergeants were to operate the radio for the five A-20s destined for Montreal. The other four pilots were male. It was obvious that none of the noncoms had ever *seen* a woman fly a military plane. From the sudden silence when I appeared and the grim set of his jaw, it was also obvious that disciplined Stamp had been taking a bit of ribbing. It presaged to be one long, disagreeable flight from my Palm Springs base.

Luck and some corrective measures came into play. First, my plane was ready to go, so we took off immediately, leaving the skeptics behind. Then it was time for some hedge-hopping (no witnesses a necessity) to illustrate pilot aptitude. Somewhere over the southern tip of the Sierra Nevadas, the doughty sergeant broke. "Lady, I'm convinced. You can fly. If you'll get a little altitude, I can tune in some music for you, okay?" So I relaxed while he, presumably mollified, guided us towards Albuquerque. Once on the ground, another surprise awaited him. *Girls* (WACS) were refueling the planes. They waved companionably to me and flirted gently with him. All parties were delighted. And the A-20 could not have been

A newly graduated bombardier gets his wings from his sweetheart, along with a gleaming new pair of second lieutenant's "brown" bars. Before long, the hat will have its stiffener removed so it can be crumpled and mashed into a "fifty-mission crush." Moments like this made the Army Air Forces live up to its reputation as the "glamour boy" service. But that image wouldn't count for much in a few months, when the fly boys would be under attack from intense flak and determined enemy fighters. *USAF*

Upon getting one's wings, whether as a pilot, bombardier, navigator, radioman, flight engineer, or gunner, the next stop was bomber transition at a stateside training base devoted to a specific type of aircraft. This B-17F, with standard four-digit white training numbers on the tail, heads out on a practice mission. *Albert J. Keeler*

After graduating from twin-engine advanced, Jack Havener took his first operational training unit ride in this B-26 Marauder at Drane Field, Lakeland, Florida, in October 1943. Known as the "Widow Maker" due to so many accidents, the Marauder had a higher landing speed than most bombers, demanding the utmost attention to the airspeed indicator on final approach. By the end of the war, the '26 was rated as one of the Army Air Forces' most effective aircraft. *Jack K. Havener*

30

in better hands. So I set the time for the next morning and got a ride into town. It was obvious that my "crew" needed no further assistance.

Proof indeed was the WAC send-off in the early dawn: "Bye, Louie! See ya again!" Then, since it was Saturday morning, I listened to the opera and Stamp listened to his baseball game, in between his radio reporting. We were flying "over the top." The world was beautiful and unreal, only miles of white cotton beneath the A-20 and Verdi in the ears. Then came a request. The weather sounded not too great for our destination. How about putting into "St. Joe" to check it out? Sounded like good advice, so we did. The weather did close in, and, surprise of

surprises, Staff Sergeant Stamp had a sick aunt in St. Joseph, so we RON'ed [remained overnight] in conscience. I arranged a ride into town for myself, since the sergeant assured me that his cousin would drive out for him. When I arrived at the airport the next morning, he was already there—asleep on a bench. He had to stay up all night with his sick aunt, the poor man.

We were now a real team, the best of pals, sharing a mutual admiration. I had to give him an "A" for apparent stamina—which needed no words. In fact, the only words I recall him saying to me, which were not directly related to navigation or radio, was a phrase used as the highest compliment in those long-ago days: "You ought to

Stateside practice mission. An early model B-25 is loaded with practice bombs for a trip to the range. Though trainee crews—particularly those in the hot Southwest—thought such flying would never end, the common complaint was not enough training by the time they got to the combat theaters. That the Army Air Forces produced the first-rate bomber crews it did is a credit to that service's "can do" attitude, from General Hap Arnold on down. *USAF*

be in the movies!" We returned from Montreal by different routes, and by the time I had delivered a P-39 and was back at Palm Springs again, he had been transferred. But there was a box of candy in my BOQ with the note, "Lady, I would fly with you again anytime. You're a good pilot. I told those guys too. Sincerely, Louis F. Stamp, Jr. Staff Sergeant"

Bob Gillman
B-24 pilot, advanced four engine bomber transition

We flew just about every day and some nights and started doing a lot of formation flying. We were getting to know each other individually and began melting together as a crew. Naturally, we had no doubts that our crew was the best! I got a kick when Ed Caley, our top turret gunner and assistant engineer, told me that some of our guys had made bets with some men on another crew that we could fly a closer formation than them on today's scheduled formation flight. After takeoff, we formed up on the right wing of the lead ship (number two position), while they were on the left wing.

Now, as it happened, I loved to fly formation and worked very hard learning to fly tight and smooth. You must learn to almost

A fledgling F-10 Mitchell crew heads out over the Colorado flatlands from Peterson Field on a practice photo mission. The trimetrigon camera equipped B-25 was an ideal mapping platform—stable, long-ranged, and easy to fly. *Ole C. Griffith*

Being a Women Airforce Service Pilot (WASP) was every bit as thrilling as these WASPs in front of a Lockheed Lodestar at the Army Air Forces Fighter Gunnery School, Foster Field, Victoria, Texas, late 1944 seem to think it is. When the WASPs were phased out in December 1944, most offered to stay on for nothing as long as they could fly the fighters, bombers, and transports they had come to love. From left to right are Pauline S. Cutler, Dorothy Erhardt, Jennie M. Hill, Etta Mae Hollinger, Lucille R. Cary, Jane B. Shirley, Dorothy H. Beard, and Kathryn L. Boyd. Their jobs included ferrying aircraft, towing targets, and instrument instruction. Of the 1,104 women who became WASPs, forty-one were killed in the line of duty. *USAF*

A veteran bomber transition B-17D was pulled off the line to star as *Mary Ann* in one of the better wartime films on the Army Air Forces—*Air Force*, starring John Garfield. The film followed the fortunes of a single Fort from its flying into the attack on Pearl Harbor to the invasion of Wake Island. *Mary Ann* is seen here after the filming, back at her training field, on 6 April 1943. *USAF*

anticipate the need to add or reduce power *before* you actually begin to slide slowly back or forward, and I was getting this down to a science. Tom would watch my every move closely and would get so frustrated when he could see my hand moving the throttles forward ever so slightly and wondered why, because he could not see that we were falling back. Rather, we did not move at all, or, I could sense that we were about to drop back and would add a little power and, again, we didn't move at all.

As crews headed overseas, they often took mascots with them, though that was strictly against Army regulations. There had to be very few cats in the world that could live with the in-flight noise of a B-25, but pilot Ole Griffith proved the point by snapping the 90th Photo Mapping Squadron cat in flight over Peru in 1944. *Ole C. Griffith*

It was very smooth today, and I kept inching closer and closer, "sticking the wing tip in the waist window," as it used to be called, until I was satisfied, then held it right there, even during turns. Actually, close formation flying is really dangerous, especially among low time pilots in 65,000-pound large airplanes. Once a heavy aircraft starts moving, especially in the wrong direction, you have no way of "putting on the brakes" to stop the movement. Midair collisions were not uncommon, especially in combat, where every aircraft took off well over gross weight and was very hard to handle in formation. After we landed, our guys were smiling and told us the next day that they made a few bucks.

Corrine Wall
widow of B-24 copilot Jack Wall, 392nd Bomb Group

Words can never express the feelings families have when their young men are sent out to kill or be killed—no matter how noble the cause may seem to be—for there is no winner as the cream of that generation dies. Only by living through this period can anyone really feel the pains of war.

A son missing for a year, constant hope that he'll be found. Asking for help from the Red Cross to find information and then having their reply blocked just prior to reaching you. Needing your other son to hold as you grieve for the lost one, but not being able to do so. Knowing your son would never have been flying and would possibly still be alive had you never signed parental permission papers. Replacing the little flag in the window that had two blue stars (two sons in the service) with two flags—one with a blue star and one with a gold star (one killed).

A baby who would never know her father. A body returned six years after death with only officials stating he was your son. Many years of movies being made that glorified war and not being able to watch them because the pain was still so real. These things are so private, and yet we who remember *must* convey them to our sons and daughters, for only through God can we have life, and that abundantly!

John Gabay
B-24 tail gunner, advanced bomber transition

When I completed armament school at Salt Lake City, I was shipped to Tucson, Arizona, to join a B-24 Liberator training group. I would have preferred B-17s, but it didn't matter too much as long as I got on a crew

One of the major jumping off points for the European Theater of Operations was Goose Bay, Labrador, where the base ground crew is giving this B-25 the standard treatment for snow and ice prevention: Cover the whole thing with tarps, let it snow or sleet like mad, then pull off the tarps. It sure beat having the aircraft stranded and out of action for an indefinite period of time. *Morris Davidson via Richard Davidson*

and started flying. I was anxious to find out what kind of crew I was assigned to, and it wasn't long before I found out. We met under the wing of the ship. I was the tail gunner and armorer. Then we met our officers: Lieutenant Huie, the pilot, from Ark-ansas; Lieutenant Kemp, our bombardier, from Chicago; Lieutenant Glickman, our navigator, also from Chicago. No copilot was assigned to us. The reason was that our pilot was such a poor flyer that we always had an instructor for a copilot. Our navigator was another beauty. He couldn't find the field one day and took us into Mexico. But our bombardier took the cake. We were supposed to be on a night practice bombing mission over the desert. Instead, he dropped a 100-pound smoke bomb through the roof of a house in the suburbs of Tucson. Our enlisted men

had the highest marks in the group; our officers were the lowest.

Roy Kennett
B-24 radio operator, advanced bomber transition

You know, I didn't even want to be a radio operator. I wanted to be a gunner, and I was a *good* gunner. Little did I know the only one on a B-24 who doesn't have a gun is the radio operator. I went to school at Fort Myers and got a top-notch shooting record, but they told me "You've got to have another technical school. You can't be just a gunner. You need something in conjunction with that." I'd heard that Armorer's School was in a mudhole down in Biloxi, Mississippi, and the engineers went to some God-awful place near Brownsville, Texas. Now radio school

A B-17 on the way to Europe about to touch down at Goose Bay, Labrador, 1942. The North Atlantic Ferry Route was absolutely crucial to the quick movement of men and aircraft into the combat zones. Though often fraught with severe hazards and some of the world's worst weather, wartime ferrying was immensely successful. *Morris Davidson via Richard Davidson*

was in St. Louis, Illinois. So I said, "Yep! Send me to radio school. I'm going to *Saint Looey!*" I went to St. Louis just because it was the best place to go. They turned me into a gunner without a gun.

Bob Gillman, B-24 pilot, bomber debarkation pool

We spent three days at Grenier and were issued many additional items. We took off from Grenier on July 25, 1944, at 1500 and landed at Presque Isle, Army Air Base, Maine, at 1700 for additional equipment. We were certain that this would surely be our last stop in the USA, and we all felt it would be only proper that we should go into town and do a little partying. We were assigned quarters, but for some reason we were told to leave our baggage in the airplane. We all

went down to the line, got dressed, and proceeded to the main gate to see if we could get transportation to Presque Isle. However, we were stopped short by the guard, who advised us that only officers were allowed off the base; enlisted men were restricted to the base. We argued vehemently with the guard, to no avail. He had his orders. We all stepped outside then, quite upset that we could not be together as a crew to have some fun on our last night in the States.

Then one of my officers, who shall remain nameless, suggested a very simple plan that would solve this problem. We all walked down to the flight line to the airplane and dug into our baggage again. Twenty minutes later, ten officers walked back to the main gate. We never really knew if that guard recognized any of our faces. However, after proper salutes were ex-

A line of new B-17Es at Goose Bay, staging for the European Theater of Operations, 1942. These early Fortresses were the mainstay of the Eighth Air Force's early penetrations at Nazi-occupied Europe, testing German defenses as well as their abilities at daylight precision bombing, an unproven doctrine. In the years to come, thousands of men would fight and die to make precision bombing a key cog in the Allied plan to defeat Hitler. *Morris Davidson via Richard Davidson*

changed, we all caught a bus and headed to town. I took time to explain to our enlisted men what a serious offense it was to impersonate an officer, but no one seemed overly concerned. In fact, they were already enjoying returning salutes. I also told them that if anyone got into trouble and was not back in the morning, he would be left behind if we had to leave. We then separated and proceeded to have a great time. Sure, it was a stupid thing to do, but someone must have been watching over us that night, and it really brought us closer together as a crew.

Willetta Shoens
wife of B-17 pilot Bob Shoens, 100th Bomb Group

I sat at home next to the radio, devouring the newspaper, adding to the wartime scrapbook I was assembling to keep track of the missions Bob was flying. As a young wife, waiting at home, you just naturally assumed that your husband went on every raid. On March the 4, we learned that our best man had died in the first raid on Berlin. You just pray that *your* man is going to come home. You can't help but be selfish about it.

Mediterranean Theater of Operations

Bob DeGroat
B-24 pilot, 459th Bomb Group

My first flight in Italy was an adventure in itself. The first pilot and pseudo-tour director (I flew the right seat) was a veteran flier who had completed his tour and was waiting for transportation back to the States. The plane was a war-weary B-24 that had six-by-six boards in the bottom of the bomb bay and was used as a freight carrier.

The idea was to load my "green" crew aboard and show them the local area and its landmarks, so we wouldn't get lost when we were on our own. The flight was pleasant: We checked out the gold dome of the cathedral at Cerignola, took a look at the lighthouse and cliffs that make up the spur of the boot as seen on any map of Italy, and buzzed some fishing boats. All went well until we returned to make a landing.

This was an early model of the B-24 that had a warning horn that sounded if you retarded the throttles without having the landing gear locked down. There were also light indicators for the gear position. In our first attempt at lowering the gear, the horn was silent, but the indicators showed that one of the main gears was not locked. We recycled the landing gear, and this time the indicators were satisfactory, but the warning horn went off. We recycled over and over, but something always refused to check out.

We finally threw out the nose gear manually and cranked the main gear down by hand, trying to get everything locked in place properly. At last the yellow-painted main gear latches looked from the waist section to be correct. All the indicators were green, and the warning horn remained silent. I double-checked everything on the base leg, and things were fine. We turned on final, and shortly thereafter the warning horn sounded briefly, but went silent again.

We touched down gently and began to slow when the warning horn came on again as the right main gear started to retract. Suddenly the gear snapped back into place and the horn was quiet once more. The plane had slowed to what I estimate to be

The mainstay of Army Air Forces bomber operations in North Africa was the B-25 Mitchell, which was able to take the rough and tumble operations of flying through sandstorm takeoffs and harsh conditions. A B-25C attached to the 321st Bomb Group, *Oh-7*, and crew prepare to take off on a mission from their Tunisian base. *USAF*

In January 1944, when the 344th Bomb Group left as a unit with their B-26s for England on the South Atlantic Ferry Route, they had no idea they'd be stuck for almost a month in Marrakech, Morocco. After getting all the Marauders to Africa in February, the weather closed in, preventing them from making the final leg to England. What else to do but see the sites? This local bus was the most modern form of transportation available. *Jack K. Havener*

sixty to seventy miles per hour, when the horn again came on, and the left main gear retracted completely into the wing. The left wing tip hit the ground, causing the wing to crack at the root and drag to the rear at an odd angle. The nose gear broke off. The upper turret came off its track and swung by its guns between the pilot and me.

I flipped the switches off and unbuckled to get out. The engineer had gone out the top hatch like a rocket, run down the wing, and was a quarter mile away. There was all kinds of dust in the air, but I couldn't detect any smoke, fumes, or fire (but I wasn't far behind the engineer). They towed the wreckage to the bone yard, and I never heard anything but thanks for getting rid of that lemon.

That's not where the story ended. One, the officers of each crew had a tent in the olive orchard up on the hill that they called home. It was late fall and our newly erected tent had no heater. The holdup was the lack of a hard-to-find petcock to control the flow of captured German gasoline into our rudimentary stove. After our crash landing, the dust had not yet settled before my bombardier was back in the plane trying to pry a petcock out with his bare hands.

Then I made my next landing in Italy. To this point, I had never made a normal landing on a gravel runway. The first landing, as indicated above, was a noisy affair, so you can imagine my first thoughts when loose gravel was kicked up against the bottom of the fuselage as I let the nose wheel down in

After the first B-17s had arrived in North Africa, combat damage quickly took its toll, a preview of things to come. Quickly stripped of useful items to keep others flying, this 97th Bomb Group hulk was put to good use as a training aid for ditching, an ever-present possibility regardless of theater of operation. These 414th Squadron crewmen were a part of the unit's move up through Algeria and Tunisia in 1942 and 1943. *USAF*

Mt. Vesuvius rumbles in the distance beyond this 47th Bomb Group A-20 Havoc and some 31st Fighter Group Spitfire Vs at Pomigliano, Italy, in late 1943. When the volcano finally erupted in 1944, it virtually destroyed the 340th Bomb Group's B-25s, something the Luftwaffe was never able to pull off. *William J. Skinner*

a normal landing. My hair stood on end for a second, as I thought I had another collapsed gear.

Philip Ardery
B-24 squadron commander, 389th Bomb Group

Before I started combat, the most important question in my mind was how I would take it. I knew I had no more courage than the average American, but I had studiously followed the methods suggested by psychologists to overcome fear. Early in my flying career I discovered that when you have an airplane in your hands and you feel yourself getting scared, the first thing you must do is force yourself to relax. If you become tense, you completely lose that all-important feel of the controls that gives advance warning of what the ship is likely to do. You know what kind of glide to set for landing. You know whether you have enough speed to clear the tree ahead of you, or you know if you try to clear it, you will stall out at a critically low altitude. Then you must plan to point the nose of your ship down and let the tree take a wing off to break the forward motion as the plane pancakes it. I have prayed

Red Cross girl Helen Ellor serving coffee and doughnuts to a tired bunch of 320th Bomb Group Marauder crews on Corsica after a mission in 1944. There was nothing quite so beautiful as the sight of these wonderful gals, always ready with a smile and some conversation. That such lambs survived in a den of wolves was a tribute to their stamina and dedication. *Joseph S. Kingsbury*

for a greater capacity to keep cool in pinches, because I know that panic may be the equivalent of suicide. If I maintain calm, I think there is a good chance I can land an airplane in any sort of terrain without injuring myself.

My first few missions hit me just about the way I thought they would. Sometimes I was scared, but on the easier runs I didn't feel much more than a pleasant exhilaration. Still, when the flak started breaking right against my airplane, or when I saw the enemy fighters practically flying through our waist windows, I could feel my pulse rise. Particularly, if I saw one of our ships filled with friends of mine sprout flames for a few seconds and then blow up—which wasn't uncommon—the icy fingers I hated would reach right around my heart. I would shut my eyes for a brief instant, pray for a little more nerve, and then say to myself, "R-e-l-a-x, you jerk!" My temples would pound, but I would keep my hands flexible and easy of motion and feel. I've heard lots of pilots tell of narrow escapes and say, "Things happened so fast I didn't have time to get scared." I found no matter how fast things happened I always had time to get scared.

A number of the raids were rough enough to keep some of the boys from sleeping at night for sweating out the next one. But, there again, I was lucky. When I got my feet on the ground after one mission, I rarely had trouble sleeping because of the next one. The raids went quickly. That, too, was another factor to help. We didn't have too much time to sit around and think about the next mission. Another thing that helped was

"My sack, Corsica, 1944," remembered Joe Kingsbury, a 320th Bomb Group B-26 pilot. All the comforts of home, from bedside canteen to pierced-steel plank (PSP) for a floor. *Joseph S. Kingsbury*

After the 320th Bomb Group got settled on Sardinia in 1944, the officers' club was under construction in no time. With some very talented nose artists in the group, the mural decorations quickly took on the form of desired companions. It wasn't home, but it wasn't bad. *Joseph S. Kingsbury*

44

that we suffered absolutely no limitations of weather. Sometimes the haze was very heavy over the Mediterranean; but the sky was always clear at our base, and we never had to cancel a mission because of cloud over the target.

Bob Gillman
B-24 pilot, 456th Bomb Group

The weather was clear as briefed, as we climbed slowly up to 25,000 feet. Looking down at the detail on the ground, it began to sink in that this was *enemy territory*, and we were heading toward the worst target in the world—the Ploesti oil refinery. The total briefed round trip time was seven hours and twenty-five minutes, and we would be flying tight formation all the way. Ed List saw that I was able to fly good formation from the right seat and asked me to fly a lot. This gave him a break and kept me busy, with

less time to worry about what was happening. Intense and accurate flak was briefed, and some fighter attacks were expected. The Germans knew by now where we were going and would be ready and waiting for us.

The element of fear began to grow within me as we continued onward, and I could see the whole crew beginning to tense up. I had not expected that my "baptism of fire" would begin at this target! But I quickly reasoned, as I would do many times again, that nothing could be changed. There were no choices here but to go on. We had been flying now for about three and a half hours, and it was very cold. Fatigue was becoming noticeable, and we would soon be approaching the target area. Actually, the Ploesti oil refinery complex was spread over many square miles, and individual targets within the complex would be assigned to the various groups. As fear began to grow, I had a fleeting thought about how it must be like to be the enemy on the ground looking up at this armada of hundreds of bombers about to drop thousands of tons of death and destruction down upon them.

The weather today was crystal clear as we pressed on closer and closer. However, there was no way of knowing that there was nothing that could possibly prepare us for what was about to take place. At twenty to twenty-five miles away we could clearly see some weather ahead over the target, as we could see dark clouds forming. This was surely strange, since the weather had been so clear, as it was briefed to be. As we got closer, we could begin to see that something was very strange about the cloud formations. They seemed to be constantly moving! It reminded me of the grand finale at a Fourth of July fireworks, when everything is exploding at once. Then it hit me! *My God, it wasn't clouds at all—but barrage flak!* The Germans knew where we were going, and their radar-controlled 88 and 105mm anti-aircraft guns had our altitude "nailed." So they just kept throwing it up continuously. We were able to see the groups going in

Missouri Mule heads out with other 320th Bomb Group Marauders on a mission in 1945. Joseph S. Kingsbury

The bombs from eighteen B-26 Marauders of the 320th Bomb Group begin to impact on the bridge and approaches of Manjua, Italy, 1944. Though seldom reported, medium bombers like the B-26 flew at low altitude through intense flak to deliver their bombs accurately, as clearly evident here. To get such results, losses were often high. *Joseph S. Kingsbury*

Little friend! An 86th Fighter Group P-47D Thunderbolt escorts a formation of 320th Bomb Group Marauders home, 1945. What a sight! No bomber crewman, even if he did think the fighter boys got all the girls, ever felt so good as when a fighter sidled up to take care of any Luftwaffe intruders. *Joseph S. Kingsbury*

ahead of us getting clobbered, with B-24s going down all around. It became instantly obvious to me that by flying large formations of bombers through flak like that, the ones that came out the other side would purely and simply be the *lucky* ones. Skill would have little to do with it.

We touched down at base after seven hours and twenty-five minutes in the air on the nose. The best way to describe my feelings as we got out of the plane was that I was completely drained, both physically and mentally. The thought ran through my brain, "*So this is what it is to fly a combat mission!*"

Bud Abbot
B-17 pilot, 483rd Bomb Group

The P-38s used to really enjoy coming over and buzzing our field, in addition to the big headquarters building. All the guys lived in tents, and all our tents were down in a little meadow, down a little slope from the headquarters building. All the officers' tents were down in one area, and then, over on the other side of the headquarters building, were the enlisted men. The officers' tents were kind of on a little slope and out by themselves. The '38s used to love to come in and buzz our area. They'd come in real low, and then they'd throw it up and blow dust

Sometimes bombers were used to take the brass to appointments within the combat zone—and what brass this is! Generals Dwight D. Eisenhower and Mark Clark talk in front of Ike's B-17 in late 1943, as the Allies were attempting to gain a foothold on the Italian boot. *William J. Skinner*

A diverted B-17 ready to help move the 31st Fighter Group to their next field, late 1943. Bombers were often detached to serve as transports when units had to be moved quickly. *William J. Skinner*

all over everything. They created quite a ruckus.

We were unable to get field stoves for our tents, so we were quite chilly at night in the spring. We found a bunch of fifty-gallon drums, cut them in half, turned them upside down, cut a little hole in the front of them, and then buried a number ten can full of gravel and sand in the ground. We scrounged some aluminum tubing off a wrecked airplane, and we had a five-gallon

Jerry can. We put that tubing into the Jerry can, ran it under ground, under the tent floor. We didn't have a floor in our tent; it was just dirt. We ran this tube in there and put it in the can. Then you could open the vent in the five-gallon gas can, and it would run the gasoline into that can. It would run in there and drip on the rocks in the can. When you lit it, you had a fire.

Of course, that would put out some smoke and fumes and stuff, so we found a

48

The dreaded, deadly German 88mm flak gun. This one at Salerno has a number of American kills marked by white circles on the barrel. The 88 was Germany's most effective flak cannon, with just the right balance of range and punch, capable of reaching right up to the American bomber streams. Flak was by far the most dreaded of enemy weapons, since there was no way to tell if a hit was on the way. At least fighters could be tracked and fired back at. *William J. Skinner*

whole bunch of cast-iron pipe; apparently, they had been planning to lay some water pipe somewhere. It was about, oh, four inches. The filler top on the top of the fifty-gallon drum, that pipe would fit just right over it, so we'd stick the pipe right up through the top of the tent. The only trouble was that the pipes were about twenty-five feet long. So the pipe stuck way up in the air. The smoke and fumes and stuff would go out there. A '38 never hit one of them, but one of our crews was up flying a B-17 on a maintenance hop or something like that with no ammunition, no bombs on board, and decided to come in and buzz the area.

He came in real low, and the ball turret hit one of those smoke stacks. The stack didn't break, but it tumbled, end over end, right over the row of tents, flattening about six or eight of them, plus the one that he hit. Fortunately, everybody was out on a mission and nobody was in any of the tents, so no one got hurt. But the ball turret came off of the airplane and fell over into an olive orchard. The guy that was flying wound up getting court martialed, I think. Everybody was mad at him for a long time, because they came back from a mission, all pooped out and ready to hit the sack, and their tents were laying on the ground! It was quite a mess.

Bob DeGroat
B-24 pilot, 459th Bomb Group

Take a bunch of young fellows who are flying life-and-death combat nearly every

49

A stripped-down combat veteran B-17F at Foggia-Main, Italy, June 1944. Though such tired war-weary planes couldn't be used in combat any more, they served as transports and general "hack" aircraft until so worn out they had to be pushed aside. *Fred E. Bamberger*

Life around the bomber bases in Italy was a continual draw for Fifteenth Air Force crews. The Italian people, though very poor from the ravages of war, were always happy to welcome Americans into their lives, as this 483rd Bomb Group pilot discovers near the base at Sterparone, southeast of Foggia. *James C. Leigh via Mrs. M. M. Leigh/Jim Dietz*

50

day, give them their war toys and tell them to go play, and the exuberance of youth tends to show. Our gunnery missions usually got lower and lower to the surface of the water. The gunners, however, soon learned that bullets ricochet at unpredictable angles off the waves, even back at them, so they cut that short.

Buzzing was always fun, so I had lots of encouragement from the crew. A badge of accomplishment was getting low enough to have water spray on the bomb bay doors.

The Italian fishing boats were fair game. The fishermen would see those four big en-

gines bearing down on them, and there would be a mad scramble to let the sails down before the prop wash could blow the boat over as the bomber just cleared the mast. I even saw a few fishermen dive over the side.

I actually only buzzed a fishing boat once. My better judgment returned, and although I loved the sensation of speed from being that low, I left the fishermen to their livelihood. Others were as addicted as I was, and I heard speculation about whether or not it was possible to squeeze a B-24 between the lighthouse and the cliffs at the fa-

A formation of 483rd Bomb Group Forts climb out of Sterparone, Italy, for an attack on Germany. James C. Leigh via Mrs. M. M. Leigh/Jim Dietz

Noble Holbert and John McArthur make some repairs at their palatial digs on 759th Squadron officers row at Giulia, near Cerignola, home of the 459th Bomb Group. Yes sir, this was living. Well, at least the tents each had a small stove. *James Wilson via 459th Bomb Group Assn.*

mous spur on the boot of Italy if you banked the plane to ninety degrees. I cannot verify that anyone ever tried.

Lyle McCarty
B-24 pilot, 459th Bomb Group

Weather proved a serious problem off and on during the entire stay of the 459th in Italy—worse, of course, during the winter months. Besides the problem of flying in and out of a field essentially devoid of navigational aids (Giulia Field boasted a nondirectional radio beacon, and that put it a notch above almost any other field in Italy), the targets were often hidden beneath an undercast. Also, the Germans employed smoke generators to obscure targets, especially oil refineries. To enable the group to strike their targets under these conditions of poor or no visibility, "Mickey" ships were introduced and used for group and squadron lead and sometimes deputy lead aircraft. These planes were radar equipped (the ball turret was replaced by a radome) and carried an additional navigator trained in the use of the Mickey equipment. Bombing accuracy

Liberators of the 459th Bomb Group pulling vapor trails as they climb out of Italy over the Alps for Germany. The group arrived in the theater in January and February 1944 and got a Distinguished Unit Citation for leading the 304th Bomb Wing 23 April 1944 mission through fighters and flak to the aircraft factory at Bad Voslau. *James Wilson via 459th Bomb Group Assn.*

was a bit ragged, but the radar was used quite effectively to establish positions while flying to and from the targets. Mickey craft were originally bare aluminum, but later they were painted a light gray to distinguish them from the other planes.

Ken Kailey
C-47 pilot, 8th Troop Carrier Squadron

I think that troop carrier was just about the best deal in the Army Air Forces. Although the C-47 was not among the "fast and flashy" aircraft, it was solid, dependable, and easy to fly—and so very forgiving. It's still around today, isn't it! While the bombers and fighters did their same old routine each time—fly to 30,000 feet, suck on oxygen for hours, drop the bombs, and re-

Lieutenant Jack Evans, a B-24 pilot with the 759th Squadron, 459th Bomb Group, has just finished shining his shoes . . . on a board . . . in the middle of the mud at Giulia. Now where is he going to go? Why did he bother? *James Wilson via 459th Bomb Group Assn.*

53

Navigator John D. McArthur and pilot Noble G. Holbert make their way through the mud at Giulia, home of the 459th Bomb Group at Cerignola, Italy. About the only way to beat the stuff was to wear those large flying boots over your shoes, then take off the boots when entering a tent, building, or the airplane. *James Wilson via 459th Bomb Group Assn.*

By the time the Fifteenth Air Force had become firmly established in Italy, the country became another "aircraft carrier" similar to England, as this field full of bombers near Rome clearly shows. *James Wilson via 459th Bomb Group Assn.*

54

turn to same old field—we had variety. You might say that we were in the Sightseeing Corps. We flew low enough to see things, and we got to land at the other end and look around. Very casual—we were told to fly to point "A," pick up a load, and take it to point "B." No flight plan to file, no assigned altitude. And if we wanted to stray off course a bit to check something out, no problem. Besides that, they weren't shooting at us all the time.

We pretty much covered the European theater—I got to visit France, London, Casablanca, Cairo, Athens, and most of the major cities in Italy. In addition, we viewed most of the points in between from the air. And the most thankful part of all is that I'm still here today!

Bob DeGroat
B-24 pilot, 459th Bomb Group

Before we had our own plane, a B-24G called *Cherry II,* we were usually assigned Number 614, a B-24J. Unfortunately, it had a balky number three engine that was difficult to start. Several times it caused us to be

A 759th Squadron, 459th Bomb Group, Ford-built B-24M waits on its PSP hardstand at Giulia in 1944 for the next mission. The four-leaf clover on the nose was one of the squadron's symbols, carried on several Liberators. *James Wilson via 459th Bomb Group Assn.*

Patches **was another of the 459th Bomb Group's veteran Liberators. She survived the war and made it back to Altus, Oklahoma, only to be scrapped.** *Claude Porter via 459th Bomb Group Assn.*

real late, requiring "cleaning up" on the move, although we never missed our proper order in the procession. Semi-humorously, our copilot named the engines after former girlfriends according to how hard they were to get started.

Philip Ardery
B-24 squadron commander, 389th Bomb Group

When a group lost heavily on one or two raids, there was a natural strain on the morale of the remaining combat crews. It was hard for the boys coming back to go to quarters that were practically vacant—quarters that had been full a few hours before. It wore on their nerves to go to the club and find the place more filled with the ghosts of those who had gone than the presence of the few who remained. General Doolittle was a savvy guy about this particular hardship. I heard a story about a visit

A 489th Squadron, 340th Bomb Group B-25J at Capodocino, Naples, November 1944. The 340th had been decimated by the eruption of Mt. Vesuvius but came back strong to maintain its place as one of the theater's most effective medium bomb groups. Originally attached to the Ninth Air Force in North Africa, the group transferred to the Twelfth Air Force and continued to hit tactical targets through the end of the war. *Fred E. Bamberger*

he made to one of the groups that had lost nearly everyone on a single raid. The incident happened just after the unit had been filled up with replacements following a similar occurrence only a few weeks before. The general, as was his custom, flew his own fighter plane to the base and went unannounced to pay a visit to the officers club.

It was late evening, and the bar was open. A lone lieutenant was solemnly drinking a beer. The general stepped up beside him and ordered one. The lieutenant, noticing who the newcomer was, turned to the star-bearing little flyer and said, "What're you doing up here, General? Lookin' over our morale?"

The general smiled. "Not at all. I try to get around to visit all my groups every now and then. I didn't have much to do in headquarters this afternoon, so I decided I'd fly up and pay you a call."

"You know, General," the lieutenant continued, "Funny thing, morale. Ours is okay till the high-ranking generals start coming around lookin' it over. Then it just goes all to hell."

The general laughed, chatted with the officer a while, went out, climbed in his ship, and flew off. Yes, General Doolittle was a savvy guy. He was hard when the situation called for that, but when he left that group that day he knew that there was enough

A veteran 484th Bomb Group B-24 on the way out of Torretto, another of the Fifteenth Air Force Liberator bases near Cerignola. The group got two Distinguished Unit Citations. They earned the first on 13 June 1944 for hitting the marshaling yards at Innsbruck after a heavy smoke screen prevented dropping on the primary target at Munich. The second citation honored their 21 August 1944 bombing of Vienna without fighter escort. *Lieutenant Colonel J. Pool via David W. Menard*

fighting spirit in the handful of flying men left to give proper inspiration to the new bunch of replacements he was sending in.

Bob DeGroat
B-24 pilot, 459th Bomb Group

I remember one occasion being overloaded with six 1,000-pound bombs instead of the usual ten 500-pounders. On another we had to take off downwind. Power lines diagonally crossing that end of the runway forced me to bank and fly down them until I had enough altitude to clear. The tower wisely decided to change the direction of takeoff after three of us had problems. We circled the field while the whole bomb group reassembled at the other end of the runway.

Jim Bakewell
B-24 nose turret gunner, 459th Bomb Group

In August 1944, as a nose turret gunner on a mission over Blechhammer, Germany, I had something happen to me that never happened on any of my other missions. On the bomb run with very rough flak, at approximately the time for "bombs away," I suddenly had an extremely intense urge to urinate. There was no way to wait until we had pulled off the target; I had to do it immediately. With great effort, I stood up with my five-foot-eleven frame hunched up against the Plexiglas roof and doubled over in a "half-moon" shape. With greater effort, I extracted my "apparatus" through my heavy

Headquarters, Twelfth Air Force, Peretola, Italy, November 1944. Many war weary bombers ended up as headquarters hacks, stripped of armament. This early model "clean" B-25 sits next to a newer B-25J of the 321st Bomb Group. *Fred E. Bamberger*

flying suit and flak jacket (I still don't know how I did so), and I proceeded to make a "direct hit" on the Plexiglas covering the front of my turret. All hell was breaking loose outside our plane, but I didn't care about the flak or anything else. I had to do what I had to do. As I settled back down into my seat, I figured the bombardier would "chew me out," but he never said a word. I discovered that the fluid had frozen on the Plexiglas, and apparently he never saw what happened.

When we landed and were standing outside of our plane, eating doughnuts and drinking coffee served by the Red Cross girls, an armorer or crew chief came along and said, "Who is the nose turret gunner on this plane?" I admitted that I was and walked with him to look at the turret per his request. He said, "What in the hell are those stains on the Plexiglas?" I said that I didn't know, but suggested that maybe we hit a bird on the way in for landing, and that caused the stains. He said, "The stains are not on the outside, but inside." I replied that I had absolutely no idea what could have caused such an amazing thing. It was my suggestion that he talk to the bombardier and see if he knew anything about it. Whether the armorer or crew chief ever did so, I do not know, but just in case he remembers this episode after forty years, I confess that I was the culprit.

Bob DeGroat
B-24 pilot, 459th Bomb Group

I always felt sorry for the copilot. The first pilot invariably had the controls on the bomb run and was, therefore, occupied. The copilot, on the other hand, had very little to do but watch the flak and enemy fighters. Unless your box was leading the Fifteenth Air Force formation, the surprise for the enemy as to our target for the day was over, and the copilot could see the intense flak curtain that we would eventually have to go through (no matter where we went in the sky first). Those minutes must have seemed

59

The ground crew of a 460th Bomb Group Liberator readies bombs for the next mission at Spinazzola, south of Cerignola, Italy. The group got a Distinguished Unit Citation for leading the 55th Bomb Wing through adverse weather and heavy enemy fire to bomb the airfield and aircraft repair facilities at Zwolfaxing, Austria, on 26 July 1944. *USAF*

like hours. The copilot may have been the bravest man on any bomber crew.

A. H. Albrecht
B-25 pilot, 319th Bomb Group

I was fortunate enough to fly twenty-five B-26 and six A-26 missions in addition to twenty in the B-25—which was much easier to fly than either of the others. I flew my first B-25 combat mission with a total time of 100 hour's training, but I never felt comfortable with a B-26 till I had 300 hours of first-pilot time. The B-25J was much easier to fly.on one engine; the B-26 barely flew on one, but the A-26 did nicely. Takeoff and landing were easy by comparison with the B-26, and formation flying was easier in the Mitchell than either of the others. The B-26 was the hardest to fly but the most rugged. The A-26 was a superb airplane—same bomb load as the others but forty miles per

hour faster; two or three man crew; single-engine performance exceptional. The B-25 had no problems with oil coolers (the B-26 was bad in this way) and none with propellers, whereas the B-26's propellers could run away. The B-25's Wright Cyclone engines were much noisier than the Pratt & Whitneys in the other two, and the B-25 had much less room everywhere than the B-26.

Philip Ardery
B-24 squadron commander, 389th Bomb Group

Part of my reaction to my luck and general combat experience was to sense a resurgence of religion. Fellows who hadn't attended services in years found themselves going to Sunday services. My religion didn't take me to these services with regularity, but I went occasionally, not only for myself but to let the men in my squadron know I

Headquarters, Twelfth Air Force, Peretola, Florence, Italy, on VE-Day, May 1945. The conglomeration of bombers, fighters, trainers, and transports made the place more than interesting, particularly for headquarters pilots who wanted a variety of flying time. *Fred E. Bamberger*

Bari, Italy, on the Adriatic coast, served as a major repair and replacement depot for the Twelfth and Fifteenth Air Forces, so it was usually crowded with a number of types, old and new. *Fred E. Bamberger*

didn't consider attendance a sign of weakness. I felt if they saw me there it might help some of them to go who wanted to but were kept from going out of embarrassment.

In my case, religion made me say short prayers before going to sleep at night and sometimes during a fleeting instant at the height of combat. I think this undoubtedly made me a better combat officer. It comforted me so that I could sleep before missions, even though I had been briefed for the next mission and knew the assignment of the morning might be my last. It helped me to say to myself with complete calm: "You can't live forever. You have had a great deal in your life span already, much more than many people ever have. You would not shirk the duty tomorrow if you could. Go into it calmly; don't try too hard to live. Don't ever give up hope; never let the fear of death strike panic in your mind and paralyze your reason. Death will find you sometime, if not tomorrow. Give yourself a chance." And then I would remember that very appropriate sentence of Shakespeare: "Cowards die many times before their deaths; the valiant never taste of death but once."

Bob Gillman
B-24 pilot, 456th Bomb Group

I am in a state of euphoria, since this is my last mission, and each of the crew have been joking about how nice it would be if I would volunteer to fly additional missions until they are finished too. Fat chance! I feel as though an enormous weight has just been lifted from my back, and it's really hard to believe that I will not be flying any more combat missions. What a thrill to bring the

A 450th Bomb Group Liberator on takeoff at Florence, April 1945. The 450th was based at Manduria, east of Taranto, as a part of the 47th Bomb Wing. Though the Liberator was often overshadowed by its more famous stable mate, the B-17, the type was built in larger numbers (more than 18,000) than any other American aircraft. *Fred E. Bamberger*

formation over the field for the last time, peeling off in turn and landing.

After evening chow, I invite the crew to come to our tent for a few drinks to join me in celebrating my final mission. I must also remember to write to my family tonight to give them the good news. I am sure that this great feeling will be with me for quite a while. I have not even begun to think about what my plans will be, except that I will be able to spend more time with my extracurricular flying activities. It is such a great feeling and a great relief not to be aroused at 0530 in the morning to fly another mission, but, strangely, I feel just a twinge of guilt. I am concerned about my crew having to fly

with someone else, and I sweat them out each mission until they return.

Ralph "Doc" Watson
wing commander, Fifteenth Air Force

Italy 0730 P.M.

Thanksgiving Day

November 23, 1944

Dear Little Sis,

I only wish that I could be there with you tonite to comfort you, instead of having to write you from thousands of miles away. I will try and tell you all I can.

I was notified last night of Gordon's death. Early this morning, I got into my Mustang and flew down to his base.

A 450th Bomb Group B-24 taxies out at Florence, April 1945. The flight engineer is at the top hatch to help guide the pilots on the ground, a normal procedure across the Army Air Forces. *Fred E. Bamberger*

I got in touch with Lieutenant Sanderson, Sergeant Spindle, and Sergeant Nelson, who had been with Gordon and who had successfully bailed out. The rest of the crew didn't get out. The accident happened yesterday morning at about eight o'clock. I talked with the squadron doctor and the three boys for a long time, finding out all of the details that I could. When the ship hit, Gordon was thrown clear but was badly broken up and died instantly. All three of the boys landed nearby in their parachutes and a few seconds later everybody was taken to the hospital.

When I got down to the field this morning, they were having the funeral at the American Cemetery for the Fifteenth Air Force fliers. Gordon was buried in Plot L, Row 12, Grave 1723. Chaplain Golden, the group chaplain, conducted the services. The chaplain had gone down from the group. The caskets were draped with the American flag, and it was a beautiful little cemetery with an American flag waving over all. I knelt down by myself and prayed to God over Gordon's grave.

They informed me that the bodies would be sent back to America after the war

if you so desire. I have the location, and all the graves are well marked with concrete markers.

I then saluted the flag and went back to the field and flew back to his group. There, I gathered up Gordon's personal things and brought them back here with me. I will send them to you in a little box—the rest will be sent home by the army. I am enclosing his ring in this letter; he had it on when they crashed. His bracelet and his Bible, which he had with him, are in the box with your letters and pictures.

Midge, honey, my heart goes out to you, and I cannot begin to express my feelings and sympathy by this letter. I only hope that you will take it like a good flier's wife, which you are, and be proud, knowing that Gordon died as a hero fighting for his country, and that the little boys and girls now growing up may enjoy the freedom and privileges which America is fighting for. I know that you loved him dearly, Midge, and I know that he lived and breathed for you. It is God's will, Margaret, and I pray to Him that you will be strong. God bless you always, my dear little sweet sister.

Words seem so futile, but I will always be where you may lean on my shoulders, God willing.

Always, your brother,
Ralph

Fresh from the States, these brand new B-24s lined up, ready for assignment to a bomb group, at Capodocino, Naples, in November 1944. At this point in the war, American industry was building aircraft at such a furious rate that these new aircraft were often stored. Replacement had finally overtaken combat losses, something unheard of earlier in the war.
Fred E. Bamberger

A 450th Bomb Group B-24M, built at Ford's Willow Run plant, taxies out at Florence in April 1944. The group began combat operations with the Fifteenth Air Force in January 1944, going straight into "Big Week" over Germany in February and winning a Distinguished Unit Citation in the process for pressing through bad weather, fighters, and flak to get bombs on target. *Fred E. Bamberger*

An Army Air Forces OA-10A Catalina at Foggia, May 1945. There was no more wonderful sight than one of these "Dumbos" coming in to pick up a crew that had ditched at sea. Often unheralded, Army Catalina crews braved some of the most intense enemy fire to rescue airmen in distress. *Fred E. Bamberger*

The Flight Section, Headquarters Twelfth Air Force, Peretola Field, Florence, Italy, May 1945. Yep, this was all there was. A working, moving air force rarely had time to build fine buildings or worry about the comforts of home. If this got the job done, then why waste time building anything more complicated? *Fred E. Bamberger*

Officers of the 344th Bomb Group watch with detached curiosity as a caravan weighs in at the scales outside the walls of Medina, Morocco. Such diversion was a welcome respite from the tents these men lived at their field in Marrakech while waiting to depart for England, March 1944. *Jack K. Havener*

67

CHAPTER 3

Life in the ETO

Sam Wilson

ground echelon, 17th Bomb Group (letter home, October 1942)

I'm sorry I can't tell you . . . when we first arrived, how we traveled and where we are. However, I can say that England is really beautiful—everything is so neat and orderly. The trains are just like in the movies—only no sleeping accommodations except luxury trains, no dining cars. Sunday we visited Cambridge, which is quaint—no buildings are over three stories. The streets are cobblestone and run in every damned direction! The lower-class English rather resent us; however, the middle class and upper bend over backwards being nice to us.

We are at one of the finest airdromes; the accommodations are excellent. In fact they beat those of my former station. Virginia creeper, ivy, and honeysuckle grow on many of the structures, and there are lawns, roses, and poplars. A few observations on the customs. We're taking to "tea" wonderfully . . . the Bank of England (Lloyds?) representative changed our money. I can't make

change yet; they have a god-awful system.

The Scotch people we have met are really swell, more like Yanks.

We have to watch our slang. Have already had a few misunderstandings that way.

The British version of toilet tissue is equivalent to the rotogravure section of the Sears Roebuck catalogue. There are no oranges. We will soon be eating American food tho' I like English food, but they have tried to cook our dishes and have flopped so far. But their hospitality extended that far!

The English people have taken a terrible beating in the air raids, and many people show it. When they play, they play hard, though they have very high spirits and rarely speak of the war except in passing, or else of the end of it. They have no doubts as to an English victory.

The British WAAFs [Women's Army Air Force] are taken very seriously and do a good job. We paled up with a few at a pub, and they knew our latest songs and some slang. . . . the English seem to feel that our

High Street and the town square, Diss, the village closest to the 100th Bomb Group at Thorpe Abbots, East Anglia. These old towns, particularly their pubs, became hubs of activity for Americans. *Arnold N. Delmonico*

When the Army Air Forces "invaded" England, many units were based near the food-providing farms (so crucial for the war effort) that dotted the nation. Here, the 322nd Bomb Group's Marauders nestle next to Bacon Farm, Stebbing, September 1943. The group was the first to fly B-26s from Britain, beginning 14 May 1943. *USAF*

A train pulls into the station at Eye where a few Americans wait to board. Such weather was the norm rather than the exception. *Arnold N. Delmonico*

Ninth Air Force Marauder pilot Jack Havener in his sack at Stanstead, just north of Bishops Stortford, home of the 344th Bomb Group from March through September 1944. This was livin', brother . . . and that was no joke, particularly compared to the tents, mud, and grit of most other theaters of war. *Jack K. Havener*

high pay will buy up everything in the way of luxuries; one British major said to me that if we kept drinking at the rate we were (really very little on American standards) all the Scotch in England would be gone in a month! So you can see, we are rightly called "crazy Yanks" (they call us Yanks whatever we are).

The blackouts are terrific, 100 percent all over. I've bumped into lampposts a hundred times and said politely "beg your pardon."

In conclusion, I'm well, I'm happy. . . . I like the country, the people, and a fraction of the customs.

If you send a package, make it the size of a shoe box. I'd like some pine nuts, stamps, and airmail stationery. I'll write soon again.

All my love,
Sam

Ben Smith

B-17 radio operator, 303rd Bomb Group

We were hardly down and checked in before our new airplane was taken away from us, never to be seen again. This was quite a shock, especially to Bachman. We had even named the airplane. Our morale took a nose-dive. For the first time, the realization

71

A cross-country jaunt across the English farmland, full of railroad crossings like this one at a country rail station. *Mark Brown/USAFA*

began to steal over us that we were not something special. We were not Chick's Crew—we were "fresh meat," replacements, soon to be gobbled up by the voracious appetite of the air war like all those who had gone before. A chill rain was falling. We huddled together dejectedly, full of gloomy foreboding.

John Gabay
B-17 tail gunner, 94th Bomb Group

When we came back from a raid, usual-ly between 4:00 and 5:00 P.M., we were picked up by a truck or jeep and brought to the interrogation shack. After that, to the mess hall for chow, then to the armament shack to clean our guns. We got back to the barracks between 8:00 and 9:00 P.M., exhausted. My raids averaged eight hours and forty minutes in the air. So when we finally got back to our barracks, the thing uppermost in our minds was to crawl into the sack and go to sleep.

Although a war was in progress, as far

as we were concerned, everything centered around our barracks. It was located at the very end of the base, surrounded by woods in the back and open fields in the front. The base road ended at our front door. Across the road were the washroom and showers. A perfect setup. When the truck came to pick us up for a raid, it had to turn around in the fields. Directly across the fields (about 200 yards) was a tar road. If you went left on the road for about two miles, you ended up in the town of Bury St. Edmunds. But if you went right for about a mile, you hit an Eng-

lish pub, standing out in the middle of nowhere. When we were sure there wasn't a raid the next day, we drew straws to see who would go to the pub for a barracks bag full of bottled beer. The same guy always drew the short straw, and he never caught on. It was no easy task coming back with a sack full of beer—and riding a bicycle. If he broke a bottle or two, which he occasionally did, everyone would bawl him out, and the poor guy would always apologize. A few months later he was shot down, and we all missed him. Not because we loved him, but because we

Regardless of wartime pressures and bombing raids, Piccadilly Circus remained a flurry of activity, both day and night, attracting Americans based across the United Kingdom. *Byron Trent*

73

Maintenance area, 94th Bomb Group, Bury St. Edmunds. Nissen huts and large, freestanding hangars were easy to build and dotted Eighth Air Force fields in England like runaway weeds. Though such temporary structures were cursed for letting in so much of the cold and wet English weather, they were far better than the tents that typically housed Ninth Air Force groups. *Byron Trent*

The 333rd Bomb Squadron living area at Bury St. Edmunds, 1944. Nissen huts were cold and drafty, and it was amazing how attached one could get to a coal-burning pot-bellied stove. *Byron Trent*

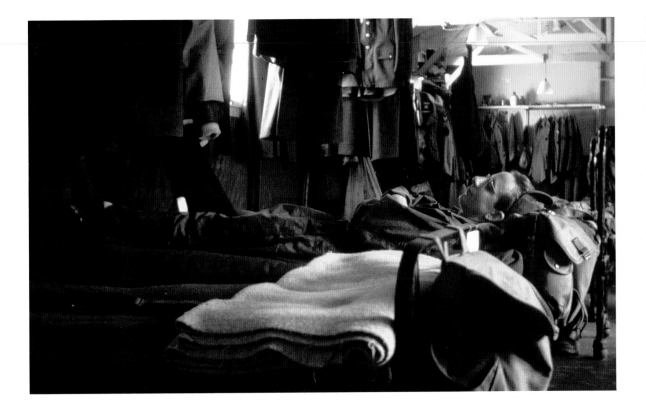

Hitting the sack became a pastime at which most became more than adept. Sleep was often a rare commodity, and one learned to drop off whenever there was a moment to spare, as is evident here in a 489th Bomb Group barracks at Halesworth. *Wallace A. Portouw via Roger Freeman*

would have to look for another live one. The next day we got six new rookies so we made sure one of them always got the short straw—and they never found out. Hard to believe!

Some nights when we were drinking beer, one of the comedians would drink a toast to the guys who were shot down. It was always a comical takeoff of an old World War I movie. It would start out very solemn, and then turn into a roast—especially if the guys didn't leave any cigarettes or candy in their foot lockers. What really cracked us up was when the clown giving the toast couldn't remember the names of the guys being toasted. Not very good copy for a movie or the folks back home, but that's the way it was—no dramatics, no sadness, no hearts and flowers.

John Ramsey
B-17 navigator, 493rd Bomb Group

In 1938, I began to write to a pen-friend, Miss Joan Green, in Leeds, Yorkshire. After a year or two we lost contact. However, Joan's address stayed somewhere in the back of my mind, and after I arrived in the United Kingdom and became settled in at Debach in September 1944, I wrote Joan, knowing she probably wondered what had become of me as the war unfolded. She and her mother both wrote back urging me to come to Leeds at the first opportunity. There was much hesitation because I knew about rationing in England, besides which the rail connections were very vague. There were no regular advertised schedules, probably for security reasons. I finally decided to give it a try, and, after the first time, made the trip

Captain John Meyers in the 386th Bomb Group chow tent at St. Trond, Belgium, early 1945. When the Ninth Air Force moved to the Continent in late 1944, it left behind all vestiges of real comfort. Few groups had more than tents to begin with. Life in the field was a series of quick moves and constant bad weather. *John H. Meyers*

frequently, but I never got to Leeds by the same route twice! When I boarded the train at Ipswich, it was with the understanding that the conductor would tell me where to get off to make the first connection. Then in the next station I'd ask someone which train to get on, and the next conductor would tell me where to get off again, and so on to Leeds.

On one occasion in the bitter cold winter of 1944–45, I had an interesting encounter.

It was so cold that at each stop I would buy a cup of tea and two or three of those hard little cookies or crackers. The tea wasn't just to drink—by holding the cup between my hands I could warm them, as there was no heating in the carriages. On one leg of the journey I found myself in a compartment with a young Royal Air Force sergeant. His insignia indicated he was an aircrew member, and I immediately felt that I had a friend. However, I tried without success to

In spite of the usual rough living conditions, there were times when a dream came true. After living in tents up through the Mediterranean, the officers of the 320th Bomb Group were assigned this chateau at Longecourt, France, in early 1945. *Joseph S. Kingsbury*

Unfortunately, the 340th Bomb Group enlisted men had to pitch their tents in the snow and ice behind the officers' chateau at Longecourt. Army life never seemed to be fair for noncoms, a fate most endured with resignation.
Joseph S. Kingsbury

A local resident near the base at Eye, England, trades some good-natured conversation with one of the 490th Bomb Group's pilots. Though the common description of the Yanks was "overpaid, oversexed, and over here," for the most part, the Americans and the British got along very well.
Arnold N. Delmonico

strike up conversation. He would only answer my questions with a very curt "yes" or "no." At the next station we both changed trains, and I heard him mention that he was going to the Bradford area. I knew Bradford was near Leeds, so I stuck to the young sergeant like wallpaper—you better believe I was having a hard time with the English accents trying to understand directions.

When we set off again there was an older man sitting opposite us in the compartment who noticed my attempts to engage the Royal Air Force sergeant in conversation. He explained that British enlisted personnel do not converse with officers except to answer questions and then as briefly as possible. This older man then pointed out to the young sergeant that the Yank was trying to be friendly and that he, the sergeant, was not being properly polite. The Royal Air Force man relaxed after that and was soon all smiles. He proved to be as curious about the Eighth Air Force as I was about Royal Air Force Bomber Command.

He was a Lancaster gunner and had completed a tour of duty but was hoping that his pilot could pull a few strings so that he could remain on operations. He felt that if he was grounded he might end up in "the pits," the coal mines, which I assume was his

Buzz job! A 379th Bomb Group Fort clips the grass at Mt. Farm to give the 7th Photo Group boys something to talk about. Though strictly prohibited, and not a little dangerous, buzzing was considered great sport among all Army pilots, particularly at the finish of a combat tour. *Robert Astrella*

Sick bay, 65th US Army General Hospital. Eighth Air Force personnel used these hospitals with alarming frequency. *Arnold N. Delmonico*

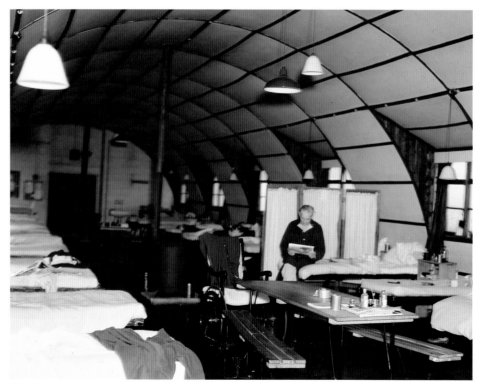

peacetime job. He was fascinated by our going to targets in broad daylight while I couldn't imagine milling around in darkness in the midst of other aircraft. We talked about how interesting it would be to trade places for one mission.

As the journey wore on, it became apparent that at the rate of progress we were making I was not going to arrive in Leeds until two or three o'clock in the morning. I asked if anyone in the compartment might recommend a hotel close to the rail station. Immediately a woman said that there should be no need to find a hotel as she was sure that any householder to whom I explained my predicament would be happy to find me a bed for the night, further suggesting that when I got to Leeds I should "knock someone up." I was momentarily taken

aback by this statement, as in American slang it means making someone pregnant. This was the first time I had heard this expression from a Britisher but quickly realized that the woman was telling me to go bang on a door.

At the same time my newfound Royal Air Force friend invited me to go home with him if I didn't mind getting off at Bradford, taking a bus with him to a smaller place, and walking a mile. He pressed me, but I had to decline. I knew how few rations these people got. For example, my friends the Greens had nine people in their home and could only buy two eggs a week. I was also aware that the sergeant's family was not aware he was coming on leave, and I could picture the scene when he arrived unexpectedly in the wee hours with a Yank in tow. His offer was appreciated more than he probably realized, but I begged off on the grounds that my leave time was too short, which was true.

That night was spent at the Queens Hotel, an act for which Mrs. Green scolded me soundly when I arrived next day. Felt badly about the Royal Air Force man's offer as I probably hurt his feelings in declining. I wish I had gotten his name and address, and I often wonder if he survived the air war.

Bob Morgan
B-17 pilot, 91st Bomb Group

When we went overseas, the British built these temporary fields for us. On a practice mission we tore the runway all to pieces, so we couldn't use it, and were grounded until we found another place to go. Our group commander, Colonel Wray, was a very versatile person who was able to do a lot of things. He heard about this base at Bassingbourn, an old British permanent base with brick houses and all the fineries near the town of Royston. He went down to visit it on his own without permission from

One of the Eighth's early 97th Bomb Group veterans, a B-17E, JW-M, now turned into a war-weary hack for the 92nd Bomb Group. Stripped of armament and combat equipment, the Fort was almost like a fighter to fly when compared to a '17 at full gross weight. *Robert Astrella*

81

After being transferred to the 92nd Bomb Group at Bovingdon, this B-17E introduced crews to the procedures on in-theater combat flying. It then made its way around as a staff transport, ending up with the 100th Bomb Group. *Robert Astrella*

the higher command, and there was nobody using it. He went back to the base and moved us down there without any orders! General Eaker found out about it, and Colonel Wray nearly got court martialed, but they finally said, "You're there. All right, stay there." We ended up with the best base in England, no question about it, living pretty high on the hog.

Jack Havener
B-26 pilot, 344th Bomb Group

"How's the ankle this morning, Lieutenant?" The GI medic was all smiles as he brought me a cup of coffee and the morning *London Daily Express*. I told him it was still throbbing, but as long as I kept it elevated, it wasn't so bad. I was in the small base hospital of the 344th Bomb Group (M) at Stansted-Mountfichet, Essex, England, recuperating from a flak wound received the

day before. Sipping the coffee, I leafed through the *Express*, looking for some news of our mission. All I could find was an article on the third page:

FORTS AND LIBS ON BIG STRIKE

21 June 1944—Over 1,000 Flying Fortresses and Liberators of the U.S. Eighth Air Force struck telling blows on Hitler's Germany yesterday. Factories and strategic targets deep within the Reich were pounded with tons of high explosives and incendiaries in the continuing air battle. Walls of flak were encountered and the Luftwaffe put up a tremendous defensive effort with all types of fighter aircraft. The Eighth Fighter Command reported fourteen enemy fighters knocked down to only three lost in the more than four hundred of our planes escorting the bombers. Twenty-eight bombers failed to return to their home bases

As in no era before or since, aircraft nose art was the hallmark of World War II, as *Lilly Ann* demonstrates. Aircraft in the European Theater of Operations were graced by nose art of all forms, on all types of aircraft, but the bomber was the ideal canvas. *Robert Astrella*

after the raids but the gallant airmen of the Eighth are already preparing for another strike tomorrow. Mediums of the Ninth Air Force were also out.

"Mediums were also out!" I exclaimed to a navigator in the next bed. "Why in the hell does the Eighth get all the recognition? We're in this war too!" Shifting his weight off his bandaged hip he replied, "Hell's fire, Johnny, don't you know? They've got Clark Gable and Jimmy Stewart on their team!"

Ben Smith
B-17 radio operator, 303rd Bomb Group

There was almost no distinction between officers and noncoms. The lowest grade on a crew was staff sergeant. Often the bombardier was a noncommissioned officer. The officers and men went on pass together and chummed with each other. There was not much saluting or military formality except in formations held for decorations or visiting dignitaries. An officer in charge of our squadron was called the ground CO [commanding officer] or adjutant. He managed to stay drunk most of the time. He didn't bother us, and we didn't bother him. I recall only one inspection of the barracks while I was there. I don't know what prompted that one.

We seldom wore uniforms. Our dress

Alice Blue Gown was indeed a lovely lady, managing to take her crews through sixty-seven missions with the 851st Squadron, 490th Bomb Group, out of Eye. *Arnold N. Delmonico*

was flight coveralls and leather A-2 jackets. We clomped around a lot in our flight boots, always when we went to the latrine or some short distance, because they were warm. We either went bareheaded or wore the leather fleece-lined gunners' caps. I can recall wearing my flight coveralls for days at a time without taking them off. I would sleep in them too. We cleaned our ODs [wool uniforms] in aviation gas. Consequently, we smelled like gasoline when we were dressed up to go on pass.

If we wanted to take a shower, we had to go a considerable distance to the showers. There was never any hot water. It was just

too much trouble and a very punishing experience, so nobody bothered. Sponge baths had to do. After a time we couldn't smell ourselves; or we thought we smelled all right, because everybody else smelled that way.

We had a few English radios that were continually malfunctioning. The BBC was dry as dust; the Armed Forces Network was what we listened to. The AFN was the best link we had to home as they played a lot of good jazz, featuring the big name bands of that era. We listened to Axis Sally a lot. She would call some guy's name in the 92nd Bomb Group and tell him his wife was dating a lot. It probably was the truth. We

thought these little gems were funny as hell; they delighted us to no end. Far from damaging our morale, these broadcasts from the enemy were a source of great pleasure to us.

Each crewman had his favorite pinups on the wall behind his bunk. These were highly prized and usually came from *Yank* magazine. The favorites were Betty Grable, Chili Williams in the two-piece polka dot bathing suit, and Rita Hayworth in a silk negligee—the picture that was in *Life* magazine. Sometimes the movie stars sent autographed photos in response to requests. I had one of Ginger Rogers that she had signed. A friend gave it to me. I still have it. I never saw a lewd picture as this was before pornography killed off the pinup.

In the barracks there was a never-ending poker game. George Kepics, our ball turret gunner, was always a big winner. Every month or so he would send home nearly a thousand dollars. He was a rich man when the war was over. We warned the other guys, but they would play with him anyway. The problem was that George was a pro, and they were a bunch of turkeys. There was al-

ways a Shylock in every squadron, and most of the guys stayed in hock to him, mostly because of George. The Shylock's interest rates would have shocked any loan shark back in the States. Of course, if the Shylock went down, all debts were paid, but there was always another to take his place.

Paradoxically, our tenuous existence had the effect of ridding us of the twin sins of covetousness and avarice. The men on the combat crews were completely unselfish. They shared everything—nothing else would have made sense. When someone got a box from home, it was opened right on the spot and shared by all. Nothing was hoarded except whiskey. We loved for the Jewish boys to get boxes from home, because theirs were the best—full of salami, knockwurst, gefiltefisch, pumpernickel, bagels, kosher dills, and all kinds of great things from the "deli," plus the inevitable Manischewitz. The flight crews were also generous with their English friends, sharing an endless booty of chewing gum, chocolates, silk hose, and cigarettes with them. A few boorish fellows attempted to use these goodies to bargain for

Traffic at Mt. Farm. One of the 92nd Bomb Group's B-17E hacks runs up prior to takeoff as the 7th Photo Group control jeep heads back to the line and a visiting Royal Air Force pilot walks in from his de Havilland Dominie. *Robert Astrella*

A 490th Bomb Group Fort, *Love 'em All*, on takeoff at Eye, late 1944. The basis of the nose art was copied from the Alberto Vargas July 1943 *Esquire* magazine gatefold. Copies of this art ended up on literally hundreds of aircraft before the war was over. *Albert N. Delmonico*

the favors of the English girls, but only the most insensitive ones responded to such degrading behavior. When I was in England in 1977, many people would come up and say, "I was one of the little kids who begged chewing gum from the Yanks through the fence."

No one really cared about money. It was completely irrelevant to our existence. When a crew was going on pass, the hat was passed, and everyone would throw in a few pounds. The crew would have a sizable pot to leave with but would return to base without a cent. The Shylock preyed upon these improvident chaps. Really he was very necessary. Since I didn't care for poker, I sent $100 home every month to be saved for me. I don't know why I was saving it. I didn't think I would ever get to spend it. When I came back to the States, a small fortune awaited me.

One function always well attended was sick call. It was not that the fellows were sick; it was the delightful medicine they served: terpinhydrate, called by its aficionados "GI Gin." It was cough syrup with

codeine in it. A guy could get bombed with a couple of swallows. There was always a long line with a lot of phony coughing going on.

Lalli Coppinger
Red Cross Club volunteer hostess

Maybe, in our ignorance, we in Britain had expected Americans to be more like ourselves. After all, didn't they speak the same language—more or less—and didn't they used to be British? A little World War II British guidebook on "Meeting the Americans" reminded us that they had also once fought a war to get away from us, and although they might not be thought of exactly as foreigners, the little book explained that they certainly weren't another kind of Englishman either!

Getting to know the Americans was a memorable highlight of the war. They provided excitement and brought fun back into our lives at the time we most needed it, when we were suffering greatly from the deprivations of the years of war. They livened up our dreary towns and introduced a new world to us.

We learned to understand each other's cultural differences, but were also surprised to find out how much alike we were in many ways. When we opened up our homes and hospitality to them, they responded wholeheartedly and gradually became a very large part of our lives. Many were in England for as long as three years, plenty of time to form a special bonding and lasting friendships.

The GIs had a great liking for children, who needed no encouragement to make their acquaintance. Their faces would light up when their American friends dug down into their pockets and brought out never-ending supplies of candy and chewing gum. No one will ever forget the catch phrase, "Any gum, chum?"

Bob Morgan
B-17 pilot, 91st Bomb Group

Though I flew the airplane, the rest I left up to the other nine members, and they did a great job. And the tenth and eleventh member: my crew chief. I couldn't tell you a nut from a bolt as far as a B-17 is concerned. All I knew was when she would fly, what she would do, what I could do with her, and what she would do for me. And fortunately enough, what she could do was one of the reasons I lived through it. Some others were not so fortunate.

The Army Air Forces decided to make a documentary of combat, which ended up being named *Memphis Belle* after our airplane. The main purpose was to send it back to the people in the United States and show them what was going on in Europe at that time since this was very early in our participation in World War II. There was a great deal of controversy about the B-17 being able to do the job that the Army Air Forces thought it could do, particularly with men like Eighth Air Force commander General Ira Eaker. There were strong feelings that it couldn't be done. The British pooh-poohed us. They said that there was no way that you could go out and daylight bomb with that airplane or any other airplane and not have casualties so high that it would not be profitable or the net results beneficial.

I must say for the first three or four

months I was there I was kind of questioning myself whether it could be done. We had to learn the hard way. There were no books or training in the United States, except how to fly the airplane, that told us exactly what we had to do. Every mission we learned, and we started to write the manual for combat flying over Europe. It was tough. We lost eighty-two percent of our group in the first three months. When you start looking at those figures, you realize how fortunate we were, and how fortunate I was to live through it. It was rough, but we learned, and, little by little, the job got done.

Memphis Belle was made by the famous movie director William Wyler, who did some great movies, including *Mrs. Miniver* and *The Best Years of Our Lives*. He knew what he was doing as far as shooting film, but he had never been in a position where they were shooting back at him! He flew five mis-

Warner Brothers had its most famous cartoon character painted on a number of aircraft, including this 490th Bomb Group B-17. The aggressive, wisecracking rabbit with the New York accent seemed to be a perfect representation of how aggressive Army aircrews viewed themselves. Cockiness was an integral part of remaining sane through an insane war in which the odds of surviving a combat tour were low. *Albert N. Delmonico*

Staff Sergeant Vern Woodward, a waist gunner with the 97th Bomb Group, is a long way from Greenwich, New York—and he doesn't look all that happy about it. Though this kind of hands-on training could be boring and uncomfortable, particularly if they left you in the Channel for a while, it proved essential. Coming down in the water was dreaded, particularly in the winter. Learning how to get into a raft, then crank the "Gibson Girl" emergency radio, often meant the difference between life and death. *USAF*

sions on our airplane, and we got to know him pretty well. We admired him more than anybody else on the crew because here he couldn't shoot back at all, and he was running around the airplane, sticking his camera out, taking pictures! All of the footage didn't come from what he did. He gave out over two hundred 16mm cameras to the various groups, saying, "Now, if you get a chance, when you're not shooting your guns or whatever you're supposed to be doing, if you get a chance, take some film." And they did, resulting in this documentary. Then he gave the cameras to each one that took shots for him. He was a great guy. . . . I was really very fond of William Wyler. They gave him the air medal for those five missions.

I visited his home in Hollywood after the war. In his trophy room he had his Oscars all around, but right in the middle he had that air medal. He was more proud of that than he was of all his Oscars. And we were proud of him and the job he did. It was an unusual documentary done for the time because it was done in color. Most photography in World War II, in the early stages particularly, was done in black and white. This made it even more important. On some things in the film (not the shots in combat, not the scenes on the ground, but shots of the high command strategic planning of a particular mission—our twenty-fifth mission) they lied a little bit, I'm sure because they were pretty sure the Germans would get a copy of *Memphis Belle*. They wanted to make them think that we had all those airplanes on that drawing board up there— which we didn't, by any means, at that time. Of course we did later on, and the job done

after I left was even more fantastic. We were just the neophytes and the beginners. We did our part. . . . but we were glad to get back home.

John Ramsey
B-17 navigator, 493rd Bomb Group

In January 1945, members of our crew were sent to rest homes for a week, the four officers going to Eynsham Hall near Oxford. On Sunday the Yanks at the hall were transported to various places of worship, and the party I joined went to a small Methodist church in the town of Witney. We were ushered to seats on the left side of the sanctuary as one faced the chancel. There was a balcony along the full length of the opposite side, and in the end closest to the chancel was a group of children who had remained after Sunday school for the church service. The text of the sermon was introduced by the pastor's listing several leave-taking expressions, including "Adios," "Au revoir," the British expression of the day "God bless," and what he thought was the predominant American expression, "So long." He then asked the children in the balcony which expression they thought was the nicest and most meaningful. Obviously he expected their reply to be "God bless," which would lead him nicely into his sermon. Those kids looked down at the dozen or so Yanks in their proper dress uniforms and shouted as one, "So long." Whether it was the novelty of having Yanks in the congregation or just that natural rapport that seemed to exist between the US servicemen and the British kids didn't matter, but those kids really made the day for some homesick young

Nose art took on almost every imaginable form, as this 446th Bomb Group B-24 at Bungay demonstrates. *Albert R. Krassman*

Lieutenant A. J. Wood sits in the cockpit of his B-26 Marauder at Stanstead in mid-1944. The 344th Bomb Group had an outstanding nose artist who seemed to have no trouble painting just about anything on metal. *Jack K. Havener*

Yanks. We almost stood up and saluted our young friends. Needless to say, it took some adroit maneuvering on the part of the pastor to get back on track with his sermon.

Ben Smith
B-17 radio operator, 303rd Bomb Group

We didn't fly all the time. We would fly a mission, lick our wounds for a few days, then fly again. The weather was our worst enemy or friend, depending on how one looked at it. It kept us grounded a lot. This didn't bother anybody but a few brave souls. I was always glad to see the mission scrubbed because of bad weather. It meant I had another day to live.

When not flying, at four o'clock each afternoon we would go to the Red Cross for tea

October 1944. An absolutely stunning example of the 344th Bomb Group artist's ability to transfer the July 1943 Alberto Vargas *Esquire* gatefold to a Marauder. The aircraft was named *Valkyrie*, and here it waits to go on the next mission from the group's new base at Cormeilles-en-Vexin, France, which was coded Station A-59 by the Ninth Air Force. *Jack K. Havener*

The honcho nose artist in the 487th Bomb Group at Lavenham was Sergeant Duane Bryers. *Tondelayo* is an excellent example of his skill with paint. *Mark Brown/USAFA*

and crumpets, a rather tame repast for the aerial gunners. I grew quite fond of tea. It gave one a nice little pick-up. I thought tea a very civilized custom; in fact, we tended to ape a lot of the things the British did. They were not to be deterred from their tea. I am told British soldiers would make tea while they were being shelled. I was once in a barber's chair in Northampton when the town clock struck tea time. The barber left me sitting there in the chair with a partial hair cut as he went out for tea. Of course, he begged my pardon first.

When one of the 446th Bomb Group's nose artists had finished this beautiful girl, he began to paint the name *Black Magic* behind her. But he misjudged and ended up with only enough room for *Black M*. That didn't make much sense, so later he painted it out with fresh olive drab paint that is clearly visible on the original faded paint. *Albert R. Krassman*

Classy Chassy was a well-used name for wartime aircraft, certainly put to good use on this 446th Bomb Group Liberator out of Bungay. *Albert R. Krassman*

At times, names were bad omens. *Lassie Come Home* didn't make it back on 4 November 1944, and it was not only the single loss from the 446th Bomb Group but the only loss from the entire strike force. *Albert R. Krassman*

CHAPTER 4

Mission

Fritz Nowosad

group engineering officer, 384th Bomb Group

Typically I would be told at about 10:00 P.M. that I had to put up airplanes for a maximum effort mission. Work was taking place on the aircraft continually. . . . there was no eight-hour day. The group engineering officer would come around and say, "How many airplanes have you got serviceable?" I might say the best I could give was eight. Then he would go around the other squadrons and if everybody else had only eight, there would be only thirty-two of the needed fifty for the raid. So, he would come around again and say, "I need more." I would survey my boards and see which aircraft could be made ready if I concentrated men on these, then come back with, "Perhaps I can give you twelve." He would go around again, maybe get forty-six, then return around midnight or one o'clock in the morning saying, "You've got to give me thirteen airplanes." That's when the trouble began. "I can't give you thirteen airplanes. . . . I went

overboard giving you twelve." No use. "Look, I need thirteen to meet the requirement, and that's the end of it."

We would start to pull bits off other aircraft to make up the one serviceable one. My speech to the crew chief would go something like, "I don't care what you do, but I want that airplane working." How they did it sometimes, I don't know, but when I came back they would be replacing the cowlings, the engine would be fixed, and the crew chief would say, "Captain, it's ready to go." Borrowing, stealing, scrounging—somehow the airplane would always be made ready. GI ingenuity was unbelievable. They could put a B-17 together out of pieces, spray a serial number on it, and you would never know how it got there.

Pecos Reeves

B-17 ground crewman, 100th Bomb Group

It is very hard to say how we ground crew felt when our plane failed to return from a mission. We were never given any in-

A pair of 322nd Squadron, 91st Bomb Group B-17Fs climb to join the formation on the way to Germany in mid-1943. In spite of prewar faith in the ability of bomber formations to protect themselves from fighter attack, the opposite proved to be the case. Statistically the most dangerous place to be in combat that year, whether on the ground or in the air, and regardless of theater, was inside a bomber over Germany. *USAF*

B-17Fs of the 401st Squadron, 91st Bomb Group, low over England in early 1943. Based at Bassingbourn, the 91st was one of the pioneer Eighth Air Force heavy bomb groups, the first to attack a target in the Ruhr-Hamm area on 4 March 1943. Without extensive fighter escort through that year, the going was rough indeed. *USAF*

formation as to what might have happened. We would just stand around until dark, and, when there seemed like there was no hope, we would go help some other crew or go to the barracks. The next morning we would go to the flight line, hoping it would be sitting on the hardstand, but we knew better. You could count on it that you would be getting another aircraft in just a little while. If it was a new one, we would start stripping it, test fly it, and wonder how the new crew would accept us.

We knew that when the crew got in that machine in the morning, the chances of us never seeing them again were very real and likely. I just don't know how those guys did it. I never heard a whimper or a cry, and I only heard of one man in the 100th who refused to go. I guess there were more; I don't

know. Our world and war was on that flight line. We never saw our officers or superiors unless they needed something. The aircraft was ours and ours alone until the flight crews came out and taxied out in it. We pulled all the pre-flights and post-flights on it. I never saw an air crew pre-flight one. They took our word for it: no questions asked, no problems.

Hubert Cripe
B-24 pilot, 453rd Bomb Group

Holding brakes to twenty-five inches mercury, brakes off, and the agonizing, slow roll of takeoff. Sweat, baby, sweat. Wide open throttles and 4,800 horses in the Pratt & Whitneys bellowed their song. Cool Hand Luke, the engineer, calmly called airspeed: sixty, sixty-five, seventy, eighty, ninety, ninety-five, one hundred. Holy Smokey, I can already see the end of the runway! Come on, baby: one-ten, one-twelve, one-fifteen, one-eighteen, one-twenty. Keep that nose down and get all that speed you can. At a hundred and twenty miles per hour I eased back pressure on the wheel, the heavy plane lightened, and we were airborne. Some terrific load—we can scarcely climb. "Gear up!" I screamed. "Gear up," came Russ's assuring answer, and the big gear swung outward and upward into the nacelles. Russ reset the manifold pressure and rpm, then milked up the flaps. At a hundred and fifty miles per hour we started climbing.

Robert Keir
B-17 tail gunner, 401st Bomb Group

We were the third ship to take off. We had just become airborne when the Fort

nosed up and the left wing dropped. We seemed to be going around in a big curve, and my first reaction was that our pilot was pulling a fancy maneuver. I got down on my left knee to look out the side window of the radio room in time to see the left wing throwing up dirt and sparks. Didn't have to be told we were in trouble, and, expecting a crash, I turned to brace against the radio room door. As I did, it swung open, and at first I thought someone was coming through. I held it and looked into the bomb bay, but there was nothing to see except those twelve 500-pounders. I shut the door and braced

myself against it and realized the pilot had got us off the ground. The engines were groaning, and I knew things were still very wrong. I glimpsed some guys standing by a hangar and wondered why I couldn't be there at this moment.

The plane struck the ground again, then cleared, but it was plain we weren't going to make it. I gripped the beading around the edge of the open radio room gun hatch and thought of trying to jump out, but things were going past too fast. Then we hit the ground hard, tail first, and I found myself looking out where the tail had been. Pieces

Bag of Bolts, **a 450th Squadron, 322nd Bomb Group B-26B, low over the Essex countryside, September 1943. The 322nd flew the first Marauder missions in the European Theater of Operations, paving the way through painful experience for a record that gave the B-26 the lowest loss rate of any Army Air Forces type in the war.** *Roland B. Scott*

Though not as well known as their Army counterparts, the US Navy flew the antisubmarine version of the B-24, the PB4Y. This PB4Y-1 out of England is hunting subs in the Bay of Biscay, 1944. In the face of strong enemy fighter resistance, Navy crews did a creditable job of sinking German U-boats. *National Archives via Stan Piet*

The 388th Bomb Group on the way back to Knettishall after hitting tactical targets at Brest, 26 August 1944. *Tactical* was another word for supporting the troops on the ground as they moved forward across the Continent. Arguments raged over whether this lengthened or shortened the war by pulling the bombers off their strategic targets deep inside the Third Reich. *Mark Brown/USAFA*

of fuselage were flying off and bulkheads were moving around and the ball turret was crushed up inside. The wreck was slowing, but I kept thinking about those bombs just the other side of that plywood door. A final big lurch and we came to a stop. I could see the reflection of flames on the aluminum skin.

I heard Musser say, "Let's get the hell out of here," as he jumped up and stepped over Cohen, who was lying by the ball turret. I walked over him too and out the fuselage side entrance. Cohen followed, and we all went around to the front of the wing and saw that the plane had hit a barn. The pilot had clambered out. He had blood running down his face. I was going back to get the bombardier and navigator, but the pilot said

they were dead and we should get clear before the bomb load went up. We ran down the field towards the village. A man stuck his head out of the first house and said, "Did you hear a bang?" I said, "You gonna hear another one in a minute." We told him to get his family out and down the road. There was a straw stack in the field near the road, and we all got behind that.

People were now coming down the road like a load of refugees. I took a look back at the plane and saw it was burning fiercely. There was nothing the crash wagon could do but let it burn and get people away from neighboring houses. Then, about fifteen minutes later, there was one hell of a boom and for a moment the clouds in the sky turned red. Pieces started to fall, the heavy

Next page
Major Byron Trent, commanding officer of the 333rd Squadron, 94th Bomb Group, Bury St. Edmunds, with one of his B-17s. Close up, it was easy to see that individual unit markings were painted on as quickly as possible, without primer or multiple coats of paint. There just wasn't much time to do otherwise. *Byron Trent*

bits first and then the lighter pieces, which seemed to take a few minutes to come down. Many of the houses in the village were wrecked by the blast, but no one was seriously injured. The bombardier and navigator survived too, so all the crew escaped with their lives, if not without injury.

John Gabay
B-17 tail gunner, 94th Bomb Group

Wilhelmshaven, Germany, 3 February 1944 (ship number 846). Target: sub pens. It seems we made this raid the hard way, under very bad weather conditions. We had complete ten tenths cloud cover up to 20,000 feet. We had fairly good escort for a while. We ran into heavy but not so accurate flak as we crossed the enemy coast. On the bomb run, the bomb bay doors stuck, so Mike had to crank them down—in time to drop on target. Flak was heavy, but over on our left. We were to come out by way of the North Sea. A sleet storm reached our altitude, and we couldn't see to stay in formation, so we got orders that everyone was on their own. Ice was forming on our wings as we let down through the storm.

The last thing I saw before the weather enveloped us was a Fort running into the tail of another . . . chewed it up so bad the gunner fell out over the North Sea. I couldn't see anything else as the weather closed in around us. We dove at great speed trying to get to warmer air. The ice soon broke away from the wings, and we didn't hit anything—so far so good! We broke out through the clouds about 200 feet over the North Sea along the Frisian Islands. Now plenty of 20mm were bursting around the tail and left waist—couldn't see where it was coming

from. Then weather opened up and we saw soldiers running for their gun positions. We opened up on them—saw about twenty go down like rag dolls—and got out of there fast. Was a bumpy ride home. Found myself in midair several times.

Roy Kennett
B-24 radio operator, 392nd Bomb Group

Now, when we released the bombs, I was down on the catwalk. Bomb bay doors were open, and the bombs were gone. Then I had to say, "Bombs away, Sir!" Big deal, right? On the first mission I flew, I was a substitute radio operator; their guy had taken a hit, so I flew with this other crew. In fact, it was the first day we got to Wendling and the 392nd. Now their waist gunner was a big, tall, blonde guy, and it was his job to tell the pilot when the bomb bay was clear. He was a good guy, but he had a heck of a stutter. Well now, we're leaving the target, and he's down on the catwalk calling to the captain. We're all listening for him to say, "Bombs away,

Late 1944. A 385th Bomb Group B-17G climbs out from Great Ashfield and heads for Germany. *Clark B. Rollins, Jr.*

Wading through flak on the bomb run, as seen by a tail gunner in a 385th Bomb Group B-17 in late 1944. The twin smoke trails are from the target markers released by the lead aircraft. *Clark B. Rollins, Jr.*

Sir." So he says, "Ba-ba-ba-bob-ba-bob-bo . . . (Silence.) The goddamn things are gone, Sir!" That was a tough mission, but we all broke up over that one.

Ed Leighty
B-17 waist gunner, 447th Bomb Group

I shall never forget the briefing for that mission, the first daylight attack on Berlin. The intelligence officer was a big man; he looked as if he had lived a good life. He pulled back the curtain over the wall map, and there was the target marked out by a long wool string from England to Germany. "Men," he said pointing with his stick, "today you will bomb Berlin." I don't know about any men being there in the room, but I know there were a lot of frightened boys.

Ben Smith
B-17 radio operator, 303rd Bomb Group

After three missions, I was beginning to swagger a bit. I went out of my way to paint lurid pictures of aerial combat to the green crews coming in as replacements. Really there was no need to exaggerate. The empty beds in the huts were silent witnesses to that fact. I suppose veteran warriors from time immemorial have sought to frighten their novice companions. But none was more vocal than I was in describing the maniacal fury of the German opposition. This bombastic euphoria was of short duration, however. It had been rumored in the squadron that we would be one of the lead crews after Captain Brinkley's crew finished their tour. This belief was reinforced when a bird

A 367th Squadron, 306th Bomb Group Fort climbs out from Thurliegh as it passes directly over Benson Airfield, Oxfordshire. *Ben Marcilonis via Roger Freeman*

The 490th Bomb Group heads into Germany, far from home. *Albert N. Delmonico*

colonel flew with us on one of our early missions, ostensibly to look us over. When we came off the target, it was my job to look in the bomb bay and see that all the bombs had cleared the racks. On this mission the flak was really coming up, so I hastily looked in the bomb bay, closed the door, and yelled, "Bomb bay clear." I had seen no bombs. When we got down from altitude and were out over the Channel, I started through the catwalk, and, to my horror, half the bombs were in the bomb bay and still fully armed. Since we were nearing the English coast, Chick and the colonel decided to land with the bombs. They were too costly to jettison. We flew back to the 303rd and landed safely. Chick made a perfect landing. Thank God

he did. I knew I was going to catch hell. For some reason the colonel did not chew me out, but I could see he was sore as hell. I had really blown it. We heard nothing more about "lead crews," and my crew members blamed me for the fact that we were passed over. I had endangered the whole crew needlessly, and I felt awful about it. I was completely deflated, a condition which became me more than my previous swaggering. When we were down, Chick looked at me and said, "For Chris's sakes, Smitty," but that's all he ever said.

Marauders of the 495th Squadron, 344th Bomb Group marshal at A-59, Cormeilles-en-Vexin, France, in October 1944 for takeoff against targets in the Cologne area as the Allied armies push toward Germany. *Jack K. Havener*

A well-worn 386th Bomb Group Marauder over occupied France, 1944. At this point, war paint wasn't much of an issue. If it stayed on, fine; if it didn't, so what. *John H. Meyers*

Captain John Meyers with his 386th Bomb Group B-26G *La Paloma* at A-60, Beaumont-sur-Oise, late summer 1944. One look at a Marauder head-on gave a good idea of why it was so fast. *John H. Meyers*

Roy Kennett

B-24 radio operator, 392nd Bomb Group

There could have been about 155 fighters in the area, but not all attacking our particular group. They were Focke-Wulf 190s. Now an Fw 190 looks a lot like our P-47s—it's got that oval configuration with a slight dihedral to the wings, and the Fw 190 looks just like it. We thought they were ours—until they started shooting at us. We had been escorted by P-38s, and they had just left us because their range wasn't long enough. The P-47s were supposed to pick us up. All I remember is that their wings sparkled. It looked like they had headlights, and they were turning them on and off on the leading edge of the wing.

All of a sudden, all hell broke loose. When we got hit, a fire broke out in the airplane, and it spread into the bomb bay. So I went down into the bomb bay and tried to get the fire out—it was around the bombs because we still had our bombs in the aircraft. The bomb bay went open while I was on the catwalk. The fire was just tremendous by that time, and there was no chance of getting it out. It was all over everything. Gasoline was pouring down into the bomb bay and was feeding the fire, so I looked upwards toward the flight deck. . . . the copilot was standing there motioning for me to get out. I walked up out of the bomb bay into that well that goes into the command deck, grabbed my parachute, and snapped it on. I grabbed at Krushas's feet a couple of times and yanked on them. Then I turned around on the catwalk and rolled out of the bomb bay.

Krushas was in his turret when it got shot out and it was inoperable. He looked down and saw fire around his feet, so he crawled out of his turret and looked around for me. I was gone, so he said, "If it's no place for Kennett, then it's no place for me." He grabbed his chute, snapped it on, and jumped out too. He said, when he got out,

103

the pilot and copilot were both in their seats trying to fly the airplane. Now back in the waist, where Hatton was, Smitty had one waist gun and Hatton had the other waist gun. Rowlett was in the tail and Oliver Schmelzle was in the ball turret. I can't remember if the ball turret was hurt or not, but they got the turret up into the waist of the airplane and got Schmelzle out. And the airplane still hadn't gone down! The tail gunner got out of the tail section and came back into the waist. I don't know if it was three minutes, five minutes, or ten minutes, but it was more than just a few seconds.

So then all four were around the camera hatch. Smitty told me that Hymie Hatton

The 457th Bomb Group begins to pull contrails as it crosses into enemy airspace, late December 1944. No one liked to see these plumes of vapor coming from the exhaust of each engine; they virtually pointed German fighter pilots and flak gunners to their targets. *Leslie R. Peterson*

Pulling some maintenance at Mendlesham on the 34th Bomb Group's *Ole Timer*, a 391st Squadron ship, while there's a respite between missions. *Mark Brown/USAFA*

was down on his knee, right alongside the open camera hatch, motioning for Schmelzle and Rowlett to jump. Smitty was standing up right beside Hymie. Schmelzle and Rowlett were just standing there and wouldn't jump, so then Hatton jumped. Smitty went right down alongside the hatch and tried to get Rowlett to jump, but he just stood there. Just about that time, the ship snapped into a spin. It threw Smitty halfway out. He said to me, "The last thing I saw when I looked back was Schmelzle and Rowlett stuck to the bulkhead by centrifugal force." Then the slipstream tore him out.

Now, the sound of being pulled out into the slipstream—you'd almost have to hear

it, and a person telling you probably can't describe it either. The best way I can think of to describe what happens when you first jump out of an airplane is this: If you're traveling down the road in an automobile and you throw a piece of paper out the window, you notice how it flutters and turns and does all kinds of whirligigs, and then all of a sudden it just calms down and very gently floats down to ground. Well, the initial reaction to a jump is very much the same. When I rolled off that catwalk and into the slipstream, it just turned me every which way but loose for a few minutes. Then it sort of comes down to your normal falling speed— around 120 miles per hour. But you have no

Changing engine number two, 18th Squadron dispersal, 34th Bomb Group, Mendlesham, 1945.
Mark Brown/USAFA

105

Forts of the 18th
Squadron, 34th Bomb
Group spread across
their dispersal points
at Mendlesham.
Eighth Air Force
airfields were laid out
in excellent fashion,
making it easy to taxi
aircraft from each
squadron to the active
runway, yet remain
dispersed enough to
avoid extreme
vulnerability to enemy
attack. A walk—even a
bike ride—around a
base took awhile.
Mark Brown/USAFA

sensation of falling, because you have no reference point. If you fall off a ladder, you can see the house go by. When you're five miles up in the air, you're not passing anything (although there were pieces of airplanes falling down all around you). It isn't noisy; you don't hear anything but the wind whistling next to your ears. I know when I first came back, I told my father I had glided for over four miles before I pulled the ripcord.

Jack Havener
B-26 pilot, 344th Bomb Group

Uncle Sam always wanted value for his dollar, and this certainly applied to the payloads of World War II bombers. A combat overload was more the rule than the exception, especially with the B-26s, which we regularly flew off at 40,000 pounds, gross, when the manufacturer's maximum recommendation was 37,000 pounds. Every bomber pilot's dread was the loss of an engine on or soon after takeoff. We B-26 men were almost conditioned into believing that if this happened a crash was inevitable. Confidence was maintained because you hoped it only happened to the other guy. This time it didn't—it happened to me!

On 12 September 1944 our group was briefed to bomb strong points at Foret de Haye near Nancy, France. I was flying *Terre Haute Tornado* with First Lieutenant William R. Hunter as my copilot. I had flown copilot for Hunter a few days previous in his regular lead ship, and now he was flying co for me in my regular one. On these extra missions, we normally carried our regular crew with the exception of the bombardier and the navigator. Lead bombardiers were zealously relegated to lead missions only, so this routine gave wing position bombardiers a chance for extra missions also. On this one we had one of the few remaining sergeant bombardiers on board, Phil Dolce. Likewise, since we were flying a wing position, we didn't need a navigator.

We had just taken off to the northeast and were about halfway through the first turn to join up with the balance of the flight on our left, when the right engine started sputtering and losing power. We were only at about 1,000 feet, and as we frantically clawed the pedestal controls, trying to get some life back into the engine, we realized we had a serious problem. Naturally we couldn't gain altitude, so we abandoned the attempt to join up with the flight and turned on the downwind leg of the traffic pattern, trying to maintain flying speed.

When it was obvious that the engine would not respond, I gave Hunter the order to feather the prop. By the time I had trimmed for single-engine operation we were still losing altitude, so I gave Sergeant John Skowski, our engineer-gunner, the signal to pull the emergency bomb salvo release. He always stood between the two pilot seats on takeoff to keep an eye on the instruments. He immediately reached up and pulled the release to dump the four 1,000-pounders we were carrying, turned around to watch the bomb bay doors open and snap shut after the salvo, and greatly relieved the tension in the cockpit when he yelled, "We got a haystack, Lieutenant!"

Hunter kept calling out airspeed as we continued on the downwind leg and called the tower, informing them of our situation and requesting permission to land immediately. In a very cool tone the tower operator came back, telling us he had a formation still taking off and could we please hold for a bit until all the ships were off? Hunter and I stared across at one another in disbelief, and he replied, "Hell no! We're on one engine just above stalling speed, and we're coming in if we have to land on the taxi strip!" His ruddy face turned even redder as he blasted this to the tower in a manner that only Willy could do.

We were so low (no more than 500 feet) that we couldn't see the field to our left but knew we were on a correct downwind heading and would begin our approach turn when we sighted the St. Giles church steeple at Great Hallingbury just off the southwest

Eighth Air Force Station 134, Eye, in the Suffolk countryside, home of the 490th Bomb Group. *Mark Brown/USAFA*

end of the runway a couple miles. Then pre-stall vibrations set in, and I told Hunter, "We can't make it. Let's land on the RAF fighter field just ahead of us." Before he could answer, the Royal Air Force field loomed ahead where tractors were pulling mowing machines across the center of the grass. How do you decide what to do in a situation such as this? Sacrifice two lives on the ground in hopes of saving six in the aircraft, possibly wiping out the aircraft in the process, or save the two on the ground and try for the good old Stanstead runway? The Royal Air Force field was Sawbridgeworth, by the way.

As if reading my thoughts, Hunter said, "We've got to make it! Just keep her from stalling and do a flat pylon turn around the steeple!" I agreed and began a gentle turn to the left with the steeple as my bearing point. Not wanting to lose any more altitude than necessary, I kept the turn very shallow and silently prayed a thanks to Mr. Ransom,

This 490th Bomb Group B-17G has just turned off the active runway at Eye after a mission and heads for its hardstand. *Mark Brown/USAFA*

my primary flight school instructor, for drilling into me the intricacies of a correct pylon turn. As a result, we rounded out the turn just southwest of the steeple and homed in on it to the northeast, looking for the end of the runway.

It's hard to believe, but my top-turret gunner, Sergeant J. E. Smith, who had dropped out of his turret and crawled into the navigator's chair when the engine quit, swore that I lifted the right wing to clear the St. Giles steeple. This done, I had Hunter drop the gear and flaps at the same time, and I chopped the throttle over the end of the runway, still managing to unwind the trim and keep her straight. With my preoccupation in winding out lateral trim, I didn't have time to adjust elevator trim on the round-out (flat as it was) and can thank Hunter for helping me pull back on the control column to keep us from going in too steeply.

Luckily, we had consumed enough time during our slow-flying transit of the traffic pattern to allow the rest of the formation to take off, and the runway was clear for the landing with the crash trucks, the ambulances, and the inevitable group commander's jeep racing down alongside us as we touched down and braked to a halt about halfway down the strip. The usual ground-kissing ritual was performed by the entire crew after we exited the aircraft, and my right arm was quivering from the crew shaking my hand. Sergeant Raymond C. Sanders, my radio gunner, says it was the only time he ever kissed a man when he planted a big one on my cheek. Under the circumstances, I didn't mind at all.

The colonel's jeep careened up, and he uncoiled that big frame and strode over to me. I thought, "Oh, oh, I'm going to catch hell now for aborting." Aborting with questionable cause was a no-no in the 344th, and

Bomb dump, 490th Bomb Group, Eye, England, late 1944. *Mark Brown/USAFA*

lately there had been some obvious incidents of "featheritis." My emergency was legitimate, and I was prepared to tell him so.

I saluted, and returning it, he asked, "What happened, son?" I related how she'd cut out after takeoff, and, despite all action by my copilot, she kept losing power so we had to salvo and shut her down. To my surprise, he stuck out that big paw and said, "Congratulations, Son. You did a magnificent job of bringing her in and saving the airplane and your crew!" I was almost too taken aback to murmur, "Thank you, Sir," as he shook my hand. I stood transfixed as he

turned on his heel, climbed back in the jeep, and motioned his driver to move out, yelling to us all to go over to the flight surgeon for a shot of whiskey as he peeled away.

Just at that time, Staff Sergeant Jerry Reed, our crew chief, and the technical sergeant line chief arrived and were looking at the suspect engine and giving me jaundiced glances, so I opted to go with the aircraft as it was being towed back to the hardstand to try to find out what had caused the loss of power. Back at the hardstand, as the line chief ran the engine up to full power time and again with no drop in manifold

A 490th Bomb Group Fort begins a turn off the active runway at Eye after the long trip home from Germany. Flying B-24s, then B-17s, the 490th was one of the few good-luck groups in the Eighth, with one of the lowest combat loss rates. *Mark Brown/USAFA*

pressure or the faintest hint of a sputter, I had the uneasy feeling that he was thinking, "Well, another pilot with featheritis." The next time he ran her up there was a definite sputtering and loss of manifold pressure. This repeated itself on subsequent run-ups, and he admitted that there seemed to be fuel starvation.

Subsequent investigation revealed a perforated carburetor diaphragm, which prompted a maintenance directive to go out and all engines in the group were checked for this fault. I never did find out how many more were faulty, but I know that they found some on other aircraft and consequently all diaphragms were replaced. It was one of those quirks that doesn't show up on a ground check but only manifest themselves under full power load in flight. I was vindicated!

After a meal at the mess, Hunter and I and an intelligence officer took off in the Ox-

ford Airspeed to plot the location of the jettisoned bombs. Retracing our previous calamitous flight pattern, as best we could, we found that Skowski was right. We had completely demolished a large haystack in a farmer's field but had caused no other damage or injury. Of course, the bombs hadn't been armed, so the haystack had been clobbered by impact alone. The armament crew went out and retrieved the bombs, and our personnel officer made arrangements with the farmer to pay for the damage.

By the time we were ready to take off in the Oxford, I had recovered from the shock of the experience but had developed a bad case of the jitters, so had prevailed upon Hunter to fly the Oxford. Old steel-nerved Willy rose to the occasion, and as we were starting our left turn after takeoff, I slyly reached over and pulled the right throttle back just enough to create a noticeable loss of rpm, yelling, "Oh, no! Not again!" Hunter's startled look changed into a grin as he saw what I was doing, and we laughed like idiots, bleeding off plenty of pent up emotions.

Johnny Miller
B-17 waist gunner, 100th Bomb Group

The 6 March 1944 mission to Berlin was a slaughter for our group. Most of our planes didn't make it back. It was so quiet. The men spoke in low, almost inaudible tones, if they spoke at all. There were many that wandered off by themselves wanting to be alone in their grief. Others, their eyes moist, stood silently. And many drank more than usual

At the end of the war, the Eighth Air Force was tasked with dropping a different kind of ordnance—food—on Holland. The Dutch were starving, and the quickest way to meet the need, until ground links could be set up, was to air-drop the food. This 34th Bomb Group B-17G, northwest of Amsterdam, is on the way back from Utrecht in May 1945. *Mark Brown/USAFA*

Our Baby, an 839th Squadron, 487th Bomb Group Fort with another of Alberto Vargas's famous *Esquire* girls on the nose, climbs out of Lavenham to drop napalm on the last German troop strongholds at Royan, near Bordeaux, 15 April 1945. *Mark Brown/USAFA*

The view from the tower at Snetterton Heath. Flying Fortresses of the 96th Bomb Group taxi out for takeoff, late 1944. This scene was duplicated across England, in everything but the aircraft markings, for three years, dozens of times each day. *Mark Brown/USAFA*

The 100th Bomb Group's airfield, Thorpe Abbots, mid-1944. *Lady Geraldine* has just been shut down in its hardstand after a mission, and the crew is trying to stretch the kinks out as cigarettes are lit up. A six-by-six truck and jeep stand ready to take them to interrogation. *Mark Brown/USAFA*

that evening. Lieutenant Colonel John Bennett, our squadron CO but now commanding officer of the group, grasping for some words to say, said the Eighth had lost less than ten percent. But his voice sounded strange, and his words trailed off.

I was living in the spare gunner's hut at the time, and for fifteen days following that raid on Berlin, I was alone in that hut! Everyone I knew was either killed or taken prisoner. *Less than two months* after joining my group, I became the oldest gunner in my outfit. I was seventeen years old.

A new engine has just been hung on the 100th Bomb Group's *Boss Lady* at Thorpe Abbots. The prop, in full feather position for positioning on the engine prop shaft splines, is getting its last bolts tightened before a ground check. *Mark Brown/USAFA*

CHAPTER 5

Combat

Ben Smith
radio operator, 303rd Bomb Group

I recall that I used to lie awake in bed dreading the time when I would have to lay it on the line or forever be lost in the infamy of disgrace (I learned later that I was not the only one). This was so real to me. Outwardly, I was lighthearted and jovial, well liked by my friends. They thought I was a pretty cool customer, but inside I was sick, sick, sick! My bravado was sort of a rallying point, though phony as a three-dollar bill. I wore a "hot pilot's" cap, smoked big black cigars, and drank boilermakers. The only one who wasn't fooled was me.

Richard Fitzhugh
B-17 pilot, 457th Bomb Group

Our bombardier crawled through the top turret one time on the way to pull the pins on the bombs (the engineer would have to step down and get out of there). And going through there, he caught some part of his flying equipment on the trigger that makes the turret go round and round. The harder he pulled, the faster this thing went, just beating him to a pulp. The harder he tried to get out, the faster that thing went. Finally the engineer came to his rescue, and they got him disentangled from that thing. I thought we were going to lose a bombardier that day.

John Gabay
B-17 tail gunner, 94th Bomb Group

16 October 1943: Today was a sad one. Our radio man, Charley Gunn, went on his first raid with another crew and all hands failed to return. There was a cablegram waiting for him—his wife gave birth to a baby boy. He'll never know.

Roy Kennett
B-24 radio operator, 392nd Bomb Group

After the plane took off and we made formation, you had to maintain radio silence. So I didn't have anything to do. As soon as we got over enemy territory, that was it. All I did was sit there. Sometimes that's the scariest thing—to be just helpless. My job

A B-17 navigator at his station. I guess the Army Air Forces photographer didn't think to hide the still propeller visible through the window, but this is still an excellent look at how a navigator went to war in the Eighth Air Force. *USAF*

was to take over if someone else was hit; I would take over his position. Thank God I never had to do that—until the very last mission, and then it was over.

Al Keeler
B-17 copilot, 95th Bomb Group

We were returning from a bombing mission to Trzebinia, Poland, and were well within friendly territory, descending through 10,000 feet on our way to land at our "shuttle raid" base at Poltava in the heart of the Ukraine. Our aircraft, *Full House* (so named because of its serial number: 2977797), with the appropriate five-card display on our nose, was leading the high squadron. I was the copilot. As we de-

Almost home, 26 August 1944. After hitting Brest, the 388th Bomb Group lets down over the English countryside on the way in to Knettishall. *Mark Brown/USAFA*

Not until 1945 did the Eighth get some Army OA-10A Catalinas to supplement the Royal Air Force's air-sea rescue (ASR) aircraft. Unfortunately, red tape kept them from arriving earlier. Still, the 5th Emergency Rescue Squadron put them to good use, losing two, one to enemy fire. This Cat is paying a visit to the 4th Fighter Group at Debden. *F. M. "Pappy" Grove*

One of the most welcome sights of the war, if you were an airman down in the English Channel—a Royal Air Force rescue High Speed Launch at the dock ready to cast off. The Royal Navy was also a part of the ASR fleet with similar Rescue Motor Launches. These brave air force and navy sailors meant business, at times taking extreme risks to get to crews, even using the cannon on the bow if that's what it took. These fast PT-boat types, based at Harwich and Great Yarmouth, performed the majority of wartime rescues at sea. *F. M. "Pappy" Grove*

An 18th Squadron, 34th Bomb Group B-17G sits out an approaching storm while visiting Mt. Farm. *Robert Astrella*

parted 9,500 feet, I called over the interphone, "Copilot going off oxygen," meaning that I would remove my oxygen mask and change to a throat mike for the lower altitude.

Suddenly, a small oxygen explosion occurred under the base of the top turret gunner, Staff Sergeant Ray Rich. Immediately the cockpit filled with smoke. The pilot, First Lieutenant George Dancisin, who was still hooked to his oxygen tube and helmet headset, bolted out of his left seat, separating his oxygen hose, headset cord, and oxygen mike cord. Since this occurred as I was changing to my headset and throat mike, no other crew members had interphone contact with the cockpit. After Danny left his seat, I was

immediately flying the aircraft. The smoke became so dense I could hardly breathe. Fortunately, our B-17 had a small window vent panel on the front windscreen that could be opened. I grabbed for it and immediately the slipstream from the open panel helped clear the instrument panel so I could check our altitude. We were in a loose formation, so I peeled away from the group in a sharp right turn—no place for a burning aircraft that might explode and take some other aircraft down with it. I leveled the aircraft at a safe distance in line with the rest of the group.

The cockpit became even more drafty as Danny, who had climbed down into the nose, had told the navigator, First Lieutenant Frank Morrison, and the bombardier, First

Lieutenant Foster Sherwood, to bail out through the lower nose hatch. Why Danny did not bail out then I'll never know. Evidently, it suddenly dawned on him that he was the pilot and there were other crew members still in the aircraft! He came back up to the cockpit and said, "Rube [my nickname], we're bailing out!" I had reached for my chest pack to buckle it on while Danny was down in the nose. No chute! We always hung our chest packs on the back of each other's seat for easier access to grab them. Danny had taken my chute and climbed back down into the nose preparing for bailout. I reached in back of Danny's seat, and evidently in the melee, Danny's chute had fallen off its hook. Through the smoke, I

A 95th Bomb Group Fort just airborne at Horham, August 1944. *Albert J. Keeler*

A part of the 412th Squadron, 95th Bomb Group crew of *Full House* on top of their B-17G at Horham, summer 1944. (Left to right): right waist gunner Staff Sergeant Bob Rogers, ball turret gunner Staff Sergeant Leo Makelky, top turret gunner Staff Sergeant Ray Rich, radio operator Technical Sergeant Alyre "Joe" Comeau, and tail gunner Staff Sergeant Larry Stevens. *Albert J. Keeler*

First Lieutenant Albert Keeler was copilot on the 412th Bomb Squadron's *Full House* from April to August 1944. Like most Army Air Forces pilots, he left peacetime pursuits (in this case studying to become a music teacher at Ithaca College, New York) to enter flight training. By the time he had completed thirty-five missions, flying had firmly taken hold, and Al made the Air Force a career, flying another combat tour in Korea in the process. *Albert J. Keeler*

Lieutenant Colonel Harry G. "Grif" Mumford was one of the original members of the 95th Bomb Group's air echelon when they arrived in England in early April 1943 after flying their Forts across the South Atlantic Ferry Route. He served as commanding officer of the 412th Bomb Squadron, 95th Bomb Squadron operations officer, and then group air executive officer; he also led the 95th during the first try at bombing Berlin on 4 March 1944. *Albert J. Keeler*

reached down and felt a back harness moving—Rich! I yelled, "Hey, Rich, find me a chute!" We always carried spares in the lower cockpit area. He threw one up to me and, at about the same time, located a fire extinguisher. After a couple of squirts of the CO2 bottle, the fire was out under the turret.

Just as the smoke was clearing, the door to the front of the bomb bay opened. It was Technical Sergeant Langford, the engineer, with a large fire extinguisher. He had been riding as waist gunner and had smelled smoke in the rear of the aircraft. He couldn't make interphone contact with the cockpit, so he had grabbed the big fire extinguisher and crawled between the bomb racks with *no chute* on, because he couldn't climb through the racks with it on and still carry

the extinguisher. What guts! With the fire out and cleared, I rejoined the formation and checked in with the lead, advising them that we were OK to continue back to Poltava with no emergency landing requirement. After the smoke cleared from the turret area, the base of Rich's turret was red hot! Some of the flames had blasted against the fuel transfer valves and burned some of the paint off the nameplate! Rich's chute, which he had buckled on during the incident, had one end of its packing burned out! Rich had minor burns on his hands.

I put Rich in the left seat, and we continued on back to land at Poltava. Danny came back up to the cockpit and stood between our seats, stone silent and ashen white. When we got on the ground, we later

Next page
Aircraft commander of the 95th Bomb Group B-17G *Full House*. First Lieutenant George Dancisin was twenty-three years old here in the summer of 1944 at Horham, a world away from his Stateside job in a zipper factory. *Albert J. Keeler*

found out that Morrison and Sherwood had been located by the Russians and would be returned to Poltava. Danny and I discussed the whole incident. I was pissed off, because so many of us were deserted in a burning aircraft, and I wanted to recommend Rich for an award, since he got the fire out, saving the rest of us. We were near the end of our combat tour. This had been our thirty-second mission. With two more missions back to England, via Foggia, and probably "milk runs" (they were!), we decided to forget the whole deal. There might have been a lot of questions asked, and Danny, who had been a fine pilot, might have had a rough time of it if the facts had come out.

Frank Morrison
B-17 navigator, 95th Bomb Group

I think most crews in the 95th could be described as crews of "extreme camaraderie." I had to make up three missions as the result of being hospitalized and, again, three more as a result of a parachute jump. I have seen a blow-up color photo of the crew sitting by the runway at Horham, waiting for my make-up plane to return. On my thirty-fourth mission, the balance of the crew already having flown thirty-five, we all received a good scare. I guess I would have to say that 26 August 1944 was a day when it could have gone either way.

We took a series of flak hits over the target at 26,000 feet, and with two engines out and a broken oxygen line, we could not take evasive action to escape the extremely heavy ground fire. We began to gradually lose altitude, and we called for a fighter escort. Almost at once those beautiful P-51s

95th Bomb Group crew of *Full House* outside their Nissen hut briefing room at Horham, summer 1944. Back row: pilot First Lieutenant George Dancisin, navigator First Lieutenant Frank Morrison, right waist gunner Staff Sergeant Bob Rogers, bombardier First Lieutenant Foster Sherwood, and tail gunner Staff Sergeant Larry Stevens. Front row: copilot First Lieutenant Al Keeler, radio operator Technical Sergeant Alyre "Joe" Comeau, top turret gunner Staff Sergeant Ray Rich, and ball turret gunner Staff Sergeant Leo Makelky. *Albert J. Keeler*

appeared and stayed right on our wing tips as we limped for the coast. The Me 109s just loved to get a wounded B-17 alone, but they surely didn't want to tangle with a couple of P-51s. As we reached the Channel, we were down to near 1,000 feet, and the pilot gave the order to jettison all expendable cargo. That seemed to be just enough to let us land at the first fighter base on the English shore. My estimation of B-17 pilots, which was already good, went up 1,000 percent. If they were good enough to be in the 95th, they were good enough for me.

Meanwhile, back at Horham, my crew was watching the squadron return as usual, and all the planes were accounted for except one, and that was the one I was flying with that day. They hurried over to question some of the other crews and were told of us losing altitude with two feathered props and being unable to keep up with the formation. When they went back to the Quonset, I guess it was a pretty sad evening. At last we were furnished a ride from the fighter base back to Horham. When I walked into the Quonset, there were some damp eyes among these so-called "tough" sergeants. I will say that the "welcome" was followed by one helluva party. And then I received the icing on the cake. The following day I was notified by Colonel Carl Truesdell that I might just be trusting my luck a bit too far, and if I so desired, I could go home with the rest of the crew, even though I had only flown thirty-four missions, and they had flown thirty-five. I have never met Colonel Truesdell

The 344th Bomb
Group climbing out of
Stanstead, England,
for a support mission,
June 1944. *Jack K.
Havener*

The 7th Bomb
Squadron's *Flying
Dutchmen* gets some
much needed post-
mission maintenance
at Mendlesham, home
of the 34th Bomb
Group. *Mark
Brown/USAFA*

With one B-24 on the
runway about to
release brakes, the
493rd Bomb Group
marshals for takeoff at
Debach, June 1944.
Mark Brown/USAFA

since that day, but I've always had a soft spot in my heart for him. Again that night, we had one of those parties to remember.

Richard Fitzhugh
B-17 pilot, 457th Bomb Group

On the missions we didn't have any food, so they'd give us a big square of chocolate for the crew. One great, big solid piece of chocolate. On the way back, the engineer would break this up and pass it out for a little nourishment. Sometimes it would get so cold—it might be seventy below up there—

that he would take the fire ax and lay this chocolate down on the sheet metal floor of the B-17 and hammer on it. The first time I heard him doing that, I thought he was firing the guns up there. He'd bang on that thing and break it up, but then it was so cold you couldn't hardly put it in your mouth.

John Gabay
B-17 tail gunner, 94th Bomb Group

History of ship number 846, named *Lucky 13* by ground crew: Lawrence Kersey, Don MacConnell, Leroy Kriest. First B-17G

Two 490th Bomb Group Forts are already on the runway at Eye with a third on short final, while the next squadron is on initial approach for the overhead break to landing. By this time in the winter of 1944–45, the Eighth Air Force had worked out an excellent recovery procedure with minimum spacing between landing bombers. An entire group could land in short order if everyone was sharp; and everyone usually was, since landing was considered the test of a pilot's ability. *Mark Brown/USAFA*

to be assigned to 331st Squadron on 28 October 1943. Twenty-fifth mission on 11 March 1944. Fiftieth mission 28 June 1944. First G to make fifty missions in 94th. Made "war weary" on 11 October 1944. Seventy-eight missions, 935 hours. Two large Ws painted on rudder. Will go to sub depot for major overhaul after 1,000 hours. Went on first and only shuttle mission to Africa after Regensburg raid. Fifteen engine changes, three oil coolers, two superchargers, one wing tip, one outer wing panel, two inner gas tanks, one rudder, one elevator, one right stabilizer, one rudder control cable, one tail wheel, seven tire changes, two de-icer boots, one patch on Plexiglas nose, hundreds of patches, one flat on landing, running off runway into mud. Spent all night getting it changed.

Bob Morgan
B-17 pilot, 91st Bomb Group

It was a great airplane for a number of reasons. The first is that it would take a lot of punishment—a lot of punishment. I can vouch for that, and I'm sure any other B-17 pilot that flew the airplane in combat can say the same thing. I flew B-29s in the Pacific after I left the European theater, and people have asked me to compare the '29 and the '17. The '29 would never have lasted in Europe, and there was a thought to take it over there at one time. It could never have taken the punishment the '17 did. We lost more B-29s from mechanical failure than we did from the Japanese. If it had been in Europe, it would have been a dead dog. It was a great airplane, don't get me wrong, but the '29 was built for a particular purpose: long-

Late June 1944. Flying gear is spread across a hardstand at Debach, where the crew of *Katrinka*, a 493rd Bomb Group B-24H, gets ready for a mission—the aircraft's eighth, judging by the seven bombs painted on the nose. *Mark Brown/USAFA*

range, Saipan and Guam to Japan. It could carry a big load, but it was not the airplane that could take the punishment from the accurate German antiaircraft and the German fighters.

I get a little flak once in a while from B-24 pilots, and I have friends who flew the B-24. The prettiest sight in combat when we went over France and Germany was to see a B-24 group, 'cause if we saw a B-24 group, we knew the German fighters would not pick on us so badly that day. That's not a nice thing to say, but it is, honestly, truthful.

Besides the B-17, there was one other factor—the Norden bomb sight. A lot of people overlook that fact. The British didn't have it; no one else had it but us, and it was accurate. I'll always remember one mission

in January of 1943. We were the lead ship going over Lorient to bomb some submarine pens from 26,000 feet. The photographs showed that the main impact point of the first bomb was ten feet from the center of the target the bombardier was supposed to hit. That is pretty accurate. They awarded him an air medal for that particular raid.

Bob DeGroat
B-24 pilot, 459th Bomb Group

On one mission, while still over enemy territory, a P-51 slid in and flew formation off my left wing. A voice on the radio casually asked, "Big Brother, mind if I join you?" His engine was running rough and in this situation our guns would be able to cover him. It was a chance for us to protect him for

Some 487th Bomb Group B-17Gs taxiing back in at Lavenham after the 15 April 1945 mission to Royan, France. *Mark Brown/USAFA*

The 446th Bomb Group begins to come alive as the sun rises at Bungay, winter 1944–45. *Albert R. Krassman*

a change. He left us at the head of the Adriatic.

Bud Guillot
B-24 waist gunner, 392nd Bomb Group

The first time we saw a P-51 escort, we almost shot them down. We were on a mission to a six-engine bomber school, and it was over the other side of Munich—a long haul for us. Most of our fighters couldn't go that far, so we thought they were Me 109s. Instead of coming up beside us and slowly moving in, they came in nose first from six o'clock. It was a new aircraft, and we were new, so we didn't recognize them. In the blink of an eye we would have opened up on them. Lark Morgan, our tail gunner, called

up to Kamy and said, "Hey, there's four ships back here—I can't identify them." Kamy said, "Well, watch them and if they come in too close, shoot the hell out of them!" Lark looked back. "They're getting too damn close!" So Kamy said, "Go get 'em." Just then they rocked their wings up to identify themselves. I think they were new at their jobs too, otherwise they wouldn't have gotten that close to a bomber's tail!

Louis Kandl
B-17 pilot, 96th Bomb Group

On all our raids of not too great a length, P-47s give us cover. We could kiss every one of them; they're that good. Many a Fortress crew owes their lives to these buzz boys. They stick to you like glue when you're crippled.

George Meshko
B-17 waist gunner, 96th Bomb Group

Returning over our base, we buzzed the field and shot off two boxes of flares—about 200 rounds—to celebrate the completion of our combat tour. Our tail gunner was firing a Very pistol out the waist window and lobbed one right into the control tower. We all got a big kick watching the "brass" scramble. Our pilot, Lieutenant Thompson,

A 490th Bomb Group B-17 revs up for takeoff, as other Forts taxi up to the active runway at Eye, winter 1944–45. *Arnold N. Delmonico*

129

Invasion stripes never did wear very well, but no one really cared by the time the D-day invasion was history, as this 596th Squadron, 397th Bomb Group B-26B, *Dee Feater*, reveals while flying over the English landscape during late 1944. *Charles E. Brown/Royal Air Force Museum*

put on a real show for us—swabbing the field back and forth. What happy warriors we were in the B-17 that afternoon. We landed after nine hours aloft. I thought for sure we would never see England again since I had never expected to get back.

There at our hardstand to congratulate us on our tour completion were all our buddies, ground crew, and even the brass. As we came tumbling out of our ship, we were greeted with laughter, tears, hugs, back slapping . . . silent prayers.

In the wee hours of the morning, our gallant crew crawled in loose formation, leaving strange contrails across some muddy plowed fields from the combat club to our Nissen hut. Our tour completed, the only thing left was the hangover.

John Gabay

B-17 tail gunner, 94th Bomb Group

Cazuax, France, 27 March 1944 (ship number 540). Target: airdrome. Can't believe this is the last mission. Made it back OK. Had a celebration in the barracks. I was the first to finish from the barracks—fifty-two didn't make it.

Very short final, full flaps, coming back on the power. The B-24J *Betta Duck*, 7th Squadron, 34th Bomb Group, about to touch down. Wrinkled skin was a standard feature on Liberators, even new ones, but it never seemed to bother anyone. *Arnold N. Delmonico*

The 34th Bomb Group on the way back across the North Sea from a food drop mission to Utrecht, Holland, early May 1945. *Mark Brown/USAFA*

Ready to leave on a May 1945 food drop mission with the 385th Bomb Group, 3rd Air Division, headquarters photo officer Captain Mark Brown is dressed in regulation Army Air Forces flying gear—except for the Royal Air Force Type C helmet, which was much prized among American flyers. Thanks to this man, one of the finest collections of Eighth Air Force Kodachrome slides has been preserved for future generations. A look through the credits on these pages is ample testimony to his talent with a camera. *Mark Brown/USAFA*

Ready to drop food on Utrecht, Holland, in the first days of May 1945, the 385th Bomb Group has bomb bay doors open, wheels down, and partial flaps to get the bombers as slow as possible. Though this appeared to be safe enough, the slow speeds were very dangerous, particularly when flying in formation and making steep turns. Some of the Forts stalled out, and men were killed in this "biscuit bombing" campaign. *Mark Brown/USAFA*

Early May 1945. A 7th Squadron, 34th Bomb Group Fort leaves the Dutch coast on the way back to England from a food drop to Utrecht. *Mark Brown/USAFA*

CHAPTER 6

Fighters and Flak

Bob Kennedy
B-17 tail gunner, 303rd Bomb Group

It was a really nice day, as weather went for Germany. I sat back, enjoyed the view, and tried to acclimate myself to my new surroundings, not the least of which were the optical gun sight—my very first time in the tail with the same. Things up to, and including, the Initial Point run during which I had buried myself in the flak suit, naturally sitting on the apron to help later-life sexual adventures. Flak seemed neither heavy nor accurate. Off the run I started stowing things away while glancing rearward to see how the following group was doing. There was no following group—period! We'd heard no alarming "bandits in the area" call, which came when some group nearby was getting clobbered. I was still relaxed, looking rearward, when I picked up what looked like a dozen or so flashes pretty far back, like little flashbulbs going off. The only problem was I didn't know what it was! Later, after many conversations, we decided that I'd seen the Jerry fighters in the center of the wide,

sweeping left turn they made, when the sun glanced off their canopies.

Suddenly, all hell broke loose! A '17 to our rear began belching flames from number two engine and started peeling off. All this time there was *no* radio warning of attack. I stared in amazement as what looked like a hundred blurry shapes came in, all (in my mind) aiming directly at us. I was trying to get my helmet on when little firecrackers began breaking around the tail and the blurry shapes turned into fighters with wings and cowlings flickering with little lights. I tried to get my guns unlimbered; then some reflex action, probably terror, made me yell to the pilot, "Curley, the whole damn Luftwaffe is out here—*pull her up!*" What happened then took me and the waist gunner completely out of the action, but very probably saved our lives!

Neither I nor any of the crew had ever been on a '17 being yanked up and down—twice. Imagine the most vicious roller coaster ride possible, take off the restraints, load a bunch of goods around you, and you're in a

The 7th Photo Group's *Miss Nashville* was the only B-25 to serve in combat with either the Eighth or Ninth Air Force. Though originally sent to England in March 1943 to begin forming a Mitchell combat group, the bomber ended up doing communications work until it lost its original olive drab camouflage. According to Ed Hoffman of the 381st Air Service Squadron, crew chief Staff Sergeant Hicks asked for permission to strip and polish her. It was given, so he and his crew did the job; then a Varga Girl was painted on each side with the name. When Eighth Air Force commander Jimmy Doolittle—who had led the famous 1942 bombing raid on Tokyo in a B-25— *continued on next page* visited Mt. Farm, he couldn't resist flying the Mitchell for an hour. Later the plane was painted overall gloss black. White invasion stripes were added on the night of June 5, 1944, and the B-25 carried stripes below the wings and fuselage for the rest of its career. In August 1944 it flew thirteen night photo missions over V-weapons sites on the Channel coast. It was then relegated to carrying photos to Twelfth Army Headquarters as that army advanced across France. On 26 October 1944 it was heading for Hamm, a small forward field near Luxembourg City, where it dropped off its intelligence cargo. After takeoff for Mt. Farm, the B-25 was fired on and hit near Trier. Pilot Lieutenant Bob Kraft began looking for a field. Upon approaching Chalons-sur-Marne, France, the bomber burst into flame, but he got it down. The aircraft skidded off and into a tree, killing Kraft and the engineer, Sergeant Hicks. The copilot, Lieutenant Madden, was thrown clear, though he was badly burned. *Robert Astrella*

loose but confined space. That's it! I was smashed up and almost through the roof. Everything loose—flak suit, escape bag, shoes, helmet—all flew up and down with me and ended up in a heap flopping with me on the floor. Then before I could do much of anything, up, then down again! I fell over backwards, narrowly missing the seat horn with my crotch. This time, to give an idea of the sheer violence of the whiplashes, the ammunition on the right storage bin somehow jumped out and about five feet of heavy .50-caliber ammo added to the mess.

On my hands and knees, I tried to free my oxygen tube (caught in the ammo mess), get a glove back on (torn loose by the gun butts), and get the flak suit off me, along with the ammo, all at the same time. I glanced for a second out the right window and saw the crew coming out the waist of the nearest '17 off our left horizontal stabilizer. Still frantic to be able to move and breathe, in the next second I glanced up again and there sat—and I mean *sat*—an Fw 190 right off our left stabilizer, so close I could have wing-walked over to him. He must have just finished firing, because a yellow-white cloud of smoke came back from somewhere front like.

I think terror just took control because I can remember crawling over to the little exit door and putting on my chute (still in one piece) and just sitting, gasping oxygen, and praying to all gods I could think of, hoping I didn't miss any. Nothing, but nothing, happened. The plane still flew. I looked past the tail wheel housing and saw the waist gunner still alive and trying to get to his feet. Turned out he was pretty banged up during

the roller coaster ride. Getting a semblance of courage back, I tried to get the mess straightened out and my guns at least operative. Did some and finally mustered enough guts to look rearward and see how many Germans were still mad at our dear little tiger-tailed '17.

Nothing—pure, unadulterated, empty sky. I searched for our trailing squadron '17s. All gone. Pretty far below I could see one "falling leafing" all over the place. That was it! This time I really concentrated on finding the trailing group. Nothing—no group. Whatever segment of the Eighth this was—Wing, Division, or the whole Eighth— I had to face one fact: We were the last plane in the last formation. A *real* tail-end Charlie! About this time, I became aware that my radio wasn't working, got that straightened up, and called up front. Turned out they'd given up on me, and the waist hadn't heard anything since the famous "Pull her up." I told the pilot the situation, but he didn't believe that the rest of the squadron was gone. He did eventually.

The rest of the mission was routine except right after the onslaught when I was seeking to find *anything* in back of us. The call came in: "Fighters, twelve o'clock level coming in fast." Before I could get to my guns again, three or four P-51s flashed past to my left, really going all out. The pilot called that we were getting fighter cover front and rear and, this time, not German. I asked him if there was anything up front of us as there wasn't a *damn* thing in back of us. He assured me that we and the lead plane were closing up on another squadron

(probably the 359th). But the sky sure was empty—all the way back.

I remember the pilot being chewed out for not using proper squadron landing procedures—and him telling them there was no squadron. Also the copilot "browning out" (losing bowel control) when, as he said, an Me 109 was so close he could kiss the Jerry pilot.

I can't remember one damn thing after the landing. *Nothing*. No battle damage inspections, no talking with the crew, and even nothing about the debriefing. Crazy, impossible, but true—a complete blank.

One thing sure about the mission. The Luftwaffe pilots were skilled operators. They didn't slash in but approached slowly and deliberately. They taught us a lesson for our few remaining missions—*alertness*. Never again did we relax—not ever!

Hans Iffland
Me 109 pilot, IV/JG 3

Normally we got up at about 6:00 A.M. and reported to the operations building at 6:30, where we had our breakfast. Officers and NCOs sat around chatting, some playing cards, others writing letters or reading books.

There were several rooms and offices in the operations building, as well as the main briefing room. There was a large gridded map on one wall of the waiting room, where the position of the bomber stream was marked when it began to come in. Next to the map was a large board with all of the pilots' names, their victory scores, which operations they had flown in, and when pilots had had to break off operations prematurely for any reason. So one could see at a glance which pilots had pressed on with their attacks, and which were liable to break away at the least sign of engine or other trouble. Obviously, if a man had engine trouble and returned early four times in a row, questions would be asked. The board also showed who was sick or wounded, who was on leave, etc.

While waiting, I would play cards or ping-pong.

By mid-summer 1944, the early G-model Fortresses were beginning to show some serious wear, clearly evident on this 750th Squadron, 457th Bomb Group '17 from Glatton. *Robert Astrella*

137

This 554th Squadron, 386th Bomb Group B-26B from Great Dunnow, late summer 1944, has already seen a steady amount of action with the Ninth Air Force. The group hammered at a long list of strategic and tactical targets before being transferred to the Continent in October 1944. *Robert Astrella*

When the bombers were reported coming in, we had three states of readiness. First was 30 Minute Readiness: *"Achtung, Achtung, Achtung, Achtung, eine Durchsage: Ab sofort 30 Minuten Bereitschaft!"* This was a loose form of readiness, and meant only that the pilots were not allowed to leave the airfield. Normally martial music was played over the loudspeakers, and the announcements would interrupt this. Next readiness state was 15 Minute Readiness order as before, but *"15 Minuten Bereitschaft!"* Then came more music. On this order the pilots walked to the Staffel readiness rooms; next, they went to their aircraft dispersed around the airfield. Earlier in the day, each aircraft had been run up by the ground crewman, so each was ready for action, fully fueled up and armed. Each aircraft carried a drop tank under its belly. The engine had been warmed up first thing in the morning. At this stage, the pilots put on their life jackets and other flying clothing (though this was

often worn throughout the day).

Next stage was Cockpit Readiness: *"Achtung, Achtung, ab sofort, Sitzbereitschaft!"* The pilots walked over to their aircraft and climbed in, strapped on their parachutes, did up their seat harnesses, pulled on their helmets, and did up their radio connectors. Each Messerschmitt already had the large crank handle in place, sticking out the starboard side of the engine, ready for the engine to be started.

At Cockpit Readiness, the pilots could hear the fighter broadcasts via a telephone line plugged into each aircraft. Cockpit Readiness usually lasted no more than ten to fifteen minutes, though it could last for as much as an hour. For me, the minutes between being ordered to Cockpit Readiness and being given the order to take off were the most terrible of all. After the order came to get airborne, one was too busy to think about one's possible fate. But waiting to go, with nothing to do but think about what

might happen—that was the most terrible time of all. Would one still be alive that evening, or was this the beginning of one's last day? My own greatest fear was that I might be seriously wounded, with permanent injuries. Death was, of course, a fear, but that would have been the end. The thought of being left a cripple for the rest of one's life was, for me, the greatest fear of all.

At 11:37 came the order to scramble. A single green flare rose up from the operations building. The scramble takeoff was normal for a German fighter unit, with the aircraft of the three Staffeln and the Stab unit dispersed at four points equidistant around the airfield. On the order to scramble, two crewmen hopped onto the wing of the Messerschmitt and began turning the crank handle to get the heavy flywheel of the inertia starter revolving. They wound the crank faster and faster, then the pilot pulled a handle beside his right knee to clutch in the engine, which usually coughed a couple of times before starting with a throaty roar. After engine starting, the Stab took off first, straight out of their dispersal point. As they passed the center of the air-

field, the tenth Staffel, situated ninety degrees to the left around the perimeter of the airfield, began its takeoff run. Then the eleventh, then the twelfth Staffeln. After takeoff, the Stab turned left, circling the airfield, and climbed away, collecting the tenth, eleventh, and twelfth Staffeln rapidly behind it. Once the Gruppe had assembled, the leader, Major Friedrich-Karl Mueller, swung it around to a southeasterly heading for Magdeburg.

When we were within about 800 meters of the bombers, we felt ourselves safe from the enemy fighters and had only the bombers' return fire to worry about. At such a range it was difficult to tell a Mustang from a Messerschmitt, and both would be shot at by the bombers' gunners. Our orders were to help the Destroyers punch through the screen of escorts, so that they could engage the bombers. I remember seeing the bomber formation like a swarm of insects in the distance.

It was terrible to have to attack the bombers, which opened fire at very long ranges (about 800 meters), while our Messerschmitts had only limited ammuni-

Ridden hard and put away wet, *Our Gal Sal* flew over 100 missions with the 100th Bomb Group out of Thorpe Abbots and finished the war to fly back home, only to be scrapped. Bob Shoens and his crew flew this Fortress to Berlin and back on 6 March 1944, the first all-out daylight mission to the German capital. *Robert Astrella*

An 18th Squadron, 34th Bomb Group B-24H from Mendlesham at rest with a trusty guard in front. It was not unusual for dogs to fly on missions, though this practice was strictly forbidden by Army Air Forces brass. Some dogs had their own oxygen masks and flying suits, and one was even rumored to have flown the low-level mission to Ploesti with the 44th Bomb Group. *Robert Astrella*

tion—we had to hold fire until within about 300 or 400 meters. This interception on 6 March 1944 was one of my first operational head-on attacks against an enemy bomber formation. The head-on attack was adopted because it was a more cost-effective way of engaging the bombers. When we attacked from the rear, there was a long period of overtaking when the enemy gunners were shooting at us, but we were not within range to fire at them. As a result, we sometimes lost more fighters than we shot down bombers. When we attacked from head-on, we were able to fire for only about one second, but the bombers were big, and we were relatively so small, that we were far more likely to hit them than they were likely to hit us. Our tactic was to attack by Staffeln in line abreast, so that the enemy bombers could not concentrate their fire against any one of us.

During the firing run, everything happened very quickly. We were flying at about 450 kilometers per hour, and the bombers were flying at about 380 kilometers per hour, so closing speed was 800 to 900 kilometers per hour. After firing my short burst at one of the B-17s, I pulled up over it. I had attacked from slightly above, allowing a slight deflection angle and aiming at the nose. We knew that just a single hit with a 3cm explosive round would have devastating effects anywhere on the nose, but it was hardly possible to aim so accurately during the brief firing pass. I aimed at the nose, but saw the flashes of my rounds exploding against the Fortress's port wing root. And the whole time, we could see the tracer

rounds from the bombers flashing past us. I saw four or five rounds exploding around the wing root.

As I pulled up over the bomber, I dropped my left wing to see the result of my attack and to give the enemy gunners the smallest possible target at which to aim. I had also to pull up to get out of the way of the fire of the other Staffeln of the Gruppe coming in behind me. Of course, I did not want to ram the B-17. I saw the port wing of the B-17 slowly begin to fold up, and the bomber went down. Then I was out the back of the formation, and my main concern was to join up with other Messerschmitts of the Gruppe for the next attack.

On this day we knocked down thirteen bombers in return for only one of our fighters wrecked, and none of our pilots was killed or wounded. It seemed that we really were able to overcome the massive numerical superiority enjoyed by the enemy. We were astounded by our success, which gave us all new hope. We felt we really had grasped the problem of dealing with the great formations of bombers.

I tried to join up with machines from my Staffel, which carried white numbers. The eleventh Staffel had yellow numbers. If one was alone, one was highly vulnerable to attack from the Mustangs, and many of our fighters were lost that way. The Gruppe pulled around in a sweeping turn to the left of the formation, and then the fighters sped, flying a course parallel to and slightly above the bombers, overtaking them out of gun range as they moved into position for a second head-on attack. It was very important to deliver the second attack in line abreast with sufficient aircraft. If one or two attacked alone, the bombers would concentrate their fire on these, and that was extremely dangerous. Our orders were to continue attacking the bombers so long as we had ammunition and fuel. It was frowned upon if undamaged fighters returned with

This 332nd Squadron, 94th Bomb Group B-17G has had its chin and ball turrets removed to gain a little more performance—a clear sign of the air superiority the Eighth Air Force enjoyed in the last months of 1945. At this point in the war, the extra weight and drag was deemed more a hindrance than a help. *Robert Astrella*

The 93rd Bomb Group on the way to hit front line targets at Ahrweiler, Germany, 24 December 1944. The lead aircraft is a pathfinder, equipped with radar in place of the ball turret. *Glenn A. Tessmer*

fuel and ammunition remaining. Even if we had only ten rounds of cannon ammunition left, we were expected to deliver another attack against the bombers.

I came in for my second attack, but the target bomber made a slight turn, causing my rounds to miss. At the time of the first attack, the bombers had been flying in close formation. Now there were gaps in the formation, and the bombers were flying further apart so the pilot would have more room to maneuver. The B-17 snaked from side to side when I opened fire; it was enough to make the rounds miss during the brief firing pass. Then I was out of ammunition.

The most dangerous part of the engagement was getting through the screen of escorts. On this day we had done so without difficulty. Our orders were to engage the enemy fighters only when we had to. Otherwise we had to concentrate our attack on the bombers, which represented the greatest danger to our country. The only exception was when we were escorting the Destroyers.

Once one was out of ammunition, it was important to join up with other German fighters, because it was very dangerous if one was attacked by American escorts. If there were four or five of us together, the Americans would be more careful about attacking us. Also, being short of fuel, it was important to fix our position and decide where we were going to land.

On breaking away from the bombers, we went down in a rapid descent to about 200 meters to get well clear of the enemy fighters. At that altitude our camouflaged aircraft were very difficult to see from high above, while we could see the enemy machines silhouetted against the sky. A 200- to 300-meter altitude also gave us good R/T range, so we could contact our base. Sometimes we flew back even lower than that and climbed only when we wished to call our base to make sure it was safe for us to land there, since it might have come under enemy attack. When we arrived back over Salzwedel, we flew low over the airfield, and those pilots who claimed victories waggled their wings. I saw another aircraft in front of me doing it; then I did it. We knew we had been successful even before we landed. When we were overtaking the bombers for our second attack, we had seen some going down, others streaming fuel or smoke. One went down about 1,000 meters and then ex-

Cpls. Larry Roth and Wallace Merquardt move their radio-equipped control jeep out to the active runway at Mendlesham as a 34th Bomb Group Lib follows. Radio-equipped jeeps and mobile towers were an immense help in moving bombers and fighters to takeoff position in an orderly manner. *USAF*

143

Patches and *Sleepy Time Gal*, B-17Gs of the 532nd Squadron, 381st Bomb Group, climb out over England in late summer 1944. *USAF*

ploded. Another was on fire, and parachutes were coming from it. If there was a burning machine in the formation, the others would have to pull away from it in case it exploded. It made a vivid impression.

After landing and taxiing to the Staffel dispersal, the first to meet me was my mechanic. He had seen me rock my wings, and when I had shut down the engine and opened the hood, he stood by the trailing edge of the wing, clapped his hands above his head, shouted, *"Herr Leutnant, gratuliere!"* and offered me a cigarette. Obviously, if a pilot scored a kill, that counted for the mechanic also; it meant he had done a good job preparing the machine. No shortage of

cigarettes for the Luftwaffe; we were looked after very well as regards food and drink. I do not remember any problems when we operated in Germany, though there had been some difficulties in getting supplies through when we were in Italy.

When I reached the Gefechtsstand, our commander, Major Mueller, was already there receiving the reports from his pilots. I awaited my turn, then marched to the table. I clicked my heels, saluted, and proudly said, *"Melde gehorsamst. Vom Einsatz zurück. Eine Fortress abgeschossen!"* Then I explained how I had hit it and seen the wing fold up on the port side before it went down. *"Ach, das war Ihrer! Hab ich gesehen!"* ex-

A 91st Bomb Group crew chief, Master Sergeant Herbert H. Roberts, has just guided his Fort to a stop at Bassingbourn, late summer 1944. Though there was a defined chain of command up and down the enlisted and officer ranks, a crew chief made the final decision about the availability and condition of his airplane. In reality, it belonged to him, and though the aircraft commander could walk around, jiggle a few things, and kick the tires, if he wanted to know the exact status of the airplane, he asked the crew chief. *USAF*

claimed one of the other pilots. This was important, for without a witness, it was very difficult to get credit for a victory. Several other pilots said the same thing: The bomber had gone down in a spectacular manner, and several pilots remembered seeing it. *"Gratuliere!"* smiled Mueller. After me, other pilots reported kills. Each one was marked on the board beside the pilot's name, so soon it was clear we had had a very successful day.

Salzwedel was a permanent Luftwaffe airfield. Mueller announced, when the Gruppe was stood down from readiness,

"Tonight we celebrate!" After a bath and changing out of my sweaty flying suit, I was at the officers Kasino for dinner at 7:00 P.M. Jagdgeschwader 3 had links with the Henkell wine company, which ensured that the we never ran short of wine. Whenever a pilot was killed, it was usual for the Kommandeur to deliver a short requiem after dinner; then the pilots drank a toast to his memory before hurling their glasses (special cheap ones!) into the fireplace. But there had been no losses on this day.

The party would have gone on until after midnight, but it came to an end when

A wounded crewman is taken out the waist window of *Liberty Lib*, 458th Bomb Group, Horsham St. Faith, mid-1944. The Dodge ambulance doors are open, and there are more men yet to be offloaded. *USAF*

Mueller said, "Jungs, that's enough. We must be ready again tomorrow." At a Luftwaffe officers' party we did not have violent games. We sang songs (*not* Nazi party songs!): *"Es ist so wunder wunder schön, hoch in den blauen Luftigen Hohen"; "Oh, du schöner We-e-esterwald"; "Auf der Luneburger Heide, in den wunderschönen Land."* One of the officers would accompany the songs on a guitar. A pleasant comradely evening, with the officers steadily getting more and more drunk, then off to bed.

Bud Guillot
B-24 waist gunner, 392nd Bomb Group

You know, it's funny. You look back and you only remember the crazy things. Everything else just gets blacked out. There's always that moment, though, when for the first time in your life, you realize, "Someone is trying to kill me." It's a strange feeling. We were just kids—maybe eighteen to twenty-one years old. I've always heard people say, "If you're not afraid in combat, you're crazy!" I wasn't afraid in combat. My time was when I saw my name on the bulletin board, and I knew I was going to fly a mission the next day. It's hard to say why, but that's the way it was.

For example, the first time we flew through flak on the way to the target, I was sitting on some ammo cans watching the white puffs of 88mm flak come up. The first burst came away out in front of us and the next one was behind us. I said to myself, "Wow, this is going to be easy. These guys aren't very good." Well, little did I know they had just bracketed us. They had just zeroed

Just about all the Eighth Air Force top brass, and then some, you'd want to see in one spot during the 11 April 1944 visit of Supreme Allied Commander Dwight Eisenhower to the 4th Fighter Group at Debden. In front of the officers club are (left to right) Brigadier General Jesse Auton (65th Fighter Wing commander), Ike, Lieutenant General Carl "Tooey" Spaatz (US Strategic Air Forces Europe commander), Lieutenant General James H. Doolittle (Eighth Air Force commander), Major General William Kepner (VIII Fighter Command commander), and Colonel Don Blakeslee (4th Fighter Group commander). *USAF*

in on our altitude and direction. All hell broke loose below us and I never sat down on a mission again.

John Gabay
B-17 tail gunner, 94th Bomb Group

Munster, Germany, 11 November 1943 (ship number 846). It seemed at first to be a pretty easy mission. As we entered the Dutch coast we were met with light flak. Then our P-47s showed up, and we had no trouble at all until we reached the target. Flak wasn't too heavy, but our bomb bay doors wouldn't open. We finally got them open and got rid of the bombs in Germany. Our escort stayed with us as long as they could, engaging in several dogfights. They had to leave us over Holland and then the fun began.

About fifty Fw 190s and Me 109s attacked us from every direction. We couldn't close our bomb bay doors so they picked on us, thinking we were crippled. One Fw dove straight down from one o'clock high and let go with his cannons. He put a hole in our left wing big enough to crawl through. He also blew off a piece of the vertical stabilizer over my head. The Fort on our wing burst into flames and only five got out—one chute was on fire. They were from our barracks. A 109 came directly at me, and I know I hit him, as he rolled over in a dive and disappeared. Another one came in low at eight o'clock, and Chauncey, our ball gunner, hit him and he

When *5 Grand* (the 5,000th B-17 built by Boeing) went to war, it carried the company employees' autographs all the way to the 96th Bomb Group at Snetterton Heath. Here the B-17 makes a shakedown flight over England before getting painted with the group identification letter (square C), individual call letter (H), red vertical fin stripes on the tail, and squadron codes (BX) on the fuselage. *5 Grand* must have been a lucky ship; after seventy-eight missions, it went home to end up in the scrap yard. *USAF*

burst into flames and went down.

Several Fw 190s kept coming in at the tail, and I hit one. He rolled over, and I lost him. The Fort on our other wing burst into flames and went into a spin. Didn't see any chutes. Flak burst under our ship and concussion knocked us up about fifty feet. As we reached the Channel, an Fw 190 followed up low at five o'clock, and Chauncey knocked him into the water. We made it back OK, but our new ship was a wreck. This was our crew's first raid together.

Philip Ardery
B-24 squadron commander, 389th Bomb Group

I would like to correct a frequent fallacy made by writers describing bombing raids. The noise a bomber pilot hears is awful, but that noise isn't the loud noise of shells burst-

ing. The pilot is encased in many thicknesses of clothing—even his head is almost completely covered. Tightly clamped against his ears are his headphones, built into his helmet. Out of these headphones comes most of the noise he hears. The horrible screaming is the noise of the radio-jamming apparatus of the enemy. It is like a death cry of the banshees of all the ages. On our missions it usually started faintly in our headphones as we neared the enemy coast and grew louder and louder. A pilot had to keep the volume of the receiver turned up high in order to hear commands over the air through the bedlam of jamming. After a few hours of it, I felt that I would go crazy if I didn't turn the volume down. I would turn it down when I was out of the target area, but I knew when I did that I might be missing an important radio order or a call from another ship asking for help or direction in one way or another.

We could hear the firing of our own guns. Chiefly we could hear the top turret. In addition to the noise of the top turret we could hear the nose guns, the waist guns, the ball turret, and finally the tail turret. We really couldn't hear the tail turret, but after we had ridden in our bombers for a while there was a peculiar faint vibration that would run down the skin of the ship and up the seats to let us know little Pete Peterson of Fowble's crew was warming up his guns. When Pete's guns chattered, some Nazi always regretted it. And when I felt the vibrations of his guns coming through the seat of my pants, it was like someone scratching a mosquito bite in the middle of my back.

But then about the flak. You could hear it—faintly. When flak was very near you could see the angry red fire as the shells exploded before the black smoke formed. You could hear the bursts sounding like *wuff, wuff, wuff* under your wings. You could see the nose of the ship plowing through the smoke clouds where the bursts had been. You could hear the sprinkle of slivers of shrapnel go through the sides of the ship if they were hitting close to you. I always said that if you hear the flak—if you get the *wuff, wuff, wuff*—and really hear it over the screaming of the radio and other sounds, then it is deadly close. You don't realize the terror it strikes into some airmen's hearts until you've had your own plane shot to hell a few times. I laughed at Franco's flak coming through Gibraltar. It wasn't much flak, but I wouldn't laugh six months later when I had seen more of it.

Friedrich Stehle
Me 410 pilot, II/ZG 26

If we attacked the bombers from behind, we could really work on them—if we were left alone by the enemy escorts. You really had to work on those bombers; it was very seldom that you knocked them down with the first burst. Sometimes you would sit behind a bomber and fire off all your ammunition into it, and it would not move. It would just keep going.

If you were attacked by a Mustang, you could only pray and hope your gunner shot well. I had a few tricks I could throw in, and perhaps they saved me. My Viennese gunner, Unteroffizier Alois Slaby, was very experienced, and he knew exactly when the enemy fighter was about to fire. He would say, "Not yet—not yet. Now!" and I would chop the throttles, and the 410 would decelerate very rapidly. If we were lucky, the fighter would go screaming past us. Sometimes I would put the 410 into a skid with the wings level, and the enemy rounds would flash past the wing tip. We knew that if we could buy a little time, that often meant survival. Once the escorts had dropped their tanks, they could not fight for very long near Berlin. They had to break off and return to England.

At 28,000 feet, the Me 410 was only just about flying. It could not maneuver much. Even at full throttle, we would be overtaking the enemy bombers at only about thirty miles per hour. As a result, it took us a long time to get ourselves into firing position. Fighting in the Me 410 was a bit like entering the Kentucky Derby on a cart horse!

Sky marker smoke trails from the preceding formation drift beneath a 329th Squadron, 93rd Bomb Group Liberator heading for Ahrweiler, Germany, 24 December 1944. *Glenn A. Tessmer*

By the end of the war, aircraft of the Eighth, Ninth, Twelfth, and Fifteenth Air Forces were operating over Germany. Though air superiority was a reality, Luftwaffe pilots continued to mount heavy opposition, particularly in the form of the jet-propelled Messerschmitt 262. This 320th Bomb Group B-26G got back to its French base with this damage from an Me 262's 30mm cannons. *Joseph S. Kingsbury*

John Gabay
B-17 tail gunner, 94th Bomb Group

Kiel, Germany, 13 December 1943 (ship number 846). Target: heart of city. We flew up through the North Sea and just as we entered the enemy coast, about forty Ju 88s appeared out of nowhere. They flew alongside our formation on both sides, but just out of range. After several minutes of this, they began to peel off, and four of them attacked our ship from the tail, one at a time. The flame from the cannons, tracers from their machine guns, and rockets from under their wings made the situation a bit hairy. All I could do, besides being scared, was to spray each one as they came in and call for evasive action.

I hit the second one, and he rolled over and burned. I saw my tracers slam into the cockpit of the third. I may have hit the pilot, as the ship started to go out of control. I poured more into it, knocking off the canopy under the nose. It looked like a leg hung out of the ship for an instant, then fell out. Then the ship went into a spin. More Ju 88s flew alongside of us, out of range. Some of them waved to us. It was shaky waiting for them to attack. Then they came at us. Our pilot used plenty of evasive action, and all guns were firing. The ball turret in the ship next to us was blown out. Several ships were hit hard. We had several flak holes, machine gun holes, and a couple of 20mm cannon holes in the right wing. A squadron of P-38s showed up for a change, and the bandits scattered.

One bomb got hung up in the bomb bay, but C. L. managed to dump it after a few

minutes. Leo was annoyed that I didn't put in any claims. I don't like the hassle. Today—December *13;* Our Crew—*number 13*; bombs away at *1300*. Another lucky day.

Lowell Watts
B-17 pilot, 388th Bomb Group

Then the flak hit us. They didn't start out with wild shots and work in closer. The first salvo they sent up was right on us. We could hear the metal of our plane rend and tear as each volley exploded. The hits weren't direct. They were just far enough away so that they didn't take off a wing or the tail or blow the plane up. . . . they would just tear a ship half apart without completely knocking it out. Big, ragged holes appeared in the wings and fuselage. The copilot was watching nothing but instruments, waiting for that telltale story on some instrument that would indicate a damaged or ruined engine, but they kept up their steady roar, even as the ship rocked from the nearness of the hundreds of flak bursts.

Missouri Mule **with the 320th Bomb Group over Dôle, France, 1945.** *Joseph S. Kingsbury*

151

Bombs away! The 320th Bomb Group bombs through clouds, 1945. They hit an eighty-five-foot rail bridge. *Joseph S. Kingsbury*

John Gabay

B-17 tail gunner, 94th Bomb Group

Bremen, Germany, 16 December 1943 (ship number 037). Target: docks—heart of the city. We were supposed to have plenty of escort—P-38s, P-51s, and P-47s, but we were late and missed them. When we saw the P-38s, they were passing us on their way home—not a nice feeling. Flak over the target was extra heavy. The sky was black with flak burst smoke, and I could smell it through my oxygen mask. The noise was cruel and the concussions were murderous. Every ship in the group must have had flak holes—we had plenty.

When we came out of the target area, the fighters were waiting for us. I never saw so many. They were hiding over the stale flak smoke. Our crew led the Eighth Air Force on this raid. We had two direct attacks at the tail, but they didn't press them. The low group in our wing got hit very hard. One of the Forts blew up. The Jerry that got him gave some exhibition of flying. He was something special. We had a British radar officer on board. His job was to confuse the German radar. It didn't work.

The weather over the Channel was bad and especially over our field. We made the landing on the first try but nearly collided with another Fort. There were two crack-ups later on. Our ship was a mess—full of holes. I thought the crew chief was going to cry. We were told at interrogation that Bremen put up more flak today than any city up to now. Big deal!

John Gabay

B-17 tail gunner, 94th Bomb Group

Brunswick, Germany, 10 February 1944 (ship number 498). Target: heart of city. I don't know how to start this one. I'm very tired. They told us at briefing the plan was to send 200 Forts deep into Germany as a decoy to lure up enemy fighters so our escort could try to knock out the Luftwaffe. It didn't turn out that way. As soon as we crossed the enemy coast, we ran into swarms of enemy fighters (at interrogation everyone agreed over 300 fighters at one time pounded our group). I knew we were really in trouble when about 150 of our escort showed up and immediately dropped their belly tanks so they could mix it up with the enemy. That meant they couldn't stay with us very long—and the raid was just beginning.

The Luftwaffe must have put up every fighter they had—Me 109s, 110s, 210s, 410s, Ju 87s, 88s, Fw 190s, and a new type of Focke-Wulf. We had '47s, '51s, and '38s. But

A bomber pilot's dream—a new Douglas A-26B Invader from the 416th Bomb Group, early 1945. The first Invaders entered combat with the Ninth Air Force on 19 November 1944. From the start, pilots knew they had a hot rod, with ten forward-firing .50-caliber guns, a bomb load of 4,000 pounds, and a top speed of 355 miles per hour. *Robert Astrella*

no Spits. Fighters hit us from every angle. I saw Forts and fighters blowing up, Forts and fighters going down smoking and burning, wings coming off, tails coming off, the sky full of parachutes, white and checkered. One guy floated into a low Fort—he was churned up by the propellers and took the Fort with him. It just rolled over into a dive. The sky was so full of tracers, 20mm cannon shells exploding, and even rockets. Steel was ripping into our ship with sickening sounds. There were times when I was afraid to shoot for fear of hitting one of our own planes or some poor guy in a parachute.

We were leading the high squadron of nine planes—only two of us got back. They attacked the tail four abreast and four deep, sixteen at a time. Their wing guns lit up like Luna Park. These guys were not fooling. There were countless dogfights. The P-47s at times were badly outnumbered, but they did a great job and stayed with us until the very last minute. A couple of them asked for a heading home and said they were sorry they had to leave, but they were very low on fuel. When they left, the fighters became even more aggressive—if that was possible. All guns were firing at the same time—the whole ship was vibrating. I was shooting at everything that came in range. I think I hit a few but was too busy to see what happened as another attack was already starting, then another, etc. I know Chauncey got an Fw 190. Ju 88s flew over us dropping aerial bombs, but they weren't effective. At one time there must have been 200 fighters above us in dogfights. I saw two P-47s go down, but I saw the '47s shoot down several Jerries.

The battle let up for about five minutes and about that time Chambers, our bombardier, called out large formations of fighters at twelve o'clock high. We all thought they were our escort coming in force from England to help. But it turned out to be Fw 190s and Me 109s—about 150 of them. Now the fun really began. We had no more escort. Forts and fighters were going down all

The 391st Bomb Group at Asch (Y-29), Belgium, April 1945. The A-26 had a fighter pilot's cockpit with one set of controls, all easily within reach—and it was light on the controls compared to almost any other bomber. Even though the Invader was only in combat for just over five months, it proved to be a very lethal ground-attack aircraft. *John Quincy via Stan Wyglendowski*

around us. Our ship got slammed with 20mm cannon and machine gun slugs—a miracle none of us were hit. At the end of the battle, twenty P-47s showed up and put up a magnificent battle. Flak over the target was heavy, but not bad on the way home. We made it back OK, but there are a lot of empty beds tonight. This old Fort really took a beating—I don't know how it stayed in the air. The damage: half the nose blown out; six feet of the vertical stabilizer blown off; tail cables severed; all my windows blown out; one 20mm went through left side of tail above my hands and blew up just outside my window. All in all, ground crew counted 136 holes.

John Gabay
B-17 tail gunner, 94th Bomb Group

Pas de Calais, France, 13 February 1944 (ship number 498). Target: rocket sites. We did squadron bombing today. Our crew led the low squadron. Each squadron had different targets. We flew over six or seven flak areas. Flak wasn't very heavy, but what they

threw was right in there—medium to light but very accurate. It killed a navigator in our squadron. I didn't see any fighters—friendly or otherwise—on the way in, but I could hear every burst of flak. Maybe I'm thinking too much about flak. At least with fighters you can fight back. France looked so peaceful and quiet until bombs away. Forts were coming and going, dropping bombs on their own individual targets. I wondered what the heck was so important down there. The ground was covered with bomb bursts and once in a while a big explosion—a hit, I guess! One B-24 got hit bad by flak and flew in our formation all the way home. Coming back we saw some fighters near the Channel, but they ignored us. Thanks a lot.

John Flottorp
B-17 pilot, 390th Bomb Group

Engineering surveyed the damage and determined the aircraft beyond economical repairs. We had landed without brakes with the right tire burned badly after having to crank the gear down. Seventeen 20mm en-

try holes were counted along with numerous machine gun bullet holes and too many flak holes to count. The number three engine had the crankcase holed, the oil cooler shot away, a runaway prop, and a fire. The number four engine turbo waste gate had been hit and jammed in a partial power position. On one of the last attacks it had been hit again, and the top of one cylinder and valves were knocked out. Both numbers one and two had burned valves and pistons from overboosting and overheating but had held together. The bomb bay had been holed and the life raft compartment blown out. The vertical fin had collected seven 20mm hits that opened up the skin, looking like Swiss cheese the rats had been at, but the spar structure was not appreciably damaged. The main wing spar on the right wing had been virtually severed in two places along with the right aileron cables.

Each crew member had his own narrow escape. The tail gunner had a stoppage in one of his guns. He raised the armor plate and bent far forward to clear a jammed car-tridge when a 20mm round slammed through from side to side where his head had been the instant before. It did not explode but left him a hole whistling by each ear. The waist and radio room had been sieved by flak and fighter fire, but no one got a scratch. The top turret gunner was firing at an attacking fighter at a high angle when a machine gun slug came through the turret Plexiglas, just missing his head. His helmet, goggles, and oxygen mask saved him from cuts from the Plexiglas fragments. The navigator, down in the nose, had his throat mike strap cut by a flak fragment leaving only a minor scratch on his neck.

We were just one crew who were inordinately lucky. The good Lord had other plans for us that day. The incredibly tough B-17 also deserves much credit.

Lowell Watts
B-17 pilot, 388th Bomb Group

I noticed the windshield and the top of the cockpit was gone, and I was sitting out in the gentle breezes. I could tell we rolled

With the A-26C came a clear plexiglass nose for a bombardier. The 386th Bomb Group gave up their beloved Marauders for these Invaders in St. Trond, Belgium, spring 1945. Within a very short time the group was sold on the new bomber. Richard H. Denison

A 386th Bomb Group A-26B over France, spring 1945. About the only real drawback to the new Invader was poor visibility to the side and down because the plane's engines extended forward of the cockpit. In the Marauder, the pilot sat far ahead of the engines,. *Richard H. Denison*

over upside down. My safety belt had been unbuckled so I fell away from the seat, but held myself in with the grasp I had on the control wheel. After a few weird sensations, I was pinned to the seat, unable to move or even raise my hand to pull off the throttles or try to cut the gas to the inboard engines. Flames now swept past my face, between my legs, and past my arms as though sucked by a giant vacuum.

John Gabay
B-17 tail gunner, 94th Bomb Group

February 9: Kersey and I got up to preflight at 4:00. Lieutenant Anderson and crew was to fly ours. As we got ready to start engines, the left waist gun went off—hit the tail gunner, who was outside, in the head. He was knocked down, and when we got to him, he was bleeding badly. We gave him first aid, and by then the ambulance came and took him away. I cleaned up the mess afterwards and found pieces of meat and brains. They operated on him and took out the shell casing that had pierced his skull. Luongo gave a pint of blood for transfusion. The doctor says he will live. This is the first time we've had an accident. The bullet was an incendiary that went through the door, then the trim tab on the elevator before it hit Millinger. Mission was scrubbed, so the damage was repaired today.

Ben Smith
B-17 radio operator, 303rd Bomb Group

We got out and looked her over. It was unbelievable. We had taken a savage mauling, and she was one more lacerated lady. That morning our bomber had been a lovely girl without blemish. The ground crews could do wonders with a shot-up B-17, but they had their work cut out for them with that one. Sometimes when one was shot up too badly, they made her a "hangar queen" and cannibalized parts off her. I remember the ground crew laid some rueful looks on us.

Bob DeGroat
B-24 pilot, POW Stalag Luft IIIA

It is sometime after midnight and pitch black. The air is humid and pungent, almost physically thick. I am accustomed to the smell, but if I had to describe it, I would say that it is equal parts of unwashed human/animal smells, masonry mildew, filthy ancient straw ticking, and unwashed clothing that has been worn every day for months. The lingering odors from Kriegie fat lamps, cooking devices fed from shaved bed boards, dried weed roots, or anything else short of rocks that can be found to burn are also evident.

As my eyes gradually become accustomed to the murk, I begin to make out the forms of the bunk blocks, four square and three tiers high. They are arranged in the familiar cubical pattern, allowing a wide aisle down the center of the barracks.

I become aware of a constant shuffle and passage of prisoners up and down the aisle, even at this hour. They represent the steady stream of men headed for the latrine that becomes a part of the Kriegie night life. When solid food is scarce, the addition of extra liquid helps to give a feeling of semi-fullness, but the penalty, of course, is paid in added trips to relieve the pressure. The diet in general affects various people differently. Some are in a situation of never-ending diarrhea; on the other hand, some find that if it's inconvenient to go today, just wait until tomorrow. But the liquid must be relieved on schedule, so I prepare to join the shuffling procession.

I am lucky. I have a top bunk. Although potentially the foul air rises, the roof is a good ten feet above me, and the air seems better up here. I also don't have any claustrophobia-causing bodies lying above me, and I don't have a constant number of groggy, semi-sleepwalkers climbing down over me to join the nightly procession to the "john."

I gently move my two three- by five-foot, threadbare blankets to the side. I grab my jacket . . . actually a Polish army coat that has been cut off at the waist and redesigned into a unique Eisenhower jacket. I carefully move to sit up. There are two reasons for moving with care. One is that if you sit up too suddenly, you might faint. The other and more important reason is that each of us is issued only three bed boards to support our thin straw mattress tick. I use one under my shoulders, another under my hips, and the third about at my calves. If I get any weight in the wrong place, there is a real danger of falling through into the bunk below. I swing my feet over and climb down to the floor, trying to avoid stepping on the hands and arms of my lower bunk mates.

I am dressed in my jacket, underpants, and shoes. It is a cool spring night out, and I'll be shivering by the time I return, but the barracks is almost hot with human-animal

The Twelfth Air Force's 320th Bomb Group marshaling for takeoff at Longvic, 1945. Unlike the heavy bomb groups of the Eighth and Fifteenth Air Forces, the Ninth and Twelfth Air Forces hopped from one base to another across Europe as the tactical battle lines moved. It was a gypsy's life with tents, mud, and dust being the norm.
Joseph S. Kingsbury

heat and I'll warm up quickly when I return. I try not to wear outer apparel to bed as there is almost no way to clean or wash anything, and it will have to last indefinitely.

Outside there are a few hooded lights, but the buildings stand out in long, low silhouette against the lighter sky. Directly ahead, at right angles to the row of barracks buildings, and well elevated on a manmade berm, is the latrine. It is really just a many-holed, brick outhouse and smells just as you would imagine. The Germans send the "honey wagon" around periodically in an effort to prevent overflow. I grope through the blackness to an available empty hole.

As I head back to the barracks, the fresh air is sharp. I can see my breath. I am shivering.

When I open the door, I have to pause to let my eyes adapt to the gloom, but also find that I'm almost subconsciously taking a deep breath before plunging into the thick,

overpowering atmosphere inside. I shuffle back to my bunk and climb up. I carefully arrange my body over the bed boards and drop off to sleep until the next latrine call. I average, like everyone else, about four times a night.

The entire barracks comes to life about 7:00 A.M. Prisoners are getting dressed, making conversation with bunk mates, or just puttering at unimportant things as only people who have no schedule and too much time on their hands can do.

At 8:00 comes "tea." This is kindly called "ersatz tea," but I have my suspicions that it is really water stained a bit with tree bark. It comes in a huge wooden tub lugged from the kitchen by four men using a carrying pole. It is placed in a convenient open spot in the barracks, and the appointed barracks rationer takes over. He uses an "official" instrument—a soup can wired to a stick handle.

The men in the barracks are organized into ten cubicles of twelve to eighteen men each. For purposes of food rationing, a meticulous log is kept, and the order of the cubicles is rotated at each issue so that the first becomes last and the last gradually works up to first. If there are any seconds left to be given out, they start exactly where they left off the last time; not just with the correct cubicle, but with the exact man within that cubicle.

I get in line with Cubicle No. 9, and shortly I am issued my Campbell's soup can ration of warm ersatz tea. I pour half into a cup for leisurely sipping; it is warm and tasteless, but it looks like tea. The other half I keep in my pot and use for a comfortable shave; it saves fuel needed to heat the water and is much better than a cold shave when your only blade is dull as a hoe.

About 9:00 A.M., when everything settles down again, it is time for *"Appell."* This is the first head count of the day. I join the formation in front of the barracks along with the rest of the men. Each of the six barracks within this compound has its own formation. When we are all formed, guards are sent through each barracks to check that they are empty. Then the numbers are laboriously counted, with a guard passing down both the front and back of each formation simultaneously to make sure no inmate changes position.

In the old days, in warmer weather, we made a game of being uncooperative, what we called "baiting the goon." The uniforms of the prisoners are so mixed and nonstandard that there is no longer any real attempt to keep the British separated from the Norwegians, or the Poles, or us Americans. The best the guards can do is some kind of total count.

Return to the barracks is followed by the daily cleanup period. There is no official inspection, but cubicle leaders are constantly aware of the devastation that any contagion could bring, due to the tenuous resistance within the group. Floors are swept, beds are made, and on bright days, an attempt is made to air the area, clothing, and bedding.

With my chores done, I am free until noon. There's a couple of cold water sinks at the back of the barracks, and I find space there to rinse out my spare socks. They are about the only spares that I possess. That done, I hunt up a couple of bunk mates, and we go outside to get in our daily exercise walk. We are not preparing for the Olympics; we are just trying to slow down the deterioration. The rest of the morning is spent chatting in leisurely groups in the sunshine on the sheltered side of the building.

About noon, our wooden tub from the kitchen arrives for the second time. This time it is soup. The official story is that it is dehydrated vegetables, but for most of us it is simply "grass soup." I assemble with my cubicle in our proper order in line, and in due course, I receive my soup can allotment of grass soup. Today, on whim, I drain the liquid off and drink the bitter, rather evil-looking stuff in hopes that it has some nutritional value. Next, I take the grass part of the soup and, in my turn at the cubicle stove (ingeniously made out of crimped and bent tin cans from lush Red Cross parcel days), I fry the grass to a less limp state. It tastes different, if not much better.

Next page
The 458th Bomb Group crew of *Arise My Love and Come With Me* at Horsham St. Faith unfortunately lost part of their wonderful Varga calendar girl (January 1944) when additional armor plate was installed for the copilot. *USAF*

Now our bread ration arrives. I am the official cutter for cubicle number 9. The ration for our fifteen men today is a loaf and a half. A loaf is about the size of the average raisin bread loaf at today's supermarket, but it is very wet, very sour, very dark, and many times heavier. As I measure and estimate, trying to take every little bump and indentation into account, the rest of my cubicle mates watch me closely with a lot of shifting of weight from one foot to the other, but they do not say a word to interrupt my concentration. When I have finally arranged fifteen equal slices or lumps of bread (including crumbs) around the edge of the cubicle table and have noted a few heads nodding in agreement out of the corner of my eye, I ask for a volunteer. The volunteer turns his back to the table, and as I point at random to one of the piles, he gives a number between one and fifteen. I then number the piles clockwise consecutively from that number and point. Each man claims his ration, having gotten it as fairly and objectively as we can arrange.

Sometimes, at infrequent intervals, another ration occurs along with the bread. Several times we had four or five potatoes per man, each the size of a golf ball, though they were shot through with black spots and mostly rotten. We are not that lucky today.

At this point, the average Kriegie starts the long preparation of his "big" meal of the day, designed to coincide with the arrival of the evening tea ration. I am no different. Today I slowly and carefully whittle my precious bit of sour, dark bread into as many wafer-thin pieces as I can manage, while gobbling up the crumbs as they fall. Then, with my time on the stove, I very carefully toast each piece lightly to drive out some of the wetness and hopefully some of the sourness as well. To boost my sagging morale, I go all out. I dig into my hoarded reserve for that little bit of German jam that I horse traded from a guard one day with a couple of the most valuable trading devices of World War II: the American cigarette. I coat each sliver with a fine film of jam—just enough to taste—and my banquet is ready. There seems to be something therapeutic about spreading both the preparation and the consuming of food over the greatest possible span of time, and I am prepared now to spread the act of eating almost nothing over the best part of the evening. I count success in strange ways these days.

About 5:00 P.M. we are called out for our second *"Appell."* I fall into my accustomed position in the formation out front and wait to be counted with the rest. This time there is a lot of explosive German shouting, excited gestures, and scurrying of guards through the barracks. Something has gotten screwed up in the head count. All I can do is wait. It could be someone has been removed for questioning, and the word did not get around. It could be just a bad count by the guards, or more likely, it is someone in a dark corner of the latrine, too miserable to get out for formation. Things finally get resolved.

Almost immediately upon return to the barracks, the evening "tea" arrives. Going through the usual ritual, I get my ration and take it along with my beautiful stack of jam-garnished wafers to a corner of the cubicle table. This is the best time of the day—the social time of the day. Lots of drawn-out conversation, lots of drawn-out eating. It is the best way to disguise the lack of bulk and calories in the diet.

Night falls, and this is the nervous time. We are waiting for the "bird." The bird is the almost nightly reading of the BBC news. One of the Norwegian prisoners has a crystal radio set contained in a wearable upper-tooth bridge (it can now be told). From this, our captured war correspondent (we have one in camp) makes up a news release for the camp. With the release complete, a reader will go from barracks to barracks and read the latest war news. At these times we have our own brand of security, with guards posted to prevent interruptions or discovery.

The news tonight is good. All European fronts are progressing. Of almost equal interest is the war in the Pacific and its developments.

Lights out is 9:00 P.M. Until that time, I wander outside for some fresh air and to discuss the bird with some others. Sometimes we are lucky enough to get in on an RAF bombing show to the north towards Berlin. Under those conditions, the guards try to force us all inside, but there is no show tonight.

At 9:30 the fat lamps are out, and conversation gradually dies out as well. I head for the cold water sinks and do what washing up I can. Back at the bunk, I remove my outer clothing and climb under my two meager blankets. I can hear a little movement here and there in the barracks, but most prisoners have learned to fall asleep easily. I will too.

CHAPTER 7

Little Friends

Clarence E. "Bud" Anderson
P-51 pilot, 357th Fighter Group

It seemed we were always outnumbered. We had more fighters than they did, but what mattered was how many they could put up in one area. They would concentrate in huge numbers, by the hundreds at times. They would assemble way up ahead, pick a section of the bomber formation, and then come in head on, their guns blazing, sometimes hitting the bombers below us before we knew what was happening.

In the distance, a red-and-black smear marked the spot where a B-17 and its ten men had been. Planes still bearing their bomb loads erupted and fell, trailing flame, streaking the sky, leaving gaps in the bomber formation that were quickly closed up. Through our headsets we could hear the war, working its way back toward us, coming straight at us at hundreds of miles per hour. The adrenaline began gushing, and I scanned the sky frantically, trying to pick out the fly speck against the horizon that might have been somebody coming to kill us, trying to see him before he saw me, looking, squinting, breathless.

Francis "Lefty" Grove
P-51 pilot, 4th Fighter Group

Nineteen October 1944, P-51 VF-T, FO number 1249A, Escort "Libs" to Mainz. On way home rounded up four B-24 stragglers and one B-17 and escorted them home. Made no note in my log book, but do remember one badly damaged B-24 kept calling for close escort. I remember sliding in close, and they kept calling closer, closer. Finally they said good—and I was between the tail and wing, flying formation. They said they'd keep their eyes peeled for bogies and tell me where. I could see the crew, and I hoped they weren't trigger happy—their voices were certainly not calm on the trip home. And fortunately we spotted no Huns. When we made landfall after crossing the Channel, I broke off and headed home. Another reminder—how grateful to be a fighter pilot.

Mid-summer 1944. One of the working checker-nosed Thunderbolts of the 78th Fighter Group based at Duxford, which was a Royal Air Force base "loaned" to the Americans. Airplanes in combat didn't last long. Dick Sharpe was lost in this one on a strafing mission to targets in the Netherlands area, 3 September 1944. The 78th was known for eight-ship line abreast takeoffs on the large grass expanse at Duxford, getting the entire group into the air in record time. *USAF*

The first American escort fighter to arrive in England (late December 1942) was the Republic P-47C Thunderbolt. Not until 10 March 1943 did the 4th Fighter Group fly the large fighter's first mission, a cautious sweep into France. This 56th Fighter Group P-47C runs up in England during that time. The 56th and 78th Fighter Groups flew their first mission on 8 April. The white nose and tail stripes were applied to help friendly crews distinguish the P-47 from the similar-looking Fw 190. *Charles E. Brown/Royal Air Force Museum*

164

John Gabay
B-17 tail gunner, 94th Bomb Group

When a red alert was on (that meant a raid the next day), we'd fill up the two tiny belly stoves with coal, put out the lights, and try to sleep. About 3:00 A.M., some guy would come in, switch on the lights, and scream out the names of the men going on the raid while ducking a few army shoes. We'd get dressed in about five minutes to keep from freezing, as the stoves were out and the barracks cold, damp, and miserable. We would file outside into the waiting truck amid mumbled gripes and curses.

The truck would take us to the mess hall for breakfast, then to the briefing room. (Before entering this room, you had to identify yourself to two MPs with machine guns.) We'd take our seats, and the usual chatter would be going on, but as soon as the briefing officer came on stage, the silence would

be deafening. He would walk over to the large covered map in the center of the stage and pull the curtain off. If the line to the target was a long one, the moans and whistles filled the room. Then the briefing would begin. We didn't pay much attention to the weather report or the amount of flak batteries and fighters we would encounter along the way—these reports were always wrong. But we did pay attention to the length of the raid, the altitude, the type of bomb load, and most of all the escort. The few times we were to get the English Spitfire escort, the men would boo, but they would cheer whenever we would get Polish Spits. The English were very poor at escort duty—they never seemed to get the hang of it.

On one occasion, our group was getting shot up by about twenty Me 109s. A few minutes later twenty-seven British Spitfires showed up and half the German fighters

The ground crew of Lieutenant F. M. "Lefty" Grove's 4th Fighter Group P-51C Mustang get the aircraft ready for a morning mission, Debden, mid-1944. With the arrival of the Mustang came the range and capability the Eighth Air Force had needed since the very start of the bombing effort. With fighters able to go all the way to the target and back, the Luftwaffe was stopped in its tracks. *F. M. Grove*

A 48th Squadron, 14th Fighter Group P-38J Lightning on short final at Triolo, Italy, winter 1944–45. The P-38 had the range and firepower to make an excellent escort fighter, and it did a sterling job for the Ninth, Twelfth, and Fifteenth Air Forces. Unfortunately, it suffered from continual mechanical failures with the Eighth Air Force over Europe and was withdrawn in favor of the P-51. Lack of adequate cockpit heat was the most common complaint from pilots. *James M. Stitt, Jr.*

A 325th Fighter Group Mustang pulls up alongside a B-25 to provide some escort before breaking off for home base in Italy, fall 1944. The Mustang did well in all theaters of war. A pilot's airplane with an excellent cockpit, strapping into a '51 was like pulling on a pair of pants. *James M. Stitt, Jr.*

Fighter pilots—God bless 'em. First Lieutenant Bob Flynt and Captain Jim Stitt, 37th Squadron, 14th Fighter Group, Triolo, Italy, late 1944. The fighter boys always seemed to be without a care in the world, never lacked for girls, knew where the hooch was, and were so cocky that the bomber boys loved to hate them. All that didn't make a whisker's difference when a bomber was under attack by German fighters and a Little Friend showed up to keep the wolves at bay. *James M. Stitt, Jr.*

166

plowed into them and chased them, shooting down several Spits. Then the German fighters grouped up and continued to clobber us. It would not be fair to judge the Royal Air Force on these few incidents. They certainly proved themselves as great aerial fighters throughout the war, but they just weren't good at escorting American bomb-ers.

From the briefing room we went to see the chaplain, Father Joe Collins, and either got a blessing or went to group confession, then walked to the locker room and picked up our flight clothes and parachutes. Then to the squadron armament shack for our guns, which we checked out and cleaned thoroughly. Then we'd climb into the truck

There was no mistaking the 4th Fighter Group's Mustangs with their blazing red noses. Lieutenant Bob Dickmeyer's *Jan* rests in its sandbagged revetment on the outer perimeter of Debden. *Larry Hendel*

Freddie F. Ohr's 52nd Fighter Group P-51D *Marie* at Capodocino, Naples, November 1944, when the Mustang reigned supreme across Europe. *Fred E. Bamberger*

A 64th Squadron, 57th Fighter Group P-47D taxies in at Grosseto, Italy, December 1944. The Thunderbolt was equally at home escorting bombers or dropping bombs at close range. Its rugged construction and excellent Pratt & Whitney R-2800 engine made it one of the safer places to be in the air. *Fred E. Bamberger*

P-51Ds of the 364th Fighter Group running up for takeoff at Honington, August 1944. Each fighter carried two 110-gallon drop tanks, which added a good four hours' range at cruise power. This allowed the Mustang to roam Europe at will, a war-winning capability. *Mark Brown/USAFA*

and ride out to our plane where we would put in our guns (in the dark) and complete dressing. Then we would sit under the wings, smoke a cigarette, and wait for about five minutes for the officers to arrive. When they arrived there were always a few wise cracks; then the pilot would ask if everything was OK. If there were no problems, we would climb into the plane and wait for the signal flare to start the engines. At no time, from briefing until we were airborne, did we mention the target.

A 63rd Squadron, 56th Fighter Group P-47D taxies out at Boxted, mid-1944, with two 150-gallon drop tanks. At the normal cruise of 100 gallons per hour, this gave an extra three hours' flying time—absolutely essential to put the thirsty Thunderbolt deep into enemy territory. The 56th, unlike the other Eighth Air Force fighter outfits, decided to stay with its '47s rather than trade them in for Mustangs. *Mark Brown/USAFA*

A P-47D yet to be assigned to a line fighter group, pays a visit to Mt. Farm with a fresh set of theater markings and invasion stripes. The bubble canopy on later Thunderbolts gave pilots excellent all-round visibility, an absolutely crucial asset in air-to-air combat. *Robert Astrella*

A war-weary P-47D of the Eighth Air Force's Air Sea Rescue Squadron, later the 5th Emergency Rescue Squadron. Though the airplane has had some hard use, it has been retrofitted with a Malcolm Hood, an outstanding addition for searching at sea. From May 1944 through the end of the war, the rescue squadron devoted full time to rescuing pilots at sea. The '47s were fitted with droppable dinghies and sea markers and were a more than welcome sight for a guy floating in frigid water with nothing more than a Mae West. *Robert Astrella*

One of the most vexing of problems for Eighth Air Force planners was obtaining accurate weather information, particularly over the Continent. In April 1944, the 802nd Reconnaissance Group (P) was formed with reverse Lend-Lease Mosquito Mk. XVI bombers. The unit became the 25th Bomb Group (Recon) by August. These fast "Mossies", painted in PRU Blue with red tails (to keep friendly fighters from thinking they were Me 410s), were ideal to range ahead of the bomber stream, reporting weather and target strikes, taking photos of special areas, and (late in the war) dropping radar-blinding chaff ahead of the attacking formations. The happy pilots of these beautiful de Havilland all-wood wonders initially came from the almost forgotten P-38 pilots of the 50th Fighter Squadron who had been left in Iceland by the 14th Fighter Group since mid-1942 sitting boring alert. *Robert Astrella*

Hairless Joe, the P-47D Thunderbolt of legendary 56th Fighter Group ace David C. Schilling, who ended the war with twenty-two and one half air-to-air and ten and one half ground kills. With the group since it was formed in June 1941, Schilling was made commander of the 62nd Squadron, then group executive officer by August 1943. He began his string of victories with two kills on the 9 October 1943 mission to Emden. When group commanding officer Colonel Hubert "Hub" Zemke took over the 479th Fighter Group in August 1944, Schilling was given command of the 56th, a position he held until tranfering to the 65th Fighter Wing the next January. Aggressive and capable, Dave Schilling was one of the finest fighter pilots of World War II. *Robert Astrella*

The 339th Fighter Group flew in combat with the Eighth Air Force for just under a full year—30 April 1944 to 21 April 1945—and managed to score a total of 239.5 air-to-air and 440.5 ground kills, almost all under the command of one man, Colonel John B. Henry, Jr. This 504th Squadron Mustang

172

was an early P-51B in the group, originally Vern Blizzard's *Punkie*. When Duane Larson was assigned the aircraft, it was renamed *Swede* as a reflection of his family origins. *Robert Astrella*

A 22nd Squadron, 7th Photo Group P-51K taxies out on the eastern perimeter track at Mt. Farm, March 1945. After suffering a string of recce aircraft losses to German fighters, the group was assigned its own fighter escort, beginning January 1945, in the form of Mustangs. At this point in the war American industry was pouring out an almost unlimited supply of aircraft. *Robert Astrella*

When fighters had seen their day and managed to last through enough combat to be classified "war weary," they were usually herded off to some other form of useful service. This veteran P-47C from Atcham, Shrewsbury, early 1944, was with the 551st Fighter Training Squadron, where it introduced pilots fresh from the States to VIII Fighter Command tactics and doctrine. *Robert Astrella*

CHAPTER 8

Home

Richard Fitzhugh
B-17 pilot, 457th Bomb Group

After my combat tour, they sent me to a redeployment pool of some kind. I believe the name of the place was Stoke, a miserable-looking place, cold, with tarpaper shacks, in December during the Battle of the Bulge. News was very bad at that time. I somehow felt kind of bad about going home, so I called up my squadron commander and got him on the phone, and I told him that I was willing to come back and do some more flying if he needed me, because I'd heard over the radio or something that B-17s had landed all over the continent there. The whole Eighth Air Force was all over creation. He told me to leave well enough alone, so I caught a C-54 back to the States.

We stopped at the Azores, and an interesting thing I noticed there, while taxiing out, were the locals were eating out of the garbage cans of the kitchen. I'd never seen that before. Then Bermuda. Bermuda was spectacular. We flew at night and came in there in the morning. Beautiful, beautiful pink sand and blue water. I still have the newspaper-this was January 1945—*The Bermuda Gazette,* McKinley Field.

We landed at Washington National. This was an Air Transport Command C-54, and so we went through a processing line. When it got to my turn, the corporal sitting there says, "Are you married or single?" And I asked him what difference did that make? And he says, "Well, if you're single, you go to Atlantic City, New Jersey for R&R, but if you're married, you get to go to Miami Beach." It was snowing in Washington at that time. I'd been freezing to death for a long time in England, and I didn't want to go to Atlantic City, so I said, "I'm married." I really wasn't married. So he signs me up for Miami Beach. My mother was living in Washington at the time, so this was very convenient.

I went home, and first thing I did was call up Alice, my wife-to-be, and tell her that we had to get married in a hurry. She said, "When?" and I said, "Well, next week! I've got to be married before I report in to my

A stripped-down and slick B-26 Marauder on short final at Gablingen Airdrome near Augsburg, Germany, fall 1945. When everyone else went home, a few Americans were left as a part of the occupation forces, and life became pretty boring. This Marauder was "requisitioned" by the 355th Fighter Group as their "Whiskey Wagon," and it was sent on a number of important missions to bring back food and drink. It was ideal for fighter pilots used to fast cruising speeds. And the '26 could really go without the extra drag and weight of turrets, armor plate, and bombs. *Alexander C. Sloan*

This was the awesome, terrible price Germany paid for going to war: Münster, Germany, just after the surrender. Though controversy raged from the start over the effectiveness of American daylight bombing, no one argued against bombing as a crucial part of overall victory. *Mark Brown/USAFA*

The remains at the southwest end of Villacoublay Airfield, just outside Paris. This field came under continual bombing attack until the Germans finally retreated in mid-1944. Afterward, it was nearly impossible to clean up the damage and rebuild the hangars. Many years elapsed before the field was once again back to prewar civil standards. *Mark Brown/USAFA*

next station." So she said, "Well, I'll tell my mother." She agreed, but I'm not sure her mother did. She was working in Columbia, South Carolina, at the time, and her home was Manning, South Carolina. So I bought the rings, went on down to Columbia and got her. Of course, I didn't have a car; in fact, I didn't even know how to drive a car. I didn't have a driver's license. I finished a combat tour in the B-17, but I never learned to drive a car.

We took the bus to Manning, which was about, I guess, an hour away. Some of her friends had a car, but there were a bunch of them, and we couldn't all get in the car. Somebody bought the wedding cake in Columbia. You couldn't get a cake that size, I don't think, in Manning. So we had the cake, and, being an independent person, I said, "We'll take the bus, and we'll take the cake." So Alice and I got on the bus with the cake. She had a suitcase, I had a suitcase, and that's all we had.

The bus broke down after about thirty minutes, so the driver let everybody out on the highway. Here I am, standing there with my suitcase, a wife-to-be, and a cake. I'm out there thumbing a ride to our own wedding! Then her friends came by, so we figured that we could really all get in there after all. I sat on somebody's lap, had the cake on my lap; and we all made it to the wedding. I don't think too many people have to hitchhike to their own wedding!

Bob Morgan
B-17 pilot, 91st Bomb Group

When General Eaker told us we could come back to the States as our twenty-sixth mission, we really didn't know what we were in for. All we knew was we were going home. We came back; we landed at Bradley Field, then flew on to Washington, D.C.'s National Airport as our first official stop. General Hap Arnold was there, and as we approached the field, through air traffic control he told us to buzz the field. Well, for Robert Morgan, that is a real license to steal. We did a pretty good buzz job. He also gave us full license during this three-month tour of the United States to buzz any place we wanted. So, needless to say, I had a good

Though they were glad to get out of combat and go home, few aircrews had any idea that their wonderful steeds of war would be discarded as so much scrap to be turned back into pots and pans . . . or to be simply broken apart, carted away, and buried. This forlorn B-26 Marauder at Herzogenaurach, Germany, is only a short time away from being chopped up, burned, and buried on the spot, late 1945. The work was given at minimal wages to local Germans, many of whom had been active fighter pilots. They were astonished at being paid by Americans for doing something they had tried so hard to do six months before. *Herbert R. Rutland, Jr.*

Heading home. A mixed bag of Forts from the 94th, 34th, and 490th Bomb Groups gather at Bury St. Edmunds after VE-day to fly back to the United States with as many servicemen aboard as can fit. Flying former combat aircraft back across the Atlantic was an ideal way to bring masses of former combat crews home without creating a massive tie-up of ships and transport aircraft. Afterwards the

177

aircraft were useless. Upon arrival in the United States, they were flown to one of many bone yards to await civilian buyers or the smelter's torch. *Byron Trent*

Altus, Oklahoma, August 1945. B-24s from the 459th Bomb Group, Fifteenth Air Force, and other units sit in the Midwest sun awaiting their fate. Virtually all of the aircraft were scrapped within a year or two. *Claude Porter*

Old Ironpants awaits its fate at Altus, Oklahoma, August 1945. The Liberator was not a favorite of civilian postwar buyers looking for usable aircraft. As a result, almost all the Liberators were scrapped, much to the heartbreak—or delight—of the pilots who flew them. *Claude Porter*

time—a real good time. Asheville is still talking about it! If you've ever been up there and seen the courthouse and city hall, we managed to get a wing between the two of them. This was a lot of fun, and we enjoyed it. I must say, though, that, at the end of the three months, I felt like I'd been through combat again. I was ready to go to the Pacific.

Jack Havener
B-26 pilot, 344th Bomb Group

"What a disgraceful way to go!" These were my words after watching a newsreel in March of 1946 showing the demolition of surplus B-26s at Landsburg, Germany. The camera stopped in front of one ship being stripped of equipment prior to the attachment of dynamite packs to the wing roots for separation from the fuselage. I recognized the airmen removing the radio gear as members of the 497th Bomb Squadron, 344th Bomb Group, as the camera panned to the left and showed the nose art name to be *Terre Haute Tornado*. Rising up in my seat, I exclaimed, "That's my ship!" and much to my wife's embarrassment, continued to moan, "Oh no—Oh no!" throughout the balance of the newsreel. Needless to say, I didn't enjoy the feature picture that followed. After flying in that aircraft for some thirteen months, it was quite a shock to see her pushed up into a scrap heap by a bull-dozer.

Bob DeGroat
B-24 pilot, 459th Bomb Group

People sometimes ask about my feelings concerning the civilian death and destruction our bombing caused. Although I was aware that this was undoubtedly happening, the fact that it was unintentional probably salved my conscience. All briefings were for military or industrial targets, and the view of destruction from 25,000 feet was usually a column of black smoke erupting through an undercast. I was also a bit hardened by the death and destruction I witnessed among the planes around me. It became an unemotional everyday job with attached personal risk.

Fred Weiner
POW, Stalag Luft VI

It didn't take long to get back into the life in America. Yeah, you wanted to get started, you wanted to be a part of civilian life. While I was still in uniform, I met Edith. I wanted to get married, to get a job— so it didn't take long to get going. There are some things that are hard to tell somebody about the fun we had in the prison camps. In order to go steady with me, Edith prom-ised to let her friends meet the guy before she got serious with him. We had a double date at the Paramount to see Frank Sinatra. So, don't ask—we're in a line and have to wait two hours to get in. We're talking, and it turns out the other guy was a POW at Stalag 17B. Here I was a POW from Stalag Luft

VI, so we started in with the stories—laughing and telling anecdotes about the prison camp life. Well, people gathered all around us to hear us talk. We could hear them in the background saying, "Didn't they say they were in a prison camp?"

Home! **What a sight for sore eyes in 1946 after several years overseas—Grand Central Station in Los Angeles. What a city in which to get off the train and get reacquainted with American life.** *Alexander C. Sloan*

Could there be a better place for a serviceman to find out that American girls were still the prettiest in the world than the beach at Playa del Rey, south of Los Angeles? Home at last. *James C. Leigh via Mrs. M. M. Leigh/ Jim Dietz*

179

Index

AIR COMMAND

FIGHTERS AND BOMBERS OF WORLD WAR II

Jeffrey L. Ethell

Lowe & B. Hould
Publishers

This edition published in 1997 by Lowe and B. Hould, an imprint of Borders, Inc., 515 East Liberty, Ann Arbor, MI 48104 Lowe & B. Hould Publishers is a trademark of Borders Properties, Inc.

FIGHTER COMMAND first published in 1991 by Motorbooks International Publishers & Wholesalers, 729 Prospect Ave, PO Box 1, Osceola, WI 54020-0001 USA

© Jeffrey L. Ethell, 1991

All rights reserved. With the exception of quoting brief passages for the purposes of review no part of this publication may be reproduced without prior written permission from the Publisher

Motorbooks International is a certified trademark, registered with the United States Patent Office

The information in this book is true and complete to the best of our knowledge. All recommendations are made without any guarantee on the part of the author or Publisher, who also disclaim any liability incurred in connection with the use of this data or specific details

We recognize that some words, model names and designations, for example, mentioned herein are the property of the trademark holder. We use them for identification purposes only. This is not an official publication

Library of Congress Cataloging-in-Publication Data Available
ISBN 0-681-22745-1

On the front cover: The Republic P-47D Thunderbolt was powered by an air cooled, radial eighteen cylinder Pratt & Whitney R-2800 Double Wasp engine that enabled the big fighter to reach maximum speeds of 428 miles per hour. *Warren Bodie*

On the frontispiece: Copilot Lieutenant William C. Rowland from New Castle, Pennsylvania, off to war from England in a B-24. Relationships on the flight deck could be good, could be bad. A great deal depended upon the attitude of the aircraft commander in the left seat. Some gave their copilots half of the flying time, while others were of the "gear up, flaps up, shut up" variety. *USAF*

Printed in Hong Kong

Contents

Introduction

By the end of World War II the US Army Air Forces stretched across the globe with a seemingly endless supply of aircraft, aircrew and ground crew. American industrial might and military training, in a few short years, had geared up from lethargy to a frenzy of mass production. Seldom are the sheer numbers ever mentioned, and even then they are so large as to be incomprehensible.

From 1 July 1940 to 30 August 1945 the United States manufactured 299,293 aircraft. Of those, 69,118 were for the US Navy and in the massive Lend-Lease effort to supply the Allies, over 43,000 aircraft were sent to the Soviet Union and Great Britain. By comparison, the United Kingdom built 128,835 aircraft from 1939 to 1945, Germany rolled out 113,514 (53,728 of which were fighters) and Japan produced 58,834 from 1941 to 1945.

As astonishing as it seems today, 9,535 P-38s were built at an average cost of $97,147 each; 15,579 P-47s for $85,578 apiece; 14,490 P-51s for $51,572 each; 12,677 B-17s for $204,370 each; 18,188 B-24s for $215,516 per copy; and on the list goes.

To man these aircraft the USAAF trained 193,440 pilots and washed out another 124,000 from 1 July 1939 to 31 August 1945 while training over 400,000 aircrew to man the bombers and transports with bombardiers, navigators, gunners, flight engineers and other specialists. To support every one man in combat, the AAF had to field sixteen noncombat personnel. There were seven ground crew for every man who flew and four ground technical specialists for every one man in the air.

How well were these men paid? In 1944 a private got $50 a month, a staff sergeant $96, a master sergeant $138. Yearly pay for a second lieutenant was $1,800, a major got $3,000, a bird colonel $4,000 and a four-star general $8,000.

By June 1944 here's what it cost to outfit the average fighter pilot: gloves $1.74, goggles $10.74, sun glasses $3.25, helmet $1.16, A-2 jacket $8.12, winter flying jacket $25.00, summer flying suit $8.50 and Mae West $10.00.

There never was, and there never will be, another flying armada to equal the wartime US Army Air Forces.

From this war machine emerged but 35,000 fighter pilots supported by highly competent and technically savvy ground crews.

As much as it made their fellow bomber pilots furious, fighter pilots were the glamor boys of the "Air Corps"—in spite of a name change to AAF in 1941, the older, more romantic term stuck throughout the war, even in official documents and reports. The dashing fighter pilot in his leather jacket, fifty-mission "crush" hat and silk scarf was idolized by the press and chased by the girls. But when a bomber was in serious trouble, the feisty "Little Friend" was a savior . . . fighter pilots were welcome at bars or pubs and told they could not pay for a single drink. There isn't a bomber crewman alive who didn't heave a massive sigh of relief at the sight of a Lightning, Thunderbolt or Mustang over enemy territory.

Certainly the AAF had a tough time dealing with these aggressive men who flew single-seat aircraft, relying on themselves and their skill—"you can always tell a fighter pilot, but you can't tell him much." By his very nature, a fighter pilot had to believe that he was the best at what he did, that no one else could fly a plane like he could, that the enemy was going to die in a dogfight, that the other guy was going to "auger in" and kill himself through some stupid mistake.

Otherwise, he would never have gone to war alone at 30,000 feet, deep in enemy territory, looking for enemy aircraft to shoot down or flak-infested airdromes to shoot up. The pilot who loved flying single-seat aircraft with no crew to rely on was often the one who tore apart the local base officer's club for a good time or threw the commanding general in the pool. The exceptional wartime fighter pilot had little patience with peacetime flying and the social climbing required for promotion.

In the background sat the hard-working ground crew. Though they never got the glory, they basked in the satisfaction of giving their pilots the best maintenance possible. A kill was earned by the whole team but when "their" airplane came back all shot up, the crew chief and his men would listen impatiently while the pilot had some tall explaining to do.

Beneath all the banter and the caste system which kept officer and enlisted man apart, the Army fighter outfits were the epitome of teamwork, both on the ground and in the air. The fighter was, for the most part, overshadowed by prewar faith in the ability of the strategic bomber to survive enemy attack. Until the escort fighter arrived, bombers were hacked down in ever-increasing numbers. Nowhere was this more evident than in the European Theater of Operations (ETO) when, by the end of 1943, the Eighth Air Force bomber offensive was close to being stopped by the Luftwaffe.

Though the Republic P-47 Thunderbolt had been covering the bombers through most of 1943, its lack of range left the "Big Friends" alone deep in enemy territory. With the arrival of the Lockheed P-38 Lightning in late 1943, then the North American P-51 Mustang in early 1944, the fortunes of war changed as Eighth AF commanding general Jimmy Doolittle turned his fighter pilots loose under the command of Gen. Bill Kepner. No longer restricted to escorting within visual range of the bombers, fighter pilots roamed Germany at altitude and on the deck to destroy the Luftwaffe and the Wehrmacht; from that point, the outcome of the air war was a foregone conclusion. The tactical fighter units of Gen. Pete Quesada's Ninth Air Force came into their own as they supported the ground forces deep into Germany, strafing and bombing everything in sight.

In the Mediterranean Theater of Operations (MTO) American fighter pilots were thrown into the meat grinder of North Africa at the end of 1942 to face an experienced enemy. The campaign moved slowly up to Sicily and Italy as the "soft underbelly of Europe" proved to be anything but. Fighter groups of the Twelfth and Fifteenth Air Forces provided escort deep into Germany from the south and then went after targets on the ground under the leadership of Generals Ira Eaker and Nate Twining.

Though the exploits of these fighter pilots and their crews are well known, they are set in a sepia-toned memory for later generations. The first batches of experimental color film from Kodak were hard to find, leaving photographers with little choice but to record events in black and white. This book will change that memory and give the reader the first full-blown exposure to outstanding color photography of pilots and ground crews as they lived their lives, accompanied by the vivid narration of first-person recollection.

A fortunate few managed to scrounge up some rolls of Kodachrome and record what was going on around them, among them the coauthor of this book, Bob Sand. Many of the photos are his, and they come to life with his recollections written at the time in a diary and in letters home, which his parents saved. Bob had one continual request—send more Kodachrome when it could be found.

Like most enlisted ground crew, Bob led what he considers to be an unspectacular life in the propeller shop, then as a member of a P-51 ground crew, in the 55th Fighter Group, first at Nuthampstead, then at Wormingford, England. Just after his arrival in England, he wrote his parents on Thanksgiving 1943, "I've shot up one roll of [Kodachrome] film, and while this roll contains nothing spectacular, I hope it is the beginning of something that may have a little interest later on. I'm a little worried about light conditions. I only shoot when sun is bright." No wonder—the film had an ASA of around 12!

That was the beginning. Bob's uncanny eye for using a camera often led to him being ridiculed for carrying the thing around all the time. Fortunately, for those of us who were born later, he did not let that stop him. The result is, without question, some of the finest wartime photography in existence. In many ways this book is his lasting testament to life in a fighter group during World War II.

The narrative portions of the 55th Group in the air, written by former pilot Arthur L. Thorsen, are vibrantly alive, adding yet another dimension to Bob's photos. Thanks to Gen. Regis Urschler for sending a copy of Art's unpublished manuscript, "The Fighting 55th." With Art's kind permission we have been

7

able to let the reader fly along with him and live the life of a fighter pilot.

Other unpublished memoirs were provided by 339th Fighter Group pilot James R. Hanson, who chronicled his career in the AAF, through Korea to his days flying for Piedmont Airlines, and Gilbert C. Burns, Jr., a 50th Fighter Group pilot who was in the thick of Ninth Air Force ground support activity. Without question the Thorsen, Hanson and Burns manuscripts deserve to be published; they put the reader straight back into the emotion of those times. Should a publisher reading this book be sufficiently impressed with what they read from these men, we would welcome an inquiry to put the parties together.

Had it not been for the 55th Fighter Group Association editor Chet Patterson, none of this would have been possible. After seeing a video tape of his presentation using Bob's slides, I prevailed upon him to put me in touch with Bob and this project was born. He then sent several excellent editions of the 55th newsletter, along with his own recollections, thus rounding out our look at the group in wartime England.

Once the project got under way, we attempted to broaden its scope and made a series of requests to people who had taken color slides during the war. With typical generosity, many responded.

The exceptional understanding of Duane J. Reed, curator of special collections in the US Air Force Academy Library, will long be remembered. He provided access to the outstanding Mark H. Brown photography collection, and his assistant, Robert Troudt, was always willing to help us find what we needed. John Woolnough, editor of the *Eighth Air Force News,* sent his collection of wartime color slides which had come from a number of veterans. That opened more doors in finding 357th Fighter Group veteran Jim Frary and 386th Bomb Group pilot Byron Trent, both of whom sent their precious original slides.

As usual, Bob Kuhnert of the 355th FG Assn. came through in his usual selfless fashion and copied Alexander C. "Cal" Sloan's fabulous slide collection, as well as sending several of his favorite issues of *Mustang,* the group newsletter which he so ably edits, and some of his own recollections. Cal was attached to the 1066th Signal Company at Steeple Morden with the 355th. He kept his camera with him as well.

Through the generosity of the 4th FG Assn.'s Charles E. Konsler, we found 4th Fighter Group veterans Edward B. Richie, Joseph B. Sills and Donald E. Allen. Ed, along with sons Mark and Alan, reloaned Ed's fantastic collection of wartime slides, as did Joe and Don.

Through the friendship of P-51 owner Joe Scogna we were put in contact with 356th Fighter Group pilot Herbert R. Rutland, Jr., who took his camera along with him over Germany in the cockpit of his Mustang for some of the most stunning combat color photography to come out of the war, as well as some poignant memories of leaving the fighter pilot's life at the end of the war. Jack and Jan (Houston) Monaghan jumped in with relish to tell of their days in the 55th Fighter Group from the enlisted man's side and through the eyes of a Red Cross girl in a world of men.

Richard H. Perley, and Philip Savides sent slides of their Ninth Air Force, 50th Fighter Group tours of duty, while Gil Burns passed on some of Phil's wartime recollections. Another Ninth Air Force pilot, Arthur O. Houston of the 368th Fighter Group, provided exceptional slides, as he has always has.

Thanks to the willingness of 14th Fighter Group ground crewman Ira Latour and 31st Fighter Group pilot William J. Skinner, the book was able to branch out into coverage of North Africa and the MTO through the many slides they took during their time overseas. Many thanks to Chris Davis for introducing us to William Skinner. Through leading fighter historian Steve Blake, these were added to by Walter E. Zurney who flew with the 82nd Fighter Group and managed to get a roll of Kodachrome in the process.

In searching out recollections from people who had served in fighter units, we found several to be more than willing to jump in. Eric V. Hawkinson, editor of the 7th Photo Group Journal, sent numerous issues with great stories of the unheralded job of recon flying and George Lawson, former 7th Photographic Reconnaissance Group commander and president of the Eighth Air Force Historical Society, put his support behind the project as well. The irrepressible Jack Ilfrey (USAAF class of '41 with my dad, Erv Ethell) opened the 20th Fighter Group archives to send the late John Hudgens' color shots while Leo D. Lester of the 56th Fighter Group Association and Robert H. Powell, Jr., of the 352nd Fighter Group Association interrupted their own association projects to help. Thanks, also, to James Starnes of the 339th Fighter Group Association for history and photos.

Fellow historians Roger Freeman, David Menard, Larry Davis, Samuel Sox, Tom Hitchcock of Monogram Aviation Publications, Bill Hess, Pete Bowers, Dana Bell and Robert DeGroat supplied rare material from their archives while Melissa Kaiser, Dan Hagedorn, Larry Wilson and Mark Avino helped me gain continual access to the National Air & Space Museum (NASM) USAAF color collection.

Then there were the vets themselves who recalled those unforgettable days: William B. Bailey, Duane W. Beeson, Arthur O. Beimdiek, William Bell, Donald J.M. Blakeslee, Marvin Bledsoe, Wayne K. Blickenstaff, John Blyth, Henry W. Brown, Dan Burrows, Thomas J.J. Christian, Jr., Harry Corey, Harry J. Dayhuff, James H. Doolittle, Ervin C. Ethell, Edward B. Giller, Herman Greiner, Walter Hagenah, John B. Henry, Jr., Mark E. Hubbard, Stanley A. Hutchins, Norman W. Jackson, Herbert E. Johnson, Robert S. Johnson, Thomas H. Jones, Claiborne H. Kinnard, Jr., Heinz Knoke, Jean Landis, Don Larson, Jack Lenox, Daniel M. Lewis, Walker M. Mahurin, Chester Marshall, Joe L. Mason, V. K. Meroney, John C. Meyer, Erwin Miller, John Most, John B. Murphy, Elmer W. O'Dell, Ben Rimerman, Robb Satterfield, David C. Schilling, Frank C. Shearin, Jr., Ernst Schroeder, Robert Shoens, Bert Stiles, Avelin P. Tacon, Jr., Harrison B. Tordoff, Ralph P. Willett, Paul Wingert and Hubert Zemke.

The Eighth Air Force tactics manuals, *The Long Reach* and *Down to Earth*, put together by VIII Fighter Command Generals Bill Kepner and Francis Griswold in 1944, added a great deal to placing the reader straight into those times with on-the-spot recollections of serving fighter pilots who described the events as they took place.

For keeping Bob supplied with Kodachrome we would like to thank his parents, Oscar and Rosa Sand, and his friends Violet and Archie Gerry.

For encouragement, we thank George Cockle, McCauley Clark and Danny Morris.

For retyping a massive portion of the manuscript for her dad, we thank Jennie Ethell.

We particularly want to thank our wives, Bettie Ethell and Donna Sand, for their unwavering support.

To all of you, we express our warmest thanks for making the days of Fighter Command come alive again.

Jeff Ethell,
Bob Sand

9

Chapter 1

So You Want to Be a Fighter Pilot?

William Bell, *AT-6 flying cadet*

Once we got into advanced training with a hot 600 hp airplane, we flying cadets considered it the hot rod we never could afford during the Depression. We would cruise about the Texas plains after dark, harassing train crewmen to the point of serious injury. We would spot a slow freighter ambling along a track, fly ahead of it for several miles, turn and meet the locomotive at cab level, and wait until we were right on the engine before turning on one landing light. The engineer would *know* that he couldn't stop in time to avoid a *sure* collision, and order the fireman to jump before the "other train" hit. The engineer

A fighter! During the last few hours of advanced training a select few Cadets were allowed to log their last solo time in an older model pursuit ship. Others who went on to fighter transition had to wait until graduation and getting wings. This obsolete Curtiss P-40B was flown from Luke Field, Arizona, in 1942. That it had seen better days was irrelevant to a pilot moving up from an AT-6. *USAF*

10

Stateside Mustang transition appears to agree with these fledgling fighter pilots, fresh out of advanced training in late 1943. The AT–6 and A–20 in the background form part of the base's complement of aircraft as well. Judging from the exhaust trail on the P–51A, the fighters were ridden hard and put away wet. *USAF*

promptly slammed on the brakes and ground the wheels flat as the AT-6 roared overhead and we hightailed it back to base with our night flying training completed. This was great sport for both Army and Navy pilots.

John Most, *AT-6 flying cadet*

As students we'd play a game during formation flying—the wingman had to get his wingtip as close as possible to the leader's fuselage . . . between his wing and his tail . . . and not hit him.

Robb Satterfield, *AT-6 flying cadet*

For all local flying we had a tower officer, usually a first lieutenant, to handle emergencies and back up the enlisted tower personnel. One day this boy captain was tower officer, a recent overseas returnee with many ribbons and fairly well impressed with himself. Suddenly, over the radio comes the message, 'King Uncle, King Uncle (Williams Tower)! This is Yoke Three Four! My engine just quit! What shall I do?' Our captain hero wades through the sergeants and corporals, grabs the mike, and says, 'Yoke Three Four, this is *Captain* Snodgrass [meaning your troubles are all over, I'm here]. Stay calm, mister. What is your position?' The cadet came back, 'King Uncle, this is Yoke Three Four. I'm still on the ramp. I haven't taxied out yet.' At this, our captain turns instant red and tried to melt into the floor. He was a rather subdued fellow—for maybe three days.

Robb Satterfield, *AT-6 pilot*

I was on the morning schedule as a recently commissioned pilot, which meant from about 0600 till noon on the flight line. Just at noon a beautiful brand new P-51D, first bubble '51 any of us had seen, came over the field at about 1,500 feet, did a roll, entered the pattern, landed and parked at base ops about 150 yards away. As the super fighter enthusiast in the gang, I grabbed up about four or five friends and we headed down to ops to see the Mustang. As we got within about 100 feet of the bird, the pilot, in summer flying suit, stepped out on the wing, took off the helmet and shook out *her* long blond curls! That did it. We halted in our tracks, spun on our heels and strode back to squadron ops,

Barbara Jane Erickson (in the cockpit) is congratulated by Evelyn Sharp, 6th Ferry Group, Women's Auxiliary Ferrying Squadron (WAFS) after delivering a P-51A to Long Beach, California, in early 1943. Much to the consternation of many male fighter pilots, as the war went on the number of women pilots grew until the Women Airforce Service Pilots (WASPs) were formed in July 1943. Sharp was later killed in the crash of a P-38, while Erickson survived the war to win an Air Medal for her outstanding ferry service. *USAF*

The AT-6 was the first dose of real horsepower given to Army Air Force Cadets and they took to the beefy trainer with unbridled enthusiasm, much to the horror of local townspeople who were constantly buzzed and chased at all hours of the day and night. It was intoxicating to ride behind 600 horsepower with the canopy slid back and the landing gear tucked up. A pilot's first taste of "rat racing" in trail, leader trying to shake those following, came with the Texan. *USAF*

five very unhappy 19 to 22 year old 2nd lieutenants.

Jean Landis, *Women's Airforce Service Pilot*

Reactions to a woman climbing out of a P-51 were varied, mostly startled. Once I flew into a field that was off limits but the weather was bad and I had a slight mechanical problem so I called in and asked for permission to land. I kept radioing, "P-51 ready to land; awaiting final landing instructions." It was sort of garbled and they kept asking me to call in again and again. Finally, they said, "Waggle your wings if you receive." Then, "Lady, the only thing we see up there is a P-51." They couldn't believe it—they were looking for a Piper Cub or something. Finally, when I landed, what a welcome I got. Word got around that a gal was flying that thing. They were darlings. By the time

Airacobra training at Hamilton Field, California, for the 357th Fighter Group before shipping out to England to join the Eighth Air Force in July 1943. Group CO Col. Edward S. Chickering's P-39 is being started by the ground crew the hard way—with the hand crank to get the inertia starter going. *NASM*

13

I had taxied up to the line, following the little Follow Me truck, there were lots of guys around to see what kind of woman was flying this P-51. They'd never heard of us, the WASPs. **James R. Hanson,** *fighter transition*

My first flight in the 'Cobra is tremendous. I'm all strapped in and the crew chief gives me the clear signal. When I press my heel to the starter, there's a squeal, then a couple cylinders bark and with a few shakes from nose to tail the 12 cylinder Allison comes to life with a roar. You can feel the fuselage twist as the long driveshaft takes up the torque. My instructor gives me the thumbs up and waves me out.

As I roll into position I really appreciate the forward visibility and advance the throttle. The take-off is a real joy . . . a simple flip of the toggle switch brings the gear up. I was prepared for the solid feel of a fighter

Army Air Corps pilots dreamed of flying the hot ships after getting out of advanced training. When a new Lightning like this one would show up and dazzle the Flying Cadets, there would be a rush for the few fighter slots available. This hot rock shows real fighter pilot savoir-faire for the troops (more likely the photographer) by stepping into his '38 with the engines running. *NASM*

this time, having been one of the lucky ones to have flown the P-40 for six hours. Except for the solid feel, everything else is different. In the P-40 the whole airplane seems to spread out ahead of you since you sit behind the long nose and back over the trailing edge of the wing. Here in the '39, sitting high over the leading edge, I feel like the wings are strapped onto my hips. The climb is better and the controls are lighter. It's everything I've dreamed about. There are some scattered clouds up here to play with and then I do some steep turns, a roll, and pull vapors off the wingtips.

Frank C. Shearin, Jr., *P-38 pilot, fighter transition*

During the course of four ship P-38 student navigation flight (one instructor and three students), positions were changed to where I was leading the second element with a student on my wing. It was a beautiful day and the sun made the cockpit cozy. After approximately 20 minutes, I noticed my wingman slowly leave the formation up and to the right. Over the radio I yelled, "Bartlett!" The wings of his aircraft fluttered and he returned to the formation. Shortly thereafter he left the formation again—slowly up and to the right. Again I yelled, "Bartlett!" with the same reaction. His wings fluttered and he returned to the formation. Upon landing I asked him why he left the formation. He replied, "The sun made me sleepy, so I trimmed the aircraft to fly up and to the right in case I fell asleep. I didn't want to fall asleep and run into you."

Ervin C. Ethell, *P-63 pilot and gunnery instructor*

During the maneuvers in the California desert while serving as a practice antiaircraft target, I decided to show the ground pounders how us Army pilots could fly. Roaring over the makeshift airfield adjacent to the bivouac, I came in on the deck, pulled the nose up and started a slow roll. As I got upside down the nose fell through—I wasn't going to make it. Shoving with all my might, both feet on one rudder and both hands on the stick, I got the P-63 reversed in what must have been a reverse snap roll but she was shuddering on the edge of a stall as I pulled back on the stick. I just missed the commanding general's tent but proceeded to blow it down on top of him with my considerable prop wash. Sand, tumbleweeds and who knows what else formed a wake behind me as I tried to keep from mushing in, hovering in ground effect—for some unknown reason the fighter stayed airborne, slowly regaining flying speed.

I calmed down enough to quit shaking and headed back for Muroc, knowing I was going to get court martialed for sure. After landing I took a look under my airplane, sure the belly must have dragged the desert, miraculously missing the prop. No damage but I had to pick quite a few tumbleweeds out of the small air scoop on the belly. The worst was yet to come—as was usual after a sortie, I had to take the Jeep and drive out to the general's tent for a debrief on the day's results. When I arrived his first words to me were, "You blew my tent down!" Bracing for the chewing out, I saw him break into a wide grin and

say, "Can you come back tomorrow and do that great show again?"

Thomas E. Maloney, *P-38 pilot, fighter transition*

I'll never forget my P-38 instructor, Capt. Erv Ethell, a North Africa combat veteran. After he briefed us on the mission for the day, we would get in a jeep or command car and he would have us each dropped off at our planes. He would be the last to get to his. No matter how fast you would climb up, get in your chute and crank that old bird up, when we got the engines started and taxied out, he would always be out at the head of the taxi strip waiting on us. Naturally, this got to be quite a game we played but by the end of our three weeks training he would still beat us out just as badly as at first. I naturally got very proficient at this with continued practice and as the P-38 got to be a part of me, but in my best days, I'm sure Captain Ethell would still be out on the end of the runway waiting for me since we later found out he contorted his arms, hands and fingers in such a way that he could start both engines at once. Us hot rock, brand new shavetail fighter pilots found out we had some things to learn.

Andy Anderson, *AT-6 student*

I was once privileged to see one of the Chinese trainees land his Curtiss P-40 on the taxiway adjacent to the parking area. Somehow he became disoriented and put it down, just as a weaving class of AT-6s was working their way into the parking areas. There must have been five or six AT-6s S-ing when the P-40 touched down coming at them head-on, at about ninety miles per hour. I was told later that the tower operators were going out of their collective minds trying to get the Chinese fighter pilot to go around, this before he touched down. Story has it that he kept responding to their instructions by replying, 'Loger, loger, loger.' In any event, the AT-6s—all of them saw him coming and either dived into the parking area or plunged out onto the mat to let him get by. He managed to get it stopped and all those cadets in the AT-6s survived without a dented wingtip.

Pete Vandersluis, *AT-6 instructor*
The first student I had got on the wobble pump and the primer, then

A fighter transition P–39D Airacobra on the line at Page Field, Ft. Myers, Florida in March 1943. *William J. Skinner*

Who cares if this is a staged AAF public relations shot? No question this Flying Cadet at Luke Field, Arizona, 1941, is happy to climb into the hot rod he could never afford during the depression. Only *this* one has wings and 600 hp under the hood. *USAF*

The expression says it all ... Though the P–39 was not greatly loved by most who flew it in combat, when it was the first fighter given to a new shavetail second looie out of Advanced, it was "hawg heaven." This instructor at Ft. Myers, Florida seems to mirror his students' enthusiasm—or relish what he is about to introduce them to. *William J. Skinner*

backfired the engine which caught fire. Every time he would hit the primer and the wobble pump, the flames went higher around the cowl and I was yelling at him to stop priming. I opened the throttle and tried to pull the mixture to idle cut-off. Of course with the lock on the mixture in the front cockpit, I couldn't do it and I'm yelling at him to pull the mixture to idle cut-off. The flames really started spreading, so about then I yelled, "Get out!," turned off everything, threw my shoulder harness and seat belt off, left my chute on and jumped out. As I jumped up on the step, the shoulder harness caught in my parachute and my foot came off the step. I came down on the canopy rail you know where, went headfirst over and hung with my head about a foot from the ground, upside down by my shoulder harness.

It wasn't more than a few seconds, before I was covered with foam from head to toe from the fire truck. That was my first check ride. The student was so rattled he failed and washed out.

James R. Hanson, *BT-13 student*

Just below I saw a BT do a slow roll—when it got inverted someone fell out. I heard the student yell over the radio. "My instructor fell out, my instructor fell out!" The plane scooped out but the cadet was really shook up. I told him to just fly the plane and go back to the field, then I dropped down and watched the instructor come

down in his chute and land in the trees. I radioed his position. When we got to him after his recovery we found that he got a cut lip and a lot of razzing from his fellow instructors.

Chester Marshall, *PT-19 student (from his book* Sky Giants Over Japan *by Chester Marshall, Apollo Books, 1984)*

Then came the slow roll. By this time I was concentrating deeply on the movements and instruments and I failed to realize that strange things were beginning to happen in my cockpit. That is, until we started into inverted flight. First, there was a floating sensation. I surmised that was associated with the slow roll feeling. But as the maneuver progressed, I departed farther from my seat. By the time the plane was upside down I was flapping in the breeze *outside the cockpit,* or at least 99% of my body was. Luckily, during my abrupt departure, I locked the toes of my right foot under the top edge of the cockpit and tightened my one-hand death grip on the stick.

Slip stream and gravitation came close to winning the struggle, but the instructor somehow overpowered my deadweight grip on the stick and flipped the plane upright. Embarrassed, I plopped into the cockpit, headfirst.

After verifying that all was well, the instructor broke into uproarious laughter, muttering something about the funniest sight he had ever seen,

and he bellowed over the tube: "I'll bet you never forget to fasten your safety belt again." He was right. I didn't.

Charles A. Lindbergh, *P-38 pilot, 475th Fighter Group*

Science, freedom, beauty, adventure: what more could you ask of life? Aviation combined all the elements I loved. There was science in each curve of an airfoil, in each angle between strut and wire, in the gap of a spark plug or the color of the exhaust flame. There was freedom in the unlimited horizon, on the open fields where one landed. A pilot was surrounded by beauty of earth and sky. He brushed treetops with the birds, leapt valleys and rivers, explored the cloud canyons he had gazed at as a child. Adventure lay in each puff of wind.

I began to feel that I lived on a higher plane than the skeptics on the ground—one that was richer because of its very association with the element of danger they dreaded, because it was freeer of the earth to which they were bound. In flying, I tasted a wine of the gods of which they could know nothing. Who valued life more highly, the aviators who spent it on the art they loved, or these misers who doled it out like pennies through their antlike days? I decided that if I could fly for ten years before I was killed in a crash, it would be a worthwhile trade for an ordinary lifetime.

17

Chapter 2

Mud, Sand, and Sweat: North Africa and the MTO

Ervin C. Ethell, *P–38 pilot, 14th Fighter Group*

During a sweep near Tunis we discovered, after turning around for Maison Blanche, we had overextended our range so we'd have to land and refuel. It was late in the evening and as nightfall settled, we received a vector from the British to land at Bone, a field manned by the now friendly French with no runway lights. Open five gallon cans were half filled with dirt and soaked with gasoline. When lit they gave a reasonably good outline of the landing strip.

As each P–38 landed the pilot was signaled to brake, get out and leave his aircraft unmoved until

Three 308th Fighter Squadron officers ponder the L-shaped slit trench they have just excavated from the North African hard pan. The trench had not existed the previous night when the unit experienced its first German air raid on the field at Korba, near Cape Bon, Tunisia. Left to right are "Dutchy" Holland, Dick Hurd and Don Walker. The three men had it finished before sundown. *William J. Skinner*

The 14th Fighter Group's North African bases during 1942 were barren stretches of Tunisian desert. Pilots and ground crews lived in tents or holes and food was the major topic of conversation. *Ira Latour*

daylight. After getting out of my ship, *Tangerine*, I walked to the rear instead of the nose as I usually did. The next morning I found my nosewheel less than three feet from the edge of a 200 foot cliff overlooking the sea.

Arthur O. Beimdiek, *P-38 pilot, 14th Fighter Group*

In North Africa if the supply people got the mail through, they had done a good job, even if the food and ammunition didn't make it. At the

forward bases, they flew almost everything in with C-47s. These pilots told us the lead C-47 carried the mail; the rest of our supplies came in the others. The lead plane with the mail landed first. If he made it safely on our

An RAF air-sea rescue Walrus sits ready at Korba, Cape Bon, Tunisia. These lumbering biplanes were a most welcome sight across Europe and the Mediterranean when a downed flier was sitting in a raft or bobbing in his Mae West. Tragically, the pilot of this aircraft was killed during the first German air raid on Korba in May 1943, leaving the American 31st Fighter Group without rescue support until another pilot was transferred in. *William J. Skinner*

American fighter pilots in the Mediterranean had a fantastic form of recreation very seldom matched in other theaters of war—flying captured enemy aircraft. Occupying one enemy airfield after another, units would find numerous enemy aircraft left behind. This Me 109 was reworked by 31st Fighter Group mechanics in their spare time, put back in airworthy shape and flown by the pilots to compare performance. The 109 was painted overall sand yellow in order to make it conspicuous when in the air; no one wanted to get shot down while hot rodding in the Messerschmitt. *William J. Skinner*

Americans were in for some colorful culture changes overseas. When Bill Skinner arrived in North Africa he met this friendly water vendor on the streets of Casablanca, Morocco, complete with goatskin bladder and drinking cups. *William J. Skinner*

19

usually muddy field, the rest would come in. If not, at least we got our mail.

Thomas H. Jones, *P-38 pilot, 82nd Fighter Group*

I'll never forget my first combat field in North Africa and the surrounding area—looked like something out of *Grapes of Wrath.* Wash hanging on lines and tent roofs—chickens tied with string to tent ropes and eggs lying in the helmet liners by the tent doors—all belonging to P-38 jocks who had done some trading with the "Arabs," as North African natives were labeled. Chickens and eggs for mattress covers, which the Arabs prized, cut arm holes in and wore.

William J. Skinner, *Spitfire pilot, 31st Fighter Group*

At Pomigliano we were assigned some beautiful four-story-high apartments formerly used by Italian factory workers. When the Germans would come over at night to bomb Naples, which they did with monotonous regularity, they came right over the apartments. Mt. Vesuvius was right behind us, which was always lit up, so the bombers would pass over the volcano, make a turn of so many degrees, wait so many seconds, then drop their bombs. Naples couldn't get out of the way, and the Germans were bound to hit something.

Another 31st Fighter Group recreational vehicle—*Wacky Macchi,* a captured Italian Macchi C.202 Folgore. The Macchi was the equal of any fighter in the theater. Unfortunately, it didn't fly for long due to lack of compatible hydraulic fluid and no spare tires. *William J. Skinner*

Though it was unusual for Spitfire pilots to see a heavy bomber up close, B-24D *Bathtub Bessie* made an unscheduled landing at the 308th Fighter Squadron's base in North Africa while trying to get back to base, 1943. *William J. Skinner*

Termini, Imerese Airfield, the 31st Fighter Group's base on the north coast of Sicily . . . as Bill Skinner remembered, "Leetle mud in Sicily. Knothaid tried to go through." A Dodge command car, which seemed to be able to go through anything, comes to the rescue and pulls a jeep from the thick, slimy, sucking slough. *William J. Skinner*

Flak was going up all over . . . we'd go up on the roof and watch . . . it was like the 4th of July. Every once in awhile night fighters would go up there—we'd see tracers going back, tracers going up. Once we heard a bomber wind up and go down with a big boom. A big cheer! Later we found out it was an A-20, which was no plane to be night fighting in. We didn't know if he was hit or got vertigo.

Norman W. Jackson, *P-38 pilot, 14th Fighter Group*

By the time I had 30 hours of combat, I had bailed out, crash landed in the desert, come home on one engine and brought one more home so

August 1943, Cape Milazzo, Sicily. A 308th Fighter Squadron Spitfire Mk. VIII with a 90 gallon auxiliary fuel tank sits in front of a doctor's vineyard villa. Flying missions from such a sylvan setting pointed up the incongruity of war, but no one thought about it much. Quarters such as these were a break from tents and barren open stretches. *William J. Skinner*

Bob Hope and his main morale booster, Frances Langford, giving it their best at Palermo, Sicily, 1943, for members of the 31st Fighter Group. *William J. Skinner*

Cape Milazzo, Sicily, September 1943. Bill Skinner dejectedly looks over his first Spitfire Mk. VB, now broken and bent beyond repair. The 308th Fighter Squadron had moved up to this forward area field to cover the invasion of Italy. The dry dust kicked up through the Marston mat pierced steel planking became a nightmare. Taxiing through the choking dust, Bill stopped to clear the area ahead but wingman Ed Fardella behind couldn't see a thing and ran his Spit right up the back of his leader. Unfortunately Ed's fighter was equipped with a metal rather than a wood prop. Instead of breaking apart it proceeded to chop the tail, then dig in just behind the cockpit. Fardella's spinner was almost in Skinner's cockpit when he realized what was happening and cut the engine. *William J. Skinner*

shot up that it was junked. There was talk of presenting me with the German Iron Cross.

William J. Skinner, *Spitfire pilot, 31st Fighter Group*

Our Spitfires and the P-51Bs that replaced them had the same Rolls-Royce Merlin engine, but the P-51 had a laminar flow wing which gave it 10 mph more speed straight and level and much greater fire power with .50 caliber machine guns. When strafing a target with the Mustang it seemed like I'd never run out of ammunition while the Spit had 120 rounds each for the two cannon and 350 for each .303, which was a good gun but didn't have much power. But the Spit had excellent maneuverability and rate of climb and no restrictions on maneuvers performed. The British never gave us any flight manuals, just word of mouth. We'd ask these guys what we could or couldn't do and they'd say, "Hell, you've got a fighter plane; you can do anything you want . . . straight down, full throttle . . . put your feet on the upper rudder pedals and pull back as hard as you can.

Bill Skinner takes a pensive look at his Spitfire Mk. V after returning to the 31st Fighter Group base at Montecorvino, Italy on 1 October 1943 after covering the landings at Salerno. An 88 mm flak shell went off between him and his wingman, putting a sizeable dent in his Spit. *William J. Skinner*

23

Nothing's going to happen." You couldn't do that with many other planes.

However the Spit was short ranged, even with the 90 gallon auxiliary belly tank. It was good for escorting A-20s, B-25s, B-26s, but we didn't have the range to escort the heavy bombers, and that's where the '51 came in.

For the average fighter pilot, if you got in trouble, you were better off in the Spit than the '51. Your chances of surviving were better because you could maneuver out of tight spots. I got in a situation where I was tangling with six Me 109s and I didn't get a bullet hole in the plane. Four I could keep track of . . . they bounced us when I was flying on a friend's wing.

My radio was out and I kept trying to tell him these guys were coming in . . . I just couldn't wait any longer so I broke into them. We went head-on for several passes and I got a couple of hits on one of them but it didn't seem to bother him too much. We finally broke it off. I wasn't too happy but I didn't feel as uncomfortable as I would have in a '51.

308th Fighter Squadron pilots wait in front of their mess hall in the early morning sunlight for the truck to take them back to their field at Pomigliano, Italy. The building used to house the local workers' nursery before the Allied invasion. *William J. Skinner*

24

The Spitfire was a fun plane to fly—there was nothing to worry about. It looked nice, it felt nice, it flew nice—it didn't take very long before you felt very comfortable in it. The narrow landing gear didn't seem to make any difference on landing— the AT-6 was much worse. The Spit had no tendency to ground loop.

The pilots in my squadron weren't too happy about giving up their Spits for '51s. They were used to the Spit and knew what it would do while the Mustang was sort of an unknown thing. Unfortunately the 31st Group had to build up P-51 time on missions without any real transition . . . that's not really the place to learn your limitations. But they were looking forward to the '51 in another way because it had the range . . . after

A 308th Fighter Squadron Spitfire Mk. VB at sunset looking toward Mt. Vesuvius at Pomigliano, Italy. Though the deep chin dust filter under the spinner kept engines healthy, it cut performance significantly. *William J. Skinner*

all, we were fighter pilots and we wanted to get into a fight. Flying patrol so much and never getting into a dogfight could get pretty old . . . the '51 assured you were going to run into something on almost every mission. You had a well-built plane, good firepower, the range and if you kept your head up and didn't let the Germans get behind you, your chances of surviving were pretty good.

Arthur O. Beimdiek, *P-38 pilot, 14th Fighter Group*
Some nights the Germans would drop various things. They dropped metal prongs that no matter how they fell on the ground, there would be one sharp prong straight up. In the tall grass, they could blow tires when taxiing a plane. They also dropped booby trap pens and pencils. You pick one up, unscrew it, and you lose a couple of hands. I was sitting at the

Fighter pilots look at a 487th Bomb Squadron, 340th Bomb Group B-25 in amazement just after the Mitchell crash landed on the 31st Fighter Group runway at Pomigliano, Italy. The left engine was ripped off and several of the crew were hurt. It was one thing to fly escort for the bombers and quite another to see up close what happened when they had been shot up. *William J. Skinner*

Jerry Carver stands in front of Bill Skinner's 308th Squadron Spit
Lonesome Polecat, Pomigliano, Italy, 1944. *William J. Skinner*

Donald Firoved and Ralph Francis use their Spitfire for some relaxation while waiting for engine start time before a mission. *William J. Skinner*

Though the Spitfire was smaller than most fighters, ground crew with a will could find a way to get into even the most difficult spaces, as these 308th Fighter Squadron men prove. *William J. Skinner*

When the 308th Fighter Squadron's ground crew managed to get a relatively undamaged Italian training plane airworthy, it became their own to do with as they wished. Pilots taught a few enlisted men how to fly it, and from then on, it was for enlisted men only—and they flew it

with great enthusiasm. Officers look on at Pomigliano, Italy, as *Achtung* is run up during a maintenance check. So successful was this effort that the aircraft went from field to field as the group moved, remaining an enlisted hack until it wore out. *William J. Skinner*

flagpole base and noticed a fountain pen on the ground. I told the guy with me to back off, took out my .45 automatic and hit it first shot. It was a perfectly good pen.

Barrie Davis, *P-51 pilot, 325th Fighter Group*

New pilots coming to our fighter group were invariably cocky to the point that they were dangerous to themselves. They thought the Luftwaffe was finished and that the P-51 could quickly and easily kill anything else that flew. To modify the attitude of newcomers, we used a war

Examining a newly arrived Merlin engine still mounted in the crate, 308th Fighter Squadron CO Maj. Walt Overend (right), Lieutenant Rodmyre (kneeling) and Lieutenant Roche waste no time in getting it assigned to one of the unit's Spitfires. *William J. Skinner*

29

weary P-40 which our squadron somehow acquired. I was in charge of putting new pilots through a quick, intensive training program, and the final flight included a mock dogfight with the new pilot of a P-51 pitted against one of us flying the P-40. I can tell you that until a pilot knows the strengths and weaknesses of both airplanes, the P-40 can make the P-51 look outclassed. Using all of the P-40's strengths, an innovative pilot could outfly a P-51 at low altitudes until the P-51 jockey finally realized that there was something more to fighting in the air than simply having the best airplane. At that point the new pilot became ready to listen to everything we had to say.

Paul Wingert, *P-38 pilot, 14th Fighter Group*

Flying at 10,000 feet, the squadron was greeted with a heavy barrage of flak. The squadron commander immediately started evasive action, but on the second barrage my aircraft was hit. I nursed it along as far as possible but within a few minutes both engines were dead. Not knowing my exact position, I rolled the aircraft over and bailed out, hoping I was over friendly territory. Falling for what seemed like eternity, I was able to locate the D-ring and gave it a hard pull. When the

The 308th Fighter Squadron chow line at Castel Volturno, Italy, February 1944. Everyone was still living in tents but at least the food got better when the Allies became established on the mainland. *William J. Skinner*

parachute opened, I was falling in a head-down position, causing it to stream and the shroud lines to wrap around my legs. With the chute streaming overhead I started to work frantically to untangle my legs—after getting them off I was then able to turn upright in the harness.

Tugging frantically on the shroud lines, I managed to make the parachute flare open, abruptly slowing my descent. By the time the chute opened properly, I was less than a thousand feet above the ground with very little time to orient myself—could only hope for the best as the ground came up to meet me.

An American infantry squad, for days in the mud of Italy with nothing but cold rations, were lining up for their first hot meal. As the cook yelled, "Come and get it," I landed at the head of the chow line. Dazed and shaken up from the bailout and somewhat hard landing, I still knew a good thing when I saw it so I unbuckled my chute harness, brushed myself off, smiled a big smile to everyone, picked up a mess kit and proceeded to be the first one through the chow line. I had parachuted into friendly territory by about half a mile.

Jack Lenox, *P-38 pilot, 14th Fighter Group*

I flew my third mission as wingman to group commander Col. O. B. Taylor. During a dive onto a formation of Me 109s I made a turn to

A 307th Fighter Squadron, 31st Fighter Group Spitfire Mk. IX sits ready for the day's mission. *William J. Skinner*

the left, losing sight of my leader. I observed black smoke trailing from the Me 109 I was firing at, but was unable to observe more as I continued my dive to outrun a 109 firing at me. Passing through about 15,000 feet, I was able to pull out of my dive and blacked out in the dive recovery. The next thing I knew, I was at 20,000 feet, alone, and trying to find someone to attach myself to. Seeing another P-38 in the same predicament, I

Lt. Bill Skinner, 308th Fighter Squadron, sits in his Spitfire awaiting the order to "press" and start engines in the early morning, Italy, 1944.
William J. Skinner

joined formation with the P-38 as his wingman and discovered it was the group commander! When we returned home, Col. Taylor commented on how we had become involved in the fight, and although he was all over the sky I had followed him and ended up in place on his wing. Of course I had no idea he was in the other P-38—all I was looking for was a wing to nest on.

Thomas H. Jones, *P-38 pilot, 82nd Fighter Group*
I well remember my first mission. After take-off and climb over the sea, some jock above and ahead of me cleared his four .50s with a burst of fire, as we always did, and the empty casings rattled off my windscreen, scaring the hell out of me. Thought the Jerries had me zeroed in and I was gonna be shot down!

12 February 1944. Bill Skinner's wingman stands in front of his leader's Spitfire Mk. VIII after landing at Castel Volturno, Italy, and points to the second kill he has just helped Skinner make. Victories were often hard to come by; this was the only kill made by an American pilot in the Mediterranean Theater that day. There was good reason for the wide smile. *William J. Skinner*

In March 1944 Mt. Vesuvius erupted and covered the surrounding area with lava cinders, destroying the 340th Bomb Group's B-25s near Pompeii and generally doing more damage than all the Luft-waffe's air raids. This was the view from Naples harbor. *William J. Skinner*

In March 1944, at Castel Volturno Airfield, Italy, the 308th Fighter Squadron lets go of its beloved Spitfires for new Mustangs, and are assigned a new mission. With the arrival of P-51s the 31st Group was transferred from the Twelfth to the Fifteenth Air Force for long range bomber escort duties which would take the group into combat over Germany itself. Though the P-51B and the unit's Spitfires both had Packard-built Rolls-Royce Merlin engines, the differences in the two aircraft are manifold. *William J. Skinner*

American Spitfire pilots with the 31st Fighter Group get a look at their first replacement P-51B at Castel Volturno, Italy, March 1944. The Mustang opened up the long range escort mission for the unit's pilots but they were not enthusiastic in the least about losing their maneuverable Spits. It would take some time and an increasing opportunity to shoot down enemy aircraft to make them forget the elegant British fighter. *William J. Skinner*

Bill Skinner's crew chief, Donald Firoved, and armorer, Ralph Francis, stand by their faithful *Lonesome Polecat* without much concern for the P-51B running up in the background. It was hard on all 31st Fighter Group personnel to let go of their proven Spitfires. *William J. Skinner*

Heading out from Foggia, Italy, for a mission with the 97th Squadron, 82nd Fighter Group are Lt. Billie B. Watson, Maj. Steve Stone and Capt. George Marvin. *Walter E. Zurney*

An 82nd Fighter Group Lightning departs from Foggia, Italy, on a
bomber escort mission in 1944. *Walter E. Zurney*

Flying from the mud and shacks of Foggia, Italy, *Taffy* was 1st Lt. Walter Zurney's 97th Squadron, 82nd Fighter Group Lightning—and his second love. *Walter E. Zurney*

Mud, mud, mud . . . Foggia, Italy, during the spring thaw of 1944. P-38 maintenance was never easy, but the weather often made it close to impossible. Work stands would sink into the gumbo and aircraft would be bogged down into a mush that could swallow things forever. Ground crews would wear a set of oversize boots out to the plane, then leave them on the ground or on the stands before stepping up onto the wing or into the cockpit. This P-38J of the 48th Squadron, 14th Fighter Group, has seen its share of use, and there hasn't been enough time to paint the right spinner. *Ira Latour*

1st Lt. Walter Zurney sits in his P-38 after his fiftieth and last mission. Zurney was one of the rare breed of sergeant pilots later commissioned as flight officers before going off to combat. *Walter E. Zurney*

A red-tailed P-51D of the all-black 301st Fighter Squadron, 332nd Fighter Group in November 1944. Though segregated from their fellow fighter pilots and often subjected to biased criticism, as 332nd pilot Louis R. Purnell recalled, "When you fly, nothing else matters. I could have been flying for the devil and it wouldn't have mattered." Not one bomber was lost in the time the 332nd provided escort for the Fifteenth Air Force's bomb groups. *Fred Bamberger via David W. Menard*

Fred F. Ohr's 2nd Fighter Squadron, 52nd Fighter Group P-51D with his six kills stenciled on the side. Originally equipped with reverse lend-lease Spitfires and sent from England to the Mediterranean, the 52nd later converted to Mustangs and became a part of the long-range escort units covering the Fifteenth Air Force. *Fred Bamberger via David W. Menard*

Chapter 3

Brother, It Was Rough in the ETO

Erwin Miller, *P-47 pilot, 4th Fighter Group*

When we strapped into a Spitfire we felt snug and part of the aircraft; the Thunderbolt cockpit, on the other hand, was so large that we felt if we slipped off the god damned seat we could break a leg! We were horrified at the thought of going to war in such a machine: we had enough trouble with the Focke-Wulfs in our nimble Spitfire Mk. Vs; now this lumbering seven-ton monster seemed infinitely worse.

Gradually, however, we learned how to fight in the Thunderbolt. At high altitude, she was a "hot ship" and very fast in a dive; if anyone tried to escape from a Thunderbolt by diving, we had him cold. Even more important, at last we had a fighter with the range to penetrate deeply into enemy territory—where the action was. So, reluctantly, we had to give up our beautiful little Spitfires and convert to the new juggernauts. The war was moving on and we had to move with it.

My heart remained with the Spitfire. The mere sound or sight of a Spitfire brings deep feelings. She was such a gentle little airplane, without a trace of viciousness. She was a dream to handle in the air.

Arthur L. Thorsen, *P-38 pilot, Eighth AF Replacement Training Unit*

I had always felt that getting shot down was part of this game and I dwelt on that possibility so much it began to disturb my sleep. I was having a recurring nightmare that started one night on the *Aquatania,* during the crossing. The dream would begin peacefully enough with me at the controls of a P-38 and in a group formation with other ships, penetrating enemy territory. Suddenly we were under attack by Jerries and we careened around the sky, firing, turning, and spinning out.

I was on the tail of a Focke-Wulf 190 and was just getting my sights lined up when the loud banging of machine gun bullets on metal started tearing my aircraft apart. I had not

kept my tail clear and another Jerry was making me pay for the blunder. As my ship began disintegrating, I popped the canopy and nonchalantly stepped out into space. I fell for a few seconds and then seeing that I was clear of the debris I pulled the ripcord of my parachute. A few seconds passed, nothing happened, no parachute. Now frantic, I twisted my head and looked up to see what was wrong with the chute. A cold hand clutched at my gizzard, for there was no parachute—just dirty laundry streaming from my back pack. Long johns, dirty socks, pillow cases, even a red nightshirt.

As always, I awoke with a snort, clammy sweat covering my body. I felt I was getting a heavenly message and swore I would never bail out. I made a pact with myself that, should the time come when I was shot up badly, I would not leave the aircraft as long as there was a response of any kind from the controls. After all, P-38s belly in just as easy as they land on wheels.

Sunset at Nuthampstead, the 55th Fighter Group's initial home with
the Eighth Air Force in England. *Robert T. Sand*

Socked in at Wormingford, 22 December 1944. This 55th Fighter Group P-51D's crew chief was Roger Fraleigh, assisted by Nick Lippucci. Fraleigh was awarded a medal for his aircraft flying the most missions without mechanical failure. The Mustang was later lost in action on 20 February 1945. *Robert T. Sand*

55th Fighter Group Lightnings taxi out and take off on a mission in late December 1943. Pilots were already numb with frosted instruments and fingers, then had to climb into the minus 50 degree Fahrenheit temperature at altitude with virtually no cockpit heat. "This was always an agonizing moment for all," said Bob Sand, "particularly at this period, as the Allison engines and Curtiss electric propellers were not as dependable as the [P-51's] Merlins and Hamilton props. This agony was particularly true for the propeller men. The chief and crew could turn away when they saw their ship take off, then pray that all would go well for the hours ahead, and to a safe return. Only then was he sure he had done everything right to protect the life of his pilot. The propeller men, however, could not rest easy until *every ship* was off safely and had returned safely. And when *any* ship was lost unaccountably, there remained a little nagging question." *Robert T. Sand*

Herbert E. Johnson, *P-38 pilot, 20th Fighter Group*

The P-38 requires a far greater knowledge of its mechanical and aerodynamic characteristics on the part of the pilot than normally required to fly fighters.

If jumped on the deck the best evasive maneuver is a tight level turn. Due to the beautiful stall characteristics of the '38, you can turn much tighter without the danger of spinning than any German craft.

Hubert "Hub" Zemke, *P-38, P-47 and P-51 pilot and fighter group commander*

I was fortunate enough to have flown the P-51, P-47 and P-38 in combat and to have led fighter groups with all three.

P-51—By far the best air-to-air fighter aircraft of the three below 25,000 feet. A very good long-range radius of action for the type of work we did in Europe. The acceleration from slow cruise to maximum performance was excellent compared to the competition.

Its rate of roll was good and it maneuvered easily to a learned hand. Dive and acceleration were rapid. Visibility in all directions was very ample for the need. As an instrument aircraft it was a bit touchy. It could be overactive in turbulence.

On armament it carried sufficient machine guns. Why I say this is that after viewing numerous combat films where pilots often fired at extreme range or overdeflected, I came firmly to the conclusion that one fought for a combat position of 10 degrees or less deflection. At close range—250 yards or less—there is no doubt what could happen when the trigger was depressed. It was a matter of ducking the flying pieces after that. This was drilled into the skulls of all pilots.

P-47—A rugged beast with a sound radial engine to pull you along.

Heavy in fire power that chewed up the opponent at close ranges. Best suited and likewise adopted in the ground support role, as everything in the armament arsenal was hung on its sturdy wings.

Accelerated poorly and climbed not too much better from a slow airspeed. Once a good high cruising speed was attained, the P-47 could pretty well stand up with the competition.

Strangely the rate of roll and maneuverability was good at high speeds. In fact, the aircraft had many a forgiving feature and reliability. With its high altitude supercharger its performance at altitude—above 24,000 to 25,000—appeared superior to the other two U.S. Army Air Corps fighters in the theater. At high altitude this fighter's level speed, better climb and more solid response to control reflected the tactics that the 56th Fighter Group developed early in combat.

Swinging the compass on a 55th Fighter Group P-38 at Nuthampstead, dawn, 2 January 1944. *Robert T. Sand*

It should not be overlooked here that the P-47—once it gained altitude—could exceed any of the contenders in speed of entering a dive with a very good "zoom" recovery to altitude again.

Naturally, a fighter pilot endeavors to fight his aircraft from the strengths of his machine's performance rather than from its weaknesses. With this in mind, I repeatedly impressed upon the 56th's fighter pilots that our tactics were to "hit and recover, hit and recover." If one couldn't get the opponent by an altitude of 15,000 feet, then break off and recover to altitude again.

In this respect it was stressed that the element leader, who initiated the attack, pressed in viciously. If he missed his attack, it was his responsibility to set up his wingman to press through for a cleanup kill on the dive. If the wingman's follow-through failed, a zoom recovery by the element leader to give high cover and a position for a second attack often resulted.

This one, two punch tactic was continued into refinement of the entire

20th Fighter Group Lightnings at Wittering in December 1943 when the type was new to the ETO. Harry Bisher's *Kitty* is the second aircraft from the left. *Air Force Museum*

The 364th Fighter Group lines up for takeoff at Honington, England, in the late summer of 1944. The tension generated by pre-mission jitters would normally give way to a sense of power as the Merlin engines were run up to 61 in. of manifold pressure and 3000 rpm for takeoff. From that point on, leaders were intent on joining with the other flights, and wingmen had no other world but keeping tight formation from brake release until ready to scan for bogies once in enemy territory. *Mark H. Brown/USAFA*

group's tactical employment, wherein the first or lead squadron was designated the Assault or Strike squadron, the second designated Support or Follow Through squadron which flew a bit higher, and the third which flew still higher, became the Reserve or High Cover Squadron.

Though the 56th received criticism for this conservative policy of not bouncing below 15,000 feet,

until the introduction of the paddle blade propeller and water injection to the R-2800 engine there was considerable effort to refine tactics and coordination of the entire group formation. The tactic worked.

About the highest engagement I recall was just over 35,000 feet. Here the P-47 still performed fairly well while the enemy (Me 109s) had dropped off considerably. In about one

turn with the group, the opponents were falling off in spins or split-S-ing for denser air mass. Then the enemy fell into the trap of being overhauled by the superior diving speed of the P-47. The P-51 and P-38 also employed these tactics but to a lesser degree in dive performance to the P-47.

As an instrument flying platform, the P-47 proved to be better than the

A brand-new P-51D upon arrival at the 355th Fighter Group's home base of Steeple Morden, England, mid-1944. The only markings applied at the air depots after assembly were black bands on wings and tail and a black nose. *Alexander C. Sloan via Bob Kuhnert, 355th FG Assn.*

48

P-51 but probably not as good as the P-38. Though not equipped for icing conditions, with carburetor heat the engine pulled the bulk through.

As to fire power, the eight .50 caliber machine guns were ample proof of a real punch either in aerial combat or on a strafing run. Once dive bombing was learned, the P-47 consistently came up with flying colors.

P-38—Though this aircraft had virtues, for me it was the poorest of the three U.S. Army fighters in the European Theater. The fact that the extreme cold at altitude affected its performance hardly endears the machine. The turbosuperchargers were controlled by an oil regulator. At altitude the oil had a tendency to congeal, which caused serious

Though all bubble canopy Mustangs were delivered natural metal without camouflage paint, there was skepticism about flying shiny aluminum aircraft that flashed in the sun like mirrors. The 357th Group decided to paint its aircraft in the field, sometimes in regulation olive drab and other times in RAF green which was made available by the English. Clearly, Julian H. Bertram's *Butch Boy* got this treatment when Joe Broadhead flew it as *Master Mike*. Note the chipped paint and the long stream of oil from the engine breather exit below the word "Butch." *Alexander C. Sloan via Bob Kuhnert, 355th FG Assn.*

Lt. Marvin W. Arthur with his *Blondie* at Debden, England, home of the 4th Fighter Group. As crew chief Don Allen remembered, "We were supposed to use kerosene to wash oil and soot off the planes, but it usually wasn't on site . . . thus we took a bucket of 140 octane gas and washed the junk off. It's a wonder we weren't all blown sky high. Youth . . . thinks it's invulnerable!" *Donald E. Allen*

Thunderbolts from the 78th Fighter Group just after landing; external tanks are gone, a Mae West is hanging on the machine guns, pilots are donning A-2 jackets (which were worthless for flying in the frigid higher altitudes) and walking off the kinks from sitting cramped up for so long. The paddle-bladed propellers shown here resulted in a major performance increase for the P-47, giving much improved rate of climb and acceleration. *Mark H. Brown/USAFA*

Maj. Claiborne H. Kinnard, Jr.'s first *Man O' War* just after the 354th Fighter Squadron commander got his first kill on 29 March 1944. The standard ETO white nose and bands on wing and tail have been applied, as well as the Malcolm Hood over the cockpit in place of the factory-installed "chicken coop" panels. The white paint was supposed to help identify American fighters from their German counter-parts, but aircraft continued to be lost to friendly fire. The Spitfire-style bubble canopy was a major improvement that pilots found outstanding in all respects, allowing them to actually lean out over the canopy rail and look behind. *Alexander C. Sloan via Bob Kuhnert, 355th FG Assn.*

problems. On two occasions I recall, when entering combat with enemy single seaters it was a case of life and death to get away and survive, though I had started with the advantage.

On both occasions the engines either cut out completely or overran rpm limitations as the throttles were cut or advanced. It was enough just to regulate the engines and control the aircraft without entering combat.

The second serious limiting factor that detracted from the P-38's combat capability was its steep diving restriction—estimated at about 375 mph. A common tactic of the Luftwaffe single seaters was to split-S for the clouds or the deck. Oftentimes their head-on attacks on the bomber formations saw them roll over and dive for the deck to confuse and outdistance the flexible machine gunners. P-38s had little chance to pursue. When on defense, it can be easily understood that a dive to safety was the best maneuver for longevity.

Another factor to degrade the P-38's combat capability was its identification factor. The eyes of a pilot often picked up specks in the distance that could not be immediately identified as friend or foe. These were reported in as "bogies." Appropriate tactical maneuvers were taken to prevent bogies from having the advantage of a subsequent attack. In the case of the P-38 the twin booms and slab elevator gave this aircraft's identity away—as far as the eye could see.

It was also necessary for the P-38 pilot to do much more weaving to look down over the two engines that lay on each side of the cockpit. A better cockpit heating system could have been provided as my feet always froze at altitude.

Taken alone, the above statements would conclude that the P-38 had no outstanding features . . . it did! As a gun platform, it was steady as a shooting stand. With two engines, there was no torque. With a little trim for buildup of speed (in a dive), a pilot could ride directly into a target.

As to the armament installation, I have seen no better. Four machine guns and one cannon in a tight pocket directly in front of the pilot. This armament being so closely aligned to the sight of plane of the gunsight required no convergence of fire as necessitated in fighters having their guns placed in the wings.

Though the P-38 had a wheel instead of the proverbial stick, this was no handicap—controls were light and response was excellent.

Relative to load carrying capacity, the aircraft could take off with just about anything. I've taken off with a thousand pound bomb under each wing and cruised with ease. On fuel consumption, the P-38 enabled us to cruise out to combat areas deep in Germany without the anguish of not having enough "petrol" to return home.

A tricycle landing gear made it much easier for a junior pilot to "spike the kite" on the runway and chalk up another landing. This was also an advantage in taxiing—a large engine and cowling did not deter from forward vision.

Harrison B. Tordoff, *P-47 pilot, 353rd Fighter Group*

We loved the P-47 for its toughness and reliability. It was heavy and looked cumbersome but in the hands of a good pilot, it could turn and climb with an Me 109 or an Fw 190. And nothing could outdive it. We had pilots bring back tree branches and tops of telephone poles in the wings of their '47s. A few even came home with top cylinders shot off. It could be belly landed in a forest, if necessary. On an open field, it crash-landed about as well as it landed on wheels. Pilots learn to appreciate this sort of toughness. The eight .50 caliber machine guns were devastating on ground or air targets and the plane was a very stable gun platform. On the negative side, the '47 burned fuel at full power at 450 gallons/hour, if I remember right. It only carried about 350 gallons internally. It got nose light in a stall, and nose heavy in a dive—had a very nasty spin—violent and hard to stop. I spun out of a slow turn at high altitude with full wing tanks once, by accident, while trying to keep in formation on a combat mission. It tore the wing tanks off and scared hell out of me. But the general way I felt in a '47 was invincible. I had complete faith in the plane and would excuse its shortcomings to anyone.

Marvin Bledsoe, *P-47 pilot, 353rd Fighter Group (from his book* Thunderbolt, *Van Nostrand Reinhold, 1982)*

The target for the day was a railroad tunnel that the heavy bombers had been unable to destroy. The Germans were rushing reinforcements toward the beachhead at night, using this particular railroad track. The fighters' job was to go in low and destroy the tunnel.

The air was charged with excitement when we entered the

51

briefing room. I was nervous, my insides kept whirling around, and I was scared as hell. The instant the briefing was over I raced for the latrine, where I felt my stomach turning inside out.

As we headed to our planes my mouth was dry. I found it hard to breathe and almost impossible to swallow. My stomach was doing flip-flops; I was terrified.

In the cockpit of the Thunderbolt I felt somewhat better. How I loved to fly that airplane!

This takeoff of our fighter squadron was a thrilling spectacle. Every engine started at the same moment in one huge roar. The planes taxied out toward the runway in close formation, then seemed to pause and huddle together at the extreme end, wing tips and twirling props bare inches from the ships next to them. Each squadron lined up on a different runway, waiting its turn to take off. When the last airplane of the first squadron started down, the group

Cameron Hart's 63rd Fighter Squadron P-47D warms up in the foreground as the 56th Fighter Group lines up for takeoff from Boxted, England, in late 1944. It was not unusual for variations of the squadron insignia to be used for nose art, as can be seen on Hart's Thunderbolt. *Mark H. Brown/USAFA*

operations officer fired a flare from the tower, signaling the second squadron to give their engines the gun. They crossed the intersection an instant behind the last ship that had taken off on the other runway.

My flight leader's ship taxied by and I moved into position alongside him. My ground crew gave me a final "thumbs up" as we headed out to the runway.

The frightened feeling had passed. I felt a surge of pride that I was a member of a combat fighter squadron and was flying the most powerful fighter ship in the world.

Chet A Patterson, *P-38 pilot, 55th Fighter Group*

Because of the losses in P-38 units someone at Lockheed thought the pilots didn't known how to fly it so they sent over Tony LeVier. As far as I was concerned, he did nothing that I couldn't do or nothing that I hadn't

56th Fighter Group commander Col. David C. Schilling's P-47D fitted with rocket tubes for the increasing ground attack work that took place after D-Day. When the 56th elected to remain the only Eighth Air Force fighter group flying Thunderbolts after the rest transitioned to Mustangs, a number of non-standard and colorful camouflage schemes began to appear in place of the GI-issue olive drab and gray or natural metal. Not only did it set the Wolfpack apart, but it served as a vent for artistic license in trying out the effective use of paint in combat. *Mark H. Brown/USAFA*

53

Sheep in wolf's clothing—a P-47 of the 65th Fighter Wing Detachment B, Air-Sea Rescue Squadron, at Boxted in Mid-1944. Later redesignated the 5th Emergency Rescue Squadron, the unit was equipped with war-weary (note WW on tail) P-47Ds to drop smoke markers and dinghy packs near downed airmen. Though not quite as glamorous as flying fighters in combat, the unit did an exceptional job, flying an effective 3,520 of 3,616 sorties in aiding some very desperate men. *Mark H. Brown/USAFA*

The 335th Fighter Squadron dispersal area, 4th Fighter Group home base, Debden, with the sun low on the horizon. With drop tanks hung, canopies open and engines run up, last-minute polishing of wind-screens takes place as the "kites" are being readied for the next "show." *Joseph B. Sills*

seen around the airfield by our own men. Had it been my choice of what he did, I would have had him fly some two hours at 28,000 feet, then tangle with me at 15,000 feet instantly. Then we would see how well he could fly when he was frozen.

As an example, Bushing, who did not like combat, was up leading the 338th Squadron and had to urinate. Well, by the time you got out of your shoulder harness, the parachute straps and through four more layers of clothes (tank suit, pinks, long johns and shorts) you found your peter was

Up for some proficiency time on 2 June 1945, almost a month after the war in Europe ended, 354th Fighter Squadron, 355th Fighter Group pilots fight to hold formation in some very rough air. From front to back: Stan Silva in WR-B *My Catherine*, WR-V, WR-S (bar), Clay Kinnard's former WR-A, WR-T (bar), Glenn Beeler in WR-L (bar), Don Langley in WR-C *Lil Curly Top*. Just outside camera range were Jimmy Jabara in WR-P (bar) and James O'Neill. Moments later they had a mid-air and both managed to bail out successfully. *Alexander C. Sloan via Bob Kuhnert, 355th FG Assn.*

about one half inch long at that altitude. Well anyway, Bushing let go in the relief tube and at that very moment someone hollered, "Bogies on the right!" Bushing turned to the right and madly looked for the bogies, and though it was a false alarm, by the time his heart stopped pumping and

he looked back at the dashboard, he could see only frosted instruments.

To be sure things were working properly, he had to take off his gloves and with his fingernails scrape off the frost on the important instruments. When he got back to the field the P-38, once it got on the ground,

turned into a hot box even in England. So by the time he taxied up to the hard stand and shut down the engines the urine had melted and heated up to probably 110 degrees. By tradition, the crew chief climbed on the aircraft as soon as you killed the engines and opened the canopy. In this case, just as

With a puff of oil smoke, Lieutenant Erickson cranks up the 55th Fighter Group Lightning normally assigned to Capt. Jerry H. Ayers.
Robert T. Sand

Capt. Jerry Ayers' P-38 gets a going over at Nuthampstead in late 1943. *Robert T. Sand*

he opened it, he slammed it down when he got a whiff of what was there. Bushing had not noticed it as he had been wearing his oxygen mask.

Edward B. Giller, *P-38 pilot, 55th Fighter Group*

Returning to England with considerable undercast always presented a severe problem of location. We had only four channels of VHF which were always crowded. Once over England we could only let down straight ahead until you could see the ground. The other P-38 groups were operating with the same problem as the 55th. But one thing we liked about the P-38 was its instrument flying ability.

Flying around 30,000 feet resulted in extreme fouling of the plugs in the Allison engine as well as a great number of thrown rods and swallowed valves. Needless to say, a P-38 on a single engine was in an unenviable condition. Our record during this period was very poor, about 1.5 Germans shot down to each American lost to all causes.

This was the world's coldest airplane and we tried every combination of suit, glove and heater imaginable, including some that

Phil Savides, suited up and ready to go at the 313th Squadron, 50th Fighter Group parachute shop in Nancy, France, 1944. The Ninth Air Force's Thunderbolts flew some of the most effective, and most dangerous, ground support missions of the war. *Phil Savides*

Lt. George D. Green, 4th Fighter Group, with his Mustang in mid-1944. When squadron mate Pierce McKennon bailed out of his P-51 near Berlin on 18 March 1945, Green set his P-51 down in a nearby field, threw the chute out, put McKennon in the seat, got on his lap and took off. Sharing one oxygen mask, they made it all the way back to Debden. *USAF/NASM*

would short out and give you a hot foot. We were so cold sometimes, we did not even want to fight.

The twin tails provided positive recognition for the Germans at distances greater than we could see them. Therefore, our initial engagements were always at a disadvantage. We were forced to go to very high altitudes, 30,000 feet to 35,000 feet. Even so, the Germans flew way above us. The Germans would escape by a split-S maneuver from these altitudes and the P-38 could not follow due to compressibility.

The maintenance on the P-38 was something to behold. The engines were extremely closely-cowled with much piping and no space. The mechanics did a magnificent job with extremely long hours of trying tediously to fix coolant leaks, rough engines, etc. It was truly a crew chief's

nightmare. The plane employed oleo shocks on all three landing gear struts. These had a habit of leaking as soon as it got cold and required considerable maintenance to reinflate. The turbo supercharger regulator had a delightful habit of freezing at high altitude, resulting in only two throttle settings . . . 10 inches of mercury, which would not sustain flight, or 80 inches which would blow up a supercharger. I recall one very cold day over the Ruhr Valley [in Germany] where both the pilots and the regulators were so frozen that, in spite of heavy flak in that vicinity, we let down to 3,000 feet to warm up both us and the airplanes.

Harry R. Corey, *P-51 pilot, 339th Fighter Group*
Weather, the other enemy, is a factor in any form of combat. The Romans built roads in Britain, not out

of civic pride, but to increase the mobility of their legions. Air combat involves a third dimension, because the cloud cover can range from 100 to over 2,000 feet. Winds aloft, that can reach 70 to 90 mph, are a fourth dimension. We lost eleven pilots (thirteen planes) due to adverse weather. This was more than we lost to the Luftwaffe. Seven pilots had less than two months of combat experience. Five of these were operational for one month or less. Frequently missions were flown without ever seeing the ground between take off and landing. If coupled with the loss of radio contact, this could lead to disaster.

We lost two pilots under these same circumstances. It was a long mission (7 hours) to Posnan, Poland. (One element became separated from its squadron during combat and were last heard from in the direction of

Maj. Pierce W. "Mac" McKennon's P-51D on the line at Debden with the 335th Squadron, 4th Fighter Group. This was the second of his *Ridge Runner* Mustangs with the Arkansas razorback on the side and his string of victories. On 18 March 1945 he bailed out of this fighter near Berlin and was picked up by Gearge Green. *Joseph B. Sills*

Though similar in appearance to his earlier Mustangs, Pierce McKennon's *Ridge Runner III* had a slightly different razorback hog, more victory markings and the two parachutes added for his successful escapes after going down in enemy territory. Here Mac poses with his colorful mount just after it replaced the one he left in Germany. This aircraft was eventually crash-landed in France on 17 April 1945 by another pilot. *Joseph B. Sills*

59

Southampton.) They called for a bearing to our base, which was forty degrees or northeast. Their transmission was weak and they did not respond. Their leader's receiver may have been out, or more likely, they were too low over the Channel to receive. The English Channel is only 110 miles south of our base. A strong wind from the north could easily cause them to drift that far south during a long mission. They went out to sea with very little fuel left.

After an escort mission to Halle, near Leipzig, the bombers returned via

Front office—the wartime cockpit of a P–38J Lightning. On the left are the red-balled throttles, prop pitch controls and mixture levers. Behind the control yoke in the center is the main switch box and armament selectors with the magneto switches on the upper left. The machine gun and cannon triggers are on the wheel grips, while the red dive flap switch is on the left brace and the white microphone button is on the right brace. The printed placards on the yoke are dive limiting speeds (left) and power and flap settings (right). The flap handle is just to the right of the yoke, mounted on the right side of the cockpit just in front of the radio and electrical controls. Oxygen regulator and controls are mounted on the center floor between the rudder pedals.

60

a southern route. Our escort left them at Hersfeld, south of Kassel. They made landfall out near Dieppe, on the deck under a 100% cloud cover. This put them on a northerly course for home across the English Channel. All three pilots in one flight were lost when they apparently came upon the cliffs of the Isle of Wight too late to successfully pull up. They must have spun in, as one was found on the Isle, one on the beach at low tide, and the third crashed near Nuthampstead.

The Cliffs of Dover presented a similar hazard. However, most pilots still favored coming home on the deck when the weather was bad. If we let down over East Anglia we would be competing for space with a few hundred bombers and other fighters. If you happened to go past the base before breaking out you could meet up with a barrage balloon. The most important key was to establish a rate of descent (or climb) before entering the clouds. This relieved pressure on the controls and helped to avoid the very slow imperceptible movements that can confuse your inner ear, cause vertigo and put the seat of your pants in conflict with your instruments. Half of our losses can be attributed to vertigo. During the let down we would call home for a heading from our homing station and get an altimeter setting. In addition to correcting for any change in pressure, it provided a slight margin for error because our base was about 50 feet above sea level.

It was also a good idea to have an alternate plan in case the radio failed. My system was to pick up the main road from Norwich to London. Turn left down the road until I came to my special roundabout. Then a hard

right due west for two minutes, let down the gear, flaps and look for a green flare. On one occasion, I had to warn my flight that there was a Jug [P-47] in our traffic pattern. Then, once again, we were safely down on that good old grass field. Except that this time we were at Duxford! Their folks were kind enough to point out the direction to Fowlmere, about four miles west.

Of course one could fly 5 minutes in any direction in East Anglia and find an Air Base. This was very helpful on one mission when the ceiling was especially low. Capt. Richard Olander led Red Flight and I had White Flight tucked in behind and below so tightly that I was inside Red four. We came down from 20,000 feet and shortly after we made land fall, we came over the end of a paved runway. They were shooting up green flares. Olander called for us to take spacing for landing and no one argued. We made one circle keeping the field off my left wing tip. When I got back to the flares we set them down. I was enjoying the roll and the cool breeze, when I saw them on my left. The other four planes had landed on the second runway and we were heading for the intersection. Fortunately, we had good spacing so that a little throttle allowed us to alternate every other plane at the intersection. It was show time at Wormingford, near Colchester, which we subsequently learned was the home of the 55th FG. After we came inside and the coffee was poured, their control tower officer came in with the startling news that we had landed on intersecting runways! Someone in the back of the room said, "We always land that way at a strange field." That

plus the hot coffee had reduced the adrenaline levels and chased from our minds any thoughts of what might have been or how narrow the margin between success and disaster can be.

Robert T. Sand, *Propeller shop, 55th Fighter Group*

Sometimes, for reasons I don't know—probably an unseated gas cap—the P-38 would start syphoning out its gasoline. From the ground it looked like a long plume of mist coming from the wing.

One day, as the planes were droning around the field getting into formation for a mission, a group of ground crew members were in the radio shack listening to the conversations of the pilots. Suddenly, they heard this: "Pete, you'll have to abort! You are syphoning fuel!" No answer. Then, a little more urgently, "Pete! Abort! Abort! You are syphoning fuel!" Finally a sheepish voice came on, "Aw hell. No I'm not. I forgot to go to the bathroom and I'm just taking a leak."

Arthur L. Thorsen, *P-38 pilot, 55th Fighter Group*

We flew through a fierce anti-aircraft barrage and the gunners had just enough lead on [John] Landers to get me instead. Suddenly, amidst the deafening explosions, my aircraft was pitched nearly upside down. I don't know how I righted the ship so close to the ground without crashing. There must be some kind of unknown skill that surfaces in times of disaster to give your mind and body an instantaneous reaction impulse. I had no time to check my damage, for shells were exploding all around me. I pushed the nose forward, aware that I was using all my strength on the left rudder, to keep the aircraft level. I was cutting the grass and went through what I perceived to be a baby fruit orchard, cutting saplings with the leading edge of my wing like they were stalks of sunflowers.

Eventually the firing ceased and I saw, with horror, that my right propeller had only one blade and was windmilling. I immediately cut the switch to that engine and trimmed the ship. Then I noticed blood dripping on my lap. I put my hand to my head and my right eyebrow felt mushy. My goggle was smashed. My left eye was

stinging and I opened and closed each eye alternately. I could see! I looked at the right engine. It appeared to be gutted.

I couldn't believe it! I was helpless, with one engine shot out and no escort. Meat on the table for any Hun aircraft that should spot me . . . There was nothing else to do, but try to make it back to England alone, on one engine. If I get jumped on the way, I'll just bail out, hide in a haystack somewhere with an armload of cabbages and wait for the invasion. I put my hand on my forehead again.

The bleeding seemed to have stopped, but I had the impression my right eyebrow was gone.

With the ship trimmed up now, it seemed to be handling okay. I twisted my head to examine my plexiglas canopy. There were no holes in it. No holes anywhere in the cockpit that I could see, but some bits of flak must have come in from somewhere. I was on a compass heading of 290 degrees and doing 180 miles an hour. If I stayed on the deck, I might not be spotted. I saw the Meuse River coming up and the city of Namur on

Sitting in its hardstand at Boxted, *Pat* from the 56th Fighter Group's 63rd Fighter Squadron warms up for a mission in 1944. The black and white invasion stripes were painted on all Allied aircraft the night before D-Day in order to prevent friendly gunners from shooting at the wrong guys in the heat of battle. It still didn't seem to stop them. As the months went by and the Allies were firmly established on the Continent, the stripes slowly disappeared, first from the tops of the aircraft, then from the undersides of the wings and finally from below the fuselage. *Mark H. Brown/USAFA*

my right. I wasn't picking up flak anymore and surmised I was too low for the Jerry radar to detect me.

Time passed, my single engine droning smoothly. I was beginning to feel good. I passed between Brussels and Lille and was soon crossing out over the Channel at Dunkirk. I had made it! I was now approaching London and several Spitfires joined me, flying formation. The pilots studied my aircraft and then, with a wave, they were gone again. I hit the mike button and called Fusspot, our control at Wormingford. I explained my condition. They acknowledged and assigned me a specific runway to land on. Four miles from home! I had made it, but not quite!

Things started going wrong at that moment. I felt a lurch as my landing gear came down. I hadn't touched my landing gear lever. The extra drag was killing my air speed. I

goosed the good engine and the aircraft wanted to roll. I couldn't use more power. I was going down! My altimeter read 800 feet! My nose was down too low and the ship wasn't responding to its elevators. I quickly locked my shoulder straps and rolled trim tabs, but too late. The ship was wobbling as the nose came up slightly, then I hit a telephone pole, snapping it like a match stick. It caromed me into another. It, too, snapped! I had the nose up, but the ship went skidding into the roof of some kind of building and I was lost in a shower of debris. Then the ship hit the ground and bounced up again, becoming engulfed in flying stones, dirt and several tons of turnips. I thought the ship would explode and released my harness and canopy, but as the ship bounced the canopy slammed back and drove me down into the cockpit again. My bell was rung, but I still knew what was

going on and pushed the canopy up and scrambled free of the wreckage, still expecting it to explode. It didn't.

I managed to run about fifty feet from the crash and fell down. My legs didn't seem to want to work anymore. Suddenly I was aware of a civilian running to me. I started to yell a warning to him to stay back, the ship might explode, but then, I noticed he was carrying a bottle, which I took to be scotch, and decided to let him approach and we'd brave the explosion together. Right behind him came a lady I assumed to be his wife. She was carrying a cup of tea, and they commenced to arguing over what I should have, the scotch or the tea. I felt it incumbent upon me to settle this family argument, so I grabbed the bottle, took a long pull of what was, indeed, scotch and then washed it down with the tea. I smiled my thanks to both of them. . . . I had one last look

Lt. Robert Schmidt has just pulled the mixture on his *Tar Baby* after a mission with the 356th Fighter Group in April 1945. His crew chief is already up on the wing to get the first report of how the show went, and more importantly, to ask whether pilot had any "squawks" on the aircraft. *Herbert R. Rutland, Jr.*

A meeting of fighter group commanders at Debden on 23 March 1945 to plan support for the Rhine River crossing. In this lineup are Mustangs from the following groups: 359th, 20th, 353rd, 357th and an F-5 Lightning from the 7th Photo Group. *Edward B. Richie*

The next row of aircraft at Debden on 23 March 1945 were from these groups: 355th, 361st, 339th, 364th, 55th and 356th. Certainly VIII Fighter Command allowed their pilots to carry some of the most colorful markings since von Richthofen's Flying Circus. *Edward B. Richie*

64

at my dead bird, lying out there in the turnip patch. It had gotten me home with its last gasp. It was like saying goodbye to a very dear friend.

Elmer W. O'Dell, *P-51 pilot, 363rd Fighter Group*

I destroyed an aircraft on my first mission. Unfortunately, it was a P-51. I was taking off on my leader's wing when I blew a tire and swerved toward him. Kicking opposite rudder, I avoided the collision, but by the time I got straightened out I didn't have enough speed or runway to get airborne. I cut the switches, held the stick in my gut, and closed my eyes. The plane ran off the field, across the sunken road which sheared off the gear, dropped on two full wing tanks, skidded across a field, tore off the left wing on a stump, and wound up with its nose in a chicken coop. I was told later that I killed a crow in a hedge along the road and two chickens in the coop. The Mustang was rugged. I didn't even get a scratch.

Arthur L. Thorsen, *P-38 pilot, 55th Fighter Group*

As I shaved and showered for the Officer's Club dance, I thought how fortunate I was, being in the Army Air Corps. We fight a clean war. We have a change of clothes whenever we wish. We eat well. We sleep between

The 56th Fighter Group lines up for takeoff from Boxted. In the foreground Russell Westfall runs up his P-47D *Amaposa II. Mark H. Brown/USAFA*

sheets on soft mattresses, and we carry on at the Officer's Club after duty hours. We fly from four to six hours per mission and we're through for the day. We fly magnificent aircraft that we could never even climb into in civilian life and rarely do we see the bloody side of combat. The bomber crews do, but fighter pilots are alone and are spared that shock. If one of our pilots is wounded, he would faint from loss of blood, long before he could be attended to and crash in enemy territory. Without a doubt, this must have been what happened to many of our missing friends. But we had a habit of not accepting the loss of a comrade as final. We just said that he was transferred to another group. Apart from that, however, we led a good life.

Arthur L. Thorsen, *P-38 pilot, 55th Fighter Group*

With more experience I was becoming more comfortable with the job. My green was wearing off. It occurred to me that I was no longer trembling when I got into an airplane for a mission, but only when I was crawling out of the cockpit, after a mission. The mission briefings were no longer leaving an anvil in my stomach. Things were becoming routine, for I believe I convinced myself that the only Jerry that could clobber me would be the one I didn't see.

I hoped this attitude would continue. I was more afraid of doing something less than honorable, than I was of facing the German. I told myself I would never abort a mission, no matter how life threatening it was, unless I legitimately had mechanical problems. There were those, not only

in my group, but other groups too, who would purposely ride their brakes, taxiing to the runway for a mission takeoff and have their brakes lock up, prohibiting a takeoff. Others would accidentally drop belly tanks on the taxi strip or imagine a more than 100 rpm mag drop upon running up their engines. Both cases sufficient reason to abort.

No one was really fooled, but even if these ploys worked, the pilot guilty of them had to live with his own conscience. I realized I was drawing closer to the men who flew the missions without complaint, or trickery. It was not a case of heroics on anyone's part, it was simply an attitude of, "If the other guys are doing it, so can I."

Arthur L. Thorsen, *P-38 pilot, 55th Fighter Group*

I ventured another look away from Wyche's ship. P-38s were assembling from all directions as we headed over the North Sea back to England. I was amazed at the outcome of [my first] mission. We tangled with the Germans, had a dogfight and I was still alive. How about that? It was strange how abruptly the fight ended. Then again, perhaps it wasn't. The Jerries could break combat anytime they wanted to by heading for the deck—which is what they did. Our job was to stay with the bombers until relieved. . . .

I was suddenly very hungry, and remembering a chocolate bar I had tucked away in the shin pocket of my flying suit, I reached down for it, unaware that, in so doing, I had pulled the yoke back into my lap. My ship climbed. When I straightened up and

relaxed my hold on the yoke, the ship levelled off 500 feet above the group.

I looked around, a cold hand clutching my heart. There wasn't a ship in the sky! *My God!,* I thought. *Where is the group?* Perhaps something happened back at Kiel and the group turned back to give assistance. I was panic-stricken—all alone over the North Sea.

I made a steep 180 degree turn and headed back to the target area, then I heard a voice on the R/T. It was the Colonel.

"Who is that silly bastard that made a 180?" he inquired.

I knew that had to be me and I was elated at the sound of so friendly a voice. I made another 180 and could see the group 500 feet below and ahead of me. Saved! I pushed the throttles forward, dipped the nose and took my place next to Wyche as fast as I could.

Wyche came over the R/T very quietly, "Arthur, Arthur, Arthur," he chuckled.

Geez, I thought, how could I be so dumb? If I am to have any hope of surviving this war, I had better grow up fast. I had to be about the greenest of all the replacements that came with me to the 55th. How could any combat pilot be in a dogfight and not see a single German? I learned much later that phenomenon was not too uncommon. . . .

Later, in the 38th ready room, Wyche looked at me, quizzically, "What the hell happened back there?" he asked. "Why did you turn back?"

"I don't know," I replied, searching for an excuse. "I think I blacked out!"

"Blacked out?" he repeated. "Flying straight and level?"

66

"I guess I was mostly confused," I admitted.

Marvin Bledsoe, *P-47 pilot, 353rd Fighter Group (from* Thunderbolt*)*

Blick [Capt. Wayne Blickenstaff] motioned to me to tighten up the formation. I suspected he wanted to put on a show for the guys on the ground, so I tucked my wing in as close to his as I could. As we roared over the field, we were mere inches apart and less than six feet off the ground. We buzzed the runway, and I knew we were looking good. I stayed close as Blick made a sharp, sweeping turn and came in for a landing. My wheels touched the ground almost with his. We pulled off the runway together, and as I taxied off to my parking area Blick gave me the thumbs-up sign.

The ground crew ran out to meet me, waving and jumping up and down as I pulled into the revetment. I was their personal weapon against the Germans, and I made it back in one piece. The crew chief leaped up on the wing even before I had killed the motor. The prop was still turning over when he got the canopy open and pounded me on the back.

"Jeez, I'm glad to see you, lieutenant. We were really sweating you out. Our last pilot got knocked down on his first mission. God damn, but it sure looked good seeing you and the captain buzz the field in formation."

By now the other crew members had gathered around, congratulating me on coming back alive. They pumped my hand and patted me on the back. I felt like a hero.

This 357th Fighter Group P-51K was flown from Leiston by the 362nd Squadron's Jim Gasser. *Butch Baby* sits in the background. *Alexander C. Sloan via Bob Kuhnert, 355th FG Assn.*

Chapter 4

Overpaid, Oversexed and Over Here

Robert T. Sand, *propeller shop 55th Fighter Group*

September 6, 1943

Just had our first boat drill. On our way to "A" Deck we passed through some of the luxury parts of the ship. We were dumfounded, after experiencing the conditions we have lived under here. Beautiful halls, corridors and staterooms. A super lounge and dining room.

All this used by officers and nurses. We never saw such a lot of good looking girls in uniform. Most are usually rugged. The officers are clean and shaved, and allowed the company of the girls. These conditions are probably necessary, but it makes us feel like cattle—or as I heard a British officer describe it, "—running around like a bunch of bloody pigs!" Some of us now wish we had either gone to OCS [Officer Candidate School], or that we were women!

September 7, 1943

We had to go up on "A" deck while our deck was scrubbed today. Lots of officers and nurses. They had
68

all the room in the world (until *we* arrived). They all looked so fresh and clean, the officers clean shaven, alongside us unshaven cattle.

Most of my gang had to go thirteen hours without going to a latrine, due to the strict traffic regulations on the boat. I've only been able to wash once since boarding. Haven't shaved. A few have shaved, showered and washed by breaking rules. Very few.

We are now in the compartment, stinking, hot and sweaty again. Have only eaten one meal in 48 hours, so maybe supper will go down tonight. Here it comes! . . . .

Chicken is just one of the meals served on china plates to officers and nurses, who were also officers. They even have a choice of menu, beautiful green upholstered chairs, fancy tables, etc.

There was a near mutiny, if noise means anything, by the men this morning, when the galley turned us down on seconds of anything.

September 13, 1943

On my way down to one of the galley store rooms to pick up a case of "C" rations, I saw several *tubs* full of steaks; beautiful, red, thick cuts, apparently for officers, as we had a sort of vegetable stew. It was fairly good at that. Cooked cabbage was the vegetable, as usual. Fooey!

September 1943

This morning began the pains of reassembling our personal equipment. Then the stealing which had already been rampant this whole voyage turned into the worst outrage of mass thievery I have ever seen. Barracks bags, bedrolls, guns, clothing, *everything*, stolen left and right. Some things were recovered, many things not. Someone got Rod's [Fraleigh] gas mask, and while I was standing right by it, someone stole my breakfast "C" ration for tomorrow. I also lost a hand towel. Recovered my spoon and fork, used and dirty, that was taken from my kit the first day. Also my soap dish, the soap used. Everywhere there are messkits lying about, which had

4th Fighter Group ace Don Gentile engages in a fighter pilot's favorite
pastime. *USAF/NASM*

been used once, then thrown aside, and someone else's used.

Jack Monaghan, *maintenance supply, 55th Fighter Group*

When we landed in Greenock, Scotland, we learned an interesting British regulation. I am not sure if this is still true but at that time no foreigner could land on British shores carrying any arms or ammunition. As we came off the troop transport, the *Orion*, a British ship, we had to hand over our arms and ammunition to someone aboard ship before we went down the gangplank to the dock. The guns and ammunition were collected on the deck, were lowered over the side to another British vessel and brought to shore and handed back to us again so that no foreigner carried arms and ammunition onto British shores. We had to identify our weapons by serial number when they returned our arms.

Robert T. Sand, *propeller shop, 55th Fighter Group*

When the Group arrived at Nuthampstead, England, in September of 1943, the weather was already turning cold and soggy. Like most wartime airfields, this one was hastily constructed by the English and widely dispersed on farmland, connected by existing country roads. For living quarters, we enlisted men were assigned to a small area consisting of about four Nissen huts for barracks, one Nissen hut for an orderly room, a latrine a dozen yards from the huts. They were shelter indeed, which front line infantry would have considered palatial, I am sure. It is also true that they were bare, uninsulated metal, drafty and dimly lit. Small wattage bulbs were used to conserve scarce energy, and there was always a shortage of fuel for the tiny stove that tried unsuccessfully to heat the frigid air that lay over England for most of

those two years. Usually a sea of gumbo mud surrounded these buildings. The barracks were connected by sidewalks, but the latrine was not. It was a challenge to make the crossing without having your boots sucked into the gumbo and sometimes the trip was too urgent to stop and retrieve them.

The showers were separate little buildings quite some distance from the barracks area. The stories coming back to us about the showers filled us with foreboding, but the time soon came when a shower was essential.

This is what we found: The time of day left for showers was after work, and after chow, so the trip to the shower building was a long walk through blackness, with the careful flicking on and off of a penlight to stay on sidewalk or road. From out of the cold dark night we entered a room nearly as dark. Steam swirled out of the open door and was torn away by

Huddled into Hut 16 at Nuthampstead, Technical Sergeant Hoch writes home, 28 March 1944. *Robert T. Sand*

Wormingford, 12 May 1944. Red Cross doughnut girls were loved by almost everyone who came in contact with them. They were always ready with a smile, an encouraging word and the simple presence of a woman in a man's world. *Robert T. Sand*

70

the night breeze. The inside had shower heads, not stalls, arrayed along one or two sides of the room. The rest of the room contained rows of benches for changing clothes. These were made of 1″x1″ slats, as were the floor sections which were now floating in confusion on three or four inches of dirty, soapy water, on which also floated soggy cigarette butts and all manners of paper scraps. All drains were plugged.

Home for 55th Fighter Group ground crewman Sgt. Bob Sand, who slept in the top bunk of this cot at Wormingford. *Robert T. Sand*

Just below the prop maintenance shops at Wormingford sat this windmill, built in that late 1700s. England at war was a nation of contrasts. *Robert T. Sand*

We did as the others were doing, climbed on the benches and commenced a balancing act of removing clothing, rolling it into a ball and stashing it with the shoes on the driest part of the bench. Stowed the clean long handled underwear the same way, hoping it would not fall into the soup. Same with the towel. We reluctantly stepped down on the skittery floating platforms and sloshed our way to the shower heads, barely visible in the dim, steamy light. Here, men were shrieking. One because his shower was dispensing ice cold water, and the one next to him because his was scalding hot. They tried running back and forth to temper the pain a bit. I found one which was all plugged up except for a couple of holes which sent out a needle spray of very hot water.

When the installers had finished the plumbing, all handles were removed from the heat controls, supposedly to conserve hot water. Mechanics soon learned to bring pliers when they showered.

Anyway, the struggle with soap, washcloth, towel, and the balancing act of trying to dress atop the by now soggy benches, without dropping things in the water, was epic and unforgettable. Over the months these conditions gradually improved, but it was little solace when we knew the officers were bathing in Roman tiled sunken baths smothered in bubbles and listening to Vera Lynn singing the latest songs while beautiful houris adjusted the water temperature with solid gold knobs and scraped their skin with whalebone after anointing them with oil.

Well, I have to admit that the part about the officers came through the grapevine and may differ in some details, but I can attest to every word of the enlisted men's experience firsthand.

Marvin Bledsoe, *P–47 pilot, 353rd Fighter Group (from* Thunderbolt*)*

It was always dark when we got up. It was invariably wet with fog outside our Nissen huts, and cold as cold could be inside or out. Night and day the English air chilled me to the bone. Right after my arrival, I wrote and asked [my wife] Harriet to make a flannel sleeping outfit for me with feet, mittens and a hood for my head. She added rabbit ears to the hood, and I was teased unmercifully about my "bunny suit." But from then on I slept warmly.

Chet A. Patterson, *P–38 pilot, 55th Fighter Group*

The 338th Squadron had reserved a room in one of the nicer hotels in London. It had two bedrooms and a sitting room. As each flight went in for their R&R the room just kept rotating with the flights.

Once as four men were getting into an elevator a young, very attractive lady got in with them. Immediately each man tuned in hoping for a date for the evening. She seemed very pleased with the attention. As the elevator stopped at her floor, the men almost said in unison, "Would you like to come up to our room for a drink?"

She said, "Yes," and as far as the pilots were concerned the chase was on. When she got to the room each man was jockeying for position. It seems her father was in the Parliament and she had studied to be a ballet dancer before the war started.

Somehow the conversation got into ballet dancing and she was asked to show a couple of movements. She accepted the challenge.

In trying to demonstrate, she decided she had to shed her heavy clothes. So, in bra and panties, she gave the pilots a demonstration and I don't think they ever saw any of the dance steps. An outsider watching this would wonder who was the "chassee" and who was the "chaser."

She pointed to one of the pilots, said, "Follow me," and headed for one of the bedrooms. That left three broken hearts wondering why they were not chosen. Not too long after that the door opened and she came out to choose another pilot while the first man crashed on the sofa. This was repeated till all four were shot down.

So for the next two days of leave no one left the room and the woman should have but didn't get her fill of young, eager pilots. When they left they asked her to stay for the next flight that would be following them.

This went on for several flights. I felt something was wrong with the way the fellows were returning after their leaves. The normal was a few hangovers with attached headaches, somewhat depressed because the leave wasn't long enough, etc. Everyone seemed to have a big smile and no hangovers. I asked Dr. Randy Garnett to check up on what was going on.

He came back to tell me what was happening at the hotel. As soon as I heard I got a car and along with Dr. Garnett we headed for London. In my mind if she was a German agent she could put the 338th Squadron out of business if she had a social disease. I wanted Dr. Garnett to check her right away and he was a GYN so this was right down his line.

Dr. Garnett gave her a clean bill of health and said she was a nymphomaniac. In the taxi taking her back to the hotel we told her to let us know if she ever went outside the squadron. Otherwise she was free to stay in the room and I was sure the men would bring her special treats.

This went on for over a month and then one day she just disappeared. I knew something changed for the next flight came back with bo-que headaches, assorted hangovers and obvious signs of depression.

Robert T. Sand, *Propeller shop, 55th Fighter Group*

The second Christmas passed as another workday for us, but spirits weren't too low. We had a pretty good turkey dinner Christmas Day. Christmas Eve was a milling, informal party, or parties, in all the huts and we

On the six-mile stretch of road from Colchester to the 55th field at Wormingford sat this old flour mill, a constant reminder of changing times. *Robert T. Sand*

had quite a lot of beer and spirits, and snacks assembled from packages from home. I got a little tight, but not like last year.

Even got to decorate a Christmas tree this year (for the day room). Christmas paper stuffed with balls of newspaper and tied with ribbons made decorations, also a blue cellophane bow, a few little Santas robbed from another home-sent tree, and a few salvaged icicles. The tree is about five feet tall and sits on a table. Surgical cotton serves as a snow base, and snow patches on tree, and shredded radar f.u. (foul up) tinfoil for sparkles. Our communications officer donated us a string of lights made up of gunsight bulbs, painted, but it didn't burn very brightly, and soon burned out. With another soldier I helped cut some red berries on a side road and some holly at the nearby minister's estate, and with the leftover limbs of the Xmas tree, we did a pretty nice job of decorating the day room. We

used the radar tinfoil about the same as you use colored straws by tying bunches of it to form pretty flared out disks.

Arthur L. Thorsen, *P-38 pilot, 55th Fighter Group*
We were assigned to various shacks and issued three iron hard pillows, to be used as a mattress. We called them biscuits. We also received blankets made, it seemed, of steel wool and thorns. I was gradually beginning to feel better instead of worse, for I reasoned that if I were eventually shot down and taken prisoner, prison camp couldn't possibly be a greater hardship than this.

Chet A. Patterson, *P-38 pilot, 55th Fighter Group*
There were some billets on Wormingford called the VIP quarters. It housed some 20 or 25 men and was a Quonset hut built in the form of a T.

The horizontal bar of the T was the largest portion and had the rooms. The vertical shape was much smaller and contained the showers, johns and washstands. There were four large rooms for two on the corners while the rest of the rooms were small individual units. Dr. Randy Garnett and I were roommates and had been close personal friends since the days of Port Angeles.

We had a dance held in the Officer's Club when they invited English girls from the Land Army to the party. The weather was bad and forecast for getting worse so you might say it was a "maximum effort" for all the officers. There were no holds barred for they knew they could sleep in the next day.

I don't know how many scored in this encounter but two men in the VIP quarters ended up with girls in their room. Obviously it was a mutual attraction for both sexes and they did what came naturally. In the wee hours

There was nothing more popular than Bob Hope's touring USO show which made its way across the globe through all theaters of war. As Bob Sand recalled, "Bob Hope's pin-up girls got more attention from GIs than Bob Hope . . . gee, they looked good!" *Robert T. Sand*

An ironmonger's wagon passing through Colchester seems out of place when compared to the modern fighter ironmongery on nearby airfields. *Robert T. Sand*

London's Piccadilly Circus in 1945 was a constant magnet for Yanks on leave. *Byron Trent*

of the morning one of the girls had to go to the john. Her partner told her to just leave the door ajar and feel her way down the hall, turn left and then left again at the next opening. Naturally she was to return the same as we had a very strict blackout. Only the john area had a dim light.

I guess this noise of her leaving the room also caused the other girl to decide to do the same thing and she happened to be in the next room. She got the same instructions, however this room was closest to the john. Now there [were] two doors left ajar so when the first girl got back she entered the first room and closed the door. The second girl did the same thing. As long as both couples were awake (the beds were single cots) they again did what came naturally. Mind you they all had met for the first time and with a little liquor to dim their senses no one noticed any difference.

When dawn came and there was sufficient light, one of the girls awoke to look into a face of a total stranger. She let out a wild yell and this woke everyone in the building (soundproofing was not a requirement for these buildings).

Randy and I jumped up and ran to the rooms. One of the cardinal rules was no rough stuff at any time. By the time we got there the second gal awoke with the shout and she too was screaming. The two pilots were totally confused. Fortunately, though the women accused the men of switching, of course the pilots were each in their own room.

After separating the pilots and the women we finally figured out what happened. It was hard not to laugh right then but it was still a bitter experience to the women. We had them gather their clothes and had them taken home by the squadron jeep.

Robert T. Sand, *P-51 ground crew, 55th Fighter Group*

I live in a Nissen hut, which is the British prototype of a Pacific hut. We have a little coal stove, but still, they aren't exactly warm, and the wind leaks through. Have an iron cot, with a three section mattress of unresisting material. I sleep on the mattress and over me are two American Army blankets, two gray British blankets (one folded double to give an extra layer), my overcoat, my Mackinaw, and sometimes my sweater and leather sheep jacket. No sheets. The wool tickles one's face all night. The pillow is a round cylinder of horsehair and dried camel dung (well, maybe not) and is covered by a coarse, sack-like slip. I removed over half its stuffing, and it's not bad now.

In spite of the fact that this sack (bed) is bringing back my old rheumatism, I am always reluctant to leave it in the morning.

Jan Houston Monaghan, *Red Cross girl, 55th Fighter Group*

The base at Wormingford was overrun with dogs . . . all kinds: big ones, little ones, with long legs, short legs, long tails, no tails, cute and cuddly and ugly as sin. They would come into the Red Cross Club and climb up in the chairs to sleep. Most of the time they were filthy and made the upholstery, such as it was, filthy too. The men thought I was a mean gal because I would go through the club and tip the chairs to make the dogs fall out and then I shooed them outside. The fellows didn't seem to mind giving up chairs to dogs, but I thought that was ridiculous. Whenever an announcement was made over the Tannoy [public address system] to the effect, "All dogs that are not registered will be put to sleep," every guy would hasten to adopt a dog and have it registered. The dog population grew and grew and I fought a losing battle with the chairs.

Robert T. Sand, *Propeller shop, 55th Fighter Group*

It may sound funny, but the byword over here is "It's *rough* in the ETO!" Fact is, mister, when the ETO G.I. reads of your troubles back home, he just laughs. Income tax? "Boy, ain't that tough!" he chuckles. Rationing? "It'd be a pleasure!" he says. Prices? Well, Uncle Sam takes care of our clothing account pretty well, though the styles are rather limited. But I've heard of G.I.s paying as much as twenty-five shillings for one dozen eggs, and mister, that is more than five good old American dollars. Ninety cents a dozen is a more common price in the country, *if* you *know* someone, and are very *lucky*. Try and get them!

Rationing, eh? No whipping cream over there? Hm! Well, there's none over here either, or commercial cream . . . or milk! Condensed milk is used for our coffee, powdered milk for the cereal. We don't complain . . . but! Our favorite food back home, ice cream, is a very rare thing over here, and cannot be obtained in public at all. When we do get it in the mess hall, it tastes like canned milk, but we consider it a gala occasion.

We don't have butter at every meal, and about half the butter (by my guess) has been canned butter, with a large percentage of cottonseed oil to help it withstand warm temperatures. It does! It refuses to spread on anything. Won't melt on hot foods, and it leaves a coating in one's mouth that is very unpleasant. We've learned to pass it up if we recognize it though the day may come when we'll be glad to get it.

Have you ever heard of "C" rations, mister? Ever tasted 'em? Well, it's a sort of finely chopped hash, with a certain taste and feeling in your mouth. Ask any G.I. who has lived over here what he thinks of them! Oh! for a good, cold bowl of crackers and milk!

[Breakfast] comes this way to a G.I. . . .

He is awakened by the C.Q. (charge of quarters) at a plenty early hour, and after battling with his apprehension of the icy air outside his finally warmed pile of blankets, overcoats, jackets, sweaters, overalls, etc., he drags himself out and pulls on the layers of shapeless clothing that characterize the Army mechanic. Then, if he remembers his childhood training, he sloshes his way to the almost deserted wash-house to dash some ice water (there is only one kind) into his face, a quick towel rub with cold, numbed hands, a few hurried strokes of the toothbrush, and

Local pubs became very popular, very quickly. These GIs from the 355th Fighter Group are clearly enjoying the ancient English tradition of paying one's respects to the local publican and his wife by having a pint. *Alexander C. Sloan via Bob Kuhnert, 355th FG Assn.*

then back to the hut to make up the sack (they just *aren't* beds over here) and sweep up a bit. Finally, with an envious look at the few G.I.s fortunate enough to be able to sleep in, he grabs the ever-present messkit and goes out into the darkness towards the mess hall.

The road is narrow, and a dozen times he has to step off onto the slippery, muddy shoulder, averting his head to try ineffectually to shield his face from the fine shower of mud as Army vehicles hurtle past.

A few minutes' walk and he reaches the mess hall, only to find that the chowline extends from fifty to a hundred yards outside the door. So, he stands with his back to the wind, and tucks his mess gear into his jacket to warm it up a little from the heat that is in his body, if any.

And here is one of the evils of the Army . . . "Sweating out the chowline." What a long-gone dream, that—the days we used to only walk into the next room to find bright china plates, and shiny silverware on a clean, white table! Most G.I.s would trade you all your troubles for just that!

Anyway, the shivering G.I. hunches up in his jacket, and moving one step at a time, sometimes stopping for a while, he gradually moves toward his first goal, which is the shelter of the doorway. Once inside, he starts the juggling act of removing his gloves and cap, stuffing them into pockets, trying to untie the messkit bag, and unsnap the handle of the canteen cup before the line passes the fruit juice, which is placed near the door. Gulping the juice down so he will have the cup ready for coffee, he unsnaps the messkit, which sometimes

requires a sharp bang on the table, causing the messkit to open with such explosive force everyone in the chowline jumps. And there isn't a chowline in which at least one messkit doesn't slip from someone's grasp and explode with a clatter of dancing knives, forks, etc., across the floor.

With practiced motions, the G.I. pokes knife, fork and spoon into a pocket, balances messkit and messkit lid in the fingers of the left hand, tucks the cup under the left arm, and is finally ready to serve himself. If something special is on the menu, such as real eggs, the cooks wisely do not trust the individual to serve himself. The food is in large containers placed on a counter some fifteen feet long, and the line splits, forming a line on each side of the counter.

Let's see, what does the G.I. have for breakfast this morning? It's an unusually good one, and there is more variety than usual. Pancakes! Happy Day! The rightfully *un*happy K.P. flops two pancakes onto the G.I.'s proffered messkit lid. Next he helps himself to a ladle of syrup. Then with a long, two-tined fork, he chases a piece or two of bacon floating in three inches of melted fat. Since the man on the other side is doing the same thing, it practically amounts to a duel. After a minute or two of exasperating effort he decides he didn't want any bacon anyway. It looks a lot different than the home kind variety, too.

Next is the cold cereal. It looks something like the old familiar Wheaties we once knew, but upon the application of milk it instantly assumes all the properties of a soggy pulp. Nor does it seem to be "flavored with additional salt and malt extract,"

because it is quite tasteless. Then comes the milk, which he ladles out steaming hot, with a surface foam, and many little powder-lumps which look like rice on the surface of the cereal.

Now things are getting tricky, especially if yours is the old model messkit with the shallow lid. You can't keep lid and kit on the same level, and you are either spilling syrup from one or milk from the other. There is even fruit this morning. Cooked, dried apricots. Now where to put 'em? Oh, well, they look as tough as leather, and your mouth puckers just thinking how sour they are. Let's skip 'em.

There is almost always butter with hotcakes, so again he does the chasing act with a two pronged fork, trying to capture elusive cubes of butter floating in a pan of water. O.K. Now he no longer needs his right hand, so he retrieves the cup from under his arm, and a K.P. fills it with coffee.

Balancing is at a critical stage, now. Hold your finger on the cup-handle latch, because if it slips out it will dump the entire contents on the floor so quickly you never fail to be astonished, and worse. He half squats to get the cup under the condensed milk spout, and the K.P. gives it a quick squirt. With his other hand the K.P. tosses an enormous slab of light brown bread onto the kit, or cup, if you want it at all, and the G.I. is ready to eat.

Well, not quite. Getting a place to sit is another matter. He looks up and down the long line of tables and finally spots a place only about five men from the outside end of the table. With his heart in his mouth, he carefully steps out in that direction, trying to make shoulders and arms glide smoothly, and trying to avoid the bumping of the constant streams of heavy traffic.

Squeezing in between two rows of leather clad backs he gingerly sidesteps towards his goal, hoping no one decides suddenly to stand up, and hoping that if someone does, he's a smaller guy than himself.

Ah! Now, he sets his cup down, pushes aside the crusts of bread left by the last three men, and contemplates what to do about the ever present puddle of milk or fruit juice in the middle of the space. Finally, he sets his gear as much to one side of it as possible and then climbs awkwardly over the bench, knocking his neighbor's elbows with his knees as he does so.

Meanwhile the aluminum messkit is draining the heat from the food with alarming rapidity. The food is seldom very hot in the first place, as it must be cooked hours ahead of time, and kept in the large pots and pans until serving time. Only very recently has our own shift of cooks provided a can of warm water at the head of the serving line, for taking the outdoor's chill from the messgear . . . this helps considerably.

Now, he is ready to eat. He pleads above the noise for the sugar (yes, we still have sugar, very coarse, but plenty good enough). It finally reaches him, and usually his worst fears are realized . . . it is what is commonly known in G.I. circles as "cinched." This means that if he uses any of it, it's a darn cinch that the next one to use it will have to refill it, so according to Army courtesy, he is bound to forestall this tragedy by filling the sugar tin himself. Complicated, but customary. The movements about the table of such table-supplied foods are as strategically planned [as] a game of chess, each man craftily trying to avoid being the recipient of a "cinch."

But, the G.I. has it, so he struggles out of his seat, picks up the little sugar tin and beats his way to the sugar barrel for a refill. When he gets back, his food is only lukewarm, so he gulps it down as fast as possible before it gets completely cold.

Just eating is quite a job. Since you have on your bulky clothing (sheepskin jacket, and sometimes sheepskin pants) you find that every movement of your arms tends to knock utensils one way or another, and your scarf keeps trying to trail in the food. When you raise a spoonful of food to your mouth, the stiff jacket goes up with it so that the collar blocks the way. You try tucking it in different ways, but finally end up holding it down with your left hand.

A welcome final destination on leave—the American Red Cross Service Club at the Bull Hotel, Cambridge. *Alexander C. Sloan via Bob Kuhnert, 355th FG Assn.*

Rainbow Corner, the American Red Cross Club on Shaftsbury Avenue, just off Piccadilly Circus in London. *Alexander C. Sloan via Bob Kuhnert, 355th FG Assn.*

Finally the G.I. drinks his coffee, which doesn't taste like the old homemade coffee, then he threads lid, knife, fork and spoon onto the messkit handle, and heads for the steamy washing room. After emptying scraps into a garbage can, he gets into one of the lines, each leading to three huge kettles, beneath which smoky coal fires are burning. The first is soapy water (except when we run out of soap), the second contains disinfectant, and the third a final rinse in hot water. All goes well here except when the meal is of a greasy nature, or the water is not hot, or there is no soap, or you drop part of your gear into one of the deep kettles.

Then, slipping and sliding in the mud, the ETO soldier goes around to the front of the messhall, meanwhile assembling mess gear, cap, gloves, etc., and joins the crowd waiting for the chowtruck—"bus" to you. Everyone tries to find some shelter in the lee of the little Nissen shack, but there isn't room for everyone, and shoes pick up heavy gumbo with every step.

Just like any bus back home, it seems that fate decrees that the bus must pull out just the moment before you get there. So, everyone huddles and waits. There is horseplay and talk. I know how crowded busses are at home, but you should see ours! The moment our particular truck comes into sight with a clattering roar of the exhaust, there is a mad rush towards it long before it stops, and a seething battle to get on it. The mob bails into the back of the truck, which is equipped with some steps made by our shop, and in the wink of an eye, the benches lining each side are filled and G.I.s are sitting on other G.I.s'

laps, and then every available inch of standing space, leaning space, squatting space, is taken up and then some more are crowded on. For a time we used a truck designed to carry eighteen men, and we've counted as many as forty-four coming out of it. Now we use a roomier truck, but still just as proportionately packed. Until MP law clamped down recently the steps and tail gate were loaded in a swaying bulge of humanity hanging on for dear life.

There are no upholstered seats in these busses, no windows, and no light when crowded. If you are toward the front, all you can see are faintly dimmed, disconnected parts of human beings . . . a nose, a jaw, a hand, someone's back, a foot. The driver is an unmerciful guy with a mania for making his cargo as uncomfortable as possible by starting fast, stopping fast and swinging fast around the curves. The mob swings and sways, desperately trying to maintain balance by grasping anything possible, even a neighbor, whose own balance is equally precarious. Sometimes you are shocked to find that a bodyless head is protruding from between your knees, or that a foot has found its way into your lap.

If you happen to be sitting anywhere near the back of the truck, you are favored by a fine spray of mud that clouds glasses, and leaves one whole side of you a glistening coat of brown mud. In spite of this, it is all endured in a spirit of good humor, and most complaints are good-natured.

The thing is, this whole procedure is repeated with little change, except for menu, and weather conditions, three times a day, day in and day out.

It has lost its novelty, if it ever had any.

Jan Houston Monaghan, *Red Cross girl, 55th Fighter Group*

On July 6, 1944, one month after D-day, I arrived on the base at Wormingford and met Nelle Huse with whom I would work for the next seventeen months. After I unpacked, Nelle took me to the Aero Club and introduced me to the British staff, showed me around and described my particular responsibilities as Program Director. When we went back to our quarters, I asked, "What do we do now?"

"Well," Nelle said, in her soft southern drawl, "the girl who was here before you always went to the Officers' Club for cocktails before dinner."

"Is that what you do? Do we have to?" I wanted to know.

"No, I don't go because I don't drink," Nelle replied.

"You don't? Neither do I!" I exclaimed, delighted to find a non-drinking buddy and so cocktails at the Officers' Club never became a part of our daily routine. We ate our meals there, helped to decorate the club for their dances and always attended since dancing partners were needed, but most of our time was spent with the enlisted men. The Officers had their club and the Red Cross Aero Club provided a place for the enlisted personnel to meet.

Nelle was everyone's love and her beautiful photogenic smile had won her distinction as one of the beauties at the University of Alabama. She married Lt. John Huse, a West Point graduate, in 1940 when he was at Lackland Field, San Antonio,

81

Texas. John was in the Philippines at the time of Pearl Harbor and was shot down over Java in early 1942.

"One day in our Red Cross office someone mentioned an article in a recent paper about a flyer being found alive in a jungle when he had been presumed dead. A wistful expression crossed Nelle's face prompting me to ask, 'You wish that could be your John, don't you, Nelle?'

" 'Yes,' she said sadly, 'but it's impossible because the other men in his outfit saw John crash and they buried him there in Java. I had letters from his commanding officer and others telling me all about it.' "

Robert T. Sand, *Propeller shop, 55th Fighter Group*

August 3, 1944 was one of those rare, beautiful autumn days, and little

The wheat field behind the work line at Wormingford the day after the GI shocking of August 3, 1944. *Robert T. Sand*

work to do. A small crew of English farmers showed up and began shocking the turned and dried rows of wheat. Gradually, G.I.s drifted over to the fence to watch. Many were ex-farm workers, and watched longingly as the few men made slow progress on the big field, and talked nostalgically of harvests they remembered. Suddenly one man could stand it no longer, jumped the fence, and plunged into the work, setting an example of speed and enthusiasm that must have astonished the English men.

This was too much for the watching G.I.s and, as if obeying a World War I order to "go over the top," a whole army of frustrated farmers leaped over the fence and soon covered the entire field, with arms flailing, everyone competing to tie and stack faster than the others. It was a fantastic scene. I always wondered what the English farmers thought as they saw this wild horde advancing pell-mell across their field towards them and demanding binding twine. That entire field was shocked so fast it was unbelievable, and a happier crew you never saw.

Jan Houston Monaghan, *Red Cross girl, 55th Fighter Group*
The living quarters for the Red Cross girls were at the end of the Commissary building where the rats spent the day gorging themselves and then, at night, came down to our end and played tag. They slid down the Nissen Hut roof, squealing and scampering until they woke us up at night. Nelle would get so mad she threw her shoes at the sloping ceiling.

The rats gnawed holes along the baseboard about which we complained about to the English

maintenance crew. They simply said, "No use patching the holes, they'll only make more."

We covered the holes with stacks of bricks, some stacks were two feet high. Once a rat died on a nest of babies in the wall behind the bathtub. The smell of dead rats became so overpowering, we had to give up taking baths until someone could come, move the tub, make a hole in the wall and remove the nest. Another rat died behind one of our brick piles in the guest room. I was away on leave and when I returned, I asked Nelle if she'd had the rat taken away.

"Oh, yes," she replied, casually, "I did it myself. I just took a couple of sticks, lifted up the rat and carried it to the garbage bin." Dainty little Nelle continually amazed me.

Gilbert C. Burns, Jr, *P-47 pilot, Fighter OTU*
On July 16, 1944, I took off from the OTU at Atcham, England with no particular objective in mind. The razorback P-47 was 41-6237, an old one, one of the first few hundred made at Farmingdale, New York. Its cost then was about $85,000. When a fighter pilot flies, he is supposed to keep his head turning, constantly watching in all directions. The reason, of course, being that no enemy aircraft could approach and catch you by surprise.

I was flying in the vicinity of Shrewsbury and my mind was not on flying, but on other things. I was not looking around, but staring straight ahead. I had "my head up my ass." I happened to turn my head to the left and lo and behold, what was sitting close to my left wing but a Spitfire. It had come up and caught me

unawares. I was quite embarrassed and I am sure the Spitfire pilot was quite pleased about it. I took a close look at the pilot and there was blond hair coming down from beneath a white flying helmet. A girl! One of the English ATA ferry pilots. I knew that those girls were great pilots. I had seen them slow roll on take-off from our airfield. I had seen them in Hurricanes fly across our field only a few hundred feet up and inverted.

So this blonde ATA pilot must have felt pretty proud after catching me asleep at the wheel, and she dove off down to the left. Being more than annoyed with myself, I jumped on her tail and followed her down. She led a merry chase on the deck, but I clung to her. We were circling a huge tree in a vertical bank when suddenly my engine stopped. I glanced at the fuel gauges; they checked out OK, so with what power I had left, I pulled up a few hundred feet to look for a crash landing site. God was with me because there was a field off to the left and in I went. I turned off the ignition, shut the gas line off, put the flaps down, wheels up, trying to come in as slowly as possible.

I hit the ground tail first and crash-slid to a stop. Releasing my oxygen connection, radio cable and safety belt, I jumped out and started running in case the plane decided to blow. I looked back over my shoulder at the plane while I was running and what was chasing me but a bull! I kept running and came to a barbed wire fence that surrounded the field. With the bull coming up fast, I jumped over the fence. Going over the barbs ripped the seat of my flying suit and drew blood on my behind. This was to be my only "wound" of the war.

A jeep was sent for me finally and I returned to base. After telling my CO the story I asked him, in jest, if that "wound" would qualify me for a Purple Heart. He quickly informed me that they did not give medals for chasing blondes.

Jan Houston Monaghan, *Red Cross girl, 55th Fighter Group*

Christmas Day 1944 was one day none of us will forget. The weather had been 'socked in' for days and the planes had been unable to give air support to the Battle of the Bulge, but Christmas morning dawned clear, cold and bright. The sky was filled with planes from one horizon to the other, in layers as high as the eye could see. Everything in England that could fly was in the air that day heading for the continent.

As I stood staring at the spectacle, I found myself praying, "Oh God, it's Christmas . . . watch over those at the other end . . . and help us find peace someday. . . ."

A few years later I mentioned that Christmas at a meeting and a young woman in the group said, "I remember that Christmas too . . . I was at the other end. . . ."

Robert T. Sand, *Propeller shop, 55th Fighter Group*

I got my first view of an air raid from the target itself. Have seen others, but never before from the middle. It was indeed a rather awesome spectacle. But more than anything, I was impressed by the people themselves. The shows had just let out, and the already thronged streets were mobbed, when the wailing sirens shrieked out the

English farmhouses such as this one were not primarily something of historical interest to GIs. Here a USAAF officer and his enlisted driver are on a serious mission in the East Anglian countryside—hunting and bartering for fresh eggs. *Mark H. Brown/USAFA*

familiar rising and falling tone that is "red alert." Did people head for the shelter and undergrounds? Did the double-deck buses, the taxis stop, or turn out their lights? Or were traffic lights turned off? Hell, no! Everything went on its merry way; the people crowding and laughing in utter disregard for any danger from above.

At first there were a few flickers on the horizon, then they gradually grew closer, until you could hear the whoom! whoom! of the concussions. I can't tell at a distance the difference between bombs and anti-aircraft guns. Only when searchlights broke out right around us did the streets begin to clear somewhat of pedestrians. The noise and flashes grew greater and greater till it was for all the world like a terrific thunderstorm. Then all of a sudden there was a violent "bloom-bloom-bloom!" from an anti-aircraft battery right near us. A couple of feet from me I heard one girl say to her girlfriend, "I'm *scared*, aren't you?" The other answered, "Yes," and they said little more. And other girls and guys barged back and forth, laughing and talking. The buses kept plugging along. I was part of quite a crowd of curious gathered in a semi-sheltered place where we could see everything well.

A tall, respectable-looking gent leaned down and kissed his wife and said, "Don't worry, dear, it's all right."

We couldn't see the planes, but we could follow their course by the pin-pricks of light, high overhead, that spelled death, and we could sometimes hear the engines. It passed on to a moderate distance, growing muffled. Some of the people passed on, but I stayed to see it all. Soon the barrage grew closer, and was right on

us again, and new people were standing by me. A tall, middle-aged woman was standing near, and I decided she wasn't young enough to think I was trying to proposition her if I spoke to her.

"This beats me. If anything like this occurred back home, there wouldn't be a soul on the street, or a light, or a vehicle running."

The conversation continued about like this. (Meanwhile, my knees were doing a jitterbug number.)

The lady: "Well (boomety-boom-boom!) we've grown so used (boom, boom, boom!) so used to it, you (boom-bloom!) see."

Me (or I—one of us, anyway): "Yes, but how can anyone get so used to it that it doesn't bother them? After all (boom!) that's a lot of high-power stuff going off, and with the shrapnel falling and all?"

The lady: "Yes, but they know when it is bad enough to head for shelter. They don't like shelters. They are afraid of indirect hits, and of being trapped. You are safer in the open. I usually watch this from my hotel roof, but the lift isn't running right now."

For the third time the bombers are coming back. The sky is a constant blaze of flashes. The din is terrific. The lady watches unperturbed: "They seem to (boom, boom, boom!) be coming back (wham! bloom!) again. This is a (blam! Wham blam!) this is a rather (Whoom!) a small (wham, blam, boom!) a small affair tonite."

I faint! Mentally, anyway.

However, when I got back here, one or two of the porters (or janitors) had been watching it from the roof, and seemed to have quite a bit of

news to report, but I couldn't get close enough to hear it.

Tomorrow the paper will say, if anything, "Enemy aircraft were over London last night. One old lady in a nursing home was killed. Some anti-aircraft firing was heard."

Radio news says fifty bombers reached the outskirts of London, but only ten penetrated to the center. Six reported shot down so far. Pfui! Only ten bombers! What is ten or fifteen tons of bombs? Pfui! I still say it is much.

Arthur L. Thorsen, *P–38 pilot, 55th Fighter Group*

[During a London air raid] someone shouted, "Let's get down in the bloody cellar where the bloody wine is kept!" There was no panic. The party guests, mostly English, were used to this sort of thing and slipped out of the [hotel] suite in small groups. Those raids were nothing compared to the blitz of 1940 and '41, and only occurred with lengthy intervals between.

The door to one of the bedrooms slammed open and Penn came out with only one pant leg on. Staggering around, trying to get his other leg into his pants, he said, "Those goddam Jerries! Their timing is always rotten." Ethel followed him out of the bedroom, buttoning her blouse.

"Nice party," she said, "Where's Jackie?"

"Went out with the others." I replied. "She might have gone to the cellar."

"Not Jackie," said Ethel, "she's a queer one. Likes to watch the raids. She's probably out in front of the hotel."

Woods, Jaklich, and DesVoignes were gathering up the remaining bottles. "Let's go watch the show with Jackie," suggested Jaklich. We all agreed that was a good idea and left the suite. The only person left behind was correspondent Leatherby, asleep in a corner, in a drunken stupor.

By the time we reached street level, the first bombers were coming over, some getting caught in searchlights. Then the anti-aircraft opened up and the sky came alive with orange flashes. The bombers were hitting the dock area at the Victoria embankment again. One bomb seemed very close, hitting a building on Bedford Street to our right. It did a half roll in the air.

Not all of the party went to the shelters. Some of the RAF fliers and their girlfriends had joined us on the curb. We all sat there, enjoying the show the same as folks back home would enjoy a fireworks display. We began passing the bottles around as pieces of shell casings fell to the street with loud clatters. The whole exercise seemed to be a variation on the "chicken" game. Everyone sweated their way through it, none wanting to be the first "chicken" to run for a shelter. In about ten minutes the "all clear" sounded and we went back to the suite. No one else returned, so the party broke up. . . .

I wasn't really tired and did not go directly to my room. Instead, I took the elevator down to the ground floor and stepped out into the night. There was a red glow in the sky over the docks and another over Bedford Street. Curious, I walked down the Strand toward Bedford. Turning the corner, I could see the bombed building burning and being attended to by firefighters. As I approached, ambulances went racing back and forth. Some civilians were standing in groups on the periphery of the burning building, and, noticing one gentleman standing alone, I stepped to his side.

He was well dressed with bowler hat and umbrella and he was cursing quietly to himself.

"Did everyone get out?" I asked.

"Very few," he replied, "and they're in pretty bad shape. This was a WAAF barracks. Women's Auxiliary Air Force, you know. They manage the barrage balloon in Victoria Gardens."

"Can we help?"

"'fraid not. We'd only be in the way. Those chaps know their business better than we. There's not much left of the ladies, I'm afraid. Look there!" and he pointed with his umbrella to an object lying in the glow of the fire. I saw what appeared to be a bloody human spine.

Robert T. Sand, *propeller shop, 55th Fighter Group*

As far as I know, there were no bomb shelters [at the time] at Nuthampstead. Certainly none in our barracks area. Almost right away we

The Orderly Room crew at Nuthampstead, the 55th Fighter Group's first base, December 1943. Mud was a constant in England, getting into everything imaginable and miring down even the most elaborate anti-gumbo devices. Corporal Horn snaps Captain Boggess' picture as (right to left): Sergeant Laque, Sergeant Fladung, Staff Sergeant Golden and Corporal Anderson look on. *Robert T. Sand*

The 55th Group mess hall during lunch at Wormingford, 7 May 1944. Upper non-coms were issued bikes but the lower-ranking enlisted men had to buy theirs. *Robert T. Sand*

began to wonder if it wouldn't be nice to have some. Most histories I have read of WWII in Britain say there were no significant air raids by the Germans over England after the Blitz. It would have been hard to convince us of that fact in Nuthampstead in late 1943 or early 1944.

One night we were awakened by a series of explosions that seemed mighty close. Our instructions in case of an air raid were to crawl under our cots until it was over. Very few did so, whether out of bravado, or futility, I don't know. The corrugated metal of our huts was mighty thin, and the flashes showing thru the edges of our blacked out windows were not very reassuring. I don't remember any display of fear, though it was pretty obvious that we were the target of the moment.

Next morning revealed that the raiders had literally driven down our runway dropping hundreds of incendiary stick bombs and quite a number of canister type incendiary bombs. The runway was pocked, but no serious damage was done, and all was quickly patched and the runways were soon in use again. As far as I know, none of our planes or installations was hit, and no one was injured. We must have been unloaded on after failure to reach a prime target. Or—were *we* it?

Robert T. Sand, *P-51 ground crew, 55th Fighter Group*

With one notable exception, no one ever used our air raid shelter for its intended purpose. That would be "chicken." Instead it was used for parking bicycles and tossing beer bottles. The one exception was the night I kissed the world goodbye. At

night, as was most frequent, the alert sounded and was ignored by everyone as usual. I was out with my camera and was shocked to see a buzz bomb heading straight for us from a direction 90 degrees from the usual heading. I think there was a frantic call on the Tannoy speaker to "seek shelter." In any case, it was coming fast at what seemed to be not far above tree top level.

A few hundred feet before reaching our road, the clatter of the engine suddenly stopped and the red eye stopped blinking. Knowing most of them were set to dive immediately, I hit the ground and wondered what the end would be like. After a few seconds and I was incredibly still alive, I took my hands from my ears (if it landed nearby I didn't want to lose my eardrums!) and could hear the machine whistling in a low, fast glide into a slight valley below our area, and explode. Was I scared? Yes!

But, getting back to the air raid shelter. For the first time everyone was alarmed enough to take the "seek shelter" seriously, and according to what I was told, there was a sudden invasion of the shelter (sensibly, I might add) followed by great pandemonium as bare feet found broken glass, and legs tangled with bicycle frames, resulting in our most serious injuries as a result of buzz bombs.

Arthur L. Thorsen, *P-38 pilot, 55th Fighter Group*

I don't know why I was selected for the job, but our squadron commander Major Mark Shipman picked me, I think, because he did not want to endanger the life of one of his veteran pilots. I was more expendable.

The job called for aerobatics on the deck—that is ground level. Now I could do aerobatics just about as well as the next pilot, but it's much more comfortable at ten or twenty thousand feet. Rolling on the deck required ultra precision. The slightest mistake and you've "bought the farm." Combat stunting I could accept; unnecessary stunting, I felt was the domain of all the mental minus marks in the service.

I flew to a field north of London, which was a replacement depot for bomber crews who had recently arrived from training fields in the States. There existed at this station a very serious morale problem as the incoming bomber crews were made instantly aware of the high mortality rate of their brethren who had arrived earlier. Bomber Command, indeed, was suffering heavy losses. To counter this pit of despair the bomber crews found themselves in, senior officers in their infinite wisdom, decided that an air show would turn the situation around.

After landing, I taxiied behind a jeep to a designated hardstand, shut the engines down and climbed into the jeep to be driven to the Operations Shack. On the way I saw hundreds of air crew members lined up parallel to the runway I had just landed on. A flight of B-17s were preparing to take off.

At the Operations building, I reported to the officer in charge of the show, a Colonel Wilson. He introduced me to two other pilots he had been talking to. They had also been selected to take part in the impending rat race. I did not retain their names as my mind was on the challenge that lay ahead, but one, a little fellow with a moon face and a cock of the barnyard strut, was a P–51 Mustang pilot. The other officer, a P–47 Thunderbolt pilot, was a stocky, freckle-faced redhead who was rather quiet and seemed about as pleased with this assignment as I was.

Colonel Wilson said, "I'm not going to tell you boys what to do. I'm sure you can cook up something yourselves. All I ask is that you give these bomber boys something to cheer about. Show them the kind of protection they'll get when those 109s start squirting at them! Show them how you can handle those crates, but do it on the deck. You'll take off in twenty minutes. The heavies are giving them a show right now!" With that, he turned to speak to another group of officers, who were there, apparently, as spectators.

"Well," little Mustang pilot said, "I'll lead this thing." That was just about what I expected him to say.

Nelle Huse wears an officer's sheepskin jacket. She was already a widow, having lost her husband in action in the South Pacific. Nelle died shortly after attending a 55th reunion with Jan and Jack Monaghan. *Robert T. Sand*

Jan Houston brings her coffee urn in the backseat of a Jeep, and a generous portion of sunshine for the troops. *Robert T. Sand*

88

"Here's what we'll do. We'll take off in formation. Thunderbolt on my left, Lightning on my right." Thunderbolt pilot and I looked at each other in tacit agreement that this little runt was a fruitcake. At that moment the flight of B-17s roared down the runway at low level. When the noise subsided, Mustang pilot continued, "We'll climb to 5,000 feet, then I'll peel off, Thunderbolt second and Lightning last, all line astern. I'll pull her out on the deck and roll her right in front of the tower. You fellas' do the same."

Thunderbolt pilot and I looked at each other again. Now we were positive Mustang pilot was a fruitcake. We were all three second lieutenants so neither of us outranked the other where a question of leadership was involved. It was just that Mustang pilot was a pushy type and we were foolish enough to let him take charge. He was still babbling, "Then we'll pull up, get a little sky beneath us and do a loop, coming out of it right on the deck again, balls out! From then on, it'll be follow the leader. I'll lead. Okay?"

We both nodded to him and he lighted up a cigar that was too big for him and strolled over to a window where he could watch the heavies. Thunderbolt pilot looked at me and winked. I guess neither of us cared if Mustang pilot wanted to lead the show and have his moment of glory out front. There was still some time to kill, so Thunderbolt pilot and I sat on a bench fronting a row of lockers lining the wall at one end of the room. "You got to hand it to the little guy." he said. "He's an eager beaver. If he lives long enough, he'll be a general some day."

"He's a fruitcake," I said, and we each fired up a cigarette. At that moment a sturdy looking individual in a greasy flying suit approached, opened a locker and started getting out of his flying suit. He was a good deal older than us, probably in his early forties, stood about five ten, had a strong jaw, a thin black mustache and a day old beard. He was wearing no rank. "Hi Mac!" I greeted, "Are you flying in this stupid air show too?"

He smiled, amiably and said, "No, I just flew in to watch. Are you the fighter boys I came here to see?"

"That's right," I replied, "and it's just about time for us to get started!"

"Good luck!" he said, and Thunderbolt pilot and I walked off. Strangely, Thunderbolt pilot seemed to be walking at attention.

"Geez!" he said to me out of the corner of his mouth, "Didn't you know who that was?"

"No," I replied, nonchalantly, "He's just another pilot, isn't he?"

"Christ, no! Not *just* another pilot. That's General Bill Kepner, Commander of the whole VIII Fighter Command! He's our boss!"

I went into shock. "Good God!" I moaned, "and I called him 'Mac.' Let's get the hell out of here before he gets my name and outfit!"

"Don't worry about him," smiled Thunderbolt, "He's a great guy. He probably got a big kick outa' you."

Outside of operations, we found the little Mustang pilot waiting for us in a Jeep. "Let's use 'C' channel," he said, "In case I want to talk to you guys, okay?"

"Okay!" said I and Thunderbolt pilot in unison as we climbed into the Jeep. Shortly, we were out where our three ships were parked on the hardstands about a quarter of a mile from the tower. The ground crews had checked them over thoroughly and topped off the gas tanks. We dropped off the Thunderbolt pilot at his ship and he winked at me again as he got out of the Jeep.

"Cheers," he said, and walked over to his ship. We pulled over to the next hardstand where the little fellow's Mustang was parked. He got out.

"Let's keep a real tight formation when we climb outa' here, then loosen it up when we go down on the deck, okay?"

"Okay!" I said, and the Jeep driver put his machine in gear and took me over to where my Lightning was crouched. The crew chief, a staff sergeant, met me. "All set?" I asked.

"Yes sir. She's a fine ship. I sure hope you fellows can buck up these air crews. Their morale isn't so hot right now."

"We'll do what we can," I said. "But to tell you the truth, Sergeant, my morale isn't so hot either." His jaw dropped and I am sure he expected a pep talk from me, but he helped me into the cockpit and into my parachute harness and shortly I was turning the engines over. I turned the radio to channel C.

Mustand pilot was already jabbering, "Got the tower okay for takeoff. Let's go boys." He pulled his Mustang out of his hardstand and taxiied in front of me, whereupon I pulled out and followed him down the taxi strip. Thunderbolt pulled out behind me. At the end of the runway, we stopped to run up our engines and check the magnetos. My engines checked out fine and apparently the others did too. We pulled out onto the runway and started our takeoff roll in formation. We were soon airborne with our wheels coming up immediately. Suddenly Mustang "fruitcake" peeled up in a tight left turn, almost driving the Thunderbolt into the ground. Thunderbolt had to slide under the Mustang and came up on my left wing. Now we were in echelon. *It's going to be a long afternoon,* I thought.

After several hundred feet of climbing, Thunderbolt slid into position on Mustang's left wing. At 5,000 feet and east of the field, the radio came to life, "Okay boys, I'm going in!" It was Mustang pilot and he peeled off and pushed into a thirty degree dive, lined up on the runway from which we had just taken off.

One of the barracks at Steeple Morden, the 355th Fighter Group base in East Anglia. The cots weren't great, but when you were always tired it didn't seem to matter. *Alexander C. Sloan via Bob Kuhnert, 355th FG Assn.*

90

A wonderful sight—the Churchill Club adjacent to Westminster Abbey in London meant some companionship and a welcome for Yanks away from home. *Mark H. Brown/USAFA*

Usually the only way to London, or any other distant destination from East Anglia, was by train. Here a train pulls into the station at Royston. *Alexander C. Sloan via Bob Kuhnert, 355th FG Assn.*

VE Day (Victory in Europe), 1945. The village of Thetford in East Anglia is festooned with Union Jacks and bustling with celebration. In the center of Eighth Air Force activity during the war, Thetford was enjoyed by crews who would pass through and stop to soak up the history and hospitality. *Mark H. Brown/USAFA*

Thunderbolt followed him by about ten ship lengths and I rolled over at an identical spacing and followed Thunderbolt.

On the way down I could see the hundreds of air crew members on the ground, watching the show. I hoped they would enjoy it. Now Mustang was levelling off on the deck and went into his roll. Suddenly a huge flame blossomed out on the runway where Mustang had been and Thunderbolt pulled out of his dive.

"Jesus Christ!" I shouted to myself, "The silly bastard let the stick come back too soon!" I had levelled off now and the Thunderbolt pulled up on my right wing. As we circled the field, I could see fire trucks, Jeeps and a meat wagon race out to where the burning and smoking wreckage lay strewn on the runway. Meat wagon hell, I thought, they'll need a vacuum cleaner to pick the little guy up.

Suddenly the radio crackled. It was Thunderbolt pilot: "I don't believe it!" he cried, "What do we do now? Fool around up here, or what?"

I punched the mike button, "Piss on it!" I shouted, "I'm going home!"

"Sounds like a good idea," he replied, "Good luck!" and he peeled off and set a heading for his home field. I did the same.

All the way back I felt sorry, more for the air crews that needed some encouragement, than I did for the Mustang pilot. What a job we did for their morale. On the other hand, looking at it realistically, we reinforced their belief that not everyone survives this war. The experience brought back to me the words of an old RAF ditty:

A poor aviator lay dying,
At the end of a bright, summer day;
His comrades had gathered around him
To carry his pieces away.

The aircraft was stacked on his wishbone,
His machine gun was wrapped 'round his
    head;
A spark plug he wore on each elbow,
It was plain he'd quickly be dead.

He spit out a valve and some gaskets,
And stirred in the sump where he lay;
To mechanics who 'round him came
    sighing,
These are the brave words he did say.

"Take the magneto out of my stomach,
And the butterfly valve off my neck;
Tear from my liver the crankshaft,
There's a lot of good parts in this wreck.

"Take the manifold out of my left eye,
And the cylinders out of my brain;

Take the piston rods out of my kidneys,
And assemble the engine again."

Jan Houston Monaghan, *Red Cross girl, 55th Fighter Group*
In November 1944 Red Cross headquarters in London decided it was time to move Nelle [Huse] to another base where they needed a good director and to make me director at Wormingford. But when the men heard about it, they got up a petition with over 800 signatures requesting that Nelle stay at Wormingford. Headquarters gave in and I was delighted because we worked well as a team and I dreaded the thought of her leaving.

Later our teamwork prompted the commanding officer to come to us at the time he first learned the base was moving to Germany as part of the Airforce of Occupation. He asked us to accompany the base and wanted our reply before he made the official announcement to the men. Then he could say "And the Red Cross girls are coming along." We felt very honored to be recognized in that way and were happy to pack up the club and move to Kaufbeuren, Germany.

Chapter 5

Ground Crews

Robert T. Sand, *propeller shop, 55th Fighter Group*
The men who worked on the line consisted of everything from saints to knaves. They did share one thing in common: total dedication to their jobs and to the safety of the men who flew their airplanes. This means everyone from the line chief, who was a master sergeant, down to the privates. The mechanics were concerned that the engines could survive a 900 mile trip

The ground crew for Lt. William "Hank" Gruber services *Cooter* at Leiston, England, home of the 357th Fighter Group. *J. E. Frary*

94

Crew Chief T/Sgt. Roger Fraleigh and Sgt. Bob Sand on the line at
Wormingford, home of the 55th Fighter Group. *Robert T. Sand*

at peak performance. The radio men knew that communication during the long flights, and during combat, was a matter of life or death. Armorers, too, were very conscious of the fact that all machine guns must work smoothly, bomb racks must release belly tanks or bombs when commanded, or the plane would be greatly handicapped in combat. During those years up to the end of the war, I never knew a man who didn't do his best.

Whenever there was any kind of crash, or a plane failed to return from a mission, the crew of that plane was in a state of great apprehension until proven that no maintenance fault was the cause. The propeller department was even more concerned because it worked on every plane in the squadron. Not only the fighter planes, but the training planes and the officers' own "air taxis."

When we could, we watched every plane take off, and when possible watched them land. This was particularly so when combat missions were involved. At the end of a mission we anxiously awaited the reports from the crew chiefs all down the line, hoping for a clear report.

We still remember the anxiety we felt regarding the [P-38's] Curtiss-Electric constant speed propeller. It was a clever design but prone to troubles. On some planes the carbon brushes that carried the circuits from the static engine to the rotating propeller wore out excessively fast or sometimes snapped off. Sometimes electrical relays failed, or points would carbon up, or fuse together. An

The right engine on this 55th Fighter Group P-38 has just stopped turning at Wormingford. During a massive dogfight with German fighters, the Lightning had a mid-air collision with another of the unit's fighters, which did not come home. The left engine is feathered and the ground crew are clearly astonished at what they see. *Robert T. Sand*

96

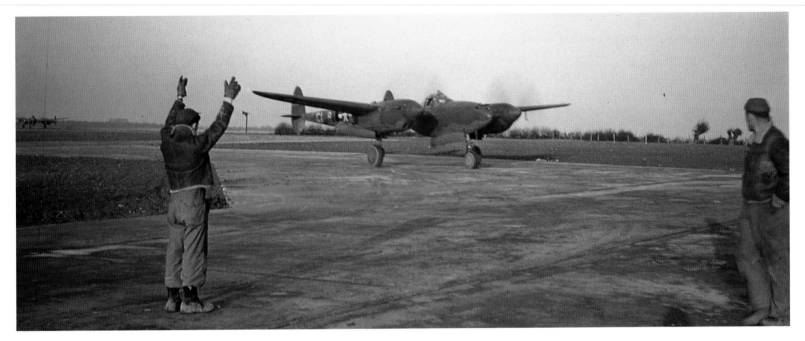

Nuthampstead, 27 December 1943. T/Sgt. Roger Fraleigh spots his P–38, flown by Lt. Ernest Marcy, as fellow ground crew member Nick Lippucci looks on. *Robert T. Sand*

Bonds between ground crew and pilot became very strong in spite of the distinct divisions the Army made between enlisted men and officers. Crew Chief Sgt. Don Allen and pilot Lt. Marvin Arthur, 4th Fighter Group, stand in front of their *Davey Lee,* named after Arthur's son. Allen had crewed the Mustang during Clarence Boretsky's entire tour, when it was named *Meg,* then repainted the nose art for Arthur and stayed on as crew chief. Ground crews came to have an uncanny ability for keeping their aircraft in top shape. *Donald E. Allen*

When major inspections were due, the maintenance hangar crew became involved in the process with the regular ground crew. The Mustangs of the 4th Fighter Group, as with most Eighth Air Force units, were exceptionally well cared for. Here Don Allen shares a moment with hangar crew mechanic Chuck Bowen. Don is wearing the highly prized sheepskin jacket which fighter pilots found impossible to wear in the confines of the P-51's cockpit. *Donald E. Allen*

improper connection could cause one propeller to increase pitch and the other to decrease pitch. Even worse it was possible that one prop could feather up entirely—or if an engine failed and needed the prop feathered but failed to work, could cause that prop to windmill causing a great drag on that side of the airplane, with disastrous results.

The fact that we had Harold Melby, one of the best prop men in the Army Air Force, to head up our department accounts for the fact that as far as we know, our planes had no accidents due to prop failure. He would frequently have us review every wiring connection, every adjustment to bell-crank control, all governor and relay tolerances over and over so they

would be indelibly fixed in our minds. Then he would test us, and boy! We'd better get it right! We didn't resent this discipline as we were well aware of what a critical difference it could make.

Eventually we could pat ourselves on the back because both the Curtiss-Electric and the Hamilton Standard propeller reps who called on

Don Allen (right) and his best buddy in the service, Jerry Byrge, served as crew for *Blondie,* Marvin Arthur's new Mustang that replaced *Davey Lee.* Allen's talent for nose art is more than evident here. He was responsible for most of the outstanding nose art in the 4th Fighter Group's 334th Fighter Squadron. *Donald E. Allen*

us from time to time told us we were the best prop crew in the UK, and that they didn't call on us to teach us anything, but to learn from us. *That* was our best medal! Of course, they may have told that to *all* the girls. We took it at face value, though.

Kermit Riem, our second in charge, was also a meticulous and sharp trouble-shooter. He could easily have headed up his own department, but as it was he made an ideal fellow crew member. Aside from that, he helped our morale with his cheerful nature and sense of humor. Why shouldn't he? He had a great gal back home whom he married before going overseas. Harold found his bride in England and was married there. Both couples are still dancing up a storm every week!

Arthur L. Thorsen, *P-38 pilot, 55th Fighter Group*
When I got out on the line, I found Sergeant Harmon tracing down a hydraulic leak that my aircraft had

Lt. Col. Everett W. Stewart helps a passenger strap into the 4th Fighter Group's first two-seater Mustang at Debden. This war-weary P-51B, converted by T/Sgt. Woody Jensen, carried all three squadron colors on the rudder and WD-2 on the side. It was a huge success with ground crew, not to mention girlfriends smuggled in by pilots who wanted to make the ultimate impression. *Edward B. Richie*

developed. While he was busy at that task, I put in a little more cockpit time to refresh my memory on the location of all switches and instruments. It might seem strange that after more than 230 hours in the aircraft, I would still have to familiarize myself with what made it go [but] when you're spending hours, weaving over the bombers, you can't pass the time examining your cockpit setup. I was a slow study to begin with and felt pretty lucky I knew where all the instruments were and how to use them.

Every time I caught Sergeant Harmon's eye, he seemed to be grinning. Once he said, "Found a shell hole in your right, rear boom the other day, Lieutenant. It's patched up now." I crawled out of the airplane and went back to inspect the repair job, feeling a slight flutter under my breast bone. "Want me to fix you up with another rear view mirror?" he asked.

"What's that supposed to mean?" I grinned, sheepishly.

"Just that someone must have snuck up on you while you had your head up your can."

I appreciated the high level of respect that my fatherly crew chief had for young officers and after receiving a brief lecture on how to care for "his" airplane, I was allowed to pedal my bicycle back to the barracks area.

Robert T. Sand, *P-51 ground crew, 55th Fighter Group*
Have rather enjoyed the change in jobs since being put on a [P-51] crew. The hours of work are slightly longer, but I can see where the prop man has the most work, which is a revelation to me, after all of the ribbing we have always taken. I can see now that the ribbing was a defensive mechanism. And as to deserving ratings, I am more sure than ever that myself and Stivason were

Debden sported one of the most colorful Mustangs flying when the 335th Squadron's converted, war-weary two-seater P-51B was painted the same overall red carried on the group's aircraft noses. Though it was technically an OTU (operational training unit) aircraft used for pilot familiarization, it saw more use giving rides to ground crews who deserved a taste of what they had worked so hard to keep flying. *Edward B. Richie*

treated unjustly by denying us our authorized ratings of staff sergeant and buck sergeant respectively when we had P–38s.

The ratings were given to other departments in which they were not authorized. Now, however, with single engine ships, we have more ratings than would ordinarily be allowed, so chances are even less of getting anywhere. It isn't the money so much, but the fact that I still pull all the details of a raw recruit while all of my old buddies have long ago graduated from that realm.

Jack Monaghan, *maintenance supply, 55th Fighter Group*

Just before D-day everybody on the base was a painter—officers, enlisted men. Everybody from top to bottom was out on the line painting black and white stripes on the wings and bodies of all the planes so they could be identified by our troops as they were landing on D-day. In the process everything was shut down. Nobody could get on or off the base.

Unfortunately there were some girls from neighboring farms who had

Damn great Merlin out front . . . that's how most Mustang pilots felt about the Packard-built Rolls-Royce engine that pulled them into combat. Lt. Robert E. Woody's 355th Fighter Group P–51B, *Woody's Maytag,* swallows up crew chief Bill Gertzen during some routine maintenance at Steeple Morden. *Alexander C. Sloan via Bob Kuhnert, 355th FG Assn.*

lost cows on the base. They—and their cows—were put in quarantine and could not go home. The next thing we knew there were a bunch of farmers storming onto the base to see the commanding officer, demanding their daughters be allowed to go home. They were quickly put in quarantine also. They finally quieted down enough to listen to what was happening. The day they had been waiting for all the years was finally here. When they registered what was going on, they stayed put.

It so happened that same night a heavy fog rolled in and our group found they were painting not only our own planes but those of two or three British squadrons that had found their own bases closed in the fog and ours was the only place they could land. I don't know how long or how many planes we painted but we had our own outfit—the 38th, 338th and 343rd—plus two or three squadrons of British bombers and some night fighters. Everybody was tired but glad the invasion was at last starting.

Every now and then as we painted, we would stop because we could hear the buzz bombs chugging straight down the middle of the runways and we waited to see what would happen. Buzz bomb engines might cut out and they might go a mile or two or they might stop dead and come straight in. We never knew. Everyone would stop painting while the buzz bomb chugged over our field and went on. We never did know where some of them hit.

Robert T. Sand, *propeller shop 55th Fighter Group*

When P–38s were pioneering the long distance fighter sweeps, of course the kidneys didn't stop working on these many hours long flights, so Lockheed included a urinal dubbed a relief tube. This consisted of a stiff, cylindrical tube of black rubber, designed to fit the average pilot. From this a smaller flexible tube led to the underside trailing edge of the wing. There it exited into a little fairing with an opening of a couple of square inches facing away from the

Dawn seeps through the fog and into a 55th Fighter Group maintenance hangar at Wormingford, 19 May 1944. P–38s that have required major work during the night will be pulled out on the line by the Cletrac tug near the door. This amazing little tracked vehicle could pull just about anything through mud, snow and slime. *Robert T. Sand*

slipstream, hence causing a vacuum to evacuate the tube. Evidently the designer had not flight tested it.

After one of these grueling missions, a very tired pilot dragged himself out of the plane, saying to his crew chief, "Causey, can't you do something about this relief tube? I had to take a leak and it came back and soaked my pants and made a helluva mess!"

The pilot stalked wearily to the jeep, leaving the crew chief scratching his head. After giving it a good think, he went to the engineering shack, got a piece of sheet aluminum, some snips, a drill and some rivets. He then fashioned a sort of reverse scoop like half of a funnel, and attached it in place of the former tiny one. The new one was like four or five inches across at the large end facing to the rear.

"This should solve the problem," he mused, then forgot all about it.

When the pilot returned from the next mission, the crew chief raised the canopy and started releasing the pilot's harness, to be greeted with, "Causey, what in hell did you do to that relief tube? When I had to take a leak I got the damn thing within 6 inches of my peter, and Whap!, it popped right in, and when I finished I thought I'd *never* get it out again!"

So, we all made special trips to see this engineering marvel. We noted, though, that no other pilots requested this modification. The poor crew chief never did get a medal for innovation.

Arthur L. Thorsen, *P-38 pilot, 55th Fighter Group*

I landed at Wormingford and taxied to my hardstand where Sergeant Harmon and the rest of my crew waited for me. The ground crews are very special people. They watch you take off for a mission, then wait in the dispersal area for your return, greeting you with broad smiles of relief. All of the pilots are touched by this display of faithfulness and affection, and though few of them will comment on it, the warm feeling between pilot and crew is there, nevertheless.

When I shut down my engines and cut the switches, I began to tremble, first mildly, then growing in intensity. I was bathed in sweat and soon realized I was too weak to crawl out of the cockpit. Sergeant Harmon and Sergeant Shieny had to help me out of the cockpit, then off the wing of the aircraft and onto the waiting truck that would take me back to the 38th Squadron pilot's room. As the truck pulled away, Sergeant Hadsel, my armorer, noticing that the tape had been blown away from the muzzles of my guns, gave me a thumbs up sign. The ground crews delight in their

This is what close formation practice resulted in at times. M/Sgt. "Heine" Ziegler, A flight line chief, and crew chief T/Sgt. Richard Bock change the damaged rudder, Bob Sand helped replace the pro- peller on the other ship. Both Mustangs were lucky to make it back. *Robert T. Sand*

pilot's claims, because it's their ship and they're just as proud as if they squeezed the triggers themselves.

As the truck rumbled along, I wondered about my seizure of trembling. It must be some kind of delayed action. It was fear, of course, and that was the strange part of it all. It occurred to me that, while in the air and even in combat, I was not afraid, but as soon as I was safe on the ground, fear set in. I wondered if the others in the truck felt the same way now, but I didn't ask.

Jan Houston Monaghan, *Red Cross girl, 55th Fighter Group*
Every morning we took turns driving our little Hillman car around the line with coffee for the men who were "sweating out" the planes. Sometimes we had to pull off on the side as the planes taxied by before takeoff but usually they were long gone and the Red Cross coffee van provided a welcome break in the dreary waiting period. The hardest time for the men was when the planes were coming home and theirs was not among them. Ground crews became very possessive of their planes and pilots and never forgot them. Pilots, in return, never forgot their lives

The 56th Fighter Group Thunderbolts on the line at Boxted in late summer, 1944. Drop tanks have been spread around for use at the numerous hardstands and the aircraft are slowly coming back up to operational status for the next mission. *Mark H. Brown/USAFA*

depended on the careful maintenance of their planes by their crews.

When the winter winds whistled across the airfield, Nelle and I found our slacks and jackets weren't very warm. Feeling sorry for the shivering Red Cross girls, the men at Air Corps Supply issued us leather fleece-lined flying suits and boots that were no longer being worn by the pilots since P-51s replaced the P-38s. We resembled funny brown bears as we plodded around but were we warm!

Our coffee van was always received with smiles and the question, "How's the coffee?" and sometimes I would have to admit, "It tastes like the shavings from the pencil sharpener but you can warm your hands on the cup."

Robert T. Sand, *P-51 ground crew, 55th Fighter Group*

Ground personnel were gleeful targets for playful pilots, and more than once I hit the sod or dove off my bike as a P-51 streaked down the perimeter track at close to 400 mph with prop tips only about a foot above the asphalt. I remember once as we got up and were dusting ourselves off, someone said, "Good God, did you notice we were looking down on *top* of his wing!" Another time I was on my bike in an exposed area on the perimeter when I saw this guy coming in a long power dive. I thought it was for scaring hell out of me, but he apparently didn't have that in mind as he passed at a respectable distance. Strange, but those buzz jobs remain among my fondest memories of those days. It was pure envy!

Jack Monaghan, *maintenance supply, 55th Fighter Group*

Two fellows called Younger and Rampke were old buddies from way

A 62nd Squadron, 56th Fighter Group P-47D is getting a thorough going over before its next mission over enemy territory. All eight machine guns have been removed for servicing and ammo sits ready to be loaded from the wooden boxes in front of each wing and the fuel truck is running. Soon the drop tanks will be hung and the fighter will be ready. *Mark H. Brown/USAFA*

With drop-tank crates spread across the field at Honington, 364th Fighter Group ground crew bring their P-51Ds back to operational status. The enlisted men who kept the Eighth Air Force's fighters airworthy rarely got a full-night's sleep. Up long before the pilots, they would make sure their assigned aircraft were loaded and run-up. After group takeoff they supposedly had some time to sleep, but nervous worry about their pilots and aircraft would make them "sweat out" the mission and pace the field until the first sight of returning fighters. After the mission the aircraft required extensive attention, often late into the night when the entire cycle started again. *Mark H. Brown/USAFA*

back. They had gone into the service together and always went to town together. One night they were out on the town and when they returned to the base, Rampke was stopped by the MPs. He gave them some lip and was promptly arrested and thrown in the brig.

As it so happened, Younger was slow getting out of the truck and Rampke was gone by the time he got there. When he learned what had happened to Rampke, Younger promptly went to the squadron area and got on the phone. He called the MPs. A Captain was on duty that night, and he said to them, "You have a man there by the name of Sergeant Rampke. I want him out of the Brig now. This is Colonel Younger on the base and I want him released immediately."

The MPs had no idea who Colonel Younger was, they'd never heard of him but they released Rampke anyhow because a colonel had told them to.

From that day on T/Sgt. Ralph Younger was called The Colonel.

Robert E. Kuhnert, *radio line chief, 355th Fighter Group*

As radio maintenance line chief, it was my responsibility to see that the communications equipment (VHF radio, SCR-522) was operable in all

Crew chief S/Sgt. Don Allen sits on the wing of Lt. Clarence L. Boretsky's 4th Fighter Group P-51D *Meg*. Metal drop tanks have been placed on the ground, ready for installation. As Allen recalled, "There were a few sandbag revetments for parking the 'kites' at Debden but most sat out in the open, some on concrete pads, others on the interlocked metal sheeting. Metal drop tanks were usually ready to go, complete with two little glass elbows on each to provide the 'breakaway' when released from the bomb rack." *Donald E. Allen*

squadron airplanes. Our technicians worked long hours, cold nights to keep the equipment operable.

Major Claiborne H. Kinnard came to us as 354th Fighter Squadron CO in late 1943 (from the 356th FG). He had problems with his ears, as later confirmed by our squadron flight surgeon, Dr. R. A. Fontenot. Kinnard was grounded for a short time because of it.

On many missions Major Kinnard returned complaining that he could not hear. My communications officer, Lt. Stan Clark, twisted the field phone immediately after mission de-briefing to ask what was wrong with Major Kinnard's airplane. A check-out immediately after the plane landed usually revealed a perfectly working radio. My reply to my boss was, "Nothing wrong, sir; his radio works fine."

After several such complaints, followed by the same response from me—which was not being accepted by Major Kinnard, nor by a frustrated Lieutenant Clark—I was finally given a stern order: "Find something wrong with it and fix it!"

Needless to say, there was much activity in an attempt to find something wrong and fix it. We tried many different receivers, resulting in no apparent difference. We checked wiring harness bundles, changed dynamotors (radio power supply), strung a new co-ax cable from radio set to antenna. We even added a

Capt. Jerry H. Ayers, 55th Fighter Group, has just landed at Nuthampstead in the early evening of 29 November 1943 after getting his first kill. Crew Chief T/Sgt. Ralph Sexton (left) and assistant Sgt. "Irish" O'Flaherty are intent on hearing the full story upon climbing up onto the P–38 after shutdown. *Robert T. Sand*

The Mary N II gets washed down, scrubbed and scoured by its crew chief at Debden. Whatever it took, the ground crews did, not only to keep the aircraft running, but to keep them looking like polished race cars. Note the oil trail from the engine breather tube on the side of the cowling. This usually spread back across the fuselage, but the crewman has already cleaned it off to just short of the leading edge, most likely with high-octane fuel. Red tape has been placed over the .50 caliber machine gun muzzles after reloading. *Edward B. Richie*

second antenna (the IFF antenna) to the receiver, in case he was experiencing blocking by wing or tail.

Nothing changed; the radio worked fine but pilot Kinnard could not hear away from base. To satisfy the order handed down we turned to our "4th Echelon Shop," which performed heavy, internal maintenance on equipment which could not be done on the line. S/Sgt Warren Brainard and his workmates devised a solution. They added a separate tube, another stage of amplification, to a receiver, increasing audio power output to rival the "boom boxes" today's youth carry around.

Eureka! Problem solved! Major Kinnard can hear. We kept that one specially-modified receiver for him alone. When it needed maintenance it was removed from the airplane, checked, and returned to his airplane only. All other airplanes were maintained by a "black box" swap procedure from the supply of repaired radios on our shop shelf.

In my frustration to find a solution I mentally hatched a fiendish method which I threatened to employ.

Ground crew mix with pilots of the 55th Fighter Group after the unit's return from what turned out to be the Eighth Air Force's biggest mission of World War II, 24 December 1944. From left to right: M/Sgt. Robert Tudor (line chief), S/Sgt. Nick Lippucci, S/Sgt. Fred Rumley, T/Sgt. Roger Fraleigh (crew chief of CG-R behind), Cpl. Herb Heichelbech, Sgt. "Frog" Sheen, Lt. Bob Maloney, Maj. John D. Landers (38th Squadron CO) and S/Sgt. Francis O'Leary. Landers is clearly happy about the 38th scoring four of the Group's fifteen confirmed kills that day. *Robert T. Sand*

(I voiced the threat in very close circles, well away from the CO, else I might still be breaking rocks at Leavenworth.) My ingenious procedure would have been to connect a wire to the 300 volt output of the dynamotor, string it unnoticed into the cockpit, under the pilot's seat, and connect it to a fine wire circle in the pilot's relief tube. My medical hypothesis was that if he used the relief tube at altitude the resultant jolt would surely clear his ears. (I have had no confirmation of this procedure from the medical community.)

Happily for all concerned—especially a certain technical sergeant—the highly advanced experimental procedure was not needed: the problem was solved through a more orthodox and acceptable approach.

Jan Houston Monaghan, *Red Cross girl, 55th Fighter Group*

Since only the pilots flew on a fighter base, there were a lot of boring hours for the ground crews. We tried at the Red Cross Club to find different types of programs: concerts, lectures, dances, snooker and ping-pong tournaments to satisfy the varied interests of the men. Birthday parties each month for those with birthdays had the traditional ice cream and cake. Sometimes when we heard that an officer had a birthday, we would invite him to our Red Cross office for "afternoon tea" with special sandwiches and cake.

One day I said to Nelle [Huse], "Tomorrow is Colonel [Elwyn] Righetti's birthday. Let's invite him for a really nice tea."

"We have too much to do this week, Jan, we don't have time for that tomorrow," said Nelle. "We'll do something special for him next week."

I always wondered afterwards . . . if we'd invited him, would he have come? And if he had come, he wouldn't have flown that day. But he flew . . . on his birthday . . . and was shot down.

Arthur O. Beimdiek, *P-38 pilot, 14th Fighter Group*

I had much compassion for my crew chief and the others too. Stop and think about it. If their plane did not make it home, they never knew, for sure, whether it was their fault or the enemy's. After one raid, I was so full of holes I stopped at a base called Ferriana which was south of Constantine [in northern Algeria]. The rest of the flight went on home. When I didn't peel off with the others, they told me my crew chief sat on an ammunition box and cried like a baby. The others in the flight told him I sat down for emergency patching and would be along later. When I got back, he was waiting for me with a bottle he had been saving.

Jan Houston Monaghan, *Red Cross girl, 55th Fighter Group*

When the Red Cross snack bar was especially busy, we knew the mess that night must have been inedible. We spent many hours in the evening visiting with fellows in the snack bar, listening to their gripes, sharing their homesickness, admiring pictures of their girlfriends, wives, children, and rejoicing with them when they had good news from home.

Sometimes on dance nights or after weekend passes, fellows would show up three sheets to the wind from a few too many drinks. We quickly learned to laugh with the funny ones as we moved them to the door, to manipulate the argumentative ones and to maneuver with gentle persuasion the mean drunks. We rarely had a problem but if we did, we had plenty of willing helpers standing by.

Chapter 6

Nose Art

Robert T. Sand, *propeller shop, 55th Fighter Group*
During those first weeks at Nuthampstead I did a few "nose art"

jobs for some of the pilots. One was for Captain Joe Myers. He took me to his plane and described what he wanted.

"I want a skull, as gruesome as you can make it. Have blood dripping all over it, and, under the skull, written in blood, put 'Journey's End.'"

Propeller shop Sergeant Bob Sand did some five nose art paintings for 55th Fighter Group P-38s, including *Texas Ranger* for group CO Col. Jack S. Jenkins. Another pilot bellied the original plane in and the armament door was transferred to Jenkins' new Lightning, as is evident here due to the missing section of painted-on rope. "My main memory," recalls Sand, "is of working on this all night a couple of nights and of my boss' displeasure at my not showing up for work til 9 a.m." *Robert T. Sand*

Capt. Joseph Myers' *Journey's End* of the 38th Squadron, 55th Fighter Group, painted by Sgt. Bob Sand. The crew stands in front of the Lightning, 18 November 1943; left to right: Nick Lippucci, armorer K. P. Bartozeck, crew chief J. D. "Dee Dee" Durnin, assistant crew chief Fred Rumley (known as a most persuasive philosopher on *any* subject). *Robert T. Sand*

112

I was appalled, but I was also awed by the fact that he was one of the most admired and daring of our pilots, and also by those bright and shiny captain's bars.

I stammered that I thought the idea was much too gory.

"Well, you can leave off the blood on the skull, but will you write 'Journey's End' in blood?"

The talent was doubtful, and I didn't have the proper colors for the job, but, of course, I said I would try.

One day, from across the dispersal area, I looked up to see a P–38 wallowing in a stall only about fifty feet off the ground. It dropped from my sight and a big cloud of what I first thought to be smoke, but turned out to be dust, appeared.

Later, when I was free to go to the scene, I entered the area with my camera. It was chaos. The '38 had come down, colliding with a fuel tanker truck, turning it over on its back, bounced into at least one parked P-38, perhaps two, and came to rest upside down, partly on one of the P-38s. 150 octane gasoline had poured in a fast-spreading lake over the entire area. The pilot was hanging by his harness, stunned and unable to free himself. Men from the line ran in across the gasoline-soaked ground. One shut off switches and disconnected the battery, as some motors were still sparking. At least two men opened the canopy, and, taking the weight of the pilot on their shoulders, unsnapped the harness and eased him to the ground. Observing first aid procedures as well as possible, but expecting the gasoline to go up any second, they dragged or carried him beyond the danger area and laid him on a blanket.

According to angry crew members who had been on the scene, and who told me this part of the story, the rescuers were not commended for their deed, but actually "chewed out" by the doctor for moving an injured man. This in spite of the fact that they, and all of us, had taken first aid

Skylark IV was painted on Maj. Mark W. Shipman's Lightning by Bob Sand. Yet to be added was one Italian fascist symbol from a kill during Shipman's tour with the 48th Fighter Squadron in North Africa. Standing to the left is armorer Sergeant Westman, with crew chief T/Sgt. "Fox" Nelson, 18 November 1943. *Robert T. Sand*

Capt. Jerry H. Ayers stands with his crew in front of *Mountain Ayers,* one of Bob Sand's favorite creations. "This was a labor of love, partly because I, like everyone else, had great respect and admiration for Capt. Ayers. He was a real, and unassuming, gentleman. He was so appreciative, which was not usually the case with others. These quite crude efforts were done on very cold nights, with runny paints, usually not being completed until four or five a.m., and a full work day before and after at the regular job, and without pay, out of respect for the men who were putting their lives on the line. So, a 'thank you' was like a pat on the head to a puppy. It made one glow! The enlisted men were saddened by Capt. Ayers' ear problems, which restricted his flying career. In our estimation he was an extremely talented pilot. The old mountaineer, by the way, outlasted all the other insignias. We figured that he had at least 150 missions over enemy territory, some sort of record." *Robert T. Sand*

Nooky Booky IV was flown by 357th Fighter Group ace Leonard K. "Kit" Carson. Unable to get into Leiston due to poor weather, several of the unit's P-51s landed at Wormingford on Christmas Day 1944 after escorting bombers over Germany. *Robert T. Sand*

115

Originally the mount of 357th Fighter Group pilot Arval J. Roberson, *Passion Wagon* was passed on to Charles E. Weaver, then given to yet another pilot. The early morning frost, 26 December 1944, has retained the chill of the cold Christmas holiday missions flown by the Eighth Air Force. Ground crew would shortly be trying to get the Mustangs ready to head back to Leiston from Wormingford. Bob Sand had to help: "My memory is of washing down iced wings and tail surfaces with rags and gallons of ethylene glycol, and frozen bare hands." *Robert T. Sand*

courses, and knew the risk. There just was no choice. They deserved a medal.

The pilot had a sore neck and back for a while, then returned to flying duty. He expressed his gratitude to his rescuers, whose names I once knew, but have forgotten. It would be nice to find that this young man had survived the war, was still alive, and could tell us this story himself.

So, coming upon the crash scene just described, what do I see in the middle of all this carnage, and the cause of all this mess, but Joe Myers' plane, *Journey's End*. Here was this badly damaged plane upside down and partially supported by another P-38. Its twin tails pointed crazily to the sky—and plainly, upside down, on its nose, the perfect title for this scene, "Journey's End."

It made such a fantastic subject that I lined it up in the viewfinder of my little Kodak Pony and prepared to snap the picture of a lifetime. Then an alarm buzzer went off in my head. "Whoa! You may get into trouble here. There may be a security violation you don't even know about."

So, regretfully, I lowered the camera and the scene went un-recorded.

James R. Hanson, *P-51 pilot, 339th Fighter Group*

As we fly on towards France I find myself humming the music from Ravel's "Bolero" to the steady throb of my beautiful Rolls-Royce engine. The music seems to fit right in with the smooth throb of the engine which is like drums in the background. The ever increasing tempo and volume of the music matches my increasing tension as we approach the enemy coast. The music builds and gets faster until finally it seems to spin wildly and

crash into silence. Just as we've crossed inland several bursts of flak break the spell and I'm back to reality. I have the name for my plane now, *Bolero*.

Robert T. Sand, *Propeller shop, 55th Fighter Group*

One time I had the ignominy of watching a P-38 belly in which had one of my nose art jobs painted on its armament door. This was *Texas Ranger* made for Col. Jack S. Jenkins. Colonel Jenkins allowed a friend to borrow the plane, and he bellied it in at another field. The armament door was retrieved and installed on Colonel Jenkins' new P-38 with the missing parts of the lariat smudged in hastily by someone else. This plane came to a bad end too, and may have been the one I saw belly in. It seems there was a third plane this happened to. I found that armament door in a stack of

Charles W. Reed flew *Princess Pat* with the 63rd Fighter Squadron, 56th Fighter Group. In the background another group P-47 still carries the white nose marking which adorned all Eighth AF fighters until various colors were chosen to differentiate groups from each other. *Alexander C. Sloan via Bob Kuhnert, 355th FG Assn.*

When Lt. Marvin Arthur had crew chief S/Sgt. Don Allen paint the nose art on his new aircraft, he wanted it named after his wife, Blondie. Here Don admires his vision of loveliness and, as he recalls, *Blondie* "was the name of his wife, but the painting was strictly from my imagination—sexy, but covered. It appears I got a new sheepskin jacket to go with the new plane. It seemed we only discarded this garb for about six weeks in mid-summer. It felt good to be warm when the pesky wind was always blowing." *Donald E. Allen*

scrap aluminum, undamaged, but disgraced. I'm sure it was bad for Colonel Jenkins' morale, and it didn't do mine any good either.

Much later, when P-38s were being retired and replaced by P-51s, I felt exonerated when a P-38 carrying my whimsy of nose art *Mountain Ayers* was cited for having made at least 150 missions over enemy territory, which was considered to be a sort of record, at least in our outfit.

This was made for Capt. Jerry H. Ayers. When he left the plane, others flew with his logo.

Well, at least the good and the bad neutralized each other!

Capt. Jim Duffy greets the 354th Fighter Squadron mascot bulldog "Yank" shortly after landing at Steeple Morden in his *Dragon Wagon*. According to Bob Kuhnert, the well-bred English canine, whose sire was owned by Winston Churchill, was bought at a dog show in Duxford by Buck Wrightam, Harold Berg and I. C. Myers. Buck decreed he would be the squadron mascot, suggesting all personnel be called "The Bulldogs." Squadron CO Claiborne Kinnard liked the idea, put the existing unit bulldog logo in a circle and placed "The Bulldogs" across the Statue of Liberty in the background, thus creating the definitive 354th Squadron patch issued to the troops. "Bulldogs" was painted above the exhaust stacks on many of the unit's P-51s. After the war Myers brought Yank home in his duffle bag. Yank was sedated before the trip to avoid alerting inspectors. They made it safely to Camp Shanks, then home to Seymour, Missouri. *USAF/NASM*

118

Ted Lines' first *Thunder Bird,* a P-51B, gets the nose art treatment. The motif was natural for the 4th Fighter Group pilot because he came from Mesa, Arizona, with its rich American Indian heritage. *Edward B. Richie*

Though this nose art did not belong to his P–38, Lt. Alvan DeForge is clearly delighted to stand next to it on the 82nd Fighter Group line at Foggia, Italy. *Walter E. Zurney*

The nose art on Lt. Albert P. Knafelz' 62nd Fighter Squadron, 56th Fighter Group P-47D was fanciful and poignant at the same time— *Staglag Luft III . . . I Wanted Wings. Mark H. Brown/USAFA*

Lt. Arthur R. Bowers in the cockpit of his P-51D *Sweet Arlene.* Don Allen painted the nose art from a snapshot of Bowers' wife. *Donald E. Allen*

Col. Dave Schilling, commander of the 56th Fighter Group, taxies out for a mission in his camouflaged P-47D, which bears the "Li'l Abner" comic strip character "Hairless Joe." The 56th had several Thunder-bolts adorned with Al Capp's creations, each done in impeccably faithful style to the originals. *Mark H. Brown/USAFA*

Leland P. "Tommy" Molland's 308th Fighter Squadron Spitfire Mk. VIII *Fargo Express* in Italy, January 1944. The single white swastika denotes a confirmed kill while the black swastikas stood for probables. By the time Molland ended his tour, he had a total of 11 confirmed kills—four in Spitfires, seven in Mustangs. *William J. Skinner*

withdraw, we would indirectly aid the bombers by preventing attack after we would normally leave. There is no set thumb rule as to how far you can leave the bombers because the tactics and the strategy of the situation are mentally weighed and thought out on the scene of the engagement and can never be predicted prior to a mission. . . .

Being on the offensive all of the time and attacking, although more than normal risk is involved, will give a Group higher scores and lower losses in any engagement, because aggressiveness on our part shakes the enemy to such a degree that he becomes excited and discouraged.

Mark E. Hubbard, *P-38 pilot, 20th Fighter Group*

Under no circumstances should there be less than two airplanes working together as one man cannot

Contrails in the sky above Wormingford on 11 December 1944. *Robert T. Sand*

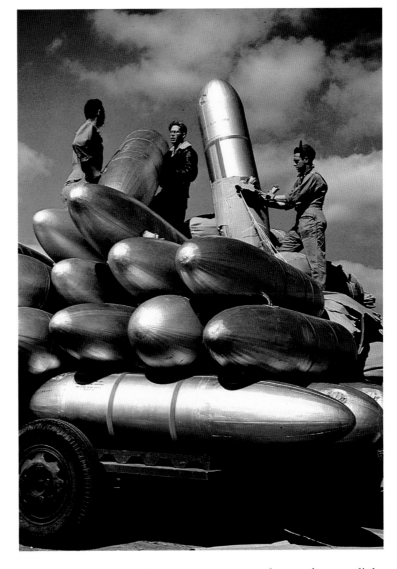

Compared to their metal counterparts, paper drop tanks were light and easy to handle; just climb up the stack and toss them down. Unloading this batch are, left to right, S/Sgt. Robert G. Keich, Cpl. Howard Middlemas and Sgt. Michael H. Moran. *USAF/NASM*

protect his own tail, and 90% of all fighters shot down never saw the guy who hit them.

Walker M. Mahurin, *P-47 pilot, 56th Fighter Group*

In my opinion aerial combat isn't half of what it is shown to be in the movies. Most of us have some sort of an idea formed in our heads when we finally get into a combat theater. We like to think that the battle will assume proportions equal to those of the movies. You know how it is—one pilot sees the other, they both grit their teeth to beat hell, and finally the deadly combat begins with violent maneuvering by both parties. This field of thought is entirely erroneous. The combat usually takes place at a hell of a speed; the enemy plane is only seen for a few seconds. In nine cases out of ten the victor never sees his victim crash. As a result of the wrong idea, the new pilot first sees a Jerry ship, goes in to attack hell bent for election, and winds up feeling futile as the dickens. [I know] because I've done it myself many times. In fact, I've blown some darned good chances by just that sort of attack.

The conclusion I draw from this is that no combat is worthwhile unless the attacking pilot does his work in a very cool and calculating way. I don't do it that way myself, but I think that if I have got things pretty well figured out before I make a bounce, I stand a much better chance of bagging that guy I'm going down after. The cardinal points in an attack are first, be sure of your own position. See that

Mission planning in the operations hut. No one really liked to spend the long hours necessary, but it was absolutely vital to getting the job done. *USAF/NASM*

there are no Jerries around to make an attack on you. Secondly, make sure that you know what the Hun is doing. Try to figure out what you would do if you were in his position. Third, try to get up sun on him. This is extremely important, because once the element of surprise is lost the Jerry is about ten times as difficult to bring down. Even if he is not surprised, he still can't see into the sun—so the chances of getting to him before he can make a turn are pretty darned good. Last, close right up his old rudder and let go. Then he'll be a dead Hun. Now, these are what I consider to be the most important points of combat, even though I don't [always] practice them myself, at least I try to.

Before I ever saw a Jerry, I used to spend hours just sitting in the old sack thinking up just exactly what I would do if the Jerry were in such and such a position, and what I would do if he were doing something else. I think that it all paid in the long run. A couple of times I have been fortunate in running into just the situation I had dreamed of at one time or another. Then, I didn't have to think. I just acted, because I had mentally been in that very position before. I believe it helped. At least I would advocate it. I

Taxiing past the drop tank farm at Boxted, this 56th Fighter Group P–47D is ready to head for Germany as its crew chief looks on. *Mark H. Brown/USAFA*

129

still do it, and I hope that I run into a couple more of the dream castles, because it pays big dividends. At the same time, I don't always imagine what I would do if I were making the attack. I have it all figured out, also, when the Hun is on my tail. It can

happen anytime and sometimes has. I know that I don't consider the dreaming time wasted. It's a lot of fun, too.

In regard to looking behind and around, I realize that it is a subject that has been harped on by every guy

that has ever spent one measly hour on a combat operation. It is an absolute necessity. The result is most obvious. The Hun will never bag an American fighter if the Yank sees him coming in time to take proper evasive action. It is still a bad thing to spend

The 356th Fighter Group spread out and pulling contrails on long-range escort in early 1945. Tanks have not yet been dropped. *Herbert R. Rutland, Jr.*

Deep in Germany, 1945. A 356th Fighter Group P–51D on long-range escort has yet to drop its external tanks as pilots scan for enemy aircraft. *Herbert R. Rutland, Jr.*

130

all one's time looking behind. The idea behind fighter aircraft is that they will seek out the enemy and destroy him. A pilot will never accomplish this aim by looking behind him all the time. He must divide all his time to where it will do him the most good. If he knows that there are Huns above him, then, sure, look above and behind, but if he thinks the Hun is below him, then, for God's sake look in front and down. When you spot the Jerry go down and get him. Everyone knows about this subject so I think that I've said enough.

One thing that I believe should be stressed by all means is the reading of the mission reports of every group. Those daily summary reports that we get the next day after each mission are the most important of all the printed matter in our intelligence office. Both the bomber and fighter reports are good, because it is easy to see just what tactics the enemy has used against us. Also, it is easy to note just what changes have been made in previous days. I usually use this stuff to formulate some plan of attack that I would use if I were the German controller.

Sometimes it works. I know that I got my first victory from reading the mission reports turned in by Gene Roberts. On the day he first got a couple of Jerries, he put in the mission reports how the Jerry was lining up far out to the side and making head-on attacks on the bomber formation. Gene just happened to mention exactly how far away from the bombers the Jerries were. On August 17th [1943] I went out to the spot where Gene found his and I got two of them out there. Now, I'm a firm believer in the reports. So, I advocate

that all pilots read them. I kind of wish that accounts of the engagements were just a little more complete.

The next most important thing is the duty of all the positions in a squadron. I've been fortunate in that I have always been in a hitting position—leading a flight. I still think that it is the wingman who counts. I couldn't shoot down a thing if I were worrying about whether or not I had a wingman. He is the most important guy in the squadron. It is up to the wingman to cover his element leader no matter what. Sure, I know it's tough to sit back and tell a guy that he is clear behind so he can shoot down a Jerry. But look at it this way. Sooner or later the guy you're following around is going to be through with his tour. That'll leave a vacancy. The guy who will fill it will be the guy who has been giving the perfect job as a wingman. He will then get the chance to shoot, and probably will have profited by following a good shot around. Then, too, he will realize just what an important job the wingman has.

A good wingman is worth his weight in API [armor piercing incendiary ammunition]. So, for the wingmen, stick close to the man you fly with. Watch behind and let him look out in front. Fly well, and you will get to do all the shooting you want soon enough. I know I don't have to say a word about the leaders, because I've tried to beat all of them out of an attack from time to time, and it's almost impossible to get through the maze of Thunderbolts who have beaten me to the draw.

The last thing that I can stress is training. I think that my group probably does more training than any

other in the ETO. At least, it seems that way to me. I've been training ever since I got to the group and I imagine I'll continue to do so 'till the war is over. It really pays. Every worthwhile hour in the air is the most valuable thing I know of. After all, we are fighting for our lives. What's more, we are fighting for the most valuable thing in the world—Freedom. I think that these two things are well worth a little practice. Aerial camera gunnery is absolutely the most valuable training a man can get. Almost exactly like the real thing, only play with our own ships. Next in importance comes formation—both tactical and close. A good formation flyer will almost manufacture gasoline—something of which we don't have enough as it is. Third comes acrobatics, because a guy who knows what his airplane will do won't have to worry about how to make it do it when he could use the time shooting down a Hun. Fourth, anyone knows just how good a red-hot outfit looks when they take off and land. They really look good. This is all done by practice and don't think they don't feel proud of themselves when they do make good landings and take-offs. I know, because I'm in one of those red-hot outfits, and it makes me feel good as hell. The same old axiom applies:

"Anything worth doing is worth doing well."

Besides aerial camera work, I don't know of a thing that closely parallels shooting in combat. I certainly wish I did. My shooting is probably the worst in the whole Air Force. I know that most of us feel the same. Jerry Johnson is probably the best shot in the Air Force, but he

Capt. Robert Schmidt's *Tar Baby* cruises back home with the 356th Fighter Group after an escort mission. *Herbert R. Rutland, Jr.*

When pilots finished their tours and moved on, their aircraft were passed to successive pilots. Here Capt. Jack "Wild Bill" Crump flies the same aircraft Bob Schmidt named *Tar Baby*. Crump adorned the P-51 with a painting of his pet coyote, which flew several missions with him before being accidentally run over. *Herbert R. Rutland, Jr.*

Inbound to England from Germany, April 1945, 356th Fighter Group P-51Ds flown by Jack Crump, Nunzio B. Ceraolo and Don Jones are

viewed from Herb Rutland's position as No. 2 in the flight. *Herbert R. Rutland, Jr.*

won't tell me how he does it. I have to get close enough to the Hun to reach out and club him before I can hit him. Usually, even that won't work. But, boy if I knew how to practice shooting, I would spend all my waking hours at it. If we, and I speak of the Air Forces as a whole, could only shoot perfectly we would double our score with no effort at all. When the man does come forth who has invented a way of simulating combat, complete with shooting down the target, then we will win the air war hands down.

Hubert "Hub" Zemke, *P–47 pilot, 56th Fighter Group*

A fighter pilot must possess an inner urge to do combat. The will at all times to be offensive will develop into his own tactics. . . .

Learn to break at the proper time to make a head-on attack. The enemy doesn't like it. Don't run. That's just what he wants you to do. He can't help from getting right behind you if you are moving away. When caught by the enemy in large force the best policy is to fight like hell until you can decide what to do next.

V. K. Meroney, *P–47 pilot, 352nd Fighter Group*

When we get replacements, they know practically nothing of the many

Before the pilot can get out of his Mustang at Wormingford, 55th Fighter Group personnel climb up and gather around to hear what the Christmas Eve 1944 mission to Germany was like. From left to right, Sergeant Woods (assistant crew chief), Lieutenant Miller (engineering officer), Lieutenant Grimmer (communications officer), Master Sergeant Stone (flight chief) and, at bottom, Zuckerman (radio man). *Robert T. Sand*

133

things that go towards making a good fighter pilot. Their training, before we get them, is a headache in itself; what with all the safety precaution and all that they have back in the States. . . .

I believe the main things are . . . teamwork . . . confidence in your leaders, your ships, and that old fighting heart.

Kill the bastards!!!

John C. Meyer, *P-47 pilot, 352nd Fighter Group*

Showing a willingness to fight often discourages the Hun even when he outnumbers us, while on the other hand I have, by immediately breaking for the deck on other occasions, given the Hun a "shot in the arm," turning his half-hearted attack into an aggressive one.

I do not like the deck. This is especially true in the Pas-de-Calais area [in northern France]. I believe that it may be used effectively to avoid an area of numerically superior

E/A [enemy aircraft] because of the difficulty in seeing an aircraft on the deck from above. With all silver planes this excuse is even doubtful. The danger from small arms fire especially near the coast is great. I realize that I differ from some of my contemporaries in this respect, but two thirds of our Squadron losses have been from enemy small arms fire. . . . When an aircraft is below 8,000 feet over enemy territory, it [should] be just as low as possible. Twenty feet above the ground is too high. . . .

I am not a good shot. Few of us are. To make up for this I hold my fire until I have a shot of less than 20 degrees deflection and until I'm within 300 yards. Good discipline on this score can make up for a great deal.

Robert S. Johnson, *P-47 pilot, 56th Fighter Group*

A lot of green pilots fly good combat formation for the first, second or third mission. If they see no enemy,

many of them get cocky and think combat is a cinch. They relax and maybe get away with it several trips over enemy territory—then it happens. The first enemy they see or have contact with knocks them down, simply because they didn't see the enemy. They were too relaxed to kick the airplane rudders or roll the ship up on a wing and look behind and above them as well as straight ahead or at their leaders. It's much easier and better to come home tired with a sore neck from looking constantly in every direction and being tired from constantly skidding sideways to look behind and around you than it is to leave the thing you *sit on* over enemy territory. Once in a while it's good business to put a wing tip up just over the sun and look around it too. Often there is plenty of company there.

Never let a Jerry get his sights on you. No matter whether he is at 100 yards or 1,000 yards away, 20 mm will carry easily that far and will

Back from what turned out to be the biggest mission of the war, 24 December 1944, with 2,046 bombers and 853 fighters sent out against targets in western Germany, pilots of the 55th Fighter Group listen on the ramp at Wormingford as Lieutenant Koenig tries to describe what it was like. The no smoking near aircraft rule was routinely broken under the pressure of wartime flying. *Robert T. Sand*

A pilot and navigator, 94th Bomb Group, check their watches before takeoff. *Robert T. Sand*

easily knock down a plane at 1,000 yards. It is better to stay at 20,000 feet, than it is to pull up in his vicinity at a stalling speed. If he comes down on you pull up into him and 9 times out of 10, if you are nearly head-on with him he'll roll away to his right.

Then you have him. Roll on to his tail and go get him. If he tries to turn with you and can out turn you, pull the nose up straight ahead and kick rudder and stick toward him and you can slice to the inside of him. The enemy thinks then that you are turning inside him and tries to dive away and outrun your bullets!

Try this and any other trick you think of in friendly combat.

Anytime you lose your wing man or leader, you've lost 75% of your eyes and fighting strength. Jerries will

Field maintenance on the 94th Bomb Group's *Mighty Mike* at Bury St. Edmonds. Ground crews at bomber bases had a massive job in keeping aircraft combat ready, and much of the work was performed in the open at the assigned hardstand. Only the seriously damaged aircraft were pulled into the hangars. *Byron Trent*

shoot at anyone. Never think you're a favorite to them. Anyone can get it, some of the best have gotten it. So keep your eyes open.

Harry J. Dayhuff, *P-47 pilot, 78th Fighter Group*

If the Hun is right on your tail do something quick and violent. (As one of our pilots once said when the first he was aware of a Hun were the tracers going by his shoulder, "I put the stick in one corner and the rudder in the other. I don't know what happened but when I came out the Hun wasn't there any longer.")

If outnumbered, dive like hell (that is in a Thunderbolt—other fighter types may prefer other methods).

If the Hun is in shooting range always keep the ball going in each corner—never give him an opportunity to line up his sights. Remember this slows you up though. . . .

Most successful offensive actions come with superior speed and altitude coupled with surprise. Always use the sun or blind spots to obtain surprise.

Duane W. Beeson, *P-51 pilot, 4th Fighter Group*

I think the most important one thing to a fighter pilot is speed! The faster an aircraft is moving when he spots an enemy aircraft, the sooner he will be able to take the bounce and get to the Hun. And it's harder for him to bounce you if you are going fast. . . .

Never give the Hun an even break. If you have any advantage on him, keep it and use it. So, when attacking, I would say, plan to

overshoot him if possible; hold fire until within range, then shoot and clobber him down to the last instant before breaking away. It's sorta like sneaking up behind and hitting him with a baseball bat.

Official AAF History

It is difficult to escape the conclusion that the air battles did more to defeat the Luftwaffe than did the destruction of the aircraft factories.

Arthur L. Thorsen, *P-38 pilot, 55th Fighter Group*

The briefing room was large, but it was filled to capacity. All of the chairs were occupied and there were some small groups, standing. They must have gotten everyone up for this briefing, I thought. Someone said, "Don't tell me they're gonna' send us on a 'do' in this soup! I had to go on instruments just to walk over here!" This was greeted with good-natured, but weak laughter.

As the intelligence and weather officers gathered at the dais, I looked over the scores of pilots who were engrossed in animated chatter. It was easy, I thought, to tell the veterans from the beginners. You could recognize them by their eyes. Veterans' eyes were surrounded by wrinkled and sunburned flesh. They all appeared to be wearing tan bandits' masks. Below the eyes and where the oxygen masks covered the lower halves of their faces, the flesh was white. On the other hand, pilots fresh from the States had pink, unwrinkled faces. In the briefing room now, the veterans seemed to outnumber the beginners, but not by much.

I suddenly realized I was studying the faces of the men more intently with each briefing. It was as if I didn't know who was coming back again and wanted that one last look to remember them by. I shook myself, fighting a wave of depression. I hated being maudlin.

Maj. Todd Crowell of Headquarters Squadron, standing at the back of the room suddenly barked "Ten-hut!" and everyone came out of their chairs to stand at attention. Everyone that is, except Don Penn. He didn't know how. Shepard maintained that Penn really knew how to stand at attention, it was always his clothes that were 'at ease.' Now Colonel [Jack] Jenkins called out "At ease!" and stepped up on the dais.

The men relaxed, but did not sit down. Jenkins turned and faced them, studying the expressions on the faces of the pilots gathered there. Finally, he said, quietly, "Be seated, gentlemen." There was a shuffling of feet as the men resumed their seats. Jenkins turned, picked up a pointer and stepped to the red curtain covering the wall map. Quickly he drew the curtain aside and one could see the crimson ribbon stretching from our field at Nuthampstead to deep in Germany. There was a low, but audible mass intake of breath followed by a score or more of loose bowels. The target was Berlin!

Colonel Jenkins began speaking. "Your eyes aren't playing tricks on you gentlemen," he said, "The target is Berlin! Right in Hitler's back yard!" He tapped Berlin with the pointer and continued, "The weather is pretty foul, but I'm sure we can get through. We'll have full belly tanks, but we'll want to fly pretty lean all the way in, just to make sure. We're flying target support, so if we're engaged and have to dump tanks, we won't make rendezvous and that won't be too good for our 'Big Friends.'

"This is a maximum effort and fighters from all the other groups will be participating, either with us on target support, or escort on penetration or withdrawal. So look sharp! Most of the planes up there will be ours. Don't shoot any of them down!" A sprinkling of chuckles filled the room as Jenkins continued. "Takeoff will be at 0930 . . . rendezvous at 1200. Tom will give you the lowdown now on what you may expect."

Maj. Tom Welch, chief of the intelligence group, got to his feet and took the pointer from Jenkins. "Well, boys," he began, "this one's a doozy. If you don't get a little excitement out of this one, you're not really trying. Our intelligence reports are that the Jerries have moved more 88s into the Amsterdam area, so you'll get more

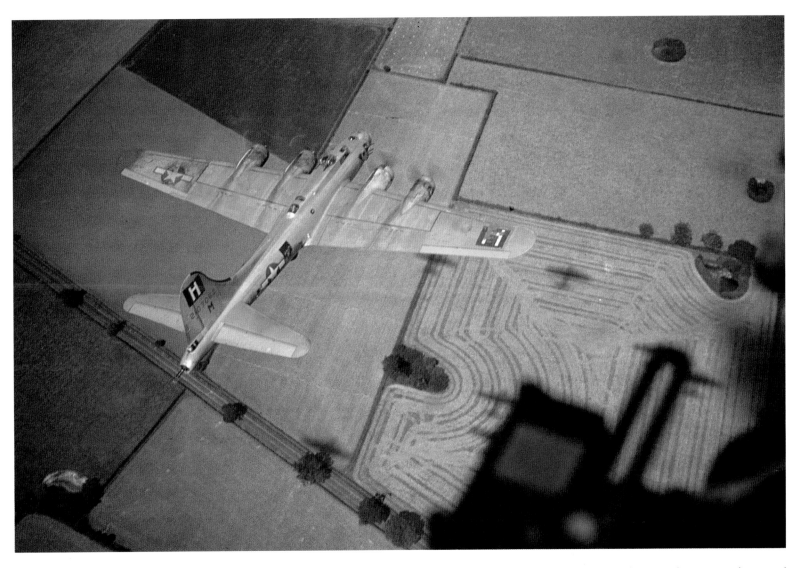

The lead B-17 of the 388th Bomb Group takes the formation home to Knettishall after attacking Brest, France, 26 August 1944. The "Big Friends" flew into the roughest of conditions and the wear and tear was evident on their aircraft. This Fort has a replacement wing panel from a camouflaged sister ship, deeply stained engine nacelles and flaking paint. *Mark H. Brown/USAFA*

than the usual amount of flak going in. It'll get heavier here at Hanover." He tapped both places with his pointer, "More at Stendal and everything including the toilet seat at Berlin itself. Going in, you'll probably encounter fighters here at Hanover." He tapped the spot with his pointer. "Look for them again at Oschersleben and Brunswick. Be sure to check out escape kits with your squadrons before you go. Any questions?"

"Yes sir!" A tall, gangly pilot from the 338th Squadron stood up. "What about some good news?" he asked.

"Certainly," replied Welch, "Spam sandwiches for all when you return! Good luck!" With that he handed the pointer to the Weather Officer and sat down. So did [the] gangly pilot from the 338th.

Jenkins again: "Gentlemen, as you can easily see outside, the weather stinks, so don't lose sight of the flights up ahead of you on takeoff, or we'll never form up. For more on the weather problem, here's our weather merchant."

There were scattered boos and hisses as the weather officer made his report.

"Visibility is down to a little more than a half mile," he said, "so you won't see the end of the runway. It should improve some when you come back. The stuff thins out at 18,000 feet and you should be in the clear by 20,000 feet. Temperature at 20,000, minus 52 degrees. The soup should taper off by the time you reach Osnabruck, with bright sunshine and unlimited visibility the rest of the way to the target. This is indeed an instrument mission, gentlemen, but I

138

see no icing conditions." He was given a round of boos as he sat down.

Colonel Jenkins came forward again. We synchronized watches and he said, "We'll form up at 5,000 feet before we head out. That's all gentlemen. Good luck!"

Taking off . . . was a bit hairy. One no sooner got his wheels up when the ground began to disappear in the fog. We began a slow, climbing turn to the left, forsaking the more colorful peel-up of clearer days. My eyes moved continuously between my instruments and Captain Wyche's ship, for I was flying his wing again. I could barely discern ships just ahead and those who took off first were swallowed up completely in the deadly mist. In school we were never taught to fly a tight formation in this stuff. It would have sent air safety officers screaming to their mistresses, for comfort.

The weather wrapped around us like a fuzzy cocoon. It was like flying through a bottle of milk. Soon we were at 5,000 feet. Then 10,000. I snapped on my oxygen mask. Berlin! Gay Berlin! Will we ever get there to dance the oom-pah-pah on the Reichstag? The radio was silent. Good discipline. If anyone was spinning in, he wasn't telling the others about it. Silence, save for the drone of the engines. They sounded good and I blessed my crew chief, Sergeant Harmon. I chanced a look through the windscreen. Nothing. We were in a ghostly purgatory waiting for something to happen.

How many hours will it take to fly through this stuff? How do we find the ground when we get back home? Drone, drone! The engines still sounded good. I wondered if others

were having mechanical difficulties. I looked at my altimeter, 24,000 feet! What did old Lieutenant Cold Front say? We'd be in the clear by 20,000 feet? How can you tell that by wetting your finger and sticking it out the window? 24,000 feet and the stuff was as thick as ever. The engines droned sweetly. If we didn't see land soon, they would put me to sleep. I looked at my wrist watch. 1055. We should be crossing in at The Hague now. Better brace yourself for a flak barrage, I told myself. But nothing happened. The minutes ticked by. It was 1130. No flak, no anything. We were flying in a void, detached from the world. I checked my altimeter. We had climbed to 30,000 feet and we were still in the soup. I felt a slight touch of vertigo. I shook myself and began to sing. It was another little RAF ditty I had picked up in some vile den.

The minstrels sing of an
English King, that lived many
years ago
He ruled his land with an iron
hand, but his mind was weak
and low.
He loved to hunt the royal stag
that roamed the royal wood,
But better he loved the pleasure
of—pulling his royal pud.
All hail the bastard king of
England.

It was a rather foul song, but it gave me comfort. Drone, drone! The engines were accompanying me. By the time I got to, "The Queen of Spain was a glamorous dame and an amorous dame was she," vertigo left me, so I abandoned the wretched song. I looked at my wristwatch. 1145. We should be making rendezvous soon, but what good would it do? You couldn't find your behind with both hands in this solid soup.

Suddenly we broke clear, into sunny unlimited visibility. It was like being thrown off a cliff. We popped out of the muck and there was a 30,000 foot drop to the ground below us. There were only a few P-38s in front of us and one behind. Where in hell did they all go? Then on my right and left, other P-38s popped into the clear and began assembling around us. I looked behind me. The other two ships of our flight were not there. I counted those that were. Sixteen. Only sixteen of us got through. Sixteen out of 45 that started and there wasn't a bomber in sight.

My nerves were pushed almost beyond endurance from the long instrument flight . . . my imagination had me colliding with another P-38. . . . [After spotting some 110s and 190s we] once again picked up a heading for England, plunging into the wall of stratocumulus that obliterated the continent. Back on instruments again . . . all the way to England and Nuthampstead. When we arrived at 1500 hours, the field was socked in and we circled, trying to find it through the muck. Then someone on the ground with a high I.Q. dispatched a jeep-load of flare shells and two enlisted men with pistols to the end of the field where they took up positions on each side of the runway and proceeded to fire flares straight up. Beautiful! We could see the flares. All we had to do was land between the two flare pistols popping off, methodically. Everyone landed safely.

Glenn T. Eagleston, *P-51 pilot, 354th Fighter Group*

We were all pretty aroused at the debriefing. We were happy that this milestone was past and we had gone in and bombed hell out of the German capital, we thought at the time, without too much loss to ourselves. In all we went to Berlin four times that week and I've never been so tired in my life—6 hour missions one right after the other just knocked the 'coon pee right out of you. I'd swear I could have given you the serial number off my oxygen bottle and dinghy pack by reading it off my left cheek.

Bert Stiles, *B-17 copilot, 91st Bomb Group (from his book* Serenade to the Big Bird, *W. W. Norton & Co., 1952)*

We were like old men. It seemed like the sun had gone out of the world. I looked in the mirror and a haggard mask of a face stared back at me. The eyes were bright. And the veins were cleanly etched in the whites, and the pupils were distended. We were all like that. "I'm gonna get grounded," Sam said. "They're trying to kill us off."

We'd been in the group twelve days. The first four days we did

The 493rd Bomb Group's B-24s line up for takeoff from Debach in the summer of 1944. *Mark. H. Brown/USAFA*

nothing. The next eight, we flew. Grant had a thin face anyway, but by then it was like an ax. Bird was impossible to get along with; neither of them could sleep.

I could sleep. Or maybe it was a form of death. I would stretch out in my sack and feel my muscles give way completely. There was no pleasure in it. They just went flat and lifeless. And then my nerve endings would die for a while, until Porada came to wake us up.

"Breakfast at two. Briefing at three." He was always nice about it. Quiet and easy and insistent.

I would lie there and the glare of the light would smash back into my mind. Somewhere in the Reich today. Somewhere in that doomed land. There was a movie named *Each Dawn I Die*. It was like that.

After I got my clothes on, and out into the night, it was better. I'd stand still and look away at the stars and ask Lady Luck to bring me back

home. Just ask her. Just hoped she'd stay with me another day. One day at a time. Taking one day at a time we got through it.

Don Larson, *C-47 pilot, 444th Troop Carrier Group*

I've lost all conception of time lately. Between working all nights planning these missions, flying most of the day, and listening to the British government switch from Greenwich to British Standard to British Summer to

Old Baldy sits in its 486th Bomb Group revetment at Sudbury while being serviced for the next day's mission. *Mark H. Brown/USAFA*

This 490th Bomb Group B-24 is in the process of being brought up to operational status for the next mission. Bombs have been "dropped" off onto the ground for loading into the open bomb bays. They also make handy bike stands. Deicer boots on the leading edges of the wings have been removed for summer flying. *Mark H. Brown/USAFA*

View across the 490th Bomb Group bomb dump at Eye Peninsula. These 1,000 pound and 500 pound general purpose bombs await loading into the Group's Forts. *Mark H. Brown/USAFA*

Double British Summer Time, and then back down the scale—I usually didn't even know the date or month.

Well, I guess you've read about the "commitment of the first airborne army." Mostly, I still can't talk about it—but as the communiques say, I lost "some" friends. My crew chief, for whom I have a great deal of affection, as we've been together since Sedalia, was badly wounded.

One oil tank, hydraulic tank, electric system and all radios were shot up, to say nothing of forty-something holes, one as big as a baseball bat, right through my roof. Oh, yes, my side window was smashed, about three inches from my head, and that, too, somehow missed me. I wasn't scared though—Haw! Two days later, when they quieted me down, I told 'em just what happened.

So many things happened there in such a short time that it seems like a bad dream. In fact, one of the radio operators talked about "flak sandwiches" all that night in his sleep.

I know now for certain that when the pressure is really on you fly by instinct alone. Once, when we were hit, my co-pilot and I were both flying the ship 'cause we *knew* the other one was dead, yet we were unaware of the other's pressure on the controls. When you watch the formation ahead of you getting hell, ships crazily burning, spiraling, exploding, knowing that in a fraction of a second it will be shifted on you, it brings on a feeling that cannot be described as mere fear—it paralyzes the brains, turns muscles to jelly—and God and instinct alone take care of man.

I now have personal effects scattered with rear echelons in Italy, France, and two bases in England—that is also why mail never finds us—can't catch up with us. A.T.C. [Air Transport Command] brings the mail, and when A.T.C. catches up with the troop carrier it will be 'cause the war's over and there's nowhere left to go. Told you that A.T.C. stands for "Allergic to Combat," didn't I?

The 100th Bomb Group has just returned to Thorpe Abbots from Germany—with casualties. The "meat wagon" was on the scene quickly as engines were shut down and the wounded offloaded. *Mark H. Brown/USAFA*

Robert Shoens, *B-17 pilot, 100th Bomb Group*

Somewhere over France one of the crew asked, "Has anyone seen our escort lately?" Suddenly it was obvious that no one had. The chatter stopped. You could feel the tension rise. It wasn't long before there appeared ahead of us what looked like a swarm of bees, fighters several miles off but coming at us, dozens of them. It became obvious in a few seconds that we were their target as they came straight at us. It apparently didn't bother them that our greatest fire power was straight ahead. In an instant they went right through us. In that instant eight of nine planes in the high squadron were gone. The group lead aircraft had a six foot gap in his vertical stabilizer.

As pilot you don't see much; you are busy keeping your aircraft in position, but a glance through the overhead window told me the high squadron was gone. On our right wing was a crew from our barracks. Their

A 486th Bomb Group B-17G climbs out over England in the spring of 1945. The war was almost over but the Big Friends continued to hammer the German war machine. *Alexander C. Sloan via Bob Kuhnert, 355th FG Assn.*

143

entire wing was on fire. Before they could get out, there was nothing there. By the end of the third attack we were all alone! One aircraft from the entire group? It couldn't be, yet, there we were.

As we circled the field after getting home we could see a lot of empty spaces and we knew we were at least one of the few. We landed and when we taxied to our space, we found our squadron commander waiting for us. He was crying. We were stunned to learn that we were the only aircraft to return to the field and only one of four to make it back to England out of the original group of 20 aircraft. Of the 8th Air Force aircraft lost over Germany that day we had lost almost 25% of them. What do you say, what do you do when your squadron commander is crying and wants to know what happened? You do the same thing he is doing.

Stanley A. Hutchins, *B-24 pilot, 484th Bomb Group*

I desperately tried to transfer into P-38s and did everything that a 19 year old could think of to shake B-24 dust off my feet. Tolerantly the 15th Air Force said fine, just finish your bomber tour first. The B-24, and my escapist attitude toward it, ruined my "feel" so that it took 10 hours of dual to check me out in an AT-6 in July 1945. I am grudgingly grateful to the B-24 for bringing me home over those 11 months in combat, still I never got to live my dream of rat racing an Me 109 into the ground.

Robert E. Kuhnert, *radio line chief, 335th Fighter Group*

Ward Douglass, forming up with the 358th Fighter Squadron one day in the familiar base-circling pattern, accidentally dropped a full wing tank directly over Bassingbourn Airdrome. The tank went through the mess hall

roof, spraying avgas throughout the kitchen. Luckily, there were no casualties. The 91st Bomb Group C.O. sent the following cryptic message to our 355th Group C.O.: "We are not the enemy."

James R. Hanson, *P-51 pilot, 339th Fighter Group*

Knowing that we are now headed out for the real thing, for the first time, is beyond description. We circle the field to get everyone into set course formation. It's a beautiful, sunny day with about 3/10ths clouds at about 8,000 feet. It's a great feeling to look around the formation, knowing who is in each plane, guys you've flown with and lived with in the States and now together doing the job you were trained for and in the airplane you had hoped to fly.

Crossing out over the North Sea, Col. Hayes calls, "Oilskin, feet are wet." I know that a lot of us are

The 388th Bomb Group has just returned to Knettishall from bombing Brest on 26 August 1944 and ground crews are already servicing and refueling this Flying Fort, the lead ship of the high squadron that day. *Mark H. Brown/USAFA*

taking a long look at the beautiful green English countryside, thinking that it is going to be home from now on. We climb steadily on up to 20,000 feet. Up ahead I can see the French and Belgian coast. We make landfall near Dunkirk. I've read enough about that place. The sky is clear and blue and the land below looks so green and peaceful with those scattered, puffy clouds . . . then wham bang, it's flak at 7 o'clock. There it is for the first time . . . doesn't look dangerous . . . just appears like magic, black and umbrella shaped, fading away quickly to a gray smoke as it drifts back behind. We make some evasive turns and nothing really comes close to us but I really get a stab of excitement each time I hear that call of "Flak!"

Back to the hardstand, this 490th Bomb group B-17G heads down the taxiway at Eye after turning off the active runway upon completion of another trip over enemy territory. *Mark H. Brown/USAFA*

Terre Haute Tornado, a B-26 Marauder of the 344th Bomb Group, at rest in England. Generally speaking, fighter pilots found escorting Marauders and A-26 Invaders to be far easier than escorting the heavy four-engine types. This was due primarily to equal cruising speeds, which eliminated the fighters having to weave over the bomber formation. *Mark H. Brown/USAFA*

145

Chapter 8

Huns

Ernst Schroeder, *Fw 190 pilot,*
Jagdgeschwader 300
    I catch sight of the glittering reflections of the sun on the uncamouflaged American bombers,

off to the left and at the same altitude, about 25,000 feet. Still a long way away, the stately enemy formation crosses in front of us from left to right. I carefully search the sky for enemy

escorts, but I can make out only three or four condensation trails above the bombers.
    Curving round, the Sturmgruppe is now directly in front of me, about

Though several different aircraft were manufactured by Willy Messerschmitt's company, the use of his name among Americans usually meant a single machine, the Me 109. Built in multiple versions, 109s flew in combat from the Spanish Civil War through the end of World War II, giving Allied pilots a rough time when flown by skilled pilots. "Black 12," an Me 109 G–10/R2, flew with 2./NAG 14 at the end of the war. *Ralph Woolner via Monogram Aviation Publications*

150 yards below; I have a grandstand view of the attack as it unfolds. The bombers open up with a furious defensive fire, filling the sky with tracers as we move in at full throttle. At 300 yards the main body of the Fw 190s opens up with their 20 mm and 30 mm cannon, the murderous trains of high explosive shells streaking out towards the Liberators. Within seconds two of the giant aircraft have exploded into great fireballs, while several others have caught fire and are falling out of formation.

On either side of me my Schwarm comrades fire like mad and score hit after hit on their targets. Looking around, I see the sky is like a

When pilots in the MTO encountered Me 109s, it did not follow that they were necessarily flown by Germans. Several Italian *Regia Aeronautica* units were equipped with 109s and flown throughout the war against the Allies. This Me 109 G-6/trop at Sciacca, Sicily was attached to the 365ª Squadriglia, 150° Gruppo until the Italian capitulation on 8 September 1943. *William J. Skinner*

147

An Fw 190 G–3, fighter-bomber version of the famous Focke-Wulf, sits at Montecorvino Airfield, near Salerno, Italy in 1943. *William J. Skinner*

chaotic circus: whirling and fluttering pieces of aircraft, an entire wing falling complete with engines and propellers still turning, several parachutes and some of our aircraft battling with the few P-38 escort fighters that have reached us.

Arthur L. Thorsen, *P-38 pilot, 55th Fighter Group*

I was turning tight with the German now and my ship trembled and buffeted slightly. I couldn't pull enough deflection on him, but I had him, he had no place to go. He couldn't dive and if he climbed, he was finished. All he could do was try to out turn me. We could turn like this forever, I thought and quickly dumped ten percent flaps. My ship reared up and turned on its wingtip. I was out turning the Jerry. I opened fire and saw strikes around the cockpit and left wing root. The thrill of the chase is hypnotic. Your body tingles. You feel you have wings of your own. You make funny noises to yourself. You strain against your shoulder straps as if that will give you more momentum. You begin to tremble with the knowledge that the German ship ahead of you, is yours. You can take him. You don't think of shooting a human being, you just shoot at a machine. Air combat is strictly that impersonal.

The German was not done yet and rolled out quickly to starboard, sucking in his stick and pulling vapor streamers from his wing tips. I rolled with him, but he had me by a second and I lost my deflection. We were in a vertical turn now and the centrifugal force was pushing me hard into the seat. I was about 150 yards astern of him when his ship filled my gun sight. I pulled through and opened fire. I could see strikes on his engine and pieces flew off. Then a long stream of glycol poured from his engine and I knew he was finished. He suddenly pulled out of the turn, went into a steep climb, popped his canopy and bailed out. We were very low, almost too low for bailing out. I followed him down and his chute must have popped just as his feet hit the ground.

I began a series of turns to clear my tail and couldn't see an airplane in the sky. Then I noticed, as I was turning at low level, scores of Parisians dancing around the roof tops and throwing their berets in the air, as if cheering what they had been watching. I chuckled as I turned the nose of my ship toward home.

Heinz Knoke, *Me 109 pilot, Jagdgeschwader 11*

I jumped into the cockpit for my second mission of the day. The mechanics climbed up on the right

A deadly opponent, this Focke-Wulf Fw 190 D-9 flew with II./JG 6 as "Black 12," in 1945. An upgraded version of the radial-engined 190, the "Dora 9," had an inline liquid-cooled V-12 engine with a circular radiator in front, giving it the nickname "long nose" in both American and German squadrons. In all respects the 190 D-9 was the equal of its American counterpart, the P-51D. *Ralph Woolner via Monogram Aviation Publications*

wing with the heavy starting handle and began winding up the inertia starter. As I sat there in the cockpit, canopy open, the nose pointing north, I noticed two aircraft coming straight for me from the east, very low. American fighters! I threw off my straps and scrambled out of the cockpit, shouting "Tiefangriff!" to the two mechanics. They were not quick enough, just standing there looking around, while I was already out of my 109 and diving into a small ditch nearby. Finally Kretchmer jumped down, a few steps behind me, but the second mechanic was still standing on the wing, looking to see what was happening.

At that moment the bullets started flying all around us. The aircraft was hit several times, with six or seven holes in and around the cockpit . . . the canopy was smashed. Then I heard the cries from the second mechanic. He lost three fingers from his right hand and had one shot through his buttock. Then the Mustangs flashed close overhead at 20 meters and were away—I could see their muzzle flashes. . . .

Shortly after 2200 I got on my bicycle and pedaled in the darkness the one and a half kilometers from the

Though less maneuverable than single engined fighters, the Messerschmitt 110 had to be approached with care if a skilled gunner manned the rear seat. This Me 110 G–2 of II/2G 1 at Montecorvino, Italy, 1943, is painted in the unit's colorful *Wespe* (wasp) insignia. *William J. Skinner*

150

airfield to the small guesthouse where my wife and infant daughter were staying. It was a funny kind of war. Each evening I went home to my wife.

She was asleep and I think I was a little bit drunk when I got there. I just got undressed and climbed into bed with my wife. Sleepily she turned around and said, "Hey, are you drunk? What have you been up to?" I said, "We've had a lot of work." She rolled over and went back to sleep. I was up before she awoke—had to be at the Staffel between 5 and 6 AM.

That day had been one of the most exciting, exhausting and frightening day's fighting I had ever had. I had battled with fighters, knocked down a bomber, made a crash-landing on one wheel, been in a plane shot up on the ground, lost one of our ground crewmen wounded, gone into action a second time, lost my wingman, returned to base and got drunk.

John B. Murphy, *P-51 pilot, 359th Fighter Group*

My first impression when I saw the jet plane was that I was standing still. It seemed hopeless to try to attempt to overtake them, but my actions were prompted by a curiosity to get as close to them as possible. I believe that will be the reaction of every pilot that comes in contact with them.

Hermann Greiner, *Me 110 pilot, Nacht Jagdgeschwader 1*

Just as I got airborne after being scrambled, I could hardly believe my eyes. There, at a height of 200 meters (100 above me), a B–17 was flying straight towards me with two fighters flying loose escort. I pulled the stick back, made a steep turn to the left and opened fire at it right away, even before I had time to retract my landing gear and flaps, which put me

on the edge of my Messerschmitt's capabilities. With so little speed, there was grave danger that my machine would stall out and fall into a spin. As I held my plane on the edge of a stall and fired, the Fortress was so badly hit that it was forced to make a belly landing. The enemy fighters were then closing in so I had to dive under them, get into my own airfield's flak defenses and land to escape. Later I found out that six or seven of the ten Americans in the bomber had escaped without injury.

Walter Hagenah, *Fw 190 pilot, Jagdgeschwader 3*

To be sure of bringing down a bomber it was essential that we held our fire until we were right up close against the bombers. We were to advance like Frederick the Great's infantrymen, holding our fire until we could see "the white of the enemy's eyes."

One of the most potent German aircraft of the war, the Messerschmitt Me 262 jet fighter presented a real challenge to AAF fighter pilots. Fortunately a combination of tactics and numbers allowed Mustang units to engage and down 262s on a regular basis, though when the jets did get through to the bombers they proved to be extremely effective. This EJG 2 aircraft sits at Lechfeld in 1945. *Byron Trent*

Chapter 9

On the Deck

Frances H. Griswold, *CO, VIII Fighter Command*

Since the beginning of this war the profit and loss on the proposition of fighter aircraft attacking ground targets has been the subject of professional debate and pilot discussion. Small profit to shoot up two or three trucks or a couple of machine guns for the loss of a valuable aircraft and pilot. Worse still when two, three, four go down over one well-dispersed enemy A/D [airdrome] or, as on the days of our large-scale attacks by the whole

A 313th Fighter Squadron, 50th Fighter Group Thunderbolt just about to touch down at Nancy, France, in the winter of 1944. In spite of the rough weather conditions on the Continent, Ninth AF aircraft operated continually in support of the First and Third Armies. *Phil Savides*

Amidst the bare base rubble at Nancy, France, the ground crew of Phil Savides' 50th Fighter Group P–47D *Juicy Lucy* gets things ready for the next mission. The Ninth Air Force turned the Thunderbolt into the finest ground attack weapon on the Allied side under the leadership of Gen. Elwood "Pete" Quesada. *Phil Savides*

Command, twenty-five or more may be MIA [missing in action]. In addition to the loss of these planes and pilots is the unfortunate fact that our best, our outstanding leaders and fighters who had yet to meet their match in any enemy they could see, have gone down before the hidden gunfire or light flak incident to a ground attack. Duncan, Beeson, Beckham, Gerald Johnson, Gabreski, Juchheim, Andrew, Hofer, Goodson, Schreiber, Millikan, Carpenter, the list could go on.

For equal numbers engaged, four times as many pilots of this Command are lost on ground attack as in aerial combat. Light flak will ring an A/D [airdrome] or an M/Y [marshalling yard]. Flak cars will open up in the middle of a train. A truck convoy, with sufficient warning, may be a hornet's nest. Every target of special value to the enemy will be heavily defended and may exact its price.

Where then is the profit? The answer is the successful invasion and the victorious battle of France. The answer is our flight of many a heavy bomber mission without challenge by enemy fighters, and the presence of our hordes of bombers and fighter-bombers over our troops in Normandy. The roads of France, strewn with enemy wreckage, reply, and an enemy starving for oil, ammunition, supplies, reinforcement could answer with deep feeling.

Donald J.M. Blakeslee, *P-51 pilot, CO, 4th Fighter Group*
I use terrain—hills, gullies, and trees—for cover, and such airdrome installations as hangars, etc., to screen my approach. I never come right in on an airdrome if I can help it. If I have

154

planned to attack an airdrome beforehand, I pick an I.P. [initial point] some 10 miles away—some easily recognizable place. I have my course from there to the drome worked out. Once in the air, I take my boys right past the airdrome as if I had no intention of attacking it at all. At my I.P. I let down and swing back flat on the deck. I usually try to have another check-point on the course from my I.P., not far from the airdrome, and when I pass that I know I am definitely coming in on the right field. I don't like to end up on an airdrome before I realize I am even coming to one. But once I hit the drome, I really get down on the deck. I don't mean five feet up; I mean so low the grass is brushing the bottom of the scoop.

After the attack on the field, stay on the deck for a good mile beyond the drome before pulling up. The break should consist of rudder yawing. Never cock a wing up. If you must turn on the drome, do flat skidding turns. Don't give the Hun a better target to shoot at.

I prefer to get down low and shoot up at any aircraft on the ground rather than come in high and shoot down. Usually I fire a short burst from long range and correct for it as I come in.

In general, my pilots and I realize ground strafing involves a greater risk than shooting Huns down in the air. But it seems to be quite as important. Besides, we get more fun out of strafing ground targets instead of airfields—no one really likes to attack these.

I want to say a word about tactics. My feeling is that there is entirely too much emphasis placed on

methods of strafing and on so-called tactics. Strafing is a simple process. You pick a target and shoot it up. As long as you are comfortable and get away with it, that's all there is to it. Every pilot probably has a different idea on how to do it. A general rule just can't be laid down, for one method is probably no better than another.

Philip Savides, *P-47 pilot, 50th Fighter Group*
Juicy Lucy was a hand-me-down P-47 which I received without question just as a poor kid puts on the jacket of his older brother. No one told me who was the previous pilot nor did I ever ask about him. The plane outlasted the war, I believe, but I left Europe without saying goodbye to her.

In my recollections, we (or at least I) often flew different planes. It seems to me that even after I was assigned *Juicy Lucy* I frequently flew other aircraft, although she was ready for flight. Why that should be, I cannot explain. Maybe, because I was easy going and did not demand or reject certain aircraft, *Lucy* was assigned to another pilot on some flights while I found myself in the one which he, for some whim, found unacceptable.

In spite of what might appear to be a disinterest in a particular P-47, I developed an enduring affection for the breed. Sure, there was that obvious obesity coupled with a drinking problem and the undeniable fact that she glided like a flat iron and looked—head on—like a flying toilet seat. Yet, I'm grateful for the chance I had to pilot the Thunderbolt. It was a mighty fine, mighty machine.

Thomas J.J. Christian, Jr., *P-51 pilot, CO, 361st Fighter Group*

Usually, a successful fighter attack against a ground target requires less skill, more nerve, and as precise an estimate of the situation as an air-to-air attack. We say *usually* because there are exceptions; for example, successful fighter-bombing is a specialized sport which requires considerable practice and skill; moreover, it does not take any courage to shoot up an undefended target (provided that you know beforehand that the target *is* undefended); and, it is often much easier to make a proper estimate of a ground situation than it is to make one of an air situation because, in many cases, we are afforded prior knowledge of the target conditions.

The latter is never true in air-to-air combat.

Ben Rimerman, *P-47 pilot, CO, 353rd Fighter Group*

A few main points to remember are that a definite target should always be selected before the approach to the attack should be made. The target should be worth what you have to pay, meaning that it is foolish to lead a flight into a heavily defended airdrome to shoot up an old, beat-up Fieseler Storch if that is all you can see. Remember that the approach and break away may vary in a hundred different ways, but in each attack you must, at a normal range, fly comparatively straight and hold your pip on the target long enough to do the job you started on. For that short

moment in any attack, you might as well forget flak and everything and concentrate on sighting; otherwise there is no point in carrying a lot of heavy .50 cal. slugs around in your guns all the time.

William B. Bailey, *P-47 pilot, 353rd Fighter Group*

The first few times a new pilot goes down on a ground target he is probably just plain scared. He feels there are hundreds of hidden guns which will open up on him at any moment. Naturally, this mental attitude will reflect on the firing accuracy of the individual concerned. He will invariably come in too fast, too high, or too low, slipping and skidding without much thought of hitting the target until he is closing so

Strafing run! Gun camera film from a 78th Fighter Group Mustang records part of the biggest day's bag by an Eighth AF fighter group during the war—125 German aircraft were claimed destroyed, nine by group CO John Landers, on 16 April 1945 on airfields in Czecho-slovakia. Total Eighth Air Force claims were an incredible 752 aircraft. The He 111 in the foreground is already burning smartly as .50 caliber hits register on and around the next German aircraft.

fast he has only the briefest interval to fire.

The first step in overcoming these errors is to instill in the pilot a sense of security. This is done by proper briefing, giving him an accurate knowledge of the existing flak installations, making arrangements for flak spotters, whose job it is to neutralize the flak, and to assign adequate top cover for the operation.

Wayne K. Blickenstaff, *P-47 pilot, 353rd Fighter Group*
Train busting is a great sport.

Joe L. Mason, *P-51 pilot, CO, 352nd Fighter Group*
On trains and convoys where you encounter no return fire, you must make every bullet count. Our ammunition is belted with five rounds of tracer fifty rounds from the end of the belt. We have a rule that you will not shoot past that tracer on a ground target—we lost some 109s one day because not a damn soul in the group had any bullets left. And good shooting is good shooting regardless of the target, and good shooting is what kills Germans.

On specific assigned targets I think bombing with fighters is O.K. I'm partial to dive bombing, as I think it's as accurate as any. Anything less than 1,000 pounds is not too much good on bridges. On all bridges we've bombed, we have only been successful in dropping one span. I'm sorry to have to admit it, but it seems to be the truth. Bombing with a fighter aircraft is one hundred percent personal skill, and it's just like playing basketball— the more you practice, the more baskets you can sink. We in the VIII Fighter Command have not had the

156

time, ranges, or equipment to practice fighter bombing to even approach the degree which could be obtained. But we are basically an escort outfit, and, in that, we have had sufficient practice to come closer to perfection. The score board shows that. You can mess up a lot of railroad by flying straight and level and dropping one bomb at a time. If done right, one group can break the tracks every ¼ mile for about fifty miles. That should drive the Hun nuts trying to fix it; it's not a permanent injury, but it makes him mad as hell. A good fighter-bomber pilot can hit his target from any dive angle at any altitude; that is what takes practice.

A fighter pilot who doesn't want to shoot his guns is no fighter pilot. I continuously have to warn them about non-military targets; the angle they shoot so it won't kill half the French in France, etc.

Shooting up convoys, and especially staff cars and dispatch riders, is considered great sport.

Avelin P. Tacon, Jr., *P-51 pilot, CO, 359th Fighter Group*
It is impossible to attack ground targets without having to pull up as the nose of the Mustang rides pretty well down at high speed. If the nose isn't far enough down, you can use 10 degrees of flaps, which is permissible up to 400 mph. This will bring your guns down on the ground right in front of you.

As for bombing, we much prefer dive bombing. Skip bombing is something we are not at all enthusiastic about. Probably because we can't hit a damn thing that way. The only thing we consider a skip bomb target is a tunnel mouth. All of

the bridges we have skip bombed have had low river banks and our bombs have just tumbled cross-country for about a mile before exploding.

Dive bombing is something else. We've gotten pretty accurate with dive bombing since we've had the Mustangs. By starting our dive from about 8,000 feet and releasing about 4,000 feet, we can get pretty good results. Particularly on bridge approaches and marshalling yards. Flak doesn't bother us much dive bombing, as we have plenty of speed. We like to dive bomb individually if there isn't any heavy flak bothering us.

As to the danger—everyone agrees that in strafing you're bound to get it in the end if you do enough of it, but that by being smart and taking every advantage, you can prolong it somewhat.

John B. Henry, Jr., *P-51 pilot, 339th Fighter Group*
Because of the extreme vulnerability of the P-51 airplane to any kind of damage, it is considered by most of our pilots that attacks on ground targets are not worth the risk unless those targets are poorly defended and are extremely vulnerable to .50 caliber fire.

After a long lull, when no opposition has been encountered from the Luftwaffe in the air, a couple of missions of ground strafing, despite the risk, does a lot for the morale of the pilots. Just to fire their guns and to know they are doing some damage boosts their spirits and tides them over until the next batch of Jerries comes to meet us in the air.

Incidentally, most of our airplanes have only four guns and usually at least one or two of them are jammed and useless. One of our "pet peeves" against this airplane is its lack of fire power in combat models prior to the "D" series.

Henry W. Brown, *P-47 pilot, 355th Fighter Group*

We had been escorting some bombers part of the way to Berlin. We were on our way home when I saw this airfield. There were four Junkers 88s parked in a line, with a lot more strung out around the field. I called them in on my radio. I was plenty green, but I sure wanted to shoot at some swastikas.

We didn't know much about ground strafing; no one in the outfit had ever done it. We got down real low, from about five miles out, and we gave it full throttle. We hopped over trees and buildings, going like hell, and we missed the field. We had to make a sharp left turn, all five of us. That screwed us up. Instead of being the second in line, I became the fourth.

The first guy blew up a Ju 88 right away. We still were real low.

The second guy opened up on the next Ju 88 in line. It began to burn just as he went over it. I thought he was going to crash into it. His tail did scrape the top of it. He was too close to fire at the third one, so he took the fourth. He shot the hell out of it, but it didn't burn—not right away.

I took the third one. It blew up. Just like that; real quick. I flew through the smoke of the first one to get to it. It was like going through a tunnel. Then I kicked the rudder and squirted at one that was parked to one

Just about everything you could hang on a fighter in 1944—metal drop tanks, 500-pound bombs and .50 caliber bullets. *USAF/NASM*

A Thunderbolt is loaded for a ground attack mission over France in support of advancing Allied armies. S/Sgt. Robert E. Robinson rearms the four .50s in the left wing as M/Sgt. James H. McGee and Sgt. John A. Koval move a 500 pound bomb onto the wing shackle. *USAF/NASM*

side. The flame shot out of it like water from a hose, out of its right side, and then [came] the biggest puff of black smoke I'd ever seen.

The flak was there the very first time. The minute we started at the field, they opened up on us. I knew that was bad, but I hadn't done any strafing before, so I really didn't know how bad that was. When they're firing at you right away, one attack is always enough. The odds get higher and higher every time.

But we made another attack. That was the roughest I've ever seen. Tracers and explosive cannon shells were popping all around us, like a rain of golf balls. We got some more planes, but it was like juggling a dozen ice picks, trying to shoot at the planes, and trying to shoot at the gun emplacements, going through all the smoke, trying to keep from crashing into something, moving as fast as we could. . . .

We didn't see the first boy after we started our second pass. I guess we left him there, somewhere. So there were three of us.

Two of us pulled away after that second pass. That had been murder. But the third guy was too excited to realize that his radio had been shot

The bomb dump, not a place for the weak-hearted. No wonder it was covered with camouflage netting. *USAF/NASM*

Capt. Dick Perley in front of the 313th Fighter Squadron operations tent at Toul-Ochey, near Nancy, France, before a mission. *Richard H. Perley*

158

out, and he didn't know he was making a third attack by himself. But he did [make the attack].

Every gun on that field was concentrated on him. Somehow he got through. He climbed up and joined us, and we started home. Then I saw another airfield with a couple of planes on it. I tore across it real fast, and set one on fire and kept right on going. I looked back—and damned if this third guy hadn't followed me!

He was climbing up to rejoin us again when the flak went after him once more. This time he really caught hell. One burst exploded right under his tail. Just as he called and told me he had been hit, another burst put some shrapnel through the rear of his cockpit canopy. Pieces hit him in the back of the head, in five different places, but he was a hard-headed boy. It just stunned him for a couple of seconds.

The other guy and I talked him back to England, telling him he'd make it okay, and wondering to ourselves what was keeping his plane in the air. But he made it. He ground-looped when he landed, but he got out of the plane and was sitting on the grass when the ambulance got to him.

That plane . . . you had to see it to believe it. I don't think there was three feet of it that didn't have a hole in it, and the gas tank was bone dry.

They picked the shrapnel out of the guy's head, and the next morning he was on the flight line again, wrestling with everybody!

Claiborne H. Kinnard, Jr., *P-51 pilot, CO, 355th Fighter Group*

Boy, it was better than any movie ever made. Just before we met the bombers, south of the target, fourteen Messerschmitt 109s came streaming along. I wanted to hold the group as intact as possible so we could do the most damage to Ober-whatchacallit, so I told Jonesy to take them. He and his boys knocked down five, got two

probablies, and damaged one. The rest of the Jerries got out of there. Jonesy and his squadron rejoined us near the target.

We took the Libs across and went down with the bombs. I streamed across the field once, at about 6,000 feet, to look it over good, and spot the gun emplacements. On the way I planned my runs. Boy, I'm telling you; things looked too good to be true! All the south and east side was literally covered with airplanes, like sitting ducks!

A big wall of smoke was rolling up from the hangars, and we used that to screen our approach. Soon as we busted through it, we started shooting. One twin-engined job blazed up in front of me right away.

We got to work in earnest. I looked behind me once, and boy, what a sight! I saw two German planes blow up; there was smoke and fire all over; guys pulling up firing, dodging each other, some going up, some

Lt. Robert C. Bucholz was killed in action in this 4th Fighter Group Mustang, *Suzy*, on 9 April 1945 when the group was strafing Munich-Brunnthal airdrome in Germany. Hit by flak, the P-51 went in before he had a chance to bail out. *Mark H. Brown/USAFA*

Maj. Pierce W. "Mac" McKennon runs up his *Ridge Runner III* at Debden, April 1945. Though he was forced to bail out twice, as indicated by the small parachutes behind the razorback boar, Mac managed to return to the 4th Fighter Group each time and get back on flying status. Crew chief Joseph B. Sills was constantly amazed at his pilot's energy and aggressiveness. *Joseph B. Sills*

diving, and all that smoke and fire. It was the damnedest thing I've ever seen. But there were a couple of surprises coming up.

I circled the field about the fourth attack, and passed over two batteries of heavy guns. It was that high altitude stuff. I couldn't help but grin, because I could see the gunners just standing there, their heads turned toward the field, with guns too big to use on us. They couldn't depress them enough to hit us.

I started to circle once more, and all hell broke loose on the field. I looked up and saw a little formation of our bombers going right over us, all but one. He had a wing gone, and was spinning down. I thought I'd lost my mind. I reckon they had gotten lost from the main bunch. Luckily, no one was hit badly.

We worked a little longer, and then the Jerries stopped vibrating and came out of their holes. They started pouring flak at us like water out of a firehose. We were about out of ammunition, and the place looked like a junkyard anyway, so we started home.

On the way out, seven Focke-Wulf 190s jumped out of the clouds behind us and started looking mean. I only had four ships with me. The group had split up. We turned suddenly and charged toward them, trying to look just as mean, or meaner. They ran. It was a good thing; I don't know what the hell we'd have done if they hadn't left. We didn't have any ammunition.

You know, I sure was proud of those boys. It may take time, but you can't keep those kids from winning. I don't know exactly what it is—but they've got it. Four of 'em were

starting across that field when those late bombers started unloading on it. One of 'em got a six inch hole in his wing from a bomb fragment, but they kept right on attacking and came around for more. One even thought that delayed action bombs were going off—but he kept right on going anyway. Maybe that's the answer. Nothing can stop them. They just keep right on going.

Jack Monaghan, *maintenance supply, 55th Fighter Group*

After all the long-range escort work we had been doing, the pilots became accustomed to carrying belly-tanks of fuel. As the war moved farther and farther into France and Germany, the fighters would go off carrying bombs for ground support instead of wing tanks with fuel. Some of the pilots would forget that because they had become accustomed to switching to wing-tanks as soon as they were off the ground. Unfortunately bombs on the wings don't carry fuel and they would go straight in. I don't know how many fighters we lost that way. It was pretty grim watching them pulling into the air and then suddenly see them wheeling down wing over wing to crash and burn. A couple of times when we finally reached the plane, we found the pilot standing there watching it burn.

Philip Savides, *P-47 pilot, 50th Fighter Group*

In the spring of 1945 I led a flight and dove down alone to strafe a retreating German convoy. While at low level, just as I was exulting in the find we had (it was a long, important looking string of trucks), I saw what

looked like red-hot golf balls arcing through the air, saw a field full of undisguised light antiaircraft guns, and in a second felt a couple of explosions.

I don't know what I hollered over the radio, but I attempted to let the guys know that I didn't expect anyone to join me. My right wing was showing flame from the cockpit out about half the length of the wing and the engine was pouring black smoke against the windscreen. Clearly the engine was not putting out power as it should and I prepared to get out of what appeared to be a doomed Thunderbolt.

I let go of the canopy, threw out my maps (didn't they always do that in the Hollywood movies?) and tore off and threw overboard my helmet, oxygen mask and earphones. In spite of the flame streaming back eight or ten feet from the trailing edge of the right wing, that was the side I decided to jump out of. With harness off and my hair flying in the smoke, I suddenly realized that the wing fire had stopped and it dawned on me that the engine was still running and the controls were intact. Besides, who would want to bail out in the area where you've just strafed?

If I could just put a few miles between me and that column of trucks before I had to parachute. . . . The engine sounded odd and continued to pour dense black smoke against the windshield and I had the impression that the power plant would soon quit altogether or catch on fire. Increased throttle seemed to do little good in my struggle to gain altitude, but I found that the plane performed better when I manually increased the rpm. Before long I had gained a few hundred feet and with the better perspective began to look for a flat spot to make my belly landing. It would be tough to bring it down because the engine continued to belch dark oil smoke which condensed on the windscreen, making it impossible to see straight ahead.

A check of the instruments revealed that I had zero hydraulic pressure, but every thing else read OK. What really had me on edge, though, was that smoking engine. How long could it pump oil overboard like that without either running dry or starting a fire? Obviously the Germans had poked a hole in one of the front cylinder banks and with each stroke of the piston, my lubricant was spurting out of the damaged cylinder and being driven back by the air stream to sizzle into smoke as it struck the adjacent cylinders.

Although the film of oil kept creeping up on my windshield, obscuring my forward vision, I began to feel pretty comfortable. If the engine should seize from lack of oil, I could make a belly landing and if the vapor should flame, I had enough altitude to roll her over and drop out in my chute.

My wingman gave me the once over and helped with the heading toward home, but we couldn't talk because I had tossed away my helmet. I was unable to reach the spare headset which was supposed to be stowed under the seat. That flight continued to progress in my favor. At the moment I was first hit, I thought the only salvation was a low-level parachute jump into the hands of bitter enemies. Then perhaps we could get away a little to a bit of flat land in enemy territory for a belly landing.

Next—oh, you magnificent engine!—we made it to friendly territory and finally there is the field. My wingman called the tower for clearance to land straight in and the controller responded that he couldn't yet see the planes, but he did have my smoke in sight!

I had been pampering the power for 45 minutes since I was hit and never did believe it would turn for more than another minute, so I resolved that I would land on the first pass and avoid the strain of another climb. Reasoning that I had no hydraulic fluid and that I was shot up in the area of the landing gear, I decided to land wheels up beside the runway on the right. I cut the power and as I neared the field I began to realize I was too high and too hot. How ironic—after 45 minutes of praying that the aircraft would fly fast and high, I now wanted to slow down and drop.

I was over the end of the runway with about 100 feet and 150 mph. When I saw only half of the runway remained ahead of me, I eased the stick forward and flew the plane

The 50th Fighter Group's Thunderbolts dispersed across the forward operating field near Nancy, France. *Richard H. Perley*

into the dirt at about 150 mph. Thunderbolts with the gear up are inclined to land a little longer than those whose wheels are down! The deceleration forced my body forward with my head tipped forward as if I were trying to look at my knees. (The next morning, when dressing, I noticed I had a pink stripe in front of each shoulder where I been thrown against the shoulder harness.)

As the plane stopped, I got out so fast I don't remember undoing the harness and I believe the plane was rocking back toward the tail as I ran straight off the right wing tip (why the right side?). The ambulance guys drove up and were looking in the cockpit when I turned around and walked back to the plane. When I got there, one of them asked me where

Lt. Dick Perley leans against the only contraption conceived by man that could overcome "General Mud," the mighty Cletrac, at Toul-Ochey airfield near Nancy, France, winter 1944–45. Like other Ninth Air Force fighter groups, the 50th operated, for the most part, from unprepared areas covered by pierced steel planking (PSP), living in tents and trying to find enough heat. *Richard H. Perley*

the pilot was. I had left there so quickly that he hadn't even seen me as they were driving toward the spot. The prop blades were each neatly and uniformly bent backwards around the engine.

Gilbert C. Burns, Jr., *P-47 pilot, 50th Fighter Group*

My fifth combat mission changed my viewpoint on combat flying in many ways. The first four missions I had flown mechanically. The hands and feet flew the plane, the finger squeezed the trigger, doing automatically all the things I had been taught. But this mission got me thinking.

I thought about *killing.*

I had killed the rear gunner in an Me 110 by rote. Very nonchalantly, like brushing my teeth. However, when I killed three flak gunners, I was mentally and acutely aware of just what had occurred. I had seen their bodies being blown apart and was keenly concerned that I had done something serious. I had a mental reaction.

I thought about being *wounded.*

I heard a pilot say on radio after he had pulled up from the airfield that he was hit in the knee and that he could not stop the blood from flowing. He wanted to bail out and hoped he could find a German doctor. From that day onward, during every mission, I wore four loose tourniquets around my upper arms and thighs. I thought that if I was hit I could just take up on the tourniquets, as they were already in place.

I thought about being *captured.*

The stories we had heard were not pretty. The civilians in Germany understandably hated us for bombing and strafing their towns and unintentionally killing many of their own. We had heard rumors of our captured fliers being tied to horses' tails by the ankles, dragged through the streets and stoned and beaten by the civilians. True or not, these stories now prompted me to further protect myself in case of a bail out.

My Colt .45 automatic pistol was my first concern. I set up some bottles as targets 50 feet away and began firing practice. Not one bottle could I hit. I tried at 25 feet with the same bad results. When at 10 feet I was not good, I put the .45 in my barracks bag and forgot about it. I managed to obtain a .38 Colt long barrel six shooter with an 8 inch barrel. A minimum of practice showed that with this weapon I was quite good and so carried it on my hip on the rest of my missions. I would have preferred carrying a Luger. If I did bail out and was evading and ran out of ammunition, cartridges for the Luger would be easier to come by. I found out years later that all the local German police carried Lugers. But at Toul, France, a Luger was not available.

Also at that time the German High Command learned that American pilots were carrying .45s. They were quite concerned about this, with visions of a flier descending in his parachute, blasting away with his .45. What they did not know was that nine out of ten pilots couldn't hit the broad side of a barn with it. They had nothing to fear about the Colt .45.

164

Chapter 10

Photo Recon

Ralph P. Willett, *F-5 crew chief, 3rd Photo Group*

The ground haze that was lifting from the field under the weak rays of winter sun uncovered a bee-hive of activity on the line of this forward aerodrome. Mechanics in greasy coveralls swarmed around the sleek lines of the photo plane; a lumbering, red-flagged gasoline truck scurried up and deposited its fuel. Camera technicians inserted the film magazines and set shutter speeds and lens openings. The crew chief nonchalantly climbed up to the pilot's housing and abstractly began polishing the canopy of the cockpit, all the while keeping a sharp watch on the activities about him.

Everything was set now, but he continued polishing the smooth lucite in even, round, unhurried motions, keeping the rhythm set by his jaws. At last the pilot, a small young fellow, half the age of the crew chief, drove up; even his padded flying clothes did not obliterate the impression of extreme youth. Quickly he climbed to the wing of the plane, silently accepted the mechanic's aid in settling himself in his cockpit and quickly became engrossed in the manipulation of the myriad of switches and dials in front of him. The previously tested engines turned over quickly with a start, coughed once or twice, and settled down to a deep throttle roar that spoke of unbridled power.

Throwing up clouds of dust, the plane taxied out to the runway and soon was hurtling into space. Unfettered now, the plane began making great circles, climbing, always climbing, until it became an unbelievably small speck against the blue-gray winter sky. The crew chief, jaws still working unhurriedly, cloth clutched in his closed fist, followed the plane until it abruptly swung north and was lost from view and then turned and walked away.

No, there is no full blown action at a photo recon base, but there is drama. The drama of an individual pitted alone against unknown opposition, of machines and men working as one organ, of callousness born of necessity; there is the drama of accomplishment; of several hundred men working with dogged insistency, impersonally and yet with the human element, laughing at their own situation when it could become no worse; of C-rations, seas of mud, cold tents without cots, goldbricks and eager-beavers, religious services and poker games.

John Blyth, *Spitfire pilot, 7th Photo Group*

When I heard that we were getting enough Spitfires to equip one squadron, I asked to be transferred. I had dreamed since high school of flying a Spitfire and now it was becoming a reality. My first mission in the Spitfire Mark XI was in April 1944. I went in at 36,000 ft. and was thrilled by the Spit's performance. It exceeded my expectations because it was so much more than the Mark V I had flown locally. The 1,650 hp Rolls-Royce Merlin really made a difference. I loved its response at

A well-worn F–5A Lightning in synthetic haze paint, with cameras instead of guns in the nose. *Fred Bamberger via David W. Menard*

This recce Lightning has a uniform blue haze color scheme which was applied over a black lacquer base coat. The "Photo Joes" wanted to blend in with their environment as much as possible. *National Archives via Dana Bell*

altitude and didn't mind that it only had one engine.

I don't know about other pilots, but to me the English Channel was like an invisible wall. At some point one passed from being relatively safe to entering the unknown. Mentally, each of us probably handled it differently, but flying alone and unarmed was quite different than flying with others. Actually, I was usually busy climbing on course and navigating while crossing the channel and tried not to think about it. Oftentimes part of the mission would be on instruments making navigation more difficult. We often had several targets to photograph, making at least three runs over each, all the while watching for German fighters or our own fighters that figured a Spitfire in this deep must have been captured.

On the way home, it was almost guaranteed that we would face a headwind. Sometimes it seemed forever to reach the English Channel. If I was low on fuel, I would land at RAF Bradwell Bay or RAF Manston stations to refuel and make a bathroom stop. A cramped cockpit at -50 degrees is not the most comfortable work place. At altitude, the heater in the Spitfire or F-5 wasn't much good.

From April 1944 to October I flew 36 missions in the Spitfire. The F-5 had been limited for a period to shorter missions because of problems. It became the mission of the Spits to fly the deeper penetrations and subsequently, I flew missions to Berlin, Munich and eastern and central areas of Germany. Most of these were at 30,000 ft. or above. If the contrails were at 22,000 ft. (winter) I would go to 36,000 or 38,000. In the

summertime, I would usually hit contrails and then drop to around 30,000 ft. The buzz bomb sites on the coast of France were flown at 15,000 ft.

All of my missions were unarmed and without fighter escort. Robert R. Smith and Waldo Bruns failed to return from a mission to the Polish border. Glenn Wiebe was then sent in and he failed to return. It was then decided to send in Spitfires. Three of us were to go in at thirty minute intervals. Walt Simon was to go to the synthetic oil refinery at Brux, Czechoslovakia. I was next going to Ruhland synthetic oil refinery (Polish border) and Kermit Bliss would be behind me. We refueled at RAF Manston for maximum fuel. I was at 30,000 ft. on the way in and could hear the German radar pick me up. I could hear it build up and fade on my headset. Being in the middle, I figured they would intercept Walt first. My thoughts were of the three that hadn't come back and what might have happened to them. Also, Glenn Wiebe and I had started first grade together in Dallas, Oregon, and what a coincidence it might be if the Germans also got me.

Near Dresden I saw a factory that had been bombed and figured I would make a pass across it and save someone a trip. It probably saved my life! As I rolled into a turn to align the target and turned on my cameras, I noticed an aircraft diving and closing rapidly on my tail. He must have been above me and I missed him. At first I thought it was a jet because of the black exhaust trail. It was an Me 109 with a yellow prop spinner and yellow and orange checkered nose. There might have been others. In a Spit, the

throttle was full forward at altitude so I pushed full forward on the propeller control to pick up speed. I flew straight and level and played like I didn't see him. He probably figured he had another victory for the Fatherland and was about to squeeze the trigger when I pulled back abruptly on the stick. Then and there we must have parted company. When I rolled into a turn and looked down, he was underneath me. The climb at that altitude surprised me. Any other evasive maneuver and he probably would have nailed me. I then remembered my cameras and turned them off.

For a short time I didn't know my location. I ended up over Brux, which was on fire, and took pictures, went on to Ruhland, both my other targets and returned to Manston with only several gallons of fuel remaining. I was put in for the DFC but was turned down. The 7th PRG had to be the most poorly decorated unit in the 8th Air Force.

Dan Burrows, *F-5 pilot, 7th Photo Group*

On 20 April 1944, I was operations officer of the 22nd Squadron, and recall that the spring weather was good over England and Europe. Good enough to complete a mission and Doc [Malcolm D. Hughes] was planning to announce his return to Mount Farm by improving the low fly-by over the Intelligence building after his first ops flight exactly ten months earlier.

George Nesselrode and I learned of this from his crew chief and had been monitoring his position with the tower and Base Ops. We positioned ourselves at a vantage point in front of the Intelligence briefing building, having first discussed jumping in a jeep and driving out to mid-field, but thought better of it—too inviting a target. Looking to the southwest we saw the silhouette of the F-5 banking down over the far perimeter, level out and then *disappear!* We knew the field had a rise in the center, but up until then, never realized you could hide behind it. We knew then that Doc was serious, and as he popped into view cutting grass at a high rate of speed, it was obvious he was heading straight for us, and it would not be prudent to remain in the line of flight.

George let out a whoop, threw his hat in the air, and we departed rapidly at a ninety degree angle. It couldn't have been more than two seconds when I heard what sounded like 20 mm cannon fire—glancing over my left shoulder I saw the F-5 tail booms disappear over the back of the building. Knowing that the maintenance hangar was just a short distance behind, we braced for the crash and explosion. Instead we saw the plane pulling up into a climbing left turn, heading back toward the runway, but making a strange ffft-fft-fft sound.

By then George and I had stopped, marveling at the seeming miracle, when something equally astonishing occurred. The door to the Intelligence building flew open and a ghost appeared, a fearful apparition all in white, waving its arms, making strange sounds and surrounded by what seemed a cloud of mist. George and I stood with our mouths open, until we slowly recognized the earthly form of "Pappy" Lytton Doolittle, the patriarchal Intelligence Officer of the 13th Photo Squadron. It was subsequently found that he was covered with plaster dust, and he and Capt. Walt Hickey, 27th Photo Intelligence Officer, thought they'd been hit by a V bomb, but only Pappy suffered a slight cut on the forehead.

By now, troops who had been witnessing the show started showing up, wondering what had happened, and we had brushed Pappy off and explained the situation. He mentioned something about [being] eligible for a Purple Heart. We realized that Doc had landed, and watched as he taxied toward the Ops ramp, with *one prop feathered*, no simple feat in itself.

Nesselrode and I ran over as Doc braked to a stop, opened the canopy, stepped out on the wing and said, "Let's see you bastards beat *that* one!"

A 3rd Photo Group F-5A Lightning comes in to land in Italy, 1944. The synthetic haze blue paint was designed to make the recce aircraft basically invisible until very close range. The color blended in quite well at high altitude. On solo flights, without armament, it was important that they avoid enemy fighters. *Peter M. Bowers via Dana Bell*

The need for accurate weather reporting over the Continent resulted in the formation of the 25th Bomb Group (Recon), which flew fast de Havilland Mosquito Mk. XVIs from April 1944 to the end of the war. The 25th's Mosquitos flew out in advance of bomber formations to report weather and target strikes but also to take photos and fly chaff screening missions for the bombers. This Mossie was attached to the Group's 653rd Bomb Squadron. *Edward R. Richie*

Doc told me later that as he started his pull up to go over the Intelligence building, he mushed slightly—just enough so that one prop struck the flat roof, pulling him down. Of course, this required desperate action, since he was looking straight at the 381st hangar, so he hauled back on the wheel, at the same time noticing severe vibration. He knew if he didn't do something quickly, he would literally lose an engine. Everything was shaking so badly that the instruments were unreadable. Taking a deep breath, he reached to the left and feathered a prop. Fortunately, he made the correct selection—the rest, for him, was a piece of cake. . . .

The briefing room [was] in a shambles, plaster and white dust everywhere, with neon lights hanging by one chain, the other end resting on the table. There were three gashes in the ceiling, where, amazingly, the prop had not hit any of the large support beams and it was obvious that the blade tips had to have been a few inches inside the room. . . .

The Group Commander, George Lawson, told me, "I rushed over to survey the damage, and immediately instructed the engineers to start repair on the gashes in the roof. Speed was essential if Doc's latest antic was to be suppressed. Of course, something of this magnitude was not about to be kept quiet and soon enough Wing Headquarters had people at Mount Farm making noises about 'court martial, loss of wings and other nasty punitive measures.' My rebuttal was 'why ground a talented pilot, when we need him here to fight the war and not stuck in some office back in the boondocks?' Since our losses were running about 33% and we needed pilots, the argument stood up."

My recollection is that he was grounded for 30 days and afterward contributed to the war effort until the spring of 1945. . . . Doc was lucky in more ways than one—when it comes right down to it, Wing could have got him for breaking and entering!

German divisional order, 1944

Enemy aerial photo reconnaissance detects our every movement, every concentration, every weapon, and immediately after detection, every one of these objectives is smashed.

An F–6C Mustang of the 15th Tactical Reconnaissance Squadron on the European continent in late 1944. Most tac recon outfits had Malcolm Hoods fitted to their razorback F–6s for better visibility. The camera port in the rear plexiglass panel is just visible, along with at least four kill markings. Flown primarily at low level, tactical reconnaissance was hazardous but thrilling and because the recce version of the Mustang retained its guns, self-defense resulted in numerous kills. *Ralph Woolner via Monogram Aviation Publications*

An F–5 Lightning of the 3rd Photo Group on short final to its base in Italy. *Peter M. Bowers*

An F–5 Lightning climbing for altitude. *Lockheed*

Chapter 11

Ruptured Duck

Herbert R. Rutland, Jr., *P-51 pilot, 356th Fighter Group*

When the war ended in Europe, my fighter group in England was disbanded, and I found myself in Germany with the occupation forces. We were engaged in moving troops back and forth in transport planes operating out of a remote airfield near the town of Illesheim, [then I was] transferred to R–29, the airfield at Herzogenaurach.

As flying had been curtailed, pilots had to wait their turn to get an occasional flight. In the meantime, some turned up with motorcycles, delighting in roaring down the narrow roads in close formation at high speed. More than one ox-cart took to the ditch upon hearing the approach of the crazy Americans. After numerous complaints and a growing casualty list, the base commander called a halt to this pastime.

Monday was laundry day at the base. Arms bare to the elbows, the female DPs [displaced persons] would gather the woolen uniforms and scrub them in tubs of pure aviation gasoline. One day a loud explosion sounded from my barracks, and smoke filled the building. When the smoke cleared and it was determined that no serious injuries had been incurred, one of the DPs admitted to breaking the rules: she had moved the tub inside, out of the cold. We dubbed the cheerful, young Polish girl "Blockbuster"—the same name given by the British to their largest bomb.

The base was not without social activity, and periodically a gala was held at the non-commissioned officers' club. Young ladies from throughout the area were invited to attend. More often, the entire female population descended upon the base. The prospect of food, drink, and dancing lured many on foot over long distances. As they began their long trek home in the darkness, most could be seen holding morsels of leftovers or candy bars. If some of the ladies appeared more buxom than upon their arrival, it was likely that cigarette butts had been collected and stored in consideration of the smokers at home.

By the spring of 1946, the 354th Fighter Group [based at R–29] no longer existed as a fighting unit. Most of its members had returned home, and a large number of its P–51s had been systematically turned into scrap upon orders from above. German civilians hired to assist in the demolition had every reason to believe that the Americans were truly out of their minds: those of us who had flown and loved those beautiful machines watched in dismay as the explosive charges were placed and then set off. It was like a knife in the heart.

On May 1, 1946, I climbed into one of the remaining Mustangs and headed south for the Alps. As I cruised among the snowcapped peaks, I found myself, by habit, searching the sky behind me for little specks that might be unfriendly planes. Touching down back at "Herzo," I completed my last flight as a fighter pilot.

171

June 1945. The war in Europe is over and the Mustangs of the 55th Fighter Group are lined up for inspection at Wormingford. Slowly each fighter group in the AAF would drift back to peacetime status, men would go home, units would be transferred or disbanded and the massive number of aircraft would be scrapped. *Robert T. Sand*

As GIs roamed Germany they came across numerous yards of wrecked or scrapped Luftwaffe aircraft. This dump at Kaufbeuren airfield, Bavaria, contained quite an assortment of machines that were shot up or sabotaged by retreating Germans, and 55th Fighter Group mechanics found it fascinating to compare the aircraft with what they had been working on. Bob Sand recalls, "The line chiefs took to these shattered planes, patched some up and got them running. The enlisted men had been promised flying lessons in American light observation planes, which never materialized, so some of the men were hot to fly their resurrected planes, but probably wisely, were given thumbs down. However, they were given permission to taxi them when the field wasn't busy. I'll never forget one pretty powerful twin engine plane. The guy would get at one end of the runway, rev the engines high, lift off the brakes and go roaring down the runway, then brake so he could stop at the end of the runway and start the opposite way. As a long frustrated flyer, how I commiserated with that man. Still, it was a pleasure to look down on these planes after looking up at them so often in England." *Robert T. Sand*

As the months of occupation wore on in Germany, groups were decommissioned and aircraft slowly stripped to keep others flying. The derelicts, such as *Pard* of the 359th Fighter Group sitting on a field in Germany, were painful viewing for pilots and ground crews as they watched their once-vital birds get plucked. When personnel were released from active duty and sent home on accumulated service points, they were entitled to sew a small eagle and wreath within a diamond emblem on the sleeves of their uniforms. This quickly became known as a "ruptured duck." symbolizing both men and machines as they were discarded from what used to be the world's mightiest air force. *Fagen via Dave Menard*

Happy Warrior, a Ninth Air Force P–47D, has been put out to pasture in Germany. National, unit and personal markings have been painted over. *Fagen via Dave Menard*

On this page and following page
The sad end of the once-proud 354th Fighter Group's Mustangs at Herzogenaurach, Germany. Germans were hired to chop the P-51s down, then burn them—a task they would have given anything for the chance to do just months before. It puzzled them even more than the Americans who were left to watch. *Herbert R. Rutland, Jr.*

175

176